FOREWORD

There are few resources that have meant as much to me, both directly and indirectly, as the *UK Christian Handbook*. As the role of my work in television and the media has expanded, and frequently as the scratchings of different projects develop, this is one of the books I turn to. It has helped to clarify and fill foundations, develop avenues and often offered inspiration. The listings are generous, the categories fruitful and within each entry lies the potential to explore and enlarge another perspective of the Christian experience.

I was delighted to be approached by the Christian Research Association to write the foreword for this edition. I am sure I echo the words of many when I express my sincere thanks to those who work so hard year after year putting this book together.

We herald the Millennium and I see many Christian groups preparing and pooling their wits. Their aim is to create a celebration in which all whom they embrace have a joyful experience in a moment of history which cannot be repeated. I hope that this Millennium edition of the *UK Christian Handbook* facilitates and inspires all of us to strive for ideals in working, growing and celebrating together, not just now but for life.

Diane Louise Jordan

Diane Louise Jordan
Television and radio broadcaster

ACKNOWLEDGMENTS

This is the Millennium edition of the first, simple volume of both information and statistics which was compiled in 1972 and published a few months later. It evolved into the *UK Christian Handbook*. With over 6,000 entries in the *Handbook*, along with several tables and indexes, there is a hugh volume of work for those involved in the compilation and we are grateful for the commitment to excellence and accuracy and determination which have been evidenced by the staff of Christian Research and others involved in the production of this volume.

A volume like this demands detailed work under pressure to meet the strict time schedule and we would like to record our thanks to those who stuck at their task:

Victoria Poynter	Assistant Editor, who did much of the editing and entering of data
Pamela Poynter	who sold advertising and handled administration
Yvonne Parfett	who administered book orders and took on additional duties to free others for work on the *Handbook*
Keith Poynter and Rachael Iden	who assisted with the data entry and organisation of the entries
Joan Cheeseman and Margaret Barrett	who made nearly all the reminder phone calls and helped in the mailing of forms
Peggy Hale	who worked on the many mailings involved.

The *Handbook* also involves several others in a demanding workload often under strict time constraints and we want to thank them:

Vernon Blackmore	for compiling the list of additional web sites
Jeff Bonser	for compiling the list of television and radio stations
Brian Clews	for advice and information on the Millennium section
Lynn Elias	for the painstaking task of cross-checking proofs against original forms
David Longley	whose advice is invaluable and proofreading meticulous
John Marcus	for days of work on the database which holds the information
Lesley Reynolds	for researching and contacting potential new entries
Pat Wraight	for additional editing

Matthew Gavan and Jim Henderson at WestKey for the typesetting, and James Catford, Jeremy Yates-Round, Kathryn Porter, Monica Green and others at HarperCollins*Religious* working with us as co-publishers.

Thank you also to all who are listed in this volume, for completing forms, sending faxes, answering phone calls, and in other ways helping to ensure the information contained here is as up to date, comprehensive and accurate as possible.

We pray that as always, this new edition will serve the Kingdom well – that is our motive in producing it.

Peter Brierley	Managing Editor
Heather Wraight	Editor

CRITERIA FOR INCLUSION

Organisations are normally only listed in this volume if they:

1. Are *Trinitarian*, that is, they accept the historic formulary of the Godhead as the three eternal persons, God the Father, God the Son and God the Holy Spirit, in one unchanging Essence. A fuller statement is available on request.
2. *Offer a definitive Christian product, service or function*, that is the nature of their output or work reflects their belief and could not be adequately performed without it.
3. *Do not operate or trade under their own individual name* (musical artistes, evangelists and similar occupations apart), so that their listing represents an identifiable organisation, however small, rather than the work or interest of one or two persons.
4. *Work in a wide geographical area*, that is they are serving the wider Body of Christ and not only one local church. Individual churches are usually only included if they are also the headquarters for their denomination in the UK.

Specific ministries within organisations are only included separately upon payment of a fee.

In spite of the above, the Editors reserve the right to make the final decision as to the inclusion of any organisation, and to the information included about each organisation. The editors have not verified whether each entry fulfils all the criteria.

INFORMATION COLLECTION

Prior to the production of this edition each organisation listed in the previous edition was sent a form asking for up-to-date details of its work. A reminder letter was sent to each organisation which did not respond to the initial mailing. Reminders by telephone and/or fax were subsequently made to ensure that the data is as up-to-date as possible.

Organisations not previously listed, because either newly formed or unintentionally omitted from earlier volumes, were researched in a variety of ways and sent similar forms. These organisations were not reminded if they did not respond.

Information received up to July 1999 has been included.

Categories
The basic details of each organisation listed in this volume are shown once, under the most appropriate category. As many organisations have activities in more than one group, a number will be found in more than one category.

Scope
While every effort has been made to be comprehensive, and to include organisations relevant to this publication, no responsibility can be taken by the Editors for the omission of an organisation. The inclusion of an organisation does not necessarily imply agreement by the Editors with its work.

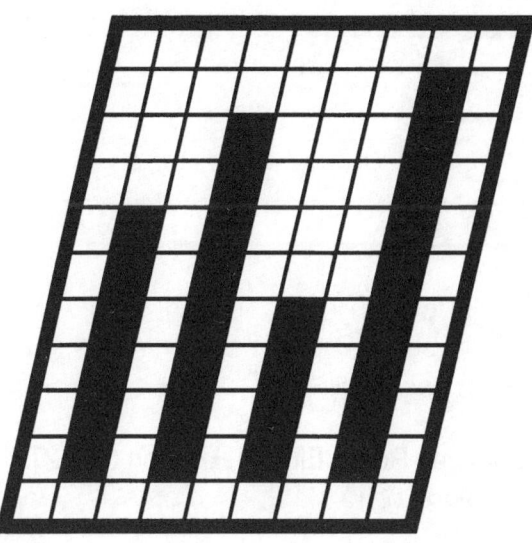

Benefits of belonging to the Christian Research Association

- Receive ***Quadrant* Free** six times a year - 'Information to Steer By' delivered to your door
- **Discount** on ***UK Christian Handbook*** - Corporate members 50%, Personal 25%
- **Discount** on our **seminars** - or we could bring them to you!
- Come **Free** to a Members' Briefing - held alternate years at different locations
- Have access to key **information** - use your Information Token to ask us questions
- Buy from our regular **booklist** - titles carefully chosen for Christian leaders
- Network with our **Membership list** - get in touch with key people

HOW TO JOIN

Choose from three easy ways:

Either photocopy this form, complete it and send it to the address below. Remember to include a credit card number or a cheque (payable to Christian Research).

Or phone on 020 8294 1989 between 9.30-12.30 or 1.30-5.00 Monday to Friday. Have your credit card details ready.

Or photocopy this form, complete it (including credit card details) and fax it on 020 8294 0014.

Cost Corporate membership is for churches or organisations.

Please tick one	**Personal** 1 year	**Personal** 2 years	**Corporate** 1 year	**Corporate** 2 years
Address in UK	☐ £20	☐ £38	☐ £48	☐ £94
Outside UK	☐ £25	☐ £47	☐ £58	☐ £110

(Please use block capitals)

Name________________ Title Rev/Dr/Mr/Mrs/Ms/Other________

Church/organisation________________

Address ________________

____

Post Code ________________ Tel ________

Denomination ________________

Credit card: ☐ Access/Master Card ☐ Visa

Card No: ☐☐☐☐ ☐☐☐☐ ☐☐☐☐ ☐☐☐☐

Expiry Date: ☐☐☐☐

Signature ________________

Christian Research Association, Vision Building, 4 Footscray Road, Eltham, London SE9 2TZ
Tel: 020 8294 1989 Fax: 020 8294 0014

CONTENTS

CONTENTS BY SUBJECT

This list contains Section names and subjects which are part of a Category name in this or the previous edition. See also the Main Index on Page 627, which includes hundreds of additional subject entries.

UNDERSTANDING THIS BOOK

CONTENT

Contents are listed in the Table of Contents on Page 7

The Millennium edition of the *UK Christian Handbook* contains two new sections. The previous eight sections have been retained, each of which can be identified by a thumb tab:

Accommodation	(A)
Books	(B)
Churches	(C)
Evangelism	(E)
Media	(M)
Overseas	(O)
Services	(S)
Training	(T)

In addition a special **Millennium** (thumb tab 2000) section can be found at the start of the book.

At the end of the book the previous section Other Useful Information & Addresses has been expanded and re-named **Extra Information** to create the tenth section (thumb tab X).

Within each section are various **categories**. A completely new category in this edition is:

> **Organisations for People with Disabilities** on Page 410. All entries which were in **Blind Organisations** in the previous edition have been moved to this category, along with some from **Social Service & Welfare Organisations**.

In addition another category has been re-organised:

> **Creation and Environment Movements** has been split into **Creation Movements** and **Environmental Movements**.

The Handbook essentially lists organisations in the UK which would ascribe to the Trinitarian position described on Page 4. The groups included in **Other Churches and Religious Headquarters** and **Multi-Faith Organisations** were previously listed in an appendix to the **Church Headquarters** category. The majority of these do not satisfy the Trinitarian criterion for inclusion and have therefore been moved to Section X, Extra Information, all of which (except the Late Entries) are non-Trinitarian organisations which are included for information purposes.

Other material has also been added to the volume:

> A list of **helpline** numbers has been added to the Extra Information section.
> Contributors were given the option of including Mobile phone numbers.

ENTRIES

Layout

Entries are printed in a solid block of text, with the information always in the same order. Research has shown that people use the *Handbook* most often for four key items. These always appear in the same position in an entry:

> Name of organisation starts the entry, in **bold**
>
> Address immediately follows the organisation name
>
> Chief Executive Officer starts a new line, immediately below the organisation name and address, with the actual title in *italic*
>
> Phone and fax numbers are always on the last line of entry.

Lists

Fourteen categories have some information which does not fit into a standard entry, such as number of beds in the Accommodation section. Such information is given in a list at the start of the appropriate category. The following categories have such lists:

Bookshops on Page 134
Camping, Caravan & Outdoor Centres on Page 62
Conference Centres, Guest Houses & Hotels on Page 67
Hostels on Page 89
Missionary Sending Churches (Direct) on Page 351
Missionary Societies on Pages 328–350
Newspapers & Periodicals on Page 310
Publishers on Page 169
Residential Homes for Disadvantaged People on Page 104
Residential & Nursing Homes for Elderly People on Page 107
Retreat Centres on Page 121
Sheltered Housing on Page 129
Theological Colleges & Bible Schools (Residential) on Page 500
Theological Colleges & Bible Schools (Non-residential) on Page 509

Where no relevant information is available, an organisation is listed in the category but not included in the list.

Abbreviations

E = estimated
M = men
n/a = not answered, not available, not applicable or unknown
W = women

Symbols

🄴 = Email address
☎ = telephone number
📠 = fax number
* = member of Evangelical Alliance or Evangelical Missionary Alliance
† = Information not updated since last edition.

HOW TO FIND WHAT YOU WANT

If you know –	Use:
Organisation's current name	Main Index on Page 627
Organisation's previous name	Main Index on Page 627
Name of Chief Officer	Main Index on Page 627
Magazine's name	Main Index on Page 627
Postcode, county or town where located	Location Index on Page 569
Postcode, county or town and kind of work	List at start of appropriate category
Particular type of work undertaken	Contents in alphabetical order on Page 8
General type of work undertaken	Contents by Section on Page 5
Local name or address	Contents by Section or Location Index
Subject of data needed (eg schools)	Subject in Main Index on Page 627

In desperation, you are always welcome to telephone Christian Research on 020 8294 1989.

QUICK GUIDE TO MEANING OF ENTRIES

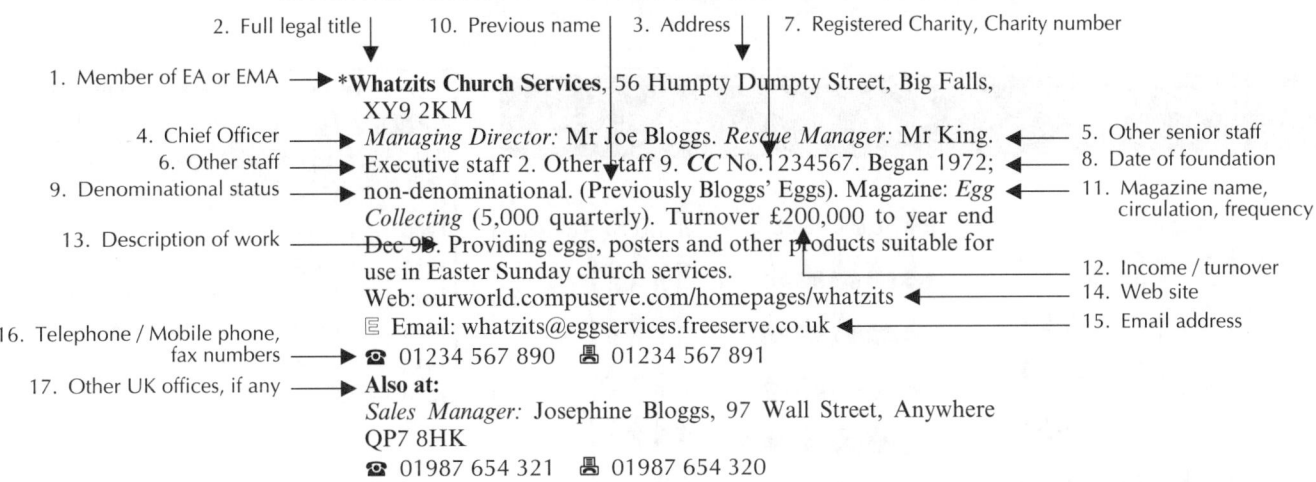

2. Full legal title | 10. Previous name | 3. Address | 7. Registered Charity, Charity number

1. Member of EA or EMA → *__Whatzits Church Services__, 56 Humpty Dumpty Street, Big Falls, XY9 2KM
4. Chief Officer → *Managing Director:* Mr Joe Bloggs. *Rescue Manager:* Mr King. ← 5. Other senior staff
6. Other staff → Executive staff 2. Other staff 9. *CC* No.1234567. Began 1972; ← 8. Date of foundation
9. Denominational status → non-denominational. (Previously Bloggs' Eggs). Magazine: *Egg Collecting* (5,000 quarterly). ← 11. Magazine name, circulation, frequency
Turnover £200,000 to year end Dec 98. ← 12. Income / turnover
13. Description of work → Providing eggs, posters and other products suitable for use in Easter Sunday church services.
Web: ourworld.compuserve.com/homepages/whatzits ← 14. Web site
Email: whatzits@eggservices.freeserve.co.uk ← 15. Email address
16. Telephone / Mobile phone, fax numbers → ☎ 01234 567 890 🖷 01234 567 891
17. Other UK offices, if any → **Also at:**
Sales Manager: Josephine Bloggs, 97 Wall Street, Anywhere QP7 8HK
☎ 01987 654 321 🖷 01987 654 320

LAYOUT OF ENTRIES

1. *A preceding asterisk indicates membership of the Evangelical Alliance or Evangelical Missionary Alliance, who have published or co-published the *UK Christian Handbook* since its inception. See Pages 000 and 000 for a full list of their group members.

† A preceding dagger indicates that no return was received or contact made and the information given may therefore be unreliable.

2. Organisation name is in **bold** and is usually the full legal title.

3. Correct postal address given is for the UK office. The address gives the Post Town and Postcode. There is considerable difficulty relating Postcodes to old Counties or new Unitary Authorities and Administrative Areas. Therefore this edition uses only Postcode towns, a list of which can be found on Page 000 at the start of the Location Index.

4. The Chief Executive Officer is given together with his/her actual designation (in *italics*). No academic degrees or other professional qualifications are shown except for Principals of Theological Colleges and Bible Schools. No title is shown for those belonging to the Society of Friends, and for others who requested the omission of a title. Normally only one name is shown.

5. Organisations with larger income/turnover were given the option of including a second or third name and designation. For missionary societies the international chief officer is included where known, but correspondence should normally be addressed to the first named person.

6. UK Staff numbers are as at 1st January 1999 and normally relate to full-time personnel only. Some organisations indicated part-time personnel and these have been combined to count as full-time equivalents. If there are no full-time staff, any part-time or voluntary staff are indicated as such. Executive or Admin (administrative) staff are usually those in management positions, while Other staff is not defined and may include a wide range of roles including clerical or manual.

7. *CC* indicates that the organisation is registered with the Charity Commission, and where known the Charity number follows immediately.

8. "Began xxxx" gives the year of foundation of the present or originating organisation.

9. Denominational status of organisation may be one of three: denominational (naming the denomination), interdenominational/ecumenical/evangelical, or non-denominational. No definition is given on the questionnaire for these categories.

10. If the organisation has changed its name recently, the previous name will be found in the entry in brackets. If it has changed its name in the last 10 years, the old name is usually included in the Main Index.

11. Magazine name is given in *italics* followed by the circulation and frequency in brackets.

12. Income/Turnover. The term Turnover has been used throughout this volume, but for some organisations it refers to income. This figure relates to the latest (published) Income and Expenditure Account for the United Kingdom, and the month and year to which it refers is indicated. Where not known this is assumed to be December 1998.

13. Description of work is a maximum of 15 words and is the last item in the block of information.

14. Web site address is listed after the description of work. It will also be found in the Web site list on Page 000. In most cases the site address is listed on one line, but in the occasional case where it is too long for one line, it should be treated as one continuous number. Web addresses are preceded by http:// but as this is automatically included by most Web Browsers it has not been printed for every web address. Lower case is used throughout.

15. Email address is on the penultimate line of an entry. In most cases these are listed on one line, but in the occasional case where the address is too long for one line, it should be treated as one continuous number. Lower case is used throughout.

16. Telephone, mobile phone and fax numbers are always on the last line of the main entry. New code numbers introduced in June 1999 and which must be used after April 2000 have been included.

17. Other UK Offices or additional information (eg Suffragan Bishops and Archdeacons for Church of England Dioceses) follow below the main entry.

FIGURE 2.12.1
Total Church Members, Churches and Ministers, UK, 1900–2000

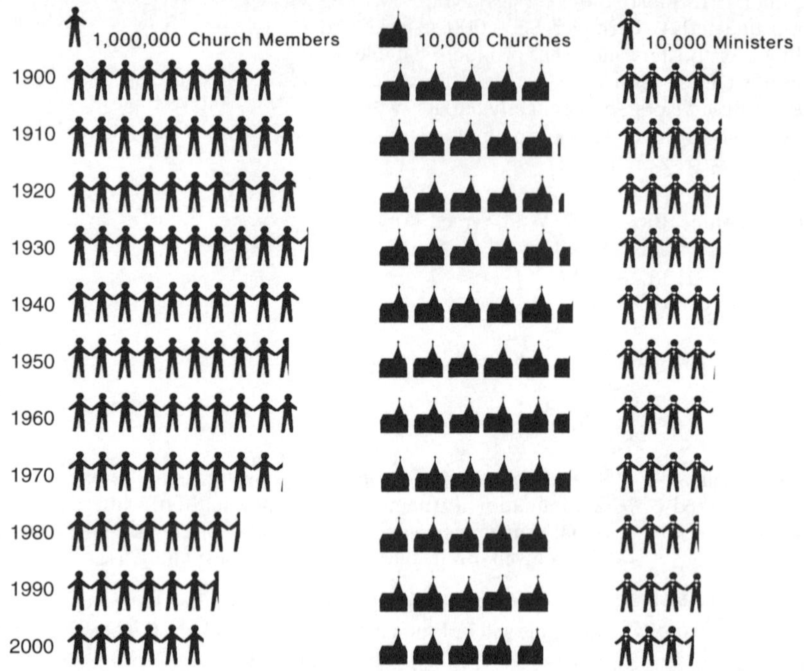

TABLE 2.12
Total UK Members, Churches and Ministers 1900–2000

	Membership	Churches	Ministers
1900	8,663,826	48,988	45,408
1910	9,703,961	51,244	45,273
1920	9,802,669	52,035	44,037
1930	10,357,153	54,059	43,700
1940	10,017,230	54,928	45,002
1950	9,613,984	54,671	41,654
1960	9,917,845	54,760	41,211
1970	9,079,403	53,215	39,281
1980	7,528,995	49,838	35,694
1990	6,624,051	49,595	36,896
2000	5,861,796	48,695	33,709
1991	6,537,669	49,467	37,073
1992	6,525,262	49,280	37,079
1993	6,475,621	49,290	36,853
1994	6,400,667	49,216	37,046
1995	6,283,073	49,094	36,213
1996	6,065,415	48,977	34,856
1997	6,031,372	49,020	34,446
1998	6,012,231	48,759	34,157

FIGURE 2.12.2
Rates of change for UK Churches 1900–2000

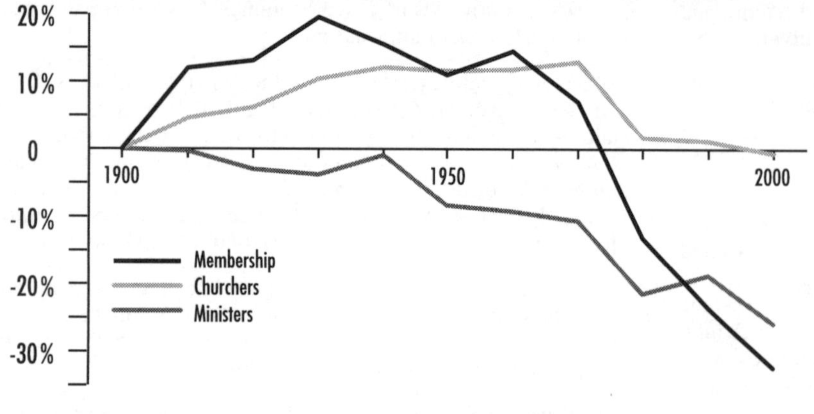

The membership figures in **Table 2.12** are illustrated in **Figure 2.9.1. Table 2.12** and **Figures 2.12.1** and **2.12.2** show that the 20th century may be divided into three parts as far as the church is concerned:

- 1900-1930 when church membership and numbers of congregations were growing, although not as it happens the number of ministers
- 1930-1960 when the church was largely static, although in reality membership slightly declined and then recovered because of a massive influx of Irish labourers in the 1950s most of whom were Catholic
- 1960-2000 when church membership has dropped 40%, a net 6,000 churches have closed, and there are 7,500 fewer ministers.

At its peak in 1930, the 10 million plus church members were 31% of the adult population, whereas by 2000 it will have fallen to 12%.

The number of adults per church in the population in 1900 was 500, which rose to 620 by 1930, to 710 by 1960, and will be 970, virtually double the 1900 figure, by the year 2000.

When the number of ministers was highest, in 1900, they each had 190 members on average. By 1930 that had become 240, the same figure as in 1960, whereas by the 2000 it will be back to 170, showing that the number of leaders did not rise as fast as membership at the beginning of the century and is not shrinking as fast as membership at the end.

3.2 TOTAL BRITISH MISSIONARIES

FIGURE 3.2.1 Total British Missionaries 1980–1999

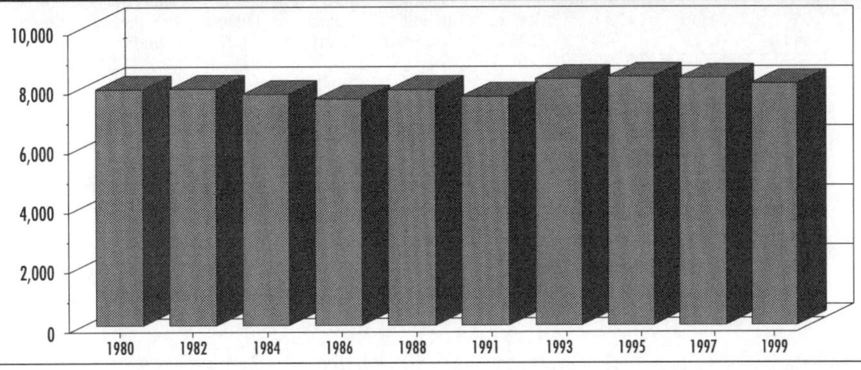

TABLE 3.2 Total British Missionaries 1980–1999[2]

	1980	1982	1984	1986	1988	1991	1993	1995	1997	1999
Anglican Societies	1,428	1,319	1,068	1,044	1,088	998	940	912	906	919
Roman Catholic Societies[1]	1,799	1,783	1,717	1,588	1,723	1,625	1,540	1,496	1,396	1,287
Other Denominational Societies	1,080	1,114	1,203	1,276	1,267	1,215	1,191	1,261	1,243	1,261
Interdenominational Societies	3,058	3,212	3,315	3,218	3,351	3,346	4,116	4,160	4,220	4,125
Direct Sending Churches	560	512	452	469	478	491	480	508	529	513
Total	7,925	7,940	7,755	7,595	7,907	7,675	8,267	8,337	8,294	8,105

[1] Numbers include those serving in the UK [2] This includes estimates for missing data

FIGURE 3.2.2 British Missionaries by Denomination

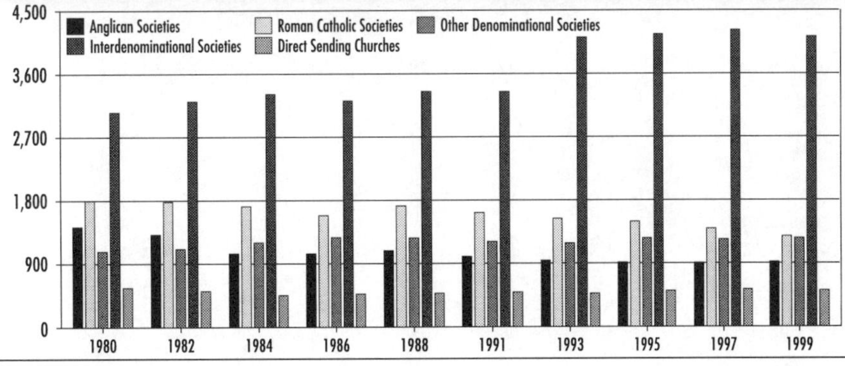

The total number of British missionaries, shown in **Table 3.2**, and illustrated in **Figure 3.2.1**, declined slightly between 1997 and 1999, falling by 189 people or 2% of the total. Similar variations have occurred on the year by year figures over the last 20 years, and is nothing unusual on this occasion. The overall number of missionaries serving overseas in 1999 is virtually the same as the total in 1980, 2% higher, varying from a high in 1995 of 8,300 to a low in 1986 of 7,600. Figures for earlier years are not available.

British missionaries are those serving overseas, mostly in cross-cultural settings, but includes some working in the UK (often amongst immigrants), and those on home leave.

Figure 3.2.2 depicts the detail of **Table 3.2** and shows the growth in the number serving in Interdenominational Societies, that is, societies whose missionaries come from a variety of denominational backgrounds. They do not give up their denominational allegiance in serving with such societies, but are those preferring to serving with such a society to one whose missionaries are *only* of one denomination.

The number serving with Interdenominational Societies has increased by over a third, 35%, in the 19 years shown in the Table. Those in Anglican Societies have seen a decline of over a third, 36%, in the same period, partly because of the much smaller number of missionaries now serving in India. Roman Catholic missionaries have likewise declined 28%.

The line "Direct Sending Churches" gives the total number of missionaries sent out directly by individual churches, who do not work overseas under the auspices of a missionary society. They have dropped 8% in the same period.

Other Denominational Societies, that is, those working within a specific denomination (such as the Methodist Church World Church Office or the Pentecostal Assemblies of God World Ministries) have seen an increase of 18% between 1980 and 1999.

Part of the reason for this change is because many of the Interdenominational Societies are evangelical, and it is this sector which is growing, as **Table 3.6.6** shows. In 1995, the first year such an analysis was undertaken, 63% of serving missionaries were with societies in membership with the Evangelical Missionary Alliance, now called Global Connections. In 1999 the percentage was 75%.

TABLE 1: SUMMARY OF ORGANISATIONS BY FOUNDATION DATE, STAFF & FACILITIES

Category	Number[1]	Date of Foundation Percentage Founded: Before 1920	1920–1985	After 1985	Percentage with no Full Time Staff	Staff Percentage of: Admin Staff	Other Staff	Total Number of Full-time Staff	Average Number	Percentage with: Fax/ Phone	E-mail Address	Web site
		%	%	%	%	%	%			%	%	%
Millennium Organisations	24	*0*	*0*	*100*	*75*	*25*	*75*	29	5	*54*	*54*	*42*
Accommodation												
Camping, Caravan & Outdoor Centres	59	*0*	*64*	*36*	*7*	*23*	*77*	561	10	*76*	*54*	*31*
Conference Centres	243	*5*	*63*	*32*	*12*	*31*	*69*	2,430	11	*61*	*35*	*17*
Hospices	6	*17*	*83*	*0*	*0*	*35*	*65*	1,148	164	*83*	*33*	*33*
Hostels	160	*16*	*40*	*44*	*7*	*31*	*69*	2,622	18	*53*	*20*	*12*
Housing Associations	28	*7*	*54*	*39*	*11*	*6*	*94*	6,013	231	*82*	*43*	*25*
Residential Homes for Disadvantaged People	31	*0*	*45*	*55*	*13*	*20*	*80*	541	20	*45*	*16*	*6*
Residential & Nursing Homes for Elderly People	165	*6*	*38*	*56*	*2*	*11*	*89*	5,266	32	*58*	*12*	*0*
Retreat Houses	119	*26*	*59*	*15*	*13*	*45*	*55*	979	9	*54*	*28*	*14*
Sheltered Housing	26	*0*	*38*	*62*	*4*	*100*	*0*	13	1	*4*	*0*	*0*
TOTAL ACCOMMODATION	**849**	***10***	***51***	***39***	***9***	***18***	***82***	**19,581**	**25**	***57***	***26***	***13***
Books												
Bible Distributors	14	*57*	*36*	*7*	*21*	*36*	*64*	140	12	*93*	*64*	*50*
Bookshops	530	*4*	*68*	*28*	*12*	*41*	*59*	1,938	4	*62*	*34*	*16*
Libraries	14	*50*	*14*	*36*	*14*	*40*	*60*	98	8	*64*	*50*	
Publishers of Books	121	*21*	*45*	*34*	*12*	*43*	*57*	1,695	16	*84*	*69*	*38*
Other Literature Producers & Distributors (Primarily in the UK)	102	*12*	*48*	*40*	*29*	*14*	*86*	1,118	15	*68*	*58*	*29*
TOTAL BOOKS	**781**	***10***	***61***	***29***	***14***	***35***	***65***	**4,989**	**7**	***67***	***43***	***22***
Churches												
Cathedrals	82	*4*	*1*	*95*	*99*	*100*	*0*	2	2	*71*	*28*	*16*
Chaplaincies	21	*33*	*38*	*29*	*10*	*92*	*8*	670	30	*67*	*19*	*5*
Church Headquarters	751	*34*	*27*	*39*	*22*	*92*	*8*	4,944[2]	13	*61*	*34*	*18*
Church Organisations	142	*29*	*51*	*20*	*51*	*49*	*51*	613	8	*60*	*38*	*18*
Councils of Churches	76	*3*	*45*	*52*	*63*	*41*	*59*	188	7	*41*	*30*	*8*
Evangelical Fellowships (Inter-Church)	36	*0*	*25*	*75*	*86*	*75*	*25*	8	2	*17*	*28*	*3*
Religious Orders (Anglican)	16	*69*	*25*	*6*	*6*	*0*	*100*	39[3]	0	*38*	*19*	*0*
Religious Orders (Roman Catholic)	55	*62*	*27*	*11*	*0*	*0*	*100*	658[3]	0	*65*	*22*	*11*
TOTAL CHURCHES	**1,179**	***28***	***30***	***42***	***39***	***78***	***22***	**7,122**	**14**	***58***	***32***	***15***
Evangelism												
City & Town Missions	41	*51*	*27*	*22*	*5*	*41*	*59*	694	15	*61*	*44*	*22*
Evangelistic Agencies (Primarily in the UK)	187	*13*	*46*	*41*	*14*	*39*	*61*	3,498	20	*73*	*68*	*42*
Evangelists (Independent)	31	*0*	*61*	*39*	*19*	*88*	*12*	49	2	*48*	*45*	*19*
Teaching & Preaching Agencies	17	*12*	*24*	*64*	*18*	*70*	*30*	40	2	*71*	*47*	*18*
TOTAL EVANGELISM	**276**	***17***	***43***	***40***	***13***	***40***	***60***	**4,281**	**16**	***68***	***61***	***35***
Media												
Art & Craft Product Suppliers	38	*0*	*55*	*45*	*11*	*37*	*63*	263	8	*66*	*29*	*8*
Design, Layout & Editorial Services	50	*2*	*30*	*68*	*8*	*37*	*63*	265	6	*88*	*70*	*28*
Media Producers	63	*0*	*48*	*52*	*11*	*29*	*71*	406	7	*90*	*83*	*40*
Media Services	78	*0*	*54*	*46*	*13*	*40*	*60*	327	5	*78*	*59*	*23*
Musical & Theatrical Performers	105	*0*	*33*	*67*	*43*	*75*	*25*	243	4	*56*	*63*	*17*
Musical & Theatrical Services	71	*1*	*37*	*62*	*24*	*56*	*44*	303	5	*79*	*54*	*34*
Newspapers & Periodicals	154	*26*	*41*	*33*	*40*	*33*	*67*	630	7	*84*	*71*	*48*
Photographers	4	*0*	*50*	*50*	*0*	*80*	*20*	5	1	*25*	*50*	*0*
Video, Film & Cassette Libraries & Suppliers	21	*0*	*52*	*48*	*38*	*50*	*50*	50	4	*71*	*57*	*24*
TOTAL MEDIA	**584**	***7***	***42***	***51***	***27***	***41***	***59***	**2,492**	**6**	***77***	***64***	***31***
Overseas												
Evangelistic Agencies (Overseas)	26	*0*	*58*	*42*	*27*	*37*	*63*	166	9	*77*	*81*	*38*
Literature Producers & Distributors (Overseas)	22	*9*	*59*	*32*	*32*	*32*	*68*	151	9	*77*	*68*	*18*
Missionary Sending Churches (Direct)	8	*25*	*50*	*25*	*0*	*100*	*0*	533	67	*75*	*88*	*25*
Missionary Societies	221	*55*	*30*	*15*	*4*	*87*	*13*	922[4]	27	*88*	*58*	*32*
Missionary Support Organisations	136	*18*	*46*	*36*	*25*	*33*	*67*	1,072	10	*78*	*65*	*30*
Relief & Development Agencies	65	*0*	*31*	*69*	*22*	*15*	*85*	989	19	*88*	*78*	*42*
TOTAL OVERSEAS	**478**	***31***	***38***	***31***	***15***	***75***	***25***	**3,833**	**22**	***84***	***65***	***32***

1. Excluding multiple entries
2. Excluding serving ministers
3. Excluding members
4. Excluding serving members

TABLE 1: SUMMARY OF ORGANISATIONS BY RELIGIOUS AFFILIATION & INCOME

Category	Number[1]	Percentage registered with Charity Commission	Religious Affiliation Percentage who are Anglican	Roman Catholic	Other Denominations	Inter[2]	Income/Turnover Estimated Total £'000	Percentage[3]
		%	%	%	%	%		%
Millennium Organisations	24	17	4	0	4	92	£144	8
Accommodation								
Camping, Caravan & Outdoor Centres	59	73	10	0	14	76	£8,387	75
Conference Centres	243	53	11	2	16	71	£39,541	56
Hospices	6	100	0	0	0	100	£17,900	83
Hostels	160	96	5	7	39	49	£38,504	47
Housing Associations	28	82	0	4	25	71	£128,347	86
Residential Homes for Disadvantaged People	31	84	0	6	35	59	£7,051	45
Residential & Nursing Homes for Elderly People	165	79	5	4	56	35	£31,073	12
Retreat Houses	119	87	37	39	8	16	£12,833	32
Sheltered Housing	26	100	0	0	96	4	£520	4
TOTAL ACCOMMODATION	**849**	**76**	**11**	**8**	**31**	**50**	**£284,182**	**42**
Books								
Bible Distributors	14	100	0	0	0	100	£55,370	57
Bookshops	530	61	6	4	13	77	£64,340	42
Libraries	14	79	57	7	7	29	£420[4]	7
Publishers of Books	121	36	7	8	19	66	£16,421	20
Other Literature Producers & Distributors (Primarily in the UK)	102	44	5	3	15	77	£50,068	40
TOTAL BOOKS	**781**	**56**	**7**	**5**	**14**	**74**	**£186,201**	**38**
Churches								
Cathedrals	82	9	54	26	21	0	£19,157	9
Chaplaincies	21	57	29	19	24	28	£813	33
Church Headquarters	751	36	18	11	70	1	£98,204	6
Church Organisations	142	61	41	15	34	10	£19,339	44
Councils of Churches	76	33	0	1	22	77	£4,803	49
Evangelical Fellowships (Inter-Church)	36	19	0	0	14	86	£454	28
Religious Orders (Anglican)	16	94	81	6	0	13	£900	6
Religious Orders (Roman Catholic)	55	98	0	100	0	0	£4,253	5
TOTAL CHURCHES	**1,179**	**42**	**23**	**18**	**45**	**14**	**£147,925**	**18**
Evangelism								
City & Town Missions	41	80	2	0	49	49	£13,581	83
Evangelistic Agencies (Primarily in the UK)	187	86	2	2	22	74	£49,561	61
Evangelists (Independent)	31	48	6	0	61	33	£730	23
Teaching & Preaching Agencies	17	53	0	0	59	41	£629	47
TOTAL EVANGELISM	**276**	**79**	**3**	**1**	**33**	**63**	**£64,502**	**59**
Media								
Art & Craft Product Suppliers	38	3	5	5	16	74	£13,188	37
Design, Layout & Editorial Services	50	8	0	0	22	78	£10,426	44
Media Producers	63	38	0	5	8	87	£14,274	51
Media Services	78	15	4	1	22	73	£13,107	49
Musical & Theatrical Performers	105	22	1	2	40	57	£2,832	29
Musical & Theatrical Services	71	32	1	1	18	80	£12,506	44
Newspapers & Periodicals	154	32	7	6	31	56	£9,089	8
Photographers	4	0	0	0	0	100	£600[4]	33
Video, Film & Cassette Libraries & Suppliers	21	48	14	0	5	81	£1,034	43
TOTAL MEDIA	**584**	**25**	**4**	**3**	**24**	**69**	**£77,059**	**32**
Overseas								
Evangelistic Agencies (Overseas)	26	88	0	0	19	81	£3,603	69
Literature Producers & Distributors (Overseas)	22	86	0	0	9	91	£7,604	82
Missionary Sending Churches (Direct)	8	88	0	0	50	50	£5,002	63
Missionary Societies	221	91	6	48	12	34	£144,010	98
Missionary Support Organisations	136	84	11	5	16	68	£47,949	76
Relief & Development Agencies	65	89	0	5	26	69	£105,498	74
TOTAL OVERSEAS	**478**	**88**	**6**	**24**	**16**	**54**	**£313,667**	**86**

1. Excluding multiple entires
2. Interdenominational/non-denominational/Ecumenical/Evangelical
3. Percentage of organisations on which total figure is estimated
4. Based on previous entry

TABLE 1: SUMMARY OF ORGANISATIONS BY FOUNDATION DATE, STAFF & FACILITIES (CONTINUED)

Category	Number[1]	Date of Foundation Percentage Founded: Before 1920	1920–1985	After 1985	Percentage with no Full Time Staff	Staff Percentage of: Admin Staff	Other Staff	Total Number of Full-time Staff	Average Number	Percentage with: Fax/ Phone	E-mail Address	Web site
		%	%	%	%	%	%			%	%	%
Services												
Addictions & Rehabilitation Services	38	*5*	*45*	*50*	*13*	*27*	*73*	468	13	*55*	*32*	*13*
Animal Welfare Organisations	6	*17*	*67*	*16*	*67*	*100*	*0*	2	1	*17*	*0*	*0*
Benevolent Organisations	50	*34*	*40*	*26*	*46*	*66*	*34*	494	18	*50*	*30*	*18*
Buildings & Church Design	17	*6*	*47*	*47*	*6*	*27*	*73*	144	9	*94*	*53*	*12*
Children's Care & Adoption Societies	23	*48*	*30*	*22*	*4*	*5*	*95*	5,223	201	*78*	*35*	*13*
Computer & Business Services	56	*2*	*32*	*66*	*16*	*49*	*51*	431	8	*80*	*80*	*45*
Counselling Organisations	75	*0*	*25*	*75*	*21*	*72*	*28*	473	7	*49*	*33*	*17*
Creation Movements	5	*0*	*60*	*40*	*40*	*50*	*50*	14	5	*40*	*20*	*80*
Organisations for People with Disabilities	23	*17*	*35*	*48*	*26*	*5*	*95*	1,137	67	*61*	*57*	*30*
Environmental Movements	5	*0*	*40*	*60*	*60*	*100*	*0*	12	4	*60*	*80*	*80*
Ethnic Minority Associations	27	*11*	*41*	*48*	*33*	*23*	*77*	148	8	*59*	*41*	*7*
Financial Services	59	*19*	*46*	*35*	*10*	*17*	*83*	1,684	28	*85*	*46*	*19*
Furnishings, Fabric & Church Interiors	43	*19*	*47*	*34*	*5*	*17*	*83*	654	15	*95*	*56*	*44*
Health & Healing Organisations	37	*11*	*49*	*40*	*11*	*29*	*71*	1,214	33	*65*	*51*	*22*
Information & Telephone Organisations	32	*3*	*59*	*38*	*31*	*52*	*48*	81	4	*72*	*47*	*34*
Marketing & Fundraising Services	18	*0*	*17*	*83*	*11*	*56*	*44*	64	4	*100*	*78*	*17*
Marriage Ministries	23	*0*	*48*	*52*	*48*	*66*	*34*	35	3	*70*	*74*	*52*
Personnel Consultancy and Placement	16	*0*	*44*	*56*	*0*	*64*	*36*	58	3	*75*	*88*	*38*
Prayer Fellowships	33	*12*	*55*	*33*	*55*	*51*	*49*	47	3	*39*	*39*	*18*
Printers	15	*7*	*53*	*40*	*7*	*44*	*56*	192	14	*93*	*20*	*7*
Professional Christian Groups	97	*11*	*53*	*36*	*60*	*60*	*40*	121	3	*68*	*64*	*37*
Pro-Life Organisations	5	*0*	*60*	*40*	*40*	*27*	*73*	45	15	*60*	*60*	*60*
Reconciliation Groups	37	*8*	*65*	*27*	*43*	*62*	*38*	271	12	*68*	*57*	*30*
Research & Development Organisations	29	*0*	*52*	*48*	*28*	*41*	*59*	134	6	*86*	*79*	*55*
Social Associations	47	*4*	*60*	*36*	*60*	*30*	*70*	237	12	*51*	*53*	*38*
Social Service & Welfare Organisations	80	*21*	*44*	*35*	*15*	*22*	*78*	9,222	121	*79*	*43*	*20*
Travel: Agents, Services, Tour Operators	48	*4*	*58*	*38*	*6*	*63*	*37*	579	12	*92*	*67*	*35*
Youth Organisations	91	*20*	*53*	*27*	*21*	*77*	*23*	2,508	32	*74*	*68*	*41*
TOTAL SERVICES	**1,035**	***12***	***46***	***42***	***27***	***28***	***72***	**25,692**	**31**	***70***	***53***	***29***
Training												
Bible Study Agencies	15	*13*	*73*	*14*	*33*	*42*	*58*	66	7	*60*	*80*	*33*
Conventions, Bible Weeks, Exhibitions and Festivals	27	*11*	*52*	*37*	*37*	*37*	*63*	147	8	*56*	*59*	*44*
Educational Agencies	69	*12*	*46*	*42*	*32*	*34*	*66*	343	7	*74*	*55*	*30*
Educational Resource Centres	23	*22*	*48*	*30*	*0*	*48*	*52*	146	6	*91*	*48*	*22*
Teaching English as a Foreign Language Schools	10	*0*	*50*	*50*	*0*	*23*	*77*	123	12	*100*	*90*	*70*
Theological Colleges & Bible Schools (Residential)	93	*49*	*40*	*11*	*1*	*56*	*44*	2,259	23	*87*	*69*	*42*
Theological Colleges and Bible Schools (Non-residential)	57	*14*	*49*	*37*	*9*	*73*	*27*	546	10	*75*	*74*	*40*
Training Centres & Services	100	*5*	*37*	*58*	*15*	*39*	*61*	729	8	*78*	*65*	*26*
TOTAL TRAINING	**394**	***20***	***44***	***36***	***15***	***51***	***49***	**4,359**	**12**	***78***	***65***	***35***
GRAND TOTAL 1999	**5,600[2]**	***15***	***41***	***44***	***28***	***41***	***59***	**72,378**	**19**	***69***	***44***	***23***
GRAND TOTAL 1997	5,515	*17*	*51*	*32*	*20*	*35*	*65*	69,832	16	*57*	*20*	*8*
GRAND TOTAL 1995	5,593	*22*	*57*	*21*	*19*	*34*	*66*	64,333	14	*48*	*3*	*n/a*
GRAND TOTAL 1993	5,215	*18*[3]	*41*[4]	*41*[5]	*20*	*36*	*64*	57,133	14	*40*	*n/a*	*n/a*
GRAND TOTAL 1991	4,738	*17*[3]	*43*[4]	*40*[5]	*22*	*36*	*64*	62,012	17	*26*	*n/a*	*n/a*
GRAND TOTAL 1988	4,074	*19*[3]	*24*[4]	*57*[5]	*24*	*38*	*62*	48,781	16	*3*	*n/a*	*n/a*
GRAND TOTAL 1986	3,580	*19*[3]	*26*[4]	*55*[5]	*27*	*38*	*62*	45,944	14	*n/a*	*n/a*	*n/a*

1. Excluding multiple entries
2. Excluding 48 Late Entries and 528 addresses of Other Organisations
3. Founded before 1900
4. Founded 1900-1975
5. Founded after 1975

TABLE 1: SUMMARY OF ORGANISATIONS BY RELIGIOUS AFFILIATION & INCOME (CONTINUED)

Category	Number[1]	Percentage registered with Charity Commission	Religious Affiliation Percentage who are Anglican	Roman Catholic	Other Denominations	Inter[2]	Income/Turnover Estimated Total £'000	Percentage[3]
		%	%	%	%	%		%
Services								
Addictions & Rehabilitation Services	38	92	3	5	37	55	£9,930	58
Animal Welfare Organisations	6	17	17	0	17	66	£21	83
Benevolent Organisations	50	94	38	8	22	32	£171,171	74
Buildings & Church Design	17	18	12	0	0	88	£22,110	41
Children's Care & Adoption Societies	23	100	9	48	17	26	£76,946	74
Computer & Business Services	56	13	0	0	20	80	£13,879	57
Counselling Organisations	75	76	1	1	31	67	£3,473	71
Creation Movements	5	80	0	20	0	80	£178	80
Organisations for People with Disabilities	23	91	9	9	22	60	£17,318	65
Environmental Movements	5	80	0	0	40	60	£272	80
Ethnic Minority Associations	27	67	0	15	19	66	£2,168	59
Financial Services	59	27	10	0	24	66	£288,935	63
Furnishings, Fabric & Church Interiors	43	2	2	0	12	86	£24,960	44
Health & Healing Organisations	37	95	16	5	14	65	£16,838	76
Information & Telephone Organisations	32	50	9	16	19	56	£1,277	34
Marketing & Fundraising Services	18	6	6	0	0	94	£2,123	56
Marriage Ministries	23	74	17	13	26	44	£566	70
Personnel Consultancy and Placement	16	31	0	0	31	69	£1,946	63
Prayer Fellowships	33	55	3	3	15	79	£873	61
Printers	15	13	7	0	0	93	£6,333	47
Professional Christian Groups	97	60	6	7	9	78	£4,457	55
Pro-Life Organisations	5	0	0	0	0	100	£1,650	40
Reconciliation Groups	37	54	3	16	11	70	£4,803	62
Research & Development Organisations	29	69	10	0	10	80	£3,171	52
Social Associations	47	43	0	13	11	76	£6,734	64
Social Service & Welfare Organisations	80	90	6	14	21	59	£191,775	69
Travel: Agents, Services, Tour Operators	48	15	0	0	10	90	£72,028	54
Youth Organisations	91	87	13	7	27	53	£63,828	58
TOTAL SERVICES	**1,035**	**59**	**8**	**7**	**18**	**67**	**£1,009,774**	61
Training								
Bible Study Agencies	15	93	0	7	7	86	£920	67
Conventions, Bible Weeks, Exhibitions and Festivals	27	59	4	4	26	66	£3,991	52
Educational Agencies	69	70	7	6	17	70	£7,994	62
Educational Resource Centres	23	78	35	4	17	44	£2,357	48
Teaching English as a Foreign Language Schools	10	60	0	0	20	80	£1,755	70
Theological Colleges & Bible Schools (Residential)	93	85	17	12	34	37	£20,969	26
Theological Colleges and Bible Schools (Non-residential)	57	72	18	4	33	45	£5,973	37
Training Centres & Services	100	73	4	3	21	72	£12,000	57
TOTAL TRAINING	**394**	**75**	**11**	**6**	**25**	**58**	**£55,963**	47
GRAND TOTAL 1999	**5,600[4]**	**55**	**9**	**8**	**33**	**50**	**£2,139,843**	45
GRAND TOTAL 1997	5,515	59	12	9	18	61	£1,821,793	51
GRAND TOTAL 1995	5,593	54	14	9	19	58	£1,872,198	50
GRAND TOTAL 1993	5,215	58	14	9	18	59	£1,418,337	53
GRAND TOTAL 1991	4,738	55	11	10	18	61	£1,112,135	54
GRAND TOTAL 1988	4,074	48	10	10	16	64	£774,583	55
GRAND TOTAL 1986	3,580	48	11	11	14	64	£586,395	51

1. Excluding multiple entires
2. Interdenominational/non-denominational/Ecumenical/Evangelical
3. Percentage of organisations on which total figure is estimated
4. Excluding 48 Late Entries and 528 addresses of Other Organisations

EVANGELICAL ALLIANCE MEMBER GROUPS

= Organisation in membership of the Evangelical Alliance which is not listed in the UK Christian Handbook. All other organisations are listed in the UK Christian Handbook and have an asterisk (*) against their entry.

The 174 Trust
40:3 Trust

A Rocha Trust
A.T.Bell Insurance Brokers Ltd
Abernethy Trust Ltd
ACET – Aids Care Education & Training
The Acorn Christian Healing Trust
Act For Christ
Action International Ministries (UK)
#AD Productions
Adept Design
ADMINISTRY
Adullam Homes Housing Association
AFD Enterprises
#Africa
#African Revival Ministries UK
AGAPE
#Agapé Outreach
Aid to Romania
#All for Jesus Ministries
All Nations Christian College
Ambassadors for Christ
Ambassadors in Sport
#Amersham Christian Housing Association
Amethyst Centre For Alcohol Concern
Anchor Recordings Limited
Anglo Japanese Christian Ministries
Anorexia and Bulimia Care
Anthony Collins Solicitors
Anvil Trust
The Apostolic Church
#Aquasports
Aquila Housing Association
Arts Centre Group Limited
Ashburnham Christian Trust
Assemblies of God in Great.Britain.& Ireland
#Assemblies of God Property Trust
Assist Europe
#Association of Biblical Counsellors
Association of Christian Teachers (Scotland)
Association of Christian Teachers
At Home in the Community Ltd

The Baptist Union Mission Department
The Baptist Union of Scotland
The Barn Christian Association For Youth
Barnabas Trust Ltd
Barnabus Project
Bar-N-Bus Trust
Bawtry Hall
BeaconLight Trust
Beckenham & Penge Evangelical Fellowship
Beechwood House Rehabilitation Centre
Betel of Britain
#Bethany (Shropshire) Trust
Bethany Christian Trust
Bethany Ministries
#Bethel Vision Ministries
#Beulah
#Bible Life Family Ministries
#Bible Ministry College International
The Bible Network
Bible Society
Bible Text Publicity Mission
Big Ideas Trust
Birmingham Bible Institute
Birmingham City Mission
Black Christian Civic Forum UK
Blessed Hope of Christ (Evangelical Ministries)
Bournemouth & Poole Bible Convention
Bournemouth Conference Centre Ltd (Slavanka)
Bournemouth Y.M.C.A.
The Boys' Brigade
The Breakout Trust
Breakthrough
Brent Evangelical Alliance
Brentwood & District Evangelical Fellowship
Bridge Christian Community
#Bridges
#Bridges International
Brighton & District Evangelical Alliance
Brighton & Hove Town Mission
Bristol Evangelical Alliance
#Bristol International Student Centre
#Bristol University Christian Union
#British National Temperance League
British Youth for Christ
Bromley Evangelical Fellowship
Brunel Manor Christian Centre

Café.Net
Caladine Stevens
The Campaigners
#Campbeltown Joint Churches Mission Committee
#Cantercare
Capernwray Missionary Fellowship
CARE
The Care Centre
Care For The Family
Care in Crisis
Careforce
Causeway(Prospects)
Centre for Christ Trust
Centre For International Christian Ministries
Challenge Publishing
Chapter & Verse Christian Bookshop
#Cheltenham Youth for Christ
A Child Is Born
Children Worldwide
Children's Evangelism Ministry UK
Chinese Church Support Ministries
Christ for All Nations
#Christ for England School
Christ for the Nations UK
Christian Alliance Housing Association
Christian Book Centre
Christian Camping International UK
Christian Communication Network
Christian Concern, Crewe
Christian Contact
Christian Copyright Licensing
Christian Deaf Link
#Christian Discipleship International
Christian Education – Europe
Christian Endeavour Union of Great Britain & Ireland
Christian English Language Centre
#Christian Faith Ministries
Christian Fellowship Ministry
Christian Focus Publications
Christian Friendship Fellowship
Christian Guidelines
Christian Haven Trust
The Christian Housing Trust
Christian Impact – *see* London Institute for Contemporary Christianity
Christian Insurance
Christian International Relief Mission
Christian Link Association for Single Parents (CLASP)
Christian Literature Crusade
Christian Media Centre Ltd
Christian Medical Fellowship
Christian Motorcyclists Association (UK)
Christian Mountain Centre
Christian Police Association
Christian Publicity Organisation
Christian Research Association
Christian Resources Exhibitions
Christian Resources Projects
The Christian Schools' Trust
Christian Solidarity Worldwide
Christian Support for the Persecuted
#Christian Surfers UK
Christian Television Association
Christian Victory Group-I Care Project
Christian Viewpoint
Christian Vision
Christian Vocations
Christian Women Communicating International Inc. UK
Christian Youth Enterprises
#Christians Against Poverty
Christians in Business – see Christian Resources Centre
Christians in Caring Professions
Christians in Entertainment
Christians in Property
Christians in Science
Christians in Sport
Christians Involved in Derbyshire Schools
Chrysalis Arts Trust
Church of England Evangelical Council
Church of God – Western Europe
Church of God of Prophecy Trust
#Church of Ireland Evangelical Fellowship
Church of Scotland Board of Social Responsibility

Church Pastoral Aid Society
#Churches in Communities
Church's Ministry Among Jewish People
Cities Network – Scotland
#City Light Trust
City of Belfast YMCA
#Clarion Community Development Trust
Clerkenwell Medical Mission
Cliff College
C.net
The Co-Labourers
Coastline Christian Resources
Come Back to God Campaign
Commission – Christian Radio
Community Bible Study – UK
Compassionate Response
#Connections
Cornerstone
#Cornerstone College
#Council of Christians in Commerce
Counselling & Prayer Trust
Countess of Huntingdon's Connexion
Counties
Courage
Covenant Ministries International
Covenanters
Creation Resources Trust
Creation Science Movement
Creative Publishing
Credit Action
Criss Cross
Crocus Ministries
Cross Rhythms
Crossroads Christian Counselling Service
Crusaders Union
Crying Out Loud Trust
Crystal Clear Audio
Cutting Edge Productions
CVG Television
CWR (Crusade For World Revival)

Darash Trust
Daventry Contact
#Dawn (Scotland)
#Daybreak Drug Abuse Project
Daybreak Mission
#Days of Wonder Trust
Dayspring Ministries – Mitcham
DCI Trust
Deaf Christian Network
Deo Gloria Trust
Derbyshire Village Mission
#The Albert Dicken Charitable Trust
Disabled Christians Fellowship
Dominion International Opera Trust
Don Summers Evangelistic Association
#Dudley Stationery Ltd

Eagle
Eagle Ministries
East European Literature Advisory Committee
The East to West Trust
Edinburgh City Mission
Elam Ministries
#Eleos Charitable Trust
Elim Church Headquarters – Ireland
Elim Pentecostal Church Headquarters
Elim Pentecostal Church Headquarters Scotland
Ellel Ministries
Elm Tree Farm Christian Conference Centre
#Elmgrove Centre
Elsdon Mailing
Ethos Communications Ltd
European Christian Mission
Eurovangelism
Evangelical Concern for People with Disabilities
Evangelical Christians for Racial Justice
Evangelical Contribution Northern Ireland
Evangelical Environmental Network
#Evangelical Ministries
Evangelical Peacemakers
#Evangelical United Relief Organisation
Evangelical Urban Training Project
Evangelism Explosion (GB) Ltd
The Evangelism Fellowship
Evangelism Today
The Evangelization Society (TES)
#Eyukamba Foundation

The Faith Mission
Family Foundations Trust
Family Life Foundation
The Family Trust
#Fanning The Flames
Farmers' Christian Postal Service
FCS Cassette Services
Fegans Child & Family Care
Fellowship Finders
Fellowship of Christian Magicians
Fellowship of Churches of Christ
Ffald-y-Brenin Trust
Field Lane Foundation
Finnish Lutheran Mission
Food for the Hungry UK
Forerunner Charitable Trust
The Fountain Gate Community
#Four Twelve Ministries
France Mission Trust
Frank Wright Mundy & Co. Ltd
Free Church of England
Free Church of Scotland
Free Methodist Church in the UK
#Freedom Road Ministries
#Freedom Unlimited
Friends of Turkey (UK)
Full Gospel Business Men's Fellowship International
#Full Gospel Business Men's Fellowship – Bath
Functional English
Fusion
Fellowship for Evangelising Britain's Villages
Fylde Evangelism

#GHOBE Ministries
Gaines Christian Youth Centre
George Muller Foundation
#Gerry Fuller Financial Services
Gilead Foundations Training Centre
The Girls' Brigade England & Wales
Glasgow City Mission
Global Care
Go To The Nations Link
Going Public
Good News Centre Ltd
Good News Crusade
Good News Video Centre
#The Good Shepherd Trust
#The Good Soil Trust
Gospel Cards
#Grampian Evangelical Fellowship
Grandma's
#Great Commission Training Centre
Ground Level Ministry Team
Group for Evangelism and Renewal
Growing Through.....
Guernsey Evangelical Fellowship
Guildford YMCA Ltd
Gypsies for Christ

HCJB – UK
The Haggai Institute
#Hants & Dorset Christian Youth Camp
Hard of Hearing Christian Fellowship
Harvesters Trust
Havering Mission 2000
Headway
#Headway Ireland
Healthcare Christian Fellowship
Heart of England Outreach
Hebron Trust
Helping Hand
The Heralds Trust
#Hesters Way Family Project
Hi Kids!
Home Evangelism
#Homeland Deliverance Centre
#The Hope Foundation
Hope Now Ministries
Hope UK
#Hospital Christian Fellowship of Wales
Hothorpe Hall Conference Centre
Hour of Revival Association
Hove YMCA
Hull Evangelical Alliance
#Hull Youth for Christ

ICI Bible Study
Ichthus Christian Fellowship (HQ)
#Ichthus Community Projects Ltd
Ichthus Motor Mission
#Ignite
Impact Giving UK Trust
Independent Methodist Connexion Churches
Inn Christian Ministries
Institute for Communication & Development Studies
Integrity Music (Europe) Ltd
Intercessors for Britain
INTERDEV UK
#Interface
Interhealth
Interlink Haven
International Student Christian Services
International Bible Society (UK)
International Bible Training Institute
International Christian College
International Films
International Gospel Outreach
International Media for Ministry
International Mission Project
International Teams UK
International Training Network
Interserve Scotland
Inverness & District Evangelical Alliance

Member Bodies

Inverness Crisis Pregnancy Centre
#Inverness Ladies Christian Coffee Club
Ipswich Christian Youth Ministries
#Ipswich Partnership of Evangelical Churches
#Irish Christian Endeavour Union
Irish Christian Study Centre – *see* Belfast Bible College
Irish Mission
The Island Churches of Guernsey Festival Chorus
#Isle of Wight Keswick Association.

Jews For Jesus
Jews for Jesus (UK)
John Grooms Association for Disabled People
John Grooms Housing Association
Joshua Generation
Jubilee Action
Jubilee Centre

#Kent Baptist Association
The Kestrel Trust
The Keswick Convention
Key Services
KeyChange Charity
Kingdom Creative
Kings Communications
King's Lynn Evangelical Alliance
KingsCare
Kingsway Communications Ltd

#Label of Love Limited
Latin Link UK
Lay Witness Movement
#Leaders' Prayer Fortress Ministry
The Legacie Trust
#Lenchwood Christian Centre
Leyton Evangelical Fellowship
Librarian's Christian Fellowship
Life for the World Trust
#Lifeline Ministries
Lifestyle International
#Lighting Fires
Link Ministries
Link Romania
Links International
Living Waters Christian Centres
Living Waters Discipleship & Healing Trust
#The Local EA in the Forest (LEAF)
London & Home Counties Festival Male Voice Praise
London Baptist Association
London Bible College
London Mennonite Centre Trust
Lydia Fellowship (HQ)
Lydia House Trust

Macedonian Evangelical Trust
#Mainstream-Baptists for L & G
Mallon De Ministries
#Malvern Bible Ministry
Manchester City Mission
Manchester Network (ECMA)
#Maranatha Ministries
March for Jesus
#Marpe Shalom Trust
Marriage Ministries International
Marriage Resource
Marriage Review
MasterPlan Publishing Ltd
Mattersey Hall
Matthew Project
MAXCO Trust
Medina Valley Centre
Message to Schools Trust
#Methodist Church Resources Centre
#Mevagissey Christian Fellowship
Michael Roberts Charitable Trust
Mid-Cotswold Evangelical Alliance
#Midwales Christian Holiday Centre
#Midweek in Bristol
Mildmay Mission Hospital
Mill Grove
Mill House Trust
Mimeistry UK
Mission Aviation Fellowship
Mission Care
Mission Doncaster
Mission for Christ-Rural Evangelism
Mission in Hounslow Trust
Mission Supplies Ltd
The Mission Team
Mission To Eastern Europe
#Mission To London
Mission to Marriage
#Missions To Prisons (NGM Trust)
Moorlands College
Morrison Reprographics
Mulberry House
Multiply Christian Network

The Navigators
Nazarene Theological College
#Nehemiah Housing Association
The Nehemiah Project
#"NEST, The New Start Trust U.K"
#The Net
#Net Trust
New English Orchestra
New Frontiers International
New Generation Ministries – see NGM
New Hope Trust
New Testament Church of God
NISSI in Health
Norfolk Broads Summer Cruise
#North West Region of Christian Endeavour
Northants Association of Youth Clubs
#Northern Evangelical Trust
Norwich YMCA
Not Yet
Novi Most International
#Nucleus

Oak Hill Theological College
Oasis Trust
Off The Fence
Old Baptist Union
#The Olive Tree Centre
Olivet English Language School
OMS International
Open Air Campaigners Ministries
Operation Mobilisation (HQ)
Orpington & District Evangelical Council
Outlook Trust
#Outreach Unlimited....
#Overcomers (Scotland)
Overseas Council: TEAM
Overseas Fellowship of Nigerian Christians
Paisley & District Evangelical Alliance
Luis Palau Evangelistic Association
Paraclete Christian Network International
Partnership
Partnership Missions
Passion
PCCA Christian Childcare
Pecan Ltd
Pennefather Christian Medical Communications Trust
People of God
Peterborough Alliance of Christian Evangelical
#The Philippi Trust
The Philo Trust
Pilgrim Hall Christian Trust
Pilgrims Hall Fellowship Ltd
Pioneer Trust
Plumbline Ministries
#Plymouth City Mission
The Pocket Testament League
#Poole Bible Training Centre
Portsmouth Evangelical Fellowship
#Positive Parenting Publications
Post Office & Telecommunications Christian Association
#Power & Glory Day Ministry
#Praise Celebration Trust
Pray for Revival
Prayer For The Nation
#Premier Network Ministries
Premier Radio
#Presbyterian Church in Ireland-Board of Social Witness
Presbyterian Youth Board (Ireland)
#Preston Evangelical Network
Prison Fellowship – Scotland
Prison Fellowship England & Wales
Prison Fellowship Northern Ireland
Probation Service Christian Fellowship
Project Evangelism
Prospects
#The Protekton Trust
The Public Transport Scripture Text Mission
Purley & Andover Christian Trust

#ROPE Charitable Trust
Radiant Life Ministries
Radstock Ministries
#Ramparts Christian School
#Rayleigh Christian Ministries Trust
REACH Merseyside
Reach Out Ministries
Reachout Trust
Reconciliation Ministries International
Redcliffe College
#Redeemed Christian Church of God
Reelife Recordings
Regents Theological College
Reprotec (Office Solutions) Ltd
Resurrection Theatre Company
#Rhema Consultants Ltd
Rhos-Llyn Christian Centre
Richard Miller Audio Systems
Ridley Hall Theological College
River of Life Trust
Rodd & Marco-The Acts Drama Trust
Romanian Aid Fund
Romanian Missionary Society
Royal Sailors' Rests

Rural Sunrise
Rushworth Literature Enterprise

#St Christopher's One World Group
St John's College – Durham
St John's College – Nottingham
#St Mary Magdalene School
The Salmon Youth Centre in Bermondsey
Salt & Light Ministries
Saltbox Christian Centre
Saltmine Trust
The Salvation Army (UK)
#Salvation Army Candle Project
Sanctuary Counselling and Training
Scottish Christian Alliance Ltd
Scottish Crusaders
#Scottish Gospel Outreach
Scripture Gift Mission Incorporated – *see* SGM
Scripture Union
Scripture Union Scotland
Seacare (Christian Care Projects)
Seamen's Christian Friends Society
SEAN International
Seed BMI
Send the Light Ltd
Servants Fellowship International
Servants to Asia's Urban Poor
Shaftesbury Society
Share Trust
Sightlink *see* Fellowship for Visually Handicapped
SIM International (UK)
Soapbox Communications Trust
#The SOAR Trust
Social Workers' Christian Fellowship
Solent Christian Trust
The Soteria Trust
South Asian Concern
South Bristol Christian Centre
South Bristol Outreach Trust
South East Essex Evangelical Alliance
#South Wales Christian Outreach Trust
#South Wessex Evangelical Alliance
South West London Asian Outreach
Southampton Action For Employment
Southampton Asian Christian Outreach
Southampton City Mission
Southampton Evangelical Alliance
Southeast Asian Outreach
Southport Methodist Holiness Convention
#Southwark For Jesus
Sovereign Giving
Sovereign World Trust
#Sowers Prayer Fellowship
Spinnaker Trust
#Spirit Led Ministries Network
Spitalfields Crypt Trust
Spotlight Wales
Spring Harvest
#Springboard Coventry
Springdale College
Springs Dance Company
SPUC Evangelicals
Spurgeons College
Stamps for Evangelism
The Stapleford Centre
Stepping Stones Christian Training Project
The Stepping Stones Trust
Stewardship Services (UKET)
Stress and Life Trust (SALT)
#Stroud & District Evangelical Alliance Fraternal
Summer Crusades Trust
#Sunrise Video Productions
Swanwick Ladies Conference
Swindon Evangelical Alliance
#Switch Active Help Project

Tandem TV & Film Limited
Taunton Evangelical Alliance
#TBF Thompson Ministries
Teachers For China
#Team Thrust for the Nations (UK)
Tearfund
Teen Challenge (Newport & Gwent)
Teen Challenge UK
Teeside Evangelical Alliance
Telephone Prayer Chain Ministry
#Thamesdown Youth For Christ
There Is Hope
Third Wave Group of Companies
Through The Roof
Time Ministries International
Tiverton & District Evangelical Fellowship
#Together For Sheffield
Together For The Harvest
#Torbay Evangelical Fellowship
Torch Trust for the Blind
Touchstones (London & South East)
#Tower Hamlets Evangelical Alliance
Toxteth Evangelical Association
Toy Box Charity
Trans World Radio
#Tredegar & District Free Church Council
Trinity Care plc
Trinity College
True Freedom Trust
#The True Vine Prayer Fellowship
Tunbridge Wells Fellowship of Evangelicals
The Turnpike Trust
The Twenty Five Trust
Twenty Thirty
Tynddol Trust

UCCF Business Study Group
United Christian Broadcasters – *see* UCB
United Free Church of Scotland
Universal Prayer Group Ministries
#Upminster Christ.Ent.Ltd (Fools)
#Urban Action – North Manchester
Urban Presence
U-Turn Anglia Trust

Victory Tracts & Posters
Video Bible Teaching Ministry
#Vine Care Pregnancy Crisis Centre
#Vinesong
Vision Broadcasting Ministries
#Vision Crusades Trust
The Viva Network
Viz-a-Viz
Voice of Renewal UK International

#Wales Awake
Wallington Missionary Mart & Auctions
Wanstead & Woodford Evangelical Council
#Watford New Hope Trust
Wayside Training Centre
Wellspring Christian Trust
#Wellspring Trust
Wesleyan Reform Union
#West Ham Central Mission
#Wight Evangelical Alliance Fellowship
Willow Creek Association – UK – *see* WCA-UK
#Wirral Christian Drugs Action
#Wolverhampton Evangelical Fellowship
Women's Aglow Fellowship – Northern Ireland
Women's Aglow Fellowship – Britain
Won Across
Word Entertainment Ltd – *see* Word Music and Publishing
Word of Life
World Action Ministries
World Emergency Relief
World Horizons
#World Literature Crusade
World Vision UK
WorldShare
#Worldwide Christian Publications
Worldwide Harvest Ministries

Yeldall Christian Centres
Youth for Christ – Northern Ireland
Youth Ministries International
Youth With A Mission
Youth With A Mission – Liverpool
Youth With A Mission – Scotland
Youth With A Mission – Northern Ireland

The Zacharias Trust
#Zephaniah Trust

In addition to the member organisations listed above, the Evangelical Alliance at 8th June 1999 had 44,887 personal members, 3,066 church members and 729 other group members, plus churches whose denomination is in membership.

EVANGELICAL MISSIONARY ALLIANCE

Member Bodies of the Evangelical Missionary Alliance are asterisked (*) against their entry in the *Handbook*

Full members (124)
ACET (AIDS Care, Education & Training)
Action International Ministries UK
Action Partners Ministries
AE Evangelistic Enterprise
Africa Inland Mission
Agapé Ministries Ltd
All India Mission
Ambassadors for Christ Britain
Anglo-Japanese Christian Ministries
AOG World Ministries
Apostolic Church
Arab World Ministries
Areopagus Romania Trust
Asia Link
Baptist Missionary Society
Belgian Evangelical Mission
Bible Mission International
Bible Society
Book Aid
Care For Mission
Cedars
China Ministries International
Chinese Church Support Ministries
Christian Blind Mission (UK)
Christian International Relief Mission
Christian Literature Crusade
Christian Medical Fellowship
Christian Outreach (CORD)
Christian Publicity Organisation
Christian Research
Christian Vocations
Christians in Action
Christians in Communications
Church Mission Society
Crosslinks
Crusaders
East African Ministries Trust
Edinburgh Medical Missionary Society
Elam Ministries
Emmanuel International Ltd
Europe Now
European Christian Mission (Britain)
FEBA Radio
Fellowship of Faith for the Muslims
Focus Radio
FOI Ministries
France Mission Trust
The Free Methodist Church UK
Frontiers
GAP International
Global March for Jesus
Global Outreach UK
Gorakhpur Nurseries Fellowship
Gospel Broadcasting System Ltd
Gospel Printing Mission
Haggai Institute
Latin Link
Links International
Media Associates International
Medical Missionary Association
Medical Service Ministries
The Messianic Testimony
Mid-Africa Ministry (CMS)
Middle East Christian Outreach
Middle East Media
Mission Aviation Fellowship
Mission Encouragement
Mission Supplies
The Navigators
North West Frontier Fellowship
Novi Most International
Oasis Charitable Trust
OMF International (UK)
OMS International
Open Doors with Brother Andrew
Operation Mobilisation
Overseas Council TEAM
People International
Pocket Testament League
Prayer Fellowship for South Asia
Preacher's Help
Presbyterian Church in Ireland
Qua Iboe Fellowship
Radio Worldwide
Radstock Ministries
Red Sea Mission Team
Release International
Romanian Aid Fund
Rushworth
Samaritan's Purse International Ltd
Scripture Union
Servants to Asia's Urban Poor
SGM International
Sierra Leone Mission
Sightlink
SIM International (UK)
Slavic Gospel Association
South American Mission Society
South Asian Concern
Southeast Asian Outreach
Stamps for Evangelism
TASK (Training & Advice for Service in the Kingdom)
Teachers for China
Tearfund
The Leprosy Mission
Titus Ministries Worldwide
Trans World Radio
UFM Worldwide
Vision International Healthcare Ltd
The Viva Network
Wallington Missionary Mart & Auctions
WEC International
WMA-UK
World Gospel Mission
World Horizons
World in Need
WorldShare
Worldwide Missions Outreach Ministries
Worldwide Missionary Convention
Wycliffe Associates (UK)
Wycliffe Bible Translators
YWAM England
Zambesi Mission

Member Colleges (20)
All Nations Christian College
Belfast Bible College
Bible College of Wales
Birmingham Bible Institute
Evangelical Theological College of Wales
Faith Mission Bible College
International Christian College
International Training Network
London Bible College
Moorlands College
Nazarene Theological College
Oxford Centre for Mission Studies
Redcliffe College
Regents Theological College
Southall School of Languages & Missionary Orientation
St John's Extension Studies
Tilsley College
Trinity College
Veritas College

Affiliated Members (4)
Antioch Mission
Finnish Lutheran Mission
Gospel Missionary Union
Worldteam UK

MEMBER BODIES OF:

CHURCHES TOGETHER IN BRITAIN AND IRELAND

An asterisk (*) in this list indicates membership of the World Council of Churches

Full Members (32)
*Baptist Union of Great Britain
Cherubim and Seraphim Council of Churches
*Church in Wales
*Church of England
*Church of Ireland
*Church of Scotland
Congregational Federation
Council of African and Afro-Caribbean Churches
Council for Oriental Orthodox Christian Churches
Free Churches' Council
*Greek Orthodox Church
Independent Methodist Churches
International Ministerial Council of Great Britain
Joint Council for Anglo-Caribbean Churches
Lutheran Council of Great Britain
*Methodist Church
*Methodist Church in Ireland
*Moravian Church
New Testament Assembly
*Presbyterian Church of Wales
Religious Society of Friends Britain Yearly Meeting
Roman Catholic Church in England and Wales
Roman Catholic Church in Scotland
*Russian Orthodox Church
Salvation Army UK Territory
*Scottish Congregational Church
*Scottish Episcopal Church
*Serbian Orthodox Church
*Undeb Yr Annibynwyr Cymraeg (Union of Welsh Independents)
*United Free Church of Scotland
*United Reformed Church
Wesleyan Holiness Church

Bodies in Association (23)
Action by Christians Against Torture
Association of Centres of Adult Theological Education
Association of Interchurch Families
Centre for Black and White Christian Partnership
Christian Council on Ageing
Christian Education Movement
Christianity and the Future of Europe
Church Action on Poverty
Churches' Council for Health and Healing
Churches' East West European Relations Network
Ecumenical Committee for Corporate Responsibility
Feed the Minds
Fellowship of St Alban and St Sergius
Iona Community
Irish School of Ecumenics
Living Stones
National Association of Christian Communities and Networks
National Christian Education Council
New Assembly of Churches
William Temple Foundation
Women's Inter-Church Council
YMCA
YWCA

Associate Members (2)
Roman Catholic Church in Ireland
Seventh Day Adventist Church

THE CHURCHES' COMMISSION ON MISSION

Member Bodies (37)
Baptist Missionary Society
Baptist Union of Great Britain
Catholic Church in England and Wales [1]
Catholic Fund for Overseas Development
Catholic Institute for International Relations
Centre for Black and White Christian Partnership
Cherubim and Seraphim Council of Churches
Christian Aid
Christian Education Movement
Christians Abroad
Christians Aware
Churches' Commission on Overseas Students
Church in Wales
Church Mission Society Ireland
Church of England
Church of Scotland
Feed the Minds
Free Church Federal Council
Grassroots
Greek Orthodox Church
Independent Methodist Churches
International Ministerial Council of Great Britain
Interserve
Irish Missionary Union
Leprosy Mission
Methodist Church
Methodist Church in Ireland
Presbyterian Church of Wales
Salvation Army (UK Territory)
Scottish Congregational Church
Scottish Episcopal Church
Selly Oak School of World Mission
Society of Friends/Quaker Peace Service
Union of Welsh Independents
United Reformed Church
World Conference – a Family of Christian Youth Organisations
YMCA

[1] Denominational organisations (eg mission societies) are included in this membership

RELIGION IN BRITAIN 1900 TO 2000

Dr Peter Brierley, Executive Director,
Christian Research

"God is losing market share, awareness, trial and repeat purchase"[1].

"There is no logical quantitative connection between the number of people who go to church and those who recognise within themselves a spiritual need, even if it surfaces only occasionally. You might as well say that the only people interested in politics are those who go to meetings or are members of a political party"[2].

INTRODUCTION

The above quotations give the false impression that religion, or at least Christianity the majority religion, is about to fade out in this country. Not at all! They mislead because they give no indication of the huge numbers of people who profess to be religious, nor do they indicate that the *rate* of change is relatively small. There are far more Christians around than people think, and likely to be so for the foreseeable future.

"Religion" is a comprehensive word which can stir the deepest emotions – witness Northern Ireland. At the same time it can stretch the finest intellect – "theology" it used to be said was "the queen of the sciences". Durkheim gives three aspects of religion – belief, practice and affiliation; we will briefly look at all three in this Introduction. The first is internal, measured usually by asking people individually; the second and third are external and at least theoretically measured by observation.

Religious statistics are relatively few, and are not spread equally across these three measures, nor uniformly across the century. Since the observable presence of religions other than Christianity has only been a phenomena of recent decades, most of the data relate to Christianity. In addition, key data is missing for some years, and is estimated where necessary. Nor is the data comprehensive – some denominational data, especially for the many smaller denominations, is simply not available for early decades. Some data, like membership, is collected according to different definitions[3], or at different times of the year[4].

MEASURING RELIGIOUS PEOPLE: COMMUNITY

There are three broad ways of counting religious people – their community, their membership and their attendance. The first two would both come under Durkheim's concept of affiliation. Looking first at Community[5], we here focus mainly on data for the Trinitarian churches[6]. Table 1 gives estimated figures for the Trinitarian church community, made up of the baptised population for the Anglicans[7] and Roman Catholics and estimates for the other denominations, and for all other religions (Jews, Hindus, Muslims, Sikhs and others) and Non-Trinitarian churches. There is one other source for the total religious picture for 1900, but not unfortunately for intermediate years – David Barrett's *World Christian Encyclopedia*[8]. He suggests a higher number of Anglicans (25.1 million) and a higher total figure for Other Protestants (9.5 against 7.2 in Table 1) making Christians 97% of the population. This appears unreasonably high.

Table 1: Christian and Religious Community in millions in the UK 1900–2000

Year	Anglican	Roman Catholic	Presbyterian	Methodist	Baptist	Others[2]	TOTAL Christian Number	TOTAL Christian % Pop[3]	Other Religions	TOTAL Number	TOTAL % Pop[3]
1900	23.1	2.5	3.2	1.7	0.7	1.6	**32.8**	*86%*	0.2	**33.0**	*86%*
1910	25.4	2.7	3.4	1.8	0.8	1.8	**35.9**	*85%*	0.3	**36.2**	*86%*
1920	26.3	2.9	3.5	1.7	0.8	1.8	**37.0**	*84%*	0.4	**37.4**	*85%*
1930	27.1	3.2	3.5	1.8	0.8	1.8	**38.2**	*83%*	0.5	**38.7**	*84%*
1940	27.6	3.5	3.5	1.7	0.8	1.8	**38.9**	*82%*	0.7	**39.6**	*83%*
1950	28.5	4.0	3.5	1.7	0.7	1.7	**40.1**	*80%*	0.8	**40.9**	*81%*
1960	27.6[1]	4.8	3.5	1.7	0.6	1.7	**39.9**	*77%*	1.1	**41.0**	*78%*
1970	27.8[1]	5.4	3.1	1.5	0.6	1.6	**40.0**	*72%*	1.9	**41.9**	*75%*
1980	27.7	5.7	2.8	1.4	0.6	1.6	**39.8**	*71%*	2.6	**42.4**	*75%*
1990	26.6	5.6	2.7	1.4	0.6	1.7	**38.6**	*67%*	3.6	**42.2**	*73%*
2000	25.6	5.8	2.6	1.3	0.5[1]	1.9	**37.7**	*64%*	4.5	**42.2**	*71%*

[1] Revised figure [2] Independent, Orthodox, Pentecostal, New and Other Churches
[3] Including Northern Ireland population prior to 1921

Table 1 indicates that there is a considerable number of Christian people in the United Kingdom, and that although their percentage in the population has decreased throughout the century, their actual numbers remain considerable. The critical estimates in the above Table are for the Church of England – its baptised population is very difficult to assess. Table 1 suggests a 2 million drop in the last 20 years which if discounted would make the Christian percentage of the population 67% in 2000 instead of 64%. Note also the growth of Catholics in the last 50 years, due to immigration, and the small but real impact of the New Churches in the Other column for 1990 and 2000.

The rise of the other religions in the latter third of the twentieth century is apparent also from this Table making the number of religious people in the population almost static. Thus this Table does not suggest the demise of religion in the UK, but rather a slow change to include faiths other than Christianity and a relatively stationary number of religious people which is not growing as the population increases. The percentages given in this Table are similar to the percentages who say they believe in God.

MEASURING RELIGIOUS PEOPLE: MEMBERSHIP

Unlike the religious community, there is much data on church membership, almost too much. In 1999 there were 247 different denominations in the UK, a figure which has considerably increased since the first count of 97 in 1977[9]. As just three of these – the Church of England, Roman Catholic Church in England and the Church of Scotland – accounted for 64% of total membership in 1995, it may be seen how relatively small are the other 240, yet cumulatively important. (It also may be seen how *institutional* church life stands in the UK, part of the culture we share with Europe, the only continent where it is so, reflecting perhaps our history of Empire – institutionalism in essence – through the last two millennia[10].)

Part of the problem of measuring across the century is that many of the smaller denominations did not publish figures of membership in early years; they have been assessed comprehensively only since 1970, but Robert Currie is an excellent source for many of the detailed figures, and not just for the 20th century[11]. A summary of the main figures is published in *Religious Trends* No.2 2000/2001. One other attempt has been made to fill in these gaps[12], but a comprehensive assessment has only been made with the production of *Religious Trends* No.2 2000/2001 from which these members come. Note that the unit has changed from millions to thousands. The Roman Catholics do not have any figures corresponding to membership. They call their community figures membership, so their figures below relate to Mass attendance, a convention long followed in the *UK Christian Handbook*, initially at their request.

Table 2: Christian and Religious Membership in thousands in the UK 1900–2000

Year	Anglican	Roman Catholic	Presbyterian	Methodist	Baptist	Others²	TOTAL Christian Number	% Pop³	Other Religions	TOTAL Number	% Pop³
1900	3,241	1,912¹	1,649	849	360	644	**8,664**	*33%*	164	**8,828**	*34%*
1905	3,336	1,965¹	1,739	908	417	726	**9,091**	*33%*	171	**9,262**	*34%*
1910	3,480	1,995¹	1,766	918	412	733	**9,704**	*33%*	179	**9,833**	*34%*
1915	3,871	2,064¹	1,783	900	403	761	**9,782**	*32%*	183	**9,965**	*33%*
1920	3,820	2,107¹	1,816	877	399	779	**9,803**	*31%*	194	**9,997**	*31%*
1925	4,120	2,176¹	1,852	911	404	825	**10,288**	*31%*	202	**10,490**	*31%*
1930	4,166	2,190¹	1,829	918	400	854	**10,357**	*29%*	209	**10,566**	*30%*
1935	4,124	2,205¹	1,840	894	391	838	**10,292**	*29%*	227	**10,519**	*29%*
1940	3,911	2,232¹	1,822	862	376	814	**10,017**	*27%*	244	**10,261**	*28%*
1945	3,670	2,247¹	1,790	815	352	808	**9,682**	*26%*	258	**9,940**	*26%*
1950	3,444	2,432¹	1,796	809	334	799	**9,614**	*25%*	270	**9,884**	*25%*
1955	3,397	2,567	1,827	798	320	809	**9,773**	*25%*	375	**10,148**	*26%*
1960	3,341	2,845¹	1,814	789	317	812	**9,918**	*24%*	471	**10,389**	*26%*
1965	3,174	2,793¹	1,791	761	290	839	**9,648**	*23%*	580	**10,228**	*25%*
1970	2,987	2,746	1,951	673	272	843	**9,272**	*22%*	732	**10,004**	*24%*
1975	2,298	2,525	1,718	602	238	679	**8,060**	*19%*	885	**8,945**	*21%*
1980	2,180	2,455	1,437	540	239	678	**7,529**	*17%*	1,088	**8,617**	*19%*
1985	1,896	2,281	1,322	497	242	705	**6,943**	*15%*	1,300	**8,243**	*18%*
1990	1,728	2,198	1,214	478	230	776	**6,624**	*14%*	1,527	**8,151**	*17%*
1995	1,785	1,914	1,088	434	223	841	**6,285**	*13%*	1,800	**8,085**	*17%*
2000	1,657	1,722	979	387	209	908	**5,862**	*12%*	1,962	**7,824**	*17%*

¹ Estimate ² Independent, Congregational, Orthodox, Pentecostal, New & Other Churches
³ Adult population, including Northern Ireland population prior to 1921

Table 2 shows that church membership is always much less than the community figure, from over a third (37%) at the beginning of the century to a fifth (20%) at the end. The pattern exhibited in this Table is typical however of most individual denominations – membership grew in absolute terms from 1900 to the 1930s, despite the First World War. It dropped a little in the depression of the 1930s, and the Second World War (despite the thesis that war often helps people turn to God[13]) in the 1940s, but recovered a little (mostly because of immigration) in the 1950s. The really big drops occurred in the "Swinging Sixties" and the 1970s, though perhaps half a million of this is definitional change[14], since when the decline has continued at a high but slightly lesser pace. The growth of Other Churches in the latter part of the century is easily observable in Table 2, but, important though it is, is not of sufficient magnitude to offset large losses elsewhere. Why the decline was so great in the 1970s is not known; it could be partly the age factor (a lot of older members died), it might have been a disillusionment with religion because of educational changes, or a change in the loyalty of the middle classes, the impact of widespread television in leisure habits, or the increase in sporting events (which has certainly been one cause of the decline in the later decades).

Likewise the growth in Other Religions is obvious in the last third of the century, again mainly through immigration. This increase does not however totally offset the decline in the Christian churches.

It is important to realise that this decline in membership parallels the decline in membership of many other institutions in the latter part of the 20th century. Thus while the Christian church membership in the UK may have decreased 21% between 1980 and 2000, the decline in the Trade Union movement over the same period was 55%. Dr Grace Davie deliberately subtitles her book[16] "Believing without Belonging" to describe this societal, not just religious, change. It is, she says, "the most significant feature of British, and indeed European, religion at the turn of the millennium."[17]

Hidden in the Others column is the fact that while some denominations have remained fairly static over the 20th century, others have decreased, and three especially have grown – the Orthodox, New and Pentecostal Churches. All three have seen the starting of many new congregations in the last 30 years, all have relatively small congregations with often authoritative leadership unburdened by a dominant hierarchy in terms of local freedom for action, with a specific spirituality. The rapid growth of these three indicates the danger of proclaiming the death of God or the Christian Church in Britain.

MEASURING RELIGIOUS PEOPLE: ATTENDANCE

A visible behavioural manifestation of a person's religious belief is their attendance at religious services or meetings. But attendance has not been measured very often, although numbers of communicants for the Anglican[18] and Presbyterian churches are available since 1900. The first count of attendance was in 1851 as part of the Census of Population in England and Wales; depending on how the figures are taken, the percentage attending church that day was 39%, *including* those who went two or three times[19]. (If the same percentage of "twicers" which were counted in 1903 applied in 1851, then this figure would reduce to 24% of the population in church that Sunday). Robin Gill has spent much time analysing these figures in detail[20].

One major large scale study of London[21] was undertaken by the *Daily News* between November 1902 and November 1903. This sought to count everyone entering every place of

Table 3: Religious Belief and Disbelief in Britain since 1940

Year	Believe in ...							Do not believe in ...					
	God	God as Spirit	Jesus as Son of God	Life after death	Devil	Exchange... dead[1]	Ghosts	God	Jesus as a man[2]	Life after death	Devil	Exchange.. dead[1]	Ghosts
	%	%	%	%	%	%	%	%	%	%	%	%	%
1940+[3]	*81*	*38*	*68*	*49*	*24*	*15*	*15*	*n/a*	*18*	*21*	*54*	*59*	*64*
1960s	*78*	*39*	*62*	*49*	*28*	*n/a*	*n/a*	*10*	*22*	*23*	*52*	*n/a*	*n/a*
1970s	*70*	*38*	*n/a*	*37*	*20*	*11*	*19*	*15*	*n/a*	*42*	*70*	*79*	*73*
1980s	*71*	*39*	*49*	*43*	*24*	*14*	*28*	*18*	*38*	*40*	*64*	*77*	*65*
1990s	*71*	*40*	*n/a*	*44*	*26*	*14*	*32*	*27*	*n/a*	*42*	*67*	*80*	*58*

[1] Exchange messages with the dead
[2] Jesus as just a man/story
[3] 1940/50s

worship in a specific Borough of London for every service, counting a different Borough each week. The conclusion of the report's author is interesting: "The outstanding lesson of the Census is that the power of preaching is undiminished. Wherever there is the right man in the pulpit there are few, if any, empty pews"[22]. *Excluding* twicers, the percentage of the population who attended church in London was 19% each Sunday, 43% of whom were Church of England, 43% Free Churches, 8% Roman Catholic, and 6% "other services". Whether this 19% applied throughout the whole country is of course not known.

A Mass-Observation survey in 1948/49 found that 15% of the population attended church[23]. In 1979 the English Church Census found 12% of the population (11% of adults and 14% of children) attended on an average week[24], and the 1989 Census 10%[25]. The Welsh Church Census of 1982 found 15% of the population (13% of adults and 21% of children[26]); the Welsh Churches Survey of 1995 9% (9% of adults and 8% of children[27]). In Scotland in 1984 17% of the population (17% of adults and 19% of children) attended weekly[28]; by 1994 this was 15%[29]. No survey of church attendance has been undertaken in Northern Ireland.

Putting these together indicates that Scotland is more religious than Wales (if church attendance is the judge of religiousness), and Wales more than England in the 1980s but not 1990s. The figures as a whole indicate that there has been a decline in church attendance over the century, but this decline is in fact very small and slow (if the London figure of 1903 is taken for the whole country). To reduce from 19% in 1903 to 15% in 1951 to 12% in 1979 to 10% in 1989 and an estimated 8% in 2000[30] is a decline of 0.6% compound per annum. However at current attendance levels, there is a decline of over 2,000 people per week, half of whom are under 20 years of age[31]. But, as before, whilst the decline is real, it shows a huge residual strength, more than is generally realised.

Of great importance in earlier years was the numbers attending Sunday School, which reached their peak in the 1880s[32]. "In 1957, 76% of those over 30 had at some time attended Sunday School"[33]; in 1992 it was 41%, "many of whom would now be over 50"[34]. Historical figures across the century have been collated[35]. The 1989 English Church Census collected Sunday School figures by denomination and county, showing about 7% of children then attended[36]. Many studies have been undertaken by Leslie Francis on young people[37, 38, 39].

BELIEF

Religion is notoriously difficult to define but at its most basic it is a system of beliefs and practices in response to God or gods[40]. The core of much religious literature is a description of or an exhortation to belief, but attempting to measure what is believed and by whom only began in any coherent way with the development of the market research industry just before the Second World War. A list of all the studies which included religious questions has been compiled[41], and analysed[42] by those answering such questions both positively and negatively. Table 3 extracts both sets of answers for data measured first in the 1940/50s.

Much could be written about the figures in Table 3; they suggest that what has happened since the Second World War is not so much a relatively small decline of religious belief in Britain but rather a much greater increase of disbelief. This supports the thesis of this Introduction that Christianity is more widely spread in the population than is commonly supposed, but also indicates that the divide between Christian and non-Christian is becoming sharper.

Other measurements of belief have been largely confined to the huge European Values Systems Study in 1981[43, 44] and 1990[45, 46]. Their results are not dissimilar to Table 3, but include like measurements for other countries in Europe and beyond.[47]

It could be argued that belief is reflected in the number of baptisms, confirmations and church marriages. Some of the

Table 4: Estimated number of church buildings or congregations by denomination 1900–2000

Year	Anglican	Roman Catholic	Presbyterian	Baptist	Independent	Methodist	New and Pentecostal	Orthodox and all Others	TOTAL Number	Per 10,000 pop.	Members per church
1900	20,079	2,272	5,923	4,424	7,015	7,404	0	1,871	**48,988**	12.8	177
1910	20,707	2,566	5,988	5,048	7,231	7,772	2	1,930	**51,244**	12.2	189
1920	20,976	2,765	6,117	4,990	7,184	8,121	26	1,856	**52,035**	11.8	188
1930	21,152	3,075	5,857	5,107	7,588	8,507	402	2,371	**54,059**	11.7	192
1940	21,393	3,452	5,399	5,104	7,568	8,891	782	2,339	**54,928**	11.5	182
1950	20,956	3,850	5,090	5,045	7,287	9,249	809	2,385	**54,671**	10.9	176
1960	20,677	3,972	4,822	4,882	7,181	9,613	1,092	2,521	**54,760**	10.4	181
1970	20,417	4,058	4,409	3,588	7,280	9,950	1,358	2,155	**53,215**	9.6	171
1980	19,399	4,156	5,920	3,317	4,294	8,517	2,013	2,222	**49,838**	8.8	151
1990	18,823	4,334	5,492	3,438	4,101	7,625	3,291	2,491	**49,595**	8.6	134
2000	18,307	4,276	5,074	3,430	3,889	6,746	4,467	2,506	**48,695**	8.2	120

relevant data on baptisms is available across the century, and is given in *Religious Trends* No.2 2000/2001. The figures show that over three-quarters of infants were baptised up to 1960, a percentage which had slipped to just under half by 1990, although it rose to 50% for the years 1993 to 1995[48]. The size of these percentages supports a huge sub-culture of belief, and Christian belief at that.

Confirmation figures for the Church of England suggest that 6% of 15 to 19 year olds were confirmed up to 1960, with a decreasing percentage thereafter[49]. About 40% of those baptised were confirmed about 15 years later, a percentage which again held up to 1960, but had decreased to half that figure by 2000.

Belief may also be said to be reflected in the proportions getting married in a religious building, invariably a church or synagogue prior to 1980. 85% of all marriages in England and Wales had a religious ceremony in 1900, a percentage which had declined to 74% by 1930, 70% by 1960, 53% by 1990 and an estimated 40% by 2000[50]. There are two trends to be noted. With the increasing incidence of divorce, many divorcees re-marrying either can't or don't wish to re-marry in church, reducing the proportion of religious marriages. In 1993 for instance 64% of those marrying for the first time were married in church. Secondly, since 1996 it has been legal to marry in places other than a registered religious building or registry office; many couples now choose other settings, some of whom might previously have married in church. The majority of religious marriages are Church of England (79% in 1900, 64% in 2000), followed by the Roman Catholics (5% in 1900, 19% in 2000). About 7% are Methodist, 2% Baptist, 2% Congregational, 2–4% Other Protestants, and 1% Jewish. Detailed historical figures are available[51], as are figures for Scotland[52] and Northern Ireland[53], some are given in *Religious Trends* No.2.

72% of people are cremated at death, virtually all with a religious ceremony. Most of the other 29% are buried likewise.

A number of studies have looked at young people's beliefs. Leslie Francis has surveyed 500 secondary school pupils every 4 years by asking them 24 questions about Christianity, some positive and some negative[55]. They show fewer agreements with positive statements on the church (27% in 1974, 14% in 1994), prayer (44% and 27%) and God (42% and 26%), but continue to agree about Jesus (32% to 25%).

CHURCH BUILDINGS

One other church series may be of interest – the number of church buildings[56] (or congregations where groups do not meet in an ecclesiastical building).

Table 4 (previous page) shows a remarkable consistency in the number of churches in the UK in the 20th century, the number varying between 49,000 and 57,000, the peak in 1930. The increase due to the New and Pentecostal Church planting philosophy may be seen in the later years in the All Others column.

Whilst the number of churches has not kept up with population growth, the size of each church has kept above 150 people for the first 90 years, only dropping in the 1990s as societal disaffection with membership began to make inroads on church membership also. These figures, and the earlier ones, do not support Bryan Wilson's secularisation thesis of behaviour without belief; rather belief persists even if some religious behaviour decreases. They do however support David Martin's forecast in the rise of small denominations and an increase in implicit religion.

FULL-TIME CHURCH PEOPLE

The number of full-time clergy across all denominations in 1900 is estimated as 45,408. In 1980 there were 35,700, but this is estimated to drop by 6% to 33,700 in 2000[57]. As well as these serving the church in the UK there were also 7,900 missionaries of all denominations serving overseas in 1980, 8,100 by 1999; 37% of these serve in Africa, 28% in Asia and India, and 19% in Europe[58].

8% of the ministers were female in 1990, 13% in 1994, against 58% of missionaries in 1991 and 57% in 1995[59], reflecting something of the desire for women to serve even if unable to enter the ordained ministry in the UK. It will be interesting to see how much these proportions will change subsequent to the ordination of women by the Church of England in 1994. The age of clergy in the Church of England is available for various years[60] – about half are between 45 and 60 – but is not available for missionaries.

In summary then, in the Millennium, Britain will have a smaller Christian core valuing integrity, a continuing wider vaguer Christian penumbra, with a religious fringe beyond that including the other religions. Belief will be real for the few, but disappearing in the many. It will be a different world from the one grandfather even imagined, but still one where faith is worth having!

NOTES

1. Skywalker, Luke, April/May 1998 issue, article "Ethics in Business", *Ethos* magazine.
2. McLeish, Robert, 1996, *Word on the Box*, Paternoster Publishing, Carlisle, edited by David Porter, Page 9.
3. Thus, for example, the Church of England Electoral Roll, used here as a proxy for membership, is measured by the number of people who have signed the Roll, the qualifications being that they have lived in the parish (or attended the church) for at least six months and are over 15 years of age (it used to be 16 years). Baptist membership on the other hand counts, in the main, those adults who have been baptised by immersion. Pentecostals ask for evidence of a person being born again, living an upright Christian life for at least six months, and speaking in tongues.
4. Thus the Church of England collect attendance figures usually in May, or May and other times of the year, the Roman Catholics use the last Sunday in October, and the Methodists the end of the year. Whilst these are real differences, the speed at which religious statistics normally change are sufficiently slow for these timing differences to be inconsequential.
5. Community is taken as all those who belong, or are affiliated, or in any way associated, however vaguely, to a religion. It would include those baptised as babies, for example, even if they have nothing to do with a church subsequently in later life.
6. Trinitarian churches are those who accept the historic formulary of the Godhead as the three eternal persons, God the Father, God the Son and God the Holy Spirit, in one unchanging Essence. Groups not included are listed in Brierley, P W, 1999, *Religious Trends* No 2, 2000/2001 edition, Christian Research and HarperCollins*Religious*, London, Pages 10.2-5.
7. Op cit (Item 6), Table 2.7
8. Barrett, Rev Dr David, 1982, *World Christian Encyclopedia*, Oxford University Press, Oxford, United Kingdom Table 1, Page 699
9. Op cit (Item 6) Table 8.14.3
10. This is followed through in more detail in Brierley, P W, 1998, *Future Church,* Monarch Publications, Crowborough.

11. Currie, Robert, Gilbert, Alan, and Horsley, Lee, 1974, *Churches and Churchgoers*, Oxford University Press, Oxford, Appendices.
12. Hadaway, C Kirk, and Marler, Penny Long, *The Measurement and Meaning of Religious Involvement in Great Britain,* paper unpublished at time of writing.
13. Op cit (Item 11).
14. A major component of the decline in the 1970s is the decrease in the Church of England membership. These figures, based on the Electoral Roll, went through a key definition change in 1972, whereby all on the Roll had to sign afresh after every six years. This meant that those who had moved away or deceased were automatically taken off. This pruning was especially marked when it first took place in 1972. See also op cit (Item 6), Figure 8.5.4.
15. Brierley, Dr P W, editor, 1997, *Religious Trends* No. 1, 1998/99, Christian Research and Paternoster Publishing.
16. Davie, Dr Grace, 1994, *Religion in Britain since 1945*, Blackwell, Oxford.
17. Op cit (Item 15), Foreword, Page 0.3.
18. Op cit (Item 6), Table 8.4.1
19. Mann, Horace, 1854, *Religious Worship in England and Wales*, Census of Great Britain 1851, George Routledge & Co., London.
20. See for example Professor Robin Gill, 1993, *The Myth of the Empty Church*, SPCK, London.
21. Richard Mudie-Smith, 1904, *The Religious Life of London*, Hodder and Stoughton, London.
22. Ibid., Page 7.
23. Report of Mass-Observation survey in 1949, published originally in *British Weekly*, Jan/Feb 1949, and also in Winter, 1952, edition of *Vision*, Vol III, No 1, Journal of the Free Church of England, Page 1. Original report in the Mass-Observation Archive in the University of Sussex, Brighton.
24. Brierley, Dr P W, 1980, *Prospects for the Eighties,* Volume 1, Bible Society, London, and 1983, Volume 2, MARC Europe, London.
25. Brierley, Dr P W, 1991, *'Christian' England*, MARC Europe, London.
26. Brierley, Dr P W, and Evans, Byron, 1983, *Prospects for Wales*, Bible Society and MARC Europe, London
27. Gallacher, Dr John, 1997, *Challenge to Change*, The Results of the 1995 Welsh Churches Survey, Bible Society, Swindon.
28. Brierley, Dr P W, Macdonald, Fergus, 1985, *Prospects for Scotland*, MARC Europe, London, and the National Bible Society of Scotland, Edinburgh.
29. Brierley, Dr P W, Macdonald, Fergus, 1995, *Prospects for Scotland 2000*, Christian Research, London, and the National Bible Society of Scotland, Edinburgh.
30. Op cit (Item 15), Table 2.12.1.
31. Brierley, Dr P W, 2000, *The Tide is Running Out*, Christian Research and HarperCollins, London.
32. Laquer, Thomas, 1976, *Religion and Respectability*, chapter "Sunday Schools and Working Class Culture".
33. Martin, Professor David, 1967, *A Sociology of English Religion*, New York, Page 42.
34. Brierley, Dr P W, 1993, *Reaching and Keeping Teenagers*, Monarch Publications, Crowborough.
35. Brierley, Dr P W, 1989, *A Century of British Christianity*, MARC Monograph No. 14, MARC Europe, Page 48
36. Brierley, Dr P W, 1991, *Prospects for the Nineties*, MARC Europe, London.
37. Francis, Professor Leslie J, 1984, *Teenagers and the Church*, Collins, London.
38. Francis, Professor Leslie J, and Kay, William, K, 1995, *Teenage Religion and Values*, Gracewing, Leominster.
39. Francis, Professor Leslie J, Kay, William K, Kerbey, Dr Alan, and Fogwill, Olaf. Editors, 1995, *Fast-moving Currents in Youth Culture*, Lynx, Oxford.
40. Smart, Ninian, 1983, article in *A New Dictionary of Christian Theology*, editors Richards, Alan, Bowden, John, SCM Press Ltd., London.
41. Maunder, W F, editor, 1987, *Reviews of United Kingdom Statistical Sources: Religion*, Volume XX, section by Field, Dr C D, "Non-recurrent Christian Data" lists all surveys up to 1982, Pergamon Press, Oxford.
42. Gill, Professor Robin, 1999, *Churchgoing and Christian Ethics*, CUP.
43. Abrams, Mark, Gerard, David, Timms, Noel, editors, 1985, *Values and Social Change in Britain*, Studies in the Contemporary Values of Modern Society, MacMillan Press, Basingstoke.
44. Harding, Stephen, and Phillips, David, 1986, *Contrasting Values in Western Europe*, Unity Diversity and Change, Studies in the Contemporary Values of Modern Society, MacMillan Press, Basingstoke.
45. Barker, Dr David, Halman, Loek, and Vloet, Astrid, 1992, *The European Values Study 1981-1990*, Summary Report, Gordon Cook Foundation.
46. Ester, Peter, Halman, Loek, and de Moor, Ruud, editors, 1994, *The Individualizing Society*, Value Change in Europe and North America, Tilburg University Press, The Netherlands.
47. A summary may be found in op cit (Item 15), Table 2.5.2. See also the July 1997 issue of *Quadrant*, Christian Research, London.
48. Op cit (Item 15), Table 2.5.1.
49. Op cit (Item 35), Table 13.
50. Op cit (Item 35), Table 30 up to 1960, and op cit (Item 6), Table 4.7.1 thereafter.
51. *Marriage Series*, FM2, Number 16, Table 3.8(a), published initially by the Office for Population Censuses and Surveys, and now by the Office for National Statistics.
52. Op cit (Item 35), Table 31.
53. See for example, Brierley, P W, editor, 1994, *Irish Christian Handbook*, 1995/96 edition, Christian Research, London, Table 23.
54. Op cit (Item 6), Table 4.8.1.
55. Francis, Professor Leslie, 1996, *Drift from the Churches*, University of Wales Press, Appendix 3.
56. Taken from appropriate Tables in op cit (Item 6)
57. Op cit (Item 6), Table 2.12
58. Op cit (Item 6), Table 3.2 and Figure 3.5.1.
59. *UK Christian Handbook* 1989/90 edition Tables 8b and 34, 1994/95 edition Table 9b; op cit (Item 15), Table 3.10.
60. Op cit (Item 6), Table 5.4.

MILLENNIUM

MILLENNIUM SUPPLEMENT

This Millennium Section has been specially compiled for this edition of the *UK Christian Handbook*. Much of the material was supplied by Brian Clews of **Anno Domini**. In addition, organisations in the rest of the *Handbook* were given the opportunity to submit details of events and resources which they would like listed in this section.

INTRODUCTION

Is your church ready for the next millennium? This has been the question **Anno Domini** has been asking over the last two years. The Evangelical Alliance set up Anno Domini with the chief objective that the Name of Jesus be central to all that is done to celebrate the year AD2000. This is being done by increasing awareness of ideas and projects that can be employed for this time of celebration and encouraging churches to get involved in a variety of initiatives for their local community.

Through the pages of this special supplement it is hoped that the information on the main national projects, the lists of ideas for story-telling and suggested packages of celebration will encourage churches and all Christians to put Jesus Christ at the heart of the millennium. The projects outlined here are grouped into four sections: story-tellers, celebration, prayer, and special initiatives. Contact details for organisations set up specifically for the millennium can be found on pages 34, 35. Page numbers are given for organisations listed elsewhere in the *Handbook*

STORY-TELLERS

Up and down the country many good ideas have been developed by gifted people to help tell the story of the most important person who ever lived. They encourage Christians to become effective in telling this most wonderful of stories, and to offer to their neighbours and friends a variety of ways of hearing that story.

Fanfare For a New Generation is aimed at local churches with the objective of ongoing church growth in the new millennium. By means of a Millennium Challenge pack, *Making Sunday Best,* Fanfare has identified 10 practical goals designed as a 'health check' to help local churches become more welcoming, relevant and challenging. The book *New Era, New Church*, by Steve Chalke and Sue Radford, offers practical ideas for implementing these goals.

Through surveys and audits, the church is enabled to assess the steps necessary to attract newcomers to services and to use January 2nd, the first Sunday in AD2000, to invite the community to come and see the 21st century church in action. The evening of January 2nd culminates in a major national celebration aimed at putting Jesus Christ centre stage and calling the whole nation back to its Christian roots.

Fanfare is also encouraging churches to get more involved with local schools through its *Generation to Generation* manual aimed at church leaders and activists. It is designed to enable local churches to support the schools in their community, raise the profile of Christians in education, build bridges in communities and invest in the lives of young people.

A different way to tell the story is through a new musical, **Hopes and Dreams,** devised by Rob Frost and featuring music by Paul Field, with three new hymns from Graham Kendrick. Imaginative and often humorous drama has been scripted by Stephen Deal, which expands the words of the Lord's Prayer and relates them to the millennium. The objective of the initiative is to encourage local churches to get together and present the programme in their own area during AD2000. It is an ideal opportunity to share gifts, skills and resources in a combined outreach to local communities in a culturally relevant way and to encourage individuals to consider Jesus and their own 'hopes and dreams' for a new millennium.

Another musical form of outreach is Roger Jones' (Christian Music Ministries page 183) musical, **Snakes and Ladders**. The plot follows the ups and downs of God's people through history, slithering down in sin and disobedience, and being lifted by God's grace. Commencing in the Garden of Eden, and passing through Old Testament history, the audience experiences Noah's Ark, the lives of Abraham and Isaac, Jacob's ladder and the tales of Moses. The final death and resurrection of Jesus represents the only ladder by which people can reach the end of the game of life.

This musical not only provides an opportunity to take friends and neighbours to a performance at its nearest point in its 37-city tour, but also to participate, as the organisers are looking for singers to form the choir at each venue.

A new film, **Jesus the Christ,** has been produced as another form of outreach. A joint initiative between The Visual Bible (page 322) and Army of Ants (page 257), this full length feature film is created from the NIV version of the book of Matthew with the key roles played by Christians – Bruce Marchiano's portrayal of a joyful Jesus is refreshing to say the least! Shot on location in the Middle East, it is as different as it is possible to be from the Luke based **Jesus** film so the projects are compatible.

A 23 minute video version of this film, for door-to-door evangelism, is endorsed by Sir Cliff Richard, Archbishop George Carey, Rev Steve Chalke and evangelist J.John, well known names to many non-churchgoers. In addition, a schools pack gives six 60 minute lessons for Key Stages 3 and 4 focusing on the birth, teachings, miracles, death and resurrection of Jesus. This pack and a five week Seeker Group kit have been produced in association with Viz-a-Viz (page 270), and all the resources are available from Christian Publicity Organisation (page 183).

The original **Jesus** film (page 263) based on the Gospel of Luke that has been seen by 1.6 billion people worldwide has been developed into the **Jesus Video Millennium Adventure.** It also allows people to explore the meaning of the millennium in the privacy of their own homes. When distributed by churches covering a whole area the **Jesus** video is being made available at a subsidised price of £1 a copy. A special introduction and ending has been added to highlight the relevance of Jesus to today's society. The videos are distributed to homes on the understanding that the church can return later with an opinion questionnaire.

A project aimed primarily at schools is **JC2000 The Millennium Arts Festival for Schools.** This will enable over 15,000 schools to celebrate the real meaning of the millennium by creating school productions which apply the words and actions of Jesus to the issues of today. It is a curriculum linked RE and Arts project launched in 1998 with the backing of Church Leaders and Education Ministers and is the only Government backed initiative to explore the Christian origin of the millennium. The project brings together RE, Drama, Dance, Art and Music.

This highly flexible project can be adapted to be suitable for any school and can be used in the classroom or as the basis for a full school production. There will also be the opportunity to perform at local events, at 9 regional festivals in England, national festivals in Scotland, Wales and Northern Ireland and a spectacular UK-wide event to be held in June 2000 at The Royal Albert Hall.

During the beginning of the new millennium, **The Passion Event**, a spectacular performance on the life of Christ, will be touring worldwide, including the UK. **Passion** will present a unique and highly innovative retelling of the story of Jesus Christ to an international and predominantly secular audience. Churches and individuals are invited to help support an education and training programme that will bring school and college students to special matinee performances.

Passion acknowledges that the story of Jesus Christ is at the heart of Western society and influences each generation in new and profound ways. It will reproduce the story in a modern and sophisticated way in keeping with the advances in technology and art. It will be a highly populist entertainment accessible to anyone familiar with the modern grammar of film and pop, while faithfully following the New Testament accounts. The audience will be transported to the beginning of the first millennium but return to the third to help us understand why this first century carpenter started the clock by which we set our lives.

On a more personal level there is **Y2000** an evangelism tool using the letter **Y** – an ancient Christian symbol for the Trinity – to raise curiosity and provoke questions such as, "Y 2000?", "Y the millennium?", "Y the Party?" Through Y lapel pins, posters, car stickers and other resources and activities, Christians have the opportunity to open doors which help them point their neighbours and friends to Christ. In a simple, powerful and effective way, Y2000 answers the significant question – "What made one man so unique that the whole of history became dated from his birth?"

The answer is provided through a range of resources centred on 5 different pictures, each based on the Y symbol, that convey the uniqueness of Christ. These resources create opportunities to tell the story of Christ in personal and community wide settings. A church resources pack includes an eight-week evangelistic course, seeker service outlines, a children's holiday club, and a series of preaching themes based on the five Y pictures. It is aimed at aiding interchurch cooperation and giving existing church activity a millennium cutting edge.

From videos, or candles (Pendlebury's Church Candles, page 426), to personal invitations, there is a desire to penetrate every home in the country with some form of gift for the millennium. What could be more appropriate than a copy of the gospel? **Millennium Gospels** (available from Christian Publicity Organisation page 183) meet that need in a unique way. A company in Bath have subsidised the printing of millions of high quality gospels and are making them available at extremely low prices. Produced on art paper, with a gold or silver cover the NIV version in English has been produced first but versions in other languages will also be available. The four gospels are each packaged in a special memento fashion that will be both inspirational and a keepsake as well as ideal for mass distribution. A special pack, being made available for schools to give out, includes a torch beacon for millennium Eve celebrations.

We want to celebrate this story and the fact that this very special Person still lives to impact the hearts of men, women and children all over the globe, 2000 years after his birth. From humble beginnings, Jesus Christ became *KING OF KINGS AND LORD OF LORDS*, fully deserving a year of birthday celebrations during his 2000th anniversary.

CELEBRATION

Beacon Millennium – 31st December 1999. A date destined to become an important milestone in our history. Beacons have been part of our cultural heritage for thousands of years and have often been used to pass on news of major events in our history. What more significant event than the 2000th anniversary of Jesus' birth? Everyone in Britain is invited to join in celebration by means of beacons lit the length and breadth of the nation. Lighting times will be coordinated, starting in the Scottish Isles and leading up to a midnight lighting of the final bonfires along the meridian line. Fireworks and candles will feature in civic events affording an opportunity for churches to play a major role in helping local and national communities to reflect and celebrate.

Churches are being encouraged to take part in these local events by the lighting of beacons so that the world's most important birthday can be heralded by worshipping communities as part of a time of prayer and praise.

An initiative of Churches Together in England is **A New Start**. *The New Start Millennium Moment* project is designed to see a candle and the *Millennium Resolution* card in every household for use in the last 30 minutes of 1999 as a gift from the local church. Churches are invited to participate in three key areas of faith into and during the year 2000:

A New Start at Home encourages a locally based nation-wide debate asking what kind of Britain we want for the next century.

A New Start With God creates ideas for mission and evangelism in the new millennium. It challenges the churches to forge a link in people's minds between AD2000, the name of Jesus Christ, and the possibility of personal meaning and public hope.

A New Start for the World's Poor gives ideas for bringing hope to all humanity with practical action to free people from poverty and injustice. Resources identify existing Christian action and list 10 steps by which churches can work to make a difference.

After that all important midnight hour that starts the New Year, **Celebration 2000** invites all of a Christian persuasion to bring their friends and family at 12 noon Saturday, January 1st to their local Cathedral, Church or Chapel for a 15 minute ecumenical act of devotion. The services will celebrate the birth of Christ, giving thanks for the second millennium and seeking a blessing on the third. Churches possessing bells will celebrate with a peal of bells during the service.

Later that day, at 3pm January 1st **All the World Sing Praise** is an ecumenical initiative to launch praise parties to welcome in the new millennium in every time zone and capital of the world. As parties go this should be some party, but the **Worlds' Biggest Birthday Party – Pentecost 2000** is being planned from 10th – 21st June (see A Child is Born Charitable Trust). Groups of churches are being encouraged to invite their entire community to a grand party which may incorporate music and drama. While it is hoped that there will be parties in every village, town and city, the focus is planned for Blackheath by Greenwich Royal Park, with the Royal Observatory as the reference place for time. The Blackheath party will take place in the replica Crystal Palace, which will be built on the zero meridian line. It is planned that the Party will be the culmination of a period of twelve months of gathering gifts from all over the nation for the children of the world of the third millennium. The organisers are also producing "A Child Is Born" Bible, in partnership with the International Bible Society (page 133).

The first day of the great party, June 10th AD2000, has been designed **Jesus Day.** A huge international response is expected to the call from **Global March for Jesus** (page 262) for a day of joyful praise and united prayer spanning the nations. Global Praise Marches over the last decade have seen 50 million people in 117 nations participating in this worldwide parade of witness. Jesus Day AD2000 will potentially see the largest ever gathering of Christians around the world with nearly 200 countries expected to join in.

It's About Time is the name given to a group of initiatives from Greenwich Evangelical Leaders to encourage and resource the churches of Greenwich and East London in preparation for the influx of millennium visitors to the Dome and the area. Hospitality projects, Jesus Video distribution, street drama, multi-language literature and training schemes are all included. They may also be able to advise how to start up similar town-wide initiatives elsewhere.

All this, and much more, is very encouraging, but no one is going to throw a switch on December 31st in 1999 and create a new set of circumstances with which to confront the church. Rather, the church is still trying to catch up with the changes of the 1990's whilst the nation at large is being challenged with an ever increasing pace of life and a burgeoning uncertainty concerning unemployment, family life and prosperity.

How to reach out to a more free thinking nation which buys more heavily into short-termism, with a message that has thousands of years of history and an unlimited future of hope, is the sort of question the future-proof church of tomorrow will be asking today. The backing to all this must be ...

PRAYER

A nationwide prayer initiative, **Million for the Millennium**, comes from the Assemblies of God, Apostolic and Elim Pentecostal Churches. It's aim, to see 20,000 people pray for revival for at least 10 minutes each day through 1999, would give a minimum of 1,000,000 hours of prayer for our nation.

In a similar initiative on April 6th 1997, it was 1,000 days to the end of 1999. All across the United Kingdom, special services of prayer were held for our nation. With the prompting of churches in the Greenwich area, the Evangelical Alliance felt it appropriate to call the church in our nation to continue praying throughout these 1,000 days in what became the **1,000 Day Prayer Count-down.** The prayer programme was subsequently relaunched on August 19th 1998 at which point there were 500 days to go. A brochure lists major Christian millennium projects, three prayers of unity and seven other items for prayer concerning the state of our nation and the work of the Church. With all this activity, how many churches and individuals have been and continue to be faithful in praying for this special time in our nation?

SPECIAL INITIATIVES

A major ecumenical project, **Songs for the New Millennium**, has resulted in an exciting music resource that brings together nearly 200 songs, as well as prayer and liturgy, based on themes such as justice and peace, church as community and the celebration of God's world and people.

Using a combination of new and established writers the music encompasses a variety of styles ranging from calypso to Celtic, through to modern hymns. **Songs for the New Millennium** offers a refreshing approach to worship that expresses the struggles as well as the triumphs of faith and helps reflect and inspire our contemporary world and spiritual lives.

For something quite different, **Pilgrim Walks,** (see Meridian Millennium Way Project) aim to prepare body mind and spirit for the next millennium. A week-long pilgrimage to early Christian and Celtic sites across the British Isles has been organised and in addition, a 2 hour guided walk along the Meridian Line, *Cross Over the Line,* will teach about the Christian significance of Greenwich sites in the context of the millennium. In mid 2000, **Jubilee 2000 Walk** is being organised along the Meridian Way with representatives of all the Meridian Line nations.

Christians are sometimes lost for words when the hoped-for opportunity to share their faith occurs. ICC (page 294) has created a low cost, give away cassette, **Time to Make a Difference,** to help churches and individuals tell the story of Jesus through personal testimony.

In recent years the week of Valentine's Day has afforded an opportunity for churches to focus on the foundations of marriage. From 14th February AD2000, **Millennium Marriage Week,** will be an ideal occasion for highlighting the God-given institution of marriage to our 21st century communities (see National Marriage Week page 438). A chance to be creative in uplifting the values of biblical family life are all possible through special media events, training courses, services and counselling opportunities.

As there will be a shortage of accommodation in London during the millennium events, the **Christian Host Project** plans to make available 3,000 rooms in Christian homes, including offering to hosts full training in hospitality and witnessing. A supporting gospel literature campaign in many languages is included

In the midst of the celebrations and partying, there will be many people with little understanding of the Jesus story. **The Open Book**, a joint initiative between Bible Society (page 132) and Churches Together in England (page 241), aims to shape an appropriate public theology which 'opens the Book to the culture and the culture to the Book.' The aim is to encourage renewed interest in and a more meaningful encounter with Scripture, as the story of God's relationship with the world: the story of who we are, why we are here, and how we discover our shared vocation as people created in the image of God.

Project 2000 is an initiative of Global Care (page 384) focusing on the needs of children at risk in AD2000. Global Care wants to celebrate the 2000th birthday of Jesus Christ by giving tangible help to thousands of innocent, suffering children and to recruit 2,000 new supporters to help the world's neediest children.

With all these activities there are expected to be many enquirers wanting to know more about the Christian faith without giving their names to a local church. **The Christian Enquiry Agency** (page 431) offers an anonymous response system on behalf of churches, and produces a wide range of literature, beer mats, posters etc encouraging people to write off for more information.

The Shaftesbury Society (page 468), Tearfund (page 367) and the Evangelical Alliance (page 234) aim to impact local communities through **Rebuilding Community.** The project plans to develop the quantity and quality of local church-linked social action. They want to stimulate and build local church confidence in the fact that they can make a difference and that new partnerships formed locally, regionally and nationally have a vital contribution to make.

To implement this vision, a large coalition of national Christian organisations, denominations, church movements and key individuals are working together. A range of resources, models and thinking is planned to enable local churches to take relevant action. Community weeks, an information website, and the opportunity to develop new initiatives under a national umbrella are to be made available.

Anno Domini, set up by the Evangelical Alliance, is seeking to create awareness in churches and ministries of the available Christian projects and celebrations to mark the new millennium. Through presentations, training days, a quarterly news letter and the use of *The Millennium Wall,* (a major project display utilised at Bible weeks and exhibitions) **Anno Domini** has conducted an awareness campaign for over two years with the declared objective to make Jesus central to the millennium.

The celebrations and initiatives contained in this supplement will not in themselves transform the church of our nation into the 21st century community of faith we all long to be. But adopting some of them will create a foundation for future change that will potentially position us alongside those we wish to reach as they too stand before a new era in their own frailty and fears.

AD2000 presents an ideal opportunity for the Christian, with a destiny that is assured, to be the banner to which friends and work colleagues turn in their world of uncertainty. A church that takes the road to visibility and high profile acknowledgement of its 2000th birthday will have asked the right questions and found the right answers.

Our hope is that the reader of this special section of the *UK Christian Handbook* will have been inspired by a number of the creative ideas contained and that it will have provided at least some of the answers.

MILLENNIUM ORGANISATIONS

All the World Sing Praise, New Life, 60 Wickstead Avenue, Luton LU4 9DP
Director: n/a. Began n/a. No magazine. Turnover n/a. Ecumenical initiative to launch praise parties across the world.
☎ 01582 571 011

***Anno Domini**, PO Box 680, Maidenhead SL6 9ST
Project Director: Mr Brian Clews. Began 1997. An initiative of the Evangelical Alliance. No magazine. Turnover n/a. Making Jesus central to the millennium by creating awareness in churches and ministries of Christian projects.
Web: www.eauk.org
Email: anno.domini@dial.pipex.com
☎ 07071 202 000 Fax 01628 525 314

Avon Silversmiths Ltd, 10 Avenue Road, Bishop's Stortford CM23 5NU
Chairman: Mr Michael McCarthy. Executive staff 1, Other staff 5. Began 1994; interdenominational. No magazine. Turnover n/a. Manufacturing church silver plate and giftware, new millennium products.
Web: www.church-silver.co.uk
Email: mike@church-silver.co.uk
☎ 01279 508 084 Fax 01279 831 828

Beacon Millennium, PO Box 1718, Fordingbridge SP6 3SB
Contact: Mr Bruno Peek. Began n/a. No magazine. Turnover n/a. Celebration by means of beacons lit across the nation with a final lighting of bonfires.
Email: henrywilkinson@beacon.dircon.co.uk
☎ 01725 518 810 Mobile: 0468 350 804

Celebration 2000, The Open Churches Trust, c/o The Really Useful Group Ltd, 22 Tower Street, London WC2H 9NS
Trust Administrator: Brigadier Adam Gurdon. Executive staff 2. ***CC*** Began n/a; interdenominational. No magazine. Turnover n/a. On January 1st 2000 Christians will be persuaded to join together for ecumenical services to celebrate Christ's birth.
Web: www.merseyworld.com/faith/html_file/octhead.htm
Email: oct@reallyuseful.co.uk
☎ 020 7240 0880 Fax 020 7240 1204

***A Child Is Born Charitable Trust**, 16 Belmont Hill, Lewisham, London SE13 5BD
Trustee: Mr Raymond Hall. No other staff. ***CC*** No.1066783. Began 1997; non-denominational. No magazine. Turnover £2,000 to year end Mar 99. Events and donations enabling giving to the children of the world of the third millennium.
Web: www.achildisborn.org.uk
Email: admin@achildisborn.org.uk
☎ 020 8318 9233 Fax 020 8463 0634

Christian Host Project, 53 St John's Park, Blackheath, London SE3 7JW
Contact: Mr Louis Alexander. Began n/a. No magazine. Turnover n/a. Establishment of rooms in Christian homes for people who need accommodation in London during the millennium season.
☎ 020 8305 1027

Fanfare for a New Generation, 115 Southwark Bridge Road, London SE1 0AX
Director: Gill Harper. Began 1998; interdenominational. No magazine. Turnover n/a. Ten practical millennium goals for churches; advising how to be more welcoming, relevant and challenging.
☎ 020 7450 9070 Fax 020 7450 9060

Hopes and Dreams, One Voice, The Methodist Church, Tolverne Road, Raynes Park, London SW20 8RA
Director: Rev Dr Rob Frost. Began n/a; interdenominational. No magazine. Turnover n/a. Musical devised by Rob Frost and featuring music by Graham Kendrick and Paul Field.
Email: rob.frost.team@dial.pipex.com
☎ 020 8944 5678 Resources: 020 8288 1961
Fax 020 8947 5152

It's About Time, London City Mission HQ, 175 Tower Bridge Road, London SE1 2AH
Administrator: Mr George Hider. Staff 2. Began n/a. Magazine: *It's About Time Bulletin* (5,000 quarterly). Turnover £10,000 to year end Dec 98. Encouraging and resourcing churches in Greenwich/East London to prepare for the influx of visitors to the area during the millennium.
Web: www.lite.co.uk/its-about-time
Email: lcm.uk@btinternet.com
☎ 020 7407 7585 Fax 020 7403 6711

JC2000 – The Millennium Arts Festival for Schools, 4 Hazlitt Mews, London W14 0JZ
Project Manager: Mr David Senior. ***CC*** Began n/a; non-denominational. No magazine. Turnover n/a. Nationwide festival in which schools/communities can participate by using drama, dance, art and music.
Web: www.jc2000.org
☎ 020 7371 3716 Fax 020 7371 3790

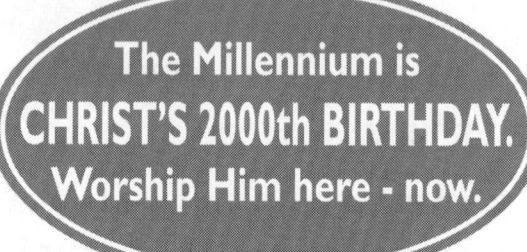

Jesus Day, Global March for Jesus, Waverley Abbey House, Waverley Lane, Farnham GU9 8EP
UK Coordinator: Mr Keith Marchant. Began n/a. No magazine. Turnover n/a. June 10th AD2000 will see a day of joyful praise and united prayer spanning the nations, events planned nationwide.
Web: www.gmfj.org
Email: 100572.323@compuserve.com
☎ 01252 784 774 Fax 01252 784 775

Jesus the Christ, 11 Pinkerton Court, Lambourne Grove, Kingston upon Thames KT1 3SG
Contact: Mr David Taylor. Began n/a. Joint project of Visual Bible Society and Army of Ants. No magazine. Turnover n/a. Feature film about Jesus made to be shown in local cinemas and publicised by local churches.
Web: www.armyofants.org
☎ 020 8549 6014

***JESUS Video Project**, Fairgate House, Kings Road, Tyseley, Birmingham B11 2AA
Director: Mr John Arkell. Other staff 8. *CC* Began 1967; interdenominational. Part of Agapé. No magazine. Turnover: included in Agapé. Video with range of training/support resources, starter pack, leadership briefings, advice, companion magazine.
Email: jvp@agape.org.uk
☎ 0121 765 4404 Fax 0121 765 4065

Meridien Millennium Way Project, 58 Geoffrey Road, London SE4 1NT
Project Manager: Mr David Pott. Began n/a; non-denominational. No magazine. Turnover n/a. Pilgrim walks along the zero meridian to prepare the walker in body, mind and spirit for the next millennium.
Email: jerry.whitehead@virgin.net
☎ 020 8692 8271

Millennium Gospels, Downwood, Claverton Down Road, Bath BA2 6DT
Distributor: Mr Robert Hicks. Began 1998; interdenominational. Published with Christian Publicity Organisation. No magazine. Turnover n/a. Each of the gospels packaged in a special memento fashion; nationwide distribution.
☎ 01225 445 121

Million for the Millennium, 55 Fidlas Avenue, Llanishen, Cardiff CF4 5NZ
Contact: Rev Kevin Tugwell. Began 1998; Assemblies of God. No magazine. Turnover n/a. Nationwide initiative to see 20,000 people pray for revival for ten minutes each day to make a million hours of prayer.
☎ 01222 757 312

A New Start, Millennium Office, Church House, Great Smith Street, London SW1P 3NZ
Contact: Rev Stephen Lynas. Other staff 4. Began 1995; Anglican. Magazine: *Millennium News* (Circulation n/a every four months). Turnover n/a. Inviting churches to participate in three areas of faith during the year 2000; home, God, the World's poor.
Email: millennium@mission.u-net.com
☎ 020 7898 1435 Fax 020 7893 1432

The Passion Event, ABC Interactive, Kelso House, Lansdown, Bath BA1 5SH
Organiser: Mr Alexander Best. Began n/a; interdenominational. No magazine. Turnover n/a. Jesus' life, death and resurrection told through witnesses to his life using technology and music.
☎ 01225 466 900

Prayer Countdown, PO Box 680, Maidenhead SL6 9ST
Director: Brian Clews. Began 1997; non-denominational. No magazine. Turnover n/a. 1000 Days to the Millennium prayer countdown, praying throughout this time for the nation; prayer brochures available.
☎ 07071 202 000

Sing'Fest' 2000, 6 Hall Crescent, Sawston, Cambridge CB2 4SR
Co-ordinator: Mr Michael Lovell. No other staff. Began n/a. No magazine. Turnover n/a. Worldwide singing festival for the year 2000 celebrating Christ; local singing events can be involved.
Web: www.singfest2000.org
Email: enquiries@singfest2000.org
☎ 01223 833 452

Snakes and Ladders, Christian Music Ministries, 325 Bromford Road, Birmingham B36 8ET
Writer: Mr Roger Jones. Executive staff 3, Other staff 4. Began 1983. No magazine. Turnover n/a. Musical following the ups and downs of God's people through history, touring nationwide.
Email: roger@cmm.org.uk
☎ 0121 783 3291 Fax 0121 785 0500

Songs for the New Millennium, 37 Haymers Avenue, Hull HU3 1LL
Contact: Jenny Mash. Began n/a; ecumenical. Support from Greenbelt, URC, Methodists, CAFOD and Baptist Union. No magazine. Turnover n/a. Creating a major worship songbook of new songs, capturing the millennium mood for worship.
Email: admin@image-on.demon.co.uk
☎ 01482 445 570 Fax 01482 341 813

***Y 2000 – Using the Millennium to make Jesus Known**, PO Box 94, Chessington KT10 2YJ
Director: Mr Peter Meadows. Executive staff 1, Admin staff 1. Began 1997; interdenominational. No magazine. Turnover n/a. Providing resources to help people make Jesus known based on the ancient Christian symbol Y.
Web: www.y-2000.com
Email: info@y-2000.com
☎ 020 8287 3147 Fax 020 8286 3700

GENERAL MILLENNIUM EVENTS

Listed by date and alphabetical order of event

Date from:	Event	Venue	Organisation	Contact no.	Page
1999 onwards	Genesis Expo; permanent exhibition	Portsmouth	Creation Science Movement	023 9229 3988	410
	Gospel Celebration, multi media followed by 2 week gospel proclamation	Chatsworth Park, Derbyshire	Cliff College	01246 582 321	503
	Local events, services & pilgrimages	Brighton	Old Roman Catholic Church of Great Britain	01273 554 260	224
	Millennium-in-the-Fields. Year-long celebration & exploration in the Royal Parish Church	London	St Martin-in-the-Fields	0207 930 0089	
	Pilgrimage/National Celebration	Llangeitho, Ceredigion	Presbyterian Church of Wales	029 2049 4913	225
	Target Millennium – 3 year social challenge initiative to set targets for change	Throughout Birmingham; special events in the Symphony Hall & NIA	Target Millennium Office	0121 233 2155	
1999 – May 2000	Forge The Link – co-ordinated poster campaign	Croydon	Churches Together in Croydon	0208 657 4880	
1999 – June 2000	Devon, various events co-ordinated by the Churches Millennium Group	Local area	Tiverton & District Evangelical Fellowship	01884 820 210	247
	Scottish programme of prayer & celebration	Throughout Scotland	Scottish Churches' House	01786 823 588	86
	Staffordshire's Millennium Celebrations	Various Stafford locations	Saltbox Christian Centre	01782 814 417	268
1999 – Dec 2000	Various services celebrating the Millennium; including Christmas Day mass & Easter vigils	Southwark Cathedral	Roman Catholic Archdiocese of Southwark	020 7928 2495	201
1999 – 2001	Research into popular meanings of Millennium	Middlesex (distance learning)	Centre for the Study of Implicit Religion & Contemporary Spirituality	020 8362 6220	518
From Jan 2000					
	2000 in 2000 Leadership Training (the training of 2000 leaders)	10 nations overseas	Proclaimers International	01603 260 222	267, 521
	Calling on every home in the area	Brighton & Hove	Brighton & Hove Town Mission	01273 609 484	254
	Dawn Project; visiting secondary schools	London Borough of Bromley	Spinnaker Trust	020 8295 2070	269
	Distribution of 2 million Bibles & Scripture books to the Chinese Church	China	Open Doors with Brother Andrew	01865 300 300	327
	Dorset, various events throughout the year	Local areas	Churches Together in Dorset	01305 264 416	241
	England, various events throughout the year	Nationwide; please contact Stephen Lynas for full list	Archbishops' Officer for the Millennium/Churches Together in England	020 7898 1435	231, 241
	Exhibitions, public mystery plays, marches/processions, lectures & services	Various local areas around North London	Churches Together in North London	020 8959 7246	242
	Hexham & Newcastle, various events throughout the year	Local area; please contact Fr Paul Southgate for full details	Roman Catholic Diocese of Hexham & Newcastle Millennium Committee	01670 712 476	200
	International Conference for senior pupils	Lendrick Muir Centre	Scripture Union Scotland	0141 332 1162	269

Date from:	Event	Venue	Organisation	Contact no.	Page
	London, various events throughout the year	London; please contact David Saville for full list	Church of England Diocese of London	020 7932 1100	208
	Performance projects	Schools, churches, theatres, art centres nationwide	Springs Dance Company	020 8289 8974	303
	Pilgrim 2000	The Holy Land	McCabe Pilgrimages	020 8675 6828	472
	Project ARK 2000; short term shelter for homeless in church buildings	Brighton & Hove churches	Off The Fence	01273 420 657	266
	R.E & the Millennium; encouraging Millennial projects to develop RE in schools		Culham College Institute & the St Gabriel Programme	01235 520 458	456
	Special services & concerts to celebrate the Millennium	Cathedral Church of St Peter & St Wilfrid, Ripon	Church of England Cathedral Church of St Peter & St Wilfrid, Ripon	01765 602 072	192
	Ten Commandments mission series	Bath, Beaconsfield, Coventry, St Albans	The Philo Trust	01923 286 286	261
	Ten Cubed – A community theatre project for the millennium	Theatres & community venues in Deptford & Greenwich	Kettle of Fish Theatre	020 8691 9782	300
	West Midlands, various events	Across the West Midlands	United Reformed Church: West Midands Province	0121 783 1177	229
	Word and Spirit Conference	The Evangelical Theological College of Wales	The Evangelical Theological College of Wales	01656 645 411	504
2001 – 2010	Decade for a Culture of Peace & Non-Violence for Children in the World	Wales; through local cells of Cymdeithas Y Cymod Yng Nghymru	Cymdeithas Y Cymod Yng Nghymru (Fellowship of Reconciliation, Wales)	01938 500 631	454
May/June 2001	50th Anniversary of Emmaus Bible School Celebrations	Wirral, Merseyside	Emmaus Bible School UK	0151 327 1172	326

MILLENNIUM EVENTS

Listed by date and alphabetical order of event

Date	Event	Venue	Organisation	Contact no.	Page
1999					
Nov 28th – Dec 19th	Conclusion of 1000 Day Prayer Countdown	Nationwide	Evangelical Alliance	020 7207 2115	234
DECEMBER					
	Carol concerts	Nationwide	Mainstage Management Agency	020 8555 5510	308
	Millennium Weekend	Kinmel Hall, Clwyd	Kinmel Hall Christian Trust	01745 833 450	80
2nd	New Year Celebration	High Leigh Conference Centre, Herts	The Network	01271 817 093	462
9th	Jesus 2000	Walsall	Walsall Christian Centre	01922 648 058	
23rd	Christmas 2000 House Party & Millennium Celebration	Winford Manor, Bristol	Omega – Winford Manor	01275 472 262	83
26th	Assembly/ Convocation of Prayer	Coleg Y Baya	Presbyterian Church of Wales Youth & Children's Centre	01678 520 565	481
26th – Jan 4th	Millennium Skiing Holiday	Switzerland	Gold Hill Holidays	01753 880 753	471
27th – Jan 3rd	Package Holiday for Edinburgh Hogmanay	Edinburgh	Ben Doran Guest House	0131 667 8488	72
28th – Jan 3rd	New Year Study Conference	Capernwray Hall, Carnforth, Lancs	Capernwray Missionary Fellowship of Torchbearers	01524 733 908	370
28th – Jan 2nd	Y2K Youth Camp	Quinta Centre, Oswestry	Word of Life Ministries	01324 558 535	482
29th – Jan 2nd	Millennium Celebration	Holland House, Pershore	Holland House	01386 860 330	125
29th – Jan 1st	Millennium Conference	Germany	Christian Businessmen's Committee (CBMC)	020 7404 6970	258
29th – Jan 2nd	New Year Millennium House Party	Burstone Manor, Devon	Burstone Manor, Centre for Christ Trust	01363 822 61	73
29th – Jan 5th	Family Celebration Week; children's activities, adult worship	Elm House Centre, Leyburn	The Jonas Trust	01969 624 900	80
30th – Jan 6th	Millennium Desert Escape	Sinai	Wind, Sand & Stars Ltd	020 7433 3684	475
31st – Jan 1st	Church & Community party	Mayflower Centre, London	Mayflower Family Centre	020 7476 1171	265
31st – Jan 1st	Lighting up of Norwich	Norwich	Cathedral Church of the Holy and Undivided Trinity, Norwich	01603 218 308	192
31st – Jan 1st	Millennium Retreat	Trefeca, Powys	Presbyterian Church of Wales	029 2049 4913	225
31st – Jan	Service of repentance and affirmation	Edgehill Theological College, Belfast	Edgehill Theological College	028 9066 5870	503
31st	Choral Eucharist	Birmingham Cathedral Church of St Philip	Birmingham Cathedral Church of St Philip	0121 236 4333	191
31st	Gospel & Poster Campaign, musical & special services	Borough of Brent	Brent Churches 2000	0208 902 1729	
31st	House Party	Gartmore House, Stirling	Gartmore House Conference & Activity Centre	01877 382 991	77
31st	Live Family Event; link up with Chatham Islands (other side of the world)	Rochester Cathedral Church of Christ and the Blessed Virgin Mary	Rochester Cathedral Church of Christ and the Blessed Virgin Mary	01634 843 366	192
31st	Mass for the Millennium; 8pm	Metropolitan Cathedral of St George, Southwark	Metropolitan Cathedral of St George, Southwark	020 7928 5256	190
31st	Millennium Eve; evening of fun & celebration; praying in the new millennium; late night praise	Woodcroft Christian Centre	Woodcroft Christian Centre	01291 624 114	88
31st	Millennium service	Southwark Cathedral & King's College	Southwark Cathedral & King's College, London	020 7407 3708	193
31st	Millennium Moment & following prayer service	Birmingham Cathedral	Birmingham Churches Together	0121 643 6603	240
31st	Party, prayers & Millennium candles	Bradford Cathedral	Bradford Cathedral	01274 777 724	191
31st	Welcome service to the Millennium	Liverpool Cathedral	Liverpool Cathedral	0151 709 6271	192

Millennium Events

Date	Event	Venue	Organisation	Contact no.	Page
JANUARY 2000					
	Conference on Middle East	London Colney	Christians Aware	0116 254 0770	372
	Official opening after restoration of a new Orthodox Church	Manod, Blaenau Ffestiniog	Orthodox Church in Wales	01766 831 272	224
– May 2000	Timewarp 2000 – education performance for years 5 & 6; assemblies	Launch at Barbican, York, then throughout York region	St Michael's Chambers	01904 639 767	
MILLENNIUM DAY					
1st	All the World Sing Praise	Global praise party	New Life (Faith Alive Youth Ministry)	01582 571 011	261
1st	Celebration 2000 – noon services & national peal of bells	Throughout UK	Celebration 2000	020 7240 0880	34
1st	Choral Eucharist	Birmingham Cathedral Church of St Philip	Birmingham Cathedral Church of St Philip	0121 236 4333	191
1st	Church bells to be rang at noon	Throughout the UK	Central Council of Church Bell Ringers	01428 628 790	459
1st	Cover to Cover Bible Read	St Peters Port, Guernsey	The Island Churches Guernsey Festival Chorus	01481 650 04	300
1st	Local events, outreach & services	Greenwich & East London	It's About Time (London City Mission)	020 7407 7585	34
1st	Local events, outreach & services	Southampton	Southampton Millennium Festival	023 8051 6005	
1st	Peel of bells (noon) followed by short service	Carlisle Cathedral Church of the Holy and Undivided Trinity	Carlisle Cathedral Church of the Holy and Undivided Trinity	01228 523 335	191
1st	Prayers for the Millennium; noon	Metropolitan Cathedral of St George, Southwark	Metropolitan Cathedral of St George, Southwark	020 7928 5256	193
1st	Service (noon) & party (4pm)	Warde Aldam, Pontefract	Warde Aldam Christian Nursing Home	01977 643 697	120
1st	Youth celebration	Scinajoki, Finland	David Lyle Morris	020 8658 2152	302
2nd	Bible reading/teaching/ bringing Christian leaders together	Coleg Y Baya	Presbyterian Church of Wales Youth & Children's Centre	01678 520 565	481
2nd	County Ecumenical & Civic Service	Truro Cathedral	Churches Together in Cornwall	01872 273 154	241
2nd	Ecumenical service (10.30am)	Carlisle Cathedral Church of the Holy and Undivided Trinity	Carlisle Cathedral Church of the Holy and Undivided Trinity	01228 523 335	152
2nd	Millennium Challenge Services	Throughout UK	Fanfare for a New Generation	020 7450 9070	34
2nd	National Millennium Service	Waterfront, Belfast	Methodist Church in Ireland: Enniskillen & Sligo District	No phone	222
2nd	Praise in the Park	Crawley, West Sussex	St Andrew's Church	01293 538 699	
2nd	Songs of Praise	Transmission from Millennium Stadium, Cardiff	Church in Wales Diocese of Llandaff & BBC Religious Programmes	029 2057 8899 & 0161 200 2020	202, 532
2nd	World Day of Praise for Jesus Christ with world satellite link	Churches worldwide	Christian Communications Commission	0115 930 7552	292
7th – 12th	Time to Pray	Cliff College, Sheffield	Cliff College	01246 582 321	503
9th	All Day Celebration	Brentwood International Centre	Brentwood & District Evangelical Fellowship	01277 202 722	246
9th	Millennium Praise	Fort Regent, Jersey	Churches Together in Jersey	01534 861 386	242
10th	Christian Celebration Day	Cardiff City Centre	Church in Wales Diocese of Llandaff	029 2057 8899	202

Date	Event	Venue	Organisation	Contact no.	Page
10th – 13th	International Preaching Conference: Preaching Christ for a New Millennium	University of Kent, Canterbury	College of Preachers	01778 422 929	493
12th, 13th	Health and Justice; evening event	Southwark Cathedral & King's College	Southwark Cathedral & King's College, London	020 7407 3708	193
16th – June 11th	Season of Prayer	Various	Saltbox Christian Centre	01782 814 417	268
19th – 21st	A Dialogue Encounter for the New Millennium; Tony Campolo & Leslie Griffiths	To be confirmed	Belfast Central Mission	028 9024 1917 (Rev David Kerr)	254
24th – 28th	The Ages of Man; pageant	Blackburn Cathedral Church of St Mary	Blackburn Cathedral Church of St Mary	01254 514 91	191
29th	2000th Birthday Party	Bells Sports Centre, Perth	Scottish Crusaders	0141 331 2400	481
FEBRUARY					
2nd	Completion of Bishop's pilgrimage to every church in the Diocese	Cathedral Church of All Saints, Wakefield	Church of England Diocese of Wakefield	01924 255 349	211
5th	Festival for St Albans Deanery	St Albans Cathedral	St Albans Cathedral and Abbey Church	01727 860 780	192
7th – 14th	Millennium Marriage Week	Nationwide events, workshops and seminars	National Marriage Week	01202 849 000	437
13th – 15th	Hymn – Psalm a Song Marathon	St Peters Port, Guernsey	The Island Churches Guernsey Festival Chorus	01481 650 04	300
15th – 17th	Senior Leaders' Conference	High Leigh Conference Centre, Hoddesdon	Christian Research	020 8294 1989	456
MARCH					
7th	They Think It's All Over – results of the English Church Attendance Survey	Norwich	Christian Research	020 8294 1989	456
8th	They Think It's All Over – results of the English Church Attendance Survey	Derby	Christian Research	020 8294 1989	456
8th, 9th	Staying Human; evening event	Southwark Cathedral & King's College	Southwark Cathedral & King's College, London	020 7407 3708	193
9th	They Think It's All Over – results of the English Church Attendance Survey	Birmingham	Christian Research	020 8294 1989	456
10th	They Think It's All Over – results of the English Church Attendance Survey	Bath	Christian Research	020 8294 1989	456
10th – 12th	Millennium Deaf Christians Weekend Conference	Northampton	Christian Deaf Link UK	Fax: 01277 632 558	410
18th	Golden Jubilee Festival	London, to be announced	The London & Home Counties Festivals of Male Voice Praise	020 8688 1346	301
19th	Festival for Hertford Deanery	St Albans Cathedral	St Albans Cathedral and Abbey Church	01727 860 780	192
20th	They Think It's All Over – results of the English Church Attendance Survey	Manchester	Christian Research	020 8294 1989	456
21st	Bicentenary of the birth of Cardinal Newman	The Oratory, Edgbaston	The Friends of Cardinal Newman	0121 454 0496	235
21st	They Think It's All Over – results of the English Church Attendance Survey	Newcastle	Christian Research	020 8294 1989	456
22nd	They Think It's All Over – results of the English Church Attendance Survey	Leeds	Christian Research	020 8294 1989	456

Millennium Events

Date	Event	Venue	Organisation	Contact no.	Page
APRIL					
	Millennium pilgrimage	Sinai	Wind, Sand & Stars Ltd	020 7433 3684	475
	Visit to Egyptian monasteries	Egypt	Christians Aware	0116 254 0770	372
Apr – Aug	Tall Ships 2000	Southampton, Bermuda, Boston, Halifax, Amsterdam	Morning Star Trust	01634 403 890	65
Easter weekend	Easter Conference	Haverford West Congregational Church	Congregational Federation Youth (CF Youth)	0115 941 3801	478
Spring	Millennium studies; 20 week evening course	Holland House, Pershore	Holland House	01386 860 330	125
Spring	Students will be planting over 200 trees	Minstead	Minstead Training Project	023 8081 2297	105
1st – Oct	Musical drama, daily performances	St Alfege's, Greenwich	Greenwich Beta	0208 858 3006	
1st – Nov 4th	Lambeth Palace Millennium Opening; guided tours	Lambeth Palace, London	Project Manager: Dr John Ledger	Lambeth Palace, London SE1 7JU	205
4th	They Think It's All Over – results of the English Church Attendance Survey	Hertfordshire	Christian Research	020 8294 1989	456
5th	They Think It's All Over – results of the English Church Attendance Survey	Central London	Christian Research	020 8294 1989	456
6th	They Think It's All Over – results of the English Church Attendance Survey	Guildford	Christian Research	020 8294 1989	456
7th – 9th	Pilgrim's Progress	Lantern Arts Centre	Lantern Arts Centre	020 8944 5794	300
7th – 9th	Weekend Get Together	Methodist Church, Stamford	British Association of Christian Bands	01483 760 904	304
12th, 13th	The Causes of Illness & the Role of Doctors; evening event	Southwark Cathedral & King's College	Southwark Cathedral & King's College, London	020 7407 3708	193
21st	Passion Play (cast of 1000)	Greenwich Park on Good Friday	Greenwich Beta	0208 858 3006	
21st – 24th	Alive 2000 Festival Weekends	Cornhill Manor, Pattishall, Northampton	Jesus Fellowship	01327 349 991	218
26th – 30th	CBMC International Convention	Chicago, USA	Christian Businessmen's Committee (CBMC)	020 7404 6970	258
29th	Special Service; 11am	Canterbury Cathedral	Guild of Church Musicians	01883 743 168	235
MAY					
	Lecture	Southwark Cathedral	South London Industrial Mission	020 7928 3970	256
21st	Priestfield 2000; worship event	Priestfield Stadium, Gillingham	Churches Together in Medway & Inn Christian Ministries	01634 581 019 (ICM)	263
26th – 29th	Ecumenical Conference	Brentwood International Centre	Darash Trust	01277 374 844	518
27th	Celebration Day	Goodwood Racecourse, Surrey	Churches Together in Sussex	01444 456 588	243
28th – June 18th	Meridian Millennium Way	Walking along the Meridian	Youth with a Mission UK (David Pott)	020 8692 8271	35
29th	National Celebration Eucharist	NEC Birmingham	Briefing, Catholic Media Office	020 7828 8709	431

Date	Event	Venue	Organisation	Contact no.	Page
JUNE ASCENSION DAY	Ascension Day service	Wells Cathedral	Bath and Wells Diocesan Education Retreat Centre	01749 670 777	496
	Major East London Celebration	Barking Abbey Grounds	Essex Churches Consultative Council	01702 342 327	243
	Millennium Sunday School day trip	Wales	Sunday Schools Council for Wales	01248 382 947	496
	Pentecost 2000 Radio Project	Nationwide	CACLB – Churches Advisory Council for Local Broadcasting	01702 348 369	431
	St Olave's Festival	To be announced	Norwegian Church and Seamen's Mission	020 7237 5587	224
	Stepping Out 2000	Peak District, Derbyshire	Cliff College	01246 582 321	503
	Visit to Zimbabwe	Zimbabwe	Christians Aware	0116 254 0770	372
	Youthquake 2000	Winchester Cathedral	Winchester Diocesan Youth	01962 844 644	482
	Zambesi River bike ride		Help International	024 7661 1244	384
1st – 8th	Preparation – Jubilee Year; retreat	Cold Ash Centre	Cold Ash Retreat & Conference Centre	01635 865 353	124
3rd	Scotfest; speaker Ann Graham Lotz	SECC Glasgow	Telephone Prayer Chain Ministry	0141 332 6382	442
3rd	Thanksgiving Mass	Polish Church, 2 Devonia Road, London	Polish Institute of Catholic Action	020 8563 0206	415
4th	Diocesan pilgrimage to Walsingham	Walsingham	Roman Catholic Diocese of East Anglia	01508 492 202	200
6th	5th All Britain Festival	Waterfront Hall, Belfast	The London & Home Counties Festivals of Male Voice Praise	020 8688 1346	301
7th, 8th	Culture, Personality & Mental Health; evening event	Southwark Cathedral & King's College	Southwark Cathedral & King's College, London	020 7407 3708	193
9th – 11th	Derby Cathedral's Millennium Commission; musical drama for young people	Derby Assembly Rooms	Contact: Martin Von Fragstein	01332 290 771	192
9th – 11th	Gateshead Festival Weekend	Gateshead International Stadium	Churches Regional Commission	0191 482 3158	
9th – 12th	8th LBMC Europartners Convention	Basel, Switzerland	Christian Businessmen's Committee (CBMC)	020 7404 6970	258
PENTECOST 2000					
10th	Jesus Day; global street celebration of Christ's millennium	London, Liverpool, Edinburgh, Cardiff, Belfast	Global March for Jesus	01252 784 774	262
	Solemn Eucharist; Archbishop of York	London Arena, Docklands	Forward in Faith	020 7976 0727	235
	LOCAL CELEBRATIONS				
10th	Aspley; March & Celebration	Aspley		0115 932 9402	
	Bedford: exhibition, festivals & celebrations	Bedford	Bedford Church Leaders (Miracle Church of God)	01234 215 081	222
	Bingham March for Jesus	Bingham	Contact: Bryan Erde	01949 876 037	
10th – 11th	Buckinghamshire; Exhibition & celebration, worship led by Graham Kendrick	Buckinghamshire County Showground	Churches Together in Buckinghamshire	01844 275 822	
10th	Chester; Walk of Witness		Contact: Canon Michael Rees	01244 347 500	
	Christchurch March for Jesus	Quayside	Contact: John Ryan	01202 471 773	
	Derby & District	Derby Market Place	Contact: Terry Garley	0115 932 9402	
	Edinburgh: special exhibitions (series)	Edinburgh	Wilson Memorial Church	gwsmith@clara.net	

Millennium Events

Date	Event	Venue	Organisation	Contact no.	Page
10th – 11th	Exeter; Carnival & special service	Exeter Cathedral	Contact: Michael Selman	01392 272 450	191
10th	Gloucester	Cheltenham Racecourse	Event & Management	01242 245 444	306
	Leicester Millennium Praise	Victoria Park	Contact: Rev Barbara Stanton	01858 880351 & 0116 273 0400	
	Lincoln: special service	Lincoln Cathedral	Contact: Ven A Hawes	01529 304 348	
	Liverpool March for Jesus	Liverpool		07711 556 3690	
	Livingston: pageant Event; choirs, bands, etc	Almondvale Stadium	Catholic Press & Media Office	0141 221 1168	431
	London March for Jesus	London	Contact: Keith Marchant	01252 784 774	
	Mossley: events & special services	Mossley, Greater Manchester	St George's and Churches in Mossley	01457 832 219	
	Norwich March for Jesus	City Centre	Contact: Rev Robin Hewetson	01263 880 6020	
	Ockbrook & Borrowash; Carnival, street theatre		Contact: Terry Garley	0115 932 9402	
	Plymouth March for Jesus		Contact: Nick McKinnel	01752 772 139	
	Purbeck March for Jesus		Contact: John Barry	01929 423 308	
	Sandringham; special birthday party	Grounds of the castle	Contact: Rev Robin Hewetson	01263 880 6020	
	West Bridgford; Family Fun Day		Contact: David Bignell	0115 923 2034	
11th	Basildon	Gloucester Park	Basildon Christian Council	01277 656 344	
	Bath	Victoria Park	Bath City Churches	01225 872 903	
	Beverley	Beverley Market Square	Contact: Mark Hutton	01482 652 999	
	Birmingham: Jesus Christ – The Hope for a New Millennium; open air guest event	Cannon Hill Park	Birmingham Churches Together, contact: Mark Fisher	0121 643 6603	240
	Blandford: jamboree		Contact: Hugh Trenchard	01258 452 397	
	Brean: joint service		Contact: Robin Dixon	01225 872 903	
	Bridgwater: united Act of Praise	West Somerset Railway	Bridgwater Churches Together	01225 872 903	
	Bridport: united ecumenical service		Contact: Jenny Jenkins	01308 482 559	
	Cambridge: party, parade and prayer	Cambridge City Centre	Contact: Frank Himsworth	01223 356 047	
	Chard: united celebration		Contact: Robin Dixon	01225 872 903	
	Clevedon: worship & family picnic		Clevedon Churches Together	01225 872 903	
	Dorchester		Contact: Val Potter	01305 264 416	
	East London	Barking Abbey	Contact: Rev David Hardiman	01702 342 327	
	Gainsborough: carnival & Songs of Praise		Contact: Rev Kevin Clark	01427 612 427	
	Gillingham		Contact: Alan Norman	01747 823 069	
	Great Yarmouth: carnival	Great Yarmouth seafront	Contact: Rev Robin Hewetson	01263 880 602	
	Herne Bay Ecumenical Praise	Kings Hall, preceded by seafront celebrations	Contact: Michael Bowers	01227 375 154	
	Ilkeston All Together Day: open air service, picnic & fun afternoon	Ilkeston	Contact: Michael Brueck	0115 932 0057	
	Isle of Wight	County Showground	Contact: Ven Mervyn Banting	01983 884 432	
	Leeds	Victoria Gardens	Contact: Canon Graham Smith	0113 245 2036	
	Lowestoft		Contact: Rev Robin Hewetson	01263 880 602	
	Malvern: Pentecost Praise including Hopes & Dreams	Three Counties Showground	Churches Together in Malvern/Dudley & Worcestershire Ecumenical Council (DWEC)	01886 812 483 & 01684 574 346	243

Date	Event	Venue	Organisation	Contact no.	Page
	Mansfield Churches & Civic celebration		Contact: Graham Knott	01623 625 999	
	Matlock: open air service		Contact: Paul Newman	01629 582 804	
	Milton Keynes	Aylesbury Showground	Milton Keynes Christian Council	01908 311 310	244
	Minehead		Contact: Robin Dixon	01225 872 903	
	Norfolk	Mannington Hall	Contact: Rev Patrick Foreman	01603 754 643	
	Peasdown: mission & unity event		Peasdown Churches Together	01225 872 903	
	Plymouth: open air celebration	Plymouth Hoe	Contact: Nick McKinnel	01752 772 139	
	Preston: 'That's the Spirit'	North End Football Ground	Churches Together in Lancashire	01254 852 860	242
	Redcar	Redcar Racecourse	Churches Together in Redcar	01642 483 896	
	Salisbury: united service	Salisbury Cathedral	Contact: Tony Thorpe	01722 411 102	193
	Scarborough	Scarborough Cricket Ground	Contact: Gerry Strefford	01723 373 645	
	Shepton Mallet: worship & family picnic		Contact: Robin Dixon	01225 872 903	
	Southampton: Pentecost Party		Southampton Churches Millennium Trust	023 8077 1515	
	Stoke-on-Trent; Stadium Celebration	Port Vale Football Club	Saltbox Christian Centre	01782 814 417	268
	Wareham: united service	Quayside	Contact: Angela Salter	01929 550 011	
	Watchet: joint act of worship		Watchet Churches Together	01225 872 903	
	West Moors: united service		Contact: Janet Parker	01202 892 413	
	Weymouth: open air service		Contact: Jane Taylor	01305 815 119	
	Yeovil	Huish Park	Churches Together in Yeovil	01935 425 452	
	York	Museum Gardens	Contact: Robin Watson	01904 639 767	
	OTHER EVENTS				
11th	Opportunity for churches to reach out to communities by short-term radio services	Over the air-waves!	Premier Radio, CACLB, Trans World Radio & the Radio Authority	020 7316 1300 01702 348 369 0117 925 1775	286, 431, 367
	Tent Evangelism	Cobham, Surrey	Pioneer	01252 784 733	224
11th – Harvest	Peace Banquets	Various locations, UK & abroad	The Word for Life Trust	01590 645 216	256
12th – 14th	Spring Conference	Hothorpe Hall, Leicestershire	TES (The Evangelization Society)	01793 481 444	270
12th – 14th	Local Broadcasting Conference	Hayes Conference Centre, Derbyshire	CACLB – Churches Advisory Council for Local Broadcasting	01702 348 369	431
14th	Festival for Bedford Deanery	St Albans Cathedral	St Albans Cathedral and Abbey Church	01727 860 780	192
14th	Time 2 Change	Salisbury Market Square	Contact: Tony Thorpe	01722 411 102	
15th	The National Football Cup Final	To be announced	The National Football Cup	01923 819 932	266
16th – 24th	Cathedral Bike Ride: pilgrimage with multi-media services at each cathedral en route	Dunblane to Glasgow	Classic Bike Tours	01506 825 803	
17th	Celebration 2000 & Stepping Out 2000	Chatsworth Park, Derby;	Cliff College; contact Philip Clarke for details	01246 582 321	503
17th	Church Leaders Prayer Pilgrimage	Various points around Surrey Invitation only	Churches Together in Surrey (please contact Ecumenical co-ordinator)	020 8394 0536	243
18th	Catch the Dream	Tatton Park, Cheshire	Roman Catholic Diocese of Shrewsbury & Church of England Diocese of Chester	0151 652 9855 & 01244 620 444	201, 206
19th – 27th	Breakthrough 2000; tent conference	Oliver's Mount, Scarborough	Breakthrough	01725 378 045	246

Millennium Events

Date	Event	Venue	Organisation	Contact no.	Page
21st – 24th	International Church Music Festival	Coventry Cathedral	Coventry Cathedral	024 7622 7597	191
22nd – 28th	Community Participation (Part 1); Biblical expositions & workshops	Greatfields Hall, King Edwards Road, Barking	Institute for Community and Development Studies	020 8507 2603	519
24th	Gathering 2000	Farnborough Hill, Portsmouth	Diocesan Co-ordinator	01489 572 479	209
	Gathering 2000	Newham, London	Plaistow Christian Fellowship	020 7476 4863	
27th – 29th	Alive 2000 Festival Weekends	Cornhill Manor, Pattishall, Northampton	Jesus Fellowship	01327 349 991	218
27th – 30th	Celebration Weekend	Cliff College, Sheffield	Cliff College	01246 582 321	503
JULY					
	Cotswold Way bike ride		Help International	024 7661 1244	384
	Jesus for the 3rd Millennium; annual summer conference	High Leigh Conference Centre, Herts	The Modern Churchpeople's Union	020 8932 4379	237
	Millennium studies; 20 week evening course	Holland House, Pershore	Holland House	01386 860 330	125
	Oberammergau Passion play holidays	Germany/Austria	MasterSun	020 8942 9442	474
	Summer School	Yorkshire	Christians Aware	0116 254 0770	372
– Aug	Message 2000 Project; sports ministry sector	Manchester	Ambassadors in Sport	01204 363 606	257
1st	Bradwell Pilgrimage	Bradwell-on-Sea	Essex Churches Consultative Council	01702 342 327	243
2nd	County Celebration Worship	Rase Showground, Stoneleigh	Coventry and Warwickshire Ecumenical Council	024 7635 2551	243
3rd – 10th	Expanding the horizons of nursing – a Christian perspective; conference	Heriot Watts University, Edinburgh	Nurses Christian Fellowship International	01622 753 111	450
14th – 16th	Come Celebrate: Experience of Family – Past, Present & Future	Location unknown	Flame – Family Life & Marriage Education	01622 755 014	437
14th – 16th	Hearts on Fire 2000; Gala night (15th); rededication & celebration (16th)	Glastonbury Abbey	Hearts on Fire (Christian Arts Promotions)	01454 319 447	488
15th – 16th	Medieval Mystery Plays re-enactment & arrival of Christianity in the Channel Islands	Jersey	Churches Together in Jersey	01534 861 386	242
15th – 20th	Ireland Youth Camp	Co. Clare/Tipperary, Ireland	Faith Alive Youth Ministry	01707 664 687	261
17th – Aug 5th	Coventry Mystery Plays	Coventry Cathedral ruins	Coventry Cathedral	024 7622 7597	191
21st, 22nd	Alive 2000 Jesus Celebration	Sixfields Stadium, Northampton	Jesus Fellowship	01327 349 991	218
22nd – 29th	Derwent Week	Cliff College, Sheffield	Cliff College	01246 582 321	503
24th – 30th	National Pathfinder Conference	Scotland	Seventh-day Adventist Pathfinder Club	01923 672 251	482
24th – 31st	International Conference	Strasbourg	International Ecumenical Fellowship	01576 610 341	494
27th – 29th	Family Holiday Conference	Living Waters, North Wales	British Reformed Fellowship	028 7082 3913	231
28th – Aug 6th	Soul Survivor The Message 2000	Manchester	Soul Survivor	01923 333 331	482

Millennium Events

Date	Event	Venue	Organisation	Contact no.	Page
AUGUST					
	Family Conference	Loughborough	Evangelical Fellowship of Congregational Churches	01482 860 324	215
	International Convention	Penygroes, South Wales	The Apostolic Church International Convention	01792 473 992	487
	Power of Jesus around the World; churches Millennium convention	Lira, Uganda	Inn Christian Ministries	01634 581 019	263
2nd – 8th	Soul Survivor The Message 2000	Manchester	Soul Survivor	01923 333 331	482
25th – 26th	Convention 2000 (Tom Houston speaking)	Stirling University	United Free Church of Scotland	0141 333 3435	228
27th – Sept 3rd	Saints Uprising; gathering on Christianity's cradle isle	Halls & churches of Lindisfarne	Lindisfarne Mustard Seed Project	01289 389 249	520
28th	Millennium Day of Prayer	Ambless Society headquarters; phone in prayer requests	Ambless Society	028 6632 0320 (10 am – 10 pm)	463
29th – Sept	Weaving new cloth symposium	Lindisfarne	Lindisfarne Mustard Seed Project	01289 389 249	520
SEPTEMBER					
	Mississippi River bike ride		Help International	024 7661 1244	384
	Mouthpeace; evangelistic/ performing arts team	Sydney Olympics	Grassroots	020 8441 0642	262
9th	Let There Be – book launch	To be announced	McCrimmon Publishing Co Ltd	01702 218 956	177
23rd	Creative Christianity Conference	Worth Abbey, Sussex	The Framework Trust	01293 824 840	274
24th	16th Anniversary of Ambless	St Andrew's Parish Church, Killyman	Ambless Society	028 6632 0320	463
30th	Alive 2000 Wembley Praise Day	Wembley Conference Centre, London	Jesus Fellowship	01327 349 991	218
OCTOBER					
	Bike Ride	Israel	Edinburgh Medical Missionary Society	0131 313 3828	357
	Choral concert/poetry reading	Abbey Church, Shrewsbury	Feather Books	01743 872 177	174
	Pilgrimage	Rome	Polish Institute of Catholic Action	020 8563 0206	415
	Prism of Praise	Midlands (to be announced)	Music and Worship Foundation	01252 614 604	308
4th, 5th	Living Well, Dying Well, evening event	Southwark Cathedral & King's College	Southwark Cathedral & King's College, London	020 7407 3708	193
7th	Free to Live service	Guildford Cathedral – 10.30 am Worth Abbey – 3.30 pm Invitation only	Churches Together in Surrey	020 8394 0536	243
7th	Millennium Festival of Praise	Fairfield Halls, Croydon	London Emmanuel Choir	01737 350 637	301
9th	Provincial Service	Worcester Cathedral	United Reformed Church: West Midands Province	0121 783 1177	229
10th – 14th	UBS World Assembly	Midrand, South Africa	United Bible Societies World Service Centre	01189 500 200	133
13th – 15th	UK Educators Conference	Hebron Hall, Cardiff	Association of Christian Teachers of Wales	01656 734 118	444
21st – 23rd	Ecumenical Music Conference	The Hayes, Swanick	Methodist Church Music Society; sponsored by Pratt Green Trust	0114 235 1085	236
29th – 1st Nov	Irish Weekend for 2000 AD	Castlewellan Castle, Co.Down	Audio Visual Ministries	028 4476 8007	516

Date	Event	Venue	Organisation	Contact no.	Page
NOVEMBER					
	Desert trek, 3 week	Sinai	Wind, Sand & Stars Ltd	020 7433 3684	475
	Pilgrimage	Holy Land	Reliance World Travel Ltd	020 7489 0571	474
	Snakes & Ladders – Roger Jones musical	Milton Keynes	Milton Keynes Christian Council	01908 311 310	244
29th – Dec 6th	A New Beginning; retreat	Cold Ash Centre	Cold Ash Retreat & Conference Centre	01635 865 353	124
14th	Britten's War Requiem	Coventry Cathedral	Coventry Cathedral	024 7622 7597	191
16th – 23rd	Diocesan pilgrimage	Holy land	Church of England Diocese of Blackburn	01254 544 21	205
17th	Celebration of 800th Anniversary of St Hugh of Lincoln	Lincoln Cathedral	Churches Together in All Lincolnshire	01522 520 984	242
22nd, 23rd	Health in the City, evening event	Southwark Cathedral & King's College	Southwark Cathedral & King's College, London	020 7407 3708	193
27th	Christ of the Universe carol concert	Middlesex University, Bounds Green campus	Churches Together in North London	020 8959 7246	242
DECEMBER					
	Christmas 2000 – Multi media creation story, laser images on water screens, carols & fireworks	Castle Gardens, Rochester, Kent	Avril Sime	01634 849 304	
31st	Singfest 2000 – Global Christian singing festival event	Various	Sing'Fest'2000	01223 833 452	35
2001					
APRIL					
13th – 16th	Alive 2001 Festival Weekends	Cornhill Manor, Pattishall, Northampton	Jesus Fellowship	01327 349 991	218
MAY					
12th	Plymouth Royal Marines Band	Plymouth Pavillions	Royal Sailors' Rest (RSR)	023 9229 6096	468
18th – 24th	Community Participation (Part 2); Biblical expositions & workshops	Greatfields Hall, King Edwards Road, Barking	Institute for Community and Development Studies	020 8507 2603	519
28th – 31st	Alive 2001 Festival Weekends	Cornhill Manor, Pattishall, Northampton	Jesus Fellowship	01327 349 991	218
JUNE					
11th – 13th	Local Broadcasting Conference	Hayes Conference Centre, Derbyshire	CACLB – Churches Advisory Council for Local Broadcasting	01702 348 369	431
JULY					
3rd – 7th	World Congress: Communication – from confrontation to reconciliation	Netherlands	World Association for Christian Communication	020 7582 9139	381
Summer/ Autumn	City Reaching Event	London Borough wide	Passion	020 7586 3044	495
AUGUST					
27th – 30th	Alive 2001 Festival Weekends	Cornhill Manor, Pattishall, Northampton	Jesus Fellowship	01327 349 991	218
OCTOBER					
6th	Alive 2001 Wembley Praise Day	Wembley Conference Centre, London	Jesus Fellowship	01327 349 991	218

MILLENNIUM SECTION: RESOURCES

Listed by date of publication and alphabetical order of item

AVAIL-ABLE 1999

Item	Description	Organisation	Contact no.	Page
10 Resolutions to make for the Millennium	Replycard & Beermat	Christian Enquiry Agency	020 7523 2123	431, 258
2000 Church Year Planner	New calendar and ASB & PB Sunday titles	Decade Ministries	01235 833 030	260
2000 Years – the Christian Faith in Britain	Visual history book for children with full-colour spreads	Lion Publishing	01865 747 550	177
2000 years of classic Christian prayers	Collection for public & private use; Ed. Owen Collins	HarperCollins	020 8741 7070	174
Aberdeen & the Great Jubilee of the year 2000	Leaflet & video showing the preparations in the Roman Catholic Diocese of Aberdeen	Roman Catholic Diocese of Aberdeen	01224 208 944	199
Abolition 2000 pack	Pack of materials to help lobby/ pray for abolition of nuclear weapons	Pax Christi	020 8203 4884	455
AD Booklet	History of 2000 years of British Christian people	Lord's Day Observance Society (Day One Publications)	01372 728 300	265
AD: Milestones to the Millennium	Full colour survey of the way in which Christians have left a lasting mark on UK society by Brian Edwards	Day One Publications	01372 728 300	174
AD Musical	Resources, music and scripts for time-travel musical for 7-11 year olds	Paul Banderet	01923 679 605	
All the time in the world	Interactive childrens book 6+ years	Summit Publishing	01908 614 777	180
All the World Praise manual	Manual to help prepare global children's praise party	All the World Sing Praise Project (Faith Alive Youth Ministry)	01582 571 011	34, 261
Anthology	Book by E. Banyard	National Christian Education Council (NCEC)	0121 472 4242	157
Archbishops Millennium Message, The	By George Carey	HarperCollins	020 8741 7070	174
Artwork brochure	Photo images plus information of church textiles, banners, icons, etc; Millennium theme	Jacquie Binns	020 8874 0895	276
As the Millennium approaches	For schools use; material for discussion and activity	McCrimmon Publishing Co Ltd	01702 218 956	177
As the Millennium approaches	Study pack in 7 sessions for parishes & groups	McCrimmon Publishing Co Ltd	01702 218 956	177
Awaiting the Millennium	History of thought about the end times	IVP	0115 978 1054	155
Banners	Wide range of colourful hangings on heavyweight natural fabric	McCrimmon Publishing Co Ltd	01702 218 956	177
Banners	Numerous with Millennium messages relating to Jesus; vinyl material	The Banner Company	01297 444 665	276
Beermats/Coasters	Set of 4; Gospel on back detailing Jesus' birth, life, death & resurrection	Through Faith Missions	01954 210 239	270
Belfast Millennium Gospel Folder	To be distributed in large housing areas of Belfast	Belfast City Mission	028 9032 0557	254
Beyond the Millennium	Prophetic look at the end of the second millennium of Christianity; by John Bird	McCrimmon Publishing Co Ltd	01702 218 956	177
Bible Truth Explained	Millennium Gospels follow-up booklet	Christian Publicity Organisation	01903 264 556	183
Biblical reflections on the Political economy of Jubilee	by Pat Logan	Southwark Diocesan Board for Church in Society	020 7403 8686	210
Bulletin	Essential Christian Media Guide	Send The Light	01228 512 512	187

Item	Description	Organisation	Contact no.	Page
Calendar	Bible texts relating to the Millennium	British Israel Bible Truth Fellowship	01963 371 137	492
Calendar card	White or coloured, with one side the customer's own design	Hoplon Plastic Cards	0121 561 2472	185
Year 2000				
Candle in the Dark	Musical play for schools for the millennium	Loxwood Press	01903 824 174	177
Candles	Distribution of Millennium candles	Pendleburys Church Candles	020 8809 4922	426
Cards	Turvey Abbey's Millennium range in 8 designs	McCrimmon Publishing Co Ltd	01702 218 956	177
Carols 2000	CD & Song book	Mainstage Management Agency	020 8555 5510	308
Catching the Dream	Study course (5 part) helping churches to be ready for practical implications of gospel sharing	Action of Churches Together in Scotland	01786 823 588	240
Celebrating the Millennium in the Local Church	Practical suggestions for congregations by Michael Rees	Grove Books	01223 464 748	174
Celebrating the Christian Centuries	Collection of Christian writings from each century through 2 millennia; by A. Mayes	Society for Promoting Christian Knowledge	020 7387 5282	179
Challenge 2000 – An Advent Calendar for the Millennium	Traditional style, but inviting child to take up a challenge for the Millennium year; for Key Stage 2	Bible Reading Fellowship	01865 748 227	171
Christian Promotional News	Promotional ideas for celebrating the new Millennium	Kingscourt Enterprises	01923 248 154	277
Christianity – an introduction to the Catholic faith	Overview & guide sponsored by Catholic students at Oxford University	Family Publications	01865 514 408	174
Christians in Last Days	Audio & video tapes featuring talks by Roger Forster, Ken McCreavy & Keith Gerner	Audio Visual Ministries	028 4476 8007	516

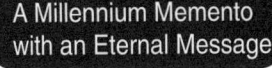

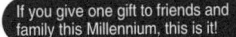

Item	Description	Organisation	Contact no.	Page
Christmas cards & leaflets	Heralding 2nd Advent of Jesus	Christian Communications Commission	0115 930 7552	292
Christmas card	Millennium theme	Ambless Society	028 6632 0320	463
The Church – Relic of a Bygone Age?	Evangelistic booklet	Christian Publicity Organisation	01903 264 556	183
Colour edition Mark's Gospel	Good News Bible version	The National Bible Society of Scotland	0800 526 910	186
Colour edition Luke's Gospel	Good News Bible version	The National Bible Society of Scotland	0800 526 910	186
Concerned to care, commitment to share	Manual on sharing your faith	Keith Wills Evangelism Trust	01204 399 363	273
Countdown	Millennium information for Surrey churches	Churches Together in Surrey	020 8394 0536	243
Disciple	Discipleship course	Counties	01373 823 013	260
Discover Y	5 small group sessions ideal for Lent 2000	Y2000	020 8287 3147	35, 271
The Dome of Heaven	Publication by Lavinia Byrne	Hodder Headline plc	020 7873 6000	176
Equigas (Based on New Start at Home)	Christian not-for-profit equitable billing company to help those on low income	Ebico Ltd	01344 425 412	
Ethical investment pack	Materials to help us look at how we can invest our money ethically	Pax Christi	020 8203 4884	455
Evangelistic booklet		Time for Truth	01562 824 337	270
Evangelistic folder	Celebrating the Millennium . . . 2000 years of history; the Millennium bug . . . when the chips are down in Y2000	TELit	0131 554 0339	188
Extreme	All age worship album	Kingdom Creative	01903 523 171	480
Five Minutes to Midnight	Gospel Tract	St Matthias Press	020 8942 0880	178
Furnishing brochure	Church furnishing specifically with Millennium theme	Vanpoulles Ltd	020 8668 6266	427
Generation to Generation Manual	Workbook helping churches to work alongside schools to raise awareness of Christianity in education	Fanfare for a New Generation	020 7450 9070	34
Gift product catalogue	Millennium theme	Ambless Society	028 6632 0320	463
Gift Millennium Gospel	Hardback Gospel with Reform introduction and millennium prayers	Reform	0114 230 9256	238
Giftware	Mugs, fridge magnets, keyrings	Igwit	01925 269 763	277
Gospels, Millennium editions	Large range of each of the gospels; softback and hardback in NIV, AV & CEV versions; children's also available	Christian Publicity Organisation	01903 254 556	183
Grace and Mortgage	Studying the language of faith and pervasive power of debt	Darton Longman & Todd	020 8875 0155	174
HarperCollins book of sermons from 2000 years, The	Compiled by John Thornton & Katherine Washburn	HarperCollins	020 8741 7070	174
Hearts on Fire brochure	Explanation of the Hearts on Fire vision in Glastonbury	Hearts on Fire	01454 319 447	488
History and Purpose of the Old Roman Catholic Church	Re-issue of the history with re-appraisal of purpose	Old Roman Catholic Church	01273 554 260	224
Hodder Celebration of Christianity, The		Hodder & Stoughton	020 7873 6000	176
Holy Bible	Contemporary English Version	The National Bible Society of Scotland	0800 526 910	186
Hope for Europe	Articles & testimonies from leading Europeans; New Testament for professional people	Christian Businessmen's Committee (CBMC)	020 7404 6970	258
Hope for the New Millennium	Reworking of David Pawson's previous book on the Second Coming	Monarch	020 8959 3668	177
Hope for the Millennium	Publication by David Pawson	Hodder Headline plc	020 7873 6000	176

Item	Description	Organisation	Contact no.	Page
Hopes & Dreams	Thriller by Rob Frost with Celtic edge; accompanies 40-city multimedia presentation	Monarch	020 8959 3668	177
IDEAS	Free Guide	Send The Light	01228 512 512	187
Images of Jesus	Classic posters of Great Master paintings of Christ with booklet of teachers' notes/classroom activities	Church House Publishing	020 7898 1451	172
Images of Jesus	Contemporary posters of Jesus stressing his encounters with people; artists from a variety of cultures	Church House Publishing	020 7898 1451	172
In Him We Move Vol. I Creative Dancing in Worship	Practical dances for individuals, congregations, those with disabilities; recommended by Cliff Richard & Margot Fonteyn	Cedar Dance & Solway Publications	01691 791 486	298
In Him We Move Vol. II Manual of Creative Dances for Worship	Practical dances for individuals, congregations, those with disabilities; recommended by Cliff Richard & Margot Fonteyn	Cedar Dance & Solway Publications	01691 791 486	298
Inspiration for a New Beginning	Words of the Millennium Resolution supported by quotations from Christian thinkers around the world	Lion Publishing	01865 747 550	177
Into the Millennium	Set of 8 colour posters by the Benedictine nuns of Turvey Abbey	McCrimmon Publishing Co Ltd	01702 218 956	177
Iona Community worship and prayer book		Wild Goose Publications	0141 440 0985	180
It's About Time – Millennium evangelism	Full colour tract	Christian Publicity Organisation	01903 264 556	183

Item	Description	Organisation	Contact no.	Page
It's About Time	Full colour brochure available to all churches; over 30 organisations advertising resources	London City Mission & It's About Time	020 7407 7585	255, 34
Jesus 2000	Range of products; posters, cards, folders, bookmarks, mugs, keyrings, T-shirt, window strips, pins, souvenir teaspoons, etc	Christian Publicity Organisation	01903 264 556	183
Jesus Through Art	Life and teaching of Jesus designed for Art & RE syllabi; activities & material included	RMEP, Hymns Ancient & Modern	01603 612 914	176
Jesus 2000 Exhibition	For local church outreach; a 'Dome at Home' pack	Christian Publicity Organisation	01903 264 556	183
Jesus and Jubilee: the Kingdom of God and our New Millennium	by Laurie Green, Bishop of Bradwell	Jubilee 2000 and Urban Theology Unit	020 7401 9999 0114 243 5342 (UTU)	384, 523
Jesus at the Millennium	The evidence for Jesus; evangelistic booklet	Christian Publicity Organisation	01903 254 556	183
Jesus Files, The	Resource pack for churches and schools	Church House Publishing	020 7898 1451	172
The Jesus Story	Close-up look at the 'Millennium Man' through stories, sketches and poems, to be booked for events	Lance Pierson Performances	020 7731 6544	302
Join in the Jubilee	Practical course to help your church prepare for the Millennium	Church in Wales Publications	029 2070 5278	172
Journey to the Millennium and Beyond	Reflections, prayers & poems of Christian women	McCrimmon & National Catholic Womens Network	01702 218 956 020 7834 1186	177, 237
Jubilee Challenge series	Videos & books concerning the Trinity and the Millennium	Missionary Society of St Columban	01564 772 096	362
Juice	New Music Reviews	Send The Light	01228 512 512	187
Just In	Best Guide to Christian Books, Music & Media	Send The Light	01228 512 512	187
Lent book for 2000	Group or individual study	CTBI Publications	020 7620 4444	172
Let There Be . . . Praying the New Millennium	Modern prayers & reflections inspired by the Millennium Resolution; posters planned	McCrimmon Publishing Co Ltd	01702 218 956	177
Listening to the Millennium	Workbook for small groups	Acorn Christian Healing Trust	01420 478 121	428
Liturgical Manual	Pamphlet	The Society of King Charles the Martyr	01947 600 766	239
Lord and His Prayer, The	Analysis of the meaning in the Lords Prayer with particular reference to debt and forgiveness, by Tom Wright	Society for Promoting Christian Knowledge	020 7387 5282	179
Lord's Prayer Anthology	Book by D. Hilton	National Christian Education Council (NCEC)	0121 472 4242	157
Luke – the Book	Luke's gospel in a modern format for distribution to school pupils (9 – 14)	The Bible Society in Northern Ireland	028 9032 6577	132
Making the most of the Millennium	Workbook with resources, ideas & information for celebration & mission	Church Pastoral Aid Society	01926 458 458	259
Man Behind the Millennium JESUS video	Open and close to the original Jesus video	JESUS Video Project	0121 765 4404	263
Managing & Leading	Challenges for Church & Society	MODEM	01273 493 172	458
Master of the Millennium	Plan of 6 sermons	Breath Ministries	01892 514 112	428
Meaning of Millennium, The	Short study of Millennium in the book of Revelation	Grove Books	01223 464 748	174
Meditations for Advent 1999: Children's version	Material for young people by the youth service at Coleg Y Bala	Presbyterian Church of Wales	029 2049 4913	225
Meditations for Advent 1999	by Rev Elfed & Nefydd Roberts	Presbyterian Church of Wales	029 2049 4913	225
Message for the Millennium	Teachings of Jesus in 40 daily readings with notes	Bible Reading Fellowship	01865 748 227	171

Item	Description	Organisation	Contact no.	Page
"Millennium"	Evangelistic tract using the Millennium as an opportunity for the gospel, in English, French (possibly Spanish, Portuguese)	Gospel Printing Mission	020 8597 2140	327
Millennium booklist	93 titles illustrated in colour	Christian Book Promotion Trust	01223 300 065	182
Millennium & The Book of Revelation, The	Sets the Millennium in Revelation in context of historical and serious thought	Lutterworth Press	01223 350 865	177
Millennium Calendar	52 door advent calendar style countdown, one door per week	National Council for Christian Education (NCEC)	0121 472 4242	177
Millennium edition of FCPS magazine	Significant events in farming past; facing the future; evangelistic thrust	Farmers Christian Postal Service	01255 508 492	184
Millennium edition of Luke's Gospel	For children, for distributing in schools	Scripture Union Northern Ireland	028 9045 4806	269
Millenium Flag	Designed to compliment Christian initiatives, to raise awareness, with New Start Link	J W Plant & Co	0113 248 0454	
Millennium Meltdown	Book by Grant Jeffrey	Harvest Field Distributors	01302 367 868	185
Millennium & New Age	Christian tract	Birmingham Gospel Outreach	0121 478 2952	182
Millennium New Start – Healing the Past	Prayers & liturgies	Lindisfarne Mustard Seed Project	01289 389 249	520
Millennium Pack	Pack including The Jesus Files, Curriculum ideas, worship ideas, general ideas & contacts	Church House Publishing	020 7898 1451	172
Millennium Pack	Resource pack for companies	Boys' Brigade	01442 231 681	476
Millennium Package	Posters, booklets, cards for churches, communities, groups	St Paul Multimedia Productions	01753 577 629	288
Millennium Planning Pack	Material on communications, planning & PR tips	The Teal Trust	01670 717 452	523

2000

Item	Description	Organisation	Contact no.	Page
Millennium Poster Book	Photocopiable posters of all the pictures from the Millennium Calendar	National Council for Christian Education (NCEC)	0121 472 4242	177
Millennium Praise	Booklet of 6 hymns	Breath Ministries	01892 514 112	428
Mustard seed versus McWorld	Reinventing Christian Life and Mission for a New Millennium by Tom Sine	Monarch	020 8959 3668	177
Mystery of Joseph, The	Translation from French for pre-millennium year of God, by Dominique Philippe	Family Publications	01865 514 408	174
A New Start?	Hopes & Dreams for the new Millennium by Rob Frost & David Wilkinson; how to make a new start with notes & ideas	Hodder Headline plc	020 7873 6000	176
New Start Worship Vol 1	Worship resources, themes, readings, prayers on photocopiable sheets; Annunciation to Advent	NS2000 & Bible Society	01793 418 100	132
New Start Worship Vol 2	Second volume of worship resources covering Advent to Epiphany	NS2000 & Bible Society	01793 418 100	132
New Testament, special edition	NIV version	Hodder Headline plc	020 7873 6000	176
New Testament & Psalms, pocket edition	Contemporary English Version	The National Bible Society of Scotland	0131 337 9701	133
New Era, New Church?	10 New Millennium Challenge goals; practical ideas by Steve Chalke & Sue Radford	HarperCollins	020 8741 7070	174
NIV Millennium Bible	£2.99 in cartons of 24	International Bible Society	01483 306 869	133
Now you see it: An introduction to Gospel Magic	Book designed to help Christians communicate the Gospel through conjuring	Keith Wills Evangelism Trust	01204 399 363	273
Peace & Truth	Articles on significance of the millennium	Sovereign Grace Union	01773 608 431	274
Pilgrim to Rome	An A-Z of Rome giving details about interesting points; H J Richards	McCrimmon Publishing Co Ltd	01702 218 956	177
Pilgrim to the Holy Land	Revised edition to the best-selling handbook of the Holy Land; H J Richards	McCrimmon Publishing Co Ltd	01702 218 956	177
Pilgrim 2000 Brochure	Outline of major church venture – 2000 pilgrims from churches across UK	McCabePilgrimages	020 8675 6828	472
Posters	Colourful and vibrant artwork of the nuns of Turvey Abbey; each one includes a Scriptural reference	McCrimmon Publishing Co Ltd	01702 218 956	177
Prayer booklet & card	Repentance, thanksgiving & commitment; Christ our Light prayer	Church of England Diocese of Wakefield	01924 255 349	211
Prayer – God's Resource	Workbook on prayer	Keith Wills Evangelism Trust	01204 399 363	273
Race for the Millennium	Analysis, theology and a programme for action in the search for racial equality	Church House Publishing	020 7898 1451	172
Religious Trends No. 2	Church and other statistics for the past 100 & 1,000 years	Christian Research	020 8294 1989	172
Re-rooting	Getting a handle on the future without losing your grip on the past	Monarch	020 8295 3668	177
Resource book/ Video	Ideas for home based outreach	Christian Viewpoint	01374 370 775	259
Rolls of visuals	For family services and school assemblies	Decade Ministries	01235 833 030	260
Salvation Tract	Poster	Victory Tracts and Posters	020 8656 2297	188
Sanctity of King Charles	Pamphlet	The Society of King Charles the Martyr	01947 600 766	239
Sceneset	Interactive CD Rom; pictures of places, customs, artefacts, etc in 12 Bible lands	Bible Scene Multimedia	01234 781 946	320
Schools Resources	Series of 5 Key Stage 1-3 learning themes & assemblies for Key Stage 2	Church in Wales Publications	029 2071 2413	172

Item	Description	Organisation	Contact no.	Page
Seeker Service Ideas	5 creative presentations based on the Y2000 theme	Y2000	020 8287 3147	271
So who is this Jesus?	Documentary video about the person and life of Jesus	Contact for Christ & Christian Television Association	020 8651 6246 & 01275 851 222	184, 285
Songs for the new Millennium	Ecumenical songbook containing many new worship songs that challenge current worship styles. Words and music; words edition and music CD	Church House Publishing, CJM Music Ltd & National Society for Promoting Religious Education	020 7898 1451 & 01675 466 254 020 7898 1000	172, 298, 393
Special birthday card	For the birthday of Jesus Christ	Cards of Encouragement	01629 580 321	276
Spirit Alive	Set of 8 colour posters by Sr Sheila Gosney	McCrimmon Publishing Co Ltd	01702 218 956	177
Stations of the Cross	Book of meditations on debt themes linked to the passion & death of Christ	CAFOD	020 7733 7900	382
Stories for the Millennium: Why the fuss?	Gift book for 8-13 year olds; life of Jesus plus other writings from contemporary Christians	Scripture Union	01908 856 188	179
Stories for the Millennium	Children's book to be distributed free to pupils in Plymouth	Christian Resources Project in conjunction with Scripture Union	01908 856 188 01752 224 012	292, 179
Stories for 2000: Why the fuss?	Retold Bible story & explanation of the Millennium; 4-7 years olds	Scripture Union	01908 856 188	179
Straight down the line	Mission poster focusing on countries down to the zero meridien	Evangelical Missionary Alliance	020 7207 2156	373
Ten Minute Miracle Plays	Medieval Miracle Plays adapted for school use; full guidance given (9+); Creation, Noah, Nativity, etc	Bible Society	01793 418 100	171
Ten Minute Miracle Plays for Easter	2 more plays concentrating on the events of the Passion and Easter	Bible Society	01793 418 100	171
Tertio Millennio Adveniente	Full text of the Pope's letter about the Great Jubilee Year	Catholic Truth Society	020 7640 0042	171
A Thousand Years of Christian Verse	Compiled by Joseph Pearce	Hodder Headline plc	020 7873 6000	176
Through the Year with the Celtic Saints	Bible readings; biographical studies	Northumbria Community Trust Ltd	01289 388 235	126
The Time of Your Life	Poetry performance taking a humorous journey through life, ideal for use at meal events, coffee mornings, etc	Lance Pierson Performances	020 7731 6544	302
Time to make a difference	Audio cassette featuring Cliff Richard, Jonathan Edwards, Steve Chalke, etc. Evangelism resource.	ICC – International Christian Communcations	01323 647 880	294
A Time to Plant	Resources pack for Millennium Trees Fund	Methodist Relief & Development Fund	020 722 8010	385
Time to Think	Pre-Millennium tract	Christian Publicity Organisation	01903 264 556	183
Time Lord	Poster	Christian Enquiry Agency	020 7523 2123	258
Timeline Assembly Book	How Christianity has influenced culture, history & spiritual life over 2000 years; for school assemblies	RMEP (Hymns Ancient & Modern)	01603 612 914	176
Traditional Anglican churches	Millennium directory	Church in Danger	01485 528 664	232
UFOs and the New Millennium	Evangelistic booklet	Christian Publicity Organisation	01903 264 556	183
The Uncancelled Mandate	by Bishop John V Taylor; 4 Bible studies on the Christian Mission approaching the Millennium	Church House Publishing	020 7898 1451	172

Item	Description	Organisation	Contact no.	Page
The Unconquerable Hope	Examination of reconciliation & a re-evaluation of its place & role in the 21st century society	Old Roman Catholic Church	01273 554 260	224
Videos	Provision of a video to every school	Staffordshire Plus Ecumenical Council	01992 475 932	245
Vigilantes in the crows nest	Concerning the new millennium; science, the Bible, end of the universe & the fate of humanity	Chyvounder Consolidated Publishing	01872 865 844	172
Visions of the Future	Bible prophecy; evangelistic booklet	Christian Publicity Organisation	01903 264 556	183
Web site launch	Free downloadable materials to help churches/leaders with evangelism, outreach, growth	Not Yet	01670 503 847	266
Welcome to the Millennium	Christian tract	Birmingham Gospel Outreach	0121 478 2952	182
Who is Jesus?	Full drama video, 23 minutes	Army of Ants	01628 481425	257
Why 2000? – The man behind the Millennium	Gospel of Luke (CEV) with additional material in magazine format	Contact for Christ	020 8651 6246	184
Why 2000? 'The Man Behind the Millennium'	Magazine style version of Luke's gospel and testimonies; video available	JESUS Video Project	0121 765 4404	263
Why 2000?	Small booklet for young children about why Jesus came	Clifford Frost Ltd	020 8540 2396	280
Word of Life Calendar 2000	Scripture text picture calendar with texts in English and one of several African languages	Word of Life	0161 628 4051	487
Worship 2000 – Celebrating a New Millennium	Substantial section of worship resources, 20 messages from world leaders, hymns, songs. Bishop Peter Atkins	HarperCollins	020 8741 7070	174

Item	Description	Organisation	Contact no.	Page
Y Now? Millennium projects for children	Resource book with material for holiday club, school assemblies & other activities	Scripture Union in association with Y-2000	01908 856 188 (SU)	179
Y Course, The	Evangelistic series including videos, 8 weeks	Y2000	020 8287 3147	271
Y2000 Personal Pack	Y lapel pin & accompanying resources for evangelism	Y2000	020 8287 3147	271
Year 2000 Millennium website	http://users.powernet.co.uk/cia/YEAR2000 Educational information with a Christian perspective	Anno Domini 2000 Designs	0121 449 4679	279

AVAIL-ABLE JAN 2000

Item	Description	Organisation	Contact no.	Page
2001 – a Faith Odyssey, booklet	A demographic and spiritual heritage guide for churches	South East Essex Churches	01702 540 255	
Anno Domini Magazine	Back issues of Evangelical Alliance Millennium quarterly 'ideas' magazine	Anno Domini	07071 202 000	34
British Israel Bible Truth Fellowship magazine articles	Historic and prophetic relating to Millennium in the Bible	British Israel Bible Truth Fellowship	01963 371 137	492
Churches Together Collection	The New Start Churches Together Hymn and Song Book	Kevin Mayhew Ltd	01449 737 978	177
Commitment to Diversity: Catholics and Education in a changing world	Collection of essays	St Mary's, Strawberry Hill	020 8240 4198	507
Directory of Catholic Diocesan Children's Societies & other caring services	Details of the work of member agencies for children and families in need	Catholic Child Welfare Council	020 8203 6323	232
Directory of millennium activities in Kent	Activities organised by churches in Kent	Churches Together in Kent	01732 761 766	242
Forge the Link posters	Poster series forging a link between the year 2000 and the name of Jesus	Christian Publicity Organisation	01903 264 556	183
Gathering 2000 Guide	Web site helping with planning a Gathering	Gathering 2000	www.firstfruit.net/gathering	
Hi Kids!	Christian Telephone Stories and a club for 6-12 year olds	Hi Kids!	020 7386 8638	480
Jesus 2000 Exhibition	18 panels on the life of Jesus, for churches & schools	Christian Publicity Organisation	01903 264 556	183
'Joshua Generation'	Book about the shape of leadership for the 3rd Millennium	Joshua Generation	020 8947 1313	494
Light in the Darkness	Exploring the meaning of the millennium through stories, visuals, worksheets and drama	Scottish Churches Millennium	0131 225 5722	
London Church Leaders Guide	List of all Millennium celebrations in London	London Church Leaders	01932 355 464	
Making and Using Banners	Making and use of banners in Millennium celebrations	Brian Clews Services	07071 202 000	399
March for Jesus Resources	Official Jesus Day books, manuals, shirts, flags, caps and balloons	Brian Clews Services	07071 202 000	399
Meeting Hindus	Education	Christians Aware	0116 254 0770	372
Millennium Celebration Toolkit	Practical information for organising a local event	All Local Authority offices		
Millennium edition of Areopagus guide to Christian publications	Booklet listing editors' requirements for freelancers	Areopagus	No telephone	311
Millennium Gift Catalogue	Party products with Christian designs for children and adults	Woodcote International Ltd	01753 642 924	
Millennium Man Booklet	Give-away evangelism booklet by escapologist Steve Legg	Christian Publicity Organisation	01903 264 556	183
Millennium Marriage Week Support Pack	Encouraging couples to make a new commitment for a new millennium	National Marriage Week & Christian Publicity Organisation	01202 849 000 & 01903 264 556	438, 183

	Item	Description	Organisation	Contact no.	Page
	The Millennium Sign (for outside churches)	"The Millennium is Christ's 2000th birthday. Worship Him here – now"	Signs of Cheshire	01606 451 87	Advert, 34
	Mustard Seed Directory	Directory of church-linked homelessness projects in Scotland	Scottish Churches Housing Agency	0131 226 2080	468
	National Prayer Resource	Programme of prayer for spiritual revival	Assemblies of God, Apostolic & Elim Pentecostal Churches	029 2075 7312 01792 473 992 01242 519 904	195, 196, 215
	Pentecost 2000 Radio Project Information & Training pack	Resource for churches wanting to set up temporary radio stations during Pentecost 2000	CACLB – Churches Advisory Council for Local Broadcasting	01702 348 369	431
	Pocket Testaments with Psalms	Commemorating 2000 years since the birth of Jesus	The Gideons International in the British Isles	01455 554 241	133
	Resource Catalogue	List of scores, music and words for Christian musicals and messages	Christian Music Ministries	0121 783 3291	183
	Rural Worship Resource Book		Christian Rural Concern	020 8657 0831	493
	Sharing Ideas	A list of Millennium ideas for RE teachers	Culham College Institute	01235 520 458	456
	S.T.E.P (Strategic Training for End-Time Preparedness)	Leadership Training programme by correspondence	Hosanna Family Churches	No telephone	325
	The Tide is Running Out	Analysis by Peter Brierley of the English Church Attendance Survey and its implications for Christianity	Christian Research	020 8294 1989	172
	Yews for the Millennium	Largest propagation programme for ancient Yews ever	The Conservation Foundation	020 7591 3111	
AVAIL-ABLE FEB 2000	'Faith in Britain's Future'	Christianity and public policy in next century	Conservative Christian Fellowship	020 7896 4245	460
MARCH	English edition of Cryu Katolicki	Roman Catholic Church in the life of Poland	Polish Institute of Catholic Action	020 8563 0206	415
	'What on earth happened to the A.D in 2000?'	Gospel presentation	World Team UK	020 8769 6343	271
APRIL	Desert Spirituality	Book about understanding desert spirituality	Northumbria Community Trust Ltd	01289 388 235	126
	Scotfest Recipe Book	Promoting the Scotfest event in Glasgow with contributions from eminent Christians	Telephone Prayer Chain Ministry	0141 332 6382	442
JUNE	People in Rural Development, 3rd edition	Book with new co-authors Jakonda & Wibberley	RURCON	01983 566 770	377
OCTO-BER	Biblical Christianity explained to Muslims	Answering most asked questions of Muslims	World Team UK	020 8769 6343	271
	Feather Books Collection of New Hymns	Hymns & church music	Feather Books	01743 872 177	174
	Poetry Church Anthology	Collection of Christian poems & prayers	Feather Books	01743 872 177	174
MAY 2001	Cross-sector Partnership in Christian Ministry Training	Manual on a ministry research on how/where Pentecostal churches may work with academic institutions	Institute for Community and Development Studies	020 8507 2603	519

MILLENNIUM TIME LINE

1/11/99	Got your Y2000 materials yet? (020 8287 3147)
2/11/99	Requested your Fanfare 'New Millennium' Challenge Pack yet? (020 7450 9070)
2/11/99	Ordered you Millennium Candles? (020 7898 1425)
3/11/99	Obtained your New Millennium Song Book for Christmas services? (01482 444 832)
	Scheduled your Open Book campaign? (01793 418 100)
12/11/99	50 days to go!
13/11/99	Contacted Christian Publicity Organisation for special millennium literature for local delivery? (01903 264 556)
14/11/99	Decided where YOU are going to be on New Year's Eve?
15/11/99	Scheduled your New Start themes for next year's services? (020 7898 1435)
1/12/99	Planned your visit to The Passion Event? (01225 466 900)
2/12/99	Checked out your local Beacon party for 31st December? (1725 518 810)
3/12/99	Fixed dates for your Hopes & Dreams presentations in AD2000? (020 8288 1961)
4/12/99	Invited EVERYONE you know to your First Millennium Sunday service?
31/12/99	Timed Beacon events throughout the UK. Midnight in capital cities.
	New Start Millennium Moment, in numerous settings.
1/1/00	Noon – Attend local Celebration 2000 service, with national peal of bells (020 7240 0880)
	Is there an 'All the World Sing Praise' service nearby? (01582 571 011)
2/1/00	Your own 'Making Sunday Best' service.
	World Day of Praise for Jesus Christ at a church near you (0115 930 7552)
	Services of rededication, Scotland.
	2.30 – Special Millennium Services in London, Cardiff, Belfast and Edinburgh.
	Tune into the first Songs of Praise on the new millennium (0161 200 2020)
	Evening – Fanfare Extravaganza from Birmingham (020 7450 9070)
February	Have your Millennium Gift Gospels for your neighbours been delivered? (01903 264 556)
	Ordered your copy of 'The Tide is Running Out'? (020 8294 1989)
	Planned your Pentecost Sunday event yet?
14 – 19/2/00	Millennium Marriage Week (01202 849 000)
Feb & March	JC2000 Regional Festivals. Is your school taking part? (020 7371 3716)
March	Jesus videos in every home in time for Easter? (0121 765 4404)
April	Selected your March for Jesus venue? (01252 784 774)
	Scheduled your Discover Y course? (01903 264 556)
May	Got your Jesus Day T shirt? (01628 525 314)
June	Find out where your local Peace Banquet is being held (01590 645 216)
10/6/00	Global Jesus Day – March for Jesus
	Have you found out what your local town is doing for Pentecost?
10 – 21/6/00	World's Biggest Birthday Parties (020 8318 9233)
11/6/00	Pentecost Sunday
	Take the opportunity to reach the community over local radio airwaves (020 7316 1300)
28/8/99	Phone in your prayer requests for the Millennium Day of Prayer (01365 320 320)
Aug – Nov	Further Y2000 campaign? (020 8287 3147)
	Cinema booked for 'Jesus the Christ' season? (020 8549 6014)
	Gospel distribution?
	New Start with God programme? (020 7898 1435)
Dec	Christmas 2000 extravaganza
31/12/00	Opportunity for candles and resolution again

A

ACCOMMODATION

CAMPING, CARAVAN & OUTDOOR CENTRES

By Country and Postcode area (see Page 569 for explanation)
Organisations which did not supply any of this information are not listed here

S = single rooms **D/T** = number of bed spaces in double/twin rooms **L** = number of bed spaces in rooms larger than double
TS = total bed spaces (not number of rooms) **DR** = Day Room, the capacity of the largest room suitable for group use
⇌ = nearest Railway station ⊖ = nearest London Underground station

Postcode	Location	Name	S	D/T	L	Other		TS	DR	Railway Station
ENGLAND										
Anglia										
CM 9	**Maldon**	Fellowship Afloat Charitable Trust	n/a	n/a	n/a			36	60	⇌ Witham
NR12	**Norwich**	The Horstead Centre	2	4	29			35	30	⇌ Norwich or Hoveton & Wroxham
RM 4	**Romford**	Mansfield Outdoor Centre	-	-	-	non-residential		-	40	⊖ Hainault
Midlands										
DE 6	**Ashbourne**	Dovedale House	-	10	50			60	60	⇌ Derby
NN 7	**Northampton**	Yardley Hastings Centre	3	8	30			41	70	⇌ Northampton
NN 9	**Wellingborough**	Frontier Centre	-	6	18	camping	68	92	50	⇌ Wellingborough
North East										
DL11	**Richmond**	Marrick Priory Outdoor Education and Residential Centre	n/a	n/a	n/a			38	30	⇌ Darlington
DL12	**Barnard Castle**	The Kingsway Adventure Centre	n/a	n/a	n/a			42	-	⇌ Darlington
DL13	**Bishop Auckland**	YMCA, Weardale House	-	-	60			60	60	⇌ Durham
HG 3		West End Outdoor Centre	-	16	44			60	-	⇌ Harrogate
North West										
CA16	**Appleby-in-Westmorland**	Knock Christian Centre & Dun Fell Christian Trust	-	4	56			60	-	⇌ Appleby or Penrith
CW10	**Middlewich**	Middlewich Narrowboats	n/a	n/a	n/a	2 narrowboats		24	n/a	⇌ Sandbach
LA20	**Broughton-in-Furness**	Kepplewray Centre	2	18	30			50	75	⇌ Foxfield
LA22	**Ambleside**	Victor Training	n/a	n/a	n/a			n/a	n/a	
LA23	**Windermere**	Packway House	-	-	-	apartments	5	5	-	⇌ Windermere
South Central										
OX 8	**Witney**	Adventure Plus	n/a	n/a	n/a	+ camping		100	100	⇌ Oxford
PO18	**Chichester**	Christian Youth Enterprises Sailing Centre	-	6	30			36	40	⇌ Nutbourne or Bosham
PO21	**Bognor Regis**	Copthorne Caravans	n/a	n/a	n/a	12 holiday caravans		52	-	⇌ Bognor Regis
PO30	**Newport**	Medina Valley Centre	-	10	64			74	80	⇌ Ryde Esplanade
PO33	**Ryde**	Crusader Centre, Westbrook	-	20	80			100	75	⇌ Ryde Esplanade
SO30	**Southampton**	YMCA National Centre, Fairthorne Manor	-	96	64	camping	180	340	60	⇌ Botley
South East										
BN17	**Littlehampton**	Climping Centre	-	-	-	camping	80	80	-	⇌ Littlehampton
ME 4	**Chatham**	Morning Star Trust	n/a	n/a	n/a			14	-	⇌ Chatham
TN11	**Tonbridge**	Carroty Wood	n/a	n/a	n/a			198	-	⇌ Tonbridge
TN14	**Sevenoaks**	Halls Green	n/a	n/a	n/a			101	-	⇌ Sevenoaks
South West										
EX16	**Tiverton**	Palfreys Barton Caravans	-	-	-	6 berth caravans		24	-	⇌ Tiverton Parkway
EX33	**Braunton**	St George's House	n/a	n/a	n/a			46	-	⇌ Barnstaple
GL15	**Lydney**	Viney Hill Christian Adventure Centre	-	-	-	camping	50	50	-	⇌ Lydney
PL26	**St Austell**	Trencreek Farm Holiday Park	-	-	-	self-catering units camping pitches	43 200	243	-	⇌ St Austell
PL27	**Wadebridge**	The Laurels, Holiday Cottages & Campsite	6	8	-			14	28	⇌ Bodmin Parkway
WR 6	**Worcester**	Gaines Christian Youth Centre	1	26	88			115	120	⇌ Worcester Shrub Hill
NORTHERN IRELAND										
BT33	**Newcastle**	YMCA, Greenhill	-	8	40	tents	88	136	-	*Rail:* Newry
SCOTLAND										
DD11	**Arbroath**	Windmill Christian Centre	2	8	35			45	-	⇌ Arbroath
DG7	**Castle Douglas**	Barcaple Christian Outdoor Centre	-	-	46			46	-	⇌ Dumfries
IV20	**Tain**	Tarbat Free Church Caravan Site	-	-	-	caravans	35	35	-	⇌ Fearn or Tain
KA27		Abernethy Trust Arran	1	2	38			41	-	⇌ Ardrossan Harbour
PA29	**Tarbert**	Port Ban Caravan Park	-	-	-	caravans	125	125	250	⇌ None near
PA39	**Ballachulish**	Glencoe Outdoor Centre	-	2	33			35	50	⇌ Fort William
PA67	**Isle of Mull**	Camas Adventure Camp	-	-	16			16	20	⇌ Oban
PH10	**Blairgowrie**	Compass Christian Centre	-	4	46	self-catering	10	60	-	⇌ Perth (30 miles)
PH14	**Perth**	Teen Ranch Scotland	n/a	n/a	n/a			66	-	⇌ Dundee or Perth
PH21	**Kingussie**	Badenoch Christian Centre	-	36	-			36	-	⇌ Kingussie or Aviemore
PH22	**Aviemore**	Alltnacriche Christian Centre	1	8	33			42	-	⇌ Aviemore
PH25	**Nethy Bridge**	Abernethy Trust Nethy Bridge	-	60	20			80	120	⇌ Aviemore
PH33	**Fort William**	Discovery Cruising	-	-	-	6-berth yachts	12	12	-	⇌ Fort William
TD 9	**Newcastleton**	Whithaugh Park	n/a	n/a	n/a			188	-	⇌ Carlisle
WALES										
LL23	**Bala**	Quest Achievement Centre	-	6	24			30	30	⇌ Wrexham
LL39	**Arthog**	Min-Y-Don Christian Adventure Centre	3	14	30	self-catering flat	3	50	60	⇌ Fairbourne
LL45	**Llanbedr**	CMC Pensarn Harbour	1	4	30			35	50	⇌ Porthmadog
		The Ranch Outdoor Discovery Centre	-	4	36			40	40	⇌ Pensarn (Gwynedd) or Barmouth
SA 3	**Swansea**	St Madoc Christian Youth Camp	1	10	70			81	-	⇌ Swansea
SA44	**Llandysul**	The Long Barn	-	2	29	flat	3	34	30	⇌ Carmarthen
SY23	**Aberystwyth**	Tynddol Challenge Centre	-	-	30			30	30	⇌ Aberystwyth

CAMPING, CARAVAN & OUTDOOR CENTRES

By Alphabetical Order

*Abernethy Trust Ardeonaig**, Killin FK21 8SY
Centre Director: Mr Philip A Simpson. *Deputy Centre Director:* Mrs Rosemary K Simpson. Executive staff 1, Other staff 15. ***CC*** No.SCO 06270. Began 1984; non-denominational. (Previously Ardeonaig Outdoor Centre). Turnover £212,000 to year end Oct 98. Fully staffed residential centre offering courses for groups to develop leadership and team skills.
Web: www.abernethytrust.org.uk
Email: abernethytrustardeonaig@compuserve.com
☎ 01567 820 523 🖷 01567 820 955

Abernethy Trust Ardgour, School of Adventure Leadership, Ardgour, Fort William PH33 7AD
Centre Director: Mr Barry Edmondson. Admin staff 2, Other staff 6. ***CC*** No.SCO 06270. Began 1992; interdenominational. (Previously Ardgour Outdoor Centre). Turnover £80,000 to year end Dec 98. Providing a one year instructor training course and schools and youth group multi-activity programme.
Web: www.abernethytrust.org.uk
Email: abernethytrustardgour@compuserve.com
☎ 01967 411 222 🖷 01967 411 222

Abernethy Trust Arran, Shiskine, Brodick KA27 8EW
Centre Director: Mr Peter W Jones. Admin staff 3, Other staff 8. ***CC*** No.SCO 06270. Began 1981; interdenominational. (Previously Arran Outdoor Centre). Turnover £150,000 to year end Dec 96. Residential outdoor centre offering multi-activity and environmental studies courses.
Web: www.abernethytrust.org.uk
Email: abernethytrustarran@compuserve.com
☎ 01770 860 333 🖷 01770 860 301

*Abernethy Trust Nethy Bridge**, Nethy Bridge PH25 3ED
Executive Director: Mr J Lorimer Gray. *Development Director:* Mr P A Simpson. *Centre Director:* Mrs M R Gray. Admin staff 5, Other staff 30. ***CC*** No.41055. Began 1971; interdenominational. (Previously Abernethy Outdoor Centre). Turnover £1,000,000 to year end Oct 98. Group of residential Christian outdoor centres using its people, properties and programmes to share Christ.
Web: www.abernethytrust.org.uk
Email: admin@abernethytrust.org.uk
☎ 01479 821 279 🖷 01479 821 162

Adventure Plus, Church Lane, Witney OX8 6LA
Director: Mr Jonathan Cox. *Secretary:* Mr Malcolm Dick. Admin staff 3, Other staff 1. ***CC*** No.802659. Began 1990; interdenominational. (Previously Fair Glade Trust). Turnover £104,000 to year end Dec 98. Adventure holidays, expeditions and training courses for young people, schools and adults.
☎ 01993 703 308 🖷 01993 708 433

Alltnacriche Christian Centre (Scripture Union), Lynwilg, Aviemore PH22 1PZ
General Director: Rev David Clark. Admin staff 2, Other staff 2. ***CC*** No.35168. Began 1988; interdenominational. Turnover £70,000 to year end Mar 97.
☎ 01479 810 237 🖷 01479 811 388

Badenoch Christian Centre, Kincraig, Kingussie PH21 1QD
Manager: Mrs D Lamb. Other staff 2. ***CC*** Began 1976; Church of Scotland, but open to all. Turnover £59,000 to year end Sept 98. Self-catering outdoor centre for outreach.
Email: badenoch@dial.pipex.com
☎ 01540 651 373 🖷 01540 651 373

Barcaple Christian Outdoor Centre, Ringford, Castle Douglas DG7 2AP
Executive Director: Mr David Grout. *Centre Director:* Mrs Sue Grout. Admin staff 3, Other staff 12. ***CC*** No.SCO 08771. Began 1983; non-denominational. Turnover £202,751 to year end Dec 98.
Email: david@barcaple.sol.co.uk
☎ 01557 820 261 🖷 01557 820 261

A

Camas Adventure Camp (Iona Community), Bunessan PA67 6DX
Manager: Warden, Iona Community's Island Centres. Admin staff 1. ***CC*** No.SCO 03794. Began 1938; ecumenical, Church of Scotland based. Turnover n/a. A Christian adventure camp, where outdoor adventure facilitates inner adventure, personal relationships and environmental awareness.
Web: www.iona.org.uk
Email: ionacomm@iona.org.uk
☎ 01681 700 367/01681 700 404

***Carroty Wood (Barnabas Trust Holiday Centres)**, Carroty Wood, Higham Lane, Tonbridge TN11 9QX
Centre Manager: Mr Michael Wells. Admin staff 1, Other staff 2. ***CC*** No.276346. Began 1978; interdenominational. Turnover £193,000 to year end Mar 98. Outdoor centre for holidays for young people and conferences. Youth groups, churches and schools.
Email: headoffice@barnabas.org.uk
☎ 01732 354 690 🖷 01732 360 429

Chapel Farm Caravan Park, Little Asby, Appleby-in-Westmorland CA16 6QE
Proprietor: Mr Williams. Admin staff 2. Began 1980; interdenominational. Turnover £20,000 to year end Dec 94. Caravan park including 5 caravans to let.
☎ 0153 962 3665

***Christian Mountain Centre,** Tremadog, Porthmadog, Gwynedd LL49 9PS
Centre Director: Mr Richard Mayhew. Admin staff 1, Other staff 9. CC Began 1967; non-denominational. Turnover £96,000 to year end Dec 96.
☎ 01766 512 616 🖷 01766 512 616

***Christian Youth Enterprises Sailing Centre**, The Gerald Daniel, Chidham, Chichester PO18 8TE
Director: Mr Norman Doney. *Centre Manager:* Mr Gavin Jones. Admin staff 2, Other staff 6. ***CC*** No.293781. Began 1986; non-denominational. Turnover £125,000 to year end Dec 98. Watersports activity centre catering for groups, schools and individuals on holiday, courses and field studies.
Web: ourworld.compuserve.com/homepages/cye
Email: cye@compuserve.com
☎ 01243 573 375 🖷 01243 574 992

The Cirdan Sailing Trust, Fullbridge Wharf, Maldon CM9 7LE
Chief Executive Officer: Mr Nicholas Back. Executive staff 1, Other staff 10. ***CC*** No.288366. Began 1983; Anglican. Turnover £250,000 to year end Dec 99. Providing groups of young people the challenge of sailing large historic vessels.
☎ 01621 851 433 🖷 01621 840 045

***Climping Centre (Barnabas Trust Holiday Centres)**, Brookpit Lane, Climping, Littlehampton BN17 5QU
Centre Manager: Mr Michael Wells. Admin staff 1. ***CC*** No.276346. Began 1978; interdenominational. Turnover £16,000 to year end Mar 98. Seasonal centre mainly May-Sept, youth groups, schools, church groups.
Email: headoffice@barnabas.org.uk
Bookings: Carroty Wood, Higham Lane, Tonbridge TN11 9QX
☎ 01732 354 690 🖷 01732 360 429

For additional information see List on Page 62

***CMC Pensarn Harbour**, Pensarn Harbour, Llanbedr LL45 2HS
Centre Director: Mr Richard Mayhew. Admin staff 1, Other staff 9. ***CC*** No.1060275. Began 1967; non-denominational. (Previously Christian Mountain Centre). Turnover £160,000 to year end Dec 98. Residential outdoor activity centre, catering for all ages and abilities, catering for up to 50.
Email: cmcpensarn@aol.com
☎ 01341 241 646 / 241 718 🖷 01341 241 646 / 241 718

Compass Christian Centre, Glenshee Lodge, Blairgowrie PH10 7QD
Director: Mr Gordon Roy. *Bookings Secretary:* Mrs Kitty Clare. Admin staff 2, Other staff 14. ***CC*** No.40441. Began 1967; interdenominational. Turnover £167,253 to year end May 98. Skiing and outdoor activity centre also offering environmental studies and team building.
Email: compass@compasschristian.co.uk
☎ 01250 885 209 🖷 01250 885 309

Copthorne Caravans, Rose Green Road, Bognor Regis PO21 3ER
Proprietors: Mr Tony & Mrs Lindsay Leney. Admin staff 2, Other staff 3. Began 1945; non-denominational. Turnover n/a. Holiday caravan park. Static caravans for hire, and privately owned caravans. No animals.
☎ 01243 262 408

***Crusader Centre, Westbrook**, Westbrook, Oakhill Road, Ryde PO33 1PU
Director: Mr Stephen R Foster. Admin staff 1, Other staff 4. ***CC*** No.223798. Began 1947; interdenominational. Turnover £200,000 to year end Dec 98. Young people.
Web: web.ukonline.co.uk/members/crusaders/
Email: westbrook.isleofwight@btinternet.com
☎ 01983 811 118 🖷 01983 616 335

Discovery Cruising, Quiraing, Onich, Fort William PH33 6SB
Skipper: Mr Melville Paton. Admin staff 1. ***CC*** No.SCO 15412. Began 1986; interdenominational. Turnover £35,000 to year end Nov 98. Skippered cruises on the west coast of Scotland, particularly for young people and students.
Web: www.discoverycruising.co.uk
Email: info@discoverycruising.co.uk
☎ 01855 821 371 Mobile: 07050 294 159
🖷 01855 821 371

Dovedale House (Residential Centre for Young People), Ilam, Ashbourne DE6 2AZ
Warden: Mr Arthur J Hack. *Deputy Warden:* Mr Martin Stephens. Other staff 6. ***CC*** No.522677. Began 1966; Anglican but open to all. Turnover £135,000 to year end Dec 98. For young people and adult groups.
☎ 01335 350 365 🖷 01335 350 441 (office hours)

Fellowship Afloat Charitable Trust, The Sail Lofts, Woodrolfe Road, Tollesbury, Maldon CM9 8SE
Director: Mr David Hillyer. Admin staff 3, Other staff 7. ***CC*** No.1059143. Began 1966; non-denominational. Turnover £140,000 to year end Mar 98. Sailing, environmental studies, craft activities. Boatyard and berthing facilities, residential outdoor activities.
Web: www.mccom.co.uk.fact/
Email: info@fact.kemc.co.uk
☎ 01621 869 779 (Office) 868 113 (Centre)
🖷 01621 869 771

***Frontier Centre (Barnabas Trust Holiday Centres)**, Addington Road, Irthlingborough, Wellingborough NN9 5UH
Centre Manager: Mr Chris Shrimpton. Admin staff 4, Other staff 20. ***CC*** No.276346. Began 1983; interdenominational. Turnover n/a. Accommodation for groups wanting conference facilities or for youth organisations wanting outdoor activities.
Email: frontier@barnabas.jireh.co.uk
☎ 01933 651 718 🖷 01933 651 893

Gaines Christian Youth Centre, Whitbourne, Worcester WR6 5RD
Director: Mr Graham Woods. *Director:* Mrs Susan Woods. Admin staff 3, Other staff 7. ***CC*** No.1057267. Began 1963; non-denominational. Turnover £150,000 to year end Dec 98. Fully-catered residential youth centre with many safe, exciting on-site activities.
☎ 01886 821 212 🖷 01886 822 042

Glencoe Outdoor Centre, Glencoe, Ballachulish PA39 4HS
Centre Director: Mr Chris Williams. Admin staff 4, Other staff 8. Began 1988; non-denominational. Turnover £138,000 to year end Mar 98.
Email: gocjezza@aol.com
☎ 01855 811 350 🖷 01855 811 644

***Halls Green (Barnabas Trust Holiday Centres)**, Halls Green Centre, Hale Oak Road, Weald, Sevenoaks TN14 6NQ
Centre Manager: Mr Marcus Cameron. Admin staff 1, Other staff 1. ***CC*** No.276346. Began 1978; interdenominational. Turnover £77,000 to year end Mar 98. Outdoor centre for holidays for young people and conferences.
☎ 01732 463 212 🖷 01732 463 212

The Horstead Centre, Rectory Road, Horstead, Norwich NR12 EP
Warden: Mrs Val Khambatta. Executive staff 1, Other staff 5. ***CC*** No.303986. Began 1970; Anglican. Turnover £70,000 to year end Dec 98. Residential study/activity centre for young people to develop their physical, mental and spiritual capacities.
Web: www.zoo.co.uk/~horstead.centre
Email: horstead.centre@zoo.co.uk
☎ 01603 737 215 🖷 01603 737 494

Kepplewray Centre, Broughton-in-Furness LA20 6HE
Chief Executive: Rev Tim Montgomery. *Programme Manager:* Mr Taff Bowles. Executive staff 1, Other staff 7. ***CC*** No.1015762. Began 1993; ecumenical. Turnover £110,000 to year end Jun 98. Activity, education, conference and holiday centre for disabled and able-bodied people together.
Web: www.kepplewray.org.uk
Email: stay@kepplewray.org.uk
☎ 01229 716 936 🖷 01229 716 938

The Kingsway Adventure Centre, Alston Road, Middleton-in-Teesdale, Barnard Castle DL12 0UU
Principal: Mr Adam Hearn. Admin staff 1, Other staff 2. Began 1990; non-denominational. Turnover £60,000 to year end Apr 99. Outdoor activity centre, holidays for groups and individuals.
Web: www.bigfoot.com/~kingsway
Email: kingsway@bigfoot.com
☎ 01833 640 881 🖷 01833 640 155

Knock Christian Centre & Dun Fell Christian Trust, Knock, Appleby-in-Westmorland CA16 6DL
Manager: Mr Trevor Watson. No full-time staff. ***CC*** No.510095. Began 1979; evangelical. Turnover n/a. 10 canoes on trailers, climbing wall and pool/tennis tables available; indoor and outdoor activities.
☎ 01768 361 762
Bookings: *Booking Secretary:* Mrs R Murray, 74 Lyndhurst Road, Brighouse HD6 3RX
☎ 01484 715 070 🖷 01484 722 561

The Laurels, Holiday Cottages and Campsites, Whitecross, Wadebridge PL27 7JQ
Owners: Mr & Mrs Laing. No full-time staff. Began 1986; non-denominational. Turnover £32,000 to year end May 96. Providing holiday cottages and campsite.
☎ 01208 813 341

***Lendrick Muir Centre (Scripture Union)**, Rumbling Bridge, Kinross KY13 0QA
Centre Director: Malcolm Webb. Admin staff 5, Other staff 8. ***CC*** Began 1999; interdenominational. Turnover: first year of operation.
☎ 01577 840 164

The Long Barn, Penrhiw, Capel Dewi, Llandysul SA44 4PE
Proprietors: Mr Tom & Mrs Eva Cowcher. Admin staff 2, Other staff 2. Began 1989; non-denominational. Turnover £3,600 to year end Mar 98. Bunkhouse accommodation on working farm.
☎ 01559 363 200 🖷 01559 363 200

Mansfield Outdoor Centre, Manor Road, Lambourne End, Romford RM4 1NB
Manager: Mr Greg Barton. Other staff 10. ***CC*** No.220085. Began 1989; interdenominational. Turnover £100,000 to year end Apr 98. Outdoor activities, personal development for young people/young adults from inner cities and within London.
☎ 020 8500 3047 🖷 020 8559 8481

Marrick Priory Outdoor Education and Residential Centre, Richmond DL11 7LD
Warden: Dr Roger Hopper. *Deputy Warden:* Miss Cilla Withers. Admin staff 3, Other staff 8. ***CC*** Began 1970; Anglican-based but interdenominational. Turnover £160,000 to year end Mar 98. Residential centre, with educational, conference and outdoor pursuits facilities for church and secular groups.
Email: marrick@mpriory.demon.co.uk
☎ 01748 884 434

***Medina Valley Centre for Outdoor Education**, Dodnor Lane, Newport PO30 5TE
Executive Director: Mr Peter Savory. Admin staff 2, Other staff 9. ***CC*** No.236153. Began 1963; interdenominational. Field studies GCSE/A-level, Geography/Biology; sailing courses for schools/individuals; church and youth holidays/retreats.
Web: www.medinavalleycentre.org.uk
Email: info@medinavalleycentre.org.uk
☎ 01983 522 195 🖷 01983 825 962

Middlewich Narrowboats, Canal Terrace, Middlewich CW10 9BD
Proprietor: Mr Christopher Cliff. Executive staff 2, Other staff 3. Began 1971; non-denominational. Turnover £270,000 to year end Oct 98. Self-drive holidays on the inland waterways of north-west England and north Wales.
Web: www.middlewichboats.co.uk
Email: midboats@globalnet.co.uk
☎ 01606 832 460 🖷 01606 737 912

Min-Y-Don Christian Adventure Centre, Arthog LL39 1BZ
Administrator: Mrs Elizabeth Boot. Admin staff 2, Other staff 4. Began 1961; interdenominational. Turnover £65,000 to year end Jan 98. Activity holidays (licensed activity provider), retreats, conferences, family weeks, school parties.
☎ 01341 250 487/433 🖷 01341 250 686

Morning Star Trust, Crews Quarters Offices, Chatham Historic Dockyard, Chatham ME4 4TZ
Administrator: Mr Tim Millward. Admin staff 1, Other staff 3. ***CC*** No.328320. Began 1981; interdenominational. Turnover £82,000 to year end Dec 97. Off-shore sail training for young people; 62ft gaff ketch; Duke of Edinburgh award; tall ships events.
Email: mornstar@globalnet.co.uk
☎ 01634 403 890 🖷 01634 403 890

Packway House, Crook Road, Bowness-on-Windermere, Windermere LA23 3NE
Managers: Mr & Mrs John Parsons. Admin staff 1. Began 1971; non-denominational. Turnover n/a. Self-catering apartments.
☎ 01539 443 532

Palfreys Barton Caravans, Cove, Tiverton EX16 7RZ
Proprietor: Mrs J Withers. Staff n/a. Began n/a; interdenominational. Turnover n/a.
☎ 01398 331 456 🖷 01398 331 456

Port Ban Caravan Park, Kilberry, Tarbert PA29 6YD
Owners: The Sheldrick family. Admin staff 1, Other staff 3. Began 1967; interdenominational. Turnover £10-50,000 to year end Dec 96.
☎ 01880 770 224/388 🖷 01880 770 388

Quest Achievement Centre, Gwern Genau, Arenig, Bala LL23 7PB
Manager: Mr Tim Jones. Other staff 2. ***CC*** No.501648. Began 1971; non-denominational. (Previously Quest Farmhouse and Adventure Centre). Turnover £38,000 to year end Dec 98. Providing accommodation for youth groups, with the options of catering and adventure activities.
Email: sam@the-jones.freeserve.co.uk
☎ 01678 520 735

***The Ranch Outdoor Discovery Centre**, Bryn-y-Moel, Llanbedr LL45 2HU
Centre Director: Mr Andy Whittaker. Admin staff 3, Other staff 1, Volunteers 6. ***CC*** No.803431. Began 1973; interdenominational. Turnover n/a. Provision of residential facilities to assist young people develop physically, mentally and spiritually.
Web: members.xoom.com/the_ranch
☎ 01341 241 358 🖷 01341 241 530

A

St George's House (Christian Outdoor Centre), Georgeham, Braunton EX33 1JN
Manager: Mr Martin Larrington. Admin staff 2, Other staff 6. *CC* No.279046. Began 1978; interdenominational. Turnover £80,000. Outdoor centre schools clubs for educational courses; climbing, surfing, kayaking, waterskiing, biking, sailing, abseiling, etc.
☎ 01271 890 755

St Madoc Christian Youth Camp, Llanmadoc, Gower, Swansea SA3 1DE
Camp Managers: Mr & Mrs Steve & Julie Jenkins. *CC* No.260655. Began 1944; non-denominational. Turnover n/a. For self-contained youth groups.
☎ 01792 386 291

Tarbat Free Church Caravan Site, Portmahomack, Tain IV20 1YL
Manager: Rev John MacLeod. Admin staff 1, Other staff 2. *CC* Began 1955; Free Church of Scotland. Turnover £13,000 to year end Dec 97. 35 holiday caravans (touring and static).
Web: www.highlander.zetnet.co.uk/tfc/caravan
Email: tarbat@bigfoot.com
☎ 01862 871 467 Fax 01862 871 467

†Teen Ranch Scotland, Ballindean House, Inchture, Perth PH14 9SF
Trustees: Mr Robert & Mrs Jenny Ockenden, Mr Allan McCulloch. Admin staff 3, Other staff 12. *CC* Began 1984; interdenominational. Turnover £100,000 to year end Jan 91. Activity Centre for young people offering a diverse range of activities and interests.
☎ 01828 686 227

Trencreek Farm Holiday Park, Hewaswater, St Austell PL26 7JG
Proprietor: Mr Steve Kendall. Admin staff 2, Other staff 2. Began 1990; interdenominational. Turnover n/a.
☎ 01726 882 540

***Tynddol Challenge Centre**, Cwmystwyth, Aberystwyth SY23 4AG
Director: Mr Robin Morris. Admin staff 3, Other staff 6. *CC* No.1019827. Began 1986; interdenominational. Turnover n/a. Activity-based holidays with Christian teaching for young people, schools and families (particularly single-parent families).
Email: tynddolcc@aol.com
☎ 01974 282 618

Victor Training, Dovedale House, 6 Compston Street, Ambleside LA22 9DP
Managing Director: Mr David Hendrickse. Executive staff 1, Other staff 1. Began 1991; interdenominational. No magazine. Turnover £24,000 to year end Apr 98. Outdoor activities and team building for business, church and youth organisations.
Email: hendrickse@bigfoot.com
☎ 01539 432 748 Mobile: 07767 603 848 Fax 01539 432 692

Viney Hill Christian Adventure Centre, The Vicarage, Viney Hill, Lydney GL15 4NA
Warden: Capt Stephen Hunt. Began 1983; Anglican. Turnover £4,000 to year end Dec 90. May to September only.
☎ 01452 410 022 Fax 01452 308 224

West End Outdoor Centre, Whitmoor Farm, West End, Summerbridge, Harrogate HG3 4BA
Proprietor: Mrs Margaret Verity. Admin staff 1, Other staff 1. Began n/a; non-denominational. Turnover £25,000 to year end May 98. Self-catering.
Web: www.yorkshiremet.co.uk/accgde.westend
☎ 01943 880 207 Fax 01943 880 207

***Whithaugh Park (Barnabas Trust Holiday Centres)**, Newcastleton TD9 0TY
Centre Manager: Mr David Jenner. Admin staff 2, Other staff 1. *CC* No.276346. Began 1989; interdenominational. Turnover £176,000 to year end Mar 98. Outdoor centre for young people and conferences; for youth groups, churches and schools.
☎ 01387 375 394 Fax 01387 375 661

Windmill Christian Centre, Millgate Loan, Arbroath DD11 1QG
Centre Manager: Mrs Dorothy Parsons. Executive staff 1. *CC* No.SCO 22258. Began 1998; interdenominational. Turnover: first year of operation. Providing self catering accommodation for Christian groups who have Bible teaching as part of programme.
Web: www.netlink.co.uk/users/dk/arbroath/windmill/
Email: windmill@dk.sol.co.uk
☎ 01241 434 455 Fax 01241 434 466

Yardley Hastings Centre, National Youth Resource Centre, Castle Ashby Road, Yardley Hastings, Northampton NN7 1EL
Chaplain: Rev Liz Byrne. *Centre Administrator:* Mrs Janet Nicholls. Executive staff 3, Administrative staff 2. Began 1992; United Reformed. Turnover £150,000 to year end Dec 98. Encouraging and training Christians to reach full potential in body, mind, spirit through events, activities.
Email: nyrc@surfaid.org
☎ 01604 696 307 Fax 01604 696 030

†YMCA, Weardale House, Ireshopeburn, Bishop Auckland DL13 1HB
Warden: Mr Simon Graham. *Deputy Warden:* Mr Dave Jones. Admin staff 3, Other staff 10. *CC* Began 1988; interdenominational. Turnover £150,000 to year end Jan 96.
☎ 01388 537 479 Fax 0191 385 2267
Bookings: YMCA Office, Herrington Burn, Houghton le Spring DH4 4JW
☎ 0800 591 527 Fax 0191 385 2267

†YMCA, Greenhill, Donard Park, Newcastle BT33 0GR
Centre Director: n/a. Admin staff 5, Other staff 25. *CC* Began 1974; interdenominational. (Previously Glen River YMCA). Turnover £250,000 to year end Mar 94.
Email: tim@ymca-ire-dnet.co.uk
☎ 028 4472 3172 Fax 028 4426 009

YMCA National Centre, Fairthorne Manor, Curdridge, Southampton SO30 2GH
Director of Operations: Mr Chris Hand. Other staff 19. *CC* Began 1947; interdenominational. Turnover n/a.
☎ 01489 785 228 Fax 01489 798 936

YMCA, National Centre, Lakeside, Ulverston LA12 8BD
Director: Mr Jim Dobson. *Director of Training:* Mr Steve Taylor. Admin staff 10, Other staff 100. *CC* No.212810. Began 1951; non-denominational. Turnover £1,140,000 to year end Mar 98. Outdoor education and training, holidays, conferences.
Email: admin@lakeside.ymca.org.uk
☎ 01539 531 758 Fax 01539 530 015

For additional information see List on Page 62

CONFERENCE CENTRES, GUEST HOUSES & HOTELS

By Country and Postcode area (see Page 569 for explanation)
Organisations which did not supply this information are not listed here

S = single rooms **D/T** = number of bed spaces in double/twin rooms **L** = number of bed spaces in rooms larger than double
TS = total bed spaces (not number of rooms) **DR** = Day Room, the capacity of the largest room suitable for group use
⇌ = nearest Railway station ⊖ = nearest London Underground station

Postcode	Location	Name	S	D/T	L	Other		TS	DR	Railway Station
ENGLAND										
Anglia										
CM 5	**Ongar**	Mulberry House	15	18	1			35	80	⇌ Brentwood ⊖ Epping
CM15	**Brentwood**	Pilgrims Hall	4	6	-			10	55	⇌ Brentwood
EN11	**Hoddesdon**	High Leigh Conference Centre	99	94	38			231	220	⇌ Broxbourne
IP16	**Leiston**	Sizewell Hall Ltd	5	26	49			80	150	⇌ Saxmundham
IP25	**Thetford**	Letton Hall	-	22	103	1 flat, caravans, tents	-	125	-	⇌ Norwich
IP28	**Bury St Edmunds**	Hengrave Hall Centre	13	22	43			78	100	⇌ Bury St Edmunds
NR20	**Dereham**	Moor Farm Holidays	6	12	-			18	-	⇌ Norwich
NR26	**Sheringham**	Greenhedges	-	-	30			30	50	⇌ Sheringham
		Keychange Holiday and Conference Centre	5	8	3			16	35	⇌ Sheringham
		Ye Homesteade	2	10	10			22	40	⇌ Sheringham
NR27	**Cromer**	The Pleasaunce	5	22	53	self-catering bungalow	5	85	50	⇌ Cromer
		Tudor Christian Guest House	3	14	7			24	24	⇌ Cromer
NR33	**Lowestoft**	Fairhavens Christian Guest House	1	2	3		6	12	-	⇌ Lowestoft
NR34	**Beccles**	Ringsfield Hall	2	8	49	cottage	1	60	50	⇌ Beccles
PE37	**Swaffham**	Carey House: The Pickenham Centre	-	8	11			19	45	⇌ Downham Market
London										
E 14	**London**	The Royal Foundation of St Katharine	15	4	-			19	40	*Docklands* Limehouse ⊖ Shadwell
EC1V	**London**	Central Conference Centre	-	-	-	non-residential		-	200	⊖ Old Street or Barbican
N5	**London**	Foreign Missions Club	26	30	2	flats	18	77	45	⇌ Highbury and Islington ⊖ Highbury and Islington
N 14	**London**	Oak Hill	30	20	-	flats	6	56	-	
SE 1	**London**	World Mission Association Ltd	-	-	-	non-residential		-	180	⇌ Waterloo ⊖ Waterloo
SW16	**London**	Streatham Christian Conference Centre	-	-	-	non-residential		-	300	⇌ Streatham or Streatham Common
SW1P	**London**	Emmanuel Centre	-	-	-	non-residential		-	1,000	⊖ St James Park
W1M	**London**	St Paul's Church	-	-	-	non-residential		-	260	⊖ Bond Street
W2	**London**	Ashley, Tregaron and Oasis Hotels	12	58	30			100	-	⇌ Paddington ⊖ Paddington
		Lancaster Hall Hotel Ltd	3	80	67			150	200	⇌ Paddington ⊖ Paddington or Lancaster Gate
		Redland House Hotel	7	18	6			31	-	⊖ Marble Arch
W10	**London**	Latymer Christian Centre	n/a	n/a	n/a			3	200	⇌ Paddington ⊖ Latimer Road
WC1E	**London**	Quaker International Centre	18	16	13			47	70	⇌ Euston ⊖ Euston Square or Goodge Street
Midlands										
B 15	**Birmingham**	Queen's, Birmingham, The Ecumenical Foundation for Theological Education	54	4	-	one bed flats	2	60	80	⇌ Selly Oak
B 29	**Birmingham**	Sion Catholic Community for Evangelism	20	10	5			35	75	⇌ Selly Oak
B 60	**Bromsgrove**	Wadderton Conference Centre	26	10	-			36	50	⇌ Barnt Green
CV 7	**Coventry**	Nettle Hill Training and Conference Centre	-	12	43			55	120	⇌ Coventry
CV33	**Leamington Spa**	The Southam Centre	-	-	32			32	-	⇌ Leamington Spa
CV37	**Stratford-upon-Avon**	Welford Hill Farm	-	16	-			16	36	⇌ Stratford-upon-Avon
DE 4	**Matlock**	Alison House Training and Conference Centre	10	22	-			32	35	⇌ Cromford
		Willersley Castle Hotel & Conference Centre	11	66	21			98	106	⇌ Cromford
DE55	**Alfreton**	The Hayes Conference Centre	169	210	41			420	400	⇌ Alfreton or Derby
DY14	**Kidderminster**	Pioneer Centre & Forest Lodge	7	32	206			245	250	⇌ Kidderminster
LE 8	**Leicester**	Arnesby Christian Conference Centre	-	22	-			22	30	⇌ Leicester
LE17	**Lutterworth**	Hothorpe Hall	2	64	57			123	200	⇌ Market Harborough
NG 9	**Nottingham**	St John's College	53	4	-	+ self-contained flats		57	180	⇌ Nottingham or Derby
NN 3	**Northampton**	King's Park Conference & Sports Centre	-	100	-			100	200	⇌ Northampton
NN 9	**Wellingborough**	Frontier Centre	n/a	n/a	n/a			n/a	n/a	⇌ Wellingborough
NN14	**Kettering**	Fellowship of Reconciliation, England	-	12	-	+ tents, caravans		12	50	⇌ Kettering or Peterborough
NN29	**Wellingborough**	Knuston Hall	20	32	6			58	60	⇌ Wellingborough
WV 6	**Wolverhampton**	Badger House	2	22	-			24	40	⇌ Codsall
North East										
BD 7	**Bradford**	St Columba's Horton Outreach	-	-	-	non-residential		-	n/a	⇌ Bradford Forster Square
BD23	**Skipton**	Parcevall Hall	7	22	-			29	30	⇌ Skipton or Ilkley
		Scargill House Ltd	16	66	8			90	80	⇌ Skipton
DH 1	**Durham**	St John's College	120	20	-			140	300	⇌ Durham
DL 8	**Leyburn**	The Jonas Trust	-	54	24			78	80	⇌ Darlington
DN 9	**Doncaster**	Epworth Old Rectory	-	4	-			4	-	⇌ Crowle or Doncaster
DN10	**Doncaster**	Bawtry Hall	10	50	10			70	120	⇌ Doncaster or Retford
DN32	**Grimsby**	Ice House Christian Centre	-	-	-	non-residential		-	800	⇌ Grimsby Town
HG 4	**Ripon**	Lindley Educational Trust Ltd	35	32	-			67	70	⇌ Thirsk
NE19	**Newcastle upon Tyne**	YMCA, Otterburn Hall	30	70	30			130	200	⇌ Newcastle
NE26	**Whitley Bay**	Livingstone Christian Centre	-	-	30			30	30	*Metro:* Whitley Bay
NE43	**Stocksfield**	The Boys' Brigade Training Centre	n/a	n/a	n/a			62	n/a	⇌ Stocksfield
NE49	**Haltwhistle**	Featherstone Castle	-	-	-	self-catering	80	80	-	⇌ Haltwhistle
S 11	**Sheffield**	Whirlow Grange Conference & Training Centre	20	20	-			40	120	⇌ Sheffield or Dore

Conference Centres, Guest Houses & Hotels

Postcode	Location	Name	S	D/T	L	Other	TS	DR	Railway Station
S 32	**Hope Valley**	Cliff College Conference Complex	n/a	n/a	n/a		286	n/a	⇌ Grindleford
S 33	**Hope Valley**	Hollowford Centre	1	-	67		68	60	⇌ Hope
TD15	**Berwick-upon-Tweed**	Cambridge House	4	4	-		8	-	⇌ Berwick-upon-Tweed
		Marygate House	20	2	21		43	40	⇌ Berwick-upon-Tweed
TS12	**Saltburn-by-the-Sea**	Brockley Hall	4	30	52		86	80	⇌ Saltburn
YO 7	**Thirsk**	Hollybush Christian Fellowship and Convention Centre	n/a	n/a	n/a		n/a	n/a	⇌ Thirsk
YO11	**Scarborough**	Selbourne Licensed Hotel	1	14	19		34	34	⇌ Scarborough
		Southlands Hotel	6	100	6		112	150	⇌ Scarborough
YO13	**Scarborough**	Wydale	10	32	16		58	60	⇌ Scarborough
YO21	**Whitby**	Moorlands	13	30	8		51	60	⇌ Whitby
		Sneaton Castle Centre	58	24	38		120	140	⇌ Whitby or Scarborough
YO22	**Whitby**	Fairhaven Country Hotel	2	8	11		21	26	⇌ Whitby
YO62	**York**	Redcar Farm	16	8	3		28	55	⇌ York or Malton or Thirsk
North West									
CA 3	**Carlisle**	Kingstown Hotel	-	14	3		17	-	⇌ Carlisle
CA 7	**Wigton**	Blaithwaite Christian Centre	3	22	86		111	200	⇌ Wigton
CA11	**Penrith**	Lattendales	5	18	-		23	-	⇌ Penrith
CA12	**Keswick**	Bassenfell Manor Christian Centre	-	12	57	disabled holiday flat 2	71	70	⇌ Carlisle or Penrith
		Keswick Convention Centre	1	8	32		41	60	⇌ Penrith
CW 5	**Nantwich**	Regents Park Conference Centre	9	26	15		50	100	⇌ Nantwich
FY 1	**Blackpool**	Kelvin Hotel	1	10	4		15	-	⇌ Blackpool North
FY 2	**Blackpool**	Palm Court Hotel	n/a	n/a	n/a		130	90	⇌ Blackpool North
LA 2	**Lancaster**	Littledale Hall	n/a	n/a	n/a		n/a	n/a	⇌ Lancaster
LA 4	**Morecambe**	Silverwell Christian Hotel	1	20	13		34	35	⇌ Morecambe
LA 6	**Carnforth**	Capenwray Hall	-	20	190		210	250	⇌ Carnforth or Lancaster
LA 8	**Kendal**	Damson Dene Hotel	6	64	8		78	70	⇌ Windermere
LA11	**Grange-over-Sands**	Abbot Hall	19	50	34		103	110	⇌ Kents Bank
		Boarbank Hall	20	10	-	+ nursing home 30	60	50	⇌ Grange-over-Sands
		Highway Trust, Thornleigh	6	26	20		52	55	⇌ Grange-over-Sands
LA22	**Ambleside**	Rydal Hall	10	30	16	+ campsite 350	56	150	⇌ Windermere
PR 9	**Southport**	Beach House Private Hotel	6	12	10		28	-	⇌ Southport
SY 8	**Ludlow**	Bishop Mascall Centre	16	8	24		48	100	⇌ Ludlow
SY10	**Oswestry**	Coed-y-Go Farm Holiday Centre	-	64	36	cottages 10	110	-	⇌ Gobowen
		Quinta Christian Centre	6	54	200	+ camping 150	410	400	⇌ Chirk or Gobowen
SY13	**Whitchurch**	Cloverley Hall	5	28	106		139	150	⇌ Whitchurch (Salop)
WA 6	**Warrington**	Foxhill	15	12	4		31	80	⇌ Frodsham or Runcorn
South Central									
HA 1	**Harrow**	St Mary's Church House	-	8	4		12	15	⇌ Harrow-on-the-Hill ⊖ Harrow-on-the-Hill
HA 5	**Pinner**	The Grail Centre	n/a	n/a	n/a		25	-	⇌ Hatch End ⊖ Pinner
HA 6	**Northwood**	London Bible College	69	24	-		93	250	⊖ Northwood
HP14	**High Wycombe**	Wycliffe Centre	9	38	43		90	200	⇌ High Wycombe
OX 7	**Oxford**	Cotswold View Guest House	2	24	14		40	30	⇌ Kingham
OX11	**Didcot**	Baptist House	-	-	-	non-residential	-	120	⇌ Didcot Parkway
OX12	**Wantage**	Charney Manor	10	20	-		30	45	⇌ Didcot Parkway
PO19	**Chichester**	Chichester Institute of Higher Education	218	40	-		258	350	⇌ Chichester
PO36	**Sandown**	Rowanhurst Christian Hotel	1	12	21		34	45	⇌ Lake
PO38	**Ventnor**	Delamere	1	6	8		15	-	⇌ Shanklin
		Hotel Picardie	2	14	5		21	-	⇌ Shanklin
		St Andrew's Hotel	-	14	9		25	-	⇌ Shanklin
		St Rhadagunds	5	12	87		104	-	⇌ Shanklin
PO39	**Totland Bay**	Sandford Lodge Hotel	1	8	3		12	15	⇌ Lymington Pier
RG23	**Basingstoke**	The Holy Trinity Malshanger Trust	1	12	18		31	30	⇌ Basingstoke
SL 1	**Slough**	King's Church Business Centre	-	-	-	non-residential	n/a	1,000	⇌ Slough
SL 4	**Windsor**	The Eton Dorney Centre	-	2	33		35	35	⇌ Windsor and Eton Riverside or Burnham
SN 4	**Swindon**	Legge House	1	6	26		33	40	⇌ Swindon
SO24	**Alresford**	Winchester Diocesan House	6	34	9		49	n/a	⇌ Alton or Winchester
South East									
BN 6	**Hassocks**	North Acres Farm (Streat Trust)	1	4	15		20	30	⇌ Plumpton or Hassocks
BN21	**Eastbourne**	Ansvar Conference and Holiday Centre	-	8	12		20	24	⇌ Eastbourne
		Grays Hotel	-	10	4		14	-	⇌ Eastbourne
BN22	**Eastbourne**	Ranworth Christian Hotel	5	8	16		29	-	⇌ Eastbourne
		Seven Sisters Christian Guest House	n/a	n/a	n/a		6	-	⇌ Eastbourne
CT 6	**Herne Bay**	Herne Bay Court Evangelical Centre	24	52	74		150	140	⇌ Herne Bay
GU 9	**Farnham**	CWR	1	14	28		43	100	⇌ Farnham
GU29	**Midhurst**	YMCA, Dunford House	13	22	9		44	60	⇌ Haslemere or Chichester
RH 5	**Dorking**	Felbury House	-	30	16		46	60	⇌ Gomshall
RH13	**Horsham**	Family Foundations Trust Ltd	-	2	62		64	100	⇌ Horsham
RH19	**East Grinstead**	Neale House Retreat and Conference Centre	n/a	n/a	n/a		44	150	⇌ East Grinstead
TN2	**Tunbridge Wells**	Alan Gardiner House	-	-	-	non-residential	-	40	⇌ Tunbridge Wells
TN3	**Tunbridge Wells**	Burrswood Christian Centre for Healthcare and Ministry	6	10	-	conference centre 40	56	-	⇌ Tunbridge Wells
		The Oast Houses	3	10	40		53	60	⇌ Etchingham
TN15	**Sevenoaks**	Oak Hall	3	22	55		80	100	⇌ Otford or Sevenoaks
TN22	**Uckfield**	Annan Court	-	-	-	camping 150	150	200	⇌ Lewes, Uckfield or Haywards Heath
		Pilgrim Hall Christian Hotel & Conference Centre	22	30	68		120	130	⇌ Uckfield
TN25	**Ashford**	Elm Tree Farm Christian Conference Centre	-	10	30		40	-	⇌ Ashford (Kent)
TN33	**Battle**	Ashburnham Christian Trust	20	116	72		208	220	⇌ Battle
TW 8	**Brentford**	St Paul's Church & Parish Centre	-	-	-	non-residential	-	350	⇌ Brentford ⊖ Northfield
TW16	**Sunbury-on-Thames**	Sunbury Court	n/a	n/a	n/a		90	110	⇌ Hampton
		Sunbury Court Recreation Centre	-	10	100		110	110	⇌ Hampton

	Location	Name	S	D/T	L	Other	TS	DR	Railway Station
South West									
BA 2	**Bath**	Carfax Hotel	14	50	-		64	35	Bath Spa
BH 1	**Bournemouth**	The Lansdowne Centre	-	-	-	non-residential	-	220	Bournemouth
		Roysdean Manor Hotel	n/a	n/a	n/a		100	-	Bournemouth
BH 4	**Bournemouth**	Daybreak Guest House	-	6	16		22	-	Bournemouth
		The Golden Sovereigns Hotel	1	4	18		23	-	Bournemouth
		New Horizon Hotel	3	20	24		47	47	Bournemouth
		Silverthorn Hotel	3	10	-		13	-	Bournemouth
BH 5	**Bournemouth**	Undercliff Private Christian Hotel	8	24	22		54	60	Bournemouth
BH 6	**Bournemouth**	Slavanka	6	76	18		100	100	Bournemouth
BH19		Bella Vista Hotel	-	6	12		18	-	Wareham
	Swanage	St Brides Hotel	-	8	17		25	-	Wareham
BH23	**Christchurch**	Moorlands College	4	90	-	+ touring vans, tents	94	200	Christchurch
BS 9	**Bristol**	Trinity College Conference Centre	55	2	4		61	150	
BS15	**Bristol**	Wick Court Centre	-	4	54		58	-	Bristol Temple Meads
BS21	**Clevedon**	Cavell Christian Guest House	5	12	19		36	40	Yatton
BS23	**Weston-super-Mare**	Ashcroft Guest House	1	4	9		14	-	Weston-super-Mare
		Highbury Hotel	n/a	n/a	n/a		123	90	Weston-super-Mare
DT 3	**Weymouth**	The Briary	-	6	-		6	-	Weymouth
EX 6	**Exeter**	Broomhill Conference Centre	1	24	14		39	48	Exeter St Davids
		Sheldon Centre	8	18	26		52	-	Exeter St Davids
EX 8	**Exmouth**	Haldon Court Christian Hotel and Conference Centre	6	36	56		98	120	Exmouth
EX10	**Sidmouth**	Sidholme	30	72	30		132	130	Exeter or Honiton
EX12	**Seaton**	Peacehaven Christian Centre	4	4	26		34	34	Axminster
		Upcott	n/a	n/a	n/a		34	-	Axminster
EX14	**Honiton**	Westcott Farm Christian Holiday Centre	31	18	-		49	80	Honiton
EX17	**Crediton**	Burstone Manor, Centre for Christ Trust	1	20	30		51	70	Exeter or Crediton or Lapford
EX22		Bennetts	-	-	-	5 apartments, cottage 22	22	-	Liskeard
	Holsworthy	Yellowland Farm	-	4	7		11	-	Exeter St Davids
EX34	**Ilfracombe**	Keswick House	n/a	n/a	n/a		25	30	Barnstaple
		Lee Bay Hotel	4	50	6		60	100	Barnstaple
		Lower Campscott Farm	1	2	-	self-catering 31	34	-	Barnstaple
		Trimstone Manor Hotel	2	12	3		17	80	Barnstaple
EX35	**Lynton**	Lee Abbey Fellowship	18	74	25		117	120	Barnstaple
EX39	**Bideford**	The Mount	2	10	4		16	13	Barnstaple
GL15	**Lydney**	Lindors Country House	3	44	20		67	70	Lydney
GL54	**Cheltenham**	Glenfall House	10	36	-		46	50	Cheltenham
HR 4	**Hereford**	Mellington House	1	10	-	flats 3	14	-	Leominster
PL19	**Tavistock**	The Watering Hole Holiday Centre	-	20	-	3 cottages 25	45	-	Plymouth
PL27	**Wadebridge**	Lowenna Manor	6	32	62		100	100	Bodmin Parkway
		Trevanion House	4	22	-		26	20	Bodmin Parkway
PL29	**Port Isaac**	Corestin Christian Guest House	1	8	14		23	-	Bodmin Parkway
TA 4	**Taunton**	Harnham Farmhouse	-	2	12		14	-	Taunton
TA 5	**Bridgwater**	Hill House Christian Centre	2	4	60		66	150	Bridgwater
TA24	**Minehead**	Mayfair Hotel	2	14	12		28	-	Taunton
		Westholme Holiday Conference Centre	10	26	7	self-catering flats 9	52	60	Taunton
TQ 1	**Torquay**	Brunel Manor	18	20	21	4 cottages 91	150	230	Teignmouth
TQ 4	**Paignton**	Glencoe Holiday Flatlets	-	-	-	5 flats 25	25	-	Paignton
		Park Hotel	n/a	n/a	n/a		115	-	Paignton
		Seaford Sands Hotel	4	10	20		34	65	Paignton
TQ11	**Buckfastleigh**	Buckfast Abbey	5	10	5		20	150	Newton Abbot or Totnes
TQ12	**Newton Abbot**	Rora Christian Fellowship Trust	6	28	18	+ camping 1,500	1,552	-	Newton Abbot
TQ14	**Teignmouth**	Thornley House	8	6	10		24	40	Teignmouth
TR 2	**Truro**	Trewince Manor	85	140	-	self-catering chalets	225	70	St Austell or Truro
TR 7	**Newquay**	Newquay Christian Guest House	2	8	4		14	20	Newquay
TR11	**Falmouth**	Crill Manor Hotel	-	12	-		12	-	Falmouth Town
		Falmouth Beach Resort Hotel and Conference Centre	16	176	69		261	300	Falmouth Town
TR26	**St Ives**	Lamorna Christian Guest House	4	20	9		33	33	Carbis Bay
		Treloyhan Manor	16	46	38		100	80	St Ives
WR 2	**Worcester**	St Mary's House	10	4	5		19	30	Worcester Foregate Street
WR12	**Broadway**	House of the Open Door Community	n/a	n/a	n/a		45	100	Evesham
WR14	**Malvern**	Day of Salvation Ministries	35	18	6		59	200	Malvern Link
NORTHERN IRELAND									
BT31	**Castlewellan**	Castlewellan Castle Christian Conference Centre	1	8	121		130	130	*Rail:* Belfast
BT33	**Newcastle**	Glenada Holiday and Conference Centre	-	54	-		54	150	*Rail:* none near
BT34	**Newry**	Kilbroney Centre	1	2	74		77	-	*Rail:* Newry
BT47	**Londonderry**	YMCA, Londonderry	10	-	-		10	270	*Rail:* Londonderry
BT54	**Ballycastle**	Corrymeela	-	110	-		110	150	*Rail:* Ballymoney
BT56	**Portrush**	Castle Erin Christian Holiday & Conference Centre	3	80	6		89	250	*Rail:* Portrush
BT66	**Craigavon**	YMCA, Lurgan	-	-	-	non-residential	-	25	*Rail:* Lurgan
BT71	**Dungannon**	Benburb Conference Centre	16	26	-		42	200	*Rail:* Portadown
SCOTLAND									
EH 9	**Edinburgh**	Ben Doran Guest House	1	8	20		29	-	Edinburgh
EH21	**Musselburgh**	Carberry	14	36	42		92	100	Edinburgh or Musselburgh
FK 1	**Falkirk**	Falkirk Christian Centre	n/a	n/a	n/a	non-residential	n/a	100	Falkirk Grahamston
FK 8	**Stirling**	Gartmore House Conference and Activity Centre	4	40	106	+ 6 caravans	150	300	
FK15	**Dunblane**	Scottish Churches' House	13	40	-		53	80	Dunblane
G2	**Glasgow**	Adelaides	2	12	10		24	500	Glasgow: Central or Queens Street
IV2	**Croy**	Kilravock Castle Christian Trust	4	12	9		25	200	Inverness or Nairn
		Kilravock Granary Christian Youth Centre	-	-	46		46	200	Inverness or Nairn
IV 3	**Inverness**	Park Guest House	2	6	3		11	-	Inverness
IV41	**Kyleakin**	Dunringell Hotel	3	16	21		40	42	Kyle of Lochalsh
ML12	**Biggar**	Maranatha Christian Centre	-	16	54		70	70	Lanark or Carstairs

A

Conference Centres, Guest Houses & Hotels

Postcode	Location	Name	S	D/T	L	Other	TS	DR	Railway Station
PA33	Dalmally	Eredine House	2	4	-	self-catering cottages 8	14	50	None near
PA76	Isle of Iona	Bishops House	3	20	-		23	24	Oban
PH 2	Perth	Perth Christian Centre	-	-	-	non-residential	n/a	130	Perth
PH 7	Crieff	St Ninian's Centre	22	28	36		86	90	Perth or Gleneagles or Dunblane
PH 8	Dunkeld	Waterbury Guest House	1	4	7		12	12	Birnam or Dunkeld
PH16	Pitlochry	Atholl Centre	2	22	8		32	60	Pitlochry
PH22	Aviemore	The Rowantree Restaurant & Guest House	3	-	7		10	-	Aviemore
PH33	Fort William	The Lodge on the Loch Hotel	2	28	12		42	-	Fort William
TD9	Hawick	Balcary House Christian Conference and Ministry Support Centre	1	8	36		45	80	Carlisle or Edinburgh
WALES									
CF31	Bridgend	Bryntirion Christian Conference Centre	-	86	14		100	90	Bridgend
CF64	Dinas Powis	Hebron Hall Ltd Christian Conference Centre	n/a	n/a	n/a		92	-	Dinas Powis
LD 2	Builth Wells	Bron Wye Guest House	1	6	4		11	10	Builth Road
LD 3	Brecon	Coleg Trefeca	-	38	-		38	60	Abergavenny
LL19	Prestatyn	Homefield	2	6	27		35	-	Prestatyn
LL22	Abergele	Kinmel Hall Christian Trust	48	280	750		1,078	-	Rhyl
		Living Waters	2	24	114		140	120	Colwyn Bay
LL23	Bala	Bryn-y-Groes Christian Conference Centre	-	6	70		76	70	Ruabon or Wrexham
LL28	Colwyn Bay	St Winifreds	4	60	6		70	60	Colwyn Bay
LL30	Llandudno	Beth-Eden Christian Guest House	5	12	10		27	37	Llandudno
		Bodlondeb Castle (Epworth Hotels)	n/a	n/a	n/a		110	80	Llandudno
		Fairhaven Christian Hotel	2	18	0		20	20	Llandudno
		Plas Brith Guest House	-	6	16		22	22	Llandudno
LL32	Conwy	Beechwood Court	2	52	98		152	72	Llandudno Junction
LL35	Aberdovey	Frondeg Country Guest House	-	4	6		10	-	Aberdovey
LL36	Tywyn	Glanmor Christian Holiday and Conference Centre	8	24	38		70	60	Tywyn
LL43	Talybont	Llys Andreas Christian Holiday Centre	2	8	10		20	20	Talybont
LL53	Pwllheli	Olgra	-	4	24		28	28	Pwllheli
		Pendorlan	2	2	16		20	-	Pwllheli
NP 6	Chepstow	Woodcroft Christian Centre	-	4	46		50	50	Chepstow
SA 3	Swansea	Nicholaston House	n/a	n/a	n/a		n/a	n/a	Swansea
SA19	Llanwrda	Carmarthenshire Rural Missionary Centre	-	14	10	1 cabin 4	28	-	Llandeilo
SA43	Cardigan	Croft Farm Celtic Cottages	-	-	-	2 cottages 34	34	40	Haverfordwest
		Gorslwyd Farm	1	42	4		48	60	Carmarthen or Aberystwyth
		Rhos-Llyn	5	8	-		13	-	Carmarthen
SA71	Pembroke	Haven Christian Holiday Centre	2	20	43		65	150	Pembroke
SY15	Montgomery	Pentrenant Hall	-	2	50	+ tents 150	202	60	Newtown (Powys)
SY16	Newtown	Cefn Lea Park Midwales Christian Holiday and Conference Complex	-	300	100		400	500	Newtown (Powys)
CHANNEL ISLANDS									
GY 1	Guernsey	Les Cotils Ecumenical Centre	5	8	3		16	-	
JE 3	Jersey	Biarritz Methodist Hotel	21	80	6		107	100	
		Highlands Hotel Ltd	20	60	13		93	100	

CONFERENCE CENTRES, GUEST HOUSES & HOTELS

By Alphabetical Order

Abbot Hall (Christian Guild Holidays), Kents Bank, Grange-over-Sands LA11 7BG
Manager: Mr Tim Rogers. Staff n/a. Began 1916; ecumenical. Turnover n/a.
☎ 01539 532 896 🖷 01539 535 200

***Adelaides**, 209 Bath Street, Glasgow G2 4HZ
Centre Director: Mr Sandy Meiklejohn. *Minister:* Rev Jack Quinn. Executive staff 2, Other staff 18. Began 1992; Baptist. Turnover £350,000 to year end Dec 98. Guesthouse, auditorium, nursery, church and café.
☎ 0141 248 4970

Alison House Training and Conference Centre, Intake Lane, Cromford, Matlock DE4 3RH
Warden: Mr Bill Pepper. *Assistant to Manager:* Mr David Palmer. Admin staff 3, Other staff 7. *CC* No.1057232. Began 1968; interdenominational. (Operated by Toc H). Turnover £110,000 to year end Mar 98.
☎ 01629 822 316

***Allen Gardiner House**, Pembury Road, Tunbridge Wells TN2 3QU
Financial & Adminstrative Secretary: Mr Philip Tadman. Admin staff 2. *CC* No.221328. Began 1970; Anglican. (South American Mission Society). Turnover n/a. Non-residential.
☎ 01892 538 647 🖷 01892 525 797

Annan Court, Easons Green, Uckfield TN22 5RE
Administrator: Catherine Butler. Other staff 5. Began 1975; interdenominational. Turnover £150,000 to year end Dec 98.
☎ 01825 840 387 🖷 01825 840 910

Ansvar Conference and Holiday Centre, NBV House, 29 St Leonards Road, Eastbourne BN21 3UU
Manager: Mrs Marianne Williams. Admin staff 1, Other staff 3. Began 1980; non-denominational. Turnover n/a.
☎ 01323 722 439 🖷 01323 739 355

***Arnesby Christian Conference Centre**, St Peter's Road, Arnesby, Leicester LE8 5WJ
Wardens: Mr & Mrs R D Wainwright. No other staff. *CC* Began 1974; non-denominational. Turnover £4,700. Residential accommodation for children and youth. Day conferences for all.
☎ 0116 247 8392

For additional information see List on Pages 67–70

***Ashburnham Christian Trust**, Ashburnham Place, Battle TN33 9NF
Resident Director: Mr Brian M Betts. *Conference Manager:* Mr Nigel Coleman. *Administrator:* Mrs Jennifer Oldroyd. Admin staff 6, Other staff 19. ***CC*** No.212755. Began 1960; non-denominational. Turnover £800,000 to year end Apr 98.
Web: www.ashburnham.org.uk
Email: mail@ashburnham.org.uk
☎ 01424 892 244 🖷 01424 892 243

Ashcroft Guest House, 13 Clevedon Road, Weston-super-Mare BS23 1DA
Proprietor: Mrs Daphne Hill. Admin staff 2. Began 1981; interdenominational. Turnover £22,000 to year end Dec 98.
☎ 01934 621 737

Ashley, Tregaron and Oasis Hotels, 15 Norfolk Square, London W2 1RU
Proprietor: Mr William J George. Admin staff 4, Other staff 5. Began 1967; non-denominational. Turnover n/a.
☎ 020 7723 3375/9966 🖷 020 7723 0173

Atholl Centre, Atholl Road, Pitlochry PH16 5BX
Director: Mr Gavin Graham. Admin staff 1, Other staff 5. ***CC*** Began 1970; interdenominational. Turnover £110,000 to year end Dec 96.
Email: info@atholl-bap-cen.u-net.com
☎ 01796 473 044 🖷 01796 473 844

Badger House, Badger, Burnhill Green, Wolverhampton WV6 7JR
Warden: Wing Commander Dan Gleed. Executive staff 1, Other staff 5. ***CC*** No.1002371. Began 1991; non-denominational. Turnover £65,000 to year end 98. Conference and holiday centre open to all but primarily for the armed forces.
Web: www.charitynet.org/~cornelius
Email: 100600.3061@compuserve.com
☎ 01746 783 226 🖷 01746 783 226

Balcary House Christian Conference and Ministry Support Centre, Buccleuch Road, Hawick TD9 0EH
Manageress: Miss Jane Cameron. Executive staff 4, Other staff 3. ***CC*** No.SCO 014546. Began 1986; non-denominational. People with a Mission Ministries. Turnover n/a. Conference, retreat and holiday facilities for groups, families and individuals. Bookshop, video library, landscaped garden.
☎ 01450 372 966 🖷 01450 377 732

Baptist Holiday Flats, 1 The Esplanade, Minehead TA24 5BE
Company Secretary: Mrs Christine Lawrence. Admin staff 2, Other staff 1. ***CC*** Began 1907; Baptist. (Previously Westholme Holiday Conference Centre). Turnover n/a. Open all year.
☎ 01643 703 473 🖷 01643 703 473

Baptist House, 129 Broadway, Didcot OX11 8XD
Centre Manager: Mr Jonathan Spiller. Admin staff 6. Began 1989; Baptist. Turnover £142,412 to year end Oct 98. Non-residential.
Email: baptisth@rmplc.co.uk
☎ 01235 517 700 🖷 01235 517 715

Bassenfell Manor Christian Centre, Bassenthwaite, Keswick CA12 4RL
Manager: Mr Chris Davison. Admin staff 4. ***CC*** No.283247. Began 1984; interdenominational. Turnover £60,000 to year end Mar 98. Group self-catering holidays, also children's adventure holidays and walking holiday provided.
Email: manager@bassenfellmanor.freeserve.co.uk
☎ 01768 776 366 📠 01768 776 366

***Bawtry Hall**, Bawtry, Doncaster DN10 6JH
Manager: Mr Drew Bryce. *Conference Co-ordinator:* Mrs Margaret Scott. Admin staff 4, Other staff 8. ***CC*** No.225364. Began 1989; interdenominational. Turnover £275,000 to year end Dec 97. House and grounds offering residential and day conference facilities. Also office accommodation.
Web: ourworld.compuserve.com/homepages/bawtry_hall
Email: bawtry_hall@compuserve.com
☎ 01302 710 020 📠 01302 710 027

Beach House Private Hotel, 4 Knowsley Road, Southport PR9 0HG
Owners: Mr Edward & Mrs Janice James. No other full-time staff. Began n/a; non-denominational. Turnover n/a.
☎ 01704 500 100

Beechwood Court (CE Holiday/Conference Centre Ltd), Mountain Road, Conwy LL32 8PY
Managers: Mr John & Mrs Beth Bowgett. Staff n/a. ***CC*** No.1039170. Began n/a; interdenominational. Turnover n/a. Providing accommodation all year for holidays, conferences, retreats and outreach.
Web: www.marketsite.co.uk/beechwd
☎ 01492 593 405 📠 01492 593 404

Bella Vista Hotel, Burlington Road, Swanage BH19 1LS
Proprietor: Mr Michael Hayes. Executive staff 2, Other staff 2. Began n/a; non-denominational. Turnover £50,000 to year end Oct 98. Small private hotel catering for family holidays and short breaks.
Email: bella.vista@cwcom.net
☎ 01929 422 873 📠 01929 426 220

Ben Doran Guest House, 11 Mayfield Gardens, Edinburgh EH9 2AX
Proprietor: Dr Joseph Labaki. Executive staff 1, Other staff 3. Began 1996; interdenominational. Family-run B & B.
Web: www.asper.co.uk/bendoran.html
Email: bendoran.guesthouse@virgin.net
☎ 0131 667 8488 📠 0131 667 0076

Benburb Conference Centre, 89 Miltown Road, Benburb, Dungannon BT71 7LZ
Manager: Ms Noilin Mullin. Admin staff 2, Other staff 4. ***CC*** Began n/a; Roman Catholic. Turnover n/a.
☎ 028 3754 8170 📠 028 3754 8113

Bennetts, Whitstone, Holsworthy EX22 6UD
Proprietor: Mr David Olivant. Other staff 2. Began 1986; non-denominational. Turnover £20,000 to year end Mar 98. Self-catering holidays in country house; apartments and cottage.
Email: bennetts@olivant.surfaid.org
☎ 01288 341 322

Beth-Eden Christian Guest House, 4 West Parade, Llandudno LL30 2BB
Proprietors: Lionel and Doreen Phillips. Other staff 5. Began 1972; independent evangelical. (Previously Emmaus Christian Guest House). Turnover n/a. Ten en-suite rooms, ministry and fellowship daily.
☎ 01492 877 057

Biarritz Methodist Hotel, Le Mont Sohier, St Brelade's Bay, Jersey JE3 8EA
General Manager: Mr Duncan O'Neill. Full-time staff 2. Began 1959; Methodist. Turnover £550,000 to year end Dec 98.
☎ 01534 742 239 📠 01534 747 433

Bishop Mascall Centre (Hereford Diocesan Centre), Lower Galdeford, Ludlow SY8 1RZ
Director: Rev Graham Earney. *House Manager:* Miss Janet Haynes. Admin staff 2, Other staff 5. ***CC*** Began 1980; Anglican but open to all. Turnover £150,000 to year end Dec 98. Residential and day conference centre.
☎ 01584 873 882 📠 01584 877 945

Bishops House, Isle of Iona PA76 6SJ
Wardens: Mr & Mrs Michael & Erica Meehan. Admin staff 2, Other staff 4. ***CC*** Began 1894; Episcopalian. Turnover £90,000 to year end Oct 98.
Email: b/hiona@aol.com
☎ 01681 700 800 📠 01681 700 801

Blaithwaite Christian Centre, Wigton CA7 0AZ
Centre Manager: Mr David Bowie. Admin staff 2, Other staff 6. Began 1969; interdenominational. Turnover £105,000 to year end Apr 99.
☎ 01697 342 319

Boarbank Hall, Grange-over-Sands LA11 7NH
Superior: Sister Hannah Campbell. Admin staff 5, Other staff 60. ***CC*** No.233499. Began 1921; Roman Catholic. Augustinian Sisters. Turnover n/a. Nursing home, guest house, centre for private retreats, willing to help anyone in need.
☎ 01539 532 288 📠 01539 535 386

For additional information see List on Pages 67–70

Bodlondeb Castle (Epworth Hotels), Church Walks, Llandudno LL30 2HH
Manager: Mrs H Farrell. Admin staff 2, Other staff 10. Began 1931; non-denominational. Turnover £198,000 to year end Feb 98.
☎ 01492 876 411 🖷 01492 877 047

The Boys' Brigade Training Centre, Broomley Grange, Hindley Road, Stocksfield NE43 7RX
Manager: To be appointed. Other staff 5. ***CC*** No.505386. Began 1976; interdenominational. Turnover £125,000 to year end Feb 97. Residential centre for youth, church and community-based organisations.
☎ 01661 842 299 🖷 01661 842 071

The Briary, Osmington, Weymouth DT3 6EH
Owners: Mr Anthony & Mrs Irene Scott. No other staff. Began 1974; non-denominational. Turnover n/a. Small Christian guest house providing Christian fellowship and help or rest to the needy.
☎ 01305 833 747 🖷 01305 833 747

Brockley Hall (CE Holiday/Conference Centre Ltd), Glenside, Saltburn-by-the-Sea TS12 1JS
Centre Manager: Mr David Brooking. Admin staff 1, Other staff 9. ***CC*** No.1039170. Began 1934; interdenominational. Turnover £150,000 to year end Dec 98.
☎ 01287 622 329 🖷 01287 622 329

Bron Wye Guest House, 5 Church Street, Builth Wells LD2 3BS
Proprietors: Mr Martin & Mrs Ros Wiltshire. No other full-time, staff. Began 1985; non-denominational. Turnover n/a.
☎ 01982 553 587

Broomhill Conference Centre, Foxhole Hill, Christow, Exeter EX6 7PJ
Managers: Mr & Mrs P Chapman. Admin staff 2, Other staff 3. ***CC*** No.1045587. Began 1974; interdenominational. Turnover n/a. Conferences, holidays and retreats.
☎ 01647 252 488

***Brunel Manor**, Watcombe Park, Torquay TQ1 4SF
General Manager: Mr Geoff Bishop. *Development Manager:* Mr Barry Shorto. Admin staff 8, Other staff 26. ***CC*** No.209651. Began 1942; interdenominational. (Previously Brunel Christian Centre). Turnover £520,000 to year end Sept 98. Hotel and conference centre for holidays, conferences and retreats.
Web: www.brunel-manor.org.uk
🖃 Email: brunelmanor@demon.co.uk
☎ 01803 329 333 🖷 01803 311 857

Bryntirion Christian Conference Centre, Bryntirion House, Bridgend CF31 4DX
Warden: Mr Kevin Olsen-Vetland. Other staff 4. ***CC*** No.517324. Began 1970; non-denominational. Turnover £75,000 to year end Feb 96.
🖃 Email: 100667.1273@compuserve.com
☎ 01656 652 714

Bryn-y-Groes Christian Conference Centre, Bryn-y-Groes, Bala LL23 7YE
Warden/Manager: Mr Peter Hallsworth. Admin staff 1, Other staff 3. ***CC*** Began 1960; non-denominational. Turnover £78,000 to year end Jan 96.
☎ 01678 520 752 Mobile: 07860 882 276

†**Buckfast Abbey**, St Mary's Abbey, Buckfast, Buckfastleigh TQ11 0EE
Liaison Officer: Mr Trevor Jarvis. ***CC*** Began 1882; Roman Catholic. Turnover n/a.
☎ 01364 642 519 Ext 237

***Burrswood Christian Centre for Healthcare and Ministry**, Burrswood, Groombridge, Tunbridge Wells TN3 9PY
Director: Dr Gareth Tuckwell. *Senior Chaplain:* Rev Michael Fulljames. Executive staff 10, Other paid staff 120, Voluntary staff 130. ***CC*** No.229261. Began 1948; Anglican. Dorothy Kerin Trust. Turnover £2,327,207 to year end Dec 97. Acute short stay non-surgical hospital, church, hydrotherapy pool, bookshop, tea room.
Web: www.burrswood.org.uk
🖃 Email: admin@burrswood.org.uk
☎ 01892 863 637 🖷 01892 863 623

***Burstone Manor, Centre for Christ Trust,** Bow, Crediton EX17 6LB
Resident Administrators: Mr & Mrs Gary & Mary Lee. Admin staff 1, Other staff 2. ***CC*** No.270327. Began 1977; interdenominational. Turnover £90,000 to year end Dec 98. A Christian holiday, retreat and conference centre.
☎ 01363 822 61

Cambridge House, Holy Island, Berwick-upon-Tweed TD15 2SQ
Warden: Mr Ian Mills. Executive staff 4. ***CC*** No.500051. Began 1970; interdenominational. Part of the Marygate Trust. Turnover n/a.
☎ No telephone
Bookings: Marygate House, Holy Island, Berwick-upon-Tweed TD15 2SD
☎ 01289 389 246 🖷 01289 389 246

For additional information see List on Pages 67–70

***Capenwray Missionary Fellowship of Torchbearers**, Capenwray Hall, Carnforth LA6 1AG
Managing Director: Rev Mark Thomas. *Company Secretary:* Mr David Bell. Admin staff 8, Other staff 25. *CC* No.1073139. Began 1999; interdenominational. (Previously Capenwray Hall). Turnover £1,000,000 [as Capenwray Hall] to year end Dec 98. Residential Bible school, residential conferences, overseas holidays, correspondence, book sales and holidays.
Web: www.capernwray.co.uk
Email: info@capernwray.co.uk
☎ 01524 733 908 🖷 01524 736 681

Carberry, Musselburgh EH21 8PY
Warden: Mr Bill Alcorn. Executive staff 3, Other staff 19. *CC* No.SCO 24381. Began 1966; non-denominational. (Previously Carberry Tower). Magazine: *Carberry News* (1,500 half-yearly). Turnover £350,000 to year end Dec 98. Providing courses and conference facilities.
Web: dspace.dial.pipex.com/carberry
Email: carberry@dial.pipex.com
☎ 0131 665 3135/3488 🖷 0131 653 2930

Carey House: The Pickenham Centre, North Pickenham, Swaffham PE37 8LG
Director: Mr Peter Gillett. Staff n/a. *CC* No.1009279. Began 1974; interdenominational. Turnover: n/a. Retreat and conference centre, prayer house, intercession meetings, teaching seminars, Alpha and away days.
Email: pickenham@clara.co.uk
☎ 01760 440 561 🖷 01760 440 561

Carfax Hotel, 13 Great Pulteney Street, Bath BA2 4BS
General Manager: Mrs Sylvia Back. Admin staff 2, Other staff 16. *CC* Began 1945; Salvation Army. Turnover £260,000 to year end Mar 94. Also day nursery.
Email: carfaxhotel@compuserve.com
☎ 01225 462 089 🖷 01225 443 257

Carmarthenshire Rural Missionary Centre, Ty Brasil, Crugybar, Llanwrda SA19 8TE
Directors: Mr & Mrs John R Richards. Admin staff 2. *CC* No.502821. Began 1973; interdenominational. Turnover £22,200 to year end Dec 97. For evangelical ministers, church groups, missionaries and their families.
☎ 01558 650 213

Castle Erin Christian Holiday & Conference Centre, Castle Erin Road, Portrush BT56 8DH
Manageress: Miss Ann Doherty. Admin staff 2. Began 1926; interdenominational. Turnover n/a.
☎ 028 7038 22744

***Castlewellan Castle Christian Conference Centre**, Castlewellan BT31 9BU
Managers: Rev & Mrs Andrew Forson. Other staff 4. *CC* Began 1975; interdenominational. Cloverley Centres. Providing residential conference facilities for church groups, youth groups, school and activity groups.
☎ 028 4477 8733

Cavell Christian Guest House, 1 Elton Road, Clevedon BS21 7RA
Managers: Mr George & Mrs Daphne Hamnett. Other staff 2. Began 1996; non-denominational. Turnover n/a. Holidays/B&B accommodation/conferences. Transport available from house.
☎ 01275 874 477 / 342 938

***Cefn Lea Park Midwales Christian Holiday and Conference Complex**, Dolfor, Newtown SY16 4AJ
Partner: Mr David Morgan. Admin staff 3, Other staff 7. Began 1978; interdenominational. Conference venue, also summer family holidays and available for school groups.
Web: www.cefnlea.wyrecompute.com
Email: cefnlea@wyrecompute.com
☎ 01686 625 275 🖷 01686 626 122

Central Conference Centre, 90 Central Street, London EC1V 8AQ
Conference Centre Manager: Mr Vim Vimal. Admin staff 6, Other staff 20. *CC* No.207497. Began 1732; non-denominational. St Luke's Parochial Trust. Turnover n/a. Providing facilities for non-residential conferences, seminars, theatre productions etc.
Email: cenconcen@aol.com
☎ 020 7250 4144 Mobile: 07721 499 024 🖷 020 7251 8689

Charney Manor, Charney Bassett, Wantage OX12 0EJ
Manager: Sheila Terry. *Courses Administrator:* Clare Hayes. Admin staff 3, Other staff 5. *CC* No.237267. Began 1947; Religious Society of Friends. Turnover £140,000 to year end Dec 98. Programme of courses and retreats.
Web: www.quaker.org.uk/charney.html
Email: charneymanor@quaker.org.uk
☎ 01235 868 206

Chichester Institute of Higher Education, Bishop Otter Campus, College Lane, Chichester PO19 4PE
Conference Officer: Ms Jacqueline Chirat. Admin staff 106, Other staff 110. *CC* Began n/a; Anglican. (Previously West Sussex Institute of Higher Education). Turnover n/a.
Web: www.chihe.ac.uk
Email: conference@chihe.ac.uk
☎ 01243 816 070 🖷 01243 816 081

The Children's Society, Wadderton Conference Centre, 37 Greenhill, Blackwell, Bromsgrove B60 1BL
Centre Manager: Mr David L Steed. Other staff 6. *CC* Began 1982; Anglican. Turnover £180,000 to year end Dec 98.
☎ 0121 445 4716 🖷 0121 447 7384

For additional information see List on Pages 67–70

Christian Guild Holidays, Derwent House, Cromford, Matlock DE4 5JG
General Manager: Mr Geoff Griffiths. Began 1910; ecumenical. (Previously Methodist Guild Holidays Ltd). Turnover n/a. Hotels/conference centres in Grange-over-Sands, Derbyshire Dales, St Ives (Cornwall), Sidmouth, Whitby, Wye Valley.
Web: www.cgholidays.co.uk
Email: cgholidays@aol.com
☎ 01629 580 550 Fax 01629 580 025

Cliff College Conference Complex, Calver, Hope Valley S32 3XG
Director: Mr Maurice Houghton. *Administrative Assistant:* Miss Helen Hollingworth. Admin staff 1, Other staff 5. Began 1965; Methodist but open to all. Turnover £265,501 to year end Aug 98.
Email: outreach@cliff.sheffield.ac.uk
☎ 01246 582 321 Fax 01246 583 739

Cloverley Hall Conference Centre, Whitchurch SY13 4PH
Manager: B Hieber. *Group Administrator:* D E Burton. Admin staff 1, Other staff 5. ***CC*** No.528419. Began 1968; non-denominational. Cloverley Centres. Turnover £190,000 to year end Sept 98. Residential Christian conference centre for churches, Christian groups; full board.
Email: ben&nicky@cloverleyhall.swinternet.co.uk
☎ 01948 890 688 Fax 01948 890 366

Coed-y-Go Farm Holiday Centre, Morda, Oswestry SY10 9AD
Manager: Mr David Arnott. Admin staff 1, Other staff 2. Began 1980; interdenominational. Turnover £80,000 to year end Nov 96.
Web: ourworld.compuserve.com/homepages/davidarnott1
Email: davidarnott1@compuserve.com
☎ 01691 656 037 Mobile: 07710 246 226

Coleg Trefeca, Trefeca, Brecon LD3 0PP
Wardens: Rev Gethin Rhys, Dr Fiona Liddell. Admin staff 4, Other staff 4. ***CC*** No.258456. Began 1968; Presbyterian Church of Wales. Turnover £119,995 to year end Dec 97. Lay training centre of Presbyterian Church of Wales and ecumenical conference and retreat centre.
Web: ebcpcw.org.uk/pcwtrefeca.html
Email: fiona.gethin@btinternet.com
☎ 01874 711 423 Fax 01874 711 423

***Corestin Christian Guest House**, 11 The Terrace, Port Isaac PL29 3SG
Proprietors: Mr & Mrs George Oxley. Admin staff 2. Began 1983; interdenominational. Turnover £32,000 to year end Dec 98. Holidays, ministry.
☎ 01208 880 267

Corrymeela, 5 Drumaroan Road, Ballycastle BT54 6QU
Centre Director: Mr Colin Craig. Admin staff 7, Other staff 14. ***CC*** Began 1965; non-denominational. Turnover £500,000 to year end Mar 98.
☎ 028 7076 2626 Fax 0128 7076 2770

Cotswold View Guest House, Nether Westcote, Kingham, Oxford OX7 6SD
Directors: Mr Anthony & Mrs Hazel Gibson. Began 1985; non-denominational. Turnover £75,000 to year end Dec 96.
☎ 01993 830 699 Fax 01993 830 699

Crill Manor Hotel, Budock Water, Falmouth TR11 5BL
Proprietor: Mr Peter Roberts. Admin staff 2, Other staff 8. Began 1993; non-denominational. Turnover £175,000 to year end Apr 98.
☎ 01326 211 880 Fax 01326 211 229

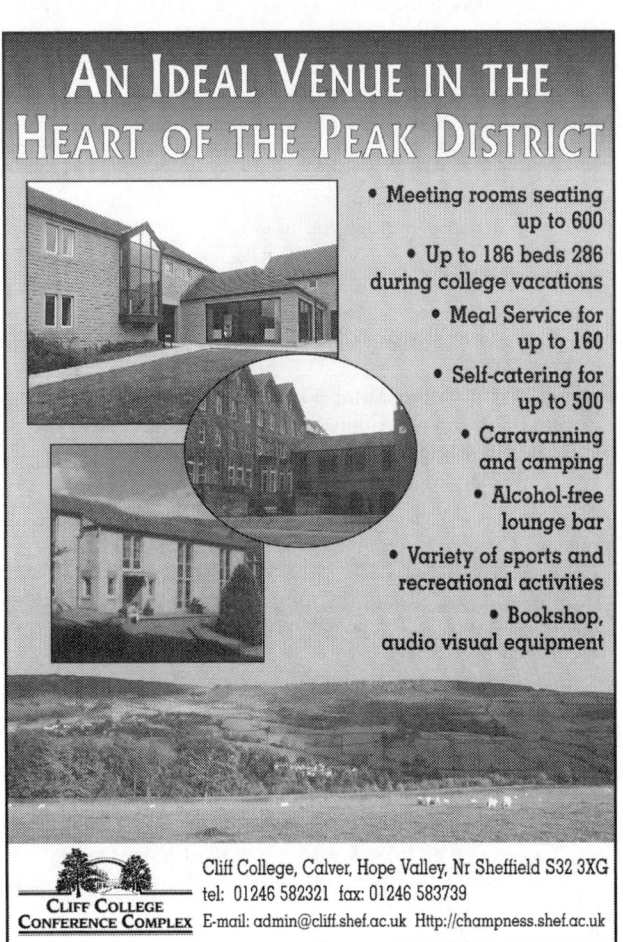

For additional information see List on Pages 67–70

Croft Farm Celtic Cottages, Croft, Cardigan SA43 3NT
Proprietors: Mr Andrew & Mrs Sylvie Gow. Began 1988; non-denominational. Turnover n/a. Self-catering cottages complemented by indoor heated pool, sauna, jacuzzi, gym. Friendly farm animals.
Web: www.webscape.co.uk/farmaccom/wales/pembrokeshire/croft-farm/
☎ 01239 615 179 🖷 01239 615 179

Damson Dene Hotel (Epworth Hotels), Crosthwaite, Kendal LA8 8JE
Manager: Mr Paul Roebuck. Admin staff 3, Other staff 12. Began 1993. Interdenominational. Turnover £435,000 to year end Feb 98.
☎ 01539 568 676 🖷 01539 568 227

Day of Salvation Ministries Ltd, International Gospel Centre, Ranelagh Road, Malvern WR14 1BQ
Director: Mr Gordon Leveratt. Executive staff 2, Other staff 4. Began 1994; non-denominational. No magazine. Turnover £37,000 to year end Oct 98. Residential conference centre and B&B.
Web: www.dofs.mcmail.com
Email: dofs@mcmail.com
☎ 01684 568 241 Mobile 07767 898 568 🖷 01684 577 317

Daybreak Guest House, 6 Herbert Road, Alum Chine, Bournemouth BH4 8HD
Proprietors: Mr Neil & Mrs Anne Rumsey. No other staff. Began 1984; interdenominational. Turnover £31,000 to year end Dec 90.
☎ 01202 761 055

Delamere, Belle Vue Road, Ventnor PO38 1DB
Proprietors: Mr & Mrs John Dodds. No full-time staff. Began 1987; non-denominational. Turnover n/a. Guesthouse open to all.
☎ 01983 852 322

Dunringell Hotel, Kyleakin IV41 8PR
Managers: Mr & Mrs Ian & Marion MacPherson. Admin staff 2, Other staff 9. Began 1963; non-denominational. Turnover n/a. Hotel with restaurant offering Christian fellowship (evening worship), and some holiday fellowship weeks with speakers.
☎ 01599 534 180

***Elm Tree Farm Christian Conference Centre**, Mersham, Ashford TN25 7HS
Owner: Mr David Pickford. Full-time staff 1. ***CC*** No.263429. Began 1974; interdenominational. Turnover £26,000 to year end Mar 98. Mainly for people aged 15 to 25.
☎ 01233 720 200 🖷 01233 720 522

Emmanuel Centre, 9 Marsham Street, London SW1P 3DW
Contact: Mrs Irene Liau. Other staff 1. Began 1997; interdenominational. Turnover n/a. Providing non-residential facilities for day conferences, seminars and workshops for up to 1,000 people.
Email: emmanuel_central@dial.pipex.com
☎ 020 7222 9191 🖷 020 7233 1276

Epworth Old Rectory (The home of the Wesleys), 1 Rectory Street, Epworth, Doncaster DN9 1HX
Warden: Mr Colin Barton. Other staff 2. Began 1954; Methodist. Turnover n/a. John Wesley's boyhood home, built 1709. Open to public, guided tours, portraits, Methodist memorabilia, accommodation.
☎ 01427 872 268

Eredine House, Eredine, SE Lochaweside, Dalmally PA33 1BP
Manager & Owner: Mrs Joyce Goel. Other staff 2. Began 1993; interdenominational. Turnover £26,000 to year end Dec 98. Car essential.
☎ 01866 844 207

The Eton Dorney Centre, The Vicarage, Lake End Road, Dorney, Windsor SL4 6QS
Warden: Mr Ged Pearce. Admin staff 1, Other staff 3. ***CC*** No.305994. Began 1971; Anglican but interdenominational. Turnover £60,000 to year end Dec 96. Residential youth centre.
Email: dorney@globalnet.co.uk
☎ 01628 662 823

Fairhaven Christian Hotel, 3 Craig-y-don Parade, Promenade, Llandudno LL30 1BG
Proprietors: Mr & Mrs J K Hammond. No full-time staff. Began 1991; non-denominational. Turnover £55,000 to year end May 98.
☎ 01492 878 447 🖷 01492 870 185

Fairhaven Country Hotel, The Common, Goathland, Whitby YO22 5AN
Proprietors: Mr Keith & Mrs Clare Laflin. Admin staff 2, Other staff 2. Began 1989; interdenominational. Turnover n/a.
☎ 01947 896 361

Fairhavens Christian Guest House, 8 Wellington Esplanade, Lowestoft NR33 0QQ
Partners: Mr & Mrs Keith Clarke, Mr & Mrs Eric Mattless. No other staff. Began 1972; interdenominational. Turnover n/a.
☎ 01502 574 927

Falkirk Christian Centre, 1 Glebe Street, Falkirk FK1 1HX
Secretary: Mr John Todd. No full-time staff. ***CC*** No.SCO 16770. Began 1987; non-denominational. Turnover £7,000 to year end Dec 98. Non-residential.
Web: www.yell.co.uk/sites/falkirk-christianctr/
☎ 01324 621 320

Falmouth Beach Resort Hotel and Conference Centre, Gyllyngvase Beach, Seafront, Falmouth TR11 4NA
General Manager: Mr David Glover. *Chairman:* Mr David Evans. Admin staff 14, Other staff 86. Began 1976; non-denominational. Turnover £2,600,000 to year end Oct 98. Resort hotel and conference centre, fitness suite and health club.
Web: members.aol.com/falbeach
Email: falbeach@aol.com
☎ 01326 318 084 🖷 01326 319 147

***Family Foundations Trust Ltd**, Dalesdown, Honeybridge Lane, Dial Post, Horsham RH13 8NX
Manager: Mr Alex Parsons. Other staff 1. ***CC*** No.284006. Began 1987; non-denominational. Turnover n/a. Largely self-catering.
☎ 01403 710 712

Featherstone Castle, Haltwhistle NE49 0JG
Owner: Mr John M Clark. Other staff 1. Began 1961; non-denominational. Turnover n/a. For young people and students, self-catering.
☎ 01434 320 202

For additional information see List on Pages 67–70

Felbury House, Holmbury St Mary, Dorking RH5 6NL
Chief Executive: Richard Bowden. *Centre Director:* Mr John Fidgett. Admin staff 3, Other staff 7. ***CC*** No.803697. Began 1973; interdenominational. Turnover £120,000 to year end Mar 98.
Email: surrey.youthclubs.uk@ukonline.co.uk
☎ 01306 730 929 🖷 01306 730 610

Fellowship of Reconciliation, England, The Eirene Centre, The Old School, Clopton, Kettering NN14 3DZ
Co-ordinator: Mr Robert Drost. *Administrator:* Mr Brian Harder. Executive staff 1, Admin staff 1. ***CC*** No.207822. Began 1914; interdenominational. Magazine: *Reconciliation Quarterly* (800 quarterly), *Peacelinks* (1,500 every two months). Turnover £112,052 to year end Dec 96. Promoting spiritual development, witness and service; reconciling all people with God and with each other.
Web: www.gn.apc.org/fore
Email: fellowship@gn.apc.org
☎ 01832 720 257 🖷 01832 720 557

Foreign Missions Club, 20 Aberdeen Park, Highbury, London N5 2BJ
Managers: Mr David & Mrs Beryl Littlehales. Admin staff 4, Other staff 10. ***CC*** No.227866. Began 1893; interdenominational. Turnover £200,000 to year end Dec 96. Quiet atmosphere, free on-street parking in private road.
Email: 100307.1206@compuserve.com
☎ 020 7226 2663 🖷 020 7704 1853

Fountain Springs, Glenfeadon House, Portreath, Redruth TR16 4JU
Proprietor: Pastor Anthony Keast. Family run. Began 1997; non-denominational. Turnover n/a. Hotel promoting healing, counselling, teaching ministry, Holy Land tours, messianic roots in Biblical feasts.
☎ 01209 842 650 🖷 01209 842 650

Foxhill (Chester Diocesan Conference Centre), Foxhill, Tarvin Road, Frodsham, Warrington WA6 6XB
Wardens: Ian & Sue Cameron. Admin staff 3, Other staff 5. ***CC*** Began 1969; Anglican. Turnover £100,000 to year end Dec 96.
☎ 01928 733 777 🖷 01928 731 422

†**Frondeg Country Guest House**, Copperhill Street, Aberdovey LL35 0HT
Owners: Mr & Mrs P Needham. No other staff. Began 1986; non-denominational. Turnover n/a.
☎ 01654 767 655 🖷 01654 767 655

Frontier Centre (Barnabas Trust Holiday Centres), Addington Road, Irthlingborough, Wellingborough NN9 5VH
Centre Manager: Mr Chris Shrimpton. Admin staff 4, Other staff 20. ***CC*** No.803431. Began 1983; interdenominational. Turnover n/a. Accommodation for groups wanting conference facilities or for youth organisations wanting outdoor activities.
Email: frontier@barnabas.jireh.co.uk
☎ 01933 651 718 🖷 01933 651 893

Gartmore House Conference and Activity Centre, Gartmore, Stirling FK8 3RS
Director: Peter Sunderland. ***CC*** No.528419. Began 1997; non-denominational. Cloverley Centres. Turnover £100,000. Activity and conference centre activities designed for over 35 year olds. Full board and self-catering.
Web: www.gartmore.uk.com
Email: mail@gartmore.uk.com
☎ 01877 382 991 Mobile: 07850 368 969 🖷 01877 382 725

†**Glanmor Christian Holiday and Conference Centre**, 3 Marine Parade, Tywyn LL36 0DE
Director: Mr Glyn Morgan. Admin staff 4, Other staff 6. Began 1981; interdenominational. Turnover n/a.
☎ 01654 710 253

Glenada Holiday and Conference Centre, 29 South Promenade, Newcastle BT33 0EX
Manager: Mr Dan Connor. ***CC*** Began 1900; interdenominational. Turnover £100,000 to year end Mar 98. Holidays, conferences, training and retreats. Groups.
Web: www.glenada.org.uk
Email: info@glenada.org.uk
☎ 028 4472 2402 🖷 028 4472 6229

Glencoe Holiday Flatlets, 7 Esplanade Road, Paignton TQ4 6EB
Proprietor: Mrs P J Ayles. No other staff. Began 1971; interdenominational. Turnover n/a.
☎ 01803 557 727 🖷 01803 666 512

Glenfall House, Mill Lane, Charlton Kings, Cheltenham GL54 4EP
Warden: Mrs Ann Murgatroyd. Admin staff 6, Other staff 12. ***CC*** No.1029239. Began 1992; Anglican. Turnover £280,000 to year end Dec 96. Accommodating mainly adults.
Email: glenfall@surfaid.org
☎ 01242 583 654 🖷 01242 251 314

The Golden Sovereigns Hotel, 97 Alumhurst Road, Alum Chine, Westbourne, Bournemouth BH4 8HR
Owners: Mr & Mrs Michael & Lyn Weetman. No full-time staff. Began 1989; non-denominational. Turnover n/a.
Email: goldensov@aol.com
☎ 01202 762 088 🖷 01202 762 088

For additional information see List on Pages 67–70

Gorslwyd Farm, Tanygroes, Cardigan SA43 2HZ
Proprietors: Mr Bob & Mrs Jennie Donaldson. Other staff 1. Began 1982; Free Evangelical. Turnover n/a. Self-catering cottages adapted for disabled people.
☎ 01239 810 593

The Grail Centre, 125 Waxwell Lane, Pinner HA5 3ER
Warden: Miss Pat Hawes. Admin staff 1, Other staff 1. ***CC*** Began 1931; Roman Catholic. Magazine: *In Touch* (1,200 quarterly). Turnover n/a. Accommodation for those on courses or retreats.
☎ 020 8866 0505/2195 🖷 020 8866 1408

Grays Hotel, 18 Elms Avenue, Eastbourne BN21 3DN
Owners/Managers: Mr & Mrs R Waring. Began 1986; Methodist. Turnover n/a. Family run.
☎ 01323 723 539

Greenhedges, 15 Augusta Street, Sheringham NR26 8LB
Bookings Manager: Mrs D Burns. Admin staff 1, Other staff 1. ***CC*** No.250682. Began 1966; non-denominational. Turnover £10,000 to year end Dec 98. Self-catering Christian holiday house. Base for SU mission and youth evangelism in North Norfolk.
Email: bobcumber@compuserve.com
☎ 01263 825 918
Correspondence: Bob Cumber, Sheringham CSSM Trust, 16 St Nicholas Place, Sheringham NR26 8LF
Email: bobcumber@compuserve.com
☎ 01263 823 517 🖷 01263 822 862

Haldon Court Christian Hotel and Conference Centre, 34 Douglas Avenue, Exmouth EX8 2HB
Managers: Mr Paul & Mrs June Lambert. Live in staff 2, Temporary staff (Summer) 4. Began 1957; interdenominational. Turnover £300,000 to year end Nov 98.
☎ 01395 263 836

†**Harnham Farmhouse**, Montys Court, Norton Fitzwarren, Taunton TA4 1BT
Proprietors: Major & Mrs Anthony C W Mitford-Slade. Admin staff 2, Other staff 1. Began n/a; non-denominational. Turnover n/a. Mainly self-catering, B&B available at Montys Court.
☎ 01823 432 255

Haven Christian Holiday Centre, 1 Westgate Hill, Pembroke SA71 4LB
Managers: Mr & Mrs Colin & Jennie Whittaker. Admin staff 2, Other staff 4. ***CC*** Began 1979; interdenominational. Turnover £50,000. Group holidays, retreats and seminars; listed building opposite Pembroke Castle.
Web: www.havencentre.freeserve.co.uk
Email: managers@havencentre.freeserve.co.uk
☎ 01646 685 469

The Hayes Conference Centre, Swanwick, Alfreton DE55 1AU
General Manager: Mr Brian Cupples. Admin staff 9, Other staff 76. ***CC*** No.1056604. Began 1911; non-denominational. Part of The Christian Conference Trust – see also High Leigh Conference Centre. Turnover n/a. Serving Christian, charity and educational groups.
Web: www.cct.org.uk
Email: peter@cct.org.uk
☎ 01773 526 000 🖷 01773 540 841

Hebron Hall Ltd Christian Conference Centre, Cross Common Road, Dinas Powis CF64 4YB
Manager: Mr Roger Waggett. Admin staff 4, Other staff 20. ***CC*** No.514184. Began 1983; interdenominational. Turnover n/a.
☎ 029 2051 5665 🖷 029 2051 5776

Hengrave Hall Centre, Hengrave, Bury St Edmunds IP28 6LZ
Warden: Sister Jill. *Administrator:* James Crowe. Admin staff 14, Other staff 10. ***CC*** No.268715. Began 1974; ecumenical. Turnover £300,000 to year end Aug 98. Run by ecumenical community of reconciliation.
Web: www.hengravehallcentre.org.uk
Email: co-ordinator@hengravehallcentre.org.uk
☎ 01284 701 561/2 🖷 01284 702 950

Herne Bay Court Evangelical Centre, Canterbury Road, Herne Bay CT6 5TD
Manager: Mr D Paul Mitchell. Admin staff 2, Other staff 15. ***CC*** No.528419. Began 1948; interdenominational. Cloverley Centres. Turnover £400,000 to year end Sep 98. Full board.
Email: evangelicalsathernebaycourt@compuserve.com
☎ 01227 373 254

High Leigh Conference Centre, Lord Street, Hoddesdon EN11 8SG
Manager: Mr Ian Andrews. Admin staff 5, Other staff 39. Began 1922; non-denominational. Part of The Christian Conference Trust – see also The Hayes Conference Centre. Turnover n/a. Serving Christian, charity and business groups.
Web: www.cct.org.uk
Email: ian@hleigh.globalnet.co.uk
☎ 01992 463 016 🖷 01992 446 594

For additional information see List on Pages 67–70

Highbury Hotel, Atlantic Road, Weston-super-Mare BS23 2DL
Manager: Miss Helen Peart. Admin staff 6, Other staff 20. Began 1938; non-denominational. Turnover £320,000 to year end Feb 95. 52 Bedroom licensed hotel/restaurant.
☎ 01934 643 133/621 585 🖷 01934 612 978

Highlands Hotel Ltd, La Corbiere, Jersey JE3 8HN
Hotel Manager: Mr T Anderson. Admin staff 2, Other staff 20. Began 1966; interdenominational. Turnover £430,000 to year end Oct 96. Open April to October.
Web: www.hlands.dircon.co.uk
Email: hlands@dircon.co.uk
☎ 01534 744 288 🖷 01534 747 273

Highway Trust, Thornleigh, The Esplanade, Grange-over-Sands LA11 7HH
Managers: David & Susanna Mycock. Admin staff 4, Other staff 12. ***CC*** Began 1973; interdenominational. (Previously Thornleigh). Turnover £172,800 to year end Dec 98.
☎ 01539 532 733 🖷 01539 536 088

Hill House Christian Centre, Hill House, Otterhampton, Bridgwater TA5 2PT
Manager: Mr Alexander Cox. Admin staff 2, Other staff 3. ***CC*** No.1037604. Began 1976; interdenominational. Bristol Christian Youth Trust. Turnover n/a.
☎ 01278 652 289

***Hollowford Centre, Lindley Educational Trust Ltd**, Castleton, Hope Valley S33 8WB
Centre Manager: Mr Bill Wade. *Managing Director:* Mr Derek Handforth. *Director of Training:* Liz Dales. Admin staff 3, Other staff 19. ***CC*** No.247662. Began 1970; non-denominational. (Previously Lindley Lodge). Turnover £700,000 to year end Mar 98. Training company offering residential premises and facilities to church, school and like organisations.
Email: billwade@hollowford.lindley.org
☎ 01433 620 377 🖷 01433 621 717

***Hollybush Christian Fellowship and Convention Centre**, Hollybush Farm, Newsham, Thirsk YO7 4DH
Administrator: Mrs June Brown. Other staff 1. Began 1968; interdenominational. (Previously Hollybush Bible Week). Magazine: *Newsletter* (Circulation n/a monthly). Turnover £100 to year end Apr 98. Providing refreshment and teaching for Christians. Resourcing the Church through outreach and mission. Hire of facilities.
Email: junehollyb@aol.com
☎ 01845 587 386 🖷 01845 587 103

The Holy Trinity Malshanger Trust, Malshanger, Basingstoke RG23 7EU
Wardens: Mr John & Mrs Jane Lavers. No other staff. ***CC*** Began 1982; Anglican. Turnover £20,000 to year end Dec 98.
Email: matthew.costley@htb.org.uk
☎ 01256 782 171 🖷 01256 584 8536

Homefield – Methodist Holiday and Conference Centre, 74 Gronant Road, Prestatyn LL19 9HW
CC No.248521. Began 1948; Methodist. Turnover n/a. Holidays, church away weekends and conferences.
☎ 01745 854 164 🖷 01745 854 164

Hotel Picardie, Esplanade, Ventnor PO38 1JX
Proprietors: Mr & Mrs Brian Sparks. Admin staff 2. Began 1986; non-denominational. Turnover n/a.
☎ 01983 852 647

For additional information see List on Pages 67–70

A

*__Hothorpe Hall Christian Conference Centre__, Theddingworth, Lutterworth LE17 6QX
Director: Mr B D Dunning. *Office Manager:* Mrs Elizabeth Stribley. Admin staff 7, Other staff 14. Began 1984; non-denominational. Turnover £582,602 to year end Nov 97. Christian conference holiday and retreat centre.
Web: www.hothorpe.co.uk
Email: office@hothorpe.co.uk
☎ 01858 880 257 Fax 01858 880 979

House of the Open Door Community, Childswickham House, Childswickham, Broadway WR12 7HH
Founders: Mr & Mrs Roy Hendy. Community members 24. ***CC*** No.1064343. Began 1978; interdenominational. Turnover n/a. Annual discipleship training course, summer camps for teenagers, prison ministry, music/drama team.
Email: hod.secretary@ndirect.co.uk
☎ 01386 852 084 Fax 01386 858 751

*__Ice House Christian Centre__, Victor Street, Grimsby DN32 7QN
Director: Rev Eric T Carter. Admin staff 2. ***CC*** No.509169. Began 1981; interdenominational. Turnover n/a. Promoting the Christian faith by mission, celebration, concert and teaching programmes. Non-residential.
☎ 01472 349 917 Fax 01472 349 244

The Jonas Trust, Elm House Centre, Redmire, Leyburn DL8 4EW
Co-Managers: Mr George Lihou, Mr Peter Gallant. Executive staff 2. ***CC*** No.1049167. Began 1995; interdenominational. Turnover £250,000 to year end Sep 97.
Web: www.users.globalnet.co.uk/~jonas
Email: jonas@globalnet.co.uk
☎ 01969 624 900

Kelvin Hotel, 98 Reads Avenue, Blackpool FY1 4JJ
Owner/Occupier: Mrs Yvonne A Duckworth. No other staff. Began 1988; Salvation Army. Turnover n/a. Small, private hotel, family run.
☎ 01253 620293

*__Keswick Convention Centre__, Skiddaw Street, Keswick CA12 4BY
Convention Secretary: Mr Mark Smith. Admin staff 6, Other staff 1. ***CC*** No.225557. Began 1987; interdenominational. Turnover £57,000 to year end Aug 97. Self-catering.
Email: kesconv@aol.com
☎ 01768 772 589 Fax 01768 775 276

Keswick House, Torrs Park, Ilfracombe EX34 8AY
Resident Proprietors: Mr & Mrs Adrian Wand. No full-time staff. Began 1952; non-denominational. Turnover n/a. Holiday guest house.
☎ 01271 863 929

*__Keychange Holiday and Conference Centre__, 5 St Nicholas Place, Sheringham NR26 8LF
Managers: Mr & Mrs Alan & Marion Slater. Full-time staff 4, Part-time staff 3. ***CC*** No.1061344. Began 1920; interdenominational. (Previously The Dyke Holiday Home). Turnover n/a. Summer holidays, out of season breaks, conference and weekend retreats, Christmas and Easter house parties.
☎ 01263 822 053

Kilbroney Centre, 15 Kilbroney Road, Rostrevor, Newry BT34 3BH
Warden: Rev Jim Sims. Admin staff 2, Other staff 6. ***CC*** Began 1975; Church of Ireland. Turnover £50,000 to year end Dec 96. For young people.
☎ 028 3073 8293

Kilravock Castle Christian Trust, Kilravock Castle, Croy IV2 7PJ
Manager: Mr G Denton. Other staff 2. ***CC*** No.SCO 9834. Began 1967; interdenominational. Turnover n/a.
☎ 01667 493 258

Kilravock Granary Youth Centre, Kilravock Castle, Croy IV2 7PJ
Manager: Mr G Denton. Other staff 2. ***CC*** No.SCO 9834. Began 1969; interdenominational. Turnover n/a.
☎ 01667 493 258

*__King's Church Business Centre__, King's Centre, 673 Galvin Road, Slough SL1 4QN
Manager: Mr Knolly Shadrache. Executive staff 1, Other staff 2. Began 1994; non-denominational. (Previously Ambassador Productions). Turnover £50,000 to year end Mar 98. Promoting Christian literature; non-residential conference centre for up to 1,000 people.
Email: info@kingscentre.com
☎ 01753 786 300 Fax 01753 739 683

*__King's Park Conference and Sports Centre__, Kings Park Road, Moulton Park, Northampton NN3 6LL
Conference Centre Director: Mr Derek Redpath. Admin staff 5, Other staff 20. ***CC*** No.803431. Began 1989; interdenominational. Turnover n/a.
Email: n.a.y.c@dial.pipex.com
☎ 01604 493 111 (Conference Centre) Fax 01604 493 559

Kingstown Hotel, 246 Kingstown Road, Carlisle CA3 0DE
Proprietors: Mr & Mrs P M White. Part-time staff 1. Began 1988; Anglican. Turnover n/a.
☎ 01228 515 292

*__Kinmel Hall Christian Trust__, Kinmel Hall, Saint George, Abergele LL22 9DA
Administrator: Mr Stephen Morris. *Trustee:* Group Captain R Boggia. Admin staff 2, Other staff 7. ***CC*** No.279383. Began 1979; interdenominational. Turnover £100,000 to year end Aug 98. Christian conference and holiday centre, groups from 20-400, self-catering or full board.
Email: kinmelhall@breathmail.net
☎ 01745 833 450 Mobile: 07710 692 969 Fax 01745 822 900

Knuston Hall, Irchester, Wellingborough NN29 7EU
Principal: Mr J R Herrick. Admin staff 4, Other staff 10. Began 1951; non-denominational. Turnover n/a.
☎ 01933 312 104 Fax 01933 357 596

*__Lamorna Christian Guest House__, Boskerris Road, Carbis Bay, St Ives TR26 2NG
Proprietor: Mr Tony Seymour. Admin staff 2. Began 1960; interdenominational. Turnover n/a.
☎ 01736 795 967

Lancaster Hall Hotel Ltd, 35 Craven Terrace, Lancaster Gate, London W2 3EL
Manager: Mr U Maynard. Admin staff 4, Other staff 34. Began 1973; interdenominational. (Subsidiary trading company of The German YMCA). Turnover £1,152,000 to year end Dec 98.
☎ 020 7723 9276 Fax 020 7706 2870

*__The Lansdowne Centre__, Lansdowne Baptist Church, Lansdowne Road, Bournemouth BH1 1SB
Administrator: Mr Malcolm Fox. Admin staff 1, Other staff 2. ***CC*** Began 1985; Baptist. Turnover n/a. Non-residential.
☎ 01202 297 977

For additional information see List on Pages 67–70

Lattendales, Berrier Road, Greystoke, Penrith CA11 0UE
Wardens: Joan & David Ellison. Admin staff 2, Other staff 2. *CC* No.264223. Began 1973; Religious Society of Friends but open to all. Turnover £44,000 to year end Mar 90.
☎ 01768 483 229 🖷 01768 483 058

***Latymer Christian Centre**, 116 Bramley Road, Kensington, London W10 6SU
Centre Manager: Robin Meadows. Other staff 2. *CC* No.221948. Began 1974; non-denominational. Part of the Shaftesbury Society. Turnover £59,000 to year end Mar 98.
Email: latymer@clara.net
☎ 020 8969 2290 🖷 020 8960 5468

***Lee Abbey Fellowship**, Lynton EX35 6JJ
Warden: Rev Bob Payne. *Centre Manager:* Rev Andrew McCausland. *Accountant:* Mr Stephen Scoffield. Admin staff 19, Other staff 60. *CC* No.227322. Began 1945; Anglican. Magazine: *Rapport* (4,500 quarterly). Turnover £750,000 to year end Dec 98. Christian holiday and conference centre which aims to serve and renew the church.
Web: www.leeabbey.org.uk
Email: bookings@leeabbey.org.uk
☎ 01598 752 621 🖷 01598 752 619

†**Lee Bay Hotel**, Lee, Ilfracombe EX34 8LP
Manager: Mr Julian Turner. Admin staff 4, Other staff 30. Began 1991; non-denominational. Turnover n/a.
Web: manorgroup.uk
Email: info@manor.romgroup.co.uk
☎ 01271 867 600 🖷 01271 863 956
Bookings: Trimstone Manor Hotel, Trimstone, West Down, Ilfracombe EX34 8NR
☎ 01271 862 841

Legge House, Church Hill, Wroughton, Swindon SN4 9JS
Managers: Mr Ted & Mrs Sue Knight. No other staff. *CC* No.305602. Began 1968; Anglican. Turnover £30,000 to year end Dec 98. For young people.
Web: www.legge-house.demon.co.uk
Email: ted-sue-knight@legge-house.demon.co.uk
☎ 01793 813 273 🖷 01793 814 582

Les Cotils Ecumenical Centre, St Peter Port, Guernsey GY1 1UU
Manager: Mr M Tangey. Other staff. *CC* Began n/a; ecumenical. Turnover n/a.
☎ 01481 727 793 🖷 01481 701 062

Letton Hall, Shipdham, Thetford IP25 7SA
Director of Trust: Mr P J Carroll. Admin staff 2, Other staff 4. *CC* No.279817. Began 1980; interdenominational. Turnover £145,000 to year end Dec 98.
Email: petercarroll@lettonhall.freeserve.co.uk
☎ 01362 820 717 🖷 01362 820 877

†***Lindley Educational Trust Ltd**, Swinton Castle, Masham, Ripon HG4 4JH
Managing Director: Mr Derek Handforth. Admin staff 20. *CC* Began 1950; interdenominational. Turnover £700,000 to year end Mar 97. Personal development training centre.
☎ 01765 689 254 🖷 01765 689 604

Lindors Country House (Christian Guild Holidays), St Briavels, Lydney GL15 6RB
Manager: Mr Alan & Mrs Sandra Irving. Staff n/a. Began 1953; ecumenical. Turnover n/a.
☎ 01594 530 283 🖷 01594 530 559

Littledale Trust, Littledale Hall, Lancaster LA2 9EY
Directors: Mr Stuart & Mrs Wendy Rushton. Executive staff 2, Other staff 7. *CC* No.328268. Began 1989; interdenominational. Turnover £92,000 to year end Nov 98. Bringing wholeness and rest to leaders, individuals, family groups, retreats, counselling service, training programmes.
Web: www.doveuk.com/littledale
Email: littledale@compuserve.com
☎ 01524 770 266 🖷 01524 771 553

†***Living Waters**, Dolwen, Abergele LL22 8AY
Director: Rev David Philpott. Admin staff 1, Other staff 10. *CC* Began 1981; interdenominational. Turnover £193,000 to year end Aug 96.
☎ 01492 680 256 🖷 01492 680 267

Livingstone Christian Centre, Baptist Church, Park Parade, Whitley Bay NE26 1DT
Administrator: Miss Betty King. No full-time staff. Began 1983; Baptist. Turnover £8,000 to year end Dec 98. Self-catering accommodation for groups.
☎ 0191 252 4426

Llys Andreas Christian Holiday Centre, Llys Andreas, Talybont LL43 2AU
Managers: Mr John & Mrs Carol Lowther. Other staff 1. *CC* No.1011969. Began 1985; interdenominational. Turnover n/a.
☎ 01341 247 213

For additional information see List on Pages 67–70

The Lodge on the Loch Hotel, Onich, Fort William PH33 6RY
Manager: Mr Iain Coulter. Admin staff 6, Other staff 4. Began 1977; non-denominational. Turnover n/a.
Web: www.freedomglen.co.uk
Email: reservations@freedomglen.co.uk
☎ 01855 821 237 🖷 01855 821 238

A

***London Bible College**, Green Lane, Northwood HA6 2UW
Conference Manager: Val Edwards. No separate staff. ***CC*** No.312778. Began 1943; interdenominational. Turnover included in London Bible College. 11 conference rooms accommodating 2-250. Day conference facilities throughout the year, residential college vacations only.
Email: val.edwards@londonbiblecollege.ac.uk
☎ 01923 456 000 🖷 01923 456 001

Lowenna Manor (CE Holiday/Conference Centre Ltd), Rock, Wadebridge PL27 6NP
Centre Director: Mr W Lafebre-Bailey. *Deputy Director:* Mr William Armstrong. Admin staff 3, Other staff 12. ***CC*** No.1039170. Began 1968; interdenominational. Turnover £100,000 to year end Oct 98. Open Easter to late autumn; conferences, seminars, house and school parties, families.
☎ 01208 862 230
Correspondence: 4 Sautridge Close, Slattocks, Middleton, Manchester M24 2UB
☎ 01706 355 359

Lower Campscott Farm, Lee, Ilfracombe EX34 8LS
Proprietor: Mrs Margaret Cowell. Staff n/a. Began 1981; Baptist. Turnover n/a.
☎ 01271 863 479 🖷 01271 867 639

Maranatha Christian Centre, John's Loan, Biggar ML12 6AH
Managers: Herbie & Jacqui Darrah. Admin staff 2, Other staff 2. ***CC*** Began 1986; interdenominational. Turnover n/a.
☎ 01899 220 960 🖷 01899 220 960

Marygate House, Holy Island, Berwick-upon-Tweed TD15 2SD
Warden: Mr Ian Mills. Executive staff 4. ***CC*** No.500051. Began 1970; interdenominational. Turnover £75,000 to year end Dec 96. Providing group and individual programmes appropriate to Holy Island.
Web: www.lindisfarne.org.uk/marygate/
Email: ian@marygateho.freeserve.co.uk
☎ 01289 389 246 🖷 01289 389 246

Mayfair Hotel, 25 The Avenue, Minehead TA24 5AY
Joint Proprietors: Mr Jakob & Mrs Anne Segenhout. Other staff 2. Began 1977; non-denominational. Turnover n/a. Non-smoking.
☎ 01643 702 719

Mellington House, Broad Street, Weobley, Hereford HR4 8SA
Proprietor: Rev Mervyn N Saunders. No full-time staff. Began 1986; non-denominational. Turnover £30,000 to year end Apr 99. Guesthouse, self-catering flats.
☎ 01544 318 537

Mercer House (Exeter Diocesan Conference Centre), Exwick Road, Exwick, Exeter EX4 2AT
Wardens: Mr & Mrs Williams. Executive staff 2. Began 1983; Anglican. (Previously Mercer House Training Centre). Turnover £46,000 to year end Dec 98. Conference centre for the Exeter Diocese.
Web: freespace.virgin.net/graeme_james.williams/mercer.htm
Email: graeme_james.williams@virgin.net
☎ 01392 219 609

Moor Farm Holidays, Moor Farm, Foxley, Dereham NR20 4QN
Manager: Mr Paul Davis. Admin staff 2, Other staff 2. Began 1992; interdenominational. Turnover n/a.
☎ 01362 688 523 🖷 01362 688 523

Moorlands (Christian Guild Holidays), 16 North Promenade, Whitby YO21 3JX
Managers: Mr & Mrs John & Kathryn Key. Began 1955; ecumenical. Turnover £187,000 to year end Jan 98.
☎ 01947 603 584 🖷 01947 821 668

***Moorlands College**, Sopley, Christchurch BH23 7AT
The Principal: Rev Dr Steve Brady. Other staff 1. ***CC*** Began 1948; interdenominational. Turnover n/a. Available college vacations.
Web: www.moorlands.u-net.com
Email: conference@moorlands.ac.uk
☎ 01425 672 369 🖷 01425 674 162

The Mount, Northdown Road, Bideford EX39 3LP
Owners: Mr & Mrs Andrew & Heather Laugharne. No full-time staff. Began 1953; non-denominational. Turnover £40,000 to year end Dec 98. One room suitable for wheelchairs.
☎ 01237 473 748

***Mulberry House**, High Ongar Road, Ongar CM5 9NL
Centre Administrator: Peter Crispin. Admin staff 1, Other staff 5. ***CC*** No.282667. Began 1981; non-denominational. (Previously Woodford Wells Ministry Trust). Turnover £200,000 to year end Dec 96. Training and retreats.
Email: md@pfe.co.uk
☎ 01277 365 398 🖷 01277 365 353

Neale House Retreat and Conference Centre (St Margaret's Convent), Moat Road, East Grinstead RH19 3LB
Warden: Sister Lucy SSM. Admin staff 3, Other staff 2. ***CC*** No.231926. Began 1977; Anglican. Turnover £50-100,000 to year end Dec 96. Residential religious weekends and educational day conferences.
☎ 01342 312 552 🖷 01342 312 552

†**Nettle Hill Training and Conference Centre**, Brinklow Road, Ansty, Coventry CV7 9JL
Manager: Mr Robert Sherwin. Other staff 6. ***CC*** No.328513. Began 1990; non-denominational. Turnover n/a.
☎ 024 7662 1899 🖷 024 7660 2992

New Horizon Hotel, 7 Alumdale Road, Alum Chine, Bournemouth BH4 8HX
Owner: Mrs M A Pickworth. Other staff 4. Began 1990; non-denominational. Turnover n/a.
☎ 01202 761 087

†**Newquay Christian Guest House**, Parkenbutts, St Columb Minor, Newquay TR7 3HE
Owner: Mr Philip Martyn. Admin staff 1, Other staff 1. Began 1987; non-denominational. Turnover n/a.
☎ 01637 879 115 🖷 01637 878 973

Nicholaston House, Penmaen, Gower, Swansea SA3 2HL
Resident Managers: Mr & Mrs Derek & Anne Styants. Admin staff 2. ***CC*** No.700248. Began 1988; interdenominational. Turnover £22,000 to year end Dec 97. Conferences, holidays, teaching and training courses, fellowship-building activities.
☎ 01792 371 317 🖷 01792 371 317

For additional information see List on Pages 67–70

*__North Acres Farm (Streat Trust)__, North Acres, Streat, Hassocks BN6 8RX
Owners: Mr John & Mrs Valerie Eastwood. Admin staff 2. ***CC*** No.268602. Began 1970; non-denominational. Turnover n/a.
☎ 01273 890 278 Mobile: 07930 753 907

Oak Hall, Otford Manor, Otford, Sevenoaks TN15 6XF
Director: Mrs Judy Mayo. Staff n/a. Began 1966; non-denominational. Turnover n/a. Special rates for missions.
☎ 01732 763 131 🖷 01732 763 136

Oak Hill, Chase Side, Southgate, London N14 4PS
Conference Co-ordinator: Mrs Helen Archer. Executive staff 2, Admin staff 6. ***CC*** No.310031. Began 1932; Anglican. Specialising in conferences for organisations and training events.
Web: www.oakhill.ac.uk
Email: helena@oakhill.ac.uk
☎ 020 8449 0467 🖷 020 8441 5996

The Oast Houses, Ewhurst Lane, Northiam, Rye TN31 6HL
Director: Rev Mark Lucas. Executive staff 1, Other staff 4. ***CC*** No.801479. Began 1993; non-denominational. Turnover £110,000 to year end Dec 98. Providing residential and non-residential conferences, retreat facilities; training courses by arrangement.
Web: easyweb.easynet.co.uk/oast.houses/
Email: info@oast.houses.easynet.co.uk
☎ 01797 253 311 🖷 01797 253 314

†**Olgra (Cambrian Coast Evangelical Trust)**, Strydfawr, Abersoch, Pwllheli LL53 7DT
Bookings Secretary: Mrs Jane M Picken. No full-time staff. ***CC*** Began 1969; interdenominational. Turnover n/a. Self-catering.
☎ No telephone
Bookings: Pengwern, Lon Sarn Bach, Abersoch, Pwllheli LL53 7ER

Omega – Winford Manor, Winford, Bristol BS40 8DW
Prior: Rev Canon Peter Spink. *Administrator:* Mr James Fahey. Admin staff 3, Other staff 3. ***CC*** No.280512. Began 1980; Anglican/ Roman Catholic. Magazine: *Omega News* (2,500 every four months). Turnover £196,000 to year end Mar 97. Contemplative community of men/women. Retreats, seminars, individual spiritual direction, arts, healing, conferences, residential home.
Web: members.aol.com/omegatrust/omega/omega.html
Email: omegatrust@aol.com
☎ 01275 472 262 🖷 01275 472 065

Palm Court Hotel (Epworth Hotels), 166 Queen's Promenade, Bispham, Blackpool FY2 9JP
Manager: Mrs Stephanie Barker. Admin staff 2, Other staff 12. Began 1949; non-denominational. Turnover £200,000 to year end Feb 98.
☎ 01253 353 414 🖷 01253 355 936

Parcevall Hall (Bradford Diocesan House), Skyreholme, Appletreewick, Skipton BD23 6DG
Warden: Miss Florence Begley. Admin staff 1, Other staff 4. ***CC*** No.247858. Began 1962; Anglican. Turnover £112,000 to year end Dec 98. Retreat and Conference Centre, ecumenical, but run by the Anglican Church.
☎ 01756 722 13/722 83 🖷 01756 720 656

Park Guest House, 51 Glenurquhart Road, Inverness IV3 5PB
Owner: Mrs Irene Robertson. Other staff 1. Began 1987; non-denominational. Turnover £35,000 to year end Apr 98.
☎ 01463 231 858

†**Park Hotel (Epworth Hotels)**, Esplanade Road, Paignton TQ4 6BQ
Manager: Mrs Suzzanne Schofield. Admin staff 3, Other staff 18. Began 1965; non-denominational. Turnover £348,000 to year end Feb 95.
☎ 01803 552 505 🖷 01803 557 856

Peacehaven Christian Centre, Harepath Hill, Seaton EX12 2TA
Owner: Mr Graham P Board. Admin staff 1, Other staff 3. Began 1984; non-denominational. Turnover n/a. Accommodation for singles, families and groups. Ministry and accommodation for those in need.
☎ 01297 216 81

*__Pendorlan (Cambrian Coast Evangelical Trust)__, Lon-y-Traeth, Nefyn, Pwllheli LL53 6EF
Bookings Secretary: Rev Canon Dick Browning. No full-time staff. ***CC*** Began 1969; interdenominational. Turnover £4,780 to year end May 96. Self-catering.
Bookings: Llwyn Rhug, Ffordd Dewi Sant, Nefyn, Pwllheli LL53 6EG
☎ 01758 720 834

*__Pentrenant Hall__, Church Stoke, Montgomery SY15 6TG
Partner: Rev Peter A Rees. Other staff 3. Began 1984; interdenominational. Turnover n/a. Teaching, holiday centre.
☎ 01588 620 450 Mobile: 07703 221 577 🖷 01588 620 150

Perth Christian Centre, 28 Glasgow Road, Perth PH2 0NX
Manager: Mr John Cameron. Executive staff 23, Other staff 10. ***CC*** No.SCO 14546. Began 1986; non-denominational. Turnover n/a. Non-residential; coffee shop; bookshop; video library.
Email: mervynpwamm@btinternet.com
☎ 01738 639 792 🖷 01738 622 928

*__Pilgrim Hall Christian Hotel & Conference Centre__, Easons Green, Uckfield TN22 5RE
Executive Directors: Mr & Mrs Michael Lee. Admin staff 5, Other staff 25. ***CC*** No.262561. Began 1971; interdenominational. Turnover £400,000 to year end Dec 98.
Email: pilghall@aol.com
☎ 01825 840 295 🖷 01825 840 017

*__Pilgrims Hall__, Ongar Road, Brentwood CM15 9SA
Leader: Mr Peter F Garratt. Admin staff 2, Other staff 8. ***CC*** No.257216. Began 1968; non-denominational. Turnover £70,000 to year end July 98. Conferences, teaching, training, retreats, counselling.
☎ 01277 372 206 🖷 01277 375 590

Pioneer Centre & Forest Lodge, Cleobury Mortimer, Kidderminster DY14 8JG
Centre Director: Mr Ryland Robertshaw. *Centre Manager:* Mrs Carole Moreton. Admin staff 3, Other staff 25. ***CC*** No.803431. Began 1991; interdenominational. Turnover n/a. Residential activity and conference centre, mainly but not exclusively for young people.
Email: pioneercentre@hotmail.com
☎ 01299 271 217 🖷 01299 270 948

Plas Brith Guest House, 38 Church Walks, Llandudno LL30 2HN
Proprietor: Mr Roy Thurley. Executive staff 2. Began 1989; non-denominational. Turnover n/a.
☎ 01492 879 991

The Pleasaunce (CE Holiday/Conference Centre Ltd), Harbord Road, Overstrand, Cromer NR27 0PN
Manager: Mrs A Powell. Full-time staff 12. ***CC*** No.1039170. Began 1936; interdenominational. Turnover £180,000 to year end Oct 96.
☎ 01263 579 212 🖷 01263 579 212

For additional information see List on Pages 67–70

A

Quaker International Centre, 1 Byng Place, London WC1E 7JH
Co-ordinator: Peter Coats. Admin staff 3, Other staff 4. ***CC*** Began n/a; Religious Society of Friends. Turnover n/a.
Email: qic@btinternet.com
☎ 020 7387 5648 🖷 020 7383 3722

Queen's, Birmingham, The Ecumenical Foundation for Theological Education, Somerset Road, Edgbaston, Birmingham B15 2QH
Principal: Rev Peter Fisher. Lecturers 10, Other staff 4. ***CC*** No.528989. Began 1828; ecumenical. Turnover n/a.
Email: queens_college@compuserve.com
☎ 0121 454 1527 🖷 0121 454 8171

Quinta Christian Centre, Weston Rhyn, Oswestry SY10 7LR
Centre Manager: Mr Peter Bevington. Other staff 6. ***CC*** No.528419. Began 1985; interdenominational. Cloverley Centres. Turnover £200,000 to year end Sept 98. Self-catering or assisted catering.
☎ 01691 773 696 🖷 01691 774 687

Ranworth Christian Hotel, 86 Pevensey Road, Eastbourne BN22 8AE
Proprietors: Mr Colin & Mrs Daphne Marchant. Other staff 4. Began 1987; non-denominational. Turnover £33,600 to year end Apr 97.
Email: famarchant@aol.com
☎ 01323 733 520 Mobile: 07961 899 992

Redcar Farm, Hospitality Pastoral Office, Ampleforth, York YO62 4EN
Administrator: Jan Fitzallen-Howard. Staff n/a. ***CC*** No.1026493. Began 1973; Roman Catholic. Turnover n/a. Youth accommodation, field studies, church groups (confirmation etc).
Email: pastoral@ampleforth.org.uk
☎ 01439 766 889 🖷 01439 766 755

Redland House Hotel, 52 Kendal Street, London W2 2BP
Owners: Mr & Mrs H Newlands. Admin staff 2, Other staff 4. Began 1961; non-denominational. Turnover n/a.
☎ 020 7723 7118 🖷 020 7402 9049

***Regents Park Conference Centre**, London Road, Nantwich CW5 6LW
Manager: Ms Ann Sylvester. Admin staff 2, Other staff 6. ***CC*** No.251549. Began 1987; Elim, but open to all. (Previously Nantwich Christian Conference Centre). Turnover £117,000 to year end Dec 98. Varied accommodaton for church groups, missionary societies, specialist conferences, etc.
Web: www.regents.ac.uk
Email: admin@regentstc.freeserve.co.uk
☎ 01270 610 800 🖷 01270 610 013

***Rhos-Llyn**, Penparc, Cardigan SA43 2AB
Directors: Mr Dick & Mrs Heather Perfect. Other staff 2. Began 1980; non-denominational. Turnover n/a. Self-catering.
☎ 01239 614 501

***Ringsfield Hall**, Beccles NR34 8JR
Wardens: Ross Ashley, Mr Chris Walton. Other staff 3. ***CC*** No.264013. Began 1972; interdenominational. Turnover n/a. Short-term accommodation for churches, schools, youth groups and families; retreats.
☎ 01502 713 020 🖷 01502 710 615

Rora Christian Fellowship Trust, Rora House, Halford, Liverton, Newton Abbot TQ12 6HZ
Trust Administrators: Mr Malcolm & Mrs Christine Ford. Executive staff 2, Other staff 8. ***CC*** No.268281. Began 1970; interdenominational. Turnover £47,500 to year end Mar 93.
Email: mcoleg@globalnet.co.uk
☎ 01626 821 746 🖷 01626 821 586

Rowanhurst Christian Hotel, 88 Sandown Road, Lake, Sandown PO36 9JX
Proprietors: Mr Peter & Mrs Eileen Atkinson. No other staff. Began 1984; non-denominational. Turnover n/a.
☎ 01983 402 663

The Rowantree Restaurant & Guest House, Loch Alvie, Aviemore PH22 1QB
Owner: Mr George Orr. Other staff 2. Began 1993; non-denominational. Turnover n/a.
☎ 01479 810 207 🖷 01479 810 207

The Royal Foundation of St Katharine, 2 Butcher Row, London E14 8DS
Master: Rev Ron Swan. Staff n/a. ***CC*** Began 1147; Anglican. Turnover £100,000 to year end Mar 98.
Email: michael@stkatharine.demon.co.uk
☎ 020 7790 3540 🖷 020 7702 7603

Roysdean Manor Hotel (Epworth Hotels), 5 Derby Road, Bournemouth BH1 3PT
Manager: Mr Clive Rowe-Evans. Admin staff 3, Other staff 16. Began 1952; non-denominational. Turnover £327,000 to year end Feb 98.
☎ 01202 554 933 🖷 01202 780 916

Rydal Hall (Carlisle Diocesan Conference and Retreat House), Ambleside LA22 9LX
Warden: Rev Dr Michael Kitchener. *Administrator:* Rev David Simon. Admin staff 5, Other staff 11. Began 1963; Anglican. Turnover £400,000 to year end Dec 98. Volunteer Christian community serving its holiday, conference and retreat guests in a prayerful environment.
Web: users.aol.com/rydalhall
Email: rydalhall@aol.com
☎ 01539 432 050 🖷 01539 434 887

St Andrew's Hotel, Belgrave Road, Ventnor PO38 1JH
Proprietors: Mr and Mrs Mick Young. Part-time staff 7. Began n/a; non-denominational. Turnover £70,000 to year end Dec 98. All rooms en-suite, parking, non-smoking throughout. Church groups welcome.
☎ 01983 852 680

***St Brides Hotel**, Burlington Road, Swanage BH19 1LS
Proprietors: Mr & Mrs A Elliott. No other staff. Began 1985; Baptist. Turnover £50,000 to year end Nov 98.
☎ 01929 425 011

St Columba's Horton Outreach, St Columba's Church, St Margaret's Place, Bradford BD7 3AW
Manager: Mrs Hilary Greed. Executive staff 1, Other staff 5. ***CC*** Began 1983; Anglican. Turnover £100,000 to year end Dec 98. Non-residential conference centre, restaurant; care of elderly, disabled, people with special needs.
Web: www.bradford.anglican.org/bfd/col
☎ 01274 502 536

***St John's College, Durham**, South Bailey, Durham DH1 3RJ
Deputy Bursar: Mr Martin Clemmet. Admin staff 10, Other staff 30. ***CC*** No.113496. Began 1909; Anglican. Turnover £133,000 to year end July 94.
☎ 0191 374 3500 🖷 0191 374 3573
Bookings: 3 South Bailey, Durham DH1 3RJ
☎ 0191 374 3566

***St John's College, Nottingham**, Chilwell Lane, Bramcote, Beeston, Nottingham NG9 3DS
Bursar: Mr Terry Sheppard. Admin staff 2, Other staff 8. ***CC*** No.1026706. Began 1970; Anglican. Turnover £50,000 to year end Aug 98.
Web: www.stjohns-nottm.ac.uk
Email: college@stjohns-nottm.ac.uk
☎ 0115 925 1114 🖷 0115 943 6438

St Mary's Church House, Church Hill, Harrow HA1 3HL
Administrator: To be appointed. No full-time staff. Began n/a; Anglican. Turnover n/a.
☎ 020 8422 8409

St Mary's House, Stanbrook Abbey, Callow End, Worcester WR2 4TD
The Warden: To be appointed. Staff n/a. ***CC*** No.234722. Began 1986; Roman Catholic. Turnover n/a. Providing a place for rest and spiritual refreshment in a Benedictine context of prayer.
☎ 01905 830 307

St Ninian's Centre, Comrie Road, Crieff PH7 4BG
Director: Rev Dr Adrian Varwell. Executive staff 3, Other staff 11. ***CC*** No.SCO 14279. Began 1958; Church of Scotland and interdenominational. Magazine: *Crieff Comment* (800 every four months). Turnover £230,000 to year end Dec 98. Hosting conferences, training events, youth programmes, retreats and holidays.
☎ 01764 653 766 🖷 01764 655 824

***St Paul's Church**, Robert Adam Street, London W1M 5AH
Co-ordinator: Miss Liza Yiannopoulos. Admin staff 1, Other staff 2. ***CC*** Began 1988; Anglican. No magazine. Turnover £26,500 to year end Dec 96. Providing day and evening conference and reception facilities. Non-residential.
☎ 020 7935 5941 🖷 020 7224 6087

St Paul's Church & Parish Centre, St Paul's Road, Brentford TW8 0PN
Administrator: Ms Virginia Luckett. Admin staff 1, Other staff 4. Began 1991; Anglican. Magazine: *The Grapevine* (Circulation n/a monthly). Turnover £100,000 to year end Dec 96. Non-residential conference centre.
Email: stpaulsbrentford@btinternet.com
☎ 020 8568 7442 🖷 020 8569 7864

St Rhadagunds (CE Holiday/Conference Centre Ltd), St Lawrence, Ventnor PO38 1XQ
Manager: Mr Harry Morgan. Admin staff 2, Other staff 8. ***CC*** No.1039170. Began 1934; interdenominational. Turnover £250,000 to year end Nov 98. 7 holiday centres.
☎ 01983 852 160
Correspondence: *Director:* Mr David W Smith, The Nook, Cockey Moor Road, Starling, Bury BL8 2HD
☎ 0161 764 1889

St Winifreds (CE Holiday/Conference Centre Ltd), 35 Marine Drive, Rhos-on-Sea, Colwyn Bay LL28 4NL
Manager/Host: Mr & Mrs James Hogg. Other staff 12. ***CC*** No.1039170. Began 1912; interdenominational. Turnover £300,000 to year end Feb 94.
☎ 01492 544 128 🖷 01492 544 460

***Sandford Lodge Hotel**, 61 The Avenue, Totland Bay PO39 0DN
Proprietors: Gerard Bootle & Valerie Hutson. Admin staff 2. Began 1988; non-denominational. Turnover £29,000 to year end Jan 96.
☎ 01983 753 478

Scargill House Ltd, Kettlewell, Skipton BD23 5HU
Warden: Rev Keith Knight. Admin staff 12, Other staff 26. *CC* No.228031. Began 1959; Anglican. Turnover £400,000 to year end Dec 96. Holidays, conferences, retreats, renewal.
Web: ds.dial.pipex.com/scargill.house/
✉ Email: scargill.house@dial.pipex.com
☎ 01756 760 234 🖷 01756 760 499

Scottish Churches' House, Kirk Street, Dunblane FK15 0AJ
Warden: Mr Brian Baker. Admin staff 2, Other staff 10. *CC* No.SCO 13196. Began 1961; ecumenical. Turnover £100,000 to year end Dec 95.
☎ 01786 823 588 🖷 01786 825 844

Seaford Sands Hotel, 17 Roundham Road, Paignton TQ4 6DN
Proprietors: Mr Stanley & Mrs Carol Gill. Admin staff 6, Other staff 3. Began 1988; Anglican. (Previously Torbay Christian Hotel). Turnover £160,000 to year end Oct 98.
☎ 01803 557 722 🖷 01803 526 071

***Selbourne Licensed Hotel**, 4 West Street, Scarborough YO11 2QL
Owner: Mr Michael Broddle. Executive staff 3. Began 1986; Methodist. Turnover £45,000 to year end Apr 99. Hotel catering for couples or family holidays giving a time of refreshment from usual work.
☎ 01723 372 822 🖷 01723 372 822

Seven Sisters Christian Guest House, 3 Halton Road, Eastbourne BN22 7HL
Proprietors: Mr Philip & Mrs Mary Baldwin. No full-time staff. Began 1992; non-denominational. Turnover £10,000 to year end May 98. Providing homely holiday accommodation.
☎ 01323 721 776

Sheldon Centre, Dunsford, Exeter EX6 7LE
Warden: Mr Carl Lee. Admin staff 3, Other staff 6. *CC* No.327394. Began 1977; interdenominational. Turnover n/a. Self-catering residential accommodation for groups.
☎ 01647 252 752

Sidholme (Christian Guild Holidays), Elysian Fields, Sidmouth EX10 8UJ
Manager: Mr Jonathan Oldroyd. Staff n/a. Began 1931; ecumenical. Turnover n/a.
☎ 01395 515 104 🖷 01395 579 321

Silverthorn Hotel, 10 Herbert Road, Alum Chine, Bournemouth BH4 8HD
Proprietors: Patrick & Sue Sanderson. No other staff. Began 1986; Anglican. Turnover n/a.
☎ 01202 766 204

Silverwell Christian Hotel, 20 West End Road, Morecambe LA4 4DL
Owner: Mr Graeme Last. Other staff 1. Began n/a; non-denominational. Turnover n/a.
☎ 01524 410 532

Sion Catholic Community for Evangelism, Sion House, Greenland Road, Selly Park, Birmingham B29 7PP
President: Rev Pat Lynch CSD. *Director:* Mr Peter Moran. Executive staff 30, Other staff 5. *CC* No.327967. Began 1984; Roman Catholic but open to all. Magazine: *The New Century* (700 half-yearly). Turnover £250,000 to year end Apr 98.
Web: www.btinternet.com/-sioncommunity
✉ Email: sioncommunity@btinternet.com
☎ 0121 414 1648 Mobile 07860 621 794 🖷 0121 414 1076

Sizewell Hall Ltd, Leiston IP16 4TX
Executive Adviser: Mr Victor Jack. Other staff 5. *CC* No.269157. Began 1975; interdenominational. Turnover £135,000 to year end Dec 98. Self-catering and camping.
☎ 01728 830 715 🖷 01728 833 275
Bookings: The Homestead, Drinkstone, Bury St Edmunds IP30 9TL

***Slavanka (Bournemouth Conference Centre)**, 42 Belle Vue Road, Southbourne, Bournemouth BH6 3DS
Manager: Mr Anthony Hallam. *Chairman:* Rev John Simmons. Executive staff 2, Other staff 5. *CC* No.237157. Began 1929; interdenominational. Turnover £230,000 to year end Dec 98.
✉ Email: slavanka@btinternet.com
☎ 01202 424 151 🖷 01202 421 190

Sneaton Castle Centre (Order of the Holy Paraclete), Sneaton Castle, Whitby YO21 3QN
Centre Manager: Mr Christopher Andrews. Admin staff 4, Other staff 6. *CC* No.271117. Began 1998; Anglican. Turnover n/a. Day or residential conferences.
✉ Email: sneaton@globalnet.co.uk
☎ 01947 600 051 🖷 01947 603 490

†**The Southam Centre**, School Street, Southam, Leamington Spa CV33 0PL
Managers: Mr & Mrs G Heighton. No full-time staff. ***CC*** Began 1977; Anglican. Turnover n/a. For young people.
☎ No telephone
Bookings: 21 Dalkeith Avenue, Bilton, Rugby CV22 7NN
☎ 01788 815 514

Southlands Hotel (Epworth Hotels), West Street, South Cliff, Scarborough YO11 2QW
Manager: Miss Elaine Stewart. Admin staff 3, Other staff 15. Began 1996; non-denominational. Turnover £500,000 to year end Feb 98.
☎ 01723 361 461 🖷 01723 376 035

*__Streatham Christian Conference Centre__, 22 Lewin Road, Streatham, London SW16 6JR
Senior Pastor: Rev Mike Wood. Executive staff 2, Other staff 3. Began 1996; Baptist. Turnover n/a. Non-residential centre for private seminars to major conferences; catering available on request.
Email: streathambaptist@charis.co.uk
☎ 020 8769 1515 🖷 020 8677 3486

Sunbury Court, Lower Hampton Road, Sunbury-on-Thames TW16 5PL
Manager: Mr A W Packham. Admin staff 2, Other staff 14. ***CC*** Began 1920; Salvation Army. Turnover n/a.
☎ 01932 782 196

Sunbury Court Recreation Centre, Harfield Road, Sunbury-on-Thames TW16 5PT
Manager: Mr A W Packham. Staff n/a. ***CC*** Began n/a; Salvation Army. Turnover n/a. Self-catering only.
☎ 01932 786 198

Thornley House, Thornley Drive, Teignmouth TQ14 9JH
Proprietor: Mr James H Chivers. Admin staff 1, Other staff 4. Began 1988; non-denominational. Turnover n/a.
☎ 01626 775 270 🖷 01626 775 270

Treloyhan Manor (Christian Guild Holidays), St Ives TR26 2AL
Managers: Mr Richard & Mrs Claire Foxton. Staff n/a. Began 1948; ecumenical. Turnover n/a.
☎ 01736 796 240 🖷 01736 798 377

Trevanion House, Trevanion Road, Wadebridge PL27 7JY
Proprietors: Dr Michael & Mrs Christine Todd. Seasonal staff 15. Began 1991; non-denominational. Turnover n/a. Registered care home specialising in holiday provision, adult learning disabilities, full package, care/escorted activities.
Email: trevanion@dial.pipex.com
☎ 01208 814 903

Trewince Manor, Portscatho, Truro TR2 5ET
Owner: Mr Peter Heywood. Admin staff 2, Other staff 5. Began 1985; non-denominational. Turnover £390,000 to year end Dec 97.
☎ 01872 580 289 🖷 01872 580 694

†**Trimstone Manor Hotel**, Trimstone, West Down, Ilfracombe EX34 8NR
Owner: Mr D A Turner. Admin staff 2, Other staff 3. Began 1976; interdenominational. Turnover n/a.
Web: manorgroup.uk
Email: info@manor.romgroup.co.uk
☎ 01271 862 841

*__Trinity College Conference Centre__, Trinity College, Stoke Hill, Stoke Bishop, Bristol BS9 1JP
Principal: Rev Canon David Gillett. ***CC*** Began 1972; Anglican and interdenominational. Day or residential conferences, weddings, retreats, in peaceful setting with easy access and ample parking.
Web: www.trinity-bris.ac.uk
Email: conf@trinity-bris.ac.uk
☎ 0117 968 2803 🖷 0117 968 7470

*__Tudor Christian Guest House__, 6 Cliff Avenue, Cromer NR27 0AN
Working Partners: Mr Ivor & Mrs Shirley Charsley. No other staff. Began 1983; interdenominational. Turnover n/a.
☎ 01263 512 337

Undercliff Private Christian Hotel, Undercliff Road, Boscombe, Bournemouth BH5 1BL
Proprietor: Mr C Wheeler. Other staff 4. Began 1910; interdenominational. Turnover £125,000 to year end June 98.
☎ 01202 395 484

Upcott, Old Beer Road, Seaton EX12 2PZ
Wardens: Mr & Mrs Paul & Chrystal Milton. Admin staff 2, Other staff 4. ***CC*** No.285783. Began 1969; interdenominational. Turnover £75,000 to year end Dec 98.
Email: avctupcott@aol.com
☎ 01297 217 49

Waterbury Guest House, Birnam, Dunkeld PH8 0BG
Proprietors: Mr & Mrs Brian & Caroline Neil. No other staff. Began 1987; non-denominational. Turnover £30,000 to year end Apr 98.
Email: brian@waterbury.demon.co.uk
☎ 01350 727 324 🖷 01350 727 023

The Watering Hole Holiday Centre, Morwell, Tavistock PL19 8JH
Proprietors: Pastor Colin & Mrs Joy Bond. Admin staff 3. Began 1987; Community Church. Turnover £25,000 to year end Apr 90.
☎ 01822 833 844 🖷 01822 833 688

Waverley Abbey House (KLM & Pioneer People), Waverley Lane, Farnham GU9 8EP
Conference Co-ordinator: To be appointed. Executive staff 3, Other staff 46. ***CC*** No.294387. Began 1987; interdenominational. Turnover £2,500,000 to year end Dec 98.
Email: training@cwr.org.uk
☎ 01252 784 733 🖷 01252 784 732

Welford Hill Farm, Welford on Avon, Stratford-upon-Avon CV37 8AE
Manager: Mrs Meryl Stanley. Executive staff 1, Other staff 1. Began 1993; non-denominational. Turnover £15,000 to year end Dec 96.
Web: www.wwww.uk.com
Email: wel@welford.co.uk
☎ 01789 750 565 🖷 01789 751 901

Westcott Farm Christian Holiday Centre, Westcott Farm, Sheldon, Honiton EX14 0QS
Proprietor: Mr Philip Roberts. Admin staff 1. Began 1977; non-denominational. Turnover £30,000 to year end Apr 98. Self-catering, camping and caravans.
☎ 01404 841 238

Whirlow Grange Conference & Training Centre (Diocese of Sheffield), 484 Ecclesall Road South, Whirlow, Sheffield S11 9PZ
General Manager: Mr Jonathon Green. Admin staff 2, Other staff 4. ***CC*** Began 1953; Anglican. Turnover £280,000 to year end Dec 98.
☎ 0114 236 3173 📠 0114 262 0717

Wick Court Centre, Wick, Bristol BS15 5RB
Director: Mrs Ann Garner. Admin staff 2, Other staff 2. ***CC*** No.279910. Began 1980; non-denominational. Turnover £63,000 to year end Dec 96. For social/environmental education.
☎ 0117 937 3562

Willersley Castle Hotel & Conference Centre (Christian Guild Holidays), Cromford, Matlock DE4 5JH
Managers: Mr Bill & Mrs Carol-Anne Alcorn. Staff n/a. Began 1928; ecumenical. Turnover n/a.
☎ 01629 582 270 📠 01629 582 329

Winchester Diocesan House, Old Alresford Place, Alresford SO24 9DH
Warden: Mrs Penny Matthews. Admin staff 3, Other staff 7. ***CC*** Began 1964; Anglican. Turnover n/a.
Email: old.alresford.place@dial.pipex.com
☎ 01962 732 518 📠 01962 732 518

***Woodcroft Christian Centre**, Woodcroft, Chepstow NP6 7PZ
Manager: Rev Malcolm Purdy. Admin staff 1. ***CC*** No.237401. Began 1974; interdenominational. Turnover n/a. Self-catering, young people and students. Activity holidays, conferences, teaching, retreat. Some caravans/tents during summer.
☎ 01291 624 114

World Mission Association Ltd, Partnership House, 157 Waterloo Road, London SE1 8XA
Facilities and Services Manager: Mr Richard A Hummerston. ***CC*** No.297154. Began 1987; Anglican. Turnover n/a.
☎ 020 7928 8681

***Wycliffe Centre**, Horsleys Green, High Wycombe HP14 3XL
Conference/Services Manager: Mrs Beverly Johnston. Admin staff 3, Other staff 8. ***CC*** No.313854. Began 1973; interdenominational. Associated with Wycliffe Bible Translators. Turnover £100,000 to year end Oct 96.
Email: accommodation-uk@wycliffe.org
☎ 01494 482 521/ 01494 682 201 📠 01494 483 297

Wydale (York Diocesan Centre), Wydale, Brompton-by-Sawdon, Scarborough YO13 9DG
Warden: Mr Peter Fletcher. Admin staff 3, Other staff 10. ***CC*** Began 1963; Anglican. Turnover £198,000 to year end Dec 96.
☎ 01723 859 270

Ye Homesteade (CE Holiday/Conference Centre Ltd), 60 Cliff Road, Sheringham NR26 8BJ
Hosts: Mr & Mrs Harold & Kate Willimott. Other staff 4. ***CC*** No.1039170. Began 1936; interdenominational. Turnover £207,000 [overall company] to year end Jan 95.
☎ 01263 822 524 📠 01263 824 373

Yellowland Farm, Holsworthy EX22 7BN
Manager: Mrs Hilary Cheers. No full-time staff. Began 1984; non-denominational. Turnover n/a. Self-catering.
☎ 01409 253 659

YMCA, Dunford House, Midhurst GU29 0DG
General Manager: Mrs Pauline Dey. Admin staff 2, Other staff 12. ***CC*** No.212810. Began 1951; non-denominational. Turnover £270,000 to year end Mar 96. Conference and training centre venue, residential facilities, historic house set in 60 acres of grounds.
☎ 01730 812 381 📠 01730 817 042

†**YMCA, Londonderry**, 51 Glenshane Road, Drumahoe, Londonderry BT47 3SA
General Secretary: Mr Mark Patterson. *YMCA Administrator:* Mrs Isobel Smith. Admin staff 1, Other staff 20. ***CC*** No.NI 15660. Began 1865; interdenominational. Turnover £110,000 to year end Mar 97.
Web: niweb.com/org/ymca
☎ 028 7130 1662 📠 028 7130 1662

YMCA, Lurgan, 42d High Street, Lurgan, Craigavon BT66 8AU
Development Officer: Mr Andrew Soye. Admin staff 2, Other staff 4. ***CC*** No.X 052/88. Began n/a; interdenominational. Turnover £75,000. Personal and social development including cross community work with 'at risk' youth. Non-residential.
Email: andy@ymca-ire.dnet.co.uk
☎ 028 3832 1025

YMCA, Otterburn Hall, Otterburn, Newcastle upon Tyne NE19 1HE
Director: Mr Chris Jones. Admin staff 3, Other staff 28. ***CC*** No.701937. Began 1947; non-denominational. Turnover £1,000,000 to year end June 96.
☎ 01830 520 663 📠 01830 520 491

HOSPICES

By Alphabetical Order

Martin House Hospice for Children, Grove Road, Clifford, Wetherby LS23 6TX
Administrator: Mrs A Somerscale. Executive staff 4, Other staff 50. ***CC*** Began 1984; non-denominational. Magazine: *Martin House News* (120,000 half-yearly). Turnover n/a. Respite and terminal care for children with life threatening disorders, and their families. Bereavement support. 9 beds and family accommodation.
☎ 01937 845 045 📠 01937 541 363

***Mildmay Hospital UK**, Hackney Road, Shoreditch, London E2 7NA
Director: Barbara Dicks. *Director of Clinical Services:* Dr Jeanette Meadway. Executive staff 4, Other staff 150. ***CC*** No.292058. Began 1985; interdenominational. (Previously Midmay Mission International). Magazine: *Highlights* (8,000 half-yearly). Turnover £4,000,000 to year end Mar 98. Specialist AIDS hospice care for men, women and children; independent Christian charitable hospital.
Web: www.mildmay.org.uk/mild.int
✉ Email: dicksb@dial.pipex.com
☎ 020 7613 6312 📠 020 7729 8498

St Christopher's Hospice, 51 Lawrie Park Road, Sydenham, London SE26 6DZ
Medical Director: Dr Robert Dunlop. *Administrator:* Mr Christopher Clark. *Chief Nurse:* Mr Andrew Knight. Executive staff 6, Other staff 360. ***CC*** No.210667. Began 1967; interdenominational. Magazine: *Annual Report* (10,000 annually). Turnover £7,000,000 to year end Mar 95. Control of pain and family support for patients with advanced cancer and other diseases.
☎ 020 8778 9252 📠 020 8659 8680

St Leonards Hospice, 185 Tadcaster Road, York YO24 1GL
Chief Executive: Mr Steven Harker. *Clinical Care Services Manager:* Mrs Sue Spence. *Medical Director:* Dr Sarah Anderson. Executive staff 4, Other staff 90. ***CC*** No.509294. Began 1984; interdenominational. Magazine: *St Leonards Hospice Newsletter* (3,000 quarterly). Turnover £1,000,000 to year end Mar 98. Specialist palliative care for in-patients, day care and out-patients.
☎ 01904 708 553 📠 01904 704 337

Saint Mary's Hospice, 176 Raddlebarn Road, Selly Park, Birmingham B29 7DA
Chief Executive: Mr David Johnson. Staff 120, Volunteers 250. ***CC*** Began 1979; non-denominational. No magazine. Turnover £2,600,000 to year end Mar 99. 27 beds. Home care, day care, bereavement support, education centre..
☎ 0121 472 1191 📠 0121 472 5075

Trinity Hospice, Clapham, 30 Clapham Common, North Side, London SW4 0RN
Administrator: Ms M Morton. Executive staff 10, Other staff 100. ***CC*** No.1013945. Began 1891; interdenominational. Magazine: *Annual Report* (6,000 annually). Turnover £3,300,000 to year end Mar 99. Providing help to people with advanced illness and a limited life expectancy.
Web: www.trinityhospice.org.uk
✉ Email: enquiries@trinityhospice.org.uk
☎ 0207 787 1000

HOSTELS

By Country and Postcode area (see Page 569 for explanation)
Organisations which did not supply any of this information are not listed here

S = single rooms **D/T** = number of bed spaces in double/twin rooms **L** = number of bed spaces in rooms larger than double
TS = total bed spaces (not number of rooms) **DR** = Day Room, the capacity of the largest room suitable for group use
⇌ = nearest Railway station ⊖ = nearest London Underground station

Postcode	Location	Name	S	D/T	L	Other	TS	DR	Railway Station
ENGLAND									
Anglia									
AL 2	**St Albans**	SPEC Centre	-	40	20		60	70	⇌ Radlett or St Albans
AL 7	**Welwyn Garden City**	YMCA	115	-	34		149	-	⇌ Welwyn Garden City
CB 1	**Cambridge**	YMCA	75	75	-	bedsits 18 flatlets 11	200	150	⇌ Cambridge
CB 4	**Cambridge**	Link House Trust	15	20	-	overseas students	35	-	⇌ Cambridge
CM 0	**Southminster**	Asheldham Youth Church	-	-	36		36	-	⇌ Southminster
IP 4	**Ipswich**	Lyndon House	40	-	-	for men	40	-	⇌ Ipswich
IP28	**Bury St Edmunds**	Hengrave Hall Youth Centre	n/a	n/a	n/a		41	-	⇌ Bury St Edmunds
IP33	**Bury St Edmunds**	YMCA	23	-	-		23	-	⇌ Bury St Edmunds
NR 2	**Norwich**	YMCA	90	-	-		90	-	⇌ Norwich
NR22	**Walsingham**	Elmham House	53	70	6		129	100	⇌ King's Lynn or Norwich
NR26	**Sheringham**	Canaan Christian Centre	-	2	15		17	-	
PE 3	**Peterborough**	YMCA	156	-	-		156	80	⇌ Peterborough
PE30	**King's Lynn**	YMCA	n/a	n/a	n/a		30	-	⇌ King's Lynn
RM 7	**Romford**	YMCA	150	-	-		150	100	⇌ Romford ⊖ Dagenham East or Elm Park
RM 9	**Dagenham**	YWCA	38	-	-		38	-	⇌ Dagenham
WD 1	**Watford**	YMCA	n/a	n/a	n/a		177	-	⇌ Watford Junction

Hostels

Postcode	Location	Name	S	D/T	L	Other		TS	DR	Railway Station
London										
E1	London	Hopetown Residential Centre	n/a	n/a	n/a	for women, 9 flats		104	-	⊖ Aldgate East
E1	London	Booth House	n/a	n/a	n/a	direct access, minimal support for men		170	-	⊖ White Chapel
E13	London	House of the Divine Compassion	n/a	n/a	n/a	for homeless people		14	-	⊖ Plaistow
E14	London	Riverside House	11	4	75			90	-	*Docklands:* Westferry
E17	London	Christian Alliance Hostel, Walthamstow	14	-	-			14	-	⇌ Walthamstow Central ⊖ Walthamstow Central
		YMCA,Waltham Forest	148	-	-			148	-	⇌ Walthamstow Central ⊖ Walthamstow Central
EC1Y	London	YMCA, City	n/a	n/a	n/a			111	-	⇌ Old Street ⊖ Barbican
N5	London	Newington Court	50	-	-			50	-	⇌ Canonbury ⊖ Manor House
N8	London	YMCA, Hornsey	n/a	n/a	n/a	special needs		158	-	⊖ Turnpike Lane or Finsbury Park or Archway
N10	London	Chester House	n/a	n/a	n/a			124	-	⊖ Bounds Green or Highgate
N16	London	The Alliance Club	n/a	n/a	n/a			132	-	⇌ Essex Road or Canonbury ⊖ Highbury & Islington
NW1	London	Elgood House Hostel	39	-	-			39	-	⇌ Marylebone ⊖ Edgware Road
		Marylebone Project	n/a	n/a	n/a	for homeless women		101	-	⇌ Marylebone ⊖ Marylebone
		Poor Servants of the Mother of God	45	18	6			69	-	⇌ Euston ⊖ Euston
NW2	London	German Catholic Social Centre	1	4	12			17	40	⊖ Kilburn
NW3	London	International Students Hostel	17	2	16			35	-	⊖ Hampstead
NW4	London	Pillar of Fire Church	22	8	20			50	-	⇌ Hendon
NW6	London	Conway House	47	28	24			99	-	⊖ West Hampstead
SE1	London	Christian Alliance Hostel, Waterloo	35	86	-			121	-	⇌ Waterloo ⊖ Waterloo
		Lena Fox House	n/a	n/a	n/a	medium stay		34	-	⇌ London Bridge ⊖ London Bridge
SE5	London	John Kirk Centre	n/a	n/a	n/a	for young men		22	-	⇌ Denmark Hill
SE16	London	Bermondsey Homeless Centre	n/a	n/a	n/a	for men		44		⇌ London Bridge ⊖ London Bridge
SE18	London	International Students' Housing Society	83	10	-	flats	32	166	-	⇌ Woolwich Arsenal
SW7	London	More House	n/a	n/a	n/a			84	-	⊖ South Kensington or Gloucester Road
SW17	London	Friendship House	87	-	-			87	-	⇌ Tooting ⊖ Tooting Broadway
SW19	London	YMCA, Wimbledon	110	-	-			110	-	⇌ Wimbledon ⊖ Wimbledon or South Wimbledon
SW1P	London	St Louise Irish Centre Hostel	57	68	-			125	-	⇌ Victoria ⊖ St James's Park
W1H	London	St Vincent's Hostel	43	26	-			69	90	⊖ Baker Street or Bond Street or Oxford Circus
W1P	London	YMCA, London, Indian Student Hostel	98	10	6			114	200	⊖ Warren Street or Great Portland Street
WC1B	London	YWCA, London, Holborn	173	92	-			265	-	⊖ Tottenham Court Road
WC1H	London	International Lutheran Student Centre	64	14	-	flats	2	80	50	⇌ Kings Cross or St Pancras ⊖ Russell Square
W2	London	Christian Alliance Hostel, Pembridge Square	19	10	-			29	-	⊖ Notting Hill Gate
W2	London	Homeless Centre	n/a	n/a	n/a	for men		80	-	n/a
W5	London	Moullin House	-	50	-			50	-	⇌ Ealing Broadway ⊖ Ealing Broadway
		YMCA, Ealing & District	130	26	-			156	120	⇌ Ealing Broadway ⊖ Ealing Broadway or South Ealing
W8	London	Lee Abbey International Students' Club	67	82	31			180	60	⊖ Earls Court or Kensington High Street
Midlands										
B1	Birmingham	Birmingham City Mission	5	-	-	medical wing	40	45	-	⇌ Birmingham New Street
B4	Birmingham	William Booth Lane Social Service	n/a	n/a	n/a	for men	-	143	-	
B 15	Birmingham	YWCA, Edgbaston	92	-	-	flats	2	94	-	⇌ Birmingham New Street
		YWCA, Edgbaston, Audrey Achurch Wing	106	-	-			106	-	⇌ Birmingham New Street
		YWCA, Edgbaston, Lady Churchill House	64	-	-			64	-	⇌ Birmingham New Street
B 20	Birmingham	Lyncroft House	n/a	n/a	n/a	for mothers for children	10 26	36	-	⇌ Hamstead
B 27	Birmingham	Pamela House	n/a	n/a	n/a	for women		n/a	n/a	⇌ Acocks Green
B 29	Birmingham	Methodist International House	38	12	-			50	-	⇌ Birmingham New Street
B 98	Redditch	YMCA	185	-	-			185	100	⇌ Redditch
CV 1	Coventry	YMCA	94	-	-			94	-	⇌ Coventry
CV32	Leamington Spa	Christian Alliance Hostel	20	-	-			20	28	⇌ Leamington Spa
DE14	Burton-on-Trent	YMCA	48	-	-			48	-	⇌ Burton-on-Trent
DE24	Derby	YMCA	25	-	-	flatlets	57	82	-	⇌ Derby
LE 2	Leicester	YMCA	n/a	n/a	n/a			78	-	⇌ Leicester
NG 1	Nottingham	Sneinton House	n/a	n/a	n/a			70		⇌ Nottingham
NG 1	Nottingham	YMCA, Nottingham	n/a	n/a	n/a	for young people		80	-	⇌ Nottingham
NN 1	Northampton	Phoenix House, YWCA	34	-	-			34	100	⇌ Northampton
ST 4	Stoke-on-Trent	Vale Street Hostel	56	-	8			64	-	⇌ Stoke-on-Trent
WV 1	Wolverhampton	Little Brothers of the Good Shepherd	90	6	-			96	-	⇌ Wolverhampton
North East										
DL 1	Darlington	Tom Raine Court	55	-	-	+ rehabilitation unit	n/a	55	-	⇌ Darlington
DN 1	Doncaster	YMCA	26	-	-			26	-	⇌ Doncaster
DN32	Grimsby	YMCA	71	-	-			71	150	⇌ Grimsby Town
DN32	Grimsby	Brighowgate Social Service Centre	n/a	n/a	n/a			60	-	⇌ Grimsby Town
HG 4	Ripon	YMCA	21	-	-			21	136	⇌ Harrogate
HU 1	Hull	William Booth House	119	-	35			154	-	⇌ Hull
LS 1	Leeds	Saint George's Crypt	22	2	-			24	50	⇌ Leeds
LS13	Leeds	Mount Cross Families Centre	-	-	-	family units	32	32	-	⇌ Leeds
LN 2	Lincoln	YMCA	95	-	-			95	120	⇌ Lincoln Central
NE 1	Newcastle upon Tyne	City Road Social Service Centre	n/a	n/a	n/a	for men		66	-	*Metro:* Byker
NE 6	Newcastle upon Tyne	Gaughan Close Centre	n/a	n/a	n/a	for women		n/a	n/a	*Metro:* Walkergate
S6	Sheffield	Netherlea Social Service Centre	n/a	n/a	n/a	for men		100	-	⇌ Sheffield
S10	Sheffield	YMCA	90	-	-	flats	10	100	-	⇌ Sheffield
SR1	Sunderland	High Street Hostel	n/a	n/a	n/a	for men and women		50	-	⇌ Sunderland

Postcode	Location	Name	S	D/T	L	Other		TS	DR	Railway Station
North West										
BD3	**Bradford**	Lawley House Social Service Centre	n/a	n/a	n/a	for men	90	102	-	Bradford Interchange
						resettlement project	12			
BL1	**Bolton**	Duke Street Hostel	n/a	n/a	n/a	for homeless men		72	-	Bolton
CA12	**Keswick**	Braithwaite Methodist Youth Centre	-	-	26			26	-	Penrith
		Carlisle Diocesan Youth Centre	-	8	28			36	36	Penrith
		Castlerigg Manor	8	12	45			75	75	Penrith (18 miles)
		Kestrel Lodge Residential Centre	-	4	29			33	5	Carlisle or Penrith
CH41	**Birkenhead**	YMCA,	50	-	-			50	-	Birkenhead Central
CW 2	**Crewe**	YMCA	50	32	-			82	60	Crewe
L3	**Liverpool**	Ann Fowler House	40	-	-	for women		40	-	Liverpool Lime Street
L8	**Liverpool**	Christian Alliance Hostel	52	-	-	self-catering		52	-	Liverpool Lime Street
L13	**Liverpool**	Prescot Road Hostel	40	-	-			40	-	Liverpool Lime Street
LA21	**Coniston**	St Andrew's Youth Centre	-	8	40			48	100	Ulverston or Windermere
M14	**Manchester**	Christian Alliance Hostel	18	8	-			26	-	Manchester Piccadilly
M3	**Salford**	James Street Centre Hostel	n/a	n/a	n/a	for homeless men	-	38	-	Salford Central or Salford Crescent
M 4	**Manchester**	Mary and Joseph House	-	-	40			40	-	Manchester Piccadilly
		Methodist International House	n/a	n/a	n/a			62	-	Manchester Piccadilly
M 15	**Manchester**	Wilmott Street Hostel	n/a	n/a	n/a			115	-	Manchester Oxford Road
OL12	**Rochdale**	Providence House	n/a	n/a	n/a	for men		74	-	Rochdale
WA 1	**Warrington**	James Lee House	n/a	n/a	n/a	for men		52	-	Warrington Bank Quay
WA 3	**Warrington**	YMCA	50	33	8			124	-	Birchwood or Warrington Bank Quay
WA 9	**St Helens**	Salisbury House	n/a	n/a	n/a	for men		64		St Helens Central
WA10	**St Helens**	YMCA	120	-	-			120	100	St Helens Central
South Central										
PO 1	**Portsmouth**	Catherine Booth House	n/a	n/a	n/a	cluster flats	6	36	-	Portsmouth & Southsea
		YMCA	93	20	130			243	120	Portsmouth Harbour
RG30	**Reading**	YMCA	30	30	-			60	100	Reading
SN 1	**Swindon**	Davis House	-	-	-	9 flats	112	112	100	Swindon
SO14	**Southampton**	Mountbatten Social Services Centre	n/a	n/a	n/a	for men		55	-	Southampton Central
SO14	**Southampton**	Christian Alliance Hostel	8	-	-	homeless young people	14	22	-	Southampton Central
SP10	**Yeovil**	Christian Alliance, Andover	8	-	-			8	-	Andover
South East										
CR 0	**Croydon**	YWCA	77	56	-			133	-	East Croydon
CT 9	**Margate**	The Christian Housing Trust	19	-	-	special needs		19	-	Margate
GU 1	**Guildford**	Christian Alliance Hostel	24	16	-			40	-	Guildford
		YMCA	114	12	-			126	-	Guildford
TN 1	**Tunbridge Wells**	Christian Alliance Hostel	16	-	-			16	-	Tunbridge Wells
TN38	**St Leonards-on-Sea**	Christian Alliance Hostel	10	-	-			10	-	St Leonards Warrior Square
South West										
BA 1	**Bath**	YMCA	32	58	4			180	30	Bath Spa
BA20	**Yeovil**	Christian Alliance Hostel	12	-	-			12	-	Yeovil Junction or Yeovil Pen Mill
BA21	**Yeovil**	Christian Alliance Hostel	n/a	n/a	n/a	+ flats	6	18	-	Yeovil Junction or Yeovil Pen Mill
BH 1	**Bournemouth**	YMCA	63	-	-			63	-	Bournemouth
BS 2	**Bristol**	Little George Street Social Service Centre	n/a	n/a	n/a	for men		96	-	Bristol Temple Meads
BS 8	**Bristol**	Methodist International House	32	8	-			40	-	Bristol Temple Meads
BS23	**Weston-super-Mare**	Christian Alliance Hostel	12	-	-			12	-	Weston-super-Mare
BS25	**Winscombe**	Barton Children's Centre and Conference Centre	5	6	59			70	-	Bristol Temple Meads or Weston-super-Mare
EX 1	**Exeter**	YWCA	67	-	-			67	-	Exeter St Davids
EX 4	**Exeter**	Christian Alliance Hostel	13	-	-			13	-	Exeter Central
EX 8	**Exmouth**	Christian Alliance Hostel	12	-	-			12	-	Exmouth
		YWCA	44	-	-	flats for disabled	2	46	75	Exmouth
GL50	**Cheltenham**	YMCA	62	-	-			62	-	Cheltenham Spa
PL 1	**Plymouth**	Devonport House Social Service Centre	n/a	n/a	n/a	for men		69	-	Devonport
PL20	**Yelverton**	Buckland Monachorum Hostel	-	6	20			26	-	Plymouth
TR18	**Penzance**	YMCA	3	6	80			89	100	Penzance
WR 2	**Worcester**	YMCA	60	2	-			62	-	Worcester Forgate Street or Worcester Shrub Hill
NORTHERN IRELAND										
BT14	**Belfast**	Glen Alva Families Centre	-	-	-	family units	14	14	-	*Rail:* Belfast Central
		Thorndale Centre	4	-	-	family units	21	25	-	*Rail:* Belfast Central
SCOTLAND										
DD 1	**Dundee**	Strathmore Lodge	n/a	n/a	n/a	8 resettlement flats		54	-	Dundee
DD 2	**Dundee**	Clement Park House	n/a	n/a	n/a	5 family units		20	-	Dundee
EH 1	**Edinburgh**	Cunningham House	n/a	n/a	n/a			35	-	Edinburgh
EH 3	**Edinburgh**	Frances Kinnaird House	6	8	32			46	-	Edinburgh
EH 5	**Edinburgh**	Ashbrook Social Service Centre	n/a	n/a	n/a			16	-	Edinburgh
G1	**Glasgow**	Hope House Social Services Centre	n/a	n/a	n/a			121	-	*Underground:* St Enoch
		Wallace of Campsie House Social Services Centre	40	-	-	disabled flats	2	52	-	Glasgow Central
						2 cluster flats	10			
G5	**Glasgow**	William Hunter House Social Services Centre	5	12	20			37	37	*Underground:* Bridgestreet
PA15	**Greenock**	Fewster House Social Services Centre	n/a	n/a	n/a	men (direct access)	22	34	-	Greenock Central
						residential care wing	12			Greenock Central
		Inverclyde Families Centre	n/a	n/a	n/a	family units	25	25	-	Aviemore or Kingussie
PH21	**Kingussie**	Glen Feshie Hostel	-	-	12			12		
WALES										
CF1	**Cardiff**	Bute Street Social Service Centre	n/a	n/a	n/a	men		88	-	Cardiff Central
CF3	**Cardiff**	YWCA	19	-	-			19	-	Cardiff Central

A

HOSTELS

By Alphabetical Order

A

***The Alliance Club**, Newington Green, London N16 9QH
Warden: Mr P Clarke. *Bursar:* Mr Alexander A Anteyi. Admin staff 4, Other staff 6. ***CC*** No.212325. Began 1963; non-denominational. Turnover £370,000 to year end Dec 96. For overseas students.
Email: allianceclub@btinternet.com
☎ 020 7226 6085 Fax 020 7704 2486

Ashbrook Social Service Centre, 492 Ferry Road, Edinburgh EH5 2DL
Officer-in-Charge: Captain Mark Holder. Admin staff 3. ***CC*** Began n/a; Salvation Army. Turnover n/a. Women.
☎ 0131 552 5705

Asheldham Youth Church, 28 The Promenade, Maylandsea, Southminster CM3 6AR
Warden: Mr Brian Jiggins. Admin staff 1. ***CC*** Began 1976; Anglican. Turnover £15,200 to year end Mar 98. Self-catering residential centre, young people.
☎ 01621 743 536
Correspondence: The Vicarage, 6 Bakery Close, Tillingham, Southminster CM0 7TT
☎ 01621 778 017

Barton Children's Centre and Conference Centre, Barton, Winscombe BS25 1DY
Chairman: Mr M J Hardwick. Admin staff 1. ***CC*** No.220253. Began 1884; non-denominational. Turnover n/a. Purpose built premises for children's and group holidays and children in need.
☎ No telephone
Bookings: 20 Southfield Road, Westbury-on-Trym, Bristol BS9 3BH
☎ 0117 962 1757 Fax 0117 962 1757

Bermondsey Homeless Centre, 122 Spa Road, Bermondsey, London SE16 3SH
Officer-in-Charge: Captain David Hubbell. Admin staff 4. ***CC*** Began n/a; Salvation Army. Turnover n/a. Accommodation for men.
☎ 020 7237 1107 Fax 020 7394 6193

Birmingham City Mission, Washington Court, Washington Street, Birmingham B1 1SE
Senior Manager: Mr David Curnock. Admin staff 2, Other staff 23. ***CC*** No.1051023. Began 1979; interdenominational. Turnover £390,000 to year end Mar 98. Direct access for 43 single male/females. Support, detox, resettlement services. Care centre: food, advice.
Web: www.internet-pilots.com/city_missions/
Email: mission@globalnet.co.uk
☎ 0121 643 6182

Booth House, 153 Whitechapel Road, London E1 1DP
Team Leader: Captain Nigel Collins. Admin staff 6. ***CC*** Began n/a; Salvation Army. Turnover n/a. For men.
☎ 020 7247 3401

Catherine Booth House Residential Centre, 1 Aylward Street, Portsmouth PO1 3PH
Officer-in-Charge: Mrs Jean Hunt. Admin staff 4. Other staff 8. ***CC*** Began 1959; Salvation Army. Turnover n/a. Cluster flats for homeless men.
☎ 023 9273 7226

William Booth House, Social Service Centre, 2 Hessle Road, Hull HU1 2QQ
Officers-in-Charge: Captains Paul and Margaret Hardy. Executive staff 5. ***CC*** Began n/a; Salvation Army. Turnover n/a. For men, women and children.
☎ 01482 225 521/226 289 (Office)
☎ 01482 227 037 (Quarters) Fax 01482 322 483 (Office)

William Booth Lane Social Service Centre, William Booth Lane, Birmingham B4 6HA
Officers-in-Charge: Captains Timothy & Ruth Dykes. Executive staff 4. ***CC*** Began n/a; Salvation Army. Turnover n/a. For men.
☎ 0121 236 6554/236 7135 Fax 0121 523 4742

Braithwaite Methodist Youth Centre, The Methodist Church, The Green, Braithwaite, Keswick CA12 4QR
Warden: Mr Philip Bullen. No full-time staff. ***CC*** Began 1980; Methodist. Self-catering.
☎ 01768 778 507
Bookings: Carlton House, 6 Southey Street, Keswick CA12 4EF
☎ 01768 774 314

Brighowgate Social Service Centre, Brighowgate, Grimsby DN32 0QW
Officer-in-Charge: Mr Michael Hardy. Admin staff 3. ***CC*** Began n/a; Salvation Army. Turnover n/a. For men and women.
☎ 01472 242 648 Fax 01472 250 209

Buckland Monachorum Hostel, Yelverton PL20 7LY
Chairman Hostel Committee: Rev Jon Bush. No full-time staff. ***CC*** No.257055. Began 1981; interdenominational. Devon and Cornwall Baptist Association. Turnover £6,000 to year end Dec 95. Self-catering for youth groups.
☎ 01752 342 101

Bute Street Social Service Centre, 240 Bute Street, Cardiff CF1 5TY
Officer-in-Charge: Captain Eric Dowling. Admin staff 3. ***CC*** Began n/a; Salvation Army. Turnover n/a. Accommodating 88 men.
☎ 029 2048 0187 Fax 029 2048 0708

***Canaan Christian Centre**, 21 Holt Road, Sheringham NR26 8NB
Director: Miss Eve Smith. Admin staff 1. ***CC*** No.284117. Began 1978; interdenominational. Turnover £31,730 to year end Apr 96. Short-term accommodation for needy families, homeless and abused women and children. Holiday accommodation all year.
☎ 01263 824 300

Carlisle Diocesan Youth Centre, The Rectory, Threlkeld, Keswick CA12 4RT
Warden: Rev B Rothwell. No full-time staff. ***CC*** No.520363. Began 1950; Anglican. Turnover £29,000 to year end Dec 98. Self-catering accommodation in the Lake District for youth organisations, churches and other organisations.
Web: www.btinternet.com/~cdyc
Email: bryan.rothwell@btinternet.com
☎ 01768 779 714

For additional information see List on Pages 89–91

Castlerigg Manor, Manor Brow, Keswick CA12 4AR
Bookings Officer: Mr John Gallagher. Admin staff 8. *CC* No.254331. Began 1970; Roman Catholic. Turnover n/a. For young people.
Email: xlj55@dial.pipex.com
☎ 01768 772 711

Centenary House, 2 Victoria Street, Belfast BT1 3GE
Officer Chaplain: Lieut Howard Russell. Admin staff 3. *CC* Began n/a; Salvation Army. Turnover n/a. Accommodation for men, also charity shop.
☎ 028 9032 0320/9024 7304 Fax 028 9043 4944

Chester House, 1 Chester House, Pages Lane, Muswell Hill, London N10 1PR
Warden: Mr Andy Parkins. Admin staff 3, Other staff 10. *CC* Began 1960; Methodist. Turnover £553,595 to year end Aug 98. Halls of residence for students.
Email: chester.house@virgin.net
☎ 020 8883 8204 Fax 020 8883 0843

***The Christian Alliance Housing Association, Andover**, 70 Junction Road, Andover SP10 3QX
Senior Project Worker: Ms Eileen Lambert. Other staff 2. *CC* No.293232. Began n/a; interdenominational. Turnover £38,776 to year end Dec 98. Self-catering for 8 young single people.
☎ 01264 336 199

***The Christian Alliance Housing Association Hostel, Exeter**, The Grapevine Centre, 1 Culverland Road, Exeter EX4 6JH
Manager: Miss Ruth Pierce. Other staff 5. *CC* No.293232. Began n/a; interdenominational. Turnover £138,676 to year end Dec 98. Self-catering for 13 vulnerable young mothers and babies.
☎ 01392 218 044

***The Christian Alliance Housing Association Hostel, Exmouth**, St Andrew's House, St Andrew's Road, Exmouth EX8 1AS
Manager: Mrs Ruth Brinsden. Other staff 5. *CC* No.293232. Began 1995; interdenominational. Turnover £86,201 to year end Dec 98. Self-catering housing for vulnerable young mothers and babies and 6 young single people with mental health difficulties.
☎ 01395 223 737

***The Christian Alliance Housing Association Hostel, Exmouth**, St Saviour's House, Church Street, Exmouth EX8 1PE
Manager: Mrs Ruth Brinsden. Staff 1. *CC* No.293232. Began n/a. Turnover £5,954 to year end Dec 98. 8 move-on flats for young single people.

***The Christian Alliance Housing Association Hostel, Guildford**, Mulberry House, 32 Epsom Road, Guildford GU1 3LE
Manager: Miss Erica Brown. Other staff 4, Voluntary staff 1. *CC* No.293232. Began 1986; interdenominational. Turnover £158,018 to year end Dec 98. Self-catering for 40 single women aged 16 to 45.
☎ 01483 577 375

***The Christian Alliance Housing Association Hostel, Leamington Spa**, Binswood Lodge, 44 Binswood Avenue, Leamington Spa CV32 5SG
Senior Manager: Mrs Kathleen Farmer. Other staff 3. *CC* No.293232. Began 1920; interdenominational. Turnover £102,837 to year end Dec 98. Self-catering facilities for 20 single women and girls and vulnerable young mothers and babies.
☎ 01926 335 402

***The Christian Alliance Housing Association Hostel, Leamington Spa**, Warford Lodge, 79 Radford Road, Leamington Spa CV32 1NE
Project Manager: Mrs Tracy Webb. Began n/a. Turnover £65,604 to year end Dec 98. Houses 4 ex-care single young people.
☎ 01926 771 921

***The Christian Alliance Housing Association Hostel, Liverpool**, Mildmay House, 6 Blackburne Place, Liverpool L8 7PQ
Manager: Mr Leslie Simnor. Other staff 7. *CC* No.293232. Began n/a; interdenominational. Turnover £337,459 to year end Dec 98. Self-catering for 52 young single people.
☎ 0151 709 1417

***The Christian Alliance Housing Association Hostel, London (Pembridge Square)**, Dashwood House, 6 Pembridge Square, Bayswater, London W2 4ED
Manager: Ms Moira McGreevy. Other staff 3. *CC* No.293232. Began 1920; interdenominational. Turnover £150,905 to year end Dec 98. Medium-term, for women aged 16 to 30.
☎ 020 7229 7848

***The Christian Alliance Housing Association Hostel, London (Walthamstow)**, Stephen House, 1b Copeland Road, Walthamstow, London E17 9DB
Manager: Mr W Quigg. Other staff 3. *CC* No.293232. Began n/a; interdenominational. Turnover £101,131 to year end Dec 98. Self-catering for young single homeless.
☎ 020 8509 1090

***The Christian Alliance Housing Association Hostel, London (Waterloo)**, 2 Secker Street, Waterloo, London SE1 8UF
Manager: Rev Bruce Duncan. Other staff 8. *CC* No.293232. Began 1978; non-denominational. Turnover £474,830 to year end Dec 98. Self-catering for 121 single young people aged 18 to 30 years in cluster flat system.
Web: www.dircon.co.uk/~genesis/CACW/
Email: cac@genesis.org.uk
☎ 020 7450 4601 Fax 020 7401 9945

***The Christian Alliance Housing Association Hostel, Manchester**, The Limes, 76 Daisy Bank Road, Victoria Park, Manchester M14 5GL
Manager: Mr James Rogers. Other staff 6. *CC* No.293232. Began 1920; interdenominational. Turnover £204,233 to year end Dec 98. Self-catering for 26 young single people.
☎ 0161 224 5883

***The Christian Alliance Housing Association Hostel, St Leonards**, Turner House, 6 Pevensey Road, St Leonards-on-Sea TN38 0JZ
Manager: Mrs Carol Sawatzky. Other staff 3. *CC* No.293232. Began n/a; interdenominational. Turnover £67,148 to year end Dec 98. Self-catering for 10 vulnerable young mothers and babies.
☎ 01424 442 480

***The Christian Alliance Housing Association Hostel, Southampton**, Kingsley House, 64 Alma Road, Southampton SO14 6UX
Manager: Ms Stacey Taylor. Other staff 5. *CC* No.293232. Began 1920; interdenominational. (Previously Kingsley House). Turnover £146,572 to year end Dec 98. Self-catering for young people and separate unit for mothers and babies.
☎ 023 8055 0131

A

For additional information see List on Pages 89–91

A

***The Christian Alliance Housing Association Hostel, Tunbridge Wells**, Calverley Hill, 6 Clarence Road, Tunbridge Wells TN1 1HE
Manager: Mrs Anne Johnson. Other staff 2. ***CC*** No.293232. Began 1920; interdenominational. Turnover £90,576 to year end Dec 98. For 16 girls or single mothers and babies.
☎ 01892 530 676

***The Christian Alliance Housing Association Hostel, Weston-super-Mare**, 20 Graham Road, Weston-super-Mare BS23 1YA
Manager: Mrs Pat Ephgrave. Other staff 5. ***CC*** No.293232. Began n/a; interdenominational. Turnover £120,809 to year end Dec 98. Self-catering for 12 vulnerable young mothers and babies.
☎ 01934 612 810

***Christian Alliance Housing Association Hostel, Yeovil**, Christopher House, 93 Preston Road, Yeovil BA20 2DN
Manager: To be appointed. Admin staff 3, Other staff 3. ***CC*** No.293232. Began 1993; non-denominational. (Previously Hebron). Turnover £66,189 to year end Dec 98. For homeless people aged 16 to 30 with special needs.
☎ 01935 411 021

***The Christian Alliance Housing Association Hostel, Yeovil**, Elsinore, 57 The Avenue, Yeovil BA21 4BW
Manager: To be appointed. ***CC*** No.293232. Began n/a. Turnover £23,084 to year end Dec 98. 6 move-on flats housing 12 young single people.
☎ No telephone

***The Christian Housing Trust**, 38 Sweyn Road, Margate CT9 2DT
Trust Manager: Mr Paul K Trumble. Admin staff 1, Other staff 4. ***CC*** No.1005330. Began 1988; interdenominational. Turnover £145,000 to year end Mar 98. 19 furnished bed-sits providing care and support to homeless people with mental health problems.
☎ 01843 290 583

City Road Social Service Centre, 39 City Road, Newcastle upon Tyne NE1 2BR
Officers-in-Charge: Majors Alan and Brenda Austin. Admin staff 4. ***CC*** Began n/a; Salvation Army. Turnover n/a. For men.
☎ 0191 233 9150 🖷 0191 232 5521

Clement Park House Social Service Centre, Dundee Homelessness Project, Clement Park, Lochee, Dundee DD2 3JQ
Officer-in-Charge: Mrs Elizabeth Cowan. ***CC*** Began n/a; Salvation Army. Turnover n/a. Accommodating men and women; family units.
☎ 01382 611 452

Conway House, 20 Quex Road, Kilburn, London NW6 4PG
Manager: Mr Aidan Kane. Admin staff 10, Other staff 21. ***CC*** Began 1974; Roman Catholic. Turnover n/a. For young men new to London (mostly Irish).
☎ 020 7624 2918

Cunningham House, 205 Cowgate, Edinburgh EH1 1JH
Unit Manager: Jean Simpson. Other staff 18. ***CC*** Began n/a; Church of Scotland. Turnover n/a. Vulnerable single adults.
☎ 0131 225 4795 🖷 0131 220 1354

Davis House Social Service Centre, Turl Street, Swindon SN1 1EF
Officers-in-Charge: Captains Gary & Rosemary Chatburn. *Assistant Officer-in-Charge:* Major Tim Wicker. Admin staff 5, Other staff 45. ***CC*** Began 1981; Salvation Army. Turnover £900,000 to year end Mar 98.
☎ 01793 531 107 🖷 01793 423 820

Devonport House Social Service Centre, Park Avenue, Devonport, Plymouth PL1 4BA
Officers-in-Charge: Captains Stephen & Deborah Melvin. Admin staff 5. ***CC*** Began n/a; Salvation Army. Turnover n/a. Accommodation for 69 men.
☎ 01752 562 170/564 545 🖷 01752 605 901

***Duke Street Hostel**, Duke Street, Bolton BL1 2LU
Officer-in-Charge: Capt J Watchorn. Admin staff 3, Other staff 30. ***CC*** No.214779. Began 1959; Salvation Army. Turnover n/a. Direct access hostel for homeless men.
☎ 01204 394 499

Elgood House Hostel (Church Army), 84 Bell Street, London NW1 6SP
Warden in charge: To be appointed. Admin staff 6. ***CC*** No.226226. Began 1882; Anglican. Turnover n/a. For women.
☎ 020 7402 4971

Elmham House (Pilgrim Bureau), Friday Market, Walsingham NR22 6EG
Director: Rev A Williams. Admin staff 6, Other staff 10. ***CC*** No.265755. Began n/a; Roman Catholic. Turnover n/a. Accommodation for visitors to national shrine.
Web: www.walsingham.org.uk
Email: rcnatshrine@aol.com
☎ 01328 820 217

Fewster House Social Service Centre, 10 Terrace Road, Greenock PA15 1DJ
Officers-in-Charge: Captains Dean & Alison Logan. Executive staff 3. ***CC*** Began n/a; Salvation Army. Turnover n/a. Direct access for men and residential care wing.
☎ 01475 721 572

Ann Fowler House Social Service Centre, Fraser Street, Liverpool L3 8JX
Officer-in-Charge: Captain Biddle. Admin staff 3, Other staff 11. ***CC*** Began 1959; Salvation Army. Turnover n/a. For homeless women.
☎ 0151 207 3815 🖷 0151 207 3495

***Frances Kinnaird House (Scottish Christian Alliance)**, 14 Coates Crescent, Edinburgh EH3 7AG
Manager: Miss J Laidlaw. Other staff 2, Voluntary staff 1. ***CC*** No.SCO 021765. Began 1945; interdenominational. Turnover £70,000 to year end Mar 94. Mainly female students and young workers during term, visitors during holidays.
☎ 0131 225 3608

Friendship House Shaftesbury Housing, 1 St Nicholas Glebe, Rectory Lane, Tooting, London SW17 9QH
Estate Manager: Miss Kelly Andrews. Other staff 4. ***CC*** Began 1968; interdenominational. (Previously Friendship House London Student Housing). Turnover £500,000-1,000,000 to year end Dec 96. Primarily for overseas students.
☎ 020 8672 2262
Also at *Estate Manager:* Mrs Sandy White, Friendship House, 13 Breakspears Road, Brockley, Lewisham, London SE4 1XW
☎ 020 8672 2262
And: *Estate Manager:* Mrs Sandy White, Gilmore House, 113 Clapham Common, Northside, London SW4 9SN
☎ 020 8672 2262

Gaughan Close Centre for Women, Gaughan Close, Walker, Newcastle-upon-Tyne NE6 3RR
Officer-in-Charge: Captain Yvonne Holland. Admin staff 2. ***CC*** Began n/a; Salvation Army. Turnover n/a. Accommodating 18 women.
☎ 0191 224 1509

For additional information see List on Pages 89–91

German Catholic Social Centre, Lioba House, 40 Exeter Road, London NW2 4SB
Social Worker: Miss Adelheid von Oy. Other staff 4. ***CC*** No.261117. Began 1952; Roman Catholic. Magazine: *Unterwegs – invia* (500 every two months). Turnover n/a. Personal help and advice, social activities, au pair placement service, and hostel accommodation for 17.
☎ 020 8452 8566

Glen Alva Families Centre, 19 Cliftonville Road, Belfast BT14 6JN
Officer-in-Charge: Mr William Wilson. Staff 3. ***CC*** Began n/a; Salvation Army. Turnover n/a. Accommodation in family units.
☎ 028 9035 1185 🖷 028 9035 2265

Glen Feshie Hostel, Kincraig, Kingussie PH21 1NH
Owner: Jean Hamilton. No full-time staff. Began 1985; non-denominational. Turnover n/a.
☎ 01540 651 323

David Gray House (Probation Hostel), 6 Drury Terrace, Douglas IM2 3HY
Officers-in-Charge: Captains Lynden & Julie Gibbs. Admin staff 2. ***CC*** Began n/a; Salvation Army. Turnover n/a. Accommodating 10 people on probation, also day care centre.
☎ 01624 662 814 Day care centre: 01624 675 702
🖷 01624 613 787

Heaton Street Hostel, Heaton Street, Blackburn BB2 2EF
Officer-in-Charge: Captain D Coates. Admin staff 5, Other staff 20. ***CC*** Began 1959; Salvation Army. Turnover £42,000 to year end Apr 98. For homeless, elderly and people with mental health problems.
☎ 01254 677 338 🖷 01254 692 471

Hengrave Hall Youth Centre, Bury St Edmunds IP28 6LZ
Warden: Sister Katie. No full-time staff. ***CC*** No.268715. Began 1974; interdenominational. Turnover n/a. Simple self-catering accommodation for anyone.
☎ 01284 754 537 🖷 01284 702 950

High Street East Social Service Centre, 5 High Street East, Sunderland SR1 2AU
Associate Officers-in-Charge: Lieutenants Leon & Susan Dean. Admin staff 6, Other staff 20. ***CC*** Began 1982; Salvation Army. Turnover n/a.
☎ 0191 565 5411 🖷 0191 514 7576

Hope House Social Service Centre, 14 Clyde Street, Glasgow G1 5JH
Officers-in-Charge: Captains Robert & Ruth Deans. Executive staff 4. ***CC*** Began n/a; Salvation Army. Turnover n/a. Accommodation for 121 men and women.
☎ 0141 552 0537

Hopetown Residential Centre (Women), 60 Old Montague Street, Whitechapel, London E1 5LF
Team Leader: Major Margaret Halbert. Staff 50. ***CC*** No.215174. Began 1931; Salvation Army. Turnover n/a. Providing care of elderly, direct access (homeless women), minimum support, support services.
☎ 020 7377 6429 🖷 020 7375 0637

House of the Divine Compassion (Society of St Francis), 42 Balaam Street, Plaistow, London E13 8AQ
Contact: Brother Julian. No other staff. ***CC*** Began 1894; Anglican. Turnover £25,000 to year end Dec 98.
☎ 020 7476 5189

Hull International House, 96 Westbourne Avenue, Kingston upon Hull HU5 3HY
Joint Wardens: Mrs Loretta Lynch, Mrs Janet Woolley. Admin staff 2, Other staff 5. ***CC*** Began 1961; Methodist. Turnover n/a. For overseas students.
Web: www.methodist.org.uk/hih
☎ 01482 342 104 🖷 01482 447 729

William Hunter House Social Service Centre, 70 Oxford Street, Glasgow G5 9EP
Officers-in-Charge: Captains Robert & Ruth Deans. Executive staff 3. ***CC*** Began n/a; Salvation Army. Turnover n/a. 25 flats for families and individuals, 1 disabled.
☎ 0141 429 5201

Huntly House, Social Service Centre, 1 Huntly Place, Inverness IV3 6HA
Officer-in-Charge: Mr Alexander Campbell. Staff n/a. ***CC*** Began n/a; Salvation Army. Turnover n/a. For men and women.
☎ 01463 234 123 🖷 01463 717 469
Resettlement Project: *Assistant Officer-in-Charge:* Mr Alexander Frame, 3 Huntly Place, Inverness IV3 6HA. Accommodating 22 in 10 units.

International Lutheran Student Centre, 30 Thanet Street, London WC1H 9QH
Warden: Mr David Ward. Admin staff 3, Other staff 10. ***CC*** No.232042. Began 1963; Lutheran. Turnover £200,000 to year end Dec 93. For post-graduate students. Some summer vacancies.
Web: www.lutheran.org.uk
Email: ilscaccomm@lutheran.org.uk
☎ 020 7388 4044 🖷 020 7383 5915

International Students Hostel (Sisters of St Dorothy), 99 Frognal, Hampstead, London NW3 6XR
Sister-in-Charge: Sister Pauline Taylor. Admin staff 2, Other staff 5. ***CC*** No.266436. Began 1968; Roman Catholic. Turnover £40,000 to year end Dec 96. For full-time female students, young female tourists.
☎ 020 7794 6893 🖷 020 7435 0724

International Students' Housing Society, International House, 109 Brookhill Road, London SE18 6RZ
Director: Mr B M Siderman. *Chairman:* Rev J B Preston. Admin staff 3, Other staff 21. ***CC*** No.15977. Began 1963; interdenominational. Turnover £372,512 to year end Apr 98. Student hostel, accommodation, single and married students (families with up to 2 children), vacation visitors.
☎ 020 8854 1418 🖷 020 8855 9257

Inverclyde Families Centre, 98 Dalrymple Street, Greenock PA15 1BZ
Officer-in-Charge: Auxiliary-Captains Douglas & Eileen Shankster. Executive staff 4. ***CC*** Began n/a; Salvation Army. Turnover n/a. 25 family units.
☎ 01475 783 608

James Lee House Social Service Centre, Brick Street, Howley, Warrington WA1 2PD
Officers-in-Charge: Captains D & J Lees. Admin staff 4. ***CC*** Began n/a; Salvation Army. Turnover n/a. For men.
☎ 01925 636 496 🖷 01925 230 334

James Street Centre Hostel, James Street, Salford M3 5HP
Team Leader: Miss Valerie Haynes. Admin staff 6, Other staff 12. ***CC*** Began 1959; Salvation Army. Turnover n/a. For homeless men.
☎ 0161 831 7020 🖷 0161 834 3699

For additional information see List on Pages 89–91

†**John Kirk Centre**, Thompsons Avenue, Camberwell, London SE5 0YG
Homeless Services Team Manager: Bob Bailey. Admin staff 3, Other staff 20. ***CC*** No.221948. Began 1991; interdenominational. (Shaftesbury Society, Homeless Project). Turnover n/a. Short stay, for homeless young men.
☎ 020 7703 6787

Kestrel Lodge Residential Centre, High Close Farm, Bassenthwaite, Keswick CA12 4QX
Manager: Mr Terry Beckham. No full-time staff. Began 1974; non-denominational. Turnover £15,000 to year end Apr 98. Christian holiday hostel for groups to organise their own programme and enjoy the Lake District.
Web: www.kestrel98.freeserve.co.uk
Email: peter@kestrel.freeeserve.co.uk
☎ 01768 776 455

Lawley House Social Service Centre, 371 Leeds Road, Bradford BD3 9NG
Officer-in-Charge: Captain David Johnston. Executive staff 3. ***CC*** Began n/a; Salvation Army. Turnover n/a. Accommodation for 90 men and resettlement project for 12.
☎ 01274 731 221 Fax 01274 738 839

Lee Abbey International Students' Club, 57 Lexham Gardens, London W8 6JJ
Warden: Rev David Weekes. *Assistant Warden/Personnel:* Mrs Jean Weekes. *Administrator:* Gordon MacBean. Admin staff 7, Other staff 34. ***CC*** No.23667. Began 1964; Anglican but interdenominational. Turnover £855,501 to year end Aug 98. Home from home for students of all faiths or none, staffed by a Christian community.
Web: www.leeabbeylondon.freeserve.co.uk
Email: studentsclub@leeabbeylondon.freeserve.co.uk
☎ 020 7373 7242 Fax 020 7244 8702

Lena Fox House, 40 Crimscott Street, London SE1 5TE
Homeless Services Team Manager: Carrie Sommerton. Admin staff 3, Other staff 20. ***CC*** No.221948. Began 1991; interdenominational. (Shaftesbury Society, Homeless Project). Turnover n/a. For homeless young men aged 16–26.
☎ 020 7237 1286 Fax 020 7231 8713

Link House Trust, 17 Chesterton Road, Cambridge CB4 3AL
Wardens: Mr & Mrs K Heywood. Admin staff 2. ***CC*** No.296226. Began 1987; interdenominational. Turnover £150,000 to year end Dec 98. For international graduate students.
Email: linkhouse@aol.com
☎ 01223 572 290
Also at: 95 Gilbert Road, Cambridge CB4 3NZ

Little Brothers of the Good Shepherd, Good Shepherd Centre, 27 Thornley Street, Wolverhampton WV1 1JS
Vicar General: Rev Brother David Lynch. Community 6. Began 1971; Roman Catholic. Turnover n/a. For homeless men.
☎ 01902 773 721 Fax 01902 712 495

Little George Street Social Service Centre, Little George Street, Bristol BS2 9EL
Officer-in-Charge: Mr Bramwell Tout. Admin staff 3. ***CC*** Began n/a; Salvation Army. Turnover n/a. Accommodation for 96 men.
☎ 0117 955 2821 Fax 0117 954 1595
Rough Sleepers' Initiative Outreach Team
☎ 0117 935 1255

Lyncroft House, 99 Handsworth Wood Road, Handsworth, Birmingham B20 2PH
Officer-in-Charge: Captain Suzanne Lowe. Executive staff 3. ***CC*** Began n/a; Salvation Army. Turnover n/a. For mothers and children.
☎ 0121 357 9936 (Quarters) Fax 0121 523 4742

Lyndon House, 107 Fore Street, Ipswich IP4 1JZ
Officer-in-Charge: Major Hazel Wilson. Staff n/a. ***CC*** Began 1959; Salvation Army. Turnover n/a. Direct access hostel for homeless men.
☎ 01473 251 070 Fax 0143 225 613
Training flats: 12 St Clements Church Lane, Ipswich IP4 1JH 12 flats

†**Mary and Joseph House**, 34 George Leigh Street, Ancoats, Manchester M4 5DG
Manager: n/a. Admin staff 10. ***CC*** Began 1965; Roman Catholic foundation but interdenominational. Turnover n/a. For homeless men.
☎ 0161 236 2519

Marylebone Project, 1 Cosway Street, London NW1 5NR
Warden-in-Charge: n/a. Staff n/a. ***CC*** No.226226. Began 1881; Anglican. (Previously Emergency Hostel). Turnover n/a. Hostel accommodation and day centre facilities for single homeless women.
☎ 020 7262 3818 Fax 020 7402 8752

†**Methodist International House, Birmingham**, 52 Oakfield Road, Selly Park, Birmingham B29 7EQ
Warden/Manager: Mrs Maureen A Osborne. Admin staff 1, Other staff 4. ***CC*** Began 1955; Methodist. Turnover £90,000 to year end Aug 97. For full-time overseas students.
☎ 0121 472 0109

The Methodist International House, Bristol, Rodney House, Clifton Down Road, Clifton Village, Bristol BS8 4AL
Warden: Mr Mark Tubey. Admin staff 1, Other staff 5. ***CC*** Began 1957; Methodist. Turnover n/a. For students of all faiths, nationalities and ages.
☎ 0117 973 5179

Methodist International House, Manchester, 68 Daisy Bank Road, Victoria Park, Manchester M14 5QP
Warden: Mr Colin Morton. Admin staff 4. ***CC*** Began 1956; Methodist. Turnover n/a. Licenced hall of residence for 62 post graduate students (mainly from overseas) studying at universities in Manchester.
Email: mih@manchester68.freeserve.co.uk
☎ 0161 224 8041 Fax 0161 225 0823

More House, 53 Cromwell Road, London SW7 2EH
Warden: Sister Francoise Georgeault. *Bursar:* Miss P J Mitchell. Admin staff 2, Other staff 5. ***CC*** No.229051. Began 1950; Roman Catholic. (See also London University Catholic Chaplaincy). Turnover n/a. Part of Canonesses of St Augustine Trust. For university students; holiday guests in summer.
☎ 020 7584 2040 Fax 020 7581 5748

Moullin House, 24 Mount Park Road, Ealing, London W5 2RT
Warden: Mr Colin Pratt. *Assistant Warden:* Mr Michael Walmsley-Cotham. Admin staff 2, Other staff 1. ***CC*** Began 1951; Methodist. Turnover £200,000 to year end June 98. International house for students and young workers.
☎ 020 8997 4343 Fax 020 8991 0254

For additional information see List on Pages 89–91

Mount Cross Families Centre, 139 Broad Lane, Bramley, Leeds LS13 2JP
Officer-in-Charge: Captain Theresa Maunder. Executive staff 3. ***CC*** Began n/a; Salvation Army. Turnover n/a. Family units and Spring Grove Resettlement Unit.
☎ 0113 257 0810 (Office) 0113 257 7552 (Annexe)

Mountbatten Social Service Centre, 57 Oxford Street, Southampton SO14 3DL
Officers-in-Charge: Majors Robert & Barbara Davies. Admin staff 3. ***CC*** Began n/a; Salvation Army. Turnover n/a. Accommodation for men.
☎ 023 8063 7259/3508 🖷 023 8022 3868/8033

Netherlea Social Service Centre, Adelphi Street, Netherthorpe, Sheffield S6 3DX
Officer-in-Charge: Major Albert and Major Margaret Sutton. Executive staff 4. ***CC*** Began n/a; Salvation Army. Turnover n/a. For men.
☎ 0114 272 5158

*__Newington Court__, Newington Court, 1 Collins Road, London N5 2UF
Manager: Khalda Saleem. Admin staff 4, Other staff 4. Began 1912; Baptist. Turnover £100,000 to year end Dec 98. For women aged 18 to 35.
Web: www.goodnews.co.uk/newcourt
Email: newcourt@btinternet.com
☎ 020 7359 2495 🖷 020 7288 1913

Pamela House Women's Hostel (Birmingham City Mission), 38 Flint Green Road, Birmingham B27 6QA
Senior Manager: Mrs Christine Saunders. Admin staff 1, Other staff 6. ***CC*** No.1051023. Began 1991; interdenominational. Turnover n/a. For single, homeless women; help with benefits, rehabilitation, rehousing; emotional support, homely atmosphere.
Web: www.internet-pilots.com/city_missions/
Email: mission@globalnet.co.uk
☎ 0121 706 5567

Parkway Homeless Centre, 12 Inverness Terrace, Bayswater, London W2 3HU
Officer-in-Charge: Brother Michael Bartlett. Admin staff 3. ***CC*** Began n/a; Salvation Army. Turnover n/a. For men.
☎ 020 7229 9223

*__Pillar of Fire Church__, 19 Brent Street, Hendon, London NW4 2EU
Administrator: Rev Bernard Dawson. *Assistant Administrator:* Rev F Sherman Grove. Admin staff 3. ***CC*** No.1015529. Began 1915; Pillar of Fire. Magazine: *British Isles Pillar of Fire* (600 every two months). Turnover £120,000 to year end Dec 96. For international students.
Email: bernard.dawson@lineone.net
☎ 020 8202 3219/7618 Mobile: 07767 356 307
🖷 020 8202 3277

Poor Servants of the Mother of God, 70 Euston Square, London NW1 1DJ
Warden: Sister Anne Redmond. Admin staff 1, Other staff 3. ***CC*** Began 1945; Roman Catholic. Turnover n/a. For women aged 18 to 25.
☎ 020 7387 5855 🖷 020 7935 8969

Prescot Road Hostel, 380 Prescot Road, Liverpool L13 3DA
Officer-in-Charge: Captain Neil Denyer. Other staff 22. ***CC*** Began 1989; Salvation Army. Turnover n/a. Direct access hostel for homeless men.
☎ 0151 228 0925

Providence House Social Service Centre, High Street, Rochdale OL12 0NT
Officer-in-Charge: Major John Luce. Admin staff 4. ***CC*** Began n/a; Salvation Army. Turnover n/a. Accommodation for men and a charity shop.
☎ 01706 645 151 🖷 01706 759 466

Tom Raine Court Social Service Centre, Coburg Street, Darlington DL1 1SB
Officers-in-Charge: Major Malcolm & Major Sylvia Walters. Other staff 3. ***CC*** Began 1987; Salvation Army. Turnover n/a.
☎ 01325 489 242 🖷 01325 465 603

Raisdale Centre for Adolescents, 605 Parkhouse Road, Barrhead, Glasgow G78 1TE
Officer-in-Charge: Mr Gilbert Esson. Executive staff 3. ***CC*** Began n/a; Salvation Army. Turnover n/a. Accommodation for 15 boys.
☎ 0141 881 1130

*__Riverside House__, 8 Greig House, 20 Garford Street, London E14 8JG
Officer-in-Charge: Mrs Janet Hancock. Admin staff 6, Other staff 4. ***CC*** No.215174. Began 1928; Salvation Army. Turnover n/a. For 90 homeless men.
☎ 020 7987 1520 🖷 020 7536 1603

St Andrew's Youth Centre, The Vicarage, Yewdale Road, Coniston LA21 8DX
Warden: Rev Mark Cannon. Admin staff 1, Other staff 2. ***CC*** Began 1981; Anglican. Turnover £40,000 to year end Dec 98. Residential centre for a wide variety of groups.
Email: mark.cannon@btinternet.com
☎ 01539 441 262

†**Saint George's Crypt**, Great George Street, Leeds LS1 3BR
Senior Social Worker: Mr Peter Sanders. *Administrator:* Mr Tony Beswick. Executive staff 5, Other staff 29. ***CC*** No.250016. Began 1930; Anglican. Magazine: *Prayer Diary* (Circulation n/a quarterly). Turnover £450,000 to year end Dec 96. Providing night centre, family centre, 3 hostels.

St Louise Irish Centre Hostel, 33 Medway Street, London SW1P 2BE
Manageress: Sister Rosalie. Admin staff 3. ***CC*** Began 1981; interdenominational. Turnover n/a. For women.
☎ 020 7222 2071 🖷 020 7976 0569
Headquarters: The Irish Centre, 52 Camden Square, London NW1 9XA

St Vincent's Hostel, 14 Blandford Street, London W1H 3HA
Manager: Miss Carol Joseph. Other staff 4. Began 1938; Roman Catholic. Turnover £147,182 to year end Dec 98. For women aged 18 to 30.
☎ 020 7224 3616 🖷 020 7388 7900

Salisbury House Social Service Centre, Parr Street, St Helens WA9 1JU
Officers-in-Charge: Captains Graham & Inga Longmore. Admin staff 5. ***CC*** Began n/a; Salvation Army. Turnover n/a. For men.
☎ 01744 243 02 🖷 01744 730 289

Sneinton House Social Service Centre, 2 Boston Street, Nottingham NG1 1ED
Officers-in-Charge: Majors Richard & Ellen Cushing. Admin staff 4. ***CC*** Began n/a; Salvation Army. Turnover n/a. For men.
☎ 0115 950 4364 🖷 0115 950 9605

For additional information see List on Pages 89–91

A

SPEC Centre, Shenley Lane, London Colney, St Albans AL2 1AF
Manager: Mr David Satchell. Admin staff 2, Other staff (voluntary) 18. *CC* Began 1993; Roman Catholic. Turnover n/a. For people aged 15 to 30.
☎ 01727 828 888
For people aged 9–15 The Loft @ SPEC, All Saints Pastoral Centre, London Colney, St Albans AL2 1AF
☎ 01727 828 888 🖷 01727 822 927

Strathmore Lodge Social Services Centre, 31 Ward Road, Dundee DD1 1NG
Officer-in-Charge: Mr Kenneth Darroch. Admin staff 2. *CC* Began n/a; Salvation Army. Turnover n/a. Accommodation for 54 people including 8 resettlement flats.
☎ 01382 225 448 🖷 01382 203 404

Thorndale Families Centre, Duncairn Avenue, Antrim Road, Belfast BT14 6BP
Officers-in-Charge: Captains Adrian & Beverly Stringer. Admin staff 4. *CC* Began n/a; Salvation Army. Turnover n/a. Family units and women's hostel.
☎ 028 9035 1900 🖷 028 9035 1310

Vale Street Hostel, Vale Street, Stoke-on-Trent ST4 7RN
Officer-in-Charge: Capt T Dykes. Admin staff 3, Other staff 25. *CC* Began 1987; Salvation Army. Turnover n/a.
☎ 01782 744 374 🖷 01782 749 512

Wallace of Campsie House Social Service Centre, 30 East Campbell Street, Glasgow G1 5DT
Officer-in-Charge: Captain Valerie Merser. Executive staff 3. *CC* Began n/a; Salvation Army. Turnover n/a. Single and cluster flats for men and women; 2 for disabled.
☎ 0141 552 4301 🖷 0141 552 5910

Willow House Social Service Centre, Willow Street, Fobney Street, Reading RG1 6BD
Officers-in-Charge: Captains Paul & Christine Kingscott. Admin staff 4. *CC* Began n/a; Salvation Army. Turnover n/a. Men and women.
☎ 0118 959 0681 🖷 0118 959 8663

Wilmott Street Social Service Centre, 1 Wilmott Street, Chorlton-on-Medlock, Manchester M15 6BD
Officers-in-Charge: Captains John & Jean Middleton. Admin staff 6, Other staff 25. *CC* Began 1977; Salvation Army. Turnover £750,000 to year end Dec 98. Direct access hostel for homeless men.
☎ 0161 236 7537 🖷 0161 237 9782

YMCA, Bath, Broad Street Place, Bath BA1 5LH
Chief Executive: Mr Tony Teasdale. Admin staff 12, Other staff 48. *CC* No.250549. Began n/a; interdenominational. Turnover n/a.
Email: ymcabath@intecc.co.uk
☎ 01225 460 471 🖷 01225 462 065

YMCA, Birkenhead, 56 Whetstone Lane, Birkenhead CH41 2TJ
Executive Director: Mr S Larmour. *Treasurer:* Alan D Richards. Admin staff 5, Other staff 20. *CC* No.1000601. Began 1874; interdenominational. Turnover £350,000 to year end Dec 98. For young adults.
Web: www.btinternet.com/~s.larmour
Email: s.larmour@btinternet.com
☎ 0151 647 8123/9115 🖷 0151 650 1944

***YMCA, Bournemouth**, Delta House, 56 Westover Road, Bournemouth BH1 2BS
Director: Mr B Crawford. *Chairman:* Mr Bill Hood. Admin staff 10, Other staff 31. *CC* No.250619. Began n/a; interdenominational. Turnover £800,000 to year end Dec 98. Special needs hostel, youth and community facilities.
Email: bmouthymca@aol.com
☎ 01202 290 451 🖷 01202 314 219

YMCA, Burton, 5 Borough Road, Burton-on-Trent DE14 2DA
General Secretary: Mr Martin Pearse. Admin staff 11. *CC* No.517232. Began 1985; interdenominational. Turnover £280,000 to year end Mar 99. Accommodating young, homeless people aged 16 to 30.
☎ 01283 538 802
Also at: James Court, James Street, Burton-on-Trent DE14 3ST
☎ 01283 511 103
And: Milton House, Milton Street, Burton-on-Trent DE14 1EP
☎ 01283 511 165

YMCA, Bury St Edmunds, Batt House, 56 Westgate Street, Bury St Edmunds IP33 1QG
General Secretary: Mrs Ruth Hammond. Other staff 7. *CC* No.802285. Began 1989; interdenominational. Turnover £50,000 to year end Mar 97. Provides self-catering accommodation for 23 young people aged 16 to 28.
☎ 01284 701 697

YMCA, Cambridge, Queen Anne House, Gonville Place, Cambridge CB1 1ND
Executive Director: Mr Robert Higginbottom. *Programme Director:* Mr Nigel Fenner. *Housing Director:* Mr George Cordeiro. Admin staff 11, Other staff 39. *CC* No.250193. Began 1855; interdenominational. Turnover £1,122,390 to year end Mar 96.
Web: www.pcug.co.uk/ymca/regions/central/project/cam0.html
Email: 106440.1655@compuserve.com
☎ 01223 356 998 🖷 01223 312 749

YMCA, Cheltenham, Vittoria Walk, Cheltenham GL50 1TP
Chief Executive: Mr Adrian Sharpe. *ACE (Housing):* Mrs Cathy Lowe. Admin staff 5, Other staff 23. *CC* No.250195. Began 1855; interdenominational. Turnover £448,000 to year end Apr 98. Hostel and community centre with sports, health and fitness facilities.
Web: www.cheltenhamymca.org.uk
☎ 01242 524 024 🖷 01242 232 635

YMCA, Coventry, 11 The Quadrant, Warwick Road, Coventry CV1 2EJ
Residential Manager: Mr Leonard Allan. Admin staff 6, Other staff 26. *CC* Began 1889; interdenominational. Turnover £280,000 to year end Dec 90.
☎ 024 7625 7312 🖷 024 7663 2587

YMCA, Crewe, Two-Ways, Gresty Road, Crewe CW2 6EL
General Secretary: Mr Norman Littler. Admin staff 8, Other staff 12. *CC* Began 1984; interdenominational. Turnover £343,000 to year end Mar 99. For single people aged 16 to 30.
Web: ymca-crewe.demon.co.uk
☎ 01270 257 673 🖷 01270 586 200

YMCA, Derby, London Road, Wilmorton, Derby DE24 8UT
General Secretary: Mr Anthony Gratton. *Programme Manager:* Mr Kevin Newton. Admin staff 8, Other staff 21. *CC* No.1049904. Began 1847; interdenominational. Turnover £400,000 to year end Mar 98. Short and medium stay for young men and women. Also youth and community facilities.
Email: derbyymca@derbyymca.demon.co.uk
☎ 01332 572 076 🖷 01332 572 596

For additional information see List on Pages 89–91

YMCA, Doncaster, Goodall House, 31 Wood Street, Doncaster DN1 3LW
Hostel & Housing Manager: John Mackie. Admin staff 2, Other staff 2. ***CC*** Began 1989; interdenominational. Turnover £100,000 to year end Mar 98. For young single people.
☎ 01302 342 148 🖷 01302 342 148

YMCA, Grimsby and Cleethorpes, Peaks Lane, Grimsby DN32 9ET
Chief Executive: Mr Hywel Roberts. *Housing Officer:* Mrs Pat Donald. *Programme Manager:* Robyn Laurie. Admin staff 3, Other staff 32. ***CC*** No.1058613. Began 1906; interdenominational. Turnover £506,000 to year end Dec 98. Helping young people, particularly at times of need, regardless of gender, race, ability or faith.
☎ 01472 359 621 🖷 01472 340 086

*__YMCA, Guildford__, Bridge Street, Guildford GU1 4SB
Executive Director: Mr Alex Cloke. Admin staff 30, Other staff 50. ***CC*** No.295314. Began 1989; interdenominational. Turnover £1,400,000 to year end Mar 98. Youth organisation, housing, support, counselling, youth cafe, arts, information and advice, training, opportunities, development.
Email: admin@guildford.ymca.org.uk
☎ 01483 532 555 🖷 01483 537 161

YMCA, Hornsey, 184 Tottenham Lane, London N8 8SG
General Secretary: Mr Louis A Lewis. *Hostel Manager:* Rev Ben O Badejo. *Programme Manager:* Mr Ian Burks. Other staff 70. ***CC*** No.209492. Began 1929; interdenominational. Turnover £800,000 to year end Mar 97. For young homeless people with special needs.
Email: ben.ymca@dial.pipex.com
☎ 020 8340 2345 🖷 020 8340 2345

†**YMCA, King's Lynn**, Columbia Way, King's Lynn PE30 2LA
Manager: Mr Terry Harsant. Admin staff 6, Other staff 2. ***CC*** Began 1867; interdenominational. Turnover n/a. For homeless young people.
☎ 01553 769 496

*__YMCA, Leicester__, Leicester Southfields College, Aylestone Road, Leicester LE2 7LW
General Secretary: Mr Kevin Williams. Admin staff 8, Other staff 40. ***CC*** No.213513. Began 1844; interdenominational. Turnover n/a. For young homeless people aged 16 to 25.
☎ 0116 224 2058

YMCA, Lincoln, St Rumbold's Street, Lincoln LN2 5AR
Chief Executive: Mr Dean Bell. Admin staff 10, Other staff 22. ***CC*** No.243017. Began 1969; interdenominational. Turnover £500,000 to year end Dec 97. Providing housing, fitness and charity shop services to young people in need.
Web: www.ymca.org.uk
Email: admin@lincoln.ymca.org.uk
☎ 01522 888 200 Mobile: 07970 155 756
🖷 01522 888 201

YMCA, London, City, Luwum House, 8 Errol Street, London EC1Y 8SE
Chief Executive: Mr Andy Wilson. *Deputy Chief Executive:* Mrs Sally Yousif. *Chairman:* Mr Peter Ellis. Staff 33. ***CC*** No.1053864. Began 1988; interdenominational. Turnover £850,000 to year end Mar 96. Hostel for young people in housing need and detached youth work project.
☎ 020 7628 8832 🖷 020 7628 4080

YMCA, London, Ealing & District, 25 St Mary's Road, Ealing, London W5 5RE
Chief Executive: Mr Kevin Williams. *Housing Manager:* Miss Jenny Aris. *Pastor:* Mr Graham Jarrett. Admin staff 12, Other staff 119. ***CC*** No.1058593. Began 1877; interdenominational. Turnover £1,800,000 to year end Mar 98. For students, homeless and special needs young people, employment training, advice and counselling.
Web: www.ymca.org.uk/
Email: ealingymca@btinternet.com
☎ 020 8579 6946 🖷 020 8579 1129
Also at: 14 Bond Street, Ealing, London W5 5AA
☎ 020 8579 8996 🖷 020 8840 8203

YMCA, London, Indian Student Hostel, 41 Fitzroy Square, London W1P 6AQ
General Secretary: Mr S Kakarda. Admin staff 4, Other staff 18. ***CC*** Began 1920; interdenominational. Turnover £862,000 to year end Dec 98. For students and trainees.
Email: indianymca@aol.com
☎ 020 7387 0411 🖷 020 7383 7651

YMCA, London, Waltham Forest, 642 Forest Road, Walthamstow, London E17 3EF
General Secretary: Mr David Myles. Admin staff 4, Other staff 110. ***CC*** No.803442. Began 1970; interdenominational. Turnover £1,008,002 to year end Mar 98. Housing and community services.
Web: wforest.ymca.org.uk
☎ 020 8520 0931 🖷 020 8521 8581

YMCA, London, Wimbledon, 200 The Broadway, Wimbledon, London SW19 1RY
General Secretary: Mr Stewart Page. Admin staff 13, Other staff 36. ***CC*** No.250637. Began 1875; interdenominational. Turnover £1,500,000 to year end Sept 96. For people aged 18 to 25.
☎ 020 8542 9055 🖷 020 8542 1086

*__YMCA, Norwich__, 48 St Giles Street, Norwich NR2 1LP
General Secretary: Mr John Drake. *Hostel Director:* Mr Ed Vaughn. Admin staff 40. ***CC*** No.801606. Began 1856; interdenominational. Turnover £1,000,000. For the unemployed and homeless youth; day camps, community programmes, job training.
☎ 01603 620 269 🖷 01603 762 151

YMCA, Nottingham, 4 Shakespeare Street, Nottingham NG1 4FG
Chief Executive: Mr Will Wakefield. Admin staff 5, Other staff 40. ***CC*** No.243044. Began 1871; interdenominational. Turnover £510,000 to year end Mar 98. For people aged 18 to 30.
Email: admin@nottm.ymca.org.uk
☎ 0115 956 7600 🖷 0115 956 7601

YMCA, Penzance, The Orchard, Alverton, Penzance TR18 4ET
Chief Executive: Mr David Smith. Admin staff 7, Other staff 7. ***CC*** Began 1893; interdenominational. Turnover £120,000 to year end Jan 94.
Web: www.cornwall.co.uk/ymcapenzance
Email: penz-ymca@hotmail.com
☎ 01736 365 016 🖷 01736 365 016

YMCA, Peterborough, The Cresset, Rightwell, Bretton, Peterborough PE3 8DX
Chief Executive: Mr Richard Long. Admin staff 6, Other staff 36. ***CC*** Began 1989; interdenominational. Turnover £735,000 to year end Dec 98.
☎ 01733 269 621

For additional information see List on Pages 89–91

A

*YMCA, Portsmouth**, Chaucer House, Isambard Brunel Road, Portsmouth PO1 2NN
Chief Executive Officer: Mr Tom Kennar. *General Manager:* K A Deane. Admin staff 10, Other staff 25. ***CC*** No.250632. Began 1855; interdenominational. Turnover £260,000 to year end Mar 98. Also children's (after school) work, youth work.
Email: tomkennar@aol.com & kadeanymca@msn.com
☎ 023 9286 4341 Fax 023 9229 3276

YMCA, Reading, Marlborough House, 34 Parkside Road, Reading RG30 2DD
Chief Executive: Mr Vic Hills. *Residential Secretary:* Mr Bob Sadler. *Programme & Youth Development Worker:* Mr Steve Gunn. Admin staff 10, Other staff 20. ***CC*** Began 1846; interdenominational. Turnover £600,000 to year end Mar 98. For people aged 16 to 35.
☎ 0118 957 5746

†**YMCA, Redditch**, Church Hill Centre, Loxley Close, Redditch B98 9JG
General Secretary: Mr Ian Barcham. Admin staff 4, Other staff 12. ***CC*** Began 1978; interdenominational. Turnover n/a. For singles and couples aged 18 to 35.
☎ 01527 597 885 Fax 01527 597 885

†**YMCA, Ripon**, Water Skellgate, Ripon HG4 1BQ
General Secretary: Mr D Gardener. Admin staff 1, Other staff 1. ***CC*** Began 1916; interdenominational. Turnover £56,000 to year end Mar 92.
☎ 01765 607 609

YMCA, Romford, Rush Green Road, Romford RM7 0PH
General Secretary: Mr Pip Wilson. Senior staff 9, Other staff 84. ***CC*** No.299947. Began 1844; interdenominational. Turnover £2,000,000 to year end Dec 96.
Email: romfordymca@mcmail.com
☎ 01708 766 211 Fax 01708 754 211

YMCA, St Helens, North Road, St Helens WA10 2TJ
Executive Director: Mr A Chick. Admin staff 8, Other staff 70. ***CC*** No.517144. Began n/a; interdenominational. Turnover £2,000,000 to year end Mar 98. Mainly for special needs.
Email: admin@st.helens.ymca.org.uk
☎ 01744 225 29

YMCA, Sheffield, 11 Broomhall Road, Broomhall, Sheffield S10 2DQ
Chief Executive: Mr David Reynolds. *Company Secretary:* Mr Neville Chambers. *Housing Director:* Mr Chris Litherland. Staff 75. ***CC*** No.243410. Began 1855; interdenominational. Turnover £850,000 to year end Mar 98. Housing, leisure facilities, foyer project, children's services and meeting rooms.
☎ 0114 268 4807 Fax 0114 268 3472

YMCA, Warrington, Hamnett Court, Ainscough Road, Birchwood, Warrington WA3 7PL
Chief Executive: Mr Keith Fletcher. Other staff 3. ***CC*** Began 1981; interdenominational. (Previously Birchwood YMCA, Warrington). Turnover £200,000 to year end Mar 98. Self-contained flats (furnished).
☎ 01925 821 996 Fax 01925 811 342

YMCA, Watford, Charter House, Charter Place, Watford WD1 2RT
Housing Services Manager: Ms S Kiddell. Admin staff 30, Other staff 60. ***CC*** Began 1886; interdenominational. Turnover £1,230,000 to year end Mar 98.
Email: watfordymca@intecc.co.uk
☎ 01923 353 600 Fax 01923 353 606

YMCA, Welwyn/Hatfield, Maynard House, Peartree Lane, Welwyn Garden City AL7 3UL
General Secretary: Mr Michael J Fairbeard. Admin staff 3, Other staff 27. ***CC*** No.1065875. Began 1967; interdenominational. Turnover n/a.
Web: www.intecc.co.uk/ymca
Email: welwyn-ymca@intecc.co.uk
☎ 01707 327 930 Fax 01707 377 993

YMCA, Worcester, Henwick Road, St John's, Worcester WR2 5NS
Director: Miss C Daniels. Admin staff 1, Other staff 7. ***CC*** No.250213. Began 1869; interdenominational. Turnover n/a.
☎ 01905 423 197 Fax 01905 929 8292

YWCA, Cardiff, 126 Newport Road, Roath, Cardiff CF3 5EP
Director: Ms Jane Huyton. Staff n/a. ***CC*** No.217868. Began n/a; interdenominational. Turnover n/a.
☎ 01222 497 379 Fax 01222 497 379

YWCA, Croydon, Alexandra Residential Club, 32 Dingwall Road, Croydon CR0 2NB
Manager: Mrs Suzie Hale. Staff n/a. ***CC*** Began 1985; interdenominational. Turnover n/a. For people aged 17 to 25.
☎ 020 8688 0289

YWCA, Dagenham, 1 Vineries Close, Heath Way, Dagenham RM9 5DA
Director: Mrs Heather Pembroke. Executive staff 2, Other staff 3. ***CC*** No.217868. Began n/a; interdenominational. Turnover n/a.
☎ 020 8595 8672

YWCA, Edgbaston, 27 Norfolk Road, Edgbaston, Birmingham B15 3PY
Project Manager: Mrs Mary Capewell. Admin staff 4, Other staff 7. ***CC*** No.217868. Began 1967; interdenominational. Turnover n/a. For homeless.
☎ 0121 454 8134

YWCA, Edgbaston, Audrey Achurch Wing, Audrey Achurch Wing, 5 Stone Road, Edgbaston, Birmingham B15 2HH
Housing Project Co-ordinator: Dee McClenaghan. ***CC*** No.217868. Began n/a; interdenominational. Turnover n/a.
☎ 0121 440 2924 Fax 0121 440 2076

YWCA, Edgbaston, Lady Churchill House, Lady Churchill Wing, 1 Stone Road, Birmingham B15 2HH
Acting Manager: Azam Haramy. Admin staff 2, Other staff 3. ***CC*** Began n/a; interdenominational. Turnover n/a.
☎ 0121 440 5345

YWCA, Exeter, Mortimer House, Grendon Road, Exeter EX1 2NL
Manager: Ms Pauline Jewall. Admin staff 3, Other staff 2. ***CC*** No.217868. Began 1977; interdenominational. Self-contained flats.
☎ 01392 259 992

YWCA, Exmouth, Alexandra House, 59 Imperial Road, Exmouth EX8 1AU
Manager: Mr Jeremy Drew. Admin staff 3, Other staff 4. ***CC*** No.217868. Began 1986; interdenominational. Turnover n/a. For people aged 16 to 25.
☎ 01395 279 702

For additional information see List on Pages 89–91

YWCA, London, Holborn, Helen Graham House, 57 Great Russell Street, London WC1B 3BD
Housing Project Manager: Miss Janet Boyle. Admin staff 6, Other staff 12. ***CC*** No.217868. Began 1985; non-denominational. Turnover n/a. Transient accommodation (limited) for single people aged 18 to 30.
☎ 020 7430 0834

YWCA, Northampton, Phoenix House, 17 Castilian Street, Northampton NN1 1JU
Housing Project Manager: Miss Sarah Reed. ***CC*** No.217868. Began n/a; interdenominational. Turnover n/a. Safe, supported accommodation for young women aged 16 to 26 with needs in addition to housing.
☎ 01604 635 090 🖷 01604 239 706

For YWCA's in the following towns please contact the YWCA headquarters on page 484.

Aberystwyth
Altrincham
Ambleside
Blackburn
Bournemouth
Chester
Coventry
Harlow
Harrow
Hull
Ipswich
Kirkcaldy
Leeds
Leicester
Liverpool
London (other than Holborn)
Manchester
Moseley
Newcastle upon Tyne
Nottingham
Oxford
Plymouth
St Helens
Sheffield
Southampton
Taunton
Watford
Winchester
Windsor
Wolverhampton
York

A

HOUSING ASSOCIATIONS

***Adullam Homes Housing Association Ltd**, Pool House, Arran Close, Great Barr, Birmingham B43 7AD
Chief Executive: Mr Rob Taylor. Executive staff 4, Other staff 186. ***CC*** No.326743. Began 1972; non-denominational. Magazine: *Lifebuilder* (4,000 half-yearly). Turnover £5,804,000 to year end Mar 96. Providing housing care and support for people with special needs.
Web: adullum.org.uk
☎ 0121 358 3818 🖷 0121 358 6188

Baptist Housing Trust, 23 Hillway, Westcliff-on-Sea SS0 8QA
Secretary: Mr J Barfield. No other staff. ***CC*** No.1031620. Began 1994; Baptist. (Previously Baptist Housing Association Charitable Fund). No magazine. Turnover £58,000 to year end Mar 98. Supporting the charitable work of English Churches Housing Group by funding housing and associated amenities.
☎ 01702 473 373

Battersea Churches and Chelsea Housing Trust, Estra House, Station Approach, Streatham, London SW16 6HW
Chief Executive: Ms Jan Tomlinson. *Finance Director:* Mr White Edeubie. *Housing Services Director:* Mr Bob Thompson. Executive staff 5, Other staff 55. ***CC*** Began 1967; interdenominational. Magazine: *Report* (Circulation n/a annually). Turnover £4,500,000 to year end Mar 98. Community based association providing affordable homes for those in housing need; some special needs housing.
☎ 020 8664 4000 🖷 020 8664 4001

***CAHA Christian Alliance Housing Association Ltd**, Exton Street, London SE1 8UE
Chief Executive: Mr Richard Brook. Executive staff 5, Admin staff 6. ***CC*** No.293232. Began 1985; interdenominational. (Previously Christian Alliance). No magazine. Turnover £2,500,000 to year end Dec 98. Sharing the Gospel of Christ with practical care through provision of residential accommodation for those in special need.
☎ 020 7620 1455

Thomas Chalmers Housing Association Ltd, 15 North Bank Street, Edinburgh EH1 2LS
Secretary: Mr Iain D Gill. Other staff 2. ***CC*** Began n/a; Free Church of Scotland. No magazine. Turnover £175,000 to year end Mar 98. Providing special needs housing.
☎ 0131 226 5286 🖷 0131 220 0597

†***A Christian Haven Trust**, 24 Dunraven Road, West Kirby, Wirral CH48 4DS
Director: To be appointed. Executive staff 1. ***CC*** Began 1987; non-denominational. Magazine: *Newsletter* (Circulation n/a occasionally), *Prayerletter* (Circulation n/a monthly). Turnover £2,400 to year end Mar 93. Providing Christian homes where those with spiritual and physical needs can find care and help.
☎ 0151 625 9337

Christian Projects Ltd, 15 Musters Road, West Bridgford, Nottingham NG2 7PP
Chief Executive: Mr David G Henderson. Executive staff 3. Began 1987; interdenominational. No magazine. Turnover n/a. Developing nursing homes for elderly people.
☎ 0115 945 5485 🖷 0115 982 1919

***Church Army**, Independents Road, Blackheath, London SE3 9LG
Chief Secretary: Capt Philip Johanson. *Director of Finance:* Mr John Welsh. *Director of Personnel:* Mr Ray Viney. Executive staff 9, Other staff 600. ***CC*** No.226226. Began 1882; Anglican. Magazine: *Share it!* (55,000 quarterly). Turnover £7,600,000. Providing residential homes for elderly people.
Email: information@churcharmy.org.uk
☎ 020 8318 1226 🖷 020 8318 5258

English Churches Housing Group, Sutherland House, 70 West Hendon Broadway, London NW9 7BT
Chief Executive: Mr Ed Wood. Executive staff 7, Other staff 1400. ***CC*** Began n/a. (Baptist Housing Association (1966) and Church Housing Association (1924) merged 1991). No magazine. Turnover n/a. Providing general family housing, sheltered housing for the elderly and supported housing schemes for single homeless people.
☎ 020 8203 9233 🖷 020 8203 0092
Also at: Provident House, Burrell Row, Beckenham BR3 1AT
☎ 020 8650 0066
And: Central House, 32 High Street, London E15 2PD
☎ 020 8519 4028
And: Devonshire House, Devonshire Avenue, Street Lane, Leeds LS8 1AY
☎ 0113 269 7151
And: 170 Plymouth Grove, Manchester M13 0AF
☎ 0161 273 3755
And: 18b Ley Court, Barnett Way, Gloucester GL4 7RT
☎ 01452 372 505
And: Highfield Court, Highfield Farm, Church Lane, Madingley, Cambridge CB3 8AG
☎ 01954 210 616

Eothen Homes Ltd, J31 Eleventh Avenue North, Team Valley, Gateshead NE11 0NJ
General Manager: Mrs J M Hearl. Admin staff 3, Other staff 110. ***CC*** No.223262. Began 1950; interdenominational. No magazine. Turnover £1,464,000 to year end Mar 96. Residential care homes for the elderly; 108 people in three locations.
☎ 0191 491 5300 🖷 0191 487 0859

The Fairfield Trust, Fairfield, Huxtable Hill, Torquay TQ2 6RN
Chairman: Rev Alex W H Dick. No full-time staff. ***CC*** No.266699. Began 1974; non-denominational. No magazine. Turnover £28,000 to year end Oct 97. Providing residential flats in Devon for 18 clergy and missionaries retired or on leave.
☎ 01803 605 126

*__The Gilead Foundation__, Risdon Farm, Okehampton EX20 3AJ
General Manager: Pastor Ian Samuel. Executive staff 9, Other staff 14. ***CC*** No.1002909. Began n/a; evangelical. No magazine. Turnover £200,000 to year end Apr 98. Meeting the needs of hurting lives through residential Christian training and work. Four centres; 70 people.
☎ 01837 851 240 🖷 01837 851 520

Grace and Compassion Benedictines, St Benedict's, 1 Manor Road, Kemp Town, Brighton BN2 5EA
Prioress General: Mother Mary Garson. Religious sisters 191. ***CC*** No.1056064. Began 1954; Roman Catholic. (Previously House of Hospitality Ltd). Magazine: *Our Lady's Newsletter* (6,000 quarterly). Turnover £1,839,000 to year end Sept 98. Residential homes, sheltered flats, nursing unit for 300 people in caring environment across southern England.
Web: max.roehampton.ac.uk/link/aandb/gcb.htm
Email: generalate@graceandcompassion.co.uk
☎ 01273 680 720 🖷 01273 680 527

*__John Grooms Housing Association__, 50 Scrutton Street, London EC2A 4XQ
Chief Executive: Mr David Harmer. *Finance Director:* Mr William Phillips. *Chairman:* Mr Ernest Picton. Executive staff 5, Other staff 62. ***CC*** Began 1970; interdenominational. Magazine: *Grooms News* (50,000 half-yearly). Turnover £4,213,000 to year end Mar 98. Specialist builder of housing for people with physical disabilities.
Web: www.johngrooms.org.uk
Email: housing@johngrooms.org.uk
☎ 020 7452 2000 🖷 020 7452 2001

Habitat for Humanity Belfast, Farset Enterprise Park, 638 Springfield Road, Belfast BT12 7DY
Director: Mr Peter Farquharson. Executive staff 1, Other staff 9. ***CC*** No.XR 18070. Began 1994; non-denominational. No magazine. Turnover £500,000 to year end Apr 98. Building homes for low-income families in partnership with individuals, communities, churches and businesses.
Email: belfast@habitatni.co.uk
☎ 028 9024 3686 🖷 028 9033 1878

Habitat for Humanity Great Britain, The Malt House, 25 Bridge Street, Banbury OX16 8PN
Director: Mr David Stapleton. *Community Development Officer:* Mr Bruce Thomson. Executive staff 8. ***CC*** No.1043641. Began n/a; interdenominational. Magazine: *Newsletter* (Circulation n/a quarterly). Turnover £220,000 to year end Mar 98. Assists local communities to build affordable houses with and for low-income families in housing need.
Web: www.habitat.org
Email: 106076.1056@compuserve.com
☎ 01295 264 240 🖷 01295 264 230

*__KeyChange__, 5 St George's Mews, 43 Westminster Bridge Road, London SE1 7JB
Chief Executive: Mr David Shafik. Executive staff 6, Other staff 110. ***CC*** No.1061344. Began 1920; interdenominational. (Previously Christian Alliance). Magazine: *KeyChange News* (4,000 every five months). Turnover £1,410,324 to year end Mar 98. Providing residential care for frail elderly and supported accommodation for vulnerable, homeless people.
Web: www.keychange.org.uk
Email: info@keychange.org.uk
☎ 020 7633 0533 🖷 020 7928 1872

KMC, 96 Clarendon Road, London W11 2HR
Manager: Ms Karen O'Donnell. No other full-time staff. Began 1997; interdenominational. No magazine. Turnover n/a. Managing and letting residential property in London, primarily for Christians.
☎ 020 7229 0696 🖷 020 7229 0696

Manchester Methodist Housing Group, Hopeleigh, 1 Fairhope Avenue, Salford M6 8AR
Chief Executive: Stephen Porter. ***CC*** No.19564. Began n/a; Methodist. No magazine. Turnover n/a. Providing rented accommodation, low cost homes for purchase, housing management services.
Email: manchester.methodist@mmhg.org.uk
☎ 0161 707 7147 🖷 0161 707 7300

Methodist Homes for the Aged, Epworth House, Stuart Street, Derby DE1 2EQ
Chief Executive: Mrs Barbara Leighton. *Senior Chaplain:* Rev Albert Jewell. Executive staff 47, Other staff 1300. ***CC*** No.218504. Began 1943; Methodist. Magazine: *At Home* (35,000 half-yearly). Turnover £24,600,000 to year end Mar 98. Caring for over 2,000 older people in residential homes and sheltered housing.
☎ 01332 296 200 🖷 01332 296 925

Pilgrim Homes, Nasmith House, 175 Tower Bridge Road, London SE1 2AL
Chief Executive: Mr P A Tervet. Executive staff 10, Other staff 202. ***CC*** No.242266. Began 1807; non-denominational. (Previously Aged Pilgrims' Friend Society). Magazine: *Quarterly* (5,000 quarterly), *Annual Report* (3,000 annually). Turnover £3,800,000 to year end Dec 96. Providing sheltered housing, residential care and nursing for 372 elderly Protestant Christians in 12 locations.
Email: pilgrimhomes@compuserve.com
☎ 020 7407 5466 🖷 020 7403 5433

Retired Baptist Ministers Housing Society Ltd, Baptist House, PO Box 44, 129 Broadway, Didcot OX11 8RT
Manager: Rev Paul Henstock. Executive staff 1. ***CC*** No.21462. Began 1975; Baptist. No magazine. Turnover £935,700 to year end Sep 98. Providing accommodation for retired Baptist ministers and missionaries.
☎ 01235 517 700 🖷 01235 517 715

St Christopher's Fellowship, 217 Kingston Road, Wimbledon, London SW19 3NL
Chief Executive: Mr Jonathan J M Farrow. *Personnel and Administration Manager:* Mr R Axe. Executive staff 3, Other staff 90. ***CC*** No.207782. Began 1870; non-denominational. No magazine. Turnover £2,953,880 to year end Mar 98. Providing support for vulnerable young people (16-22) and residential care for severely abused children aged 4–12. 30 projects across London.
Web: www.users.dircon.co.uk/~st-chris
Email: st-chris@dircon.co.uk
☎ 020 8543 3619 🖷 020 8544 1633

St Vincent's Family Housing Association Ltd, 24 George Street, London W1H 5RB
Secretary: Mrs R Everidge. Executive staff 1. Began 1965; non-denominational. No magazine. Turnover £150,000 to year end Dec 97. Providing accommodation for families, young couples and elderly.
☎ No telephone

Salvation Army Housing Association, 18 Thanet Street, London WC1H 9TR
Chief Executive: Mr Richard Smillie. Executive staff 4, Other staff 96. ***CC*** Began 1959; Salvation Army. No magazine. Turnover £15,751,000 to year end Mar 98. Constructing and letting flats, houses and hostels for people in need.
Web: www.saha.org.uk
Email: richardsmillie@saha.org.uk
☎ 020 7388 2025 🖷 020 7388 9525
Also at: 33 Chorley New Road, Bolton BL1 4QR
☎ 01204 360 500 🖷 01204 360 509
And: Jarodale House, 7 Gregory Boulevard, Nottingham NG7 6LD
☎ 0115 985 6637 🖷 0115 956 5385
And: 39 Bath Road, Swindon SN1 4AS
☎ 01793 541 635 🖷 01793 420 159
And: Sophia House, 214 High Road, London N15 4NP
☎ 020 8885 6100 🖷 020 8885 6101
And: Triangle House, Bath Lane, Newcastle upon Tyne NE4 5SW
☎ 0191 260 6130 🖷 0191 260 6131

***Scottish Christian Alliance**, 3 Nethercairn Place, Newton Mearns, Glasgow G77 5SZ
Director: Mr Daniel McPhail-Smith. Executive staff 4, Other staff 9. ***CC*** No.SCO 21765. Began 1993; interdenominational. (Previously KeyChange Scotland Ltd). No magazine. Turnover £190,000 to year end Mar 98. Presenting the Gospel of Jesus Christ principally through offering accommodation.
☎ 0141 571 3804 🖷 0141 571 3804

Shaftesbury Housing Group, Shaftesbury House, 87 East Street, Epsom KT17 1DT
Chief Executive: Mr Jeffrey Cackett. ***CC*** No.19574 Began 1970; non-denominational. Magazine: *Shaftesbury Housing News* (4,500 quarterly). Turnover £32,000,000 to year end Dec 98. Providing quality affordable homes for people whose needs cannot be met in the commercial housing market.
☎ 01372 727 252 🖷 01372 736 800

Springboard Housing Association Ltd, 2a Claughton Road, Plaistow, London E13 9PN
Chief Executive: Jakki Moxham. *Housing Director:* Mrs Lynn Vickery. *Finance Director:* Mr Keith Hickey. Executive staff 5, Other staff 650. Began 1971; non-denominational. Magazine: *Newsletter* (7,500 n/a). Turnover £24,982,000 to year end Mar 98. Providing general and special needs housing in East London, Hertfordshire and Essex. Over 5,000 homes.
Email: 100651.3510@compuserve.com
☎ 020 8475 0033 🖷 020 8503 4286

***Trinity Care plc**, 15 Musters Road, West Bridgford, Nottingham NG2 7PP
Chief Executive: Mr David G Henderson. *Director of Care:* Dr Mervyn Suffield. Executive staff 5, Other staff 1500. Began 1987; non-denominational. Magazine: *Trinity Times* (Circulation & frequency n/a). Turnover £13,814,000 to year end Mar 98. Developing, managing nursing homes and apartments for elderly people; bungalows for people with a learning disability.
Email: enquiry@trinitycare.co.uk
☎ 0115 945 5485 🖷 0115 982 1919

YMCA, London, Lambeth, 40 Stockwell Road, London SW9 9ES
Chief Executive: Mr Malcolm Bruce. Staff 14. ***CC*** No.294069. Began 1957; interdenominational. Turnover £1,600,000 to year end Mar 98.
Email: ymca_international@msn.com
☎ 020 7501 9795 🖷 020 7501 8005

RESIDENTIAL HOMES FOR DISADVANTAGED PEOPLE

Homes which did not supply this information are not listed here

≠ = nearest Railway station ⊖ = nearest London Underground station

A

Name, Town	Type of resident	Number	Railway Station
Aquila Housing Association, Gateshead	homeless young women	7	≠ Newcastle
Ashfield Court, Sutton-in-Ashfield	learning difficulties, challenging behaviour	n/a	≠ Sutton Parkway
Ashlar House, Leeds	adults with autism	8	≠ Leeds
Badgers, Leigh-on-Sea	learning disabilities	9	≠ Leigh-on-Sea
Bethany Christian Trust, Edinburgh	homeless people	18	≠ Edinburgh
Bethany House Hostel, Glasgow	homeless men	14	≠ Glasgow Queen Street
Christian Home, Hornchurch	physically handicapped	12	⊖ Dagenham Heathway
Crossways Community, Tunbridge Wells	mental health problems	0	≠ Tunbridge Wells
Gilven House, Glenrothes	homeless women	15	≠ Markinch
Good News Family Care, Buxton	families in need	n/a	≠ Buxton
The Havens Guild, London N3	learning disabilities, elderly	19	⊖ Finchley Central
Holme Hall, York	adults with any disability	47	≠ Goole
Jericho Benedictines, Edinburgh	mental health problems	20	≠ Edinburgh
The Langley House Trust			
Bedford	ex-offenders	9	≠ Bedford
Bradford	ex-offenders	15	≠ Bradford Forster Square
Cheltenham	ex-offenders	15	≠ Cheltenham
Coventry	ex-offenders, drug addictions	23	≠ Coventry
Lancaster	ex-offenders	17	≠ Lancaster
Otterbourne	ex-offenders	18	≠ Winchester
Poole	ex-offenders	14	≠ Poole
Ramsbottom	ex-offenders, drug addictions	14	≠
Reading	ex-offenders	12	≠ Reading
Strood	ex-offenders	19	≠ Rochester
Taunton	ex-offenders	18	≠ Taunton
Wakefield	ex-offenders	14	≠ Wakefield Westgate
Wing	ex-offenders	23	≠ Oakham
Living Springs, Stourbridge	families, child protection	n/a	≠ Stourbridge
The Lodge Trust, Oakham	learning disabilities	20	≠ Oakham
Mayflower Centre, Plymouth	learning disabilities	15	≠ Plymouth
Minstead Training Project, Lyndhurst	learning disabilities	23	≠ Ashurst New Forest
Moorfield House, Liverpool	young adults with learning disabilities	24	≠ Maghull
Our Lady's House, London SE22	women, mental health problems	12	≠ North Dulwich
PROSPECTS, Reading	learning disabilities	110	≠ Reading
Redheugh Day Centre, Kilbirnie	learning difficulties	17	≠ Glengarnock
St Michael's Fellowship, London SE24	families	5	≠ Herne Hill
St Michael's Fellowship, London SE24	families	5	≠ Loughborough Junction
St Michael's Fellowship, London SW2	adolescent mothers and babies	8	≠ Streatham Hill or Tulse Hill
Salem Court, Llandudno	mental illness	12	≠ Llandudno
Springboard Housing Association, SE England	special needs housing	5,000	n/a
Springfield Lodge, London SE5	male ex-offenders	n/a	≠ East Dulwich
W J Thompson House, Belfast	male ex-offenders	16	*Rail:* Belfast Great Victoria Street
Trinity Care, nationwide	learning disabilities	n/a	n/a
Victory Outreach UK HQ	ex-offenders, addictions	36	≠ Newport (Gwent)
Wayside (A KeyChange initiative)	homeless women	16	≠ Reigate
Westhaven, Glasgow	adults with epilepsy	16	≠ Rutherglen
Yeldall Homeless Projects, Hayes	homeless adults, ex-offenders, addictions	28	≠ Hayes and Harlington

RESIDENTIAL HOMES FOR DISADVANTAGED PEOPLE

See also Addictions & Rehabilitation Centres on Page 330

***Aquila Housing Association**, 169 Coatsworth Road, Bensham, Gateshead NE8 1SQ
General Manager: Mrs Marjorie Webster. Executive staff 1, Other staff 5. *CC* No.24582. Began 1984; non-denominational. No magazine. Turnover £74,000 to year end Dec 98. For homeless young women.
Email: j.webster@cablenet.co.uk
☎ 0191 477 1870 Fax 0191 443 0038

***Ashfield Court**, Stoneyford Road, Sutton-in-Ashfield NG17 2DR
Home Manager: John Greentree. Other staff n/a. Began 1999; interdenominational. Trinity Care plc. No magazine. Turnover n/a. For people with learning difficulties or challenging behaviour.
☎ 0115 945 5485 Fax 0115 982 1919

Ashlar House, 76 Potternewton Lane, Leeds LS7 3LW
General Manager: Mr S Haddock. *Day Services Manager:* Mr Stephen Smith. Executive staff 4, Other staff 18. *CC* No.1047981. Began 1988; interdenominational. No magazine. Turnover £363,500 to year end Mar 97. Long-term care and development of adults with autism.
☎ 0113 226 2700 (home) 0113 245 2736 (day services)
Fax 0113 226 2700

Badgers, 53 Rayleigh Avenue, Leigh-on-Sea SS9 5DN
Manager: Mr Greg Mellusco. Other staff 30. *CC* No.207493. Began 1993; non-denominational. No magazine. Turnover n/a. Supported by the Field Lane Foundation. For people with learning disabilities.
☎ 01702 526 027

*__Bethany Christian Trust__, Bethany Hall, 18 Jane Street, Edinburgh EH6 5HD
Director: Rev Alan Berry. Other staff 85. ***CC*** No.SCO 03783. Began 1983; interdenominational. Magazine: *Bethany Newsletter* (4,000 quarterly). Turnover £1,600,000 to year end Apr 98. Short, medium and long-stay housing with care to resettle homeless people into the community.
Email: bethanycc@msn.com
☎ 0131 554 4071 🖷 0131 554 4071
Also at: Bethany House, 12 Coupar Street, Edinburgh EH6 6HH
☎ 0131 467 1010 🖷 0131 467 1010
And: Bethany Christian Centre, 6 Casselbank Street, Edinburgh EH6 5HA
☎ 0131 554 4071 🖷 0131 554 4071
And: Bethany Supported Housing, 5 Casselbank Street, Edinburgh EH6 5HA
☎ 0131 553 1119 🖷 0131 553 1119

*__Bethany House Hostel (Scottish Christian Alliance)__, 36 Muslin Street, Glasgow G40 4AP
Administrator: Rev A Webster. Admin staff 3, Other staff 10. ***CC*** Began n/a; interdenominational. No magazine. Turnover n/a. Self-referral hostel for homeless men with an alcohol problem.
☎ 0141 554 2497 🖷 0141 554 2497

Christian Home for the Physically Handicapped, 58 Purbeck Road, Hornchurch RM11 1NA
Organiser: Mr Ronald G Albon. All voluntary staff. ***CC*** No.326182. Began 1981; interdenominational. Magazine: *Newsletter* (600 quarterly). Turnover £30,906 to year end Mar 98. Long and short stay.
☎ 01708 443 169

Crossways Community, 8 Culverden Park Road, Tunbridge Wells TN4 9QX
Manager: Mr Martin Granger. Executive staff 2, Other staff 8. ***CC*** No.1007156. Began 1967; interdenominational. No magazine. Turnover £300,000 to year end Jan 99. Working with 34 people suffering from mental health problems in 2 residential settings.
☎ 01892 529 321

Esther Community (A Key Change Project), 12 Queen's Terrace, St David's, Exeter, Devon EX4 4HR
Manager: Mr Andrew Lyle. Project staff 4. **CC** Began 1998; interdenominational. Turnover n/a. For direct access, vulnerable homeless women.
☎ 01392 272 983 🖷 01392 272 983

*__Gilven House, Scottish Christian Alliance Hostel, Glenrothes__, Gilven House, 22 Iona Park, Glenrothes KY7 6NU
Wardens: Rev John and May Cropley. Other staff 2. ***CC*** No.SCO 21765. Began 1920; interdenominational. No magazine. Turnover £38,000. Hostel for homeless women teaching Christian principles and bringing Christ to them in the Gospel.
☎ 01592 744 849

Good News Family Care (Homes) Ltd., Charis House, Hardwick Square East, Buxton SK17 6PT
Administrator: Ms Hazel Guest. *Public Relations Officer:* Mr Keith Jones. Executive staff 5, Other staff 20. ***CC*** No.1042386. Began 1994; evangelical. Magazine: *Charis News* (Circulation n/a quarterly). Turnover £100,000. Offering help and support to families in need.
Web: www.king-fisher.co.uk/familycare
Email: familycare@king-fisher.co.uk
☎ 01298 247 61 Mobile: 07774 159 157 🖷 01298 270 27

†**The Havens Guild**, 95 Hendon Lane, Finchley, London N3 3SH
Home Manager: Ms Iris Jebri. Other staff 37. ***CC*** No.207493. Began 1982; non-denominational. No magazine. Turnover n/a. Supported by the Field Lane Foundation. For elderly people and those with learning disabilities.
☎ 020 8346 7303

Holme Hall, New Road, Holme-on-Spalding-Moor, York YO43 4BS
Matron: Mrs Lynda Muscroft. Admin staff 3, Other staff 90. ***CC*** No.1052076. Began 1979; Roman Catholic. Sue Ryder Homes. No magazine. Turnover £755,000 to year end Dec 98. For people aged over 18 with a wide range of disabilities and conditions.
☎ 01430 860 904 🖷 01430 860 591

Jericho Benedictines, Jericho House, 53 Lothian Street, Edinburgh EH1 1HB
Superior: Rev James Ferguson. Admin staff 7, Other staff 40. ***CC*** Began 1970; Roman Catholic. No magazine. Turnover n/a. For those with serious mental health problems.
☎ 0131 225 8230

The Langley House Trust, PO Box 181, Witney OX8 6WD
Chief Executive: Mr John Adams. *Promotions Officer:* Mr Paul Langley. Admin staff 8, Other staff 90. ***CC*** No.290059. Began 1958; interdenominational. Turnover n/a. Providing residential care and rehabilitation for ex-offenders in a Christian environment.
Email: langley_house@cin.co.uk
☎ 01993 774 075 🖷 01993 772 425

*__Living Springs__, Bridgnorth Road, Stourton, Stourbridge DY7 6QY
Manager: Jane Chapman. Other staff n/a. ***CC*** No.701674. Began n/a; interdenominational. No magazine. Turnover n/a. Support and assessment of families including social service referred cases involving child protection concerns.
☎ 01384 872 817 Mobile: 07801 255 171 🖷 01384 872 817

The Lodge Trust, The Lodge, Market Overton, Oakham LE15 7PL
Chief Executive: Mr Roy Palframan. *Care Manager:* Miss Elizabeth Irvine. Staff 25. ***CC*** No.516835. Began 1985; evangelical. No magazine. Turnover £400,000 to year end Mar 96. Providing a home and place of work for adults with learning disabilities.
☎ 01572 767 234

Mayflower Centre, Courtfield Road, Plymouth PL3 5BB
Officer-in-Charge: Captain Beverley Riley. Admin staff 2. ***CC*** Began n/a; Salvation Army. No magazine. Turnover n/a. For adults with a learning disability, residential and day centre.
☎ 01752 660 302

Minstead Training Project, Minstead, Lyndhurst SO43 7FT
Project Director: Mr Martin Lenaerts. *Administrator:* Mr Stephen Cole. Other staff 39. ***CC*** No.1053391. Began 1986; non-denominational. No magazine. Turnover £692,000 to year end Apr 98. Offering training in work, life and social skills to young people with learning disabilities.
☎ 023 8081 2297

Moorfield House, Melling, Liverpool L31 1AQ
Manager: Miss Susanne Lamkin. *Project Director:* Mr D Lamkin. Admin staff 3, Other staff 17. Began 1985; Christian Brethren. No magazine. Turnover £500,000 to year end Aug 98. For young adults with learning difficulties.
☎ 0151 549 2100 🖷 0151 546 6828

For additional information see List on Page 104

Notintone Place Family Rehabilitation Unit, Notintone Place, Sneinton, Nottingham NG2 4OQ
Unit Manager: Ms Yvonne Miller. *CC* Began n/a; Salvation Army. No magazine. Turnover n/a. Accommodation for 4 families.
☎ 0115 950 3927 🖷 0115 959 8604

A

†**Our Lady's House**, 212 Lordship Lane, London SE22 8LR
Housing Manager: To be appointed. Executive staff 4, Other staff 3. Began 1989; non-denominational. St Vincent's Family Housing Association. No magazine. Turnover n/a. For women recovering from mental health problems.
☎ 020 8299 0250

***PROSPECTS for People with Learning Disabilities**, PO Box 351, Reading RG1 7AL
Chief Executive: Mr Peter Levell. *Director of Living PROSPECTS:* Miss Maureen Wise. *Director of Causeway PROSPECTS:* Mr Tony Phelps-Jones. Executive staff 4, Other staff 186. *CC* No.1060571. Began 1976; interdenominational. (Previously A Cause for Concern). (See also Causeway PROSPECTS). Magazine: *Better Prospects* (10,000 half-yearly). Turnover £3,500,000 to year end Mar 99. Providing residential support, day services, development opportunities and spiritual ministry for people with learning disabilities.
Email: info@prospects.org.uk
☎ 0118 950 8781 🖷 0118 939 1683

Redheugh Day Centre for Adults with Learning Difficulties, Dipple Road, Kilbirnie KA25 7JX
Officer-in-Charge: Mrs Patricia Simpson. *CC* Began n/a; Salvation Army. No magazine. Turnover n/a. Accommodation for 17 people.
☎ 01505 683 233

St Michael's Fellowship, Herne Hill, 46 Herne Hill, London SE24 9QP
Project Manager: Ms Anna Kraus. Other staff 5. *CC* No.1035820. Began 1992; interdenominational. No magazine. Turnover n/a. Accommodating vulnerable families where there are child protection issues.
☎ 020 7738 4242

†**St Michael's Fellowship, Herne Hill**, 84 Herne Hill Road, London SE24 0AN
Project Manager: Ms Shelagh Gilliver. Other staff 5. *CC* No.1035820. Began 1980; interdenominational. No magazine. Turnover n/a. For parents with dependency problems.
☎ 020 7733 8153

St Michael's Fellowship, Streatham, 52 Palace Road, Streatham, London SW2 3NJ
Project Manager: Ms Mona Monahan. Other staff 5. *CC* No.1035820. Began 1972; interdenominational. No magazine. Turnover n/a. Self-catering.
☎ 020 8671 1252

***Salem Court**, Tygwyn Road, Llandudno LL30 2QR
Proprietor: Rev Pam Wright. *Manager:* Mr Bell Lloyd-Williams. Admin staff 2, Other staff 6. Began 1988; interdenominational. No magazine. Turnover £120,000 to year end May 98. Residential care for those suffering or recovering from mental illness or a dependency problem.
Web: salemcourt.co.uk
Email: pwright@salemcourt.u-net.com
☎ 01492 877 024 Mobile: 07850 180 420

Springboard Housing Association Ltd, 2a Claughton Road, Plaistow, London E13 9PN
Chief Executive: Jakki Moxham. *Housing Director:* Mrs Lynn Vickery. *Finance Director:* Mr Keith Hickey. Executive staff 5, Other staff 650. Began 1971; non-denominational. Magazine: *Newsletter* (7,500 n/a). Turnover £24,982,000 to year end Mar 98. Providing general and special needs housing in East London, Hertfordshire and Essex. Over 5,000 homes.
Email: 100651.3510@compuserve.com
☎ 020 8475 0033 🖷 020 8503 4286

Springfield Lodge, 1 Grove Hill Road, Camberwell, London SE5 8DF
Officer-in-Charge: Mr John Griggs. Admin staff 3. *CC* Began n/a; Salvation Army. No magazine. Turnover n/a. Resettlement centre for 25 men.
☎ 020 7274 7188 🖷 020 7737 7707

W J Thompson House, 426 Antrim Road, Belfast BT15 5GA
Director: Mr David Farrow. Resident social workers 6, Other staff 2. Began 1984; Presbyterian Church in Ireland. No magazine. Turnover £150,000 to year end Dec 98.
☎ 028 9037 0923 🖷 028 9077 5177

***Trinity Care plc**, 15 Musters Road, West Bridgford, Nottingham NG2 7PP
Chief Executive: Mr David G Henderson. *Director of Care:* Dr Mervyn Suffield. Executive staff 5, Other staff 1500. Began 1987; non-denominational. Magazine: *Trinity Times* (Circulation & frequency n/a). Turnover £13,814 to year end Mar 98. Developing and managing nursing homes/apartments for elderly people; bungalows for people with a learning disability.
Email: enquiry@trinitycare.co.uk
☎ 0115 945 5485 🖷 0115 982 1919

***Victory Outreach UK HQ**, The Bush Hotel, High Street, Abertillery NP3 1DD
Directors: Rev David & Mrs Dinah Sansome. Admin staff 2, Other staff 7, Volunteers. *CC* No.291611. Began 1984; Pentecostal. No magazine. Turnover n/a. Providing Christian homes for young people in need, ex-offenders, homeless, drug-dependants, alcoholics and abused.
☎ 01495 212 516

***Wayside (A KeyChange initiative)**, Wayside, 42 Croydon Road, Reigate RH2 0PQ
Manager: Mrs Etta Colville. Project staff 4. *CC* Began 1996; interdenominational. No magazine. Turnover n/a. For vulnerable, homeless women.
☎ 01737 248 304 🖷 01737 248 304

***Westhaven**, 2 Upper Bourtree Drive, High Burnside, Rutherglen, Glasgow G73 4EH
Unit Manager: Mrs Elizabeth Gibb. Full-time staff 8. *CC* No.SCO 24366. Began n/a; Church of Scotland. No magazine. Turnover n/a. For 16 epilepsy sufferers.
☎ 0141 634 4563

***Yeldall Homeless Projects**, 2 Barnhill Lane, Hayes UB4 8HD
Director: Rev Graham Duncan. *Executive Director:* Mr David Partington. Staff 10. *CC* No.1000038. Began 1989; non-denominational. (Previously Yeldall Christian Centres Homeless Project). Part of Yeldall Christian Centres. No magazine. Turnover £199,000 to year end Mar 99. For young homeless adults, ex-offenders and people with drug/alcohol problems in Hillingdon, Hounslow.
Email: ycc@patrol.i-way.co.uk
☎ 020 8845 9651 🖷 020 8862 1166

For additional information see List on Page 104

RESIDENTIAL & NURSING HOMES FOR ELDERLY PEOPLE

By Country and Postcode area (see Page 569 for explanation)
Organisations which did not supply any of this information are not listed here

S = single rooms **D/T** = number of bed spaces in double/twin rooms **Total** = total bed spaces (not number of rooms)
⇌ = nearest Railway station ⊖ = nearest London Underground station

Postcode	Location	Name	S	D/T	Other		Total	Railway Station
ENGLAND								
Anglia								
CO12	**Harwich**	Alexandra House	21	10			31	⇌ Dovercourt
CO14	**Walton on the Naze**	The Ernest Luff Homes Ltd	n/a	n/a			66	⇌ Frinton
		Singholm	n/a	n/a			39	⇌ Walton-on-Naze
IP1	**Ipswich**	Norwood	n/a	n/a	Registered beds		38	⇌ Ipswich
IP14	**Stowmarket**	Finborough Court Pilgrim Homes	-	-	care	6	49	⇌ Stowmarket
					nursing	14		
					sheltered flatlets	29		
IP33	**Bury St Edmunds**	The Martins	n/a	n/a	with dementia		36	⇌ Bury St Edmunds
MK16	**Newport Pagnell**	Westbury	n/a	n/a	dementia care		30	⇌ Milton Keynes Central
MK40	**Bedford**	The Dorothea Trust	16	-			16	⇌ Bedford
NR1	**Norwich**	Cromwell House	n/a	n/a	Registered beds		38	⇌ Norwich
NR20	**Dereham**	Eckling Grange Ltd	-	-	residential	45	123	⇌ Norwich
					nursing care beds	20		
					sheltered bungalows	58		
NR28	**North Walsham**	The Mildred Duff Memorial Eventide Home	n/a	n/a			25	⇌ North Walsham
NR32	**Lowestoft**	Harleston House	n/a	n/a			25	⇌ Lowestoft
NR33	**Lowestoft**	The Dell	17	10			27	⇌ Oulton Broad
SG5	**Hitchin**	Elmside	33	-			33	⇌ Hitchin
SG6	**Letchworth**	Trembaths	n/a	n/a	residential and nursing		40	⇌ Letchworth
SS9	**Leigh-on-Sea**	Eastwood Lodge	n/a	n/a			35	⇌ Rayleigh
London								
E1	**London**	Rawson Eventide Home	n/a	n/a			34	⊖ Whitechapel
N10	**London**	The Meadow	31	4	with dementia		35	⊖ Highgate
SE1	**London**	South London Mission	n/a	n/a			38	⊖ Borough
SE13	**London**	Glebe Court	n/a	n/a			41	⇌ Lewisham
SE26	**London**	Rookstone Eventide Home	n/a	n/a			32	⇌ Sydenham
SW4	**London**	Alver Bank Residential Home	25	2	sheltered housing	8	59	⊖ Clapham Common
					independent housing	24		
SW20	**London**	St Theresa's Home	n/a	n/a			18	⇌ Wimbledon ⊖ Wimbledon
W4	**London**	St Mary's Convent and Nursing Home	-	-	residential	23	59	⇌ Chiswick ⊖ Turnham Green
					nursing home	36		
W11	**London**	The Sheppard Trust	n/a	n/a			34	⊖ Holland Park
Midlands								
B12	**Birmingham**	St Vincent's Homes	28	-			28	⇌ Birmingham New Street
CV13	**Nuneaton**	Hornsey Rise Memorial Home	-	-	care	33	39	⇌ Nuneaton
					sheltered single	2		
					sheltered double	4		
CV32	**Leamington Spa**	Homewood	n/a	n/a			35	⇌ Leamington Spa
CV37	**Stratford-upon-Avon**	Cedar Lawn	n/a	n/a			35	⇌ Stratford-upon-Avon
DY9	**Stourbridge**	The Cedars Christian Residential Home	20	-			20	⇌ Stourbridge
LE2	**Leicester**	Aigburth	30	2			32	⇌ Leicester
LE5	**Leicester**	Evington Home	-	-	care	16	52	⇌ Leicester
					nursing	13		
					sheltered flatlets	23		
NG2	**Nottingham**	Notintone House	n/a	n/a			38	⇌ Nottingham
NG5	**Nottingham**	St Andrew's Lodge	-	-	Nursing	80	160	⇌ Bulwell
					EMI	80		
NG7	**Nottingham**	Churchfield Christian Care Centre	-	-	Nursing	36	76	⇌ Nottingham
					EMI	36		
					Terminal	2		
					YPD	2		
NG9	**Nottingham**	Queenswood	n/a	n/a			41	⇌ Nottingham or Beeston
NG12	**Nottingham**	Oakfield Eventide Home	n/a	n/a			34	⇌ Radcliffe
NG17	**Sutton-in-Ashfield**	Stoneyford Christian Nursing Home	n/a	n/a	Nursing		60	⇌ Sutton Parkway
ST6	**Stoke-on-Trent**	Claybourne	n/a	n/a			36	⇌ Stoke-on-Trent
WS1	**Walsall**	Acorn Retirement Home	n/a	n/a			18	⇌ Walsall
WV3	**Wolverhampton**	Engelberg	n/a	n/a			32	⇌ Wolverhampton
North East								
DH8	**Consett**	St Mary's Convent Rest Home	20	-			20	⇌ Durham
DN6	**Doncaster**	St Anne's Rest Home	25	-			25	⇌ Doncaster
HG2	**Harrogate**	Berwick Grange	n/a	n/a			33	⇌ Harrogate
HU10	**Hull**	Willersley House	n/a	n/a	Registered beds		35	⇌ Hessle
LN6	**Lincoln**	Stones Place	31	-			31	⇌ Lincoln Central
LS29	**Ilkley**	Glen Rosa	n/a	n/a	with dementia	47	47	⇌ Ilkley
NE3	**Newcastle upon Tyne**	Eothen Homes Ltd	35	2			37	⇌ Newcastle
NE23	**Cramlington**	Harwood Court	33	2			35	⇌ Cramlington
NE26	**Whitley Bay**	Eothen Homes Ltd	23	6	sheltered flats	4	33	*Metro:* Whitley Bay
S7	**Sheffield**	Overdale Retirement Home	23	2			25	⇌ Sheffield
S32	**Sheffield**	Moorland House	n/a	n/a	Registered beds		33	⇌ Hathersage
S64	**Mexborough**	Swallow Wood Christian Nursing Home	-	-	Residential	3	43	⇌ Mexborough
					Nursing	40		
SR7	**Seaham**	Brackloon House Pilgrim Homes	n/a	n/a			17	⇌ Seaham

Residential & Nursing Homes for Elderly People

Postcode	Location	Name	S	D/T	Other		Total	Railway Station
WF9	Pontefract	Warde Aldam Christian Nursing Home	-	-	residential	20	120	South Elmsall
					Nursing	60		
					EMI	40		
YO12	Scarborough	Priceholme	32	-			32	Scarborough
North West								
BB2	Blackburn	Nazareth House	48	8			56	Blackburn
BL8	Bury	Epworth Grange	32	-			32	*Metrolink:* Bury
CH41	Birkenhead	Wirral Christian Centre Trust	n/a	n/a			39	Birkenhead Central
CH46	Wirral	St Marks Nursing Home	n/a	n/a			50	Moreton
CH62	Wirral	Oaklands Lodge	20	-			20	Bromborough
CH63	Wirral	Bebington Christian Nursing Home	-	-	EMI	24	39	Bebington
					YPD	15		
CH66	South Wirral	Mayfields	n/a	n/a	dementia care		36	Ellesmere Port
FY8	Lytham St Annes	Jubilee Nursing Home	15	-			15	Ansdell and Fairhaven
		Starr Hills	n/a	n/a	Registered beds		41	Ansdell and Fairhaven
L17	Liverpool	Fulwood Park	n/a	n/a	Registered beds		34	Aigburth
M6	Salford	Concern in Action Housing Association	-	-	nursing	16	20	Salford Central
					residential	4		
PR2	Preston	Bethany House	n/a	n/a			15	Preston
PR8	Southport	Connell Court	31	-			31	Birkdale
		The Gables Pilgrim Homes	-	-	care/sheltered housing	15	18	Southport
					sheltered single	1		Buxton
					sheltered double	2		
PR9	Southport	Orleans Residential Home	17	6			23	Southport
SK17	Buxton	The Hawthorns Eventide Home	n/a	n/a	for men and women		35	Buxton
TF10	Newport	The Cottage Christian Nursing Home	-	-	residential	10	50	Telford Central
					Nursing	40		
WA 6	Warrington	Frodsham Christian Nursing Home	-	-	Nursing	40		Frodsham
					EMI	30		
WA14	Altrincham	Handsworth	n/a	n/a	Registered beds		35	Altrincham
WA16	Knutsford	The Willows Christian Nursing Home	-	-	residential	3	63	Mobberley
					Nursing	40		
					EMI	20		
South Central								
HP11	High Wycombe	Keep Hill Rest Home	n/a	n/a	frail elderly		9	High Wycombe
GU22	Woking	Marie Carlile House	17	4			21	Woking
		Woodbank	n/a	n/a			39	Woking
GU27	Haslemere	Shottermill House Pilgrim Homes	-	-	care	27	32	Haslemere
					sheltered flatlets	5		
GU35	Bordon	Ashley House	n/a	n/a			30	Alton or Farnham or Liss
OX4	Oxford	St John's Home	30	4			34	Oxford
OX12	Wantage	Framland Pilgrim Homes	1	2	care/sheltered housing	21	24	Didcot Parkway
		St Katharine's House	-	-	residential	52	75	Didcot Parkway
					Nursing	23		
PO18	Chichester	Westhampnett Private Nursing Home	14	6			20	Chichester
PO20	Chichester	Nyton House	19	8			27	Barnham
		The West Wittering Private Nursing Home	14	14			28	Chichester
PO21	Bognor Regis	Greenways	33	-			33	Bognor Regis
PO40	Freshwater	Green Meadows	n/a	n/a			31	Lymington Pier
SL9	Gerrards Cross	Rock House	37	-	single flats	10	49	Gerrards Cross
					double flats	2		
SN15	Chippenham	Leonora Home	-	-	sheltered single	6	14	Chippenham
					sheltered double	8		
SO23	Winchester	Winchester Home	-	-	sheltered single flatlets	6	6	Winchester
SO53	Eastleigh	Chandler's Ford Christian Nursing Home	-	-	residential	3	48	Eastleigh
					Nursing	45		
South East								
BN2	Brighton	Brighton and Lady Anne Treves Memorial	-	-	care	7	37	Brighton
					nursing	12		
					sheltered flatlets	18		
BN5	Henfield	Terry's Cross House	n/a	n/a			20	Horsham
BN14	Worthing	The Priory	41	2			43	West Worthing
BR1	Bromley	Bromley and Sheppard's Colleges	-	-	flats	40	40	Bromley North or Bromley South
		St Raphael's Christian Care Home	-	-	residential	38	49	Bromley North
					Nursing	11		
BR4	West Wickham	Burrell Mead	n/a	n/a			20	West Wickham
CT5	Whitstable	Cliff Dene	n/a	n/a	Registered beds		33	Whitstable
CT8	Westgate-on-Sea	St Mildred's Court Eventide Home	n/a	n/a			23	Westgate-on-Sea
RH2	Reigate	Dovers	34	4			38	Reigate
SM2	Sutton	Eothen Homes Ltd	24		nursing home	14	38	Sutton
SM6	Wallington	Ryelands	n/a	n/a	Registered beds		36	Wallington
TN2	Tunbridge Wells	Milward House	-	-	care	13	45	Tunbridge Wells
					nursing	15		
					sheltered flatlets	17		
		Rosset Holt Retirement Home	18	-			18	Tunbridge Wells
		Sunset Lodge	n/a	n/a			27	Tunbridge Wells
TN39	Bexhill-on-Sea	Richmond	n/a	n/a	Registered beds		38	Bexhill
South West								
BA1	Bath	Stratton House	28	2			30	Bath Spa
BA2	Bath	Smallcombe House	n/a	n/a	men and women		30	Bath Spa
					flats	2		
					respite places	2		
BA5	Wells	Cathedral View Nursing Home	-	-	residential	3	54	Castle Cary or Bath Spa
					Nursing	51		

Postcode	Location	Name	S	D/T	Other		Total	Railway Station
		Wookey Hole Nursing Home	-	-	Nursing	44	88	Castle Cary or Bath Spa
					EMI	44		
BH8	**Bournemouth**	Exton Court	n/a	n/a			15	Bournemouth
BH15	**Poole**	Maidment Court	n/a	n/a	Registered beds	35	35	Poole
BS6	**Weston-super-Mare**	The Müller Homes for the Elderly	22	2			24	Weston-super-Mare
	Bristol	Ruth Cowell Home	n/a	n/a			23	Bristol Temple Meads
BS14	**Bristol**	Whitchurch Christian Nursing Home	n/a	n/a			50	Bristol Temple Meads
BS23	**Weston-super-Mare**	Dewdown House	n/a	n/a			40	Weston-super-Mare
BS40	**Bristol**	Omega – Winford Manor	13	30	flats	5	49	Bristol Temple Meads
					cottage	1		
DT9	**Sherborne**	Bible Fellowship Eventide Trust	11	2			13	Sherborne
EX8	**Exmouth**	Hulham House Eventide Home	n/a	n/a	men and women		24	Exmouth
EX8	**Exmouth**	Moreton	n/a	n/a	Registered beds		35	Exmouth
EX10	**Sidmouth**	Rose Lawn Retirement Home	n/a	n/a			18	Honiton
PL7	**Plymouth**	St Vincent's Nursing Home	12	8			20	Plymouth
TQ1	**Torquay**	Walmer House Retirement Home	n/a	n/a			19	Torquay
TQ14	**Teignmouth**	Charterhouse Christian Residential Home	n/a	n/a			20	Teignmouth
TR11	**Falmouth**	Langholme	n/a	n/a	Registered beds		36	Falmouth Town
WR5	**Worcester**	Worcester Christian Nursing Home	-	-	Nursing	50	90	Worcester Foregate Street
					EMI	30		
					YPD	10		
NORTHERN IRELAND								
BT18	**Holywood**	Sir Samuel Kelly Memorial Eventide Home	n/a	n/a			32	*Rail:* Holywood
SCOTLAND								
AB1	**Aberdeen**	Rubislaw Park	30	-			30	Aberdeen
AB3	**Stonehaven**	Clashfarquhar House	20	-			20	Stonehaven
AB10	**Aberdeen**	Ashley Lodge Home	38	4			42	Aberdeen
AB31	**Banchory**	Bellfield Home	21	12			33	Aberdeen
AB33	**Aberdeen**	Balmedie House	18	6			24	Aberdeen
DD5	**Dundee**	Duneaves Home	18	-			18	Dundee
DG1	**Dumfries**	Devorgilla House Home	20	-			20	Dumfries
EH5	**Edinburgh**	Eagle Lodge Eventide Home	n/a	n/a			30	Edinburgh
EH9	**Edinburgh**	Sunnyside Home	n/a	n/a	also sheltered housing		30	Edinburgh
EH9	**Edinburgh**	The Elms Home	41	-			41	Edinburgh
	Edinburgh	Morlich House	n/a	n/a			23	Edinburgh
EH14	**Edinburgh**	Davidson House	n/a	n/a			30	Edinburgh
EH15	**Edinburgh**	Queen's Bay Lodge	22	8			30	Edinburgh
EH19	**Bonnyrigg**	Nazareth House, Bonnyrigg	26	14			40	Edinburgh
EH20	**Loanhead**	Mayburn House Home	24	4			28	Edinburgh
EH34	**Tranent**	Tyneholm House Nursing Home	n/a	n/a			34	Edinburgh
EH41	**Haddington**	Florabank Home Ltd	n/a	n/a			20	Edinburgh
EH42	**Dunbar**	St Andrew's Home	13	-			13	Dunbar
FK2	**Falkirk**	St Margaret's	30	-	with dementia		30	Polmont
G12	**Glasgow**	Baxter House Home	44	22			66	Glasgow Queen Street
G32	**Glasgow**	Tollcross Mansionhouse	n/a	n/a			22	Carntyne
G42	**Glasgow**	Queen Mary House Home	24	4			28	Crosshill
G44	**Glasgow**	Williamwood House	20	10			30	Muirend
G46	**Glasgow**	Eastwoodhill Home	37	-			37	Giffnock
G84	**Helensburgh**	Clyde View Home	28	-			28	Helensburgh
IV2	**Inverness**	Cameron House	26	4	for confused people		30	Inverness
IV12	**Nairn**	Whinnieknowe Home	21	3			24	Nairn
IV25	**Dornoch**	Oversteps Home	11	8			19	Ardgay
IV51	**Portree**	Budhmor Home	30	-			30	Kyle of Lochalsh
KA 7	**Ayr**	Cumnor Hall Home	27	-			27	Ayr
KA22	**Ardrossan**	South Beach House Home	35	10			45	Ardrossan South Beach
KA36	**Kilmarnock**	Dunselma Home	23	4			27	Ayr
KW14	**Thurso**	Achvarasdal Home	16	6			22	Thurso
KY6	**Glenrothes**	Leslie House Home	27	2			29	Markinch
ML3	**Hamilton**	Wellhall Home	25	4			29	Hamilton West
ML11	**Lanark**	Auchlochan Trust	70	20	larger rooms	10	111	Hamilton Central
					flats	11		
PA5	**Johnstone**	Adams House	-	-	long term	28	30	Johnstone
					respite care	2		
PA23	**Dunoon**	Invereck Home	21	4			25	Gourock
PA28	**Campbeltown**	Auchinlee Home	19	-			19	None near
PH12	**Blairgowrie**	Belmont Castle Home	28	-			28	Perth
PH16	**Pitlochry**	Chequers Home	22	2			24	Pitlochry
ZE1	**Shetland**	Walter and Joan Gray Home	16	16			32	None near
WALES								
CF4	**Cardiff**	Northlands Eventide Home	-	-	men and women	28	33	Cardiff Central
					respite place	1		
					day-care	4		
CF6	**Penarth**	Homesdale Eventide Home	16	4			20	Penarth
CF64	**Dinas Powis**	Bethel House	n/a	n/a			39	Dinas Powis
	Penarth	Morel Court	30	-			30	Penarth

RESIDENTIAL & NURSING HOMES FOR ELDERLY PEOPLE

See also Sheltered Housing on Page 129.

A

***Achvarasdal Home**, Reay, Thurso KW14 7RR
Unit Manager: Mrs Alison Cook. Admin staff 1, Other staff 17. *CC* No.SCO 24366. Began n/a; Church of Scotland. Turnover n/a.
☎ 01847 811 226

***Acorn Retirement Home**, 102 Birmingham Road, Walsall WS1 2NJ
Proprietor: Mr Lloyd Davies. *Deputy Manager:* Miss Ruth Greenfield. Executive staff 4, Other staff 23. Began 1986; interdenominational. Turnover £232,000 to year end Apr 99.
☎ 01922 624 314 Mobile 07767 426 700 🖷 01922 634 549

***Adams House**, 136 Auchenlodment Road, Elderslie, Johnstone PA5 9NX
Unit Manager: Mrs Janet Smith. Admin staff 1, Other staff 32. *CC* No.SCO 24366. Began 1992; Church of Scotland. Turnover n/a.
☎ 01505 337 322 🖷 01505 337 872

Aigburth, 21 Manor Road, Oadby, Leicester LE2 2LL
Home Manager: Mrs Sarah Haines. Staff n/a. *CC* Began 1963; Methodist. Methodist Homes for the Aged, open to all. Turnover n/a.
☎ 0116 271 5086 🖷 0116 271 4288

Alexandra House, Marine Parade, Dovercourt, Harwich CO12 3JY
Home Manager: Mrs Eileen Tutssel. Staff n/a. Began 1962; Methodist. Methodist Homes for the Aged, open to all. Turnover n/a.
☎ 01255 503 340 🖷 01255 554 693

Alver Bank Eventide Home, West Road, Clapham, London SW4 7DL
Officers-in-Charge: Auxilliary Captains Edward & Doreen Bland. Admin staff 3, Other staff 14. *CC* Began 1959; Salvation Army. Turnover n/a. Men and women.
☎ 020 7627 8061 🖷 020 7720 2150
Sheltered Housing: 1 Alver Court, Alver Bank, West Road, Clapham, London SW4 7DH
Independent Housing: *Liaison Officer:* Brigadier Clifford Honeyball, 2 Mayfield Close, West Road, Clapham, London SW4 7DH

***Arden Valley Christian Nursing Home**, Bearley Cross, Wootton Wawen, Solihull B95 6DR
Home Manager: Carole Underwood. Other staff 60. Began 1997; interdenominational. Trinity Care plc. Turnover n/a.
Email: ardenvalley@trinitycare.co.uk
☎ 01789 731 168 🖷 01789 731 883

Ashley House, 56 Forest Road, Bordon GU35 0XT
Project Manager: Mr Brian Gavigan. Staff 35. *CC* Began 1987; interdenominational. Care division of the Shaftesbury Housing Group. Turnover n/a.
☎ 01420 489 877 🖷 01420 474 445

***Ashley Lodge Home**, 253 Great Western Road, Aberdeen AB10 6PP
Unit Manager: Mr Bill Campbell. Other staff 35. *CC* No.SCO 24366. Began 1950; Church of Scotland. Turnover n/a.
☎ 01224 585 558

***Auchinlee Home**, Campbeltown PA28 6EN
Unit Manager: Miss Jill Slater. Admin staff 2, Other staff 17. *CC* No.SCO 24366. Began n/a; Church of Scotland. Turnover n/a.
☎ 01586 552 568

Auchlochan Trust, Auchlochan House, New Trows Road, Lesmahagow, Lanark ML11 0JS
Manager: Mr Andrew Brown. Admin staff 6, Other staff 120. *CC* Began 1974; interdenominational. Turnover n/a.
☎ 01555 893 592 🖷 01555 894 919

***Balmedie House**, Balmedie, Aberdeen AB33 8XU
Unit Manager: Mrs Sheila Crowe. Other staff 22. *CC* No.SCO 24366. Began 1937; Church of Scotland. Turnover n/a.
☎ 01358 742 244

***Baxter House Home**, 8 Lowther Terrace, Glasgow G12 0RN
Unit Manager: Mr James Lindup. Admin staff 1, Other staff 46. *CC* No.SCO 24366. Began n/a; Church of Scotland. Turnover n/a.
☎ 0141 334 1231

***Bebington Christian Nursing Home**, Heath Road, Bebington, Wirral CH63 2HB
Business Manager: Mr John Wilson. Other staff n/a. Began 1987; interdenominational. Trinity Care plc. Turnover n/a.
Email: bebington@trinitycare.co.uk
☎ 0151 609 1100 🖷 0151 608 9098

***Bellfield Home**, 1 Dee Street, Banchory AB31 3XS
Unit Manager: Mrs Sandra Johnston. Admin staff 1, Other staff 19. *CC* No.SCO 24366. Began 1971; Church of Scotland. Turnover n/a.
☎ 01330 822 692

***Belmont Castle Home**, Meigle, Blairgowrie PH12 8TH
Unit Manager: Mrs Sheila Murray. Admin staff 1, Other staff 28. *CC* No.SCO 24366. Began n/a; Church of Scotland. Turnover n/a.
☎ 01828 640 244

Berwick Grange, 5 Otley Road, Harrogate HG2 0DJ
Home Manager: Miss Margaret Boland. Other staff 28. *CC* Began 1946; Methodist. Methodist Homes for the Aged, open to all. Turnover n/a.
☎ 01423 566 196 🖷 01423 536 790

Bethany House, Gamull Lane, Ribbleton, Preston PR2 6TQ
Matron: Miss Marian Hughes. *Chairman of the Trust:* Rev Edwin Holland. Admin staff 1, Other staff 13. *CC* No.511538. Began 1987; non-denominational. Turnover £143,000 to year end Mar 98. For committed, elderly Christians.
☎ 01772 792 226 🖷 01772 792 226

Bethel House, Cross Common Road, Dinas Powis CF64 4YB
Manager: Mrs Betty Iveson. Admin staff 5, Other staff 30. *CC* No.514184. Began 1983; interdenominational. Hebron Hall Ltd. Turnover £314,000 to year end Apr 98.
☎ 029 2051 3162

For additional information see List on Pages 107–109

Bible Fellowship Eventide Trust, Gainsborough House, 48 Gainsborough, Milborne Port, Sherborne DT9 5BB
Housekeeper: Corrinne Vaughan. Other staff 3. ***CC*** No.273736. Began 1978; evangelical. Turnover £10,000–50,000 to year end Dec 98.
☎ 01963 250 684
Correspondence to: *Secretary:* Derrick Nadal, 4 Manor Gardens, Barnstone, Nottingham NG13 9JL
☎ 01949 860 416

Brackloon House Pilgrim Homes, Melbury Street, Dawdon, Seaham SR7 7NE
Manager: Mrs L Yule. Other staff 11. ***CC*** No.242266. Began 1984; non-denominational. Turnover n/a.
☎ 0191 581 7253 🖷 0191 581 0988

Bradbury Eventide Home, 2 Roots Hall Drive, Southend-on-Sea SS2 6DA
Officer-in-Charge: Captain Mary Boyd. Admin staff 3. ***CC*** Began n/a; Salvation Army. Turnover n/a. Accommodation for men and women; disabled places.
☎ 01702 435 838

Brighton and Lady Anne Treves Memorial Pilgrim Homes, 35 Egremont Place, Brighton BN2 2GB
Manager: Mr D Couling. Other staff 24. ***CC*** No.242266. Began 1879; non-denominational. Turnover n/a.
☎ 01273 606 940 🖷 01273 692 640

Bromley and Sheppard's Colleges, Chaplain's House, Bromley College, London Road, Bromley BR1 1PE
Chaplain & Clerk to the Trustees: Rev Edward Morrow. Admin staff 2, Other staff 4. ***CC*** No.210337. Began 1666; Anglican. Turnover £164,508 to year end Dec 96. Providing unfurnished flats for widow(er)s of Anglican clergy and retired Anglican clergy and their spouses.
☎ 020 8460 4712 🖷 020 8460 4712

***Brookfield Christian Care Home**, Little Bury, Oxford OX4 5UY
Home Manager: Wendy Champion. Other staff 100. Began 1999; interdenominational. Trinity Care plc. Turnover n/a.
Email: brookfield@trinitycare.co.uk
☎ 01865 779 888 🖷 01865 779 444

***Budhmor Home**, Portree IV51 9DJ
Unit Manager: Mrs Evelyn Marquis. Admin staff 1, Other staff 17. ***CC*** No.SCO 24366. Began n/a; Church of Scotland. Turnover n/a.
☎ 01478 612 012

Burrell Mead, 47 Beckenham Road, West Wickham BR4 0QS
Head of Home: Mrs June Parke. *Chairman:* Mr Alan Bowen. Admin staff 1, Other staff 30. ***CC*** No.16397 Began 1964; Baptist. Turnover £302,500 to year end Aug 98.
☎ 020 8776 0455

***Cameron House**, Culduthel, Inverness IV2 4YG
Unit Manager: Mr Donald MacAskill. Admin staff 2, Other staff 26. ***CC*** No.SCO 24366. Began n/a; Church of Scotland. Turnover n/a. For confused people.
☎ 01463 243 241

***Cathedral View Nursing Home**, 19 Wookey Hole Road, Wells BA5 2NN
Home Manager: Linda Hallet. Other staff 64. Began 1995; interdenominational. Trinity Care plc. Turnover n/a.
Email: cathedralview@trinitycare.co.uk
☎ 01749 674 137 🖷 01749 676 921

Cedar Lawn, Cedar Close, Stratford-upon-Avon CV37 6UP
Home Manager: To be appointed. Staff n/a. ***CC*** Began 1975; Methodist. Turnover n/a. Methodist Homes for the Aged, open to all.
☎ 01789 205 882 🖷 01789 292 752

The Cedars Christian Residential Home, 22 Redlake Road, Pedmore, Stourbridge DY9 0SA
Proprietor: Mrs Carole Jenkins. Admin staff 2, Other staff 30. Began 1983; interdenominational. Turnover n/a.
☎ 01562 882 299

***Chandler's Ford Christian Nursing Home**, Winchester Road, Chandler's Ford, Eastleigh SO53 2GL
Home Manager: Mrs Ann Jones. Other staff 70. Began 1995; interdenominational. Trinity Care plc. Turnover n/a.
Email: chandlersford@trinitycare.co.uk
☎ 023 8026 7963 🖷 023 8026 7980

Charterhouse Christian Residential Home, Second Drive, Dawlish Road, Teignmouth TQ14 8TL
Proprietors: Mr David & Mrs Joan Pope. Other staff 14. Began 1988; interdenominational. Turnover £200,000 to year end Jan 95. For elderly, mentally handicapped, infirm people.
☎ 01626 774 481

***Chequers Home**, 12 Atholl Road, Pitlochry PH16 5DH
Unit Manager: Mrs R Boa. Admin staff 2, Other staff 19. ***CC*** No.SCO 24366. Began n/a; Church of Scotland. Turnover n/a.
☎ 01796 472 521

***Churchfield Christian Care Centre**, Millers Court, Radford, Nottingham NG7 3DP
Home Manager: Ian Davidson. Other staff 93. Began 1989; interdenominational. Trinity Care plc. Turnover n/a.
Email: churchfield@trinitycare.co.uk
☎ 0115 942 2317 🖷 0115 979 0074

***Clashfarquhar House**, Robert Street, Stonehaven AB3 2DJ
Unit Manager: Mrs Brenda Fraser. Admin staff 5, Other staff 21. ***CC*** No.SCO 24366. Began n/a; Church of Scotland. Turnover n/a.
☎ 01569 762 438

Claybourne, Turnhurst Road, Chell, Stoke-on-Trent ST6 6LA
Home Manager: Annemarie Walton. Other staff 52. ***CC*** No.21854. Began 1998; Methodist. Methodist Homes for the Aged, open to all. Turnover n/a. Specialist dementia care.
☎ 01782 790 500 🖷 01782 832 642

Cliff Dene, 11 Marine Parade, Tankerton, Whitstable CT5 2BQ
Home Manager: Ms Jennifer Charlton. Staff n/a. ***CC*** No.21854. Began 1946; Methodist. Methodist Homes for the Aged, open to all. Turnover n/a.
☎ 01227 273 209 🖷 01227 265 690

***Clyde View Home**, 12 East Montrose Street, Helensburgh G84 7HP
Unit Manager: Mr Swaran Rakhra. Admin staff 2, Other staff 21. ***CC*** No.SCO 24366. Began n/a; Church of Scotland. Turnover n/a.
☎ 01436 674 529

Coed Craig, Tan y Bryn Road, Rhos-on-Sea, Colwyn Bay LL28 4AD
Home Manager: Mrs Jean Cheeseman. Staff n/a. ***CC*** Began 1994; Methodist. Methodist Homes for the Aged, open to all. Turnover n/a. Residential and dementia care.
☎ 01492 544 075 🖷 01492 543 353

For additional information see List on Pages 107–109

Concern in Action Housing Association, Hamilton House, King Street, Salford M6 7GY
Manager: Mr E Costello. Other staff 52. ***CC*** Began 1979; non-denominational. Turnover n/a.
☎ 0161 736 3189 🖷 0161 736 4886

Connell Court, 22 Weld Road, Southport PR8 2DL
Home Manager: Mrs Doreen Whitlow. Staff n/a. ***CC*** Began 1976; Methodist. Methodist Home for the Aged, open to all. Turnover n/a.
☎ 01704 560 657 🖷 01704 551 983

A

***The Cottage Christian Nursing Home**, Granville Road, Newport TF10 7EQ
Home Manager: Christine Blakemore. Other staff 74. Began 1995; interdenominational. Trinity Care plc. Turnover n/a.
☎ 01952 825 557 🖷 01952 820 883

Cromwell House, Cecil Road, Norwich NR1 2QJ
Home Manager: Mr Jeffrey Carnell. Staff n/a. ***CC*** No.21854. Began 1969; Methodist. Methodist Homes for the Aged, open to all. Turnover n/a.
☎ 01603 625 961 🖷 01603 660 581

***Cumnor Hall Home**, 18 Racecourse View, Ayr KA7 2TY
Unit Manager: Mr Wilson Meredith. Other staff 32. ***CC*** No.SCO 24366. Began n/a; Church of Scotland. Turnover n/a.
☎ 01292 266 450

Davidson House Eventide Home, 266 Colinton Road, Edinburgh EH14 1DT
Officer-in-Charge: Mr Francis Watts. Admin staff 4. ***CC*** Began n/a; Salvation Army. Turnover n/a. Men and women.
☎ 0131 441 2117

The Dell, 45 Cotmer Road, Oulton Broad, Lowestoft NR33 9PL
Manager: Mrs Betty Muffett. Admin staff 3, Other staff 17. Began 1955; Seventh-Day Adventist. Turnover n/a.
☎ 01502 572 591

***Devorgilla House Home**, 33 George Street, Dumfries DG1 1EH
Unit Manager: Mrs Anne MacLeod. Admin staff 1, Other staff 18. ***CC*** No.SCO 24366. Began n/a; Church of Scotland. Turnover n/a.
☎ 01387 254 007

Dewdown House, 64 Beach Road, Weston-super-Mare BS23 4BE
Officer-in-Charge: Major Dorothy Crosswell. Staff n/a. ***CC*** Began 1959; Salvation Army. Turnover n/a.
☎ 01934 417 125

The Dorothea Trust, 32 Park Avenue, Bedford MK40 2LR
Manager: Mr M O'Searle. Staff n/a. ***CC*** Began 1968; interdenominational. Turnover n/a.
☎ 01234 359 103 🖷 01234 342 116

Dovers, 9 Doversgreen Road, Reigate RH2 8BU
Home Manager: Ms Glenys Scadden. Other staff 61. ***CC*** No.207493. Began 1948; non-denominational. Turnover n/a. Supported by the Field Lane Foundation.
☎ 01737 244 513

***The Downs Christian Nursing Home**, Laburnam Avenue, Hove BN3 7JW
Home Manager: Glynis Whitmore. Other staff 50. Began 1999; interdenominational. Trinity Care plc. Turnover: first year of operation. Care for frail elderly.
Email: thedowns@trinitycare.co.uk
☎ 01273 746 611 🖷 01273 737 314

The Mildred Duff Memorial Eventide Home, 73 Happisburgh Road, North Walsham NR28 9HD
Officer-in-Charge: Major Jean Bradley. Executive staff 4. ***CC*** Began n/a; Salvation Army. Turnover n/a. For men and women.
☎ 01692 403 292 🖷 01692 404 778

***Duneaves Home**, 7 Claypotts Road, Broughty Ferry, Dundee DD5 1BX
Unit Manager: To be appointed. Other staff 13. ***CC*** No.SCO 24366. Began n/a; Church of Scotland. Turnover n/a. For ladies.
☎ 01382 738 559

***Dunselma Home**, 55 Main Road, Fenwick, Kilmarnock KA36 6DR
Unit Manager: Miss Agnes Neil. Admin staff 1, Other staff 21. ***CC*** No.SCO 24366. Began n/a; Church of Scotland. Turnover n/a.
☎ 01560 600 218

Eagle Lodge Eventide Home, 488 Ferry Road, Edinburgh EH5 2DL
Officer-in-Charge: Major Jeanette Parker. Admin staff 4. ***CC*** Began n/a; Salvation Army. Turnover n/a. Men and women.
☎ 0131 551 1611 🖷 0131 552 5673

Eastwood Lodge, 61 Rayleigh Avenue, Eastwood, Leigh-on-Sea SS9 5DN
Home Manager: Mrs Jill Woolsenden. Other staff 49. ***CC*** No.207493. Began 1957; non-denominational. Turnover n/a. Supported by the Field Lane Foundation.
☎ 01702 525 200 🖷 01702 523 533

***Eastwoodhill Home**, 238 Fenwick Road, Giffnock, Glasgow G46 6UU
Unit Manager: Mrs Sally Marney. Admin staff 1, Other staff 21. ***CC*** No.SCO 24366. Began n/a; Church of Scotland. Turnover n/a.
☎ 0141 638 5127

Eckling Grange Ltd, Norwich Road, Dereham NR20 3BB
Manager: Mr Peter Baldwin. Admin staff 6, Other staff 85. ***CC*** No.251534. Began 1960; interdenominational. Turnover £828,000 to year end Mar 98. Residential and nursing Christian care home and sheltered accommodation for the elderly.
Email: eckling.grange@btinternet.com
☎ 01362 692 520 🖷 01362 690 278

***The Elms Home**, 148 Whitehouse Loan, Edinburgh EH9 2EZ
Unit Manager: Mrs E Waddell. Admin staff 1, Other staff 24. ***CC*** No.SCO 24366. Began n/a; Church of Scotland. Turnover n/a.
☎ 0131 447 4924

Elmside, Elmside Walk, Hitchin SG5 1HB
Home Manager: To be appointed. Staff n/a. ***CC*** Began 1966; Methodist. Methodist Homes for the Aged, open to all. Turnover n/a.
☎ 01462 451 737 🖷 01462 454 298

Engelberg, Ash Hill, Compton, Wolverhampton WV3 9DR
Home Manager: Mrs Lettie Harris. Staff n/a. ***CC*** Began 1966; Methodist. Methodist Homes for the Aged, open to all. Turnover n/a.
☎ 01902 206 13 🖷 01902 713 587

For additional information see List on Pages 107–109

Eothen Homes Ltd, Newcastle, 45 Elmfield Road, Gosforth, Newcastle upon Tyne NE3 4BB
Warden: Mrs Janet McKenzie. Staff 25. *CC* Began 1950; interdenominational. Turnover n/a.
☎ 0191 213 0707

Eothen Homes Ltd, Sutton, 31 Worcester Road, Sutton SM2 6PT
Warden: Mrs Margaret Honey. Staff 25. *CC* Began 1950; interdenominational. Turnover n/a.
☎ 020 8642 2830

Eothen Homes Ltd, Whitley Bay, Park Gardens, Whitley Bay NE26 2TX
Warden: Mrs Anne Goodwin. Staff 25. *CC* Began 1950; interdenominational. Turnover n/a.
☎ 0191 297 0707

Epworth Grange, 1 Chirmside Street, Bury BL8 2BX
Home Manager: Mrs Eileen Burns. Staff n/a. *CC* Began 1990; Methodist. Methodist Homes for the Aged, open to all. Turnover n/a.
☎ 0161 761 7500 🖷 0161 763 6630

The Ernest Luff Homes Ltd, 2 Luff Way, Garden Road, Walton on the Naze CO14 8SW
Manager: Mr Derek Carpenter. Admin staff 1, Other staff 55. *CC* No.1045920. Began 1950; interdenominational. Turnover n/a. Sheltered care.
☎ 01255 679 212

Evington Home Pilgrim Homes, Grocot Road, Evington, Leicester LE5 6AL
Manager: Mrs J Leach. Other staff 21. *CC* No.242266. Began 1954; non-denominational. Turnover n/a.
☎ 0116 273 8131

†**Exton Court**, 44 Portchester Road, Bournemouth BH8 8JZ
Manager: Mr Jonathan Ooi. Admin staff 9. Began 1982; interdenominational. Turnover n/a.
☎ 01202 555 472

Finborough Court Pilgrim Homes, Pilgrims' Way, Finborough, Stowmarket IP14 3AX
Manager: Mrs L Durrant. Other staff 24. *CC* No.242266. Began 1982; non-denominational. Turnover n/a.
☎ 01449 676 336 🖷 01449 672 408

Florabank Home Ltd, 18 Florabank Road, Haddington EH41 3LR
Manager: Mr W Smith Flett. Admin staff 3, Other staff 80. *CC* Began 1984; interdenominational. Turnover n/a.
☎ 01620 823 259 🖷 01620 823 006

Framland Pilgrim Homes, Naldertown, Wantage OX12 9DL
Manager: Mrs M Mayo. Other staff n/a. *CC* No.242266. Began 1986; non-denominational. Turnover n/a.
☎ 01235 769 876 🖷 01235 762 090

***Frodsham Christian Nursing Home**, Chapelfields, Frodsham, Warrington WA6 7BB
Home Manager: Mrs Caroline Durrant. Other staff 84. Began 1996; interdenominational. Trinity Care plc. Turnover n/a.
Email: cdurrant@trinitycare.co.uk
☎ 01928 734 743 🖷 01928 734 745

Fulwood Park, 19 Fulwood Park, Aigburth, Liverpool L17 5AD
Home Manager: Miss Katherine Kelly. Staff n/a. *CC* No.21854. Began 1948; Methodist. Methodist Homes for the Aged, open to all. Turnover n/a.
☎ 0151 727 3840 🖷 0151 726 0983

The Gables Pilgrim Homes, 9 Westcliffe Road, Southport PR8 2BW
Manager: Mrs E Isaacs. Other staff 8. *CC* No.242266. Began 1986; non-denominational. Turnover n/a.
☎ 01704 563 183 🖷 01704 563 188

Glebe Court Eventide Home, 2 Blackheath Rise, Lewisham, London SE13 7PN
Officer-in-Charge: Mr John Mills-Darrington. Admin staff 3. *CC* Began n/a; Salvation Army. Turnover n/a. Men and women.
☎ 020 8297 0637 🖷 020 8852 7298

Glen Rosa, 24 Grove Road, Ilkley LS29 9PH
Home Manager: Ms Karolyn Johnson. Staff n/a. *CC* No.21854. Began 1947; Methodist. Methodist Homes for the Aged, open to all. Turnover n/a.
☎ 01943 609 604 🖷 01943 817 363

Green Meadows, Colwell Road, Freshwater PO40 9SN
Home Manager: Mr Tony Blunden. Staff n/a. *CC* Began 1963; Methodist. Methodist Homes for the Aged, open to all. Turnover n/a.
☎ 01983 752 589 🖷 01983 755 623

Greenways, 227 Hawthorn Road, Bognor Regis PO21 2UW
Home Manager: Mrs Lynne Mitchell. Other staff 25. *CC* Began 1948; Methodist. Methodist Homes for the Aged, open to all. Turnover n/a.
☎ 01243 823 732 🖷 01243 826 309

Hall Grange, Shirley Church Road, Shirley, Croydon CR9 5AL
Home Manager: Mrs June Parke. Staff n/a. *CC* No.21854. Began 1972; Methodist. Methodist Homes for the Aged, open to all. Turnover n/a.
☎ 020 8654 1708 🖷 020 8654 4982

Handsworth, Cheshire, West Road, Bowdon, Altrincham WA14 2LA
Home Manager: Margaret Drury. Staff n/a. *CC* No.21854. Began 1971; Methodist. Methodist Homes for the Aged, open to all. Turnover n/a.
☎ 0161 928 5314 🖷 0161 929 9048

***Harleston House**, 115 Park Road, Lowestoft NR32 4HX
Officer-in-Charge: Mr John Worsfold. Admin staff 3, Other staff 19. *CC* No.226226. Began 1947; Anglican. Church Army. Turnover n/a.
☎ 01502 574 889

Harwood Court, Highburn, Cramlington NE23 6AZ
Home Manager: Mrs Margaret Danielson. Staff n/a. *CC* Began 1969; Methodist. Methodist Homes for the Aged, but open to all. Turnover n/a.
☎ 01670 712 492 🖷 01670 735 626

The Hawthorns Eventide Home, Burlington Road, Buxton SK17 9AR
Officer-in-Charge: Mrs Nicolette Chatfield. Admin staff 3. *CC* Began n/a; Salvation Army. Turnover n/a.
☎ 01298 237 00 🖷 01298 736 24

Holt House Eventide Home, Headlands Drive, Hilton Lane, Prestwich, Manchester M25 9YF
Officer-in-Charge: Major Carol Sharrard. Admin staff 3. *CC* Began n/a; Salvation Army. Turnover n/a. Men and women.
☎ 0161 773 0220 🖷 0161 798 6428

†**Homesdale Eventide Home**, 1 Homesdale Place, Penarth CF6 2BB
Head of Home: Mrs S Mattey. Admin staff 3, Other staff 13. *CC* Began 1955; interdenominational. Turnover n/a.
☎ 029 2070 7881

For additional information see List on Pages 107–109

A

Homewood, 19 Kenilworth Road, Leamington Spa CV32 5TR
Home Manager: Mrs Sandra James. Staff n/a. ***CC*** Began 1951; Methodist. Methodist Homes for the Aged, open to all. Turnover n/a.
☎ 01926 423 519 🖷 01926 421 758

Hornsey Rise Memorial Home Pilgrim Homes, Wellsborough, Nuneaton CV13 6PA
Managers: Mr & Mrs P Willis. Other staff 20. ***CC*** No.242266. Began 1974; non-denominational. Pilgrim Homes. Turnover n/a.
☎ 01455 290 219 🖷 01455 292 867

Hulham House Eventide Home, 16 Booth Way, Exmouth EX8 4PS
Officer-in-Charge: Mrs Christine Costello. Admin staff 3. ***CC*** Began n/a; Salvation Army. Turnover n/a. Accommodation for men and women.
☎ 01395 263 369

***Invereck Home**, Sandbank, Dunoon PA23 8QS
Unit Manager: Miss Sheila J Kerr. Admin staff 1, Other staff 19. ***CC*** No.SCO 24366. Began n/a; Church of Scotland. Turnover n/a.
☎ 01369 706 231

Jubilee Nursing Home (A KeyChange initiative), 51 Clifton Drive, Fairhaven, Lytham St Annes FY8 1AL
Matron: To be appointed. Admin staff 1, Other staff 10. ***CC*** Began 1992; interdenominational. Turnover n/a.
☎ 01253 735 491 🖷 01253 735 491

***Keep Hill Rest Home**, 7 Keep Hill Drive, High Wycombe HP11 1DU
Care Management Partner: Mrs Maria Edmondson. Executive staff 1, Other staff 5. Began 1983; non-denominational. Turnover £100,000 to year end Jun 98. For frail elderly.
☎ 01494 528 627

Sir Samuel Kelly Memorial Eventide Home, 39 Bangor Road, Holywood BT18 0NE
Officer-in-Charge: Mr James Hewitt. Admin staff 3. ***CC*** Began n/a; Salvation Army. Turnover n/a. Men and women.
☎ 028 9042 2293 🖷 028 9042 7361

Langholme, Arwenack Avenue, Falmouth TR11 3JP
Home Manager: Mrs Susan Kings. Staff n/a. ***CC*** No.21854. Began 1969; Methodist. Methodist Homes for the Aged, open to all. Turnover n/a.
☎ 01326 314 512 🖷 01326 317 577

***Lauriston Christian Nursing Home**, 40 The Green, St Leonards-on-Sea TN38 0SY
Home Manager: Larry Maurice. Other staff 82. Began 1997; interdenominational. Trinity Care plc. Turnover n/a. For frail elderly.
Email: lauriston@trinitycare.co.uk
☎ 01424 447 544 🖷 01424 447 522

Leonora Home Pilgrim Homes, Wood Lane, Chippenham SN15 3DY
Manager: Mrs B Kyte. Other staff 14. ***CC*** No.242266. Began 1974; non-denominational. Turnover n/a.
☎ 01249 651 613 🖷 01249 460 037

***Leslie House Home**, Leslie, Glenrothes KY6 3EP
Unit Manager: Mrs Jean C Ruddiman. Admin staff 1, Other staff 19. ***CC*** No.SCO 24366. Began n/a; Church of Scotland. Turnover n/a.
☎ 01592 741 228

Maidment Court, 47 Parkstone Road, Poole BH15 2NX
Home Manager: Mr Ivan Hadlington. Staff n/a. ***CC*** No.21854. Began 1972; Methodist. Methodist Homes for the Aged, open to all. Turnover n/a.
☎ 01202 674 423 🖷 01202 676 410

Marie Carlile House, Coley Avenue, Woking GU22 7BS
Officer-in-Charge: Capt James Etheridge. Admin staff 2, Other staff 20. ***CC*** No.226226. Began 1882; Anglican. Church Army. Turnover n/a.
☎ 01483 763 304

The Martins, Vinefields, Bury St Edmunds IP33 1YA
Home Manager: Mrs Alison Baggaley. Staff n/a. ***CC*** No.21854. Began 1962; Methodist. Turnover n/a. Methodist Homes for the Aged, open to all.
☎ 01284 753 467 🖷 01284 701 328

***Mayburn House Home**, 2 Hawthorn Gardens, Loanhead EH20 9EE
Unit Manager: Miss Rosemary Little. Admin staff 1, Other staff 19. ***CC*** No.SCO 24366. Began n/a; Church of Scotland. Turnover n/a.
☎ 0131 440 0299

Mayfields, Naylor Crescent, Netherpool Road, Ellesmere Port, South Wirral L66 1TP
Home Manager: Mrs Sybil Gardiner. Staff n/a. ***CC*** No.21854. Began 1997; Methodist. Methodist Homes for the Aged, open to all. Turnover n/a. Dementia care.
☎ 0151 356 4913 🖷 0151 356 4913

The Meadow, Meadow Drive, Muswell Hill, London N10 1PL
Home Manager: Mrs Kim Samuel. Staff n/a. ***CC*** Began 1965; Methodist. Methodist Homes for the Aged, open to all. Turnover n/a. Dementia care.
☎ 020 8883 2842 🖷 020 8442 1394

Methodist Local Preachers Mutual Aid Association, 89 High Street, Rickmansworth WD3 1EF
General Secretary: Mr Godfrey Talford. Executive staff 1, Other staff 98. ***CC*** No.213001. Began 1849; Methodist. Magazine: *Local Preachers' Magazine* (23,000 quarterly). Turnover £2,335,740 to year end Aug 98. Financial assistance to necessitous local preachers and their widow(er)s; providing suitable housing for elderly/infirm preachers.
Email: headoffice@lpma.demon.co.uk
☎ 01923 775 856

Milward House Pilgrim Homes, 6 Madeira Park, Tunbridge Wells TN2 5SZ
Manager: Miss M Waller. Other staff 28. ***CC*** No.242266. Began 1972; non-denominational. Turnover n/a.
☎ 01892 528 115 🖷 01892 518 802

Moorland House, Station Road, Hathersage, Sheffield S32 1DD
Home Manager: Mr Keith Farrow. Staff n/a. ***CC*** No.21854. Began 1949; Methodist. Methodist Homes for the Aged, open to all. Turnover n/a.
☎ 01433 650 582 🖷 01433 650 795

Morel Court, Raisdale Road, Penarth CF64 5BN
Home Manager: Mrs Sheila Bradbury. Staff n/a. ***CC*** Began 1975; Methodist. Methodist Homes for the Aged, but open to all. Turnover n/a.
☎ 029 2070 4811 🖷 029 2070 0987

For additional information see List on Pages 107–109

Moreton, 13 Drakes Avenue, Exmouth EX8 4AA
Home Manager: Mrs Ann Burrin. Staff n/a. ***CC*** No.21854. Began 1953; Methodist. Methodist Homes for the Aged, open to all. Turnover n/a.
☎ 01395 272 897 🖷 01395 223 716

***Morlich House**, West Pavilion B, 133 Grange Loan, Edinburgh EH9 2HL
Unit Manager: Mr Alex McClure. Admin staff 1, Other staff 20. ***CC*** No.SCO 24366. Began n/a; Church of Scotland. Turnover n/a.
☎ 0131 537 9538 🖷 0131 537 9533

***The Müller Homes for the Elderly**, 7 Cotham Park, Bristol BS6 6DA
Chief Executive: Mr J P Marsh. Executive staff 1, Other staff 20. ***CC*** No.1066831. Began 1983; interdenominational. Part of the George Müller Foundation. Magazine: *Report on the work* (4,000 annually). Turnover £265,000 to year end Feb 98.
☎ 0117 924 5001 🖷 0117 924 4855

Nazareth House, Blackburn, Preston New Road, Blackburn BB2 7AL
Mother Superior: Sister Louise. Staff n/a. ***CC*** Began 1912; Roman Catholic. Turnover n/a.
☎ 01254 530 00 🖷 01254 679 850

Nazareth House, Bonnyrigg, 13 Hillhead, Bonnyrigg EH19 2JF
Mother Superior: Rev Mother. Full-time staff 30. ***CC*** Began 1931; Roman Catholic. Turnover n/a.
☎ 0131 663 7191

Northlands Eventide Home, 202 North Road, Cardiff CF4 3XP
Officer-in-Charge: Mrs Jennifer Yarnham. Admin staff 3. ***CC*** Began n/a; Salvation Army. Turnover n/a. Accommodating men and women, 1 residential respite place and 4 day-care places.
☎ 029 2061 9077 🖷 029 2061 7786

Norwood, 14 Park Road, Ipswich IP1 3ST
Home Manager: Mrs Carolyn Wallace. Staff n/a. ***CC*** No.21854. Began 1979; Methodist. Methodist Homes for the Aged, open to all. Turnover n/a.
☎ 01473 257 502 🖷 01473 216 697

Notintone House Eventide Home, Sneinton Road, Nottingham NG2 4QL
Officer-in-Charge: Major Cynthia Clay. Admin staff 3. ***CC*** Began n/a; Salvation Army. Turnover n/a. Men and women.
☎ 0115 950 3788 🖷 0115 950 2060

Nyton House, Nyton Road, Westergate, Chichester PO20 6UL
Proprietors: Mr P & Mrs Mary Davis. Admin staff 3, Other staff 40. Began 1983; Christian Brethren. Turnover £600,000 to year end Apr 98.
☎ 01243 543 228 🖷 01243 543 228

Oakfield Eventide Home, 107 Bingham Road, Radcliffe-on-Trent, Nottingham NG12 2GP
Officer-in-Charge: Miss Ruth Castles. Admin staff 3. ***CC*** Began n/a; Salvation Army. Turnover n/a. Men and women.
☎ 0115 933 2316 🖷 0115 933 2274

Oaklands Lodge, Flat 40, 11 Plymyard Avenue, Eastham, Wirral CH62 6EL
Matron: Mrs Stephanie Sumbler. Admin staff 3, Other staff 45. ***CC*** Began 1986; interdenominational. Turnover n/a.
☎ 0151 334 1054

Omega – Winford Manor, Winford, Bristol BS40 8DW
Prior: Rev Canon Peter Spink. *Administrator:* Mr James Fahey. Admin staff 3, Other staff 3. ***CC*** No.280512. Began 1980; Anglican/ Roman Catholic. Magazine: *Omega News* (2,500 every four months). Turnover £196,000 to year end Mar 97. Contemplative community of men/women. Retreats, seminars, individual spiritual direction, arts, healing, conferences, residential home.
Web: members.aol.com/omegatrust/omega/omega.html
Email: omegatrust@aol.com
☎ 01275 472 262 🖷 01275 472 065

Orleans Residential Home for Elderly Christians, 8 Lathom Road, Southport PR9 0JA
Owner Managers: Mr & Mrs Jim McCallum. Admin staff 2, Other staff 23. Began 1988; non-denominational. Caring for elderly Christians in an atmosphere of love, interest and consideration.
☎ 01704 530 440 🖷 01704 549 995

***Overdale Retirement Home (A KeyChange initiative)**, 29 Kenwood Park Road, Sheffield S7 1NE
Manager: Mrs Ruth Brown. Admin staff 2, Other staff 33. ***CC*** No.700301. Began n/a; interdenominational. (Previously The Christian Alliance Home for Elderly). Turnover n/a.
☎ 0114 255 0257

***Oversteps Home**, Earls Cross Road, Dornoch IV25 3PJ
Unit Manager: Mrs Elizabeth Finlayson. Admin staff 2, Other staff 13. ***CC*** No.SCO 24366. Began n/a; Church of Scotland. Turnover n/a.
☎ 01862 810 393

A

Priceholme, Givendale Road, Scarborough YO12 6LE
Home Manager: Mrs Josephine Williams. Staff n/a. ***CC*** Began 1963; Methodist. Methodist Homes for the Aged, open to all. Turnover n/a.
☎ 01723 361 022 🖷 01723 500 159

The Priory, South Street, Tarring, Worthing BN14 7ND
Acting Home Manager: Ms Iris Jebri. Other staff 41. ***CC*** No.207493. Began 1951; non-denominational. Turnover n/a. Supported by the Field Lane Foundation.
☎ 01903 237 027

***Queen Mary House Home**, 52 Queen Mary Avenue, Glasgow G42 8DT
Unit Manager: Miss Janice Gillespie. Admin staff 2, Other staff 20. ***CC*** No.SCO 24366. Began n/a; Church of Scotland. Turnover n/a.
☎ 0141 423 2736

***Queen's Bay Lodge**, 49 Milton Road East, Edinburgh EH15 2NN
Unit Manager: Mrs Elizabeth Bennett. Admin staff 1, Other staff 30. ***CC*** No.SCO 24366. Began 1962; Church of Scotland. Turnover n/a.
☎ 0131 669 2828

Queenswood, Cliffgrove Avenue, Beeston, Nottingham NG9 4DP
Home Manager: Mrs Irene Webb. Staff n/a. ***CC*** Began 1975; Methodist. Methodist Homes for the Aged, open to all. Turnover n/a.
☎ 0115 922 1037 🖷 0155 943 6245

Rawson Eventide Home, 153 Whitechapel Road, London E1 1DP
Officers-in-Charge: Captains Alex & Janet Bishop. Admin staff 4. ***CC*** Began n/a; Salvation Army. Turnover n/a. Accommodation for men.
☎ 020 7247 9560

Richmond, Collington Lane East, Bexhill on Sea TN39 3RJ
Home Manager: Mrs Shirley Kent. Staff n/a. ***CC*** No.21854. Began 1970; Methodist. Methodist Homes for the Aged, open to all. Turnover n/a.
☎ 01424 217 688 🖷 01424 210 242

Rock House (Gold Hill Housing Association Ltd), Rock House, Austenwood Lane, Chalfont St Peter, Gerrards Cross SL9 9DF
Executive Manager: Mr Gordon Clifford. *Acting Head of Home:* Miss Pauline Gilchrist. Staff n/a. ***CC*** Began 1966; Baptist. Turnover £546,000.
☎ 01753 882 194

Rookstone Eventide Home, Lawrie Park Crescent, Sydenham, London SE26 6HH
Officer-in-Charge: Mrs Christine Fell. Admin staff 3. ***CC*** Began n/a; Salvation Army. Turnover n/a. Accommodation for men and women.
☎ 020 8778 0317 🖷 020 8778 5822

Rose Lawn Retirement Home (A KeyChange initiative), All Saints Road, Sidmouth EX10 8EX
Manager: Mrs Margaret Field. Admin staff 1, Other staff 8. ***CC*** Began n/a; interdenominational. Turnover n/a.
☎ 01395 513 876 🖷 01395 579 519

***Rosset Holt Retirement Home (A KeyChange initiative)**, Pembury Road, Tunbridge Wells TN2 3RB
Manager: Mrs Marylin Luck. Admin staff 1, Other staff 12. ***CC*** Began n/a; interdenominational. Turnover n/a.
☎ 01892 526 077

***Rubislaw Park**, Rubislaw Park Road, Aberdeen AB1 8DA
Unit Manager: Mr Bill Campbell. Admin staff 1, Other staff 19. ***CC*** No.SCO 24366. Began n/a; Church of Scotland. Turnover n/a.
☎ 01224 310 641

Ruth Cowell Pilgrim Homes, 3 Belvedere Road, Bristol BS6 7JG
Manager: Mrs J Jacob. Other staff 18. ***CC*** No.242266. Began 1968; non-denominational. Turnover n/a.
☎ 0117 973 0553 🖷 0117 970 6913

Ryelands, 15 Beddington Gardens, Wallington SM6 0JF
Home Manager: Mrs Catherine Finn. Staff n/a. ***CC*** No.21854. Began 1946; Methodist. Methodist Homes for the Aged, open to all. Turnover n/a.
☎ 020 8647 6837 🖷 020 8647 8542

***St Andrew's Home**, 34 High Street, Dunbar EH42 1JH
Unit Manager: Ms Moira Fenning. Admin staff 1, Other staff 12. ***CC*** No.SCO 24366. Began n/a; Church of Scotland. Turnover n/a.
☎ 01368 862 474

***St Andrew's Lodge**, Riber Crescent, Basford, Nottingham NG5 1LP
Home Manager: Chris Davis. Other staff 119. Began 1994; interdenominational. Trinity Care plc. Turnover n/a.
Email: cdavis@trinitycare.co.uk
☎ 0115 924 5467 🖷 0115 924 5485

†**St Angela's Residential Care Home**, 5 Litfield Place, Clifton, Bristol BS8 3LU
Matron: Sister Marie-Louise Levern. Other staff 15. ***CC*** No.229049. Began 1920; Roman Catholic. Turnover £3,000 to year end Mar 96.
☎ 0117 973 5436/5518

St Anne's Rest Home, Grange Lane, Burghwallis, Doncaster DN6 9JL
Managers: Janet Willis, Ann Holland. Other staff 10. ***CC*** Began 1986; Roman Catholic. Turnover £220,000 to year end Dec 98. For ladies.
☎ 01302 700 319 🖷 01302 708 752

St John's Home, St Mary's Road, Oxford OX4 1QE
Head of Home: Miss Mollie Burns. Admin staff 1, Other staff 41. ***CC*** Began 1874; Anglican. Turnover £378,000 to year end Mar 90.
☎ 01865 247 725 🖷 01865 247 920

St Katharine's House, Ormond Road, Wantage OX12 8EA
Warden: Commander Robin House. *Nursing and Care Manager:* Mrs Elizabeth Cranham. *Sister in charge:* Sister Mary Jennifer. Admin staff 5, Other staff 71. ***CC*** No.240513. Began 1848; Anglican. Turnover £992,000 to year end Mar 99. Residential and nursing accommodation for elderly ladies in Christian ethos within Anglican community.
☎ 01235 762 739 🖷 01235 772 105

***St Margaret's**, St Margaret's Crescent, Polmont, Falkirk FK2 0UP
Unit Manager: Miss Catherine Cairns. Admin staff 2, Other staff 26. ***CC*** No.SCO 24366. Began n/a; Church of Scotland. Turnover n/a. For people with senile dementia.
☎ 01324 716 149 🖷 01324 711 841

For additional information see List on Pages 107–109

A

†***St Marks Nursing Home**, Leasowe Road, Moreton, Wirral CH46 3RE
Manager: Mrs Evelyn Epton. Other staff 34. ***CC*** No.700269. Began 1987; Elim Pentecostal. Wirral Christian Centre Trust. Turnover n/a.
☎ 0151 605 1240 🖷 0151 606 0051

St Mary's Convent Rest Home, Ebchester, Consett DH8 0QD
Sister Superior: Sister Josephine. Admin staff 6, Other staff 6. ***CC*** Began 1934; Roman Catholic. Turnover n/a.
☎ 01207 560 288

St Mary's Convent and Nursing Home, Burlington Lane, Chiswick, London W4 2QE
Sister Superior: Sister Jennifer Anne. Admin staff 2, Other staff 70. ***CC*** Began 1910; Anglican. Turnover £888,250 to year end Mar 98. Guest house and nursing home for women.
☎ 020 8994 4641 🖷 020 8995 9796

St Mildred's Court Eventide Home, 114 St Mildred's Road, Westgate-on-Sea CT8 8RL
Officer-in-Charge: Major Lynda Snaith. Admin staff 3. ***CC*** Began n/a; Salvation Army. Turnover n/a. For men and women.
☎ 01843 831 407

***St Raphael's Christian Care Home**, 32 Orchard Road, Bromley BR1 2PS
Home Manager: Miss Lisa Shemilt. Other staff 74. Began 1996; interdenominational. Trinity Care plc. Turnover n/a.
Email: straphaels@trinitycare.co.uk
☎ 020 8313 1377 🖷 020 8460 1710

St Theresa's Home, 12 Lansdowne Road, London SW20 8AN
Matron: Mrs Channon. Staff n/a. ***CC*** Began n/a; Roman Catholic. Turnover n/a. Congregation of the Sisters of St Anne.
☎ 020 8879 7366 🖷 020 8879 1070

St Vincent's Homes, 102 Moseley Road, Birmingham B12 0HG
Principal: Mr John Moroney. Admin staff 4, Other staff 24. ***CC*** No.512992. Began 1901; Roman Catholic. Turnover £250,000 to year end Mar 92.
☎ 0121 773 7696

St Vincent's Nursing Home, 79 Fore Street, Plympton St Maurice, Plymouth PL7 INE
Administrator: Sisters of Charity. Admin staff 2, Other staff 40. ***CC*** No.215027. Began 1944; Anglican. Turnover n/a. For sick and terminally ill patients.
☎ 01752 336 205

The Sheppard Trust, 12 Lansdowne Walk, London W11 3LN
Director: Mr O J Wingate. *Assistant to the Director:* Mrs B V Ray. Admin staff 4, Other staff 3. ***CC*** No.205924. Began 1855; Anglican. Turnover £220,000 to year end Dec 98. Providing unfurnished sheltered flats for gentlewomen aged over 65 of limited means.
☎ 020 7727 5500 🖷 020 7727 7730

Shottermill House Pilgrim Homes, Liphook Road, Haslemere GU27 1NX
Manager: Mrs D Eldrett. Other staff 21. ***CC*** No.242266. Began 1990; non-denominational. Turnover n/a.
☎ 01428 661 034 🖷 01428 645 233

Singholm, 41 Naze Park Road, Walton on the Naze CO14 8JW
Home Managers: Mr Denis Bradshaw, Rita Dowdeswell. Other staff 49. ***CC*** No.207493. Began 1953; non-denominational. Turnover n/a. Supported by the Field Lane Foundation.
☎ 01255 675 842

Smallcombe House Eventide Home, Oakwood Gardens, Bathwick Hill, Bath BA2 6EJ
Officers-in-Charge: Auxiliary-Captains M & J Doyle. Admin staff 4. ***CC*** Began n/a; Salvation Army. Turnover n/a.
☎ 01225 465 694 🖷 01225 465 769

***South Beach House Home**, 7 South Crescent Road, Ardrossan KA22 8DU
Unit Manager: Mrs Gladys Watt. Admin staff 1, Other staff 25. ***CC*** No.SCO 24366. Began n/a; Church of Scotland. Turnover n/a.
☎ 01294 468 234

†**South London Mission**, Cluny Place, London SE1 4QU
Warden: Sister Pat Soule. Staff 2. Began 1968; Methodist. Turnover n/a.
☎ 020 7407 2014

Springboard Housing Association Ltd, 2a Claughton Road, Plaistow, London E13 9PN
Chief Executive: Jakki Maxham. *Housing Director:* Mrs Lynn Vickery. *Finance Director:* Mr Keith Hickey. Executive staff 5, Other staff 650. Began 1971; non-denominational. Magazine: *Newsletter* (7,500 n/a). Turnover £24,982,000 to year end Mar 98. Providing general and special needs housing in East London, Hertfordshire and Essex. Over 5,000 homes.
Email: 100651.3510@compuserve.com
☎ 020 8475 0033 🖷 020 8503 4286

Starr Hills, Ansdell Road South, Ansdell, Lytham St Annes FY8 5PG
Home Manager: Ms Lesley Standing. Staff n/a. ***CC*** No.21854. Began 1948; Methodist. Methodist Homes for the Aged, open to all. Turnover n/a.
☎ 01253 735 037 🖷 01235 732 466

Stones Place, Skellingthorpe Road, Lincoln LN6 0PA
Home Manager: Mrs Dorothy Moran. Staff n/a. ***CC*** Began 1972; Methodist. Methodist Homes for the Aged, open to all. Turnover n/a.
☎ 01522 680 295 🖷 01522 697 625

***Stoneyford Christian Nursing Home**, 173 Stoneyford Road, Sutton-in-Ashfield NG17 2DR
Acting Home Manager: Penelope Bowman. Other staff 112. Began 1989; interdenominational. Trinity Care plc. Turnover n/a. Nursing care incorporating spiritual and physical well-being.
Email: stoneyford@trinitycare.co.uk
☎ 01623 441 329 🖷 01623 511 558

Stratton House, 16 Park Lane, Bath BA1 2XH
Home Manager: Mrs Carol Britton. Staff n/a. ***CC*** Began 1953; Methodist. Methodist Homes for the Aged, open to all. Turnover n/a.
☎ 01225 421 196 🖷 01225 443 432

Sunnyside Home Eventide Home, 75 South Oswald Road, Edinburgh EH9 2HH
Officer-in-Charge: Mrs Heather Marriott. Admin staff 4. ***CC*** Began n/a; Salvation Army. Turnover n/a. Also sheltered housing, categories 1 and 2.
☎ 0131 667 6831/2 🖷 0131 667 1516

Sunset Lodge Eventide Home, Pembury Road, Tunbridge Wells TN2 3QT
Officer-in-Charge: Captain Alma Thomas. Admin staff 3. ***CC*** Began n/a; Salvation Army. Turnover n/a. Men and women.
☎ 01892 530 861 🖷 01892 533 769

For additional information see List on Pages 107–109

***Swallow Wood Christian Nursing Home**, Wath Road, Mexborough S64 9RQ
Home Manager: Margaret Mardy. Other staff 59. Began 1992; interdenominational. Trinity Care plc. Turnover n/a.
Email: swallowwood@trinitycare.co.uk
☎ 01709 571 477 Fax 01709 585 505

Terry's Cross House, Brighton Road, Woodmancote, Henfield BN5 9SX
Wardens: Mr Norman & Mrs Edna Bartley. Other staff 3. ***CC*** No.1011373. Began n/a; Anglican. Turnover £88,622 to year end May 98. For retired Anglican clergy, lay workers and missionaries.
☎ 01273 492 821

***Tollcross Mansionhouse**, 601 Tollcross Road, Glasgow G32 8TF
Unit Manager: Mrs Isabella Sharpe. Admin staff 1, Other staff 19. ***CC*** No.SCO 24366. Began n/a; Church of Scotland. Turnover n/a.
☎ 0141 778 5406

Trembaths, Talbot Way, Norton, Letchworth SG6 1UA
Home Manager: Mr Alan Dickinson. Staff n/a. ***CC*** No.21854. Began 1989; Methodist. Methodist Homes for the Aged, open to all. Turnover n/a. Nursing and residential care.
☎ 01462 481 694 Fax 01462 485 606

***Trinity Care plc**, 15 Musters Road, West Bridgford, Nottingham NG2 7PP
Chief Executive: Mr David G Henderson. *Director of Care:* Dr Mervyn Suffield. Executive staff 5, Other staff 1500. Began 1987; non-denominational. Magazine: *Trinity Times* (Circulation & frequency n/a). Turnover £13,814 to year end Mar 98. Developing and managing nursing homes and apartments for elderly people and bungalows for people with a learning disability.
Email: enquiry@trinitycare.co.uk
☎ 0115 945 5485 Fax 0115 982 1919

***Tyneholm House Nursing Home**, Pencaitland, Tranent EH34 5DJ
Proprietor: Mrs Romy Newell. *Proprietor:* Mr Paul Newell. *Matron:* Mr David Small. Admin staff 3, Other staff 47. Began 1986; non-denominational. Turnover £514,000 to year end Oct 98. Short or long stay. Inclusive holidays for elderly or disabled.
☎ 01875 340 708 Office: 01361 890 291 Fax 01875 341 240

Villa Adastra Eventide Home, 79 Keymer Road, Hassocks BN6 8QH
Officer-in-Charge: Major Ruth Curtis. Admin staff 3. ***CC*** Began n/a; Salvation Army. Turnover n/a. Men and women.
☎ 01273 842 184 Fax 01273 845 299

Walmer House Retirement Home (A KeyChange initiative), 6 Ash Hill Road, Torquay TQ1 3HZ
Administrator: Mrs Barbara Barrett. Admin staff 2, Other staff 12. ***CC*** Began n/a; interdenominational. Turnover n/a.
☎ 01803 292 734

For additional information see List on Pages 107–109

A

***Walter and Joan Gray Home**, Main Street, Scalloway, Shetland ZE1 0XJ
Unit Manager: Mrs Rosemary Blain. Other staff 13. ***CC*** No.SCO 24366. Began n/a; Church of Scotland. Turnover n/a.
☎ 01595 880 691

***Warde Aldam Christian Nursing Home**, Westfield Lane, South Elmsall, Pontefract WF9 2JX
Home Manager: Evelyn Horsfall. Other staff 75. Began 1995; interdenominational. Trinity Care plc. Turnover n/a.
Email: wardealdam@trinitycare.co.uk
☎ 01977 643 697 🖷 01977 643 452

***Wellhall Home**, 60 Wellhall Road, Hamilton ML3 9DL
Unit Manager: Miss Joyce Foster. Admin staff 2, Other staff 22. ***CC*** No.SCO 24366. Began 1957; Church of Scotland. Turnover n/a.
☎ 01698 286 151

The West Wittering Private Nursing Home, Pound Road, West Wittering, Chichester PO20 8AJ
Matron: Mrs Joy Hillary. Admin staff 3, Other staff 21. Began 1975; non-denominational. Turnover n/a.
☎ 01243 513 373 🖷 01243 511 177

Westbury, Westbury Lane, Newport Pagnell MK16 8QW
Head of Home: To be appointed. Staff n/a. ***CC*** No.21854. Began 1989; Methodist. Methodist Homes for the Aged, open to all. Turnover n/a. Dementia care provision.
☎ 01908 210 885 🖷 01908 218 428

Westhampnett Private Nursing Home, Westhampnett House, Westhampnett Road, Chichester PO18 0NT
Proprietors: Mr P & Mrs Mary Davis. Admin staff 3, Other staff 30. Began 1978; Christian Brethren. Turnover n/a.
☎ 01243 782 986

***Whinnieknowe Home**, Mill Road, Nairn IV12 5EN
Unit Manager: Mrs Agnes Lafferty. Admin staff 2, Other staff 20. ***CC*** No.SCO 24366. Began n/a; Church of Scotland. Turnover n/a.
☎ 01667 452 387

†*Whitchurch Christian Nursing Home, 95 Bristol Road, Whitchurch, Bristol BS14 0PS
Home Manager: Mrs Tina Bradshaw. Other staff 22. Began 1996; interdenominational. Trinity Care plc. Turnover n/a.
☎ 01275 892 600 🖷 01275 832 675

Willersley House, 85 Main Street, Willerby, Hull HU10 6BY
Home Manager: Mrs Barbara Bond. Staff n/a. ***CC*** No.21854. Began 1963; Methodist. Methodist Homes for the Aged, open to all. Turnover n/a.
☎ 01482 653 353 🖷 01482 659 668

***Williamwood House**, Strathtay Avenue, Netherlee, Glasgow G44 3YA
Unit Manager: Mrs Moira Jack. Admin staff 1, Other staff 22. ***CC*** No.SCO 24366. Began n/a; Church of Scotland. Turnover n/a. For people with senile dementia.
☎ 0141 637 1168

***The Willows Christian Nursing Home**, Warford Park, Faulkners Lane, Mobberley, Knutsford WA16 7AR
Home Manager: Pat Crook. Other staff 85. Began 1995; interdenominational. Trinity Care plc. Turnover n/a.
Email: pcrook@trinitycare.co.uk
☎ 01565 880 180 🖷 01565 880 068

Winchester Home Pilgrim Homes, 36 Arthur Road, Winchester SO23 7EA
Warden: Mrs G Procter. Staff n/a. ***CC*** No.242266. Began 1899; non-denominational. Turnover n/a.
☎ 01962 853 236

***Wirral Christian Centre Trust, Residential Home**, Woodchurch Road, Birkenhead CH41 2UE
Manager: Mrs Evelyn Epton. Other staff 14. ***CC*** No.700269. Began 1983; Elim Pentecostal. Turnover n/a. Also day nursery.
☎ 0151 653 8307 🖷 0151 653 4600

Woodbank, Hollybank Road, Hook Heath, Woking GU22 0JP
Home Manager: Mrs Marion Nianko. Staff n/a. ***CC*** Began 1952; Methodist. Methodist Homes for the Aged, open to all. Turnover n/a.
☎ 01483 773 684 🖷 01483 730 698

***Woodlands Christian Nursing Home**, Middlewood Road, Poynton SK12 1SH
Home Manager: Graham Seddon. Other statt 85. Began 1998; interdenominational. Trinity Care plc. Turnover n/a.
Email: gseddon@trinitycare.co.uk
☎ 01625 877 112 🖷 01625 877 113

***Woodleigh Christian Care Home**, Norfolk Drive, Mansfield NG19 7AG
Home Manager: Rita Cooper. Other staff 64. Began 1988; interdenominational. Trinity Care plc. Turnover n/a.
Email: woodleigh@trinitycare.co.uk
☎ 01623 420 459 🖷 01623 460 381

***Wookey Hole Nursing Home**, School Hill, Wookey Hole, Wells BA5 1BZ
Acting Home Manager: Lauren Biggs. Other staff 54. Began 1995; interdenominational. Trinity Care plc. Turnover n/a.
Email: wookeyhole@trinitycare.co.uk
☎ 01749 670 119 🖷 01749 673 542

***Worcester Christian Nursing Home**, London Road, Red Hill, Worcester WR5 2LG
Home Manager: Mrs Alison Skeet. Full-time staff 79, Part-time staff 13. Began 1997; interdenominational. Trinity Care plc. Turnover n/a.
Email: alisonskeet@worcester.trinitycare.co.uk
☎ 01905 354 000 Mobile: 0788 585 6428 🖷 01905 357 353

For additional information see List on Pages 107–109

RETREAT CENTRES

By Country and Postcode area (see Page 569 for explanation)
Organisations which did not supply any of this information are not listed here

S = single rooms **D/T** = number of bed spaces in double/twin rooms **L** = number of bed spaces in rooms larger than double
TS = total bed spaces (not number of rooms) **DR** = Day Room, the capacity of the largest room suitable for group use
⇌ = nearest Railway station ⊖ = nearest London Underground station

Postcode	Location	Name	S	D/T	L	Other		TS	DR	Railway Station
ENGLAND										
Anglia										
AL2	**St Albans**	All Saints Pastoral Centre	72	48	-			120	120	⇌ Radlett
		SPEC Centre	n/a	n/a	n/a			60	-	⇌ Radlett
CB1	**Cambridge**	Mill Green House	-	2	-			2	30	⇌ Audley End or Cambridge
CB7	**Ely**	Bishop Woodford House	32	2	3			37	50	⇌ Ely
CB8	**Newmarket**	Sisters of St Louis	4	8	-			12	-	⇌ Newmarket
CM3	**Chelmsford**	Diocesan House of Retreat	22	2	-	self-catering cottage	5	29	30	⇌ Chelmsford
		Diocesan Pastoral Centre, The Barn	7	8	-			15	60	⇌ Chelmsford
MK43	**Bedford**	Priory of Our Lady of Peace and Monastery of Christ our Saviour	8	8	-			16	40	⇌ Bedford
NR20	**Dereham**	The Old Bakery	3	10	-			13	15	⇌ Norwich
NR35	**Bungay**	All Hallows Community Retreat Houses:								
		All Hallows House	3	6	-			9	-	⇌ Norwich or Beccles or Diss
		Holy Cross House	11	-	-			11	-	⇌ Norwich or Beccles or Diss
		St Gabriel's Centre	26	48	56			130	-	⇌ Norwich or Beccles or Diss
		St Mary's Lodge	-	-	-	non-residential		-	n/a	⇌ Norwich or Beccles or Diss
		St Michael's Centre	18	8	-			26	-	⇌ Norwich or Beccles or Diss
		St Raphael's Centre	-	-	-	non-residential		-	40	⇌ Norwich or Beccles or Diss
		Quiet Waters Christian Retreat House	1	14	-			15	25	⇌ Halesworth
PE17	**Huntingdon**	Houghton Chapel Retreat	-	2	28			30	50	⇌ Huntingdon
PE18	**Huntingdon**	St Francis' House	17	6	-			23	18	⇌ Huntingdon
PE32	**King's Lynn**	Massingham St Mary Retreat Centre	10	20	-	self-catering bungalows	2	30	30	⇌ Kings Lynn
London										
E2	**London**	Society of St Margaret	6	2	-			8	25	⇌ Liverpool Street ⊖ Liverpool Street
N14	**London**	Benedictine Centre for Spirituality	6	6	-			12	100	⊖ Oakwood
NW7	**London**	Damascus House	63	24	-			87	100	⇌ Mill Hill Broadway ⊖ Mill Hill East
SE4		The Fountain Gate Community	-	-	-	non-residential		-	n/a	⇌ Greenwich
SW15		Kairos Centre	7	4	12			23	120	⇌ Putney Bridge
SW19	**London**	Marie Reparatrice Retreat Centre	29	-	-			29	45	⇌ Wimbledon ⊖ Wimbledon
Midlands										
B61	**Bromsgrove**	Community for Reconciliation	4	16	18			38	60	⇌ Longbridge
B98	**Redditch**	Berean Place	n/a	n/a	n/a			n/a	40	⇌ Redditch
CV33	**Leamington Spa**	Offa House	17	12	-	cottage	8	37	50	⇌ Leamington Spa
DE7	**Ilkeston**	Morley Retreat and Conference House	24	10	-			34	34	⇌ Derby
DE56	**Ripley**	Convent of St Laurence	24	6	-			30	-	⇌ Belper
LE7	**Leicester**	Launde Abbey	15	42	-			57	50	⇌ Oakham
LE67	**Coalville**	Mount St Bernard Abbey	20	-	-			20	-	⇌ Loughborough
NN6	**Northampton**	Ecton House	27	2	-			29	100	⇌ Northampton or Wellingborough
ST15	**Stone**	Shallowford House	15	48	-			63	40	⇌ Stafford or Norton Bridge
WS15	**Rugeley**	Crocus Ministries	-	-	-	non-residential		-	n/a	⇌ Rugeley Trent Valley
North East										
DH8	**Consett**	Minsteracres Retreat Centre	n/a	n/a	n/a			70	-	⇌ Riding Mill
H3	**Harrogate**	Barrowby House	9	22	-	flat	2	33	60	⇌ Harrogate
LN2	**Lincoln**	Edward King House	5	22	3			30	80	⇌ Lincoln Central
LS29	**Ilkley**	Myddelton Lodge	29	20	-			49	70	⇌ Ilkley
NE44	**Riding Mill**	Shepherds Dene	7	28	-			35	40	⇌ Riding Mill
NE66	**Chatton**	Northumbria Community Trust Ltd	n/a	n/a	n/a			n/a	n/a	⇌ Berwick upon Tweed
YO21	**Whitby**	St Oswald's Pastoral Centre	8	8	-			16	40	⇌ Sleights
YO62	**York**	The Grange	16	8	4			28	55	⇌ York or Malton or Thirsk
North West										
BB7	**Clitheroe**	Whalley Abbey	2	30	6			38	100	⇌ Whalley
CA4	**Carlisle**	The Bernard Delany OP Ecumenical and Peace Centre	4	2	15			21	-	⇌ Carlisle
CH1	**Chester**	Chester Retreat House	23	2	-			25	30	⇌ Chester
CH48	**Wirral**	Sisters of Jesus Way Retreat House	8	4	-			12	-	⇌ West Kirby
CW2	**Crewe**	Wistaston Hall Oblate Retreat Centre	2	36	6			44	150	⇌ Crewe
L15	**Liverpool**	Cenacle Retreat and Conference Centre	-	-	-	non-residental		25	-	⇌ Liverpool Lime Street
L35	**Prescot**	Loyola Hall - Jesuit Spirituality Centre	46	2	9			57	100	⇌ Rainhill
LA2	**Lancaster**	Littledale Trust	1	12	24	flat	3	40	50	⇌ Lancaster
LA5	**Carnforth**	Monastery of Our Lady of Hyning	5	30	-			35	35	⇌ Carnforth
M16	**Manchester**	Cenacle Retreat and Conference Centre	-	-	-	non-residential		-	n/a	⇌ Manchester Victoria or Manchester Piccadilly
SK10	**Macclesfield**	Savio House	36	2	32			70	64	⇌ Macclesfield
SK23	**Stockport**	Whaley Hall Community of the King of Love	3	26	3			32	-	⇌ Whaley Bridge
SY14	**Malpas**	St Joseph's Retreat and Conference Centre	36	16	-			52	50	⇌ Chester or Whitchurch (Salop)

Retreat Centres

Postcode	Location	Name	S	D/T	L	Other		TS	DR	Railway Station
South Central										
HA8	**Edgware**	Convent of St Mary at the Cross	n/a	n/a	n/a			8	50	⇌ Mill Hill Broadway ⊖ Edgware
OX2	**Oxford**	The Cherwell Centre Ltd	13	16	-			29	50	⇌ Oxford
OX12	**Wantage**	St Mary's Convent	14	2	-			18	-	⇌ Didcot Parkway or Oxford
OX18	**Oxford**	Burford Priory	4	8	-			12	30	⇌ Charlbury or Oxford
OX33	**Oxford**	Stanton House	5	10	-			15	20	⇌ Oxford
PO17	**Fareham**	Park Place Pastoral Centre	31	22	6			59	200	⇌ Fareham
PO33	**Ryde**	Quarr Abbey	9	-	-			9	-	⇌ Ryde Esplanade
RG9	**Henley-on-Thames**	Congregation of Marian Fathers	13	66	133			212	250	⇌ Henley-on-Thames
RG14	**Newbury**	Elmore Abbey	4	-	-			4	-	⇌ Newbury
RG17	**Hungerford**	St Cassian's Centre	5	58	-	cottage	1	64	50	⇌ Kintbury
RG18	**Newbury**	Cold Ash Retreat and Conference Centre	28	6	-			34	40	⇌ Thatcham
SL4	**Windsor**	Clewer Spirituality Centre	28	-	-	twin	4	36	40	⇌ Windsor and Eton Riverside or Windsor Central
SL5	**Ascot**	Ascot Priory	n/a	n/a	n/a		20	20	40	⇌ Ascot or Bracknell
SO4	**Southampton**	The Montfort Missionaries and Daughters of Wisdom	17	2	-			19	60	⇌ Southampton Central
SO31	**Hindhead**	Cenacle Retreat House	21	18	-			39	40	⇌ Haslemere
South East										
BN3	**Hove**	The Monastery of Christ the Saviour	1	-	-	mainly non-residential		1	12	⇌ Brighton
BN6	**Hassocks**	Priory of Our Lady	18	14	4			36	40	⇌ Hassocks
BR4	**West Wickham**	Emmaus Retreat and Conference Centre	9	64	-	2 flats	5	77	80	⇌ Hayes or Bromley South or East Croydon
CT12	**Ramsgate**	Minster Abbey Retreat/Guesthouse	8	4	4			16	40	⇌ Minster
GU22	**Woking**	St Columba's House	24	2	-			26	50	⇌ Woking
GU34	**Alton**	Alton Abbey	15	2	-			17	20	⇌ Alton
KT3	**New Malden**	Marist Sisters	10	18	-			28	-	⇌ New Malden
ME20	**Maidstone**	The Friars Aylesford	20	-	12	twin	68	100	100	⇌ Aylesford or Maidstone East
RH1	**Redhill**	Wychcroft	11	22	3			36	40	⇌ Redhill
RH10	**Crawley**	The Monastery of the Holy Trinity	6	-	-			6	-	⇌ Three Bridges
TN15	**Sevenoaks**	Society of Retreat Conductors	20	-	-			20	25	⇌ Swanley
TN33	**Battle**	Ashburnham Prayer Centre	1	20	-			21	60	⇌ Battle
TW10	**Richmond**	St Michael's Convent	13	4	-			17	30	⇌ Richmond ⊖ Richmond
South West										
BA3	**Bath**	The Ammerdown Centre	30	12	-	self-catering flat family rooms	2 5	65	80	⇌ Bath Spa
		Bainesbury House	1	-	16			17	-	⇌ Bath Spa
BA6	**Glastonbury**	The Abbey House	18	18	-			36	50	⇌ Castle Cary or Bristol Temple Meads
BA12	**Warminster**	St Denys Retreat Centre	16	6	-			28	25	⇌ Warminster
BH24	**Ringwood**	Crow Hill Day Retreat Centre	n/a	n/a	n/a			n/a	30	⇌ Bournemouth
BS40	**Bristol**	Omega - Winford Manor	13	30		flats cottage	5 1	49	0	⇌ Bristol Temple Meads
DT2	**Dorchester**	Hilfield Friary	13	2	-			15	50	⇌ Sherborne
GL4	**Gloucester**	Prinknash Abbey	5	-	-			5	-	⇌ Cheltenham or Stroud or Gloucester
		St Peter's Grange, Prinknash Abbey	4	18	-			22	45	⇌ Cheltenham or Stroud or Gloucester
TA13	**South Petherton**	The Community of St Francis	14	4	-	self-catering cottage	5	23	40	⇌ Crewkerne
TQ11	**Buckfastleigh**	Buckfast Abbey	4	8	-			12	50	⇌ Newton Abbot or Totnes
TR12	**Helston**	Trelowarren Christian Fellowship	2	20	8			30	100	⇌ Redruth
WR6	**Worcester**	Glasshampton	4	-	-			4	-	⇌ Worcester: Foregate Street or Shrub Hill
WR10	**Pershore**	Holland House	18	6	-			32	50	⇌ Evesham
NORTHERN IRELAND										
BT30	**Downpatrick**	Tobar Mhuire	10	10	-			20	30	*Bus:* Downpatrick
BT34	**Newry**	Dromantine	n/a	n/a	n/a			200	-	*Rail:* Newry
		Our Lady of Apostles Retreat House	43	50	-			93	60	*Bus:* Rostrevor (*Rail:* Newry)
BT36	**Belfast**	St Clements Retreat House	54	32	-			86	-	⇌ Belfast Central
BT48	**Londonderry**	Iona Carmelite Retreat Centre	60	40	-			100	-	⇌ Londonderry
SCOTLAND										
DG2	**Dumfries**	Kinharvie House	11	10	9			30	30	⇌ Dumfries
G71	**Glasgow**	Craighead Spirituality Centre	30	-	-			30	40	⇌ Blantyre or Hamilton
IV30	**Elgin**	Pluscarden Abbey	24	4	-			32	50	⇌ Elgin
KA28	**Millport**	The College	n/a	n/a	n/a			n/a	n/a	⇌ Largs
PA33	**Dalmally**	Craig Lodge	n/a	n/a	n/a	for young people		n/a	n/a	⇌ Dalmally
PA76	**Isle of Iona**	Macleod Centre and Iona Abbey	3	26	66			95	140	⇌ Oban
PH2	**Perth**	Mission and Renewal Centre	38	16	-			54	50	⇌ Perth
WALES										
LD2	**Builth Wells**	The Rowan Tree Centre	3	10	-			13	-	⇌ Builth Road
LD3	**Brecon**	Llangasty Retreat House	10	6	-			16	25	⇌ Abergavenny
LL17	**St Asaph**	St Beuno's	n/a	n/a	n/a			45	40	⇌ Rhyl
LL21	**Corwen**	Coleg Y Groes	0	10	5			15	20	⇌ Wrexham
LL26	**Llanrwst**	Pencraig Arthur Christian Retreat, Conference and Holiday Centre	2	12	-			14	25	⇌ Llanrwst
LL30	**Llandudno**	Loreto Centre	31	12	-			43	160	⇌ Llandudno
LL34	**Penmaenmawr**	Noddfa Spirituality Centre	32	-	-			32	-	⇌ Penmaenmawr
NP5	**Monmouth**	Tymawr Convent	9	6	-			15	20	⇌ Newport (Gwent) or Chepstow
SA65	**Fishguard**	Ffald-y-Brenin Retreat Centre	5	6	8	flat/cottage	6	25	50	⇌ Fishguard Harbour or Whitland
SA70	**Tenby**	Caldey Abbey	18	2	-			20	-	⇌ Tenby
SY22	**Meifod**	Canolfan Cristionogol Anenwadol Cymru	-	-	-	non-residential		-	50	⇌ Welshpool

RETREAT HOUSES

For Religious Orders see also Religious Orders (Anglican) on Page 248, Religious Orders (Roman Catholic) on Page 249, Missionary Societies on Page 352.

The Abbey House (Bath and Wells Diocesan Retreat & Conference Centre), Chilkwell Street, Glastonbury BA6 8DH
Warden: Mr D Hill. Admin staff 2, Other staff 5. *CC* No.224866. Began 1931; Anglican but open to all. Turnover n/a. For groups and individuals.
☎ 01458 831 112 🖷 01458 831 893

All Hallows House (All Hallows Community Retreat Houses), Belsey Bridge Road, Ditchingham, Bungay NR35 2DT
Contact: Guest Sister. Staff n/a. *CC* No.230143. Began 1855; Anglican. Turnover n/a. Offering a programme of retreats throughout the year; church groups, fellowships, individuals; full board.
☎ 01986 892 840

All Saints Pastoral Centre, Shenley Lane, London Colney, St Albans AL2 1AF
Director: Rev Vladimir Felzmann. Other staff 15. *CC* Began 1973; Roman Catholic. Turnover n/a.
☎ 01727 822 010 🖷 01727 822 880

Alton Abbey, Beech, Alton GU34 4AP
Bursar: n/a. Community n/a. *CC* No.229216. Began 1884; Anglican. Turnover n/a.
☎ 01420 562 145/ 563 575

The Ammerdown Centre, Radstock, Bath BA3 5SW
Convenor: Sister Carolyn Wicks. Executive staff 5, Other staff 12. *CC* No.1010244. Began 1973; ecumenical. Magazine: *Newsletter* (Circulation n/a half-yearly). Retreat, conference centre and holiday facilities.
Web: www.midsomernorton.co.uk/smallpages/ammerdown.htm
Email: centre@ammerdown.freeserve.co.uk
☎ 01761 433 709 🖷 01761 433 094

Ascot Priory (Society of the Holy Trinity), Priory Road, Ascot SL5 8RT
Warden: Rev Philip Ursell. Staff n/a. *CC* Began n/a; Anglican. Turnover n/a.
☎ 01344 885 685 🖷 01344 885 685

***Ashburnham Prayer Centre**, Ashburnham Place, Battle TN33 9NF
Resident Director: Mr Brian M Betts. *Conference Manager:* Mr Nigel Coleman. *Administrator:* Mrs Jennifer Oldroyd. Admin staff 6, Other staff 19. *CC* No.212755. Began 1960; non-denominational. Turnover £800,000 to year end Apr 98.
Web: www.ashburnham.org.uk
Email: mail@ashburnham.org.uk
☎ 01424 892 244 🖷 01424 892 243

Bainesbury House, Downside Abbey, Stratton on the Fosse, Bath BA3 4RH
Warden: Rev Christopher Calascione. Run by community. *CC* No.232548. Began 1795; Roman Catholic. Turnover n/a. Benedictine; self-catering.
☎ 01761 235 135 🖷 01761 235 124

†Barrowby House (Ripon and Leeds Diocesan Retreat and Conference Centre), Kirkby Overblow, Harrogate HG3 1HY
Warden: Mr Derek Hewitson. Admin staff 1, Other staff 4. *CC* No.249860. Began 1950; Anglican. Turnover n/a.
☎ 0113 288 6240 🖷 0113 288 6428

Benedictine Centre for Spirituality, 29 Bramley Road, Oakwood, London N14 4HE
Director: Rev Anthony Smithwick OSB. Administrative staff 2, Community 15. *CC* No.265126. Began 1995; Roman Catholic but ecumenical. Turnover n/a. Day, residential and personal retreats, interfaith.
☎ 020 8449 2499

Berean Place (Berean Trust), Bordesley Park Farm, Beoley, Redditch B98 9BH
Centre Director: Mr Andrew Nicholls. Admin staff 2, Other staff 2. *CC* No.801668. Began 1987; interdenominational. Turnover £25,000 to year end Oct 94. Non-residential.
☎ 01527 638 78 🖷 01527 615 27

†The Bernard Delany OP Ecumenical and Peace Centre, Froddle Crook, Armathwaite, Carlisle CA4 9SY
Director: Ms Alice Stephens. No full-time staff. Began 1970; ecumenical. Turnover n/a. Ecumenical dialogue work for world-wide co-operation; human rights; emancipation of women.
☎ 01228 613 84

Bishop Woodford House (Ely Diocesan Retreat and Conference Centre), Barton Road, Ely CB7 4DX
Warden: Miss Mary Russell. Full-time staff 2. *CC* No.230573. Began 1973; Anglican. Turnover £100,000 to year end Dec 98.
☎ 01353 663 039

†Buckfast Abbey, St Mary's Abbey, Buckfastleigh TQ11 0EE
Guestmaster: Rev Fr Peter Morgan. *CC* Began 1882; Roman Catholic. Turnover n/a.
☎ 01364 642 519 Ext 237

Burford Priory, Priory Lane, Burford, Oxford OX18 4SQ
Prior: Very Rev Stuart Burns. Community 9. *CC* No.479317. Began 1941; Anglican. Turnover n/a. Benedictine community.
☎ 01993 823 605

Caldey Abbey, Caldey Island, Tenby SA70 7UH
Guestmaster: n/a. Admin staff 3. *CC* Began 1929; Roman Catholic. Turnover n/a.
☎ 01834 842 632 🖷 01834 845 942

Canolfan Cristionogol Anenwadol Cymru, Hen Gapel John Hughes, Pont Robert, Meifod SY22 6JA
Guide: Nia Rhosier. No full-time staff. *CC* No.1001418. Began 1993; non-denominational. Ecumenical centre of Christian renewal and unity for Wales. Turnover n/a. For those seeking deeper understanding of Christian spirituality.
☎ 01938 500 631

Cenacle Retreat and Conference Centre, Lance Lane, Wavertree, Liverpool L15 6TW
Warden: The Retreat Secretary. Community n/a. *CC* Began n/a; Roman Catholic but ecumenical. Turnover n/a. Day retreats for groups of 30 persons.
☎ 0151 722 2271

Cenacle Retreat and Conference Centre, 28 Alexandra Road South, Whalley Range, Manchester M16 8HU
Community 5. *CC* No.232928. Began 1888; Roman Catholic but open to all denominations. Turnover n/a. Non-residential.
☎ 0161 226 1241 🖷 0161 226 3170

Cenacle Retreat House, 48 Victoria Road, Netley Abbey, Southampton SO31 5DQ
Superior of Community: Sister Superior. Community n/a. *CC* No.232928. Began 1912; Roman Catholic. Turnover n/a.
☎ 023 8045 3718

A

The Cherwell Centre Ltd, 14 Norham Gardens, Oxford OX2 6QB
Director: Sister Carolyn Green. Other staff 6. *CC* No.2702845. Began 1971; Roman Catholic. Turnover n/a. Retreats and Conference centre.
Email: cherwell@enterprise.net
☎ 01865 552 106 📠 01865 558 183

Chester Retreat House, 11 Abbey Square, Chester CH1 2HU
Warden: Sister of the Community of the Holy Name. Other staff 3. *CC* No.248968. Began 1925; Anglican. Turnover n/a. Providing space and atmosphere for people in quietness to grow closer to God.
☎ 01244 321 801

Clewer Spirituality Centre, Hatch Lane, Windsor SL4 3QR
Administrator: Mr Robert Langton. Admin staff 1, Other staff 3. *CC* No.236939. Began 1852; Anglican. Turnover £36,500 to year end June 98. Retreats, quiet days, religious conferences.
☎ 01753 868 602 📠 01753 868 602

Cold Ash Retreat and Conference Centre, The Ridge, Cold Ash, Thatcham RG18 9HU
Directoress: Sister Noreen McGlynn. Staff n/a. *CC* No.249515. Began 1979; Roman Catholic. Turnover n/a. Retreats: Preached, individually-guided, massage and private. Conferences: Ecumenical, ministry, in-service training, educational.
☎ 01635 865 353

Coleg Y Groes, Corwen LL21 0AU
Wardens: Rev Heather Fenton, Rev Margaret Harvey. No other staff. Began 1985; Anglican. Turnover n/a. Individually guided and private retreats; 30 day Ignation exercises by arrangement; holidays; quiet space.
☎ 01490 412 169

The College, Millport (Argyll Diocesan Conference Centre), Isle of Cumbrae KA28 0HE
Warden: Rev Tony Burdon. Staff 3. *CC* No.SC 23281. Began 1851; Scottish Episcopalian. Turnover £38,000 to year end Oct 98. Retreat House and conference centre for groups and individuals.
Web: www.sol.co.uk/s/sedat/millport.htm
Email: tccumbrae@argyll.anglican.org
☎ 01475 530 535 📠 01475 530 204

Community for Reconciliation, Barnes Close, Malthouse Lane, Chadwich, Bromsgrove B61 0RA
Company Secretary: Rev John Johansen-Berg. Executive staff 2, Other staff 4. *CC* No.295113. Began 1984; ecumenical. Turnover £67,181 to year end Mar 98. Conference retreat training centre with residential community, evangelistic missions, peacebuilding East Africa, Croatia, reconciliation UK, overseas.
Web: ourworld.compuserve.com/homepages/communityforreconciliation
Email: johnjoberg@aol.com
☎ 01562 710 231 📠 01562 710 278

The Community of St Francis, Manor House, Compton Durville, South Petherton TA13 5ES
Warden: Sister Guardian. Other sisters 9. *CC* No.286619. Began 1905; Anglican. Turnover £48,000 to year end June 98.
☎ 01460 240 473 📠 01460 242 360

Congregation of Marian Fathers, Fawley Court, Henley-on-Thames RG9 3AE
Father Superior: Rev T Wyszomierski. Members 28. *CC* No.251717. Began 1950; Roman Catholic. Turnover n/a. Pastoral, retreats, functions, weddings and christenings. Museum, historical house and gardens. Student exchange schemes.
Email: marian_f@dircon.co.uk
☎ 01491 574 917

Convent of St Laurence, Field Lane, Belper DE56 1DD
Mother Superior: Rev Mother. Admin staff 13. *CC* No.220282. Began 1874; Anglican. Turnover n/a. Retreats and quiet days.
☎ 01773 822 585

Convent of St Mary at the Cross, Priory Field Drive, Hale Lane, Edgware HA8 9PZ
Mother Abbess: Mother Mary Zelent. Other staff 3, Community 12. *CC* No.209261. Began 1866; Anglican. Turnover n/a. Benedictine community providing guest house. Day Conference Centre; care for the disabled and elderly.
☎ 020 8958 7868 📠 020 8958 1920

Craig Lodge, Dalmally PA33 1AR
Senior Manager: Mr Stephen Roche. Executive staff 2, Other staff 5. *CC* No.SCO 23023. Began 1995; Roman Catholic, but open to all. Magazine: *Craig News* (2,500 annually). Turnover £100,000 to year end Dec 98. A house of prayer and reflection with special ministries to the young and disadvantaged.
Web: www.craiglodge.org
Email: stephen@craiglodge.freeserve.co.uk
☎ 01838 200 216 📠 01838 200 622

Craighead Spirituality Centre, Bothwell, Glasgow G71 8AU
Director: Rev Brian McClorry. Other staff 8. *CC* Began 1916; Roman Catholic. Turnover n/a. Retreats and courses based on the spiritual exercises of Ignatius Loyola.
☎ 01698 285 300/282 420 📠 01698 891 014

***Crocus Ministries**, 6 Moorcroft, Colton, Rugeley WS15 3ND
Director: Mrs Norma Heasman. Admin staff 2. *CC* No.1046184. Began 1995; non-denominational. Turnover n/a. Providing rest, training, listening ears and intercession for leaders in Christian ministry.
Web: almac.co.uk/personal/rheasman/crocus.htm
Email: crocus@clara.co.uk
☎ 01889 582 650

†**Crow Hill Day Retreat Centre**, Bradbury Cottage, Crow Hill, Ringwood BH24 3DQ
Wardens: Mr Brian & Mrs Claire Skelley. No other staff. Began 1983; Methodist. Turnover £1,600 to year end Aug 96.
☎ 01425 470 310

†**Damascus House**, The Ridgeway, Mill Hill, London NW7 1HH
Director: Sister Ellen Flynn DC. Admin staff 4, Other staff 15. *CC* No.803465. Began 1972; Roman Catholic. Turnover £350,000 to year end Dec 92.
☎ 020 8959 8971 📠 020 8906 4573

Diocesan House of Retreat, The Street, Pleshey, Chelmsford CM3 1HA
Warden: Rev John T Howden. *Assistant Warden:* Mr Derek Gruender. Admin staff 3, Other staff 10. *CC* No.249505. Began 1919; Anglican. Turnover £102,000 to year end Dec 98.
☎ 01245 237 251 📠 01245 237 594

Diocesan Pastoral Centre, The Barn, New Hall, Boreham, Chelmsford CM3 3HT
Run by: The Barn Team. Staff n/a. *CC* No.229288. Began 1986; Roman Catholic but open to all. Turnover n/a. Retreats & other courses, spiritual direction & prayer guidance, residential accommodation for group or individuals.
☎ 01245 451 760 📠 01245 464 348

†**Dromantine**, Newry BT34 1RY
Superior: Rev William Foley. Staff n/a. Began n/a; Roman Catholic. Turnover n/a.
☎ 028 3028 2224

For additional information see List on Pages 121–122

Ecton House (Peterborough Diocesan Retreat and Conference Centre), Church Way, Ecton, Northampton NN6 0QE
Warden: Rev Stephen Evans. Admin staff 2, Other staff 16. Began 1968; Anglican. Turnover £150,000 to year end Dec 98.
Email: evanssj@globalnet.co.uk
☎ 01604 406 442 📠 01604 787 052

Edward King House, The Old Palace, Minster Yard, Lincoln LN2 1PU
Warden: Rev A Adkins. *Duty Manager:* Mrs Sue Brennan. Admin staff 3, Other staff 6. *CC* No.517930. Began 1960; Anglican. Turnover £142,000 to year end Mar 98. Day and residential conference and retreat centre for church and the wider community.
Web: www.lincoln.anglican.org/ekh/
Email: ekh@oden.org.uk
☎ 01522 528 778 📠 01522 527 308

Elmore Abbey, Church Lane, Speen, Newbury RG14 1SA
Abbot: Rt Rev Basil Matthews. No full-time staff. *CC* Began 1914; Anglican. Turnover n/a. Benedictine monastery, for men.
☎ 01635 330 80

Emmaus Retreat and Conference Centre, Layhams Road, West Wickham BR4 9HH
Director: Sr Celia Beale. Admin staff 4, Other staff 9. *CC* Began 1979; Roman Catholic but open to all. Turnover n/a. Directed, preached and private retreats, quiet days, spiritual direction. Conference facilities.
☎ 020 8777 2000 📠 020 8777 2022

***Ffald-y-Brenin Retreat Centre**, Pontfaen, Fishguard SA65 9UA
Wardens: Mr & Mrs Vic & Lilian Davidson. *CC* No.516594. Began 1985; interdenominational. Turnover £35,000 to year end Dec 97. Self-catering for individuals, families and groups.
Email: fy.b@virgin.net
☎ 01348 881 382 📠 01348 881 419

***The Fountain Gate Community**, 58 Geoffrey Road, Brockley, London SE4 1NT
Director: Mr David Pott. Executive staff 3. *CC* No.264078. Began 1996; non-denominational. Part of YWAM. Turnover £1,200 to year end Dec 98. Committed to community, hospitality, stillness, celebration, helping families, leading retreats and pilgrimages especially for Millennium.
☎ 020 8694 2220 📠 020 8694 2220

The Friars Aylesford, Aylesford, Maidstone ME20 7BX
General Manager: Mr Norman Harlow. Admin staff 10, Other staff 38. *CC* No.1068518. Began 1242; Roman Catholic but open to all. Turnover n/a.
☎ 01622 717 272 📠 01622 715 575

Glasshampton, Shrawley, Worcester WR6 6TQ
Staff n/a. *CC* Began n/a; Anglican. Turnover n/a.
☎ 01299 896 345

The Grange, Pastoral Office, Ampleforth Abbey, York YO62 4EN
Administrator: Jan Fitzallen-Howard. Staff n/a. *CC* No.1026493. Began 1973; Roman Catholic. Turnover n/a.
Email: pastoral@ampleforth.org.uk
☎ 01439 766 889 📠 01439 766 755

Hilfield Friary, Dorchester DT2 7BE
Guest Brother: n/a. Staff n/a. *CC* Began 1921; Anglican. Turnover n/a.
Email: hilfielduk@aol.com
☎ 01300 341 345 📠 01300 341 293

Holland House, Cropthorne, Pershore WR10 3NB
Warden: Mr Peter Middlemiss. *Deputy Warden:* Miss Liz Palin. Admin staff 2, Other staff 2. *CC* No.504839. Began 1945; interdenominational. Turnover £155,000 to year end Dec 97. Providing a venue for residential and non-residential courses; retreat, conference, and laity centre.
Web: www.users.surfaid.org/~laycentre
Email: hollandhouse@laycentre.surfaid.org
☎ 01386 860 330 📠 01386 861 208

Holy Cross House (All Hallows Community Retreat Houses), Belsey Bridge Road, Ditchingham, Bungay NR35 2DT
Contact: Guest Sister. Staff n/a. *CC* No.230143. Began 1855; Anglican. Turnover n/a. Offering a programme of retreats throughout the year; available to church groups, fellowships, individuals; full-board.
☎ 01986 894 092

Houghton Chapel Retreat, Chapel Lane, Houghton, Huntingdon PE17 2AY
Wardens: Mr Gerald & Mrs Sue Feakes. No other staff. *CC* Began 1986; United Reformed. Turnover n/a.
Email: vw18@dialpipex.com
☎ 01480 469 376/468 535

Iona Carmelite Retreat Centre, Termonbacca, Londonderry BT48 9XE
Prior: Very Rev Sean Conlon. Other staff 7. Began 1982; Roman Catholic. Turnover n/a.
☎ 028 7126 2512 📠 028 7137 3589

Iona Community – Macleod Centre and Iona Abbey, Isle of Iona PA76 6SN
Warden, Iona Abbey: Rev Brian Woodcock. *Deputy Warden, MacLeod Centre:* Ms Jan Sutch Pickard. Admin staff 7, Other staff 30. *CC* No.SCO 03794. Began 1938; ecumenical, Church of Scotland based. Magazine: *The Coracle* (8,000 quarterly). Turnover £1,040,000 to year end Dec 98. Christian experiment and renewal; prayer, politics, peace and healing in common life; creating community.
Web: www.iona.org.uk
Email: ionacomm@iona.org.uk
☎ 01681 700 404 📠 01681 700 460

Kairos Centre, Mount Angelus Road, London SW15 4JA
Director: Sister Mary Ward. Community members 3, Other staff 5. *CC* No.227961. Began 1869; Roman Catholic but open to all. (Previously Maryfield Convent). Turnover £70,000 to year end Mar 99. Retreat and conference centre offering a range of resources for retreats, conferences, meetings, courses.
Web: www.kairoscentre.demon.com.uk
Email: maryward@kairoscentre.demon.com.uk
☎ 020 8788 4188 📠 020 8788 4198

Kinharvie House, New Abbey, Dumfries DG2 8DZ
Director: Rev Ronald McEwan. Admin staff 3, Other staff 4. *CC* No.SCO 00565. Began 1953. Turnover n/a.
Email: kinharvie.hse@aol.com
☎ 01387 850 433 📠 01387 850 465

Launde Abbey (Leicester Diocesan Retreat House and Conference Centre), Launde Abbey, East Norton LE7 9XB
Warden: Rev Graham Johnson. *Deputy Warden:* Mr John Flood. Admin staff 3, Other staff 19. *CC* Began 1958; Anglican. Turnover £235,000 to year end Dec 98.
Web: webleicester.co.uk/customer/laundeabbey/welcome.htm
Email: laundeabbey@leicester.anglican.org
☎ 01572 717 254 📠 01572 717 454

A

Littledale Trust, Littledale Hall, Lancaster LA2 9EY
Directors: Mr Stuart & Mrs Wendy Rushton. Executive staff 2, Other staff 7. ***CC*** No.328268. Began 1989; interdenominational. Turnover £92,000 to year end Nov 98. Bringing wholeness and rest to leaders, individuals, family groups, retreats, counselling service, training programmes.
Web: www.doveuk.com/littledale
Email: littledale@compuserve.com
☎ 01524 770 266 🖷 01524 771 553

Llangasty Retreat House, Brecon LD3 7PJ
Warden: Mr Dannatt. Admin staff 1, Other staff 2. ***CC*** No.1060743. Began 1954; Anglican. Turnover n/a.
☎ 01874 658 250 🖷 01874 658 328

†**Loreto Centre (Institute of the Blessed Virgin Mary)**, Loreto Centre, Abbey Road, Llandudno LL30 2EL
Sister-in-charge: Sister Brigid Kenny. Community 5. ***CC*** Began 1851; Roman Catholic. Turnover £56,000 to year end Dec 94.
☎ 01492 878 031

Loyola Hall – Jesuit Spirituality Centre, Warrington Road, Rainhill L35 6NZ
Director: Rev David Birchall. *Bursar:* Mrs Sheila Hanley. Admin staff 4, Other staff 20. ***CC*** No.230165. Began 1923; Roman Catholic. Turnover £100,000 to year end Dec 98. Ecumenical retreat house/conference centre with beautiful grounds. Extensive programme of retreats and courses.
Web: home.clara.net/loyola
Email: loyola@clara.net
☎ 0151 426 4137 🖷 0151 431 0115

Marie Reparatrice Retreat Centre, 115 Ridgway, London SW19 4RB
Sister Superior: Rev Sister. Admin staff 2, Other staff 3. ***CC*** No.233640. Began 1957; Roman Catholic. Turnover n/a.
☎ 020 8946 1088 🖷 020 8947 9820

Marist Sisters, 55 Thetford Road, New Malden KT3 5DP
Provincial: Sister Monica O'Brien. Staff n/a. ***CC*** Began 1858; Roman Catholic. Turnover n/a.
Email: marist@saqnet.co.uk
☎ 020 8949 1355 🖷 020 8336 0193

Massingham St Mary Retreat Centre, Little Massingham, King's Lynn PE32 2JU
Retreat Director: Sister Margaret Devine. Staff n/a. ***CC*** No.234925. Began 1962; Roman Catholic. Turnover £100,000 to year end Dec 98. Retreats, quiet days, away days, mass centre, deaneries, spiritual direction, counselling.
☎ 01485 520 245

Mill Green House, Mill Green, Horseheath, Cambridge CB1 6QZ
Retreat Leaders & Administrators: Mr Graeme & Mrs Sue Walker. No other staff. Began 1986; ecumenical. Turnover £1,000 to year end Dec 94.
☎ 01799 584 390 🖷 01799 584 390

Minster Abbey Retreat / Guesthouse, Minster, Ramsgate CT12 4HF
The Guest Sister: Sister A Erwin. Community 10. ***CC*** Began 1937; Roman Catholic. Turnover n/a.
☎ 01843 821 254

Minsteracres Retreat Centre, Minsteracres Retreat Centre, Consett DH8 9RT
Rector: Rev Mark White. Community 7, Other staff 7. ***CC*** No.234436. Began 1967; Roman Catholic. Turnover n/a.
☎ 01434 673 248 🖷 01434 673 540

Mission and Renewal Centre, St Mary's, Kinnoull, Perth PH2 7BP
Rector: Rev P Gallagher. Admin staff 2, Other staff 3. ***CC*** Began 1869; Roman Catholic. Turnover £200,000 to year end Apr 98. Retreats and renewal courses.
Email: coplosa@aol.com
☎ 01738 624 075 🖷 0738 442 0171

The Monastery of Christ the Saviour, 23 Cambridge Road, Hove BN3 1DE
Prior: Rev Brian. No full-time staff. ***CC*** Began 1985; Anglican. Turnover n/a.
☎ 01273 726 698

Monastery of Our Lady of Hyning, Hyning, Warton, Carnforth LA5 9SE
Prioress: Sister Mary Lucy. Community 13, Other staff 3. ***CC*** Began 1974; Roman Catholic. Turnover n/a.
☎ 01524 732 684 🖷 01524 720 287

The Monastery of the Holy Trinity (Community of the Servants of the Will of God), Crawley Down, Crawley RH10 4LH
Father Superior: Rev Fr Gregory. Community n/a. Began 1950; Anglican. Turnover n/a. Traditional monastic liturgy with instruction in the life of prayer, especially use of Jesus prayer.
☎ 01342 712 074

The Montfort Missionaries and Daughters of Wisdom, Lyndhurst Road, Ashurst, Southampton SO4 2DU
Male staff 5, Resident sisters 3. ***CC*** No.1050485. Began 1981; Roman Catholic. (Previously Saint Joseph's House of Prayer). Turnover £28,000 to year end Dec 98.
☎ 023 8029 2337

Morley Retreat and Conference House, Church Lane, Morley, Ilkeston DE7 6DE
Wardens: John & Jackie Carey. Admin staff 4, Other staff 1. ***CC*** Began 1959; Anglican. Turnover £170,000 to year end Dec 97.
Web: www.btinternet.com/~treasure/aml/morley/
☎ 01332 831 293

Mount St Bernard Abbey, Coalville LE67 5UL
Abbot: Rev John Moakler. Staff n/a. ***CC*** Began 1835; Roman Catholic. Turnover n/a. Order of Cistercians of the Strict Observance.
☎ 01530 832 298 / 832 022 🖷 01530 814 608

Myddelton Lodge, Langbar Road, Ilkley LS29 0EB
Director: Rev Laurie Hulme. Admin staff 1, Other staff 14. ***CC*** Began 1922; Roman Catholic. Turnover n/a.
Email: myddeltonlodge@compuserve.com
☎ 01943 607 887 🖷 01943 817 830

Noddfa Spirituality Centre Convent of the Sacred Heart of Mary, Conwy Old Road, Penmaenmawr LL34 6YF
Retreat Programmer: To be appointed. Admin staff 3, Other staff 5. ***CC*** No.232190. Began 1970; Roman Catholic. Turnover n/a. Parish retreats.
☎ 01492 623 473 🖷 01492 622 517

Northumbria Community Trust Ltd, Nether Springs, Hetton Hall, Chatton NE66 5SD
Directors: Rev Roy Searle, Rev Trevor Miller. Executive staff 2, Admin staff 3, Other staff 17. ***CC*** No.28395. Began 1988; interdenominational. Magazine: *CAIM* (1,500 quarterly). Turnover £200,000 to year end Dec 98. Dispersed Christian community. Mother house – Nether Springs, open to visitors, retreatants, pilgrims, seekers.
Email: northumbriacommunity@bigfoot.com
☎ 01289 388 235 🖷 01289 388 510

For additional information see List on Pages 121–122

Offa House (Coventry Diocesan Retreat and Conference Centre), Offchurch, Leamington Spa CV33 9AS
Wardens: Revs Michael & Sharon Simpson. Admin staff 2, Other staff 7. *CC* Began 1962; Anglican. Turnover £160,000 to year end Dec 98. Retreats for individuals and groups, conferences for church organisations, parishes and groups.
☎ 01926 423 309 🖷 01926 330 350

The Old Bakery, Hindolveston, Dereham NR20 5DF
Owner: Rev Percy Gandon. No other staff. Began 1983; Anglican. Turnover n/a. Retreats and healing ministries for groups and individuals.
☎ 01263 861 325

Omega – Winford Manor, Winford, Bristol BS40 8DW
Prior: Rev Canon Peter Spink. *Administrator:* Mr James Fahey. Admin staff 3, Other staff 3. *CC* No.280512. Began 1980; Anglican/Roman Catholic. Magazine: *Omega News* (2,500 every four months). Turnover £196,000 to year end Mar 97. Contemplative community of men/women. Retreats, seminars, individual spiritual direction, arts, healing, conferences, residential home.
Web: members.aol.com/omegatrust/omega/omega.html
Email: omegatrust@aol.com
☎ 01275 472 262 🖷 01275 472 065

Our Lady of Apostles Retreat House, 11 Greenpark Road, Rostrevor, Newry BT34 3EY
Sister-in-Charge: Sister Eugenius. Admin staff 2. *CC* Began 1976; Roman Catholic. Turnover £228,000 to year end Apr 94.
☎ 028 3027 38333 🖷 01693 739 454

†**Park Place Pastoral Centre**, Winchester Road, Wickham, Fareham PO17 5HA
Secretary: Sister M Frances. Admin staff 10, Other staff 3. *CC* No.250185. Began 1968; Roman Catholic. Turnover n/a.
☎ 01329 833 043 🖷 01329 832 226

***Pencraig Arthur Christian Retreat, Conference and Holiday Centre**, Pencraig Arthur, Llanddoget, Llanrwst LL26 0DZ
Proprietor: Rev John Farrimond. No full-time staff. Began 1984; Methodist/Ecumenical. Turnover n/a. Retreats/holidays.
☎ 01492 640 959

†**Pluscarden Abbey**, Elgin IV30 8UA
Guestmaster: Br Gabriel Potter. *Women: Warden:* Dom Finbar Boyle. Community 25. *CC* Began 1948; Roman Catholic. Turnover £80,000 to year end Dec 93. Benedictine.
☎ 01343 890 257 🖷 01343 890 258

†**Prinknash Abbey**, Cranham, Gloucester GL4 8EX
Guestmaster: Rev Stephen Horton. Admin staff 1. *CC* No.232863. Began 1928; Roman Catholic. Turnover n/a. For men.
Web: www.brunel.co.uk//davidw//.prinknash.html#1
☎ 01452 812 455

Priory of Our Lady, Sayers Common, Hassocks BN6 9HT
Secretary: The Sister Secretary. Community n/a. *CC* Began 1972; Roman Catholic. Turnover n/a.
☎ 01273 832 901

†**Priory of Our Lady of Peace and Monastery of Christ our Saviour**, Turvey Abbey, Turvey, Bedford MK43 8DE
Mother Prioress: Sister Zoe Davis. *Superior:* Dom Gregory van der Kleij. Community 18. *CC* No.246754. Began 1981; Roman Catholic. Magazine: *Turvey Chronicles* (Circulation n/a quarterly), *One in Christ* (Circulation n/a quarterly). Turnover n/a. Benedictine Monastery. Spiritual, intellectual, artistic and practical activities.
☎ 01234 881 432 🖷 01234 881 538
And: Turvey Mews, Turvey, Bedford MK43 8DH
☎ 01234 881 211

†**Quarr Abbey**, Ryde PO33 4ES
Guestmaster: Rev Matthew Tylor. Community 20. *CC* No.218731. Began 1908; Roman Catholic. Turnover n/a. For men.
☎ 01983 882 420

Quiet Waters Christian Retreat House, Flixton Road, Bungay NR35 1PD
Team Leaders: Mr & Mrs Andrew & Geraldine Farley. Admin staff 2, Other staff 4. *CC* No.269866. Began 1985; non-denominational. Turnover £41,500 to year end Sept 98.
Email: quiet_waters@btinternet.com
☎ 01986 893 201

The Rowan Tree Centre, The Skreen, Erwood, Builth Wells LD2 3SJ
Director: Rev Mary Lewis. Staff n/a. Began 1983; interdenominational. (Previously The Skreen). Turnover n/a.
Email: marylewis@btinternet.com
☎ 01982 560 210 🖷 01982 560 470

St Beuno's, Spiritual Exercises Centre, St Asaph LL17 0AS
Director: Rev Tom McGuinness. Admin staff 10. *CC* No.230165. Began 1848; Roman Catholic. Turnover n/a. Training centre in Ignatian spirituality.
Email: stbeunos@aol.com
☎ 01745 583 444 🖷 01745 584 151

St Cassian's Centre, Kintbury, Hungerford RG17 9SR
Director: Brother Benet Conroy. Staff 15. *CC* No.232632. Began 1946; Roman Catholic. (De La Salle Brothers). Turnover n/a. Mainly for people aged 15 to 18 in school groups.
Email: kintbury@aol.com
☎ 01488 658 267 🖷 01488 657 292

St Clements Retreat House, 722 Antrim Road, Belfast BT36 7PH
Superior: Father Brendan Kane. Team 4. Began n/a; Roman Catholic. Turnover n/a.
Web: www.reds-belfast.com
Email: st.clements@reds-belfast.com
☎ 028 9077 6500/771799 🖷 028 9077 5924

St Columba's House, Maybury Hill, Woking GU22 8AB
Director: Rev Paul M Jenkins. Admin staff 1, Other staff 3. *CC* No.240675. Began 1968; Anglican. (Owned by St. Peter's Convent, Woking). Turnover £35,000 to year end Dec 96. Retreat and conference centre with two liturgical spaces. Religious and secular groups, individuals, businesses.
Email: retreats@st.columba.org.uk
☎ 01483 766 498 Mobile: 07973 848 941 🖷 01483 740 441

St Denys Retreat Centre, 2 Church Street, Warminster BA12 8PG
Retreat Secretary: n/a. Admin staff 1, Other staff 2. *CC* No.233026. Began 1879; Anglican. Turnover n/a. Open retreats and parish groups, individually guided groups.
☎ 01985 214 824

St Francis' House, Hemingford Grey, Huntingdon PE18 9BJ
Warden: Mrs Sue Smith. Admin staff 2, Other staff 6. *CC* No.232670. Began 1950; Anglican. (Administered by the Community of the Resurrection, Mirfield). Turnover n/a.
☎ 01480 462 185

St Gabriel's Centre (All Hallows Community Retreat Houses), Belsey Bridge Road, Ditchingham, Bungay NR35 2DT
Contact: Convent Secretary. Other staff 8. *CC* No.230143. Began 1855; Anglican. Turnover n/a. Offering a programme of retreats throughout the year; available to church groups, fellowships, individuals; full-board.
☎ 01986 892 749

For additional information see List on Pages 121–122

A

St Joseph's Retreat and Conference Centre, Tilston Road, Malpas SY14 7DD
Run by community. ***CC*** Began 1974; Roman Catholic but open to all. Turnover n/a.
☎ 01948 860 416 🖷 01948 860 055

St Mary's Convent, Wantage OX12 9DJ
Sister-in-Charge: n/a. Community n/a. ***CC*** No.240513. Began 1848; Anglican. Turnover n/a.
☎ 01235 760 170

St Mary's Lodge (All Hallows Community Retreat Houses), Belsey Bridge Road, Ditchingham, Bungay NR35 2DT
Contact: Guest Sister. Staff n/a. ***CC*** No.230143. Began 1855; Anglican. Turnover n/a. Offering a programme of retreats throughout the year; available to church groups, fellowships, individuals; self-catering, silent.
☎ 01986 892 731

St Michael's Centre (All Hallows Community Retreat Houses), Belsey Bridge Road, Ditchingham, Bungay NR35 2DT
Contact: Convent Secretary. Other staff 5. ***CC*** No.230143. Began 1855; Anglican. Turnover n/a. Offering a programme of retreats throughout the year; available to church groups, fellowships, individuals; full-board.
☎ 01986 892 749

St Michael's Convent (Community of the Sisters of the Church), 56 Ham Common, Richmond TW10 7JH
Mother Superior: Sister Anita. Admin staff 2, Other staff 3. ***CC*** No.271790. Began 1870; Anglican. Turnover n/a.
☎ 020 8940 8711 🖷 020 8332 2927

St Oswald's Pastoral Centre (Order of the Holy Paraclete), Sleights, Whitby YO21 1RY
Run by sisters. ***CC*** No.271117. Began 1983; Anglican. Turnover £50,000-100,000 to year end Dec 98. Opportunities for retreat, study and quiet.
☎ 01947 810 496

†**St Peter's Grange, Prinknash Abbey**, Cranham, Gloucester GL4 8EX
Warden: Rev Alphege Stebbens. Other staff 3. Began 1973; Roman Catholic Benedictine. Turnover n/a.
Web: www.brunel.co.uk//davidw//-prinknash.html#1
☎ 01452 813 592

St Raphael's Centre (All Hallows Community Retreat Houses), Belsey Bridge Road, Ditchingham, Bungay NR35 2DT
Contact: Convent Secretary. Staff n/a. ***CC*** No.230143. Began 1855; Anglican. Day groups only. Turnover n/a. Offering a programme of retreats throughout the year; available to church groups, fellowships, individuals; self-catering.
☎ 01986 892 749

Savio House, Ingersley Road, Bollington, Macclesfield SK10 5RW
Rector: Rev Michael T Winstanley. Admin staff 4, Other staff 6. ***CC*** Began n/a; Roman Catholic but open to all Christian groups. Turnover £210,000 to year end Dec 98.
☎ 01625 573 256 🖷 01625 560 221

Shallowford House (Lichfield Diocesan Retreat and Conference House), Stone ST15 0NZ
Warden: Mr D O T Rowlands. Admin staff 2, Other staff 8. ***CC*** Began 1939; Anglican. Turnover n/a.
☎ 01785 760 233 🖷 01785 760 390

Shepherds Dene (Newcastle and Durham Retreat House and Conference Centre), Riding Mill NE44 6AF
Warden: Mr P J Dodgson. Admin staff 1, Other staff 6. ***CC*** No.700258. Began 1946; Anglican. Turnover £125,000 to year end Dec 98. For churches, other groups and individuals.
Email: shepherds-dene@newcastle.anglican.org
☎ 01434 682 212 Mobile: 07970 215 667

Sisters of Jesus Way Retreat House, Red Acre, 24 Abbey Road, West Kirby, Wirral CH48 7EP
Run by community. ***CC*** No.509284. Began 1979; interdenominational. Turnover n/a. For guests seeking quiet rest fellowship, Sisters lead small day groups, small groups for prayer planning.
☎ 0151 625 8775

Sisters of St Louis, The Old Stable House, 3 Sussex Lodge, Fordham Road, Newmarket CB8 7AF
Director: Sister Margaret Duggan. Admin staff 1, Other staff 2. ***CC*** No.255245. Began 1912; Roman Catholic. Turnover n/a.
☎ 01638 667 190

Society of Retreat Conductors, Stacklands Retreat House, West Kingsdown, Sevenoaks TN15 6AN
Administrator of House: Rev David Rogers. Admin staff 1, Other staff 2. ***CC*** No.246045. Began 1927; Anglican but interdenominational. Turnover n/a. Ignatian retreats for groups and individuals.
☎ 01474 852 247

Society of St Margaret, St Saviour's Priory, 18 Queensbridge Road, London E2 8NS
Rev Mother: Mother Elizabeth. Community 18. ***CC*** Began 1866; Anglican. Turnover n/a.
☎ 020 7739 9976

South Park Community Trust, Brook Place, Bagshot Road, Chobham, Woking GU24 8SJ
Administrator: Ms Patricia Beall Gavigan. Executive staff 3, Other staff 12. ***CC*** No.292294. Began 1985; ecumenical. No magazine. Turnover n/a. Hospitality and prayer; conference and retreat centre.
☎ 01276 857 561 🖷 01276 857 561

SPEC Centre, Shenley Lane, London Colney, St Albans AL2 1AF
Directors: Mr David Satchell, Mrs Sandra Satchell. Staff n/a. Began n/a; Roman Catholic. Turnover n/a. For people aged 15 to 30.
☎ 01727 828 888
The Loft @ SPEC Centre, *Director:* Catriona Fletcher
Began 1998. For young people aged 9 to 15
☎ 01727 828 888 🖷 01727 822 927

Stanton House, Stanton St John, Oxford OX33 1HQ
Warden: Rev Ray Atwood. Other staff 4. ***CC*** No.275205. Began 1978; interdenominational. Turnover £67,000 to year end Dec 98. Offering space and quiet for spiritual rest, refreshment and renewal, also day group facilities.
☎ 01865 358 807

†**Tobar Mhuire**, Crossgar, Downpatrick BT30 9EA
Superior: Rev Charles Cross. Admin staff 2, Other staff 3. ***CC*** Began 1982; Roman Catholic. Turnover n/a.
☎ 028 4483 0242

For additional information see List on Pages 121–122

Trelowarren Christian Fellowship, Mawgan, Helston TR12 6AD
Wardens: Mr Colin & Mrs Avril Rogers. Resident staff 4, Other staff 2. *CC* No.269444. Began 1976; non-denominational. Turnover £50,000 to year end Dec 96.
☎ 01326 221 366

Tymawr Convent, Lydart, Monmouth NP5 4RN
Guest Hostess: n/a. Staff n/a. Began 1914; Church in Wales. Turnover n/a.
☎ 01600 860 244

Whaley Hall Community of the King of Love, Whaley Hall, Reservoir Road, Whaley Bridge, Highpeak SK23 7BL
Guardian: Rev Neil R Smith. Admin staff 1. *CC* No.271207. Began 1972; non-denominational. Turnover n/a. Hospitality and retreats for individuals, religious caring and arts organisation, for personal re-creation, development, support.
Email: the guardiansckl@compuserve.com
☎ 01663 732 495

Whalley Abbey (Blackburn Diocesan Conference & Retreat House), Whalley, Clitheroe BB7 9SS
Manager: Mrs Dinah Critchley. Admin staff 2, Other staff 10. *CC* No.247647. Began 1926; Anglican but open to all. Turnover n/a.
☎ 01254 822 268 🖷 01254 824 227

Wistaston Hall Oblate Retreat Centre, 89 Broughton Lane, Crewe CW2 8JS
Director: Very Rev Collum Connelly. Other staff 3. *CC* Began 1943; Roman Catholic. Turnover n/a.
☎ 01270 568 653 🖷 01270 650 776

†**Wychcroft (Southwark Diocesan Retreat House)**, Bletchingley, Redhill RH1 4NE
Warden: n/a. Staff n/a. *CC* Began 1960; Anglican. Turnover n/a.
☎ 01883 743 041

SHELTERED HOUSING

Organisations which did not supply any of this information are not listed here

⇌ = nearest Railway station ⊖ = nearest London Underground station

Name, Town	Number		Railway Station
Aldersgate, Nuneaton	Units	33	⇌ Nuneaton
Callin Court, Chester	Units	34	⇌ Chester
Charles Court, Tunbridge Wells	single rooms	9	⇌ Tunbridge Wells
	double/twin rooms	8	
Church Court, Midsomer Norton	Units	19	⇌ Bath Spa
Coles Court, Tunbridge Wells	single rooms	13	⇌ Tunbridge Wells
	double/twin rooms	5	
Derham Court, Yatton	Units	16	⇌ Yatton
Edina Court, Wisbech	Units	31	⇌ Peterborough or Kings Lynn
Epworth Court, Swindon	Units	23	⇌ Swindon
Field Court, York	Units	29	⇌ York
Gowan Park, Arbroath	Units	15	⇌ Arbroath
Grace Court, Folkestone	Units	26	⇌ Folkestone Central
The Hawthorns, Ellesmere Port	Units	40	⇌ Ellesmere Port
Hinton Court, Guisborough	Units	31	⇌ Middlesbrough
Jubilee Cottage Trust, Lytham St Annes	Places	17	⇌ St Annes-on-the-Sea
Naylor Court, Ellesmere Port	Units	20	⇌ Ellesmere Port
The Paddock, Muswell Hill	Units	26	⊖ Highgate
Pilgrims' Court, Newcastle upon Tyne	Units	40	⇌ Newcastle
St Andrew's Court, East Kilbride	Units	32	⇌ East Kilbride
Southcroft, Sheffield	Units	36	⇌ Sheffield
Taransay Court, Glasgow	Units	36	⇌ Glasgow Central
Tranquility Court, Leeds	Units	21	⇌ Cross Gates
Walcot Court, Bath	Units	36	⇌ Bath Spa
Wesley Court, Edinburgh	Units	28	⇌ Edinburgh
Wesley House, Lancaster	Units	42	⇌ Lancaster
West Court, Banbury	Units	21	⇌ Banbury
Woodlands, Penrith	Units	26	⇌ Penrith

SHELTERED HOUSING

See also Residential & Nursing Homes for Elderly People on Page 110.

Aldersgate, Nuneaton, Rose Lane, Nuneaton CV11 5TR
Scheme Manager: Mrs Hilary Mountney. Staff n/a. *CC* Began 1989; Methodist. Methodist Homes for the Aged, open to all. Turnover n/a. Independent living for older people.
☎ 024 7664 2330

Callin Court, Grey Friars, Chester CH1 2NW
Scheme Manager: Mrs Carol Ward. Staff n/a. *CC* Began 1983; Methodist. Methodist Homes for the Aged, open to all. Turnover n/a. Independent living for older people.
☎ 01244 315 252 🖷 01244 322 416

Charles Court, Pembury Road, Tunbridge Wells TN2 3QQ
Warden: Mr George Stoten. *CC* Began n/a; Salvation Army. Category 2. Turnover n/a.
☎ 01892 547 439

Church Court, Midsomer Norton, Church Lane, Midsomer Norton, Bath BA3 2JA
Scheme Manager: Mrs Madeline Edwards. Staff n/a. *CC* Began 1978; Methodist. Methodist Homes for the Aged, open to all. Turnover n/a. Independent living for older people.
☎ 01761 414 927

Coles Court, Kingswood Road, Tunbridge Wells TN2 4UJ
Warden: To be appointed. Staff n/a. *CC* Began n/a; Salvation Army. Category 1. Turnover n/a.
☎ 01892 529 078

Derham Court, Yatton, High Street, Yatton, Bristol BS19 4DW
Scheme Manager: Mrs Julia Sinclair. Staff n/a. *CC* Began 1982; Methodist. Methodist Homes for the Aged, open to all. Turnover n/a. Independent living for older people.
☎ 01934 835 443

A

Edina Court, Wisbech, 57 Harecroft Road, Wisbech PE13 1RL
Scheme Manager: Anne Crofts. Staff n/a. *CC* Began 1986; Methodist. Methodist Homes for the Aged, open to all. Turnover n/a. Independent living for older people.
☎ 01945 463 419

Epworth Court, Swindon, Bath Road, Swindon SN1 4BA
Scheme Manager: Mr Martin Clarke. Staff n/a. *CC* Began 1987; Methodist. Methodist Homes for the Aged, open to all. Turnover n/a. Independent living for older people.
☎ 01793 612 006

Field Court, York, Hempland Lane, Heworth, York YO31 0DN
Scheme Manager: Mrs Jean Feavers. Staff n/a. *CC* Began 1991; Methodist. Methodist Homes for the Aged, open to all. Turnover n/a. Independent living for older people.
☎ 01904 430 147

Gowan Park, Arbroath, Gowan Street, Arbroath DD11 2BN
Scheme Manager: Mrs Glenise Burns. Staff n/a. *CC* Began 1985; Methodist. Methodist Homes for the Aged, open to all. Turnover n/a. Independent living for older people.
☎ 01241 879 432

Grace Court, Folkestone, Grace Hill, Folkestone CT20 1HG
Scheme Manager: Anne Boughton. Staff n/a. *CC* Began 1988; Methodist. Methodist Homes for the Aged, open to all. Turnover n/a. Independent living for older people.
☎ 01303 241 551

The Hawthorns, Ellesmere Port, Naylor Crescent, Netherpool Road, Overpool, Ellesmere Port L66 1TW
Scheme Manager: Mrs Rita Louden. Staff n/a. *CC* Began 1997; Methodist. Methodist Homes for the Aged, open to all. Turnover n/a. Independent living for older people.
☎ 0151 356 4870

Hinton Court, Union Street, Guisborough TS14 6HN
Scheme Manager: Mrs Patricia Robinson. Staff n/a. *CC* Began 1988; Methodist. Methodist Homes for the Aged, open to all. Turnover n/a. Independent living for older people.
☎ 01287 636 719

†***Jubilee Cottage Trust (A KeyChange initiative)**, 143 St Andrews Road South, Lytham St Annes FY8 1YB
Warden: Mrs J Hogan. Admin staff 1. *CC* No.1061344. Began 1978; interdenominational. Turnover £20,000 to year end Mar 97. Sheltered flats.
☎ 01253 725 056

Naylor Court, Ellesmere Port, Rossmore Road West, Ellesmere Port CH66 1SY
Scheme Manager: Mrs Pamela Ashton. Staff n/a. *CC* Began 1984; Methodist. Methodist Homes for the Aged, open to all. Turnover n/a. Independent living for older people.
☎ 0151 355 8896

The Paddock, Muswell Hill, Meadow Drive, Muswell Hill, London N10 1PL
Scheme Manager: Jackie Argent. Staff n/a. *CC* Began 1987; Methodist. Methodist Homes for the Aged, open to all. Turnover n/a. Independent living for older people.
☎ 020 8444 1050

Pilgrims' Court, Newcastle upon Tyne, Eslington Terrace, Jesmond, Newcastle upon Tyne NE2 4RL
Scheme Manager: Christine Ackinclose. Staff n/a. *CC* Began 1985; Methodist. Methodist Homes for the Aged, open to all. Turnover n/a. Independent living for older people.
☎ 0191 281 7800

St Andrew's Court, East Kilbride, Sycamore Crescent, Greenhills, East Kilbride, Glasgow G75 9LN
Scheme Manager: Frances McCart. Staff n/a. *CC* Began 1981; Methodist. Methodist Homes for the Aged, open to all. Turnover n/a. Independent living for older people.
☎ 01355 231 248

Southcroft, Sheffield, 33 Psalter Lane, Sheffield S11 8YL
Scheme Manager: Mrs Valerie Loach. Staff n/a. *CC* Began 1989; Methodist. Methodist Homes for the Aged, open to all. Turnover n/a. Independent living for older people.
☎ 0114 255 3978

Taransay Court, Glasgow, Liddesdale Square, Milton, Glasgow G22 7BT
Scheme Manager: Miss Isobel Anderson. Staff n/a. *CC* Began 1990; Methodist. Methodist Homes for the Aged, open to all. Turnover n/a. Independent living for older people.
☎ 0141 772 5384

Tranquility Court, Leeds, 6 Tranquility Avenue, Cross Gates, Leeds LS15 8QX
Scheme Manager: Mrs Elizabeth Brook. Staff n/a. *CC* Began 1989; Methodist. Methodist Homes for the Aged, open to all. Turnover n/a. Independent living for older people.
☎ 0113 260 6948

Walcot Court, Bath, Walcot Gate, Bath BA1 5UB
Scheme Manager: Mrs Margaret Whittemore. Staff n/a. *CC* Began 1992; Methodist. Methodist Homes for the Aged, open to all. Turnover n/a. Independent living for older people.
☎ 01225 428 476

Wesley Court, Edinburgh, 13 Royston Mains Place, Granton, Edinburgh EH5 1LG
Scheme Manager: Susan Rochester. Staff n/a. *CC* Began 1982; Methodist. Methodist Homes for the Aged, open to all. Turnover n/a. Independent living for older people.
☎ 0131 552 4568

Wesley House, Lancaster, Sulyard Street, Lancaster LA1 1PX
Scheme Manager: Mr Robert McCreadie. Staff n/a. *CC* Began 1984; Methodist. Methodist Homes for the Aged, open to all. Turnover n/a. Independent living for older people.
☎ 01524 373 28

West Court, Banbury, 45 West Street, Banbury OX16 7HA
Scheme Manager: Mrs Ian Bakker. Staff n/a. *CC* Began 1986; Methodist. Methodist Homes for the Aged, open to all. Turnover n/a. Independent living for older people.
☎ 01295 258 859

Woodlands, Penrith, Bridge Lane, Penrith CA11 8GW
Scheme Manager: Mrs Patricia Davison. Staff n/a. *CC* Began n/a; Methodist. Methodist Homes for the Aged, open to all. Turnover n/a. Independent living for older people.
☎ 01768 867 490

For additional information see List on Page 129

BOOKS

B

BIBLE DISTRIBUTORS

Bible Distributors, 13 Plum Lane, London SE18 3AF
General Manager: Mr Edwin Cross. Executive staff 1, Other staff 2. ***CC*** No.1053047. Began 1976; interdenominational. Magazine: *Truth & Testimony* (2,500 every two months). Turnover £150,000 to year end July 99. Publishing Scripture portions, tracts and Bible courses, distributing Bibles.
☎ 020 8316 5389 🖷 020 8854 5963

***Bible Society (The British and Foreign Bible Society)**, Stonehill Green, Westlea, Swindon SN5 7DG
Executive Director: Mr Neil Crosbie. *Director of Mission and Theology:* Rev Dr Martin Robinson. *Commercial Director:* Dr Ashley Scott. Executive staff 8, Other staff 97. ***CC*** No.232759. Began 1804; interdenominational. Magazine: *Word in Action* (165,000 every four months). Turnover £10,140,000 [Voluntary income: £7,370,000, Sales: £2,770,000] to year end Dec 98. Making the Bible available where needed and challenging indifference to the Bible wherever it exists. Also co-ordinators of The Open Book Project.
Web: www.biblesociety.org.uk
Email: info@bfbs.org.uk
☎ 01793 418 100 🖷 01793 418 118

The Bible Society in Northern Ireland, Bible House, 27 Howard Street, Belfast BT1 6NB
General Secretary: Rev David J Campbell. *Administrative Secretary:* Mrs Anna Morton. Executive staff 1, Other staff 2. ***CC*** No.935PR11461. Began 1806; interdenominational. Magazine: *Word at Work* (4,000 frequency n/a). Turnover £350,000 to year end Dec 98. Fundraising for translation, production, distribution and use of the Scriptures.
Email: 11303.1511@compuserve.com
☎ 028 9032 6577 🖷 028 9031 1545

Bible Spreading Union, 1 Donald Way, Chelmsford CM2 9JB
Hon Secretary: Mr Stephen A Toms. No full-time staff. ***CC*** No.280847. Began 1894; interdenominational. No magazine. Turnover £28,827 to year end Aug 98. Distributing Holy Scriptures.
☎ 01245 268 815

Cambridge University Press, Edinburgh Building, Shaftesbury Road, Cambridge CB2 2RU
Bible Publishing Manager: Mr Christopher Wright. Executive staff 1, Other staff 2. ***CC*** Began 1591; non-denominational. No magazine. Turnover n/a. Publishing at all educational levels across most subjects (including religion and theology); Bibles, prayer books.
Web: www.cup.cam.ac.uk
Email: bibles@cup.cam.ac.uk
☎ 01223 325 586 🖷 01223 325 810

The Gideons International in the British Isles, Western House, George Street, Lutterworth LE17 4EE
Executive Director: Mr Desmond W Saunders. *Finance Officer:* Mr Christopher J Bryne. *Field Development Officer:* Mr Michael J Urwin. Executive staff 1, Other staff 10. ***CC*** No.221605. Began 1949; interdenominational. Magazine: *Gideon News* (44,000 quarterly). Turnover £2,656,745 to year end Dec 98. Personal witnessing and free distribution of Scriptures in hotels, hospitals, schools in 172 countries.
Web: www.gideons.org.uk
Email: hq@gideons.org.uk
☎ 01455 554 241 Fax 01455 558 267

International Bible Society (UK), 192 High Street, Guildford GU1 3HW
UK Director: Ms Sally Lambert. *Sales Director:* Mr Tim Moyler. Executive staff 2, Other staff 2. ***CC*** No.285319. Began 1992; non-denominational. (Incorporating Living Bibles International (UK)). No magazine. Turnover £230,000 to year end Dec 98. Serving the Church worldwide in evangelism and discipleship by providing low-cost editions of God's word.
Web: www.gospelcom.net/ibs/
Email: ibs_uk@eur.ibs.org
☎ 01483 306 869 Fax 01483 306 870

Lord Wharton's Charity, 30 Prentis Road, London SW16 1QD
Clerk to the Trustees: Mrs W B N Edwards. No full-time staff. ***CC*** No.200298. Began 1696; non-denominational. No magazine. Turnover £8,554 to year end Dec 97. Distributing free Bibles and prayer books to young people through Anglican and non-conformist churches.
☎ 020 8769 1924 Fax 020 8769 1924

National Bible Society of Scotland, Bible House, 7 Hampton Terrace, Edinburgh EH12 5XU
Executive Director: Rev Dr Graham Houston. Executive staff 4, Office staff 19. ***CC*** No.SCO10767. Began 1861; but Edinburgh Bible Society 1809; interdenominational. Magazine: *Word at Work* (70,000 every four months). Turnover n/a. Helping make the Word of God available to people everywhere at a price they can afford.
Web: www.nat-bible-society.org
Email: nbss@nat-bible-society.org
☎ 0131 337 9701 Fax 0131 337 0641

***Naval, Military & Air Force Bible Society**, Radstock House, 3 Eccleston Street, London SW1W 9LZ
Director: Mr Martin Hines. *Chairman:* Rev John Whitton. ***CC*** No.219055. Began 1780; non-denominational. Part of SGM International. Magazine: *SGM News* (30,000 quarterly). Turnover £157,000 to year end Dec 98. Distributing Scriptures to armed forces and merchant navy worldwide.
Email: nma@sgm.org
☎ 020 7463 1468 Fax 020 7730 0240

Open Book – contact **Bible Society**

Oxford University Press Bible Department, Great Clarendon Street, Oxford OX2 6DP
Publisher, Bibles and Worship Resources: Mr Nigel Lynn. Executive staff 2, Other staff 1. ***CC*** Began 1478; non-denominational. No magazine. Turnover n/a. Publishing of Bibles, hymn books and music, religious and theological books and software.
Web: www.oup.co.uk/
Email: lynnn@oup.co.uk
☎ 01865 556 767 Fax 01865 267 749
Also at: Distribution Services, Saxon Way West, Corby NN18 9ES
☎ 01536 741 519 Fax 01536 746 337

***SGM International**, Radstock House, 3 Eccleston Street, London SW1W 9LZ
Executive Director: Mr Bryan Stonehouse. *International Director:* Mr Hugh Davies. *International Publishing Director:* Mr David Atkinson. Executive staff 4, Other staff 36. ***CC*** Began 1888; non-denominational. (Previously Scripture Gift Mission). Magazine: *Interact* (30,000 quarterly). Turnover £2,700,000 to year end Dec 98. Distributing Bible portions in over 400 languages.
Web: members.aol.com/sgmint
Email: lon@sgm.org
☎ 020 7730 2155 Fax 020 7730 0240
Also at: 218 York Street, Belfast BT1 1GY
Email: ire@sgm.org
☎ 028 9074 5551

Society for Distributing Hebrew Scriptures, Joseph House, 1 Rectory Lane, Edgware HA8 7LF
General Secretary: Mr Eric R Browning. Executive staff 1, Other staff 6. ***CC*** No.232692. Began 1940; interdenominational. Magazine: *Lamp & Light* (6,000 every two months). Turnover n/a. Publishing and distributing Hebrew bilingual Scriptures worldwide.
Email: 106252.3131@compuserve.com
☎ 020 8952 9892 Fax 020 8381 1493

Trinitarian Bible Society, Tyndale House, Dorset Road, London SW19 3NN
General Secretary: Mr D P Rowland. *Assistant to General Manager:* Mr David Larlham. *Editorial Manager:* Mr George Anderson. Executive staff 2, Other staff 15. ***CC*** No.233082. Began 1831; non-denominational. Magazine: *Quarterly Record* (12,000 quarterly). Turnover £1,100,000 to year end Dec 98. Sale and grant of the Bible and Scripture portions in several languages throughout the world.
Web: biz.ukonline.co.uk/trinitarian.bible.society/contents.htm
Email: trinitarian.bible.society@ukonline
☎ 020 8543 7857 Fax 020 8543 6370

United Bible Societies, Europe/Middle East Regional Service Centre, Allied Dunbar House, East Park, Crawley RH10 6AS
Europe Middle East Regional Secretary: Rev A M Milloy. Executive staff 9, Other staff 14. ***CC*** No.2264875. Began 1946; interdenominational. No magazine. Turnover n/a. Developing and co-ordinating Bible Society policy in the Middle East and Europe.
☎ 01293 553 821 Fax 01293 553 839

United Bible Societies, World Service Centre, Reading Bridge House, 7th Floor, Reading RG1 8PJ
General Secretary: Rev Fergus Macdonald. Executive staff 8, Other staff 35. ***CC*** No.800058. Began 1946; interdenominational. Magazine: *UBS Bulletin* (Circulation n/a half-yearly), *The Bible Translator* (Circulation n/a quarterly). Turnover US$50,000,000 to year end Oct 95. Providing development support to national Bible Societies worldwide.
Web: www.biblesociety.org
☎ 01189 500 200 Fax 01189 500 857

B

BOOKSHOPS

By Country and Postcode area (see Page 569 for explanation)
Bookshops which did not supply any of this information are not listed here

Postcode	Location	Name	Titles Total	Titles of which Christian	Second-hand Titles Total	Second-hand Titles of which Christian	Floor Space sq ft
ENGLAND							
Anglia							
AL2	**St Albans**	McCrimmons Bookshop	10,000	10,000	-	-	250
AL3	**St Albans**	Crusader Book Centre	5,127	5,127	-	-	1,041
AL5	**Harpenden**	YWAM Books	1,000	1,000	-	-	500
CB2	**Cambridge**	Society for Promoting Christian Knowledge (SPCK)	30,000	30,000	-	-	n/a
		Wesley Owen Books and Music	3,500	3,500	-	-	680
CB7	**Ely**	Ely Cathedral Shop Ltd	2,500	1,500	-	-	1,000
		Lighthouse Christian Books and Music	3,000	3,000	200	200	750
CM2	**Chelmsford**	Christian Bookshop	10,500	10,500	-	-	500
		Elim Christian Centre Bookroom	600	600	-	-	150
CM9	**Maldon**	The Lighthouse	850	800	-	-	320
CM14	**Brentwood**	Christian Bookshop & The Edge Coffee Shop	10,500	10,500	-	-	800
CM21	**Sawbridgeworth**	Chapter and Verse	4,000	4,000	-	-	620
CO1	**Colchester**	Sign of the Fish Christian Bookshop	5,000	5,000	-	-	820
CO13	**Frinton-on-Sea**	Olive Luff Bible Bookshop Ltd	3,000	3,000	-	-	450
CO15	**Clacton-on-Sea**	Christian Bookshop Clacton Ltd	7,000	7,000	-	-	782
EN2	**Enfield**	Wesley Owen Books and Music	4,000	4,000	-	-	381
IG1	**Ilford**	The Bible Bookshop	3,500	3,500	-	-	1,000
IP1	**Ipswich**	CLC Bookshop	6,000	6,000	-	-	550
		Revelations	1,500	1,500	-	-	425
IP33	**Bury St Edmunds**	The Cathedral Shop	2,000	1,500	-	-	144
		Peter A Cook Christian Books	2,000	2,000	500	500	480
LU1	**Luton**	Luton Christian Book Centre	3,000	3,000	-	-	150
LU2	**Luton**	Hightown Christian Books	2,500	2,500	-	-	380
LU6	**Dunstable**	Christian Books	4,000	4,000	-	-	400
MK6	**Milton Keynes**	Christian Centre Bookshop	1,500	1,500	-	-	440
MK12	**Milton Keynes**	St Andrews Bookshop Ltd	3,000	3,000	-	-	400
MK40	**Bedford**	Harmony Books	5,500	5,400	100	100	450
		Wesley Owen Books and Music	3,500	3,500	-	-	620
NR1	**Norwich**	CLC Bookshop	8,500	8,500	-	-	720
		Norwich Cathedral Shop Ltd	1,000	1,000	-	-	n/a
NR2	**Norwich**	Society for Promoting Christian Knowledge (SPCK)	4,000	4,000	-	-	883
NR11	**Norwich**	Sonshine Christian Bookshop	1,800	1,800	-	-	700
NR19	**Dereham**	Green Pastures Christian Gift Shop	1,200	1,200	-	-	550
NR22	**Walsingham**	The Shrine Shop	1,500	1,500	-	-	300
NR32	**Lowestoft**	Oasis Christian Bookshop	2,000	2,000	-	-	600
PE1	**Peterborough**	Peterborough Cathedral Enterprises Ltd	950	900	-	-	200
		Peterborough Christian Books Ltd	5,000	5,000	-	-	1,000
PE9	**Stamford**	CLC Bookshop	3,000	3,000	-	-	525
PE13	**Wisbech**	GEM Books	450	450	-	-	n/a
PE17	**Huntingdon**	Christian Bookshop	1,000	1,000	-	-	225
PE19	**Huntingdon**	St Neots Christian Bookshop	2,000	2,000	-	-	650
RM1	**Romford**	Havering Christian Bookshop and Centre	7,000	7,000	-	-	1,800
RM12	**Hornchurch**	Frontline Christian Bookshop	1,000	1,000	200	200	500
SG6	**Letchworth**	The Christian Bookshop	9,000	9,000	-	-	600
SG12	**Ware**	All Nations Christian Bookshop Ltd	2,000	2,000	-	-	120
SS1	**Southend-on-Sea**	Southend Christian Bookshop Ltd	10,500	10,500	-	-	1,200
SS9	**Leigh-on-Sea**	Church Shop	1,600	1,600	-	-	576
SS14	**Basildon**	Eastgate Christian Bookshop Ltd	3,000	3,000	-	-	300
WD1	**Watford**	Wesley Owen Books and Music	3,500	3,500	-	-	683
London							
E2	**London**	Books For Life	1,500	1,500	200	200	300
E10	**London**	Good News Shop	10,000	10,000	-	-	400
E18	**London**	Wesley Owen Books and Music	4,400	4,400	-	-	691
EC1	**London**	CLC Bookshop	16,000	16,000	-	-	5,000
EC4	**London**	Protestant Truth Society Bookshop	6,000	6,000	-	-	950
N6	**London**	Metanoia Book Service	840	840	-	-	45
N9	**London**	Olive Tree	3,000	3,000	-	-	1,400
N12	**London**	Bedford Books	2,000	2,000	-	-	500
		Cornerstone	5,000	5,000	1,000	1,000	1,500
N14	**London**	Oak Hill College Bookroom	1,000	1,000	-	-	250
N16	**London**	Pendlebury's	-	-	25,000	25,000	n/a
NW1	**London**	Friends Book Centre	5,000	2,000	500	-	900
		Methodist Bookshop	6,000	6,000	-	-	576
		The Mustard Seed (Camden Town)	1,000	950	-	-	270
		SPCK Secondhand & Antiquarian Bookshop	-	-	10,000	10,000	600
SE1	**London**	The Cathedral Shop, Southwark	1,000	900	-	-	600
		Society for Promoting Christian Knowledge (SPCK)	5,000	5,000	-	-	400
		Tabernacle Bookshop	1,500	1,500	-	-	2,000
SE5		Christian City Books	1,500	1,500	300	300	400
SE12	**London**	Book AID	-	-	20,000	15,000	1,000
		Daybreak Books	1,200	1,200	-	-	76
SE18	**London**	Chapter Two	5,000	5,000	200	190	300
SE25	**London**	Spurgeon's Book Room	4,000	4,000	-	-	500
SW7	**London**	Holy Trinity Brompton Bookshop	3,300	3,300	-	-	1,000
SW16	**London**	Manna Christian Centre	5,000	5,000	-	-	700
SW19	**London**	E & W Fielder Ltd	12,000	200	-	-	n/a
SW1	**London**	Catholic Truth Society	2,000	2,000	-	-	750
		Church House Bookshop	12,000	12,000	-	-	2,000

Postcode	Location	Name	Titles Total	Titles of which Christian	Second-hand Titles Total	Second-hand Titles of which Christian	Floor Space sq ft
		St Pauls (Westminster Cathedral)	40,000	40,000	-	-	11,500
		Wesley Owen Books & Music	500	500	-	-	120
W1	London	The Good Book Café	1,000	1,000	-	-	250
		Institute for Contemporary Christianity	450	450	-	-	400
		Waterstones Bookshop incorporating Mowbrays	45,000	10,000	-	-	3,000
		Wesley Owen Books and Music	5,000	5,000	-	-	2,721
W3	London	Good News Christian Resource Centre Ltd	5,000	5,000	-	-	600
W8	London	St Paul MultiMedia	20,000	20,000	-	-	1,200
W11	London	Christian Books & Music, Kensington Temple	5,000	5,000	-	-	450
WC1	London	Dillons Bookstore (Theology Department)	2,000	2,000	500	500	n/a
	London	Salvationist Publishing and Supplies Ltd	1,300	1,200	-	-	2,300
		URC Bookshop	2,500	2,500	-	-	96
Midlands							
B21	Birmingham	Sharon Rose Bible Shop	2,000	2,000	-	-	500
B29	Birmingham	National Christian Education Council Book Sales	275	275	-	-	200
B30	Birmingham	St Andrews Bookshop Ltd	3,000	3,000	-	-	300
B90	Solihull	Revelation Books	3,000	3,000	-	-	600
B97	Redditch	Christian Word Shop	798	798	-	-	500
CV1	Coventry	Coventry Cathedral Bookshop	1,100	1,000	-	-	n/a
		Wesley Owen Books and Music	4,000	4,000	-	-	1,200
CV8	Kenilworth	Juteronomy	1,100	1,100	-	-	100
CV10	Nuneaton	YWAM Books	200	200	-	-	150
CV11	Nuneaton	The Sycamore Tree	2,000	2,000	-	-	450
CV21	Rugby	Christian Bookshop	2,000	2,000	-	-	60
CV31	Leamington Spa	Christian Book Shop	3,500	3,500	-	-	500
CV37	Stratford-upon-Avon	Jubilate Christian Bookshop Ltd	4,500	4,500	-	-	620
DE1	Derby	Derby Cathedral Shop Ltd	1,500	1,450	-	-	400
		Wesley Owen Books and Music	3,500	3,500	-	-	1,025
DE4	Matlock	Cornerstone	2,085	2,085	-	-	150
DE14	Burton-on-Trent	Linkup Christian Literature	1,800	1,800	-	-	729
DY1	Dudley	Barogha Books Ltd	2,500	2,500	-	-	1,500
DY8	Stourbridge	Living Springs	2,500	2,500	-	-	1,000
LE1	Leicester	Carley Centre Bookshop	500	500	-	-	36
		CLC Bookshop	10,000	10,000	-	-	1,195
		Society for Promoting Christian Knowledge (SPCK)	5,000	5,000	-	-	1,152
LE10	Hinckley	Christian Books (Hinckley)	2,500	2,500	-	-	252
LE11	Loughborough	Good News Centre	8,000	8,000	1,000	1,000	1,700
LE67	Coalville	Mount Saint Bernard Abbey Shop	6,000	4,000	-	-	280
NG1	Nottingham	Castlegate Bookshop	4,800	4,800	-	-	144
		Wesley Owen Books and Music	6,000	6,000	-	-	1,630
NG4	Nottingham	The Mustard Seed	1,500	1,500	-	-	600
NG7	Nottingham	Beech Avenue Bible Shop	3,000	3,000	-	-	500
		IVP Bookstall Service	350	350	-	-	120
NG9	Nottingham	Christian Book Centre	10,000	10,000	-	-	2,500
NG17	Nottingham	The Jesus Centre	3,000	3,000	-	-	1,600
NG18	Mansfield	Mansfield Christian Book Centre	n/a	n/a	n/a	n/a	900
NG24	Newark	Emmanuel Christian Bookshop	2,900	2,900	-	-	300
NN1	Northampton	Chapters	3,000	3,000	150	150	380
		The Manna House (Northampton Christian Centre)	5,000	5,000	2,000	2,000	2,400
ST1	Stoke-on-Trent	Bible Book Shop	4,000	4,000	-	-	450
		Methodist Book Centre	n/a	n/a	n/a	n/a	6,200
ST16	Stafford	Gateway Trust	6,000	6,000	-	-	800
WS1	Walsall	Wesley Owen Books and Music	3,500	3,500	-	-	975
WS13	Lichfield	Lichfield Cathedral Bookshop	5,000	4,000	-	-	725
WV2	Wolverhampton	CLC Bookshop	5,000	5,000	-	-	530
North East							
BD1	Bradford	Society for Promoting Christian Knowledge (SPCK)	10,000	10,000	-	-	2,000
BD21	Keighley	Grape Vine Bookshop	2,000	2,000	-	-	310
BD23	Skipton	Cornerstone	3,000	3,000	300	300	750
DH1	Durham	Barbican Bookroom	4,000	4,000	2,000	2,000	350
		Dillons University Bookshop	72,000	8,000	10,000	4,000	6,000
		The Cathedral Bookshop (Society for Promoting Christian Knowledge)	2,000	2,000	-	-	792
DH8	Consett	Good News Christian Book Shop and Coffee Shop	300	300	-	-	250
DL3	Darlington	Acorn Christian Bookshop	2,000	2,000	-	-	500
DL10	Richmond	Zetland Christian Bookshop	563	563	-	-	255
DL12	Barnard Castle	Book AID	-	-	5,000	5,000	800
DN1	Doncaster	Christian Outlook	3,500	3,500	-	-	450
DN10	Doncaster	Book AID	-	-	3,000	3,000	400
DN15	Scunthorpe	Kings Christian Bookshop	3,000	2,500	500	500	600
DN22	Retford	Book AID	-	-	20,000	15,000	1,000
DN32	Grimsby	Lifeline Christian Bookstore	4,500	4,500	-	-	3,000
HD1	Huddersfield	Centre Books, Crafts and Coffee Shop	5,000	5,000	-	-	7,000
HG1	Harrogate	Branchlines Christian Resource Centre	7,000	7,000	-	-	900
HG4	Ripon	The Ark Christian Bookshop	800	800	200	200	200
HU2	Hull	Good News Centre, Hull (Wesley Owen Books & Music)	5,000	5,000	5,000	5,000	1,100
HU13	Hessle	Our Lady's Bookshop	5,000	5,000	-	-	350
HU17	Beverley	Beverley Minster Shop	100	60	-	-	192
		Jacob's Well	500	500	500	150	430
HX1	Halifax	Good Life Books (GLF)	2,000	2,000	-	-	1,000
LN2	Lincoln	Advance Bookshop	6,500	4,500	-	-	700
		Society for Promoting Christian Knowledge (SPCK)	n/a	n/a	n/a	n/a	1,173
LS1	Leeds	Society for Promoting Christian Knowledge (SPCK)	n/a	n/a	n/a	n/a	355
		Wesley Owen Books and Music	5,000	5,000	-	-	1,060
LS2	Leeds	C Goodliffe Neale Ltd	6,000	6,000	-	-	300
NE1	Newcastle upon Tyne	The Bible House	7,250	5,250	-	-	1,544
		CLC Bookshop	10,000	10,000	-	-	1,980

Bookshops

Postcode	Location	Name	Titles Total	Titles of which Christian	Second-hand Titles Total	Second-hand Titles of which Christian	Floor Space sq ft
		Society for Promoting Christian Knowledge (SPCK)	9,000	9,000	-	-	1,053
NE26	**Whitley Bay**	Bethany Christian Bookshop and Coffeeshop	1,500	1,500	-	-	466
NE46	**Hexham**	Shalom The Good Book Shop	3,800	3,800	-	-	600
S1	**Sheffield**	CLC Bookshop	10,000	10,000	-	-	935
		Hallam Book Centre	1,000	1,000	-	-	500
		SPCK Sheffield Cathedral Bookshop	2,800	2,800	-	-	817
		Wesleyan Reform Union Bookshop	400	400	-	-	324
S32	**Sheffield**	Cliff College Bookshop	3,500	3,500	-	-	430
S40	**Chesterfield**	Cornerstone Bookshop and Coffee Shop	1,500	1,500	-	-	n/a
S45	**Chesterfield**	Food for Thought	1,500	1,500	-	-	240
S66	**Maltby**	Full Life Christian Book and Music Shop	400	400	-	-	600
SR5	**Sunderland**	Bridge Books & Music	3,500	3,500	-	-	872
TD15	**Berwick-upon-Tweed**	Faith Mission Christian Book Centre	5,000	5,000	-	-	250
TS1	**Middlesbrough**	CLC Bookshop	8,000	8,000	-	-	720
TS10	**Redcar**	Adeste Christian Trust	1,000	1,000	200	200	800
TS18	**Stockton-on-Tees**	Christian Literature Centre	5,000	5,000	-	-	1,028
TS25	**Hartlepool**	Christian Ministries	275	275	35	35	n/a
WF1	**Wakefield**	3's Company Bookshop	2,500	2,500	-	-	500
		Wakefield Cathedral Bookshop	350	350	-	-	130
WF5	**Ossett**	Christian Bookshop	1,600	1,600	2,000	2,000	540
WF8	**Pontefract**	Pontefract Christian Bookshop	2,000	2,000	-	-	700
WF13	**Dewsbury**	The Branch Christian Books	5,000	5,000	300	300	1,000
YO1	**York**	Barbican Bookshop	10,000	5,000	20,000	10,000	2,000
		Society for Promoting Christian Knowledge (SPCK)	10,000	10,000	-	-	1,507
		Spurriergate Centre	200	200	-	-	n/a
YO11	**Scarborough**	Immanuel Bookshop	3,000	3,000	100	100	400
YO15	**Bridlington**	Bethany Bookshop	2,000	2,000	250	250	600
North West							
BB2	**Blackburn**	Blackburn Bible Depot	200	200	100	100	1,000
BB5	**Accrington**	Abbey Book and Resource Centre	4,000	4,000	6,000	5,000	1,200
BL1	**Bolton**	Wesley Owen Books and Music	2,000	2,000	-	-	856
BL9	**Bury**	Exodus (The Rock) Ltd	5,000	5,000	1,000	1,000	1,500
CA3	**Carlisle**	Society for Promoting Christian Knowledge (SPCK) (The Cathedral Bookshop)	n/a	n/a	n/a	n/a	610
		Wesley Owen Books and Music	3,500	3,500	-	-	750
CA15	**Maryport**	The Bookshop	400	250	-	-	250
CA28	**Whitehaven**	Cornerstone Christian Bookshop	2,600	2,600	500	500	1,200
CH1	**Chester**	Chester Cathedral Shop	650	550	-	-	200
		Ravens Ltd	8,000	8,000	-	-	750
		Society for Promoting Christian Knowledge (SPCK)	4,000	4,000	-	-	902
CH41	**Birkenhead**	Christian Bookshop	8,000	8,000	-	-	750
CH44	**Wallasey**	Wallasey Christian Books	3,500	3,500	500	0	576
CH45	**Wallasey**	The Haven Christian Bookshop & Centre	500	500	-	-	540
CW1	**Crewe**	Copnal Books	-	-	15,000	2,000	700
		The Way Bookshop	n/a	n/a	n/a	n/a	432
CW9	**Northwich**	Ichthus Christian Books	2,000	2,000	-	-	390
FY1	**Blackpool**	Chapter & Verse Christian Bookshop	6,000	6,000	-	-	700
FY8	**Lytham St Annes**	Stepping Stone	5,000	5,000	-	-	500
L1	**Liverpool**	Gladstones Bookshop (Christian Media)	3,000	3,000	200	200	1,200
		St Paul MultiMedia	20,000	20,000	-	-	1,000
		Liverpool Cathedral Bookshop (SPCK)	8,500	8,200	-	-	2,000
		Wesley Owen Books and Music	3,500	3,500	-	-	865
L3	**Liverpool**	Metropolitan Cathedral Bookshop	700	600	-	-	400
L13	**Liverpool**	Bethany Books	2,000	2,000	-	-	300
L17	**Liverpool**	Aigburth Christian Bookshop	5,000	5,000	-	-	n/a
L31	**Liverpool**	Cornerstone	2,000	1,900	-	-	150
LA1	**Lancaster**	Good News Christian Bookshop	2,000	2,000	-	-	310
LA6	**Carnforth**	Capernwray Bookshop	2,000	2,000	-	-	200
LA9	**Kendal**	Market Place Books	4,000	3,500	-	-	500
LA12	**Ulverston**	Lonsdale Bible Society	3,000	3,000	1,000	1,000	500
M2	**Manchester**	Catholic Truth Society	8,500	8,500	-	-	2,800
M3	**Salford**	Cathedral Books Ltd	2,200	2,200	-	-	1,750
	Manchester	Society for Promoting Christian Knowledge (SPCK)	10,000	10,000	-	-	1,041
		Wesley Owen Books and Music	3,500	3,500	-	-	1,440
M4	**Manchester**	St Denys' Bookshop	5,000	5,000	-	-	1,200
M41	**Manchester**	Taste & See Bookshop	1,000	1,000	-	-	n/a
M43	**Manchester**	Reflections Bookshop	6,500	6,500	-	-	620
M60	**Manchester**	Christian World Centre	12,000	12,000	-	-	5,000
OL1	**Oldham**	King of Kings Christian Bookshop	2,000	2,000	-	-	350
OL6	**Ashton-under-Lyne**	Spectrum Christian Books and Gifts	2,000	2,000	-	-	360
OL12	**Rochdale**	Campaign Christian Books	1,800	1,800	-	-	360
OL15	**Littleborough**	The Vine Christian Bookshop and Coffee House	800	800	-	-	90
PR 1	**Preston**	Christian Book Centre	8,000	8,000	-	-	900
PR 7	**Chorley**	Two Worlds Christian Bookshop	3,000	3,000	-	-	400
PR 8	**Southport**	Southport Christian Book Centre	8,000	8,000	-	-	1,200
SK 1	**Stockport**	Wesley Owen Books and Music	3,500	3,500	-	-	1,185
SK10	**Macclesfield**	Christian Book Centre	250	250	-	-	140
SK11	**Macclesfield**	Wesley Owen Books and Music	3,000	3,000	-	-	689
SK17	**Buxton**	Buxton Christian Bookshop	1,750	1,750	160	160	350
SY1	**Shrewsbury**	Freemans Christian Bookshop	6,000	6,000	250	250	1,200
SY11	**Oswestry**	Oswestry Christian Bookshop	2,000	2,000	-	-	6,900
SY13	**Whitchurch**	Aletheia Ltd	4,000	4,000	-	-	100
TF3	**Telford**	Revelations	6,000	6,000	-	-	800
TF9	**Market Drayton**	St Mary's Church Bookshop	1,000	1,000	-	-	145
WA1	**Warrington**	CLC Bookshop	4,000	4,000	-	-	700
WA10	**St Helens**	The Christian Bookshop	3,000	3,000	-	-	192
WA14	**Altrincham**	Charis Books	1,000	1,000	-	-	1,000
WN1	**Wigan**	Words Bookshop	4,500	4,500	-	-	2,000

Postcode	Location	Name	Titles Total	Titles of which Christian	Second-hand Titles Total	Second-hand Titles of which Christian	Floor Space sq ft
South Central							
HA3	Harrow	Wesley Owen Books and Music	3,500	3,500	-	-	1,156
HA6	Northwood	The Christian Book Centre	2,000	2,000	-	-	300
HP16	Great Missenden	St Andrews Bookshop Ltd	6,000	6,000	-	-	1,500
OX1	Oxford	B H Blackwell Ltd (Religion Dept)	6,939	6,005	1,420	1,420	169
		St Andrews Bookshop Ltd	3,000	3,000	-	-	300
OX4	Oxford	St Andrews Bookshop Ltd	3,000	3,000	-	-	850
OX8	Witney	St Andrews Bookshop Ltd	3,000	3,000	-	-	350
OX10	Wallingford	The Fountain (Wallingford) Ltd	1,000	1,000	-	-	360
PO1	Portsmouth	Portsmouth Cathedral Bookshop	1,500	1,200	-	-	80
PO2	Portsmouth	Portsmouth Christian Book Centre	5,000	5,000	-	-	500
PO5	Southsea	Academy Books	100,000	50,000	75,000	25,000	n/a
		Acorn Book and Toy Shop	2,000	1,500	-	-	144
PO11	Hayling Island	The Bridge Centre	900	900	-	-	250
PO12	Gosport	Cornerstone Books	2,500	2,500	-	-	900
PO18	Chichester	Catholic Bible School Bookshop	1,000	1,000	-	-	25
PO19	Chichester	Living Word	3,500	3,500	150	150	500
		Society for Promoting Christian Knowledge (SPCK)	3,000	3,000	-	-	624
PO21	Bognor Regis	Living Word	2,500	2,500	100	100	600
PO30	Newport	Castlebooks	8,000	8,000	-	-	858
PO33	Ryde	Quarr Abbey Bookshop	700	700	100	100	600
RG1	Reading	Greyfriars Christian Centre	1,200	1,200	-	-	1,080
		St Andrews Bookshop Ltd	4,000	4,000	-	-	800
RG12	Bracknell	Kerith Centre Bookshop	2,200	2,200	-	-	200
RG14	Newbury	Temple Courts Christian Bookshop	2,000	2,000	-	-	300
RG40	Wokingham	St Andrews Bookshop Ltd	3,000	3,000	-	-	350
SL6	Maidenhead	St Andrews Bookshop Ltd	3,000	3,000	-	-	425
SL9	Gerrards Cross	Gold Hill Church Books	1,000	1,000	-	-	n/a
		WEC Bookroom	1,000	1,000	-	-	200
SN1	Swindon	Christian Bookshop	3,500	3,500	-	-	450
		The Rainbow Bookshop	700	700	-	-	120
		Wesley Owen Books and Music	3,500	3,500	-	-	941
SN6	Swindon	Seekers Light Trust	3,000	3,000	-	-	500
SN8	Marlborough	Mustard Seed	2,000	2,000	-	-	288
SN9	Pewsey	Pewsey Christian Bookshop	6,200	6,000	200	200	1,000
SN11	Calne	Calne Christian Bookshop	2,750	2,750	300	300	200
SN15	Chippenham	The Revelation Christian Bookshop	3,000	3,000	-	-	500
SN16	Malmesbury	Malmesbury Abbey Books Ltd	4,000	4,000	-	-	350
SO15	Southampton	CLC Bookshop	10,000	10,000	-	-	1,100
SO16	Southampton	Southern Light Ministries	800	800	100	0	100
SO19	Southampton	Mayflower Christian Bookshop	1,990	1,990	135	135	500
SO23	Winchester	Society for Promoting Christian Knowledge (SPCK)	10,000	10,000	-	-	752
SO41	Lymington	The Archway	6,500	6,500	40	40	n/a
SO51	Romsey	The Oasis Christian Centre	3,500	3,500	-	-	800
		Sozo Books	750	750	-	-	300
SP1	Salisbury	Close Harmony Ltd	170	60	-	-	30
		Society for Promoting Christian Knowledge (SPCK)	3,000	3,000	-	-	835
		Swells Bookshop Ltd	4,000	4,000	1,000	1,000	360
SP10	Andover	The Vine Trust Bookshop	2,000	2,000	-	-	400
UB6	Greenford	Perivale Christian Bookshop	5,000	5,000	-	-	850
UB8	Uxbridge	Maranatha Christian Bookshop	5,000	5,000	-	-	850
South East							
BN1	Brighton	Society for Promoting Christian Knowledge (SPCK)	3,000	3,000	-	-	600
BN3	Hove	Books Alive Christian Bookshop	4,000	4,000	-	-	500
BN11	Worthing	Wesley Owen Books and Music	3,000	3,000	-	-	750
BN21	Eastbourne	Eastbourne Christian Resource Centre	10,000	10,000	1,000	1,000	1,000
BN25	Seaford	Living Words	6,000	6,000	-	-	1,000
BR1	Bromley	Goodnews Bookshop	50	50	-	-	n/a
		Wesley Owen Books and Music	10,000	10,000	-	-	3,683
BR3	Beckenham	Churches Together in Beckenham Shop	650	650	-	-	550
BR5	Orpington	Rainbow Christian Centre	2,500	2,500	-	-	300
BR6	Orpington	The Christian Bookshop	11,000	11,000	-	-	860
CR0	Croydon	Wesley Owen Books and Music	4,500	4,500	-	-	883
CT1	Canterbury	CLC Bookshop	10,000	10,000	-	-	1,625
		Society for Promoting Christian Knowledge (SPCK)	10,000	10,000	-	-	917
CT5	Whitstable	Bethsaida Christian Bookshop	6,000	3,000	3,000	3,000	550
CT6	Herne Bay	Herne Bay Court Bookshop	300	300	-	-	144
CT9	Margate	Christian Book Centre	5,000	5,000	1,500	1,500	850
CT14	Deal	Deal Christian Resource Centre	1,500	1,500	-	-	432
DA8	Erith	Ark Christian Bookshop & Cafe	1,000	1,000	-	-	500
DA12	Gravesend	Oasis Christian Bookshop	2,600	2,600	-	-	312
DA16	Welling	CLC Bookshop	7,000	7,000	-	-	600
GU 1	Guildford	Society for Promoting Christian Knowledge (SPCK)	n/a	n/a	n/a	n/a	492
		Wesley Owen Books and Music	3,000	3,000	-	-	700
GU 2	Guildford	Guildford Cathedral Bookshop	3,000	2,900	-	-	380
GU 7	Godalming	Nathan's Christian Book Shop	3,000	3,000	-	-	645
GU12	Aldershot	The New Life Bookshop	3,500	3,500	-	-	480
GU13	Fleet	LivingStones Christian Centre	3,000	3,000	-	-	1,500
GU14	Farnborough	The Triangle	5,000	5,000	-	-	460
GU15	Camberley	High Cross Christian Bookshop	2,500	2,500	-	-	n/a
GU21	Woking	Berean Bookshop	3,000	3,000	-	-	440
GU31	Petersfield	Unity Bookshop	1,750	1,750	-	-	300
GU34	Alton	The Alton Christian Bookshop	750	200	-	-	100
		Just Looking Christian Bookshop	2,500	2,500	100	100	800
		Redemptorist Publications	3,000	3,000	-	-	6,000
KT1	Kingston upon Thames	Chapter & Verse	6,000	6,000	-	-	900
ME4	Chatham	CLC Bookshop	4,500	4,500	-	-	484
ME10	Sittingbourne	Sittingbourne Christian Bookshop	1,350	1,350	225	225	400

B

Bookshops

Postcode	Location	Name	Titles Total	Titles of which Christian	Second-hand Titles Total	Second-hand Titles of which Christian	Floor Space sq ft
ME14	Maidstone	The Christian Bookshop	10,000	10,000	-	-	n/a
ME20	Maidstone	Aylesford Priory Bookshop	2,000	1,700	-	-	750
RH2	Reigate	Christian Bookshop	2,000	2,000	-	-	400
RH4	Dorking	Dorking Christian Bookshop	3,000	3,000	1,000	1,000	550
RH10	Crawley	Dabcec Bookshop	3,000	2,700	-	-	600
		Wesley Owen Books and Music	3,000	3,000	-	-	350
RH16	Haywards Heath	Christian Book Centre	6,500	6,500	-	-	800
RH19	East Grinstead	The Open Door	6,000	6,000	-	-	700
SM1	Sutton	Wesley Owen Books and Music	6,200	6,200	-	-	1,000
SM6	Wallington	The Oasis Christian Centre	3,000	3,000	-	-	900
TN1	Tunbridge Wells	The Christian Book Shop	11,000	11,000	-	-	500
TN6	Crowborough	Good News Christian Bookshop	1,500	1,500	-	-	160
TN9	Tonbridge	The Tonbridge Christian Book Centre Ltd	11,000	11,000	-	-	1,200
TN22	Uckfield	Pilgrim Hall Bookshop	1,500	1,500	-	-	300
TN24	Ashford	Cornerstone Bookshop	1,800	1,800	-	-	473
TN33	Battle	Ashburnham Christian Trust Bookshop	1,500	1,500	-	-	300
TN34	Hastings	Pathway Books Ltd	4,000	4,000	-	-	440
TW3	Hounslow	Bridge Christian Books	4,500	4,500	-	-	900
TW9	Richmond	Wesley Owen Books and Music	3,500	3,500	-	-	620
TW18	Staines	Canaan Christian Book Centre	5,000	5,000	-	-	600
South West							
B2	Birmingham	CLC Bookshop	10,000	10,000	-	-	1,045
		Society for Promoting Christian Knowledge (SPCK)	10,000	10,000	-	-	1,150
B4	Birmingham	St Chad's Cathedral Bookshop	306	306	-	-	60
		The Book Room (Wesley Owen Books and Music)	40,000	10,000	-	-	3,000
B9	Birmingham	Birmingham City Mission Bookshop/Video Library	2,500	2,500	500	500	550
BA1	Bath	Society for Promoting Christian Knowledge (SPCK)	5,000	5,000	1,500	0	800
BA5	Wells	Wells Cathedral Publications Ltd	369	324	-	-	432
BA14	Trowbridge	Kings	250	250	-	-	n/a
BA20	Yeovil	Oasis Christian Bookshop	2,000	2,000	-	-	795
BH 1	Bournemouth	Keith Jones Christian Bookshop	20,000	20,000	500	500	2,250
		The Living Stone Bookshop	6,500	6,500	-	-	500
BH 9	Bournemouth	Bible Truth Depot	1,000	1,000	-	-	n/a
BH15	Poole	Ichthus Bookshop	300	300	-	-	320
BH19	Swanage	Swanage Christian Centre	3,500	3,500	-	-	400
BS1	Bristol	Society for Promoting Christian Knowledge (SPCK)	5,000	5,000	-	-	1,450
		Wesley Owen Books and Music	4,000	4,000	-	-	1,349
BS16	Bristol	Oasis Coffee House	1,300	1,300	-	-	500
BS18	Bristol	Family Books (Keynsham)	1,000	700	-	-	1,400
BS23	Weston-super-Mare	Wesley Owen Books and Music	n/a	n/a	n/a	n/a	735
DT1	Dorchester	Frank Herring & Sons	2,000	2,000	-	-	240
DT4	Weymouth	Weymouth Christian Books	3,000	3,000	-	-	400
DT6	Bridport	Good Books	5,000	4,000	-	-	1,200
EX1	Exeter	The Cathedral Shop	450	350	-	-	270
		Society for Promoting Christian Knowledge (SPCK)	5,000	5,000	-	-	921
		Wesley Owen Books and Music	3,500	3,500	-	-	1,154
EX4	Exeter	Book AID	-	-	3,000	1,500	500
EX16	Tiverton	New Creation Trust Christian Book and Coffee Shop	1,500	1,500	-	-	720
EX23	Bude	The Ark Angel Christian Bookshop	1,500	1,500	50	50	480
EX31	Barnstaple	Doves Christian Bookshop	4,000	4,000	-	-	1,000
EX39	Bideford	Evangel Christian Shop and Resource Centre	4,500	4,000	-	-	400
GL1	Gloucester	SPCK Gloucester Cathedral Bookshop	1,000	1,000	-	-	400
GL5	Stroud	Centre Christian Bookshop	2,500	2,500	900	900	800
GL14	Cinderford	Wye Dean Christian Centre	1,500	1,500	-	-	600
GL15	Lydney	Wye Dean Christian Centre	1,500	1,500	-	-	500
GL18	Newent	Good News Centre (Bookshop and Coffeehouse)	3,000	3,000	5,000	5,000	1,000
GL20	Tewkesbury	The Bible Bookshop	2,750	2,750	-	-	192
GL50	Cheltenham	Wesley Owen Books and Music	3,500	3,500	-	-	900
HR1	Hereford	Hereford Cathedral Shop	20	10	-	-	400
HR4	Hereford	Palace Yard Bookshop (Society for Promoting Christian Knowledge)	3,000	3,000	-	-	389
HR9	Ross-on-Wye	John Bevan (Catholic Bookseller)	0	0	10,000	10,000	1,150
PL1	Plymouth	Christian Literature Centre	5,000	5,000	-	-	500
PL15	Launceston	Aquila Fellowship Trust (The Christian Bookshop)	4,000	4,000	700	680	1,122
PL25	St Austell	Good News Crusade Bookshop	5,000	5,000	-	-	450
TA1	Taunton	Good News - TCLC	5,000	5,000	-	-	650
TA6	Bridgwater	Acorns Christian Resources	2,400	2,400	-	-	700
TQ4	Paignton	Choice Words Torbay	3,000	3,000	-	-	850
TQ11	Buckfastleigh	Abbey Bookshop	5,000	5,000	-	-	660
TQ12	Newton Abbot	Brexwise Ltd Bookshop	600	600	150	150	n/a
		Choice Words Christian Bookshop	3,000	3,000	-	-	650
TR1	Truro	Society for Promoting Christian Knowledge (SPCK)	7,500	7,500	-	-	1,218
		Sunrise (Good News Crusade)	6,000	6,000	-	-	525
		Truro Cathedral Shop	2,000	1,500	-	-	500
TR13	Helston	Living Waters Christian Bookshop	8,000	8,000	-	-	450
TR15	Redruth	Christian Book Centre	5,000	5,000	-	-	400
TR18	Penzance	The Living Word	3,000	3,000	-	-	130
TR26	St Ives	Zion Christian Books	2,000	2,000	-	-	n/a
WR1	Worcester	Ichthus Christian Bookshop	2,000	2,000	-	-	120
		Society for Promoting Christian Knowledge (SPCK)	7,500	7,500	-	-	1,234
NORTHERN IRELAND							
BT1	Belfast	APCK Book Centre	7,000	7,000	-	-	940
		Belfast Book and Bible House	800	700	-	-	1,000
		Evangelical Book Shop	10,000	10,000	5,000	5,000	900
		Faith Mission Bookshop	10,000	10,000	2,000	2,000	6,000
		Familybooks Ltd	12,000	11,000	-	-	1,450
BT4	Belfast	Belmont Christian Book Centre	3,000	3,000	200	0	n/a

Postcode	Location	Name	Titles Total	Titles of which Christian	Second-hand Titles Total	Second-hand Titles of which Christian	Floor Space sq ft
BT5	Belfast	Scripture Union Resource Centre	1,500	1,500	-	-	1,000
BT6	Belfast	Ebenezer Bible and Bookshop	1,200	1,200	450	450	675
BT7	Belfast	Methodist Bookroom	2,500	2,500	-	-	500
BT9	Belfast	Covenanter Bookshop	3,000	3,000	500	0	400
BT20	Bangor	Faith Mission Bookshop	10,000	10,000	-	-	750
BT23	Newtownards	Ards Evangelical Bookshop	20,000	20,000	-	-	1,200
BT28	Lisburn	Faith Mission Bookshop	10,000	10,000	-	-	750
BT32	Banbridge	Faith Mission Bookshop	5,000	5,000	-	-	750
BT33	Newcastle	Beulah Bookshop	4,000	4,000	300	300	300
BT34	Newry	Faith Mission Bookshop	10,000	10,000	-	-	1,500
BT39	Ballyclare	Book AID	-	-	3,000	3,000	400
		Christian Book Centre	1,000	1,000	-	-	500
BT41	Antrim	Books in Print	1,000	1,000	-	-	500
BT43	Ballymena	Faith Mission Bookshop	10,000	10,000	-	-	750
BT47	Londonderry	Faith Mission Bookshop	10,000	10,000	-	-	750
BT52	Coleraine	Mizpah Bible & Bookshop	3,500	3,500	-	-	600
BT61	Armagh	Faith Mission Bookshop	5,000	5,000	-	-	600
BT62	Craigavon	Faith Mission Bookshop	10,000	10,000	-	-	3,000
BT66	Craigavon	Faith Mission Bookshop	10,000	10,000	-	-	500
BT74	Enniskillen	Evangelical Bookshop	3,000	3,000	-	-	440
BT78	Omagh	Faith Mission Bookshop	10,000	10,000	-	-	500
BT80	Cookstown	Faith Mission Bookshop	10,000	10,000	-	-	600
BT92	Enniskillen	Oasis Bookshop	500	500	-	-	380
SCOTLAND							
AB1	Aberdeen	CLC Bookshop	10,000	10,000	-	-	2,000
		Wesley Owen Books and Music	15,000	12,500	-	-	1,973
AB2	Aberdeen	Blackwell's University Bookshop	500	500	-	-	2,000
AB10	Aberdeen	Scripture Union Bookshop	1,000	1,000	-	-	150
AB42	Peterhead	Faith Mission Christian Book Centre	10,000	10,000	-	-	500
AB43	Fraserburgh	Faith Mission Christian Book Centre	4,500	4,500	-	-	360
DD1	Dundee	CLC Bookshop	5,000	5,000	-	-	500
		Wesley Owen Books and Music	2,500	2,500	-	-	670
DD10	Montrose	The Water Pot	500	500	-	-	300
DG5	Dalbeattie	The Bible Shop	1,200	1,200	350	350	360
DG7	Castle Douglas	The Bible Shop	1,700	1,700	-	-	400
EH1	Edinburgh	James A Dickson Books (The Christian Bookshop)	7,500	5,000	5,000	5,000	444
		Free Church of Scotland Bookshop	10,880	10,880	-	-	300
		B McCall Barbour	10,000	10,000	300	300	300
EH 2	Edinburgh	Wesley Owen Books and Music	21,000	17,500	-	-	2,723
EH51	Bo'ness	Branches	300	300	-	-	450
FK1	Falkirk	Wesley Owen Books and Music	3,000	3,000	-	-	900
FK8	Stirling	Faith Mission Christian Book Centre	5,000	5,000	-	-	600
G1	Glasgow	St Paul MultiMedia	20,000	20,000	-	-	900
G2	Glasgow	Wesley Owen Books and Music	22,000	20,000	-	-	2,800
G3	Glasgow	Free Presbyterian Church of Scotland Bookroom	3,500	3,500	500	0	450
G4	Glasgow	Scripture Union Bookshop	4,000	4,000	-	-	500
G64	Glasgow	Christian Centre	1,000	1,000	-	-	150
G66	Glasgow	The Baptist Church Bookshop	2,000	2,000	-	-	300
G67	Glasgow	Cumbernauld Churches Bookshop Ltd	500	500	-	-	300
		New Dawn Bookshop and Connection Coffee House	2,000	2,000	-	-	1,200
G82	Dumbarton	Dumbarton Baptist Bookshop	1,200	1,200	-	-	450
HS1	Stornoway	Blythswood Bookshop	1,100	1,100	-	-	550
		Stornoway Religious Bookshop	1,200	1,200	-	-	360
IV1	Inverness	CLC Bookshop	4,500	4,500	-	-	430
IV2	Inverness	Wesley Owen Books and Music	4,500	4,000	-	-	1,200
IV15	Dingwall	Blythswood Bookshop	850	850	50	50	216
IV30	Elgin	Pluscarden Abbey Bookshop	500	500	100	100	430
IV51	Portree	Blythswood Bookshop	800	800	50	50	250
IV54	Lochcarron	Blythswood Bookshop	650	650	1,000	1,000	300
KA7	Ayr	Wesley Owen Books and Music	4,000	3,250	-	-	1,157
KA21	Saltcoats	Come Back to God Campaign	322	322	-	-	400
KY1	Kirkcaldy	GLO Bookshop	n/a	n/a	n/a	n/a	800
KY12	Dunfermline	Faith Mission Christian Book Centre	20,000	20,000	-	-	2,000
KY15	Cupar	The Lighthouse	2,500	2,500	-	-	160
KY16	St Andrews	The Ladyhead Bookshop	3,000	2,800	-	-	300
ML1	Motherwell	GLO Bookshop	15,491	15,491	-	-	1,500
ML3	Hamilton	SCEM Bookstore	950	950	-	-	250
PA15	Greenock	New Dawn Bookshop and Connection Coffee House	4,500	4,500	-	-	1,850
PA23	Dunoon	Dunoon Baptist Church Centre	2,000	2,000	-	-	500
PA34	Oban	Fountain Christian Books	1,100	1,100	-	-	250
PH1	Perth	The Manna House	3,000	3,000	-	-	700
PH2	Perth	Mustard Seed Bookshop	5,000	5,000	-	-	945
PH16	Pitlochry	Atholl Centre Bookshop	400	400	-	-	247
TD9	Hawick	Mustard Seed Bookshop	4,000	4,000	-	-	400
ZE1	Lerwick	Christian Bookshop, Lerwick	2,500	2,500	-	-	295
ZE2	Shetland	Christian Bookshop	750	750	-	-	54
WALES							
CF1	Cardiff	Christian Bookshop	3,500	3,500	200	200	1,000
		English, Welsh and Foreign Bible Depot	1,250	1,250	-	-	250
		Society for Promoting Christian Knowledge (SPCK)	n/a	n/a	n/a	n/a	700
CF4	Cardiff	Heath Christian Bookshop Charitable Trust	2,500	2,500	500	500	750
		The Olive Branch Christian Book & Coffee Shop	3,000	3,000	-	-	400
CF6	Penarth	Vale Christian Bookshop	2,000	2,000	-	-	400
CF31	Bridgend	Christian Bookshop	1,000	1,000	-	-	400
CF37	Pontypridd	Harvest Books and Crafts	2,000	2,000	-	-	400
CF44	Aberdare	Beulah Faith Mission & Christian Bookshop	2,000	2,000	-	-	500

Postcode	Location	Name	Titles Total	Titles of which Christian	Second-hand Titles Total	Second-hand Titles of which Christian	Floor Space sq ft
CH5	Deeside	Bethany Books	600	400	-	-	260
CH7	Mold	Good News Centre	1,000	1,000	-	-	280
LD1	Llandrindod Wells	E.M.W. Christian Books & Crafts	1,200	1,200	-	-	275
LL11	Wrexham	The Christian Bookshop	1,000	1,000	-	-	200
LL18	Rhyl	Clwyd Christian Bookshop Ltd	4,000	4,000	-	-	700
LL34	Penmaenmawr	Oasis Christian Bookshop and Tearoom	950	950	-	-	760
LL57	Bangor	Bangor Christian Bookshop	2,100	2,100	-	-	270
		RE Bookshop/Llyfrfa AG	6,000	2,000	-	-	450
NP4	Pontypool	Christian Bookshop	1,000	1,000	300	300	n/a
NP9	Newport	Christian Book and Media Centre	9,000	8,000	500	500	2,000
NP44	Cwmbran	Beacon Books and Crafts Ltd	3,250	3,250	700	700	800
SA1	Swansea	Christian Bookshop	900	900	-	-	360
		CLC Bookshop	10,000	10,000	-	-	1,195
SA14	Llanelli	The Apostolic Church Training School Bookshop	1,200	1,200	-	-	850
SA31	Carmarthen	Christian Books	550	550	-	-	12
SA34	Whitland	Christian Connections	450	450	100	100	200
SA43	Cardigan	Teifi Christian Books	1,500	1,500	250	250	260
SA61	Haverfordwest	Emmanuel Missions Bookshop	2,500	2,500	-	-	450
SA62	Haverfordwest	St Davids Cathedral Bookshop	700	700	-	-	250
SA65	Fishguard	Emmanuel Christian Bookshop	1,000	1,000	-	-	180
SA71	Pembroke	Haven Christian Bookshop	4,000	4,000	-	-	100
SY16	Newtown	Emmanuel Books and Gifts	1,200	1,200	50	50	402
SY18	Llanidloes	Bethany Books	1,000	1,000	-	-	150
SY23	Aberystwyth	Christian Bookshop	2,000	2,000	-	-	200
		St Michael's Bookshop	1,741	1,741	-	-	250
CHANNEL ISLES							
GY1	Guernsey	Good News Christian Bookshop	1,500	1,500	-	-	300
JE2	Jersey	Christian Bookshop Mission Ltd	2,000	2,000	-	-	210
ISLE OF MAN							
IM1	Douglas	Churches Bookshop	4,000	4,000	70	70	200
IM2	Douglas	The Well Bookshop & Coffee Shop	3,500	3,500	50	50	750

BOOKSHOPS

3's Company Bookshop, 3 Upper York Street, Wakefield WF1 3LQ
Manager: Mrs Bridie Watson. Other staff 1. ***CC*** No.1003233. Began 1991; interdenominational. Turnover £50,000 to year end Dec 98. Coffee shop.
☎ 01924 201 022

***Abbey Book and Resource Centre**, 188 Union Road, Oswaldtwistle, Accrington BB5 3EG
Manager: Mr A Best. Executive staff 1. ***CC*** No.517995. Began 1984; interdenominational. Turnover n/a. Coffee shop.
☎ 01254 399 299

†Abbey Bookshop, Buckfast Abbey, Buckfastleigh TQ11 0EE
Manager: Rev Fr Matthew. Other staff 3. Began n/a; Roman Catholic. Turnover £156,000 to year end Oct 92.
☎ 01364 642 882

Academy Books, 13 Marmion Road, Southsea PO5 2AT
Proprietor: Mr William H Robinson. Executive staff 1, Other staff 2. Began 1972; non-denominational. Turnover n/a.
☎ 023 9281 6632 🖷 023 9281 6632

Acorn Book and Toy Shop, 109 Palmerston Road, Southsea PO5 3PS
Director: Miss Jean Pitts. Executive staff 1, Other staff 1. Began 1988; non-denominational. Turnover n/a.
☎ 023 9282 3925

Acorn Christian Bookshop, Royal Oak Yard, Bondgate, Darlington DL3 7JD
Manager: Mr Duncan Tart. Executive staff 1, Other staff 4. Began 1995; interdenominational. (Previously Elim Christian Centre Bookshop). Turnover £150,000 to year end Dec 98. Worldwide mail order service.
Web: www.acorndirect.co.uk & www.christian.music.co.uk
Email: info@acorndirect.co.uk
☎ 01325 487 366

***Acorns Christian Resources**, 67 High Street, Bridgwater TA6 3BQ
Manager: Mrs Eileen McDonald. No other full-time, staff. ***CC*** No.1071926. Began 1988; non-denominational. (Previously Little Acorns). Part of Acorns Christian Trust. Turnover n/a.
☎ 01278 453 045 🖷 01278 453 045

Adeste Christian Trust, 8 Redcar Lane, Redcar TS10 3JF
Chairman: Mr John Ashwell. No full-time staff. ***CC*** Began 1982; interdenominational. Turnover £10,000 to year end Mar 98.
☎ 01642 480 252

Advance Bookshop, 17 Monks Road, Lincoln LN2 5HL
Proprietors: Mr David & Mrs June Pallister, Mrs Anne Winslade. Other staff 1. Began 1950; interdenominational. Turnover n/a.
☎ 01522 525 898 🖷 01522 528 188

Aigburth Christian Bookshop, 361 Aigburth Road, Liverpool L17 0BP
Manager: Mr C Barton. No full-time staff. ***CC*** No.278411. Began 1982; non-denominational. Turnover n/a. Selling Reformed Christian books. Mail order service.
☎ 0151 727 0436

†Aletheia Ltd, 11 High Street, Whitchurch SY13 1AX
Managing Director: Rev Kenneth T Lillie. Executive staff 1, Other staff 3. Began 1977; evangelical. Turnover £150,000 to year end Dec 96.
☎ 01948 663 770

***All Nations Christian Bookshop Ltd**, Easneye, Ware SG12 8LX
Manageress: Mrs Elizabeth Wright. Executive staff 1, Other staff 1. Began 1972; interdenominational. Turnover £80,000 to year end Dec 98.
☎ 01920 469 126 🖷 01920 462 997

For additional information see List on Pages 134–140

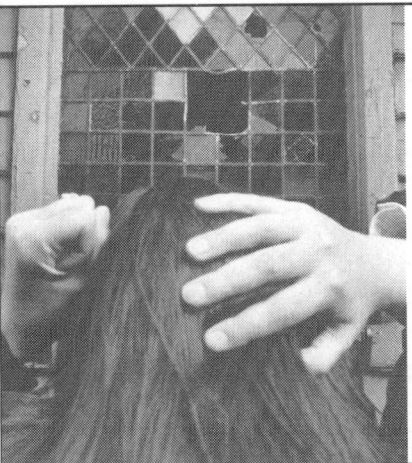

The Alton Christian Bookshop, Maranatha, 8 Hall Road, Alton GU34 2NU
Proprietor: Mr Damian Duggan. Full-time staff 1. Began 1993; interdenominational. Turnover £6,000 to year end July 96. Mail-order books; also small bookshop; supplying Christian greeting cards to repositories and shops.
☎ 01420 805 71 🖷 01420 805 71

APCK Book Centre, Church of Ireland House, 61 Donegall Street, Belfast BT1 2QH
Manager: Mr Stephen Edgar. *Senior Bookseller:* Mrs Evelyn Lewis. Other staff 4. Began 1978; Church of Ireland. (Previously Belfast Cathedral Book Centre). Turnover n/a.
Email: apck@ireland.anglican.org
☎ 028 9024 4825

†**The Apostolic Church Training School Bookshop**, Caerbryn Road, Penygroes, Llanelli SA14 7PH
Manageress: Mrs Lorraine Price. Executive staff 1. Began n/a; Apostolic. Turnover n/a.
☎ 01269 832 069

Aquila Fellowship Trust (The Christian Bookshop), 9 Westgate Street, Launceston PL15 7AB
Hon Secretary: Mr Christopher G Paxman. Executive staff 1, Other staff 2. ***CC*** No.253092. Began 1967; non-denominational. Turnover n/a.
☎ 01566 772 047

The Archway, 11 St Thomas Street, Lymington SO41 9NA
Executive staff 1, Other staff 10. Began 1984; non-denominational. Turnover £61,488 to year end Jan 98. Coffee shop.
☎ 01590 679 710 🖷 01590 679 710

Ards Evangelical Bookshop, 7 High Street, Newtownards BT23 4JN
Owner & Manager: Mr Richard M'Coubrey. Executive staff 4, Other staff 2. Began 1965; non-denominational. Turnover n/a.
Email: order@ardsbookshop.com
☎ 028 9181 7530 🖷 028 9181 5581

The Ark Angel Christian Bookshop, 4 Lansdowne Mews, Lansdowne Road, Bude EX23 8BH
Manageress: Mrs P Knight. Staff n/a. ***CC*** No.294313. Began 1986; interdenominational. Turnover n/a. Book sales, music, prayer, videos, video library, Traidcraft, sheet music, play corner.
☎ 01288 356 886

Ark Christian Bookshop & Cafe, 19 Pier Road, Erith DA8 1TA
Administrator: Mr M Harvey. Other staff 2. ***CC*** No.1044047. Began 1988; interdenominational. Turnover n/a.
Email: mickharvey@compuserve.com
☎ 01322 332 515 🖷 01322 348 249

The Ark Christian Bookshop, 3 Ripon Small Shops, Duck Hill, Ripon HG4 1BL
Owners: Mr & Mrs P Bertenshaw. No other staff. Began 1988; non-denominational. Turnover n/a.
☎ 01765 603 551

***Ashburnham Christian Trust Bookshop**, Ashburnham Place, Battle TN33 9NF
Manager: Mrs Susan Betts. No full-time staff. ***CC*** Began 1960; non-denominational. Turnover £75,000 to year end Apr 98.
Web: www.ashburnham.org.uk
Email: mail@ashburnham.org.uk
☎ 01424 892 244

†**Atholl Centre Bookshop**, Atholl Road, Pitlochry PH16 5BX
Director of Centre: Mr Gavin Graham. Other staff: see Atholl Centre. ***CC*** Began 1970; interdenominational. Turnover n/a.
☎ 01796 473 044

Aylesford Priory Bookshop, The Friars, Aylesford, Maidstone ME20 7BX
Business Manager: Mr Norman Harlow. Executive staff 1, Other staff 4. ***CC*** Began 1949; Roman Catholic. Turnover n/a.
☎ 01622 717 272 🖷 01622 715 575

Bangor Christian Bookshop, 31 Holyhead Road, Upper Bangor, Bangor LL57 2EU
Manager: Mr John P Gough. Executive staff 1, Part-time staff 2. ***CC*** No.222407. Began 1972; non-denominational. Turnover £36,035 to year end Jan 98.
☎ 01248 353 386 🖷 01248 353 386

The Baptist Church Bookshop, Kirkintilloch Baptist Church, Townhead, Kirkintilloch, Glasgow G66 3EG
Manager: Ms Elizabeth Thomson. Executive staff 2. ***CC*** Began 1985; Baptist. Turnover n/a.
☎ 0141 578 0059 🖷 0141 578 6004

Barbican Bookroom, 28 Sutton Street, Durham DH1 4BW
Manageress: Mrs Eileen Farquhar. Executive staff 1. Began 1970; interdenominational. Turnover n/a.
☎ 0191 386 3041

For additional information see List on Pages 134–140

Barbican Bookshop, 24 Fossgate, York YO1 2TA
Directors: Mr Les & Mrs Jean Bingham. Executive staff 1, Other staff 6. Began 1962; non-denominational. Turnover n/a. Supplying Christian books/resources including huge second-hand/antiquarian section; mail order anywhere. Good books wanted.
Email: barbican@cwcom.net
☎ 01904 653 643

Barogha Books Ltd, 1 Rutland Passage, Dudley DY1 1PZ
Director: Mrs Gillian Nash. *Manager:* Mrs Rita Collins. Executive staff 1, Other staff 2. ***CC*** Began 1984; interdenominational. (Previously Filling Station Christian Bookshop). Turnover n/a.
☎ 01384 213 764 Fax 01384 213 764

B

Beacon Books and Crafts Ltd, 17 North Walk, Cwmbran NP44 1PR
Manageress: Miss Tracey Downey. Executive staff 1, Other staff 2. ***CC*** No.517778. Began 1983; non-denominational. Turnover £130,000.
☎ 01633 484 587

Bedford Books, 45 Woodhouse Road, North Finchley, London N12 9ET
Manager: Andrew Franks. Executive staff 2. ***CC*** No.281838. Began 1958; non-denominational. Owned by Finchley Christian Bookshops Ltd. Turnover n/a. Remainder books, also by mail order.
☎ 020 8446 3056
Email: bedford@cornerstone4551.freeserve.uk

Beech Avenue Bible Shop, 52 Beech Avenue, New Basford, Nottingham NG7 7LQ
Manager: Mr David Hayes. Executive staff 1, Other staff 2. ***CC*** No.245132. Began 1978; interdenominational. Turnover £21,000 to year end Dec 96.
Email: cys@prima.net
☎ 0115 962 3715 Fax 0115 962 3715

Belfast Book and Bible House, 64 Ann Street, Belfast BT1 4EG
Proprietor: Mr Michael J Penfold. Executive staff 1, Other staff 3. Began 1882; non-denominational. (Previously Northern Publishing Belfast). Turnover n/a.
☎ 028 9023 0064

Belmont Christian Book Centre, 49 Belmont Road, Belfast BT4 2AA
Manager: Mr Andrew Poots. Executive staff 1, Other staff 1. Began 1987; non-denominational. Turnover n/a.
☎ 028 9065 3718 Fax 028 9065 3718

Berean Bookshop, 26 High Street, Woking GU21 1BW
Manager: Mr A Thomson. Executive staff 1, Other staff 3. Began 1956; evangelical. Turnover n/a.
☎ 01483 715 358 Fax 01483 715 358

Bethany Books, 5 Chester Road West, Shotton, Deeside CH5 1BX
Managers: Mrs Cathy Griffiths, Mrs Janice Matthews. Executive staff 2. Began 1986; non-denominational. Turnover n/a.
☎ 01244 813 532 Fax 01244 813 532

Bethany Books, 28 Uppingham Road, Liverpool L13 7BJ
Proprietor: Mr D Brian Greenhalgh. Executive staff 1. Began 1982; non-denominational. Turnover n/a.
Email: brian@ghalgh.freeserve.co.uk
☎ 0151 259 4831 Mobile: 07958 460 592

Bethany Books, 1 High Street, Llanidloes SY18 6BY
Manager: Miss C Davies. All voluntary staff. Began 1985; Church in Wales. Turnover £6,000 to year end Dec 92.
☎ 01686 412 370 Fax 01686 412 370

***Bethany Bookshop**, 48 Promenade, Bridlington YO15 2QQ
Manager: Mr Christopher J Heywood. Executive staff 2, Other staff 1. Began 1984; non-denominational. Turnover n/a.
☎ 01262 604 758

Bethany Christian Bookshop and Coffeeshop (Churches Acting Together, Whitley Bay), 26 Ilfracombe Gardens, Whitley Bay NE26 3SL
Shop Manager: Mrs Hilary Atkinson. Other staff 8. ***CC*** No.1009261. Began 1995; interdenominational. Turnover £34,000 to year end June 94. Bookshop, coffee, quiet room.
☎ 0191 297 0262 Fax 0191 297 0262

Bethsaida Christian Bookshop, 9 Tower Parade, Whitstable CT5 2BJ
Manager: Mr Robin W H Johnson. Other staff 1. Began 1980; interdenominational. Turnover n/a.
Email: rob@bethsaida.idps.co.uk
☎ 01227 265 961

Beulah Bookshop, 67 Central Promenade, Newcastle BT33 0HH
Manager: Mr G McConnell. Admin staff 1. Began 1966; Free Presbyterian. Turnover n/a.
Email: fpcmisson@aol.com
☎ 028 4472 2629

Beulah Faith Mission & Christian Bookshop, 30 Whitcombe Street, Aberdare CF44 7AU
Manager: Mr Peter Mitchell. Executive staff 1. ***CC*** No.135597. Began 1927; interdenominational. Turnover n/a.
☎ 01685 873 209

John Bevan (Catholic Bookseller), St Francis, Great Doward, Ross-on-Wye HR9 6DY
Proprietor: Mr John Bevan. Executive staff 2. Began 1974; Roman Catholic. Turnover £100,000 to year end July 97.
Email: catholicbooks@compuserve.com
☎ 01600 890 878 Fax 01600 890 888

Beverley Minster Shop, Minster Yard North, Beverley HU17 0DP
Manager: Mr R I Shaw. All voluntary staff. ***CC*** No.244976. Began 1975; Anglican. Turnover £60,000 to year end Dec 98. Sale of Christian books, artefacts and music, site specific and general souvenirs, postcards, cards, guidebooks.
☎ 01482 887 520 Fax 01482 887 520

Bible Book Shop, 17 Huntbach Street, Hanley, Stoke-on-Trent ST1 2BL
Manager: Mr Keith Galley. Executive staff 1, Other staff 1. Began 1963; interdenominational. Turnover n/a.
☎ 01782 214 709

The Bible Bookshop, 27 Clements Road, Ilford IG1 1BH
Partner: Miss Jill Black. Executive staff 1, Other staff 1. Began 1960; non-denominational. Turnover n/a. Cards, gifts, music, videos and pictures also available.
☎ 020 8478 3278 Fax 020 8478 3278

The Bible Bookshop, 11 Nelson Street, Tewkesbury GL20 5QF
Proprietor: Mrs Elizabeth Williams. No other staff. Began 1976; non-denominational. Turnover £53,000 to year end Dec 96. Coffee shop.
☎ 01684 295 546

The Bible House, 14 Pilgrim Street, Newcastle upon Tyne NE1 6QD
Manageress: Mrs B Johnson. Executive staff 1, Other staff 8. ***CC*** No.228583. Began 1864; non-denominational. Turnover £50,000 to year end Jan 94. Tapes and CDs, stationery office, supporting Bible Society.
☎ 0191 232 0335 Fax 0191 233 0869

For additional information see List on Pages 134–140

The Bible Shop, 168 King Street, Castle Douglas DG7 1DA
Manager/Owner: Mr Jim Figgis. Staff 1. Began 1996; non-denominational. Turnover £22,500. Bible specialists, music, mail order, tracts, stationery, cards.
Web: www.castledouglas.net/thebibleshop
☎ 01556 504 416 🖷 01556 504 416

The Bible Shop, 40a High Street, Dalbeattie DG5 4AA
Manager/Owner: Mr Jim Figgis. Staff 1. Began 1991; non-denominational. Turnover £5,500. Bible specialists, tracts, music, stationery, cards, coffee shop.
☎ 01556 610 549 🖷 01556 610 549

Bible Truth Depot, 18 Namu Road, Bournemouth BH9 2QU
Owner: Mr Philip Jenkins. Executive staff 1. Began 1980; non-denominational. Turnover n/a. Publishers of 'Joyful News Gospel Calendar' and other evangelical literature.
☎ 01202 516 739

***Birmingham City Mission Bookshop/Video Library**, 75 Watery Lane Middleway, Bordesley, Birmingham B9 4HN
Manager: Mr Warwick Goulding. Executive staff 1. ***CC*** No.1051023. Began 1968; interdenominational. Turnover £24,570 to year end Mar 98. Gifts, music, video library.
Web: www.internet-pilots.com/city_missions/
Email: mission@globalnet.co.uk
☎ 0121 771 0098

Blackburn Bible Depot, 10 Stansfeld Street, Blackburn BB2 2NH
Overseer: Mr Frank Thomas. No full-time staff. Began 1948; Christian Brethren. Turnover n/a.
☎ 01254 663 874

B H Blackwell Ltd (Religion Dept), 48 Broad Street, Oxford OX1 3BQ
Department Manager: Mr L J Fry. Executive staff 1, Other staff 2. Began n/a; non-denominational. Turnover n/a.
Web: www.bookshop.blackwell.co.uk
Email: extra@blackwellsbookshops.co.uk
☎ 01865 792 792 Ext 440 🖷 01865 794 143

Blackwell's University Bookshop, 99 High Street, Old Aberdeen, Aberdeen AB2 3EN
Profit Centre Manager: Mr Colin Walker. Staff n/a. Began 1879; non-denominational. (Previously Bissets Theology Department). Turnover £800,000 to year end Dec 98.
Email: aberdeen@blackwellsbookshops.co.uk
☎ 01224 486 102 🖷 01224 276 162

Blythswood Bookshop, Station Square, Dingwall IV15 9JD
Manageress: Miss M MacDougall. Executive staff 1, Other staff 2. ***CC*** Began n/a; Reformed/evangelical. (Previously Christian Bookshop). Turnover n/a.
☎ 01349 864 608

Blythswood Bookshop, Main Street, Lochcarron IV54 8YD
Manager: Mr Peter Reynolds. ***CC*** Began 1984; Reformed/evangelical. (Previously Lochcarron Christian Books). Turnover n/a.
Web: www.blythswood.org.uk
Email: reynoldsp@blythswood.org.uk
☎ 01520 722 337 🖷 01520 722 264

Blythswood Bookshop, Quay Street, Portree IV51 9DE
Contact: Mrs Anne Shaw. All voluntary staff. ***CC*** Began 1973; Reformed/evangelical. (Previously Christian Bookshop). Turnover n/a.
☎ 01478 612 198

Blythswood Bookshop, 16 Church Street, Stornoway HS1 2DH
Contact: Mr M D Maclean. Other staff (voluntary) 8. ***CC*** Began 1973; Reformed/evangelical. (Previously Christian Bookshop). Turnover n/a.
☎ 01851 702 420

***Book AID**, The Haven Christian Centre, 44 Rickamore Road Upper, Templepatrick, Ballyclare BT39 0JE
Shop Manager: Mr Frank Rea. Executive staff 1, Other staff 2. ***CC*** Began 1987; interdenominational. Turnover n/a.
☎ 028 9443 2061

***Book AID**, 5 Galgate, Barnard Castle DL12 8EQ
Shop Manager: Mr Maurice Abrahams. Executive staff 1, Other staff 2. ***CC*** Began 1987; interdenominational. Turnover n/a.
☎ 01833 630 209

***Book AID**, Bawtry Hall, Bawtry, Doncaster DN10 6JH
Shop Manager: Mr Stephen Green. Executive staff 1. ***CC*** Began 1987; interdenominational. Turnover n/a.
☎ 01777 817 101

***Book AID**, 47 Longbrook Street, Exeter EX4 6AW
Shop Manageress: Mrs Margaret Robertson. Executive staff 2, Other staff 1. ***CC*** Began 1987; interdenominational. Turnover n/a.
☎ 01902 213 002

***Book AID**, Mayeswood Road, Grove Park, London SE12 9RP
Shop Manager: Mrs Ada Hiley. Executive staff 2, Other staff 4. ***CC*** Began 1987; interdenominational. Turnover n/a. No mail to this address.
Mailing address: 271 Church Road, London SE19 2QQ
☎ 020 8857 7794 🖷 020 8653 6577

***Book AID**, North Road, Ranskill, Retford DN22 8NL
Manager: Mr Stephen Green. Executive staff 2, Other staff 4. ***CC*** Began 1987; interdenominational. Turnover n/a.
☎ 01777 817 101 🖷 01777 817 101

***Books Alive Christian Bookshop**, 86 Elm Drive, Hove BN3 7JL
Manager: Mrs Sue Puttock. Other staff 2. Began 1994; interdenominational. Turnover £50,000-100,000 to year end Dec 98.
☎ 01273 738 818 🖷 01273 738 818

***Books For Life**, Bethnal Green Mission Church, 305 Cambridge Heath Road, London E2 9LH
Manager: Mr Richard G Farrell. Executive staff 1. ***CC*** No.222262. Began 1952; non-denominational. (Previously Bethnal Green Medical Mission Books). Turnover £42,800 to year end Dec 95.
☎ 020 7729 4286

***Books in Print**, 14 New Street, Randalstown BT41 3AF
Proprietor: Rev Robert McEvoy. Other staff 3. Began 1973; non-denominational. (Previously Christian Book Centre). Turnover n/a. Printers and stationers.
Web: www.rkmcevoy.clara.net
Email: rkmcevoy@claranet.co.uk
☎ 028 9447 3195 🖷 028 9447 3195

The Bookshop, 89 Crosby Street, Maryport CA15 6BP
Manager: Joanna Varley. Executive staff 1, Other staff 1. Began 1966; interdenominational. Turnover n/a.
☎ 01900 812 363

For additional information see List on Pages 134–140

The Branch Christian Books, 17 Halifax Road, Dewsbury WF13 4AF
Manager: Mrs Heather Ward. Executive staff 1, Other staff 2. ***CC*** No.247191. Began 1984; non-denominational. Turnover £54,000 to year end Dec 94. Coffee shop.
Email: branchsch@aol.com
☎ 01924 454 750

†**Branches**, 74 Market Square, Bo'ness EH51 9NF
Co-ordinator: Mr Douglas Farmer. All voluntary staff. ***CC*** Began 1986; interdenominational. Turnover n/a.
☎ 01506 826 205

Branchlines Christian Resource Centre, 11 Commercial Street, Harrogate HG1 1UB
Proprietor: Mrs Evelyn Dowbiggin. Executive staff 2, Other staff 2. Began 1990; non-denominational. Turnover n/a.
Email: info@branchlines.freeserve.co.uk
☎ 01423 521 662 Fax 01423 521 662

Brexwise Ltd Bookshop, Rora House, Halford, Liverton, Newton Abbot TQ12 6NG
Manager: n/a. ***CC*** Began 1972; non-denominational. Turnover n/a.
☎ 01626 821 746 Fax 01626 821 586

Bridge Books & Music, 14 North Bridge Street, Sunderland SR5 1LD
Manager: Mr Rob Foreman. Executive staff 1, Other staff 3. ***CC*** Began 1974; interdenominational. (Previously Scripture Union Bookshop, Wesley Owen Books & Music). Turnover n/a.
☎ 0191 567 3544 Fax 0191 567 3544

Bridge Christian Books, Holy Trinity Church, High Street, Hounslow TW3 1HG
Manager: Cathy Allen. Other staff 2. ***CC*** Began 1983; Anglican. (Previously Bridge Centre Ltd). Turnover n/a. Coffee shop.
☎ 020 8577 0388 Fax 020 8570 8886

The Burning Light, The Farne House, Marygate, Holy Island, Berwick-upon-Tweed TD15 2SJ
Owner/Manager: Mrs Mary Fleeson. Executive staff 1, Admin staff 2. Began 1997; non-denominational. Turnover n/a. Specialising in Celtic and Monastic spirituality, drama, puppetry, youthwork.
Web: www.burninglight.co.uk
Email: shop@burninglight.co.uk
☎ 01289 389 269 Fax 01289 389 269

Buxton Christian Bookshop, 2 Market Street, Buxton SK17 6JY
Managers: Trustees. Other staff 4. ***CC*** No.1046267. Began 1985; non-denominational. Turnover £35,000 to year end Dec 98.
☎ 01298 268 43

Calne Christian Bookshop, 16 Phelps Parade, Calne SN11 0HA
Manager: Mr H J Jarvis. All voluntary staff. ***CC*** No.298889. Began 1979; non-denominational. Turnover £20,000 to year end Dec 98. Counselling occasionally available.
☎ No telephone
Correspondence: 6 Poynder Place, Hilmarton, Calne SN11 8SQ
☎ 01249 760 398

***Campaign Christian Books**, 96 Whitworth Road, Rochdale OL12 0JJ
Manager: Mr H Varney. Executive staff 2. ***CC*** No.240168. Began 1956; interdenominational. (Linked to Come Back to God Campaign). Turnover £13,500 to year end Dec 97.
Web: www.comebacktogod.org
Email: campaign@comebacktogod.org
☎ 01706 312 53

Canaan Christian Book Centre, 121 High Street, Staines TW18 4PD
Director/Manager: Mr A P Gilmour. Executive staff 1, Other staff 4. ***CC*** No.1015433. Began 1979; non-denominational. Turnover £150,000 to year end Jan 95. Coffee shop and Christian counselling. Mail order service.
Email: canaan@bigfoot.com
☎ 01784 457 194 Fax 01784 441 040

***Capernwray Bookshop**, Capernwray Missionary Fellowship of Torchbearers, Capernwray Hall, Carnforth LA6 1AG
Bookshop Manager: Mr Richard McLeish. ***CC*** No.253607. Began 1966; non-denominational. Turnover £30,000 to year end Dec 99. Christian bookshop and resource centre.
Web: www.capernwray.co.uk
Email: info@capernwray.co.uk
☎ 01524 733 908 Fax 01524 736 681

***Carley Centre Bookshop**, Wharf Street North, Leicester LE1 2AB
Manager: Mr Peter H Adams. Executive staff 1. ***CC*** Began 1984; Independent Baptist. Turnover n/a. Part of Carley Evangelical Baptist Church.
☎ 0116 253 8064

Castlebooks, 82 High Street, Newport PO30 1BH
Manageress: Mrs Susan Young. Executive staff 1, Other staff 2. ***CC*** No.274901. Began 1976; interdenominational. Turnover £145,000 to year end Dec 98.
☎ 01983 525 885 Fax 01983 521 950

Castlegate Bookshop, 4 Castlegate, Nottingham NG1 7AS
Manager: Mrs Maureen Ashdown. Executive staff 1. Began 1979; Congregational. Turnover n/a.
☎ 0115 9111 1453 Fax 0115 9111 1455

Cathedral Books Ltd, 250 Chapel Street, Salford M3 5LL
Manageress: Miss Veronica Turtle. Other staff 2. ***CC*** No.2660084. Began 1988; Roman Catholic. Turnover £143,000 to year end Aug 97. Articles of devotion.
☎ 0161 833 0092 Fax 0161 831 9799

The Cathedral Shop, Angel Hill, Bury St Edmunds IP33 1RS
Manageress: Mrs Lorna Atwell. Other staff 1. ***CC*** Began 1991; Anglican. Turnover n/a.
☎ 01284 754 933

†**The Cathedral Shop**, Exeter Cathedral, Exeter EX1 1HS
Manager: Mr David Hanson. Executive staff 2, Other staff 1. Began 1984; Anglican. Turnover n/a.
☎ 01392 271 354

The Cathedral Shop, Montague Close, London Bridge, London SE1 9DA
Manager: Miss Leslee Turner. All voluntary staff. Began 1970; Anglican. (Previously Southwark Cathedral Bookshop). Turnover n/a. Wide range of greeting cards and gifts also available.
Web: www.dswark.org
Email: cathedral@dswark.org.uk
☎ 020 7407 3708 Fax 020 7357 7389

Catholic Bible School Bookshop, Nutbourne House, Farm Lane, Nutbourne, Chichester PO18 8SD
Director: Mrs Joan Le Morvan. Executive staff 2, Other staff 4. ***CC*** No.262679. Began 1988; Roman Catholic. Turnover n/a.
Web: www.tregalic.co.uk/catholic/bibleschool/
Email: bibleschool@tregalic.co.uk
☎ 01243 371 766

For additional information see List on Pages 134–140

Catholic Truth Society, 25 Princess Street, Albert Square, Manchester M2 4HH
Manager: Mr Michael Silgram. *CC* No.1058718. Began 1891; Roman Catholic. Turnover n/a.
☎ 0161 228 0437 🖷 0161 228 0438

Catholic Truth Society, Upper Level, Princess Square, Newcastle upon Tyne NE1 8ER
Manageress: Mrs Kay Byrne. Executive staff 4. *CC* Began 1922; Roman Catholic. Turnover n/a.
☎ 0191 232 1169 🖷 0191 232 1169

†**Catholic Truth Society**, 25 Ashley Place, Westminster Cathedral Piazza, London SW1V 1PD
Shop Manager: Ms Eleanor Greenshields. Executive staff 1, Other staff 3. *CC* Began 1926; Roman Catholic. Turnover n/a.
☎ 020 7834 1363 🖷 020 7630 5166

The Centre, 4 South Street, Horsham RH12 1NR
Manager: Mr Doug Fletcher. Executive staff 1, No other paid staff. *CC* No.1038233. Began 1994; ecumenical. Turnover £200,000 to year end Dec 98. Coffee shop, listening service.
Email: booksales@horshamchristiancentre.freeserve.co.uk
☎ 01403 218 821 🖷 01403 276 483

Centre Books, Crafts and Coffee Shop, 5a Northumberland Street, Huddersfield HD1 1RL
Bookshop Manager: Mr Paul Cooper. Other staff 8. *CC* No.514595. Began 1991; non-denominational. Turnover n/a.
☎ 01484 514 088 🖷 01484 425 188

Centre Christian Bookshop, 5 London Road, Stroud GL5 2AG
Manager: Mr David Gegg. Executive staff 2, Other staff 15. *CC* Began 1981; non-denominational. Turnover £87,000 to year end Feb 98.
☎ 01453 764 713 🖷 01453 764 713

***Chapter & Verse**, 32 Fife Road, Kingston upon Thames KT1 1SU
Manager: Mr Steve Mitchell. *Partner:* Mr Peter Butler. Other staff 7. Began 1995; non-denominational. Turnover £350,000 to year end Dec 98. Internet and mail order bookshop and resource centre.
Web: www.chapterandverse.co.uk
Email: info@chapterandverse.co.uk
☎ 020 8541 0001 (Office) 0800 731 8323 (Sales freefone)
🖷 020 8547 2617

Chapter and Verse, 49 Bell Street, Sawbridgeworth CM21 9AR
Trustee: Margaret Hill. Executive staff 2, No other full-time staff. *CC* Began 1983; interdenominational. Turnover n/a.
☎ 01279 724 929

Chapter & Verse Christian Bookshop, 45 Abingdon Street, Blackpool FY1 1DH
Proprietors: Mr John & Mrs Eileen Hutchinson. Full-time staff 4. Began n/a; non-denominational. Turnover n/a.
☎ 01253 624 160

Chapter Two, 199 Plumstead Common Road, Plumstead Common, London SE18 2UJ
Principal: Mr Edwin Cross. Executive staff 3, Other staff 10. *CC* No.1053047. Began 1976; non-denominational. Turnover n/a. Fundamental dispensational bookseller specialising in Plymouth Brethren publications, Bible sales and advice.
☎ 020 8316 4972 🖷 020 8854 5963
Also at: Fountain House, 1a Conduit Road, Woolwich, London SE18 7AJ
☎ 020 8316 5389

Chapters, 2 College Street Mews, Northampton NN1 2QP
Financial Controller: Miss Sylvia Davis. No full-time staff. *CC* Began 1987; interdenominational. Turnover n/a.
☎ 01604 636 555

Charis Books, 1 Central Way, Altrincham WA14 1SB
Manager: Mr Timothy Morris. Executive staff 1, Other staff 1. Began 1988; non-denominational. Turnover £75,000 to year end Apr 98. A small bookshop and coffee shop catering for the local churches and Christian community.
☎ 0161 929 7409 🖷 0161 926 8259

Chester Cathedral Shop, 12 Abbey Square, Chester CH1 2HU
Manager: Mrs Christine R Gibbs. Other staff 1. Began 1977; Anglican. Turnover £400,000 to year end Dec 98.
Web: www.chestercathedral.org.uk
Email: shop@chestercathedral.org.uk
☎ 01244 311 586 🖷 01244 313 155

B

Choice Words Christian Bookshop, 40 Devon Square, Newton Abbot TQ12 2HH
Proprietor: Mrs Pam Brittle. Executive staff 1, Other staff 2. Began 1984; non-denominational. Turnover £100,000 to year end Dec 98. Mail order, student discounts, bookstalls and conferences.
☎ 01626 334 027 🖷 01626 334 027

Choice Words Torbay, 37 Hyde Road, Paignton TQ4 5BP
Proprietor: Mrs Pam Brittle. Executive staff 1. *CC* No.1051834. Began 1998; interdenominational. (Previously Torbay Christian Bookshop). Linked with Choice Words Newton Abbot. Turnover: first year of operation. Book agent and valued customer schemes, mail order, bookstalls and conferences, student discounts.
☎ 01803 551 316 🖷 01803 551 316

Christian Book and Media Centre, 131 Lower Dock Street, Newport NP9 1EG
Retail Manager: Geraint R Hill. Executive staff 1, Other staff 3. *CC* No.1051834. Began 1976; interdenominational. (Previously Newport Christian Bookshop (Valley Books Trust)). Division of Zionsong Ltd. Turnover £75,000 to year end Dec 96.
Email: cbmc@hill.softnet.co.uk
☎ 01633 259 222 🖷 01633 259 222

***Christian Book Centre**, 18 Rashee Road, Ballyclare BT39 9HJ
Proprietors: Mr & Mrs Harry Wilson. Staff n/a. Began 1982; non-denominational. Turnover n/a.
☎ 028 9335 2170

***Christian Book Centre**, 34 Sussex Road, Haywards Heath RH16 4EA
Co-ordinator: Mrs Paula Richardson. No full time staff. Began 1983; interdenominational. (Linked to Tonbridge Christian Book Centre). Turnover £120,000 to year end Dec 98.
☎ 01444 412 300 🖷 01444 412 300

***Christian Book Centre**, The Vicarage, Spuley Lane, Pott Shrigley, Macclesfield SK10 5RS
Director: Rev Geoffrey H Greenhough. No full-time staff. *CC* No.215332. Began 1966; non-denominational. Turnover £5,500 to year end Dec 98. Mail order.
Email: books@ggreenhough.freeserve.co.uk
☎ 01625 573 316

Christian Book Centre, 45 Northdown Road, Margate CT9 2RN
Manageress: Mrs D J Woodham. Executive staff 1, Other staff 1. Began 1975; interdenominational. Turnover n/a.
☎ 01843 226 598

For additional information see List on Pages 134–140

***The Christian Book Centre**, London Bible College, Green Lane, Northwood HA6 2UW
Manager: Miss Keren E Morrell. Executive staff 1. ***CC*** No.312778. Began 1973; interdenominational. Turnover n/a.
Email: mailbox@londonbiblecollege.ac.uk
☎ 01923 826 061

***Christian Book Centre**, 63 Chilwell Road, Beeston, Nottingham NG9 1EQ
Partner: Mr Clive Perry. Executive staff 3. Began 1966; non-denominational. Turnover n/a.
☎ 0115 925 6961

Christian Book Centre, 4 Fox Street, Preston PR1 2AB
Owner/Manager: Mr Robert Hardman. Executive staff 1, Other staff 8. Began 1968; non-denominational. Turnover n/a.
Email: cbcpreston@aol.com
☎ 01772 259 279 Fax 01772 259 279

Christian Book Centre, 13 Bond Street, Redruth TR15 2QA
Partner: Mr Chris Land. Executive staff 2. Began 1984; non-denominational. Turnover £82,000 to year end June 98. Browse and buy from website.
Web: www.icbc.co.uk
Email: mail@icbc.co.uk
☎ 01209 214 007 Fax 01209 313 191

Christian Book Shop, 2 Radford Road, Leamington Spa CV31 1LX
Proprietor: Mr David Arnold. Executive staff 1, Other staff 1. Began 1954; interdenominational. Turnover £80,000 to year end Apr 94.
☎ 01926 426 573 Fax 01926 426 573

The Christian Book Shop, 43 Monson Road, Tunbridge Wells TN1 1LU
Proprietor: Mr Gordon Hoppé. Executive staff 2, Other staff 1. Began 1890; interdenominational. (Previously S Hunt, Hunts Christian Centre). Turnover n/a. Sales and correspondence to The Christian Bookshop, Orpington.
☎ 01689 854 117 Fax 01689 851 060

Christian Books, Unit 7, Provision Market, Carmarthen SA31 1QY
Proprietor: Mr Albert Haynes. Executive staff 2. Began 1981; evangelical. Turnover n/a.
☎ 01267 234 953

Christian Books, St Mary's Gate, Dunstable LU6 3SW
Manager: Mr John Snuggs. Other staff 1. ***CC*** No.801449. Began 1982; non-denominational. Turnover £64,000 to year end Dec 96.
☎ 01582 601 945

†Christian Books (Hinckley), 58 Lower Bond Street, Hinckley LE10 1QU
Partner: Mrs Janet Newcombe. Executive staff 2, Other staff 2. Began 1976; non-denominational. Turnover n/a.
☎ 01455 230 442

Christian Books & Music, Kensington Temple, Kensington Park Road, London W11 3BY
Director: Miss Sandra Bruhn. *Buyer:* Isabella Koziel. Executive staff 3, Other staff 5. ***CC*** No.251549. Began 1982; Elim Pentecostal. Turnover £430,000 to year end Dec 98. Extensive mail order service.
Web: www.ukbusiness.com/christianbooksmusic
Email: ken-temp@dircon.co.uk
☎ 020 7727 8684 Fax 020 7727 8716

Christian Bookshop, Alfred Place, Aberystwyth SY23 2BS
Trustee: Mr Michael Keen. No full-time staff. ***CC*** Began 1975; non-denominational. Turnover n/a.
Web: www.aber.ac.uk/~emk/ap/
Email: emk@aber.ac.uk
☎ No telephone

Christian Bookshop, 14 Grange Road West, Birkenhead CH41 4DA
Manager: Mrs Elaine Thomas. Executive staff 1, Other staff 3. ***CC*** Began 1946; interdenominational. Turnover £185,000 to year end Apr 98.
☎ 0151 647 8743 Fax 0151 647 8743

Christian Bookshop & The Edge Coffee Shop, 143 High Street, Brentwood CM14 4SA
Manager: Miss Heather Snook. Other staff 2. Began 1989; interdenominational. Turnover n/a. Collecting point for Book Aid.
☎ 01277 200 044

Christian Bookshop, Bryntirion, Bridgend CF31 4DX
Manageress: Miss M Elaine Harris. Other staff 1. ***CC*** Began 1972; Evangelical Movement of Wales. Turnover £86,000 to year end Jan 94.
Email: press@draco.co.uk
☎ 01656 655 886 Fax 01656 656 095

Christian Bookshop, 7 Wyndham Arcade, St Mary Street, Cardiff CF1 1FH
Manager: Mr Stephen Potts. *Senior Sales Assistant:* Mr Robert Bennett. Executive staff 1, Other staff 2. ***CC*** No.222407. Began 1961; interdenominational. (Evangelical Movement of Wales). Turnover £108,000 to year end Dec 98. Supplying cassettes, CDs, videos and Tearcraft.
☎ 029 2022 0586 Fax 029 2022 0586

Christian Bookshop, 8 Parkway, Chelmsford CM2 0NF
Manager: Mr John Dawson. Executive staff 1, Other staff 4. Began 1977; interdenominational. Turnover n/a.
☎ 01245 257 054 Fax 01245 257 054

***Christian Bookshop Clacton Ltd**, 4 North Road, Clacton CO15 4DA
Managers: Mr Peter & Mrs Gill Ost. Executive staff 2, Other staff 2. Began 1985; Anglican. (Previously St John's Christian Books Ltd). Turnover £55,000 to year end Dec 98. Also mail order, candles, video hire, computer software and music.
☎ 01255 475 075 Fax 01255 475 075

Christian Bookshop, Great Whyte Baptist Church, Great Whyte, Ramsey, Huntingdon PE17 1HA
Manager: Rev M J Daly. No full-time staff. Began 1987; non-denominational. Turnover n/a.
☎ 01487 813 578

Christian Bookshop, Lerwick, Market Street, Lerwick ZE1 0JP
Manager: Mrs Mary Smith. No other full-time staff. ***CC*** No.SCO 26549. Began n/a; interdenominational. Turnover n/a.
☎ 01595 694 816

The Christian Bookshop, 63 Station Road, Letchworth SG6 3BJ
Manager: Mrs Edna M Brooks. Executive staff 1, Other staff 3. ***CC*** No.253478. Began 1968; non-denominational. Turnover n/a.
☎ 01462 481 285

The Christian Bookshop, 13 Brewer Street, Maidstone ME14 1RU
Manager: Mr Peter Arnold. Executive staff 1, Other staff 1. Began 1978; non-denominational. Turnover n/a.
☎ 01622 761 440 Fax 01622 761 440

For additional information see List on Pages 134–140

The Christian Bookshop, Sevenoaks Road, Pratts Bottom, Orpington BR6 7SQ
Owner: Mr Gordon Hoppé. Executive staff 1. Began 1990; non-denominational, reformed. Turnover n/a. Coffee shop.
☎ 01689 854 117 🖷 01689 851 060

Christian Bookshop, 21 Queen Street, Ossett WF5 8AS
Trustee: Mr Norman H Roe. Executive staff 1, Other staff 1. Began 1977; evangelical. Turnover n/a.
☎ 01924 260 502

***Christian Bookshop**, 23a Commercial Street, Pontypool NP4 6JQ
Shop Manageress: Mrs Amanda Hale. Other staff n/a. Began 1999; ecumenical. No magazine. Turnover: First year of operation. Counselling service, aiming to provide a centre for young people.
☎ 01495 750 680

Christian Bookshop, 90 High Street, Reigate RH2 9AP
Organisers: Mr Peter & Mrs Margaret Robinson. All voluntary staff. *CC* No.800219. Began 1983; interdenominational. Turnover n/a.
☎ 01737 247 534
Correspondence: 19 Hilltop Road, Reigate RH2 7HL

Christian Bookshop, 7 Castle Street, Rugby CV21 2TP
Manager: Joan Saunders. Executive staff 1, Other staff 2. Began 1972; interdenominational. Turnover £86,000 to year end Dec 98.
Web: ourworld.compuserve.homepages/Rugby_Fellowship/index.htm
Email: rugby_fellowship@compuserve.com
☎ 01788 542 852 🖷 01788 552 633

The Christian Bookshop, 121 Duke Street, St Helens WA10 2JG
Owner: Mrs Shelagh K Smith. Executive staff 2. Began 1968; non-denominational. Turnover n/a.
☎ 01744 274 07

Christian Bookshop, Tanglewood, Brae, Shetland ZE2 9QG
Manageress: Mrs Mary Smith. *CC* No.SCO 26549. Began 1984; non-denominational. Turnover n/a.
☎ 01806 522 649 🖷 01806 522 553

Christian Bookshop, 16e The Market, Swansea SA1 3PF
Manageress: Mrs Natasha Macdonald. Executive staff 1, Other staff 1. *CC* Began 1962; non-denominational. Turnover £82,000 to year end Jan 94.
☎ 01792 650 773

Christian Bookshop, 45 Victoria Road, Swindon SN1 3AY
Proprietors: Mr & Mrs John Black. Began 1976; interdenominational. Turnover n/a.
☎ 01793 520 528

The Christian Bookshop, 16 Central Arcade, Wrexham LL11 1AG
Manageress: Miss Julie McIntosh. Other staff 3. *CC* Began 1950; non-denominational. Turnover n/a.
☎ 01978 364 405 🖷 01978 364 405

Christian Bookshop Mission Ltd, 78 Central Market, Halkett Place, St Helier, Jersey JE2 4WL
Manager: Rev Philip Osborn. Other staff 2. *CC* Began 1972; non-denominational. Turnover £128,000 to year end Dec 98.
Email: pjourcci@ibl.net
☎ 01534 733 380 🖷 01534 808 68

Christian Centre, 21 Park Avenue, Bishopbriggs, Glasgow G64 2SN
Minister: Rev Keith Short. Executive staff 1, Other staff 2. *CC* Began 1981; non-denominational. Turnover n/a.
Email: keith@ccbishop.freeserve.co.uk
☎ 0141 762 1473 🖷 0141 772 6100

***Christian Centre Bookshop**, Strudwick Drive, Oldbrook, Milton Keynes MK6 2TG
Manageress: Mrs S Ward. Executive staff 1, Other staff 1. *CC* No.1054324. Began 1986; Assemblies of God. Turnover £43,000 to year end June 98. Counselling service, music, cards, gifts, mail order.
☎ 01908 670 655 🖷 01908 661 313

Christian City Books, 76 Bolton Crescent, Kennington, London SE5 0SE
Team Leader: Mr John Bedingfield. Admin staff 2. *CC* No.264078. Began 1993; interdenominational. Turnover n/a. Also ministry centre.
Email: dunamis@compuserve.com
☎ 020 7582 1299 🖷 020 7582 1299

Christian Connections, Pengawsai Fach, Whitland SA34 0RB
Proprietor: Mrs Iris D Staniland. Began 1987; interdenominational. Turnover n/a.
☎ 01994 240 659

Christian Literature Centre, The Upper Room, 64 Cornwall Street, Plymouth PL1 1LR
Partners: Mr David & Mrs Anne Landricombe. Executive staff 2, Other staff 3. Began 1949; non-denominational.
Email: clcply@globalnet.co.uk
☎ 01752 661 264 🖷 01752 250 815

Christian Literature Centre, 28 Wellington Street, Stockton-on-Tees TS18 1NA
Manager: Jenny Burns. Executive staff 2. Began 1977; Baptist. Coffee shop and counselling also available.
Web: www.adlib.co.uk/sbt
Email: sbt@stockton.netkonect.co.uk
☎ 01642 675 297

Christian Ministries, 102 Tristram Avenue, Hartlepool TS25 5NE
Owner: Mr David Taylor. No other full-time staff. Began 1983; non-denominational. Turnover n/a. Mobile bookshop; also Tearcraft.
Email: dave-cromwell@daveanddawn.freeserve.co.uk
☎ 01429 291 224

Christian Outlook, 44 Waterdale, Doncaster DN1 3EY
Manageress: Miss Shirley Hamilton. Executive staff 1. *CC* No.511214. Began 1983; Fellowship of Independent Evangelical Churches. Turnover £102,000 to year end Mar 94.
☎ 01302 363 033 🖷 01302 363 033

***Christian Resources Project**, 14 Lipson Road, Plymouth PL4 8PW
Administrator: Mr Michael Law. *Centre Manager:* Mrs Audrey Burnham. Executive staff 1, Other staff 2. *CC* No.281735. Began n/a; interdenominational. Magazine: *Newsletter* (Circulation n/a 5 times a year). Turnover £111,000 to year end Dec 98.
Web: business.thisisplymouth.co.uk/crp
☎ 01752 224 012 🖷 01752 224 012

Christian Word Shop, St Stephens Church, Church Green, Redditch B97 4DY
Manageress: Mrs Enid Drew. No full-time staff. *CC* No.518003. Began 1979; interdenominational. Turnover £35,000 to year end Mar 92.
☎ 01527 520 773/585 386

B

Christian World Centre, Grampian House, 144 Deansgate, Manchester M3 3ED
Operations Director: Mr John F Macdonald. Executive staff 2, Other staff 12. *CC* Began 1980; interdenominational. (Send the Light Ltd). Magazine: *Christian News World* (Circulation n/a monthly). Turnover n/a. Also restaurant, studio theatre.
☎ 0161 834 6060 🖷 0161 834 6060

Church House Bookshop, 31 Great Smith Street, London SW1P 3BN
Retail Co-ordinator: Mr Mark Clifford. Executive staff 2, Other staff 6. *CC* No.248711. Began n/a; Anglican but interdenominational. Turnover £750,000 to year end Dec 98.
Web: www.chbookshop.co.uk
Email: info@chp.u-net.com
☎ 020 7340 0280 🖷 020 7340 0278

B

Church Shop, 222 Leigh Road, Leigh-on-Sea SS9 1BP
Manageress: Mrs M Sullivan. No other staff. *CC* No.234092. Began 1978; Roman Catholic. Turnover £45,000 to year end Dec 98.
☎ 01702 710 409 🖷 01702 712 838

Churches Bookshop, Howard Street, Douglas IM1 2EQ
Manageress: Miss Ruth Cowin. Executive staff 2. Began 1971; interdenominational. Turnover n/a. Access to church and coffee lounge, counselling available.
☎ 01624 621 593

Churches Together in Beckenham Shop, 26 High Street, Beckenham BR3 1AY
Shop Manager: Mrs Maggie Turner. Executive staff 1, No other paid staff. *CC* No.1047956. Began 1995; ecumenical. Magazine: *Shoptalk* (800 every four months). Turnover £60,327 to year end Sep 98. Coffee lounge, listening ear service, advice centre.
☎ 020 8325 3806

***CLC Bookshop**, 22 Back Wynd, Aberdeen AB1 1JP
Manager: Mr Andrew Martin. Executive staff 1, Other staff 1. *CC* No.1015793. Began 1941; evangelical. Turnover n/a.
Email: 100537.2506@compuserve.com
☎ 01224 641 620 🖷 01224 626 332

***CLC Bookshop**, 51 Stephenson Street, Birmingham B2 4DH
Managers: Mr & Mrs Paul & Sue Crisp. Executive staff 2, Other staff 4. *CC* No.1015793. Began 1941; evangelical. Turnover n/a.
☎ 0121 643 6187 🖷 0121 643 2471

***CLC Bookshop**, 18 Burgate, Canterbury CT1 2HG
Manager: Mr Paul Chandler. Executive staff 1, Other staff 3. *CC* No.1015793. Began 1941; evangelical. Turnover n/a.
☎ 01227 463 535 🖷 01227 768 098

***CLC Bookshop**, 118 High Street, Chatham ME4 4BY
Manager: To be appointed. Full-time staff 1, Part-time staff 1. *CC* No.1015793. Began 1941; evangelical. Turnover n/a.
☎ 01634 843 926 🖷 01634 843 926

***CLC Bookshop**, 26 Whitehall Crescent, Dundee DD1 4AY
Manager: Mr J Collins. Executive staff 1. *CC* No.1015793. Began 1941; evangelical. Turnover n/a.
☎ 01382 226 859 🖷 01382 226 859

***CLC Bookshop**, 98 Church Street, Inverness IV1 1EP
Manager: Mr T Hunt. Executive staff 1, Other staff 1. *CC* No.1015793. Began 1941; evangelical. Turnover n/a.
☎ 01463 238 876 🖷 01463 238 876

***CLC Bookshop**, 16 St Matthews Street, Ipswich IP1 3EU
Manager: Mr Colin Waller. Executive staff 1, Other staff 1. *CC* No.1015793. Began 1941; evangelical. Turnover n/a.
☎ 01473 255 346 🖷 01473 255 346

***CLC Bookshop**, 43 Belvoir Street, Leicester LE1 6SL
Manager: Ms Naomi Thorp. Executive staff 1. *CC* No.1015793. Began 1941; evangelical. Turnover n/a.
☎ 0116 255 8481 🖷 0116 285 5283

***CLC Bookshop**, Morley House, 26 Holborn Viaduct, London EC1A 2AQ
Team Leadership Executive staff 3, Other staff 8. *CC* No.1015793. Began 1941; evangelical. Turnover n/a.
Email: clcuklond@aol.com
☎ 020 7583 4835/4837 🖷 020 7583 6059

CLC Bookshop, 10 Dundas Street, Middlesbrough TS1 1JA
Manager: Mrs Sue Screaton. Executive staff 1, Other staff 1. *CC* No.1015793. Began 1986; evangelical. Turnover n/a.
☎ 01642 247 540 🖷 01642 230 924

***CLC Bookshop**, Higham Place, New Bridge Street, Newcastle upon Tyne NE1 8AF
Manager: Miss Pauline Reay. Executive staff 1, Other staff 1. *CC* No.1015793. Began 1941; evangelical. Turnover n/a.
☎ 0191 232 5301 🖷 0191 233 0237

***CLC Bookshop**, 68 Prince of Wales Road, Norwich NR1 1LT
Manager: Mr Chris Magee. Executive staff 1, Other staff 1. *CC* No.1015793. Began 1941; evangelical. Turnover n/a.
☎ 01603 623 875 🖷 01603 623 875

***CLC Bookshop**, 103 West Street, Sheffield S1 4EQ
Manager: Mr Michael Shaw. Executive staff 1, Other staff 5. *CC* No.1015793. Began 1941; evangelical. Turnover n/a.
☎ 0114 272 4663 🖷 0114 276 5052

***CLC Bookshop**, Carlton House, Carlton Place, Southampton SO15 2DZ
Manager: Brenda Franklin. Executive staff 1, Other staff 2. *CC* No.1015793. Began 1941; evangelical. Turnover n/a.
☎ 023 8022 0844 🖷 023 8033 1013

***CLC Bookshop**, 8 St George's Street, Stamford PE9 2BJ
Manager: Mr Phil Inman. Executive staff 1, Other staff 1. *CC* No.1015793. Began 1977; interdenominational. (Previously The Ark, Stamford Christian Book Centre). Turnover n/a.
☎ 01780 755 020 🖷 01780 755 020

***CLC Bookshop**, 11 St Helens Road, Swansea SA1 4AL
Manager: Ms Moff Oldham. Executive staff 1. *CC* No.1015793. Began 1941; evangelical. Turnover n/a.
☎ 01792 654 228 🖷 01792 654 228

***CLC Bookshop**, 123 Bridge Street, Warrington WA1 2HS
Manager: Ms Debbie Pennells. Other staff 1. *CC* No.1015793. Began 1963; interdenominational. Turnover n/a.
☎ 01925 635 641 🖷 01925 635 641

***CLC Bookshop**, 13 Upper Wickham Lane, Welling DA16 3AA
Managers: Jose Seymour, Enid Perkins. *CC* No.1015793. Began 1991; evangelical. Turnover n/a.
☎ 020 8301 4641 🖷 020 8301 4641

For additional information see List on Pages 134–140

***CLC Bookshop**, 69 Worcester Street, Wolverhampton WV2 4LE
Manager: To be appointed. Other staff 2. ***CC*** No.1015793. Began 1970; interdenominational. (Previously Bible Book Shop). Turnover n/a.
☎ 01902 424 020 🖷 01902 424 020

Cliff College Bookshop, Calver, Hope Valley, S32 3XG
Manager: Mrs Eileen Bratt. Executive staff 1. ***CC*** No.529386. Began 1900; Methodist. Turnover £84,110 to year end Aug 98.
Email: bookshop@cliff.sheffield.ac.uk
☎ 01246 582 322 🖷 01246 583 739

†**Close Harmony Ltd**, Salisbury Cathedral, The Close, Salisbury SP1 2EL
Executive Manager: Mrs Renee Milner. Executive staff 3, Other staff 1. ***CC*** Began 1977; Anglican. Turnover n/a.
☎ 01722 335 188

Clwyd Christian Bookshop Ltd, 4 Bedford Street, Rhyl LL18 1SY
Manageress: Mrs Heledd Smith. Executive staff 1. Began 1969; non-denominational. Turnover n/a. Music/videos for sale and hire. Software.
Email: clwydcbc@aol.com
☎ 01745 350 994

***Come Back to God Campaign**, 21 Bradshaw Street, Saltcoats KA21 5HR
Manageress: Mrs Maureen Bunting. Executive staff 3. ***CC*** No.240168. Began 1956; interdenominational. Turnover £9,000 to year end Dec 98.
Web: www.comebacktogod.org
Email: campaign@comebacktogod.org
☎ 01294 473 022 🖷 01294 465 566

Peter A Cook Christian Books, 70 St Johns Street, Bury St Edmunds IP33 1SJ
Proprietor: Mr Peter A Cook. Executive staff 1, Other staff 2. Began 1962; non-denominational. Turnover n/a.
☎ 01284 769 517

Copnal Books, 18 Meredith Street, Crewe CW1 2PW
Partners: Mr Peter & Mrs Rose Ollerhead. Other staff 1. Began 1984; Christian Brethren. Turnover £12,000 to year end Apr 94. Second-hand bookshop.
☎ 01270 580 470

Cornerstone, 45 Woodhouse Road, North Finchley, London N12 9ET
Manager: Mr Andrew Franks. Executive staff 2, Other staff 3. ***CC*** No.281838. Began 1981; non-denominational. Head Office of Finchley Christian Bookshops Ltd. Turnover n/a. Videos, cassettes, CDs, sheet music, special orders and mail order.
Email: cs@cornerstone4551.freeserve.uk
☎ 020 8446 3056 🖷 020 8446 2227

Cornerstone, 13 Liverpool Road North, Maghull, Liverpool L31 2HB
Hon Resource Manager: Miss Isobel Turner. No full-time staff. ***CC*** No.517987. Began 1979; interdenominational. (Previously Miss Isobel Turner). Turnover £30,000 to year end June 98. Mobile bookstall, church bookstalls supplied, special orders welcome.
Web: www.merseyworld.com/cornerstone/
Email: cornmag@aol.com
☎ 0151 531 9889 🖷 0151 531 9889

Cornerstone, 2 Dale Road, Matlock DE4 3LT
Chair: Mrs Bernice Smith. No full-time staff. ***CC*** No.16603. Began 1988; non-denominational. Turnover £50,000 to year end Dec 98. Upper room available for coffee, counselling, Bible study.
Email: ebgbs@globalnet.co.uk
☎ 01629 584 296

Cornerstone, 17 Newmarket Street, Skipton BD23 2HX
Manager: Mr Jim Hope. Executive staff 1, Other staff 3. Began 1993; ecumenical. Turnover £78,000 to year end Dec 98. Coffee shop.
Web: www.raikes.demon.co.uk/sandg/
☎ 01756 793 673

Cornerstone Book and Coffee Shop, Central Methodist Church, Saltergate, Chesterfield S40 1UH
Manager: Mrs Kathryn Andrews. No paid staff. Began n/a; Methodist. Turnover n/a.
Email: 106125.2110@compuserve.com
☎ 01246 277 390

Cornerstone Books (Gosport Cornerstone Trust), 9 Bemisters Lane, Gosport PO12 1HB
Manager: Mr Richard Atkinson. No full-time staff. ***CC*** No.282517. Began 1979; non-denominational. Turnover n/a. Crisis pregnancy counselling centre.
☎ 023 9258 3824

Cornerstone Bookshop, 25 High Street, Ashford TN24 8TH
Manager: Mr Simon Trainer. Executive staff 1, Other staff 3. ***CC*** No.291001. Began 1986; non-denominational. Turnover n/a. Coffee shop, wholefood restaurant.
☎ 01233 642 874

Cornerstone Bookshop, 11 West Church Street, Buckie AB56 1BN
Manager: Mrs Gillian Simkin. Began n/a. Turnover n/a.
☎ 01542 833 647

Cornerstone Christian Bookshop, 5 Church Street, Whitehaven CA28 7AY
Manager: Mrs Sheila Coupe. Full-time staff 2, Voluntary staff 12. ***CC*** No.507105. Began 1968; interdenominational. Turnover £25,000 to year end Dec 98.
☎ 01946 695 460 🖷 01946 693 355

Covenanter Bookshop, 98 Lisburn Road, Belfast BT9 6AG
Supervisor: Rev Dr H G Cunningham. Other staff 2. Began 1961; Reformed Presbyterian Church of Ireland. Turnover n/a.
☎ 028 9066 0689

Coventry Cathedral Bookshop, 7 Priory Row, Coventry CV1 5ES
Manager: Mrs Mary Ford. Executive staff 1. ***CC*** Began 1962; Anglican. Turnover n/a.
Web: www.coventrycathedral.org
Email: information@coventrycathedral.org
☎ 024 7622 7597 🖷 024 7663 1448

***Crusader Book Centre**, 2 Romeland Hill, St Albans AL3 4ET
Manager: Mr Guy Marshall. *Assistant Manager:* Mrs Ann Byrne. Executive staff 2, Other staff 2. ***CC*** No.223798. Began 1929; interdenominational. Turnover £258,357 to year end Dec 97. Wide range of youth materials. Videos, computer software and music also available.
Email: bookcentre@crusaders.org.uk
☎ 01727 834 236 🖷 01727 848 518

Cumbernauld Churches Bookshop Ltd, 12 Ettrick Square, Town Centre, Cumbernauld, Glasgow G67 1ND
Company Secretary: Mr John D Allan. Other staff 4. ***CC*** No.SCO 02361. Began 1981; interdenominational. Turnover n/a.
☎ 01236 720 851

B

For additional information see List on Pages 134–140

Dabcec Bookshop, Christian Education Centre, 4 Southgate Drive, Crawley RH10 6RP
Manager: To be appointed. *CC* No.252878. Began 1980; ecumenical. Turnover £150,000 to year end Dec 98.
☎ 01293 571 264 🖷 01293 616 945

Daybreak Books, 68 Baring Road, Lee, London SE12 0PS
Manageress: Miss Alice Bell. Executive staff 1, Other staff 1. *CC* No.275484. Began 1977; non-denominational. Turnover £46,000 to year end Mar 97.
☎ 020 8857 1188

Deal Christian Resource Centre, 140 High Street, Deal CT14 6BE
Manager: Mr S A Boyle. Full-time staff 1. Began 1976; non-denominational. (Previously Good News Bookshop). (Linked to Tonbridge Christian Book Centre). Turnover £45,000 to year end Dec 97.
☎ 01304 363 713

B

†**Derby Cathedral Shop Ltd**, St Michael's House, Queen Street, Derby DE1 3DT
Manager: Mr A G Wilmore. Executive staff 1. Began n/a; Anglican. Turnover £125,000 to year end Jan 95.
☎ 01332 381 685

†**James A Dickson Books (The Christian Bookshop)**, 12 Forrest Road, Edinburgh EH1 2QN
Manager: Mr J Dickson. Executive staff 1, Other staff 2. Began 1970; interdenominational. Turnover n/a. New, antiquarian and secondhand theological books.
☎ 0131 225 6937

Dillons Bookstore (Theology Department), 82 Gower Street, London WC1E 6EQ
Manager Theology: Mike Long. Executive staff 1. Began n/a; non-denominational. Turnover n/a.
Email: social@dillons.co.uk
☎ 020 7636 1577 🖷 020 7580 7680

†**Dillons University Bookshop**, 55 Saddler Street, Durham DH1 3EJ
Manager: Sue Hume. Executive staff 3, Other staff 10. *CC* Began 1954; interdenominational. (Previously Society for Promoting Christian Knowledge). Turnover £1,300,000 to year end Apr 92.
☎ 0191 384 2095 🖷 0191 383 1551

Dorking Christian Bookshop, 22 West Street, Dorking RH4 1BY
Owner: Mrs Thora Saunders. No full-time staff. Began 1980; non-denominational. Turnover n/a.
☎ 01306 880 722

Doves Christian Bookshop, 65 Boutport Street, Barnstaple EX31 1HG
Manager: Mr John Adlam. Executive staff 1, Other staff 6. Began 1975; non-denominational. Turnover n/a.
☎ 01271 325 867 🖷 01271 342 810

Dumbarton Baptist Bookshop, 14 Risk Street, Dumbarton G82 1SE
Manager: Mr Richard McFarlane. Executive staff 1, Voluntary staff 6. Began 1983; Baptist. Turnover n/a.
☎ 01389 732 678

Dunoon Baptist Church Centre, Alexandra Parade, Dunoon PA23 8AB
Manager: Mrs Helen Blair. Other staff 2. Began n/a; Baptist. Turnover n/a. Coffee shop.
☎ 01369 706 665

Eastbourne Christian Resource Centre, 91 Seaside Road, Eastbourne BN21 3PL
Manager: Mr Kevin Deeley. Executive staff 2, Other staff 2. *CC* Began n/a; non-denominational. (Previously Eastbourne Bible Centre). Turnover n/a.
☎ 01323 732 070 🖷 01323 647 832

†**Eastgate Christian Bookshop Ltd**, 100 Eastgate Centre, Unit 22 Lower Gallery, Southern Hay, Basildon SS14 1AG
Principal Director: Mr Dave Omosimua. Executive staff 1, Other staff 3. Began 1988; non-denominational. Turnover n/a.
☎ 01268 282 646 / 284 402 🖷 01268 284 402

Ebenezer Bible and Bookshop, 353 Woodstock Road, Belfast BT6 8PT
Owners: Mr & Mrs Stanley McDermott. Executive staff 2. Began 1973; non-denominational. Turnover n/a.
☎ 028 9045 7048

Elim Christian Centre Bookroom, Hall Street, Chelmsford CM2 0HG
Manager: T Tween. All voluntary staff. *CC* Began 1979; Elim Pentecostal. Turnover £8,500 to year end Dec 96.
☎ 01245 358 855 🖷 01245 496 304

†**Ely Cathedral Shop Ltd**, The College, Ely CB7 4DN
Sales Manager: Mr John Simmons. Executive staff 1, Other staff 6. Began 1971; Anglican. Turnover n/a.
☎ 01353 660 345 🖷 01353 665 658

Emmanuel Books and Gifts, 47 Broad Street, Newtown SY16 2AU
Owners: Mr & Mrs A G & C M Roberts. Staff n/a. Began 1984; non-denominational. Turnover n/a.
☎ 01686 625 850 🖷 01686 626 665

Emmanuel Christian Bookshop, 32a West Street, Fishguard SA65 9AD
Manageress: Mrs Sylvia Coldrick. All voluntary staff. *CC* Began 1992; Emmanuel Holiness. Turnover n/a.
☎ 01348 875 024 🖷 01348 875 024

Emmanuel Christian Bookshop, 11c Barnby Gate, Newark NG24 1PX
Manager: Mr Ian T Lyall. Executive staff 2. *CC* No.1052628. Began 1987; Assemblies of God. (Previously Newark Christian Bookshop). Turnover £35,000 to year end Dec 98.
☎ 01636 700 412 🖷 01636 700 412

Emmanuel Missions Bookshop, 21 Market Courtyard, Haverfordwest SA61 2AL
Manageress: Mrs Carol Smith. All voluntary staff. *CC* No.215889. Began 1982; Emmanuel Holiness. Turnover n/a.
☎ 01437 763 651 🖷 01437 763 651

EMW Christian Books & Crafts, 1a Temple Street, Llandrindod Wells LD1 5DL
Manageress: Miss Gillian Davies. Executive staff 1. *CC* No.222407. Began 1974; non-denominational. (Previously Christian Books & Crafts). Turnover £27,000 to year end Dec 98.
☎ 01597 823 171

English, Welsh and Foreign Bible Depot, Stall 228, Central Market, St Mary Street, Cardiff CF1 2AU
Partners: Miss Rosemary A Evans, Miss Marilyn Palmer. Executive staff 2. Began 1910; non-denominational. Turnover £62,000 to year end May 98.
☎ 029 2022 4394

For additional information see List on Pages 134–140

Evangel Christian Shop and Resource Centre, 60 Mill Street, Bideford EX39 2JT
Proprietor: Mr Duncan Withall. Executive staff 1, Other staff 4. Began 1992; interdenominational. Turnover £80,000 to year end Jun 98.
Web: www.evangeluk.com
Email: bookshop@evangeluk.com
☎ 01237 475 395 🖷 01237 475 759

Evangelical Book Shop, 15 College Square East, Belfast BT1 6DD
Manager: Mr John Grier. Executive staff 3. ***CC*** Began 1926; interrelated trust with the Evangelical Presbyterian Church. Turnover £235,536 to year end Jan 99.
☎ 028 9032 0529 🖷 028 9043 8330

Evangelical Bookshop, 8 Dublin Road, Enniskillen BT74 6HH
Manageress: Mrs L Moffitt. Other staff 2. ***CC*** Began 1936; interdenominational. Turnover £50–100,000 to year end Dec 98.
☎ 028 6632 2400 🖷 028 6632 2400

Excelsior Books Ltd, Lewsey Church Centre, Leagrave High Street, Lewsey, Luton LU4 0ND
Managing Director: Dr Peter Warburton. Executive staff 3. Began 1994; interdenominational. (Previously The Word Services Ltd). Turnover £20,000 to year end Dec 98. Providing a retail service directly to churches, their congregations and other organisations requiring Christian products.
☎ 01582 472 724 🖷 01582 696 332

Exodus (The Rock) Ltd, 120 The Rock, Bury BL9 0PJ
Directors: Mr Bruce & Mrs Jenny Geere. Executive staff 2. Began 1979; non-denominational. Turnover £120,000 to year end Dec 98.
☎ 0161 764 4424 🖷 0161 280 9317

Exodus Books & Crafts, Champness Hall, Drake Street, Rochdale OL16 1PB
Directors: Mr Bruce & Mrs Jenny Geere. Began 1997; interdenominational. Turnover n/a.
☎ 01706 654 596 🖷 01706 654 596

Faith House Bookshop, 7 Tufton Street, Westminster, London SW1P 3QN
Bookshop Manager: Mr Patrick Jordan. *House Manager:* Mrs Jenny Miller. Full-time staff 4. ***CC*** Began 1962; Anglican. Turnover n/a.
☎ 020 7222 6952 🖷 020 7976 7180

Faith Mission Bookshop, 3 Dobbin Street, Armagh BT61 7QQ
General Manager: Mr Edward Douglas. Executive staff 1. ***CC*** Began 1990; interdenominational. Turnover n/a.
☎ 028 3752 7927

Faith Mission Bookshop, 57 High Street, Ballymena BT43 6DT
General Manager: Mr Edward Douglas. Other staff 1. ***CC*** Began 1981; interdenominational. Turnover n/a.
☎ 028 2549 443

Faith Mission Bookshop, 43 Bridge Street, Banbridge BT32 3JH
General Manager: Mr Edward Douglas. Executive staff 1. ***CC*** Began 1990; interdenominational. Turnover n/a.
☎ 01820 626 761

Faith Mission Bookshop, 1 Bingham Street, Bangor BT20 5DW
General Manager: Mr Edward Douglas. Other staff 1. ***CC*** Began 1982; interdenominational. Turnover n/a.
☎ 028 9153 222

Faith Mission Bookshop, 5 Queen Street, Belfast BT1 6EA
General Manager: Mr Edward Douglas. Other staff 7. ***CC*** Began 1889; interdenominational. Turnover n/a.
☎ 028 9023 3733 🖷 028 9023 3733

Faith Mission Bookshop, 20 Oldtown Street, Cookstown BT80 8EF
General Manager: Mr Edward Douglas. Other staff 1. ***CC*** Began 1974; interdenominational. Turnover n/a.
☎ 028 7967 66569

Faith Mission Bookshop, 20 Thomas Street, Portadown, Craigavon BT62 3NP
General Manager: Mr Edward Douglas. Other staff 1. ***CC*** Began 1972; interdenominational. Turnover n/a.
☎ 028 3833 4123

Faith Mission Bookshop, 17 High Street, Lurgan, Craigavon BT66 8AA
General Manager: Mr Edward Douglas. Other staff 1. ***CC*** Began 1977; interdenominational. Turnover n/a.
☎ 028 3832 5404

Faith Mission Bookshop, 17 Railway Street, Lisburn BT28 1XG
Manager: Miss Jean Bothwell. No other full-time staff. ***CC*** Began 1986; interdenominational. Turnover n/a.
☎ 028 9266 5888

Faith Mission Bookshop, 78 Spencer Road, Londonderry BT47 1AG
General Manager: Mr Edward Douglas. Other staff 1. ***CC*** Began 1986; interdenominational. Turnover n/a.
☎ 028 7145 137

Faith Mission Bookshop, 33 Greencastle Street, Kilkeel, Newry BT34 4BH
General Manager: Mr Edward Douglas. Other staff 1. ***CC*** Began n/a; interdenominational. Turnover n/a.
☎ 028 3076 4934

Faith Mission Bookshop, 36 Market Street, Omagh BT78 1EH
General Manager: Mr Edward Douglas. Other staff 1. ***CC*** Began 1975; interdenominational. Turnover n/a.
☎ 028 8224 1334

Faith Mission Christian Book Centre, 58 Church Street, Berwick-upon-Tweed TD15 1DU
Shop Manager: Mr Stan Forrest. Executive staff 1, Other staff 2. ***CC*** Began 1985; interdenominational. Turnover n/a.
☎ 01289 304 505 🖷 01289 304 505

Faith Mission Christian Book Centre, 4 Canmore Street, Dunfermline KY12 7PX
Manager: Mr R Purves. Executive staff 1, Other staff 3. ***CC*** Began 1976; interdenominational. Turnover n/a.
☎ 01383 720 643 🖷 01383 720 643

Faith Mission Christian Book Centre, 60 Cross Street, Fraserburgh AB43 9EL
Manager: Mrs Wendy Thom. Executive staff 1. Began 1986; interdenominational. Turnover n/a.
☎ 01346 517 088 🖷 01346 517 088

Faith Mission Christian Book Centre, 2 Erroll Street, Peterhead AB42 1PX
Manager: Mr Reg Lyon. Executive staff 1, Other staff 3. ***CC*** Began n/a; interdenominational. Turnover n/a.
☎ 01779 471 961 🖷 01779 471 961

B

For additional information see List on Pages 134–140

Faith Mission Christian Book Centre, 36 Barnton Street, Stirling FK8 1NA
Senior Sales Assistant: Mrs Edna Gibb. Executive staff 1, Other staff 3. Began 1982; interdenominational. Turnover n/a.
☎ 01786 451 152 🖷 01786 451 152

Family Books (Keynsham), 3 Temple Court, Keynsham, Bristol BS18 1HA
Bookshop Manager: Mr David Brassington. Executive staff 1, Other staff 1. Began 1984; non-denominational. Turnover n/a.
☎ 0117 986 8747

†**Familybooks Ltd**, The Spires, Church House, Fisherwick Place, Belfast BT1 6DW
General Manager: Mrs Elizabeth Bell. Executive staff 5, Other staff 2. Began n/a; Presbyterian. Turnover n/a.
☎ 028 9032 1323 🖷 028 9023 3533

E & W Fielder Ltd, 54 Wimbledon Hill Road, London SW19 7PA
Bookshop Manager: Mrs Jean Fielder. Executive staff 1, Other staff 4. Began n/a; non-denominational. Turnover n/a.
☎ 020 8946 5044 🖷 020 8944 1320

Food for Thought, 34 High Street, Clay Cross, Chesterfield S45 9DY
Manager: Mr Mick Lowry-Fields. Executive staff 1. ***CC*** Began 1986; Fellowship of Independent Evangelical Churches. Turnover n/a. Coffee shop, counselling services.
☎ 01246 866 013

***Fools Bookshop**, 14 Station Road, Upminster RM14 2UB
Manageress: Mrs Jill Warr. Admin staff 2. ***CC*** No.290260. Began 1991; interdenominational. Turnover £80,000 to year end Apr 98. Café.
☎ 01708 640 391

The Fountain (Wallingford) Ltd, 21b St Mary's Street, Wallingford OX10 0EW
Business Manager: Mrs Mary Rushton. Other staff 1. Began 1980; Community Church. Turnover n/a.
☎ 01491 839 511

Fountain Christian Books, 32 Albany Street, Oban PA34 4AL
Manager: Rev Richard Tuckley. Executive staff 2, Other staff 12. ***CC*** Began 1980; non-denominational. (Previously Christian Bookshop). Turnover £10,000 to year end Mar 98.
☎ 01631 563 741

Free Church of Scotland Bookshop, The Mound, Edinburgh EH1 2LS
Manager: Rev W D Graham. Executive staff 1, Other staff 1. Began 1950; Free Church of Scotland. Turnover £107,000 to year end Dec 97. Extensive academic range.
Email: w.d.graham@btinternet.com
☎ 0131 220 0669 🖷 0131 220 0597

Free Presbyterian Church of Scotland Bookroom, 133 Woodlands Road, Charing Cross, Glasgow G3 6LE
Manager: Miss Marion Morrison. Executive staff 1. Began 1970; Free Presbyterian Church of Scotland. Turnover £64,000 to year end Dec 98. Retailer and distributor. Second-hand titles also available.
Web: www.fpchurch.org.uk
Email: fpbookroom@compuserve.com
☎ 0141 332 1760 🖷 0141 332 4271

Freemans Christian Bookshop, 18 Wyle Cop, Shrewsbury SY1 1XB
Proprietor: Mr Stephen Lowe. Executive staff 1, Other staff 3. Began 1957; non-denominational. Turnover £190,000 to year end Jan 99. Personal service, Alpha stockist, gift vouchers, book tokens, mail order, art and craft materials stocked.
☎ 01743 233 657

Friends Book Centre, Friends House, Euston Road, London NW1 2BJ
Manager: Graham Garner. Executive staff 1, Other staff 3. ***CC*** Began 1926; Religious Society of Friends. Turnover £286,000 to year end Dec 97.
Web: www.quaker.org.uk
Email: bookshop@quaker.org.uk
☎ 020 7663 1030/1031 🖷 020 7663 1001

Frontline Christian Bookshop, 2a Newmarket Way, Hornchurch RM12 6DS
Manager: Mr Michael Robinson. Executive staff 1. ***CC*** No.1014476. Began 1987; non-denominational. Turnover n/a.
☎ 01708 440 326

Full Life Christian Book and Music Shop, 70 High Street, Maltby S66 7BN
Centre Administrator: Mr Paul Norris. Part-time staff 4. ***CC*** No.1052600. Began 1983; Assemblies of God. Turnover n/a.
☎ 01709 818 213 🖷 01709 818 213

Gateway Trust, St Mary's Mews, St Mary's Place, Stafford ST16 2AR
Manager: Mr John Bagnall. Executive staff 1, Other staff 3. ***CC*** No.702181. Began 1990; interdenominational. Turnover n/a. Music, Third World food and crafts, candles, wine, church supplies, cards.
☎ 01785 212 626

GEM Books, Christian Centre, High Road, Gorefield, Wisbech PE13 4NZ
Minister: Rev Leslie R Warren. Other staff 4. Began 1981; Pentecostal. (Part of Chapel Lodge Ministries). Turnover n/a.
Web: www.netcomuk.co.uk/~fgospelf/fgfmain.htm
Email: revles@netcomuk.co.uk
☎ 01945 870 016 🖷 01945 870 867
Also at: *Manager:* Mrs D Warren, 94 Fern Lane, Heston, Hounslow TW5 0HJ
☎ 020 8574 7369

Gladstones Bookshop (Christian Media), 18 Slater Street, Liverpool L1 4BS
Manager: Mrs Enid Tonge. Other staff 1. ***CC*** No.232909. Began 1980; non-denominational. (Previously Contact Christian Books). Turnover n/a. Conference bookstalls supplied, mail order service.
Email: gladstonet@aol.com
☎ 0151 708 9550

***GLO Bookshop**, 78 Muir Street, Motherwell ML1 1BN
Manager: Mr Geoff Ruston. Executive staff 2, Other staff 5. ***CC*** No.SCO 07355. Began 1973; non-denominational. Turnover £299,000 to year end Dec 98.
Web: members.aol.com:/gloadmin/glo.htm
Email: globooks@aol.com
☎ 01698 263 483 🖷 01698 275 418

***GLO Bookshop**, 6 Whytehouse Avenue, Kirkcaldy KY1 1UW
Manager: Mr Alec Brady. Executive staff 1, Other staff 2. ***CC*** No.SCO 07355. Began 1984; non-denominational. Turnover n/a.
☎ 01592 205 316 🖷 01592 205 316

For additional information see List on Pages 134–140

Gold Hill Church Books, Gold Hill Baptist Church, Gold Hill Common East, Chalfont St Peter, Gerrards Cross SL9 9DG
Manageress: Mrs Rita Harris. All voluntary staff. ***CC*** Began 1970; Baptist. Turnover n/a.
☎ 01753 887 173

The Good Book Café, Regent Hall, 275 Oxford Street, London W1R 1LD
Bookshop Manager: Paul Pirie. Staff n/a. ***CC*** Began 1994; Salvation Army. (Previously Regent Hall bookshop). Turnover n/a. Coffee shop, day conference facilities.
☎ 020 7629 5424/2766

Good Books, Rick Barton, Chideock, Bridport DT6 6JW
Deputy Manager: Mrs Janice Collins. Executive staff 2, Other staff 3. Began 1985; non-denominational. (Previously Good Book Services Trust). Turnover £60,000 to year end May 98. Specialising in educational resource material for physiotherapy, medical and caring professions, mail order.
Web: www.houghtonsbooks.com/goodbooks
Email: sales@houghtonsbooks.com/goodbooks
☎ 01297 489 276 🖷 01297 489 868

Good Life Books (GLF), 8 Cow Green, Halifax HX1 1JF
Manager: Mrs Beryl Hamlett. Other staff 3. Began 1973; non-denominational. Turnover £85,000 to year end Dec 98.
☎ 01422 351 361

Good News Centre (Bookshop and Coffeehouse), High Street, Newent GL18 1AN
Manager: Mr Peter A Wathen. Other staff 4. ***CC*** Began 1980; non-denominational. Turnover n/a.
Email: goodnewscentre@tesco.net
☎ 01531 821 456 🖷 01531 821 456

*__Good News Centre, Hull (Wesley Owen Books & Music)__, 67 Wright Street, Hull HU2 8JD
Bookshop Manager: Mr Adrian Wallace. Other staff 3. ***CC*** No.1015417. Began 1972; non-denominational. Turnover £165,000 to year end June 98. Coffee shop.
Email: hull@wesley-owen.com
☎ 01482 328 135 🖷 01482 324 040

Good News Centre, 47 Church Gate, Loughborough LE11 1UE
Manager: Mr Christopher C Weston. Executive staff 1, Other staff 1. ***CC*** No.512100. Began 1980; interdenominational. Turnover £155,000 to year end Dec 95. Mail order promotions, Christian resource centre, coffee shop, special events book agents.
☎ 01509 236 057 🖷 01509 236 057

Good News Centre, 11 Wrexham Street, Mold CH7 1ET
Proprietor: Mrs Geraldine R Seery. Executive staff 2. Began 1989; non-denominational. Turnover £39,000 to year end Jan 97.
☎ 01352 756 055

Good News Christian Bookshop, 1 Croft Road, Crowborough TN6 1DL
Managing Director: Mr Norman Nibloe. Other staff 4. Began 1985; non-denominational. (Linked to Tonbridge Christian Book Centre). Turnover £15,000 to year end June 98.
☎ 01892 662 136

Good News Christian Bookshop, 22 Fountain Street, St Peter Port, Guernsey GY1 1DA
Proprietor: Mrs Elizabeth Bannier. No other staff. Began 1981; interdenominational. Turnover £55,500 to year end Dec 98.
☎ 01481 728 982

Good News Christian Bookshop, 5 Mary Street, Lancaster LA1 1UW
Proprietors: Mr & Mrs Robert & Christine Hardiman. Other staff 3. Began 1987; interdenominational. Turnover £96,000 to year end Jan 98.
☎ 01524 841 655 🖷 01524 841 655

Good News Christian Resource Centre Ltd, 50 Churchfield Road, Acton, London W3 6DL
Manager: Miss Nyuk Fong Lau. Executive staff 2, Other staff 2. Began 1954; non-denominational. (Previously Good News Bookshop). Turnover n/a. Counselling and mail order services available.
☎ 020 8992 7123 🖷 020 8993 7616

*__Good News Crusade Bookshop__, 15 High Cross Street, St Austell PL25 4AN
Manager: Mr David Willis. Executive staff 1, Other staff 2. ***CC*** No.225483. Began 1960; interdenominational. Turnover n/a.
Web: www.gnc.org.uk
Email: info@gnc.org.uk
☎ 01726 639 45

Good News Shop, 654 High Road, Leyton, London E10 6RN
Managers: Mr Tom & Mrs Elizabeth Burke. Executive staff 1. Began 1981; interdenominational. Turnover n/a.
☎ 020 8539 2906 🖷 020 8539 2906

Good News - TCLC, 25 East Reach, Taunton TA1 3EP
Partner: Mr Michael A Westlake. Executive staff 1, Other staff 2. Began 1965; non-denominational. Turnover n/a. Resource centre.
☎ 01823 282 429 🖷 01823 282 429

C Goodliffe Neale Ltd, 25 Cookridge Street, Leeds LS2 3AG
Manager: Mr M Saunders. Other staff 1. Began 1953; Roman Catholic but interdenominational stock. (Previously Carmel Bookshop). Turnover n/a. Cards, gifts, church artefacts also available.
☎ 0113 245 0850 Office: 0113 245 2987 🖷 0113 245 2987

Goodnews Bookshop, 37b Blythewood Park, Bromley BR1 3TN
Manager: Mr W P Leyrie. Other staff 1. Began 1969; interdenominational. Turnover n/a.
☎ 020 8460 1470

Grape Vine Bookshop, 29 Church Street, Keighley BD21 5HT
Manageress: Mrs Ann Morrall. Executive staff 1. ***CC*** Began 1977; interdenominational. Turnover n/a.
☎ 01535 606 666

Green Pastures Christian Gift Shop, 20 High Street, Dereham NR19 1DR
Proprietor: Mr Robert Eglington. Other staff 2. Began 1996; interdenominational. Turnover £70,000 to year end Apr 98. Books, music and gifts including Tearcraft and Traidcraft, and teaching materials.
☎ 01362 697 953

*__Greyfriars Christian Centre__, Friar Street, Reading RG1 1EH
Centre Administrator: Mr John R Brown. Executive staff 1, Other staff 5. Began 1983; interdenominational. Turnover £130,000 to year end Dec 98. Coffee Shop.
☎ 0118 958 7369 🖷 0118 957 3016

Guildford Cathedral Bookshop, Stag Hill, Guildford GU2 5UP
Managers: Mrs Rosie Washbourne, Mrs Mary Pitt. Other staff 2. ***CC*** Began 1984; Anglican. Turnover n/a.
☎ 01483 565 499 🖷 01483 303 350

B

Hallam Book Centre, 22 Norfolk Row, Sheffield S1 2PA
Proprietor: Mr J F Rowan. Executive staff 2. Began n/a; Roman Catholic. Turnover n/a. Counselling services and photographic work for diocese provided. Memoriam cards.
☎ 0114 275 8225

Harkins of the Mound, 4 North Bank Street, The Mound, Edinburgh EH1 2LP
Proprietors: Mr & Mrs William Casey. No other staff. Began 1920; Roman Catholic. Turnover n/a.
☎ 0131 225 6709 🖷 0131 226 4177

Harmony Books, 82 Tavistock Street, Bedford MK40 2RP
Proprietor: Mrs Mary Shaw. No full-time staff. ***CC*** No.294509. Began 1984; interdenominational. Turnover £13,775 to year end Dec 98.
☎ 01234 210 298

B

Harvest Books and Crafts, 2 Church Street, Market Square, Pontypridd CF37 2TH
Manager: Mr Sion Herbert. Executive staff 1. ***CC*** Began 1986; interdenominational. Turnover n/a.
☎ 01443 408 962

The Haven Christian Bookshop & Centre, 142 Seabank Road, Wallasey CH45 1HG
Secretary to the Trust: Mr E J Jones. No full-time staff. ***CC*** No.510112. Began 1980; Baptist. Turnover n/a. Coffee shop.
☎ 0151 638 5910

Haven Christian Bookshop, 1 Westgate Hill, Pembroke SA71 4LB
Proprietors: Mr & Mrs Colin & Ginnie Whittaker. All voluntary staff. ***CC*** Began 1979; interdenominational. Turnover n/a. Stocking primarily second-hand books, also gifts, cards and crafts.
Email: managers@havencentre.freeserve.co.uk
☎ 01646 685 469 🖷 01646 686 893

Havering Christian Bookshop and Centre, 80 Victoria Road, Romford RM1 2LA
Manager: Mrs P Cobie. *Trustee:* Mr Colin Phillips. Executive staff 2, Other staff 4. ***CC*** No.277278. Began 1975; interdenominational. Turnover n/a. Coffee shop, mail order, conference bookstalls and video library.
☎ 01708 727 625 🖷 01708 757 758

Heath Christian Bookshop Charitable Trust, 31 Whitchurch Road, Heath, Cardiff CF4 3JN
Manager: Mr Alan White. Executive staff 1, Other staff 1. ***CC*** No.504644. Began 1975; non-denominational. Turnover n/a.
Web: www.christian-bookshop.co.uk
Email: sales@christian-bookshop.co.uk
☎ 029 2062 1794

†**Hereford Cathedral Shop**, 5 College Cloisters, The Close, Hereford HR1 2NG
Shop Manager: Mrs Alison Chambers. Executive staff 2, Other staff 6. ***CC*** Began 1976; Anglican. Turnover n/a. Cathedral gift shop.
☎ 01432 359 880 🖷 01432 355 929

Herne Bay Court Bookshop, Canterbury Road, Herne Bay CT6 5TD
Manager: Mr D Paul Mitchell. Executive staff 1. ***CC*** No.528419. Began 1949; non-denominational. Turnover n/a.
Email: evangelicalsathernebaycourt@compuserve.com
☎ 01227 373 254

Frank Herring & Sons, 27 High West Street, Dorchester DT1 1UP
Partner: Mr John Herring. Executive staff 2, Other staff 11. Began 1930; non-denominational. Turnover n/a.
☎ 01305 264 449 🖷 01305 250 675

High Cross Christian Bookshop, Knoll Road, Camberley GU15 3SY
Manager: Mrs Adriana Peacock. Executive staff 1, Admin staff 1. Began 1990; United Reformed/Methodist. Turnover £64,000 to year end Dec 98.
☎ 01276 619 61 🖷 01276 223 43

Hightown Christian Books, 67 Reginald Street, Luton LU2 7QZ
Manager: Mr John Henry Rose. Other staff 2. ***CC*** No.283511. Began 1981; interdenominational. Turnover £47,882 to year end Dec 98.
☎ 01582 725 831

HoldFast Bible & Tract Depot, 100 Camden Road, Tunbridge Wells TN1 2QP
Proprietor: Mr Nicholas R Fleet. Voluntary staff 3. Began 1991; non-denominational. Turnover £12,000 to year end Dec 98. Publishing and distributing Christian literature. Multi-media, cards, gifts, posters and music also available.
Email: hbtd@aol.com
☎ 01892 512 049

***Holy Trinity Brompton Bookshop**, Holy Trinity Church, Brompton Road, London SW7 1JA
Bookshop Manager: Rowan Miller. Executive staff 5. ***CC*** Began 1991; Anglican. Turnover £382,000 to year end Dec 98. Music, CD Rom, Alpha Resources, international publications, teaching tapes and mail order also available.
Web: dspace.dial.pipex.com/htb.london
Email: bookshop@htb.org.uk
☎ 020 7581 8255 🖷 020 7589 3390

Ichthus Bookshop, 106 Old Town Market, Poole BH15 1NZ
Owner: Miss Joyce V Smith. All voluntary staff. Began 1982; non-denominational. Turnover n/a.
☎ 01202 670 676

Ichthus Christian Books, 58 Station Road, Northwich CW9 5RB
Proprietors: Mr Peter & Mrs Sue Southern. Executive staff 2. Began 1987; interdenominational. Turnover n/a. Wide range of greetings cards, gift items and recorded music.
☎ 01606 477 67

Ichthus Christian Bookshop, 41 Broad Street, Worcester WR1 3LR
Manager: Mr Stephen Jeynes. No full-time staff. ***CC*** No.700424. Began 1985; non-denominational. Turnover n/a.
☎ 01905 295 00

Ichthus Press and Bookroom, 106 Graphic House, School Lane, Didsbury, Manchester M20 6GL
Managing Director: Mr M W Dawson. Executive staff 1, Other staff 2. Began 1976; Church of the Nazarene. Turnover n/a.
☎ 0161 445 2861 🖷 0161 434 2560

***Immanuel Bookshop**, 24 Northway, Scarborough YO11 1JL
Proprietor: Mrs Kate Close. Executive staff 1, Other staff 1. Began 1987; non-denominational. Turnover n/a.
☎ 01723 500 261 🖷 01723 500 261

For additional information see List on Pages 134–140

*__Institute for Contemporary Christianity__, St Peter's Church, Vere Street, London W1M 9HP
Bookshop Manager: Mrs Helen Parry. Other staff 1. ***CC*** No.286102. Began 1982; interdenominational. (Previously Christian Impact Bookshop). Turnover £5,000 to year end Dec 98. Christian training institute.
Email: contemporary_christianity_edu@msn.com
☎ 020 7629 3615 🖷 020 7629 1284

IVP Bookstall Service, Norton Street, Nottingham NG7 3HR
Administrator: Mrs Christine Messam. Executive staff 1. ***CC*** Began 1972; interdenominational. (Previously UCCF Bookstall Service). Turnover included in publishing division of UCCF. A service to Christian Unions.
Web: www.ivpbooks.com
Email: ivp@ivpnottm.cix.co.uk
☎ 0115 978 1054 🖷 0115 942 2694

Jacob's Well, 2 Ladygate, Beverley HU17 8BH
Owner: Dr Beryl Beynon. Executive staff 2. Began 1981; non-denominational. Turnover n/a. Coffee shop.
☎ 01482 862 185

The Jesus Centre, 14 Ashfield Precinct, Kirby in Ashfield, Nottingham NG17 7BQ
Proprietor: Mr Terry Furness. Executive staff 1, Other staff 3. Began 1979; non-denominational. Turnover £67,500 to year end Dec 98.
☎ 01623 757 427

Keith Jones Christian Bookshop, 2 Hinton Road, Bournemouth BH1 2EE
Senior Partner: Mr Colin J Bailey. *Partner:* Mr Darren Peach. Executive staff 3, Other staff 5. Began 1955; evangelical. Turnover £650,000 to year end Mar 98.
Web: www.keithjones.co.uk
☎ 01202 292 272

Jubilate Christian Bookshop Ltd, 55 Ely Street, Stratford-upon-Avon CV37 6LN
Managers: Mr Dennis & Mrs Janet Brown. Trustee/directors 5, Other staff 5, Part-time volunteers 5. ***CC*** No.1040890. Began 1986; interdenominational. Turnover £96,000 to year end July 98.
☎ 01789 298 351
Registered Office: 25 Meer Street, Stratford-upon-Avon CV37 6QB

*__Just Looking Christian Bookshop__, 8 Normandy Street, Alton GU34 1BX
Manager: Mr Bruce Stevenson. Executive staff 2, Other staff 6. Began 1994; non-denominational. Turnover £50,000 to year end Dec 98. Coffee shop.
Email: 106476.2257@compuserve.com
☎ 01420 543 354 🖷 01420 543 354

Juteronomy, 21 Talisman Square, Kenilworth CV8 1JB
Proprietor: Mrs K Shortley. Executive staff 2. Began 1980; non-denominational. Turnover £100,000 to year end Aug 98. Third world crafts, Fairtrade foods.
☎ 01926 854 721 🖷 01926 854 721

*__Kerith Centre Bookshop__, Church Road, Bracknell RG12 1EH
Manager: Mrs Heather West. Executive staff 1, Other staff 2. Began 1989; Baptist. Turnover £84,676 to year end Mar 98.
Email: bfc@kerith.co.uk
☎ 01344 862 699 🖷 01344 304 154

King of Kings Christian Bookshop, 11a Church Lane, Oldham OL1 3AN
Proprietor: Mr Robert Buckley. Executive staff 1. Began 1982; non-denominational. Turnover £35,000 to year end July 98.
☎ 0161 626 3547 🖷 0161 626 3547

Kings, 15 Church Street, Trowbridge BA14 8DW
Managers: Rev & Mrs Roger Marshall. Part time 1, volunteers 3. Began 1986; non-denominational. (Previously Manna Books). An outreach of Street Life Ministries. Turnover £60,000 to year end July 94. Coffee shop, music.
Web: www.kings-books.com
Email: kingsbooks@kings-books.com
☎ 01225 777 588 🖷 01225 777 588

Kings Christian Bookshop, 74 Frodingham Road, Scunthorpe DN15 7JW
Manageress: Mrs Mary Charlesworth. Executive staff 1, Other staff 2. ***CC*** No.505608. Began 1975; non-denominational. Turnover n/a. Coffee shop, counselling service.
☎ 01724 865 410

The Ladyhead Bookshop, 35 North Street, St Andrews KY16 9AQ
Voluntary Manageress: Mrs H G Gifford. All voluntary staff. ***CC*** No.32049. Began 1985; Anglican. Turnover £27,000 to year end Oct 98.
☎ 01334 477 886

Lichfield Cathedral Bookshop, 9 The Close, Lichfield WS13 7LD
Manager: Mrs Pauline Cox. *Gift Buyer:* Mrs Wendy Paulson. Executive staff 1, Other staff 5. Began 1975; Anglican. Turnover £250,000 to year end Dec 97. Giftware and music also available.
☎ 01543 306 150 🖷 01543 306 152

*__Lifeline Christian Bookstore__, Ice House Christian Centre, Victor Street, Grimsby DN32 7QN
Manageress: Mrs Helen M Carter. Executive staff 1, Part-time staff 4. ***CC*** No.509169. Began 1982; non-denominational. Turnover n/a. Coffee shop; videos, music, cards, candles, wine, stationery and gifts.
☎ 01472 349 917 🖷 01472 349 244

†**The Lighthouse**, 63 Bonnygate, Cupar KY15 4BY
Manageress: Mrs Jane Crockett. Other staff 3. ***CC*** No.SCO 04123. Began 1987; interdenominational. Turnover n/a.
☎ 01334 656 287

The Lighthouse, 55a East Street, Tollesbury, Maldon CM9 8QE
Chairman: Rev Keith Lovell. All voluntary staff. ***CC*** No.283085. Began 1980; interdenominational. Turnover n/a.
☎ 01621 868 088

Lighthouse Christian Books and Music, 13 Lynn Road, Ely CB7 4EQ
Manager: Mr John Peckham. Executive staff 1, Other staff 1. ***CC*** Began 1987; non-denominational. Turnover £30,000 to year end Mar 98.
Email: books@river-of-life.org.uk
☎ 01353 667 004 🖷 01353 662 179

†**Lincoln Minster Shops Ltd**, Lincoln Cathedral, Lincoln LN2 1PX
Managing Director: Mr Russell Pond. Executive staff 1, Other staff 10. ***CC*** Began 1972; non-denominational. Turnover n/a.
☎ 01522 544 544 🖷 01522 511 307

Linkup Christian Literature, 27 Bridge Street, Burton-on-Trent DE14 1SY
Manageress: Mrs Margaret I Mellor. Executive staff 1, Other staff 3, Voluntary staff. ***CC*** No.502638. Began 1972; interdenominational. Turnover £66,700 to year end Jan 98.
☎ 01283 563 661

B

For additional information see List on Pages 134–140

***Living Springs**, 105 High Street, Stourbridge DY8 1EE
Directors: Mr Robert Chapman, Mr Roger Eames. Executive staff 3, Other staff 7. *CC* No.701674. Began 1989; interdenominational. Turnover n/a. Coffee shop, counselling centre, pregnancy crisis centre.
Email: roger@livingsprings.prestel.co.uk
☎ 01384 443 636 Mobile: 07801 255 175 🖷 01384 443 636

†The Living Stone Bookshop, 44 Palmerston Road, Boscombe, Bournemouth BH1 4HS
Manageress: Mrs Lindsey Thyer. Executive staff 2, Other staff 1. Began 1989; interdenominational. Turnover n/a.
Email: 101537.1772@compuserve.com
☎ 01202 394 892 🖷 01202 394 892

B

***Living Waters Christian Bookshop**, Harbourside, Porthleven, Helston TR13 9JA
Proprietor: Mrs Helen Simmons. Executive staff 1, Other staff 1. Began 1996; non-denominational. Turnover n/a.
☎ 01326 574 446 🖷 01326 573 013

Living Word, 30 Crescent Road, Bognor Regis PO21 1QG
Owners: Mr & Mrs Tony & Lindsay Leney. Other staff 3. Began 1971; non-denominational. (Previously The Living Word Christian Bookshop). Turnover n/a. Music, videos and gifts also available.
☎ 01243 828 223 🖷 01243 828 223

Living Word, 33 West Street, Chichester PO19 1QS
Owners: Mr & Mrs Tony & Lindsay Leney. Other staff 3. Began 1975; non-denominational. (Previously The Chichester Bible Shop). Turnover n/a. Music, videos and gifts also available.
☎ 01243 780 361 🖷 01243 780 361

The Living Word, 23 Wharfside Village, Wharf Road, Penzance TR18 2GA
Manageress: Brenda Crowder. Executive staff 1. Began 1982; non-denominational. Turnover n/a.
☎ 01736 368 020

Living Words, 12 Place Lane, Seaford BN25 1LA
Owner: Mr Leslie Ayres. Executive staff 2, Other staff 3. Began 1986; non-denominational. Turnover n/a.
☎ 01323 893 699 🖷 01323 490 940

Living Stones Christian Centre, 277 Fleet Road, Fleet GU13 8BT
Manager: Glenis Allen. Full-time staff 1, Part-time staff 3. *CC* Began 1982; interdenominational. Turnover £130,000 to year end Dec 98. Coffee shop.
☎ 01252 616 038 🖷 01252 811 940

Lonsdale Bible Society, Mill Street, Ulverston LA12 7EB
Manager: Mr David Parratt. Executive staff 1. *CC* No.230656. Began 1957; non-denominational. Turnover £50,600 to year end Mar 96. Christian resource centre, primarily evangelical.
Email: david@bible-shop.freeserve.co.uk
☎ 01229 583 563

***Luton Christian Book Centre**, Church Street, Luton LU1 3JE
Manager: Overseen by Luton Pentecostal Church. Full-time staff 4. *CC* No.1054318. Began 1970; Assemblies of God. Turnover n/a.
☎ 01582 412 276

B McCall Barbour, 28 George IV Bridge, Edinburgh EH1 1ES
Managing Partner: Rev Dr T C Danson-Smith. Executive staff 2, Other staff 3. Began 1900; non-denominational. Turnover n/a. Specialist in AV Bibles. Cards, gifts and counselling service also available.
☎ 0131 225 4816

McCrimmons Bookshop, All Saints Pastoral Centre, Shenley Lane, London Colney, St Albans AL2 1AF
Proprietor: McCrimmon Publishing Company Ltd. Full-time staff 5. Began 1975; Roman Catholic. (Previously Anthony Clarke Books). Turnover n/a.
☎ 01727 827 612

Malmesbury Abbey Books Ltd, Malmesbury Abbey, Malmesbury SN16 9BA
Managing Director: Rev David Littlefair. Executive staff 2. Began 1976; non-denominational. Turnover n/a.
☎ 01666 824 339

Manna Christian Centre, 147 Streatham High Road, London SW16 6EG
Manager: Mr David Lock. Executive staff 2, Other staff 1. *CC* Began 1981; evangelical. Turnover £250,000 to year end Dec 96. Coffee shop.
Email: mannalock@mcmail.com
☎ 020 8769 8588 🖷 020 8677 0893

The Manna House (Northampton Christian Centre), St Giles Street, Northampton NN1 1JW
Director & General Manager: Mr John Nightingale. *Commercial Manager:* Joe Story. Executive staff 2, Other staff 8. *CC* No.286358. Began 1983; interdenominational. Turnover £219,000 to year end Sept 98. Also counselling and counselling training.
☎ 01604 622 666 🖷 01604 635 498

The Manna House, 240 Old High Street, Perth PH1 5QJ
Manager: Mr Derek Everett. Executive staff 1. *CC* No.SCO 12998. Began 1990; non-denominational. Turnover £63,500 to year end Jan 98. Coffee shop.
☎ 01738 638 142

Mansfield Christian Book Centre, 2 Newgate Lane, Mansfield NG18 2LF
Manager: Mrs Jackie Stevens. Executive staff 1, Other staff 1. *CC* No.1068757. Began 1978; interdenominational. Turnover £52,000 to year end Dec 94. Resource centre with video hire/sale, cassettes/CDs. Coffee bar.
☎ 01623 636 582 🖷 01623 636 582

Maranatha Christian Bookshop, 22 Windsor Street, Uxbridge UB8 1AB
Manager: Mr Geoffrey Wallace. Executive staff 3. *CC* No.801808. Began 1976; evangelical. Turnover n/a. Resource centre serving churches and individuals. Music, cards and gifts also available.
Web: www.maranathabookshop.co.uk
Email: info@maranathabookshop.co.uk
☎ 01895 255 748 🖷 01895 255 748

Market Place Books (Kendal & District Christian Literature Society), 35 Market Place, Kendal LA9 4TP
Manager: Mr J William Allen. Executive staff 2. *CC* No.505981. Began 1977; interdenominational. Turnover £135,000 to year end Jan 98.
☎ 01539 724 532 🖷 01539 724 532

Mayflower Christian Bookshop, 114 Spring Road, Bitterne, Southampton SO19 2QB
Manager: Mr Robin Lewis. Executive staff 1. *CC* No.282845. Began 1974; non-denominational. Turnover n/a.
Email: mcbs@clara.co.uk
☎ 023 8044 9398 🖷 023 8044 9398

For additional information see List on Pages 134–140

Metanoia Book Service, London Mennonite Centre, 14 Shepherd's Hill, Highgate, London N6 5AQ
Manager: Mr Will Newcomb. Other staff 1. ***CC*** No.227410. Began 1975; Mennonite. Turnover £53,000 to year end Dec 98. Focusing on Anabaptist discipleship. Sales primarily mail order.
Web: www.btinternet.com/~lmc
Email: menno@compuserve.com
☎ 020 8340 8775 🖷 020 8341 6807

Methodist Book Centre, Bemersley House, Gitana Street, Hanley, Stoke-on-Trent ST1 1DY
Manager: Mrs L Tunnicliffe. Executive staff 1, Other staff 5. ***CC*** Began 1945; Methodist. Turnover £225,012 to year end Jan 99.
☎ 01782 212 146 🖷 01782 212 146

Methodist Bookroom, Aldersgate House, 13 University Road, Belfast BT7 1NA
Manager: Mrs Joan Trew. Executive staff 1. ***CC*** Began 1974; Methodist. Turnover £54,000 to year end Dec 98.
☎ 028 9043 8700

Methodist Bookshop, 25 Marylebone Road, London NW1 5JR
Resources and Bookshop Manager: Mr Luke Curran. Executive staff 1, Other staff 3. ***CC*** Began n/a; Methodist. Turnover £150,000 to year end Dec 97.
☎ 020 7486 5502 Ext269 🖷 020 7935 1507

†**Metropolitan Cathedral Bookshop**, Cathedral Precinct, Mount Pleasant, Liverpool L3 5TQ
Manager: Mrs J Reynolds. Executive staff 1, Other staff 1. ***CC*** Began 1967; Roman Catholic. Turnover n/a.
☎ 0151 707 2109

Mizpah Bible & Bookshop, 41 Kingsgate Street, Coleraine BT52 1LD
Manageress: Mrs Ann Harrison. Executive staff 2, Other staff 2. Began 1965; interdenominational. Turnover n/a.
☎ 028 7034 3857

Mount Saint Bernard Abbey Shop, Coalville LE67 5UL
Manager: Brother Thomas Taylor. Executive staff 1. ***CC*** Began 1835; Roman Catholic. Turnover n/a.
☎ 01530 832 298 / 832 022 🖷 01530 814 608

The Mustard Seed (Camden Town), 21 Kentish Town Road, London NW1 8NH
Director: Mr Brian J Austin. Executive staff 2. Began 1973; interdenominational. Turnover n/a.
☎ 020 7267 5646 🖷 020 7916 8700

Mustard Seed, The Old Boathouse, Hillier's Yard, Marlborough SN8 1BE
General Manager: Mrs Deborah Reynolds. Executive staff 2, Other Staff 5. ***CC*** No.1015804. Began 1990; non-denominational. Turnover £85,000 to year end Mar 98. Coffee shop.
☎ 01672 511 611

The Mustard Seed, 2 Main Road, Gedling, Nottingham NG4 3HP
Owner/Manager: Mrs C Stala. Other staff 1. Began 1986; non-denominational. Turnover n/a. Handmade crafts, goods from Israel, coffee shop.
☎ 0115 987 9819 🖷 0115 987 9819

Mustard Seed Bookshop, Balcary House, Buccleugh Road, Hawick TD9 0EH
Manager: Mr Peter Edwards. Full-time staff 4. ***CC*** Began 1986; non-denominational. Turnover n/a. Video hire, music and teaching cassettes available, coffee shop with landscaped garden.
☎ 01450 372 966 🖷 01450 377 732

Mustard Seed Bookshop, Perth Christian Centre, 28 Glasgow Road, Perth PH2 0NX
Manager: Mr Peter Edwards. Executive staff 2, Other staff 3. ***CC*** No.SCO 14546. Began 1986; non-denominational. Turnover n/a. Coffee shop and video hire.
☎ 01738 639 792 🖷 01738 622 928

Nathan's Christian Book Shop, 15 Queen Street, Godalming GU7 1BA
Proprietor: Mr Allen Nathan. Executive staff 1. Began 1975; non-denominational. Turnover n/a.
☎ 01483 415 736

National Christian Education Council Book Sales, 1020 Bristol Road, Selly Oak, Birmingham B29 6LB
General Manager: Sheila Shardan. Executive staff 4, Other staff 10. ***CC*** No.211542. Began 1803; non-denominational. Turnover n/a.
Web: www.ncec.org.uk
Email: ncec@ncec.org.uk
☎ 0121 472 4242 🖷 0121 472 7575

B

*__New Covenant Bookshop__, Unit 214, Elephant and Castle Shopping Centre, London SE1 6TE
Manager: Mr Rotimi Alli-Akeju. ***CC*** No.1004343. Began 1991. Owned by New Covenant Church. Magazine: *U-turn* (2,000 quarterly). Turnover £75,000 to year end Dec 98.
☎ 020 7703 9363 🖷 020 7277 0824

New Creation Trust Christian Book and Coffee Shop, 58 Bampton Street, Tiverton EX16 6AH
Manageress: Mrs Valerie Bloxham. Staff n/a. Began 1988; non-denominational. Turnover £34,000 to year end Sept 98.
☎ 01884 255 769

*__New Dawn Bookshop and Connection Coffee House__, 36 Larch Road, Abronhill, Cumbernauld, Glasgow G67 3AZ
Manager: Miss Pauline Rough. Executive staff 1, Other staff 3. ***CC*** No.SCO 06960. Began 1997; Pentecostal. Owned by New Dawn Bookshop, Greenock. Turnover n/a. Gifts and food also available providing a link with the community.
Web: www.struthers-church.org
Email: bookshop@struthers-church.org
☎ 01236 781 102

*__New Dawn Bookshop and Connection Coffee House__, 10a Jamaica Street, Greenock PA15 1YB
Manager: Mr Chris Jewell. *Assistant:* Miss Ann Morris. Other staff 8. ***CC*** No.SCO 06960. Began 1987; Pentecostal. Turnover £230,000 to year end Dec 97. Gifts and food also available providing an effective link with the community.
Web: www.struthers-church.org
Email: bookshop@struthers-church.org
☎ 01475 729 668 🖷 01475 728 145

The New Life Bookshop, 17a St Michael's Road, Aldershot GU12 4JW
Owner: Mr Keith W Atkins. Full-time staff 1, Part time staff 1. Began 1975; non-denominational. Turnover £80,000 to year end Dec 98.
☎ 01252 311 460 🖷 01252 311 460

†**Norwich Cathedral Shop Ltd**, The Close, Norwich NR1 4EH
Manager: Mrs M A Kingham. Other staff 4. ***CC*** Began 1973; Anglican. Turnover n/a.
☎ 01603 619 920 🖷 01603 766 032

For additional information see List on Pages 134–140

Oak Hill College Bookroom, Chase Side, Southgate, London N14 4PS
Manager: Mrs Sarah Woodbridge. Other staff 1. ***CC*** No.281838. Began 1973; Anglican. Owned by Finchley Christian Bookshops Ltd. Turnover n/a. Extensive stock of titles for theological students.
Email: oh@cornerstone4551.freeserve.uk
☎ 020 8449 3162 Head Office: 020 8446 3056
📠 020 8441 3996

Oasis Bookshop, 59 Lower Main Street, Lisnaskea, Enniskillen BT92 0JD
Proprietress: Mrs Valerie Crozier. Executive staff 2, Admin staff 2. Began n/a; interdenominational. Turnover £26,000 to year end Nov 98.
☎ 028 6672 2677

B

***Oasis Christian Bookshop**, 55 Windmill Street, Gravesend DA12 1BA
Manager: Mrs Margaret Hills. All voluntary staff. ***CC*** Began 1988; Baptist. Turnover n/a.
☎ 01474 568 498

Oasis Christian Bookshop, 124 Bevan Street East, Lowestoft NR32 2AQ
Manager: Mr David Willis. Executive staff 2. ***CC*** No.279718. Began 1970; non-denominational. (Previously Lowestoft Christian Bookshop Trust). Turnover £100,000 to year end Dec 98.
☎ 01502 512 302

***Oasis Christian Bookshop and Tearoom**, Pant-yr-Afon, Penmaenmawr LL34 6BY
Manager: Mr Bill Starr. Other staff 4. ***CC*** No.1048524. Began 1995; non-denominational. Turnover n/a.
Email: oasis@oasisdwygyfylchi.freeserve.co.uk
☎ 01492 622 322

***Oasis Christian Bookshop**, 2 Park Road, Yeovil BA20 1DZ
Partners: Mr & Mrs A J Marfleet. Executive staff 2, Other staff 10. Began 1976; non-denominational. Turnover £13,000 to year end Dec 98.
☎ 01935 426 253

The Oasis Christian Centre, 25 Church Street, Romsey SO51 8BT
Manageress: Mrs Angie Nelson. Executive staff 4. ***CC*** No.295266. Began 1984; interdenominational. Turnover £110,000 to year end Sept 98.
☎ 01794 512 194 📠 01794 512 194

The Oasis Christian Centre, 2 Wallington Square, Wallington SM6 8RG
Manager: Paul Hawkins. Executive staff 1, Other staff 2. ***CC*** No.1056875. Began 1983; non-denominational. Turnover £95,000 to year end Aug 98. Crafts, gifts and software.
☎ 020 8773 1428 📠 020 8773 1428

Oasis Coffee House, 115 High Street, Staple Hill, Bristol BS16 5HF
Manager: Mr John Roberts. Staff n/a. Began 1986; non-denominational. Turnover n/a. Books, cards, gifts, crafts, Fairtrade tea and coffee, children's books and games, coffee house.
☎ 0117 956 6031 📠 0117 956 8238

The Olive Branch Christian Book & Coffee Shop, 17 Heol-Y-Deri, Rhiwbina, Cardiff CF4 6HA
Bookshop Manager: Mrs Sharon Price. Executive staff 1. ***CC*** Began 1984; non-denominational. Turnover £100-300,000 to year end Dec 98. Coffee shop.
☎ 029 2061 4659

Olive Luff Bible Bookshop Ltd, 133 Connaught Avenue, Frinton-on-Sea CO13 9PS
Manager: Mrs P McGowan. Other staff 2. ***CC*** No.289011. Began 1903; interdenominational. Turnover £75,000 to year end Mar 96. Coffee shop.
☎ 01255 674 106 📠 01255 674 106

Olive Tree, 27 North Mall, Edmonton Green Shopping Centre, Lower Edmonton, London N9 0EQ
Partner: Mr Peter Strickland. Executive staff 2, Other staff 1. Began 1991; non-denominational. Turnover n/a. Bookshop and resource centre.
☎ 020 8807 9224

The Open Door, 119 London Road, East Grinstead RH19 2EQ
Manager: Chris Gale. Executive staff 1, Other staff 2. Began 1980; non-denominational. Moving late 1999 (Linked to Tonbridge Christian Book Centre). Turnover £80,000 to year end June 94.
☎ 01342 311 333 & Contact No: 01892 654 725-Chris Gale, Manager 📠 01342 311 333

Oswestry Christian Bookshop, Lower Brook Street, Oswestry SY11 2HG
Manager: Ms Shona Stearn. Executive staff 1, Other staff 10. ***CC*** No.512756. Began 1979; evangelical. Turnover £50,000 to year end Feb 98. Coffee shop, audio, software.
☎ 01691 661 936 📠 01691 661 936

Our Lady's Bookshop, 27a Northgate, Hessle HU13 0LW
Owner: Mrs Sheila Chambers. Executive staff 1. Began 1980; Roman Catholic. Turnover £75,000 to year end Sept 98.
☎ 01482 648 779 📠 01482 641 835

Pathway Books Ltd, 34 Robertson Street, Hastings TN34 1HT
Manager: Mr Richard Butcher. Executive staff 1, Other staff 3. ***CC*** Began 1970; non-denominational. (Previously Christian Book Mission). Turnover n/a.
☎ 01424 431 387 📠 01424 442 847

Pendlebury's, Church House, Portland Avenue, Stamford Hill, London N16 6HJ
Proprietor: Mr John Pendlebury. Executive staff 1, Other staff 1. Began 1984; non-denominational. Turnover £85,000 to year end Jan 98. Second-hand theological booksellers.
Web: www.clique.co.uk/pendleburys
Email: books@pendleburys.demon.co.uk
☎ 020 8809 4922 📠 020 8809 4922

Peniel Bookshop, 49 Coxtie Green Road, Brentwood CM14 5PS
Director: Dr Carolyn Linnecar. Staff n/a. Began 1988; Pentecostal. (Previously Sharon Publications). Part of Peniel Pentecostal Church. Turnover n/a.
Web: www.aliveuk.com
☎ 01277 373 436 📠 01277 375 578

***Perivale Christian Bookshop**, 90 Bilton Road, Perivale, Greenford UB6 7BN
Director: Rev Colin E Taylor. Executive staff 1, Other staff 3. ***CC*** No.293404. Began 1984; non-denominational. (Previously Perivale Christian Centre). Turnover £56,000 to year end Dec 98.
Email: peribooks@aol.com
☎ 020 8998 2933

For additional information see List on Pages 134–140

Peterborough Cathedral Enterprises Ltd, Minster Precincts, Peterborough PE1 1XZ
Manager: Mrs Sylvia Gower. Executive staff 1. Began 1988; Anglican. Turnover £75,000 to year end Mar 96. Cathederal bookshop, gift shop and refectory.
☎ 01733 555 098 🖷 01733 524 65

Peterborough Christian Books Ltd, 68 Westgate, Peterborough PE1 1RG
Directors: Mrs Annette Smith, Mrs Ruth Grenfell. Executive staff 2, Other staff 1. Began 1978; non-denominational. Turnover £200,000 to year end Mar 98.
Email: 106054.3456@compuserve.com
☎ 01733 519 15 🖷 01733 558 520

Pewsey Christian Bookshop, The Old Rectory, River Street, Pewsey SN9 5DP
Manager: Mr R Welford. Executive staff 2. Began 1979; interdenominational. (Previously St Andrews Bookshop (SFI) Ltd). Turnover £54,000 to year end Aug 98. Specialising in books on Islam and Christianity.
Web: www.campuscc.org/sfi/
Email: 101376.2103@compuserve.com
☎ 01672 564 938 🖷 01672 564 939

***Pilgrim Hall Bookshop**, Easons Green, Uckfield TN22 5RE
Bookshop Manager: To be appointed. Executive staff 1. *CC* Began n/a; interdenominational. Turnover £30,000 to year end Dec 97.
☎ 01825 841 342 🖷 01825 841 342

Pluscarden Abbey Bookshop, Elgin IV30 8UA
Cellarer: n/a. Executive staff 1. *CC* No.SCO 13703. Began 1948; Roman Catholic. Turnover n/a. Crafts, spiritual guidance.
Web: www.celide.ndirect.co.uk/pluscarden
☎ 01343 890 257 🖷 01343 890 258

Pontefract Christian Bookshop, Unit A, Mauds Yard, Pontefract WF8 1AQ
Manageress: Mrs Pat Stephenson. No full-time staff. Began 1980; evangelical. Turnover n/a.
☎ 01977 701 405

†**Portsmouth Cathedral Bookshop**, St Thomas' Street, Old Portsmouth, Portsmouth PO1 2HH
Managers: Mr Derek & Mrs Myrna Hall. No full-time staff. Began 1983; Anglican. Turnover n/a.
☎ 023 9273 6253

***Portsmouth Christian Book Centre**, 143 New Road, Portsmouth PO2 7QS
Partner: Mr Terry Cawte. Executive staff 1. Began 1950; non-denominational. Turnover £75,000 to year end Dec 98.
☎ 023 9266 4647 🖷 023 9226 3093

Protestant Truth Society Bookshop, 184 Fleet Street, London EC4A 2HJ
Bookshop Manager: Mr George Rae. *CC* No.248505. Began 1889; interdenominational. Turnover n/a.
☎ 020 7405 4960

†**Quarr Abbey Bookshop**, Quarr Abbey, Ryde PO33 4ES
Manager: Rev Charles Fitzsimons. No full-time staff. *CC* No.218731. Began n/a; Roman Catholic. Turnover n/a.
☎ 01983 882 420

The Rainbow Bookshop, St Aldhelm's Centre, Edgeware Road, Swindon SN1 1QS
Manageress: Mrs A M Moss. Staff n/a. *CC* Began 1979; ecumenical. Turnover n/a.
☎ 01793 694 583

Rainbow Christian Centre, 87 Queensway, Petts Wood, Orpington BR5 1DQ
Partner: Miss Diana Pattison. Other staff 3. Began 1984; non-denominational. Turnover £200,000 to year end Dec 98. Office services (copying, word processing, fax transmission etc).
Email: rainbow@talk21.com
☎ 01689 821 789 🖷 01689 890 136

Ravens Ltd, 3 Delamere Street, Chester CH1 4DS
Manager: Mr John R Lane. Executive staff 2. Began 1985; non-denominational. Turnover n/a.
☎ 01244 377 696 🖷 01244 377 696

RE Bookshop/Llyfrfa AG, Welsh National Centre for Religious Education, School of Education, UWB, Normal Site, Bangor LL57 2PX
Director: Mr Rheinallt A Thomas. *Manager:* Mr Philip Wilson. Executive staff 1, Other staff 2. Began 1982; interdenominational. Turnover £225,000 to year end July 98. Covering whole field of religious, Christian and world education.
Web: weblife.bangor.ac.uk/addysg/wncre/home.htm
Email: oof@bangor.ac.uk
☎ 01248 382 952 🖷 01248 382 155

†**Redemptorist Publications**, Alphonsus House, Chawton, Alton GU34 3HQ
Executive Director: Mr James D McKell. Executive staff 3, Other staff 19. *CC* No.3261721. Began 1957; Roman Catholic/Anglican. (Previously Redemptorist Book Room). Turnover n/a.
Web: www.redempt.org
Email: rp@redempt.demon.co.uk
☎ 01420 882 22 🖷 01420 888 05

Reflections Bookshop, King Street, Droylsden, Manchester M43 6TR
Manager: Mrs Patricia Loftus. Part-time staff 5. Began 1982; Assemblies of God. Turnover n/a.
☎ 0161 292 0939 🖷 0161 370 2444

***Revelation Books**, 384 Stratford Road, Shirley, Solihull B90 4AQ
Manager: Mrs Anne Callanan. Executive staff 1, Other staff 6. *CC* No.276743. Began 1977; non-denominational. (Solihull Christian Fellowship). Turnover £130,000 to year end Mar 98. Also greetings cards, CDs, cassettes, gift items.
☎ 0121 744 1722 🖷 0121 733 3400

The Revelation Christian Bookshop, 1 River Street, Chippenham SN15 3ED
Manager: Mrs Andrea Alner. *CC* No.1015148. Began 1985; non-denominational. Turnover n/a.
☎ 01249 659 432 🖷 01249 463 227

Revelations, 13 Tower Street, Ipswich IP1 3BG
Manager: Mr James Halsall. All voluntary staff. Began 1998; non-denominational. (Previously Church Centre Ltd). Turnover n/a.
☎ 01473 256 503

Revelations, Meeting Point House, Southwater Square, Town Centre, Telford TF3 4HS
Manager: Mr Tom Pollock. Executive staff 1. *CC* No.510321. Began 1974; ecumenical. (Previously Telford Christian Council Bookshop). Turnover n/a.
☎ 01952 291 634 🖷 01952 290 617

St Andrews Bookshop Ltd, 216 Mary Vale Road, Bournville, Birmingham B30 1PJ
Manager: To be appointed. Staff 2. Began 1998; interdenominational. (Previously Mother Goose). Linked to St Andrews Bookshop Ltd, Great Missenden. Turnover £50,000 to year end Dec 98.
☎ 0121 459 2000 🖷 0121 459 7000

B

For additional information see List on Pages 134–140

St Andrews Bookshop Ltd, 61 High Street, Great Missenden HP16 0AA
Managing Director: Mr E A Barnett. Executive staff 2, Other staff 9. Began 1957; non-denominational. Head Office of St Andrews Bookshops Ltd. Turnover £500,000-1,000,000 to year end Dec 98.
☎ 01494 862 168 🖷 01494 862 068

St Andrews Bookshop Ltd, 2 Kingsway, King Street, Maidenhead SL6 1EE
Director: Mr Tony Bronnimann. Executive staff 1, Other staff 2. Began 1981; interdenominational. Linked to St Andrews Bookshop Ltd, Great Missenden. Turnover £100,000–300,000 to year end Dec 98.
☎ 01628 621 985 🖷 01628 621 985

B

St Andrews Bookshop Ltd, 50 Church Street, Wolverton, Milton Keynes MK12 5JW
Manager: n/a. Other staff 4. Began 1980; non-denominational. Linked to St Andrews Bookshop Ltd, Great Missenden. Turnover £100-300,000 to year end Dec 96.
☎ 01908 221 331 🖷 01908 221 331

St Andrews Bookshop Ltd, 57c St Clements, Oxford OX4 1AG
Manager: Mr Paul Crockett. Other staff 3. Began 1948; interdenominational. Linked to St Andrews Bookshop Ltd, Great Missenden. Turnover £100,000-300,000 to year end Dec 98.
☎ 01865 247 567

St Andrews Bookshop Ltd, Penny Farthing Place, St Ebbes, Oxford OX1 1QS
Manager: n/a. Other staff 2. Began n/a; interdenominational. Linked to St Andrews Bookshop Ltd, Great Missenden. Turnover £100,000-300,000 to year end Dec 98.
☎ 01865 247 567

St Andrews Bookshop Ltd, 60 London Street, Reading RG1 4SQ
Manager: n/a. Other staff 6. Began 1967; non-denominational. (Previously Gateway Outreach). Linked to St Andrews Bookshop Ltd, Great Missenden. Turnover £100,000-300,000 to year end Dec 98.
☎ 0118 9576 078 🖷 0118 9576 078

St Andrews Bookshop Ltd, 31 High Street, Witney 0X8 6LP
Manager: n/a. Staff 3. Began 1994; interdenominational. Linked to St Andrews Bookshop Ltd, Great Missenden. Turnover £50,000–100,000 to year end Dec 98.
☎ 01993 709 429

St Andrews Bookshop Ltd, Holme Grange Craft Village, Heathlands Road, Wokingham RG40 3AW
Manager: n/a. Other staff 3. Began 1996; non-denominational. Linked to St Andrews Bookshop Ltd, Great Missenden. Turnover £50,000–100,000 to year end Dec 98.
☎ 0118 977 6715 🖷 0118 977 6715

St Chad's Cathedral Bookshop, St Chad's Queensway, Birmingham B4 6ET
Manageress: Mrs M T Flanagan. All voluntary staff. ***CC*** Began 1960; Roman Catholic. Turnover n/a.
☎ 0121 236 9306

St Davids Cathedral Bookshop, The Deanery, The Cathedral Close, St David's, Haverfordwest SA62 6RH
Administrator: Miss Moyra Skenfield. Executive staff 1, Other staff 6. ***CC*** Began n/a; Church in Wales. Turnover n/a.
☎ 01437 721 194

***St Denys' Bookshop**, 11 Oak Street, Manchester M4 5JD
Partner: Mrs Susan Usher. Executive staff 2, Other staff 3. Began 1982; non-denominational. Turnover n/a.
☎ 0161 835 1069 🖷 0161 839 7661

St Mary's Church Bookshop, Church Street, Market Drayton TF9 1AF
Chair person: Mr Richard Light. Voluntary staff 30. Began n/a; Anglican. Turnover £10,000 to year end Oct 96. Books, bibles, cards and gifts, 11am–3pm.
☎ 01630 653 505

St Michael's Bookshop, St Michael's Church, Laura Place, Aberystwyth SY23 2AU
Manager: n/a. Staff 2. Began 1983; Church in Wales. Turnover £22,500 to year end Dec 98.
Web: www.stmikes.clara.net
Email: bookshop@stmikes.clara.net
☎ 01970 617 184 🖷 01970 610 133

St Neots Christian Bookshop, Salvation Army Hall, 64 High Street, St Neots, Huntingdon PE19 1BU
Manageress: Mrs Jean Westra. Other staff 3. ***CC*** No.57724. Began 1982; non-denominational. Turnover n/a. Coffee shop, music and gifts.
Email: westra2611@aol.com
☎ 01480 219 170

St Paul MultiMedia, 5a Royal Exchange Square, Glasgow G1 3AH
Sister-in-Charge: Sister Betty Twamley. Staff 10. ***CC*** No.296042. Began 1969; Roman Catholic. Turnover £406,000 to year end Dec 98.
Email: glasgow@stpaulmultimedia.co.uk
☎ 0141 226 3391 🖷 0141 226 4719

St Paul MultiMedia, 82 Bold Street, Liverpool L1 4HR
In charge: Sister Noreen O'Rourke. Staff 8. ***CC*** No.296042. Began 1969; Roman Catholic. Turnover £409,000 to year end Dec 98.
Email: liverpool@stpaulmultimedia.co.uk
☎ 0151 707 1328 🖷 0151 707 1371

St Paul MultiMedia, 199 Kensington High Street, London W8 6BA
In Charge: Sister Virginia Marras. Staff 10. ***CC*** No.296042. Began 1955; Roman Catholic. Turnover £772,000 to year end Dec 98.
Email: london@stpaulmultimedia.co.uk
☎ 020 7937 9591 🖷 020 7937 9910

St Pauls (Westminster Cathedral), Morpeth Terrace, Victoria, London SW1P 1EP
Managing Director: Rev S Karamvelil. *Manager:* Mr David Chapman. Executive staff 7, Other staff 7. ***CC*** No.230948. Began 1990; Roman Catholic but ecumenical stock. Turnover £1,200,000 to year end Dec 98.
Web: stpauls.ie
Email: bookshop@stpauls.org.uk
☎ 020 7828 5582 🖷 020 7828 3329

Salvationist Publishing and Supplies Ltd, 117 Judd Street, King's Cross, London WC1H 9NN
Managing Director: Lt Col Michael Williams. Executive staff 3, Other staff 45. Began 1911; interdenominational. Turnover £3,500,000 to year end Mar 98.
☎ 020 7387 1656 🖷 020 7387 3420

SCEM Bookstore, 190 Quarry Street, Hamilton ML3 6QR
SCEM Committee Member: Mr Sam Reid. No paid staff. Began 1980; Christian Brethren. Turnover n/a.
☎ 01698 282 825

For additional information see List on Pages 134–140

Scripture Union Bookshop, Didasko House, 60 Union Row, Aberdeen AB10 1SA
Manager: n/a. All voluntary staff. *CC* Began 1868; interdenominational. Turnover n/a.
☎ 01224 634 265

Scripture Union Bookshop, 9 Canal Street, Glasgow G4 0AB
Manager: Mr Norman Graham. Executive staff 1, Other staff 3. *CC* Began n/a; interdenominational. Turnover n/a.
☎ 0141 332 1162 🖷 0141 332 5925

Scripture Union Resource Centre, 157 Albertbridge Road, Belfast BT5 4PS
Manager: Mr Sam Campbell. *General Director:* Rev David Bruce. Executive staff 5, Other staff 3. *CC* Began 1954; interdenominational. Turnover £150,000 to year end Dec 98.
Web: www.suni.co.uk
Email: info@suni.co.uk
☎ 028 9045 4806 🖷 028 9073 9758

Seekers Light Trust, The Lighthouse, 40 High Street, Highworth, Swindon SN6 7AQ
Manager: Mr Anthony T Chapman. Executive staff 1. *CC* No.289860. Began 1984; non-denominational. Turnover n/a.
☎ 01793 763 337

Shalom The Good Book Shop, Central Chambers, Beaumont Street, Hexham NE46 3LS
Manager: Mrs Sandra Martin. Voluntary staff 15. Began 1996; interdenominational. (Previously Shalom Christian Bookshop, Corbridge). Turnover n/a.
☎ 01434 604 004

Sharon Rose Bible Shop, 79 Soho Road, Handsworth, Birmingham B21 9SP
Manager: Mr David Hayes. Executive staff 1, Other staff 1. *CC* No.245132. Began 1981; interdenominational. Turnover n/a.
☎ 0121 523 3289

The Shrine Shop, 2 Common Place, Walsingham NR22 6EE
Manager: Miss Brenda Taylor. Executive staff 1. *CC* No.215863. Began 1935; Anglican. Turnover n/a.
☎ 01328 820 255

Sign of the Fish Christian Bookshop, 40 Eld Lane, Colchester CO1 1LS
Proprietor: Mr Dexter Slatter. Executive staff 1, Other staff 1. Began 1967; interdenominational. Turnover n/a.
☎ 01206 579 665 🖷 01206 579 665

Sittingbourne Christian Bookshop, The Baptist Church, High Street, Sittingbourne ME10 4AQ
Manager: Ms Joan Hammond. Other staff 7. *CC* No.1070071. Began 1976; non-denominational. Turnover n/a.
☎ 01795 422 315

Sonshine Christian Bookshop, Burgh Road, Aylsham, Norwich NR11 6AJ
Manager: Mrs Dawn Lawrence. Executive staff 1. Began 1984; non-denominational. Turnover £60,000 to year end May 98.
☎ 01263 734 420

Southend Christian Bookshop Ltd, 57 London Road, Southend-on-Sea SS1 1PF
Director: Mr P J Slennett. Executive staff 2, Other staff 6. Began 1971; interdenominational. Turnover n/a.
Email: scbookshop@aol.com
☎ 01702 344 008 🖷 01702 343 749

Southern Light Ministries, 51a Wimpson Lane, Millbrook, Southampton SO16 4QF
Director: Rev Colin A Benton. Executive staff 1. *CC* No.1036409. Began 1990; Assemblies of God. (Previously Southern Light Literature). Turnover n/a.
☎ 023 8039 9894

Southport Christian Book Centre, 3 Wesley Street, Southport PR8 1BN
Proprietor: Mr T G Ellis. Executive staff 2, Other staff 1. Began 1955; non-denominational. Turnover n/a.
☎ 01704 542 226 🖷 01704 542 226

Sozo Books, PO Box 29, Romsey SO51 0YU
Partner: Mr A S Daniel. Executive staff 3. *CC* Began 1989; non-denominational. Turnover n/a. Specialising in conference and public meeting bookstalls.
Email: sozomin@msn.com
☎ 01794 323 516 🖷 01794 322 167

B

SPCK Bookshop, 3 Forum Buildings, St James Parade, Bath BA1 1UG
Manager: Mr William Hooper. Executive staff 1, Other staff 5. *CC* No.231144. Began 1983; interdenominational. (Previously Good News Media). Society for Promoting Christian Knowledge. Turnover n/a.
Email: bath@spck.org.uk
☎ 01225 466 092 🖷 01225 442 383

SPCK Bookshop, 12 Ethel Street, Birmingham B2 4BG
Manager: Mr David C Stokes. Executive staff 1, Other staff 4. *CC* No.231144. Began 1858; interdenominational. (Previously Mowbrays Bookshop). Society for Promoting Christian Knowledge. Turnover n/a.
Email: birmingham@spck.org.uk
☎ 0121 643 2617 🖷 0121 633 3459

SPCK Bookshop, 14 North Parade, Bradford BD1 3HY
Manager: Mr Nicholas Johnson. Executive staff 1, Other staff 4. *CC* No.231144. Began 1936; interdenominational. Society for Promoting Christian Knowledge. Turnover n/a.
Email: bradford@spck.org.uk
☎ 01274 728 669 🖷 01274 726 973

SPCK Bookshop, Chapel Royal, North Street, Brighton BN1 1EA
Manager: Miss Melanie Carroll. Executive staff 1, Other staff 1. *CC* No.231144. Began 1880; interdenominational. Society for Promoting Christian Knowledge. Turnover n/a.
Email: brighton@spck.org.uk
☎ 01273 328 767 🖷 01273 738 200

SPCK Bookshop, 79 Park Street, Bristol BS1 5PF
Manager: Mr Richard Greatrex. Executive staff 1, Other staff 3. *CC* No.231144. Began 1948; interdenominational. Society for Promoting Christian Knowledge. Turnover n/a.
Email: bristol@spck.org.uk
☎ 01179 273 461 🖷 01179 293 525

SPCK Bookshop, 14 King's Parade, Cambridge CB2 1SR
Manager: Mrs Christina Lang. Staff n/a. *CC* No.231144. Began n/a; interdenominational. Society for Promoting Christian Knowledge. Turnover n/a.
Email: cambridge@spck.org.uk
☎ 01223 358 452 🖷 01223 366 316

B

SPCK Bookshop, 7 St Peter's Street, Canterbury CT1 2EF
Manager: Miss Annette Ardley. Executive staff 1, Other staff 3. ***CC*** No.231144. Began 1932; interdenominational. Society for Promoting Christian Knowledge. Turnover n/a.
Email: canterbury@spck.org.uk
☎ 01227 462 881 🖷 01227 456 297

SPCK Bookshop, City Church, Windsor Place, Cardiff CF1 3BZ
Manager: Mrs Annette Sainsbury. Executive staff 1, Other staff 4. ***CC*** No.231144. Began 1937; interdenominational. Society for Promoting Christian Knowledge. Turnover n/a.
Email: cardiff@spck.org.uk
☎ 029 2022 7736 🖷 029 2022 7515

SPCK Bookshop, The Lodge, Carlisle Cathedral, Carlisle CA3 8TZ
Manager: Mr Raymond Witty. Executive staff 1, Other staff 2. ***CC*** No.231144. Began 1979; interdenominational. Society for Promoting Christian Knowledge. Turnover n/a.
Email: carlisle@spck.org.uk
☎ 01228 543 498 🖷 01228 402 857

SPCK Bookshop, 7 St Werburgh Street, Chester CH1 2EJ
Manager: Mr Ian Vollands. Executive staff 1, Other staff 3. ***CC*** No.231144. Began 1946; interdenominational. Society for Promoting Christian Knowledge. Turnover n/a.
Email: chester@spck.org.uk
☎ 01244 323 753 🖷 01244 400191

SPCK Bookshop, St Olave's Church, North Street, Chichester PO19 1LQ
Manager: Miss Barbara Scott. Executive staff 1, Other staff 2. ***CC*** No.231144. Began 1957; interdenominational. Society for Promoting Christian Knowledge. Turnover n/a.
Email: chichester@spck.org.uk
☎ 01243 782 790 🖷 01243 784 604

SPCK Bookshop, The Great Kitchen, Durham Cathedral, Durham DH1 3EQ
Manager: Mr Alan Mordue. Executive staff 1, Other staff 3. ***CC*** No.231144. Began 1954; interdenominational. Society for Promoting Christian Knowledge. Turnover n/a.
Email: durham@spck.org.uk
☎ 0191 386 2972 🖷 0191 384 2834

SPCK Bookshop, 1 Catherine Street, Cathedral Yard, Exeter EX1 1EX
Manager: Mr David Ching. Executive staff 4, Other staff 1. ***CC*** No.231144. Began 1932; interdenominational. Society for Promoting Christian Knowledge. Turnover n/a.
Email: exeter@spck.org.uk
☎ 01392 273 640 🖷 01392 495 141

SPCK Bookshop, 4 College Green, Gloucester GL1 2LR
Manager: Mr Roger Spencer. Executive staff 1, Other staff 1. ***CC*** No.231144. Began 1945; interdenominational. Society for Promoting Christian Knowledge. Turnover n/a.
Email: gloucester@spck.org.uk
☎ 01452 522 805 🖷 01452 330 447

SPCK Bookshop, St Mary's Church, Quarry Street, Guildford GU1 4AU
Manager: Mr Matthew Collins. Executive staff 1, Other staff 1. ***CC*** No.231144. Began 1979; interdenominational. Society for Promoting Christian Knowledge. Turnover n/a.
Email: guildford@spck.org.uk
☎ 01483 560 316 🖷 01483 457 173

SPCK Bookshop, Palace Yard, Hereford HR4 9BJ
Manager: Mrs Anna Evans. Executive staff 1, Other staff 1. ***CC*** No.231144. Began 1982; interdenominational. Society for Promoting Christian Knowledge. Turnover n/a.
Email: hereford@spck.org.uk
☎ 01432 266 785 🖷 01432 279 040

SPCK Bookshop, Holy Trinity Church, Boar Lane, Leeds LS1 6HW
Manager: Mrs Kay Glasby. Executive staff 1, Other staff 1. ***CC*** No.231144. Began 1983; interdenominational. Society for Promoting Christian Knowledge. Turnover n/a.
☎ 0113 244 2488 🖷 0113 243 0425

SPCK Bookshop, Pilgrim House, 10 Bishop Street, Leicester LE1 6AF
Manager: Dr Julian Scott. Executive staff 1, Other staff 3. ***CC*** No.231144. Began 1974; interdenominational. Society for Promoting Christian Knowledge. Turnover n/a.
Email: leicester@spck.org.uk
☎ 01162 854 499 🖷 01162 755 948

SPCK Bookshop, 36 Steep Hill, Lincoln LN2 1LU
Manager: Mrs Carole Burrows. Executive staff 1, Other staff 7. ***CC*** No.231144. Began 1946; interdenominational. Society for Promoting Christian Knowledge. Turnover n/a.
Email: lincoln@spck.org.uk
☎ 01522 527 486 🖷 01522 534 484

SPCK Bookshop, Liverpool Cathedral, St James Mount, Liverpool L1 7AZ
Manager: Mrs Katherine Walker. Executive staff 1, Other staff 4. ***CC*** No.231144. Began 1934; interdenominational. Society for Promoting Christian Knowledge. Turnover n/a.
Email: liverpool@spck.org.uk
☎ 0151 709 1897 🖷 0151 708 6283

SPCK Bookshop, Holy Trinity Church, Marylebone Road, London NW1 4DU
Manager: Miss Aude Pasquier. Executive staff 1, Other staff 4. ***CC*** No.231144. Began 1836; interdenominational. Society for Promoting Christian Knowledge. Turnover n/a.
Email: london@spck.org.uk
☎ 020 7388 1659 🖷 020 7388 2352

SPCK Secondhand and Antiquarian Bookshop, Holy Trinity Church, Marylebone Road, London NW1 4DU
Manager: Mr Michael Pickering. Executive staff 1, Other staff 2. ***CC*** No.231144. Began 1976; interdenominational. (Previously Charles Higham Books). Society for Promoting Christian Knowledge. Turnover n/a. Antiquarian, out of print and secondhand theology and Christian literature, maps and prints.
Email: secondhand@spck.org.uk
☎ 020 7383 3097 🖷 020 7388 2352

SPCK Bookshop, 157 Waterloo Road, London SE1 8XA
Manager: Mr Simon Lewis. Executive staff 1, Other staff 2. ***CC*** No.231144. Began 1995; interdenominational. Society for Promoting Christian Knowledge. Turnover n/a.
Email: partnership@spck.org.uk
☎ 020 7633 9096 🖷 020 7633 9096

SPCK Bookshop, 8 Ridley Place, Newcastle upon Tyne NE1 8JW
Manager: Mrs Heather Place. Executive staff 1, Other staff 3. ***CC*** No.231144. Began 1943; interdenominational. Society for Promoting Christian Knowledge. Turnover n/a.
Email: newcastle@spck.org.uk
☎ 0191 232 3466 🖷 0191 230 2265

For additional information see List on Pages 134–140

SPCK Bookshop, 19 Pottergate, Norwich NR2 1DS
Manager: Mr Steven Foyster. Executive staff 1, Other staff 2. ***CC*** No.231144. Began 1978; interdenominational. Society for Promoting Christian Knowledge. Turnover n/a.
Email: norwich@spck.org.uk
☎ 01603 627 332 🖷 01603 627 332

SPCK Bookshop, 51 High Street, Salisbury SP1 2PE
Manager: Miss Sarah Hargreaves. Executive staff 1, Other staff 3. ***CC*** No.231144. Began 1941; interdenominational. Society for Promoting Christian Knowledge. Turnover n/a.
Email: salisbury@spck.org.uk
☎ 01722 334 535 🖷 01722 414 904

SPCK Bookshop, 8 East Parade, Sheffield S1 2ET
Manager: Mr Richard Stableford. Executive staff 1, Other staff 2. ***CC*** No.231144. Began 1936; interdenominational. Society for Promoting Christian Knowledge. Turnover n/a.
Email: sheffield@spck.org.uk
☎ 0114 272 3454 🖷 0114 279 7751

SPCK Bookshop, 8 St Mary's Street, Truro TR1 2AF
Manager: Mr David Ivall. Executive staff 1, Other staff 2. ***CC*** No.231144. Began 1950; interdenominational. Society for Promoting Christian Knowledge. Turnover n/a.
Email: truro@spck.org.uk
☎ 01872 272 771 🖷 01872 260 491

SPCK Bookshop, 24 The Square, Winchester SO23 9EX
Manager: Mr William Cole. Executive staff 1, Other staff 2. ***CC*** No.231144. Began 1977; interdenominational. Society for Promoting Christian Knowledge. Turnover n/a.
Email: winchester@spck.org.uk
☎ 01962 866 617 🖷 01962 890 312

SPCK Bookshop, 105 High Street, Worcester WR1 2HS
Manager: Mr David Steel. Executive staff 1, Other staff 2. ***CC*** No.231144. Began 1937; interdenominational. Society for Promoting Knowledge. Turnover n/a.
Email: worcester@spck.org.uk
☎ 01905 243 96 🖷 01905 243 96

SPCK Bookshop, 28 Goodramgate, York YO1 7LG
Manager: Miss Rachael Franklin. Executive staff 1, Other staff 2. ***CC*** No.231144. Began 1947; interdenominational. Society for Promoting Christian Knowledge. Turnover n/a.
Email: york@spck.org.uk
☎ 01904 654 176 🖷 01904 670 931

Spectrum Christian Books and Gifts, 144 Stamford Street, Ashton-under-Lyne OL6 6AD
Manager: E J Ives. Other staff 1. ***CC*** No.509290. Began 1975; non-denominational. (Previously Jesus Family Bookshop). Turnover £60,000 to year end Jan 97.
☎ 0161 344 5991

Spurgeon's Book Room, 189 South Norwood Hill, London SE25 6DJ
Managing Director: Mr Norman E Nibloe. Executive staff 1, Other staff 1. Began 1981; Baptist. (Linked to Tonbridge Christian Book Centre). Turnover £48,000 to year end June 98.
☎ 020 8653 3640 🖷 020 8653 0850

Spurriergate Centre, St Michael's Church, Spurriergate, York YO1 9QR
Operations Manager: Simon Watterson. *Managing Director:* Mr John Marsden. Executive staff 5, Other staff 31. ***CC*** Began 1989; Anglican. Turnover £325,000 to year end Mar 97. Also restaurant, evangelism, listening, prayer.
Email: spurriergate@marsden.demon.co.uk
☎ 01904 629 393 🖷 01904 629 383

Stepping Stone, 25 Clifton Street, Lytham St Annes FY8 5EP
Manageress: Mrs Jeanette Linington. Other staff 7. ***CC*** No.515536. Began 1979; interdenominational. Turnover £100,000 to year end Jan 98. Coffee shop.
☎ 01253 735 796

Stornoway Religious Bookshop, 18 Kenneth Street, Stornoway HS1 2DR
Manager: William Forsyth. Executive staff 1. ***CC*** Began 1956; non-denominational. Turnover n/a.
☎ 01851 703 334

†**Sunrise (Good News Crusade)**, Church Walk, Truro TR1 1JH
Manager: Mr David Willis. Executive staff 2, Other staff 2. Began 1979; non-denominational. Turnover n/a.
☎ 01872 277 903

Swanage Christian Centre, The Harvest Kitchen, 36 High Street, Swanage BH19 2NU
Manageress: Mrs Pauline Werba. Executive staff 2. ***CC*** No.276495. Began 1977; non-denominational. Turnover n/a. Coffee shop.
☎ 01929 427 101

Swells Bookshop Ltd, 19 The Close, Salisbury SP1 2EE
Manager: Mr R Webb. Other staff 1, Voluntary staff 1. Began 1985; non-denominational. Turnover £108,000 to year end Mar 97. Academic theological plus mail order.
☎ 01722 326 899 🖷 01722 338 508

The Sycamore Tree, 2 Chapel Street, Nuneaton CV11 5QH
Manager: Mrs Pat Bull. Other staff 2. ***CC*** No.519317. Began 1990; non-denominational. Turnover £82,000 to year end Oct 98. Counselling, coffee shop.
☎ 024 7638 5448 🖷 024 7638 5448
Counselling: Mrs Mary Morris
☎ 024 7674 4544

Tabernacle Bookshop, Metropolitan Tabernacle, Elephant and Castle, London SE1 6SD
Bookshop Manager: Mr K C Baker. Executive staff 1, Other staff 2. ***CC*** Began 1976; non-denominational. Turnover n/a. International mail order, cassettes.
Web: www.metropolitantabernacle.org
Email: bookshop@metropolitantabernacle.org
☎ 020 7735 7076 🖷 020 7735 7989

†**Taste & See Bookshop**, 102 Irlam Road, Flixton, Manchester M41 6JT
Manager: Ms Sheila Wrigley. No other paid staff. ***CC*** Began 1994; interdenominational. (Affiliated to Maranatha Community). Turnover n/a.
☎ 0161 747 5672 🖷 0161 747 7379

***Teifi Christian Books**, Unit 2, Priory Court, Priory Street, Cardigan SA43 1BZ
Managers: Dr John & Mrs Monica Vernon. No other paid staff. Began 1994; non-denominational. Turnover £16,000 to year end Feb 98.
☎ 01239 615 516 🖷 01239 615 516

Temple Courts Christian Bookshop, 80 Bartholomew Street, Newbury RG14 7AB
Manageress: Mrs E Campbell. Executive staff 1, Other staff 1. Began 1986; non-denominational. Turnover n/a.
☎ 01635 401 21 🖷 01635 477 47

The Tonbridge Christian Book Centre Ltd, 9 Quarry Hill Parade, Tonbridge TN9 2HR
Managing Director: Mr Norman E Nibloe. Executive staff 3, Other staff 5. Began 1976; interdenominational. Turnover £170,000 to year end June 98.
☎ 01732 364 897 🖷 01732 365 437

***The Triangle**, 30 Camp Road, Farnborough GU14 6EW
Trust Co-ordinator: Mr Don Fuller. All voluntary staff. ***CC*** Began 1986; interdenominational. Turnover £85,000 to year end Aug 98.
☎ 01252 519 172 🖷 01252 519 172

Truro Cathedral Shop, Wilkes Walk, Truro TR1 2UF
Manager: Mrs Verity Barker. Part-time staff 1. Began 1987; Anglican. Turnover n/a.
☎ 01872 275 125

Two Worlds Christian Bookshop, 2 Avondale Road, Chorley PR7 2ED
Trustee: Mr W Sloan. Executive staff 4, Other staff 4. ***CC*** No.518002. Began 1978; non-denominational. Turnover £35,000 to year end Dec 98.
☎ 01257 263 880 🖷 01257 231 192

Unity Bookshop, 15 Folly Lane, Petersfield GU31 4AU
Part-time Manager: Ms Carolyn Baker. Voluntary staff 18. ***CC*** No.296533. Began 1987; interdenominational. Turnover n/a.
☎ 01730 262 572

†**URC Bookshop**, 86 Tavistock Place, London WC1H 9RT
Communications Officer: Mrs Carol Rogers. Executive staff 2, Other staff 1. ***CC*** Began n/a; United Reformed. Turnover n/a.
Email: comedi@urccompulink.co.uk
☎ 020 7916 2020 🖷 020 7916 2021

†**Vale Christian Bookshop**, 52 Plassey Street, Penarth CF6 1EN
Manager: Mrs A Edwards. No full-time staff. Began 1984; non-denominational. Turnover n/a.
☎ 029 2070 5298

The Vine Christian Bookshop and Coffee House, 6 Albert Street, Littleborough OL15 8BS
Manager: Mr Alan Duxbury. Executive staff 1. ***CC*** No.515709. Began 1981; Anglican. Turnover £50,000 to year end Mar 97. Coffee shop and counselling.
☎ 01706 374 534 🖷 01706 377 322

The Vine Trust Bookshop, 31 Bridge Street, Andover SP10 1BE
Manager: Mr Brian Percey. Executive staff 1. ***CC*** No.288706. Began 1984; non-denominational. Turnover £42,000 to year end Dec 98. Partnership with the Bridge Coffee Shop supplying literature, music, cards and gifts.
Email: valleychan@aol.com
☎ 01264 355 706 Mobile: 07770 421 535

†**Wakefield Cathedral Bookshop**, The Cathedral, Northgate, Wakefield WF1 1HG
Manager: Mr Barry Rowe. All voluntary staff. Began 1982; Anglican. Turnover £20,000 to year end Jan 97.
☎ 01924 373 923 🖷 01924 215 054

Wallasey Christian Books, 100 Liscard Road, Wallasey CH44 0AA
Managers: Mrs Lynne Clark, Rev Andrew Funnell. No full-time staff. ***CC*** Began 1985; interdenominational. Turnover £35,000 to year end Sept 98.
☎ 0151 630 5114 🖷 0151 630 5114

The Water Pot, 14 New Wynd, Montrose DD10 8RB
Manager: Miss Irene McKay. Other staff 2. Began 1992; Pentecostal. Turnover £4,000 to year end Dec 98.
☎ No telephone

Waterstones Bookshop incorporating Mowbrays, 28 Margaret Street, London W1N 7LB
Branch Manageress: Lorna Green. Executive staff 1, Other staff 11. Began 1903; non-denominational. (Previously Dillons the Bookstore incorporating Mowbrays). Turnover n/a.
☎ 020 7580 2812 Directline: 020 7436 0294
🖷 020 7637 1790

The Way Bookshop, West Street, Crewe CW1 3HE
Managers: Mrs Jill Buchan, Mrs Clarissa Shackleton. Executive staff 2. Began 1984; non-denominational. Turnover n/a. Coffee shop, counselling services can be arranged.
☎ 01270 257 623

***WEC Bookroom**, Bulstrode, Oxford Road, Gerrards Cross SL9 8SZ
Manager: Mrs Elsie Fraser. Other staff 2. ***CC*** No.237005. Began 1978; interdenominational. Turnover n/a. Also mail order.
Email: 100546.1550@compuserve.com
☎ 01753 884 631 🖷 01753 882 470

The Well Bookshop & Coffee Shop, Alpha Centre, Broadway, Douglas IM2 4EN
Manageress: Mrs Sheila Sutton. No full-time staff. ***CC*** Began 1984; non-denominational. Turnover £45,000 to year end Dec 98. Also counselling.
☎ 01624 622 284 🖷 01624 622 284

Wells Cathedral Publications Ltd, The West Cloister, Wells BA5 2PA
Manager: Mrs Elizabeth Stafford. Executive staff 3, Other staff 6. Began 1971; Anglican. Turnover n/a. Gifts, souvenirs and recordings.
☎ 01749 672 773 🖷 01749 676 543

***Wesley Owen Books and Music**, 164 Union Street, Aberdeen AB1 1QT
Manager: Mrs Sheelagh Cuthbert. Executive staff 1, Other staff 6. ***CC*** Began n/a; interdenominational. Turnover £252,000 to year end Dec 97.
Web: www.wesleyowen.com
Email: aberdeen@wesley-owen.com
☎ 01224 644 464 🖷 01224 644 989

***Wesley Owen Books and Music**, 57 Kyle Street, Ayr KA7 1RS
Manager: Mr Richard Macfarlane. Executive staff 1, Other staff 6. ***CC*** Began n/a; interdenominational. Turnover £143,000 to year end Dec 97.
Web: www.wesleyowen.com
Email: ayr@wesley-owen.com
☎ 01292 264 548 🖷 01292 264 548

***Wesley Owen Books and Music**, 30 St Loyes Street, Bedford MK40 1EP
Manager: Mr Alun Jones. Executive staff 1, Other staff 3. ***CC*** Began 1978; interdenominational. (Previously Scripture Union Bookshop). Turnover £218,000 to year end Dec 97.
Web: www.wesleyowen.com
Email: bedford@wesley-owen.com
☎ 01234 262 517 🖷 01234 262 517

For additional information see List on Pages 134–140

Wesley Owen Books and Music (The Book Room), 7 Carrs Lane, Birmingham B4 7TG
Branch Manager: Mr David J Chant. *Christian Buyer:* Mr Peter Redwood. Executive staff 1, Other staff 12. ***CC*** No.502831. Began 1893; interdenominational. Turnover £250,000 to year end Dec 95.
Web: www.wesleyowen.com
Email: birmingham@wesley-owen.com
☎ 0121 643 9235 🖷 0121 633 4311

Wesley Owen Books and Music, 129 Deansgate, Bolton BL1 1HA
Manager: Rusch Jayatunge. Executive staff 1, Other staff 2. ***CC*** Began 1963; interdenominational. Turnover £167,000 to year end Dec 97.
Web: www.wesleyowen.com
Email: bolton@wesley-owen.com
☎ 01204 532 384 🖷 01204 532 384

Wesley Owen Books and Music, 60 Park Street, Bristol BS1 5JN
Manager: Sarah Gooding. Executive staff 1, Other staff 8. ***CC*** Began 1834; interdenominational. Turnover £482,000 to year end Dec 97.
Web: www.wesleyowen.com
Email: bristol@wesley-owen.com
☎ 0117 926 4426 🖷 0117 929 4068

Wesley Owen Books and Music, 21 The Mall, Bromley BR1 1TR
Manager: Mr Dave Brown. Executive staff 1, Other staff 9. ***CC*** Began 1966; interdenominational. Turnover £460,000 to year end Dec 97.
Web: www.wesleyowen.com
Email: bromley@wesley-owen.com
☎ 020 8464 1191 🖷 020 8466 0566

Wesley Owen Books and Music, 88a Regent Street, Cambridge CB2 1DP
Manager: Anne Streeter. Executive staff 1, Other staff 4. ***CC*** Began 1984; interdenominational. (Previously Scripture Union Bookshop). Turnover £233,000 to year end Dec 97.
Web: www.wesleyowen.com
Email: cambridge@wesley-owen.com
☎ 01223 352 727 🖷 01223 352 727

Wesley Owen Books and Music, 22 Fisher Street, Carlisle CA3 8RH
Manager: Jenny Beattie. Executive staff 1, Other staff 4. ***CC*** Began 1974; interdenominational. (Previously Scripture Union Bookshop). Turnover £102,000 to year end Dec 97.
Web: www.wesleyowen.com
Email: carlisle@wesley-owen.com
☎ 01228 534 919 🖷 01228 534 919

Wesley Owen Books and Music, 44 Clarence Street, Cheltenham GL50 3PL
Manager: Mr Emil Ernst. Executive staff 1, Other staff 3. ***CC*** Began 1971; interdenominational. (Previously Scripture Union Bookshop). Turnover £183,000 to year end Dec 97.
Web: www.wesleyowen.com
Email: cheltenham@wesley-owen.com
☎ 01242 513 686 🖷 01242 228 646

Wesley Owen Books and Music, 21 City Arcade, Coventry CV1 3HX
Manager: Gina Longbottom. Executive staff 1, Other staff 7. ***CC*** Began 1978; interdenominational. (Previously The Christian Bookshop). Turnover £198,000 to year end Dec 97.
Web: www.wesleyowen.com
Email: coventry@wesley-owen.com
☎ 024 7622 2064 🖷 024 7655 3744

***Wesley Owen Books and Music**, 34 The Boulevard, Crawley RH10 1XP
Manager: Susan Attwater. Executive staff 1, Other staff 2. ***CC*** Began 1979; interdenominational. (Previously Challenge Bookshop). Turnover £103,000 to year end Dec 97.
Web: www.wesleyowen.com
Email: crawley@wesley-owen.com
☎ 01293 511 539 🖷 01293 511 539

***Wesley Owen Books and Music**, 16 Park Street, Croydon CR0 1YE
Manager: Mr James Ashton. Executive staff 1, Other staff 6. ***CC*** Began 1965; interdenominational. (Previously Scripture Union Bookshop). Turnover £339,000 to year end Dec 97.
Web: www.wesleyowen.com
Email: croydon@wesley-owen.com
☎ 020 8686 2772 🖷 020 8681 3463

***Wesley Owen Books and Music**, 48 Queen Street, Derby DE1 3GN
Manager: Mr Ian McLaren. Executive staff 1, Other staff 3. ***CC*** Began 1810; interdenominational. (Previously Scripture Union Bookshop). Turnover £258,000 to year end Dec 97.
Web: www.wesleyowen.com
Email: derby@wesley-owen.com
☎ 01332 345 936 🖷 01332 296 674

***Wesley Owen Books and Music**, 112 Nethergate, Dundee DD1 4EH
Manager: Miss Fiona Elder. Executive staff 1, Other staff 6. ***CC*** Began n/a; interdenominational. Turnover £134,000 to year end Dec 97.
Web: www.wesleyowen.com
Email: dundee@wesley-owen.com
☎ 01382 200 075 🖷 01382 200 091

***Wesley Owen Books and Music**, 117 George Street, Edinburgh EH2 4JN
Manager: Mr Graeme Campbell. Executive staff 1, Other staff 14. ***CC*** Began n/a; interdenominational. Turnover £755,000 to year end Dec 97.
Web: www.wesleyowen.com
Email: edinburgh@wesley-owen.com
☎ 0131 225 2229 🖷 0131 225 8167

***Wesley Owen Books and Music**, 111 Cecil Road, Enfield EN2 6TR
Manager: Abigail White. Executive staff 1, Other staff 2. ***CC*** Began 1955; interdenominational. Turnover £138,000 to year end Dec 97.
Web: www.wesleyowen.com
Email: enfield@wesley-owen.com
☎ 020 8363 8517 🖷 020 8366 9599

***Wesley Owen Books and Music**, 15 Paris Street, Exeter EX1 2JB
Manager: Mr Stuart Skinner. Executive staff 1, Other staff 5. ***CC*** Began 1985; interdenominational. (Previously Scripture Union Bookshop). Turnover £209,000 to year end Dec 97.
Web: www.wesleyowen.com
Email: exeter@wesley-owen.com
☎ 01392 254 024 🖷 01392 425 558

***Wesley Owen Books and Music**, 1 Glebe Street, Falkirk FK1 1HX
Manager: Mr John Marshall. Executive staff 1, Other staff 2. ***CC*** Began 1970; interdenominational. (Previously Scripture Union Bookshop). Turnover £96,000 to year end Dec 97.
Web: www.wesleyowen.com
Email: falkirk@wesley-owen.com
☎ 01324 612 955 🖷 01324 612 955

For additional information see List on Pages 134–140

Wesley Owen Books and Music, 26 Bothwell Street, Glasgow G2 6PA
Manager: Mary MacLeod. Executive staff 3, Other staff 30. ***CC*** Began 1893; non-denominational. (Previously Pickering & Inglis). Turnover n/a.
Email: glasgow@wesley-owen.com
☎ 0141 221 8913 Fax 0141 332 8680

***Wesley Owen Books and Music**, 60 Quarry Street, Guildford GU1 3UA
Manager: Dawn Rogers. Executive staff 1, Other staff 3. ***CC*** Began 1930; interdenominational. (Previously Challenge Bookshop). Turnover £168,000 to year end Dec 97.
Web: www.wesleyowen.com
Email: guildford@wesley-owen.com
☎ 01483 573 707 Fax 01483 455 214

B

***Wesley Owen Books and Music**, 11 Masons Avenue, Wealdstone, Harrow HA3 5AH
Manager: Mr Andrew Liversidge. Executive staff 1, Other staff 5. ***CC*** Began 1978; interdenominational. (Previously Scripture Union Bookshop). Turnover £187,000 to year end Dec 97.
Web: www.wesleyowen.com
Email: harrow@wesley-owen.com
☎ 020 8861 3259 Fax 020 8861 3259

***Wesley Owen Books and Music**, 23 Castle Street, Inverness IV2 3EP
Manager: Anne Hughes. Executive staff 1, Other staff 6. ***CC*** Began n/a; interdenominational. Turnover £142,000 to year end Dec 97.
Web: www.wesleyowen.com
Email: inverness@wesley-owen.com
☎ 01463 226 152 Fax 01463 237 432

***Wesley Owen Books and Music**, 3 King Edward Street, Leeds LS1 6AX
Manager: Mr Paul Walker. Executive staff 1, Other staff 6. ***CC*** Began 1968; interdenominational. (Previously Scripture Union Bookshop). Turnover £298,000 to year end Dec 97.
Web: www.wesleyowen.com
Email: leeds@wesley-owen.com
☎ 0113 245 8264 Fax 0113 244 2600

***Wesley Owen Books and Music**, 6 Roe Street, St John's Centre, Liverpool L1 1EP
Manager: Mr Andrew Stott. Executive staff 1, Other staff 4. ***CC*** Began 1973; interdenominational. (Previously Scripture Union Bookshop). Turnover £189,000 to year end Dec 97.
Web: www.wesleyowen.com
Email: liverpool@wesley-owen.com
☎ 0151 709 1029 Fax 0151 709 1194

***Wesley Owen Books and Music**, 82 High Road, South Woodford, London E18 2NA
Manager: Jan Newsom. Executive staff 1, Other staff 4. ***CC*** Began n/a; interdenominational. (Previously Dove Books). Turnover £162,000 to year end Dec 97.
Web: www.wesleyowen.com
Email: southwoodford@wesley-owen.com
☎ 020 8530 4244 Fax 020 8518 8924

***Wesley Owen Books & Music**, 3 Eccleston Street, Victoria, London SW1W 9LZ
Manager: Mr James Webster. Executive staff 1, Other staff 3. Began n/a; interdenominational. Turnover n/a.
Web: www.wesleyowen.com
Email: victoria@wesley-owen.com
☎ 020 7463 1451 Fax 020 7730 7935

***Wesley Owen Books and Music**, 3 Wigmore Street, London W1H 0AD
Manager: Mr James Webster. Executive staff 1, Other staff 12. ***CC*** Began 1926; interdenominational. (Previously Scripture Union Bookshop). Turnover £646,000 to year end Dec 97.
Web: www.wesleyowen.com
Email: london@wesley-owen.com
☎ 020 7493 1851 Fax 020 7493 4478

***Wesley Owen Books and Music**, 16 Park Green, Macclesfield SK11 7NA
Manager: Mr Julian Gittings. Executive staff 1, Other staff 3. Began 1978; interdenominational. (Previously The Christian Bookshop). Turnover £148,000 to year end Dec 97.
Web: www.wesleyowen.com
Email: macclesfield@wesley-owen.com
☎ 01625 431 684 Fax 01625 431 684

***Wesley Owen Books and Music**, 77 Bridge Street, Manchester M3 2RH
Manager: Rosalind Lysons. Executive staff 1, Other staff 5. ***CC*** Began n/a; interdenominational. (Previously Scripture Union Bookshop). Turnover £206,000 to year end Dec 97.
Web: www.wesleyowen.com
Email: manchester@wesley-owen.com
☎ 0161 834 4655 Fax 0161 839 3472

***Wesley Owen Books and Music**, 26 Heathcote Street, Nottingham NG1 3AA
Manager: Geraldine Johnson. Executive staff 1, Other staff 5. ***CC*** Began 1966; interdenominational. (Previously Scripture Union Bookshop). Turnover £230,000 to year end Dec 97.
Web: www.wesleyowen.com
Email: nottingham@wesley-owen.com
☎ 0115 950 1919 Fax 0115 941 4624

***Wesley Owen Books and Music**, 14 Eton Street, Richmond TW9 1EE
Manager: Mr Stephen Loader. Executive staff 1, Other staff 2. ***CC*** Began 1975; interdenominational. (Previously Scripture Union Bookshop). Turnover £130,000 to year end Dec 97.
Web: www.wesleyowen.com
Email: richmond@wesley-owen.com
☎ 020 8940 2915 Fax 020 8940 2915

***Wesley Owen Books and Music**, 11 Lower Hillgate, Stockport SK1 1JQ
Manager: Mr John Watkins. Executive staff 1, Other staff 4. ***CC*** Began 1976; interdenominational. (Previously Scripture Union Bookshop). Turnover £227,000 to year end Dec 97.
Web: www.wesleyowen.com
Email: stockport@wesley-owen.com
☎ 0161 480 1467 Fax 0161 477 7275

***Wesley Owen Books and Music**, 5 Grove Road, Sutton SM1 1BB
Manager: Mr Kevin Ahronson. Other staff 4. ***CC*** No.270162. Began 1974; non-denominational. (Previously Crownbooks Ltd). Turnover £176,000 to year end Dec 97.
Web: www.wesleyowen.com
Email: sutton@wesley-owen.com
☎ 020 8642 6511 Fax 020 8642 6511

***Wesley Owen Books and Music**, 11 Faringdon Road, Swindon SN1 5AR
Manager: Heather Morgan. Executive staff 1, Other staff 3. ***CC*** Began 1982; interdenominational. (Previously Scripture Union Bookshop). Turnover £120,000 to year end Dec 97.
Web: www.wesleyowen.com
Email: swindon@wesley-owen.com
☎ 01793 490 844 Fax 01793 490 844

For additional information see List on Pages 134–140

Wesley Owen Books and Music, Unit 6, The Crossing at St Paul's, Darwell Street, Walsall WS1 1DA
Manager: Mrs Joyce Clay. Executive staff 1, Other staff 6. ***CC*** Began 1969; interdenominational. (Previously Scripture Union Bookshop). Turnover £141,000 to year end Dec 97.
Web: www.wesleyowen.com
Email: walsall@wesley-owen.com
☎ 01922 631 230 🖷 01922 631 230

Wesley Owen Books and Music, The Broadway, 66 Queen's Road, Watford WD1 2LA
Manager: Mr Andrew Liversidge. Executive staff 1, Other staff 3. ***CC*** Began 1982; interdenominational. (Previously Scripture Union Bookshop). Turnover £147,000 to year end Dec 97.
Web: www.wesleyowen.com
Email: watford@wesley-owen.com
☎ 01923 248 727 🖷 01923 221 754

Wesley Owen Books and Music, 13 The Centre, Walliscote Road, Weston-super-Mare BS23 1UW
Manager: Mr Tony Hollow. Executive staff 1, Other staff 4. ***CC*** Began 1984; interdenominational. Turnover £116,000 to year end Dec 97.
Web: www.wesleyowen.com
Email: weston@wesley-owen.com
☎ 01934 418 109 🖷 01934 418 109

Wesley Owen Books and Music, 7 Chatsworth Road, Worthing BN11 1LY
Manager: Janet Ashton. Executive staff 1, Other staff 7. ***CC*** Began 1968; interdenominational. (Previously Challenge Bookshop). Turnover £200,000 to year end Dec 97.
Web: www.wesleyowen.com
Email: worthing@wesley-owen.com
☎ 01903 234 566 🖷 01903 236 857

Wesleyan Reform Union Bookshop, 123 Queen Street, Sheffield S1 2DU
General Secretary: Rev E W Downing. Executive staff 1, Other staff 1. ***CC*** No.250315. Began 1849; Wesleyan Reform. Turnover £17,494 to year end Mar 96.
☎ 0114 272 1938 🖷 0114 272 1965

Weymouth Christian Books, 25a Trinity Road, Weymouth DT4 8TJ
Co-owner: Dr John H Mann. No full-time staff. Began 1982; non-denominational. Turnover n/a.
☎ 01305 788 555

Words Bookshop, 68 Wallgate, Wigan WN1 1BA
Owner: Mrs Kathleen Cooper. Other staff 3. Began 1982; non-denominational. Turnover £80,000 to year end Mar 94.
☎ 01942 495 402 🖷 01942 820 566

Wye Dean Christian Centre, 18 Newerne Street, Lydney GL15 5RF
Director: Mr David Bowlzer. Executive staff 2, Other staff 2. ***CC*** Began 1991; non-denominational. Turnover n/a.
☎ 01594 841 907 🖷 01594 826 639

***YWAM Books**, Highfield Oval, Ambrose Lane, Harpenden AL5 4BX
Manager: Mr John Clark. full-time staff 1. ***CC*** No.264078. Began 1983; interdenominational. Turnover n/a.
Email: 106224.2334@compuserve.com
☎ 01582 463 242 🖷 01582 463 305

†*YWAM Books, The King's Lodge, Watling Street, Nuneaton CV10 0TZ
Manager: Ms Eileen Jackson. Staff n/a. ***CC*** No.264078. Began 1983; interdenominational. Turnover n/a.
Email: bookshop.kl@ywam.org.uk
☎ 024 7634 8128 🖷 024 7634 4464

Zetland Christian Bookshop, Victoria Road, Richmond DL10 4AS
Manager: Mrs Patricia Rivers. Executive staff 1, Part-time staff 2. ***CC*** Began 1984; Assemblies of God. Turnover n/a.
Email: pent.zet@privers.freeserve.co.uk
☎ 01748 823 161

Zion Christian Books, Fore Street, St Ives TR26 1HW
Manager: Mr Ralph O'Shea. All voluntary staff. ***CC*** Began n/a; Evangelical Fellowship of Congregational Churches and Countess of Huntingdon's Connexion. Turnover £18,000 to year end Dec 98.
☎ 01736 798 291

LIBRARIES

Bray Libraries Worldwide, SPCK Worldwide, Holy Trinity Church, Marylebone Road, London NW1 4DU
Administrator: Mrs Lesley Haldane. No full-time staff. ***CC*** No.231144. Began 1730; Anglican. No magazine. Turnover n/a. Small grants for Anglican parish/deanery/diocesan library development.
Web: www.spck.org.uk
Email: spckww@spck.org.uk
☎ 020 7387 5282 Fax 020 7387 3411

B

Canterbury Cathedral Library, The Precincts, Canterbury CT1 2EH
Cathedral Librarian: Mrs Sheila Hingley. Executive staff 1, Other staff 3. ***CC*** Began n/a; Anglican. No magazine. Turnover n/a. Historical library of 35,000 pre-1900 books and 8,000 20th century books.
Email: s.m.hingley@ukc.ac.uk
☎ 01227 865 247 Fax 01227 865 222

Catholic Central Library, Lancing Street, London NW1 1ND
Librarian: Mrs Joan Bond. ***CC*** No.1064460. Began n/a; Roman Catholic. No magazine. Turnover n/a. Religious subscription library open to people of all denominations.
☎ 020 7383 4333 Fax 020 7388 6675

Christian World Library, Christian Research, Vision Building, 4 Footscray Road, Eltham, London SE9 2TZ
Information Officer: Mrs Pamela Poynter. Library staff 1. ***CC*** No.1017701. Began 1983; interdenominational. No magazine. Turnover £271,600 to year end Dec 98. Statistical and other reference sources relating to the Church around the world, especially Europe.
Web: www.christian-research.org.uk
Email: admin@christian-research.org.uk
☎ 020 8294 1989 Fax 020 8294 0014

Durham Dean and Chapter Library, The College, Durham DH1 3EH
Deputy Chapter Librarian: Mr Roger C Norris. Executive staff 1, Other staff 1. Began 995; Anglican. No magazine. Turnover n/a. Historical books and Archdeacon Sharp Library of current theological books.
Email: r.c.norris@durham.ac.uk
☎ 0191 386 2489

The Evangelical Library, 78a Chiltern Street, London W1M 2HB
Librarian: Mr S J Taylor. Executive staff 1, Office staff 3. ***CC*** No.1040175. Began 1928; non-denominational. Magazine: *The Evangelical Library Bulletin* (1,500 half-yearly). Turnover £10-50,000 to year end Dec 96. Lending, reference, research and subscription library for ministers, students, authors; postal service.
☎ 020 7935 6997

Lambeth Palace Library, Lambeth Palace, London SE1 7JU
Librarian & Archivist: Dr Richard J Palmer. Executive staff 7, Other staff 4. ***CC*** Began 1610; Anglican. Magazine: *Lambeth Palace Library Review* (Circulation n/a annually). Principal library and archive for the history of the Church of England.
☎ 020 7928 6222 Fax 020 7928 7932

Partnership House Mission Studies Library, 157 Waterloo Road, London SE1 8XA
Librarian: Mr Colin Rowe. Executive staff 1, Other staff 1. ***CC*** No.297154. Began 1987; Anglican. Magazine: *Bulletin* (Circulation n/a monthly). Turnover n/a. History and theology of mission, including collections from the former CMS and USPG libraries.
Email: c.rowe@mailbox.ulcc.ac.uk
☎ 020 7928 8681 Fax 020 7928 3627

Pusey House Library, Oxford OX1 3LZ
Custodian: Rev W E P Davage. Executive staff 5. ***CC*** Began 1884; Anglican. No magazine. Turnover n/a. Church history and philosophy, theology, patristics; access by appointment.
☎ 01865 278 415 Fax 01865 278 415

St Deiniol's Residential Library, Hawarden, Deeside CH5 3DF
Warden & Chief Librarian: Rev P B Francis. Executive staff 5, Other staff 35. ***CC*** No.701399. Began 1902; ecumenical. No magazine. Turnover n/a. Residential library open to all genuine students - laity or clergy; accommodation for 44.
Web: st-deiniols.chester.ac.uk
Email: deiniol.visitors@btinternet.com
☎ 01244 532 350 Fax 01244 520 643

St Paul's Cathedral Library, St Paul's Cathedral, London EC4M 8AE
Librarian: Mr J J Wisdom. Executive staff 1. Began n/a; Anglican. No magazine. Turnover n/a. Collection of rare books; open by appointment.
☎ 020 7246 8345 / 7246 8325

***Salt Cellar Ltd**, 11a Church Lane, Oldham OL1 3AR
Manager: Mr Peter Lees. Executive staff 6, Other staff 8. Began 1990; Methodist. No magazine. Turnover n/a. Library of second-hand books, coffee shop, video hire, youth project, worship centre.
☎ 0161 628 2426

Tyndale House, 36 Selwyn Gardens, Cambridge CB3 9BA
Warden: Rev Dr B W Winter. Executive staff 5, Other staff 3. ***CC*** No.273458. Began 1944; non-denominational. Magazine: *Tyndale Bulletin* (Circulation n/a half-yearly). Turnover n/a. Residential Biblical and theological research centre and library; 12 residential and 42 non-residential.
Web: www.tyndale.cam.ac.uk
Email: librarian@tyndale.cam.ac.uk
☎ 01223 566 601 Fax 01223 566 608

Westminster Abbey Library, Westminster Abbey, London SW1P 3PA
Librarian: Dr Tony Trowles. Executive staff 2, Other staff 1. ***CC*** Began 1065; Anglican. No magazine. Turnover n/a. Archives of books and manuscripts relating to the history of Westminster Abbey; access by appointment.
Web: www.westminster-abbey.org
☎ 020 7222 5152 Fax 020 7222 6391

Dr Williams's Library, 14 Gordon Square, London WC1H 0AG
Director: Dr David Wykes. Other staff 3. ***CC*** Began 1729; non-denominational. No magazine. Turnover n/a. Part of work of Dr Williams's Trust which was established to benefit English Protestant Dissenters.
Email: 101340.2541@compuserve.com
☎ 020 7387 3727

PUBLISHERS

Listed by number of Christian titles published in 1998 (last column)
Publishers which did not supply this information are not listed here

Name	Titles 1995		Titles 1996		Titles 1997		Titles 1998	
	Total	Christian	Total	Christian	Total	Christian	Total	Christian
Kevin Mayhew	160	80	175	90	160	80	280	130
HarperCollins*Religious*	1,000	115	1,000	115	1,000	115	1,000	115
Lion Publishing plc	n/a	90	n/a	110	90	90	110	110
Hodder Headline plc	n/a	n/a	n/a	104	n/a	n/a	104	104
Sheffield Academic Press	n/a	100	n/a	100	100	100	100	100
HTB Publications with Alpha Resources	36	36	50	50	70	70	80	80
Society for Promoting Christian Knowledge (SPCK)	94	70	95	75	94	70	95	75
Cassell & Co	82	82	71	71	82	82	71	71
Feather Books	5	15	5	15	5	15	70	70
Ambassador Productions	54	47	68	62	54	47	68	62
Wild Goose Publications (The Iona Community)	42	42	60	60	42	42	60	60
Christian Focus Publications	48	48	55	55	48	48	55	55
Cyhoeddiadau'r Gair	62	62	54	54	62	62	54	54
Church House Publishing	40	40	53	53	40	40	53	53
Scripture Union	n/a	n/a	n/a	53	n/a	n/a	53	53
SCM Press Ltd	n/a	n/a	45	45	n/a	n/a	45	45
Kingsway Publications	45	45	44	44	45	45	44	44
Chapter Two (Publishing Division)	40	40	40	40	40	40	40	40
T & T Clark	n/a	40	n/a	40	40	40	40	40
Darton, Longman and Todd Ltd	n/a	n/a	40	40	n/a	n/a	40	40
Gracewing Publishing	n/a	n/a	45	43	44	42	41	40
Hymns Ancient & Modern Ltd	n/a	n/a	n/a	35	n/a	n/a	35	35
St Pauls	32	32	18	18	32	32	32	32
John Hunt Publishing	n/a	n/a	30	n/a	50	50	50	30
Bible Reading Fellowship	40	40	43	43	20	20	29	29
Grove Books Ltd	n/a	n/a	28	28	n/a	n/a	28	28
Methodist Publishing House	25	25	26	26	25	25	26	26
Eagle	23	23	24	24	23	23	24	24
Bible Society	n/a	n/a	n/a	21	n/a	n/a	21	21
Monarch Publications	31	31	21	21	31	31	21	21
New Dawn Books	n/a	n/a	n/a	n/a	18	21	18	21
Evangelical Press	15	15	15	15	20	20	20	20
NCEC/IBRA	n/a	20	n/a	20	20	20	20	20
Fellowship of Word and Spirit	13	13	15	15	13	13	17	17
Moorley's Print and Publishing Ltd	20	20	19	16	20	20	19	16
St Matthias Press	n/a	n/a	n/a	16	n/a	n/a	16	16
Stanborough Press	16	16	15	15	16	16	15	15
The Banner of Truth Trust	14	14	13	13	14	14	13	13
Sovereign World	15	15	15	15	15	15	13	13
Day One Publications	10	10	9	9	10	10	12	12
CWR (Crusade For World Revival)	11	11	7	7	11	11	11	11
The Anargyroi Press	n/a	n/a	6	10	n/a	n/a	6	10
Baptist Union Publications	n/a	n/a	10	10	n/a	n/a	10	10
Burns & Oates Ltd	n/a	n/a	10	10	n/a	n/a	10	10
Christina Press Ltd	n/a	n/a	n/a	n/a	12	12	10	10
Sessions of York, The Ebor Press	22	9	15	10	22	9	15	10
Autumn House Publishing	10	10	8	8	10	10	8	8
New Wine Ministries	24	24	18	18	10	10	8	8
Epworth Press	6	6	7	7	6	6	7	7
Bryntirion Press/Gwasg Bryntirion	n/a	n/a	n/a	6	n/a	n/a	6	6
Family Publications	3	2	7	6	3	2	7	6
Roy Hession Book Trust	n/a	5	n/a	6	5	5	6	6
Lutterworth Press	14	4	12	6	14	4	12	6
Stainer & Bell Ltd	16	7	22	6	16	7	22	6
Summit Publishing Ltd	n/a	n/a	6	6	n/a	n/a	6	6
William Temple Foundation	5	5	6	6	5	5	6	6
Handsel Press	n/a	n/a	5	5	n/a	n/a	5	5
Hayes Press	n/a	n/a	n/a	5	n/a	n/a	5	5
Janus Publishing Company	60	5	72	5	60	5	72	5
The Metropolitical Press	5	5	5	5	5	5	5	5
John Ritchie Ltd	7	7	5	5	7	7	5	5
Salvationist Publishing and Supplies Ltd	n/a	n/a	n/a	5	n/a	n/a	5	5
Action Bookshare	n/a	3	n/a	4	3	3	4	4
Ichthus Media Services Ltd	n/a	n/a	n/a	4	n/a	n/a	4	4
Plough Publishing House	5	5	4	4	5	5	4	4
Tufton Books (Church Union Publications)	4	4	4	4	4	4	4	4
Grace Publications Trust	4	4	3	3	4	4	3	3
Highland Books	8	8	11	11	8	8	3	3

Name	Titles 1995 Total	Titles 1995 Christian	Titles 1996 Total	Titles 1996 Christian	Titles 1997 Total	Titles 1997 Christian	Titles 1998 Total	Titles 1998 Christian
New City	3	3	3	3	3	3	3	3
Pentland Press Ltd	120	6	110	3	120	6	110	3
Sheed & Ward Ltd	n/a	n/a	3	3	n/a	n/a	3	3
Arthur H Stockwell Ltd	n/a	n/a	58	3	n/a	n/a	58	3
C-L Publications	n/a	n/a	n/a	n/a	2	2	2	2
CCBI Publications	2	2	2	2	2	2	2	2
Christian Year Publications	2	2	2	2	2	2	2	2
Gospel Standard Trust	3	3	2	2	3	3	2	2
John Metcalfe Publishing Trust	n/a	3	n/a	2	3	3	2	2
The Rushworth Literature Enterprise Ltd	3	3	2	2	3	3	2	2
St Stephen's Press	n/a	1	n/a	2	1	1	2	2
Bethel Publications	n/a	n/a	1	1	n/a	n/a	1	1
Bunyan Press	1	1	1	1	1	1	1	1
Chapter House Ltd	2	2	1	1	2	2	1	1
Christian Research	2	2	1	1	2	2	1	1
Chyvounder Consolidated Publishing	n/a	n/a	1	1	n/a	n/a	1	1
James Clarke and Co Ltd	1	1	1	1	1	1	1	1
Coastline Christian Resources	n/a	n/a	n/a	n/a	1	1	1	1
The Grail	1	1	1	1	1	1	1	1
Impart Books	9	n/a	5	1	9	0	5	1
Jubilate Hymns Ltd	1	1	n/a	n/a	1	1	1	1
K & M Books	n/a	n/a	n/a	1	1	1	1	1
Modern Welsh Publications Ltd	n/a	n/a	1	1	n/a	n/a	1	1
Precious Seed Publications	1	1	1	1	1	1	1	1
Quinta Press	n/a	n/a	1	1	n/a	n/a	1	1
Save The Church of England Foundation	n/a	n/a	n/a	n/a	1	1	1	1
Scripture Truth Publications	2	2	1	1	2	2	1	1
Teresian Press	n/a	n/a	n/a	n/a	n/a	n/a	1	1
Christian Education Movement	18	n/a	16	n/a	18	0	16	0
Stanley Thornes (Publishers) Ltd	4	n/a	7	n/a	4	0	7	0
R L Allan & Son Publishers	2	2	n/a	n/a	2	2	n/a	n/a
Paternoster Publishing	80	80	140	140	87	87	n/a	n/a
The Wakeman Trust	n/a	6	n/a	n/a	6	6	n/a	n/a

B

PUBLISHERS

See also Other Literature Producers & Distributors (Primarily in the UK) on Page 181, Newspapers & Periodicals on Page 311, Literature Producers & Distributors (Primarily Overseas) on Page 326.

***Action Bookshare (UK)**, PO Box 694, Rhyl LL18 1JU
UK Director: Mr Ingo Abraham. Executive staff 1. *CC* No.1058661. Began 1959; interdenominational. (Merged with Fishers Fellowship 1997). Magazine: *Impact* (2,000 every two months). Turnover £27,000 to year end June 96. Training in personal evangelism and effective follow-up to produce mature believers through Bible study.
www.actionintl.org
Email: actionuk@btinternet.com
☎ 01299 401 511 Fax 01299 405 273

ALIVE UK, 49 Coxtie Green Road, Brentwood CM14 5PS
Manager: Rev Dr Michael S B Reid. Executive staff 6, Other staff 3. Began 1988; Pentecostal. (Previously Sharon Publications). Turnover n/a.
Web: www.peniel.org
☎ 01277 373 436 Fax 01277 375 578

R L Allan & Son Publishers, 53 Bothwell Street, Glasgow G2 6TS
Manager: Mrs Margaret Milligan. *Managing Director:* Mr Nicholas Gray. Executive staff 2. Began 1863; non-denominational. Turnover £240,000 to year end Dec 98.
Email: rlallan@btinternet.com
☎ 0141 204 1285 Fax 0141 204 1285

Ambassador Productions, 16 Hillview Avenue, Belfast BT5 6JR
Contact: Mr Samuel Lowry. Full-time staff 7. Began 1980; international. Turnover n/a.
☎ 028 9065 8462 Fax 028 9065 9518

The Anargyroi Press, 42 Withen's Lane, Wallasey CH45 7NN
Editor: Father Pancratios Sanders. Executive staff 2. Began 1991; Orthodox. Turnover n/a. Publishing of books relating to the teaching of the Orthodox Church together with service books.
Email: pancratios.outlook@mcmail.com
☎ 0151 639 6509 Mobile: 07850 467 675
Fax 0151 200 6359

Apologia Publications, 5 St Matthews Road, Winchester SO22 6BX
Director: Dr Herbert H Osborn. Executive staff 1. Began 1995; interdenominational. Turnover £900 to year end Mar 98.
Web: www.apologia.free-online.co.uk
Email: hosborn@apologia.free-online.co.uk
☎ 01962 856 125 Fax 01962 856 125

Autumn House Publishing, Alma House, Grantham NG31 9SL
Managing Director: Mr Edward Johnson. Executive staff 2, Other staff 6. Began 1991; non-denominational. Turnover n/a.
☎ 01476 590 866

Avant Books, PO Box 2, Taunton TA1 4ZD
Proprietor: Stephen C Perks. Executive staff 1. Began 1988; non-denominational. Sole distributor: James A Dickson Books, Edinburgh. Turnover n/a.
Email: avantbooks@kuyper.org
☎ 01823 665 909

For additional information see List on Pages 169–170

The Banner of Truth Trust, The Grey House, 3 Murrayfield Road, Edinburgh EH12 6EL
General Manager: Mr John Rawlinson. *Editorial Director:* Rev Dr Hywel R Jones. Executive staff 4, Other staff 10. ***CC*** No.235652. Began 1957; non-denominational. Turnover n/a. Christian literature in the historic, Reformed tradition.
Web: www.banneroftruth.co.uk
☎ 0131 337 7310 🖷 0131 346 7484

Baptist Union Publications, Baptist House, PO Box 44, 129 Broadway, Didcot OX11 8RT
Manager: Mr Chris Mepham. Other staff 2. Began 1992; Baptist. Turnover n/a.
Email: admin.manager@baptist.org.uk
☎ 01235 517 700 🖷 01235 517 715

·**Bethel Publications**, Bethel, 30 Beacon Street, Lichfield WS13 7AJ
Director: Mr Philip M Horton. Executive staff 1. Began 1992; interdenominational. Turnover n/a.
☎ 01543 253 505

Bible Reading Fellowship, Peter's Way, Sandy Lane West, Oxford OX4 5HG
Chief Executive Officer: Mr Richard Fisher. *Marketing Manager:* Mrs Karen Laister. Executive staff 1, Other staff 8. ***CC*** No.233280. Began 1922; interdenominational. Imprints: Barnabas, Bible Reading Fellowship. Turnover n/a. Helping people of all ages to encounter the living God through Bible reading and prayer.
Web: www/brf.org.uk
Email: enquiries@brf.org.uk
☎ 01865 748 227 🖷 01865 773 150

***Bible Society (The British and Foreign Bible Society)**, Stonehill Green, Westlea, Swindon SN5 7DG
Executive Director: Mr Neil Crosbie. *Director of Mission and Theology:* Rev Dr Martin Robinson. *Commercial Director:* Dr Ashley Scott. Executive staff 8, Other staff 97. ***CC*** No.232759. Began 1804; interdenominational. Turnover £10,140,000 [Voluntary income: £7,370,000, Sales: £2,770,000] to year end Dec 98. Making the Bible available where needed and challenging indifference to the Bible wherever it exists.
Web: www.biblesociety.org.uk
Email: info@bfbs.org.uk
☎ 01793 418 100 🖷 01793 418 118

Bishopsgate Press Ltd, Bartholomew House, 15 Tonbridge Road, Hildenborough, Tonbridge TN11 9BH
Managing Director: Mr Ian Straker. *Sales Director:* Mr Robert Wilson. Executive staff 4, Other staff 6. Began 1800; non-denominational. Turnover £100,000+ to year end Dec 98.
☎ 01732 833 778 🖷 01732 833 090

Bryntirion Press/Gwasg Bryntirion, Bryntirion, Bridgend CF31 4DX
Managing Editor: Rev David Kingdon. Executive staff 1, Other staff 2. ***CC*** No.222407. Began 1955; non-denominational. (Previously Evangelical Press of Wales/Gwasg Efengylaidd Cymru). Turnover n/a.
Email: press@draco.co.uk
☎ 01656 655 886 🖷 01656 656 095

Bunyan Press, 23 Haslingden Close, Harpenden AL5 3EW
Manager: Mr Caleb Pearce. Other staff 1. Began n/a; non-denominational. Turnover £8,000 to year end Dec 98. Publishing Reformed books.
Email: calebpearce@yahoo.com
☎ 01582 760 545

Burns & Oates Ltd, Wellwood, North Farm Road, Tunbridge Wells TN2 3DR
Managing Director: Mr Martin De La Bedoyere. Executive staff 5, Other staff 7. Began 1847; Roman Catholic. Imprints: Burns & Oates Ltd, Search Press Ltd. Turnover n/a.
Email: searchpress@searchpress.com
☎ 01892 510 850 🖷 01892 515 903

C-L Publications, 56 Holyrood Road, New Barnet, Barnet EN5 1DG
Director: Mr Chris Hill. Executive staff 1, Admin staff 3. Began 1990; non-denominational. Magazine: *C-L Update* (300 quarterly). Turnover n/a. Opening up God's Word to prepare God's people for the end times; books, videos, tapes.
Email: keeling.anthony@btinternet.com
☎ 020 8440 0825 🖷 020 8440 0825

Candle Books, Concorde House, Grenville Place, Mill Hill, London NW7 3SA
Managing Director: Nick Jones. Staff n/a. Began n/a; interdenominational. Turnover n/a. Colour books for children and the family based on Bible stories and Christian living.
Email: coed@angushudson.com
☎ 020 8959 3668 🖷 020 8959 3678

Canterbury and York Society, 15 Cusack Close, Strawberry Hill, Twickenham TW1 4TB
Treasurer: Dr C Harper-Bill. No full-time staff. ***CC*** Began 1904; Anglican. Turnover n/a.
☎ 020 8892 0500

Cassell & Co, Wellington House, 125 Strand, London WC2R 0BB
Managing Director: Mr Phillip Sturrock. *Religious Publisher:* Mrs Ruth McCurry. *Sales Director:* Mr John Parsons. Executive staff 8. Began 1958; Roman Catholic. Imprints: Geoffrey Chapman, Mowbray. Turnover n/a.
Email: r.mccurry@cassell-press.co.uk
☎ 020 7420 5555 🖷 020 7420 8531

Catholic Truth Society, 40 Harleyford Road, Vauxhall, London SE11 5AY
General Secretary: Mr David Murphy. Executive staff 10. ***CC*** Began 1869; Roman Catholic. Imprints: CTS Publications, Catholic Truth Society. Publisher to the Holy See. Turnover n/a.
☎ 020 7640 0042 🖷 020 7640 0046

Chapter House Ltd, 53 Bothwell Street, Glasgow G2 6TS
Publisher: Mr Nicholas Gray. Executive staff 1, Other staff 2. Began 1985; non-denominational. Incorporating: Pickering & Inglis Ltd, Chapter House, R L Allan & Son. Turnover £2,500 to year end Jan 99.
Email: rlallan@btinternet.com
☎ 0141 204 1285 🖷 0141 204 1285

Chapter Two (Publishing Division), Fountain House, 1a Conduit Road, Woolwich, London SE18 7AJ
Principal: Mr Edwin Cross. *Office Manager:* Miss A Meister. Executive staff 3, Other staff 10. ***CC*** No.1053047. Began 1976; Brethren. Turnover £150,000. Propagation of Christianity by literature, outreach, Bible distribution, conferences. Worldwide distribution in many languages.
Web: www.chaptertwo.org
Email: ecross7023@aol.com
☎ 020 8316 5389 🖷 020 8854 5963

B

Christian Education Movement, Royal Buildings, Victoria Street, Derby DE1 1GW
General Secretary: Rev Dr Stephen Orchard. *Director of Publications:* Rev Colin Johnson. *Director of Professional Services:* Mrs Pamela Draycott. Executive staff 9, Other staff 9. ***CC*** No.241509. Began 1965; ecumenical. Magazine: *RE Today* (11,500 every four months), *British Journal of Religious Education* (2,500 every four months). Turnover £773,000 to year end May 98. Developing and improving Religious Education in schools and encouraging Christian reflection about education.
Email: cem@cem.org.uk
☎ 01332 296 655 🖷 01332 432 53

*Christian Focus Publications, Geanies House, Fearn, Tain IV20 1TW
Director: Mr William MacKenzie. *General Manager:* Mr Ian Thompson. *Managing Editor:* Mr Malcolm Maclean. Executive staff 4, Other staff 10. Began 1979; non-denominational. Turnover n/a.
Web: www.christianfocus.com
Email: cfp@geanies.org.uk
☎ 01862 871 011 🖷 01862 871 699

*Christian Research, Vision Building, 4 Footscray Road, Eltham, London SE9 2TZ
Executive Director: Dr Peter Brierley. *Assistant Director:* Heather Wraight. Executive staff 2, Other staff 5. ***CC*** No.1017701. Began 1993; interdenominational. (Previously MARC Europe). Turnover £271,600 to year end Dec 98.
Web: www.christian-research.org.uk
Email: admin@christian-research.org.uk
☎ 020 8294 1989 🖷 020 8294 0014

Christian Year Publications, Unit 14e, Church Farm Business Park, Corston, Bath BA2 9AP
Partner: Mr Roy and Mrs Margaret Hill. Executive staff 1, Other staff 1. Began 1988; non-denominational. Turnover n/a.
☎ 01225 874 621 🖷 01225 874 621

Christina Press Ltd, Broadway House, The Broadway, Crowborough TN6 1HQ
Publishers: Mr Tony & Mrs Jane Collins. Executive staff 2. Began 1996; interdenominational. Turnover n/a. Publishing books by women for women and discerning men.
Email: monarch@dial.pipex.com
☎ 01892 652 364 Mobile: 07771 724 117 🖷 01892 663 329

Church House Publishing, Church House, Great Smith Street, London SW1P 3NZ
Publishing Manager: Mr Alan Mitchell. *Commissioning Editor:* Mr Hamish Bruce. *Sales & Marketing Manager:* Mr Matthew Tickle. Executive staff 9. ***CC*** No.248711. Began 1923; Anglican. Turnover n/a. Official publisher of the Boards and Councils of the Archbishop's Council Church of England.
Web: www.chpublishing.co.uk
Email: publishing@c-of-e.org.uk
☎ 020 7898 1451 🖷 020 7898 1449

Church in Wales Publications, Church in Wales Centre, Woodland Place, Penarth CF64 2EX
Business Manager: Mr Hendrik Haye. Executive staff 18. ***CC*** Began 1960; Church in Wales. Turnover n/a.
Email: office@mission.churchinwales.org.uk
☎ 029 2070 5278 🖷 029 2071 2413

Chyvounder Consolidated Publishing, Coombe Lane, Bissoe, Truro TR4 8RE
Proprietor: Mr A S Darlington. No other staff. Began 1994; Methodist. Turnover n/a.
Web: www.indirect.co.uk/~chyvounder
Email: ccp@chyvounder.ndirect.co.uk
☎ 01872 865 844 🖷 01872 865 844

T & T Clark, 59 George Street, Edinburgh EH2 2LQ
Managing Director: Dr Geoffrey Green. Executive staff 3, Other staff 15. Began 1821; non-denominational. Turnover n/a.
Web: www.tandtclark.co.uk
Email: mailbox@tandtclark.co.uk
☎ 0131 225 4703 🖷 0131 220 4260

James Clarke and Co Ltd, PO Box 60, Cambridge CB1 2NT
Managing Director: Mr Adrian Brink. *Sales & Publicity Manager:* Mr Colin Lester. Executive staff 2, Other staff 4. Began 1859; non-denominational. Imprints: James Clarke, Acorn Editions, Allenson. Turnover n/a. Theology and church history.
Web: www.jamesclarke.co.uk
Email: publishing@jamesclarke.co.uk
☎ 01223 350 865 🖷 01223 366 951

*Coastline Christian Resources, 263 Arbury Road, Cambridge CB4 2JL
Director: Dr John Robertshaw. Executive staff 1. Began 1992; non-denominational. No magazine. Turnover £6,000 to year end Jan 99. Writing and publishing Bible study material.
Web: www.btinternet.com/~coastline
Email: coastline@btinternet.com
☎ 01223 355 931 🖷 01223 355 931

Covenant Publishing Co Ltd, 8 Blades Court, Deodar Road, Putney, London SW15 2NU
Chairman: Mr M A Clark. Executive staff 1. Began 1922; non-denominational. Turnover n/a.
Web: www.britishisrael.co.uk
Email: janice1@easynet.co.uk
☎ 020 8877 9010 🖷 020 8871 4770

Cressrelles Publishing Company Ltd, 10 Station Road, Colwell, Malvern WR13 6RN
Director: Mr L Smith. Staff n/a. Began 1973; non-denominational. Turnover n/a.
☎ 01684 540 154 🖷 01684 540 154

CTBI Publications, Inter-Church House, 35 Lower Marsh, London SE1 7RL
Sales Manager: Rev David Rudiger. *Bookroom Manager:* Mr Richard Bong. Other staff 2. ***CC*** No.259688. Began 1940; ecumenical. (Previously BCC Publications). Turnover n/a. Producing materials on ecumenism which arise from the work of Churches Together.
Web: www.ctbi.org.uk
Email: bookroom_ctbi@cix.co.uk
☎ 020 7620 4444 🖷 020 7928 0010

*CWR (Crusade for World Revival), Waverley Abbey House, Waverley Lane, Farnham GU9 8EP
Chief Executive: Mr John Muys. *General Manager Ministry:* Mr Sean Gubb. *General Manager Business:* Miss Lorna Browne. Executive staff 3, Other staff 43. ***CC*** No.294387. Began 1965; interdenominational. Turnover £2,500,000 to year end Dec 98. Publishing books, videos and daily devotionals including Every Day with Jesus.
Web: www.cwr.org.uk
Email: mail@cwr.org.uk
☎ 01252 784 700 🖷 01252 784 734

*Cyhoeddiadau'r Gair, School of Education, University College of North Wales, Normal Site, Bangor LL57 2PX
Director: Rev Aled Davies. Executive staff 1, Other staff 5. ***CC*** Began 1991; interdenominational. Imprints: Gydan Gilydd, Cyfres y Gair. Turnover n/a.
Web: www.bangor.ac.uk
Email: edsooe@bangor.ac.uk
☎ 01248 382 947 🖷 01248 383 954

For additional information see List on Pages 169–170

B

Darton, Longman and Todd Ltd, 1 Spencer Court, 140 Wandsworth High Street, London SW18 4JJ
Manager: common ownership company. Staff 12. Began 1959; interdenominational. Turnover n/a.
☎ 020 8875 0155 🖷 020 8875 0133

Day One Publications, No. 3 Epsom Business Park, Kiln Lane, Epsom KT17 1JF
General Secretary: Mr John Roberts. *Accountant:* Mr Mark Roberts. *Designer:* Mr Steve Devane. Executive staff 2, Other staff 10. ***CC*** No.233465. Began 1831; interdenominational. Turnover n/a.
Web: www.dayone.co.uk
Email: sales@dayone.co.uk
☎ 01372 728 300 🖷 01372 722 400

***Eagle**, 6 Leapale Road, Guildford GU1 4JX
Managing Director: Mr David Wavre. *Editorial Manager:* Mrs Lynne Barratt. Executive staff 2, Other staff 4. Began 1990; non-denominational. Imprints: Eagle. Turnover £800,000 to year end Dec 98.
Email: eagle_indeprint@compuserve.com
☎ 01483 306 309 🖷 01483 579 196

Epworth Press, Methodist Publishing House, 20 Ivatt Way, Peterborough PE3 7PG
Secretary to Editorial Committee: Rev G M Burt. No full-time staff. Began 1799; Methodist. Turnover n/a.
☎ 01733 332 202

Evangelical Press, Faverdale North Industrial Estate, Darlington DL3 0PH
General Manager: Mr John H Rubens. *Executive Director:* Mr David Clark. Executive staff 3, Other staff 9. ***CC*** No.254335. Began 1967; non-denominational. Turnover n/a. Publication and distribution of Christian literature in English, French and Russian.
Web: www.evangelical-press.org
Email: sales@evangelical-press.org
☎ 01325 380 232 🖷 01325 466 153

Family Publications, 77 Banbury Road, Oxford OX2 6LF
Director: Mr P D Riches. *Editor:* Mr Richard Brown. Executive staff 2, Other staff 3. Began 1988; Roman Catholic. Turnover £100,000 to year end Dec 98. Publishers and distributors of Catholic books about family and life issues.
☎ 01865 514 408 🖷 01865 316 951

***Feather Books**, Fairview, Old Coppice, Lyth Bank, Shrewsbury SY3 0BW
Director: Rev John Waddington-Feather. Executive staff 3, Other staff 5. Began 1980; interdenominational. Magazine: *Poetry Church* (Circulation n/a quarterly). Turnover n/a. Publishing Christian poetry, music and Christian art folios.
Web: www.feather-books.com
Email: john@feather-books.com
☎ 01743 872 177 🖷 01743 872 177

Fellowship of Word and Spirit, St Luke's Church, 28 Farquhar Road, Wimbledon, London SW19 8DA
Chairman: Rev Simon Vibert. No full-time staff. ***CC*** No.293159. Began 1983; Anglican. Turnover £2,500 to year end Apr 92.
Web: www.st-james.org.uk/sws/home.htm
Email: sws@altavista.net
☎ 020 8946 3396 🖷 020 8946 3396

Gabriel Communications Ltd, First Floor, St James's Buildings, Oxford Street, Manchester M1 6FP
Commercial Director: Mr David Bould. Other staff 56. Began 1860; Roman Catholic. Turnover n/a.
☎ 0161 236 8856 🖷 0161 236 8530

Gazelle Books, Concorde House, Grenville Place, Mill Hill, London NW7 3SA
Publishing Director: Mr Rodney P Shepherd. Executive staff 2, Other staff 1. Began 1979; interdenominational. Turnover n/a. Practical resource books for the Church and books on topical issues for a general readership.
Email: gazelle@angushudson.com
☎ 020 8959 3668 Mobile: 07970 883 910 🖷 020 8959 3678

Gospel Standard Trust, 12b Roundwood Lane, Harpenden AL5 3DD
Publications Manager: Caleb A Pearce. Executive staff 1, Other staff 1. ***CC*** No.249781. Began 1966; Strict Baptist. Turnover £27,000 to year end Dec 98. Publishing books that commend the free and sovereign grace of Almighty God.
Email: gospelstandardpublications@btinternet.com
☎ 01582 765 448 🖷 01582 469 148

Grace Publications Trust, 146 Maidstone Road, Borough Green, Sevenoaks TN15 8HQ
Hon Secretary: Mr E C Porter. No full-time staff. ***CC*** No.285237. Began 1979; Grace Baptist. Turnover £45,000.
☎ 01732 882 624
Trade enquiries: Evangelical Press, Faverdale North Industrial Estate, Darlington DL3 0PH
Email: sales@evangelical-press.org
☎ 01325 380 232 🖷 01325 466 153

Gracewing Publishing, 2 Southern Avenue, Leominster HR6 0QF
Managing Director: Mr Thomas W Longford. *Publications Manager:* Miss Jo Ashworth. *Publicity Manager:* Mrs Monica Manwaring. Executive staff 3, Other staff 3. Began 1951; non-denominational. Imprints: Gracewing. Turnover £650,000 to year end Dec 98.
Email: gracewingx@aol.com
☎ 01568 616 835 🖷 01568 613 289

The Grail, 125 Waxwell Lane, Pinner HA5 3ER
Publications Secretary: Miss Mary Grasar. Executive staff 2, Other staff 1. ***CC*** No.221076. Began n/a; Roman Catholic. Turnover n/a.
Email: waxwell@compuserve.com & grailcentre@compuserve.com
☎ 020 8866 0505/2195 🖷 020 8866 1408

Grove Books Ltd, Ridley Hall Road, Cambridge CB3 9HU
Administrator: Susanne Thompson. No other full-time, staff. ***CC*** No.327014. Began 1970; Anglican. Turnover n/a.
☎ 01223 464 748 🖷 01223 464 849

Handsel Press, Millfield, Street of Kincardine, Boat of Garten PH24 3BY
Editor: Rev Jock Stein. No full-time staff. ***CC*** No.SCO 14135. Began 1973; non-denominational. Turnover £15,000 to year end Aug 98.
Email: handsel@dial.pipex.com
☎ No telephone

HarperCollins*Religious*, 77 Fulham Palace Road, Hammersmith, London W6 8JB
Deputy Managing Director: Mr Jeremy Yates-Round. *Publishing Director:* Mr James Catford. Executive staff 2, Other staff 6. Began 1819; non-denominational. Imprints include Fount, Marshall Pickering, Liturgical, Bibles, HarperCollins. Turnover n/a.
Web: www.christian-publishing.com
Email: james.catford@harpercollins.co.uk
☎ 020 8741 7070 🖷 020 8307 4440

For additional information see List on Pages 169–170

B

Hayes Press, Essex Road, Leicester LE4 9EE
General Manager: Mr Kevin S Hickling. Executive staff 1, Other staff 5. *CC* Began 1904; non-denominational. Turnover n/a.
Web: www.tripod.hayes_press.com
Email: hayespress@btinternet.com
☎ 0116 2740 204 Fax 0116 274 0200

Roy Hession Book Trust, 3 Florence Road, Bromley BR1 3NU
General Secretary: Mr Gerry Davey. No other full-time staff. Began 1994; non-denominational. Turnover n/a. Promotes translation, publication and distribution of books by late Roy Hession worldwide.
Email: 100117.2360@compuserve.com
☎ 020 8464 0460 Fax 020 8313 1373

Highland Books, 2 High Pines, Knoll Road, Godalming GU7 2EP
Publisher: Mr Philip Ralli. Executive staff 2, Other staff 1. Began 1983; non-denominational. Turnover £50,000 to year end Dec 98.
Email: highlandbooks@compuserve.com
☎ 01483 424 560 Fax 01483 424 388

Hodder Headline plc, 338 Euston Road, London NW1 3BH
Managing Director: Mr Charles Nettleton. *Bible Editorial Director:* Ms Emma Sealey. *Religious Trade Editorial Director:* Ms Judith Longman. Full-time staff 13. Began 1868; non-denominational. Turnover n/a. Imprints: Hodder Christian Books, Hodder & Stoughton. New International Version, New International Reader's Version.
Email: religious_sales@hodder.co.uk
☎ 020 7873 6000 Fax 020 7873 6059

HTB Publications with Alpha Resources, Holy Trinity Church, Brompton Road, London SW7 1JA
Publications Manager: Mr Jonathan Gill. *Publications Co-ordinator:* Miss Catherine Bald. Other staff 2. *CC* Began 1993; Anglican. Turnover n/a.
Email: publications@htb.org.uk
☎ 020 7581 8255 Fax 020 7584 8536

Angus Hudson Ltd, Concorde House, Grenville Place, Mill Hill, London NW7 3SA
Managing Director: Mr Nick Jones. Executive staff 6, Other staff 8. Began 1976; interdenominational. Publishing imprints: Candle Books, Gazelle Books, Monarch Books. Turnover n/a. Books and Bibles in 80 languages, graphic design, specialising in coeditions, print production.
Email: coed@angushudson.com
☎ 020 8959 3668 Fax 020 8959 3678

John Hunt Publishing (incorporating Hunt & Thorpe and Arthur James Ltd), 46a West Street, Alresford SO24 9AU
Proprietor: Mr John Hunt. Executive staff 3. Began 1989; non-denominational. Imprints: Hunt & Thorpe and Arthur James Ltd. Turnover n/a. Covering the spectrum of Christian publishing: age groups, theology, denominations and markets.
Email: johnhuntpublishing@compuserve.com
☎ 01962 736 880 Fax 01962 736 881

Hymns Ancient & Modern Ltd, St Mary's Works, St Mary's Plain, Norwich NR3 3BH
Chief Executive: Mr Gordon A Knights. Other staff 50. *CC* No.270060. Began 1975; Anglican. Imprints: Canterbury Press Norwich, Hymns Ancient & Modern, SCM Press, RMEP, Church Times. Turnover n/a.
☎ 01603 612 914 Fax 01603 624 483

Ichthus Media Services Ltd, 107 Stanstead Road, Forest Hill, London SE23 1HH
Director: Mr Michael Borrett. Other staff 4. Began 1989; non-denominational. Turnover n/a.
Email: media@ichthus.org.uk
☎ 020 8699 4208 Fax 020 8291 6764

Impart Books, Gwelfryn, Llanidloes Road, Newtown SY16 4HX
Director: Mr Alick Hartley. Executive staff 1, Other staff. Began 1988; non-denominational. (Previously Gwelfryn Publications Ltd). Turnover n/a. Publishing of Bible-based puzzle books and other Christian books.
Web: www.press.mid-wales.net
Email: impart@books.mid-wales.net
☎ 01686 623 484 Fax 01686 623 784

IVP, Norton Street, Nottingham NG7 3HR
Chief Executive: Rev Frank Entwistle. *Commercial Director:* Mr Brian Wilson. Executive staff 11, Other staff 19. *CC* Began 1935; non-denominational. (Publishing division of UCCF) Imprints: Apollos, Crossway, IVP. Turnover n/a.
Email: ivp@ivpnottm.cix.co.uk
☎ 0115 978 1054 Fax 0115 942 2694

The James Begg Society, 67 Ffordd Garnedd, Y Felinheli, Caernarfon LL56 4QY
President: Rev James Gracie. No full time staff. *CC* No.SCO 25349. Began 1994; Presbyterian. Magazine: *Presbyterian Standard* (250 quarterly). Turnover £12,276 to year end Dec 98. Promoting the Reformed understanding of the Scriptures, doctrine, worship and practice.
Web: easyweb.easynet.co.uk/~jbeggsoc/jbshome.html
Email: jbeggsoc@easynet.co.uk
☎ 01248 670 260

Janus Publishing Company, 76 Great Titchfield Street, London W1P 7AF
Managing Director: Mr Sandy Leung. Executive staff 2. Began 1991; non-denominational. Turnover n/a.
Web: www.januspublishing.co.uk
Email: publisher@januspublishing.co.uk
☎ 020 7580 7664 Fax 020 7636 5756

Jay Books, Rick Barton House, Chideock, Bridport DT6 6JW
Publisher: Mr Bill Hill. Other staff 1. Began 1984; non-denominational. Imprints: Jay Books, Aquinas Books. Turnover £5,000 to year end Dec 98. Christian resource material, bookstall and copyright matters.
Web: www.houghtonsbooks.com
Email: enquiries@houghtonsbooks.com/jay
☎ 01297 489 276 Fax 01297 489 868

Jubilate Hymns Ltd, Southwick House, 4 Thorne Park Road, Chelston, Torquay TQ2 6RX
Copyright & Financial Manager: Mrs Merrilyn Williams. Executive staff 1, Other staff 1. Began n/a; interdenominational.
Email: jubilatemw@aol.com
☎ 01803 607 754 Fax 01803 605 682

K & M Books, Plas Gwyn, High Street, Trelawnyd, Rhyl LL18 6DT
Publisher: Mr Michael Kimmitt. No other staff. Began 1994; non-denominational. Turnover n/a.
Email: mrkimmitt@aol.com
☎ 01745 571 707 Fax 01745 571 707

For additional information see List on Pages 169–170

Kingsway Publications, Lottbridge Drove, Eastbourne BN23 6NT
Publishing Director: Mr Richard Herkes. *Managing Director:* Mr John Paculabo. Executive staff 6, Other staff 60. Began 1977; interdenominational. (Part of Kingsway Communications Ltd). Turnover n/a.
Email: books@kingsway.co.uk
☎ 01323 437 700 🖷 01323 411 970

Lion Publishing plc, Sandy Lane West, Oxford OX4 5HG
Managing Director: Mr Paul Clifford. *Marketing Director:* Mr Tony Wales. *Publishing Director:* Ms Rebecca Winter. Executive staff 4, Other staff 90. Began 1971; non-denominational. Turnover £6,500,000 to year end Dec 98.
Web: www.lion-publishing.co.uk
Email: custserve@lion-publishing.co.uk
☎ 01865 747 550 🖷 01865 747 568

Loxwood Press, 50 Loxwood Avenue, Worthing BN14 7RA
Directors: Mr Donald & Mrs Ruth Banks. No other staff. Began 1992; interdenominational. Turnover n/a. Music and academic monographs by Asian Christians.
☎ 01903 824 174 🖷 01903 824 376

Lutterworth Press, PO Box 60, Cambridge CB1 2NT
Managing Director: Mr Adrian Brink. *Secretary/Sales & Publicity Manager:* Mr Colin Lester. Executive staff 2, Other staff 4. Began 1799; non-denominational. Imprints: Lutterworth Press, Patrick Hardy Books. Turnover n/a.
Web: www.lutterworth.com
Email: publishing@lutterworth.com
☎ 01223 350 865 🖷 01223 366 951

McCrimmon Publishing Co Ltd, 10 High Street, Great Wakering, Southend-on-Sea SS3 0EQ
Directors: Mr Don & Mrs Joan McCrimmon. *Sales Manager:* Mr Alan Hencher. *Bookshop Manager:* Mrs Louise Madden. Other staff 8. Began 1969; ecumenical. Turnover £800,000 to year end Dec 98. Publishers/distributors of Christian books, liturgy, music, prayer, posters and cards.
Email: mccrimmons@dial.pipex.com
☎ 01702 218 956 🖷 01702 216 082

Marcham Manor Press, Appleford, Abingdon OX14 4PB
Director: Mr Gervase E Duffield. Full-time staff 3. Began 1963; non-denominational. Turnover n/a.
☎ 01235 848 319

Kevin Mayhew, Buxhall, Stowmarket IP14 3DJ
Managing Director: Mr Gordon Carter. *Chairman:* Mr Kevin Mayhew. Executive staff 5, Other staff 70. Began 1976; non-denominational. Imprints: Kevin Mayhew, Palm Tree Press. Turnover n/a.
Web: www.kevinmayhewltd.com
Email: kevinmayhewltd@msn.com
☎ 01449 737 978 🖷 01449 737 834

†**John Metcalfe Publishing Trust**, Church Road, Tylers Green, Penn, High Wycombe HP10 8LN
Managing Director: Mr John Metcalfe. Executive staff 3, Other staff 10. ***CC*** No.263381. Began 1971; non-denominational. Turnover n/a.
☎ 01494 813 174

Methodist Publishing House, 20 Ivatt Way, Peterborough PE3 7PG
General Manager: Mr Brian Thornton. Executive staff 1, Other staff 21. ***CC*** Began 1750; Methodist. Turnover n/a.
Web: www.mph.org.uk
Email: chief.exec@mph.org.uk
☎ 01733 332 202 🖷 01733 331 201

The Metropolitical Press, 10 Heathwood Gardens, Charlton, London SE7 8EP
Manager: Mr James Kirby Tomblin. No full-time staff. Began 1969; Orthodox. Turnover n/a.
Email: boc@cwcom.net
☎ 020 8854 3090 🖷 020 8244 7888

Mirfield Publications, House of the Resurrection, Mirfield WF14 0BN
Publications Secretary: Brother David Wilson. Executive staff 1. ***CC*** No.232670. Began 1958; Anglican. Turnover n/a.
☎ 01924 494 318

Modern Welsh Publications Ltd, 32 Garth Drive, Liverpool L18 6HW
Hon Secretary: Rev Dr D Ben Rees. No full-time staff. Began 1963; non-denominational. Turnover n/a.
☎ 0151 724 1989 🖷 0151 724 5691

Monarch Publications, Concorde House, Grenville Place, Mill Hill, London NW7 3SA
Editorial Directors: Tony Collins, Mrs Jane Collins. Began 1988; interdenominational. Working in partnership with Angus Hudson Ltd. Imprints: MARC, Mitre, Monarch.
Email: coed@angushudson.com
Editorial Office: Broadway House, The Broadway, Crowborough TN6 1HQ
☎ 01892 652 364 🖷 01892 663 329

Moorley's Print and Publishing Ltd, 23 Park Road, Ilkeston DE7 5DA
Managing Director: Mr John R Moorley. *Financial Director:* Mr Peter Newberry. Executive staff 4, Other staff 4. Began 1969; interdenominational. Turnover £125,000 to year end Dec 98. Publishers and printers specialising in Christian drama, school assembly material, etc. Church and charity work.
Email: 106545.413@compuserve.com
☎ 0115 932 0643 🖷 0115 932 0643

Multiply Publications, Nether Heyford, Northampton NN7 3LB
Series Editor: Mr John Campbell. Admin staff 2. Began 1997; Multiply. (Previously Jesus Fellowship Resources). Imprint of the Multiply Christian Network. Turnover n/a. Teaching and inspirational books, booklets and other literature.
Web: www.jesus.org.uk/multiply/publications
Email: books@multiply.org.uk
☎ 01327 349 992 🖷 01327 349 997

NCEC/IBRA, 1020 Bristol Road, Selly Oak, Birmingham B29 6LB
General Secretary: Rev John Gear. *Marketing Coordinator:* Mr B Morgan. *Publishing Manager:* Rev Martin Lambourne. Executive staff 3, Other staff 12. ***CC*** No.211542. Began 1803; non-denominational. (Previously Hillside Publishing). Turnover n/a.
Web: www.ncec.org.uk
Email: ncec@ncec.org.uk
☎ 0121 472 4242 🖷 0121 472 7575

New City, 57 Twyford Avenue, London W3 9PZ
Business Manager: Mr Rumold Van Geffen. Other staff 4. ***CC*** No.257912. Began 1968; interdenominational. Turnover n/a.
☎ 020 8993 6944 🖷 020 8993 6944

B

B

***New Dawn Books**, 10a Jamaica Street, Greenock PA15 1YB
Manager: Rev Hugh B Black. No full-time staff. *CC* No.SCO 06960. Began 1987; Pentecostal. Turnover n/a. Pentecostal books dealing with salvation, baptism in the Spirit, healing, deliverance and related topics.
Web: www.struthers-church.org
Email: bookshop@struthers-church.org
☎ 01475 729 668 Fax 01475 728 145

***New Hope Publications**, Faith Acres, Peterhead AB42 3DQ
Publications Director: Mr Mark Morgan. Executive staff 23. *CC* No.276520. Began 1980; interdenominational. Turnover n/a.
Web: www.newhopetrust.org
Email: info@newhopetrust.org
☎ 01779 838 251 Fax 01779 838 549

New Wine Ministries, Unit 22, Arun Business Park, Bognor Regis PO22 9SX
Partners: Mr Ed F & Dr Elizabeth Harding. Executive staff 2, Other staff 5. Began 1984; non-denominational. Turnover n/a.
☎ 01243 867 227 Fax 01243 867 292

Parish & People, The Old Mill, Spetisbury, Blandford Forum DT11 9DF
Secretary/Partner: Rev Jimmy Hamilton-Brown. No full-time staff. Began 1980; Anglican. Imprints: Parish & People, Partners. Turnover n/a. Producing the Deanery Exchange to help deaneries work more effectively.
Email: pandpeople@aol.com
☎ 01258 453 939

Paternoster Publishing, PO Box 300, Carlisle CA3 0QS
Publisher: Mr Mark Finnie. Executive staff 2, Other staff 7. *CC* No.270162. Began 1935; interdenominational. (Previously Send the Light Publishing). Imprints: Alpha, Challenge News Special, Hunt and Thorpe, OM Publishing, Paternoster Periodicals, Paternoster Press, Regnum Books, Rutherford, Solway. Turnover n/a.
Web: www.paternoster-publishing.com
Email: info@paternoster-publishing.com
☎ 01228 512 512 Fax 01228 593 388

Pentland Press Ltd, 1 Hutton Close, South Church, Bishop Auckland DL14 6XB
Chairman: Mr Nicholas Law. Executive staff 5, Other staff 4. Began 1980; non-denominational. Turnover n/a.
☎ 01388 776 555 Fax 01388 776 766

†*Plough Publishing House of the Bruderhof Communities in the UK, Darvell Bruderhof, Robertsbridge TN32 5DR
Secretary: Detlef Manke. Community 350. *CC* No.229226. Began 1936; non-denominational. Turnover n/a. Distributing literature, mainly by the Plough Publishing House in the USA.
Web: www.bruderhof.org
Email: ploughuk@bruderhof.com
☎ 01580 883 300

Precious Seed Publications, 5 Turnham Green, Penylan, Cardiff CF23 7DL
Treasurer: Mr Michael Jones. No full-time staff. *CC* No.326157. Began 1945; interdenominational. Turnover n/a. Publishing Bible study books.
☎ 029 2049 2346

Printforce Ltd, Drovers Way, Ugford, Wilton, Salisbury SP2 0EB
Director: Mr Paul Wade. Executive staff 2. Began 1983; non-denominational. Turnover n/a.
☎ 01722 743 295 Fax 01722 743 295

Prophetic Word Ministries Trust, The Park, Moggerhanger, Bedford MK44 3RW
Director: Rev Dr Clifford Hill. Executive staff 3, Other staff 5. *CC* No.326533. Began 1984; interdenominational. Magazine: *Prophecy Today* (10,700 every two months). Turnover £200,600 to year end Dec 98. Biblically-based teaching/publishing ministry; Hebraic Study Centre offering sabbaticals, courses, distance learning; residential conference facilities.
Email: pwm@the-park.u-net.com
☎ 01767 641 400 Fax 01767 641 515

†Quinta Press, Meadow View, Quinta Crescent, Weston Rhyn, Oswestry SY10 7RN
Proprietor: Dr Digby L James. No other staff. Began 1992; non-denominational and evangelical. Turnover n/a.
Web: www.cix.co.uk/~digby/qp.html
Email: quintapress@digby.cix.co.uk
☎ 01691 778 659 Fax 01691 777 638

†Redemptorist Publications, Alphonsus House, Chawton, Alton GU34 3HQ
Executive Director: Mr James D McKell. Executive staff 13, Other staff 19. *CC* Began 1954; Roman Catholic. Turnover n/a.
Email: rp@redempt.demon.co.uk
☎ 01420 882 22 Fax 01420 888 05

Regnum Books, PO Box 70, Oxford OX2 6HB
Publisher: Rev Canon Dr Vinay Samuel. Other staff 1. *CC* No.290112. Began 1986; non-denominational. Turnover n/a.
Email: regnum@ocms.ac.uk
☎ 01865 556 071 Fax 01865 510 823

John Ritchie Ltd, 40 Beansburn, Kilmarnock KA3 1RH
General Manager: Mr John Watson. *Shop Manageress:* Mrs Elizabeth Wallace. Executive staff 3, Other staff 9. Began 1880; non-denominational. Turnover n/a.
☎ 01563 536 394 Fax 01563 571 191

***The Rushworth Literature Enterprise Ltd**, 2 Dimple Lane, Crich, Matlock DE4 5BQ
General Secretary: Miss Catherine S Cheetham. Executive staff 3, Other staff 1. *CC* No.241364. Began 1953; non-denominational. Turnover £13,000 [excluding second-hand books] to year end Mar 98. Publishing and donating Christian study books to pastors in overseas countries.
Web: www.rushworth.lit.virgin.net
Email: rushworth.lit@virgin.net
☎ 01773 857 313 Fax 01773 857 313

St Matthew Publishing Ltd, 24 Geldart Street, Cambridge CB1 2LX
Director: Rev Philip Foster. No full-time staff. Began 1995; interdenominational. Turnover £19,000 to year end Sep 97. Providing materials warning the churches of the rapidly growing apostasy within them.
Web: www.phar.cam.ac.uk/stmatts/
Email: aakbb@dial.pipex.com
☎ 01223 504 871 Fax 01223 512 304

St Matthias Press, PO Box 665, London SW20 8RU
Publisher: Mr Tim Thornborough. *Staff Writer:* Mr Martin Cole. Executive staff 1, Other staff 4. Began 1990; interdenominational. Imprints: St Matthias Press, Narrowgate Press, Matthias Media. Turnover £280,000 to year end Dec 98.
Email: mattmedia@compuserve.com
☎ 020 8942 0880 Fax 020 8942 0990

For additional information see List on Pages 169–170

St Pauls, Morpeth Terrace, Victoria, London SW1P 1EP
Editorial Director: Rev S Karamvelil. Staff: members of religious order 6. ***CC*** No.230948. Began 1947; Roman Catholic. Turnover n/a.
Email: editions@stpauls.org.uk
☎ 020 7828 5582 Mobile: 07771 887 186 🖷 020 7828 3329

St Stephen's Press, 30 Oxlease, Witney OX8 6QX
Managing Director: Rev Seraphim Vanttinen-Newton. Executive staff 1, Other staff 1. ***CC*** Began 1992; Orthodox. Turnover n/a. Publishes works on behalf of the Russian Orthodox Patriarchal Church in Great Britain.
Web: www.sourozh.clara.net
☎ 01993 772 834 🖷 01993 772 834

Salvationist Publishing and Supplies Ltd, 117 Judd Street, King's Cross, London WC1H 9NN
Managing Director: Lieut-Colonel Michael Williams. Executive staff 3, Other staff 45. Began 1867; Salvation Army. Turnover n/a.
☎ 020 7387 1656 🖷 020 7387 3420

Save The Church of England Foundation, West Ella House, 15 Tunnelwood Road, Watford WD1 3SN
Chief Executive: Mr Malcolm JW Barker. Executive staff 1. Began 1979; Anglican. Turnover n/a. Campaigning for the Doctrine of the Church of England as expressed in the 39 Articles.
☎ 01923 229 045

SCM Press Ltd, 9 St Albans Place, London N1 0NX
Managing Director: Rev Dr John S Bowden. Executive staff 3, Other staff 7. Began 1929; non-denominational. Turnover n/a.
Email: scmpress@btinternet.com
☎ 020 7359 8033 🖷 020 7359 0049

Scripture Truth Publications, Coopies Way, Coopies Lane Industrial Estate, Morpeth NE61 6JN
Manager: Mr Edwin Pearsons. No other staff. ***CC*** No.223327. Began 1909. Turnover £50,000-100,000 to year end Mar 98. Publication and selling through retail and mail order of Christian literature.
Web: www.morpethnet.co.uk/scripturetruth/
Email: scripturetruth@compuserve.com
☎ 01670 511 615 🖷 01670 516 620

Scripture Union, 207 Queensway, Bletchley, Milton Keynes MK2 2EB
Director of Resourcing and Support: Mr Andrew Stockbridge. Executive publishing staff 6, Other publishing staff 29. ***CC*** No.213422. Began 1867; interdenominational. Imprints: Scripture Union, Tamarind. Turnover n/a.
Web: www.scripture.org.uk
Email: postmaster@scriptureunion.org.uk
☎ 01908 856 188 🖷 01908 856 111

Sessions of York, The Ebor Press, Huntington Road, York YO3 1HS
Publishing Manager: Mr Robert Sissons. Staff n/a. Began 1811; non-denominational. Turnover n/a.
Web: www.sessionsofyork.co.uk
Email: ebor.info@sessionsofyork.co.uk
☎ 01904 659 224 🖷 01904 637 068

Sheed & Ward Ltd, 14 Coopers Row, London EC3N 2BH
Managing Director: Mr Martin T Redfern. Executive staff 3. Began 1916; Roman Catholic. Turnover n/a.
☎ 020 7702 9799 🖷 020 7702 3583

Sheffield Academic Press, Mansion House, 19 Kingfield Road, Sheffield S11 9AS
Managing Director: Mrs Jean Allen. Staff 30. Began 1976; non-denominational. Turnover n/a.
Web: www.shef-ac-press.co.uk
Email: admin@sheffac.demon.co.uk
☎ 0114 255 4433 🖷 0114 255 4626

Silver Fish Creative Marketing Ltd, 37 Pottery Lane, Holland Park, London W11 4LY
Managing Director: Mr Stephen Jones. *Creative Director:* Mr Darren Southworth. Executive staff 5, Other staff 5. Began 1996; interdenominational. Turnover £100,000–300,000 to year end Dec 96. Providing contract publishing services for books and magazines, editorial, typesetting, graphic design, print management, distribution.
Email: silver.fish@virgin.net
☎ 020 7727 2871 🖷 020 7727 2875

Society for Promoting Christian Knowledge (SPCK), Holy Trinity Church, Marylebone Road, London NW1 4DU
Director of Publishing: Mr Simon Kingston. Executive staff 3, Other staff 14. ***CC*** No.231144. Began 1698; Anglican. Turnover n/a.
Email: publishing@spck.co.uk
☎ 020 7387 5282 🖷 020 7388 2352/1921
Also at: 7 Castle Street, Reading RG1 7SB
☎ 01734 599 011 🖷 01734 599 240

For additional information see List on Pages 169–170

Sovereign Publications, PO Box 88, Bromley BR2 9PF
Principal: Mr M Bowden. All part-time staff. Began 1977; Free evangelical. Turnover n/a. Publishing mainly books on creation and Biblical counselling.
Web: ourworld.compuserve.com/homepages/bowdenmalcolm
Email: 106012.2646@compuserve.com
☎ 020 8460 7503

Sovereign World, PO Box 777, Tonbridge TN11 0ZS
Managing Director: Mr Chris H Mungeam. Executive staff 2, Other staff 2. Began 1986; non-denominational. Turnover n/a.
Email: sovereignworldbooks@compuserve.com
☎ 01732 850 598 Fax 01732 851 077
Distribution: Unit 22, Arun Business Park, Bognor Regis PO22 9SX
☎ 01243 867 227 Fax 01243 867 292

B

Stainer & Bell Ltd, PO Box 110, Victoria House, 23 Gruneisen Road, London N3 1DZ
Managing Directors: Mr Keith & Mrs Carol Wakefield. *Publishing Director:* Mr Nicholas Williams. Executive staff 4, Other staff 6. Began 1907; non-denominational. Turnover £724,000 to year end Dec 98.
Web: www.stainer.co.uk
Email: post@stainer.co.uk
☎ 020 8343 3303 Fax 020 8343 3024

Stanborough Press, Alma Park, Grantham NG31 9SL
Manager: Mr Paul Hammond. Executive staff 5, Other staff 38. *CC* Began 1890; Seventh-Day Adventist. Turnover n/a.
Email: 101654.543@compuserve.com
☎ 01476 591 700 Fax 01476 577 144

Arthur H Stockwell Ltd, Elms Court, Torrs Park, Ilfracombe EX34 8BA
Directors: Mr R J G Stockwell, Mr P J Nicholas. Executive staff 3, Other staff 11. Began 1898; non-denominational. Turnover n/a.
☎ 01271 862 557 Fax 01271 862 988

Summit Publishing Ltd, PO Box 4065, Milton Keynes MK14 5ZE
Director: Linda Finley-Day. No other staff. Began 1995; non-denominational. Turnover n/a.
Web: www.summitpublishing.co.uk
Email: 100443.1414@compuserve.com
☎ 01908 614 777 Fax 01908 315 408

Talking Points, 2 Bishops Road, Tewinwood, Welwyn AL6 0NS
Publications Director: Mr Phil Bancroft. Executive Staff 1. Began 1992; non-denominational. Turnover n/a.
☎ 01302 538 966

William Temple Foundation, Manchester Business School, Booth Street West, Manchester M15 6PB
Executive Secretary: Rev Malcolm Brown. Executive staff 2, Other staff 3. *CC* No.528790. Began 1947; non-denominational. Turnover £100,000 to year end Dec 98.
Email: ecg-wen@mcr1.poptel.org.uk
☎ 0161 275 6534 Fax 0161 272 8663

Teresian Press, Carmelite Priory, Boars Hill, Oxford OX1 5HB
Secretary: Mrs Sandra Pooley. Executive staff 2. *CC* No.207738. Began 1985; Roman Catholic. Turnover n/a.
Web: www.carmelite.org.uk
Email: priory@carmelite.org.uk
☎ 01865 730 183 Fax 01865 326 478

Stanley Thornes (Publishers) Ltd, Ellenborough House, Wellington Street, Cheltenham GL50 1YW
List Development Manager: Mr Peter Burton. Executive staff 5, Other staff 200. Began 1986; non-denominational. (Incorporating Simon and Schuster Education). Turnover n/a.
Web: www.thornes.co.uk
Email: pburton@thornes.co.uk
☎ 01242 228 888 Fax 01242 221 914

Triumph House, 1 Wainman Road, Woodston, Peterborough PE2 7BU
Managing Editor: Mr Steve Twelvetree. Executive staff 1, Other staff 1. Began 1993; interdenominational. Turnover n/a.
☎ 01733 230 749 Fax 01733 230 751

†**Tufton Books (Church Union Publications)**, 7 Tufton Street, London SW1P 3QN
Chairman: Rev Dr R Hannaford. Executive staff 1, Other staff 2. *CC* Began 1995; Anglican. Turnover n/a.
☎ 020 7222 6952 Fax 020 7976 7180

†**The Wakeman Trust**, 5 Templar Street, Camberwell, London SE5 9JB
Chairman of Trustees: Mr Alan Polling. Other staff 3. *CC* Began 1986; non-denominational. Turnover n/a.
☎ 020 7735 7989 Fax 020 7735 7989

Westminster John Knox Press (UK Office), 2 Nursery Gardens, Tring HP23 5HZ
UK Publishing Director: Mr Philip Law. Executive staff 1. Began 1999; interdenominational. Turnover: first year of operation in UK. Publishing in all areas of theology and Biblical studies; for students, ministers and general readers.
Web: www.wjk.org
☎ 01442 382 552 Fax 01442 382 552

Wild Goose Publications (The Iona Community), Unit 15, 6 Harmony Row, Govan, Glasgow G51 3BA
Staff 4. *CC* No.SCO 03794. Began 1938; ecumenical. Turnover £150,000 to year end Dec 98.
Web: www.iona.org.uk
Email: admin@wgp.iona.org.uk
☎ 0141 440 0985 Fax 0141 440 2338

For additional information see List on Pages 169–170

OTHER LITERATURE PRODUCERS & DISTRIBUTORS (UK)

AT Publications, PO Box 14540, Dunfermline KY12 9ZD
Director: Mr Manjit Biant. Executive staff 1, Other staff 1. Began 1990; non-denominational. (Previously The Advent Truth). Magazine: *Mission Update* (3,000 half-yearly). Turnover £25,000 to year end Apr 98. Distributing books and tracts for evangelism; organising religious and health tours and seminars.
Email: adventruth@aol.com
☎ 01383 852 863 🖷 01383 852 863

*__Acts International (UK)__, Westbury-on-Trym, Bristol BS9 4LU
UK Director: Mr William D Cousins. No full-time staff. ***CC*** Began 1986; interdenominational. Magazine: *Acts Communicator* (Circulation n/a quarterly). Turnover £7,500 to year end June 92. Producing and distributing outreach leaflets speaking to felt needs in non-jargon language.
☎ 0117 962 9911

Alban Books Ltd, 79 Park Street, Bristol BS1 5PF
Managing Director: Mr Sheridan Swinson. *Operations Manager:* Ms Sue Morgan. *Marketing & Editorial Coordinator:* Ms Laura Serratrice. Executive staff 2, Other staff 4. Began 1995; non-denominational. No magazine. Turnover £750,000 to year end Dec 98. Distributing books and tapes for six publishing houses.
Web: www.albanbooks.com
Email: sales@albanbooks.com
☎ 0117 927 7750 🖷 0117 927 2785

†**AP Communications Ltd**, 11 High Street, Whitchurch SY13 1AX
Managing Director: Rev Kenneth T Lillie. Executive staff 1, Other staff 4. Began 1983; interdenominational. No magazine. Turnover n/a. Wholesaling Christian books, greeting cards, stationery.
☎ 01948 663 770 🖷 01948 663 952

Apostolic Faith Church, 66 Muscliffe Road, Winton, Bournemouth BH9 1NW
Pastor: Pastor Duncan Lee. Other staff 3. ***CC*** No.238009. Began 1910; Pentecostal. Magazine: *Showers of Blessing* (60 weekly). Turnover n/a. Publishing evangelistic booklets for use worldwide.
☎ 01202 528 270

Appleford Publishing Group, Appleford House, Appleford, Abingdon OX14 4PB
Editorial Director: Mr Gervase E Duffield. Staff 3. Began 1963; Anglican, Reformed and Evangelical. No magazine. Turnover n/a. Holding company for evangelical and academic books, magazines and pastoralia; sale of antiquarian books.
☎ 01235 848 319

Asian Books (South Asian Concern), PO Box 43, Sutton SM2 5WL
Coordinator: Mr Jayesh Patel. All voluntary staff. ***CC*** Began 1994; interdenominational. No magazine. Turnover £10,000 to year end Mar 98. Supplying Asian Christian resources and literature; over 1,100 titles in many languages; mail order only.
Email: 100126.3641@compuserve.com
☎ 020 8767 6387 🖷 020 8767 6387

Authorised Version Preservation Venture, 53 London Road, Chatteris PE16 6LW
Hon Secretary: Rev David Ellis. All voluntary staff. Began 1983; interdenominational. No magazine. Turnover n/a. Publishing and distributing literature and greetings cards to preserve the use of the Authorised Version.
☎ 01354 696 392 🖷 01354 696 392

Barnicoats, 17 Kernick Business Park, Kernick Road, Penryn TR10 9EW
Managing Director: To be appointed. Executive staff 4, Other staff 200. Began 1950; Anglican. No magazine. Turnover £10,000,000 to year end Feb 93. Book wholesaler (60,000 titles), infocado-card and calendar company.
☎ 01326 372 628 🖷 01326 376 423

Berean Publishing Trust, 4 Orchard Avenue, Whetstone, London N20 0JA
Secretary: Mr Alan Schofield. Executive staff 2, Other staff 1. ***CC*** No.232856. Began 1909; non-denominational. (Associated with Berean Forward Movement Trust). Magazine: *The Berean Expositor* (Circulation & frequency n/a). Turnover £10,000 to year end Dec 96. Publishing and distributing Bible study books and booklets.
Web: ourworld.compuserve.com/homepages/bptsales/homepage.htm
Email: bptsales@compuserve.com
☎ 020 8446 2762

B

Berith Publications, 6 Orchard Road, Lewes BN7 2HB
Manageress: Mrs Janet North. Executive staff 1. Began 1998; interdenominational. (Previously Testimony Books). No magazine. Turnover: first year of operation. Distributing and publishing books majoring on Reformation topics and Methodist Church history.
☎ 01273 472 279 🖷 01273 472 279

Bethany Christian Bookshelf, 1 Orchard Grove, Astwood Bank, Redditch B96 6BE
Manager: Mr Derek Platt. Executive staff 2. Began n/a; non-denominational. No magazine. Turnover £8,000 to year end Aug 98. Supplying Bibles and study aids by mail order.
Email: derek.platt@btinternet.com
☎ 01527 893 204 🖷 01527 893 204

The Bible & Tract Depot, 219 Mary Street, Birmingham B12 9RN
Manager: Miss O G M Everitt. No other staff. Began 1946; interdenominational. No magazine. Turnover n/a. Mail order distribution of Bible deliverance literature.
☎ 0121 440 1422

BibleLands Trading Ltd (BibleLands), PO Box 50, High Wycombe HP15 7QU
Chief Executive: Mr Andrew Jong. *Head of Trading:* Mrs D Piggott. Executive staff 1, Other staff 7. Began 1967; non-denominational. No magazine. Turnover £530,000 [to 16 months ending Apr 98]. Publishing Bethlehem Carol Sheet, Christmas cards and gifts, church folders and church-related print.
☎ 01494 521 351 🖷 01494 462 171

The Bible League Trust, Fairlea, Fron Park Road, Holywell CH8 7SP
Hon Secretary: Mrs Ruth Ward. All voluntary staff. ***CC*** No.281867. Began 1892; non-denominational. Magazine: *Bible League Quarterly* (1,200 quarterly). Turnover £8,350 to year end Dec 97. Proclaiming the inspiration, infallibility and sole sufficiency of Scripture; promoting its reverent study.
☎ No telephone

*__Bible Text Publicity Mission__, PO Box 2704, Billericay CM12 9BL
Administrator: Mr Trevor Argent. No full-time staff. ***CC*** No.235773. Began 1923; interdenominational. Magazine: *Annual Report* (650 annually). Turnover £18,500 to year end Dec 98. Displaying Bible texts to the public on railway stations, London Underground and prisons throughout UK.
☎ 01277 626 309

B

Birmingham Gospel Outreach, 21 Beeches Farm Drive, West Heath, Birmingham B31 4SD
Director: Mr Michael Simpson. Executive staff 1, Other staff 1. Began 1995; non-denominational. No magazine. Turnover n/a. Producing English and Romanian Gospel tracts, scripture memory verse cards, bookmarks, posters, evangelistic cards.
☎ 0121 478 2952 🖷 0121 478 2952

†**Blue Banner Productions**, 12 Forrest Road, Edinburgh EH1 2QN
Publisher: Mr James A Dickson. Executive staff 1. Began n/a; non-denominational. No magazine. Turnover n/a. Publishing and distributing Reformed literature especially Scottish.
☎ 0131 225 6937

Bookprint Creative Services, PO Box 827, Eastbourne BN21 3YJ
Senior Partner: Mr David Nickalls. Executive staff 2, Other staff 3. Began 1993; non-denominational. No magazine. Turnover n/a. Book production and design for publishers, Christian organisations and authors; paperbacks, hardbacks, music books, Bibles.
Email: bcs@bookprint.co.uk
☎ 01323 411 315 🖷 01323 410 461

Don Bosco Publications, Thornleigh House, Sharples Park, Bolton BL1 6PQ
Manager: Rev Michael Grix. All voluntary staff. *CC* No.233779. Began 1892; Roman Catholic. (Previously Salesian Publications (UK)). Magazine: *Salesian Bulletin* (10,000 quarterly), *Don Bosco Today* (Circulation n/a quarterly). Turnover n/a. Distributing books published mainly in USA. Salesian books available.
Web: www.salesians.org.uk
Email: mfgrix@msn.com
☎ 01204 308 811

P Brengle Crowhurst Pastoral Trust, 88 Railton Jones Close, Stoke Gifford, Bristol BS34 8BF
Secretary: Rev Peter B Crowhurst. No full-time staff. *CC* No.289620. Began 1984; interdenominational. Magazine: *Peter's Pastoral Letter* (1,000 every four months). Turnover £1,500 to year end Mar 95. Encouraging isolated believers by correspondence and publishing.
☎ 0117 979 3619

Bridge Books & Music, 14 North Bridge Street, Sunderland SR5 1AB
Chief Executives: Mr & Mrs Rob Foreman. Began 1982; interdenominational. (Previously Crown Publishing). No magazine. Turnover n/a. Distributing Christian literature to retail outlets.
Email: bridgebooks@cwcomm.net
☎ 0191 567 3544 Mobile: 07831 093 912 🖷 0191 567 3544

***By All Means Gospel Trust**, 159 Warwick Road, Solihull B92 7AR
General Secretary: Maurice J W Paine. Executive staff 1. *CC* No.231070. Began 1962; interdenominational. Magazine: *BAM News* (2,000 every two months). Turnover n/a. Greek newspaper and literature outreach; BAM booklets and Bible readings.
☎ 0121 707 4777

Carmelite Book Service, Boars Hill, Oxford OX1 5HB
Secretary: Mrs Sandra Pooley. Executive staff 1, Other staff 1. *CC* No.207738. Began 1985; Roman Catholic. No magazine. Turnover £50,000 to year end Dec 98. Specialist bookshop, mainly mail order.
Web: carmelite.org.uk
Email: priory@carmelite.org.uk
☎ 01865 730 183 🖷 01865 326 478

***Challenge**, PO Box 300, Kingstown Broadway, Carlisle CA3 0QS
Editor: Mr Donald Banks. *CC* No.270162. Began 1958; interdenominational. (Previously Challenge Literature Fellowship). See also Paternoster Publishing. Newspaper: *Challenge* (80,000 monthly). Turnover n/a. Publishing evangelistic literature; a literature mission to the UK.
Web: www.paternoster-publishing.com
Email: challenge@paternoster-publishing.com
Editorial office: 50 Loxwood Avenue, Working BN14 7RA
☎ 01908 824 174 🖷 01903 824 376

Oswald Chambers Publications Association Ltd, 2 Hunters Court, West Lane, Higher Blagdon, Paignton TQ3 3YQ
General Manager: Mrs J M Hutchison. Executive staff 1, Other staff 1. *CC* No.244995. Began 1934; non-denominational. Turnover n/a. Publishing and distributing material by Oswald Chambers.
Email: shutchison@compuserve.com
☎ 01803 550 374 🖷 01803 525 701
Registered Office: 22 Sansome Walk, Worcester WR1 1LN

Children First, Old Manse, Lightowler Street, Wibsey, Bradford BD6 1NA
Owner: Mr John M Sutcliffe. Executive staff 1, Other staff 1. Began 1999; interdenominational. No magazine. Turnover: first year of operation. Supplying Christian / high moral standard books to schools.
☎ 01274 678 157 🖷 01274 678 157

Christian Aid, PO Box 100, London SE1 7RT
Head of Publishing & Marketing: Susan Spratt. Other staff 6. *CC* No.258003. Began 1945; interdenominational. Magazine: *Christian Aid News* (230,000 quarterly). Turnover £37,928,000 to year end Mar 98. Producing materials for schools, youth, worship; policy reports, country information sheets, books.
Web: www.christian-aid.org.uk
Email: info@christian-aid.org
☎ 020 7620 4444 🖷 020 7620 0719

Christian Book Club, 18 Slater Street, Liverpool L1 4BS
Manager: Mr Peter J Lock. Executive staff 1. *CC* Began 1976; non-denominational. No magazine. Turnover n/a. Providing book service to customer's home, post free. Discount prices UK and overseas.
☎ 0151 708 9550

The Christian Book Club, Guild House, Farnsey Street, Swindon SN99 9XX
Business Manager: Mr Peter Crawshaw. Staff n/a. Began 1997; non-denominational. Magazine: *The Christian Book Club* (Circulation n/a five times a year). Turnover n/a. Offering wide range of adult and children's Christian books by mail at discount prices.
☎ 01793 548 149

Christian Book Promotion Trust, 54 Roseford Road, Cambridge CB4 2HD
Proprietor: Mr Trevor Hames. Other staff 1. *CC* No.255001. Began 1972; interdenominational. No magazine. Turnover £30,000 to year end Apr 98. Offers free illustrated booklists, encourages churches to give books to local schools and public libraries.
Web: dspace.dial.pipex.com/christian.books.direct
Email: cbd@christianbooksdirect.co.uk
☎ 01223 300 065 🖷 01223 322 277

Christian Books Direct, 54 Roseford Road, Cambridge CB4 2HD
Proprietor: Mr Trevor Hames. Other staff 1. *CC* No.255001. Began 1994; interdenominational. No magazine. Turnover £39,000 to year end Apr 98. Minimum 15% discount, bookstalls and individuals welcome.
Web: dspace.dial.pipex.com/christian.books.direct
Email: trevorhames@christianbooksdirect.co.uk
☎ 01223 300 065 🖷 01223 322 277

Christian Broadcasting Library Service, 59a Joseph's Road, Guildford GU1 1DN
Administrator: Mr J Roger Alsford. No full-time staff. *CC* No.1025090. Began 1984; non-denominational. No magazine. Turnover £24,000 to year end Dec 98. Supplying public libraries and school resource centres with free Christian books, tapes and videos.
☎ 01483 828 559

Christian Business Directories, PO Box 266, Staines TW18 4GP
Managing Directors: Katie Dodsworth & Barry Mockford. Other staff 1. Began 1997; interdenominational. Incorporating London Christian Business Directory. Turnover £40,000 to year end Dec 98. Publishing local directories around the UK advertising Christian businesses and resourcing Christians in their locality.
Web: www.cbd.org.uk
Email: info@cbd.org.uk
☎ 01784 880 022 Mobile: 07976 877 790 🖷 01784 490 031

Christian Business Pages, Heritage Publishing, Top Floor Suite, Millennium House, Lower Hall Lane, Walsall WS1 1RL
Managing Director: Mr Andrew Bell. Executive staff 2, Other staff 2. Began 1996; interdenominational. Magazine: *Christian Business Pages* (30,000 annually). Turnover n/a. Publishing a Midlands Directory of businesses and resources.
Web: www.cbpages.co.uk
Email: cb@pages777.freeserve.co.uk
☎ 01922 646 200 🖷 01922 625 752

***Christian Communications Partnership Ltd**, PO Box 17911, London SW1E 5ZR
Chairman: David Heron. *Advertising Manager:* Pamela Chaston. Other staff 4. Began 1998; interdenominational. (Previously Elm House Christian Communications Ltd and Trinity Square). Turnover £400,000 to year end Sep 98. Publishers of *Christianity* and *Youthwork*.
Web: www.youthwork.co.uk
Email: christianity@easynet.co.uk
Email: youthwork@easynet.co.uk
☎ 020 7316 1450 🖷 020 7316 1453

***Christian Education Europe**, PO Box 770, Highworth, Swindon SN6 7TU
Executive Director: Mr Arthur Roderick. Executive staff 3, Other staff 4. Began 1990; interdenominational. (Associated with The School of Tomorrow). Magazine: *Accelerator* (1,000 n/a). Turnover n/a. Starting, supporting and supplying Christian schools and home education with Bible-based curriculum and creationist literature.
Web: www.christian-education.org
Email: christianeducationeurope@compuserve.com
☎ 01793 783 783 🖷 01793 783 783

***Christian Literature Crusade**, 51 The Dean, Alresford SO24 9BJ
Wholesale Director: Mr Roger Page. Executive staff 1, Other staff 9. *CC* No.1015793. Began 1941; evangelical. Magazine: *CLC World* (6,000 every two months). Turnover n/a. International trade distribution centre for 9,000 product lines.
Email: clcwsale@aol.com
☎ 01962 733 142 🖷 01962 733 141

***Christian Media Centre**, 96 Dominion Road, Worthing BN14 8JP
Managing Director: Mr Paul Slide. *Production Director:* Mr Mike Axell. Executive staff 5, Other staff 24. Began 1980; interdenominational. Turnover n/a. Publishing Christian periodicals.
Web: www.christianherald.org.uk
Email: admin@christianherald.org.uk
☎ 01903 821 082 ISDN: 01903 537 308 🖷 01903 821 081

Christian Music Ministries, 325 Bromford Road, Hodge Hill, Birmingham B36 8ET
Directors: Mr Roger & Mrs Mary Jones. Executive staff 3, Other staff 4. *CC* No.516643. Began 1983; non-denominational. No magazine. Turnover £45,000 to year end Mar 96. Resources through mail-order catalogue, conferences, training courses and publishing and recording Roger Jones' music.
Web: www.cmm.org.uk
Email: roger@cmm.org.uk
☎ 0121 783 3291 🖷 0121 785 0500

***Christian Publicity Organisation**, Garcia Estate, Canterbury Road, Worthing BN13 1BW
General Director: Mr Roy P Barbour. *Director of Marketing:* Mr Chris Powell. *Editor:* Mr Andrew Halloway. Executive staff 3, Other staff 34. *CC* No.221462. Began 1957; non-denominational. Magazine: *CPO Catalogue* (25,000 quarterly). Turnover £2,000,000 to year end Apr 99. Supporting the Christian community through design, print and publishing, in partnership with ministries nationally and internationally.
Email: enquiries@cpo.uk.com
☎ 01903 264 556 ISDN: 01903 830 005 🖷 01903 830 066

†**Christian Publishers' Representatives**, Holy Trinity Church, Marylebone Road, London NW1 4DU
Manager: Mr Brian Keen. *Sales Administrator:* Mrs Alexandra Gunn. Executive staff 1, Other staff 6. Began 1972; non-denominational. No magazine. Turnover £3,510,000 to year end Apr 96. Representing a wide range of Christian publishers to the UK book trade.
Email: sales@spck.co.uk
☎ 020 7387 5282 🖷 020 7388 2352

Christian Weekly Newspapers Ltd, 10 Little College Street, London SW1P 3SH
Chairman: Mr Robert Leach. *CC* No.270655. Began 1976; Anglican. No magazine. Turnover n/a. Trustees of *The Church of England Newspaper*.
☎ 020 7878 1549 🖷 020 7976 0783

christianbookshop.com
Administrator: Clive Purser. No full-time staff. Began 1998; interdenominational. Administered by Christian Pastoral Aid Society. No magazine. Turnover: first year of operation. Distributing Christian literature via the internet, to support, equip and encourage church leaders.
Email: christianbookshop.com

***Christmas Letters to Prisoners**, 52a Whitehorse Lane, London SE25 6RE
Secretary: Rev Brian Wightwick. Executive staff 1. *CC* No.210053. Began 1880; non-denominational. No magazine. Turnover n/a. Sending hand-written Christmas letters to prisoners.
☎ 020 8653 3563

B

B

***Contact for Christ**, Selsdon House, 212 Addington Road, South Croydon CR2 8LD
Co-ordinator: Mr Clifford Harper. Executive staff 1, Other staff 2. ***CC*** No.243305. Began 1975; non-denominational. Magazine: *Newsletter* (7,500 annually). Turnover n/a. Personal contact and follow-up service throughout UK; publishers of outreach material.
Email: lit@deo-gloria.co.uk
☎ 020 8651 6246 🖷 020 8651 6429

Courtenay Bindery, Appleford House, Appleford, Abingdon OX14 4PB
Director: Ms Elizabeth Collie. Began 1963; non-denominational. (Part of Appleford Publishing Group). No magazine. Turnover n/a. Specialising in restoration and sale of high quality leather bcoks, antiquarian and modern.
☎ 01235 848 319

***CPAS Sales**, Athena Drive, Tachbrook Park, Warwick CV34 6NG
Marketing Manager: Clive Purser. Executive staff 4. ***CC*** No.1007820. Began 1963; Anglican. No magazine. Turnover £400,000 to year end Apr 98. Publishing and supplying leadership resources via mail order, bookshops and website.
Web: www.christianbookshop.com
Email: sales@cpas.org.uk
☎ 01926 458 400 🖷 01926 458 459

Decani Music, 30 North Terrace, Bury St Edmunds IP28 7AB
Editor/Director: Mr Stephen Dean. Executive staff 2, Other staff 2. Began 1991; non-denominational. Magazine: *The Liturgy Planner* (1,300 every four months). Turnover £100,000 to year end Dec 96. Publishing and distributing liturgy and music resources.
Web: decanimusic.uk.com
Email: decanimusic@dialdrakken.com
☎ 01638 716 579 Mobile: 07802 736 863 🖷 01638 510 390

Dorchester House Publications, PO Box 67, Rickmansworth WD3 5SJ
Director: Mr Michael de Semlyen. Executive staff 1. ***CC*** Began 1993; non-denominational. No magazine. Turnover n/a. Publishing books about Roman Catholicism and Islam in the light of the Christian Gospel.
☎ 01923 286 080 🖷 01923 286 080

Drummond Trust (Incorporating Stirling Tract Enterprise), 3 Pitt Terrace, Stirling FK8 2EY
Secretary: Mr D S Whyte. No full-time staff. ***CC*** Began 1848; non-denominational. No magazine. Turnover £20,000 to year end Dec 98. Giving financial assistance for publications of sound Christian doctrine and evangelical purpose.
☎ 01786 450 985 🖷 01786 451 360

Alan & Margaret Edwards, 10 Meteor Avenue, Whitstable CT5 4DH
Partners: Mr & Mrs Alan & Margaret Edwards. Executive staff 2. Began 1988; non-denominational. No magazine. Turnover n/a. Selling second-hand and discount priced new books by post, finding out of print titles.
Email: a.m.books@lineone.net
☎ 01227 262 276 🖷 01227 261 158

Egon Publishers Ltd, Royston Road, Baldock SG7 6NW
Managing Director: Mr John Street. Executive staff 5, Other staff 6. Began 1974; non-denominational. No magazine. Turnover £200,000 to year end Feb 90. Marketing Christian books.
☎ 01462 894 498 🖷 01462 894 660

Evangelical Sisterhood of Mary, 17 Gills Hill Lane, Radlett WD7 8DE
Sister-in-Charge: Sister Mechthild Wolf. All voluntary staff. ***CC*** No.259421. Began 1968; interdenominational. No magazine. Turnover n/a. Distributing literature, cassettes, videos by M Basilea Schlink.
☎ 01923 856 316 🖷 01923 853 255

Evangelical Tract Society (incorporating Macedonian Tracts and Urban Tracts), 48 Park Ridings, London N8 0LD
Secretary: Mr Mike Grimshaw. ***CC*** No.232773. Began 1883; non-denominational. Magazine: *Newsletter* (1,250 quarterly). Turnover £20,000 to year end Mar 99. Distributing Christian tracts, booklets and audio cassettes for evangelism.
Web: www.grace.org.uk/mission/ets/
Email: cedmu98943@aol.com
☎ 020 8881 4327 🖷 020 8881 5338

***FRC Book Services**, 126 Sutherland Avenue, Biggin Hill, Westerham TN16 3HJ
Managing Director: Mr Paul Heather. Executive staff 2. Began 1985; interdenominational. (Previously Family Reading Book Services). No magazine. Turnover £100,000 to year end July 98. Selling and distributing Christian books into non-Christian situations: shops, schools, surgeries, hotels, homes, libraries.
Email: books@frcbooks.freeserve.co.uk
☎ 01959 575 172 🖷 01959 576 445

Faith Builders, PO Box 103, Knutsford WA16 9EW
Partner: Miss Susan Spilman. Executive staff 5, Other staff 8. Began 1980; non-denominational. No magazine. Turnover n/a. Publishing and importing Christian Faith Building teaching books, audio and video tapes.
Web: www.faith-builders.co.uk
Email: enquiries@faithbuilders.co.uk
☎ 01565 654 414 🖷 01565 652 706

***Farmers Christian Postal Service**, The Manse, 7 The Ridgeway, Dovercourt, Harwich CO12 4AT
Hon General Secretary: Pastor John C Langlands. No full-time staff. ***CC*** No.251982. Began 1934; interdenominational. Magazine: *Farmers Post* (6,500 annually), *Women's Circle Magazine* (400 every four months). Turnover £4,500 to year end Dec 98. Direct mail to farmers and pastoral service to farmers and those in rural Britain with evangelistic emphasis.
☎ 01255 508 492
See also: Rural Christian Information Centre

Free Presbyterian Publications, 133 Woodlands Road, Glasgow G3 6LE
General Treasurer: Mr Roderick A Campbell. No other staff. ***CC*** No.SCO 03545. Began 1893; Presbyterian. Magazine: *Free Presbyterian Magazine* (2,000 monthly), *Young Peoples' Magazine* (1,800 monthly). Turnover £57,835 to year end Dec 97. Publication of Christian literature.
Web: www.fpchurch.org.uk
Email: gentreas@compuserve.com
☎ 0141 332 9283 🖷 0141 332 4271

Gage Postal Books, PO Box 105, Westcliff-on-Sea SS0 8EQ
Proprietor: Mr Simon A Routh. Executive staff 1, Other staff 2. Began 1971; non-denominational. No magazine. Turnover £60,000 to year end Nov 96. Buying and selling second-hand church history and theological books.
Web: home.clara.net/gagebooks
Email: gagebooks@clara.net
☎ 01702 715 133

***Gates of Praise**, Vine Christian Centre, Australian Terrace, Bridgend CF31 1LY
Administrator: Mrs Pamela Roberts. Executive staff 1, Other staff 2. ***CC*** Began 1993; non-denominational. (Previously Living Vine Fellowship). No magazine. Turnover n/a. Importing and distributing Christian literature and tapes to bookshops and churches in the UK.
Email: pastoralex@yahoo.com
☎ 01656 664 245 🖷 01656 662 252

Go Teach Publications Ltd, Unit 3T, Zan Industrial Park, Crewe Road, Wheelock, Sandbach CW11 0QD
Editorial Director: Mr Timothy Reynolds. Executive staff 2, Other staff 2. ***CC*** No.275116. Began 1946; interdenominational. No magazine. Turnover n/a. Providing quarterly Sunday School teaching materials for the aged 3 to 15 years.
Email: goteach@btinternet.com
☎ 01270 768 387 🖷 01270 768 387
Distribution enquiries and orders: *Business Manager:* Mr Brian Kuhrt, The Christian Bookshop, Sevenoaks Road, Pratts Bottom, Orpington BR6 7SQ
☎ 01689 854 117 🖷 01689 851 060

Good News Christian Books & Videos, 18 Rosamund Avenue, Wimborne BH21 1TE
Owners: Mr J A & Mrs O E Burry. No full-time staff. Began 1984; interdenominational. No magazine. Turnover £1,000 to year end Apr 98. Distributing Christian books and videos with a mobile unit and also a video recording service.
☎ 01202 880 081

Gospel Literature Outreach, 78 Muir Street, Motherwell ML1 1BN
Co-ordinator, Europe: Mr John Speirs. All voluntary staff. ***CC*** No.SCO 41802. Began 1974; Christian Brethren. Magazine: *Spearhead* (4,500 every four months). Turnover n/a. Distributing Christian literature through teams operating worldwide; church planting; training for Christian service courses.
Web: members.aol.com/gloadmin/GLO.htm
Email: gloadmin@aol.com
☎ 01698 263 483 🖷 01698 275 418

Gradwell Concepts, 197 Brodie Avenue, Mossley Hill, Liverpool L18 4RQ
Proprietor: Rev Eric G Davies. No other staff. Began 1987; evangelical. No magazine. Turnover n/a. Christian and general booksellers and out-of-print book searchers.
☎ 0151 724 1219

Harrison Trust, PO Box 47, Ramsgate CT11 9XB
Secretary: Dr Derek A Scales. No full-time staff. ***CC*** No.234959. Began 1894; Anglican. No magazine. Turnover n/a. Publishing literature to promote the principles and doctrines of the Reformation.
☎ 01843 580 542

Harvest Field Distributors, Harvest Fields, Unit 13, Wheatley Hall Business Centre, Wheatley Hall Road, Doncaster DN2 4LP
Manager: Mr Andrew Golba. Other staff 9. Began 1990; non-denominational. No magazine. Turnover n/a. Distributing to Christian bookshops Bibles, books, cards, CDs and cassettes, games, pictures and gift ideas.
☎ 01302 367 868 🖷 01302 361 006

Hoplon Plastic Cards, 1st Floor, 83 Long Lane, Halesowen B62 9DJ
Proprietor: Mr Kenneth Ball. Executive staff 1, Other staff 1. Began 1990; non-denominational. No magazine. Turnover £25,000 to year end Apr 98. Producing Scripturally-based plastic hand-held cards for evangelism and cards to customers own designs.
Web: ourworld.compuserve.com/homepages/plasticcards
Email: plasticcards@compuserve.com
☎ 0121 561 2472 🖷 0121 561 2495

Horizons Distributors, 13 Victory Grove, Audenshaw, Manchester M34 5XA
Director: Mr Colin Carson. Other staff 3. Began 1993; Assemblies of God. (Previously Reflections Distributors). No magazine. Turnover n/a. Printing and distributing Bibles, books, hymnals, baptismal and dedication certificates, cards, crafts, gifts and novelties.
Email: ccarson129@aol.com
☎ 0161 301 1162 🖷 0161 370 2494

Hosanna Books & Music Ltd, 41 Heston Road, Hounslow TW5 0QH
Director: Mrs Janet Clayton. Executive staff 2, Admin staff 2. Began 1996; non-denominational. Turnover n/a. European distributor for Harold Shaw Publishers; distributing Fisherman Bible Study Guides and books.
Web: www.hosanna.co.uk
Email: hosanna@compuserve.com
☎ 020 8737 0367 🖷 020 8737 0368

Humber Books, Rozel House, 4 St Marys Lane, Barton-upon-Humber DN18 5EX
Proprietor: Mr & Mrs P M Cresswell. No other staff. Began 1972; non-denominational. Magazine: *Antiquarian Theology* (Circulation n/a every two months). Turnover n/a. Retailing rare antiquarian and secondhand religious books and Bibles. Specialising pre-1700 imprints. International.
Web: www.netguides.co.uk/ukhumber.html
Email: humber-books@netguides.co.uk
☎ 01652 634 958 🖷 01652 634 965

Jarom Books, 18 Rigby Close, Croydon CR0 4JU
Manager: Mr Jacques R More. No full-time staff. Began 1993; non-denominational. No magazine. Turnover n/a. Publishing new Christian monographs, booklets and books.
Web: homepages.tesco.net/jacquesmore/book_cover.htm
Email: jacquesmore@tesco.net
☎ 020 8680 3635

***Kingsway Church Ministries**, Lottbridge Drove, Eastbourne BN23 6NT
Division Head: Mrs Sue Price. Other staff 9. Began 1987; interdenominational. (Previously David C Cook Resources). Part of Kingsway Communications. Magazine: *Children's ministry* (2,000 quarterly). Turnover n/a. Distributing Bible-in-Life and Scripture Press Sunday School curriculum and David C Cook Church Ministry Resources.
Email: churchministries@kingsway.co.uk
☎ 01323 437 749 🖷 01323 411 970

***Kitab**, PO Box 16, Failsworth, Manchester M35 9QL
Manager: Mr Ken Stocks. Executive staff 1, Other staff 1. ***CC*** No.250222. Began 1989; non-denominational. Owned by INTERSERVE. Magazine: *Ahl-i-Kitab* (1,000 every four months). Turnover £10,000 to year end Dec 96. Resources of Christian and secular books, videos etc, on the Muslim world, including foreign/minority languages.
Email: kitab.uk@domini.org
☎ 0161 678 6838 🖷 0161 628 4051

A M Laverty & Co Ltd, Marian House, Otley LS21 3JG
Director: Mr E C Laverty. Executive staff 2, Other staff 4. Began 1955; Roman Catholic. No magazine. Turnover n/a. Wholesale distributors of devotional and religious articles.
☎ 01943 462 032 🖷 01943 462 032

***Leadership Bookclub**, 6 Norton Street, Nottingham NG7 3HR
Bookclub Editor: Ms Kate Byrom. Executive staff 1, Admin staff 1. ***CC*** No.273458. Began 1936; non-denominational. Part of IVP. No magazine. Turnover included in IVP. Bookclub for church leaders of any denomination.
Web: www.ivpbooks.com
Email: ivp@nottm.cix.co.uk
☎ 0115 978 1054 🖷 0115 942 2694

B

B McCall Barbour, 28 George IV Bridge, Edinburgh EH1 1ES
Managing Partner: Rev Dr T C Danson-Smith. Executive staff 2, Other staff 3. Began 1900; non-denominational but fundamental. No magazine. Turnover n/a. Publishing books and greeting cards. Dr Danson-Smith is available for weekend ministry and evangelism.
☎ 0131 225 4816

Maranatha Christian Ministries Resource Centre International, PO Box 506, Portslade, Brighton BN41 2ZG
Director: Mr Eric Long. No full-time staff. Began 1987; interdenominational. No magazine. Turnover n/a. Supplying Bibles, cassettes, electronic Bibles, books, greeting cards, gifts, free local audio & video library.
☎ 01273 414 990 🖷 01273 700 116

***MasterPlan Publishing Ltd**, Thames House, 63 Kingston Road, New Malden KT3 3PB
Managing Director: Mr Bob Fleming. *Directors:* Mrs Jill Fleming, Mr Gordon Miller. Executive staff 8, Other staff 17. Began 1984; non-denominational. Turnover £5,000,000 [includes holidays division] to year end Sep 98. Distributing American Christian magazines.
Email: mplanluk@aol.com
☎ 020 8942 9442 🖷 020 8949 4396

Mourne Missionary Trust, Hor-Kesel, 4 Church Road, Carginagh, Kilkeel, Newry BT34 4QB
Director: Mr George McConnell. Executive staff 1. Began 1976; Free Presbyterian. No magazine. Turnover n/a. Bookseller, publisher and literature distributor at markets and fairs in Ulster.
☎ 028 3027 62248 🖷 028 3076 5574

National Bible Society of Scotland, Bible House, 7 Hampton Terrace, Edinburgh EH12 5XU
Sales Administrator: Miss Sharon Duncan. Executive staff 3, Other staff 8. ***CC*** Began 1861; but Edinburgh Bible Society 1809; interdenominational. Magazine: *Word at Work* (70,000 every four months). Turnover n/a. Supplying Bibles and resource materials. Mail Order and Trade sales throughout Scotland.
Web: www.nat-bible-society.org
Email: nbss@nat-bible-society.org
☎ 0800 526 910 🖷 0131 337 0641

New Life Publishing Co, PO Box 277, Sunderland SR1 1YE
Editor: Mr Peter Wreford. Executive staff 2, Other staff 5. Began 1982; interdenominational. Magazine: *Joy Magazine* (60,000 monthly). Turnover n/a. Publishers of Christian books, magazines, newspapers.
Email: editor.newlife@ukonline.co.uk
☎ 0191 568 0424 🖷 0191 568 0428

***Nova Marketing**, Lottbridge Drove, Eastbourne BN23 6NT
Sales Manager: Mr Paul Mogford. Began 1984; non-denominational. Part of Kingsway Communications Ltd. No magazine. Turnover n/a. Distributing Christian literature.
☎ 01323 437 734 🖷 01323 411 970

Onesimus Books, PO Box 463, Bristol BS99 1DH
Proprietor: Mr Chris J Mansfield. Executive staff 2, Other staff 1. Began 1986; non-denominational. No magazine. Turnover n/a. Mail order book service with 2,000 new and 6,000 second-hand titles.
Email: ones463uk@aol.com
☎ 0117 951 4794

Overseas Tract Mission, 109 Avondale Crescent, Grange, Cardiff CF1 7DF
Director: Mr Fred K Dodds. Executive staff 1, Other staff 1. Began 1940; interdenominational. No magazine. Turnover n/a. Publishing and distributing foreign Gospel literature in Britain.
☎ 029 2034 5342

***Oxfordshire Community Churches**, Area Centre, 51 West Way, Oxford OX2 0JE
Publisher: Rev Stephen Thomas. *Area Administrator:* Mr Andy O'Connell. Executive staff 15, Admin staff 4. ***CC*** No.1056921. Began 1982; non-denominational. Magazine: *Area News* (500 every two months). Turnover included in main entry. Publishers of teaching booklets.
Web: www.oxcc.u-net.com
Email: office@occ.org.uk
☎ 01865 793 003 🖷 01865 793 025

Pendle Christian Book Service, 18 Woodville Road, Brierfield, Nelson BB9 5RW
Proprietors: Rev David L White, Mr Jonathan P White. Executive staff 1. Began n/a; interdenominational. No magazine. Turnover n/a. Providing Christian book service including mail order.
Email: wwhite@provider.co.uk
☎ 01282 613 094 🖷 01282 613 094

Penfold Book and Bible House Ltd, Telford Road, Industrial Estate, Bicester OX6 0TZ
Managing Director: Mr Michael J Penfold. Executive staff 1, Other staff 3. Began 1986; non-denominational. Turnover n/a. Distributing fundamental books, cassettes and videos from USA; specialists in tracts and evangelistic materials.
Email: penfoldbooks@characterlink.net
☎ 01869 249 574 🖷 01869 244 033

Derek Prince Ministries - UK, PO Box 77, Harpenden AL5 1PJ
Director: Mr Mark Buchanan. Executive staff 3, Other staff 10. ***CC*** No.327763. Began 1983; interdenominational. No magazine. Turnover £726,000 to year end Mar 98. International producer/distributor of Biblical foundational teaching resources (books, audios, videos, radio and television broadcasting).
Web: www.derekprince.com
Email: enquiries@uk.derekprince.com
☎ 01582 466 200 🖷 01582 766 777

Protestant Truth Society Inc and the Wickliffe Preachers, 184 Fleet Street, London EC4A 2HJ
Secretary: Rev Samuel R McKay. Executive staff 6, Other staff 4. ***CC*** No.248505. Began 1889; interdenominational. Magazine: *Protestant Truth* (3,000 every two months). Turnover £65,000 to year end Mar 94. Furtherance of Christ's gospel and the promotion of the Protestant Reformed religion and faith.
☎ 020 7405 4960

***The Public Transport Scripture Text Mission**, PO Box 99, Loughton IG10 3QJ
Administrator: Mr Peter Martin. No full-time staff. *CC* No.233136. Began 1883; Protestant. No magazine. Turnover £31,014 to year end Dec 97. Displaying Scripture posters to the travelling public throughout the UK.
Email: stewardship@compuserve.com
☎ 020 8502 5600 🖷 020 8502 5333

Rosemary Pugh Second Hand Books, 59b Old Sarum Airfield, Salisbury SP4 6DZ
Owner: Mrs Rosemary M Pugh. Full-time staff 1. Began 1991; non-denominational. (Previously Pugh & Greatrex Second Hand Books). No magazine. Turnover n/a. Mail order distribution of second-hand books with 8,000 titles in stock.
Web: www.freenet.co.uk/homepages/rosemarypugh/home.html
Email: rosemarypugh@freenet.co.uk
☎ 01722 330 132 🖷 01722 338 508

Quidenham Bookservice, Carmelite Monastery, Quidenham, Norwich NR16 2PH
Manager: Sister Mary Garnet. No other staff. Began 1986; Roman Catholic but ecumenical. No magazine. Turnover £12,000 to year end Apr 98. Distributing Christian literature to Retreat Centres, religious houses and individuals.
☎ 01953 887 202

Renewal Servicing, PO Box 17, Shepperton TW17 8NU
Hon Director: Rev John Richards. All voluntary staff. *CC* No.283064. Began 1981; interdenominational. No magazine. Turnover £2,700 to year end Jan 96. Writing, printing, publication and mail-order service for Christian literature.
Web: www.renewal-servicing.freeserve.co.uk/
Email: richards@renewal-servicing.freeserve.co.uk
☎ No telephone

Russian Orthodox Bookshop, All Saints, Ennismore Gardens, London SW7 1NH
Manager: Miss Tatiana Wolff. No full-time staff. *CC* No.254025. Began n/a; Orthodox. Turnover n/a. Selling retail and mail order Orthodox books, music and icons.
Web: home.clara.net/sourozh
Email: tawolff@aol.com
☎ 020 7722 2879 (book orders only)

***Scripture Union Mail Order Department**, PO Box 764, Oxford OX4 5JF
Coordinator: Jenny Smith. *Chief Executive:* Mr Peter Kimber. Executive staff 1, Other staff 1. *CC* No.213422. Began 1867; interdenominational. Turnover n/a. Postal service for Scripture Union books and resources; 400 titles.
Web: www.scriptureunion.org.uk
Email: postmaster@scriptureunion.org.uk
☎ 01865 716 880 🖷 01865 715 152

***Send The Light Ltd**, PO Box 300, Kingstown Broadway, Carlisle CA3 0QS
Chief Executive: Mr Keith Danby. Executive staff 19, Other staff 515. *CC* Began 1963; non-denominational. Magazine: *The Bulletin* (25,000 monthly). Turnover £25,500,000 to year end Jan 98. Distributing, wholesaling, publishing and retailing of Christian books, music and software.
Email: postmaster@stl.org
☎ 01228 512 512 🖷 01228 514 949

***SGM International**, Radstock House, 3 Eccleston Street, London SW1W 9LZ
Executive Director: Mr Bryan Stonehouse. *International Director:* Mr Hugh Davies. *International Publishing Director:* Mr David Atkinson. Executive staff 4, Other staff 36. *CC* Began 1888; non-denominational. (Previously Scripture Gift Mission). Magazine: *Interact* (30,000 quarterly). Turnover £2,700,000 to year end Dec 98. Distributing Bible portions in over 400 languages.
Web: members.aol.com/sgmint
Email: lon@sgm.org
☎ 020 7730 2155 🖷 020 7730 0240
Also at: 218 York Street, Belfast BT15 1GY
Email: ire@sgm.org
☎ 028 9038 75282

Sovereign Grace Advent Testimony, 1 Donald Way, Chelmsford CM2 9JB
Hon Secretary: Mr Stephen A Toms. No full-time staff. *CC* No.261489. Began 1918; interdenominational. Magazine: *Watching and Waiting* (3,000 quarterly). Turnover n/a. Providing exposition of Bible doctrine and prophecy.
☎ 01245 268 815

SPCK Bookshops Head Office, Holy Trinity Church, Marylebone Road, London NW1 4DU
Bookshops Director: Mr Peter Cheney. *CC* No.231144. Began n/a; interdenominational. Society for Promoting Christian Knowledge. Turnover n/a. Supplying Christian books, gifts and resources through SPCK's bookshops and mail order facilities.
Web: www.spck.org.uk
Email: pcheney@spck.org.uk
☎ 020 7387 5282 🖷 020 7387 3410
Mail Order
Email: mailorder@spck.org.uk
☎ 0345 626 747 (local rate)
Also at: *SPCK Northern Regional Manager:* Mrs Dora Smith, The Great Kitchen, Durham Cathedral, Durham DH1 3EQ
Email: dsmith@spck.org.uk
☎ 0191 386 0188 🖷 0191 383 1976
And: *SPCK Southern Regional Manager:* Mrs Hazel Wray, 7 Castle Street, Reading RG1 7SB
Email: hwray@spck.org.uk
☎ 0118 959 9011 🖷 0118 951 2160

Spearhead, Unit 7, Huffwood Trading Estate, Brookers Road, Billingshurst RH14 9UR
Proprietor: Mr Jeremy Bishopp. Other staff 5. Began 1986; non-denominational. No magazine. Turnover n/a. Publishing Christian posters, cards, calendars, books; distributing Bibles, tapes, videos, posters, cards and books.
Email: spearhead@uk.iccc.net
☎ 01403 785 785 🖷 01403 785 785

Startwrite, New Life Bible Church, 1 Graham Road, Wealdstone, Harrow HA3 5RP
IT Manager: Mr John Udoh. Other staff 4. *CC* No.295876. Began 1982; non-denominational. No magazine. Turnover n/a. Specialising in leadership, counselling and teaching books; sole distributor for City Bible Publishing; audio tapes ministry.
Email: jeyu@talk21.com
☎ 020 8427 0985 🖷 020 8933 8266

Sword Publications Ltd, Summerhill Court, Lang Stracht, Aberdeen AB15 6TW
Contact: Fiona Graham. Executive staff 2, Other staff 3. *CC* No.SCO 21984. Began 1978; non-denominational. No magazine. Turnover £20,000 to year end Apr 98. Specialising in faith books. Sole distributor for Mary-Alice Isleib. Audio and video tapes ministry.
☎ 01224 326 622 🖷 01224 312 727

B

Teal Press Ltd, Unit 12, Bunns Bank, Old Buckenham, Attleborough NR17 1QD
Director: Mr A Sayers. Executive staff 3, Other staff 10. Began 1985; non-denominational. No magazine. Turnover n/a. Wholesaling Christian literature, greetings cards, stationery, gift products.
Email: the_word@tealpress.freeserve.co.uk
☎ 01953 455 718 🖷 01953 455 190

TELit, 144a Ferry Road, Edinburgh EH6 4NX
General Secretary: Mr Barry Sprott. Other staff 2. ***CC*** No.SCO 08979. Began 1990; non-denominational. Magazine: *Newsletter* (Circulation n/a quarterly). Turnover n/a. Producing thematic evangelistic literature in a contemporary format for specific places, events and everyday activities.
Web: www.users.globalnet.co.uk/~telit/
Email: telit@globalnet.co.uk
☎ 0131 554 0339 🖷 0131 554 2330

TexStyle Graphics Ltd, 18 Pendre Industrial Estate, Tywyn LL36 9LW
Managing Director: Mr M Stevens. Executive staff 1, Other staff 2. Began 1982; non-denominational. (Previously Rainbow Company). No magazine. Turnover £300,000 to year end Dec 98. Marketing Christian T-shirts and sweat shirts by mail order and at exhibitions.
☎ 01654 710 137 🖷 01654 712 461

Tim Tiley Prints, Eblana Lodge, 157 Cheltenham Road, Bristol BS6 5RR
Managing Director: Mr Timothy F T Tiley. *Administration Manager:* Mrs Margaret Tiley. Executive staff 3, Other staff 8. Began 1974; non-denominational. No magazine. Turnover £530,000 to year end Dec 98. Producing and importing verse cards, bookmarks, small posters, frames, Christian gifts and novelties.
Email: tim.tiley@virgin.net
☎ 0117 942 3397 🖷 0117 942 0433

Victory European Ministries, PO Box 204, Southfleet, Gravesend DA13 9LG
Director: Mr Roger Harris. Executive staff 1. Began 1988; non-denominational. No magazine. Turnover n/a. European distribution of books, cassettes and tracts including Dr Hobart E Freeman, Faith Ministries & Publications, Dr Russell K Tardo, Faithful Word Ministries & Publications and others.
Email: faith@victoryeuropeanmins.freeserve.co.uk
☎ 01474 833 107 🖷 01474 833 107

***Victory Tracts and Posters**, Portland Road, London SE25 4PN
Director: Mr Jack Shellard. Executive staff 1, Other staff 2. ***CC*** No.229741. Began 1945; interdenominational. No magazine. Turnover £15,171 to year end Jan 98. Publishers of salvation gospel tracts, Bible text posters and a range of answer series booklets.
Web: www.victory10.freeserve.co.uk
Email: info@victory10.freeserve.co.uk
☎ 020 8656 2297 🖷 020 8656 2582

Wesley Owen Direct, PO Box 19, Kingstown Broadway, Carlisle CA3 0BR
Manager: Mr Mick Goodman. Other staff 8. ***CC*** Began n/a; interdenominational. No magazine. Turnover n/a. Mail order department for Wesley Owen Books and Music.
Email: wesleyowen@stl.org
☎ 0800 834 315 🖷 01228 514 949

Westminsterlink, Bethany Chapel Lane, Pirbright, Woking GU24 0JZ
Secretary: Mr John Horrocks. All voluntary staff. ***CC*** Began 1986; non-denominational. No magazine. Turnover n/a. Selling tapes, journals and articles from Westminster Theological Seminary.
☎ 01483 474 286

Whittles Publishing, Roseleigh House, Harbour Road, Latheronwheel, Latheron KW5 6DW
Proprietor: Dr Keith Whittles. Executive staff 1, Other staff 2. Began 1986; non-denominational. No magazine. Turnover n/a. Distributing books on the relationship of theology to contemporary issues.
Email: whittle@globalnet.co.uk
☎ 01593 741 240 🖷 01593 741 360

***Word Music and Publishing**, 9 Holdom Avenue, Bletchley, Milton Keynes MK1 1QR
Managing Director: Mr Graham Williams. *Head of Music:* Mr Jonathan Brown. *Head of Publishing:* Mr Malcolm Down. Executive staff 12, Other staff 38. Began 1967; non-denominational. (Previously Word Publishing & Nelson Word). Magazine: *Premier* (30,000 monthly). Premier Club (books, bibles, music, videos and software).
Web: www.premieronline.co.uk
Email: info@wordonline.co.uk
☎ 01908 648 440 🖷 01908 648 592

CHURCHES

See Extra Information Section on Page 526

C

CATHEDRALS

ROMAN CATHOLIC DIOCESES

Arundel and Brighton, Cathedral Church of Our Lady and St Philip Howard, Cathedral House, Parsons Hill, Arundel BN18 9AY
Administrator: Canon Anthony Whale. ***CC*** No.252878. Began 1873.
Email: aruncath1@aol.com
☎ 01903 882 297 ℻ 01903 885 335

Birmingham, Metropolitan Cathedral Church of St Chad, Cathedral House, St Chads Queensway, Birmingham B4 6EU
Adminstrator: Rev Father Bede Walsh.
☎ 0121 236 2251

Brentwood, Cathedral Church of St Mary and St Helen, Clergy House, 28 Ingrave Road, Brentwood CM15 8AT
Administrator: Rev David Manson
☎ 01277 210 107

C

Cardiff, Metropolitan Cathedral Church of St David, Cathedral Clergy House, St David's Cathedral, Charles Street, Cardiff CF1 4SF
Administrator: Rev Bernard Whitehouse
☎ 029 2023 1407

Clifton, Cathedral Church of SS Peter and Paul, Clifton Cathedral House, Clifton Park, Bristol BS8 3BX
Parish Priest: Mgr William Mitchell. ***CC*** No.233977.
Web: www.cliftoncathedral.org.uk
☎ 0117 973 8411 Mobile: 07774 698 691 ℻ 0117 974 4897

Derry, Cathedral Church of St Eugene, Parochial House, Derry BT48 9AP
Administrator: Very Rev John Farren ADM.
☎ 028 7126 2894/365712 ℻ 028 7137 7494

East Anglia, Cathedral Church of St John the Baptist, Cathedral House, Unthank Road, Norwich NR2 2PA
Administrator: Rev Father Paul Maddison.
☎ 01603 624 615 ℻ 01603 762 512

Hallam, Cathedral Church of Saint Marie, Rectory, Norfolk Street, Sheffield S1 2JB
Administrator: Rev Father Charles Neal.
☎ 0114 272 2522 ℻ 0114 276 3861

Hexham and Newcastle, Cathedral Church of St Mary, Clayton Street West, Newcastle upon Tyne NE1 5HH
Administrator: Rev Fr Michael Campion. Began 1844.
Web: www.hexham-newcastle-diocese.org.uk/stmaryscathedral
☎ 0191 232 6953 ℻ 0191 232 0913

Lancaster, Cathedral Church of St Peter, Cathedral House Presbytery, Balmoral Road, Lancaster LA1 3BT
Administrator: Fr Alf Hayes. ***CC*** No.234331.
☎ 01524 618 60 ℻ 01524 618 60

†**Leeds,** Cathedral Church of St Anne, Cathedral House, Great George Street, Leeds LS2 8BE
Administrator: Mgr Canon Peter McGuire
☎ 0113 245 3626 ℻ 0113 245 3626

Liverpool, Metropolitan Cathedral of Christ the King, Cathedral House, Mount Pleasant, Liverpool L3 5TQ
Administrator: Mgr Canon Peter Cookson.
Email: met.cathedral@cwcom.net
☎ 0151 709 9222 ℻ 0151 708 7274

Menevia, Cathedral Church of St Joseph, Convent Street, Greenhill, Swansea SA1 2BX
Bishop: Most Rev Daniel J Mullins.
☎ 01792 652 683

Middlesbrough, Cathedral Church of St Mary, Cathedral House Dalby Way, Coulby Newham, Middlesbrough TS8 0TW
Administrator: Rev Father Gerard Smyth.
☎ 01642 597 750

Northampton, Cathedral of Our Lady and St Thomas, Cathedral House, Kingsthorpe Road, Northampton NN2 6AG
Administrator: Rev Kenneth Payne.
☎ 01604 714 556 ℻ 01604 712 066

Nottingham, Cathedral Church of St Barnabas, Derby Road, Nottingham NG1 5AE
Administrator: Mgr Tom McGovern.
☎ 0115 953 9839 ℻ 0115 953 9840

Plymouth, Cathedral Church of St Mary and St Boniface, The Cathedral House, Cecil Street, Plymouth PL1 5HW
Administrator: Rev Bartholomew Nannery.
☎ 01752 662 537

Portsmouth, Cathedral Church of St John the Evangelist, Edinburgh Road, Portsmouth PO1 3HG
Administrator: Rev David Hopgood.
☎ 023 9282 6170 ℻ 023 9283 9143

Edinburgh, Cathedral Church of St Mary, Cathedral House, 61 York Place, Edinburgh EH1 3JD
Administrator: Rev David Gemmell.
☎ 0131 556 1798 / 0027 ℻ 0131 556 4281

Salford, Cathedral Church of St John the Evangelist, Cathedral House, 250 Chapel Street, Salford M3 5LL
Administrator: Rev Brendan Curley.
☎ 0161 834 0333 ℻ 0161 834 9596

Shrewsbury, Cathedral Church of our Lady Help of Christians and St Peter of Alcantara, Cathedral House, 11 Belmont, Shrewsbury SY1 1TE
Administrator: Rev Canon Francis Pullen.
☎ 01743 362 366

Southwark, Metropolitan Cathedral of St George, Clergy House, Westminster Bridge Road, Southwark, London SE1 7HY
Administrator: Rev James Cronin. ***CC*** No.235468. Began 1848.
Email: stgeorges@rc.net
☎ 020 7928 5256

Westminster, Metropolitan Cathedral of the Most Precious Blood, Cathedral Clergy House, 42 Francis Street, London SW1P 1QW
Administrator: Mgr George Stack. ***CC*** No.233699.
Web: www.westminstercathedral.org.uk
☎ 020 7798 9055 ℻ 020 7798 9090

Wrexham, Cathedral Church of Our Lady of Sorrows, Regent Street, Wrexham LL11 1RB
Administrator: Rev Peter M Brignall. ***CC*** No.700426. Cathedral parish and hospital chaplaincy.
☎ 01978 263 943 ℻ 01978 352 277

CHURCH IN WALES DIOCESES

Monmouth, Cathedral Church of St Woolos, Stow Hill, Newport NP9 4EA
Dean: Very Rev Richard Fenwick. *Administrator:* Mr Brian Cox.
☎ 01633 212 077 🖷 01633 212 077

St Asaph, Cathedral Church of St Asaph, Cathedral Office, High Street, St Asaph LL17 0RF
Dean: Very Rev T R Kerry Goulstone. *Administrator:* Mrs M Murphy.
☎ 01745 583 429

St David's, Cathedral Church of St David and St Andrew, The Deanery, St Davids SA62 6RU
Dean: Very Rev J Wyn Evans. *Administrator:* Moyra Skenfield.
☎ 01437 720 202 🖷 01437 721 194

Swansea and Brecon, Cathedral Church of St John the Evangelist, Cathedral Close, Brecon LD3 9DP
Dean: Very Rev Geraint Hughes.
☎ 01874 623 344 🖷 01874 623 344

CHURCH OF ENGLAND DIOCESES

Bath and Wells, Cathedral Church of St Andrew in Wells, The Dean's Lodgings, 25 The Liberty, Wells BA5 2SZ
Dean: Very Rev Richard Lewis.
Email: deanwells@wellscathedra.u-net.com
☎ 01749 670 278 🖷 01749 679 184

Birmingham, Cathedral Church of St Philip, Birmingham Cathedral, Colmore Row, Birmingham B3 2QB
Provost: Very Rev Gordon Mursell. *Chapter Clerk:* Dr Andrew Page.
☎ 0121 236 4333/6323 🖷 0121 212 0868

Blackburn, Cathedral Church of St Mary The Virgin, Cathedral Close, Blackburn BB1 5AA
Provost: Very Rev David Frayne. *Chapter Clerk:* Mr T Hoyle. Turnover £200,000 to year end Dec 98.
☎ 01254 514 91

Bradford, Cathedral Church of St Peter, Cathedral Office, 1 Stott Hill, Bradford BD1 4EH
Provost: Very Rev John Richardson.
☎ 01274 777 724 🖷 01274 777 730

Bristol, Cathedral Church of the Holy and Undivided Trinity, Cathedral Office, Bristol Cathedral, College Green, Bristol BS1 5TJ
Dean: Very Rev Robert Grimley.
☎ 0117 926 4879 🖷 0117 925 3678

Canterbury, Cathedral and Metropolitical Church of Christ, Cathedral Office, Cathedral House, 11 The Precincts, Canterbury CT1 2EH
Dean: Very Rev Dr John Simpson. *Receiver General:* Brigadier John Meardon.
☎ 01227 762 862 🖷 01227 865 222

Carlisle, Carlisle Cathedral Church of the Holy and Undivided Trinity, Cathedral Office, 7 The Abbey, Carlisle CA3 8TZ
Dean: Very Rev Graeme Knowles. Treasury exhibition, shop, restaurant, education centre, disabled access.
☎ 01228 523 335 🖷 01228 548 151

Chelmsford, Cathedral Church of St Mary The Virgin, St Peter and St Cedd, Cathedral Office, New Street, Chelmsford CM1 1TY
Provost: Very Rev Peter Judd.
☎ 01245 294 480 🖷 01245 496 802

Chester, Cathedral Church of Christ and the Blessed Virgin Mary, Cathedral Office, 12 Abbey Square, Chester CH1 2HU
Dean: Very Rev Stephen Smalley. *Administrator:* Mr David Burrows. Turnover £800,000 to year end Dec 98.
Web: www.chestercathedral.org.uk
Email: office@chestercathedral.org.uk
☎ 01244 324 756 🖷 01244 341 110

Chichester, Cathedral Church of the Holy Trinity, The Deanery, Canon Lane, Chichester PO19 1PX
Dean: Very Rev John Treadgold.
☎ 01243 787 337

Coventry, Cathedral Church of St Michael, Pelham Lee House, 7 Priory Row, Coventry CV1 5ES
Provost: Very Rev John Petty. *Marketing/Promotions Officer:* Mrs C R Monks. Turnover £500,000 to year end Dec 98. Rebuilt after its destruction to the glory of God and testimony to reconciliation.
Web: www.coventrycathedral.org
Email: information@coventrycathedral.org.uk
☎ 024 7622 7597 🖷 024 7663 1448

Derby, Cathedral Church of All Saints, Cathedral Office, St Michael's House, Queen Street, Derby DE1 3DT
Provost of Derby: Very Rev Michael Perham, The Provost's House, 9 Highfield Road, Derby DE22 1GX. *Administrator:* Mr William J Hall, Cathedral Office, St Michael's House, Queen Street, Derby DE1 3DT.
Email: derby.cathedral@btinternet.com
☎ 01332 341 201 🖷 01332 203 991

Durham, Cathedral Church of Christ and Blessed Mary the Virgin of Durham, The Chapter Office, The College, Durham DH1 3EH
Dean: Very Rev John Arnold.
Web: www.btinternet.com/~durhamcathedral/
Email: durhamcathedral@btinternet.com
☎ 0191 386 4266 🖷 0191 386 4267

†Ely, Cathedral Church of The Holy and Undivided Trinity, The Deanery, The College, Ely CB7 4DN
Dean: Very Rev Michael Higgins.
☎ 01353 667 735

Exeter, Cathedral Church of St Peter, The Deanery, Exeter EX1 1HT
Dean: Very Rev Keith Jones.
Email: admin@exeter-cathedral.org.uk
☎ 01392 255 573 🖷 01392 498 769

Gloucester, Cathedral Church of St Peter and the Holy and Indivisible Trinity, The Deanery, Miller's Green, Gloucester GL1 2BP
Dean: Very Rev Nicholas Bury.
☎ 01452 524 167

Guildford, Cathedral Church of the Holy Spirit, Cathedral Office, Guildford Cathedral, Stag Hill, Guildford GU2 5UP
Dean: Very Rev Alexander Wedderspoon.
Email: info@guildford-cathedral.org
☎ 01483 565 287 🖷 01483 303 350

Hereford, Cathedral Church of the Blessed Virgin Mary and St Ethelbert, Cathedral Office, 5 College Cloisters, Hereford HR1 2NG
Dean: Very Rev Robert Willis.
Email: office@herefordcathedral.co.uk
☎ 01432 359 880 🖷 01432 355 929

Leicester, Cathedral Church of St Martin, Cathedral Office, 1 St Martins East, Leicester LE1 5FX
Provost: To be appointed.
Email: cathedral@leicester.anglican.org
☎ 0116 262 5294 🖷 0116 262 5295

Lichfield, Cathedral Church of the Blessed Virgin Mary and St Chad, Chapter Office, 19a The Close, Lichfield WS13 7LD
Dean: Very Rev Michael Yorke. Turnover £750,000 to year end Dec 98.
Web: www.lichfield-cathedral.org
Email: lich.cath@virgin.net
☎ 01543 306 100 🖷 01543 306 109

C

Lincoln, Cathedral Church of the Blessed Virgin Mary, Chapter Office, The Cathedral, Lincoln LN2 1PZ
Dean: Very Rev Alex Knight.
☎ 01522 530 320

Liverpool, Cathedral Church of Christ, The Cathedral, St James' Mount, Liverpool L1 7AZ
Dean: Very Rev Rupert Hoare (from Feb 2000). *Treasurer:* Canon Noel T Vincent.
☎ 0151 709 6271 🖷 0151 709 1112

London, Cathedral Church of St Paul, Chapter House, St Pauls Churchyard, London EC4M 8AD
Dean: Very Rev John Moses.
Web: stpauls.london.anglican.org
Email: chapterhouse@stpaulscathedral.org.uk
☎ 020 7236 4128 🖷 020 7332 0298

Manchester, Cathedral and Collegiate Church of St Mary St Denys & St George, The Cathedral, Cathedral Yard, Manchester M3 1SX
Dean: Very Rev Kenneth Riley.
Email: manchester.cathedral@btinternet.com
☎ 0161 833 2220 🖷 0161 839 6226

Newcastle, Cathedral Church of St Nicholas, The Cathedral Office, St Nicholas Churchyard, Newcastle upon Tyne NE1 1PF
Provost: Very Rev Nicholas Coulton.
Email: stnicholas@aol.com
☎ 0191 232 1939 🖷 0191 230 0735

Norwich, Cathedral Church of the Holy and Undivided Trinity, Cathedral Office, 12 The Close, Norwich NR1 4DH
Dean: Very Rev Stephen Platten.
☎ 01603 218 308 🖷 01603 766 032

Oxford, Cathedral Church of Christ, The Deanery, Christ Church, Oxford OX1 1DP
Dean: Very Rev John Drury.
☎ 01865 276 161 🖷 01865 276 238

***Peterborough,** Cathedral Church of St Peter, St Paul and St Andrew, Chapter Office, Minster Precincts, Peterborough PE1 1XS
Chapter Clerk: Bernard Kane.
☎ 01733 343 342 🖷 01733 552 465
Dean: Very Rev Michael Bunker, The Deanery, Minster Precincts, Peterborough PE1 1XS
☎ 01733 562 780 🖷 01733 897 874

Portsmouth, Cathedral Church of St Thomas of Canterbury Cathedral Office, St Thomas's Street, Portsmouth PO1 2HH
Provost: To be appointed.
☎ 023 9282 3300 🖷 023 9229 5480

Ripon and Leeds, Cathedral Church of St Peter and St Wilfrid, The Chapter House, Ripon Cathedral, Ripon HG4 1QT
Dean: Very Rev John Methuen. Worship, work & witness.
Web: www.riponcathedral.org.uk
Email: postmaster@riponcathedral.org.uk
☎ 01765 602 072

Rochester, Cathedral Church of Christ and the Blessed Virgin Mary, The Cathedral Office, Garth House, The Precincts, Rochester ME1 1SX
Dean: Very Rev Edward Shotter. Provide educational activities and guided tours for all ages and abilities.
☎ 01634 843 366 🖷 01634 401 410

St Albans, Cathedral and Abbey Church of St Alban, Cathedral Office, The Chapter House, Sumpter Yard, St Albans AL1 1BY
Dean: Very Rev Christopher Lewis. *Sub Dean:* Rev Canon Christopher Foster. *Cathedral Administrator:* Mr Nicholas Bates. Turnover £750,000 to year end Dec 98.
Web: www.stalbansdioc.org.uk/cathedral/
Email: cathedral@alban.u-net.com
☎ 01727 860 780 🖷 01727 850 944

St Edmundsbury and Ipswich, Cathedral Church of St James, Cathedral Office, Angel Hill, Bury St Edmunds IP33 1LS
Provost: Very Rev James Atwell.
Email: cathedral@btinternet.com
☎ 01284 754 933 🖷 01284 768 655

Salisbury, Cathedral Church of the Blessed Virgin Mary, The Deanery, 7 The Close, Salisbury SP1 2EF
Dean: Very Rev Derek Watson.
☎ 01722 555 110 🖷 01722 555 155

Sheffield, Cathedral Church of St Peter and St Paul, Cathedral Office, Church Street, Sheffield S1 1HA
Provost: Very Rev Michael Sadgrove.
Web: www.sheff.ac.uk/uni/projects/sheffcath
Email: sheffcath@aol.com
☎ 0114 275 3434 🖷 0114 278 0244

Sodor and Man, Cathedral Church of St German, Chapter House, 1 Kelly Close, Ramsey IM8 2AR
Bishop and Dean: Rt Rev Nöel Jones. 26 The Fountains, Ballure Promenade, Ramsey IM8 1NN.
☎ 01624 816 545 🖷 01624 816 545

Southwark, Cathedral and Collegiate Church of St Saviour & St Mary Overie, Cathedral Office, Montague Close, Southwark, London SE1 9DA
Provost: Very Rev Colin Slee. *Canon Pastor:* Rev Canon Helen Cunliffe. *Administrator:* Mrs Sarah King. Turnover £600,000 to year end Dec 98.
Web: www.dswark.org
Email: cathedral@dswark.org.uk
☎ 020 7407 3708 🖷 020 7357 7389

Southwell, Cathedral and Parish Church of the Blessed Virgin Mary, The Minster Office, Trebeck Hall, Bishop's Drive, Southwell NG25 0JP
Provost: Very Rev David Leaning.
☎ 01636 812 649 🖷 01636 815 904

Truro, Cathedral Church of St Mary, Cathedral Office, 21 Old Bridge Street, Truro TR1 2AH
Dean: Very Rev Michael Moxon. *Administrator:* Mrs Bette Owen. *Visitor Officer:* Mrs Wendy Lloyd. Turnover £557,000 to year end Dec 98.
☎ 01872 276 782 🖷 01872 277 788

Wakefield, Cathedral Church of All Saints, Cathedral Office, Northgate, Wakefield WF1 1HG
Provost: Very Rev George Nairn-Briggs.
Email: provost@nairn-briggsfreeserve.co.uk
☎ 01924 373 923 🖷 01924 215 054

Winchester, Cathedral Church of the Holy Trinity and of St Peter, Cathedral Office, 1The Close, Winchester SO23 9LS
Dean: To be appointed.
☎ 01962 857 200

Worcester, Cathedral Church of Christ and the Blessed Virgin Mary, Cathedral Office, 10a College Green, Worcester WR1 2LH
Dean: Very Rev Peter Marshall.
Email: worcestercathedral@compuserve.com
☎ 01905 288 54 🖷 01905 611 139

York, Cathedral Church of St Peter, The Deanery, Minster Yard, York YO1 7JQ
Dean: Very Rev Raymond Furnell.
☎ 01904 623 608 🖷 01904 672 002

CHURCH OF IRELAND DIOCESES

Lisburn, The Cathedral Church of Christ Church, Cathedral Office, 24 Castle Street, Lisburn BT27 4XD
Rector: Rev Sam Wright.
☎ 028 9260 2400

CHURCH OF SCOTLAND

Edinburgh, Cathedral Church of St Giles, Royal Mile, Edinburgh EH1 1RE
Minister: Very Rev Gilleasbuig Macmillan.
☎ 0131 225 9442 🖷 0131 220 4763

ORTHODOX

Antiochian Orthodox Cathedral, St George's Cathedral, 1a Redhill Street, London NW1 4BG
Priests: Father Samir Gholam, Father Michael Harper. *CC* No.801540. Began 1984. Magazine: *The Word* (Circulation & frequency n/a).
Web: www.antiochian-orthodox.co.uk
☎ 020 7383 0403 Mobile: 07801 668 785 🖷 020 7383 0403

GREEK ORTHODOX

†**Greek Orthodox Cathedral, Bayswater**, Cathedral of the Divine Wisdom, Moscow Road, London W2 4LQ
☎ 020 7229 7260 / 4643

†**Greek Orthodox Cathedral, Birmingham**, Cathedral of the Dormition of the Mother of God, and St Andrew, 8 Arthur Place, Summer Hill, Birmingham B1 3DA
☎ 0121 236 3274

†**Greek Orthodox Cathedral, Camberwell**, Cathedral of the Nativity of the Mother of God, 305 Camberwell New Road, London SE5 0TF
☎ 020 7703 0137

†**Greek Orthodox Cathedral, Camden Town**, Cathedral of All Saints, Pratt Street, London NW1 0JA
☎ 020 7485 2149

†**Greek Orthodox Cathedral, Glasgow**, Cathedral of St Luke the Evangelist, 27 Dundonald Road, Glasgow G12 9LL
☎ 0141 339 7386

†**Greek Orthodox Cathedral, Golders Green and Hendon**, Cathedral of the Holy Cross and St Michael, Golders Green Road, London NW11 8DA
☎ 020 8455 7510 🖷 020 8458 4752

†**Greek Orthodox Cathedral, Kentish Town**, Cathedral of St Andrew, Kentish Town Road, London NW1 9QA
☎ 020 7485 6385 / 0198 🖷 020 7485 9972

†**Greek Orthodox Cathedral, Shepherd's Bush**, Cathedral of St Nicholas, 60 Godolphin Road, London W12 8JW
☎ 020 8743 3968

†**Greek Orthodox Cathedral, Wood Green**, Cathedral of St Mary, Trinity Road, London N22 4LB
☎ 020 8888 2295 / 8889 1122 🖷 020 8881 4455

RUSSIAN ORTHODOX

†**Russian Orthodox Cathedral, London**, Russian Orthodox Cathedral, 67 Ennismore Gardens, London SW7 1NH
☎ 020 7584 0096 🖷 020 7584 9864

CHAPLAINCIES

Anglican Chaplaincy to the Universities, London, University Chaplaincy, 48b Gordon Square, London WC1H 0PD
Senior Chaplain: Rev Stephen Williams. Executive staff 1, Other staff 24. Began 1962; Anglican. No magazine. Turnover n/a. Providing a ministry to students and staff within London's universities.
Email: chaplaincy@admin.lon.ac.uk
☎ 020 7387 0670 Fax 020 7387 4373

Catholic Chaplaincy for Overseas Students, 16c Portland Rise, London N4 2PP
National Chaplains: Sister Pius Singleton, Rev Felix Gilfedder. Chaplaincy 3. *CC* Began 1953; Roman Catholic. No magazine. Turnover n/a. Providing religious assistance, pastoral care, accommodation, counselling; general advice, information for overseas students, pilgrimages throughout Europe.
☎ 020 8802 9673
Also at: 28 Upper Tooting Park, London SW17 7ST
☎ 020 8672 4616

C

Catholic Students International Chaplaincy, St Joseph's College, Lawrence Street, London NW7 4UZ
International Student Chaplain: Sister Gay Barry. Executive staff 1, Other staff 1. *CC* No.313519. Began 1993; Roman Catholic. No magazine. Turnover £65,000 to year end Mar 97. Providing a Catholic centre of pastoral care for international students; accommodation for 24 students.
☎ 020 8906 3850 Fax 020 8906 2979

†**Chaplaincy Services in the Royal Navy**, Room 203, Victory Building, HM Naval Base, Portsmouth PO1 3LS
Chaplain of the Fleet: Ven S J Golding. *Director-General:* Dr Charles Stewart. Full-time chaplains 75. Began 1177; 3 different sections: Anglican, Church of Scotland, Free Churches, Roman Catholic. Magazine: *Church Pennant* (2,500 quarterly). Turnover n/a. Providing ministry of the Gospel by word and sacrament to the personnel of the Royal Navy.
☎ 023 9272 7112 Fax 023 9272 7902

†**Church of England Chaplaincy in Higher Education**, Church House, Great Smith Street, London SW1P 3NZ
Secretary: Rev Paul E P Brice. Executive staff 1, Chaplains 175. *CC* Began 1550; Anglican. Magazine: *Checkout HE* (Circulation & frequency n/a). Turnover n/a. Providing personal and professional support to Anglican chaplains in universities and colleges in England.
Email: paul@boeangel.demon.co.uk & he@pb.cix.co.uk
☎ 020 7222 9011Ext413 Fax 020 7233 1094

Churches Committee for Hospital Chaplaincy, Health Care Chaplaincy Board, The Free Churches' Council, 27 Tavistock Square, London WC1H 9HH
Secretary: Rev Christine Pocock. Executive staff 2. Began 1967; interdenominational. No magazine. Turnover n/a. Inter-church health care chaplaincy consultative body.
☎ 020 7387 8413 Fax 020 7383 0150

The Guild of St Helena, Wellington Barracks, Birdcage Walk, London SW1E 6HQ
Chief Secretary: Mrs Janice Carson. Other staff 2. *CC* No.267656. Began 1875; ecumenical. Magazine: *Guild of St Helena* (Circulation n/a annually). Turnover £20,000 to year end Dec 96. Offering Christian fellowship and charitable giving to Forces' wives, families and members.
Web: www.army.mod.uk/army/press
☎ 020 7414 3461

Health Care Chaplaincy Board, Free Churches' Council, 27 Tavistock Square, London WC1H 9HH
Secretary: Rev Christine M Pocock. Began 1950; Free Church. No magazine. Turnover n/a. Official body responsible for all matters relating to Free Church health care chaplaincy work.
☎ 020 7387 8413 Fax 020 7383 0150

Hospital Chaplaincies Council (General Synod), Fielden House, Little College Street, London SW1P 3SH
Secretary and Director of Training: Rev Robert Clarke. Executive staff 2, Other staff 2. Began 1956; Anglican. No magazine. Turnover n/a. Advisory body for chaplaincy work in health care.
☎ 020 7898 1894 Fax 020 7898 1891

†**London Universities Catholic Chaplaincy**, Newman House, 111 Gower Street, London WC1E 6AR
Senior Chaplain: Rev Jim Overton. Chaplains 5, Other staff 5. *CC* No.233699. Began 1908; Roman Catholic. No magazine. Turnover n/a. Providing pastoral services to students and staff in tertiary education in London; also accommodation.
☎ 020 7387 6370

†**Lutheran Student Chaplaincy**, 30 Thanet Street, London WC1H 9QH
Lutheran Student Chaplain: Rev Heiner Hoffmann. Executive staff 1, Other staff 3. *CC* No.232042. Began 1961; Lutheran. No magazine. Turnover £40,000 to year end Dec 92. Providing pastoral care to overseas students in the UK.
☎ 020 7388 4848 Fax 020 7383 5915

†**Methodist Church, Forces Work**, 76a Countess Road, Amesbury, Salisbury SP4 7AT
Secretary: Rev J Brian Sherrington. Executive staff 1, Other staff 1. *CC* Began n/a; Methodist. Magazine: *Over To You* (2,000 half-yearly). Turnover £40,000 to year end Aug 92. Co-ordinating Methodist service chaplains and Wesley Houses.
Email: bsherringt@aol.com
☎ 01980 623 948 Fax 01980 626 660

Methodist Prison Chaplaincy, The Methodist Church, 1 Central Buildings, Westminster, London SW1H 9NH
Superintendent Methodist Chaplain: Rev William J Davies. Executive staff 1. Began n/a; Methodist. No magazine. Turnover n/a. Appointing and pastoral oversight of Methodist/Free Church chaplains to penal establishments in England and Wales.
☎ 020 7222 8010 Ext 236 Fax 020 7233 0323

†**Ministry of Defence Chaplains (Army)**, MOD Chaplains (A), Building 183, Trenchard Lines, Upavon, Pewsey SN9 6BE
The Chaplain General to the Forces: Rev Dr Victor Dobbin. Executive staff 3, Other staff 6. Began n/a; interdenominational. No magazine. Turnover n/a. Exercising the Church's ministry within the Army.
☎ 01980 615 801

The Nigerian Chaplaincy, 82 Keslake Road, London NW6 6DG
Chaplain: Ven Jacob A Ajetunmobi. Executive staff 1, Other staff 1. ***CC*** No.1031806. Began 1981; interdenominational. Mission partner with Church Mission Society. Magazine: *Announcer* (250 quarterly). Turnover n/a. Counselling Nigerian students and residents; preaching, teaching and enabling churches and mission agencies.
Email: jacajet@aol.com
☎ 020 8969 2379 Mobile: 07966 526 157
🖷 020 969 2379

·**Prison Chaplaincy**, Abell House, John Islip Street, London SW1P 4LH
Chaplain General of Prisons: Ven David Fleming. Executive staff 8, Chaplains 300. Began n/a; interdenominational. No magazine. Turnover n/a. Ensuring the provision of religious facilities within penal establishments.
☎ 020 7217 5175 🖷 020 7217 5090

Pusey House, Pusey House, Oxford OX1 3LZ
Principal: Rev Philip E Ursell. Executive staff 7, Other staff 2. ***CC*** Began 1884; Anglican. Magazine: *Annual Report* (Circulation & frequency n/a). Turnover n/a. Providing pastoral care for undergraduates, chapel services, theology and philosophy library, writing and research.
☎ 01865 278 415

RAF Chaplains Branch, HQ PTC, RAF Innsworth, Gloucester GL3 1EZ
Chaplain-in-Chief (RAF): Ven A P Bishop. Staff n/a. Began 1918; interdenominational. No magazine. Turnover n/a. Providing spiritual, moral and welfare support to the personnel of the Royal Air Force.
☎ 01452 712 612 Ext 5030 🖷 01452 510 828

Royal Naval Lay Readers Society, Room 201, Victory Building, HM Naval Base, Portsmouth PO1 3LS
Archdeacon for the Royal Navy: Ven S J Golding. ***CC*** No.251186. Began 1860; Anglican. Magazine: *Annual Report* (Circulation n/a annually). Turnover £6,000. Providing ministry of the Gospel by word and sacrament to the personnel of the Royal Navy and Royal Marines.
☎ 023 9272 7904

SCORE, PO Box 123, Sale M33 4ZA
National Director: Rev John Boyers. Executive staff 1, Admin staff 1. ***CC*** No.1005446. Began 1991; non-denominational. Sports Chaplaincy Offering Resources and Encouragement. Magazine: *Scoresheet* (1,000 every four months). Turnover £40,000 to year end Dec 98. Promoting development of effective sports chaplaincy, encouraging fruitful local church sports ministry.
☎ 0161 969 1762 🖷 0161 969 1762

†**St Wenceslaus House – Velehrad**, 22 Ladbroke Square, London W11 3NA
Chaplain: Rev Jan Lang. Executive staff 2, Other staff 1. ***CC*** Began 1964; Roman Catholic but ecumenical. Magazine: *CM Vestnik* (Circulation n/a monthly). Turnover £60,000 to year end Dec 93. Religious services, lectures, broadcasting, social services, youth activities.
☎ 020 7727 7849

C

CHURCH HEADQUARTERS, NATIONAL & LOCAL

Abundant Life Ministries, Abundant Life Centre, Wapping Road, Bradford BD3 0EQ
Team Leader: Mr Paul Scanlon. *Administrator:* Mrs Charlotte Gambill. Staff 7, Serving Ministers 8. ***CC*** No.701289. Began 1993; interdenominational. (Previously Policy Watch, Abundant Life Centre Conference Centre). Magazine: *Voice to the Nations* (5,000 quarterly). Turnover n/a.
Web: www.alcentre.force9.co.uk
Email: a.d.ministrator@dial.pipex.com
☎ 01274 307 233 🖷 01274 740 698

American Church in London, Whitefield Memorial Church, 79a Tottenham Court Road, London W1P 9HB
Senior Minister: Rev Dr Jeffrey M Powell. *Associate Minister:* Rev Steven Gaultney. Executive staff 3, Admin staff 2, Serving ministers 2. Began 1969. Part of United Reformed Church. Magazine: *Open Door* (450 monthly). Turnover £300,000 to year end Dec 98.
Email: amchurchuk@aol.com
☎ 020 7580 2791 🖷 020 7580 5013

Ancient Orthodox Church, Church House, 26 Hillside Terrace, Milton of Campsie, Glasgow G66 8BP
Patriarch Bishop Primate: Most Rev Dr Ronald T Pengilley Harwood. *Director: Highway Ministries, Scotland:* Rev Robert MacDougall. *Director: Missions:* Pastor James McCafferty. Executive staff 5, Admin staff 6, Serving ministers n/a. ***CC*** No.SCO 23385. Began 1970. No magazine.
☎ 01360 311 903 Mobile: 07703 520 789

†**Anglian Apostolic Episcopal Free Church**, Flat 5, 3 Canfield Gardens, London NW6 3JR
Proto Notarius Apostolicus: Rt Rev Dr Eric Morse. *Archbishop and Principal:* Most Rev Dr Bruno Von Ehrenberg. Executive staff 5, Serving ministers 19. Began 1840. No magazine.
☎ No telephone

Anglican Churches
See Church in Wales Page 202
Church of England Page 203
Church of Ireland Page 212
Scottish Episcopal Church Page 227

Antiochian Orthodox Parish House, 30 Chatsworth Gardens, New Malden KT3 6DW
Priest: Father Samir Gholam. ***CC*** No.801540. Began n/a. No magazine.
☎ 020 8942 9676 Mobile: 07801 668 785

***The Apostolic Church**, 24 St Helens Road, Swansea SA1 1ZH
President: Rev Warren Jones. *Administrative Secretary:* Mr Andrew Saunders. Executive staff 6, Admin staff 3, Serving ministers 85. ***CC*** No.284789. Began 1904. Magazine: *Christian Lifestyle* (1,200 quarterly).
Web: www.apostolic-church.org
Email: admin@apostolic-church.org
☎ 01792 473 992 🖷 01792 474 087

Apostolic Faith Church, 66 Muscliffe Road, Winton, Bournemouth BH9 1NW
Pastor: Pastor Duncan Lee. Other staff 3, Serving ministers 3. ***CC*** No.238009. Began 1908; Pentecostal. Magazine: *Showers of Blessing* (60 weekly).
☎ 01202 528 270

†**Apostolic Faith Church**, 95 Fenham Road, Peckham, London SE15 1AE
Pastor: Rev Victor O Okusanya. Serving ministers 9, Admin staff 4. Began 1906. Magazine: *Light of Hope* (3,000 every two months), *Higher Way* (3,000 every two months), *London News Report* (1,000 quarterly).
☎ 020 7639 9329/8897 🖷 020 7639 9329

†**Armenian Oriental Orthodox Church**, St Peter's Church, Cranley Gardens, London SW7 3BB
Primate of Armenian Church UK: Archbishop Yeghishe Gizirian. Serving ministers 3. Began 1922. No magazine.
☎ 020 7373 3565/01712449574

C

***Assemblies of God in Great Britain and Ireland**, 16 Bridgford Road, West Bridgford, Nottingham NG2 6AF
General Administrator: Mr David H Gill. Admin staff 5, Serving ministers 800. ***CC*** No.1032245. Began 1924. Magazine: *Joy* (5,000 frequency n/a).
Email: aog@netcom.co.uk
☎ 0115 981 1188 🖷 0115 981 3377

***Assemblies of God:* Central Region**, 47 Monteagle Drive, Kingswinford DY6 7RY
Chairman: Mr Paul Chamberlain. Began n/a.
☎ 01384 293 580

***Assemblies of God:* East Midlands Region**, 95 Charles Street, Newark NG24 1RN
Chairman: Mr Kenneth A Morgan. Began n/a.
☎ 01636 683 701

***Assemblies of God:* East Pennine Region**, Apple Jade, Thorpe Road, Mattersey, Doncaster DN10 5ED
Chairman: Mr Brian Quar. Began n/a.
☎ 01777 817 602

***Assemblies of God:* Eastern Region**, 48 The Parkway, Shelfield, Walsall WS4 1XB
Chairman: Mr David Poulton. Began n/a.
☎ 01922 683 828

***Assemblies of God:* Greater London Region**, Peniel Chapel, Kensington Park Road, London W11 2ES
Chairman: Mr Ray Westbrook. Began n/a.
☎ 020 7792 0300

***Assemblies of God:* Ireland Region**, 183 Greenacres, Avenue Road, Dundalk, Republic of Ireland
Chairman: Mr Peter Lynch. Began n/a.
☎ 00 353 42 33225

***Assemblies of God:* North Wales and Midlands Region**, 305 Park Lane, Poynton, Stockport SK12 1RJ
Chairman: Mr Glyn Thomas. Began n/a.
☎ 01625 871 408

***Assemblies of God:* North West Region**, 157 Spring Street, Bury BL9 0RN
Chairman: Mr Alan Robertson. Began n/a.
☎ 0161 280 5365

***Assemblies of God:* Northumbria Region**, Guildhall Manse, Sunderland Road, Horden, Peterlee SR8 4PF
Chairman: Mr Steve Cook. Began n/a.
☎ 0191 586 0356

***Assemblies of God:* Scotland Region**, 3 Cypress Grove, Denmore, Aberdeen AB23 8LB
Chairman: Mr John Strachan. Began n/a.
☎ 01224 828 379

***Assemblies of God:* South East Region**, Helvetia, 1 Milton Drive, Tunbridge Wells TN2 3DE
Chairman: Mr Colin Blackman. Began n/a.
☎ 01892 530 233

***Assemblies of God:* South Wales Region**, 50 The Ridings, Landare, Aberdare CF44 8AQ
Chairman: Mr Ken Dancer. Began n/a.
☎ 01685 881 521

***Assemblies of God:* West Country Region**, Bethshan, 68 Southfield Avenue, Preston, Paignton TQ3 1LQ
Chairman: Mr Derek Williams. Began n/a.
☎ 012803 559 366

†**Assemblies of the First Born**, St Stephen's Church, Battersea Bridge Road, London SW11 3AE
Overseer: Mr Charles Wright. No full-time staff, Serving ministers n/a. Began 1960. Magazine: *Youth Highlight* (Circulation n/a quarterly).
☎ No telephone

Associated Presbyterian Churches, PO Box 2, Gairloch IV21 2YA
Clerk of Presbytery: Rev Dr M MacInnes. Executive staff 15, Admin staff 2, Serving ministers 15. Began 1989. Magazine: *APC News* (6,000 every two months).
☎ 01463 223 983

***Association of Vineyard Churches UK & Ireland**, 23 Blagdon Road, New Malden KT3 4AH
National Director: John Mumford. Serving ministers 53, Admin staff 1. ***CC*** No.1054443. Began 1987; Vineyard. Magazine: *Equipped* (Circulation & frequency n/a).
Web: www.vineyard.uk
Email: avc@vineyard.org.uk
☎ 020 8942 8982 🖷 020 8942 8967

†**Assyrian Church of the East**, Westminster Road, Hanwell, London W7 3TU
Archdeacon: Rev Stefan Yalda. Serving ministers 2. Began 1977. No magazine.
☎ 020 8567 1814

Baptist Union of Great Britain, Baptist House, PO Box 44, 129 Broadway, Didcot OX11 8RT
General Secretary: Rev David R Coffey. *Deputy General Secretary:* To be appointed. Executive staff 25, Admin staff 24. Began 1812. Magazine: *Baptist Times* (10,000 weekly), *Baptist Leader* (3,000 every four months), *SecCheck* (5,000 every four months).
Email: baptistuniongb@baptist.org.uk
☎ 01235 517 700 🖷 01235 517 715
See also: **Baptist House** on Page 71
Baptist Times on Page 311
Baptist Union Corporation on Page 416
Baptist Union Mission and Research Department on Page 266
Baptist Union Publications on Page 171
Baptist Union Youth Office on Page 475
BMS (Baptist Missionary Society) on Page 355
Retired Baptist Ministers Housing Society Ltd on Page 103
Also see under **Baptist** in Main Index on Page 627

Baptist Union of Great Britain: **Central Area**, 4 Corton Close, Stevenage SG1 2LB
Superintendent: Rev Paul Goodliff. Serving ministers 119. Began 1915. No magazine. Comprising Bedfordshire, Bucks, Herts and Northamptonshire and North Buckinghamshire, Associations.
☎ 01438 725 819

Baptist Union of Great Britain: **East Midland Area**, 9 Wilshere Close, Kirby Muxloe, Leicester LE9 2DN
General Superintendent: Rev Peter Grange. Executive staff 1, Other staff 2, Serving ministers n/a. Began n/a. No magazine. Comprising East Midland Association.
☎ 0116 238 7012
Administrator: Mrs Rachel Tole, 232 Westdale Lane, Carlton, Nottingham NG4 4FW
☎ 0115 940 3908

Baptist Union of Great Britain: **Eastern Area**, 7 The Furrells, Linton, Cambridge CB1 6JJ
General Superintendent: Rev Paul Hills. Executive staff 1, Admin staff 3, Serving ministers 157. Began n/a. No magazine. Comprising Cambridgeshire, Norfolk, Suffolk and Essex Associations.
Email: pslsbhills@aol.com
☎ 01223 890 141

Baptist Union of Great Britain: **Metropolitan Area**, 28 Chadwick Road, Leytonstone, London E11 1NF
General Superintendent: Rev Dr Patricia Took. Executive staff 3, Admin staff 4, Serving ministers 300. Began n/a. Magazine: *Capital Vision* (10,000 half-yearly). Turnover £255,000 to year end Dec 98. Comprising London Association.
Web: ourworld.compuserve.com/homepages/cphicks/lbahome.htm
☎ 020 8530 8179
Association Secretary: Rev Peter Wortley, 235 Shaftesbury Avenue, London WC2 8EL
Email: lbaoffice@cwcom.net.com
☎ 020 7692 5592 Fax 020 7692 5593
Metropolitan Superintendent: Rev Tony Mason, 14 Nash Green, Park Avenue, Bromley BR1 4EF
☎ 020 8464 5867

Baptist Union of Great Britain: **North Eastern Area**, 14 Fairway, Clifton, York YO30 5QA
General Superintendent: Rev Ernie Whalley. Other staff n/a, Serving ministers 154. Began n/a. No magazine. Comprising Yorkshire and Northern Associations.
☎ 01904 610047 Fax 01904 781 033

Baptist Union of Great Britain: **North Western Area**, 14 Cedar Road, Great Sankey, Warrington WA5 3BU
General Superintendent: Rev Keith H Hobbs. Executive staff 2, Other staff 3, Serving ministers 125. ***CC*** No.247113. Began n/a. No magazine. Comprising North Western Baptist Association.
Email: baptnw@aol.com
☎ 01925 722 155
Secretary Rev Christopher D Haig, Latchford Baptist Church, Loushers Lane, Warrington WA4 2RP
☎ 01925 633 929

Baptist Union of Great Britain: **South Eastern Area**, 40 Ashden Walk, Tonbridge TN10 3RL
General Superintendent: Rev David L Taylor. Executive staff 1, Serving ministers 115. Began n/a. No magazine. Comprising Kent, North Downs Association and Sussex Association.
Email: vq45@dial.pipex.com
☎ 01732 355 008 Fax 01732 355 008

Baptist Union of Great Britain:* **South Wales Area, 19 Melrose Close, St Mellons, Cardiff CF3 9SW
General Superintendent: Rev Peter D Manson. Executive staff 1, Serving ministers 150. Began 1915. No magazine. Comprising East Glamorgan, Gwent and West Wales English Baptist Associations.
☎ 029 2079 5919

Baptist Union of Great Britain: **South Western Area**, 96 Honiton Road, Exeter EX1 3EE
General Superintendent: Rev Jonathan Edwards. Executive staff 1, Serving ministers 80. Began n/a. No magazine. Comprising Devon and Cornwall and Western Associations..
☎ 01392 368 360
Devon and Cornwall office *General Secretary:* Rev D J Keenan, 13 Wrefords Drive, Cowley Park, Exeter EX4 5AU
☎ 01392 431 097

Baptist Union of Great Britain: **Southern Area**, 26 Francis Gardens, Abbots Barton, Winchester SO23 7HD
Superintendent: Rev Mike Nicholls. *Association Secretary:* Rev Frank Boyd. Executive staff 3, Serving ministers 194. Began n/a. No magazine. Comprising Berkshire, Oxfordshire and East Gloucestershire, and Southern Associations.
☎ 01962 852 943

Baptist Union of Great Britain: **West Midland Area**, 137 Newhall Street, Birmingham B3 1SF
General Superintendent: Rev Brian Nicholls. *Secretaries:* Rev Barrie Smith, Rev Peter Dwyer. Executive staff 4, Admin staff 3, Serving ministers 147. Began n/a. Magazine: *WM News* (25,000 half-yearly). Comprising West Midland and Worcestershire Associations.
Email: wmba@newhallst.freeserve.co.uk
☎ 0121 212 4842 Fax 0121 212 4512

Baptist Union of Great Britain: **Western Area**, 15 Fenhurst Gardens, Long Ashton, Bristol BS41 9AU
General Superintendent: Rev Dr Roger Hayden. No full-time staff, Serving ministers 106. Began n/a. No magazine. Comprising Bristol, Gloucestershire, Wiltshire and East Somerset Associations.
☎ 01275 394 101

†**Baptist Union of Ireland**, 117 Lisburn Road, Belfast BT9 7AF
Secretary: Rev W Colville. *Missions Secretary:* Rev Derek Baxter. *Youth Secretary:* Mr Jackie Whyte. Executive staff 4, Other staff 7, Serving ministers n/a. Began 1895. Magazine: *The Irish Baptist* (3,200 monthly).
Email: buofi@aol.com
☎ 028 9066 3108 Fax 028 9066 3616

***Baptist Union of Scotland**, 14 Aytoun Road, Glasgow G41 5RT
General Secretary: Rev Bill Slack. *Superintendent:* Rev Douglas Hutcheon. Executive staff 4, Admin staff 6, Serving ministers 150. ***CC*** No.SCO 04960. Began 1869. Magazine: *Scottish Baptist Magazine* (3,000 ten times a year). For details of regional associations, contact Superintendent.
Web: www.scottishbaptist.org.uk
Email: admin@scottishbaptist.org.uk
☎ 0141 423 6169 Fax 0141 424 1422

†**Baptist Union of Wales**, Ty Ilston, 94 Mansel Street, Swansea SA1 5TZ
General Secretary: Rev Peter D Richards. *Finance Officer:* Mr Henry D Williams. Executive staff 3, Admin staff 5, Serving ministers 115. Began 1866. Magazine: *Seren Cymru* (1,000 weekly), *Cristion* (350 every two months), *Ilston Newsfile* (800 quarterly).
☎ 01792 655 468/469 893 Fax 01792 469 489

Baptist Union of Wales: **Anglesey Association**, Tyn Llwyn, Paradwys, Llangristiolus, Ynys Môn LL62 5PG
Association Secretary: Mr A Millburn. Began n/a. Turnover n/a.
☎ 01248 724 400

Baptist Union of Wales: **Arfon Association**, Llys Cerdd, Ffordd Crwys, Penrhosgarnedd, Bangor LL57 2NT
Association Secretary: Rev Olaf Davies. Began n/a. Turnover n/a.
☎ 01248 364 613

Baptist Union of Wales: **Brecon Association**, Llynfi Cottage, Pontithel, Three Cocks, Talgarth, Brecon LD3 0SA
Association Secretary: Miss Gaynor Davies. Began n/a. Turnover n/a.
☎ 01874 711 494

Baptist Union of Wales: **Carmarthen and Cardigan Association**, Minyrhos, Efailwen, Clunderwen, Sir Benfro SA66 7UZ
Association Secretary: Rev Tecwyn Ifan. Began n/a. Turnover n/a.
☎ 01994 419 310

Baptist Union of Wales: **Denbigh, Flint and Merioneth Association**, Rhyd Lafar, Glyn Ceiriog, Llangollen LL20 7EY
Association Secretary: Miss Einwen Jones. Began n/a. Turnover n/a.
☎ 01691 718 383

Baptist Union of Wales: **East Glamorgan Association**, Golygfa, 17 Ivor Terrace, Dowlais CF48 3SW
Association Secretary: Rev Eifion Wynne. Began n/a. Turnover n/a.
☎ 01685 377 896

Baptist Union of Wales: **Gwent Association**, 104 Cefn Road, Rogerstone, Newport NP1 9AS
Association Secretary: Rev Ian Tutton. Began n/a. Turnover n/a.
☎ 01633 894 424

Baptist Union of Wales: **Pembroke Association**, 50 Whitlow, Saundersfoot, Tenby SA69 9AE
Association Secretary: Rev Dr D Pusey. Began n/a. Turnover n/a.
☎ 01834 813 750

Baptist Union of Wales: **Penfro Association**, 78 Stryd Fawr, Abergwaun SA65 9AU
Association Secretary: Rev D Carl Williams. Began n/a. Turnover n/a.
☎ 01348 872 190

Baptist Union of Wales: **Radnor and Montgomery Association**, Arosfa, Hillfield, Llanidloes SY18 6ET
Association Secretary: Rev Meredith Powell. Began n/a. Turnover n/a.
☎ 01686 412 452

Baptist Union of Wales: **West Glamorgan Association**, Littlewest, Southerndown Road, Pen-y-Bont CF32 0PY
Association Secretary: Rev Euros Miles. Began n/a. Turnover n/a.
☎ No telephone

Beneficial Christ Church, 281 Rye Lane, Peckham, London SE15 4UA
Bishop: Bishop Paul Hackman. Executive staff 9, Other staff 5, Serving ministers 14. *CC* No.1028128. Began 1988. (Previously Beneficial Veracious Christ Church). Magazine: *Beneficial Trumpet* (2,500 frequency n/a).
Email: benchrist1@aol.com
☎ 020 7639 4058

The Bible Way Church of our Lord Jesus Christ Worldwide (UK), Bibleway Tabernacle, Algernon Road, Lewisham, London SE13 7AT
Diocesan Bishop: Bishop Leon E White. Executive staff 4, Trustees 5, Serving ministers 25. *CC* Began 1958. Magazine: *Bible Way Sentinel* (700 quarterly).
☎ 020 8691 3805 🖷 020 8694 0008

Born Again Christ Healing Church, 77 Beechwood Road, Hornsey, London N8 7NE
Chief Prophet: Most Rev Prophetess Fidelia N Onyuku-Opukiri. Executive staff 4, Admin staff 2, Serving ministers 5. Began 1979. Magazine: *BAV* (150 quarterly).
☎ 020 8340 9962 🖷 020 8340 9962

British Antiochian Orthodox Deanery, 16 Pightle Close, Harston, Cambridge CB2 5NN
Dean: Father Michael Harper. Serving Ministers 13. *CC* No.1057533. Began n/a. Magazine: *Newsletter* (Circulation & frequency n/a). Turnover £6,000 to year end Dec 98.
Web: www.antiochian-orthodox.co.uk
Email: 100307.540@compuserve.com
☎ 01223 872 433 🖷 01444 417 871

British Conference of Mennonites, London Mennonite Centre, 14 Shepherds Hill, Highgate, London N6 5AQ
Administrator: Mr Will Newcomb. Other staff n/a, No serving ministers. Began 1987. No magazine.
Email: menno@compuserve.com
☎ 020 8340 8775 🖷 020 8341 6807

The British Orthodox Church of the British Isles (Coptic Orthodox Patriarchate), Church Secretariat, 10 Heathwood Gardens, Charlton, London SE7 8EP
Metropolitan of Glastonbury: His Grace Abba Seraphim. Executive staff 1, Admin staff 2, Serving ministers 18. *CC* No.267387. Began 1866. Magazine: *The Glastonbury Bulletin* (1,000 every four months).
Web: www.uk-christian.net/boc
Email: boc@cwcom.net
☎ 020 8854 3090 🖷 020 8244 7888

†***Bruderhof Communities in the UK**, Darvell Bruderhof, Robertsbridge TN32 5DR
Minister: Rev John Fransham. Serving ministers 3. *CC* No.229226. Began 1936; Anabaptist. Magazine: *The Plough* (1,500 quarterly).
Web: www.bruderhof.org
Email: ploughuk@bruderhof.com
☎ 01580 883 300 🖷 01580 881 171
Also at: *Minister:* Rev Joe Staengl, Beech Grove Bruderhof, Sandwich Road, Nonington, Dover CT15 4HH
☎ 01304 842 980 🖷 01304 841 923

†**Byelorussian Autocephalic Orthodox Church**, Holy Mother of God of Zyrovicy Church, Chapel Road, Rainsough, Prestwich, Manchester M22 4JW
Administrator: Very Rev Father John Ababurko. Executive staff 2, Admin staff 2, Serving ministers n/a. Began 1948. Magazine: *Voice of the Church* (Circulation n/a half-yearly).
☎ 0161 740 8230

C.net (Cornerstone Network), Central Hall, St Mary Street, Southampton SO14 1NF
Team Leader: Mr Tony Morton. *Admin & Legal Director:* Mr Adrian Thomas. Executive staff 14, Other staff 4, Serving ministers 40. ***CC*** No.1072645. Began 1982. (Previously Cornerstone). The Cornerstone Network. No magazine.
Web: c.net.hants.org.uk
Email: info@cornerstone-network.org
☎ 023 8023 7700 🖷 023 8023 4555

Roman Catholic Bishops' Conference Secretariat, 39 Eccleston Square, London SW1V 1BX
General Secretary: Rt Rev Mgr Arthur Roche. Executive staff 4. ***CC*** No.257239. Began 1984.
☎ 020 7630 8220
See also: Roman Catholic Bishop's Conference Departments for:
Catholic Education and Formation on Page 492
Christian Life and Worship on Page 232
International Affairs on Page 232
Mission and Unity on Page 232
Responsibility and Citizenship on Page 232
Consultative Bodies:
Canon Law Society of Great Britain and Ireland on Page 232
Catholic Missionary Union on Page 370
Catholic Union of Great Britain on Page 232
Conference of Religious on Page 448
National Catholic Women's Network on Page 237
National Conference of Priests on Page 449
National Council for the Lay Associations on Page 237
Conference Agencies of the Bishops' Conference:
Apostleship of the Sea on Page 393
Catholic Child Welfare Council on Page 232
Catholic Education Service on Page 492
Catholic Fund for Overseas Development (CAFOD) on Page 382
Catholic Youth Services on Page 476
Diocesan Vocations Service on Page 234
National Catholic Fund on Page 237
Briefing on Page 311
Catholic Communications Centre on Page 284
Catholic Media Office on Page 431
Independent Catholic newspapers:
The Catholic Herald on Page 311
The Catholic Times on Page 311
The Tablet on Page 319
The Universe on Page 319
See also under **Catholic** in Main Index on Page 000

Roman Catholic **Diocese of Aberdeen (Province of St Andrews and Edinburgh)**, Bishop's House, 3 Queen's Cross, Aberdeen AB15 4XU
Bishop of Aberdeen: Rt Rev Mario J Conti. Serving ministers n/a. Began 1131. Magazine: *News* (1,000 periodically).
☎ 01224 319 154 🖷 01224 325 570
Also at: *Millennium Appeal Co-ordinator:* Mrs Joyce P Webster,
☎ 01224 208 944 🖷 01224 208 944

†***Roman Catholic*** **Diocese of Argyll and the Isles**, Bishop's House, Esplanade, Oban PA34 5AB
Bishop of Argyll & the Isles: Rt Rev Colin MacPherson. Serving ministers 33. Began 1878. No magazine.
☎ 01631 620 10

Roman Catholic **Archdiocese of Armagh**, Ara Coeli, Armagh BT61 7QY
Archbishop of Armagh & Primate of All Ireland: Most Rev Seán Brady. Executive staff 2, Serving ministers 192. Began 444. No magazine.
Email: admin@aracoeli.com
☎ 028 3752 2045 🖷 028 3752 6182
Auxiliary Bishop of Armagh: Most Rev Gerard Clifford, Annaskeagh, Ravensdale, Dundalk, Co Louth, Republic of Ireland
☎ 00 353 42 93 71012

Roman Catholic **Diocese of Arundel and Brighton (Province of Southwark)**, St Joseph's Hall, Greyfriars Lane, Storrington, Pulborough RH20 4HE
Bishop of Arundel & Brighton: Rt Rev Cormac Murphy O'Connor. Executive staff 14, Pastoral & Admin staff 28, Serving ministers 143. ***CC*** No.252878. Began 1965. Magazine: *A & B News* (5,000 monthly).
Email: bishop@rcd.ab.btinternet.com
☎ 01903 742 172 🖷 01903 746 336
Vicar General: Rt Rev Mgr Canon John Hull, Bishop's House, Upper Drive, Hove BN3 6NE
☎ 01273 506 387 🖷 01273 501 527

C

†***Roman Catholic*** **Archdiocese of Birmingham**, Archbishop's House, 8 Shadwell Street, Birmingham B4 6EY
Archbishop of Birmingham: Most Rev Maurice Couve de Murville. *Administrator:* To be appointed. Executive staff 3, Admin staff 3. Began 1850. Magazine: *Catholic News* (Circulation n/a periodically).
☎ 0121 236 9090 🖷 0121 212 0171
Auxiliary Bishop: Rt Rev Philip Pargeter, Grove House, 90 College Road, Sutton Coldfield B73 5AH
☎ 021 354 4363
Auxiliary Bishop: Rt Rev Terence Brain, 84 St Bernards Road, Olton, Solihull B92 7BS
☎ 021 706 1658

†***Roman Catholic*** **Diocese of Brentwood (Province of Westminster)**, Bishop's House, Stock, Ingatestone CM4 9BU
Bishop of Brentwood: Rt Rev Thomas McMahon.
☎ 01227 840 268
Chancellor: Very Rev Gordon Read, Cathedral House, Ingrave Road, Brentwood CM15 8AT
Admin staff 15, Serving ministers 181. Began 1917. Magazine: *Brentwood News* (Circulation n/a monthly).
☎ 01277 232 266

†***Roman Catholic*** **Archdiocese of Cardiff**, Archbishop's House, 43 Cathedral Road, Cardiff CF1 9HD
Archbishop of Cardiff: Most Rev John Aloysius Ward. Executive staff 5, Other staff 4, Serving ministers 139. ***CC*** No.242380. Began 1895. No magazine.
☎ 029 2022 0411 🖷 029 2034 5950

Roman Catholic **Diocese of Clifton (Province of Birmingham)**, St Ambrose, North Road, Leigh Woods, Bristol BS8 3PW
Bishop of Clifton: Rt Rev Mervyn Alexander.
☎ 0117 973 3072 🖷 0117 973 5913
Vicar General: Rt Rev Mgr Canon William Mitchell, Clifton Cathedral House, Clifton Park, Bristol BS8 3BX
Executive staff 2, Admin staff 11, Serving ministers 142. ***CC*** No.233977. Began 1850. No magazine.
Web: www.btinternet.com/~Diocese.Clifton
Email: bishops.secretary@btinternet.com
☎ 0117 970 6333 🖷 0117 974 4002

†*Roman Catholic* **Diocese of Clogher (Province of Armagh)**, Bishop's House, Monaghan, Republic of Ireland
Bishop of Clogher: Most Rev Joseph Duffy. Serving ministers 112. Began n/a. No magazine.
☎ 00 35347 81019

Roman Catholic **Diocese of Derry (Province of Armagh)**, Bishops House, St Eugene's Cathedral, Londonderry BT48 9AP
Bishop of Derry: Most Rev Seamus Hegarty. Serving ministers 150. Began n/a. No magazine.
☎ 028 7126 2302 🖷 028 7137 1960
Auxiliary Bishop of Derry: Most Rev Francis Lagan, 9 Glen Road, Strabane BT82 8BX
☎ 01504 884 533 🖷 01504 884 551

Roman Catholic **Diocese of Down and Connor (Province of Armagh)**, Lisbreen, 73 Somerton Road, Belfast BT15 4DE
Bishop of Down and Connor: Most Rev Patrick Walsh. Serving ministers 236. Began n/a. No magazine.
☎ 028 9077 6185 🖷 028 9077 9377
Auxiliary Bishops of Down and Connor: Most Rev Anthony Farquhar, 24 Fruithill Park, Belfast BT11 8GE
☎ 028 9077 6185
Most Rev Michael Dallat, 96 Downview Park West, Belfast BT15 5HZ
☎ 028 9077 9377

C

†*Roman Catholic* **Diocese of Dromore (Province of Armagh)**, Bishops House, Violet Hill, Newry BT35 6PN
Bishop of Dromore: Most Rev Francis G Brooks. Serving ministers 75. Began n/a. No magazine.
☎ 028 3026 2444 🖷 028 3060 496

†*Roman Catholic* **Diocese of Dunkeld (Province of St Andrews and Edinburgh)**, Diocesan Centre, 26 Roseangle, Dundee DD1 4LY
Bishop of Dunkeld: To be appointed. Lay staff 8, Serving ministers 56. Began 1878. Magazine: *Dunkeld News* (3,000 quarterly).
☎ 01382 254 53 🖷 01382 274 33

Roman Catholic **Diocese of East Anglia (Province of Westminster)**, The White House, 21 Upgate, Poringland, Norwich NR14 7SH
Bishop of East Anglia: Rt Rev Peter Smith. Admin staff 4, Serving ministers 103. Began 1976. Magazine: *The Key* (4,500 quarterly).
Email: office@east-angliadiocese.org.uk
☎ 01508 492 202/493 956 🖷 01508 495 358

Roman Catholic **Diocese of Galloway (Province of St Andrews and Edinburgh)**, 8 Corsehill Road, Ayr KA7 2ST
Bishop of Galloway: Rt Rev Maurice Taylor. *Vicar General:* Rt Rev Joseph Boyd. Executive staff 1, Serving ministers 55. Began 398. Magazine: *The Galloway Newsletter* (5,200 monthly).
Email: stninian@globalnet.co.uk
☎ 01292 266 750

†*Roman Catholic* **Archdiocese of Glasgow**, Curial Offices, 196 Clyde Street, Glasgow G1 4JY
Cardinal Archbishop of Glasgow: Most Rev Cardinal Thomas Winning. Executive staff 8, Admin staff 40, Serving ministers 589. Began 1492. Magazine: *Flourish* (15,000 monthly).
Email: glasgow_archdiocese@compuserve.com
☎ 0141 226 5898 🖷 0141 225 2600

†*Roman Catholic* **Diocese of Hallam (Province of Liverpool)**, Quarters, Carsick Hill Way, Sheffield S10 3LT
Bishop of Hallam: Rt Rev John Rawsthorne. Admin staff 7, Serving ministers 85. Began 1980. Magazine: *Hallam News* (10,000 monthly).
☎ 0114 230 9101 🖷 0114 230 5722

Roman Catholic **Diocese of Hexham and Newcastle (Province of Liverpool)**, Bishop's House, East Denton Hall, 800 West Road, Newcastle upon Tyne NE5 2BJ
Bishop of Hexham and Newcastle: Rt Rev Ambrose Griffiths. Other staff n/a, Serving ministers n/a. ***CC*** No.235686. Began 1850. Magazine: *Northern Cross* (7,200 monthly).
☎ 0191 228 0003 🖷 0191 274 0432

Roman Catholic **Diocese of Lancaster (Province of Liverpool)**, Bishop's House, Cannon Hill, Lancaster LA1 5NG
Bishop of Lancaster: Rt Rev John Brewer. Other staff n/a, Serving ministers 250. ***CC*** No.234331. Began 1924. Magazine: *The Voice* (Circulation n/a monthly).
Web: www.churchnet.ucsm.ac.uk/lancs_rc
☎ 01524 322 31 🖷 01524 849 296

†*Roman Catholic* **Diocese of Leeds (Province of Liverpool)**, Bishop's House, 13 North Grange Road, Headingley, Leeds LS6 2BR
Bishop of Leeds: Rt Rev David Konstant. Executive staff 7, Admin staff 10, Serving ministers 180. Began 1878. Magazine: *Catholic Post* (20,000 monthly).
☎ 0113 230 4533 🖷 0113 278 9890

†*Roman Catholic* **Archdiocese of Liverpool**, Archbishop's House, 87 Green Lane, Mossley Hill, Liverpool L18 2EP
Archbishop of Liverpool: Rt Rev Patrick Kelly. Other staff n/a, Serving ministers n/a. Began 1850. Magazine: *Catholic Pictorial* (15,000 weekly).
☎ 0151 722 2379 🖷 0151 737 1055
Auxiliary Bishops: Rt Rev Vincent Malone, 17 West Oakhill Park, Liverpool L13 4BN
☎ 0151 228 7637
Rt Rev John Rawsthorne, St Joseph's, Hall Lane, Wrightington, Wigan WN6 9PA
☎ 0151 709 4801

Roman Catholic **Diocese of Menevia (Province of Cardiff)**, Curial Office, 27 Convent Street, Swansea SA1 2BX
Bishop of Menevia: Rt Rev Daniel J Mullins.
☎ 01792 644 017 🖷 01792 458 641
Vicar General: Rt Rev Mgr Provost David Bottrill, Maes-Gwyn, 63 Margam Road, Margam, Port Talbot, Swansea SA13 2HR
Executive staff 3, Admin staff 3, Serving ministers 62. ***CC*** No.234168. Began 1987. Magazine: *Menevia News-Dolen Mynyw* (Circulation & frequency n/a).
☎ 01639 883 323

†*Roman Catholic* **Diocese of Middlesbrough (Province of Liverpool)**, Bishop's House, 16 Cambridge Road, Middlesbrough TS5 5NN
Bishop of Middlesbrough: Rt Rev John Crowley.
☎ 01642 818 253
Financial Secretary: Mgr J R Charlton, Curial Office, 50a The Avenue, Middlesbrough TS5 6QT
Admin staff 10, Serving ministers 100. Began 1875. Magazine: *Catholic Voice* (20,000 monthly).
☎ 01642 850 505 🖷 01642 851 404
Auxiliary Bishop: Rt Rev Kevin O'Brien, St Charles Rectory, 12 Jarratt Street, Hull HU1 3HB
☎ 01482 329 100

***Roman Catholic* Diocese of Motherwell (Province of Glasgow)**, Diocesan Centre, Coursington Road, Motherwell ML1 1PP
Bishop of Motherwell: Rt Rev Joseph Devine. *Vicar Generals:* Rt Rev John J Burns, Rt Rev Alexander Devanny. Executive staff 3, Admin staff 15, Serving ministers 140. Began 1948. No magazine.
☎ 01698 269 114

***Roman Catholic* Diocese of Northampton (Province of Westminster)**, Bishop's House, Marriott Street, Northampton NN2 6AW
Bishop of Northampton: Rt Rev Leo McCartie. Executive staff 2, Serving ministers 154. ***CC*** No.234091. Began 1850. Magazine: *The Vine* (Circulation n/a monthly).
Web: www.cableol.co.uk/diocese/
Email: mod1@cableol.co.uk
☎ 01604 715 635 Fax 01604 792 186

***Roman Catholic* Diocese of Nottingham (Province of Westminster)**, 27 Cavendish Road East, The Park, Nottingham NG7 1BB
Bishop of Nottingham: Rt Rev James J McGuinness. Admin staff 2, Serving ministers n/a. Began 1850. No magazine.
☎ 0115 947 4786 Fax 0115 947 5325

***Roman Catholic* Diocese of Paisley (Province of Glasgow)**, Roman Catholic Diocese of Paisley, 107 Corsebar Road, Paisley PA1 9PY
Bishop of Paisley: Rt Rev John Mone.
☎ 0141 889 3601
Vicar General: Rev Mgr John Cunningham, Diocesan Offices, 8 East Buchanan Street, Paisley PA1 1HS
Admin staff 3, Serving ministers 67. ***CC*** No.SCO 13514. Began 1947. No magazine.
Web: ourworld.compuserve.com/homepages/dioceseofpaisley
Email: diocese_of_paisley@compuserve.com
☎ 0141 889 3601

***Roman Catholic* Diocese of Plymouth (Province of Southwark)**, Bishop's House, 31 Wyndham Street West, Plymouth PL1 5RZ
Bishop of Plymouth: Rt Rev Christopher Budd. Other staff 23, Serving ministers 100. Began 1850. Magazine: *Diocesan Newspaper* (Circulation n/a monthly).
☎ 01752 224 414

†*Roman Catholic* Diocese of Portsmouth (Province of Southwark), Bishop's House, Edinburgh Road, Portsmouth PO1 3HG
Bishop of Portsmouth: Rt Rev Crispian Hollis. Serving ministers 150. Began 1882. No magazine.
☎ 023 9282 0894 Fax 023 9286 3086

†*Roman Catholic* Archdiocese of St Andrews and Edinburgh, Archbishop's House, 42 Greenhill Gardens, Edinburgh EH10 4BJ
Archbishop of St Andrews & Edinburgh: Most Rev Keith P O'Brien.
☎ 0131 447 3337
Diocesan Secretary: Rev Jeremy Bath, Diocesan Offices, Gillis Centre, 113 Whitehouse Loan, Edinburgh EH9 1BB
Executive staff 5, Admin staff 10, Serving ministers 130. Began 1878. Magazine: *Archdiocesan*(Circulation & frequency n/a), *Newsletter* (500 every two months).
☎ 0131 452 8244 Fax 0131 452 9153
Auxiliary Bishop of St Andrew's and Edinburgh: Rt Rev Kevin L Rafferty, 34 West Main Street, Broxburn EH52 5RJ
☎ 01506 852 040

***Roman Catholic* Diocese of Salford (Province of Liverpool)**, Wardley Hall, Worsley, Manchester M28 5ND
Bishop of Salford: Rt Rev Terence J Brain. Staff n/a, Serving ministers n/a. ***CC*** Began 1850. No magazine.
Web: www.wardleyhall.org.uk
☎ 0161 794 2825 Fax 0161 727 8592

***Roman Catholic* Diocese of Shrewsbury (Province of Birmingham)**, Laburnum Cottage, 97 Barnston Road, Barnston, Wirral CH61 1BW
Bishop of Shrewsbury: Rt Rev Brian M Noble. Staff n/a, Serving ministers 143. ***CC*** No.234025. Began 1850. Magazine: *Catholic Voice* (n/a monthly).
Email: admin@diocshr.dircon.co.uk
☎ 0151 648 0623 Fax 0151 648 0624
Bishop's Secretary: Rev Jerome Fagan, Curial Offices, 2 Park Road South, Birkenhead CH43 4UX
☎ 0151 652 9855 Fax 0151 653 5172

***Roman Catholic* Archdiocese of Southwark**, Archbishop's House, St George's Road, Southwark, London SE1 6HX
Archbishop of Southwark: Most Rev Michael G Bowen. Admin staff 4, Other staff 8, Serving ministers 492. ***CC*** Began 1850. Magazine: *Outreach* (Circulation n/a every two months).
☎ 020 7928 2495/5592 Fax 020 7928 7833
Area Bishops: Rt Rev Charles J Henderson, 6a Cresswell Park, Blackheath, London SE3 9RD
☎ 020 8318 1094
Rt Rev John Jukes, The Hermitage, More Park, West Malling, Maidstone ME19 6HN
☎ 01732 845 486
Rt Rev Howard Tripp, 8 Arterberry Road, London SW20 8AJ
☎ 020 8946 4609

†*Roman Catholic* Archdiocese of Westminster, Archbishop's House, Ambrosden Avenue, London SW1P 1QJ
Cardinal Archbishop of Westminster: To be appointed. *Private Secretary:* Rev James Curry. Admin staff 152, Serving ministers 900. Began 1850. Magazine: *Westminster Diocesan Record* (Circulation n/a regularly).
☎ 020 7798 9033 Fax 020 7798 9077
Bishop in East London: Rt Rev Victor Guazzelli, The Lodge, Pope John House, Hale Street, London E14 0BT
☎ 020 7987 4663
Bishop in Hertfordshire: Rt Rev James O'Brien, The Gatehouse, All Saints Pastoral Centre, London Colney, St Albans AL2 1AQ
☎ 01727 824 664 Fax 01727 825 955
Bishop in North London: Rt Rev Vincent Nichols, Westminster House, Watford Way, Hendon, London NW4 4TY
☎ 020 8202 3611
Episcopal Vicar in West London: Rev Peter Gilburt, 34 Whitehall Gardens, Acton, London W3 9RD
☎ 020 8993 0270
Bishop in West London: Rt Rev Patrick O'Donaghue, 112 Twickenham Road, Isleworth TW7 6DL
☎ 020 8568 7371
Episcopal Vicar in Central London: Rt Rev Mgr Harry Turner, 73 St Charles Square, London W10 6EJ
☎ 020 8960 4029

†*Roman Catholic* Diocese of Wrexham (Province of Cardiff), Bishop's House, Sontley Road, Wrexham LL13 7EW
Bishop of Wrexham: Rt Rev Edwin Regan. *Vicar General:* Rt Rev Mgr James Fealey. Admin staff 4, Serving ministers 53. Began n/a. No magazine.
☎ 01978 262 726

Celtic Orthodox Church: British Eparchy, 33 Brownlow Street, York YO31 8LW
Administrator: Father Stephen. *Metropolitan:* His Severity Metropolitan Mael France. Serving ministers 7. ***CC*** No.1064510. Began 1866. Magazine: *Parish News* (Circulation n/a monthly).
Web: www.stanne.dircon.co.uk
Email: stanne@dircon.co.uk
☎ 01904 626 599

C

*__Chinese Church in London__, 4 Mayfields, Wembley HA9 9PS
Pastor: Rev K T Tan. Serving ministers 4, Admin staff 2. ***CC*** No.273164. Began 1951; interdenominational. No magazine.
Web: www.ccil.u-net.com
✉ Email: staff@ccil.u-net.com
☎ 020 8904 9772

Christ Apostolic Church of Great Britain, 202 Page Green Terrace, High Road, Tottenham, London N15 4NP
Minister in Charge: Rev Olu Adeshia. Executive staff 16, Serving ministers n/a. Began 1979. No magazine.
☎ 020 8365 1842 🖷 020 8365 1842

Christ Apostolic Church Mount Bethel, 215 Kingsland Road, London E2 8AN
Apostle: Apostle Ayo Omideyi. Executive staff 3, Admin staff 13, Serving ministers 2. ***CC*** No.274154. Began 1974. Magazine: *Sower Outreach* (1,000 quarterly).
☎ 020 7729 4375 🖷 020 7613 4204

Christian Brethren, 52 Hornsey Lane, London N6 5LU
Executive Secretary Partnership (UK) Ltd: Dr Neil Summerton. Full-time pastoral leaders 190. Began 1828. Magazine: *Newsletter* (400 every four months). Contact details given solely as an information point.
✉ Email: summerto@hornsey.u-net.com
☎ 020 7272 0643

The Christian Community (London West), Temple Lodge, 51 Queen Caroline Street, Hammersmith, London W6 9QL
Priest: Rev Rachael Shepherd. Staff n/a. Serving ministers n/a. ***CC*** No.210905. Began 1961. No magazine.
☎ 020 8748 8388
Editor's Note: The Christian Community has previously inadvertently been included in the non-Trinitarian section of the Handbook. They have now been transferred to the Trinitarian section because they accept the Trinitarian formula of other organisations listed with the addition that they see the Son being totally involved in all aspects of the origination of the Universe, as well as the Father.

Church in Wales, 39 Cathedral Road, Cardiff CF11 9XF
Archbishop of Wales: To be appointed.
Secretary General: Mr J W D McIntyre. Executive staff 1, Admin staff 44. Began n/a. (Disestablished 1920). Magazine: *Welsh Church Life* (20,000 monthly), *Llan* (800 fortnightly).
✉ Email: postmaster@rbchurchinwales.org.uk
☎ 029 2023 1638 🖷 029 2038 7835

***Church in Wales* Diocese of Bangor**, Church in Wales, Ty'r Esgob, Bangor LL57 2SS
Bishop: To be appointed.
☎ 01248 362 895 🖷 01248 354 866
Diocesan Secretary: Ms Stella Schultz, Diocesan Centre, Cathedral Close, Bangor LL57 1RL
Executive staff 3, Admin staff 3, Serving ministers 80. ***CC*** No.249824. Began 550. Magazine: *Y Ddolen/The Link* (3,000 quarterly).
☎ 01248 354 999 🖷 01248 353 882

***Church in Wales* Diocese of Llandaff**, Llys Esgob, The Cathedral Green, Llandaff, Cardiff CF5 2YE
Bishop: Rt Rev Barry Morgan.
☎ 029 2056 2400
Secretary to Board of Finance: Mr Michael J Beasant, Heol Fair, Llandaff, Cardiff CF5 2EE
Executive staff 4, Admin staff 3, Serving ministers 189. Began 460. Magazine: *Diocesan Leaflet* (26,000 quarterly).
☎ 029 2057 8899 🖷 029 2057 6198

***Church in Wales* Diocese of Monmouth**, Bishopstow, Stow Hill, Newport NP9 4EA
Bishop: Rt Rev Rowan D Williams.
☎ 01633 263 510
Diocesan Secretary: Mr R J Tarran, 64 Caerau Road, Newport NP9 4HJ
Executive staff 4, Serving ministers 115. Began 1921. Magazine: *Monmouth Diocesan Leaflet* (12,000 quarterly).
☎ 01633 267 490 🖷 01633 265 586

***Church in Wales* Diocese of St Asaph**, Esgobty, Upper Denbigh Road, St Asaph LL17 0TW
Bishop: Rt Rev John S. Davies.
☎ 01745 583 503 🖷 01745 584 301
Diocesan Secretary: Mr Christopher Seaton, Diocesan Office, High Street, St Asaph LL17 0RD
Executive staff 2, Serving ministers 112. Began 1921. Magazine: *Diocesan News* (15,500 quarterly).
☎ 01745 582 245

***Church in Wales* Diocese of St David's**, Llys Esgob, Abergwili, Carmarthen SA31 2JG
Bishop of St Davids: Rt Rev Huw Jones.
☎ 01267 236 597 🖷 01267 237 482
Diocesan Secretary: Mr D Vincent Lloyd, Diocesan Office, Abergwili, Carmarthen SA31 2JG
Executive staff 2, Admin staff 4, Serving ministers 135. Began 590. Magazine: *Llais Dewi* (1,300 quarterly).
☎ 01267 236 145 🖷 01267 223 046

Church in Wales **Diocese of Swansea and Brecon**, Diocesan Centre, The Cathedral Close, Brecon LD3 9DP
Bishop: Rt Rev Anthony E Pierce. *Diocesan Secretary:* Major D Hugh Thomas. Serving ministers 90. Began 1923. Magazine: *Swansea & Brecon Diocesan News* (Circulation n/a quarterly).
☎ 01874 623 716 🖷 01874 623 716

Church in Wales **Provincial Assistant Bishop,** Bodfair, 3 White's Close, Abergavenny NP7 5HZ
Bishop: Rt Rev David Thomas
☎ 01873 858 780 🖷 01873 858 780

Church of Christ, 64 Grenville Road, Southcourt, Aylesbury HP21 8EZ
Editor: Mr Graham Fisher. Began n/a. The address and person given are solely as information points. Magazine: *The Christian Worker* (1,100 monthly).
Email: grahamafisher@compuserve.com
☎ 01296 421 064

Church of England Archbishops' Council and General Synod, Church House, Great Smith Street, London SW1P 3NZ
Secretary-General: Mr Philip Mawer. Full-time staff 191. Began 597. (1999). Relevant journals: *Church Times* (38,000 weekly), *Church of England Newspaper* (12,500 weekly).
Email: firstname.surname@boe.c-of-e.org.uk
☎ 020 7898 1000 🖷 020 7898 1369
See also: **Archbishop's Council – Committee for Ministry among Deaf People** on Page 410
Archbishop's Officer for the Millennium on Page 221
Association of Ordinands and Candidates for Ministry on Page 231
Board for Social Responsibility (Archbishop's Council) on Page 455
Board of Mission on Page 370
Board of Education on Page 490
Central Board of Finance of the Church of England on Page 417
Central Readers' Council on Page 232
Church Commissioners on Page 391
Churches Main Committee on Page 233
Church House Bookshop on Page 113
Church House Publishing on Page 172
Church of England Chaplaincy in Higher Education on Page 194
Church of England National Youth Office on Page 478
Church Urban Fund on Page 392
Communication Department on Page 432
The Corporation of the Church House on Page 234
The Corporation of the Sons of the Clergy on Page 392
Council for Christian Unity on Page 234
Doctrine Commission on Page 234
Dioceses Commission on Page 234
Enquiry Centre on Page 432
Legal Advisory Commission on Page 236
Liturgical Commission on Page 236
Ministry Division (Archbishop's Council) on Page 237
National Society for Promoting Religious Education on Page 393
Queen Victoria Clergy Fund on Page 394
Together with Children on Page 319
The Worshipful Company of Parish Clerks on Page 240
See also under **Church of England** in Main Index on Page 627

Church of England **Diocese in Europe (Province of Canterbury),** Bishop's Lodge, Church Road, Worth, Crawley RH10 7RT
Bishop of Gibraltar in Europe: Rt Rev John Hind.
Email: bishop@eurobish.clara.co.uk
☎ 01293 883 051 🖷 01293 884 479
Diocesan Office: *Diocesan Secretary:* Mr Adrian Mumford, 14 Tufton Street, Westminster, London SW1P 3QZ
Serving ministers 180. ***CC*** No.250186. Began 1980. Magazine: *The European Anglican* (2,000 quarterly).
Web: www.europe.anglican.org
Email: adrian@dioeurope.clara.net
☎ 020 7976 8001 🖷 020 7976 8002
Suffragan Bishop in Europe: Rt Rev Henry Scriven
Archdeacon of the Eastern Archdeaconry: Ven Jeremy Peake
Archdeacon of Gibraltar: Ven Kenneth Robinson
Archdeacon of Italy: Ven Bill Edebohls
Archdeacon of North West Europe: Ven Geoffrey Allen
Archdeacon of France: Ven Martin Draper
Archdeacon of Scandinavia and Germany: Ven David W Ratcliff
Archdeacon of Switzerland: Ven Peter Hawker

C

Church of England **Diocese of Bath and Wells (Province of Canterbury),** Bishop's Palace, Wells BA5 2PD
Bishop: Rt Rev James L Thompson.
Email: bishop@bathwells.anglican.org
☎ 01749 672 341 🖷 01749 679 355
Diocesan Secretary: Mr Nicholas Denison, The Diocesan Office, The Old Deanery, Wells BA5 2UG
Executive staff 20, Serving ministers 319. Began 909. Magazine: *The Grapevine* (62,000 monthly).
Web: www.bathwells.anglican.org
Email: general@bathwells.anglican.org
☎ 01749 670 777 🖷 01749 674 240
Suffragan Bishop of Taunton: Rt Rev Andrew Radford, Bishops Lodge, Monkton Heights, West Monkton, Taunton TA2 8LU
☎ 01823 413 526 🖷 01823 412 805
Archdeacon of Bath: Ven Robert Evens, 56 Grange Road, Saltford, Bristol BS18 3AG
☎ 01225 873 609
Archdeacon of Taunton: Ven John Reed, 4 Westerkirk Gate, Staplegrove, Taunton TA2 6BQ
☎ 01823 323 838
Archdeacon of Wells: Ven Richard Acworth, The Old Rectory, The Crescent, Croscombe, Wells BA5 3QN
☎ 01749 342 242

Church of England **Diocese of Birmingham (Province of Canterbury),** Bishop's Croft, Old Church Road, Harborne, Birmingham B17 0BG
Bishop: Rt Rev Mark Santer.
☎ 0121 427 1163 🖷 0121 426 1322
Diocesan Office: *Diocesan Secretary:* Mr Jim Drennan, 175 Harborne Park Road, Harborne, Birmingham B17 0BH
Admin staff 34, Serving ministers 300. Began 1905. Magazine: *Bulletin* (830 monthly), *In Touch* (830 monthly).
☎ 0121 427 5141 🖷 0121 428 1114
Suffragan Bishop of Aston: Rt Rev John Austin, Strensham House, 8 Strensham Hill, Moseley, Birmingham B13 8AG
☎ 0121 427 5141
Archdeacon of Aston: Ven John Barton, 175 Harborne Park Road, Harborne, Birmingham B17 0BH
☎ 0121 427 5141
Archdeacon of Birmingham: Ven John Duncan, 122 Westfield Road, Edgbaston, Birmingham B15 3JQ
☎ 0121 454 3402

C

READY
STEADY
ChurchArmy
WE CAN HELP YOU...
explore a call to train for licensed lay ministry
by providing a licensed Evangelist to work in partnership with you in your ministry
by enabling your church and its members to participate in our 'Learning to Share' - Evangelism and Church Planting course
encourage your church and its members to partner us by supporting our evangelists in their ministry across the British Isles
WHY NOT CONTACT US AT...
Church Army, Independents Road,
Blackheath, London, SE3 9LG
Tel: 020 8318 1226 Fax: 020 8318 5258
e-mail: information@churcharmy.org.uk
Registered Charity No. 226226

***Church of England* Diocese of Blackburn (Province of York)**, Bishop's House, Ribchester Road, Blackburn BB1 9EF
Bishop: Rt Rev Alan D Chesters.
Email: bishop.blackburn@ukonline.co.uk
☎ 01254 248 234 🖷 01254 246 668
Diocesan Secretary: Rev Michael Wedgeworth, Diocesan Offices, Cathedral Close, Blackburn BB1 5AA
Executive staff 10, Other staff 10, Serving ministers 246. Began 1926. Magazine: *The See* (49,000 monthly).
Web: web.ukonline.co.uk/anchorsholme/
☎ 01254 544 21 🖷 01254 667 309
Suffragan Bishop of Burnley: Rt Rev Martyn Jarrett, Dean House, 449 Padiham Road, Burnley BB12 6TE
☎ 01282 423 564
Suffragan Bishop of Lancaster: Rt Rev Stephen Pedley, Shireshead Vicarage, Whinney Brow, Forton, Preston PR3 0AE
☎ 01524 799 900
Archdeacon of Blackburn: Ven Dr John Marsh, 19 Clarence Park Blackburn BB2 7FA
☎ 01254 262 571 🖷 01254 263 394
Archdeacon of Lancaster: Ven Colin Williams, St Michael's Vicarage, Hall Lane, St Michaels-on-Wyre, Preston PR3 0TQ
☎ 01995 679 242 🖷 01995 679 747

***Church of England* Diocese of Bradford (Province of York)**, Diocesan Offices, Cathedral Hall, Stott Hill, Bradford BD1 4ET
Bishop: Rt Rev David J Smith. *Assistant Bishop:* Rt Rev Peter Vaughan. *Diocesan Secretary:* Mr Malcolm K Halliday. Executive staff 3, Admin staff 4, Serving ministers 150. Began 1919. Magazine: *Newsround* (25,000 quarterly).
☎ 01274 725 958 🖷 01274 726 343
Archdeacon of Bradford: Ven Guy Wilkinson, c/o Diocesan Office
Archdeacon of Craven: Ven Malcolm L Grundy, The Vicarage, Gisburn,Clitheroe, BB7 4HR
☎ 01200 445 214 🖷 01200 445 816

***Church of England* Diocese of Bristol (Province of Canterbury)**, Church House, 23 Great George Street, Bristol BS1 5QZ
Bishop: Rt Rev Barry Rogerson. *Diocesan Secretary:* Mrs L E Farrall. *Finance Manager:* Mr G C Ash. Admin staff 24, Serving ministers 155. Began 1524. Magazine: *Newspaper* (20,000 monthly). Turnover £5,000,000 to year end Dec 98.
☎ 0117 921 4411 🖷 0117 925 0460
Suffragan Bishop of Swindon (formerly Malmesbury): Rt Rev Michael Doe, Mark House, Field Rise, Swindon SN1 4HP
☎ 01793 538 654
Archdeacon of Bristol: Ven Timothy McClure, c/o Church House, 23 Great George Street, Bristol BS1 5QZ
☎ 0117 921 4411 🖷 0117 925 0460
Archdeacon of Malmesbury: Ven Alan Hawker, 2 Louviers Way, Fitzroy Road, Swindon SN1 4DU
☎ 01793 644 556

***Church of England* Diocese of Canterbury (Province of Canterbury)**, Lady Woottons Green, Canterbury CT1 1NQ
Archbishop of Canterbury: Most Rev & Rt Hon George L Carey. *Diocesan Secretary:* Mr David S Kemp. Executive staff 6, Admin staff 20, Serving ministers 180. Began 597. Magazine: *Outlook* (25,000 monthly).
☎ 01227 459 401 🖷 01227 450 964
Also at: *Primate of All England and Metropolitan:* Most Rev & Rt Hon George L Carey, Lambeth Palace, London SE1 7JU
☎ 020 7928 8282
Suffragan Bishop of Dover: Rt Rev Stephen Venner, Old Palace, Canterbury CT1 2EE
☎ 01227 459 382
Suffragan Bishop of Maidstone: Rt Rev Gavin H Reid, Bishop's House, Pett Lane, Charing, Ashford TN27 0DL
☎ 01233 712 950
Archdeacon of Canterbury: Ven John Pritchard, 29 The Precincts, Canterbury CT1 2EP
☎ 01227 463 036
Archdeacon of Maidstone: Ven Patrick Evans, The Old Rectory, The Street, Pluckley, Ashford TN27 0QT
☎ 01233 840 291 🖷 01233 840 759

***Church of England* Diocese of Carlisle (Province of York)**, Church House, West Walls, Carlisle CA3 8UE
Bishop: Rt Rev Ian Harland. *Diocesan Secretary:* Rev Canon Colin Hill. Executive staff 4, Other staff 10, Serving ministers 183. ***CC*** No.251977. Began 1133. Magazine: *Carlisle Diocesan News* (35,000 monthly).
☎ 01228 522 573 🖷 01228 594 899
Suffragan Bishop of Penrith: Rt Rev Richard Garrard, Holm Croft, Castle Road, Kendal LA9 7AU
☎ 01539 727 836 🖷 01539 734 380
Archdeacon of Carlisle: Ven David C Turnbull, 2 The Abbey, Carlisle CA3 8TZ
☎ 01228 230 26 🖷 01228 594 899
Archdeacon of West Cumberland: Ven Alan Davis, 50 Stainburn Road, Workington CA14 1SN
☎ 01900 661 90
Archdeacon of Westmoreland and Furness: To be appointed

C

***Church of England* Diocese of Chelmsford (Province of Canterbury)**, Bishops Court, Main Road, Margaretting, Ingatestone CM4 0HD
Bishop: Rt Rev John Perry.
Email: bishopjohn@chelmsford.anglican.org
☎ 01277 352 001 🖷 02177 355 374
Diocesan Secretary: Mr David Phillips, Guy Harlings, 53 New Street, Chelmsford CM1 1AT
Executive staff 28, Admin staff 19, Serving ministers 410. ***CC*** No.249505. Began 1914. Magazine: *East Window* (47,500 monthly), *Notice Board* (2,000 monthly).
☎ 01245 294 400 🖷 01245 294 477
Area Bishop of Barking: Rt Rev Roger F Sainsbury, Barking Lodge, 110 Capel Road, Forest Gate, London E7 0JS
☎ 020 8478 2456
Email: bishoproger@chelmsford.anglican.org
Area Bishop of Bradwell: Rt Rev Laurie Green, Bishop's House, Orsett Road, Horndon-on-the-Hill, Stanford-le-Hope SS17 8NS
☎ 01375 673 806 🖷 01375 674 222
Email: bishoplaurie@chelmsford.anglican.org
Area Bishop of Colchester: Rt Rev Edward Holland, 1 Fitzwalter Road, Lexden, Colchester CO3 3SS
☎ 01206 576 648
Email: bishopward@chelmsford.anglican.org
Archdeacon of Colchester: Ven Martin Wallace, Archdeacon's House, 63 Powers Hall End, Witham, CM8 1NH
☎ 01376 513 130
Email: a.colchester@chelmsford.anglican.org
Archdeacon of Harlow: Ven Peter Taylor, Glebe House, Church Lane, Sheering, Bishops Stortford CM22 7NR
☎ 01279 734 524
Email: a.harlow@chelmsford.anglican.org
Archdeacon of Southend: Ven David Jennings, 136 Broomfield Road, Chelmsford CM1 1RN
☎ 01245 258 257
Email: a.southend@chelmsford.anglican.org
Archdeacon of West Ham: Ven Michael Fox, 86 Aldersbrook Road, Manor Park, London E12 5DH
☎ 020 8989 8557
Email: a.westham@chelmsford.anglican.org

Church of England **Diocese of Chester (Province of York)**, Bishop's House, Abbey Square, Chester CH1 2JD
Bishop: Rt Rev Dr Peter Forster.
☎ 01244 350 864 🖷 01244 314 187
Diocesan Secretary: Mr Stephen Marriott, Church House, Lower Lane, Aldford, Chester CH1 6HP
Serving ministers 298. ***CC*** No.248968. Began 1541. Magazine: *Chester Diocesan News* (70,000 monthly).
☎ 01244 620 444 🖷 01244 620 456
Suffragan Bishop of Birkenhead: Rt Rev Michael L Langrish, Bishop's Lodge, 67 Biston Road, Oxton, Birkenhead CH43 6TR
☎ 0151 652 2741 🖷 0151 651 2330
Suffragan Bishop of Stockport: Rt Rev Geoffrey M Turner, Bishop's Lodge, Back Lane, Dunham Town, Altrincham WA14 4SG
☎ 0161 928 5611 🖷 0161 929 0692
Archdeacon of Chester: Ven Christopher Hewetson, 8 Queens Park Road, Queens Park, Chester CH4 7AD
☎ 01244 675 417 🖷 01244 681 959
Archdeacon of Macclesfield: Ven Richard J Gillings, The Vicarage, Robins Lane, Bramhall, Stockport SK7 2PE
☎ 0161 439 2254 🖷 0161 439 0878

C

Church of England **Diocese of Chichester (Province of Canterbury)**, The Palace, Chichester PO19 1PY
Bishop: Rt Rev Eric W Kemp.
☎ 01243 782 161 🖷 01243 531 332
Diocesan Secretary: Mr J M R Prichard, Church House, 211 New Church Road, Hove BN3 4ED
Executive staff 10, Other staff 29, Serving ministers 521. ***CC*** No.243134. Began 681. Magazine: *The Chichester Leaflet* (28,000 monthly), *The Chichester Magazine* (7,000 quarterly).
☎ 01273 421 021 🖷 01273 421 041
Area Bishop of Horsham: Rt Rev Lindsay Urwin, Bishop's House, 21 Guildford Road, Horsham RH12 1LU
☎ 01403 211 139
Area Bishop of Lewes: Rt Rev Wallace Benn, Bishop's Lodge 16a Prideaux Road, Eastbourne BN21 6ST
☎ 01323 648 462
Archdeacon of Chichester: Ven Michael Brotherton, 4 Canon Lane, Chichester PO19 1PX
☎ 01243 779 134
Archdeacon of Horsham: Ven William Filby, The Archdeaconry, Itchingfield, Horsham RH13 7NX
☎ 01403 790 315
Archdeacon of Lewes and Hastings: Ven Nicholas Reade, 27 The Avenue, Lewes BN7 1QT
☎ 01273 479 530

†*Church of England* **Diocese of Coventry (Province of Canterbury)**, Bishop's House, 23 Davenport Road, Coventry CV5 6PW
Bishop: Rt Rev Colin Bennetts.
☎ 024 7667 2244 🖷 024 7671 3271
Diocesan Secretary: Mrs Isobel Chapman, Church House, Palmerston Road, Coventry CV5 6FJ
Executive staff 8, Serving ministers 175. Began 1918. Magazine: *Diamond* (1,000 monthly).
☎ 024 7667 4328 🖷 024 7669 1760
Suffragan Bishop of Warwick: Rt RevAnthony Priddis, Warwick House, 139 Kenilworth Road, Coventry CV4 7AP
☎ 024 7641 6200 🖷 01203 415 254
Archdeacon of Coventry: Ven Ian Russell, 9 Armorial Road, Stivichall, Coventry CV3 6GH
☎ 024 7641 7750
Archdeacon of Warwick: Ven Michael Paget-Wilkes, 10 Northumberland Road, Leamington Spa CV32 6HA
☎ 024 7667 4328

Church of England **Diocese of Derby (Province of Canterbury)**, Derby Church House, Full Street, Derby DE1 3DR
Bishop: Rt Rev Jonathan Bailey. *Diocesan Secretary:* Mr Robert J Carey. Staff n/a, Serving ministers n/a. Began 1927. Magazine: *The DDN* (23,000 monthly).
☎ 01332 382 233
Suffragan Bishop of Repton: Rt Rev David Hawtin, Repton House, Lea, Matlock DE4 5JP
☎ 01629 534 644
Archdeacon of Chesterfield: Ven David Garnett, The Old Parsonage, Taddington, Buxton SK17 9TW
☎ 01298 856 07
Archdeacon of Derby: Ven Ian Gatford, Derby Church House, Full Street, Derby, Derbyshire DE1 3DR
☎ 01332 382 233

Church of England **Diocese of Durham (Province of York)**, Auckland Castle, Bishop Auckland DL14 7NR
Bishop: Rt Rev Michael Turnbull.
☎ 01388 602 576 🖷 01388 605 264
Diocesan Secretary: Mr Jonathan Cryer, Diocesan Office, Auckland Castle, Bishop Auckland DL14 7QJ
Executive staff 1, Admin staff 15, Serving ministers 250. ***CC*** No.248287. Began 635. Magazine: *Durham Newslink* (27,000 monthly), *Durham Network* (Circulation & frequency n/a).
Web: www.durham.anglican.org
☎ 01388 604 515 🖷 01388 603 695
Suffragan Bishop of Jarrow: Rt Rev Alan Smithson, The Old Vicarage, Hallgarth, Pittington, Durham DH6 1AB
☎ 0191 372 0225 🖷 0191 372 2326
Archdeacon of Auckland: Ven Granville Gibson, 2 Etherley Lane, Bishop Auckland, Co Durham DL14 7QR
☎ 01388 451 635 🖷 01388 607 502
Archdeacon of Durham: Ven Trevor Willmott, 15 The College, Durham DH1 3EQ
☎ 0191 384 7534 🖷 0191 386 6915
Archdeacon of Sunderland: Ven Frank White, Greenriggs, Dipe Lane, East Boldon NE36 0PH
☎ 0191 536 2300 🖷 0191 519 3369

Church of England **Diocese of Ely (Province of Canterbury)**, Bishop's House, Ely CB7 4DW
Bishop: To be appointed.
☎ 01353 662 749 🖷 01353 669 477
Diocesan Secretary: Dr Matthew Lavis, Diocesan Office, Bishop Woodford House, Barton Road, Ely CB7 4DX
Admin staff 6, Other staff 6, Serving ministers n/a. Began 1109. Magazine: *Ely Ensign* (11,000 monthly).
☎ 01353 663 579 🖷 01353 666 148
Suffragan Bishop of Huntingdon: Rt Rev John Flack, 14 Lynn Road, Ely CB6 1DA
☎ 01353 662 137 🖷 01353 669 357
Archdeacon of Ely: Ven Jeffrey Watson, St Botolph's Rectory, Summerfield, Cambridge CB3 9HE
☎ 01223 515 725 🖷 01223 571 322
Email: archdeacon.ely@ely.anglican.org
Archdeacon of Huntingdon: Ven John Beer, The Rectory, Hemingford Abbots, Huntingdon PE18 9AN
☎ 01480 380 284 🖷 01480 496 073
Email: archdeacon.huntingdon@ely.anglican.org
Archdeacon of Wisbech: Ven James Rone, Archdeacon's House, 24 Cromwell Road,Ely CB6 1AS
☎ 01353 662 909 🖷 01353 662 056
Email: archdeacon.wisbech@ely.anglican.org

Church of England **Diocese of Exeter (Province of Canterbury)**, Diocesan House, Palace Gate, Exeter EX1 1HX
Bishop: To be appointed. *Diocesan Secretary:* Mr Mark Beedell. Executive staff 6, Other staff 7, Serving ministers 302. Began 909. Magazine: *Exeter Diocesan News* (34,000 monthly).
☎ 01392 272 686
Suffragan Bishop of Crediton: Rt Rev Richard Hawkins, 10 The Close, Exeter EX1 1EZ
☎ 01392 273 509 🖷 01392 431 266
Suffragan Bishop of Plymouth: Rt Rev John Garton, 31 Riverside Walk, Tamerton Foliot, Plymouth PL5 4AQ
☎ 01752 769 836 🖷 01752 769 818
Archdeacon of Barnstaple: Ven Trevor Lloyd, Stage Cross, Whitemoor Hill, Bishops Tawton, Barnstaple EX32 0BE
☎ 01271 375 475
Archdeacon of Exeter: Ven Tony Tremlett, St Matthew's House, 45 Spicer Road, Exeter EX1 1TA
☎ 01392 425 432 🖷 01392 425 783
Archdeacon of Plymouth: Ven Robin Ellis, The Vicarage, 33 Leat Walk, Roborough, Plymouth PL6 7AT
☎ 01752 793 397 🖷 01752 774 618
Archdeacon of Totnes: Ven Richard Gilpin, Blue Hills, Bradley Road, Bovey Tracey, Newton Abbot TQ13 9EU
☎ 01626 832 064 🖷 01626 834 947

Church of England **Diocese of Gloucester (Province of Canterbury)**, Church House, College Green, Gloucester GL1 2LY
Bishop: Rt Rev David Bentley. *Diocesan Secretary:* Mr Michael Williams. Executive staff 4, Other staff 11, Serving ministers 173. ***CC*** No.162165. Began 1541. Magazine: *Together* (60,000 monthly). Turnover £5,700,000 to year end Dec 98.
Web: www.doma.demon.co.uk/glosdioc.htm
Email: church.house@glosdioc.org.uk
☎ 01452 410 022 🖷 01452 308 324
Suffragan Bishop of Tewkesbury: Rt Rev John Went, Green Acre, 166 Hempsted Lane, Gloucester GL2 5LG
☎ 01452 521 824
Archdeacon of Cheltenham: Ven Hedley Ringrose, The Sanderlings, Thorncliffe Drive, Cheltenham GL51 6PY
☎ 01242 522 923
Archdeacon of Gloucester: Ven Christopher Wagstaff, Glebe House, Church Road, Maisemore, Gloucester GL2 8EY
☎ 01452 381 528

†***Church of England*** **Diocese of Guildford (Province of Canterbury)**, Willow Grange, Woking Road, Guildford GU4 7QS
Bishop: Rt Rev John Gladwin.
☎ 01483 573 922 🖷 01483 326 63
Diocesan Secretary: Mrs Kristina Ingate, Diocesan House, Quarry Street, Guildford GU1 3XG
Executive staff 6, Admin staff 3, Serving ministers 220. Began 1927. Magazine: *The Guildford Diocesan Herald* (53,000 monthly).
☎ 01483 571 826 🖷 01483 567 896
Suffragan Bishop of Dorking: Rt Rev Ian Brackley, 13 Pilgrims Way, Guildford GU4 8AD
☎ 01483 570 829 🖷 01483 567 268
Archdeacon of Dorking: Ven Mark Wilson, Littlecroft, Heathside Road, Woking GU22 7EZ
☎ 01483 772 713 🖷 01483 757 353
Archdeacon of Surrey: Ven Robert Reiss, Archdeacon's House, New Road, Wormley, Godalming GU8 5SU
☎ 01428 682 563

Church of England **Diocese of Hereford (Province of Canterbury)**, The Diocesan Office, The Palace, Hereford HR4 9BL
Bishop: Rt Rev John Oliver. *Diocesan Secretary:* Miss Sylvia Green. Executive staff 8, Admin staff 5, Serving ministers 160. Began 676. Magazine: *The NEWS paper* (18,000 quarterly).
☎ 01432 353 863 🖷 01432 352 952
Suffragan Bishop & Archdeacon of Ludlow: Rt Rev Dr John Saxbee, Bishop's House, Corvedale Road, Craven Arms SY7 9BT
☎ 01588 673 571 🖷 01588 673 585
Archdeacon of Hereford: Ven Michael Hooper, The Archdeacon's House, The Close, Hereford HR1 2NG
☎ 01432 272 873

Church of England **Diocese of Leicester**, Bishop's Lodge, 10 Springfield Road, Leicester LE2 3BD
Bishop: Rt Rev Timothy Stevens.
☎ 0116 270 8985 🖷 0116 270 3288
Diocesan Secretary: Mr Andrew Howard, Church House, 3 St Martins East, Leicester LE1 5FX
Executive staff 15, Serving ministers 200. ***CC*** No.249100. Began 1926. Magazine: *News and Views* (Circulation n/a monthly).
Web: www.leicester.anglican.org
☎ 0116 262 7445 🖷 0116 253 2889
Archdeacon of Leicester: Ven Michael Edson, 13 Stoneygate Avenue, Leicester LE2 3HE
☎ 0116 270 4441
Archdeacon of Loughborough: Ven Ian Stanes, The Archdeaconry, 21 Church Road, Glenfield, Leicester LE3 8DP
☎ 0116 231 1632

Church of England **Diocese of Lichfield (Province of Canterbury)**, St Mary's House, The Close, Lichfield WS13 7LD
Bishop: Rt Rev Keith Sutton. *Diocesan Secretary:* Mr D R Taylor. Executive staff 23, Admin staff 22, Serving ministers 450. Began 656. Magazine: *Link* (60,000 monthly).
☎ 01543 306 030 🖷 01543 250 935
Area Bishop of Shrewsbury: Rt Rev David Hallatt, 68 London Road, Shrewsbury SY2 6PG
☎ 01743 235 867 🖷 01743 243 296
Area Bishop of Stafford: Rt Rev Christopher Hill, Ash Garta, 6 Broughton Crescent, Barlaston, Stoke-on-Trent ST12 9DD
☎ 01782 373 308 🖷 01782 373 705
Area Bishop of Wolverhampton: Rt Rev Michael G Bourke, 61 Richmond Road, Wolverhampton WV3 9JH
☎ 01902 230 08 🖷 01902 254 43
Archdeacon of Lichfield: Ven George Frost, 24 The Close, Lichfield WS13 7LD
☎ 01543 306 145
Archdeacon of Salop: Ven John Hall, Tong Vicarage, Shifnal TF11 8PW
☎ 01902 372 622 🖷 01902 374 021
Archdeacon of Stoke-on-Trent: Ven Alan Smith, 39 The Brackens, Clayton, Newcastle ST5 4JL
☎ 01782 663 066 🖷 01782 711 165
Archdeaon of Walsall: Ven Anthony Sadler, 10 Paradise Lane, Pelsall, Walsall WS3 4NH
☎ 01922 694 299 🖷 01922 694 301

Church of England **Diocese of Lincoln (Province of Canterbury),** Bishop's House, Eastgate, Lincoln LN2 1QQ
Bishop: Rt Rev Robert M Hardy.
Email: bishlincoln@claranet.co.uk
☎ 01522 534 701 🖷 01522 511 095
Diocesan Secretary: Mr Phil Hamlyn-Williams, Church House, The Old Palace, Lincoln LN2 1PU
Email: lincolndio@claranet.co.uk
Executive staff 20, Other staff 6, Serving ministers 234. Began 886. Magazine: *The Bulletin* (Circulation & frequency n/a).
☎ 01522 529 241 🖷 01522 512 717
Suffragan Bishop of Grantham: Rt Rev Alastair Redfern, Fairacre, Barrowby High Road, Grantham NG31 8NP
☎ 01476 647 22 🖷 01476 647 22
Suffragan Bishop of Grimsby: Rt Rev David Tustin, Bishop's House, Church Lane, Irby-on-Humber, Grimsby DN37 7JR
☎ 01472 371 715 🖷 01472 371 716
Archdeacon of Lincoln: Ven Arthur Hawes, Archdeacon's House, Quarrington, Sleaford NG34 8RT
☎ 01529 304 348
Archdeacon of Stow and in Lindsey: Ven Roderick Wells, Hackthorn Vicarage, Lincoln LN2 3PF
☎ 01673 860 382

C

†*Church of England* **Diocese of Liverpool (Province of York),** Church House, 1 Hanover Street, Liverpool L1 3DW
Bishop: Rt Rev James S Jones. *Diocesan Secretary:* Mr K W Cawdron. Executive staff 12, Admin staff 18, Serving ministers 287. ***CC*** No.249740. Began 1880. Magazine: *Livewire* (21,000 monthly). Turnover £6,000,000 to year end Dec 96.
☎ 0151 709 9722 🖷 0151 709 2885
Suffragan Bishop of Warrington: Rt Rev John Packer, 34 Central Avenue, Eccleston Park, Prescot L34 1NB
Archdeacon of Liverpool: Ven Robert (Bob) Metcalf, 38 Menlove Avenue, Liverpool L18 2EF
☎ 0151 724 3956
Archdeacon of Warrington: Ven David Woodhouse, 22 Rob Lane, Newton le Willows WA12 0DR
☎ 01925 229 247

Church of England **Diocese of London (Province of Canterbury),** London Diocesan House, The Old Deanery, Dean's Court, London EC4V 5AA
Bishop: Rt Rev & Rt Hon Richard Chartres. Executive staff 25. Began 314. Magazine: *London Link* (60,000 quarterly).
Email: bishop@london.clara.co.uk
☎ 020 7248 6233 🖷 020 7248 9721
Diocesan Secretary: Mr Christopher Smith, London Diocesan House, 36 Causton Street, London SW1P 4AU
☎ 020 7932 1100 🖷 020 7932 1112
Suffragan Bishop of Edmonton: Ven Peter Wheatley, 27 Thurlow Road, London NW3 5PP
☎ 020 7435 5890
Suffragan Bishop of Fulham: Rt Rev John Broadhurst, 26 Canonbury Park South, London N1 2FN
☎ 020 7354 2334
Area Bishop of Kensington: Rt Rev Michael Colclough, 19 Campden Hill Square, London W8 8JY
☎ 020 7727 9818
Area Bishop of Stepney: Rt Rev John Sentamu, 63 Coborn Road, Bow, London E3 2DB
☎ 020 8981 2323
Area Bishop of Willesden: Rt Rev Graham Dow, 173 Willesden Lane, London NW6 7YN
☎ 020 8451 0189
Archdeacon of Charing Cross: Ven W M Jacob, The Old Deanery, Deans Court, London EC4V 5AA
☎ 020 7248 6233
Archdeacon of Hackney: Ven Lyle Dennen, St Andrew's Vicarage, 5 St Andrew's Street, London EC4A 3AB
☎ 020 7353 3544
Archdeacon of Hampstead: Ven Michael Lawson, The Basement, 44 King Henry's Road, London NW3 3RP
☎ 020 7586 3224 🖷 020 7586 9976
Email: archdeacon.hampstead@dlondon.org.uk
Archdeacon of London: To be appointed
Archdeacon of Middlesex: Ven Malcolm Colmer, 59 Sutton Lane South, London W4 3JR
☎ 020 8994 8148 🖷 020 8995 5374
Email: archdeacon.middlesex@dlondon.org.uk
Archdeacon of Northolt: Ven Peter Broadbent, 247 Kenton Road, Harrow, Middlesex HA3 0HQ
☎ 020 8907 5941

Church of England **Diocese of Manchester (Province of York),** Bishopscourt, Bury New Road, Manchester M7 4LE
Bishop: Rt Rev Christopher Mayfield. *Diocesan Secretary:* Mrs J A Park. Executive staff 5, Admin staff 13, Serving ministers 319. Began 1847. Magazine: *Crux Magazine* (Circulation n/a monthly).
☎ 0161 792 2096
Suffragan Bishop of Bolton: Rt Rev David Gillett, Bishops Lodge, Bolton Road, Hawkshaw, Bury BL8 4JN
Suffragan Bishop of Hulme: Rt Rev Stephen Lowe, 14 Moorgate Avenue, Withington, Manchester M20 1HE
☎ 0161 445 5922 🖷 0161 448 9687
Suffragan Bishop of Middleton: Rt Rev Michael Lewis c/o Bishopscourt, Bury New Road, Manchester M7 4LE
☎ 0161 792 2096
Archdeacon of Bolton: Ven Lorys M Davies, 45 Rudgwick Drive, Brandlesholme, Bury BL8 1YA
☎ 0161 761 6117
Archdeacon of Manchester: Ven Alan Wolstencroft, 2 The Walled Garden, Ewhurst Avenue, Swinton, Manchester M27 2FR
☎ 0161 794 2401 🖷 0161 794 2411
Archdeacon of Rochdale: Ven Dr Mark Dalby, 21 Belmont Way, Rochdale OL12 6HR
☎ 01706 486 40

†*Church of England* **Diocese of Newcastle (Province of York),** Church House, Grainger Park Road, Newcastle upon Tyne NE4 8SX
Bishop: Rt Rev Martin Wharton. *Diocesan Secretary:* Mr Michael Craster. *Communications Officer:* Mrs Jeanne Swallow. Executive staff 11, Admin staff 6, Serving ministers 197. ***CC*** No.247233. Began 1882. Magazine: *The New Link* (13,000 monthly).
Email: church_house@newcastle.org
☎ 0191 273 0120 🖷 0191 256 5900
Suffragan Bishop of Newcastle: Rt Rev Paul Richardson, Bishops House, 29 Moor Road South, Newcastle upon Tyne NE3 1PA
☎ 0191 285 2220
Archdeacon of Lindisfarne: Ven Michael Bowering, 12 Rectory Park, Morpeth NE61 2SZ
☎ 01670 513 207
Archdeacon of Northumberland: Ven Peter Elliot, 80 Moorside North, Fenham, Newcastle upon Tyne NE4 9DU
☎ 0191 273 8245

***Church of England* Diocese of Norwich (Province of Canterbury),** Bishop's House, Norwich NR3 1SB
Bishop: Rt Rev Graham Jones.
☎ 01603 629 001 🖷 01603 761 613
Diocesan Secretary: Mr David Adeney, Diocesan House, Dereham Road, Easton, Norwich NR9 5ES
Executive staff 8, Admin staff 26, Serving ministers 268. ***CC*** No.249318. Began 630. Magazine: *Diocesan News* (6,500 monthly).
☎ 01603 880 853 🖷 01603 881 083
Suffragan Bishop of Lynn: Rt Rev Anthony Foottit, The Old Vicarage, Castle Acre, King's Lynn PE32 2AA
☎ 01760 755 553
Suffragan Bishop of Thetford: Rt Rev Hugo de Waal, Rectory Meadow, Bramerton, Norwich NR14 7DW
☎ 01508 538 251
Archdeacon of Lynn: Ven Martin C Gray, Holly Tree House, Whitwell Road, Sparham, Norwich NR9 5PW
☎ 01362 688 032
Archdeacon of Norfolk: Ven Michael Handley, 40 Heigham Road, Norwich NR2 3AU
☎ 01603 611 808
Archdeacon of Norwich: Ven Clifford Offer, 26 The Close, Norwich NR1 4DZ
☎ 01603 620 375

***Church of England* Diocese of Oxford (Province of Canterbury),** Diocesan Church House, North Hinksey, Oxford OX2 0NB
Bishop: Rt Rev Richard D Harries. *Diocesan Secretary:* Mrs Rosemary Pearce. Executive staff 10, Other staff 47, Serving ministers 481. Began 1542. Magazine: *The Door* (48,000 ten times a year).
Web: www.oxford.anglican.org
🖅 Email: diosec@oxford.anglican.org
☎ 01865 208 200 🖷 01865 790 470
Area Bishop of Buckingham: Rt Rev Michael Hill, 28 Church Street, Gt Missenden, HP16 0AZ
☎ 01494 862 173
Area Bishop of Dorchester: Rt Rev Anthony J Russell, Holmby House, Sibford Ferris, Banbury OX15 5RG
☎ 01295 780 583
Area Bishop of Reading: Rt Rev Dominic Walker, Bishops House, Tidmarsh Lane, Tidmarsh, Reading RG8 8HA
☎ 0118 984 1216 🖷 0118 984 1218
Archdeacon of Berkshire: Ven Norman Russell, Foxglove House, Love Lane, Donnington, Newbury RG13 2JG
☎ 01635 552 820
Archdeacon of Buckingham: Ven David Goldie, 60 Wendover Road, Aylesbury HP21 9LW
☎ 01296 243 269
Archdeacon of Oxford: Ven John Morrison, Archdeacon's Lodging, Christ Church, Oxford OX1 1DP
☎ 01865 204 440

***Church of England* Diocese of Peterborough (Province of Canterbury),** The Palace, Peterborough PE1 1YA
Bishop: Rt Rev Ian Cundy.
🖅 Email: bishop@peterborough-diocese.org.uk
☎ 01733 562 492 🖷 01733 890 077
Diocesan Secretary & Bishop's Chaplain: Rev Canon Richard Cattle. Staff n/a, Serving ministers n/a. Began 1541. Magazine: *Cross Keys* (Circulation n/a Monthly).
🖅 Email: chaplain@peterborough-diocese.org.uk
☎ 01733 564 448 🖷 01733 555 271
Suffragan Bishop of Brixworth: Rt Rev Paul E Barber, 4 The Avenue, Dallington, Northampton NN5 7AN
☎ 01604 759 423 🖷 01604 750 925
Archdeacon of Northampton: Ven Michael Chapman, 11 The Drive, Northampton NN1 4RZ
☎ 01604 714 015 🖷 01604 792 016
🖅 Email: michaelrchapman@compuserve.com
Archdeacon of Oakham: Ven David Painter, c/o Diocesan Office, The Palace, Peterborough PE1 1YA
☎ 01733 562 492

†***Church of England* Diocese of Portsmouth (Province of Canterbury),** Bishopswood, The Avenue, Fareham PO14 1NT
Bishop: Rt Rev Kenneth Stevenson.
☎ 01329 280 247
Diocesan Secretary: Mr Michael Jordan, Cathedral House, St Thomas Street, Portsmouth PO1 2HA
Executive staff 3, Admin staff 4, Serving ministers 135. Began 1927. Magazine: *The Link* (24,000 monthly).
☎ 023 9282 5731 🖷 023 9275 2967
Archdeacon of the Isle of Wight: Ven K. M. L. H Banting, 5 The Boltons, Wootton Bridge, Ryde, Isle of Wight PO33 4PB
☎ 01983 884 812
Archdeacon of Portsmouth: Ven Christopher Lowson, 5 Brading Avenue, Southsea, Hampshire PO4 9QJ
☎ 023 9243 2693

***Church of England* Diocese of Ripon and Leeds (Province of York),** Diocesan Office, St Mary's Street, Leeds LS9 7DP
Bishop: Rt Rev David N de L Young. *Diocesan Secretary:* Mr Philip M Arundel. Executive staff 4, Other staff 8. ***CC*** No.249860. Began 1836. Magazine: *Bishop's Letter* (21,000 monthly).
☎ 0113 248 7487 🖷 0113 249 1129
Suffragan Bishop of Knaresborough: Rt Rev Frank Weston, 16 Shaftesbury Avenue, Roundhay, Leeds LS8 1DT
☎ 0113 266 4800
Archdeacon of Leeds: Ven John Oliver, 2 Halcyon Hill, Leeds LS7 3PU
☎ 0113 269 0594 🖷 0113 269 0594
Archdeacon of Richmond: Ven Kenneth R Good, 62 Palace Road, Ripon HG4 1HA
☎ 01765 604 342 🖷 01765 604 342

***Church of England* Diocese of Rochester (Province of Canterbury),** Bishopscourt, Rochester ME1 1TS
Bishop: Rt Rev Dr Michael Nazir-Ali.
☎ 01634 842 721 🖷 01634 831 136
Diocesan Secretary: Mr Peter G H Law, Diocesan Office, St Nicholas Church, Boley Hill, Rochester ME1 1SL
Executive staff 14, Admin staff 13, Serving ministers 306. ***CC*** No.249339. Began 604. Magazine: *Rochester Link* (25,000 ten times a year).
Web: www.anglican.org.uk/rochester/
🖅 Email: dio.off@rochdiooff.co.uk
☎ 01634 830 333 🖷 01634 829 463
Suffragan Bishop of Tonbridge: Rt Rev Brian Smith, Bishop's Lodge, 48 St Botolph's Road, Sevenoaks TN13 3AG
☎ 01732 456 070 🖷 01732 741 449
Archdeacon of Bromley: Ven Garth Norman, 6 Horton Way, Farningham, Dartford DA4 0DQ
☎ 01322 864 522
Archdeacon of Rochester: Ven Norman Warren, The Archdeaconry, Rochester ME1 1SX
☎ 01634 842 527
Archdeacon of Tonbridge: Ven Judith Rose, 3 The Ridings, Blackhurst Lane, Tunbridge Wells TN2 4RU
☎ 01892 520 660

Church of England **Diocese of St Albans (Province of Canterbury)**, Holywell Lodge, 41 Holywell Hill, St Albans AL1 1HE
Bishop: Rt Rev Christopher Herbert. *Diocesan Secretary:* Mr L M Nicholls. Executive staff 7, Admin staff 5, Serving ministers 350. ***CC*** No.248887. Began 1877. Magazine: *See Round* (27,000 monthly).
Web: www.stalbans.gov.uk/diocese
Email: stalbans@cix.compulink.co.uk
☎ 01727 854 532 🖷 01727 844 469
Suffragan Bishop of Bedford: Rt Rev John H Richardson, 168 Kimbolton Road, Bedford MK41 8DN
☎ 01234 357 551
Suffragan Bishop of Hertford: Rt Rev Robin J N Smith, Hertford House, Abbey Mill Lane, St Albans AL3 4HE
☎ 01727 866 420
Archdeacon of Bedford: Ven Malcolm L Lessiter, 17 Lansdowne Road, Luton LU3 1EE
☎ 01582 730 722 🖷 01582 877 354
Archdeacon of Hertford: Ven Trevor Jones, St Mary's House, Church Lane, Stapleford, Hertford SG14 3NB
☎ 01992 581 629 🖷 01992 558 745
Archdeacon of St Albans: Ven Richard Cheetham, 6 Sopwell Lane, St Albans AL1 1RR
☎ 01727 857 973 🖷 01727 837 294

C

Church of England **Diocese of St Edmundsbury and Ipswich (Province of Canterbury)**, Bishop's House, 4 Park Road, Ipswich IP1 3ST
Bishop: Rt Rev Richard Lewis.
☎ 01473 252 829 🖷 01473 232 552
Diocesan Secretary: Mr Nicholas Edgell, Diocesan House, 13 Tower Street, Ipswich IP1 3BG
Executive staff 16, Admin staff 10, Serving ministers 167. Began 1914. Magazine: *The Church in Suffolk* (28,000 monthly).
www.stedmundsbury.anglican.org
Email: dbfstedmundsbury.anglican.org
☎ 01473 211 028 🖷 01473 232 407
Suffragan Bishop of Dunwich: Rt Rev Clive Young, 28 Westerfield Road, Ipswich IP4 2UJ
☎ 01473 222 276 🖷 01473 210 303
Archdeacon of Ipswich: Ven Terry Gibson, 99 Valley Road, Ipswich IP1 4NF
☎ 01473 250 333 🖷 01473 286 877
Archdeacon of Sudbury: Ven John Cox, 84 Southgate Street, Bury St Edmunds IP33 2BJ
☎ 01284 799 796 🖷 01284 723 163
Archdeacon of Suffolk: Ven Geoffrey Arrand, Glebe House, The Street, Ashfield-cum-Thorpe, Stowmarket IP14 6LX
☎ 01728 685 497 🖷 01728 685 969

Church of England **Diocese of Salisbury (Province of Canterbury)**, South Canonry, 71 The Close, Salisbury SP1 2ER
Bishop: Rt Rev David Stancliffe.
☎ 01722 334 031 🖷 01722 413 112
Diocesan Secretary: Rev Karen Curnock, Church House, Crane Street, Salisbury SP1 2QB
Executive staff 6, Other staff 8, Serving ministers 301. ***CC*** No.240833. Began 1075. Magazine: *The Sarum Link* (60,000 monthly).
Web: www.eluk.co.uk/spireweb
Email: 101324.1053@compuserve.com
☎ 01722 411 922 🖷 01722 411 990
Suffragan Bishop of Ramsbury: Rt Rev Peter F Hullah, Ramsbury Area Office, Sarum House, High Street, Urchfont, Devizes SN10 4QH
☎ 01380 840 373 🖷 01380 848 247
Suffragan Bishop of Sherborne: Rt Rev John D G Kirkham, Little Bailie, Sturminster Marshall, Wimborne BH21 4AD
☎ 01258 857 659
Archdeacon of Dorset: Ven Geoffrey Walton, The Vicarage, Witchampton, Wimborne BH21 5AP
☎ 01258 840 422
Archdeacon of Sherborne: Ven Paul Wheatley, The Rectory, West Stafford, Dorchester DT2 8AB
☎ 01305 264 637
Archdeacon of Wiltshire: Ven Barney Hopkinson, Sarum House, High Street, Urchfont, Devizes SN10 4QH
☎ 01380 840 373 🖷 01380 848 247

Church of England **Diocese of Sheffield (Province of York)**, Bishopscroft, Snaithing Lane, Sheffield S10 3LG
Bishop: Rt Rev John Nicholls.
☎ 0114 230 2170 🖷 0114 263 0110
Diocesan Secretary: Mr C A Beck, 95 Effingham Street, Rotherham S65 1BL
Admin staff 12, Serving ministers 206. ***CC*** No.245861. Began 1914. Magazine: *Sheffield Diocesan News* (9,000 monthly).
Web: web.ukonline.co.uk/members/trafic
Email: sheffielddiocese@ukonline.co.uk
☎ 01709 511 116 🖷 01709 512 550
Suffragan Bishop of Doncaster: Rt Rev Cyril Ashton, Bishop's Lodge, Hooton Roberts, Rotherham S65 4PF
☎ 01709 853 370 🖷 01709 852 310
Archdeacon of Doncaster: Ven Bernard Holdridge, Sheffield Diocesan Church House, 95 Effingham Street, Rotherham S65 1BL
☎ 01302 325 787
Archdeacon of Sheffield: Ven Richard Blackburn, Sheffield Diocesan Church House, 95 Effingham Street, Rotherham S65 1BL
☎ 01709 512 449 🖷 01709 512 550

Church of England **Diocese of Sodor and Man (Province of York)**, Bishop's House, Quarterbridge Road, Douglas IM2 3RF
Bishop: Rt Rev Noel D Jones.
☎ 01624 622 108
Diocesan Secretary: Hon Christopher Murphy, 26 The Fountains, Ramsey IM8 1NN
Serving clergy 22. Began 447. Magazine: *The Church Leader* (20,000 monthly).
☎ 01624 816 545 🖷 01624 816 545
Archdeacon of Man: Ven Brian Partington, St George's Vicarage, 16 Devonshire Road, Douglas, Isle of Man IM2 3RB
☎ 01624 675 430

Church of England **Diocese of Southwark**, Bishop's House, 38 Tooting Bec Gardens, Streatham, London SW16 1QZ
Bishop: Rt Revd Dr Thomas Butler.
Email: bishops.house@dswark.org.uk
☎ 020 8769 3256 🖷 020 8769 4126
Diocesan Secretary: Mr Simon Parton, Diocesan Office, Trinity House, 4 Chapel Court, Borough High Street, London SE1 1HW
Executive staff 28, Serving ministers 450. ***CC*** No.249678. Began 1905.
Email: simon.parton@dswark.org.uk
☎ 020 7403 8686 🖷 020 7403 4770
Area Bishop of Croydon: Rt Rev Wilfred D Wood, St Matthew's House100 George Street, Croydon, CR0 1PE
☎ 020 8681 5496 🖷 020 8686 2074
Email: bishop.wilfred@dswark.org.uk
Area Bishop of Kingston: Rt Rev Peter Price, Kingston Episcopal Area Office, Whitelands College, West Hill, London SW15 3SN
Email: bishop.peter@dswark.org.uk
☎ 020 8392 3742 🖷 020 8392 3743
Area Bishop of Woolwich: Rt Rev Colin Buchanan, 37 South Road, Forest Hill, London SE3 2UH
☎ 020 8669 7771 🖷 020 8669 7949
Email cob@dswark.org.uk

Archdeacon of Croydon: Ven Anthony Davies, 246 Pampisford Road, South Croydon CR2 6DD
☎ 020 8688 2943
Email: tonydavies@dswark.org.uk
Archdeacon of Lambeth: Ven Richard Bird, Kingston Episcopal Area Office, Whitelands College, West Hill, London SW15 3SN
☎ 020 8392 3742 🖷 020 8392 3743
Archdeacon of Lewisham: Ven David Atkinson, Trinity House, 4 Chapel Court, Borough High Street, London SE1 1HW
☎ 020 7403 8686
Email: david.atkinson@dswark.org.uk
Archdeacon of Reigate: Ven Martin Baddeley, 89 Nutfield Road, South Merstham, Redhill RH1 3HD
☎ 01737 642 375
Email: martin.baddeley@dswark.org.uk
Archdeacon of Southwark: Ven Douglas Bartles-Smith, 1a Dog Kennel Hill, East Dulwich, London SE22 8AA
☎ 020 7274 6767
Email: douglasbartlessmith@dswark.org.uk
Archdeacon of Wandsworth: Ven David Gerrard, Kingston Episcopal Area Office, Whitelands College, West Hill, London SW15 3SN
☎ 020 8392 3742 🖷 020 8392 3743
Email: david.gerrard@dswark.org.uk

***Church of England* Diocese of Southwell (Province of York)**, Dunham House, 8 Westgate, Southwell NG25 0JL
Bishop: Rt Rev George Cassidy. *Diocesan Secretary:* Mr P M Prentis. Executive staff 4, Other staff 9, Serving ministers 214. Began 1884. Magazine: *See* (30,000 monthly).
Email: sdbf@john316.com
☎ 01636 814 331 🖷 01636 815 084
Suffragan Bishop of Sherwood: Rt Rev Alan W Morgan, Sherwood House, High Oakham Road, Mansfield NG18 5AJ
☎ 01623 657 491
Archdeacon of Newark: Ven Nigel Peyton, 4 The Woodwards, London Road, New Balderton, Newark NG24 3GG
☎ 01636 612 249 🖷 01636 611 952
Archdeacon of Nottingham: Ven Gordon Ogilvie, 2B Spencer Avenue, Mapperley, Nottingham NG3 5SP
☎ 0115 967 0875 🖷 0115 967 1014

***Church of England* Diocese of Truro (Province of Canterbury)**, Lis Escop, Truro TR3 6QQ
Bishop: Rt Rev William Ind.
Email: bishop@truro.anglican.org
☎ 01872 862 657 🖷 01872 862 037
Diocesan Secretary: Mr B Laite, Diocesan House, Kenwyn, Truro TR1 3DU
Executive staff 1, Other staff 4, Serving ministers 140. Began 1887. Magazine: *The Coracle* (10,500 monthly).
Web: www.truro.anglican.org
☎ 01872 274 351 🖷 01872 222 510
Suffragan Bishop of St Germans, To be appointed, 32 Falmouth Road, Truro TR1 2HX
☎ 01872 273 190
Archdeacon of Bodmin: To be appointed
Archdeacon of Cornwall: Ven Rodney Whiteman, Archdeacon's House, Knight's Hill, Kenwyn, Truro TR1 3UY
☎ 01872 272 866

***Church of England* Diocese of Wakefield (Province of York)**, Bishop's Lodge, Woodthorpe Lane, Wakefield WF2 6JL
Bishop: Rt Rev Nigel McCulloch.
Email: bishop@wakefield.anglican.org
☎ 01924 255 349 🖷 01924 250 202
Diocesan Secretary: Mr Ashley Ellis, Church House, 1 South Parade, Wakefield WF1 1LP
Executive staff 10, Other staff 12, Serving ministers 200. Began 1888. Magazine: *Seelink* (37,500 monthly), *Outlook* (15,000 quarterly).
Web: www.wakefield.anglican.org
Email: 113002.1417@compuserve.com
☎ 01924 371 802 🖷 01924 364 834
Suffragan Bishop of Pontefract: Rt Rev David James, Pontefract House, 181a Manygates Lane, Sandal, Wakefield WF2 7DR
☎ 01924 250 781 🖷 01924 250 781
Archdeacon of Halifax: Ven Richard Inwood, Vicarage Gardens, Rastrick, Brighouse, Huddersfield HD6 3HD
☎ 01484 714 553 🖷 01484 711 897
Archdeacon of Pontefract: Ven Anthony Robinson, 10 Arden Court, Horbury, Wakefield WF4 6AH
☎ 01924 276 797 🖷 01924 261 095

C

†***Church of England* Diocese of Winchester (Province of Canterbury)**, Wolvesey, Winchester SO23 9ND
Bishop: Rt Rev M C Scott-Joynt.
☎ 01962 854 050 🖷 01962 842 376
Diocesan Secretary: Mr Ray Anderton, Church House, 9 The Close, Winchester SO23 9LS
Executive staff 6, Serving ministers 253. Began 676. Magazine: *Winchester Way* (Circulation n/a monthly).
☎ 01962 844 644 🖷 01962 841 815
Suffragan Bishop of Basingstoke: Rt Rev D Geoffrey Rowell, Little Acorns, Boynes Wood Road, Medstead, Alton GU34 2EA
☎ 01420 562 925
Suffragan Bishop of Southampton: Rt Rev Jonathan Gledhill, Ham House, The Crescent, Romsey SO51 7NG
☎ 01794 516 005
Archdeacon of Basingstoke: Ven John Guille, 1 The Close, Winchester SO23 9LS
☎ 01962 869 374
Archdeacon of Winchester: Ven Adrian Harbidge, The Vicarage, Church Corner, Burley, Ringwood BH24 4AP
☎ 01425 402 303

***Church of England* Diocese of Worcester (Province of Canterbury)**, Bishop's House, Hartlebury Castle, Kidderminster DY11 7XX
Bishop: Rt Rev Dr Peter Selby.
☎ 01299 250 214 🖷 01299 250 027
Diocesan Secretary: Mr J G Stanbury, The Old Palace, Deansway, Worcester WR1 2JE
Executive staff 11, Other staff 15, Serving ministers 175. *CC* No.247778. Began 679. Magazine: *Worcester Diocesan News* (30,000 monthly).
☎ 01905 205 37 🖷 01905 612 302
Suffragan Bishop of Dudley: Rt Rev Dr Rupert Hoare (until Jan 2000), Bishop's House, 366 Halesowen Road, Cradley Heath, Warley B64 7JF
☎ 0121 550 3407
Archdeacon of Dudley: Ven John R Gathercole, Archdeacon's House, 15 Worcester Road, Droitwich WR9 8AA
☎ 01905 773 301
Archdeacon of Worcester: Ven Joy Tetley, The Old Palace, Deansway, Worcester WR5 2BQ
☎ 01905 205 37

Church of England **Diocese of York (Province of York)**, The Palace, Bishopthorpe, York YO2 1QE
Archbishop of York: Most Rev David Hope.
☎ 01904 707 021
Diocesan Secretary: Mr Colin Sheppard, Church House, Ogleforth, York YO1 7JE (Relocating end 1999)
Executive staff 5, Admin staff 10, Serving ministers 339. Began 627. Magazine: *SeeN* (50,000 monthly).
☎ 01904 611 696 🖷 01904 620 375
Suffragan Bishop of Hull: Rt Rev Richard Frith, Hullen House, Woodfield Lane, Hessle HU13 0ES
☎ 01482 649 019
Suffragan Bishop of Selby: Rt Rev Humphrey Taylor, 10 Precentors Court, York YO1 7EJ
☎ 01904 656 492
Suffragan Bishop of Whitby: Rt Rev Robert Ladds, 60 West Green, Stokesley, Middlesborough TS9 5BD
☎ 01642 710 390
Archdeacon of Cleveland: Ven Christopher Hawthorn, Park House, Rosehill, Great Ayton, Middlesborough TS9 6BH
☎ 01642 723 221
Archdeacon of East Riding: Ven Peter Harrison, 139 Laburnham Avenue, Hull HU8 8PA
☎ 01482 374 257
Archdeacon of York: Ven Richard Seed, Holy Trinity Rectory, Micklegate, York YO1 1LE (from Feb 2000)
☎ 01904 623 798

C

Church of England **Provincial Episcopal Visitor – Northern Province**, 3 North Lane, Roundhay, Leeds LS8 2QJ
Bishop of Beverley: Rt Rev John Gaisford. No full-time staff. Began n/a. No magazine. Provincial Episcopal Visitor for the Province of York.
Email: 101740.2725@compuserve.com
☎ 0113 273 2003 Mobile: 07710 887 756 🖷 0113 273 2003

Church of England **Provincial Episcopal Visitor – Southern Province**, 8 Goldney, Clifton, Bristol BS8 4RA
Bishop of Ebbsfleet: Rt Rev Michael Houghton. No full-time staff. Began n/a. No magazine. Provincial Episcopal Visitor for Province of Canterbury.
☎ 0117 974 3289

Church of England **Provincial Episcopal Visitor – Southern Province**, 14 Hall Place Gardens, St Albans AL1 3SP
Bishop of Richborough: Rt Rev Edwin Barnes. No full-time staff. Began n/a. No magazine. Provincial Episcopal Visitor for Province of Canterbury.
☎ 01727 857 764 🖷 01727 763 025

†**Church of God Ground of Truth**, 91 Cairnfield Avenue, Neasden, London NW2 7PH
Bishop: Rt Rev Lionel Bailey. No full-time staff. Began 1975. No magazine.
☎ 020 8452 8863

Church of God in Christ Congregational Independent, 112 St Stephen Road, East Ham, London E6 1AA
Bishop: Rt Rev A E Lewis. Serving ministers 8. Began 1972. No magazine.
☎ 020 8471 0214 Mobile: 07930 989 852

†**Church of God of Prophecy**, 6 Beacon Court, Birmingham Road, Great Barr, Birmingham B43 6NN
National Overseer: Bishop Lesmon R Graham. Executive staff 1, Admin staff 4, Serving ministers 81. Began 1953. Magazine: *Messenger of Truth* (1,600 quarterly).
☎ 0121 358 2231 🖷 0121 358 0934

†**Church of God Reformation Movement**, Tottenham Community Church, St Anne Road, Tottenham, London N15 6NX
Chairman of Assembly: Rev Lenworth Anglin. No full-time staff. Began 1894. No magazine.
☎ 020 8884 2509

Church of Ireland, Church of Ireland House, Church Avenue, Rathmines, Dublin 6 Republic of Ireland
Chief Officer & Secretary: Mr R H Sherwood. Executive staff 5, Admin staff 27. Began n/a. (Disestablished 1869). Magazine: *Church of Ireland*(Circulation & frequency n/a), *Gazette* (6,000 weekly). Turnover n/a.
Email: rcbdub@iol.ie
☎ 00 3531 497 8422 🖷 00 3531 497 8821

Church of Ireland **Archdiocese of Armagh**, Church House, 46 Abbey Street, Armagh BT61 7DZ
Archbishop of Armagh, Primate of All Ireland and Metropolitan: Most Rev Dr Robert H A Eames. Began n/a. Magazine: *Armagh Diocesan Magazine* (Circulation n/a monthly).
Email: archbishop@armagh.anglican.org
☎ 028 3752 7144 🖷 028 3752 7823

†*Church of Ireland* **Diocese of Clogher**, The See House, 150 Ballagh Road, Fivemiletown BT75 0QP
Bishop: Rt Rev Brian D A Hannon. No full-time staff, Serving ministers 36. Began 453. Magazine: *Diocesan Magazine* (Circulation n/a monthly).
☎ 028 6652 1265 🖷 028 6652 1265
Diocesan Secretary: Very Rev Thomas R Moore, St Macartan's Cathedral, Cathedral Rectory, 10 Augher Road, Clogher BT76 0AD
☎ 028 8254 8235 🖷 028 8254 8235
Archdeacon: Ven C T Pringle, The Rectory, Rossorry, Enniskillen BT74 5NY
☎ 028 6632 2874

Church of Ireland **Diocese of Connor**, Diocesan Office, Church of Ireland House, 61 Donegall Street, Belfast BT1 2QH
Bishop: Rt Rev James Moore. *Diocesan Secretary:* Mr T N Wilson. Executive staff 2, Admin staff 6, Serving ministers 105. Began n/a. Magazine: *Connor Contact* (Circulation n/a quarterly).
☎ 028 9032 2268/3188 🖷 028 9032 1635

Church of Ireland **Diocese of Derry and Raphoe**, The See House, Culmore Road, Londonderry BT48 8JF
Bishop: Rt Rev James Mehaffey. Serving ministers 55. Began 1844. Magazine: *Vision* (10,000 quarterly).
☎ 028 7135 1206
Diocesan Secretary: Mr Geoffrey Kelly, Diocesan Office, London Street, Londonderry BT48 6RQ
☎ 028 7126 2440

Church of Ireland **Diocese of Down and Dromore**, Diocesan Office, Church of Ireland House, 61 Donegall Street, Belfast BT1 2QH
Bishop: Rt Rev H C Miller. *Diocesan Secretary:* Mr T N Wilson. Executive staff 2, Admin staff 6, Serving ministers 110. Began n/a. No magazine.
☎ 028 9032 2268/3188 🖷 028 9032 1635

†**Church of Jesus Christ Apostolic Faith**, 47 Roberts Road, High Wycombe HP13 6XB
Pastor: Mr Filbert Johnson. Staff n/a. Began 1960. No magazine.
☎ 01494 524 384

Church of Scotland, 121 George Street, Edinburgh EH2 4YN
Principal Clerk of the General Assembly: Rev Dr Finlay A J Macdonald. Executive staff 110, Serving ministers 1167. Began 1560. Magazine: *Life and Work* (125,000 monthly).
☎ 0131 225 5722 🖷 0131 220 3113
See also: **Assembly Council** on Page 233
Board of Ministry on Page 233
Board of National Mission on Page 259
Board of Parish Education on Page 493
Board of Practice and Procedure on Page 233
Board of Stewardship and Finance on Page 419
Board of Social Responsibility on Page 465
Board of World Mission on Page 000
Ecumenical Relations on Page 233
Guild on Page 233
Life & Work on Page 316
See also under **Church of Scotland** in Main Index on Page 627
Presbytery of Aberdeen: Rev Andrew M Douglas, Presbytery Clerk, Mastrick Parish Church, Greenfern Road, Aberdeen, AB2 6TR
☎ 01224 690 494 🖷 01224 690 494
Presbytery of Abernethy: Rev James A I MacEwan, Presbytery Clerk, The Manse, Nethy Bridge PH25 3DG
☎ 01479 821 280
Presbytery of Angus: Rev R J Ramsey, Presbytery Clerk, The Manse, Kirkton of Airlie, Kirriemuir DD8 5NL
☎ 01575 530 245
Presbytery of Annandale and Eskdale: Rev C Bryan Haston, Presbytery Clerk, The Manse, Gretna Green, Gretna DG16 5DU
☎ 01461 338 313
Presbytery of Ardrossan: Rev David Broster, Presbytery Clerk, St Columba's Manse, Kilbirnie KA25 7JU
☎ 01505 683 342 🖷 01505 684 024
Email: pres@davbros.demon.co.uk
Presbytery of Ayr: Rev James Crichton, Presbytery Clerk, 30 Garden Street, Dalrymple, Ayr KA6 6DG
☎ 01292 562 63
Presbytery of Buchan: Rev Rodger Neilson, Presbytery Clerk, The Manse, Hatton, Peterhead AB42 0QQ
☎ 01779 841 229 🖷 01779 841 822
Presbytery of Caithness: Rev Michael G Mappin, Presbytery Clerk, The Manse, Watten, Wick KW1 5YJ
☎ 01955 822 20
Presbytery of Dumbarton: Rev David P Munro, Presbytery Clerk, 8 14 Birch Road, Killearn, Glasgow G63 9SQ
☎ 🖷 01360 550 098
Presbytery of Dumfries and Kirkcudbright: Rev Gordon M A Savage, Presbytery Clerk, 11 Laurieknowe, Dumfries DG2 7AH
☎ 01387 252 929 🖷 01387 252 929
Presbytery of Dundee: Rev James A Roy, Presbytery Clerk, Presbytery Office, Nicoll's Lane, Dundee DD2 3HG
☎ 01382 611 415
Presbytery of Dunfermline: Rev William E Farquhar, Presbytery Clerk, Townhill Manse, Dunfermline KY12 0EZ
☎ 01383 723 835
Presbytery of Dunkeld and Meigle: Rev A B Reid, Presbytery Clerk, The Manse, Dundee Road, Meigle, Blairgowrie PH12 8SB
☎ 01828 640 278 🖷 01828 640 278
Email: ab.reid@perth.almac.co.uk
Presbytery of Dunoon: Rev Ronald Samuel, Presbytery Clerk, 12 Crichton Road, Rothesay, PA20 9JR
☎ 01700 502 797
Presbytery of Duns: Rev Alan Cartright, Presbytery Clerk, The Manse, Swinton, Duns TD1 3JJ
☎ 01890 860 228
Presbytery of Edinburgh: Rev W Peter Graham, Presbytery Clerk, 10 Palmerston Place, Edinburgh EH12 5AA
☎ 0131 225 9137
Presbytery of England: Rev W Alexander Cairns, Presbytery Clerk, St Columba's Church, Pont Street, London SW1X 0BD
☎ 0171 584 2321
Presbytery of Falkirk: Rev Duncan E McClements, Presbytery Clerk, 30 Russel Street, Falkirk FK2 7HS
☎ 01324 624 461
Presbytery of Glasgow: Rev Alexander Cunningham, Presbytery Clerk, 260 Bath Street, Glasgow G2 4JP
☎ 0141 332 6606
Presbytery of Gordon: Rev Iain U Thomson, Presbytery Clerk, The Manse, Kirkton of Skene, Westhill AB32 6LX
☎ 🖷 01224 743 277
Presbytery of Greenock: Rev David Mill, Presbytery Clerk, 105 Newark Street, Greenock PA16 7TW
☎ 01475 396 02
Presbytery of Hamilton: Rev James H Wilson, Presbytery Clerk, Presbytery Office, 18 Haddow Street, Hamilton ML3 7HX
☎ 01698 286 837
Presbytery of Inverness: n/a
Presbytery of Irvine and Kilmarnock: Rev Colin G F Brockie, Presbytery Clerk, Grange Manse, 51 Portland Road, Kilmarnock KA1 2EQ
☎ 01563 525 311
Presbytery of Jedburgh: Rev Alan Reid, 23 Langholm Street, Newcastleton TD9 0QX
☎ 01387 375 242
Presbytery of Kincardine and Deeside: Rev J W S Brown, Presbytery Clerk, 10 Forestside Road, Banchory AB31 3ZH
☎ 01330 824 353
Presbytery of Kirkcaldy: Rev Bryan L Tomlinson, Presbytery Clerk, 83 Milton Road, Kirkcaldy KY1 1TP
☎ 01592 260 315
Presbytery of Lanark: Rev Iain Cunningham, Presbytery Clerk, The Manse, Station Road, Carluke ML8 5AA
☎ 01155 771 262
Presbytery of Lewis: Rev T S Sinclair, Presbytery Clerk, Martin's Memorial Manse, Matheson Road, Stornoway PA87 2LR
☎ 01851 702 206
Presbytery of Lochaber: Rev Alan Ramsay, Presbytery Clerk, MacIntosh Manse, Plot 26, Riverside Park, Lochyside, Fort William PH33 7NY
☎ 01397 702 054
Presbytery of Lochcarron-Skye: Rev Allan I MacArthur, Presbytery Clerk, The Manse, Lochcarron, Strathcarron IV54 8YD
☎ 01520 722 278 🖷 01520 722 674
Presbytery of Lorn and Mull: Rev William Hogg, Presbytery Clerk, The Manse, Dalmally PA33 1AS
☎ 01838 200 227
Presbytery of Lothian: Mr John D McCulloch, Presbytery Clerk, Auchindinny House, Penicuik EH26 8PE
☎ 01968 675 338 🖷 01968 675 338
Presbytery of Melrose and Peebles: Rev Jack M Brown, Presbytery Clerk, St Aidan's Manse, High Road, Galashiels TD1 2BD
☎ 01896 752 420
Presbytery of Moray: Rev John Stuart, Presbytery Clerk, 1 Seaview Farm Paddock, Cummingston, Elgin IV30 2XY
☎ 01343 830 890
Presbytery of Orkney: Rev Trevor Hunt, Presbytery Clerk, The Manse, Finstown, Orkney KW17 2EG
☎ 01856 761 328 🖷 01856 761 328
Email: tghorkney@sol.com

Presbytery of Paisley: Rev David Kay, Presbytery Clerk, 6 Southfield Avenue, Paisley PA2 8BY
☎ 0141 884 3600
Presbytery of Perth: Rev Michael J Ward, Presbytery Clerk, Glencarse, Perth PH2 7NF
☎ 01738 860 816 🖷 01738 860 837
Presbytery of Ross: Rev R M MacKinnon, Presbytery Clerk, 27 Riverford Crescent, Conon Bridge IV7 8HL
☎ 01349 866 293
Presbytery of St Andrews: Rev John W Patterson, Presbytery Clerk, 34 Claybraes, St Andrews KY16 8RS
☎ 01334 473 606
Presbytery of Shetland: Rev Magnus Cheyne, Presbytery Clerk, 19 South Lochside, Lerwick ZE1 0JT
☎ 01595 693 240
Presbytery of South Argyll: Rev Roderick H McNidder, Presbytery Clerk, The Manse, Southend, Cambeltown PA28 6RQ
☎ 01586 832 74
Presbytery of Stirling: Rev Barry Dunsmore, Presbytery Clerk, St Columba's Manse, 5 Clifford Street, Stirling FK8 2AQ
☎ 01786 475 802
Presbytery of Sutherland: Rev J L Goskirk, Presbytery Clerk, The Manse, Lairg IV27 4EH
☎ 01549 402 373
Presbytery of Uist: Rev G J Elliott, Presbytery Clerk, The Manse, Dalibrugh, Lochboisdale, PA81 5SG
☎ 01878 700 265
Presbytery of West Lothian: Rev Duncan Shaw, Presbytery Clerk, St John's Manse, Mid Street, Bathgate EH48 1QD
☎ 01506 531 46
Presbytery of Wigtown and Stranraer: Rev D W Dutton, Presbytery Clerk, High Kirk Manse, Leswalt High Road, Stranraer DG9 0AA
☎ 01776 703 268

C

***Church of the Nazarene: British Isles**, South District, 29 Parkway, Westhoughton, Bolton BL5 2RY
South District Superintendent: Rev John Paton. *District Business Manager:* Mr David Barnes. Executive staff 1, Other staff 1, Serving ministers 45. Began 1908 as Pentecostal Church of Scotland, name changed 1915, united with International Holiness Mission 1952 and Calvary Holiness Church 1955. Magazine: *Holiness Today* (Circulation n/a monthly), *Nazarene News* (2,000 quarterly).
Email: jhmpaton@aol.com
☎ 01942 815 036 🖷 01942 810 613
North District Superintendent: Rev Colin H Wood, 8 Blackcroft Road, Glasgow G32 0RB
☎ 0141 778 3262 🖷 0141 778 3262

Churches of God, UK, 23 Walcott Road, Billinghay, Lincoln LN4 4EG
UK Co-ordinator: Mr James McBride. Executive staff 1, Admin staff 1, Serving ministers 2. *CC* No.283358. Began 1978. (Previously Church of God International). Magazine: *New Horizons* (2,200 every two months). Turnover £20,000 to year end Dec 98.
Web: www.cgom.org / www.abcog.org
Email: coguk@aol.com
☎ 01526 860 508

Congregational Federation, Congregational Centre, 4 Castle Gate, Nottingham NG1 7AS
General Secretary: Pastor Graham M Adams. Executive staff 1, Admin staff 3, Serving ministers 70. Began 1972. Magazine: *Congregational Quarterly* (900 quarterly), *Congregational* (7,000 every two months).
☎ 0115 911 1460 🖷 0115 911 1462

†**Congregational Union of Ireland**, 38 Edgecumbe Gardens, Belfast BT4 2EH
Secretary: Rev Malcolm Coles. No full-time staff, Serving ministers 24. Began 1829. Magazine: *The Congregationalist* (1,400 quarterly).
☎ 028 9065 3140

Continuing Church, 15 Bridge Street, Knighton LD7 1BT
Presiding Bishop: Rt Rev Dr David N Samuel. Serving Ministers 4. *CC* No.1055010. Began 1995. (Previously Church of England (Continuing)). Magazine: *Journal of the Continuing Church* (400 periodically).
Email: nama@kpws.demon.co.uk
☎ 01934 712 520 🖷 01934 712 520

Continuing Church of England (Diocese of Lambeth), 113 Fortress Road, London NW5 2HR
Secretariat: Most Rev Dominic M Pyle-Bridges. *Administrator:* Reader Michael Farrer. Admin staff 1. Began 1994; Anglican. No magazine. Turnover £2,000 to year end Dec 98. Ministering to those who wish to remain Anglican.
☎ 020 7267 4015

Coptic Orthodox Church, Allen Street, Kensington, London W8 6UX
Head of the Church: Rev Fr Bishoy Boushra Makar. Serving ministers 2. Began n/a. No magazine.
☎ 020 7937 5782 (Church) 020 8740 1621 (Rev Bishoy Makar)
🖷 020 8743 3824

Coptic Orthodox Church of Scotland, Links Street, Kirkcaldy KY1 1QE
Church Secretary: Dr S M Hakim. *Parish Priest for Scotland:* Rev Father Mark Aziz. Serving minister 1. *CC* No.SCO 018991. Began 1977. Magazine: *Maranatha* (Circulation n/a n/a).
Email: vp54@dial.pipex.com
☎ 01592 643 333 🖷 01592 643 344

†***Countess of Huntingdon's Connexion**, 69 Jubilee Road, Middleton, Manchester M24 2LT
Secretary: Mrs Marjorie J Crossley. No full-time staff, Serving ministers 19. *CC* No.232674. Began 1781. Magazine: *Voice* (750 quarterly).
☎ 0161 643 4108

†**Covenant Ministries International**, Nettle Hill, Brinklow Road, Ansty, Coventry CV7 9JL
Managing Director: Mr Ron Tempest. Executive staff 13, Other staff 20, Serving ministers 50. *CC* No.328513. Began 1977. Magazine: *Restore* (35,000 n/a).
☎ 024 7660 2777 🖷 024 7660 2992

Croatian Roman Catholic Church, 17 Boutflower Road, London SW11 1RE
Croation Catholic Mission: Rev Fr Drago Berisic. Staff n/a. Began 1969. No magazine.
☎ 020 7223 3530

Danish Church of St Katharine, 4 St Katharine's Precinct, Regents Park, London NW1 4HH
Chaplain to Seamen's Mission and Embassy: Pastor Thomas Bruun. Executive staff 2, Admin staff 2, Serving minister 1. Began 1692. Magazine: *Kirkehilsen* (2,500 quarterly).
☎ 020 7935 1723 🖷 020 7486 9737

Deeper Christian Life Ministry, 82 Borough Road, London SE1 1DN
National Overseer: Rev Pre Ovia. Other staff 7, Serving ministers 8. *CC* No.297359. Began 1985. Magazine: *Heartbeat* (circulation n/a periodically).
☎ 020 7357 7558 🖷 020 7378 8550

Dutch Church, 7 Austin Friars, London EC2N 2HA
Minister: Rev Gerard T Van Es. Other staff 2, Serving minister 1. ***CC*** No.214686. Began 1550. Magazine: *Kerknieuws* (700 monthly).
Web: www.dutchchurch.org.uk
Email: dutchchurch@compuserve.com
☎ 020 7588 1684

Elim Pentecostal Churches, PO Box 38, Cheltenham GL50 3HN
General Superintendent: Rev I Wynne Lewis. *Administrator:* Rev Bruce Hunter. *Field Superintendent:* Rev T Gordon Hills. Executive staff 5, Admin staff 16, Serving ministers 650. ***CC*** No.251549. Began 1915. Magazine: *Direction* (22,000 monthly).
Email: info@elimhq.com
☎ 01242 519 904 📠 01242 222 279

Elim Pentecostal Church: **Ireland Region**, 20 Kings Road, Belfast BT5 6JJ
Regional Superintendent: Rev E MacComb. Began n/a.
☎ 028 9065 7744 📠 028 9047 1623

Elim Pentecostal Church: **Kensington Temple**, 66 Elton Avenue, Greenford UB6 0PP
Regional Superintendent: Rev B C Richardson. Began n/a.
☎ 020 8864 4180 📠 020 8864 4180

Elim Pentecostal Church: **Metropolitan and Eastern Region**, 29 Clarendon Road, Leytonstone, London E11 1BZ
Regional Superintendent: Rev Mervyn Tilley. Began n/a.
☎ 020 8556 3229 Mobile: 07721 360 492 📠 020 8556 3582

Elim Pentecostal Church: **Midland Region**, 8 Westhall Road, Mickleover, Derby DE3 5PA
Regional Superintendent: Rev Gordon H Neale. Began n/a.
☎ 01332 515 739 Mobile: 07973 163 169 📠 01332 513 351

Elim Pentecostal Church: **North East Region**, Muirfield, Sheep Cote Road, Shrogs Wood, Brecks, Rotherham S60 4BZ
Regional Superintendent: Rev Geoff J Feasey. Began n/a.
☎ 01709 700 819 📠 01709 703 174

Elim Pentecostal Church: **North West Region**, 1 Scaife Road, Nantwich CW5 5TS
Regional Superintendent: Rev D G Woodfield. Began n/a.
☎ 01270 611 550 Mobile: 07770 692 110 📠 01270 611 560

Elim Pentecostal Church: **Scotland Region**, 146 Wishaw Road, Waterloo, Wishaw ML2 8EN
Regional Superintendent: Rev J M Dick. Began n/a.
☎ 01698 376 762 📠 01698 376 762

Elim Pentecostal Church: **Southern Region**, 7 Carsworth Way, Canford Heath, Poole BH17 8SP
Regional Superintendent: Rev M C Epton. Began n/a.
☎ 01202 381 932 📠 01202 248 786

Elim Pentecostal Church: **Wales and South West Midlands Region**, Maranatha, 135 Vivian Road, Sketty, Swansea SA2 0UP
Regional Superintendent: Rev D Denis Phillips. Began n/a.
☎ 01792 204 826 📠 01792 203 117

Emmanuel Holiness Church, 5 Ashlea Road, Pensby, Wirral CH61 5UJ
Chairman: Rev G Smethurst. Executive staff 3, Other staff 6, Serving ministers n/a. Began 1916.
☎ 0151 648 1911 📠 0151 666 1356

†**Estonian Evangelical Lutheran Church**, 67 Westbury Avenue, London N22 6SA
Head of the Church: To be appointed. *Contact:* Mr Adolph Hanssoo. Staff n/a, Serving ministers n/a. Began 1947. No magazine.
☎ 020 8889 2806

Evangelical Fellowship of Congregational Churches, PO Box 34, Beverley HU17 8YU
General Secretary: Rev Alan Tovey. *Admin Secretary:* Mr Bryan Cook. Executive staff 4, Serving ministers n/a. ***CC*** No.262802. Began 1967. Magazine: *Concern* (2,200 quarterly).
Web: www.compulink.co.uk/~digby/efccpub.html
Email: efcc@cix.co.uk
☎ 01482 860 324

Evangelical Lutheran Church of England, 28 Huntingdon Road, Cambridge CB3 0HH
Chairman: Rev K Fry. Executive staff 1. Began 1896. Magazine: *British Lutheran* (600 monthly).
☎ 01223 355 265 📠 01223 355 265

Evangelical Presbyterian Church in England and Wales, 124 New London Road, Chelmsford CM2 0RG
Clerk: Rev David L Cross. Serving ministers 3. *CC* No.801935. Began 1987. (Previously Presbyterian Association in England). Magazine: *Presbyterian Network* (700 half-yearly), *Prayer List* (375 every two months). Turnover £100,000 to year end Dec 98.
Web: www.epcew.org.uk
Email: epcew@compuserve.com
☎ 01245 450 089 🖷 01245 450 089

Evangelical Presbyterian Church in Ireland, 15 College Square East, Belfast BT1 6DD
Clerk of Presbytery: Rev Dr Robert Beckett. Executive staff 1, Serving ministers 9. Began 1927. Magazine: *Evangelical Presbyterian* (1,000 every two months).
Web: web.ukonline.co.uk/epc
Email: epc@ukonline.co.uk
☎ 028 9032 0529/9071 4820

C

***Fellowship of Churches of Christ**, 25 Robert Avenue, Erdington, Birmingham B23 5RD
Fellowship Secretary: Mrs Hazel Wilson. No full-time staff, Serving ministers 21. *CC* No.SCO 10258. Began 1842. Magazine: *Newsletter* (450 monthly).
Web: www.charis.co.uk/coc-erdington/
Email: coc-erdington@charis.co.uk
☎ 0121 373 7942

Fellowship of Independent Evangelical Churches, 3 Church Road, Croydon CR0 1SG
General Secretary: Bev Savage. *Administrator:* Mr Rod Badams. Admin staff 12, Other staff 4, Serving ministers 250. *CC* No.263354. Began 1922. Magazine: *Together* (18,000 every four months).
Web: www.fiec.co.uk
Email: fiec@btinternet.com
☎ 020 8681 7422 🖷 020 8760 5067

Fellowship of Pentecostal Holiness Churches of Great Britain, PO Box 16262, London N4 2WN
Chairman: Rev Steve Cofer. Executive staff 5. Serving ministers n/a. Began n/a. No magazine.
☎ 020 8473 4405 🖷 020 8926 9781

***The Finnish Church in London**, 33 Albion Street, London SE16 1JG
Chaplain: Very Rev Pertti Boutanen. *Chaplain/Welfare Officer:* Rev J Murtovuori. Admin staff 2, Serving ministers 4. *CC* No.283594. Began 1882. Magazine: *Horisontti* (12,000 quarterly).
Email: kirkko@ndirect.co.uk & webmaster@scj.org.uk
☎ 020 7237 1261 🖷 020 7237 1245

***The Free Church of England**, 45 Broughton Road, Wallasey, Wirral CH44 4DT
Acting Bishop Primus: Rt Rev Ken J Powell. *General Secretary:* Rev W J Lawler. Executive staff 1, Serving ministers 44. *CC* No.366710. Began 1844; Reformed Episcopal Church of England joined 1927. No magazine.
☎ 0151 638 2564 🖷 0151 638 2564

***Free Church of Scotland**, Free Church Offices, The Mound, Edinburgh EH1 2LS
Principal Clerk of Assembly: Rev Prof J L Mackay. *General Treasurer:* Mr Iain D Gill. Other staff 10, Serving ministers 105. *CC* No.SCO 12925. Began 1843. Magazine: *Monthly Record* (7,250 monthly), *The Instructor* (4,500 monthly), *From the Frontiers* (4,000 annually).
Email: freechurch@compuserve.com
☎ 0131 226 5286/4978 🖷 0131 220 0597

Free Church of Scotland: **Northern Synod**, 10 Ardbreck Place, Inverness IV2 4QQ
Clerk of Synod: Rev Innes M MacRae. No full-time staff. Began n/a. No magazine.
☎ 01463 223 175
Presbytery of Caithness and Sutherland: Rev J H MacLean, Clerk, Free Church Manse, Lairg IV27 4AZ
☎ 01549 2034
Presbytery of Inverness: Rev David C Meredith, Clerk, The Manse, Resaurie, Smithton, Inverness IV1 2NH
☎ 01463 790 743
Presbytery of Ross: Rev John MacLeod, Clerk, Free Church Manse, Portmahomack, Tain IV20 1YL
☎ 01862 871 467 🖷 01862 871 467

Free Church of Scotland: **Southern Synod**, 48 Crofthead Road, Ayr KA7 3ND
Clerk of Synod: Mr Norman Smith. No full-time staff. Began n/a. No magazine.
Presbytery of Argyll and Lochaber: Rev Gordon Mair, Clerk, Free Church Manse, Union Road, Fort William PH33 6RB
☎ 01397 702 167
Presbytery of Edinburgh and Perth: Mr Donald Jack, Clerk, 2C Summerside Place, Leith, Edinburgh EH6 4NZ
☎ 0131 554 4687
**Presbytery of Glasgow:* Rev Harry J T Woods, Clerk, Free Church House, 16 Whitehaugh Drive, Paisley PA1 3PG
☎ 0141 889 1524

Free Church of Scotland: **Western Synod,** Free Church Manse, Upper Carloway, Isle of Lewis HS2 9AG
Clerk of Synod: Rev Donald McDonald. No full-time staff. Began 1843. No magazine.
☎ 01851 643 208
**Presbytery of Lewis:* Rev James Maciver, Clerk, Free Church Manse, Garrabost, Isle of Lewis HS2 0PW
☎ 01851 870 207
Presbytery of Lochcarron: Rev Graeme Craig, Clerk, Free Church Manse, Ardelve, Kyle IV40 8DY
☎ 01599 555 372
Presbytery of Skye and Uist: Rev Alan I M Maciver, Clerk, Free Church Manse, Broadford, Isle of Skye IV49 9AE
☎ 01470 532 221

***Free Methodist Church in the United Kingdom**, 36 Fairways, Fulwood, Preston PR2 8FY
Conference Superintendent: Rev J Allan Ellershaw. Other staff 2, Serving ministers 22. *CC* No.518173. Began 1960. Magazine: *Light and Life (published in USA)* (Circulation n/a monthly). Turnover £45,000 to year end Dec 98.
☎ 01772 691 324/713 607 🖷 01772 691 324/713 607

Free Presbyterian Church of Scotland, 16 Matheson Road, Stornoway HS1 2LA
Clerk of Synod: Rev John Macleod. *General Treasurer:* Mr R A Campbell. No full-time staff, Serving ministers n/a. *CC* No. SCO 03545. Began 1893. Magazine: *Free Presbyterian* (1,900 monthly). Turnover £839,793 to year end Dec 97.
Web: www.fpchurch.org.uk
Email: gentreas@compuserve.com
☎ 01851 702 755

Free Presbyterian Church of Ulster, Church House, 356 Ravenhill Road, Belfast BT6 8GL
Clerk of Presbytery: Dr John Douglas. Executive staff 4, Admin staff 9. Serving ministers n/a. Began 1951. Magazine: *The Revivalist* (6,000 monthly), *Truth for Youth* (3,500 every two months).
☎ 028 9045 7106
Correspondence: 40 Lombard Avenue, Lisburn BT28 2UP
☎ 028 9267 4664

French Protestant Church of Brighton, c/o St John's Cottage, 4 Norfolk Buildings, Brighton BN1 2PZ
Pastor: Rev F Orna-Ornstein. Serving minister 1. *CC* No.1063644. Began n/a. Magazine: *The Bulletin* (120 every four months). Christian ministry to French-speaking persons.
☎ 01273 770 317

French Protestant Church of Canterbury, Canterbury Cathedral Crypt, 30 King Street, Canterbury CT1 2AJ
Pastor: Rev Dr Hugh R Boudin. *Secretary of the Consistory:* Mr Michael H Peters. Executive staff 1, Other staff 2, Serving ministers n/a. *CC* No.259693. Began 1550. No magazine. Maintaining French speaking reformed worship as continuation of the Walloon-Huguenot refugee congregation of the XVIth Century.
☎ 01227 456 676

French Protestant Church of London, 8 Soho Square, London W1V 5DD
Pastor: Ms Leila Hamrat. Other staff 2. Serving minister 1, Began 1550. Magazine: *Le Lien* (450 quarterly).
Email: eglisoho@globalnet.co.uk
☎ 020 7437 5311 Fax 020 7434 4579

German Christ Church, 19 Montpelier Place, London SW7 1HL
Pastor: Dr Uwe Vetter. Serving minister 1. *CC* No.251120. Began 1904. Magazine: *Gemeindebriefe* (450 monthly).
☎ 020 8876 6366 Fax 020 8876 6366

German Roman Catholic Church (St Boniface's), 47 Adler Street, London E1 1EE
Rector of Church & Mission: Rev Heinz Medoch. Serving minister 1. Began 1809. Magazine: *OASE* (500 every two months).
☎ 020 7247 9529 Fax 020 7247 3879

German Speaking Evangelical Lutheran Synod in Great Britain, German YMCA, 35 Craven Terrace, London W2 3EL
Administrator: Mr Uwe-Kai Maynard. Serving ministers 9. *CC* No.266600. Began 1955. No magazine.
☎ 020 7706 8589

The Gospel Faith Mission International, 583 Commercial Road, Stepney, London E1 0HJ
Minister in Charge: Rev Sam Olanipekun. Other staff 2. *CC* No.293765. Began 1984. No magazine. Turnover £20,000 to year end Dec 98.
☎ 020 7729 1939 Mobile 07956 875 488

Gospel Standard Strict Baptists, 8 Fairleigh Rise, Kington Langley, Chippenham SN15 5QF
Secretary: Mr H Mercer. No full-time staff, Serving ministers n/a. Began 1872. Magazine: *Gospel Standard* (1,800 monthly), *Friendly Companion* (1,300 monthly).
☎ 01249 758 877 Fax 01249 758 877

Gospel Tabernacle Assembly, 41 Upper Tulse Hill, London SW2 2SG
Pastor: Pastor Warren Reid. No full-time staff. Began 1960. No magazine.
☎ 020 7622 8803

Grace Baptist Assembly, 4 Beechwood Road, Caterham CR3 6NA
Secretary: Mr Keith A Johns. No full-time staff, Serving ministers n/a. Began 1977; but as Particular or Strict Baptists 1620. Magazine: *Grace Magazine* (2,000 eleven times a year). Arranging annual conference for churches subscribing to 1689 and/or 1966 affirmations of faith.
Email: keithajohns@lineone.net
☎ 01883 342 711 Fax 01883 342 711

Greek Orthodox Archdiocese of Thyateira & Great Britain, Thyateira House, 5 Craven Hill, London W2 3EN
Archbishop: Archbishop Gregorios. *Chancellor:* Bishop Athanasios of Tropaeou. Admin staff 7, Serving ministers 107. *CC* No.243715. Began 1922. Magazine: *Orthodox Herald* (2,000 every two months), *The Sunday Gospel* (10,000 weekly), *The Shepherd* (circulation & frequency n/a).
☎ 020 7723 4787 Fax 020 7224 9301
Assistant Bishop of Zenoupolis: Rt Rev Aristarchos, 59 Selborne Gardens, London NW4 4SH
☎ 020 8202 4821
Assistant Bishop of Kyanea: Rt Rev Chrysostomos, Greek Cathedral of St Andrew, Kentish Town Road, London NW1 9QA
☎ 020 7485 6385
Assistant Bishop of Telmissos: Rt Rev Christophoros, Greek Cathedral of St Mary, 305 Camberwell New Road, London SE5 0TF
☎ 020 7703 0137
Assistant Bishop of Diokleia: Rt Rev Kallistos, 15 Staverton Road, Oxford OX2 6XH
☎ 01865 554 023
Assistant Bishop of Tropaeou: Rt Rev Athanasios, Greek Cathedral of St Mary, Trinity Road, London N22 8LB
☎ 020 8888 2295

C

***Ground Level Ministry Team**, 257 Freeman Street, Grimsby DN32 9DW
Team Leader: Mr Stuart Bell. *Director:* Mr Dave Kitchen. Executive staff 14, Admin staff 3, Serving ministers 65. *CC* No.1001599. Began 1985; interdenominational. Magazine: *Compass* (5,000 quarterly), *Link-up* (1,200 quarterly). Turnover £180,000 to year end Dec 98. Involved in the care and growth of churches and leaders in relationship with the team.
Web: www.groundlevel.org.uk
Email: admin@groundlevel.org.uk
☎ 01472 313 388 / 240 071 Mobile 07768 757 406
Fax 01472 346 186

Hackney Pentecostal Apostolic Faith Church, 39 Middleton Road, Hackney, London E8 4PL
Leader: Pastor E M Douglas. No serving ministers. *CC* No.76175. Began 1970. No magazine.
☎ 020 7275 0074 / 020 7254 9648 Fax 020 7254 9648

†Healing Church of God in Christ, 62 Field Road, Forest Gate, London E7 9DL
No full-time staff, Serving minister 1. Began 1963. No magazine.
☎ No telephone

†Holiness Church of God, 2 Osmond Mead, Lyndis Fayne Way, Homerton, London E9 5PZ
Pastor: Pastor Casmin Allison. No full-time staff, Serving minister 1. Began 1988. No magazine.
☎ 020 8985 7009

The Holy Catholic Church (Anglican Rite), Archbishop's Office, St Mary's House, Byatts Grove, Longton, Stoke-on-Trent ST3 2RH
Metropolitan Archbishop: Most Rev Leslie Hamlett. Executive staff 1. Serving ministers n/a. Began 1992. (Previously Anglican Catholic Church: Missionary Diocese of UK). No magazine.
☎ 01782 330 743 Fax 01782 336 361

Hungarian Roman Catholic Chaplaincy, Dunstan House, 141 Gunnersbury Avenue, London W3 8LE
Senior Chaplain: Rt Rev Mgr George Tüttö. No full-time staff, Serving minister 1. Began 1948. Magazine: *Eletunk* (700 quarterly).
☎ 020 8992 2054 🖷 020 8992 2054
Also at: *Assistant Chaplain:* Rev Denes Lakatos, Hungarian Roman Catholic Chaplaincy of St Elizabeth, 5 Needwood Close, Wolverhampton WV2 4PP
☎ 01902 344 578

Hungarian Reformed Church in the UK (Presbyterian), 17 St Dunstan's Road, London W6 8RD
Minister: Rev Laszlo Kaorda. Serving minister 1. Began 1948. Magazine: *Circular Letters* (600 every four months).
☎ 020 8748 8858 🖷 020 8948 4339

Ichthus Team Ministries, 107 Stanstead Road, Forest Hill, London SE23 1HH
Team Leader: Mr Roger T Forster. Executive staff 9, Other staff 6, Serving ministers 30. *CC* No.269575. Began 1975. Magazine: *Celebration* (Circulation & frequency n/a).
Web: www.ichthus.org.uk
Email: admin@ichthus.org.uk
☎ 020 8291 4057 🖷 020 8291 6764

C

***Independent Methodist Connexion of Churches**, Office and Resource Centre, Fleet Street, Pemberton, Wigan WN5 0DS
General Secretary: Mr John Day. Admin staff 2, Serving ministers 108. *CC* No.248813. Began 1805. Magazine: *The Connexion* (2,500 monthly).
Email: 106570.2444@compuserve.com
☎ 01942 223 526 🖷 01942 227 768

Indian Orthodox (Saint Gregorios Malankara Orthodox Syrian) Church, Parumala House, 44 Newbury Road, Ilford IG2 7HD
Resident Priest: Rev Fr M S Skariah. Serving ministers 1. *CC* No.1000423. Began 1975. Magazine: *Parish circular* (150 half-yearly). Turnover £30,000 to year end Dec 98. Worship at St Andrew by the Wardrobe, Queen Victoria Street, EC4.
☎ 020 8599 3836 🖷 020 8599 3836

***International Gospel Outreach**, The Oasis, Dwygyfylchi, Penmaenmawr LL34 6PS
General Secretary: Rev Bob Searle. Executive staff 8, Other staff 4, Serving ministers n/a. *CC* No.252872. Began 1967; interdenominational. Magazine: *Christian Vision* (2,000 monthly). Turnover n/a. Network of Churches and Christian organisations.
Web: www.churches.net/userpages/oasisdwygyfylchi.htm/
Email: igo@oasisdwygyfylchi.freeserve.co.uk
☎ 01492 623 229 🖷 01492 623 229

†**International Presbyterian Church, Korean Congregation**, 37 Grove Crescent, Kingston upon Thames KT1 2DG
Minister: Rev Puk-Kyong Kim. Serving minister 1. Began 1978. No magazine.
☎ 020 8546 9945 / 020 8337 2067

International Presbyterian Church, 53 Drayton Green, Ealing, London W13 0JD
Pastor: Rev Steve Constable. Serving minister 1. Began 1971. No magazine.
☎ 020 8997 4706

***Iranian Christian Fellowship**, 158 Sutton Court Road, Chiswick, London W4 3HR
Pastor: Rev Sam Yeghnazar. Serving ministers 3. Began 1985. No magazine.
☎ 020 8995 4966

Italian Pentecostal Church, Marlborough Road, Wokin GU21 5JG
Pastor: Mr Joseph D'Aloia. Serving ministers n/a. Began 1969 Magazine: *Notiziario Pentecostale* (1,400 quarterly, Swis publication).
☎ 01932 341 653

Jesus Fellowship, Nether Heyford, Northampton NN7 3LB
Senior Pastor: Noel Stanton. Executive staff 1, Admin staff 4 Serving ministers n/a. *CC* No.80114. Began 1969. Affiliated tc Multiply Christian Network. Magazine: *Jesus Life* (25,00(quarterly), *Modern Jesus Army Streetpaper* (100,000 quar terly). Evangelical church with charismatic emphasis.
Web: www.jesus.org.uk
Email: info@jesus.org.uk
☎ 01327 349 991 🖷 01327 349 997

***The King's Church**, The King's Centre, High Street, Aldersho GU11 1DJ
Leader: Mr Derek Brown. Staff n/a, Serving ministers 10. *CC* No.281184. Began 1984; non-denominational. No magazine.
Email: kingschurch@compuserve.com
☎ 01252 333 767 🖷 01252 310 814

Kingdom Faith Church, National Revival Centre, Foundry Lane, Horsham RH13 5PX
Senior Pastor: Rev Colin Urquhart. Serving ministers 10. *CC* No.278746. Began 1992.
Web: www.kingdomfaith.com
Email: info@kingdomfaith.com
☎ 01293 851 543 🖷 01293 851 330

The Latter-Rain Outpouring Revival, 234 Hoxton Road, London N1 5LX
Overseer/Bishop: Rt Rev Dr O Parris. Executive staff 2, Other staff 5, Serving ministers 3. Began 1964. No magazine.
☎ 020 7739 5389

†**Latvian Lutheran Church**, 65 Northcote Road, Leicester LE2 3FJ
Spiritual Head & Dean: Very Rev Dean Juris Jurgis. Executive staff 5, Other staff 5. Began 1947. Magazine: *Cela Biedrs* (500 monthly), *Pie Svetavota* (475 quarterly).
☎ No telephone

Latvian Roman Catholic Church, 114 Mount Street, London W1Y 6AH
Chaplain: To be appointed. Staff n/a, Serving ministers n/a. Began 1946. Magazine: *Circular Letter* (1,500 quarterly).
☎ 020 7495 1161

Liberal Catholic Church, The Pro-Cathedral Church, 205 Upper Richmond Road, Putney, London SW15 6SQ
Presiding Bishop: Most Rev Yohannes van Alphen. *Vicar General:* Rt Rev Graham Wale. Serving ministers 23. Began 1916. Magazine: *The Liberal Catholic* (600 every four months), *The Vine* (600 every four months).
Email: lcc@gwale.force9.co.uk
☎ 01798 872 227 🖷 01798 872 227

Liberal Catholic Church Theosophia Synod, 63 The Street, Ospringe, Faversham ME13 8TW
Bishop: Rt Rev Father Gerard J Crane. Serving ministers 14. Separated from Liberal Catholic Church Main Church 1982, Began in UK 1990. No magazine.
☎ 01795 532 037

Life Changing Ministries, Bemersley House, Gitana Street, Hanley, Stoke-on-Trent ST1 1DY
Apostle & Senior Pastor: Rev Trevor Newport. Lay staff 1, Serving ministers 2. ***CC*** No.1049129. Began 1992; non-denominational. Magazine: *Life Changing News* (250 quarterly). Turnover £50,000 to year end Dec 98. Church, apostolic covering, distribution of Pastor Newport's books, audio tapes, evangelism, newletter.
Web: www.lcm.clara.net
Email: mandy@lcm.clara.net
☎ 01782 272 671 📠 01782 272 671

Lithuanian Roman Catholic Church of St Casimir, 21 The Oval, London E2 9DT
Rector: Rev John Sakevicius. Serving ministers 1. Began 1901. No magazine.
☎ 020 7739 8735

London Chinese Lutheran Church, American Church in London, 79a Tottenham Court Road, London W1P 9PA
Minister: Rev Samuel Lo. No other staff, Serving minister 1. ***CC*** Began n/a. No magazine.
☎ 020 8954 1890

London City Church Kensington Temple, PO Box 9161, London W3 6GS
Senior Minister: Rev Colin W Dye. *Superintendent:* Rev Brian Richardson. Executive staff 12, Admin staff 24, Serving ministers 127. ***CC*** No.251549. Began n/a. No magazine. Also responsible for several congregations of overseas nationals; contact for details.
Web: www.ken-temp.org.uk
Email: ken-temp@dircon.co.uk
☎ 020 8752 8600 📠 020 8896 2628

London Messianic Congregation, 12 Salcombe Gardens, Mill Hill, London NW7 2NT
Messianic Rabbi: Dr Ruth Fleischer. Executive staff 1, Serving ministers n/a. Began 1981; non-denominational. Magazine: *Yeshua Journal* (500 quarterly). Turnover £40,000 to year end Mar 97. Supporting spiritual revival among Messianic Jews; encouraging return to biblical roots for Jews and Christians.
Email: dr.rfleischer@mjaa.org
☎ 020 8959 3869 📠 020 8959 3869

Lutheran Church in Great Britain, Lutheran Church House, 9 Alma Road, Headingley, Leeds LS6 2AH
Dean: Rev Walter Jacucki. *Deputy Dean:* P Schmiege. Serving ministers n/a. Began 1961. Magazine: *Lutherans in Britain* (Circulation n/a half-yearly).
Email: lutheransinleeds@freeserve.co.uk
☎ 0113 275 9042 📠 0113 275 9042
Also at: *Deputy Dean:* Rev D Schmiege, St Anne's Lutheran Church, Gresham Street, London EC2V 7BX
☎ 020 7353 3566

Lutheran Council of Great Britain, 30 Thanet Street, London WC1H 9QH
Chairman: Very Rev Lennart Sjöstrom. Full time 5, Part time 10. ***CC*** Began 1948.
Web: www.lutheran.org.uk
Email: enquiries@lutheran.org.uk
☎ 020 7383 3081 📠 020 7383 3081

Mar Thoma Syrian Church UK Congregation, Office Mar Thoma Centre, 22 Altmore Avenue, London E6 2BY
Vicar: Rev Varughese Dhomas. Executive staff 1, Other staff 1, Serving ministers 2. Began 1957. Magazine: *Mar Thoma Messenger* (150 quarterly).
☎ 020 8471 2446

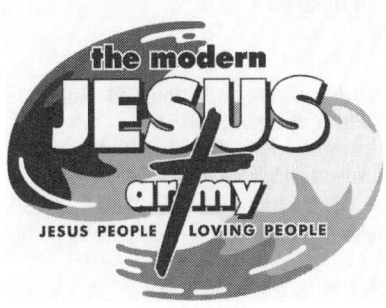

Methodist Church, Methodist Church House, 25 Marylebone Road, London NW1 5JR
Secretary of Conference: Rev Dr Nigel Collinson. Executive staff 40, Admin staff 130. Began n/a. (The Wesleyan, Primitive and United Methodist Churches united in 1932). Magazine: *Connect* (23,000 quarterly).
Web: www.methodist.org.uk
Email: co-ordsec@methodistchurch.org.uk
☎ 020 7486 5502 Fax 020 7935 1507
Co-ordinating Secretary, Unit for Church Life: Rev Dr Stephen Mosedale
Co-ordinating Secretary, Unit for Church & Society: Rev David Deeks
Co-ordinating Secretary, Unit for Family & Personal Relationships: Rev David Gamble
Co-oordinating Secretary, Unit for Service: to be appointed
Co-ordinating Secretary, Unit for Evangelism: Rev Brian Hoare

See also: **Children's Work** on Page 480
Coordinating Secretaries on Page 236
Evangelism Office on Page 236
Family and Personal Relationships on Page 236
Rob Frost Team on Page 262
Methodist Bookshop on Page 157
MAYC – Methodist Association of Youth Clubs on Page 480
Open Learning Centre on Page 521
Press Service on Page 433
Property Committee on Page 236
Public Issues on Page 236
Relief and Development Fund on Page 385
Theological Colleges and Courses on Page 237
World Church Office on Page 361
Worship & Preaching on Page 319
See also under **Methodist** in Main Index on Page 627

Methodist Church: **Birmingham District**, 36 Amesbury Road, Moseley, Birmingham B13 8LE
Chair: Rev Christina Le Moignan. Executive staff 1, Admin staff 1, Serving ministers 100. Began n/a. No magazine.
☎ 0121 449 0131 Fax 0121 449 0131
Secretary: Rev David J Easton, 2 Four Oaks Roads, Sutton Coldfield B74 2TH
☎ 0121 308 0716

Methodist Church: **Bolton and Rochdale District**, 5 Hill Side, Heaton, Bolton BL1 5DT
Chairman: Rev David B Reddish. No full-time staff, Serving ministers 45. Began n/a. No magazine.
☎ 01204 843 302 Fax 01204 843 302
Secretary: Rev Paul Martin, 16 Arkholme, Mosley Common, Worsley, Manchester M28 1ZJ
☎ 0161 790 2574

Methodist Church: **Bristol District**, Wesley Church, Wesley Slope, Frome BA11 1HP
Chairman: Rev A Ward Jones. *Secretary of the District Synod:* Rev J Carne. Executive staff 1, Serving ministers 112. Began 1739. No magazine.
☎ 0117 977 9369

Methodist Church: **Channel Islands District**, West Lea, Route des Quennevais, St Brelade, Jersey JE3 8LJ
Chairman: Rev Ian T White. Executive staff 13, Serving ministers 11. Began n/a. Magazine: *Jersey Methodist* (250 quarterly).
Email: iantwhite@cinergy.co.uk
☎ 01534 743 933 Fax 01534 498 386
Secretary: Rev Peter G Lane, Almorah, Mont Arrive, St Peter Port, Guernsey GY1 2AA
☎ 01481 728 049

Methodist Church: **Chester and Stoke-on-Trent District**, 5 Sandside Road, Alsager, Stoke-on-Trent ST7 2XJ
Chairman: Rev Brian G Powley. Executive staff 1, Serving ministers 71. Began n/a. No magazine.
☎ 01270 883 417
Secretary: Rev Andrew L Gunstone, 6 Armstrong Close, Audlem, Crewe CW3 0EB
☎ 01270 811 711

Methodist Church: **Cornwall District**, 4 Upland Crescent, Truro TR1 1LU
Chairman: Rev Dr Stephen Dawes. Staff n/a, Serving ministers 59. Began n/a. Magazine: *District Chronicle* (7,000 every four months).
☎ 01872 272 514
Secretary: Rev Howard Curnow, The Retreat, 104 Launceston Road, Callington PL17 8DS

Methodist Church: **Cumbria District**, 14 Monnington Way, Penrith CA11 8QJ
Chairman: Rev David Emison. Serving ministers 35. Began n/a. No magazine. Turnover £126,087 to year end Dec 98.
Email: david@cumbriadistrict.u-net.com
☎ 01768 866 342
Synod Secretary: Mr David Andrews, 12 Lonsdale Place, Whitehaven CA28 6DX
Email: davidjandrews@compuserve.com
☎ 01946 695 373

Methodist Church: **Cymru District**, 6 Wern Uchaf, Ffordd Cae Glas, Ruthin LL15 1EQ
Chairman: Rev R Martin Evans-Jones. Admin staff 2, Serving ministers 12. Began n/a. Magazine: *Y Gwyliedydd* (2,500 monthly).
Web: www.westwales.co.uk/methodism
☎ 01824 705 751 Fax 01824 705 751
Secretary: Rev Patrick Slattery, Heulfryn, Ffordd Tyn-y-Coed, Dolgellau LL40 2YT
☎ 01341 422 524

Methodist Church: **Darlington District**, 2 Edinburgh Drive, Darlington DL3 8AW
Chairman: Rev Graham Carter. Executive staff 1, Serving ministers 68. Began n/a. No magazine.
☎ 01325 468 119
Secretary: Mr Ian Scott, 33 Roseberry Avenue, Stokesley, Middlesbrough TS9 5HF
☎ 01642 710 772

Methodist Church: **East Anglia District**, 26 Wentworth Green, Sunningdale, Norwich NR4 6AE
Chairman: Rev Malcolm L Braddy. Admin staff 3, Serving ministers 79. Began n/a. No magazine.
☎ 01603 452 257
Secretary: Mrs Diana Sawyer, 25 Quilter Drive, Belstead, Ipswich IP8 3RB
☎ 01473 680 442

Methodist Church: **Isle of Man District**, Wesley Manse, The Crescent West, Ramsey IM8 2JN
Chairman: Rev Kenneth Britton. Serving ministers 7. Began n/a. Magazine: *Newsheet* (Circulation n/a periodically).
☎ 01624 812 385
Secretary: Rev S Caddy, 11 Bayr Grianagh, Castletown IM9 1HN

Methodist Church: **Leeds District**, 281 Otley Road, Leeds LS16 5LN
Chairman: Rev Michael J Townsend. Serving ministers 75. Began n/a. No magazine.
Email: mjt.leeds@compuserve.com
☎ 0113 278 5546 Fax 0113 274 5611
Secretary: Rev John Santry, 41 Tatefield Grove, Kippax, Leeds LS25 7LA
☎ 0113 286 2780

Methodist Church: **Lincoln and Grimsby District**, 52 St Edward's Drive, Sudbrooke, Lincoln LN2 2QR
Chairman: Rev Peter G Sulston. Executive staff 3, Admin staff 2, Serving ministers 57. Began n/a. No magazine.
☎ 01522 752 521
Secretary: Rev Gillian Riley, The Manse, 6 Ashberry Drive, Messingham, Scunthorpe DN17 3QS
☎ 01724 762 305

Methodist Church: **Liverpool District**, 49 Queen's Drive, Mossley Hill, Liverpool L18 2DT
Chairman: Rev Dr John B Taylor. *Secretary:* Rev Neil A Stubbens. Executive staff 2, Serving ministers 64. Began n/a. No magazine.
Email: liv.meth.dist@rapid.co.uk
☎ 0151 722 1219 Fax 0151 722 1219

Methodist Church: **London North East District**, 51 Beattyville Gardens, Ilford IG6 1JY
Chairman: Rev Ermal Kirby. Executive staff 2, Serving ministers 120. Began n/a. No magazine.
☎ 01708 450 146 Fax 01708 450 146
Secretary: Rev Clifford Newman, East End Mission, 583 Commercial Road, Stepney, London E1 0HJ

Methodist Church: **London North West District**, 37 Long Butlers, Harpenden AL5 1JF
Chairman: Rev W Garth Rogers. Serving ministers 94. Began n/a. No magazine.
☎ 01582 760 567
Secretary: Rev G Cornell, 6 Woodcock Hill, Kenton, Harrow HA3 0JG
☎ 020 8907 3042

Methodist Church: **London South East District**, 20 Beadon Road, Bromley BR2 9AT
Chairman: Rev Harvey Richardson. Executive staff 1, Serving ministers 105. Began n/a. Magazine: *District News-sheet* (500 half-yearly).
☎ 020 8464 2540
Secretary: Rev Jeremy Dare, 87 Lower Queens Road, Ashford TN24 8HD
☎ 01233 621 216

Methodist Church: **London South West District**, 85 Dartnell Park Road, West Byfleet KT14 6QD
Chairman: Rev R Martin Broadbent. Executive staff 1, Serving ministers 110. Began n/a. No magazine.
☎ 01932 355 784
Also at: *Secretary:* Colin A Smith, 13 Enmore Road, Putney London SW15 6LL
☎ 020 8788 1219

Methodist Church: **Manchester and Stockport District**, 15 Woodlands Road, Handforth, Wilmslow SK9 3AW
Chairman: Rev David F Willie. Serving ministers 90. Began n/a. No magazine.
☎ 01625 523 480 Fax 01625 523 480
Secretary: Rev Paul H Wilson, 22 Glebelands Road, Knutsford WA16 9DZ
☎ 01565 633 276

Methodist Church: **Newcastle upon Tyne District**, 8 Ancroft Way, Fawdon, Newcastle upon Tyne NE3 2BX
Chairman: Rev Robin E Hutt. Staff n/a, Serving ministers 105. Began n/a. No magazine.
☎ 0191 285 4163 Fax 0191 285 9250
Secretary: Rev J W Wesley Blakey, 2 Pilton Road, Westerhope, Newcastle upon Tyne NE5 4PP
☎ 0191 286 9655

Methodist Church: **North Lancashire District**, 28 Lower Greenfield, Ingol, Preston PR2 3ZT
Chairman: Rev G Michael Wearing. Staff n/a, Serving ministers n/a. Began n/a. No magazine.
☎ 01772 733 496
Secretary: Rev Andrew Horsfall, 8 Hurst Leigh Drive, Mossgate Park, Heysham LA3 2HY
☎ 01524 850 780

Methodist Church: **Nottingham and Derby District**, 37 Sutton Passey's Crescent, Nottingham NG8 1BX
Chairman: Rev Geoffrey L Clark. *Secretary:* Ms A George. Serving ministers 86. Began n/a. No magazine.
☎ 0115 978 7598 Fax 0115 978 7598

Methodist Church: **Oxford and Leicester District**, 291 Billing Road East, Northampton NN3 3LG
Chairman: Rev H Edward Lacy. Serving ministers 86. Began n/a. No magazine.
☎ 01604 301 28
Secretary: Rev Dr Martin Wellings, 11 Wodhams Drive, Brackley NN13 6NB
☎ 01280 705 601

Methodist Church: **Plymouth and Exeter District**, 18 Velwell Road, Exeter EX4 4LE
Chairman: Rev Kenneth S J Hext. Executive staff 1, Serving ministers 75. Began n/a. Magazine: *Newsletter* (Circulation n/a every four months).
Email: 101610.3066@compuserve.com
☎ 01392 272 541 Fax 01392 433 988
Secretary: Rev Peter Williamson, Fairlawne, 133 New Road, Brixham TQ5 8DB
☎ 01803 854 431 Fax 01803 854 431

Methodist Church: **Scotland District**, 20 Inglewood Crescent, East Kilbride, Glasgow G75 8QD
Chairman: Rev T Alan Anderson. Executive staff 1, Serving ministers 41. Began n/a. No magazine.
Email: taa@zetnet.co.uk
☎ 01355 237411
Secretary: Rev David Cooper, Central Hall, Tollcross, Edinburgh EH3 9BP
☎ 0131 229 7937

Methodist Church: **Sheffield District**, 65 Stafford Road, Sheffield S2 2SF
Chairman: Rev David Halstead. *Secretary:* Rev Anne Brown. Serving ministers 97. Began n/a. Magazine: *News sheet* (Circulation n/a quarterly).
Web: members.aol.com/sheffmeth/
Email: sheffmeth@aol.com
☎ 0114 281 2733 Fax 0114 281 2734

Methodist Church: **Shetland District**, Wesley Manse, 9 Hillhead, Lerwick ZE1 0EJ
Chairman: Rev Gilbert S Hall. Executive staff 1, Serving ministers 4. ***CC*** Began n/a. No magazine.
Email: gilberthall@zetnet.co.uk
☎ 01595 692 874
Secretary: Rev Colin Wilson, Westley Manse, Walls, Shetland ZE2 9PF
☎ 01595 809 210

C

Methodist Church: **South Wales District**, 12 Llwyn-y-Grant Road, Penylan, Cardiff CF3 7ET
Chairman: Rev Will Morrey. Serving ministers 50. Began n/a. (Previously Cardiff and Swansea District). Magazine: *South Wales District Issues* (4,000 half-yearly).
Email: willmorrey@enterprise.net
☎ 029 2048 6751
Secretary: Rev Graeme Halls, 63 Kingsmash Avenue, Chepstow NP6 5LY
☎ 01291 622 100

Methodist Church: **Southampton District**, 4 The Glade, Thornbury Wood, Chandlers Ford, Eastleigh SO53 5AZ
Chairman: Rev Thomas J Stuckey. Serving ministers 93. Began n/a. Magazine: *District Newsletter* (Circulation n/a quarterly).
Email: tom@sotonchr.surfaid.org
☎ 023 8027 0519

Methodist Church: **West Yorkshire District**, 19 Wentworth Court, Rastrick, Brighouse HD6 3XD
Chairman: Rev Peter Whittaker. No full-time staff, Serving ministers 65. Began n/a. Magazine: *District Newsletter* (6,000 quarterly).
Email: pwwyks@aol.com
☎ 01484 719 993 Fax 01484 720 606
Secretary: Rev Stuart J Wild, Ashfield, 37 Rawson Avenue, Halifax HX3 0LR
☎ 01422 354 610

C

Methodist Church: **Wolverhampton and Shrewsbury District**, 53 York Avenue, Wolverhampton WV3 9BX
Chairman: Rev Peter F Curry. *Secretary:* Rev Derrick R Lander. No full-time staff, Serving ministers 80. Began n/a. No magazine.
☎ 01902 424 430 Fax 01902 424 430

Methodist Church: **York and Hull District**, 13 Lawn Way, Stockton Lane, York YO3 0JD
Chairman: Rev Stuart J Burgess. Admin staff 1, Serving ministers 72. Began n/a. No magazine.
☎ 01904 424 739 Fax 01904 424 739
Secretary: Rev David Perry, 72 South Street, Hull HU16 3AT
☎ 01482 847 164

Methodist Church in Ireland, 1 Fountainville Avenue, Belfast BT9 6AN
Secretary: Rev Edmund T I Mawhinney. Executive staff 3, Serving ministers 130. Began 1738. Magazine: *Methodist Newsletter* (4,750 monthly).
Email: mci@iol.ie
☎ 028 9032 4554 Fax 028 9023 9467

Methodist Church in Ireland: **Belfast District**, Grosvenor House, 5 Glengall Street, Belfast BT12 5AD
Chairman: Rev Jim Rea MBE. Serving ministers 51. Began 1750. No magazine.
☎ 028 9045 8560 Fax 028 9043 2575
Secretary: Rev Samuel McGuffin, 10 Locksley Park, Belfast BT10 0AR
☎ 028 9065 3476

Methodist Church in Ireland: **Down District**, 16 Brooklands Road, Newtownards BT23 4TL
Chairman: Rev Robert P Roddie. Serving ministers 16. Began n/a. No magazine.
Email: robin_roddie@msn.com
☎ 028 9181 5959

Methodist Church in Ireland: **Enniskillen and Sligo District**, Ardaghowen, Sligo, Republic of Ireland
Chairman: Rev Ian D Henderson. Serving ministers 12. *CC* No.CHV 253. Began n/a. No magazine.
☎ n/a

Methodist Church in Ireland: **North East District**, 103 Station Road, Greenisland, Carrickfergus BT38 8UW
Chairman: Rev K H Thompson. Serving ministers 17. Began 1747. No magazine.
☎ 028 9085 1144 Fax 028 9085 1144
Secretary: Rev R Cooper,
☎ 01266 656 693 Mobile: 07710 945 104
Fax 01266 656 693

Methodist Church in Ireland: North West District, 9 Dergmoney Place, Omagh BT78 1HS
Chairman: Rev Peter Good. Serving ministers 11. Began n/a. (Previously Londonderry District). No magazine.
☎ 028 8224 2372
Secretary: Rev Ian Henderson, Methodist Manse, Donegal Town, Republic of Ireland
☎ 00 073 235 88

Methodist Church in Ireland: **Portadown District**, 1 Corby Drive, Lurgan, Craigavon BT66 7AF
Chairman: Rev Sean Plaland. Executive staff 1, Admin staff 1, Serving ministers 16. Began 1747. No magazine.
Secretary: Rev Westley Blair, 112a Guildford Road, Lurgan BT66 7AB
☎ 028 3832 3324

The Metropolitan Community Church, Hannington Road, Bournemouth BH7 6JT
District Co-ordinator: Rev Cecilia Eggleston. Executive staff 1, Serving ministers n/a. Began 1972. Magazine: *Eurovision* (600 quarterly).
Email: c.m.e@btinternet.com
☎ 01225 837 499 Fax 01225 837 499

Miracle Church of God in Christ, 36 Alexandra Road, Bedford MK40 1JB
Overseer: Mr Francis Vaughan. *Administrator:* Mrs Ruth Haye. Executive staff 5, Admin staff 4, Serving ministers 3. *CC* No.291224. Began 1960. No magazine. Religious organization, care of the whole man, various community work, hospital prison, ministry youth group.
☎ 01234 215 081

Moravian Church in Great Britain and Ireland, 5 Muswell Hill, London N10 3TJ
Chairman, Provincial Board: Rev W John H McOwat. Executive staff 2, Admin staff 5, Serving ministers 25. *CC* No.251211. Began 1737. Magazine: *The Moravian Messenger* (1,300 monthly), *News and Views* (400 annually).
Web: www.moravian.org.uk
Email: moravianchurchhouse@btinternet.com
☎ 020 8883 3409/1912 Fax 020 365 3371

†**Mount Zion Pentecostal Apostolic Church**, 145 Midland Road, Bedford MK40 1DW
Presiding Bishop: Rev Dr Martin Thomas. Executive staff 3, Other staff 3, Serving ministers n/a. Began 1965. No magazine.
☎ 01234 343 609 Fax 01234 343 609

Multiply Christian Network, Jesus Fellowship Central Offices, Nether Heyford, Northampton NN7 3LB
Multiply Director: Mr Huw Lewis. Admin staff 2, Other staff 2, Serving ministers 150. Began 1992; New Churches. Magazine: *Multiply Infozine* (15,000 quarterly). A growing network of independent churches and groups promoting living charismatic Christianity.
Web: www.multiply.org.uk
Email: info@multiply.org.uk
☎ 01327 349 995 📠 01327 349 997

The Mustard Seed Church, 16 Clive Road, West Dulwich, London SE21 8BY
Pastor: Rev Anthony C I Uzoka. Serving minister 1. *CC* No.1002281. Began 1987. No magazine.
☎ 020 8265 4211 / 020 7737 1626 (office)
Mobile: 07956 239 693

New Apostolic Church UK, Administration Office, 19 Southwell Park Road, Camberley GU15 3PU
District Elder: Rev Hans-Dieter Duemke. Serving ministers n/a. *CC* No.239664. Began 1948. No magazine.
☎ 01276 614 16 📠 01276 677 971

New Covenant Church, 214 Elephant and Castle Shopping Centre, London SE1 6TE
General Overseer: Rev Paul Jinadu. *National Administrator:* Rev Obafemi Omisade. *National Overseer:* Rev Niyi Kolade. Admin staff 6, Serving ministers 31. *CC* No.1004343. Began 1988. Magazine: *U-turn* (2,000 quarterly).
Email: newcovenantuk@compuserve.com
☎ 020 7277 0272 Mobile: 07899 742 851
📠 020 7277 0824

***New Frontiers International**, 17 Clarendon Villas, Hove BN3 3RE
Administrator: Mr Nigel D Ring. *International Team Leader:* Mr Terry Virgo. *National Team Leader:* Mr David Holden. Executive staff 6, Admin staff 6, Serving ministers 306. *CC* No.1006940. Began 1980. Magazine: *New Frontiers magazine* (15,000 every two months).
Web: home.ml.org/nfi
Email: nfi@n-f-i.org
☎ 01273 234 555 📠 01273 234 556

New Testament Assembly (Pentecostal), 7 Beechcroft Road, Tooting, London SW17 7BU
Presiding Bishop: Bishop ML Powell. Executive staff 4. Serving ministers n/a. Began 1961. No magazine.
☎ 020 8672 9416 / 020 8679 3565

New Testament Church of God, Main House, Overstone Park, Overstone, Northampton NN6 0AD
National Overseer: Rev Ronald O Brown. Executive staff 12, Admin staff 20, Serving ministers 243. Began 1953. No magazine.
☎ 01604 643 311/645 944 📠 01604 790 254

Non-subscribing Presbyterian Church of Ireland, 102 Carrickfergus Road, Larne BT40 3JX
Clerk to the General Synod: Rev Dr J W Nelson. *Editor:* Rev A D G Steers. No full-time staff, Serving ministers 15. *CC* Began 1910. Magazine: *The Non-subscribing Presbyterian* (1,100 monthly).
☎ 028 2827 2600

Norwegian Church and Seamen's Mission, St Olav's Church, 1 St Olav's Square, Albion Street, Rotherhithe, London SE16 1JB
Rector: Rev Helge Pettersson. Executive staff 6, Serving ministers 5. ***CC*** No.220235. Began 1692; Lutheran. Magazine: *Månedsbladet* (1,800 every two months).
Web: dspace.dial.pipex.com/londonkirken/
Email: londonkirken@dial.pipex.com & london@sifh.no
☎ 020 7237 5587 Mobile: 07860 333 512
Fax 020 7237 7280

***Old Baptist Union**, 64 Kennedy Avenue, Macclesfield SK10 3DE
Secretary: Rev C Whiteley. No full-time staff, Serving ministers 11. ***CC*** No.233642. Began 1880. Magazine: *The Link* (600 quarterly).
☎ 01625 422 404

Old Roman Catholic Church of Great Britain, 116 Brentwood Road, Hollingdean, Brighton BN1 7ES
Administrator: Very Rev James V A Phillips. Executive staff 3, Admin staff 4, Serving ministers 6. ***CC*** No.232764. Began 1908. Magazine: *One Faith* (250 half-yearly). Independent Catholic jurasdiction, traditional western liturgies.
☎ 01273 554 260 / 558 917 Mobile: 07901 644 176
Fax 01273 558 917

Orthodox Church in Wales, Orthodox Church of the Holy Protection, 11 Manod Road, Blaenau Ffestiniog LL41 4DE
Abbot: Very Rev Abbot Father Deiniol. Serving ministers 5. Began n/a. No magazine.
☎ 01766 831 272 Fax 01766 831 272

Pentecostal Revival Church of Christ, 220 Ellison Road, Streatham, London SW16 5DJ
President: Rt Rev Akinola O Ajibode. Admin staff 18, Serving ministers n/a. Began 1973. No magazine.
☎ 020 8764 2643

***The People's Christian Fellowship**, Springfield Hall, 89 Broad Lane, London N15 4DW
Pastor: Rev Joseph A Daniel. Serving minister 1. ***CC*** No.1031255. Began 1956. No magazine.
☎ 020 8801 1873

***Pillar of Fire Church**, 19 Brent Street, Hendon, London NW4 2EU
Senior Pastor: Rev Bernard Dawson. *Assistant Pastor:* Rev Gabriel Mancino. Admin staff 4, Other staff 5, Serving ministers 4. ***CC*** No.1015529. Began 1915. Magazine: *British Isles Pillar of Fire* (800 every two months). Turnover £118,000 to year end Dec 98.
Email: bernard.dawson@lineone.net
☎ 020 8202 3219/7618 Mobile: 07467 356 307
Fax 020 8202 3277

***Pioneer**, Waverley Abbey House, Waverley Lane, Farnham GU9 8EP
Team Leader: Mr Gerald Coates. Executive staff 35, Other staff 6, Serving ministers 60. ***CC*** No.327160. Began 1982. Magazine: *Compass* (5,000 quarterly), *Pioneer UpDate* (1,700 monthly). Turnover £500,000 to year end Dec 98. Church planting and care, training and evangelism, publishing and music, prayer and revival.
Web: ds.pipex.com/pioneer_trust
Email: pioneer_trust@dial.pipex.com
☎ 01252 784 733 Fax 01252 784 732

***Plumbline Ministries**, 83a High Street, Huntingdon PE18 6DP
Team Leader: Mr Simon Matthews. Executive staff 5, Admin staff 6, Serving ministers 30. ***CC*** No.327271. Began 1986. Magazine: *Newsletter* (700 every four months).
Web: www.plumbline.org.uk
Email: plumbline@plumbline.org.uk
☎ 01480 411 665 Fax 01480 414 442

Plymouth Brethren No 4, c/o Bible and Gospel Trust, 99 Green Lane, Hounslow TW4 6BW
No full-time staff. Began 1828. No magazine.
☎ 020 8577 1603

The Presbyterian Church in Ireland, Church House, Fisherwick Place, Belfast BT1 6DW
Clerk of Assembly & General Secretary: Rev Dr Samuel Hutchinson. *Financial Secretary:* Mr Hilton Henry. *Overseas Board Secretary:* Rev R J T McMullan. Executive staff 12, Admin staff 30, Serving ministers 430. Began 1662; synods united 1840. Magazine: *The Presbyterian Herald* (17,000 monthly). Turnover £50,000,000 to year end Dec 98.
Web: www.presbyterianireland.org
Email: clerk@presbyterianireland.org
☎ 028 9032 2284 Mobile: 07703 467 706
Fax 028 9023 6609

See also: **Belfast City Mission** on Page 254
Christian Irishman on Page 312
Inter-Church Relations Board on Page 236
Irish Mission on Page 263
Presbyterian Church in Ireland Overseas Board on Page 364
Presbyterian Herald on Page 317
Presbyterian Youth Board on Page 481
See also under **The Presbyterian Church in Ireland** in Main Index on Page 627

Ards Presbytery: Rev Dr Donald Watts, Clerk, 3 Second Avenue, Baylands, Bangor BT20 5JZ
☎ 028 9145 0141
Armagh Presbytery: Rev Dr J Thompson, Clerk, Greenfield Manse, 72 Newry Road, Armagh BT60 1ER
☎ 028 3752 5522
Ballymena Presbytery: Rev Joseph Andrews, Clerk, 1 Forthill Park, Ballymena BT42 2HL
☎ 028 2545 544
Belfast East Presbytery: Rev John McVeigh, Clerk, 234 Lower Braniel Road, Belfast BT5 7NJ
☎ 028 9097 5136
Belfast North Presbytery: Rev John R Dickinson, Clerk, 11 Waterloo Gardens, Belfast BT15 4EX
☎ 028 9028 9468
Belfast South Presbytery: Rev R T Anderson, Clerk, 3 Shrewsbury Gardens, Belfast BT9 6PJ
☎ 028 9066 7247
Carrickfergus Presbytery: Very Rev Dr R V A Lynas, Clerk, 19 Wheatfield Heights, Ballygally, Larne BT40 2RT
☎ 028 2858 3643
Coleraine Presbytery: Rev Ivan Hunter, Clerk, 8 Ballywatt Road, Coleraine BT52 2LT
☎ 028 7073 1310
Derry and Strabane Presbytery: Rev Dr Joseph Fell, Clerk, 19 Clearwater, Caw, Londonderry BT47 6BE
☎ 028 7131 1425
Down Presbytery: Rev James Harper, Clerk, 35 Manse Road, Ballygowan, Newtownards BT23 6HE
☎ 028 9752 8962
Dromore Presbytery: Rev J I Davey, Clerk, 2 Lisburn Road, Hillsborough BT26 6AA
☎ 028 9268 3696

Foyle Presbytery: Rev Stanley Stewart, Clerk, 68 Donagheady Road, Bready, Strabane BT82 0DE
☎ 028 7184 1320
Iveagh Presbytery: Rev I J Patterson, Clerk, 19 Shimna Road, Newcastle BT33 0AT
☎ 028 4472 3455
Newry Presbytery: Rev Stuart A Finlay, Clerk, 156 Glasdrumman Road, Annalong, Newry BT34 4QL
☎ 028 4476 8232
Omagh Presbytery: Rev J F Murdoch, Clerk, 28a Dublin Road, Omagh BT78 1HE
☎ 028 8224 2239
Route Presbytery: Rev Hugh B Wallace, Clerk, 211 Strand Road, Bushmills BT57 8XJ
☎ 028 7073 1305
Templepatrick Presbytery: Rev William D Weir, Clerk, 50 Killead Road, Crumlin BT29 4EN
☎ 028 9442 2436
Tyrone Presbytery: Rev James B McCormick, Clerk, 10 Ministers Walk, Moneymore, Magherafelt BT45 7QE
☎ 028 7974 8012

Presbyterian Church of Wales, 53 Richmond Road, Cardiff CF2 3UP
General Secretary: Rev W G Edwards. Executive staff 5, Other staff 5, Serving ministers 128. Began n/a. (First ordination 1811; incorporated 1826). Magazine: *Y Goleuad* (1,950 weekly), *The Treasury* (1,200 monthly).
Web: www.ebcpcw.org.uk
Email: ebcpcw@aol.com
☎ 029 2049 4913 🖷 029 2046 4293
East Association: Rev G Barrington, Secretary, 10 Highmead Avenue, Llanelli SA15 3SP
North Association: Rev Trefor Lewis, Secretary, 6 Wynnstay Avenue, Hen Golwyn, Bae Colwyn LL29 9DS
South Association: Rev G L Reynolds, Secretary, 18 Windermere Avenue, Roath Park, Cardiff CF2 5PQ

Protestant Evangelical Church of England, Office, 36 Shaftesbury Avenue, Worthing BN12 4EQ
Joint Co-ordinator: Rev Kenneth Whittaker. Executive staff 2, Serving ministers 5. Began 1922. (Previously Protestant Episcopal Reformed Church (The Protestant Evangelical Church of England)). Magazine: *The Cranmer Record* (100 annually).
☎ 01903 505 919

Rainbow Churches, PO Box 1908, London N4 3PY
Executive Leader: Mr Adrian Hawkes. *Administrator:* Mrs Angela Kelly. Executive staff 4, Admin staff 14, Serving ministers 11. ***CC*** No.1023328. Began 1991; affiliated to Pioneer. No magazine. Turnover £65,000 to year end Dec 98. Children, youth and adult cells, day school nursery, counselling team, homeless work, arts course.
Web: easyweb.easynet.co.uk/rain
Email: rain@easynet.co.uk
☎ 020 8885 5488 🖷 020 8885 5007

***Ransom Church of God Universal Fellowship**, 78 Albacore Crescent, Lewisham, London SE13 7HP
General Overseer: Rev Owen O Douce. Executive staff 5, Other staff 8, Serving ministers 3. Began 1965. Magazine: *Ransom Bulletin* (200 frequency n/a), *The Dove* (Circulation n/a quarterly).
Administrative Address 79 Foxborough Gardens, Brockley, London SE4 1HT
☎ 020 8690 1890

Redemption Church of God, 1 Lealand Road, Tottenham, London N15 6JS
Pastor: Pastor B W Scott. Serving minister 1. Began 1961. No magazine.
☎ 020 8802 1206 🖷 020 8802 1206

Reformed Presbyterian Church of Ireland, Cameron House, 98 Lisburn Road, Belfast BT9 6AG
Clerk of Synod: Rev A C Gregg. *Inter Church Correspondent:* Prof F S Leahy. Serving ministers 26. Began 1763. Magazine: *Covenanter Witness* (500 monthly), *The Messenger (youth)* (500 every two months).
Web: www.rpc.org
☎ 028 9066 0689

Reformed Presbyterian Church of Scotland, Magdalen Chapel, 41 The Cow Gate, Edinburgh EH1 1JR
Clerk of Synod: Rev A Sinclair Horne. Admin staff 1, Serving ministers 4. Began 1743. Magazine: *Reformed Presbyterian* (Circulation & frequency n/a). *Covenanter Witness* (3,000 Frequency n/a).
☎ 0131 220 1450

Religious Society of Friends (Quakers) in Britain, Friends House, Euston Road, London NW1 2BJ
Recording Clerk: Elsa Dicks. *Clerk, Meeting for Sufferings:* Jane Chattell. *Clerk, Britain Yearly Meeting:* Helen Rowlands. Staff 114. Began 1652. Magazine: *Quaker News* (15,000 quarterly).
Web: www.quaker.org.uk
Email: graceh@quaker.org.uk
☎ 020 7663 1000 🖷 020 7663 1001

Romanian Orthodox Church in London, St Dunstan's-in-the-West, 186a Fleet Street, London EC4A 2AE
Priest-in-Charge: Rev S P Pufulete. Executive staff 1, Serving ministers 3. ***CC*** No.269405. Began 1965. No magazine.
Email: ppufulete@compuserve.com
☎ 020 7242 6027 Mobile: 07973 308 545

Russian Orthodox Church Outside Russia, Church House, 57 Harvard Road, London W4 4ED
Presiding Bishop: Rt Rev Bishop Mark. *UK Contact:* Rev Father Vadim Zakrevsky. Executive staff 2. Began 1924. Magazine: *Orthodox Life* (Circulation n/a periodically).
☎ 020 8742 3493 🖷 020 8995 9503

†**Russian Orthodox Diocese of Sourozh**, All Saints, Ennismore Gardens, London SW7 1NH
Metropolitan: Metropolitan Anthony Bloom. Serving ministers 19. ***CC*** No.277508. Began n/a. Magazine: *Sourozh* (Circulation n/a quarterly), *Cathedral Newsletter* (Circulation n/a monthly).
☎ 020 7584 0096 🖷 020 7584 9864
Diocesan Secretary: Mrs Gillian Crow, 6 Maiden Hill Place, Dartmought Park Hill, London NW5 1HZ
Email: crow@kbnet.co.uk
Assistant Bishop of Kerch: Archbishop Anatoly 14a Bloom Park Road, Fulham, London SW6 7BG
☎ 020 7386 7837
Assistant Bishop Sergievo: Rt Rev Basil, 94a Banbury Road, Oxford OX2 6JT
☎ 01865 512 701

***Salt and Light Ministries**, c/o OCC Area Centre, 53 West Way, Oxford OX2 0JE
UK Team Leader: Rev Stephen Thomas. Executive staff 14, Other staff 4, Serving ministers 80. ***CC*** No.1071600. Began 1985; non-denominational. No magazine. Turnover £200,000 to year end Dec 90.
Email: saltandlight.u-net.com
☎ 01865 793 239 🖷 01865 248 044

C

***The Salvation Army, UK Territorial Commander**, UK Territorial Headquarters, 101 Newington Causeway, London SE1 6BN
UK Territorial Commander: Commissioner Alex Hughes. *Chief Secretary, UK:* Col Raymond Houghton. Executive staff 23. ***CC*** No.214779. Began 1865. Magazine: *The War Cry* (75,000 weekly), *Kids Alive!* (40,000 weekly), *Salvationist* (21,000 weekly). Turnover n/a.
Web: www.salvationarmy.org.uk
Email: salvationarmy@org.uk
☎ 020 7367 4500 🖷 020 7367 4728
See also: **All the World** on Page 311
Kids Alive on Page 316
The Officer on Page 317
Reliance Bank on Page 422
Reliance World Travel on Page 474
Salvation Army (International) on Page 365
Salvation Army Housing Association on Page 103
Salvation Army Social Services on Page 468
Salvation Army Youth Department on Page 481
Salvationist on Page 318
Salvationist Publishing and Supplies Ltd on Pages 160, 179
The War Cry on Page 319
See also under **Salvation Army** in Main Index on Page 627

****Salvation Army:* Anglia Division**, Barton Way, Norwich NR1 1DL
Divisional Commander: Major Howard Grottick. Executive staff 8, Admin staff 5, Serving officers 60. ***CC*** No.214779. Began n/a. No magazine.
☎ 01603 724 400 🖷 01603 506 385

****Salvation Army:* Central North Division**, Divisional Commander, 80 Eccles New Road, Salford M5 2RU
Divisional Commander: Lieut-Col Linda Bond. Executive staff 3, Admin staff 6, Serving officers 48. ***CC*** No.214779. Began n/a. No magazine.
☎ 0161 743 3900 🖷 0161 743 3911

****Salvation Army:* Central South Division**, Frays Court, 71 Cowley Road, Uxbridge UB8 2AE
Divisional Commander: Lt Col William Main. Executive staff 7, Admin staff 3, Serving officers 100. ***CC*** No.214779. Began n/a. No magazine.
☎ 01895 208 800 🖷 01895 208 811

***Salvation Army: East Midlands Division**, Paisley Grove, Chilwell, Nottingham NG9 6DJ
Divisional Commander: Major John Matear. Serving officers 102. ***CC*** No.214779. Began n/a. No magazine.
☎ 0115 983 5000 🖷 0115 983 5011

****Salvation Army:* East Scotland**, 5 East Adam Street, Edinburgh EH8 9TF
Divisional Commander: Major Robert McIntyre. Executive staff 6, Other staff 9, Serving officers 45. ***CC*** No.214779. Began n/a. No magazine.
☎ 0131 662 3300 🖷 0131 662 3311

****Salvation Army:* Ireland Division**, 12 Station Mews, Sydenham, Belfast BT4 1TL
Divisional Commander: Major George Pilkington. Executive staff 6, Other staff 13, Serving officers 46. ***CC*** No.214779. Began 1880. No magazine.
☎ 028 9067 5000 🖷 028 9067 5011

****Salvation Army*, London Central Division**, 9 Salisbury Road, Barnet EN5 4JW
Divisional Commander: Major John Wainwright. Executive staff 7, Other staff 7, Serving officers 82. ***CC*** No.214779. Began n/a. No magazine.
☎ 020 8447 1422 / 8449 4097

****Salvation Army:* London North East Division**, Maldon Roa
Hatfield Peverel, Chelmsford CM3 2HL
Divisional Commander: Lt Col David Phillips. Executive sta
10, Admin staff 6, Serving officers 80. ***CC*** No.214779. Bega
n/a. No magazine.
☎ 01245 383 000 🖷 01245 383 011

****Salvation Army:* London South East Division**, 3 West Cour
Armstrong Road, Maidstone ME15 6QR
Officer Commanding: Major David Jones. Executive staff 17
Admin staff 6, Serving officers 121. ***CC*** No.214779. Bega
1865. No magazine.
☎ 01622 775 000 🖷 01622 775 011

****Salvation Army:* North Scotland Division**, Deer Road, Woodside
Aberdeen AB24 2BL
Divisional Commander: Major David Hinton. Executive staff 6
Admin staff 5, Serving officers 36. ***CC*** No.214779. Began n/a
No magazine.
☎ 01224 497 000 🖷 01224 497 011

****Salvation Army:* North Western Division**, 16 Faraday Road
Liverpool L13 1EH
Divisional Commander: Major Geoffrey Parkin. Executive staf
7, Admin staff 7, Serving officers 75. ***CC*** No.214779. Begai
n/a. No magazine.
☎ 0151 252 6100 / 6101 (direct) 🖷 0151 252 6111

****Salvation Army:* Northern Division**, Level 3, South Wing, Regen
Centre, Gosforth, Newcastle upon Tyne NE3 3TZ
Divisional Commander: Major Ray Kirby. Executive staff 20,
Serving officers 113. ***CC*** No.214779. Began 1865. Nc
magazine.
☎ 0191 213 4100 🖷 0191 213 4111

****Salvation Army:* South & Mid Wales Division**, Eastmoors Road,
Ocean Park, Cardiff CF1 5SA
Divisional Commander: Major Michael Parker. Executive staff
6, Other staff 6, Serving officers 61. ***CC*** No.214779. Began
1878. No magazine.
☎ 029 2044 0600 🖷 029 2044 0611

****Salvation Army:* South-Western Division**, Marlborough Court, Manaton Close, Matford Business Park, Exeter EX2 8PF
Divisional Commander: Lt Col David Lambert-Gorwyn. Executive staff 9, Admin staff 9, Serving officers 49. ***CC*** No.214779. Began n/a. No magazine.
☎ 01392 822 100 🖷 01392 822 111

****Salvation Army:* Southern Division**, 6 Little Park Farm Road, Segensworth, Fareham PO15 5TD
Divisional Commander: Lt Col John Pearce-Haydon. Executive staff 9, Other staff 7, Serving officers 72. ***CC*** No.214779. Began 1865. No magazine.
☎ 01489 566 800 🖷 01489 566 811

****Salvation Army:* West Midlands Division**, 24 St Chad's, Queensway, Birmingham B4 6HH
Divisional Commander: Lt Col Ron Smith. Executive staff 7, Other staff 3, Serving ministers 97. ***CC*** No.214779. Began 1865. No magazine.
☎ 0121 212 7800 🖷 0121 236 1263

****Salvation Army:* West Scotland Division**, 4 Buchanan Court, Cumbernauld Road, Glasgow G33 6HZ
Divisional Commander: Lt Col Hugh Rea. Serving officers 80. ***CC*** No.214779. Began n/a. No magazine.
☎ 0141 779 5000 🖷 0141 779 5011

Salvation Army: **Yorkshire Division**, 1 Cadman Court, Hanley Road, Morley, Leeds LS27 0RX
Divisional Commander: Lt Col Geoff Blurton. Executive staff 7, Admin staff 13, Serving officers 121. ***CC*** No.214779. Began 1996. No magazine.
☎ 0113 281 0100 🖷 0113 281 0111

Scottish Asian Christian Fellowship, 5c Kilwinning Street, Musselburgh EH21 7EB
Pastor: Mr Shamaun Tufail. Serving minister 1. Began n/a. No magazine. Asian ethnic congregation with English, Urdu, Punjabi speaking fellowship.
☎ 0131 665 9708 🖷 0131 665 9708

Scottish Congregational Church, PO Box 189, Glasgow G1 2BX
General Secretary: Rev John Arthur. Ordained staff 2, Admin staff 2, Serving ministers 40. ***CC*** Began 1994. Comprising the Congregational Union of Scotland, the Women's Union & Scottish Congregational College. Magazine: *Focus* (5,000 quarterly).
Email: 100520.2150@compuserve.com
☎ 0141 332 7667 🖷 0141 332 8463

Scottish Episcopal Church, The Office of the General Synod, 21 Grosvenor Crescent, Edinburgh EH12 5EE
Primus: Most Rev Richard F Holloway. *Secretary General:* Mr John Stuart. *Deputy Secretary General:* Miss Pat McBryde. Executive staff 5, Admin staff 9, Serving ministers 362. ***CC*** No.SCO 13463. Began n/a. Magazine: *The Scottish Episcopalian* (6,500 ten times a year).
Email: office@scotland.anglican.org
☎ 0131 225 6357 🖷 0131 346 7247

Scottish Episcopal Church: **Diocese of Aberdeen and Orkney**, Diocesan Office, 39 King's Crescent, Aberdeen AB24 3HP
Bishop: Rt Rev Bruce Cameron. *Hon Secretary:* Mr Andrew Armstrong. *Hon Treasurer:* Canon Alex McGillivray. Admin staff 2, Serving ministers 44. ***CC*** No.SCO 22180. Began n/a. (Aberdeen 1100; Orkney 1087). Magazine: *Northern Light* (2,000 quarterly).
Email: office@aberdeen.anglican.org
☎ 01224 636 653 🖷 01224 636 186

Scottish Episcopal Church: **Diocese of Argyll and the Isles**, 25 Dublin Street, Edinburgh EH1 3PG
Bishop: Rt Rev Douglas M Cameron. *Secretary & Treasurer:* Mr C J P Hall. Executive staff 2, Serving ministers 13. ***CC*** No.SCO 05375. Began 1848. Magazine: *Argyll and the Isles* (1,450 every four months).
Web: www.argyll.anglican.org
Email: office@argyll.anglican.org
☎ 01631 556 912

Scottish Episcopal Church: **Diocese of Brechin**, The Bishop's Room, Castlehill House, 1 High Street, Dundee DD1 1TD
Bishop: Rt Rev Neville Chamberlain. *Diocesan Secretary:* Rev Gordon J H Pont. Serving ministers 28. ***CC*** No.SCO 016813. Began 1150. Magazine: *Grapevine* (Circulation n/a quarterly).
Email: office@brechin.anglican.org
☎ 01382 229 230 🖷 01382 203 446

Scottish Episcopal Church: **Diocese of Edinburgh**, Diocesan Centre, 21a Grosvenor Crescent, Edinburgh EH12 5EL
Bishop: Rt Rev Richard F Holloway. *Diocesan Secretary:* Miss Elizabeth A Brady. Executive staff 2, Admin staff 2, Serving ministers 125. ***CC*** Began 1633. Magazine: *The Edge* (1,750 five times a year).
Email: office@edinburgh.anglican.org
☎ 0131 538 7033 🖷 0131 538 7088

Scottish Episcopal Church: **United Diocese of Glasgow and Galloway**, Diocesan Office, 5 St Vincent Place, Glasgow G1 2DH
Bishop: Rt Rev Idris Jones. *Diocesan Secretary:* Mr G C Hety. Executive staff 2, Admin staff 1, Serving ministers 115. ***CC*** Began 1837. Magazine: *Glasgow and Galloway Diocesan Gazette* (6,500 quarterly).
Email: office@glasgow.anglican.org
☎ 0141 221 5720 🖷 0141 221 7014

Scottish Episcopal Church: **Diocese of Moray, Ross and Caithness**, Scottish Episcopal Church, 34 Rangemore Road, Inverness IV3 5AE
Bishop: To be appointed. *Bishop's Secretary:* Mrs Rosemary Walker. No full-time staff, Serving ministers 42. Began 1110. Magazine: *Diocesan Monthly Newsletter* (2,000 quarterly).
☎ 01463 231 059 🖷 01463 226 255
Diocesan Office: *Chancellor:* Miss Anne McGavin. 11 Kenneth Street, Inverness IV3 5NR

Scottish Episcopal Church: **Diocese of St Andrews, Dunkeld and Dunblane**, Diocesan Office, 28a Balhousie Street, Perth PH1 5HJ
Bishop: Rt Rev Michael Henley. *Diocesan Secretary:* Rev William Rootes. No full-time staff, Serving ministers 75. Began n/a. No magazine.
☎ 01738 443 173 🖷 01738 443 174

Serbian Orthodox Church Diocese of Great Britain and Scandinavia, 131 Cob Lane, Birmingham B30 1QE
Episcopal Vicar: Very Rev Milenko Zebic. Serving ministers n/a. Began 1952. Magazine: *Lazarisa* (1,500 every four months).
Email: lazarica.church@virgin.net
☎ 0121 458 5273 🖷 0121 458 4986

Seventh-Day Adventist Church, British Union Conference, Stanborough Park, Watford WD2 6JP
President: Pastor Cecil R Perry. Executive staff 24, Admin staff 54, Serving ministers 123. ***CC*** No.1044071. Began 1878. Magazine: *Messenger* (10,000 fortnightly).
Web: www.adventist.org.uk
Email: buc@adventist.org.uk
☎ 01923 672 251 🖷 01923 893 212

Seventh-Day Adventist Church: **Irish Mission Office**, 9 Newry Road, Banbridge BT32 3HF
President: Pastor A D Hodges. Began n/a.
☎ 028 4462 6361

Seventh-Day Adventist Church: **North England Conference**, 22 Zulla Road, Mapperley Park, Nottingham NG3 5BZ
President: Pastor E R Francis. Began n/a.
☎ 0115 960 6312 🖷 0115 969 1476

Seventh-Day Adventist Church: **Scottish Mission Office**, Maylea, 5 Ochilview Gardens, Crieff PH7 3EJ
President: Pastor A R Rodd. Began n/a.
☎ 01764 653 090

Seventh-Day Adventist Church: **South England Conference**, 25 St John's Road, Watford WD1 1PY
President: Pastor D W McFarlane. Began n/a.
☎ 01923 232 728 🖷 01923 250 582

Seventh-Day Adventist Church: **Trans European Division**, 119 St Peter's Street, St Albans AL1 3EY
President: Dr Bertil Wiklander. Began n/a.
☎ 01727 603 31 🖷 01727 866 312

Seventh-Day Adventist Church: **Welsh Mission Office**, Glan-yr-Afon, 10 Heol y Wern, Caerphilly CF3 3EY
President: Pastor Paul R Clee. Began n/a.
☎ 029 2088 2097 🖷 029 2088 2097

Slovene Catholic Mission, 62 Offley Road, London SW9 0LS
Chaplain to Slovenian Community in UK: Rev Stanislav Cikanek. Serving minister 1, Admin staff 1. Began 1948. Magazine: *Nasa Luc* (150 monthly).
☎ 020 7735 6655

***Spanish Evangelical Church**, 116 Bramley Road, London W10 6SU
Pastor: Pastor Candido Giraldo. Executive staff 3, Serving ministers 3. *CC* No.280694. Began 1960. Magazine: *Church Bulletin* (500 monthly).
Email: cevangelic@aol.com
☎ 020 8960 5634 🖷 020 8579 0535
Services held at: St Paul's Church, Robert Adam Street, London W1M 5AH

C

***Struthers Memorial Churches**, 33 West Stewart Street, Greenock PA15 1YB
Minister: Rev Hugh B Black. *Central Treasurer and Bookshop Manager:* Mr Chris Jewell. *Secretary:* Mr Robert M Cleary. Executive staff 8, Serving ministers 16. *CC* No.SCO 06960. Began 1955; Independent Pentecostal. No magazine. Turnover £560,000 to year end Dec 98. Evangelical outreach experiencing signs and wonders of early new testament times.
Web: www.struthers-church.org
Email: smc@struthers-church.org
☎ 01475 729 668 🖷 01475 728 145

Swahili-Speaking Christian Congregation, St Anne's Lutheran Church, Church of St Anne & St Agnes, Gresham Street, London EC2V 7BX
Pastor: Rev Paul D Schmiege. Serving ministers 2. Began 1973. No magazine.
Email: 74434.1521@compuserve.com
☎ 020 7606 4786

Swedish Church (Lutheran), 6 Harcourt Street, London W1H 2BD
Rector: Very Rev Lennart Sjöström. Executive staff 2, Admin staff 12, Serving ministers 2. *CC* No.19989. Began 1710. Magazine: *Kyrkobladet* (10,000 every four months). Religious cultural and social work for the Swedish community in the UK.
Web: www.swednet.org.uk/swedish-church
Email: office@swedish-church.org.uk
☎ 020 7723 5681 Mobile: 07785 308 067
🖷 020 7724 2178

Swiss Church in London, The Swiss Church Vicarage, 1 Womersley Road, London N8 9AE
Minister: Rev Dr Gottfried W Locher. Executive staff 2, Serving minister 1. *CC* No.234852. Began 1762. Magazine: *Swiss Church News* (1,100 n/a).
Email: swisschurch.london@btinternet.com
☎ 020 7836 1418 🖷 020 7836 1418

Swiss Evangelical Brotherhood (Evangelical Brotherhood Church), 25 Calabria Road, London N5 1HZ
Minister: Mr Henry Hanni. Executive staff 3, Serving minister 1. *CC* No.802549. Began 1960. Magazine: *The Message of Peace* (5,000 every two months).
☎ 020 7226 7341

Syrian Orthodox Church of India, 44 Newbury Road, Ilford IG2 7HD
Priest: Rev Father M S Skariah. Serving ministers n/a. Began n/a. No magazine.
☎ 020 8599 3836 🖷 020 8599 3836

Tamil Language Congregations, 35 Woodhouse Grove, London E12 6SR
Contact: Pastor G I Ebenezer. Serving ministers 11. Began 1970. No magazine. Services held at 12 places in Greater London.
☎ 020 8552 9911

Ukrainian Autocephalous Orthodox Church, 1a Newton Avenue, Acton, London W3 8AJ
Senior Priest: Very Rev Michael Holycia. Staff n/a, Serving ministers n/a. Began 1947. Magazine: *Church News* (350 quarterly).
☎ 020 8992 4689

Ukrainian Catholic Church, 22 Binney Street, London W1Y 1YN
Bishop & Apostolic Exarch: Rt Rev Michael Kuchmiak. Serving ministers 2. *CC* No.240088. Began 1947; Apostolic Exarchate in Great Britain 1957. No magazine.
☎ 020 8629 1073 / 8629 1539

Ukrainian Orthodox Church in Great Britain and Ireland (Kiev Patriarchate), 38 Gunton Road, London E5 9JS
Patriarchal Vicar General: His Lordship The Rt Rev Fr Abbot Marek Sujkowski. Admin staff 12, Serving ministers 3. Began 1995. Kiev Patriarchate. No magazine.
☎ 0780 113 8117

Union of Evangelical Churches, Eastwood Road Evangelical Church, Rayleigh SS6 7JQ
Chairman: Rev E G Blowes. *Administrator:* Rev J A Pease. Serving ministers 26. *CC* No.227498. Began 1956; but as the Peculiar People 1838. Magazine: *UEC Fellowship Link* (Circulation n/a quarterly). Associated with FIEC.
☎ 01268 742 293

Union of Welsh Independents / Annibynwr (Welsh Congregational Union), Ty John Penry, 11 St Helen's Road, Swansea SA1 4AL
General Secretary: Rev Derwyn M Jones. Executive staff 3, Other staff 2, Serving ministers 2. Began 1872. Magazine: *Y Tyst* (1,200 weekly).
☎ 01792 467 040/652 542 🖷 01792 650 647

The United Apostolic Faith Church, The Gospel Centre, Wightman Road, London N8 0LZ
Pastor: Pastor Brendan Munro. Staff n/a, Serving ministers n/a. *CC* Began 1935; Pentecostal. No magazine.
☎ 020 8374 7708 / 7709

***United Free Church of Scotland**, 11 Newton Place, Glasgow G3 7PR
General Secretary: Rev John O Fulton. *Principal Clerk:* Rev J G McPhee. Executive staff 3, Serving ministers 43. *CC* No.SCO 08167. Began 1900. Magazine: *Stedfast* (2,400 every two months). Turnover £280,000. Presbyterian Church with 70 congregations throughout Scotland.
Web: www.ufcos.org.uk
Email: ufcos@charis.co.uk
☎ 0141 332 3435 🖷 0141 333 1973

United Pentecostal Church of Great Britain and Ireland, 41 Bramley Hill, South Croydon CR2 6NW
General Superintendent: Rev James Dallas. Executive staff 5, Admin staff 2, Serving ministers n/a. Began 1958. Magazine: *Pentecostal Truth* (1,100 every two months).
Email: peter@grzeszczyk.freeserve.co.uk
☎ 020 8688 5827 🖷 020 8688 5827

United Reformed Church in the United Kingdom, 86 Tavistock Place, London WC1H 9RT
General Secretary: Rev Anthony G Burnham. Executive staff 17, Admin staff 26. Began 1972. Magazine: *Reform* (13,000 monthly).
Web: www.compulink.co.uk/~urc/urc_home.html
Email: agburnham@urc.org.uk
☎ 020 7916 2020 🖷 020 7916 2021
See also: **Fellowship of United Reformed Youth (FURY)** on Page 479
Look! Hear! on Page 316
Pilots on Page 316
Reform on Page 317
URC Bookshop on Page 164
United Reformed Church History society on Page 239
United Reformed Church International Church Relations on Page 368
See also **United Reformed Church** in Main Index on Page 627

***United Reformed Church:* East Midlands Province**, Sherwood URC, 1 Edwards Lane, Sherwood, Nottingham NG5 3AA
Provincial Moderator: Rev M G Hanson. Executive staff 4, Admin staff 2, Serving ministers 70. Began 1972. Magazine: *Newsletter* (350 half-yearly).
☎ 0115 960 9241 🖷 0115 960 9202

***United Reformed Church:* Eastern Province**, Province Office, United Reformed Church, Whittlesford, Cambridge CB2 4ND
Provincial Moderator: Rev Elizabeth Caswell. *Synod Clerk:* Mr K J Woods. *Training and Development Officer:* Mr Lawrence Bennett Moore. Serving ministers 59. Began n/a. Magazine: *Eastwords* (Circulation & frequency n/a). Turnover £568,540. Oversight and support of 150 local churches including mission strategy, property advice and training.
Web: members.aol.com/urc7/welcome.htm
Email: urc7@aol.com
☎ 01223 830 770

***United Reformed Church:* Mersey Province**, The Annexe, Trinity with Palm Grove Church, 63 Alton Road, Birkenhead CH43 1UZ
Synod Clerk: Rev Angus W Duncan. Executive staff 1, Serving ministers 70. Began n/a. Magazine: *Lookout* (6,500 every two months).
☎ 0151 653 7096

***United Reformed Church:* North Western Province**, Synod Office, Franklin Street, Patricroft, Eccles, Manchester M30 0QZ
Moderator: Rev C K Forecast. Executive staff 3, Admin staff 2, Serving ministers 95. Began 1972. Magazine: *Bridge* (Circulation n/a half-yearly).
☎ 0161 789 5583 🖷 0161 707 9117

***United Reformed Church:* Northern Synod**, 65 Westgate Road, Newcastle upon Tyne NE1 1SG
Provincial Moderator: Rev Peter I Poulter. Admin staff 4, Serving ministers 67. Began 1972. No magazine.
Email: npoffice@cix.compulink.co.uk
☎ 0191 232 1168 🖷 0191 232 1811

***United Reformed Church:* South Western Synod**, Synod Office, The Manse, Norton Fitzwarren, Taunton TA2 6RU
Synod Moderator: Rev W Raymond P Adams. Executive staff 1, Admin staff 2, Serving ministers 88. Began 1972. Magazine: *Provincial News* (1,500 half-yearly).
☎ 01823 275 470 🖷 01823 275 470
Synod Clerk: Rev Sandra K Lloydlangston, 26 Stapleton Close, Highworth, Swindon SN6 7DR
☎ 01793 762 641 🖷 01793 762 641

***United Reformed Church:* Southern Province**, Synod Office, East Croydon URC, Addiscombe Grove, Croydon CR0 5LP
Provincial Moderator: Rev D Helyar. *Synod Clerk:* Mrs C P Meekison. Serving ministers 118. Began n/a. Magazine: *Southern Link* (3,500 half-yearly).
☎ 020 8688 3730 🖷 020 8688 2698

***United Reformed Church:* Thames North Synod**, Ipalo House, 32 Great Peter Street, London SW1P 2DB
Provincial Moderator: Rev Roberta Rominger. Executive staff 3, Serving ministers 150. Began n/a. No magazine.
Web: ourworld.compuserve.com/homepages/thamesnorthurc
Email: thamesnorthurc@compuserve.com
☎ 020 7799 5000 🖷 020 7799 5555

***United Reformed Church:* Wales Province**, Provincial Office, Minster Road, Cardiff CF2 5AS
Provincial Moderator: Rev John L Humphreys. *Synod Clerk:* Mr G Griffiths. No full-time staff, Serving ministers 44. Began 1972. No magazine.
Web: www.urcwalesprovince.uk
Email: admin@urcwales.demon.co.uk
☎ 029 2049 9938 / 3606 🖷 029 2031 9177

***United Reformed Church:* Wessex Province**, Kings Road, Chandler's Ford, Eastleigh SO53 2EY
Provincial Moderator: Rev D M Wales. Admin staff 1, Serving ministers 60. Began n/a. Magazine: *Contact* (8,000 half-yearly).
☎ 023 8026 6548 🖷 023 8026 6548

***United Reformed Church:* West Midlands Province**, Digbeth-in-the-Field URC, Moat Lane, Yardley, Birmingham B26 1TW
Provincial Moderator: Rev Elizabeth Welch. *Synod Clerk:* Mr Simon Rowntree. Executive staff 1, Serving ministers 58. Began 1972. Magazine: *Connect* (5,000 frequency n/a).
☎ 0121 783 1177 🖷 0121 786 1329

***United Reformed Church:* Yorkshire Province**, Provincial Office, 43 Hunslet Lane, Leeds LS10 1JW
Provincial Moderator: Rev Arnold Harrison. *Synod Clerk:* Mr John Seager. Executive staff 2, Admin staff 2, Serving ministers 85. ***CC*** No.1068103. Began n/a. Magazine: *Province 4* (Circulation n/a every four months).
Web: dspace.dial.pipex.com/urc.yorkshire
Email: urc.yorkshire@dial.pipex.com
☎ 0113 245 1267 🖷 0113 234 1145

Universal Church of the Kingdom of God, Rainbow Theatre, 232 Seven Sisters Road, Finsbury Park, London N4 3NX
Bishop: Bishop Renato Cardoso. Staff 35, Serving ministers n/a. ***CC*** No.1043985. Began 1995; Pentecostal. Magazine: *The Sower* (5,000 every two months). Turnover n/a.
Web: www.universalchurch.org
Email: uckg@aol.com
☎ 020 7686 6000 🖷 020 7686 6008

†***Universal Prayer Group Ministries**, Edmonton Temple, 328 High Road, Tottenham, London N15 4BN
President: Rev Samson K Boafo. *Senior Pastor:* Rev Samuel Okene-Apraku. Executive staff 5, Admin staff 5, Serving ministers n/a. Began 1962. Magazine: *The Light* (700 quarterly).
☎ 020 8365 1788 🖷 020 8365

Vision International Ministries, PO Box 13256, London E12 5TH
Executive Director: Rev W Peter Morgan. Executive staff 2, Admin staff 1, Serving ministers 4. Began 1989. Magazine: *Integrity* (Circulation n/a monthly).
☎ 020 8514 5456 🖷 020 8553 1711

†**Well of Living Water Ministries**, Hado Hall, Tarves Way, Greenwich, London SE10 9QP
Minister: Mr Adam Bennett. Serving minister 1. Began 1996; Oneness Apostolic Church. No magazine.

The Wesleyan Holiness Church, Holyhead Road, Handsworth Birmingham B21 0LA
National Superintendent: Rev Kecious E Gray. Executive staff 1. Began 1958. No magazine.
☎ 0121 523 7849 🖷 0121 515 2359

***Wesleyan Reform Union**, 123 Queen Street, Sheffield S1 2DU
General Secretary: Rev John Williams. Executive staff 1, Other staff 1, Serving ministers 20. ***CC*** No.250315. Began 1849. Magazine: *Contact* (1,800 monthly).
☎ 0114 272 1938 🖷 0114 272 1965

The Worldwide Church of God (UK), Elstree House, Elstree Way Borehamwood WD6 1LU
Regional Director: Mr John A Halford. *Company Secretary* Mr Francis Bergin. *National Co-ordinator:* Mr David Silcox. Executive staff 3, Admin staff 10, Serving ministers 10. ***CC*** No.311098. Began 1957. Magazine: *The Plain Truth* (20,000 every two months).
Web: www.wcg.org/pt/uk/index.html
Email: wcgeurope@wcg.org
☎ 020 8953 1633 🖷 020 8207 1216

C

Note: The appendix previously found after this category is now on Page 526.

CHURCH ORGANISATIONS

†**Advisory Board for Redundant Churches**, Fielden House, Little College Street, London SW1P 3SH
Secretary to the Board: Dr J K West. Executive staff 2, Other staff 1. Began 1969; Anglican. Magazine: *Annual Report* (1,600 annually). Turnover n/a. Advising the Church Commissioners on the architectural and historic quality of redundant churches.
☎ 020 7222 9603

Alcuin Club, The Parsonage, 8 Church Street, Spalding PE11 2PB
Treasurer & Membership Secretary: Rev T R Barker. No full-time staff. ***CC*** No.274203. Began 1897; Anglican. Magazine: *Joint Liturgical Studies* (650 occasionally). Turnover £16,000. Promoting study of liturgy of the Christian church, especially by publication.
Email: tr.barker@cwcom.net
☎ 01775 722 675 🖷 01775 710 273

Alliance of Radical Methodists (ARM), 51 Tennyson Avenue, Swadlincote DE11 0DT
Secretary: Rev Angela Singleton. No full-time staff. Began 1971; Methodist. Magazine: *ARMprint* (500 frequency n/a), *ARM NEWS* (120 every two months). Turnover n/a. Pressure group within Methodist Church and support group for radicals within and without Methodism.
☎ 01283 217 295

The Anabaptist Network, 14 Shepherd's Hill, Highgate, London N6 5AQ
Development Worker: Andrew Francis. No full time staff. ***CC*** No.1021760. Began 1991; Baptist. Magazine: *Anabaptism Today* (300 every four months). Turnover n/a. Encouraging practice of Anabaptist principles in today's missionary church.
Email: anabnet@anmchara.surfaid.org
☎ 020 8340 8775 / 01732 453 405 🖷 01732 453 405

Anglican and Eastern Churches Association, St Mark's Vicarage, St Mark's Road, Teddington TW11 9DE
General Secretary: Rev J Philip Warner. No full-time staff. ***CC*** Began 1864; Anglican, Orthodox and Oriental Churches. Magazine: *Eastern Churches Newsletter* (750 half-yearly). Turnover n/a. Promoting the doctrinal union of the Anglican, Orthodox and Ancient Oriental Churches.
☎ 020 8977 4067 🖷 020 8977 4067
Also at: St Dunstan-in-the-West, 186 Fleet Street, London EC4A 2HR
☎ 020 7405 1929

The Anglican Association, 22 Tyning Road, Winsley, Bradford-on-Avon BA15 2JJ
General Secretary: Mr Robin Davies. No full-time staff. ***CC*** No.1002192. Began 1959; Anglican. Magazine: *Anglican Catholic* (300 half-yearly). Turnover £1,000 to year end Dec 98. Defending traditional Anglican doctrine and worship.
☎ 01225 862 965

Anglican Church Planting Initiatives, Crookes Endowed Centre, Crookes, Sheffield S10 1UB
Co-Leader: Rev Bob Hopkins. Executive staff 3, Admin staff 1. ***CC*** No.1060703. Began 1993; Anglican. Magazine: *News from Anglican Church Planting Initiatives* (1,000 half-yearly). Turnover £30,000 to year end Dec 98. Serving tomorrow's churches today by encouraging and assisting the planting of healthy missionary-minded churches.
Email: acpi@compuserve.com
☎ 0114 267 8447 🖷 0114 266 9123

Anglican Communion Office, Partnership House, 157 Waterloo Road, London SE1 8UT
Secretary General: Rev John Peterson. Executive staff 6, Other staff 6. ***CC*** Began 1969; Anglican. Magazine: *Anglican World* (20,000 quarterly). Turnover n/a. Co-ordinating body for the Anglican Communion worldwide.
Email: acc@ecunet.org
☎ 020 7620 1110 Fax 020 7620 1070

Anglican Evangelical Assembly, PO Box 93, Heaton, Newcastle upon Tyne NE6 5WL
Executive Officer: Mr Trevor Stevenson. Other staff 1. ***CC*** No.212315. Began 1982; Anglican. Magazine: *CEEC Newsletter* (Circulation & frequency n/a). Turnover: finances included under Church of England Evangelical Council. Promoting effective consultation and fostering leadership amongst Anglican evangelical leaders.
☎ 0191 240 2084 Fax 0191 240 2084

Anglican Lutheran Society, 8 Eldon Road, Bournemouth BH9 2RT
Moderator: Rev Ronald T Englund. No full-time staff. ***CC*** Began 1984; Anglican & Lutheran. Magazine: *The Window* (600 quarterly). Turnover £7,000 to year end Dec 98. Developing better understanding and closer links between Anglicans and Lutherans.
Email: englund@cap.com
☎ 01202 535 127 Fax 020 8769 2677

Anglican Renewal Ministries, 4 Bramble Street, Derby DE1 1HU
Director: Rev John Leach. Other staff 3. ***CC*** No.327035. Began 1981; Anglican. Magazine: *Anglicans for Renewal* (Circulation n/a quarterly). Turnover £125,000 to year end Dec 98. Encouraging charismatic renewal in the Church of England, through conferences, courses, consultancy and magazine.
Web: members.aol.com/armderby
Email: armderby@aol.com
☎ 01332 200 175 Fax 01332 200 185

Anglican Voluntary Societies' Forum, General Synod Office, Church House, Great Smith Street, London SW1P 3NZ
Secretary: To be appointed. Staff n/a. Began 1980; Anglican. No magazine. Turnover n/a. Promoting understanding and co-operation between Anglican Voluntary Societies, Boards and Councils of General Synod.
☎ 020 7898 1000 Fax 020 7898 1369

Anglo-Catholic Charismatic Renewal Committee, 4 Beechwood Road, Sanderstead, South Croydon CR2 0AA
Secretary: Mrs Rosemary Radley. No full-time staff. Began 1967; Anglican. No magazine. Turnover £700 to year end Dec 98. Promoting renewal in the Holy Spirit primarily in the Catholic/High Church tradition of the Church of England.
☎ 020 8657 1285

†**Apostolic Episcopal Free Churches Alliance**, Flat 5, 3 Canfield Gardens, London NW6 3JR
General Secretary: Rt Rev Eric R Morse. Other staff 3. Began n/a; interdenominational. No magazine. Turnover n/a. Promoting the traditional teachings of the Apostles and the early Christian Fathers.
☎ No telephone

The Archbishop of Canterbury's Department for Ecumenical Affairs, Lambeth Palace, London SE1 7JU
Archbishop of Canterbury's Secretary for Ecumenical Affairs: Rev Canon Richard Marsh. Executive staff 2, Other staff 3. Began 1933; Anglican. No magazine. Turnover n/a. Assisting the Archbishop on ecumenical affairs and acting ecumenically on his behalf.
☎ 020 7928 8282 Fax 020 7401 9886

Archbishop's Officer for the Millennium, Church House, Great Smith Street, London SW1P 3NZ
The Archbishop's Officer for the Millennium: Rev Stephen Lynas. Other staff 4. Began 1995; Anglican. Magazine: *Millennium News* (Circulation n/a every four months). Turnover n/a. Dealing with all matters relating to the millennium celebrations.
Web: www.2000ad.org
☎ 020 7898 1435 Fax 020 7898 1432

Association of Church Fellowships, Bickenhill House, 154 Lode Lane, Solihull B91 2HP
Head of Secretariat: Rev Canon Stanley Owen. Executive staff 2. ***CC*** Began 1960; Anglican. Magazine: *ACF National Newsletter* (1,000 quarterly). Turnover £10,000 to year end Dec 98. Encouraging Christian evangelistic charitable fellowship by fostering and forming church groups for men and women.
☎ 0121 704 9281

Association of Denominational Historical Societies & Cognate Libraries, 44 Seymour Road, London SW18 5JA
Secretary: Mr Howard F Gregg. *Convenor:* Rev Professor Alan P F Sell. No full-time staff. Began 1993; interdenominational. No magazine. Turnover n/a. Annual lecture, co-operative inter-society research, publications, conferences.
☎ 020 8874 7727

C

Association of Ordinands & Candidates for Ministry (AOCM), Via Ministry Division, Church House, Great Smith Street, Westminster, London SW1P 3NZ
Chair: Changes annually. No full-time staff. Began n/a; Anglican. Magazine: *Training for Ministry* (Circulation n/a annually). Turnover n/a. Representing the interests of Anglican Ordinands and candidates for Accredited Lay Ministry.
☎ 020 7222 9011 Fax 020 7726 7625

Baptist Historical Society, 60 Strathmore Avenue, Hitchin SG5 1ST
Secretary: Rev Stephen Copson. No full-time staff. ***CC*** Began 1908; Baptist. Magazine: *The Baptist Quarterly* (650 quarterly). Turnover £25,000 to year end Dec 98. Encouraging the study and recording of Baptist history.
Email: slcopson@dial.pipex.com
☎ 01462 431 816

Baptist Men's Movement, Engine House Cottage, Pontesford, Shrewsbury SY5 0UQ
Secretary: Mr Clifford Challinor. No other staff. ***CC*** No.250334. Began 1917; Baptist. Magazine: *World Outlook* (1,200 quarterly). Turnover n/a. Promoting faith, commitment, service and giving among Baptist men; fellowship and reconciliation worldwide.
☎ 01743 790 377

The Blue Idol / Thakeham Friends Meeting House, Coolham, Horsham RH13 8QP
Wardens: Jonathan and Julie Spencer. No other staff. Began 1691; Religious Society of Friends but open to all. Turnover n/a. Historic/Spiritual interest – visitors welcomed.
Web our world.compuserve.com/homepages/spencer_the_blue_idol/
Email: quakers@nationwide.isp.net
☎ 01403 741 241 Fax 01403 741 841

British Reformed Fellowship, 26 Caldwell Park, Portrush BT56 8PJ
Secretary: Mr Philip Rainey. No full-time staff. Began 1990; Presbyterian/Reformed. Magazine: *British Reformed Journal* (300 quarterly). Turnover n/a. Promoting Reformed faith in British Isles; organising meetings and conferences.
Email: philip.t.rainey@lineone.net
☎ 028 7082 3913

Broad Alliance of Radical Baptists, 24 Askrigg Close, Accrington BB5 6SD
Secretary: Rev Roy Parker. No other staff. Began 1968; Baptist. (Previously Baptist Renewal Group). Magazine: *The Barbarian* (100 quarterly). Turnover n/a. Encouraging awareness of radical implications of the Gospel; promoting ecumenism particularly amongst Baptists.
Email: barb@charis.co.uk
☎ 01254 393 742

Canon Law Society of Great Britain and Ireland, Westminster Metropolitan Tribunal, Vaughan House, 46 Francis Street, London SW1P 1QN
Secretary: Rev J Conneely. ***CC*** No.266263. Began 1957; Roman Catholic. Magazine: *Canon Law Society Newsletter* (Circulation n/a Members only), *Canon Law Abstracts* (1,000 half-yearly). Turnover n/a. Disseminating information concerning the Canon Law to members of the society and interested groups.
☎ 020 7798 9003

C

Roman Catholic Bishops' Conference Department for Christian Life & Worship, 39 Eccleston Square, London SW1V 1BX
Secretary, Liturgy Office: Mgr Tony Rogers. Executive staff 2. ***CC*** No.257239. Began 1984; Roman Catholic. Magazine: *Liturgy* (1,300 every two months). Turnover n/a. Concerned with pastoral liturgy, church music, art, architecture and heritage, and consecrated life.
Web: www.liturgy.demon.co.uk
Email: office@liturgy.demon.co.uk
☎ 020 7821 0553

Roman Catholic Bishops' Conference Department for Christian Responsibility and Citizenship, 39 Eccleston Square, London SW1V 1BX
Chairman: Rt Rev Peter Smith. Executive staff 6. ***CC*** No.257239. Began 1984; Roman Catholic. No magazine. Turnover n/a. Concerned with public life, employment, community relations and communications.
☎ 020 7630 8221

Roman Catholic Bishops' Conference Department for International Affairs, 39 Eccleston Square, London SW1V 1BX
Chairman: Rt Rev David Konstant. Executive staff 2. Began 1984; Roman Catholic. No magazine. Turnover n/a. Concerned with international justice, peace, development, European affairs, migrants and nuclear issues.
☎ 020 7834 5138 Fax 020 7630 5166

Catholic Child Welfare Council, St Joseph's, Watford Way, Hendon, London NW4 4TY
General Secretary: Mrs Mary Gandy. Executive staff 1, Other staff 1. ***CC*** No.274281. Began 1929; Roman Catholic. Magazine: *Newsletter* (Circulation n/a occasionally). Turnover £32,000 to year end Mar 98. Administrative umbrella body for Catholic Children's Societies and Catholic caring agencies in England, Wales and Northern Ireland.
Web: www.vois.org.uk/cathchild
Email: ccwc@compuserve.com
☎ 020 8203 6323 Fax 020 8203 6323

Catholic Record Society, 114 Mount Street, London W1Y 5AH
Hon Secretary: Dr L Gooch. No full-time staff. ***CC*** Began 1904; Roman Catholic but non-denominational. Journal: *Recusant History* (800 half-yearly). Turnover n/a. Research into post-reformation history of Roman Catholicism in England and Wales.
Web: www.catholic-history.org.uk/crs
☎ No telephone

Catholic Union of Great Britain, St Maximilian Kolbe House, 63 Jeddo Road, London W12 9EE
Secretary: Mr Peter Higgs. Began 1870; Roman Catholic. Magazine: *Annual Report* (Circulation n/a annually), *Newsletter* (Circulation n/a every four months). Turnover n/a.
☎ 020 8749 1321 Fax 020 8735 0816

Catholic Women's League, 164 Stockwell Road, London SW9 9TQ
General Secretary: Mrs Breda Ford. Part-time staff 1. ***CC*** No.250120. Began 1906; Roman Catholic. Magazine: *CWL News* (8,000 quarterly). Turnover n/a. Non-political organisation for charitable religious intellectual work, ensuring representation of Catholic interests on public bodies.
☎ 020 7738 4894 Fax 020 7737 8053

Catholics for a Changing Church, 14 West Halkin Street, London SW1X 8JS
Secretary: Mr Frank Pycroft. No full-time staff. Began 1969; Roman Catholic. (Previously Catholic Renewal Movement). Magazine: *Renew* (400 quarterly). Turnover under £10,000 to year end Apr 98. Promoting church reform and renewal in the spirit of Vatican II.
Web: www.c-c-c.freeserve.co.uk
Email: fcdp@indirect.co.uk
☎ 020 7070 2068

Central Readers' Council, Church House, Great Smith Street, Westminster, London SW1P 3NZ
Hon Secretary: Miss Pat Nappin. No full-time staff. ***CC*** No.271916. Began 1922; Anglican. Magazine: *The Reader* (9,000 quarterly). Turnover n/a. Advising Dioceses and enhancing Readers' overall contribution to the Church's ministry.
☎ 020 7898 1415/6 Fax 020 7898 1421

Christian Life Community, St Joseph's, Watford Way, London NW4 4TY
Development Worker: Ms Teresa House. Staff n/a. ***CC*** No.1056891. Began 1563; Roman Catholic but ecumenical. Magazine: *Focus* (700 monthly). Turnover £25,000 to year end Mar 98. Forming communities to help Christians integrate their lives and faith. Special characteristic is Ignatian spirituality.
Email: clcew@iname.com
☎ 020 7511 6331 Mobile: 07958 574 898

Church in Danger, PO Box 132, East Rudham, King's Lynn PE31 8QT
Director: Mr Rodney Bennett-England. No full-time staff. ***CC*** No.327963. Began 1988; Anglican. No magazine. Turnover under 10,000 to year end Dec 98. Promoting the Christian faith in accordance with the traditions and teachings of the Church of England.
☎ 01485 528 664 Mobile: 07836 357 725
Fax 01485 528 155

*__Church of England Evangelical Council__, PO Box 93, Heaton, Newcastle upon Tyne NE6 5WL
Executive Officer: Mr Frank Knaggs. Executive staff 1. ***CC*** No.212315. Began 1960; Anglican. Magazine: *CEEC Newsletter* (Circulation n/a occasionally). Turnover £13,000 to year end Mar 98. Promoting effective consultation between evangelical Anglican leaders; organising Anglican Evangelical Assembly.
Email: ceec@cablenet.co.uk
☎ 0191 240 2084 Fax 0191 240 2084

Church of God (European Office), 14 Clark's Mead, Bushey Heath, Watford WD2 3JZ
Superintendent: Rev Douglas LeRoy. Executive staff 2, Other staff 1. Began 1954; New Testament Church of God. Magazine: *European Action Report* (5,000 every four months). Turnover n/a. Maintaining links with Church of God in Europe.
☎ 020 8950 6539 🖷 020 8950 7929

Church of Ireland Men's Society, The Library, Abbey Street, Armagh BT61 7DY
General Secretary: Very Rev H Cassidy. *CC* Began n/a; Church of Ireland. No magazine. Turnover n/a. Co-ordinating work amongst men in various parishes.
Email: armroblib@aol.com
☎ 028 3752 3142 🖷 028 3752 4177

Church of Scotland Assembly Council, 121 George Street, Edinburgh EH2 4YN
The Secretary: n/a. Executive staff 1. Began n/a; Church of Scotland. Magazine: *Life and Work* (125,000 monthly). Turnover included in Church of Scotland. Assessing changing needs and priorities of the Church of Scotland.
☎ 0131 225 5722 🖷 0131 220 3113

Church of Scotland Board of Ministry, 121 George Street, Edinburgh EH2 4YN
General Secretary: Very Rev Alexander McDonald. Executive staff 11, Admin staff 7. Began n/a. Magazine: *Life and Work* (125,000 monthly). Turnover included in Church of Scotland. Recruitment, location, training and support for ordained and commissioned ministries in the Church of Scotland.
☎ 0131 225 5722

Church of Scotland Board of Practice and Procedure, 121 George Street, Edinburgh EH2 4YN
Principal Clerk: Rev Dr Finlay Macdonald. Executive staff 5, Other staff 2. Began n/a; Church of Scotland. No magazine. Turnover included in Church of Scotland. Servicing General Assembly, related church-law responsibilities, church-state relations, providing support for Moderator.
Email: pracproc@cofscotland.org.uk
☎ 0131 240 2240 🖷 0131 240 2239

Church of Scotland Church and National Committee, 121 George Street, Edinburgh EH2 4YN
Secretary: Dr Alison Elliot. Executive staff 1. Began 1919; Church of Scotland. Magazine: *Life and Work* (125,000 monthly). Turnover £27,500 to year end Dec 98. Advising General Assembly on developments in the nation's life.
☎ 0131 225 5722 🖷 0131 220 3113

Church of Scotland Ecumenical Relations, 121 George Street, Edinburgh EH2 4YN
Secretary for Ecumenical Relations: Rev Shelagh M Kesting. Executive staff 1, Admin staff 1. *CC* No.SCO 11353. Began 1994; Church of Scotland. Magazine: *Ecumenical Relations Newletter* (Circulation n/a quarterly). Turnover £100,000 to year end Dec 98. Promoting cooperation between churches of different traditions in a spirit of reconciliation and joint worship.
Email: skesting@cofscotland.org.uk
☎ 0131 225 5722 🖷 0131 220 3899

Church of Scotland Guild, 121 George Street, Edinburgh EH2 4YN
General Secretary: Mrs Alison Twaddle. Executive staff 2, Other staff 4. *CC* No.34700. Began 1887; Church of Scotland. (Previously Church of Scotland Woman's Guild). Magazine: *Newsletter* (53,000 every four months). Turnover £395,806 to year end Dec 98. Developing faith and Christian responses to current issues through worship, prayer and action.
Email: atwaddle@cofscotland.org.uk
☎ 0131 225 5722 🖷 0131 220 3113

Church of Scotland Nomination Committee, 121 George Street, Edinburgh EH2 4YN
Principal Clerk: Rev Dr Finlay MacDonald. No full-time staff. Began n/a; Church of Scotland. No magazine. Turnover included in Church of Scotland. Nominating persons to General Assembly for membership of boards and committees.
☎ 0131 225 5722

Church Patronage Trust, Truckers Ghyll, Horsham Road, Handcross, Haywards Heath RH17 6DT
Secretary: Rev K W Habershon. No full-time staff. Began 1870; Anglican. No magazine. Turnover n/a. Nominating incumbents to 120 Anglican churches.
☎ 01444 400 274

Church Society, Dean Wace House, 16 Rosslyn Road, Watford WD1 7EY
Director: Rev David Phillips. *Patronage Secretary:* Rev Alan Backhouse. Other staff 4. *CC* No.249574. Began 1835; Anglican. Magazine: *Churchman* (1,000 quarterly), *Cross+Way* (1,000 quarterly). Turnover £131,000 to year end Dec 97. Campaigning to keep the Church of England established, Protestant and Reformed. Parish patronage and support.
Web: www.churchsociety.org
Email: admin@churchsociety.org
☎ 01923 235 111 🖷 01923 800 362

†**The Church Union**, 7 Tufton Street, London SW1P 3QN
House Manager: Mrs Jenny Miller. Executive staff 1, Other staff 5. *CC* Began 1859; Anglican. Magazine: *Church Observer* (3,500 quarterly). Turnover £100-300,000 to year end Dec 96. Promoting and renewing Catholic faith and life within the Church of England and elsewhere.
☎ 020 7222 6952 🖷 020 7976 7180

Churches Commission on Overseas Students, 1 Stockwell Green, London SW9 9HP
Executive Secretary: Ms Gillian Court. No other full-time staff. *CC* No.297243. Began 1975; ecumenical. No magazine. Turnover £40,000 to year end Mar 98. Representing the churches and other Christian bodies on international students' concerns in Britain.
Email: exec@ccos.cablenet.co.uk
☎ 020 7737 1101 🖷 020 7346 5955

The Churches Conservation Trust, 89 Fleet Street, London EC4Y 1DH
Director: Miss C Cullis. Executive staff 6, Other staff 2. *CC* No.258612. Began 1969; Anglican. (Previously Redundant Churches Fund). Magazine: *Annual Report* (3,500 annually). Turnover £3,792,442 to year end Mar 98. Preserving historic Church of England churches surplus to pastoral requirements.
☎ 020 7936 2285 🖷 020 7936 2284

†**Churches Main Committee**, Fielden House, Little College Street, Westminster, London SW1P 3JZ
Secretary: Mr Derek Taylor Thompson. Other staff 1. *CC* No.256303. Began 1941; interdenominational. No magazine. Turnover £38,000 to year end Dec 94. Representing churches in their dealings with Government on matters affecting churches.
☎ 020 7222 4984 🖷 020 7233 1104

Churches' Council for Industry and Social Responsibility (ISR), St Nicholas House, Lawfords Gate, Bristol BS5 0RE
Director: Rev Canon Tim McClure. *Administrator:* Miss Gill Hiles. Executive staff 9, Other staff 1. Began 1994; ecumenical. (Previously Social & Industrial Ministry). Magazine: *ISR News* (700 every two months). Turnover £182,000 to year end Dec 97. Advising, representing and supporting churches in relating faith to life at work and in society.
Email: isr@chindsocwest.demon.co.uk
☎ 0117 955 7430

Communities Consultative Council, PO Box 17, Eccleshall, Stafford ST21 6LB
No full-time staff. *CC* Began 1975; Anglican. No magazine. Turnover n/a. Representing Church of England monks, nuns; providing information about Anglican Religious Communities, Religious Life.
☎ 020 8594 1736

Community of Aidan & Hilda, Lindisfarne Retreat, Holy Island, Berwick-upon-Tweed TD15 2SD
Guardian: Rev Ray Simpson. Executive staff 1. *CC* No.1055306. Began 1994; Anglican and ecumenical. Magazine: *The Aidan Way* (290 quarterly). Turnover £5,100 to year end Dec 98. Cradling of a Christian spirituality for today, inspired by the Celtic saints.
Web: www.john316.com/~aidan
Email: raysimpson@ndirect.co.uk
☎ 01289 389 249

The Congregational History Circle, Trinity Congregational Church, St Matthew's Road, Brixton, London SW2 1NF
Editor: Dr Alan Argent. All voluntary staff. Began 1978; Congregational. Magazine: *Congregational History Circle Magazine* (400 annually). Turnover £1,000 to year end Apr 98. Aiming to stimulate study and research into Congregational churches, ministers and members.
☎ 020 7274 5541/020 7640 8192

C

Connexion, The Manse, 11 Barns Close, Kirby Muxloe, Leicester LE9 2BA
Secretary: Mrs Angela Almond. No full-time staff. Began 1890; Baptist. (Previously Baptist Ministers and Missionaries Wives Fellowship). Magazine: *Connexion* (1,000 half-yearly). Turnover n/a. Offering fellowship and support for those married to Baptists in Ministry and Mission.
Web: visitweb.com/connexion
Email: ang@revbob.globalnet.co.uk
☎ 0116 239 2731 🖷 0116 239 5222

The Corporation of the Church House, Deans Yard, Westminster, London SW1P 3NZ
Company Secretary: Mr Colin Menzies. Executive staff 4, Other staff 21. *CC* No.213252. Began 1888; Anglican. No magazine. Turnover £2,396,000 to year end Dec 97. Operation of the administrative headquarters and conference centre of the Church of England.
☎ 020 7222 5261 🖷 020 7799 2301

Cost of Conscience, 79 Maze Hill, London SE10 8XQ
Administrator: Rev Francis Gardom. Other staff 3. Began 1986; Anglican. Magazine: *Newsletter* (3,000 occasionally). Turnover £12,000 to year end Dec 98. Welfare of all Anglican clergy unable in conscience to accept ordination of women as priests.
☎ 020 8858 7052 🖷 020 8355 0968

Council For Christian Unity, Church House, Great Smith Street, London SW1P 3NZ
General Secretary: Rev Preb Dr Paul Avis. *Administrator:* Mr Michael Patrick. Executive staff 4, Other staff 4. Began 1991; Anglican. Magazine: *Unity Digest* (600 every four months). Turnover n/a. Promoting Christian unity between the Church of England in the UK and elsewhere.
Email: ccu@chho.u-net.com.uk
☎ 020 7222 9011 🖷 020 7799 2717

†**Crown Appointments Commission**, Fielden House, Little College Street, London SW1P 3SH
Secretary: Mr A J Sadler. Executive staff 1, Other staff 1. Began 1977; Anglican. No magazine. Turnover n/a. Nominating priests for Diocesan Bishoprics to the Prime Minister.
☎ 020 7222 7010 Ext 4033

Diaconal Association of the Church of England, 95 Ballens Road, Lordswood, Chatham ME5 8PA
Secretary: Capt Neil Thomson. No full-time staff. *CC* No.1042999. Began 1988; Anglican. Magazine: *Newsletter* (200 half-yearly). Turnover £4,100 to year end Aug 98. Helping the Church of England to develop its distinctive diaconal calling and ministry.
Web: societies.anglican.org/dace
Email: secretary@dace.societies.anglican.org
☎ 07020 960 520

Diocesan Vocations Service of England and Wales, English Martyrs, 18 Garstang Road, Preston PR1 1NA
Administrator: Rev John Danson. Other staff 1. Began 1992, Roman Catholic. Turnover £25,000 to year end Dec 96. Encouraging the work for vocations to the priesthood, acting as a resource.
Email: jdanson679@aol.com
☎ 01772 558 552 🖷 01772 558 553

Dioceses Commission, Church House, Great Smith Street, London SW1P 3NZ
Secretary: Mr J David Hebblethwaite. No full-time staff. Began 1978; Anglican. No magazine. Turnover n/a. Considering proposals under the Dioceses Measure and advising on matters affecting the diocesan structures.
☎ 020 7898 1000 🖷 020 7898 1369

Doctrine Commission (General Synod), Church House, Great Smith Street, London SW1P 3NZ
Secretary: Dr Gareth Jones. Staff n/a. Began 1971; Anglican. No magazine. Turnover n/a. Advising the House of Bishops of General Synod on doctrinal questions.
☎ 020 7898 1000

†**The Ecclesiological Society**, St Andrew-by-the-Wardrobe, Queen Victoria Street, London EC4V 5DE
Chairman of Council: Mr Paul Velluet. No full-time staff. *CC* No.210501. Began 1839; non-denominational. Magazine: *Ecclesiology Today* (700 every four months). Turnover £5,000 to year end Dec 95. Studying the arts, architecture and liturgy of the Christian Church.
☎ No telephone

***European Evangelical Alliance**, Whitefield House, 186 Kennington Park Road, London SE11 4BT
Director: Mr Gordon Showell-Rogers. Executive staff 1, Other staff 3. *CC* Began 1846; interdenominational. No magazine. Turnover n/a. Uniting national evangelical alliances and other agencies to serve Christ around Europe.
Email: eeagensec@compuserve.com
☎ 020 7582 7276 🖷 020 7582 2043

***Evangelical Alliance**, Whitefield House, 186 Kennington Park Road, London SE11 4BT
General Director: Rev Joel Edwards. *Executive Director:* Mr Colin Saunders. *Public Affairs Director:* Mr Martyn Eden. Executive staff 4, Other staff 46. *CC* No.212325. Began 1846; interdenominational. Magazine: *IDEA* (55,000 five times a year). Turnover £2,230,000 to year end Mar 96. Promoting unity and co-operation among evangelical churches and organisations and providing services to them.
Web: www.eauk.org
Email: enquiry@eauk.org
☎ 020 7207 2100 🖷 020 7207 2150
Northern Ireland: 3 Fitzwilliam Street, Belfast BT9 6AW *General Secretary:* Rev David McCarthy
☎ 028 9024 7920
Wales: 20 High Street, Cardiff CF1 2BZ *General Secretary:* Rev Elfed Godding
☎ 029 2022 9822 🖷 029 2022 9741
Scotland: Challenge House, 29 Canal Street, Glasgow G4 0AD *General Secretary:* Rev David Anderson
☎ 0141 332 8700 🖷 0141 332 8704

See also: **ACUTE – Alliance Commission on Unity & Truth among Evangelicals** on Page 444
African and Caribbean Evangelical Alliance on Page 413
Alliance of Asian Christians on Page 413
Disability Network on Page 411
Evangelical Alliance Coalition on the Occult and New Spiritualities on Page 448
Evangelical Alliance Commission on Strategic Evangelism in the UK on Page 259
Evangelical Alliance Youth and Children's Unit on Page 479
Evangelical Alliance Youth Committee on Page 000
Evangelical Coalition on Drugs on Page 388
Evangelical Coalition on Educational Issues on Page 494
Groundswell on Page 262
High Rise/High Expectations on Page 263
London Leaders Consultations on page 449
Other Faiths Forum on page 238
Reaching Older People with God's Love on Page 268
See also under **Evangelical Alliance** in Main Index on page 627

Evangelical Fellowship in the Anglican Communion, 12 Foxhill, Selly Oak, Birmingham B29 4AG
International Co-ordinator: Rt Rev David Evans. No full-time staff. ***CC*** No.212314. Began 1962; Anglican. Magazine: *EFAC Bulletin* (3,000 annually). Turnover £28,956 to year end Apr 96. Fostering fellowship between Anglican evangelicals worldwide and bearing witness to Biblical and Reformation principles.
Email: samsgb@compuserve.com
☎ 0121 472 5731 🖷 0121 472 5731

Evangelical Fellowship in the Church in Wales, The Rectory, Laura Place, Aberystwyth SY23 2AU
Chairman: Rev Stuart Bell. No full-time staff. ***CC*** No.1047004. Began 1967; Anglican. Magazine: *Bulletin* (Circulation n/a quarterly). Witnessing to evangelical principles; day conferences and twice yearly meetings.
Email: efcw@stmikes.clara.net
☎ 01970 617 184 🖷 01970 610 133

Fellowship of Word and Spirit, St Luke's Church, 28 Farquhar Road, Wimbledon, London SW19 8DA
Hon Secretary: Rev Simon Vibert. No full-time staff. ***CC*** No.293159. Began 1983; Anglican. Magazine: *Orthos* (400 quarterly). Turnover n/a. Reforming Church of England for 21st Century by systematic Reformed theology and practice.
Web: www.stjames.org.uk/fws/home.htm
Email: sws@altavista.net
☎ 020 8946 3396 🖷 020 8946 3396

Forward in Faith, Faith House, 7 Tufton Street, London SW1P 3QN
National Director: Mr Stephen Parkinson. *Chairman:* Rt Rev John Broadhurst. Executive staff 1, Other staff 2. ***CC*** No.1057246. Began 1992; Anglican. Magazine: *New Directions* (18,000 monthly), *Forward Plus!* (25,000 quarterly). Turnover £150,000 to year end Dec 96. Umbrella organisation for Church of England groups opposed to the ordination of women.
Email: forwardinfaith@compuserve.com
☎ 020 7976 0727 🖷 020 7976 0737

The Friends of Cardinal Newman, The Oratory, Hagley Road, Edgbaston, Birmingham B16 8UE
Director: Rev Gregory Winterton. Executive staff 1. ***CC*** No.274474. Began 1976; Roman Catholic but ecumenical. Magazine: *Newsletter* (1,500 every four months). Turnover £10,000. Disseminating knowledge of Cardinal Newman's life, teaching and philosophy; furthering the cause of his canonisation.
Email: jhn@oratory.globalnet.co.uk
☎ 0121 454 0496 🖷 0121 455 8160

Grace Baptist Trust Corporation, 19 Croydon Road, Caterham CR3 6PA
General Secretary: Mr David J Knights. Executive staff 1, Other staff 2. ***CC*** No.251675. Began 1909; Particular Baptist (Strict Communion). (Previously Strict and Particular Baptist Trust Corporation). No magazine. Turnover n/a. Advancing Christian religion especially Particular Baptist churches practising strict communion.
☎ 01883 345 488 🖷 01883 345 488

Group for Evangelism and Renewal, 2a Chester Avenue, Poulton-le-Fylde FY6 7RY
Secretary & Treasurer: Rev Mrs Chris Vivian. No full-time staff. ***CC*** Began 1974; United Reformed. Magazine: *In Gear* (3,300 every four months). Turnover £18,500 to year end Dec 98. Promoting renewal and evangelism in the URC, emphasising again the reality and Lordship of Christ.
Web: www.gearpub.freeserve.co.uk
Email: mail@gearpub.freeserve.co.uk
☎ 01253 882 027

Guild of Church Musicians, St Katharine Cree, 86 Leadenhall Street, London EC3A 3DH
General Secretary: Mr John Ewington OBE. Executive staff 4, Other staff 2. ***CC*** Began 1888; Anglican. Magazine: *Laudate* (800 every four months). Turnover £10,000 to year end Dec 94. Examining body for Church Music for Archbishops of Canterbury and Westminster.
☎ 01883 743 168 🖷 01883 743 854

***Headway**, 4 Kingswear Avenue, Perton, Wolverhampton WV6 7RJ
General Secretary: Mr Alan Eccles. No full-time staff. ***CC*** No.298087. Began 1987; Methodist. Magazine: *Headline* (2,500 quarterly). Turnover £34,000 to year end Aug 98. Movement of Methodists committed to prayer for revival and witness to evangelical faith.
Web: www.soft.net.uk/greenhill/index
☎ 01902 744 120

The Hope Trust, 31 Moray Place, Edinburgh EH3 6BY
Secretary: Carol Hope. Executive staff 1, Admin staff 1. ***CC*** Began 1890; Church of Scotland. No magazine. Turnover n/a. Upholding the Reformed saved in Scotland and worldwide.
☎ 0131 226 5151 🖷 0131 225 2608

Incorporated Church Building Society, Fulham Palace, London SW6 6EA
Secretary: Wing Com Michael Tippen. Executive staff 3, Other staff 1. ***CC*** Began 1818; Anglican. Magazine: *Annual Report* (4,500 annually). Turnover £50,700 to year end Apr 96. Assisting with grants and loans towards building repairs to Anglican churches in England and Wales.
☎ 020 7736 3054

C

Inter-Church Relations Board, Church House, Fisherwick Place, Belfast BT1 6DW
Clerk: Very Rev Dr Samuel Hutchinson. Staff 60. Began n/a; Presbyterian Church in Ireland. No magazine. Turnover n/a. Encouraging relations with other churches, councils of churches and ecumenical organisations.
Web: www.presbyterianireland.org
Email: clerk@presbyterianireland.org
☎ 028 9032 2284 Mobile: 07703 467 706
Fax 028 9023 6609

King Edward Orthodox Trust Co Ltd, Saint Edward Brotherhood, Saint Cyprian's Avenue, Brookwood, Woking GU24 0BL
Superior: Very Rev Archimandrite Alexis. No full-time staff. ***CC*** No.284929. Began 1981; Orthodox. Magazine: *The Shepherd* (750 monthly). Turnover £6,000 to year end Apr 98. Monastic community, missionary work, care of St Edward's shrine and Orthodox Christian cemetery.
☎ 01483 487 763 Fax 01483 487763

Kingdom Faith Church Offices, Roffey Place, Faygate, Horsham RH12 4SS
Director: Rev Colin Urquhart. *General Manager:* Mr Les Mitchell. Executive staff 5, Other staff 30. ***CC*** No.278746. Began 1980; interdenominational. (Previously Kingdom Faith Ministries). Magazine: (10,000 quarterly). Turnover £2,200,000 to year end Mar 98. Promoting revival and faith in the nations through churchlife, Bible College, publications, conferences.
Web: www.kingdomfaith.com
Email: info@kingdomfaith.com
☎ 01293 851 543 Fax 01293 851 330

Legal Advisory Commission (General Synod), Church House, Great Smith Street, London SW1P 3NZ
Secretary to the Commission: Miss Ingrid E Slaughter. No full-time staff. Began 1925; Anglican. Magazine: *Annual supplements to Legal Opinions concerning the Church of England* (Circulation n/a). Turnover n/a. Advising central church bodies and diocesan authorities of the Church of England on legal matters.
☎ 020 7898 1000 Fax 020 7898 1369

Liturgical Commission (General Synod), Church House, Great Smith Street, London SW1P 3NZ
Secretary: Mr J David Hebblethwaite. No full-time staff. Began 1954; Anglican. No magazine. Turnover n/a. Advising on and preparing forms of worship in the Church of England.
☎ 020 7898 1000 Fax 020 7898 1369

***London Mennonite Trust**, London Mennonite Centre, 14 Shepherds Hill, Highgate, London N6 5AQ
Administrator: Mr Will Newcomb. *Director:* Mr Mark Thiessen Nation. Executive staff 3, Other staff 4. ***CC*** No.227410. Began 1954; Mennonite. (Previously Evangelical Mennonite Association). Turnover £140,000 to year end Dec 97. Cross Currents teaching programme, Bridge Builders conflict training, library, Metanoia book service, mediation service.
Web: www.btinternet.com/~lmc
Email: menno@compuserve.com
☎ 020 8340 8775 Fax 020 8341 6807

***Mainstream – A Word and Spirit Network**, 16 Ambleside Avenue, Rawtenstall, Rossendale BB4 6RY
Secretary: Rev Adrian Argile. No full-time staff. ***CC*** No.1490441. Began 1979; Baptist. (Previously Mainstream – Baptists for Life and Growth). Magazine: *Mainstream Newsletter* (1,800 quarterly). Turnover £3,710 to year end Apr 98. Encouraging new life and growth in Baptist churches in Britain.
☎ 01706 831 195

Methodist Church Conference Office, Methodist Church House, 25 Marylebone Road, London NW1 5JR
Secretary of Conference: Rev Dr Nigel Collinson. Began 1932. Turnover n/a. Servicing the Methodist Conference and ensuring its legislation as the Church's governing body is implemented.
Email: co-ordsec@methodistchurch.org.uk
☎ 020 7486 5502 Fax 020 7224 1510

Methodist Church Coordinating Secretaries, Methodist Church House, 25 Marylebone Road, London NW1 5JR
Coordinating Secretary: Rev Dr Stephen Mosedale. Began 1932; Methodist. Turnover n/a. Management of Methodist connexional work and leadership across the whole range of church activity.
Email: co-ordsec@methodistchurch.org.uk
☎ 020 7486 5502 Fax 020 7224 1520

Methodist Church Evangelism Office, 1 Central Buildings, Westminster, London SW1H 9NH
Secretary for Evangelism: Rev Brian R Hoare. Executive staff 1, Admin staff 1. ***CC*** Began 1996; Methodist. Restructured 1996. Magazine: *Mission in Britain* (10,000 every four months). Turnover n/a. Stimulating, supporting and resourcing Methodist churches in evangelism and church planting.
☎ 020 7222 8010 Fax 020 7233 0323

Methodist Church Family & Personal Relationships, Methodist Church House, 25 Marylebone Road, London NW1 5JR
Secretary for Family & Personal Relationships: Rev David Gamble. Began 1932. Turnover n/a. Providing coordination and resources for those involved in pastoral ministry concerning family and other relationships.
Email: co-ordsec@methodistchurch.org.uk
☎ 020 7486 5502 Fax 020 7486 7792

Methodist Church London Committee, 1 Central Buildings, Westminster, London SW1H 9NH
Secretaries: Rev Dr Stuart Jordan, Miss Diane Totkins. Executive staff 2, Other staff 2. ***CC*** Began 1861; Methodist. Magazine: *Annual Report* (5,000 annually). Turnover £500,000 to year end Dec 96. Co-ordinating Methodist work and supporting ministry and building projects in the South East Region.
Email: londoncommittee_methodist@compuserve.com
☎ 020 7222 8010 Fax 020 7799 1452

Methodist Church Music Society, 23a The Quadrant, Totley, Sheffield S17 4DB
Secretary: Mr John Bailey. All voluntary staff. Began 1935; Methodist. Magazine: *Notes* (1,100 half-yearly). Turnover n/a. Developing, enabling and encouraging vocal and instrumental worship music in all its formats throughout the Church.
☎ 0114 235 1085

Methodist Church Property Committee, Central Buildings, Oldham Street, Manchester M1 1JQ
Secretary: Rev Kenneth E Street. Executive staff 6, Other staff 17. Began 1854; Methodist. Magazine: *Property Points* (15,000 half-yearly). Turnover £1,500,000 to year end Dec 98. Providing administration, advice and financial assistance for Methodist church property.
☎ 0161 236 5194 Fax 0161 236 0752

Methodist Church Public Issues, Methodist Church House, 25 Marylebone Road, London NW1 5JR
Coordinating Secretary: Rev David G Deeks. Began 1932; Methodist. Turnover n/a. Providing for Methodism national engagement with other bodies on political, social, educational and international affairs.
Email: co-ordsec@methodistchurch.org.uk
☎ 020 7486 5502 Fax 020 7224 1520

Methodist Church Theological Colleges & Courses, Methodist Church House, 25 Marylebone Road, London NW1 5JR
Secretary for Initial Ministerial Training and Probation: Rev Kenneth Howcroft. Began 1932; Methodist. Turnover n/a. Provision of theological education and training for ministers, deacons, lay leaders and the whole church.
☎ 020 7486 5502 🖷 020 7935 2104

Methodist Sacramental Fellowship, Church Cottage 2a St Marks Road, Warle, Weston-Super-Mare BS22 0PW
General Secretary: Rev Margaret Wallwork. No full-time staff. Began 1935; Methodist. Magazine: *The Bulletin* (325 annually). Turnover £3,000 to year end Mar 96. Fostering the study and practice of theology, liturgy and ecumenism in Methodism.
☎ 01934 512 093

Ministry Division (Archbishops' Council), Church House, Great Smith Street, Westminster, London SW1P 3NZ
Director: Ven Gordon Kuhrt. Executive staff 21, Other staff 16. ***CC*** Began 1912; Anglican. (Previously Advisory Board of Ministry (General Synod)). No magazine. Turnover n/a. Advising Church of England regarding selection, training, deployment and conditions of service of candidates for ordained and lay ministries.
☎ 020 7222 9011 🖷 020 7726 7625

The Modern Churchpeople's Union, M C U Office, 25 Birch Grove, London W3 9SP
General Secretary: Rev Nicholas Henderson. No full-time staff. ***CC*** No.281573. Began 1898; Anglican. Magazine: *Modern Believing* (1,600 quarterly). Turnover £18,000 to year end Dec 98. Encouraging freedom and informed enquiry in the Church of England and Anglican Communion.
Web: www.mcm.co.uk/modchurchunion
Email: modchurchunion@btinternet.com
☎ 020 8932 4379 🖷 020 8993 5812

The Mothers' Union, Mary Sumner House, 24 Tufton Street, London SW1P 3RB
Chief Executive: Ms Angela Ridler. Executive staff 6, Other staff 36. ***CC*** No.240531. Began 1876; Anglican. Magazine: *Home and Family* (95,000 quarterly). Turnover £1,400,000 to year end Dec 95. Strengthening marriage and Christian family life; facilities for day conferences; gift shop.
Web: www.themothersunion.org
Email: mu@themothersunion.org
☎ 020 7222 5533 🖷 020 7222 1591

Movement for the Reform of Infant Baptism, 18 Taylors Lane, Lindford, Bordon GU35 0SW
Secretary: Ms Carol Snipe. No full-time staff. ***CC*** No. 1067112. Began 1986; Anglican. Magazine: *MORIB Update* (500 every four months). Turnover £1,500 to year end Dec 94. Ending indiscriminate infant baptism in the Church of England; reviewing all Christian initiation.
☎ 01420 477 508

National Association of Christian Communities and Networks (NACCAN), Community House, Eton Road, Newport NP9 0BL
Staff: Volunteer Office Co-ordinators. ***CC*** No.283972. Began 1981; ecumenical. Magazine: *Christian Community* (600 every four months). Turnover £10,000 to year end June 97. Sharing the vision of Christian community with churches and society.
☎ 01633 265486

National Catholic Fund, 39 Eccleston Square, London SW1V 1BX
General Secretary: Rt Rev Mgr Arthur Roche. Executive staff 15, Other staff 11. ***CC*** No.257239. Began n/a; Roman Catholic. No magazine. Turnover n/a. Advancing the Roman Catholic religion in England and Wales.
☎ 020 7630 8220 🖷 020 7630 5166

†**National Catholic Women's Network**, 39 Eccleston Square, London SW1V 1PD
National President: Mrs Celia Capstick. Other staff n/a. Began 1938; Roman Catholic. Magazine: *Catholic Woman* (Circulation n/a half-yearly). Turnover n/a. Co-ordinating body of Catholic women's organisations; consultative body to RC Conference of Bishops, England and Wales.
☎ 020 7834 1186 🖷 020 7834 1186

National Council for Social Concern, Montague Chambers, Montague Close, London SE1 9DA
Director: Mr Peter Carlin. Full-time staff 3, Voluntary staff 3. ***CC*** No.234801. Began 1872; Anglican. (Previously Church of England National Council for Social Concern). Magazine: *Newsletter* (Circulation n/a n/a). Turnover n/a. Producing educational materials; monitoring government policies on criminal justice, gambling, alcohol, drugs; library, information service.
Email: info@social-concern.demon.co.uk
☎ 020 7403 0977 🖷 020 7403 0799

National Council for the Lay Associations, 103 Leopold Road, Kensington, Liverpool L7 8SR
Hon Secretary: Ms Cathy Young. No full-time staff. Began 1951; Roman Catholic. No magazine. Turnover £14,000 to year end Dec 92. Co-ordinating body of national Roman Catholic lay organisations; liaison with Episcopal Conference for member organisations.
☎ 0151 263 4923

National Religious Vocation Centre, 82 Margaret Street, London W1N 8LH
Director: Sister Hilary Thompson. Other staff 1. ***CC*** No.277024. Began 1979; Roman Catholic. No magazine. Turnover n/a. Promoting vocations to the religious life in England and Wales for men and women.
☎ 020 7631 5173 🖷 020 7636 5364

New Creation Christian Community, New Creation Farmhouse, Nether Heyford, Northampton NN7 3LB
Senior Pastor: Noel Stanton. Admin staff 32. Began 1974; Jesus Fellowship. No magazine. Turnover n/a. Charismatic Christian community throughout England.
Web: www.jesus.org.uk/nccc
☎ 01327 349 991 🖷 01327 349 997

New Eclectics, St John's Vicarage, Barcroft Grove, Yeadon, Leeds LS19 7XZ
Chairman: Canon Max Wigley. No full-time staff. ***CC*** Began 1955; Anglican. (Previously Eclectics). Amalgamation of Eclectics and Senior Evangelical Anglican Clergy Conference. Magazine: *Eclectic* (600 half-yearly). For ordained and lay Anglican Evangelical leaders and their families. Annual Conference in November.
☎ 0113 250 2272

Nikaean Club, Lambeth Palace, London SE1 7JU
Honorary Secretary: Miss J R Pollard. Other staff 1. Began 1925; Anglican. No magazine. Turnover £3,500 to year end Dec 96. Extending hospitality on behalf of the Archbishop of Canterbury to church leaders from abroad.
☎ 020 7928 8282 🖷 020 7261 9836

Open Synod Group, 6 Forndon Close, Lower Earley, Reading RG6 3XR
Secretary: Dr Carole Cull. No full-time staff. ***CC*** No.297315. Began 1970; Anglican. Magazine: *OSG Magazine* (400 half-yearly). Turnover £1,500 to year end Dec 98. Enhancing and assisting the proclamation of the Gospel through the synodical process.
Email: carole.cull@drl.ox.ac.uk
☎ 01865 248 418 / 01189 617 923 🖷 01865 723 884

C

Orthodox Fellowship of St John the Baptist, 5a High Street, Blakesley, Towcester NN12 8RE
Chairman: Mr Joseph Fitzpatrick Williams. No full-time staff. ***CC*** No.1063713. Began 1979; Orthodox Magazine: *Forerunner* (250 half-yearly). Turnover £10,000 to year end Dec 98. Organising conferences, orthodox theological summer school, study weekends, day meetings and pilgrimages. Publishing directory, lectionary.
Web: www.ofsjb.org
☎ 01327 860 894

Other Faiths Forum (Evangelical Alliance), Whitefield House, 186 Kennington Park Road, London SE11 4BT
Chair: Robin Thomson. Staff n/a. Began n/a. No magazine. Turnover: finance included in Evangelical Alliance. A network for those ministering among people of other faiths in the UK.
Web: www.eauk.org
Email: members@eauk.org
☎ 020 7207 2100 Fax 020 7207 2150

C

***Oxfordshire Community Churches**, 53 West Way, Oxford OX2 0JE
Senior Pastor: Rev Stephen Thomas. *Area Administrator:* Mr Andy O'Connell. Executive staff 15, Admin staff 4. ***CC*** No.1056921. Began 1982; Salt & Light. Magazine: *Area News* (500 every two months). Turnover £1,000,000 to year end Aug 98. Group of Churches and Christian schools in Oxfordshire.
Web: www.oxcc.u-net.com
Email: office@occ.org.uk
☎ 01865 793 003 Fax 01865 793 025

***Partnership**, 52 Hornsey Lane, London N6 5LU
Executive Secretary: Dr Neil Summerton. No full-time staff. ***CC*** No. 802564. Began 1987; Christian Brethren. Including Christian Brethren Research Fellowship, Partnership Link-Up Service. Magazines: *Partnership Perspective* (450 every four months), *International Partnership perspectives* (600 annually), *Partnership Update* (1,000 half-yearly). Turnover £14,000 to year end Dec 98. Provides networking, support, encouragement, training to churches of Christian Brethren background.
Email: summerto@hornsey.u-net.com
☎ 020 7272 0643 (Evening) 01865 282 901(Office)

Pastoral Reorganization Advisory Service, 18 West Avenue, Clarendon Park, Leicester LE2 1TR
Practitioner in Pastoral Reorganisation: Mr David Gillman. Executive staff 1, Other staff 1. Began 1984; interdenominational. No magazine. Turnover n/a. Providing comprehensive independent advisory service specialising in church redundancy matters; reviews, appeals and post-closure.
☎ 0116 270 2901

Peache Trust, Truckers Ghyll, Horsham Road, Handcross, Haywards Heath RH17 6DT
Secretary: Rev K W Habershon. No full-time staff. Began 1878; Anglican. No magazine. Turnover n/a. Appointing incumbents to 45 Anglican Churches.
☎ 01444 400 274

People of God Trust, 14 West Halkin Street, London SW1X 8JS
Hon Secretary: Mr Simon Bryden-Brook. No other staff. ***CC*** No.1013830. Began 1992; Roman Catholic. No magazine. Turnover £3,000 to year end Apr 98. Promoting the Second Vatican Council's idea of renewal in the Catholic Church.
☎ 020 7235 2841 Fax 020 7823 2110

Praxis, St Matthew's House, Great Peter Street, London SW1P 2BU
Chairman: Rev Cannon Stephen Oliver. No full-time staff. Began 1990; Anglican. Magazine: *Praxis* (Circulation n/a every two months). Turnover n/a. Liturgical formation; study days and conferences on liturgy and worship.
☎ 020 7222 3704

The Prayer Book Society, St James Garlickhythe, Garlick Hill, London EC4V 2AF
Chairman: Mr C A A Kilmister. All voluntary staff. ***CC*** Began 1975; Anglican. Magazine: *Faith & Heritage* (7,000 half-yearly), *Faith & Worship* (6,500 half-yearly), *PBS Newsletter* (10,500 quarterly). Turnover £100,000 to year end Dec 92. Upholding the Book of Common Prayer, encouraging its use in Anglican churches, supporting orthodox, classic Anglicanism.
☎ 01923 824 278

Protestant Dissenting Deputies of Three Denominations, 27 Tavistock Square, London WC1H 9HH
Secretary: Rev Geoffrey H Roper. No full-time staff. Began 1732; represents Baptists, Congregationalists and United Reformed. No magazine. Turnover £600 to year end Dec 97. Defending the civil rights of non-conformists and maintaining the right of access to the throne. Annual lecture.
☎ 020 7387 8413 Fax 020 7383 0150

Protestant Reformation Society, PO Box 47, Ramsgate CT11 9XB
General Secretary: Dr Derek A Scales. No full-time staff. ***CC*** No.234959. Began 1827; Anglican. Magazine: *Newsletters* (500 quarterly). Turnover n/a. Maintaining Reformation teaching and principles in the Church of England and seeking conversion of non-Christians.
☎ 01843 580 542

Quaker Home Service, Friends House, Euston Road, London NW1 2BJ
General Secretary: Beth Allen. Executive staff 1, Other staff 16. ***CC*** Began 1978; Religious Society of Friends. Magazine: *Quaker Monthly* (2,000 monthly). Turnover n/a. Nurturing Quakers and outreach to others through conferences, correspondence, literature and advertising.
Email: betha@quaker.org.uk
☎ 020 7633 1000 Fax 020 7633 1001

Reform, PO Box 1183, Sheffield S10 3YA
Chairman: Rev Philip Hacking. Other staff 2. ***CC*** No.1036192. Began 1993; Anglican. Magazine: *Newsletter* (1,633 quarterly). Turnover £25,000 to year end Dec 98. Promoting biblically-based ideas and action for reforming the Church of England.
Web: www.reform.org.uk
Email: reform@legend.co.uk
☎ 0114 230 9256 Fax 0114 230 9256

Reformation Today Trust, 75 Woodhill Road, Leeds LS16 7BZ
Editor: Rev Erroll Hulse. All voluntary staff. ***CC*** Began 1970; Reformed Baptist. Magazine: *Reformation Today* (2,200 Frequency n/a). Turnover n/a. Distributing Reformed Baptist literature worldwide; organising conferences.
☎ 0113 261 9256 Fax 0113 261 2513

Retired Clergy Association, 12 Clouston Road, Farnborough GU14 8PN
Hon Secretary: Mr K R Lightfoot. No full-time staff. Began 1934; Anglican. No magazine. Turnover £5,603 to year end Dec 98. Encouraging retired clergy and assisting them to form groups for discussion and further study.
☎ 01252 546 486

Royal Martyr Church Union, The Priory, Pittenweem, Anstruther KY10 2LJ
Hon Secretary: W R C Miller of Pittenweem. No full-time staff. Began 1906; Anglican. Magazine: *Royal Martyr Annual* (Circulation n/a annually). Turnover n/a. Revering the memory of Charles I and bringing together descendants of Cavaliers and those interested in Caroline history.
☎ No telephone

Russian Orthodox Monastery of St Seraphim of Sarov (Orthodox Palestine Society), 158 Elmbridge Road, Perry Barr, Birmingham B44 8AE
Abbot: Very Rev Archimandrite Seraphim. *Reader:* Monk Mark. Serving ministers n/a. Began n/a. (Previously Latvian Autonomous Orthodox Church & Free Russian Orthodox Church). No magazine. Turnover n/a. Missionary spiritual centre: monastic life, prayers, advice, lectures, preaching. Also translation: French, German, Latvian, Russian.
☎ 0121 356 5176 🖷 0121 356 5176

Scottish Baptist Men's Movement, 17 Queens Terrace, Ayr KA7 1DU
Secretary: Mr T Barrie. No full-time staff. ***CC*** Began 1947; Baptist. No magazine. Turnover £4,493 to year end Dec 98. Supplying necessary books to trainee pastors overseas in countries where Baptist Missionary Society works.
☎ 01292 261 215

Scottish Catholic Archives, 16 Drummond Place, Edinburgh EH3 6PL
Keeper: Dr Christine Johnson. No full-time staff. Began 1560; Roman Catholic. (Also known as Columba House). No magazine. Turnover n/a. Listing for research purposes the records of the Scottish Catholic Church 1560-1950. Open by appointment only.
☎ 0131 556 3661

Scottish Catholic Historical Association, John S Burns & Sons, 25 Finlas Street, Glasgow G22 5DS
Chairman: Mr Campbell. All voluntary staff 4. ***CC*** Began 1950; Roman Catholic. Magazine: *The Innes Review* (500 half-yearly). Turnover n/a. Publishing Innes Review and other works relating to history of the Catholic Church in Scotland.
☎ 0141 336 8678 🖷 0141 336 3126

Scottish Church History Society, 39 Southside Road, Inverness IV2 4XA
Hon Secretary and Treasurer: Rev Peter Donald. No other staff. ***CC*** Began 1927; non-denominational. Magazine: *Records of the Scottish Church History Society* (300 annually). Turnover £3,000 to year end Dec 97. Encouraging interest and research in all aspects of Scottish Church history.
☎ 01463 231 140 🖷 01463 230 537

Scottish Episcopal Renewal Fellowship, Rose Court, Fortrose IV10 8TN
Co-ordinator: Mrs Mary MacDonell. No full-time staff. ***CC*** Began 1982; Scottish Episcopal. Magazine: *The Go-Between* (500 every four months). Turnover n/a. Seeking to manifest the fullness of the gifts and ministries of the Holy Spirit.
☎ 01381 620 250

Scottish National Tribunal, 22 Woodrow Road, Glasgow G41 5PN
Officialis: Rev James G Nicol. Executive staff 2, Other staff 21. ***CC*** Began 1970; Roman Catholic. No magazine. Turnover £96,890 to year end Dec 92. Dealing with issues of canon law, principally concerning the bond of marriage.
☎ 0141 427 3036

Simeon's Trustees and Hyndman's Trustees, c/o Mrs A Brown, 6 Angerford Avenue, Sheffield S8 9BG
Chairman: Rev Canon Michael Rees. No full-time staff. Began 1836; Anglican. No magazine. Turnover under £10,000 to year end Dec 96. Patronage trust nominating incumbents for vacant benefices in the Trust's gift.
☎ 0114 255 8522 🖷 0114 255 8522

Society for the Maintenance of the Faith, Christ Church Vicarage, 10 Cannon Place, London NW3 1EJ
Secretary: Rev Paul Conrad. No full-time staff. ***CC*** Began 1871; Anglican. Magazine: *Newsletter* (Circulation n/a occasionally). Turnover n/a. Aiming to maintain the Catholic faith within the Church of England; administration of patronage.
☎ 020 7435 6784 🖷 020 7435 6784

Society of King Charles the Martyr, Flat 5, Crinkle Court, Chubb Hill, Whitby YO21 1JU
Secretary: Rev Barrie Williams. No full-time staff. Began 1894; Anglican. Magazine: *Church and King* (500 frequency n/a). Turnover £1,000 to year end Dec 98. Promoting development to King Charles as a saint and martyr.
☎ 01947 600 766

Society of St John Chrysostom, 14 Macduff Road, London SW11 4DA
Hon Secretary: Mr John Jaques. No full-time staff. ***CC*** Began 1926; Roman Catholic but ecumenical. Magazine: *Eastern Churches Journal* (800 every four months). Turnover n/a. Making known to Western Christians the history, worship and spirituality of Eastern Christendom.
☎ 020 7720 1770

Society of St Willibrord, 57 Maltese Road, Chelmsford CM1 2PB
Secretary: Rev Ivor Morris. No full-time staff. ***CC*** Began 1908; Anglican. Magazine: *St Willibrord Newsletter* (300 half-yearly). Turnover n/a. Fostering good relationships between the Anglican Church and the Old Catholic Churches in Europe.
☎ 01245 353 914

The Strict Baptist Historical Society, 38 Frenchs Avenue, Dunstable LU6 1BH
Hon Secretary: Rev Kenneth Dix. No full-time staff. ***CC*** No.1061908. Began 1960; Strict Baptist. Magazine: *Bulletin* (150 annually), *Newsletter* (150 annually). Turnover £1,114 to year end Oct 98. Studying Baptist history; preserving books, documents and other historical material.
☎ 01582 602 242

Ukrainian Religious Society of St Sophia, 79 Holland Park, London W11 3SW
Director: Mr G I Jenkala. All voluntary staff. ***CC*** No.275483. Began 1977; Ukrainian Catholic. No magazine. Turnover n/a. Promoting religious knowledge, Christian practice and education with reference to Ukrainian Catholic Church teachings.
☎ 020 7221 1890

United Protestant Council, The Rectory, Nuffield, Henley-on-Thames RG9 5SN
Hon Secretary: Rev John F Shearer. No full-time staff. Began 1898; interdenominational. No magazine. Turnover £5,000 to year end Dec 98. Federal body supporting and co-ordinating twenty societies through corporate meetings and council.
☎ 01491 641 305

United Reformed Church History Society, c/o Westminster College, Madingley Road, Cambridge CB3 0AA
Hon Secretary: Rev Elizabeth Brown. No full-time staff. Began 1972; United Reformed. Magazine: *Journal of the United Reformed Conference Office* (500 half-yearly). Turnover £4,000 to year end Mar 96. Promoting study of Congregational and Presbyterian history, especially in England.
☎ 01223 353 997

WATCH National (Women and the Church), St John's Church, Waterloo Road, London SE1 8UF
Chair: Christina Rees. No full time staff. Began 1996; ecumenical. Magazine: *Outlook* (500 quarterly). Turnover n/a. Providing a national forum for promoting, discussing and monitoring women's ministry in the church.
Web: www.watchwomen.com
Email: chrisrees@xc.org
☎ 01763 848 822 Fax 01763 848 774

Wesley Historical Society, 34 Spiceland Road, Northfield, Birmingham B31 1NJ
General Secretary: Dr E D Graham. No full-time staff. *CC* No.283012. Began 1893; Methodist. Magazine: *Proceedings of The Wesley Historical Society* (800 every four months). Turnover n/a. Encouraging interest and research into the history and literature of all branches of Methodism.
Email: graham106364.3456@compuserve.com
☎ 0121 475 4914

Wesley's Chapel, The Museum of Methodism and John Wesley's House, 49 City Road, London EC1Y 1AU
Administrator: Mr Nigel Cowgill. Other staff 8. *CC* Began 1778; Methodist. Magazine: *Wesley's Chapel Magazine* (2,500 annually). Turnover n/a. Providing information about the Wesleys and Methodism to visitors worldwide of all denominations. Non-residential conference centre.
☎ 020 7253 2262 Fax 020 7608 3825

Westminster Interfaith, 17 Garrison Close, Hounslow TW4 5EX
Director: Mr Alfred Agius. Other staff 3. *CC* Began 1981; Roman Catholic. Magazine: *Newsletter* (850 every two months). Turnover n/a. Fostering relations between Roman Catholics and other world faiths.
Email: aagius@aol.com
☎ 020 8570 8639 Mobile: 07768 404 615
Fax 020 8570 8639

The Worshipful Company of Parish Clerks, 1 Dean Trench Street, London SW1P 3HB
Clerk of the Company: Mr B J N Coombes. Executive staff 1. Began 1274; Anglican. No magazine. Turnover £23,500 to year end Mar 98. Assisting the work of the Church in the City of London (Westminster & Southwark).
☎ 020 7222 1138 Fax 020 7233 1913

C

COUNCILS OF CHURCHES, NATIONAL, REGIONAL, COUNTY

Action of Churches Together in Scotland (ACTS), Scottish Churches House, Kirk Street, Dunblane FK15 0AJ
General Secretary: Very Rev Dr Kevin Franz. Executive staff 7, Other staff 10. *CC* No.SCO 13196. Began 1990; interdenominational. Magazine: Newsletter (Circulation n/a every four months). Turnover £304,000 to year end Dec 96. Encouraging and expressing the unity of the Christian churches in Scotland.
☎ 01786 823 588 Fax 01786 825 844

Afro-West Indian United Council of Churches, The New Testament Church of God, Arcadian Gardens, High Road, London N22 5AA
General Secretary: Rev Eric A Brown. No full-time staff. *CC* Began 1976; evangelical. No magazine. Turnover n/a. Promoting, co-ordinating and fostering Christian ideals and action between member churches and the community.
☎ 020 8888 9427 Fax 020 8888 9427

Barking Area Church Leaders' Group, 349 Westbourne Grove, Westcliff-on-Sea SS0 0PU
Secretary: Rev David Hardiman. No full-time staff. Began n/a; ecumenical. No magazine. Turnover n/a. Furthering ecumenical co-operation in the London Boroughs of Barking & Dagenham, Havering, Newham, Redbridge, Waltham Forest.
☎ 01702 342 327 Fax 01702 342 327

Birmingham Churches Together, Carrs Lane Church Centre, Birmingham B4 7SX
General Secretary: Rev Mark Fisher. Executive staff 1, Other staff 1. *CC* No.243931. Began 1951; interdenominational. Magazine: *BEN* (1,500 every two months). Turnover £44,000 to year end Dec 98. Co-ordinating body for all Roman Catholic, Anglican and Free Church denominations.
Web: ourworld.compuserve.com/homepages/revmark/
Email: revmark@compuserve.com
☎ 0121 643 6603 Fax 0121 632 5320

British Evangelical Council, Evershed House, Alma Road, St Albans AL1 3AR
General Secretary: To be appointed. Executive staff 1. *CC* No.258924. Began 1952; non-denominational. Magazine: *In Step* (10,000 half-yearly), *Foundations* (1,000 half-yearly). Turnover £56,000 to year end Aug 98. Promoting evangelical church unity and testimony, locally and nationally.
Email: becoffice@aol.com
☎ 01727 855 655

Buckinghamshire Ecumenical Council, 124 Bath Road, Banbury OX16 0TR
Ecumenical Officer: Rev Canon Derek Palmer. No full-time staff. Began n/a; ecumenical. No magazine. Turnover n/a. Furthering ecumenical cooperation within Buckinghamshire.
☎ 01295 368 201

Cambridgeshire Ecumenical Council, The Vicarage, Mingle Lane, Stapleford, Cambridge CB2 5BG
Secretary: Rev Frank Fisher. No full-time staff. Began 1988; ecumenical. No magazine. Turnover £1,300 to year end Dec 98. Intermediate body of Churches Together in England; strengthening co-operation, supporting and initiating local ecumenical partnerships.
☎ 01223 842 150

Christians Together in Devon, Grenville House, Whites Lane, Torrington EX38 8DS
Ecumenical Officer: Rev John Bradley. No full-time staff. Began n/a; ecumenical. No magazine. Furthering ecumenical co-operation within Devon.
☎ 01805 625 059

Churches Together in Bedfordshire
see Churches Together in Hertfordshire and Bedfordshire

Churches Together in Berkshire, 51 Galsworthy Drive, Caversham Park, Reading RG4 0PR
Ecumenical Officer: Rev Phil Abrey. No full-time staff. Began 1986; interdenominational. Magazine: *Broadsheet* (Circulation n/a Quarterly). Turnover n/a. Initiating, enabling and supporting efforts towards full unity in the Christian church.
☎ 01189 475 152

Churches Together in greater Bristol, 9 Lodway Close, Pill, Bristol BS20 0DE
Ecumenical Officer: Rev Brian Scott. Executive staff 1. Began 1987; interdenominational. (Previously Greater Bristol Ecumenical Council). Magazine: *Bristol Christian Quarterly* (510 quarterly). Turnover £17,236 to year end Dec 98. Fostering and oversight of regional and local ecumenical activity and action.
☎ 01275 373 488 🖷 01275 373 488

Churches Together in Britain and Ireland, Inter-Church House, 35 Lower Marsh, London SE1 7RL
General Secretary: Dr David Goodbourn. Deputy General Secretary: Rev Dr Colin Davey. Office Manager: Rev Margaret Brewster. Executive staff 13, Other staff 16. CC No.259688. Began 1990; interdenominational. (Previously Council of Churches for Britain and Ireland). No magazine. Turnover £1,000,000 to year end Dec 96. Co-ordinating the work of the churches and national ecumenical instruments and bodies.
Web: www.ccbi.org.uk
Email: gensec@ctbi.org.uk
☎ 020 7620 4444 🖷 020 7928 0010

See also: **Action of Churches Together in Scotland (ACTS)** on Page 240
Churches Together in England on Page 241
CYTUN: Churches Together in Wales on Page 243
Irish Council of Churches on Page 244

Churches Together in Cheshire, 5 Abbey Green, Chester CH1 2JH
Ecumenical Officer: Rev Canon Michael Rees. No full-time staff. Began 1975; interdenominational. Magazine: *Newsletter* (Circulation & frequency n/a). Turnover £7,500 to year end Dec 96. Encouraging co-operation, mutual support and evangelism by the churches in the county.
☎ 01244 620 444

Churches Together in Cornwall, 138 Bodmin Road, Truro TR1 1RB
Secretary: Rev Gerald M Burt. No full-time staff. *CC* No.1053899. Began 1990; interdenominational. Magazine: *Newsletter* (Circulation n/a half-yearly). Turnover £8,000 to year end Dec 96. Furthering ecumenical co-operation within Cornwall.
☎ 01872 273 154

Churches Together in Cumbria, Chapel Cottage, Hawkshead Hill, Ambleside LA22 0PW
County Ecumenical Officer: Rev Andrew Dodd. Executive staff 1. Began 1984; interdenominational. Magazine: *Cumbria Ecumenical News* (1,200 monthly). Turnover n/a. Promoting and enabling ecumencial work and witness county-wide. Social Responsibility forum.
☎ 01539 436 451

Churches Together in Derbyshire, 64 Wyndale Drive, Ilkeston DE7 4JG
Secretary: Mr Colin Garley. No full-time staff. Began 1985; interdenominational. No magazine. Turnover £800 to year end Dec 94. Furthering ecumenical co-operation within Derbyshire.
☎ 01246 413 528

Churches Together in Dorset, 22 D'Urberville Close, Dorchester DT1 2JT
County Ecumenical Officer: Mrs Val Potter. No full-time staff. Began 1990; interdenominational. Magazine: *Pilgrim Post in Dorset* (700 every four months). Turnover £10,000 to year end Dec 98. Initiating and supporting ecumenical relationships among the churches of Dorset, Poole and Bournemouth.
Web: home.clara.net/ctdorset
Email: ctdorset@clara.net
☎ 01305 264 416

Churches Together in England, 101 Queen Victoria Street, London EC4V 4EN
General Secretary: Rev Bill Snelson. *Executive Officer:* Mrs Judith Lampard. *Field Officer for the South:* Rev Roger Nunn Executive staff 5, Other staff 5. *CC* No.1005368. Began 1990; interdenominational. Magazine: *Pilgrim Post* (2,300 every two months). Turnover £906,936 to year end Dec 98. Official body enabling its 23 member churches to work together for Christian unity.
Email: <any name>@cte.org.uk
☎ 020 7332 8230 🖷 020 7332 8234
Field Officer for the North and Midlands Mrs Jenny Carpenter, Crookes Valley Methodist Church, Crookesmoor Road, Sheffield S6 3FQ
☎ 0114 268 2151 🖷 0114 266 8731

Churches Together in Gloucestershire, 3 College Green, Gloucester GL1 2LR
County Ecumenical Officer: Rev Dr David Calvert. Executive staff 1. Began 1985; interdenominational. Magazine: *Together* (Circulation n/a monthly). Turnover n/a. Fostering ecumenical relationships in the county, and links with national ecumenism.
☎ 01452 301 347

Churches Together in Greater Manchester, St Peter's House, Oxford Road, Manchester M13 9GH
County Ecumenical Officer: Sister Maureen Farrell FCJ. Executive staff 1. CC Began 1973; interdenominational. Magazine: *Together* (2,000 every four months). Turnover £34,000 to year end Apr 96. Co-ordinating the churches' service and witness within Greater Manchester.
☎ 0161 273 5508 🖷 0161 272 7172

Churches Together in Hampshire and the Isle of Wight, 71 Andover Road, Winchester SO22 6AU
Counties Ecumenical Officer: Dr Paul Rolph. Part-time staff 2. Began 1987; interdenominational. Magazine: *Newsletter* (1,400 quarterly). Turnover n/a. Forum for ecumenical matters in Hampshire and the Isle of Wight.
Email: cthi@rolph.freeuk.com
☎ 01962 849 623 🖷 01962 849 623

Churches Together in Herefordshire, Malvern View, Garway Hill, Hereford HR2 8EZ
County Ecumenical Officer: Mrs Anne Double. No full-time staff. Began n/a; interdenominational. (Previously Herefordshire Ecumenical Sponsoring Body). Magazine: *Newsletter* (Circulation n/a quarterly). Turnover £5,000 to year end Dec 99. Promoting ecumenism within the county.
☎ 01981 580 495 🖷 01981 580 495

Churches Together in Hertfordshire, High Street Methodist Church, Sish Lane, Stevenage SG1 3LS
Secretary: Rev David Butler. No full-time staff. CC No.267783. Began 1967; interdenominational. Magazine: Together (600 every four months). Turnover £7,600 to year end Dec 96. Promoting Christian unity and joint action of the churches in Hertfordshire.
☎ 01438 358 448

Churches Together in Hertfordshire and Bedfordshire, High Street Methodist Church, Sish Lane, Stevenage SG1 3LS
Secretary: Rev David Butler. No full-time staff. CC No.267783. Began 1967; interdenominational. Magazine: *Together* (1,200 every four months). Turnover £3,800 to year end Dec 96. Promoting Christian unity and joint action of the churches in Hertfordshire and Bedfordshire.
☎ 01438 358 448

Churches Together in Jersey, The URC Manse, Sion, St John, Jersey JE3 4FL
President: Rev Fred Noden. No full-time staff. Began n/a; ecumenical. No magazine. Turnover n/a. Furthering ecumenical co-operation in Jersey.
☎ 01534 861 386

Churches Together in Kent, St Lawrence Vicarage, Stone Street, Seal, Sevenoaks TN15 0LQ
County Ecumenical Officer: Rev Michael Cooke. No full-time staff. Began 1984; interdenominational. Magazine: *Together* (150 quarterly), *Directory of ecumenical contacts in Kent* (Circulation & frequency n/a). Turnover £11,400 to year end Dec 98. Encouraging and promoting ecumenism throughout the county and providing forum for church leaders.
Email: ctkent@centrenet.co.uk
☎ 01732 761 766 🖷 01732 761 766

Churches Together in Lancashire, 45 Alder Drive, Hogton, Preston PR5 0AE
Ecumenical Officer: Rev Donald A Parsons. No full-time staff. Began n/a; ecumenical. No magazine. Turnover n/a. Furthering ecumenical co-operation in Lancashire.
☎ 01245 852 860

Churches Together in Leicestershire, The Rectory, Honeypot Lane, Husbands Bosworth, Lutterworth LE17 6LY
Acting County Ecumenical Officer: Rev Barbara Stanton. No full-time staff. Began 1980; interdenominational. Magazine: *Newsletter* (Circulation n/a every four months). Turnover £12,629 to year end Dec 98. Forum for church leaders and representatives; ecumenical discussion and decision-making.
☎ 01858 880 351 🖷 0116 253 2889

Churches Together in all Lincolnshire, c/o YMCA, St Rumbold Street, Lincoln LN2 5AR
Ecumenical Development Officer: Rev John G Cole. No full-time staff. Began n/a; interdenominational. No magazine. Turnover n/a. Promoting the growth of mission and unity among churches through local and county ecumenical projects.
Web: www.ctal.org.uk
Email: ctal@surfaid.org
☎ 01522 520 984

Churches Together in Man, The Manse, 11 Bayr Grianagh, Castletown IM9 1HN
Secretary: Rev Stephen F Caddy. Staff n/a. Began n/a; interdenominational. No magazine. Turnover n/a. Local ecumenical body.
Email: caddy@advsys.co.uk
☎ 01624 822 541

Churches Together in North London, 1 Ellesmere Avenue, Mill Hill, London NW7 3EX
Chairman: Rev Dr Philip Morgan. No full-time staff. Began 1993; interdenominational. No magazine. Turnover n/a. Forum for churches of all denominations in the Boroughs of Barnet, Camden, Enfield and Haringey.
☎ 020 8959 7246

Churches Together in North West London, 185 Boston Road, London W7 2HR
Chairman: Mr Keith Browne. No full-time staff. Began 1990; interdenominational. Magazine: *Newsletter* (Circulation & frequency n/a). Turnover £1,500 to year end Dec 98. Sponsoring ecumenical resources for churches in London Boroughs of Brent, Ealing, Harrow and Hillingdon.
☎ 020 8579 5893 🖷 020 8566 0590
Ecumenical Officer: Mr Bill Boyd, 20 Rednor Avenue, Harrow HA1 1SB
☎ 020 8427 3418 🖷 020 8427 3418

Churches Together in Northamptonshire, 4 The Slade, Daventry NN11 4HH
Secretary: Mrs Christine Nelson. No full-time staff. Began n/a; ecumenical. No magazine. Turnover n/a. Furthering ecumenical co-operation within Northamptonshire.
☎ 01327 705 803

Churches Together in the North York Moors, The Vicarage, Glaisdale, Whitby YO21 2PL
Hon Secretary: Mrs Rachel Harrison. No full-time staff. Began n/a; ecumenical. No magazine. Turnover n/a. Furthering ecumenical co-operation in north east Yorkshire.
☎ 01947 897 214

Churches Together in Nottinghamshire, 35 Aylesham Avenue, Woodthorpe View, Arnold, Nottingham NG5 6PP
Secretary: Mr Alan Langton. No full-time staff. Began 1984; interdenominational. No magazine. Turnover n/a. Intermediate body between Churches Together in England and local ecumenical groups.
☎ 0115 926 9090

Churches Together in Oxfordshire, Westminster College, North Hinksey, Oxford OX2 9AT
Executive Secretary: Rev Graeme Smith. No full-time staff. Began 1986; interdenominational. (Previously Oxfordshire Ecumenical Council). Magazine: *Newssheet* (Circulation n/a every two months). Turnover n/a. Pastoral oversight of local ecumenical projects in Oxfordshire and advancement of ecumenical matters generally.
Email: g.smith@ox-west.ac.uk
☎ 01865 253 557 🖷 01865 253 417

Churches Together in Shropshire, Fern Villa, Four Crosses, Llanymynech SY22 6PR
Ecumenical Secretary: Mr Ged Cliffe. No full-time staff. Began n/a; ecumenical. Turnover n/a. Furthering ecumenical co-operation in Shropshire (except Telford).
☎ 01691 831 374

Churches Together in South London, Sisters of St Andrew, St Peter's House, 308 Kennington Lane, London SE11 5HY
Ecumenical Officer: Sister Liz Grant. No full-time staff. Began n/a; ecumenical. No magazine. Turnover n/a. Furthering ecumenical co-operation in the London Boroughs of Croydon, Greenwich, Kingston, Lambeth, Lewisham, Richmond (south), Southwark, Sutton, Wandsworth.
☎ 020 7587 0087

Churches Together in South Yorkshire, Crookes Valley Methodist Church, Crookesmoor Road, Sheffield S6 3FQ
Ecumenical Development Officer: Rev Louise Dawson. Executive staff 2. Began 1991; interdenominational. Magazine: *Update Newsletter* (700 quarterly). Turnover n/a. Encouraging and promoting local unity; sponsoring and overseeing local ecumenical partnerships in South Yorkshire.
☎ 0114 266 6156 🖷 0114 266 8731

Churches Together in Surrey, The Parish Centre, Station Approach, Stoneleigh, Epsom KT19 0QZ
Co-ordinator: Ms Rosemary Underwood. No full-time staff. Began 1976; interdenominational. Magazine: *Together* (2,000 every four months). Turnover £10,000–50,000 to year end Dec 98. Co-ordinating and enabling ecumenical activities throughout Surrey.
Email: ctsurrey@msn.com
☎ 020 8394 0536

Churches Together in Sussex, 14 Ledgers Meadow, Cuckfield RH17 5EB
Ecumenical Officer: Rev Terry Stratford. Part-time staff 1. Began 1980; interdenominational. (Previously Sussex Sponsoring Body). Magazine: *Together* (3,000 every four months). Turnover £9,300 to year end Dec 98. Co-ordinating ecumenical activity in Sussex.
☎ 01444 456 588

Churches Together in Swindon, 16 Sherwood Avenue, Melksham SN12 7HJ
Secretary: Anne Doyle. No full-time staff. Began n/a; ecumenical. No magazine. Turnover n/a. Furthering ecumenical co-operation in Swindon and surrounding areas.
☎ 01225 704 748

Churchlink West London, 30 Glencairn Drive, Ealing, London W5 1RT
Convenor: Mr Tom Flynn. No full-time staff. Began n/a; ecumenical. No magazine. Turnover n/a. Furthering ecumenical co-operation in the London Boroughs of Chelsea, Fulham, Hammersmith, Hampton, Hounslow, Kensington, Richmond (north), Spelthorne.
☎ 020 8248 9947

Council of African and Afro-Caribbean Churches UK, 31 Norton House, Sidney Road, London SW9 0UJ
Chairman: His Grace the Most Rev Father Olu A Abiola. No full-time staff. Began 1979; Pentecostal. No magazine. Turnover under £10,000 to year end Dec 98. Fostering mutual understanding and co-operation between member churches to make possible common witness and evangelism.
☎ 020 7274 5589

Coventry and Warwickshire Ecumenical Council, Horeston Grange Church Centre, Camborne Drive, Nuneaton CV11 6GU
Ecumenical Officer: David Rowland. No full-time staff. CC No.1060171. Began 1987; interdenominational. Magazine: *Newsletter* (800 every four months). Turnover £8,500 to year end Dec 97. Ecumenical forum for Coventry and Warwickshire.
☎ 024 7635 2551

CYTUN: Churches Together in Wales, 11 St Helen's Road, Swansea SA1 4AL
General Secretary: Rev Gethin Abraham-Williams. Executive staff 1, Other staff 4. CC No.246209. Began 1956; interdenominational. Magazine: CYTÛN News/Newyddion CYTÛN (4,500 every four months). Turnover £75,000 to year end Dec 96. Enabling partnership of the Churches in Wales at national and local level.
Web: www.cytun.freeserve.co.uk/
Email: gethin@cytun.freeserve.co.uk
☎ 01792 460 876 🖷 01792 469 391

Durham Church Relations Group, St Michael's Vicarage, Westoe Road, South Shields NE33 3PJ
Secretary: Rev Canon John Hancock. No full-time staff. Began 1986; interdenominational. No magazine. Turnover £3,000 to year end Dec 95. Encouraging ecumenical initiatives in the county.
☎ 01814 252 074

DWEC – Dudley & Worcestershire Ecumenical Council, The Rectory, Clifton-on-Teme, Worcester WR6 6DJ
Secretary: Rev Clifford Owen. No full-time staff. Began 1975; interdenominational. No magazine. Turnover £500 to year end Dec 96. Co-ordinating the churches' work and witness in the county of Worcestershire including Dudley.
☎ 01886 812 483

East London Church Leaders' Group, The Manse, Approach Road, Bethnal Green, London E2 9JP
Secretary: Rev Pauline Barnett. No full-time staff. Began n/a; ecumenical. No magazine. Turnover n/a. Furthering ecumenical co-operation in the London Boroughs of Hackney, Islington, Tower Hamlets.
☎ 020 8980 5278

ENFYS (Covenanted Churches in Wales), Church in Wales Centre, Woodland Place, Penarth CF64 2EX
General Secretary: To be appointed. Executive staff 1. CC No.506315. Began 1975; interdenominational. Magazine: *ENFYS Newsletter* (2,000 half-yearly). Turnover £26,000 to year end Dec 97. Being brought by the Spirit into one visible church to serve together in mission.
Email: 106074.133@compuserve.com
☎ 029 2070 5278 🖷 029 2071 2413

ENVOY (Ecumenical Network in the Vale of York), The Manor, Moss End Farm, Hawkhills, Easingwold, York YO6 3EW
Secretary: Mrs Jean Abbey. No full-time staff. Began n/a; ecumenical. No magazine. Turnover n/a. Furthering ecumenical co-operation in York and surrounding areas.
☎ 01347 838 593

Essex Churches Consultative Council, 349 Westbourne Grove, Westcliff-on-Sea SS0 0PU
Secretary: Rev D C Hardiman. No full-time staff. Began 1978; interdenominational. Magazine: *Newsletter* (1,500 every two months). Turnover n/a. Sponsoring and overseeing local ecumenical partnerships, specialist ecumenical ministries and work of Churches Together.
☎ 01702 342 327/316 305

C

The Evangelical Movement of Wales, Bryntirion, Bridgend CF31 4DX
Chief Executive: Mr G Wyn Davies. Executive staff 1, Other staff 6. CC No.222407. Began 1948; non-denominational. Magazine: Y Cylchgrawn Efengylaidd (1,000 quarterly), The Evangelical Magazine of Wales (2,000 every two months). Turnover n/a. Pursuing fellowship, evangelical unity, services of mutual benefit at church level and evangelism.
Email: press@draco.co.uk
☎ 01656 655 886 Fax 01656 656 095

Free Churches' Council, 27 Tavistock Square, London WC1H 9HH
General Secretary: Rev Geoffrey H Roper. Moderator: Rev Anthony Burnham. Executive staff 5, Other staff 5. *CC* No.236878. Began 1896; interdenominational. (Previously Free Church Federal Council). Magazine: *Free Church Chronicle* (12,000 every four months). Turnover £360,000 to year end Mar 98. Representation/co-ordination of the activities of the Free Church denominations in chaplaincy, education and ecumenical affairs.
☎ 020 7387 8413 Fax 020 7383 0150

Greater Peterborough Ecumenical Council, 61 Hall Lane, Werrington, Peterborough PE4 6RA
Secretary: Mr Frank Smith. No full-time staff. Began n/a; ecumenical. No magazine. Turnover n/a. Furthering ecumenical co-operation in Peterborough and area.
☎ 02733 321 245 / 519 15

Guernsey Council of Churches, Les Adams de Haut, St Pierre du Bois, Guernsey GY7 9LJ
Secretary: Gillian Lenfestey. No full-time staff. Began n/a; ecumenical. No magazine. Turnover n/a. Furthering ecumenical co-operation in Guernsey.
☎ No telephone

International Ministerial Council of Great Britain, 55 Tudor Walk, Watford WD2 4NY
General Secretary: Rev S M Douglas. All voluntary staff. *CC* No.269440. Began 1968; interdenominational. Magazine: *Newsletter* (Circulation n/a every four months). Turnover n/a. Ecumenical body for Christian unity in the broader aspect of Christian life without party politics.
☎ 01923 239 266

Irish Council of Churches, Inter-Church Centre, 48 Elmwood Avenue, Belfast BT9 6AZ
General Secretary: Dr David Stevens. Executive staff 1, Other staff 1. *CC* Began 1922; interdenominational. Magazine: *Irish Ecumenical News* (Circulation & frequency n/a). Turnover £79,200 to year end Dec 96. Partnership of the main Protestant churches, working in co-operation with the Roman Catholic Church.
Web: www.unite.co.uk/customers/icpep
Email: icpep@unite.co.uk
☎ 028 9066 3145 Fax 028 9038 1737

Joint Council for Anglo-Caribbean Churches, 141 Railton Road, London SE24 0LT
General Secretary: Rev Esme Beswick. Part-time staff 2. *CC* Began 1985; interdenominational. No magazine. Turnover £21,000 to year end Aug 98. Offering advice and consultancy services to member churches on administrative and social issues.
☎ 020 7737 6542

***Kent for Christ,** 37 Swalecliffe Road, Whitstable CT5 2PT
Director: Mr Tom G Poulson. No other staff. CC No.1055050. Began 1990; non-denominational. Magazine: *The Unity of the Local Church* (Circulation & frequency n/a). Turnover n/a. Encouraging the unity and witness of the local church.
☎ 01227 275 149

KEY Churches Together, The Vicarage, Skirlaugh, Hull HU11 5HE
Ecumenical Officer: Rev David W Perry. No full-time staff. Began 1981; interdenominational. (Previously Humberside Churches Council). Magazine: *Newsletter* (1,300 quarterly). Turnover £7,500 to year end Dec 98. Covering all churches in Kingston upon Hull, East Yorkshire and Scarborough/Filey area; encouraging ecumenical development.
Email: david.perry3@email.msn.com
☎ 01964 562 259 Fax 01964 563 383

The Merseyside and Region Churches Ecumenical Assembly, Friends' Meeting House, 65 Paradise Street, Liverpool L1 3BP
Ecumenical Officer: Rev Martyn Newman. Executive staff 1. CC No.519061. Began 1974; ecumenical. Magazine: Merseyside Ecumenical News (1,500 every two months). Turnover £36,000 to year end Dec 98. Enabling the churches to work together both regionally and locally.
Email: marcea@surfaid.org
☎ 0151 709 0125

Milton Keynes Christian Council, Christian Foundation, The Square, Aylesbury Street, Wolverton MK12 5HX
Ecumenical Moderator: Rev Murdoch Mackenzie. Executive staff 5, Other staff 1. CC No.293729. Began 1967; interdenominational. No magazine. Turnover £100,000 to year end Dec 98. An ecumenical body facilitating the working together of Milton Keynes' one hundred churches.
☎ 01908 311 310 Fax 01908 311 310

National Free Church Women's Council, 27 Tavistock Square, London WC1H 9HH
Secretary: Miss Pauline Butcher. Executive staff 1. *CC* No.207241. Began 1907; interdenominational. Magazine: *Free Church Chronicle* (Circulation n/a half-yearly). Turnover £4,500. Voluntary work with women, girls and the elderly; promoting social concern amongst Free Church women.
☎ 020 7387 8413 Fax 020 7383 0150

National Service Committee for Catholic Charismatic Renewal, Allen Hall, 28 Beaufort Street, London SW3 5AA
Chairman: Mr Charles Whitehead. Other staff 2. CC Began 1979; Roman Catholic. Magazine: Good News (3,500 every two months). Turnover n/a. Promoting charismatic renewal, Alpha courses in Catholic Church, prayer groups; handling enquiries; networking..
☎ 020 7352 5298 Fax 020 7351 4486
Also at: PO Box 333, St Albans AL2 1EL
☎ 01727 822 837 Fax 01727 822 837

Newcastle Church Relations Group, Pinehurst, 140 Wansbeck Road, Ashington NE63 8JE
Secretary & Treasurer: Rev Gordon Shaw. No full-time staff. Began 1965; interdenominational. No magazine. Turnover £1,400 to year end Dec 97. Sponsoring body for local ecumenical projects; co-ordination between denominations.
Email: gordon@pinehurst.demon.co.uk
☎ 01670 812 137

Norfolk Churches Together, Marsham Rectory, Norwich NR10 5PP
Executive Officer: Rev Robin Hewetson. No full-time staff. Began 1990; interdenominational. No magazine. Turnover n/a. Sponsoring body for local ecumenical partnerships to encourage churches to work together.
☎ 01263 733 249 🖷 01263 733 799

***North East Churches Association,** Hillcroft House, Sourmilk Hill Lane, Low Fell, Gateshead NE9 5RU
Chairman: Rev Brian Howell. No full-time staff. Began 1985; interdenominational. No magazine. Turnover n/a. Catalyst for churches to work together on joint projects, for mutual support and relationships.
Email: nbh2@popin.ncl.ac.uk
☎ 0191 482 3158 🖷 0191 482 3158

Somerset Churches Together, 12 Lawson Close, Saltford, Bristol BS18 3LB
Ecumenical Officer: Mr Robin Dixon. No full-time staff. Began 1983; interdenominational. (Previously Somerset and South Avon Ecumenical Council). Magazine: *Churches Together in Somerset* (1,200 quarterly). Turnover £14,000 to year end Jan 98. Encouraging and initiating ecumenical work.
☎ 01225 872 903

South Devon District of the Congregational Federation, 85 Bowden Park Road, Crownhill, Plymouth PL6 5NQ
Secretary: Mrs Greta M White. No full-time staff. *CC* No.268559. Began 1974; Congregational Federation. Magazine: *Newsletter* (30 occasionally). Turnover n/a. Mutual support group for eight congregational churches organising rallies, meetings.
☎ 01752 708 903

Staffordshire Plus Ecumenical Council, 18 Selman's Hill, Bloxwich, Walsall WS3 3RJ
Secretary: Mr Michael Topliss. No full-time staff. Began 1993; interdenominational. Magazine: *Newsletter* (1,600 every two months). Turnover n/a. Facilitating shared mission, prayer, social concern and local ecumenism; twice- yearly forum and church leaders' meeting.
☎ 01922 475 932

Suffolk Churches Together, 44 Thorney Road, Capel St Mary, Ipswich IP9 2LH
Ecumenical Officer: Rev Canon Colin Bevington. No full-time staff. Began 1970; interdenominational. No magazine. Turnover n/a. Sponsoring body for local ecumenical partnerships encouraging a deeper commitment between member churches.
Email: bevington@capel19.freeserve.com
☎ 01473 310 069 🖷 01473 310 450

Telford Christian Council, Parkfield, Park Avenue, Madeley, Telford TF7 5AB
Churches' Development Officer: Rev David Lavender. *Director of Community and Housing Projects:* Mr Alan Oliver. *Head of Personnel and Administration:* Ms June Trawter. Executive staff 13, Other staff 37. *CC* No.510321. Began 1972; interdenominational. Magazine: *Network* (Circulation n/a periodically). Turnover £700,000 to year end Dec 97. Ecumenical council for Telford, sponsoring sector ministries, local ecumenical partnerships, bookshop, community and housing projects.
Email: txc@lavenders.demon.co.uk
☎ 01952 585 731 🖷 01952 401 932

West Midlands Region Churches Forum, Carrs Lane Church Centre, Birmingham B4 7SX
General Secretary: Rev Mark Fisher. Staff n/a. Began n/a; interdenominational. No magazine. Turnover n/a. Co-ordinating body for Birmingham, Herefordshire, Shropshire, Staffordshire, Warwickshire and Worcestershire.
☎ 0121 643 6603 🖷 0121 632 5320

West Yorkshire Ecumenical Council and Sponsoring Body, Leeds Diocesan Pastoral Centre, 62 Headingley Lane, Leeds LS6 2BX
County Ecumenical Officer: Dr. Stephanie Rybak. Executive staff 1. Began 1986; interdenominational. Magazine: *Unity News* (2,000 annually), Unity Post (30,000 annually). Turnover £40,000 to year end Dec 98. Developing ecumenical witness, action and understanding; overseeing local ecumenical partnerships.
Email: stephanierybak@compuserve.com
☎ 0113 274 7912 🖷 0113 224 9998

C

Wiltshire Churches Together, 16 Sherwood Avenue, Melksham SN12 7HJ
County Ecumenical Officer: Miss Anne Doyle. No full-time staff. Began 1987; interdenominational. Magazine: Newsletter (550 quarterly). Turnover £14,000 to year end Aug 98. Oversight, care and support of local ecumenical projects and other ecumenical activities.
Email: ann.doyle@btinternet.com
☎ 01225 704 748

Women's Co-ordinating Group for Churches Together in England, c/o NFCWC, 27 Tavistock Square, London WC1H 9HH
Secretary: Miss Pauline Butcher. Moderator: Mrs Felicity Cleaves. Staff n/a. Began n/a; ecumenical. (Previously Women's Inter-Church Consultative Committee). No magazine. Turnover n/a. Sharing information.
☎ 020 7387 8413 🖷 020 7383 0150

EVANGELICAL FELLOWSHIPS (INTER-CHURCH)

****Alliance of Asian Christians**, Carrs Lane Church Centre, Carrs Lane, Birmingham B4 7SX
Executive Secretary: Mr Pradip Sudra. Executive staff 1, Other staff 3. *CC* No.1020767. Began 1989; non-denominational. In partnership with Evangelical Alliance. Magazine: *Aaeki Haae* (2,000 half-yearly). Turnover £75,000 to year end Jun 96. Support and representative organisation for Asian individuals and churches.
☎ 0121 633 4533 🖷 01902 620 811

Associating Evangelical Churches in Wales, Bryntirion House, Bridgend CF31 4DX
Secretary: Rev Peter Milsom. No full-time staff. Began 1988, interdenominational. Magazine: *Contact* (2,000 half-yearly). Turnover n/a.
Email: petermilsom@compuserve.com
☎ 01656 655 886 🖷 01656 656 095

***Bath Evangelical Fellowship**, 24 Primrose Hill, Weston, Bath BA1 2UT
Hon Secretary: Mr H Gordon Smith. No full-time staff. Began n/a; interdenominational. No magazine. Turnover n/a. Co-ordinating evangelical fellowship and work in the Bath area.
☎ 01225 429 845

***Breakthrough**, PO Box 25, Scarborough YO11 1JF
Leader: Rev David Nellist. No full-time staff. *CC* No.1052790. Began 1996; interdenominational. No magazine. Turnover n/a. Inter-church initiative encouraging leaders and churches to pray and work together for revival.
☎ 01723 378 045 Mobile: 07831 648 885
🖷 01723 503 012

†*Brent Evangelical Fellowship, PO Box 326, Wembley HA9 6HL
Chairman: Mr Henderson Springer. No full-time staff. Began n/a; interdenominational. No magazine. Turnover n/a. Co-ordinating evangelical fellowship and work in the Brent area.
☎ 020 8903 9553

***Brentwood and District Evangelical Fellowship (BADEF)**, 2nd Floor, 39 High Street, Brentwood CM14 4RH
Hon Secretary: Mrs C Hurn. No full-time staff. Began n/a; interdenominational. No magazine. Turnover n/a. Promoting fellowship between Evangelical Alliance churches in the area and coordinating joint projects.
Email: kingschurch@compuserve.com
☎ 01277 202 722

***Brighton and Hove Evangelical Fellowship**, 39 Elizabeth Avenue, Hove BN3 6WA
Chairman: Rhys Stenner. No full-time staff. Began n/a; interdenominational. No magazine. Turnover n/a. Co-ordinating evangelical fellowship and work in the Brighton area.
☎ 01273 732 111

***Bristol Evangelical Alliance**, South Bristol Centre, Churchlands Road, Bristol BS3 3PW
Secretary: Mr Les Potter. No full-time staff. Began 1965; interdenominational. No magazine. Turnover n/a. A visible and practical expression of unity God has given in Christ to Christians of all denominations.
☎ 0117 963 6329

***Bromley Evangelical Fellowship**, 49 Blackbrook Lane, Bromley BR2 8AU
Chairman: Mr James Holl. No full-time staff. *CC* Began 1970; interdenominational. No magazine. Turnover £750 to year end Dec 98. Acting as a channel for united Christian fellowship and outreach in Bromley.
☎ 020 8467 0635

***Cities Network Scotland**, Ardcraig, Bankhead Grove, Dalmeny, South Queensferry EH30 9JZ
Trustees: Mr Douglas Flett, Mr Jim Woodrow. No other staff. Began n/a; interdenominational. Magazine: *Cities Network* (Circulation & frequency n/a). Turnover n/a. Bringing together networkers from Scottish cities; providing conference events and information on the city challenge.
Email: dgj.flett@uk.iccc.net
☎ 0131 331 3310 🖷 0131 331 3310

***Criss Cross**, 291 Abbeydale Road, Sheffield S7 1FJ
Trustees: Mrs Ann Collins, Mrs D Gilbert. No full-time staff. *CC* No.1042130. Began 1994; interdenominational. Magazine: *Cross Word* (500 quarterly). Turnover n/a. Providing information, encouraging and promoting evangelical life in the City of Sheffield and surrounding area.
Email: anncollins@compuserve.com
☎ 0114 249 3956

***Eastbourne Evangelical Alliance**, Inwood, Lismore Road, Eastbourne BN21 3AX
Chairman: Rev Eddie Purse. No full-time staff. Began 1986; interdenominational. No magazine. Turnover n/a. Providing a fellowship for evangelical Christians in Eastbourne to jointly promote God's Kingdom.
☎ 01323 411 214

†Essex Protestant Council, 363 Baddow Road, Chelmsford CM2 7QF
Hon Secretary: Mr Stephen Evans. No full-time staff. Began 1982; non-denominational. No magazine. Turnover n/a. Raising a testimony on Protestant issues through correspondence, publicity, open-air and other public meetings.
☎ No telephone

***Guernsey Evangelical Alliance**, Feugre Villa, Cobo, Guernsey GY5 7TU
Secretary: Mr Jonathan Le Tocq. No full-time staff. Began 1965; interdenominational. No magazine. Turnover n/a. Deepening spiritual life of Christians in Guernsey and reaching others with the Christian gospel.
☎ 01481 528 10 Mobile: 07741 152 810

Havering Mission 2000, 108 Woodman Road, Warley, Brentwood CM14 5AZ
Chairman: Rev G Seithel. Executive staff 1. *CC* No.1051811. Began 1989; interdenominational. Turnover £1,080 to year end Mar 98. Building relationships between church leaders / member churches to encourage evangelism in London Borough of Havering.
Email: gbseithel@compuserve.com
☎ 01277 211 480 🖷 01277 211 480

***Hull Evangelical Alliance**, 17 Dene Close, Dunswell, Hull HU6 0AD
Hon Secretary: Mr M G Morfin. No full-time staff. *CC* No.212325. Began n/a; interdenominational. Magazine: *News Sheet* (Circulation n/a quarterly). Turnover n/a. Co-ordinating evangelical work and witness in Hull and district.
☎ 01482 802 186

***Inverness & District Evangelical Alliance**, 19 Bellfield Road, North Kessock, Inverness IV1 3XU
Secretary: Mr Colin Wilson. No other full-time staff. *CC* No.SCO 20725. Began 1992; interdenominational. Council of evangelical churches.
Email: colin_wilson@compuserve.com
☎ 01463 731 524 🖷 01463 731 524

***Ipswich Evangelical Fellowship**, Langdale, 22 Cuckfield Avenue, Ipswich IP3 8SA
Hon Secretary: Mr P Mills. No full-time staff. Began 1995; interdenominational. No magazine. Turnover n/a. Co-ordinating evangelical fellowship and work in the Ipswich area.
☎ 01473 710 994

***King's Lynn Evangelical Alliance Fellowship**, 11 Gloucester Road, Gaywood, King's Lynn PE30 4AB
Hon Secretary: Mr Mike Brown. No full-time staff. Began n/a; interdenominational. No magazine. Turnover n/a. Co-ordinating evangelical fellowship and work in the King's Lynn area.
☎ 01553 772 036

***Leyton Evangelical Fellowship**, 158 Twickenham Road, Leytonstone, London E11 4BH
Hon Secretary: Mr Ian Perry. No full-time staff. Began n/a; interdenominational. No magazine. Turnover n/a. Co-ordinating evangelical fellowship and work in the Leyton area of east London.
☎ 020 8926 1407

Manchester Network Evangelical Fellowship, Nazarene Theological College, Dene Road, Didsbury, Manchester M20 0GU
Chairman: Mr Geoff Lomas. Part-time staff 2. *CC* No.504453. Began n/a; interdenominational. (Previously ECMA). Magazine: *Network News* (Circulation n/a quarterly), *Network Diary (Events listing)* (Circulation n/a quarterly). Turnover £100,000 for year end Dec 98. A local evangelical fellowship of the Evangelical Alliance encouraging evangelical co-operation in the Manchester area.
Web: www.users.zetnet.co.uk/urbanpresence/network.html
Email: network@domini.org
☎ 0161 445 5738 Mobile: 07778 763 764 (Debra Green)

Mid-Cotswolds Evangelical Alliance (MCEA), 24 St George's Place, Cheltenham GL50 3JZ
Hon Secretary: Mr Wesley Boxall. *Hon Chairman:* Rev Bill O'Leary. No full-time staff. Began n/a; interdenominational. No magazine. Turnover n/a. Co-ordinating evangelical fellowship and work in the mid-Cotswold area.
☎ 01242 241 461

***Orpington & District Evangelistic Council**, 9 Dale Wood Road, Orpington BR6 0BY
Secretary: Mr Nelson D A Pallister. No full-time staff. Began 1956; interdenominational. No magazine. Turnover £1,000 to year end Dec 96. Organising evangelistic events and conventions for deepening the spiritual life among Christians in Orpington.
☎ 01689 822 495

***Paisley & District Evangelical Alliance**, 20 Gordon Street, Paisley PA1 1XD
Chairman: Mr Maurice Howson. Executive staff 1. Began 1992; interdenominational. Magazine: *Grapevine* (110 every two months). Turnover £2,000 to year end Oct 98. Co-ordinating evangelical fellowship and work in Renfrewshire.
Email: pdea@pdea.freeserve.co.uk
☎ 0141 561 0118

***The Penge and Beckenham Evangelical Fellowship**, The Vicarage, 234 Anerley Road, London SE20 8TJ
Hon Chairman: Rev M Porter. No full-time staff. Began n/a; interdenominational. No magazine. Turnover n/a. Co-ordinating evangelical fellowship and work in the Penge area.
☎ 020 8778 4800

***Peterborough Alliance of Christian Evangelicals**, 64 Hazel Croft, Werrington, Peterborough PE4 5BL
Chairman: Major John Smith. *Secretary:* Mr Peter Batiste. No full-time staff. Began 1983; interdenominational. Also Peterborough Evangelical Fellowship. No magazine. Turnover n/a. Information sharing, support group and teaching for evangelical church leaders in Peterborough and local region.
Email: pjb222@freeuk.com
☎ 01733 572 920 🖷 01733 576 541

***Portsmouth Evangelical Fellowship**, 4 Waterlock Gardens, Milton, Portsmouth PO4 8LJ
Hon Secretary: Mr Philip West. No full-time staff. Began n/a; interdenominational. No magazine. Turnover n/a. Co-ordinating evangelical fellowship and work in the Portsmouth area.
☎ 023 9273 5843

†***South East Essex Evangelical Fellowship (SEELEF)**, 29 Elizabeth Close, Hawkwell, Hockley SS5 4NQ
Hon Chairman: Rev S Kimber. No full-time staff. Began n/a; interdenominational. No magazine. Turnover n/a. Co-ordinating evangelical fellowship and work in the South East Essex area.
☎ 01702 205 939

***South Wessex Evangelical Alliance**, Delta House, 56 Westover Road, Bournemouth BH1 2BS
Chairman: Rev Mike Stear. No full-time staff. Began 1988; interdenominational. No magazine. Turnover £3,000 to year end Dec 98. Local evangelical fellowship.
☎ 01202 315 133

***Southampton Evangelical Alliance**, c/o Southampton City Mission, PO Box 649, Southampton SO15 5YB
Vice Chairman: Chris Davis. *Secretary:* Lynne Lockwood. No full-time staff. Began 1987; interdenominational. No magazine. Turnover n/a. Alliance of evangelical church leaders in the Southampton area.
☎ 023 8077 3132

***Swindon Evangelical Alliance**, 64 Griffiths Close, Swindon SN3 4NP
Hon Secretary: Mr Steve Lumb. No full-time staff. Began 1988; interdenominational. (Previously Thamesdown Evangelical Alliance). No magazine. Turnover n/a. Planning and co-ordinating inter-church evangelistic and training events within the Greater Swindon area.
☎ 01793 824 128

***Taunton Evangelical Alliance**, 12 Ashley Road, Taunton TA1 5BP
Chairman (from Feb 2000): Rev Vince Carrington. *Chairman (to Feb 2000):* Rev David Goodyear. No full-time staff. Began 1987; interdenominational. No magazine. Turnover n/a. Co-ordinating evangelical fellowship and work in the Taunton Deane area.
☎ 01823 326 400

***Teesside Evangelical Alliance**, St George's House, Spencer Road, Normanby, Redcar TS6 9BH
Administrator: George Rutter. *Chairman:* Rev Alan Leighton. No full-time staff. Began 1992; interdenominational. (Previously Cleveland Evangelical Alliance). Also Teesside Evangelical Fellowship. Magazine: *News sheet* (Circulation n/a every two months). Turnover £1,000 to year end Sept 98. Representing churches, trusts and personal members of the Evangelical Alliance in Teesside.
☎ 01642 281 182 🖷 01642 466 091

***Tiverton & District Evangelical Fellowship**, c/o Sellake Farm, Uplowman, Tiverton EX16 7DJ
Hon Chairman: Mr Mike Britton. No full-time staff. Began 1967; interdenominational. No magazine. Turnover £2,000 to year end Mar 93. Fellowship of local churches; building-up of Christians; evangelistic outreach; united services.
☎ 01884 820 210

***Together For the Harvest**, PO Box 332, Liverpool L69 1XT
Chairman: Mr John Cavanagh. Other staff 2. Began 1990; interdenominational. (Previously Merseyside Evangelical Alliance Trust). Magazine: *Leaders' Bulletin* (225 monthly), *LEF Bulletin* (260 quarterly), *Intercessors Bulletin* (300 half-yearly). Turnover £15,000 to year end Dec 98. Promoting unity and leadership and church relationships for the purpose of communicating the gospel.
Email: 100420.2571@compuserve.com
☎ Mobile: 07711 556 369

***Toxteth Evangelical Association**, 19 Glendale Close, Liverpool L8 9XT
Hon Secretary & Chairman: Rev Terry Jones. No full-time staff. Began 1973; interdenominational. No magazine. Turnover n/a. Co-ordinating and sharing in the work and witness of member churches by united action and prayer.
☎ 0151 728 8507

C

Evangelical Fellowship (Inter-Church)

*__Tunbridge Wells Fellowship of Evangelicals__, 36 Beulah Road, Tunbridge Wells TN1 2NR
Secretary: Not supplied. No paid staff. Began 1997; interdenominational. No magazine. Turnover £500 to year end Dec 98. Drawing evangelicals together for prayer, outreach and evangelism; a voice in the community.
Email: cllyallen@aol.com
☎ 01892 514 050

*__Wanstead & Woodford Evangelical Council__, 2 Gales Way, Woodford Green IG8 8NW
Secretary: Mr Dudley Doig. No full-time staff. Began 1958; interdenominational. No magazine. Turnover n/a. Promoting united events for local fellowship and evangelism.
☎ 020 8501 0062

RELIGIOUS ORDERS (ANGLICAN)

See also Retreat Houses on Page 123.

Alnmouth Friary, Society of St Francis, Alnwick NE66 3NJ
Guest brother: n/a. Members 7. *CC* No.236464. Began n/a; Anglican. No magazine. Turnover n/a. Ministry of hospitality, spiritual direction, other sacramental ministries, retreats by arrangement.
Email: alnmouthfr@aol.com
☎ 01665 830 213

C

Community of St Andrew, St Andrew's House, 2 Tavistock Road, Westbourne Park, London W11 1BA
Mother Superior: n/a. Members 10. *CC* No.244321. Began 1861. No magazine. Turnover n/a. Prayer and evangelism, carried out in parish and specialised ministry.
☎ 020 7229 2662

Community of St Clare, St Mary's Convent, 178 Wroslyn Road, Freeland, Witney OX8 8AJ
Abbess: Sister Paula Fordham. Members 12. Began 1950. No magazine. Turnover n/a. Prayer, printing, producing Communion wafers, guest house (calls about guest house, 6–7pm Mon-Sat).
☎ 01993 881 225 🖷 01993 882 434

Community of St Peter, St Peter's Convent, Maybury Hill, Woking GU22 8AE
Mother Superior: Rev Mother Margaret Paul. *Director of St Columbus' House:* Rev Paul Jenkins. *Chief Executive:* Mrs Fiona Kergoat. Members 14, Other staff 36. *CC* No.240675. Began 1861. No magazine. Turnover £900,000 to year end Dec 98. Religious community, retreats and conferences.
☎ 01483 761 137

Community of the Glorious Ascension, The Priory, Lamacraft Farm, Start Point, Kingsbridge TQ7 2NG
Prior: Brother Simon. Members 9. *CC* Began 1960. No magazine. Turnover n/a. The brothers unite a working life with monastic community life.
☎ 01548 511 474 🖷 01548 511 474

Community of the Holy Cross, Holy Cross Convent, Rempstone Hall, Rempstone, Loughborough LE12 6RG
Mother Superior: Rev Mother Mary Luke Wise. Members 9. *CC* Began 1857. No magazine. Turnover n/a. Benedictine community; producing prayer and greeting cards, and meditation leaflets.
☎ 01509 880 336

Community of the Holy Name, Morley Road, Oakwood, Derby DE21 4QZ
Provincial Superior: Jean Mary Butler. Members 145. *CC* No.250256. Began 1865. No magazine. Turnover n/a. Prayer, worship, pastoral and evangelistic work, retreat giving, counselling.
☎ 01332 671 716

Community of the Sacred Passion, Convent of the Sacred Passion, Lower Road, Effingham, Leatherhead KT24 5JP
Mother Superior: n/a. Members 25. *CC* No.800080. Began 1911. No magazine. Turnover n/a. Prayer and service in the community.
☎ 01372 457 091

Community of the Sisters of the Church, 56 Ham Common, Richmond TW10 7JH
Mother Superior: Sister Anita. Members 26. *CC* No.271790. Began 1870. No magazine. Turnover n/a. Promoting growth and fullness of life of God's people by work, worship, hospitality, education and reconciliation.
☎ 020 8940 8711 🖷 020 8332 2927
Also at: 82 Ashley Road, St Paul's, Bristol BS6 5NT
And: 10 Furness Road, Harrow HA2 0RL

†**Community of the Word of God**, 90 Kenworthy Road, London E9 5RA
Servant: Miss Jenny Brailsford. Members n/a. *CC* No.269209. Began 1972. Magazine: *Community of the Word of God magazine* (200 annually). Turnover n/a. Prayer, hospitality, service and evangelism; retreats and quiet days; involvement in work of local church.
☎ 020 8986 8511

Order of the Holy Paraclete, St Hilda's Priory, Sneaton Castle, Whitby YO21 3QN
Prioress: Sister Judith Dean. Members 68. *CC* No.271117. Began 1915. No magazine. Turnover n/a. Benedictine; education, prison and hospice chaplaincies, retreats, conferences, missions, urban priority work.
Email: ohppriorywhitby@btinternet.com
☎ 01947 602 079 🖷 01947 820 854

St Margaret's Convent, St John's Road, East Grinstead RH19 3LE
Mother Superior: Rev Mother Raphael Mary. Members 29. *CC* No.231926. Began 1855. Magazine: *St Margaret's Chronicle* (400 every four months). Turnover n/a. Prayer and service in hospitality, care of the elderly, conference and retreat facilities.
☎ 01342 323 497

Society of All Saints Sisters of the Poor, All Saints Convent, St Mary's Road, Oxford OX4 1RU
Mother Superior: Sister Helen J F Chappell. Members 14. *CC* No.228383. Began 1851. No magazine. Turnover n/a. Working with the elderly, sick children, students, the homeless. Church embroidery and small guest house.
☎ 01865 249 127 🖷 01865 726 547
Also at: All Saints House, 82 Margaret Street, London W1N 8LH
☎ 020 7637 7818 🖷 0207 636 5364

Society of St Francis, Alverna, 110 Ellesmere Road, Gladstone Park, London NW10 1JS
Provincial Secretary: Brother Angelo SSF. *Minister Provincial:* Brother Damian SSF. Members 90. ***CC*** No.236464. Began 1921. Magazine: *The Franciscan* (3,500 every four months). Turnover n/a. Franciscan community living a life of evangelism, prayer, service. 12 UK houses.
Email: damianssf@aol.com & eurprovsec@aol.com
☎ 020 8452 7285 🖷 020 8452 1946

Society of the Precious Blood, Burnham Abbey, Lake End Road, Taplow, Maidenhead SL6 0PW
Reverend Mother: Sr Elizabeth Mary. Members 25. ***CC*** No.900512. Began 1905. No magazine. Turnover n/a. Prayer and intercession; some pastoral work.
☎ 01628 604 080

Society of the Sisters of Bethany, 7 Nelson Road, Southsea PO5 2AR
Reverend Mother: Mother Gwenyth. Members 18, Other staff 3. ***CC*** No.226582. Began 1866. No magazine. Turnover n/a. Retreat work, hospitality, prayer and work for unity.
☎ 023 9283 3498

RELIGIOUS ORDERS (ROMAN CATHOLIC)

See also Retreat Houses on Page 123, Missionary Societies on Page 352.

The Abbey of Our Lady Help of Christians, Worth Abbey, Crawley RH10 4SB
Abbot: Rt Rev Stephen Ortiger. Members 28. ***CC*** No.233572. Began 1933. No magazine. Turnover n/a. Benedictine monastic community serving 5 villages and educating 380 boys aged 10 to 18.
Web: web.ukonline.co.uk/worth.abbey/homepage.htm
Email: worth.abbey@ukonline.co.uk
☎ 01342 710 310 🖷 01342 710 311

Augustinian Nursing Sisters, Ince Blundell Hall, Ince Blundell, Liverpool L38 6JL
Prioress: Sister-in-charge. Members 9, Other staff 20. ***CC*** No.251782. Began 1961. No magazine. Turnover n/a. Nursing the elderly infirm and terminally ill, sick and retired priests.
☎ 0151 929 2596 🖷 0151 929 2180

Canonesses of the Holy Sepulchre, New Hall, Boreham, Chelmsford CM3 3HT
Prioress: Sister Mary Gabriel Foley. Members 21, Other staff 150. ***CC*** No.229288. Began 1794. Founded in Belgium in 1642. No magazine. Turnover n/a. Teaching, residential, voluntary service work, spiritual direction, retreats, outreach in Catholic and Anglican parishes.
☎ 01245 467 588 🖷 01245 464 348

Canonesses Regular of St Augustine of the Lateran, St Augustine's Priory, Hillcrest Road, Ealing, London W5 2JL
Prioress: Mother Mary Gabriel. Members 10, Other staff 29. ***CC*** Began 1911. No magazine. Turnover n/a. Teaching in school, prayer, contemplation, divine offices.
☎ 020 8997 2022 🖷 020 8810 6501

The Canons Regular of Premontre (The White Canons), Our Lady of England Priory, School Lane, Storrington, Pulborough RH20 4LN
Prior: Rt Rev Andrew H Smith. Members 14. ***CC*** Began 1147. No magazine. Turnover n/a. Caring for Roman Catholics in the area; schools work; pastoral work; guest house.
Email: norbartimes@pavilion.co.uk
☎ 01903 742 150 🖷 01903 740 821

Carmelite Friars, 63 East End Road, East Finchley, London N2 0SE
Prior Provincial: Rev Piet Wijngaard. Members 50. ***CC*** No.1061342. Began 1926. No magazine. Turnover n/a. Communities of men sharing their spiritual heritage by serving the church in its various needs.
Web: www.carmelite.org
☎ No telephone

Carthusians, St Hugh's Charterhouse, Henfield Road, Partridge Green, Horsham RH13 8EB
Prior: Rev Cyril Pierce. Members 24. Began 1084. No magazine. Turnover n/a. Leading a life of prayer and worship.
☎ 01403 864 231 🖷 01403 864 231

C

Congregation of Mary, Mother of the Church, St Raphael's Convent, St Mary's Way, Brownshill, Stroud GL6 8AN
Major Superior: Sister Rose McHale. Members 23. ***CC*** No.516380. Began 1982. No magazine. Turnover n/a. Visiting sick and housebound.
☎ 01453 882 107

Congregation of the Blessed Sacrament, 4 Dawson Street, Liverpool L1 1LE
Provincial Superior: Rev James Duffy. Members 18. ***CC*** Began 1936. No magazine. Turnover n/a. Adoration shrine of the Blessed Sacrament.
☎ 0151 709 5528

Congregation of the Mission (Vincentians), Vincentian Community, 29 Eversley Crescent, Isleworth, London TW7 4LR
Regional Superior: Rev Fegus Kelly CM. Members 25. ***CC*** No.233777. Began 1853. No magazine. Turnover n/a. Parish work, chaplaincies, formation; working with the homeless, deaf.
Email: kellyf9936@aol.com
☎ 020 8560 7021 🖷 020 8568 8677

Congregation of the Sisters of St Anne, 14a The Downs, London SW20 8HS
Superior General: Sister Barbara O'Mahony. Members 18. ***CC*** No.233808. Began 1927. No magazine. Turnover £147,000. Parish assistance and home for the elderly.
☎ 020 8946 1094

Corpus Christi Carmelites, Corpus Christi House, 12 West Walk, Leicester LE1 7NA
Regional Superior: Sister Teresa Joseph. Members 8. ***CC*** Began 1908. No magazine. Turnover n/a. A contemplative lifestyle and active apostolites.
☎ 0116 255 3607

Daughters of Divine Charity, Convent of the Sacred Heart, 17 Mangate Street, Swaffham PE37 7QW
Superior: Sister Thomas-More Prentice FDC. Members 13. ***CC*** No.237760. Began 1914. No magazine. Turnover n/a. Boarding and day school for girls.
☎ 01760 245 77 / 213 30 🖷 01760 725 557

Daughters of Our Lady of Providence, Convent of Our Lady of Providence, Anstey Lane, Alton GU34 2NG
Sister-in-Charge: Sister Helen. Members 9. *CC* Began 1938. No magazine. Turnover n/a. A teaching/nursing order, undertaking any apostolate which is needed.
☎ 01420 541 545 🖷 01420 541 711

Daughters of the Cross, St Wilfrid's Convent, 29 Tite Street, Chelsea, London SW3 4JX
Provincial Superior: Sister Mary Kelly. Members 109. *CC* Began 1863. No magazine. Turnover n/a. Operating three schools, three hospitals, one home for the elderly, one home for women suffering from epilepsy.
☎ 020 7351 2117

Daughters of the Cross (of Torquay), Stoodley Knowle Convent, Anstey's Cove Road, Torquay TQ1 2JB
Mother General: Sister Benignus O'Brien. Members 47, Other staff 50. *CC* No.232014. Began 1903. No magazine. Turnover n/a. Girls' school. Education and pastoral work.
☎ 01803 293 160

C

Dominican Sisters of St Catherine of King Williams Town, St Martin's Convent, Stoke Golding, Nuneaton CV13 6HT
Area Co-ordinator: Sister Aidan Sweeney. Members 480. *CC* No. 231235. Began 1933. No magazine. Turnover n/a. Education, clinics, prisons; pastoral work, retreat work, guests.
☎ 01455 212 207

Dominican Sisters of the English Congregation of St Catherine of Siena, 21 Station Road, Stone ST15 8EN
Prioress General: Sister Angela Mary Leydon. Members 68. *CC* Began 1929. No magazine. Turnover n/a. Trying, like St Dominic, 'to praise, to bless, to preach' by prayer and service.
Email: angelaleydon@btinternet.com
☎ 01785 812 091 🖷 01785 813 852

Dominican Sisters of the Presentation, Presentation Convent, Easthampstead Road, Wokingham RG40 2ED
Superior: Sister Veronica Mary Jackson. Members 2. *CC* Began 1904. No magazine. Turnover £50,000–100,000 to year end Dec 98. Parish work, foreign student care.
☎ 0118 978 2553

Downside Abbey, Stratton on the Fosse, Bath BA3 4RH
Abbot: Dom Richard Yeo. Members 40, Other staff 150. *CC* No.232548. Began 1795. No magazine. Turnover n/a. Benedictine; teaching in school, parish work, retreat giving, academic research, publication.
☎ 01761 235 161 🖷 01761 235 124

Ealing Abbey, Charlbury Grove, Ealing, London W5 2DY
Abbot: Rt Rev Laurence Soper OSB. Community 24, Other staff 122. *CC* No.242715. Began 1897. No magazine. Turnover n/a. Benedictines; teaching in school, parish work, adult teaching in art, liturgy.
Web: members.aol.com/ealingmonk/
☎ 020 8862 2100 🖷 020 8862 2199

Franciscan Friars of the Atonement, 47 Francis Street, London SW1P 1QR
Brother-in-Charge: Rev Gerard Hand. Members 2, No other staff. *CC* Began 1957. No magazine. Turnover n/a. Mission and advisory capacity.
☎ 020 7828 4163

Franciscan Missionary Sisters, 2 Broad Road, Braintree CM7 9RS
Sister Superior: Sister Helen Connolly. Members 17. *CC* Began n/a. No magazine. Turnover n/a. Providing residential nursing care for the elderly and day nursery care for children.
☎ 01376 326 654 🖷 01376 340 401

Franciscan Missionary Sisters of Littlehampton, The Generalate St Joseph's Franciscan Convent, East Street, Littlehampton BN17 6AU
Superior General: Sister Anastasia McGonagle. Members 56. *CC* No.232931. Began 1990. No magazine. Turnover n/a. Nursing, visiting and pastoral work, parish and prison work, retreats, hostels for students.
☎ 01903 714 039 🖷 01903 731 097

Franciscan Sisters of the Immaculate Conception, St Anthony's Convent, 93 Belle Vue Road, Cinderford GL14 2AA
Sister in charge: Sister Mary Celestine McKenna. Members 12. *CC* No.35901. Began n/a. (Previously Missionary Franciscan Sisters of the Immaculate Conception). No magazine. Turnover n/a. Teaching, parish work, caring for mothers and babies and those who are mentally handicapped.
☎ 01594 822 310

Little Company of Mary, 28 Trinity Crescent, Tooting Bec, London SW17 7AE
Provincial Superior: Sister Michelle Motherway. Members 61. *CC* Began 1877. No magazine. Turnover n/a. Praying for the sick and dying, chaplaincy work and nursing where it is needed.
☎ 020 8998 0693 🖷 020 8997 3558

Little Sisters of the Assumption, 52 Kenneth Crescent, Willesden Green, London NW2 4PN
Provincial: Sister Winifred O'Brien. Members 45. *CC* Began 1880. No magazine. Turnover n/a. Supportive care for families, especially in poor areas.
☎ 020 8452 1687 🖷 020 8208 3625

Little Sisters of the Poor, St Peter's, Meadow Road, London SW8 1QH
Mother Provincial: Sister Agnes Wright. Members 150. *CC* No.234434. Began 1851. No magazine. Turnover n/a. Care until death of elderly poor people of all denominations; eight residential homes in England.
☎ 020 7735 0788 🖷 020 7820 9647

Oblate Sisters of St Francis de Sales, Convent of St Francis de Sales, Aylesbury Road, Tring HP23 4DL
Superior: Sister Mary Vincent Kowalewski. Members 6. *CC* Began 1903. No magazine. Turnover n/a. Christian education of children.
☎ 01442 822 315 🖷 01442 827 080

†**Olivetan Benedictines**, Priory of our Lady of Peace, Turvey Abbey, Turvey, Bedford MK43 8DE
Reverend Mother Prioress: Sister Zoë Davis. Members 18. *CC* No.246754. Began 1936. Magazine: *One in Christ* (Circulation & frequency n/a). Turnover n/a. Prayer, hospitality, ecumenism, liturgy, retreats.
☎ 01234 881 432 🖷 01234 881 838

Our Lady of Providence and Missionaries of Hope, Convent of our Lady of Providence, Anstey Lane, Alton GU34 2NG
Regional Superior: Sister Therese Garman. Members 9. Began 1938. No magazine. Turnover n/a. Teaching, chaplaincy, pastoral supervision, pastoral work, nursing, counselling, caring for homeless.
☎ 01420 541 545 🖷 01420 541 711

Poor Handmaids of Jesus Christ, St Boniface Convent, House of Prayer and Retreat, Doveshill Crescent, Ensbury Park, Bournemouth BH10 5BS
Sister-in-Charge: Sister Paul Snell. Members 7. *CC* No.234423. Began 1876. No magazine. Turnover n/a. Retreat/pastoral work and spiritual guidance. Group accommodation, day facilities.
☎ 01202 513 555

Poor Servants of the Mother of God, Maryfield Convent, Mount Angelus Road, Roehampton, London SW15 4JA
Superior General: Sister Rosarii O'Connor. Members 10. *CC* Began 1869. No magazine. Turnover n/a. Working in education and healthcare; social and pastoral work.
Email: smggen@compuserve.com
☎ 020 8788 4351 Fax 020 8789 9281

Presentation Brothers, 63 Bath Road, Reading RG30 2BB
Provincial Superior: Brother Richard English. *Secretary General Republic of Ireland:* Father Bede Minehane. Members 16. *CC* Began 1872. No magazine. Turnover n/a. Involved in education for the less well-off, social work.
Email: brdamian@pres-coll.i-way.co.uk
☎ 01189 572 861 Fax 01189 572 20

Presentation Sisters, Provincial House, 4 King's End, Bicester OX6 7DT
Provincial Superior: Sister Susan Richert. Members 120. *CC* Began 1836. No magazine. Turnover n/a. Christian education of youth.
Web: www.pbvmepro.clara.net
Email: pbvmepro@clara.co.uk
☎ 01869 323 660 Fax 01869 323 659

†**Prinknash Benedictines**, Prinknash Abbey, Cranham, Gloucester GL4 8EX
Abbot: Rt Rev Francis Baird. Members 21, Other staff 4. *CC* No.232863. Began 1928. Magazine: *Pax* (Circulation n/a quarterly). Turnover n/a. Prayer, study and manual work; retreats and hospitality.
Web: web.ukonline.co.uk/david.w34/davidw/_prinknash.html
Email: peter_prinknash@compuserve.com
☎ 01452 812 455 Fax 01452 813 305

Religious of St Andrew, St Peter's House, 308 Kennington Lane, London SE11 5HY
Regional Superior: Sister Diane Reynolds. Members 5. *CC* Began n/a. No magazine. Turnover n/a. Welcoming pilgrims in London and Kent for retreat time of rest and silence.
☎ 020 7587 0087 Fax 020 7793 9725
Also at: *Regional Superior:* Sister Diane Reynolds, Eden Hall, Stick Hill, Edenbridge TN8 5NN
☎ 01342 850 388 Fax 01342 850 118

Religious of the Sacred Heart of Mary, 64 Little Ealing Lane, London W5 4XF
Provincial Superior: Sister Margaret Fielding. Members 145. *CC* No.232190. Began 1849. No magazine. Turnover n/a. Pastoral and social outreach, community development, homelessness. Communities in over 20 locations..
Email: rshmlondon@aol.com
☎ 020 8567 3148 Fax 020 8579 8072

Salvatorian Sisters, 9c Boreham Road, Warminster BA12 9JR
Regional Superior: Sister Paula Langton. Members 10. *CC* No.228082. Began 1888. No magazine. Turnover n/a. Nursing, parish work and social work.
☎ 01985 217 647

Sisters of Marie Auxiliatrice, 16 Pages Lane, Muswell Hill, London N10 1PS
Regional Co-ordinator: Sister Mary Leahy. Members 23. *CC* No.230973. Began 1920. No magazine. Turnover n/a. Serving the needs of young people, especially the underprivileged.
☎ 020 8883 4577 Fax 020 8883 6299

Sisters of Mercy, Convent of Mercy, Newcastle ST5 1LH
Mother Superior: Sister Bridget English. Members 12, Other staff 2. *CC* No.233969. Began 1839. No magazine. Turnover n/a. Teaching, social work, parish work, care of the poor, sacristy work, hospital ministry.
☎ 01782 614 459

Sisters of Our Lady, Convent of Our Lady, Hall Lane, Kettering NN15 7LR
District Superior: Sister Patricia Gannon. Members 13. *CC* No.221865. Began 1933. No magazine. Turnover n/a. Administration and teaching in primary school, pastoral ministry.
Web: www.snd1.org
Email: pagannon@msn.com
☎ 01536 513 711 Fax 01536 392 599

Sisters of Providence (Ruill, sur Loir), The Mount, Wragby Road, Lincoln LN2 5SL
Regional Superior: Sister Stephanie Dalton. Members 6. *CC* Began 1896. No magazine. Turnover n/a. Dedicating their lives to God through varied ministries in the Catholic Church.
☎ 01522 540 894 Fax 01522 568 321

Sisters of Providence of Rouen, Convent of Providence, 10 Sutton Avenue, Seaford BN25 4LD
Sister Superior: Sister Odile Deswarte. Members 12. *CC* Began n/a. No magazine. Turnover n/a. Teaching in schools, parish work, visiting the sick.
☎ 01323 892 178

Sisters of St Joseph of Peace, Sacred Heart Convent, 61 Station Road, Rearsby, Leicester LE7 4YY
Provincial Superior: Sister Rosemary Reilly. Members 74. *CC* Began 1884. No magazine. Turnover n/a. Praying for and working for peace and justice; involved in nursing, teaching, hospital and prison work, pastoral work.
Email: csjpuk.prov@aol.com
☎ 01664 424 251 Fax 01664 424 195

Sisters of St Marcellina, Hampstead Towers, 6 Ellerdale Road, London NW3 6BD
Sister Superior: Sister Mirella Biondini. Members 6. *CC* Began 1955. No magazine. Turnover n/a. Boarding school for overseas girl students.
☎ 020 7435 0181

Sisters of the Christian Retreat, House of Prayer, 35 Seymour Road, East Molesey KT8 0PB
Regional Superior: Sister Melanie. Members 30. *CC* No.232567. Began 1789. No magazine. Turnover £10,000 to year end Dec 98. House of prayer, quiet days, groups welcome, self catering, counselling, prayer guides provided.
☎ 020 8941 2313 Mobile: 07789 247 905

Sisters of the Holy Family of Nazareth, Holy Family Convent, 52 London Road, Enfield EN2 6EN
Sister-in-Charge (Enfield): Sister Beata. Enfield members 15, Northampton members 7. *CC* No.234201. Began 1895. No magazine. Turnover n/a. Teaching, hospital chaplaincies, parish and pastoral work.
☎ 020 8363 4483 Fax 020 8363 2583
Also at: *Sister in charge:* Sister Mary Bozyslawa, Queen of Peace Convent, 437 Wellingborough Road, Northampton NN1 4EZ
☎ 01604 293 28

C

Sisters of the Presentation of Mary, Mount St Mary, Wonford Road, Exeter EX2 4PF
Regional Superior: Sister Guy-Marie. Members 13. ***CC*** Began 1896. No magazine. Turnover n/a. Involved in nursing, teaching, marriage tribunals, hospital and prison work, pastoral work; working with the dying.
☎ 01392 433 301 🖷 01392 490 859

Sisters of the Sacred Heart of Jesus, 6 Oakleigh Park South, Whetstone, London N20 9JU
Provincial: Sister Anniek Le Roy. Members 25. ***CC*** Began 1903. No magazine. Turnover n/a. Apostolic Religious, working in various professions: teaching, nursing, parish work, chaplaincy, social work.
☎ 020 8445 4655 🖷 020 8445 1252

Sisters of the Temple, St Angela's Convent, 5 Litfield Place, Clifton, Bristol BS8 3LU
Sister Provincial: Sister Marie-Louise Levern. Members 4, Other staff 20. ***CC*** No.229049. Began 1862. No magazine. Turnover n/a. Caring for the elderly.
☎ 0117 973 5436 🖷 0117 970 6844

C

Society of Christ, 196 Lloyd Street North, Manchester M14 4QB
Father Provincial: Rev Czeslaw Osika. Members 22. ***CC*** No.298723 Began. No magazine. Turnover n/a. Spiritual, social and cultural welfare of Poles living away from their homeland.
☎ 0161 226 1588 🖷 0161 232 0450

The Sons of Divine Providence, 25 Lower Teddington Road, Kingston upon Thames KT1 4HB
Regional Superior: Rev John C Perrotta. Members 8, Other staff 150. ***CC*** No.220608. Began 1952. Magazine: *The Bridge* (6,000 quarterly). Turnover n/a. Running daycare facilities and 7 residential homes for the elderly and those with learning disabilities.
Email: london.divineprovidence@btinternet.com.uk
☎ 020 8977 5130 / 3434 🖷 020 8977 0105

Subiaco Congregation, Ramsgate Abbey, Ramsgate CT11 9PA
Abbot: Rt Rev Laurence O'Keeffe. Members 12. ***CC*** No.245415. Began 1856. (Previously Benedictines). No magazine. Turnover n/a. Parochial and retreat work.
Email: staugabbey@aol.com
☎ 01843 593 045 🖷 01843 582 732

Trinitarian Sisters, Holy Trinity Convent, 81 Plaistow Lane, Bromley BR1 3LL
Superior: Sister J Madeleine Timmins. Members 14. ***CC*** Began 1886. No magazine. Turnover n/a. Working in the UK in parishes, prison chaplaincies and the fostering of Christian education.
☎ 020 8402 2785 🖷 020 8466 0151

Ursulines of Brentwood, Ursuline Generalate, 93 Queen's Road, Brentwood CM14 4EY
General Superior: Sister Clare Kane. Members 39, Other staff 4. ***CC*** No.223378. Began 1900. No magazine. Turnover n/a. Working in schools, residential youth centre, hospital visiting, parish pastoral work.
☎ 01277 260 156

Xaverian Brothers, 20 Belfield Road, Didsbury, Manchester M20 6BH
Regional Superior: Brother David Birtles. Members 10, Other staff 107. ***CC*** No.239240. Began 1848. No magazine. Turnover n/a. Local education and parish work.
☎ 0161 445 5273

EVANGELISM

E

CITY & TOWN MISSIONS

***Action International Ministries (UK)**, PO Box 193, Bewdley DY12 2GZ
UK Director: Mr Ingo Abraham. *Financial Director:* Mr David J Hickmar. Executive staff 1, Other staff 3. ***CC*** No.1058661. Began 1988; interdenominational. (Previously ACTION UK). Magazine: *ACTIONPOINT* (1,500 quarterly), *Street Children* (1,500 every two months). Turnover £189,000 to year end Mar 98. Reaching urban poor of the world through evangelism, discipleship, social development projects especially amongst street children.
Web: www.actionintl.org
Email: actionuk@btinternet.com
☎ 01299 401 511 🖷 01299 405 273

***The Barn Christian Association for Youth**, The Barn, Cranborne Road, Wimborne BH21 4HW
Chairman: Mr Bryan Mills. Full-time staff 1, Part-time staff 1. ***CC*** No.295519. Began 1986; interdenominational. (Previously Christian Association for Youth). Magazine: *Livewire* (800 quarterly). Turnover £40,000 to year end Sep 98. Evangelising and spreading Christianity to young people through concerts, nightlife, schools, etc. Incorporating Kingston Festivals.
Web: www.cnet.clara.net/barn/
Email: info@cafy.clara.net / barn@cafy.clara.net
☎ 01202 881 334 Mobile: 07976 632 620 🖷 01202 881 334

E

Battersea Central Methodist Mission, 20 York Road, London SW11 3QE
Superintendent: Rev Ian Field. Other staff 5. ***CC*** Began 1940; Methodist. Magazine: *Mission News* (150 monthly). Turnover £112,000 to year end Aug 98. Medical clinics, day nursery, care of elderly, welfare, cancer support centre, mental health project.
☎ 020 7207 6663 🖷 020 7924 1491

Belfast Central Mission, Grosvenor House, 5 Glengall Street, Belfast BT12 5AD
Superintendent: Rev David J Kerr. *Director of Social Work:* Mr W R Sharpe. *Minister:* Rev Gary Mason. Mission executive 7, Other staff 115. ***CC*** No.XN 46001A. Began 1889; Methodist. Magazine: *BCM in Focus* (2,000 frequency n/a). Turnover £2,000,000 to year end Dec 98. Chaplaincy, social work and counselling, street work, pastoral care, accommodation for children and elderly.
Web: www.geocities.com/heartland/meadows/3315
Email: dkerr@bcm.dnet.co.uk
☎ 028 9024 1917 🖷 028 9024 0577

Belfast City Mission, Church House, Fisherwick Place, Belfast BT1 6DW
Executive Secretary: Mr George Ferguson. *Assistant Secretary:* Mr Robin Fairbairn. Executive staff 2, Other staff 25. ***CC*** No.XN45106. Began 1827; Presbyterian. Magazine: *Annual Report* (7,500 annually). Turnover £400,000 to year end Dec 98. Evangelism: through home visitation, door to door, hospitals, prisons, open air witness, gospel, youth, children's meetings.
☎ 028 9032 0557 🖷 028 9043 9950

***Birmingham City Mission**, 75 Watery Lane Middleway, Bordesley, Birmingham B9 4HN
Executive Director: Mr Wesley Erpen. *Company Secretary:* Mr Alan Cutler. *Finance Director:* Mr Rob Warner. Executive staff 10, Other staff 50. ***CC*** No.1051023. Began 1966; interdenominational. Magazine: *Prayer Update* (6,000 monthly). Turnover £1,000,192 to year end Mar 98. Interdenominational faith mission reaching all with the Gospel by evangelistic social work.
Web: www.internet-pilots.com/city_missions
Email: mission@globalnet.co.uk
☎ 0121 766 6603 🖷 0121 766 6727

***Brighton & Hove Town Mission**, Church Building, Ashton Rise, Brighton BN2 2QR
General Secretary: Mr Tony Smith. Executive staff 1, Evangelists 3. ***CC*** No.251768. Began 1849; non-denominational. Magazine: *BHTM Newsletter* (800 quarterly). Turnover £60,000 to year end Dec 98. Training churches in evangelism; open-air witness, door-to-door visitation, homes for elderly; literature distribution.
Email: bhtmtony@aol.com
☎ 01273 609 484

Bristol City Mission Society, 12 Church Road, Thornbury, Bristol BS35 1EJ
Secretary: Mrs J M Ovens. Other staff 3. ***CC*** No.252282. Began 1826; interdenominational. Magazine: *Bristol City Mission* (250 annually). Turnover £39,000 to year end Dec 97. Supporting and resourcing churches in the Bristol area.
☎ 01454 414 727

***Bristol International Students Centre**, 45 Woodland Road, Clifton, Bristol BS8 1UT
Coordinator: Mrs Mary Morgan. Executive staff 2, Other staff 1. ***CC*** No.298035. Began 1975; non-denominational. No magazine. Turnover £30,000 to year end Aug 99. Linking students at Bristol universities and colleges with local people and each other.
Web: come.to/bisc
Email: bisc@cablenet.co.uk
☎ 0117 915 9826 🖷 0117 904 0419

British Association of City Missions, 47 Copse Hill, Brighton BN1 5GA
Hon Secretary: Mr Harold W Oakley. Staff n/a. Began 1991; interdenominational. Magazine: *Network* (Circulation & frequency n/a). Turnover n/a. Network of City Missions giving mutual support, training and sharing of resources.
☎ 01273 503 344

Coventry City Mission, PO Box 40, Coventry CV6 2PR
Director: Mr Neville Carpmail. Executive staff 1, Other staff 5. ***CC*** No.519000. Began 1983; interdenominational. Magazine: *Prayer letter* (1,200 monthly). Turnover £67,693 to year end Mar 98. Evangelistic ministry to the whole city with additional concern for those with practical needs.
Web: www.users.zetnet.co.uk/covcitymission
Email: covcitymission@zetnet.co.uk
☎ 024 7661 5931

Darlington Town Mission, 26 Teesdale Avenue, Darlington DL3 8AP
Hon Secretary: Mrs Elizabeth Ardron. Other staff 2. ***CC*** Began 1838; interdenominational. No magazine. Turnover £14,500 to year end Dec 98. Giving Christian fellowship and practical aid to needy in Darlington.
☎ 01325 461 042

Derby City Mission, 32 Quarn Drive, Allestree, Derby DE22 2NQ
Director: Mr Geoff Holland. Executive staff 1, Other staff 4. ***CC*** No.702027. Began 1989; interdenominational. Magazine: *Newsletter* (1,000 every two months). Turnover £51,444 to year end June 98. Advancing the Gospel through evangelism, practical concern to the inhabitants of Derby and suburbs.
☎ 01332 606 488 / 606 489

East Belfast Mission, 239 Newtownards Road, Belfast BT4 1AF
Superintendent: Rev Dr Gary Mason. Began n/a; Methodist. No magazine. Turnover n/a. Caring for the needy, day centre, ministry to alcoholics.
☎ 028 9045 8560 🖷 028 9045 2561

East End Mission, 583 Commercial Road, Stepney, London E1 0HJ
Minister: Rev Clifford Newman. Other staff 22. ***CC*** Began 1885; Methodist. Turnover £400,000 to year end Dec 96. Caring for vulnerable women and children, socially deprived; Opportunities Playgroup; community development work; student accommodation.
☎ 020 7790 3366

Edinburgh City Mission, 9 Pilrig Street, Edinburgh EH6 5AH
Executive Director: Rev William T Chalmers. *Administrator:* Mr Bill Staig. Executive staff 1, Other staff 11. ***CC*** No.SCO 12385. Began 1832; non-denominational. Magazine: *Sharing Life* (1,000 frequency n/a). Turnover £138,872 to year end Dec 96. Evangelistic outreach, telephone helpline and counselling service, caring for the poor, needy and homeless.
☎ 0131 554 6140

Evangelical Coalition of Urban Mission, 70 City Road, 4th Floor, London EC1Y 2BT
Secretary: Mr Michael Eastman. No other staff. Began 1980; interdenominational. Magazine: *City Cries* (500 half-yearly), *ECUM Bulletin* (400 half-yearly). Turnover £2,000 to year end Dec 98. Partnership of networks and agencies to further the evangelical thrust in urban mission.
☎ 020 7336 7744 🖷 020 7324 9900

Glasgow City Mission, Academy Park, Gower Street, Glasgow G51 1PR
Chief Executive Director: Mr Graeme M Clark. Executive staff 3, Other staff 17. ***CC*** No.SCO 001499. Began 1826; interdenominational. Magazine: *Prayer Letter* (1,700 quarterly). Turnover £490,000 to year end Dec 98. Caring for hungry and homeless people, drug addicts, street girls, children and families.
Email: mail@glasgowcitymission.com
☎ 0141 419 9090 🖷 0141 419 9222

Lambeth Mission & St Mary's (LEP), 3 Lambeth Road, London SE1 7DQ
Superintendent Minister: Rev Graham Cocking. Executive staff 1, Other staff 3. ***CC*** Began 1778; Methodist/Anglican. Magazine: *Lambeth Mission Newsletter* (1,000 every four months). Turnover £90,000 to year end Aug 98. Pastoral and community work in Lambeth and Vauxhall; day centre for homeless people.
☎ 020 7735 2166 🖷 020 7735 5814

Leeds City Mission, 61 Great George Street, Leeds LS1 3BB
Superintendent: Rev Trevor Daykin. Other staff 3. ***CC*** No.234431. Began 1837; interdenominational. Magazine: *Newsletter* (1,200 quarterly). Turnover £60,000 to year end Mar 98. Proclaiming the Gospel to the inhabitants of Leeds and district. Chaplains to prison and to police.
☎ 0113 246 0188

Liverpool City Mission, 20 Mount Pleasant, Liverpool L3 5RY
Superintendent: Rev John Scott. Executive staff 3, Other staff 8. ***CC*** No.234521. Began 1829; interdenominational. Magazine: *Voice in the City* (5,000 half-yearly). Turnover n/a. Social and evangelistic work through mission centres, telephone ministry, chaplaincies and bookshop/coffee shop.
☎ 0151 709 8866 (office) 0151 707 8555 (24hr telephone)
🖷 0151 709 8886

London City Mission, Nasmith House, 175 Tower Bridge Road, London SE1 2AH
General Secretary: Rev James McAllen. Executive staff 8, Mission staff 16, Evangelists 123. ***CC*** No.247186. Began 1835; non-denominational. Magazine: *Span* (35,000 every two months). Turnover £3,400,000 to year end Dec 97. Extending the knowledge of the Gospel among the inhabitants of London and its vicinity.
Email: lcm.uk@btinternet.com
☎ 020 7407 7585 🖷 020 7403 6711

London Methodist Mission (North West Circuit), 33 Dyne Road, London NW6 7XG
Superintendent Minister: Rev Dr Gordon Harrison. Executive staff 4. ***CC*** Began n/a; Methodist. No magazine. Turnover n/a. Inner-city ministry and community projects based on 4 church centres. Rooms available for hire.
☎ 020 7624 3075

*__Macclesfield Christian Mission__, 2nd Floor, 16 Park Green, Macclesfield SK11 7NA
Team Leader: Mrs Annie Roebuck. Executive staff 6, Other staff 2. ***CC*** No.514550. Began 1889; non-denominational. No magazine. Turnover £20,000 to year end Apr 98. Evangelistic outreach, hospital radio, mobile library, schools/youth work, café, resource to churches, elderly people's homes.
☎ 01625 616 611 🖷 01625 616 611

E

Manchester and Salford Methodist Mission, Central Hall, Oldham Street, Manchester M1 1JT
Superintendent Minister: Rev David Copley. Ministerial staff 11, Other staff 20. ***CC*** Began 1886; Methodist. No magazine. Turnover £760,000 to year end Aug 98. Proclaiming Christ in word and work in Manchester and Salford.
Email: postmaster@msmm.abel.co.uk
☎ 0161 236 5141 🖷 0161 237 1585

Manchester City Mission, Windsor Christian Centre, Churchill Way, Salford M6 5BU
Director: Mr Jonathan Stewart. *Office Manager:* Mr Michael Beere. Executive staff 2, Other staff 10. ***CC*** No.224626. Began 1837; interdenominational. Magazine: *Newsline* (3,000 frequency n/a). Turnover £194,000 to year end Dec 98. City centre and district evangelism, social concern, district visitation, literature distribution, prison and industry visiting.
Email: mancitmis@aol.com
☎ 0161 736 7959 🖷 0161 736 7963

*__Mission in Hounslow Trust__, 101a Pears Road, Hounslow TW3 1SS
Director: Mr Colin Windsor. Executive staff 1. ***CC*** No.1031597. Began 1993; non-denominational. No magazine. Turnover £73,000 to year end Dec 98. Relief of sickness, poverty; sharing the Christian message in Hounslow and surrounding areas.
☎ 020 8894 2239

Newtownabbey Methodist Mission, 35a Rathcoole Drive, Newtownabbey BT37 9AQ
Superintendent: Rev William T Buchanan. Executive staff 3, Other staff 4. ***CC*** No.XN 47068. Began 1898; Methodist. (Incorporating North Belfast Mission). Magazine: *Mission News* (700 half-yearly). Turnover £89,000 to year end Dec 98. Evangelistic outreach, worship and training, social caring, retirement flats for elderly people.
☎ 028 9085 2546 🖷 028 9085 2546

Oxford Ministry among Overseas Students (OMOS), 98 Kingston Road, Oxford OX2 6RL
Pastoral Coordinator: Mr Richard Weston. Executive staff 5, Admin staff 1. Began 1983; non-denominational. No magazine. Turnover £22,000 to year end Dec 98. Evangelism and care of international students, equipping local churches to do likewise.
Email: omos2000@aol.com
☎ 01865 552 226

Plymouth Methodist Central Hall, Eastlake Street, Plymouth PL1 1BA
Superintendent: To be appointed. Executive staff 5, Other staff 4. Began 1940; Methodist. Magazine: *Messenger* (1,500 monthly). Turnover £134,000 to year end Aug 90. City centre evangelism among young and old including day centres and chaplaincies.
☎ 01752 660 997 Fax 01752 229 911

St Giles Christian Mission, 62 Bride Street, London N7 8AZ
Superintendent: Rev David M Page. *General Secretary:* Mrs M Nwanwene. Executive staff 2, Other staff 4. ***CC*** No.208434. Began 1860; evangelical. Magazine: *Annual Report* (500 annually). Turnover n/a. Church ministry with social work in North of London.
Email: sgcm@islington22.freeserve.co.uk
☎ 020 7607 4370 Fax 020 7607 2522

E

***Shankill Road Mission**, 116 Shankill Road, Belfast BT13 2BD
Superintendent: Rev W M Campbell. Executive staff 4, Other staff 14. ***CC*** No.XN 45423. Began 1898; Presbyterian Church in Ireland. No magazine. Turnover n/a. Promoting the welfare of local people through evangelism and social witness.
☎ 028 9032 4345

Sheffield Inner-City Ecumenical Mission, 239 Abbeyfield Road, Sheffield S4 7AW
Superintendent: Rev Christine Jones. *The Furnival; Minister:* Rev Jane Grinonneau. Executive staff 4. Began 1971; ecumenical. Magazine: *Here and Now* (250 quarterly). Turnover £200,000 to year end Aug 97. Alliance of ten denominational and ecumenical churches, mission units and educational and community facilities.
☎ 0114 243 2572

South London Industrial Mission, Christ Church Industrial Centre, 27 Blackfriars Road, London SE1 8NY
Senior Chaplain: Rev John Paxton. Chaplaincy team 9, Other staff 3. ***CC*** No.801809. Began 1942; ecumenical. Magazine: *SLIMline* (150 quarterly). Turnover £41,000 to year end Dec 97. Exploring relevance of faith in industrial, commercial and service organisations and encouraging discipleship; conference facilities.
Email: slim@dswark.org.uk
☎ 020 7928 3970 Fax 020 7928 1148

South London Mission, The Central Hall, 256 Bermondsey Street, London SE1 3UJ
Superintendent: Rev John S Lampard. Executive staff 4. ***CC*** Began 1889; Methodist. Magazine: *Mission Newsletter* (300 monthly). Turnover £250,000 to year end Aug 98. Evangelism, worship, social welfare, accommodation for students and elderly women, supplementary school for 5–8 year olds.
☎ 020 7407 2014 Fax 020 7407 3885

South West London Evangelistic Mobile Unit, 56 Chestnut Copse, Hurst Green, Oxted RH8 0JJ
Hon Secretary: Mr R Reed. No full-time staff. ***CC*** Began 1947; non-denominational. Magazine: *Prayer Letter* (400 n/a). Turnover £2,000 to year end Dec 96. Open air Gospel witness.
☎ 01883 722 037

***Southampton City Mission**, Southampton SO15 5YB
Projects Director: Mr Chris Davis. Executive staff 2, Other staff 3. ***CC*** No.251142. Began 1963; interdenominational. No magazine. Turnover £70,000 to year end Sep 98. City wide evangelism through social action, schools, holiday clubs; training and teaching for churches.
Email: southampton.city.mission@dial.pipex.com
☎ 023 8077 3132 Mobile: 07789 147 010 Fax 023 8077 7040

Touchstone Centre, 32 Merton Road, Bradford BD7 1RE
Team Leader: Rev Geoff Reid. Other staff 4. Began 1989; Methodist. Magazine: *Touchlines* (450 every four months). Turnover £90,000 to year end Aug 98. City-wide community and interfaith work, student chaplaincy, resource centre.
Web: www.methodist.org.uk/touchstone
Email: touchsto@surfaid.org
☎ 01274 721 626 Fax 01274 395 324

†**Vauxhall Methodist Mission**, Worgan Street, Vauxhall, London SE11 5ED
Superintendent: Rev Lynne Mayers. Executive staff 1, Other staff 1. ***CC*** Began n/a; Methodist. No magazine. Turnover n/a. Christian pastoral and community work in Vauxhall.
Email: kan@netcomuk.co.uk
☎ 020 7587 1912

Walk of 1000 Men, 73 High Street, Coton, Cambridge CB3 7PL
Evangelists: Rev Daniel H Cozens, Rev Peter Adams. Executive staff 2, Other staff 5. ***CC*** No.801113. Began 1992; interdenominational. Also known as Through Faith Missions. Magazine: *Through Faith Prayerletter* (6,500 frequency n/a). Turnover £200,000.
Web: www.btinternet.com/~walk1000/
Email: walk1000@btinternet.com
☎ 01954 210 239 Fax 01954 211 983

West London Mission, 19 Thayer Street, London W1M 5LJ
Superintendent Minister: Rev David S Cruise. Executive staff 16, Other staff 50. Began 1887; Methodist. Magazine: *Grapevine* (400 monthly). Turnover £2,500,000 to year end Mar 98. City centre worship, university chaplaincy, day centres; projects for alcohol misusers, offenders and young homeless.
Web: www.methodist.org.uk/west.london.mission
☎ 020 7935 6179 Fax 020 7487 3965

Whitechapel Mission, 212 Whitechapel Road, London E1 1BJ
Minister: Rev Richard H Chapple. *Warden:* Mr Tony Miller. Executive staff 3, Office staff 2. ***CC*** No.227905. Began 1896; Methodist. Magazine: *Annual Report* (2,500 annually). Turnover £155,877 to year end Aug 98. Caring for homeless people, church activities.
Web: www.whitechapel.uk
Email: richard@whitechapel.org.uk
☎ 020 7247 8280 Fax 020 7377 5762

***The Word for Life Trust**, The Olive Tree, 3 Danestream Close, Milford-on-Sea, Lymington SO41 0VR
Director: Rev Elizabeth Brazell. Executive staff 1, Other staff 4. ***CC*** No.1071313. Began 1998; non-denominational. No magazine. Turnover £27,000 to year end Dec 98. Working to encourage, equip, envision and enrich local churches across the denominations.
Web: www.doveuk.com/wflt
Email: keithhawk@aol.com
☎ 01590 645 216 Mobile: 07768 864 538 Fax 01590 645 216

EVANGELISTIC AGENCIES (PRIMARILY IN UK)

'he 40:3 Trust, PO Box 403, Coventry CV3 6SW
Trust Director: Canon Ian Knox. *Trust Manager:* Mr Darren Burgess. Executive staff 5, Other staff 1. *CC* No.327205. Began 1986; interdenominational. No magazine. Turnover £120,000 to year end Sept 98. Church-based and area wide evangelism within the UK and elsewhere.
Web: ourworld.compuserve.com/homepages/40-3-trust
Email: 106342.1106@compuserve.com
☎ 024 7650 4792

.B.C. Ministries, Manor Cottage, Barras, Kirkby Stephen CA17 4ES
Evangelist: Mr Rod Readhead. Executive staff 1. Began 1999; interdenominational. No magazine. Turnover: first year of operation. Offering evangelism, encouragement, teaching, men's discipleship and outreach, missions, holiday clubs.
Email: rodredhead@aol.com
☎ 01768 341 573 Fax 01768 341 573

ction Bookshare, PO Box 694, Rhyl LL18 1JU
UK Director: Mr Ingo Abraham. Executive staff 1, Other staff 2. *CC* No.1058661. Began 1959; interdenominational. (Previously Fishers Fellowship, merged 1997). Magazine: *Impact* (2,000 every two months). Turnover £27,000 to year end June 96. Training in personal evangelism and effective follow-up to produce mature believers through Bible study.
Web: www.actionintl.org
Email: actionuk@btinternet.com
☎ 01299 401 511 Fax 01299 405 273

AD2000 Cities, Ardcraig, Bankhead Grove, Dalmeny, South Queensferry EH30 9JZ
Co-ordinator, Europe: Mr Douglas GJ Flett. No other staff. Began 1994; interdenominational. No magazine. Turnover n/a. Information on Christian city networks and groupings in UK and abroad.
Email: dgj.flett@uk.iccc.net
☎ 0131 331 3310 Fax 0131 331 3310

Agapé, Fairgate House, Kings Road, Tyseley, Birmingham B11 2AA
National Director: Mr David Wilson. *Executive Director:* Mr Evan Winter. Other staff 96. *CC* No.258421. Began 1967; interdenominational. Part of Campus Crusade for Christ International and runs Jesus Video Project. Magazine: *Agapé News* (10,000 every four months). Turnover £1,278,594 to year end June 98. Evangelism and discipleship in different segments of society; schools, universities, businesses.
Web: www.agape.org.uk
Email: jvp@agape.org.uk
☎ 0121 765 4404 Fax 0121 765 4065

Alive in Mission – Doncaster Fellowship of Churches, Mission Centre, YMCA, Wood Street, Doncaster DN1 3LH
Secretary: Ms Yvonne Cave. No full-time staff. *CC* No.518510. Began 1985; interdenominational. No magazine. Turnover £10-50,000 to year end Dec 96. Promoting local evangelism, ecumenical fellowship, Christian education and encouragement.
☎ 01302 834 937

***Ambassadors for Christ Britain**, The Elms, 61 Green Lane, Redruth TR15 1LS
British Director: Rev Colin Salter. Executive staff 1, Other staff 4. *CC* No.249782. Began 1963; interdenominational. Magazine: *AFC Britain News* (1,700 every two months). Turnover £130,000 to year end June 98. Evangelistic team working in Cornwall.
Email: afcbritain@btinternet.com
☎ 01209 217 927 Fax 01209 313 503

***Ambassadors in Sport**, Claremont House, St George's Road, Bolton BL1 2BY
Director: Mr Ray D Tucker. Executive staff 3, Other staff 5. *CC* No.1055422. Began 1990; interdenominational. Magazine: *Ambassadors in Sport 'The Goal Post'* (1,500 monthly). Turnover £100,000 to year end Dec 98. Communicating the message of Jesus Christ to all cultures through the environment of soccer.
Email: ais.uk@btinternet.com
☎ 01204 363 606 Fax 01204 364 040

Army of Ants, PO Box 4593, Kiln Farm, Milton Keynes MK8 0HH
Director: Mr Bob Davis. Executive staff 3, Admin staff 1. *CC* Began 1998; ecumenical. No magazine. Turnover: first year of operation. Helping others share their faith by providing videos of God's Word and cinema films.
Web: www.armyofants.org
Email: bob@armyofants.org
☎ 01628 481 425 Fax 01628 481 426

Associated Bus Ministries Trust, 47 Merthyr Avenue, Drayton, Portsmouth PO6 2AR
Chairman: Mr R Maclennan. Administrative staff 2. *CC* No.1002455. Began 1991; interdenominational. Magazine: *Bus Route* (3,000 every two months). Turnover £56,000 to year end Apr 98. Mobile facility for evangelism, equipped with coffee lounge, video, displays explaining the Christian message.
Email: abmndtmh@aol.com
☎ 023 9221 9490 Fax 020 8391 9231

Association of Evangelists, 15 Stirling Crescent, Horsforth, Leeds LS18 5SJ
Director: To be appointed. Executive staff 4, Other staff 1. *CC* No.266005. Began 1983; interdenominational. No magazine. Turnover n/a. An association of independent evangelists. Linked to the Metropolitan Mission in Andra Pradesh, India.
Email: assocevang@aol.com
☎ 0113 258 1183

Bath Christian Trust, 1a Forum Buildings, St James's Parade, Bath BA1 1UG
Elder: Mr Paul Wakely. Executive staff 3, Other staff 2. *CC* No.1010281. Began 1976; non-denominational. No magazine. Turnover £550,000 to year end Apr 98. Co-ordinating the work of Bath City Church and serving related churches in the region.
Web: www.bathcitychurch.org.uk
Email: enquiries@bathcitychurch.org.uk
☎ 01225 463 556

The Bible Network, 6 Clarendon House, 117 George Lane, South Woodford, London E18 1AN
Director: John Savage. Staff n/a. *CC* No.299943. Began 1985; interdenominational. (Previously Christian Mission Fellowship). Magazine: *Report* (10,000 every four months). Turnover n/a. Bible distribution and church planting.
☎ No telephone

***Big Ideas**, PO Box 39, Penarth CF64 2YH
Directors: Mr Nigel James, Mr Gary Smith. Other staff 2. *CC* No.1047757. Began 1994; interdenominational. Magazine: *Yes* (1,200 quarterly). Turnover n/a. Creative evangelism and training for churches, youth organisations; provision of performing arts.
Email: bigideas_abs@compuserve.com
☎ 029 2038 2462 Fax 029 2038 2115

Evangelistic Agencies (Primarily in UK)

***Bonneville Christian Centre**, 12 Poynders Road, London SW4 8NY
Team Leader: Rev Les Ball. Executive staff 4, Other staff 4. ***CC*** Began 1987; Baptist. No magazine. Turnover £100,000–300,000 to year end Dec 98. Evangelism, church planting in Balham, Brixton and Clapham, and overseas in India, Africa.
☎ 020 8673 0639

***Bridge Christian Community**, 135 Ravenhill Road, Belfast BT6 8DR
Leader: Ms Helen Smith. Staff n/a. ***CC*** Began 1985; interdenominational. (Previously Bridge Community Trust). No magazine. Turnover £60,000 to year end Dec 98. Providing staff, support and spiritual focus to Lower Ravenhill area of Belfast.
☎ 028 9045 9000 🖷 028 9073 9099

British Church Growth Association, The Park, Moggerhanger, Bedford MK44 3RW
Joint Executive Directors: Mrs Monica Hill, Rev Philip Walker. Executive staff 2, Other staff 1. ***CC*** No.285577. Began 1981; interdenominational. Magazine: *Church Growth Digest* (700 quarterly). Turnover £42,000 to year end Dec 98. UK Church growth specialists: emphasis on small churches, natural church development, Europe, church planting, research.
Web: www.u-net.com/~the-park
Email: bcga@the-park.u-net.com
☎ 01767 641 001 🖷 01767 641 515

The Brotherhood and Sisterhood Movement, Leamington Spa Baptist Church, Chandos Street, Leamington Spa CV32 4RN
General Secretary: Mr John C Clark. Executive staff 1. ***CC*** No.207686. Began 1875; interdenominational. Magazine: *Outlook* (1,000 every two months). Turnover n/a. Seeking to win men and women for Christ through informal worship, fellowship and community work.
☎ 01926 422 496

Catholic Missionary Society, The Chase Centre, 114 West Heath Road, London NW3 7TX
Director: Rev Paul Billington. Executive staff 10, Other staff 4. ***CC*** No.233699. Began 1902; Roman Catholic. Magazine: *Catholic Gazette* (3,000 monthly). Turnover n/a. Promotes and fosters evangelisation through parish and school missions and other initiatives in England and Wales.
Email: cms@cms.org.uk
☎ 020 8458 3316 🖷 020 8905 5780

***Causeway PROSPECTS**, PO Box 351, Reading RG1 7AL
Director: Mr Tony Phelps-Jones. Other staff 4. ***CC*** No.1060571. Began 1989; interdenominational. (Previously Causeway). (Part of PROSPECTS for People with Learning Disabilities). Magazine: *Causeway PROSPECTS Update* (500 half-yearly). Turnover £82,000 to year end Mar 99. Raising awareness, training and resource materials for effective spiritual ministry among people with learning disabilities.
Email: causeway@prospects.org.uk
☎ 0118 950 8781 🖷 0118 939 1683

***Challenge 2000**, 12a Moorland Road, Burslem, Stoke-on-Trent ST6 1DW
Co-ordinator: Mr Kevin Popely. Other staff 2. ***CC*** No.1049296. Began 1991; non-denominational. Turnover n/a. Promoting a DAWN strategy in England involving church mobilisation and multiplication.
Email: robertmountford-internet.cvm@fenetre.co.uk
☎ 01782 832 563 🖷 01782 811 938

Chapel Lodge Ministries (Go Evangelise Mission), Chapel Lodge High Road, Gorefield, Wisbech PE13 4NZ
Minister: Rev Les Warren. Executive staff 2, Other staff 2 Began 1994; Full Gospel. Magazine: *Living Water* (500 every two months). Turnover n/a. International revival and healing ministry; Christian book sales (Incorporating Gem Books).
Web: www.netcomuk.co.uk/~fgospelf/fgfmain.htm
Email: livwater@netcomuk.co.uk
☎ 01945 870 016 🖷 01945 870 867

Christian Businessmen's Committee (CBMC), 193 Fleet Street London EC4A 2AH
Chairman: Mr Steven Moussavi. No full-time staff. ***CC*** Began 1967; interdenominational. Magazine: *Contact/CBMC Newsletter*(Circulation & frequency n/a), *Businessmen & Christianity*(Circulation & frequency n/a). Turnover n/a. Sharing Christ with business and professional people.
Email: infoodspsilink.co.uk
☎ 020 7404 6970 🖷 020 7404 7017

Christian Care Ministries, 28 Dacca Street, Deptford, London SE8 3LG
Evangelist: Mrs Ethel Spiff. No full-time staff. Began 1989. No magazine. Turnover n/a.
☎ 020 8692 6374

Christian Enquiry Agency, Inter-Church House, 35 Lower Marsh, London SE1 7RL
Director: Rev Dr Philip Clements-Jewery. Executive staff 1. ***CC*** No.297393. Began 1985; interdenominational. Magazine: *Newsletter* (1,500 half-yearly). Turnover £30,000 to year end Dec 95. Dealing with enquiries on the Christian faith resulting from advertising in the media and elsewhere.
Web: www.christianity.org.uk
Email: enquiry@christianity.org.uk
☎ 020 7523 2123 (Directline)
020 7620 0718 (24hr ansaphone) 🖷 020 7928 0010

Christian Family Ministries, 32 Norfolk Road, Erdington, Birmingham B23 6NA
Director: Rev Peter Green. Executive staff 1, Other staff 1. ***CC*** No.516947. Began 1985; interdenominational. No magazine. Turnover £13,723 to year end Apr 98. Evangelistic programmes to reach the whole family; training in evangelism; conducting non-threatening marriage seminars.
Email: petecfm@aol.com
☎ 0121 350 6151 Mobile: 07778 994 016
🖷 0121 386 2218

The Christian Jew Foundation, Grove Hill Evangelical Church, Grove Hill, South Woodford, London E18 2HY
Representative & Evangelist: Rev Robert Weissman. Executive staff 1. ***CC*** No.1056947. Began 1989; (UK); interdenominational. Magazine: *Message of the Christian Jew* (300 n/a). Turnover n/a. Evangelism of Jewish people; promotion of Jewish mission work in the media; preaching.
☎ 01959 565 955 (Christian Witness to Israel)

Christian Ministries, 1 Birdlip Close, Witney OX8 6LU
Joint Directors: Rev Peter Anderson, Mr John Blanchard, Mr Derek Cleave. Executive staff 3. ***CC*** No.280172. Began 1980; non-denominational. Magazine: *Communication* (2,500 every four months). Turnover £85,000 to year end Dec 98. International ministry of evangelism and Bible teaching.
☎ 01993 702 807

Christian Student Action (Part of Agapé), Fairgate House, King's Road, Tyseley, Birmingham B11 2AA
Executive Director: Mr Evan Winter. *National Director:* Mr David Wilson. Other staff 15. ***CC*** No.258421. Began 1967; interdenominational. Magazine: *Agapé News* (10,000 every four months). Turnover included in Agapé. Evangelism and discipleship among university students.
Web: www.agape.org.uk
Email: csa@agape.org.uk
☎ 0121 765 4404 🖷 0121 765 4065

Christian Viewpoint, 14 Parkfield Road, Stourbridge DY8 1HD
National Co-ordinator: Mrs Ruth Adams. Executive staff 1. ***CC*** No.295075. Began 1966; interdenominational. Magazine: *Viewpoint* (2,500 half-yearly). Turnover £10-50,000 to year end Dec 96. Providing resources and encouragement for women to share their faith in Jesus effectively with the unchurched.
Email: 113003.345@compuserve.com
☎ 01384 370 775

Christian Viewpoint for Men, PO Box 26, Sevenoaks TN15 0ZP
Chairman: Mr Max Sinclair. Other staff 3. ***CC*** No.1071663. Began 1989; interdenominational. Magazine: *Man to Man* (2,500 frequency n/a). Turnover £60,000 to year end Dec 98. Providing training, encouragement and resources to men seeking to bring others to faith in Jesus.
Web: www.domini.org/cum
Email: maxsinclair@cvm.telme.com
☎ 01732 834 297 🖷 01732 834 298

Christian Witness Ministries, PO Box 6737, Birmingham B1 3QX
Director: Rev Oliver Joseph Raper. *General Manager:* Mr Paul Clarke. Executive staff 1, Other staff 3. ***CC*** No.1062660. Began 1998; interdenominational. No magazine. Turnover £250,000 to year end Jun 98. Reaching the unchurched through roadshows, using music, drama and contemporary preaching.
Web: www.cwm.org.uk
Email: info@cwm.org.uk
☎ 0121 687 8688 🖷 0121 687 8689

Church Army, Independents Road, Blackheath, London SE3 9LG
Chief Secretary: Capt Philip Johanson. *Director of Marketing:* Mr Nigel Edward-Few. *Director of Finance:* Mr John Welsh. Executive staff 9, Other staff 600. ***CC*** No.226226. Began 1882; Anglican. Magazine: *Share It!* (50,000 quarterly). Turnover £8,200,000 to year end Mar 98. Sharing faith through words and action, and encouraging Christians in their everyday witness.
Web: churcharmy.org.uk
Email: information@churcharmy.org.uk
☎ 020 8318 1226 🖷 020 8318 5258

Church of Scotland Board of National Mission, 121 George Street, Edinburgh EH2 4YN
General Secretary: Rev Douglas Nicol. Executive Staff 6, Full-time staff 175, Part-time staff 300. ***CC*** Began n/a; Church of Scotland. Magazine: *National Mission Update* (2,000 half-yearly). Turnover £5,000,000 to year end Dec 98. Planning and resourcing the mission and evangelism of the Church of Scotland in Scotland.
☎ 0131 225 5722 🖷 0131 226 6121

***Church Pastoral Aid Society**, Athena Drive, Tachbrook Park, Warwick CV34 6NG
General Director: Rev Canon Brian Pearson. Executive staff 9, Other staff 63. ***CC*** No.1007820. Began 1836; Anglican. Magazine: *Together* (16,000 half-yearly). Turnover £2,242,000 to year end Apr 98. Encouraging mission, resourcing leaders.
Web: www.cpas.org.uk
Email: mail@cpas.org.uk
☎ 01926 458 458 🖷 01926 458 459

Co-ordinating Group for Evangelism, 116 High Street, Harrold, Bedford MK43 7BJ
Executive Secretary: Rev Roger Whitehead. Staff n/a. ***CC*** No.1052321. Began 1990; ecumenical. No magazine. Turnover £25,000 to year end Aug 98. Co-ordinating evangelisation strategies, policies and programmes between the denominations, para-church groups and Christian agencies.
Email: gfe@harrold.demon.co.uk
☎ 01234 721 127 🖷 01294 721 127

***Come Back to God Campaign**, Adelaide College, 3 Nineyards Street, Saltcoats KA21 5HS
Director: Rev Dennis Paterson. Executive staff 9. ***CC*** No.240168. Began 1956; interdenominational. Magazine: *Teamwork* (2,000 every two months). Turnover £59,000 to year end Dec 98. Bible training college, postal enquiry, pastoral aid, conferences, radio and literature.
Web: www.comebacktogod.org
Email: campaign@comebacktogod.org
☎ 01294 463 911 🖷 01294 463 366

***Commission on Strategic Evangelism in the UK**, Whitefield House, 186 Kennington Park Road, London SE11 4BT
Chair: Rev Ian Coffey. No full-time staff. ***CC*** No.123448. Began n/a; interdenominational. An Evangelical Alliance Partnership for Change. No magazine. Turnover: finance included with Evangelical Alliance. Serving EA/EMA members through analysis, information, stimulation to complete the evangelism task in UK.
Web: www.eauk.org
Email: agreene@eauk.org
☎ 020 7207 2100 🖷 020 7207 2150

E

Community of Celebration Christian Trust, 1 Greenwood Drive, Redhill RH1 5PH
Secretary: Mrs Susan Abbott. ***CC*** No.266564. Began 1973; non-denominational. Magazine: *Newsletter* (Circulation n/a half-yearly). Turnover £108,000 to year end Mar 98. Promoting the Christian faith through support for ministry of members of Community of Celebration.
☎ 01737 761 090
Also at: 35 Cavendish Road, Redhill RH1 4AL
☎ 01737 778 760

***Cornerstone**, Cornerstone House, 5 Ethel Street, Birmingham B2 4BG
Services Director: Mr Robert Lawley. Executive staff 6, Other staff 40. ***CC*** No.510971. Began 1980; non-denominational. Magazine: *Newsletter* (1,500 quarterly). Turnover £326,187 to year end May 96. Evangelism and social action through community centres, coffee shops, hostels, children's/youth work, family care.
Email: admin@cornerstone.charis.co.uk
☎ 0121 643 1984 📠 0121 632 5136

***Counties**, 30 Haynes Road, Westbury BA13 3HD
National Administrator: Mr Ronald F Davies. *Development Secretary:* Mr Ivor Cooper. Executive staff 3, Other staff 44. ***CC*** No.264278. Began 1899; Christian Brethren. (Previously Counties Evangelistic Work). Magazine: *Forward* (6,500 quarterly). Turnover n/a. Church-based and general evangelism; Bible exhibition for churches; training department.
Web: members.aol.com/counties30
Email: counties30@aol.com
☎ 01373 823 013 Mobile: 07973 779 098 📠 01373 859 199

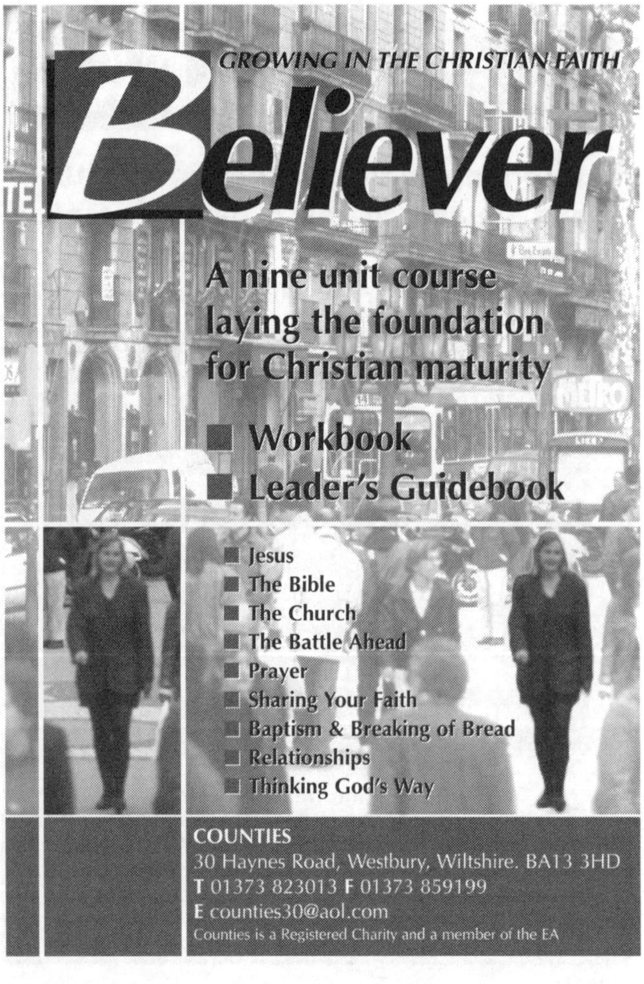

Cranmer Memorial Bible Society, PO Box 20, Bexhill-on-Se TN40 2ZH
Principle: Rev Dr Peter J Gadsden. Executive staff 2, Volun tary staff 1. ***CC*** Began 1936; non-denominational. (Previousl Cranmer Hall Bible College). Magazine: *Our Inheritanc* (2,000 quarterly). Turnover n/a. Training, Education of me from the reformed Protestant ministry.
Web: www.bt.internet.com/~gadsden/pt1/pt1
Email: gadsden@btinternet.com
☎ 01424 734 345

***Crying Out Loud Trust**, 2 Princes Crescent North, Dolla FK14 7BX
Director: Mr Eddie Williamson. Executive staff 1, Other staf 1. ***CC*** No.SCO 25267. Began 1996; interdenominational. No magazine. Turnover £25,000 to year end Dec 98. Outreach an discipleship through drama and teaching to all ages.
☎ 01259 742 425 📠 01259 724 425

The Damascus Trust, 51 Clockhouse Way, Braintree CM7 3RD
Director: Mr Andy Paine. Executive staff 1, Other staff 2. ***CC*** No.1013236. Began 1990; interdenominational. Magazine *News-Line* (1,000 quarterly). Turnover n/a. Enthusing an enabling local churches in evangelism amongst the unchurched teaching, training and establishing outreach teams.
☎ 01376 342 529 📠 01376 342 529

Miss Daniell's Soldiers' Homes, Havelock House, Barrack Road Aldershot GU11 3NP
Hon Secretary: Lt Col M Hitchcott. *Missioner:* Mr Bil Woolfall. Other staff 4. ***CC*** No.233685. Began 1861; interdenominational. No magazine. Turnover £113,000 to year en Dec 98. Providing canteen facilities as a means of introducin service personnel to the Lord Jesus Christ.
Email: mdsh@sasra.org.uk
☎ 01252 310 033 📠 01252 350 722

Day of Salvation Ministries, International Gospel Centre, Ranelagh Road, Malvern WR14 1BQ
Evangelist: Mr Gordon Leveratt. Executive staff 2, Other staf 2. ***CC*** No.1037693. Began 1992; non-denominational. Magazine: *Salvation* (500 monthly). Turnover £15,400 to year en Oct 98. Reaching out to people everywhere with the Gospe primarily through crusade evangelism (2,000 seat tent).
Web: www.dofs.mcmail.com
Email: dofs@mcmail.com
☎ 01684 568 241 Mobile: 07767 898 568 📠 01684 577 317

Decade Ministries, Grove House, Limetrees, Chilton, Didcot OX11 0HY
Director/Evangelist: Rev Roy Weaver. Executive staff 2, Other staff 3. Began 1990; Independent. Magazine: *Decade Ministries* (Circulation n/a quarterly). Turnover £53,000 to year end Oct 97. Visuals for all age worship and assemblies; planners, visual packs, posters, training, conferences; UK and USA.
☎ 01235 833 030 Mobile: 07801 515 666
📠 01235 833 030

***Deo Gloria Trust**, Selsdon House, 212 Addington Road, South Croydon CR2 8LD
Director: Mr Tim Harding. Executive staff 2, Other staff 5. ***CC*** No.243305. Began 1965; non-denominational. Magazine: *Newsletter* (7,500 annually). Turnover n/a. Projects for the promotion and defence of the Christian faith.
Email: dgt@deo-gloria.co.uk
☎ 020 8651 6428 📠 020 8651 6429

***Derbyshire Village Mission**, Epworth House, New Street, Matlock DE4 3FE
Director: Michelle Shaw. Executive staff 1, Other staff 5. ***CC*** Began 1916; non-denominational. Magazine: *DVM Newsletter* (1,300 quarterly). Turnover £19,580 to year end Apr 98. Rural ministry and evangelism with all age groups.
☎ 01629 760 735

Discovery (Part of Agapé), Fairgate House, Kings Road, Tyseley, Birmingham B11 2AA
Director: Mr Paul Duncan. Other staff 16. *CC* No.258421. Began 1983; interdenominational. Includes volunteer movement Discovery Direct. Magazine: *Agapé News* (10,000 every four months). Turnover see Agapé. Evangelism and discipleship in schools and youth groups in recognised partnership with a local church.
Web: www.agape.org.uk
Email: discovery@agape.org.uk
☎ 0121 765 4404 (Agapé) 0121 441 3364 (Discovery)
Fax 0121 765 4065

The Earls Court Project, 24 Collingham Road, London SW5 0LX
Project leader: Mr Bernhard Steenkamp. Executive staff 2, Other staff 7. *CC* No.264078. Began 1985; interdenominational. Magazine: *Earls Court Newsletter* (400 quarterly). Turnover £100,000 to year end Dec 96. Outreach to young and vulnerable people in the Earls Court area of London.
☎ 020 7370 4424

East to West, 12a High Street, Wraysbury TW19 5DB
Director: Mr Steve Holloway. Executive staff 1, Other staff 1. *CC* No.1059177. Began 1996; non-denominational. No magazine. Turnover n/a. Undertaking all age evangelism and training.
Web: www.e2w.dircon.co.uk
Email: e2w@dircon.co.uk
☎ 01784 488 000 Mobile: 07957 366 736 Fax 01784 488 300

English Lausanne Movement, c/o Christian Research, Vision Building, 4 Footscray Road, Eltham, London SE9 2TZ
Chairman: Rev Dr Derek Tidball. *Secretary:* Heather Wraight. No full-time staff. Began 1996; interdenominational. No magazine. Turnover £2,100 to year end Nov 98. Furthering the purposes, in England, of the International Lausanne movement.
☎ 020 8294 1989 Fax 020 8294 0014

Europe for Christ, 80 Victoria Road, Romford RM1 2LT
Director: Rev Colin Phillips. Executive staff 2, Other staff 5. *CC* No.278996. Began 1972; interdenominational. Magazine: *Prayer letter* (200 quarterly). Turnover £10,559 to year end Dec 98. Children's and youth missions, bookstalls, shops, video library, holidays, retreats and church planting teams.
☎ 01708 727 625 Fax 01708 757 758

***Evangelical (Youth Movement) Ministries**, 114a Holywood Road, Belfast BT4 1NU
Director: Mr David Millen. *Women's Ministry Co-ordinator:* Miss Pamela Johnston. Executive staff 4, Other staff 7. *CC* No.XN 48447. Began 1965; interdenominational. Magazine: *In Contact* (1,500 quarterly). Turnover £375,186 to year end Aug 98. Church faith planning, evangelism, discipleship, encouraging church based youth work. Focusfest conference and women's ministry.
Web: www.emins.com
Email: info@emins.com
☎ 028 9047 1100 Fax 028 9047 1190

***Evangelism Explosion**, PO Box 552, Southampton SO18 1ZL
National Director: Mr Peter Crook. Admin staff 1. *CC* No.269722. Began 1975; non-denominational. Magazine: *Update* (1,400 frequency n/a). Turnover £65,429 to year end Mar 98. Equipping churches to train their members in personal witnessing and discipleship.
☎ 023 8022 8985

Exousia Trust (Sean Stillman), PO Box 437, Reading RG30 3DF
Evangelist: Mr Sean Stillman. Executive staff 1. *CC* No.1002581. Began 1991; interdenominational. Magazine: *Newsletter* (600 half-yearly). Turnover £28,000 to year end Apr 97. Supporting the ministry of Sean and Jayne Stillman; "Bibles for Bikers".
Email: stillers@exousia.demon.co.uk
☎ 01792 480 391 Fax 01792 480 391

Faith Alive Youth Ministry, 5 Oakroyd Crescent, Potters Bar EN6 2EW
Director: Mr Cormac B O'Duffy. Executive staff 2. *CC* No.1020135. Began 1989; Roman Catholic. Turnover £15,000 to year end Aug 98. Catholic youth evangelism training teams for work in primary and secondary schools and other projects.
☎ 01707 664 687 Fax 01707 664 687
All the World Sing Praise, 60 Wickstead Avenue, Luton LU4 9DP
Email: alltheworldsingpraise@new-life.demon.co.uk
☎ 01582 571 011

***The Faith Mission**, Govan House, 2 Drum Street, Gilmerton, Edinburgh EH17 8QG
General Director: Mr Keith Percival. Executive staff 5, Other staff 100. *CC* Began 1886; non-denominational. Magazine: *Life Indeed* (8,500 every two months). Turnover n/a. Evangelistic movement geared to reach all ages in rural areas of the UK and Republic of Ireland.
Web: www.faithmission.org
Email: hq@faithmission.org
☎ 0131 664 5814 Fax 0131 664 2260
Also at: *England Director:* Mr John Townend, 10 Millgates, York YO2 6AT
☎ 01904 330 120
And: *Ireland Director:* Mr Trevor Matthews, 43a Upper Lisburn Road, Belfast BT10 0GX
☎ 028 9061 3316

***Fellowship for Evangelising Britain's Villages**, PO Box 271, Taunton TA1 1YY
Chairman: Pastor Hugh Cozens. Executive staff 3, Other staff 29. *CC* No.232793. Began 1919; interdenominational. Magazine: *Village News* (2,000 every two months). Turnover £68,000 to year end Dec 97. Assisting village churches; effective evangelism to establish groups of living witnesses for Christ.
Web: www.lineone.net/~febv
Email: febv@lineone.net
☎ 01823 321 016 Fax 01823 321 016

Fellowship of Evangelistic Ministries, 41 Ingleborough Way, Leyland PR5 2ZS
General Secretary: Rev Dr William Coppack. Executive staff 3. Began 1896; non-denominational. Turnover n/a. The proclamation of the historical, Biblical based Gospel, through its members and associates, by accreditation.
☎ 01772 436 817

The Festivals of Male Voice Praise, 90 Crookston Avenue, Glasgow G52 3PR
Secretary: Mr William Rodger. No full-time staff. Began 1934; non-denominational. Magazine: *Interlink* (3,000 quarterly). Turnover n/a. Gospel witness through the medium of male voice song and related music publications.
☎ 0141 882 2009 Fax 0141 882 2009

***Finnish Lutheran Mission**, 40 Low Hall Lane, London E17 8BE
Field Director: Ms Elisabet Elo. Executive staff 1, Other staff 3. Began 1973; Lutheran. Magazine: *Ye Sach Hai* (Circulation n/a irregularly). Turnover n/a. Bringing the Gospel to people of other faiths in the UK. Funded from Finland.
☎ 020 8925 2179 Fax 020 8925 2179

E

Frontier Year Project, Lancing Community Church, 17 Third Avenue, Lancing BN15 9PU
Training Director: Mr Simon Walker. Executive staff 3. ***CC*** Began 1985; non-denominational. No magazine. Turnover £100,000 to year end Dec 97. Training in character, gifting and skills for all ages within local churches, including 45 days theological training.
Email: fyp@bigfoot.com
☎ 01903 203 255

***Rob Frost Team**, The Methodist Church, Tolverne Road, Raynes Park, London SW20 8RA
National Evangelist: Rev Dr Rob Frost. Executive staff 4, Other staff 6. ***CC*** No.1801996. Began 1983; Methodist. Magazine: *Prayer Letter* (25,500 quarterly). Turnover n/a. Evangelism and church renewal through Seed Teams; New Creation Arts Team; student missions.
Web: www.ncl.ac.uk/~ndjs/robfrost
Email: rob.frost.team@dial.pipex.com
☎ 020 8944 5678 Fax 020 8947 5152
Easter People ☎ 020 8288 1966

***Full Gospel Business Men's Fellowship International**, PO Box 11, Knutsford WA16 6QP
Director: Mr John Walker. Executive staff 4. ***CC*** Began 1976; non-denominational. Magazine: *Voice* (17,000 every two months). Turnover £50,000 to year end Dec 97. Monthly evangelistic dinners and other outreach meetings primarily for men by 180 local Chapters (Branches).
Web: dialspace.dial.pipex.com/town/lane/kbw15
Email: fgbmfiuk@dial.pipex.com
☎ 01565 632 667 Fax 01565 755 639

***Fylde Evangelism**, 24 Daventry Avenue, Bispham, Blackpool FY2 9LB
Secretary: Mr R Palmer. No full-time staff. ***CC*** No.512580. Began 1980; interdenominational. No magazine. Turnover £750 to year end Dec 98. Arranging crusades, conventions, rallies, youth events and weekends; Bible ministry.
☎ 01253 353 926

Genesis Arts Trust, 6 Broad Court, Covent Garden, London WC2B 5QZ
International Director: Mr Nigel Goodwin. Executive staff 1, Other staff 1. ***CC*** Began 1982; non-denominational. Magazine: *Newsletter* (2,000 quarterly). Turnover n/a. Encouraging the impact of Christian faith in the professional world of arts, media and entertainment.
Email: genesisarts@btinternet.com
☎ 020 7240 6980 Fax 020 7240 6973

***Global March for Jesus**, International Office, Waverley Abbey House, Waverley Lane, Farnham GU9 8EP
International Co-ordinator: Ms Erica Youngman. *UK Coordinator:* Mr Brian Clews. Other staff 5. ***CC*** No.1008855. Began 1987; non-denominational. (Previously March for Jesus). No magazine. Turnover n/a. Serving the church worldwide in effective prayer, praise and witness through national and global events.
Web: www.newns.com/gmfj/
Email: 100572.323@compuserve.com
☎ 01252 784 774 Fax 01252 784 775

Go Ministries, 5 Monterey Drive, Havant PO9 5TQ
Director/Evangelist: Mr Mike Simmonds. Executive staff 2. ***CC*** No.276546. Began 1978; interdenominational. Magazine: *News* (600 quarterly). Turnover £8,000 to year end Mar 97. Church based evangelism and Bible teaching using preaching and multimedia graphics.
Email: gomin@surfaid.org
☎ 023 9235 6845 Mobile: 07971 235 481

***Going Public**, Glenwood Centre, Circle Way West, Cardiff CF2 6UW
Director: Mr Paul Francis. Admin staff 2, Other staff 3. ***CC*** No.1019789. Began 1990; non-denominational. No magazine. Turnover £48,000 to year end Mar 98. Evangelism to South Wales and Valleys; sex/drugs education to youth and adults; professional media services.
Web: www.company-net.co.uk/~going public
Email: gp@glenwood.cix.co.uk
☎ 029 2033 7890 Fax 029 2033 7881

***Good News Crusade**, 17 High Cross Street, St Austell PL25 4AN
Director: Rev Don Double. *Director of Administration:* Mr Tim Jones. Executive staff 4, Other staff 12. ***CC*** No.225483. Began 1960; interdenominational. Magazine: *Frontline Connections* (10,000 quarterly), *Frontline News* (2,500 quarterly). Turnover £745,497 to year end Dec 98. Evangelism through missions equipping the Church worldwide; conferences, training courses, publications.
Web: www.gnc.org.uk
Email: info@gnc.org.uk
☎ 01726 722 82 Fax 01726 698 53

Gospel Outreach International, South View House, Station Terrace, Fence Houses, Houghton le Spring DH4 6HR
Evangelist: Mr Gordon K Stoves. Executive staff 1. ***CC*** No.517006. Began 1985; interdenominational. No magazine. Turnover £5,000 to year end Mar 97. Work and training in evangelism, Bible teaching.
Email: stoves-goi@freeserve.co.uk
☎ 0191 385 6655 Fax 0191 385 8521

Billy Graham Evangelistic Association Ltd, PO Box 2032, Woodford Green IG9 5AP
Contact: Miss Jean Wilson. No full-time staff. ***CC*** Began 1956; interdenominational. Magazine: *Decision* (Circulation n/a monthly). Turnover n/a. London contact with Billy Graham and his team.
Email: 100067.1226@compuserve.com
☎ 020 8559 0342 Fax 020 8502 9062

***Grassroots**, 99 Mays Lane, Barnet EN5 2DX
Directors: Hugo & Sharon Anson. Executive staff 2, Other staff 6. ***CC*** No.1060034. Began 1997; interdenominational. Magazine: *Grassroots* (1,000 quarterly). Turnover £20,000 to year end Dec 98. Church planting, evangelism, humanitarian aid agency. Including Mouthpeace Missions.
Web: www.grassroots.org.uk
Email: info@grassroots.org.uk
☎ 020 8441 0642 Mobile: 07710 284 150
Fax 020 8449 8646

***Groundswell**, Whitefield House, 186 Kennington Park Road, London SE11 4BT
Chair: Rev Paul Harris. No full-time staff. ***CC*** No.123448. Began n/a; interdenominational. An Evangelical Alliance Partnership for Change. No magazine. Turnover: finance included with Evangelical Alliance. Promoting local missionary congregations by providing support, information, appropriate resources.
Web: www.eauk.org
Email: members@eauk.org
☎ 020 7207 2100 Fax 020 7207 2150

***Gypsies for Christ Travelling With the Romani Gospel Waggon**, 32 Ashford Road, South Woodford, London E18 1JZ
Chairman: Mr Sonnie Gibbard. Other staff 2. ***CC*** No.273789. Began 1975; interdenominational. Magazine: *Newsletter* (600 every four months). Turnover £4,000 to year end Nov 98. Co-ordinating work and evangelism amongst gypsies at home and abroad.
☎ 020 8530 2471 Fax 020 8530 2471

***Hallelujah Ministries**, 100 School Road, Wales, Sheffield S26 5QJ
Administrators: Mr Alan & Mrs Stephanie Bidwell. Executive staff 4, Other staff 4. ***CC*** No.1025529. Began 1993; interdenominational. No magazine. Turnover £42,567 to year end Oct 96. Preaching the gospel in many nations; tent crusades; radio outreach; tape ministry (prisons); aid to Uganda.
☎ 01909 770 996 🖷 01909 773 403

***Heart of England Outreach**, PO Box 470, Meriden, Coventry CV7 7YT
Director: Rev John Yates. Executive staff 4, Other staff 3. ***CC*** No.327046. Began 1979; non-denominational. Magazine: *Central Vision* (500 quarterly). Turnover £11,000 to year end Feb 99. Pioneer evangelism; training and assisting existing churches.
☎ 01676 523 050

High Adventure Ministries, PO Box 109, Hereford HR4 9XR
Administrator: Mr Peter Darg. Staff 2. ***CC*** No.327348. Began 1981; interdenominational. Magazine: *Newsletter* (Circulation n/a monthly). Turnover £35,000 to year end Dec 98. Global shortwave radio ministry with stations in Lebanon, California, Israel, Palau (South Pacific) and Germany.
Web: www.highadventure.org
Email: 101602.3273@compuserve.com
☎ 01432 359 099 🖷 01432 263 408

Holy Fools, 93 Hornes Road, Barkingside, Ilford IG6 1DQ
Director: Mr Richard James. No full-time staff. Began 1983; interdenominational. Magazine: *Foolish Times* (200 quarterly). Turnover n/a. Proclaiming the Good News through clowning and circus skills; performances and workshops.
☎ 020 8554 7986

***Home Evangelism**, Tyndale House, 3 Grange Road, Egham TW20 9QW
Field Director: Rev Robin A Wood. *Admin Director:* Mrs Diane Redwood. Executive staff 2, Other staff 2, Field staff 18. ***CC*** No.223473. Began 1874; interdenominational. Magazine: *With Tongue & Pen* (8,000 annually). Turnover £321,117 to year end Mar 98. Door-to-door evangelism; training and mobilising church teams; associate evangelists (the HEAT).
Email: robin.wood2@virgin.net
☎ 01784 432 558 🖷 01784 432 064

***Hope Now Ltd**, Croft House, Combe St Nicholas, Chard TA20 3ND
Executive Director: Mr Mike Perreau. *Founder President:* Rev Vic Jacopson. Executive staff 3, Other staff 5. ***CC*** No.293416. Began 1985; interdenominational. No magazine. Turnover £500,000 to year end Dec 98. Evangelising the gospel to the unreached and by deeds and actions showing the love of Christ.
Web: www.hopenow.org.uk
Email: mike@hopenow.org.uk
☎ Mobile: 07836 774 881

***Inn Christian Ministries**, First Floor, 64 Balmoral Road, Gillingham ME7 4QE
Director: Mr Peter Marchand. Other staff 2. ***CC*** No.1009911. Began 1989; interdenominational. Magazine: *Inn-News* (300 every four months). Turnover £17,000 to year end Feb 98. Evangelism with church planting in Uganda; resourcing churches locally, nationally and internationally.
Web: www.inn.org.uk
Email: inncm@inn.org.uk
☎ 01634 581 019 Mobile: 07710 274 825 🖷 01634 581 019

***International Gospel Outreach**, The Oasis, Dwygyfylchi Penmaenmawr LL34 6PS
General Secretary: Rev Bob Searle. Executive staff 8, Office staff 4, Field staff 270. ***CC*** No.252872. Began 1967; interdenominational. Magazine: *Christian Vision* (2,000 monthly). Turnover n/a. Fellowship of ministers, Christian workers and intercessors; worldwide team ministries; conferences, youth camps, Bible correspondence school.
Web: www.churches.net/userpages/oasisdwygyfylchi.htm/
Email: igo@oasisdwygyfylchi.freeserve.co.uk
☎ 01492 623 229 🖷 01492 623 229
Prayerline: ☎ 01492 622 473
Also at: *President:* Rev Kingsley Armstrong, 27 Crestbrooke, Northallerton DL7 8YP ☎ 01609 771 027

The International Miners' Mission, 2 Village Place, 34 High Street, Markyate, St Albans AL3 8PB
Hon General Secretary: Mr David R Shillitoe. No full-time staff. ***CC*** No.221853. Began 1906; interdenominational. Magazine: *The Safety Lamp* (400 n/a). Turnover £12,131 to year end Dec 97. Making known the saving truths of the Christian Gospel to miners and their families.
☎ No telephone

***International Student Christian Services**, 3 Crescent Stables, 139 Upper Richmond Road, London SW15 2TN
National Director: Mr Richard Weston. *Field Director:* Mr Peter Hayden. Executive staff 3, Other staff 40. ***CC*** No.326977. Began 1985; non-denominational. Magazine: *Opportunity* (2,000 quarterly). Turnover £365,000 to year end Dec 98. Evangelisation and discipleship of overseas students, working with local evangelical churches.
Web: www.iscs.org.uk
Email: info@iscs.org.uk
☎ 020 8780 3511 🖷 020 8785 1174

Into The Light, PO Box 112, Oldham OL8 2FB
Director: Mr Stephen Masood. Executive staff 1, Admin staff 1. Began 1999; non-denominational. No magazine. Turnover: first year of operation. Outreach to Muslims using the internet and other resources; distributing free literature.
Web: www.itl.org.uk
Email: steven.masood@itl.org.uk
☎ 0161 620 8991 🖷 0161 620 8991

†***Irish Mission**, Church House, Fisherwick Place, Belfast BT1 6DW
Superintendent: Rev David J Temple. Office staff 4, Field workers 10. Began 1710; Presbyterian. Magazine: *The Christian Irishman Magazine* (10,500 monthly). Turnover £300,000 to year end Dec 94. Literature, visitation, video evangelism in schools, markets, homes, churches; music/drama ministry.
☎ 028 9032 2284 🖷 028 9024 8377

***JESUS Video Project**, Fairgate House, Kings Road, Tyseley, Birmingham B11 2AA
Director: Mr John Arkell. Other staff 8. ***CC*** No.258421. Began 1967; interdenominational. Part of Agapé. Magazine: *Agapé News* (10,000 every four months). Turnover included in Agapé. Working with local churches to help every person see the JESUS video in their own home.
Email: jvp@agape.org.uk
☎ 0121 765 4404 🖷 0121 765 4065

Jesus Army (Modern Jesus Army), Nether Heyford, Northampton NN7 3LB
Senior Pastor: Noel Stanton. No full-time staff. Began 1987; Jesus Fellowship. Magazine: *Modern Jesus Army Streetpaper* (100,000 quarterly). Turnover n/a. Campaigning evangelism on streets of Britain's towns and cities; telephone helpline.
Web: www.jesus.org.uk
Email: info@jesus.org.uk
☎ 01327 349 991 Helpline: 0845 7023 199
Fax 01327 349 997

Jesus is Alive! Ministries, PO Box 5301, Southend-on-Sea SS1 1TL
Executive Director: Mr Paul Slennett. Part-time staff 6. *CC* No.1036183. Began 1994; interdenominational. No magazine. Turnover n/a. Evangelistic campaigns nationally, internationally; ministering to Jewish people, inmates of prisons, borstals; relief.
Web: www.gocin.com/jesusisalive
Email: jiaminsuk@aol.com
☎ 01702 394 077 Fax 01702 394 077

***Jews for Jesus**, 174 Finchley Road, London NW3 6BP
UK Director: Mr Jonathan Bernd. Executive staff 1, Other staff 4. *CC* No.1007336. Began 1992; non-denominational. Magazine: *Jews for Jesus Newsletter* (Circulation n/a quarterly), *Issues – A Messianic Jewish Perspective*(Circulation & frequency n/a). Turnover £202,000 to year end Dec 98. Jews for Jesus exists to make the Messiahship of Jesus an unavoidable issue for our Jewish people worldwide.
Web: www.jews-for-jesus.org
Email: enquiries@jews-for-jesus.org.uk
☎ 020 7431 9636 Fax 020 7431 6828

E

Kairos Trust, 30 St Matthews Street, Cambridge CB1 2LT
Co-ordinator: Mr Bartow Wylie. Executive staff 1, Other staff 3. *CC* No.279068. Began 1981; interdenominational. In partnership with International Student Christian Services. No magazine. Turnover £34,000 to year end Apr 98. Evangelising and discipling overseas students in Cambridge and training those involved.
Email: bartow.wylie@iscs.org.uk
☎ 01223 311 130

†**Kenneth Copeland Ministries**, Contact via Christian Research
Director of Operations UK and Europe: Mr Kim Freeborn. Executive staff 3, Other staff 10. *CC* Began 1983; non-denominational. Magazine: *Believers' Voice of Victory* (20,000 monthly). Turnover £1,261,410 to year end Dec 96. Teaching victorious Bible Christian living using believers' conventions, television, books, teaching tapes (ministry and music).

Latter Rain Ministries, Crossbasket Christian Centre, Stoney Meadow Road, Blantyre, Glasgow G72 9UE
President: Rev LaVere Soper. Executive staff 2, Other staff 4. *CC* Began 1984; interdenominational. Magazine: *Latter Rain Ministries* (3,000 quarterly). Turnover n/a. Sending and receiving teams throughout UK and Europe; Bible schools, healing crusades.
Email: 106674.2562@compuserve.com
☎ 01698 829 600 Fax 01698 824 601

Lausanne Committee for Evangelism in Ireland, The Manse, Brannockstown, Kilcullen, Curragh Camp, Co Kildare, Republic of Ireland
Chairman: Rev Robert Dunlop. No full-time staff. Began 1989; interdenominational. No magazine. Turnover n/a. Fostering and facilitating Ireland-wide evangelistic initiative.
☎ 00 353 0458 3629

Lay Witness Fellowship & House Group Evangelism, 133 Appledore Avenue, Wollaton, Nottingham NG8 2RW
Co-ordinator: Rev Thomas A Steen. Executive staff 1. *CC* Began 1973; non-denominational. Magazine: *Prayer Letter* (Circulation n/a Occasionally). Turnover n/a. Encouraging others to faith in Christ through personal witness and testimony; evangelical discussion group.
☎ 0115 928 7355

***Lay Witness Movement**, 25 Chorley Road, Standish, Wigan WN6 0AA
General Secretaries: Mr Brian & Mrs Hazel Rollins. Executive staff 2. *CC* No.328365. Began 1976; interdenominational. Turnover n/a. Spiritual stocktaking; weekends of testimony and small group discussion to strengthen churches.
Email: lwm@altavista.net
☎ 01257 422 995 Fax 01257 422 995

***The Legacie Trust**, 29 East Leys Court, Moulton, Northampton NN3 7TX
Directors: Mr Andrew & Mrs Pauline Pearson. Executive staff 2. *CC* No.292286. Began 1985; interdenominational. No magazine. Turnover n/a. Working nationally with churches in children's and family worship, also children's holiday clubs and events.
☎ 01604 493 785

***Steve Legg – The Breakout Trust**, PO Box 3070, Littlehampton BN17 5AW
Director: Mr Steve Legg. Executive staff 1, Other staff 1. *CC* No.1070960. Began 1989; interdenominational. Magazine: *Breakout Update* (1,000 quarterly). Turnover n/a. Creative evangelism in schools, colleges, universities, prisons and events in UK and abroad.
Web: www.breakout.org.uk
Email: steve@breakout.org.uk
☎ 01903 779 279 Fax 01903 779 280

Light for the Last Days, BM-4226, London WC1N 3XX
Editor: Mr Antony Pearce. No other full-time staff. Began 1989; interdenominational. Magazine: *Light for the Last Days* (5,000 quarterly). Turnover £6,000 to year end Dec 98. Producing evangelistic material, Bible studies and tapes about current affairs and prophecy.
Web: www.charitynet.org/~messianic
Email: lld@cwcom.net
☎ 020 8594 3072 Fax 020 8220 0150

Logos Ministries, 147 Albertbridge Road, Belfast BT5 4PS
Director: Rev Thomas McClean. Executive staff 2, Other staff 8. *CC* No.NI 46135. Began 1977; interdenominational. (Previously Youth Evangelical Missionary Fellowship). Magazine: *Edge* (1,500 quarterly). Turnover £98,000 to year end Dec 98. Church missions programme; youth and schools outreach; Bible teaching worldwide; training leaders for tomorrow's church.
Web: www.charis.co.uk/logos.ministries
Email: logos.ministries@charis.co.uk
☎ 02890 458 362 Fax 02890 458 362

London Hospital Ministries, 175 Tower Bridge Road, London SE1 2AH
Co-ordinator: Mr David Linley. Executive staff 1, Other staff 1. *CC* Began 1876; interdenominational. (Previously Bible Flower Mission). Part of London City Mission. Magazine: *Span* (39,000 every two months). Turnover £20,000 to year end Dec 98. Visiting patients in 20 London hospitals.
☎ 020 7407 7585

Lord's Day Observance Society (Day One Publications), No. 3 Epsom Business Park, Kiln Lane, Epsom KT17 1JF
General Secretary: Mr John G Roberts. Executive staff 2, Other staff 10. ***CC*** No.233465. Began 1831; interdenominational. Magazine: *Day One* (12,000 n/a). Turnover n/a. Evangelism; exhibitions, children's missions; Sunday observance; book publishing, selling; religious, social, political meetings; prison ministry.
Web: www.lordsday.co.uk
Email: info@lordsday.co.uk
☎ 01372 728 300 🖷 01372 722 400
Also at: Rev R Robb, 18 Rathmore Road, Limavady BT49 0DF ☎ 028 7172 2136

*****Love & Joy Ministries**, Temple of Praise, 148 Oakfield Road, Anfield, Liverpool L4 0UH
Director: Rev Dr Tani Omideyi. *Trustee:* Dr Modupe Omideyi. Executive staff 6, Admin staff 8. ***CC*** No.1050222. Began 1991; non-denominational. Magazine: *First Fruits* (500 annually). Turnover £350,000 to year end Mar 99. Reaching communities with the gospel through the medium of the arts and caring projects.
☎ 0151 475 6878 🖷 0151 475 0005

LUKE (Love UK Evangelism), LUKE Training Centre, Little Cornbow, Halesowen B63 3AJ
Director of LUKE Ministries: Mr Edward Disbury. Executive staff 15, Other staff 35. ***CC*** No.1008196. Began 1989; interdenominational. (A ministry of Operation Mobilisation). No magazine. Turnover £460,000 to year end Dec 98. Countrywide team-based evangelism, citywide campaigns, ethnic outreach, evangelistic training – local churches, foreign nationals.
Web: www.om.org
Email: postmaster@luke.om.org
☎ 0121 585 5662 🖷 0121 585 0271

Maritime Christian Ministries, 11 Worcester Road, Bootle L20 9AA
Port Missionary: Mr Stan Sherrington. Executive staff 1, Other staff 1. ***CC*** No.1071480. Began 1998; non-denominational. Magazine: *Mersey Tidings* (2,500 quarterly). Turnover n/a. Ministering to seafarers of all nations and their families, in the port of Liverpool.
Email: stanmcm@aol.com
☎ 0151 922 5543 🖷 0151 922 1415

*****Mayflower Family Centre**, Vincent Street, London E16 1LZ
Director: Mr Alan Craig. *Minister:* Rev David Gill. Other staff 16, plus voluntary staff. ***CC*** No.231370. Began 1958; Anglican/interdenominational. Magazine: *Mayflower News* (750 half-yearly). Turnover £201,000 to year end Mar 98. Church services, elderly and youth work, advice desk, charity shop, sports hall, 2 hostels, community launderette.
Email: mayflower@teleregion.co.uk
☎ 020 7476 1171 🖷 020 7511 1019

The Mega Mondo Trust, 1 Tremenheere Road, Penzance TR18 2AH
Administrator: Mr Joff Day. ***CC*** No.1032604. Began 1994; interdenominational. (Previously Network Christian Trust). No magazine. Turnover n/a. Supporting proclamation of the Gospel in UK and overseas.
Web: members.aol.com/megamondo/mmt
Email: joffday@aol.com
☎ 01736 360 350 Mobile: 07770 316 362

*****Men's Ministry (UK)**, Manor Cottage, Barras, Kirkby Stephen CA17 4ES
Board Member: Mr Rod Readhead. Executive staff 1, Other staff 1. Began 1997; interdenominational. (Previously Promise Keepers (UK)). Magazine: *Men of Vision* (3,000 every two months). Turnover n/a. Evangelism and discipling of men by resourcing the local church.
☎ 01768 341 573 🖷 01768 341 573

*****Message to Schools Trust**, PO Box 14, Cheadle SK8 2FE
Director: Mr Andy Hawthorne. *Office Manager:* Mr Rob Johnson. Executive staff 15, Other staff 5. ***CC*** No.1016357. Began 1993; interdenominational. No magazine. Turnover £250,000 to year end Aug 98. Reaching Manchester's young people with the Gospel through words, music, credible events, long-term action.
Web: www.message.org.uk
Email: info@message.org.uk
☎ 0161 491 5400 🖷 0161 491 5600

†**Mid-Sussex Christian Outreach**, Elizabeth House, 13 Heath Road, Haywards Heath RH16 3AX
Administrator: Mr Peter D Ford. No full-time staff. ***CC*** Began 1986; interdenominational. No magazine. Turnover £4,000 to year end Mar 96. Christian outreach agency promoting Christian arts in concerts, festivals; radio work; training.
☎ 01444 415 582 🖷 01444 415 587

*****Mission for Christ (Rural Evangelism)**, Guestling Lodge, 7 Martineau Lane, Hastings TN35 5DS
Executive Director: Rev Graham Ball. Executive staff 3, Other staff 4. ***CC*** No.242198. Began 1959; interdenominational. Magazine: *Action* (4,500 quarterly). Turnover £56,000 to year end Dec 98. Providing evangelism and advice, assisting the local church to share their faith with the community.
Web: www.surfaid.org/~mfcrural
Email: mfcrural@surfaid.org
☎ 01424 812 384 Mobile: 07801 334 281 🖷 01424 813 942

Mission to Mobile Homes, Bethany House, 8 Pump Square, Boston PE21 6QW
Director: Pastor Hector G Hall. Executive staff 2, Other staff 2. ***CC*** No.290932. Began 1967; non-denominational. Magazine: *Faith and Victory* (800 quarterly). Turnover n/a. Evangelising mobile home park residents, pastoral care in fellowship with Bible-believing churches.
☎ 01205 351 608 / 365 689 🖷 01205 351 608

***Mission and Research Department, Baptist Union of Great Britain**, Baptist House, PO Box 44, Didcot OX11 8RT
Head of Department for Mission and Research: Rev Derek Allan. Executive staff 3, Other staff 3. ***CC*** Began 1985; Baptist. Magazine: *Informission* (5,000 every four months). Providing research and training in holistic mission.
Web: www.baptist.org.uk
Email: mission@baptist.org.uk
☎ 01235 517 700 🖷 01235 517 715

***Missions to Prisons (NGM Trust)**, PO Box 37, Kendal LA9 6GF
Director/Head of Missions: Rev Bob Spratt. No other full-time staff. ***CC*** No.513862. Began 1974; non-denominational. (Previously Northern Gospel Message Trust). Magazine: *Prayer and Newsletter* (1,000 every two months). Turnover n/a. Ministry amongst all affected by imprisonment including prisoners, prison staff, families and local churches.
☎ 01539 720 475 Mobile: 07710 237 438 🖷 01539 720 475

E

The National Football Cup, Flat 20, 103 Langley Road, Watford WD1 3PH
Administrator: Miss Jill Freeman. Admin staff 1. Began 1992; non-denominational. Magazine: *Football Krazy* (900 four times per season). Turnover £2,000 to year end May 98. UEFA / FA affiliated competition helping Christians to evangelise teams and players on a national basis.
Email: jillntc@lineone.net
☎ 01923 819 932 Mobile: 07973 197 355 🖷 01923 819 932

Network Christian Trust, 1 Tremenheere Road, Penzance TR18 2AH
Administrator: Mr Joff Day. Staff n/a. ***CC*** No.802518. Began 1989; interdenominational. No magazine. Turnover n/a. Proclaiming the Gospel, providing housing for single young men, summer camps for young people.
Web: members.aol.com/kingch/kings
Email: joffday@aol.com
☎ 01736 360 350 Mobile: 07770 316 362 🖷 01736 360 350

†The Network Trust, 100 Lazy Hill Road, Aldridge, Walsall WS9 8RR
Trustee: Mrs Joanna Beck. No full-time staff. ***CC*** Began 1986; non-denominational. No magazine. Turnover under £10,000 to year end Dec 96. Local and national courses to equip churches for evangelism using 'Good News Down The Street'.
☎ 01922 528 30

***NGM**, Caedmon Complex, Bristol Road, Thornbury, Bristol BS35 3JA
Directors: Mr Ray & Mrs Nancy Goudie. Executive staff 3, Other staff 40. ***CC*** No.292923. Began 1981; non-denominational. (Previously New Generation Ministries). Magazine: *The Gen* (3,000 half-yearly). Turnover n/a. Engaging young people in their own culture through church planting, training and the media..
Web: www.ngm-uk.org
Email: ngm@ngm-uk.org
☎ 01454 625 577

North West Evangelistic Trust, 57 Lancaster Road, Carnforth LA5 9LE
Secretary: Mrs Christine Simpson. Other staff 10. ***CC*** No.246661. Began 1962; non-denominational. Magazine: *Newsletter* (1,000 annually). Turnover £260,000 to year end Dec 97. Evangelism through area-based schools work under the name of NISCU (Northern Inter Schools Christian Union).
☎ 01524 732 764

***Not Yet**, 18 Northbourne Avenue, Morpeth NE61 1JG
Director: Mr Anthony Brown. Executive staff 5. ***CC*** No.1058577. Began 1989; interdenominational. No magazine. Turnover n/a. Motivating Christians into mission; offering evangelism, training and imaginative ideas to local churches.
Web: www.notyet.org
☎ 01670 503 847 Mobile: 07585 069 728 🖷 01670 503 847

***Oasis Trust**, 115 Southwark Bridge Road, London SE1 0AX
International Director: Rev Steve Chalke. Executive staff 7, Other staff 60. ***CC*** No.1026487. Began 1985; interdenominational. Magazine: *Backchat* (12,500 quarterly). Turnover £1,476,869 to year end Aug 97. Demonstrating the Christian faith worldwide through working with young people, churches, the disadvantaged and homeless.
Web: www.u-net.com/oasis
Email: oasistrust@compuserve.com
☎ 020 7450 9000 🖷 020 7450 9001

***Off The Fence**, 6 Dale View, Hove BN3 8LB
Coordinator: Rev Paul Young. Executive staff 1, Other staff 1. ***CC*** No.1064139. Began 1997; interdenominational. No magazine. Turnover £19,000 to year end Mar 99. Evanglism, training, discipling, preaching, teaching, counselling, encouraging individuals and churches for outreach and social action.
Email: pwheyoung@aol.com
☎ 01273 420 657

Office for Evangelisation, 114 West Heath Road, London NW3 7TX
Director: Rev Paul Billington. Part time staff 9. ***CC*** No.233699. Began 1981; Roman Catholic. Part of Catholic Missionary Society. No magazine. Turnover n/a. Working in schools or parishes and training related to such work.
Web: officeofevangelisation.cms.org.uk
Email: cms@cms.org.uk
☎ 020 8458 3316 🖷 020 8905 5780

***One Step Forward Publications**, 20 Rufford Avenue, New Ollerton, Newark NG22 9PN
Directors: Rev David Greenaway, Mrs Margaret Greenaway. No other staff. ***CC*** Began 1964; interdenominational. No magazine. Turnover £5,040 to year end Feb 98. Ministry encouraging teaching and training local churches for effective mission and church growth.
☎ 01623 860 354

***Open Air Campaigners**, 102 Dukes Avenue, Muswell Hill, London N10 2QA
National Director: Mr David Fanstone. *General secretary:* Mrs Alice Fanstone. Executive staff 2, Other staff 23. ***CC*** No.295432. Began 1968; interdenominational. No magazine. Turnover £369,357 to year end Dec 97. Evangelising and training, chiefly in the open air, in Britain and overseas.
Web: web.ukonline.co.uk/oacministries
Email: alice.fanstone@oaci.org
☎ 020 8444 5254 🖷 020 8444 5254

Open Air Mission, 19 John Street, London WC1N 2DL
General Secretary: Mr Alan J Greenbank. Executive staff 2, Other staff 12. *CC* No.215409. Began 1853; interdenominational. Magazine: *The Master and the Multitude* (4,000 quarterly). Turnover £380,000 to year end Dec 98. Organising and encouraging open-air evangelism in the crowded places of the UK.
Web: www.btinternet.com/~oamission
Email: oamission@btinternet.com
☎ 020 7405 6135 🖷 020 7405 6135

Order of the Academy of Christ, 2 Wellington Road, Ealing, London W5 4HU
Principal: Rev Dr R S Kirby. Executive staff 1. *CC* No.800600. Began 1988; Episcopalian. Magazine: *Global Vision* (50 quarterly). Turnover £2,000 to year end Apr 98. Christian mission in the Space Age; theological education and research, emphasizing Third World culture.
Email: drrskirby@aol.com
☎ 020 8579 8026

Outlook Trust, Clare Lodge, 41 Hollybush Lane, Harpenden AL5 4AY
National Director: Miss Rhena Taylor. Part-time staff. *CC* No.1023137. Began 1992; interdenominational. No magazine. Turnover £35,500 to year end Dec 97. Evangelism among older people. Works through volunteer missionaries and local churches throughout the UK.
Email: ret@outlooktrust.nildram.co.uk
☎ 01582 760 596 🖷 01582 760 596

*__Luis Palau Evangelistic Association__, 36 Sycamore Road, Amersham HP6 5DR
European Director: Mr Nigel Gordon. Executive staff 1, Other staff 1. *CC* No.285474. Began 1979; non-denominational. Magazine: *Proclaim*(Circulation & frequency n/a). Turnover £220,000 to year end Dec 98. Responding to invitations for Crusade Evangelism with church-based preparation and follow-up.
Email: info@lpea.org.uk
☎ 01494 431 567 🖷 01494 431 428

*__Partnership Missions__, PO Box 783, Maidenhead SL6 0BL
Liaison Officer: Mrs M L Clements. No full-time staff. *CC* No.281345. Began 1981; Primarily Baptist. Magazine: *PM News* (3,000 occasionally). Turnover £50,000 to year end Dec 96. Sending lay teams to churches in the UK and abroad; study trips to Willow Creek.
Email: 101455.3267@compuserve.com
☎ 01628 633 433 🖷 01628 633 433

Pathway Ministries, 22 Elm Tree Avenue, Frinton-on-Sea CO13 0BE
Secretary: Mr Leonard A J Ashdown. Executive staff 3. Began 1996; interdenominational. No magazine. Turnover n/a. Taking the Gospel into the workplace; offering assistance to seek Christ to those involved in the occult.
☎ 01255 671 546 🖷 01255 663 380

People with a Mission Ministries, Perth Christian Centre, 28 Glasgow Road, Perth PH2 0NX
Trustees: Mr Mervyn & Mrs Jane Milne. Executive staff 27, Other staff 10. *CC* No.SCO 14546. Began 1986; non-denominational. Magazine: *Challenger* (Circulation & frequency n/a). Turnover n/a. Evangelism in Scotland; teaching and training Christians; Spring Bible School; video ministries; ministry support centres.
Email: mervynpwamm@btinternet.com
☎ 01738 639 792 🖷 01738 622 928
Also at: Balcary House, Buccleuch Road, Hawick TD9 0EH
☎ 01450 372 966 🖷 01450 377 732

*__The Philo Trust__, 60 Quickley Lane, Chorleywood, Rickmansworth WD3 5AF
Director: Mr J John. Staff 7. *CC* No.285762. Began 1981; interdenominational. Magazine: *Philo Trust Newletter* (Circulation n/a every four months). Turnover n/a. Inter-church area-wide missions teaching the Church to communicate. Mentoring young evangelists.
Web: www.philo.ndirect.co.uk
Email: jjohn@philo.ndirect.co.uk
☎ 01923 286 286 🖷 01923 286 186

*__Pocket Testament League__, Clarence Court D, Rushmore Hill, Orpington BR6 7LZ
General Director: Mr Donald Ford. *Assistant Director:* Mr Peter J Honour. Executive staff 2, Other staff 3. *CC* No.281910. Began 1908; interdenominational. Magazine: *Newsdesk* (5,000 every four months). Turnover £156,236 to year end June 98. Evangelism and scripture distribution in UK. Support in Brazil, India, Pakistan, Portugal, Spain and Yugoslavia.
Web: www.ptl.org.uk
Email: ptl@zetnet.co.uk
☎ 01689 858 066 🖷 01689 853 353

*__Proclaimers International__, Drayton Hall, Hall Lane, Drayton, Norwich NR8 6DP
Director: Rev David Tinnion. *Evangelist:* Miss Christine Green. Staff members 30. *CC* No.280469. Began 1980; non-denominational. (Previously Kerygma International Christian Ministries). Magazine: *News/Prayer letter*(Circulation & frequency n/a). Turnover £269,000 to year end Dec 98. Church, teaching, evangelism, training, spirit and word school, conferences, mobile evangelism/resource bus, overseas ministry.
Web: www.proclaim.org.uk
Email: school@proclaim.org.uk
☎ 01603 260 222 🖷 01603 261 222

*__Project Evangelism__, Murlough House, Keel Point, Dundrum, Newcastle BT33 0NQ
Director: Mr John Moxen. Executive staff 3, Other staff 4. *CC* No.XN 48651/SP. Began 1969; interdenominational. Magazine: *Newsletter* (1,500 quarterly). Turnover £66,000 to year end Mar 98. All age outreaches with teams from USA, UK; also France, Spain. Accommodation for 60 people.
Web: www.jbu.edu/projev
Email: projectmh@aol.com
☎ 028 4475 1480 🖷 028 4475 1232

The Protestant Alliance, 77 Ampthill Road, Flitwick, Bedford MK45 1BD
General Secretary: Dr Stephen J Scott-Pearson. Executive staff 3, Other staff 3. *CC* Began 1845; non-denominational. Magazine: *Reformer* (5,000 every two months), *Young Reformer* (Circulation n/a every two months). Turnover n/a. Protestant evangelistic educational body engaged in answering the teaching of Roman Catholicism.
☎ 01525 712 348 🖷 01525 712 348

Protestants Today, Sentinels Court, 130 South Coast Road, Peacehave BN10 8RD
Field Director: Rev Dr Peter J Gadsden. Executive staff 2. *CC* Began 1891; non-denominational. Magazine: *Our Inheritance* (2,000 Frequency n/a). Turnover n/a. Undertaking evangelism, seminars, Christian Heritage exhibition, literature, outreach to all ages.
Email: protestants.today@btinternet.com
☎ 01273 585 965 🖷 01273 580 084

E

The Railway Mission, Room 4, Denison House North, Hexthorpe Road, Doncaster DN4 0EL
Executive Director: Rev Philip D Gomersall. Executive staff 1, Full-time Railway Chaplains 7, Associate Chaplains 7. ***CC*** No.248988. Began 1881; non-denominational. Magazine: *Newsletter* (Circulation n/a half-yearly). Turnover £160,000 to year end Dec 98. Evangelism and pastoral caring for people and their families in the railway industry and allied groups.
Web: www.page-net.co.uk/web_sites/rmission
☎ 01302 388 445 / 0113 268 7043 Mobile: 07702 048 444
🖷 01302 388 445 / 0113 268 7043

***Rapport Trust (Servants of God Trust)**, PO Box 9, St Leonards TN37 7ZX
Director: Rev Marshall W Durrance. Executive staff 1, Other staff 5. ***CC*** No.290127. Began 1981; interdenominational. Magazine: *Newsletter* (200 quarterly). Turnover n/a. Evangelistic teaching ministry, missions, computerised information service, conferences.
Web: www.rapport.org/rap
Email: durrance@att.net & ekklesia@rapport.org
☎ 0116 212 0661 🖷 0116 212 0661

***Reaching Older People with God's Love**, Whitefield House, 186 Kennington Park Road, London SE11 4BT
Chair: Ray Adams. No full-time staff. ***CC*** No.123448. Began n/a; interdenominational. An Evangelical Alliance Partnership for Change. No magazine. Turnover: finance included with Evangelical Alliance. Networking people concerned for evangelism with/among older people; stimulating effective evangelism, promoting best practice.
Web: www.eauk.org
Email: members@eauk.org
☎ 020 7207 2100 🖷 020 7207 2150

E

Reaching The Unchurched Network, Redland House, 1 Redland Way, Aylesbury HP21 9RJ
Chairman: Rev Roger Sutton. Admin staff 1. Began 1994; interdenominational. Magazine: *Reaching The Unchurched Network* (300 quarterly). Turnover n/a. Promoting networking resources to prioritise the unchurched in the mission strategies of the Church.
Email: run@slbmandes.nildram.co.uk
☎ 01296 334 424 🖷 01296 434 143

***Reachout Trust**, 24 Ormond Road, Richmond TW10 6TH
Director: Mr Douglas Harris. Executive staff 1, Other staff 2. ***CC*** No.327346. Began 1985; non-denominational. Magazine: *Newsletter* (3,500 quarterly). Turnover £92,000 to year end May 98. Training Christians and helping those in the cults, occult and New Age come to know Christ.
Web: www.reachouttrust.org
Email: info@reachouttrust.org
☎ 020 8332 7785 🖷 020 8332 0286

Reconciliation Ministries International, Zion Christian Centre, Little Cornbow, Halesowen B63 3AJ
Evangelist: Rev Nathan Miller. Executive staff 2, Other staff 1. ***CC*** No.800894. Began 1987; interdenominational. Magazine: *Impact Missions* (Circulation n/a quarterly). Turnover £50,000 to year end Dec 98. Advancing the Christian faith and relief of the distressed.
Email: rmi@cabbinet.co.uk
☎ 0121 585 5294

Reformation Ireland: South East Antrim Reformation Movement, 1 Laral Gardens, Monkstown, Newtownabbey BT37 0LJ
Secretary: Mr Raymond Stewart. Staff n/a. Began 1986; Reformed and Calvinistic. Turnover n/a. Calling churches and individuals back to simplicity of Puritan theology practice.
☎ 028 9086 6174 Mobile: 07979 425 030

***Revival (The Hour of Revival Association)**, 13 Lismore Road Eastbourne BN21 3AY
General Secretary: Mr Ian Milmine. *Director of Programmes* Mr Patrick Woodward. Executive staff 3, Other staff 3. ***CC*** No.232509. Began 1953; interdenominational. Magazine *International Daily News Bulletin* (5,000 every two months). *Revival Newsletter* (5,000 half-yearly). Turnover £206,000 to year end Mar 97. Producing worldwide Gospel radio corrrespondance courses, cassettes, radio production facilities, Christian advertising campaigns.
Web: www.wornet.co.uk/revival.htm
Email: revival@compuserve.com
☎ 01323 725 231 🖷 01323 412 650

Rural Evangelism Network, 1 Chestnut Cottages, West End, Herstmonceux, Hailsham BN27 4NZ
Secretary: Rev Barry Osborne. No full-time staff. Began 1982; non-denominational. (Previously Federation For Rural Evangelism). Magazine: *Country Way* (4,000 every four months). Turnover n/a. Network of those involved in or concerned to promote effective rural evangelism.
Web: www.users.zetnet.co.uk/bosborne/fre.html
Email: rural.missions@zetnet.co.uk
☎ 01323 832 445 Mobile: 07958 422 297 🖷 01323 832 445

Rural Ministries, 4 Bolton Lane, Ipswich IP4 2BT
General Secretary: Mr Eddie Vass. *Administrator:* Mr John Banks. Executive staff 2, Other staff 1. ***CC*** No.200027. Began 1962; non-denominational. (Previously Datchet Evangelical Fellowship). Magazine: *Rural Challenge* (4,500 half-yearly). Turnover £114,000 to year end Mar 98. Establishing and maintaining a permanent evangelical witness in rural areas.
☎ 01473 258 743 Mobile: 07770 577 174 🖷 01473 258 743

***Rural Sunrise**, 2 The Old Forge, Gardner Street, Herstmonceux, Hailsham BN27 4LE
Director: Rev Barry Osborne. Executive staff 2. ***CC*** No.802305. Began 1988; non-denominational. (A division of Sunrise Ministries). Magazine: *Sunrise* (700 quarterly). Turnover £18,628 to year end Dec 95. Enabling and assisting rural churches in total mission and evangelism; researching and publishing related material.
☎ 01323 832 083

***Saltbox Christian Centre**, 12 Moorland Road, Burslem, Stoke-on-Trent ST6 1DW
Director: Mr Lloyd Cooke. Executive staff 2, Other staff 2. ***CC*** No.517299. Began 1982; interdenominational. Magazine: *Information Service* (1,000 monthly). Turnover £50,000 to year end Dec 96. Organising united renewal and evangelistic initiatives, concerts and schools projects.
Web: www.fenetre.co.uk/~cvm/saltbox.htm
Email: saltbox@fenetre.co.uk
☎ 01782 814 417 🖷 01782 811 938

***Saltmine Trust**, PO Box 15, Dudley DY3 2AN
Director: Mr Dave Pope. *Trust Administrator:* Miss Isobel Waspe. *Ministry Co-ordinator:* Jenny Brown. Executive staff 2, Other staff 23. ***CC*** No.1038007. Began 1980; interdenominational. Magazine: *Saltshaker News* (12,000 every four months). Turnover £600,000 to year end Mar 96. Church based missions, schools work, theatre, conference Bible teaching, worship leading.
Web: www.saltmine.org
Email: smine@ibm.net
☎ 01902 881 080 🖷 01902 881 099

Sandes Soldiers' and Airmen's Centres, 30a Belmont Road, Belfast BT4 2AN
General Secretary: Miss Hazel M Knox. Executive staff 1, Other staff 31. ***CC*** Began 1869; non-denominational. Magazine: *Forward* (3,000 quarterly). Turnover £509,438 to year end Dec 98. Offering Christian mission to the Armed Forces, especially the Army and the RAF.
Email: sandes1869@aol.com
☎ 028 9047 2717 🖷 028 9065 2592

Scottish Counties Evangelistic Movement, 916 Tollcross Road, Glasgow G32 8PE
Committee Chairman: Mr John Allan. No full-time staff. *CC* No.SCO 15845. Began 1965; Christian Brethren. Magazine: *SCEM Gen* (3,500 quarterly). Turnover £30,000 to year end Dec 96. Evangelising in Scotland.
☎ 0141 778 7399 🖷 0141 764 1401
Also at: SCEM Bookstore, 190 Quarry Street, Hamilton ML3 6QR
☎ 01698 282 825 🖷 01698 428 281

Scottish Lausanne Committee, Manse of Newhills, Bucksburn, Aberdeen AB21 9SS
Chair: Rev Norman MacIver. No full-time staff. Began 1989; non-denominational. No magazine. Turnover £600 to year end Dec 98. Furthering the purposes, in Scotland, of the International Lausanne movement.
Email: newhillsnm@aol.com
☎ 01224 716 161 🖷 01224 716 161

***Scripture Union**, 207 Queensway, Bletchley, Milton Keynes MK2 2EB
Chief Executive / Team Leader: Mr Peter Kimber. Executive staff 11, Other staff 151. *CC* Began 1867; interdenominational. Magazine: *Outreach* (65,000 every four months). Turnover £6,400,000 to year end Dec 98. Evangelising and discipling children, young people and families, through schools work, missions, holidays, Bible ministries, training, resources.
Web: www.scripture.org.uk
Email: postmaster@scriptureunion.org.uk
☎ 01908 856 000 🖷 01908 856 111
Also at: Lozells Bookshop, 92 Lozells Road, Birmingham B19 2TJ
☎ 0121 554 6471/6976

Scripture Union Northern Ireland, 157 Albertbridge Road, Belfast BT5 4PS
General Director: Rev David Bruce. Executive staff 5, Other staff 5. *CC* Began 1954; interdenominational. No magazine. Turnover £200,000 to year end Mar 96. Reaching children and young people; publishing and distributing resources and teaching materials; holiday missions and camps.
Email: info@suni.co.uk
☎ 028 9045 4806 🖷 028 9073 9758

***Scripture Union Scotland**, 9 Canal Street, Glasgow G4 0AB
General Director: David Clark. Executive staff 27, Other staff 28. *CC* No.35168. Began 1867; interdenominational. Magazine: *QSU* (8,000 frequency n/a). Turnover £2,000,000 to year end Mar 98. Working with churches, to reach Scottish school age children with Christ's Gospel.
Web: www.scriptureunionscotland.org.uk
Email: postmaster@scriptureunionscotland.org.uk
☎ 0141 332 1162 🖷 0141 352 7600

Sion Catholic Community for Evangelism, Sawyers Hall Lane, Brentwood CM15 9BX
Directors: Rev Pat Lynch CSD, Mr Peter Moran. Executive staff 30, Other staff 5. *CC* No.327967. Began 1984; Roman Catholic. Magazine: *The New Century* (2,000 periodically). Turnover £250,000 to year end Apr 98. Providing prophetic, effective and innovative approach to evangelisation within the Catholic Church.
Web: www.btinternet.com/-sioncommunity
Email: sioncommunity@btinternet.com
☎ 01277 215 011 Mobile: 07860 621 794 🖷 01277 234 401

Soapbox Communications, 3 Bank Buildings, 149 High Street, Cranleigh GU6 8BB
National Director: Rev Steve Flashman. Executive staff 1, Other staff 4. *CC* No.801584. Began 1989; interdenominational. Magazine: *On The Box* (1,200 quarterly). Turnover £270,000 to year end Dec 98. Evangelism in missions, schools, colleges, clubs, prisons; publishing, media, recording and Third World Expeditions.
Web: www.lineone.net/~soapbox
Email: soapbox@lineone.net
☎ 01483 271 015 Mobile: 07774 672 529

The Soldier's and Airmen's Scripture Readers Association (SASRA), Havelock House, Barrack Road, Aldershot GU11 3NP
General Secretary: Lt-Col M Hitchcott. Executive staff 9, Other staff 17. *CC* No.235708. Began 1838; interdenominational. Magazine: *Ready* (13,000 every four months). Turnover £544,000 to year end Dec 95. Personal evangelism in Army and RAF, linking Christian servicemen and women with fellowship.
Web: www.sasra.org.uk
Email: hq@sasra.org.uk
☎ 01252 310 033 🖷 01252 350 722

***Solent Christian Trust**, PO Box 200, Southampton SO17 2DL
Director: Mr Nick Pollard. Executive staff 1, Other staff 3. *CC* No.298170. Began 1987; interdenominational. Magazine: *Action News* (1,500 every three months). Turnover £80,000 to year end Apr 98. Outreach in universities through missions and debates and in sixth forms through conferences.
Web: www.sct.org.uk
Email: office@sct.org.uk
☎ 023 8031 5319 🖷 023 8031 5319

***Sound of the Underground**, 37 Springfield Drive, Cinderford GL14 2TE
Project Co-ordinator: Mr John Webster. Other staff 1. *CC* No.1057385. Began 1995; non-denominational. No magazine. Turnover n/a. Evangelistic roadshow involving and encouraging local churches in outreach to youth via contemporary media.
☎ 01594 824 011 Mobile: 07774 273 420
🖷 01594 827 372

***South Bristol Outreach Trust**, Churchlands Road, Bedminster, Bristol BS3 3PW
Administrator: Mr Graham J Rowles. No full-time staff. *CC* No.986627. Began 1983; interdenominational. Turnover £3,257 to year end Mar 98. Consultation service and resource centre for co-ordination of witness amongst the Christian community.
☎ 0117 963 6329 🖷 0117 963 6329

Sozo Ministries International, PO Box 29, Romsey SO51 0YU
Director: Mrs Marion Daniel. Executive staff 6, Other staff 2. *CC* No.1042420. Began 1983; non-denominational. Magazine: *Newsletter* (300 every three weeks). Turnover n/a. Preaching salvation, healing and deliverance to the church and the world.
Email: sozomin@msn.com
☎ 01794 323 516 🖷 01794 322 167

***Spinnaker Trust**, Coppice Hall, Hollingworth Road, Petts Wood, Orpington BR5 1AQ
Administrator: Mr Alan Ching. Executive staff 2, Other staff 8. *CC* No.327375. Began 1986; interdenominational. Magazine: *Spinnaker News* (1,500 quarterly). Turnover £50,000 to year end April 98. Schools and young peoples evangelism, church missions, evangelistic projects, drama and music teams.
☎ 020 8295 2070 Mobile: 07850 276 256

Spirit of '88, PO Box 67, Rickmansworth WD3 5SJ
Trustee: Mr Michael de Semlyen. Executive staff 1. *CC* No.327574. Began 1988; interdenominational. Magazine: *Spirit of '88 Bulletin* (1,250 occasionally). Turnover £20,000 to year end Dec 98. Sharing the Gospel through the anniversaries of the nation's great Christian heritage.
☎ 01923 282 333

E

Springboard, 4 Old Station Yard, Abingdon OX14 3LD
Director: Mr Martin Cavender. Other staff 5. ***CC*** No.287211. Began 1993; Anglican. No magazine. Turnover n/a. The Archbishops' initiative to encourage, renew and mobilise the Church for evangelism.
Email: springboard.uk@btinternet.com
☎ 01235 553 722 Fax 01235 553 922

Strangers' Rest Mission, 131 The Highway, London E1 9BP
Pastor: Rev Gerald Daley. Executive staff 1, Other staff 2. ***CC*** No.209117. Began 1877; non-denominational. Magazine: *Occasional Notes* (800 every four months). Turnover £14,000 to year end Sept 90. Evangelistic ministry and charitable work.
☎ 020 7488 4427

†**Street Evangelists Association**, Mandeville Cottage, Tredington, Tewkesbury GL20 7BP
Evangelist: Rev John M Heelan. Executive staff 2, Other staff 2. Began 1990; interdenominational. Magazine: *Street Life* (5,000 every two months). Turnover £200 to year end Mar 93. Street evangelism, personal evangelism and children's evangelism on the streets.
☎ No telephone

***TES (The Evangelization Society)**, Dawson House, 64 Cricklade Road, Gorse Hill, Swindon SN2 6AF
Director: Mr Ron Spillards. *Administrator:* Mr Stephen Bechervaise. Other staff 9. ***CC*** No.245273. Began 1864; interdenominational. Magazine: *Onward* (6,000 every four months). Turnover £172,000 to year end Mar 98. Providing evangelists and resources, enabling the Church to promote and maintain the Christian Faith.
Web: ourworld.compuserve.com/homepages/theevangelizationsociety
Email: theevangelizationsociety@compuserve.com
☎ 01793 481 444 Fax 01793 435 237

There is Hope, 12 Montpelier Park, Edinburgh EH10 4NJ
Chairman: Mr Jim Woodrow. No other staff. Began 1995; interdenominational. (Previously Hope for Scotland). No magazine. Turnover n/a. AD2000 And Beyond Movement in Scotland, involving tracks in communications and linked initiatives.
☎ 0131 229 0003 Fax 0131 228 8679

Through Faith Missions, 73 High Street, Coton, Cambridge CB3 7PL
Evangelists: Rev Daniel H Cozens, Rev Peter Adams. Executive staff 2, Other staff 5. ***CC*** No.801113. Began 1988; interdenominational. Magazine: *Through Faith Prayerletter* (6,500 quarterly). Turnover £200,000 to year end Dec 98. Town and parish missions; training schools for evangelism; "Walk of 1000 Men".
Web: www.btinternet.com/~walk1000/
Email: walk1000@btinternet.com
☎ 01954 210 239 Fax 01954 211 983

Time For Truth!, PO Box 1146, Kidderminster DY10 1WG
Partner: Mr John E Davis. Executive staff 2. Began 1998; interdenominational. No magazine. Turnover n/a. Encouraging Christians to reach the lost and prepare themselves for the coming of Jesus Christ.
☎ 01562 824 337 Mobile: 07958 489 994

United Beach Missions, Spring Cottage, Spring Road, Leeds LS6 1AD
Executive Officer: Mr Gordon Robertson. Executive staff 1, Other staff 1. ***CC*** No.273912. Began 1952; non-denominational. Associated with Young Life. Magazine: *Prayer Letters* (2,000 Regularly). Turnover £60,000 to year end Apr 96. Reaching families for Christ on the beaches of UK, Ireland, France and Belgium.
Web: home.aol.com/ubmhq
Email: office@ubm.org.uk
☎ 0113 230 4362 Fax 0113 230 4363
Also at: *Office Manager:* Mr Bertie Coffey, 511 Scottish Provident Buildings, 7 Donegall Square West, Belfast BT1 6JG
☎ 028 9023 1133

***Universities and Colleges Christian Fellowship (UCCF)**, 38 De Montfort Street, Leicester LE1 7GP
General Secretary: Rev Bob Horn. Executive staff 10, Other staff (including IVP) 100. ***CC*** No.273458. Began 1928; non-denominational. Magazine: *NB* (18,000 every two months). Turnover £3,700,000 to year end Apr 98. Supporting CUs in universities and colleges; evangelism; training student leaders; overseas student work; publishing (IVP).
Web: www.uccf.org.uk
Email: email@uccf.org.uk
☎ 0116 255 1700 Fax 0116 255 5672

Urban Expression, 20 Redcastle Close, Shadwell, London E1 9DQ
Coordinator: Mrs Juliet Kilpin. Executive staff 1, No other paid staff. Began 1997; non-denominational. No magazine. Turnover £14,500 to year end Apr 98. Recruiting, equipping, deploying and supporting self-financing teams to plant new churches in inner city communities.
Email: urbexpress@aol.com
☎ 020 7450 9000 Mobile: 07930 971 339
Fax 020 7450 9001

Vineyard Ministries International (UK), 37 Blagdon Road, New Malden KT3 4AH
Managing Director: Mr Christopher Whitelock. Executive staff 2, Admin staff 1. Began 1987; Vineyard Churches. Magazine: *Equipped* (Circulation n/a quarterly). Turnover n/a. Equipping the church through arranging conferences and providing teaching materials, books and worship tapes.
Email: vmguk@aol.com
☎ 020 8336 1727 Fax 020 8336 6319

***Viz-A-Viz**, Dobson House, Bentalls, Basildon SS14 3BX
General Director: Rev Dennis Pethers. *Executive Director:* Mr Jonathan Hunt. Other staff 22. ***CC*** No.1031486. Began 1993; non-denominational. Magazine: *Newsletter* (4,000 frequency n/a). Turnover £500,000 to year end May 98. Providing all-age, multi-media, evangelism, theatre, training centre, year out opportunities, schools ministry, video production.
Email: viz.a.viz@ukonline.co.uk
☎ 01268 530 531 Fax 01268 530 999

The Way to Life Ministry, Bank House, 3 High Street, Hailsham BN27 1AL
Director: Mr Dick Saunders. Other staff 4. ***CC*** Began 1965; non-denominational. Magazine: *Link Up* (10,000 monthly). Turnover £400,000 to year end Dec 90. Making Christ known through international radio outreach, Bible teaching and evangelism.
☎ 01323 842 390

***WCA-UK (Willow Creek Association - UK)**, PO Box 622, Maidenhead SL6 0YX
Chairman: Mr Patrick Mayfield. Full-time staff 3. ***CC*** No.1069726. Began 1994; interdenominational. Magazine: *Willow News* (1,000 quarterly). Turnover n/a. Helping churches to lead people to/through a relationship with Christ and build Biblically-functioning communities.
Web: www.willowcreek.org
Email: wcauk@aol.com
☎ 01628 620 602 Willow Creek Resources: 0800 592 083
Fax 01628 629 964

Women in Mission, 64 Old Shoreham Road, Brighton BN1 5DD
Chair: Mrs Davina Irwin-Clark. Executive staff 1. *CC* No.1067727. Began 1995; interdenominational. No magazine. Turnover £15,000 to year end Dec 98. Equipping and encouraging women in evangelism and mission through national and regional conferences and events.
Email: capa@compuserve.com
☎ 01273 552 267 Fax 01273 552 267

Women Reaching Women, 49 West End Avenue, Pinner HA5 1BN
Team Leader: Mrs Cynthia Pearson. No full-time staff. Began 1985; non-denominational. Magazine: *News & Views* (Circulation n/a half-yearly). Turnover n/a. Training workshops and resources to encourage evangelism at a practical level in home and community.
Email: wrw@btinternet.com
☎ 020 8866 8013

***Women's Aglow Fellowship**, 303 Blackgate Lane, Tarleton, Preston PR4 6JJ
National President: Mrs Winifred Ascroft. *Vice President of Finance:* Mrs Olwen Bird. Other staff 2. *CC* No.327825. Began 1980; interdenominational. Magazine: *Aglow* (6,500 quarterly). Turnover £250,000 to year end Dec 98. Woman to woman full Gospel evangelistic ministry; Bible studies and literature. Work in Ukraine, Belarus, Moldova.
Email: aglow.natbrit@zetnet.co.uk
☎ 01772 814 490 Fax 01772 814 490

The WorkNet Partnership, 56 Baldry Gardens, London SW16 3DJ
National Director: Geoff Shattock. Staff n/a. *CC* No.1069411. Began 1997; non-denominational. Magazine: *Quarterly Briefing*(Circulation & frequency n/a). Turnover n/a. Connecting, equipping, resourcing Christians in the workplace; faith to work resources, stress training, partnership scheme.
Web: worknetpartnership.org.uk
Email: worknetpartnership.org.uk
☎ 020 8764 8080 Fax 020 8764 3030

***World Team UK**, 10 Pringle Gardens, London SW16 1SH
Field Director: Mr Adrian Fricker. Executive staff 1, Other staff 8. *CC* No.327703. Began 1986; interdenominational. Magazine: *World Team Advance* (1,000 quarterly). Turnover £6,000 to year end Dec 96. Evangelism, discipleship and church planting in relationship with local churches among Asian population, especially Muslims.
Email: adrianfricker@bigfoot.com
☎ 020 8769 6343

World Vision for Christ, 70 Sixth Avenue, Manor Park, London E12 5PR
Director: Dr Albert Chambers. Executive staff 5. *CC* No.288179. Began 1969; interdenominational. Magazine: *Unlimited Horizons* (4,000 every two months). Turnover £48,000 to year end Dec 98. International full gospel ministry. Presenting Christ to all, regardless of colour, class or creed.
☎ 020 8478 1073 / 8514 1820 Fax 020 8553 9855

Worldwide Christian Communication Network, 54 Edgecoombe, South Croydon CR2 8AB
Director: Rev Remi Caillaux. Executive staff 1. *CC* No.1045313. Began 1995; Pentecostal. Magazine: *Victory* (Circulation n/a UK and France every two months). Turnover £90,000 to year end Mar 98. Evangelistic outreach, pastoral and Christian counselling, training.
Web: www.wccn.net
☎ 020 8405 4725 Fax 020 8405 4725

***Y 2000**, PO Box 94, Chessington KT10 2YJ
Director: Mr Peter Meadows. Executive staff 1, Admin staff 1. Began 1997; interdenominational. No magazine. Turnover n/a. Providing resources to help people make Jesus known based on the ancient Christian symbol Y.
Web: www.y-2000.com
Email: pmeadows@y-2000.com
☎ 020 8287 3147 Fax 020 8286 3700

***Youth for Christ**, PO Box 5254, Halesowen B63 3DG
National Director: Mr Roy Crowne. Executive staff 4, Other staff 120. *CC* No.263446. Began 1947; interdenominational. (Previously British Youth For Christ). Magazine: *Into View* (5,200 quarterly). Turnover £1,200,000 to year end Aug 98. Evangelistic outreach to youth through creative arts, church-based missions, schools work, community involvement and training.
Web: www.yfc.co.uk
Email: yfc@compuserve.com
☎ 0121 550 8055 Fax 0121 550 9979

***The Zacharias Trust**, The Old Malthouse, 19a Paradise Street, Oxford OX1 1LD
European Director: Mr Michael Ramsden. Executive staff 1, Other staff 2. *CC* No.1067314. Began 1998; non-denominational. Magazine: *Just Thinking* (50,000 every four months). Turnover £73,000 to year end Dec 99. Involved in evangelism, apologetics, training; aiming to reach the sceptic with the Gospel.
Web: www.rzim.com
Email: zacharias.trust@btinternet.com
☎ 01865 203 951 Fax 01865 203 950

EVANGELISTS (INDEPENDENT)

Ian and Rosemary Andrews (Citadel Ministries), PO Box 28, Chard TA20 1LT
Leader: Mr Ian Andrews. Other staff 1. *CC* No.802969. Began 1969; Independent. Magazine: *Newsletter* (Circulation n/a quarterly). Turnover n/a. Signs, wonders and teaching. Worldwide.
☎ 01460 625 42

***Hugo & Sharon Anson**, The Grassroots Office, 99 Mays Lane, Barnet EN5 2DX
Evangelists: Mr Hugo & Mrs Sharon Anson. Executive staff 2. *CC* No.1060034. Began 1981; Independent. Magazine: *Newsletter* (1,000 quarterly). Turnover n/a. Itinerant evangelistic and Bible teaching ministry; based in active church planting movement in North London.
Web: www.grassroots.org.uk
Email: hugoandsharon@grassroots.org.uk
☎ 020 8441 0642 Mobile: 07710 284 150 Fax 020 8449 8646

***Ann Baker**, 60 Earlham Grove, Weston-super-Mare BS23 3JJ
Evangelist: Miss Ann Baker. No other staff. Began 1971; Baptist. No magazine. Turnover n/a. Missions, camps, Bible teaching for children, youth, adults. Leadership training, in Great Britain and Europe.
☎ 01934 627 789

***Blessed Hope of Christ Evangelistic Ministry**, 14 Nine Acres Close, Manor Park, London E12 6AU
Evangelist: Rev William Lamptey. Full-time staff 1. Began 1993; non-denominational. No magazine. Turnover £8,000 to year end Mar 98. Holding city crusades and revivals; teaching seminars on evangelism, cults, Islam, spiritual warfare prayer, intercession.
☎ 020 8478 1769

†***Martin Blewett**, 16 Southgate, Chichester PO19 1ES
Director: Mr Martin Blewett. Executive staff 1. Began 1990; interdenominational. Magazine: *Newsletter* (250 quarterly). Turnover £10,000 to year end Apr 96. Child evangelism, school ministry, holiday clubs, open air evangelism, UK and continental Europe.
☎ 0973 690 206 📠 01243 788 706

Christopher Brown, 11 Brownings Road, Cannington, Bridgwater TA5 2RH
Evangelist: Rev Christopher Brown. No other staff. Began 1999; interdenominational. No magazine. Turnover n/a. Bible based teaching and evangelism; nationwide.
Web: www.covenant.ndirect.co.uk
Email: chris@covenant.ndirect.co.uk
☎ 01278 653 586 📠 01278 653 706

Roger Carswell, 15 Stirling Crescent, Horsforth, Leeds LS18 5SJ
Evangelist: Mr Roger Carswell. Executive staff 1. Began 1983; Independent. Magazine: *Newsletter* (2,000 quarterly). Turnover n/a. Preaching the Gospel, writing and publishing evangelistic literature.
Email: carswell77@aol.com
☎ 0113 258 1183 📠 0113 259 0647

Crossfire Trust, 95 Darkley Road, Keady, Armagh BT60 3AY
Director: Mr Ian Bothwell. Executive staff 2, Other staff 2. *CC* No.XO84085. Began 1980; Independent. (Previously Ian Bothwell (Crossfire Trust)). Magazine: *Crossfire Trust News* (700 quarterly). Turnover n/a. Reaching out to society with God's love.
Web: www.btinternet.com/~crossfire.trust/
Email: crossfire.trust@btinternet.com
☎ 028 3753 1636 📠 028 3753 8817

Leslie Edgell, 2 Beehive Lane, Ferring, Worthing BN12 5NL
Evangelist: Rev R Leslie Edgell. No other staff. Began 1960; Baptist. No magazine. Turnover n/a. Church-based Bible teaching and evangelism. Nationwide.
☎ 01903 240 455

***The Evangelism Fellowship**, PO Box 55, Stowmarket IP14 1UG
Director: Rev Don Egan. *CC* No.1049346. Began 1994; non-denominational. Magazine: *Go* (2,000 annually). Turnover £20,000 to year end Nov 98. Evangelism and Bible teaching through preaching and literature crusades in UK, France, Rwanda, Uganda, India.
Web: www.buxnet.co.uk/evangelism
Email: don@ef.buxnet.co.uk
☎ 01449 677 058

Gus Eyre (Cedarwood Ministries), 23 Warwick Road, Lytham St Annes FY8 1TX
Evangelist/Singer/Guitarist: Mr Gus Eyre. Executive staff 2. Began 1976; interdenominational. Magazine: *Newsletter* (300 every four months). Turnover n/a. Contemporary singer/songwriter and preacher. Themed audio-visual presentations for all ages; churches, prisons, students, overseas.
☎ 01253 728 465 📠 01253 728 465

Paul Gunstone, 48 St Peter's Crescent, Bexhill-on-Sea TN40 2EJ
Evangelist to the Elderly: Evangelist Paul Gunstone. Began 1981; interdenominational. Magazine: *Prayer letter* (600 quarterly). Taking the Gospel to elderly people in rest and nursing homes, hospital, private home visiting.
☎ 01424 222 224

†**Laurence Harding**, 125 Jubilee Crescent, Mangotsfield, Bristol BS17 3BD
Evangelist: Mr Laurence J Harding. No other full-time staff. Began 1979; Independent. No magazine. Turnover n/a. Child evangelism. British Isles and occasionally overseas.
☎ 0117 956 2129

***Alyn Haskey (Freedom Ministries)**, PO Box 24, Nottingham NG3 4LD
Director: Alyn Haskey. *CC* No.327526. Began 1986; interdenominational. No magazine. Turnover £15,000 to year end Mar 98. Local and itinerant evangelism and missions in schools, colleges, churches, clubs, conferences.
☎ 0115 960 5489 📠 0115 960 5489

***Ian Leitch (The Heralds Trust)**, PO Box 813, Edinburgh EH14 7LR
Evangelist/Bible teacher: Mr Ian B Leitch. Executive staff 1. *CC* No.SCO 06798. Began 1969; interdenominational. Magazine: *The Heralds Trust News Report* (1,000 quarterly). Turnover £70,000 to year end Mar 96. Evangelism and Bible teaching, New Life seminars. UK, Europe and North America.
☎ 0131 449 4440 📠 0131 449 6910

John Lewis, Gorsley Baptist Church Office, Gorsley, Ross-on-Wye HR9 7SE
Evangelist/Bible teacher: Rev John Lewis. No other full-time staff. Began 1980; Baptist but works interdenominationally. No magazine. Turnover n/a. Evangelism and Bible teaching; families, youth and men's outreach. UK and USA.
Email: gorsleychapel@msn.com
☎ 01989 720 181 📠 01989 720 312

***Graham Loader**, 62 Catlington Road, Brislington, Bristol BS4 5BP
Evangelist: Mr Graham Loader. No full-time staff. Began n/a; interdenominational. Magazine: *Prayer Bulletin* (Circulation n/a occasionally). Turnover n/a. Itinerant ministry of evangelism and Bible teaching.
Email: graham@loader62.freeserve.co.uk
☎ 0117 977 0298 📠 0117 977 0298

***Manna Ministries International**, 40 Stratheden Heights, Newtownards BT23 8TD
Founder: Mr Alan Cunningham. Executive staff 1, Admin staff 2. *CC* No.XR 15980. Began 1995; non-denominational. Magazine: *Manna Mail* (1,500 quarterly). Turnover n/a. Ministering healing, wholeness, deliverance through music, preaching God's Word, prayer, counselling.
Web: www.heartbeat-music.com/manna
Email: alanmanna1@aol.com
☎ 028 9181 0058 📠 028 9181 2275

Paul Morley, 91 Green Street, Middleton, Manchester M24 2TB
Evangelist: Mr Paul Morley. No other staff. Began 1980; Assemblies of God. Magazine: *Newsletter* (350 quarterly). Turnover n/a. Evangelism in schools, open air, missions, church planting, gospel magic. UK, Europe, Africa and India.
Email: morley54@mcmail.com
☎ 0161 653 6626 Mobile: 0860 470 812

John Pantry, 2 Conifers Close, Alresford, Colchester CO7 8AW
Musician: Rev John Pantry. No full-time staff. Began 1989; Anglican. Magazine: *Newsletter* (700 quarterly). Turnover n/a. Missions, celebrations and evangelistic concerts.
☎ 01206 824 257 Fax 01206 824 257

Andrew Pavlibeyi, St Saviour's Vicarage, 30 Eton Villas, London NW3 4SQ
Evangelist: Rev Andrew Pavlibeyi. No full-time staff. Began 1980; Anglican. No magazine. Turnover n/a. Evangelism among all ages. English and Greek speaking. UK and abroad.
Email: apavlibeyi@aol.com
☎ 020 7722 4621

Rod Readhead, Manor Cottages, Barras, Kirkby Stephen CA17 4ES
Evangelist: Mr Rod Readhead. Other staff 1. Began 1999; non-denominational. No magazine. Turnover: first year of operation. Itinerant evangelist, ministry inside and outside churches, outreach to men, missions, children's work.
Email: rodreadhead@aol.com
☎ 01768 341 573 Fax 01768 341 573

***Soteria Trust**, 23 Windsor Road, Chichester PO19 2XF
Evangelist: Mr Andy Economides. Executive staff 1, Admin staff 1. *CC* No.1040766. Began 1994; interdenominational. Magazine: *Newsletter* (550 every four months). Turnover n/a. Advancing the Gospel by evangelism, missions, training in the UK and abroad.
☎ 01243 771 494 Fax 01243 771 240

Spear Trust, 14 Hurst Way, Sevenoaks TN13 1QN
Director: Mr Roger Malstead. Executive staff 1, Other staff 1. *CC* No.277298. Began 1992; interdenominational. (Previously Reach & Teach). No magazine. Turnover n/a. Producing evangelistic films, books in Muslim languages; reaching Turkish speakers via drop-in centre, community service.
Web: domini.org/spear
Email: 70740.705@compuserve.com
☎ 01732 741 581 Fax 01732 459 918

David Stillman Evangelistic Association, PO Box 102, Reading RG30 3NP
Evangelist: Rev David Stillman. No other full-time staff. *CC* No.269396. Began 1968; interdenominational. Magazine: *Prayer and News Report* (1,000 every four months). Turnover n/a. International ministry of evangelism and Bible teaching; prison ministry in UK.
Email: davidstillman@clara.co.uk
☎ 0118 983 2221

***Don Summers Evangelistic Association**, PO Box 100, Westbury-on-Trym, Bristol BS9 4QH
Director: Rev Donald P Summers. Executive staff 1, Field staff 2. *CC* Began 1955; interdenominational. No magazine. Turnover n/a. Crusade; church planting; church missions; Mission to Mexico; radio, youth, prison evangelism; prayer ministry.
☎ 0117 962 8000

***The Twenty Five Trust**, PO Box 692, Carshalton SM5 2ZR
Director: Rev Brian Greenaway. Executive staff 1, Other staff 1. *CC* No.327483. Began n/a; interdenominational. Magazine: *Trust newsletter* (400 every two months). Turnover £32,000 to year end Aug 98. Prison evangelism, Bible teaching, schools work, crime and punishment and drug prevention, church ministry.
☎ 020 8286 9066

Keith and Maureen Venables (Living Word (Evangelistic) Ministries), 35 Croftson Avenue, Ormskirk L39 1NJ
Director: Mr Keith Venables. Executive staff 2. *CC* No.326359. Began 1976; interdenominational. No magazine. Turnover n/a. Preaching, teaching, evangelism,healing, nationwide and international.
☎ 01695 574 462

***Ian White**, 147 Old Hexthorpe, Doncaster DN4 0DX
District Evangelism Enabler: Mr Ian White. No other staff. Began 1987; Methodist. Magazine: *The White House* (300 quarterly). Turnover n/a. Evangelism and mission trainer. Children's evangelism course director – Cliff College. Projects co-ordinator (overseas) – Highway Projects.
Web: members.aol.com/sheffmeth/
Email: whitejian@aol.com
☎ 01302 850 008

***Phillip Willer (In-Sight Communication Trust)**, 76 Fore Street, Chudleigh, Newton Abbot TQ13 0HT
Evangelist: Rev Phillip Willer. No other full-time staff. *CC* No.801351. Began 1979. Magazine: *Newsletter* (200 quarterly). Turnover £10,000 to year end Mar 98. Evangelism, sport, holiday clubs, training, camps, open air, encouragement, preaching, schools.
Email: willer@in-sight.freeserve.co.uk
☎ 01626 853 693 Mobile: 07885 596 198

***Keith Wills Evangelism Trust (SPEARHEAD)**, Victoria Hall, Knowsley Street, Bolton BL1 2AS
Evangelist: Mr Keith Wills. Voluntary staff 10. *CC* No.327150. Began 1974; interdenominational. Magazine: *Spearhead Communication* (600 every four months). Turnover n/a. Helping churches to reach whole communities for Christ through an in-depth approach to evangelism.
☎ 01204 399 363 Fax 01204 399 363

Alastair Young, 51 Sharon Street, Dalry KA24 5DT
Evangelist: Mr Alastair Young. No other full-time staff. Began 1976; Christian Brethren. No magazine. Turnover n/a. Children's missions, primary school assemblies, correspondence courses for children.
☎ 01294 835 119

E

TEACHING & PREACHING AGENCIES

All-Age Christian Ministries, PO Box 55, Newport NP9 8XT
Evangelist: Mr Glyn Morgan. Executive staff 3, Other staff 4. Began 1966; interdenominational. Magazine: *Alive* (12,000 quarterly). Turnover n/a. Evangelising and Bible teaching through missions, holidays, publications, audio tapes.
☎ 01633 277 167 Fax 01633 277 167

Barratt Ministries, 114 Daisybank Road, Manchester M14 5QH
Director: Mr Maurice Barratt. Executive staff 2, Other staff 3. Began 1983; non-denominational. Magazine: *Challenge* (Circulation n/a every two months). Turnover £75,000 to year end Feb 98. Teaching discipleship, music ministry, prison work, publishing tracts/books/videos.
Web: www.members.aol.com/bminmcr/bm.htm
Email: bminmcr@aol.com
☎ 0161 224 2620 Fax 0161 224 2620

C-L Ministries, 24 The Street, Capel St Mary, Ipswich IP9 2EE
Director: Mr Chris Hill. Executive staff 1, Admin staff 3. Began 1990; non-denominational. No magazine. Turnover n/a. Preparing God's people for the Millennium and beyond; preaching, teaching, books, videos, tapes.
Email: clministries@compuserve.com
☎ 01473 311 128 Fax 01473 311 128

***Eagle Ministries**, 69 East Park Road, Blackburn BB1 8DW
Director: Mr Vincent J Purcell. Staff 2. *CC* No.1017740. Began 1988; non-denominational. No magazine. Turnover n/a. Parachurch group majoring on evangelism and discipling.
☎ 01254 521 44 Fax 01254 521 44

European Institute of Protestant Studies, The Paisley Jubilee Complex, 356 Ravenhill Road, Belfast BT6 8GL
President: Rev Dr Ian R K Paisley MP, MEP. Executive staff 1, Other staff 2. Began 1998; Free Presbyterian. Magazine: *The Battle Standard* (10,000 quarterly). Turnover n/a. Exposing the papacy; promoting, defending and maintaining the Bible and Protestantism worldwide.
Web: www.ianpaisley.org
☎ 028 9045 7106 / 8761

Evangelical Protestant Society, 26 Howard Street, Belfast BT1 6PD
General Secretary: Rev Raymond Pulman. Executive staff 1. Began 1948; non-denominational. Magazine: *Ulster Bulwark* (2,800 every two months). Turnover n/a. Propagation of protestant reformed faith and heritage, evangelism.
Email: protsoc@bizonline.co.uk
☎ 028 9032 5608 Mobile: 07802 354 530

Forthtell, 1 Grove Gardens, Boston Spa, Wetherby LS23 6BG
Convener: Mrs Sally Coulby. Executive staff 1, Admin staff 1. Began 1997; non-denominational. No magazine. Turnover n/a. Presenting Christian perspective on current issues through public meetings, rallies, the media.
☎ 01937 845 027

The Framework Trust, PO Box 199, Horley RH6 9YF
Director: Miss Terry-Anne Preston. Executive staff 1. *CC* No.1063405. Began 1997; non-denominational. Magazine: *Framework* (Circulation n/a quarterly). Turnover £4,000 to year end Feb 98. Providing communication and creative arts in worship and mission training; prayer in action network.
Email: terry-anne.preston@virgin.net
☎ 01293 824 840 Mobile: 07850 878 814 Fax 01293 824 840

***Lifestyle International Ministries**, 211 Sheldrake Drive, Ipswich IP2 9LE
International Director: Rev Eric Graham. Executive staff 1, Other staff 3. *CC* No.1071735. Began 1998; non-denominational. Magazine: *Lifestyle News* (700 quarterly). Turnover n/a. Evangelism and teaching, UK and overseas; school of ministry training ministers in developing countries.
Email: lifestyleint@cwcom.net
☎ 01473 681 298 Mobile: 07768 435 718 Fax 01473 681 298

***Paraclete Christian Network International**, 12 South Street, Lancing BN15 8AG
Executive Director: Dr Ray Whittle. No full-time paid staff. *CC* No.1019767. Began 1991; interdenominational. No magazine. Turnover £10,000 to year end Mar 99. Supporting evangelical and evangelistic work in UK and overseas; providing oversight, Bible teaching, training.
Email: paraclete@btinternet.com
☎ 01903 755 471 Mobile: 07802 790 347 Fax 01903 535 396

***Prophetic Witness Movement International**, Cherith, 139 Leyland Lane, Leyland, Preston PR5 3HE
General Secretary: Rev Colin Lenoury. *CC* No.228941. Began 1917; non-denominational. Magazine: *Prophetic Witness* (3,000 monthly). Turnover £56,000 to year end May 98. Proclaiming the return of Christ through teaching and evangelism and Christian literature.
Web: www.pwmi.org
☎ 01772 452 846 Fax 020 8502 9062

***River of Life Trust**, 50 Fountains Road, Cheadle Hulme, Cheadle SK8 7PY
Director: Miss Meriel Pinkerton. Executive staff 1, Admin staff 1. *CC* No.1056417. Began 1995; interdenominational. No magazine. Turnover £25,000 to year end Dec 98. Organising Bible teaching / evangelism workshops and seminars for the local church.
☎ 0161 439 1419 Mobile: 07778 921 098

Sovereign Grace Union, 5 Rosier Crescent, Swanwick, Alfreton DE55 1RS
General Secretary: Rev J M Brentnall. No full-time staff. *CC* Began 1914; interdenominational. Magazine: *Peace and Truth* (800 quarterly). Turnover n/a. Furthering the proclamation and defence of the doctrines of free and sovereign grace.
☎ 01773 608 431

Storehouse Ministries, PO Box 777, Bromley BR1 3XZ
Administrator: Mr Clive Pick. Executive staff 2. *CC* No.1017926. Began 1992; Pentecostal. No magazine. Turnover n/a. Teaching ministry on Biblical economics, releasing individuals, ministries and the churches into financial blessing.
☎ 020 8289 1684 Fax 020 8289 1685

The Tehillah Trust, 49 St Mary's Park, Nailsea, Bristol BS48 4RP
Administrator: Mr Julian Perkins. Executive staff 2, Admin staff 1. Began 1989; non-denominational. No magazine. Turnover £3,000 to year end Aug 98. Teaching and leading praise and worship meetings, seminars and courses including Psalmody International; music publishing.
Email: jape@living-waters.org.uk
☎ 01275 797 799 Mobile: 07839 297 639 Fax 01275 797 999

The Wesley Fellowship, Stonebridge Cottage, Back Lane, Shearsby, Lutterworth LE17 6PN
Secretary: Mr Paul S Taylor. Executive staff 1. Began 1985; interdenominational. Magazine: *The Wesley Quarterly* (250 quarterly). Turnover £3,000 to year end Mar 98. Providing a contemporary expression and interpretation of Wesleyan teaching and experience.
☎ 0116 247 8679

Andrew Wommack Ministries (Europe), PO Box 35, Coventry CV1 2DN
UK Director: Mr Ian Stewart. Executive staff 3. *CC* No.1032438. Began 1991; interdenominational. No magazine. Turnover £120,000 to year end Mar 94. Providing audio teaching tapes, Bible Study programmes, Bible correspondence courses, annual Ministers conference.
Email: wommackuk@aol.com
☎ 024 7625 1838 Fax 024 7625 1838

MEDIA

M

ART & CRAFT PRODUCT SUPPLIERS

The Andipa Gallery, 162 Walton Street, Knightsbridge, London SW3 2JL
Partner: Mr Acoris A A Andipa. Executive staff 2, Other staff 1. Began 1969; interdenominational. (Previously The Maria Andipa & Son Icon Gallery). No magazine. Turnover n/a. Dealing in fine art of Byzantine, Middle Ages and Rennaisance iconography; reproductions; lectures, exhibitions, workshops. Web: www.andipa.com
Email: art@andipa.com
☎ 020 7589 2371 🖷 020 7225 0305

The Banner Company, St Michael's Business Centre, Church Street, Lyme Regis DT7 3DB
Proprietor: Mr Mark Shurey. Executive staff 2, Other staff 2. Began 1998; non-denominational. No magazine. Turnover: first year of operation. Designers and manufacturers of vinyl banners, display panels and banner hanging systems.
☎ 01297 444 665 / 444 890 🖷 01297 444 690

Mike Barrow Agencies, 10 Mile Court, Newcastle ST5 9BY
Owner: Mr Mike Barrow. Other staff n/a. Began 1996; non-denominational. No magazine. Turnover n/a. Supplying Christian souvenirs, celtic jewellery, icons; items with customers own design / logo for special events.
☎ 01782 614 839

Bees, 12 Rutland Grove, Farnworth, Bolton BL4 9QL
Partner: Mr John Bee. Executive staff 1, Other staff 10. Began 1950; interdenominational. No magazine. Turnover n/a. Distributing the Word of God through cards and gifts.
☎ 01204 700 990 🖷 01204 792 538

M

Jacquie Binns, 1 Cargill Road, Earlsfield, London SW18 3EF
Artist/Embroiderer: Ms Jacquie Binns. No full-time staff. Began 1987; non-denominational. No magazine. Turnover n/a. Vestments and hangings richly and expertly embroidered in original designs, creating individual works of art.
Web: ourworld.compuserve.com/homepages/churchtextiles_jacquiebinns
Email: churchtextiles_jacquiebinns@compuserve.com
☎ 020 8874 0895

Boo Cards, The Woodlands, Fauld Lane, Fauld, Burton-on-Trent DE13 9HS
Designer Director: Mrs Sandra Robinson. Executive staff 3. Began 1995; Anglican. No magazine. Turnover n/a. Writing, illustrating, designing, printing range of cards with spiritual verses.
☎ 01283 520 502

Brotherhood of St Seraphim, Station Road, Walsingham NR22 6DG
Chief Officer: Brother Leon Liddament. No other staff. Began 1966; Russian Orthodox. No magazine. Turnover n/a. Painting of icons, conservation and restoration of icons and church art.
☎ 01328 820 610

Cards of Encouragement, 7 Bull Farm Mews, Bull Lane, Matlock DE4 5NB
Proprietor: Mrs Judy Barker. Executive staff 2. Began 1990; non-denominational. No magazine. Turnover £11,000 to year end Mar 98. Designing, publishing and marketing cards for spiritual encouragement, the Millennium and for use in pastoral ministry.
☎ 01629 580 321 🖷 01629 580 321

Cathcard, 49 Russell Hill Road, Purley CR8 2XB
Company Secretary: Mr T Connor. Executive staff 1, Administrative staff 2. Began 1992; Roman Catholic. No magazine. Turnover £170,000 to year end Mar 98. Publishing and selling Christian Christmas cards for a group of UK Catholic social work agencies.
Email: terry@cathchild.org.uk
☎ 020 8668 2181 🖷 020 8763 2274

Chapel House Publishing (Oxford) Limited, TBAC Business Centre, Boston House, Grove Technology Park, Wantage OX12 9FF
Managing Director: Ms Wendy Robinson. Began n/a; non-denominational. No magazine. Turnover n/a. Distribution of inspirational greetings, cards, stationery, gifts and posters.
☎ 01235 772 922

***Christian Art**, 26 Lottbridge Drove, Eastbourne BN23 6NT
General Manager: Mr Stephen H Thornett. Began 1982; interdenominational. A division of Kingsway Communications Ltd. No magazine. Turnover £500,000 to year end May 96. Wholesaling of gifts, greetings cards, jewellery, Bible covers and inspirational stationery.
Email: dwright@kingsway.co.uk
☎ 01323 437 700

Christian Craft Enterprises, Maranatha Cottages, Barras, Kirkby Stephen CA17 4ES
Director: Lilian Cook. Executive staff 1. Began 1982; interdenominational. No magazine. Turnover £3,000 to year end Dec 98. Producing distinctive personal visuals for own events in your church or group, especially evangelism.
☎ 01768 342 016

Christian Crafts, Delta Close, Norwich NR6 6BG
Managing Director: Mr John Hughes. *Buying Director:* Mrs J Wastell. Executive staff 3, Other staff 15. Began 1977; non-denominational. No magazine. Turnover £200,000 to year end Mar 98. Wholesaling witness jewellery and needlework kits to Christian bookshops.
☎ 01603 426 159 🖷 01603 486 853

***Cloisters Ltd**, Northumbria Community, PO Box 1, Wooler NE71 6YY
Designer: Ms Nancy Hammond. Staff 3. Began 1994; non-denominational. Turnover n/a. Designing and selling greeting cards, prayer cards, notelets, gift items with calligraphic Christian messages.
☎ 01289 388 235

The Cross Stitch Collection, 30 Buttermere Drive, Kendal LA9 7PA
Owner: Mrs Audrey Wilkinson. Executive staff 1, Other staff 3. Began 1995; interdenominational. No magazine. Turnover £8,000 to year end Dec 98. Supplying cross stitch kits specially designed to help churches in fundraising.
Email: audrey@adrianw.dircon.co.uk
☎ 01539 736 076 Mobile: 07831 170 798 🖷 01539 736 076

Etherea (Decorative Arts), 17 Welland Close, Crowborough TN6 3BF
Decorative Artist: Miss Kirsty Shona Whitfield. Other staff 1. Began 1997; Anglican. No magazine. Turnover n/a. Painting Christian-based murals, paint-effects, trompe l'oeil, stage sets; exterior and interior, UK and overseas.
☎ 01892 655 942 Mobile: 07957 101 421 🖷 01892 655 942

Gateway World Shop, Market Place, Durham DH1 3NJ
Manager: Ms Aileen Garden. Other staff 3. Began 1982; non-denominational. (Previously Gateway Crafts Ltd). No magazine. Turnover £80,000 to year end Dec 98. Providing a fair trade outlet for producer groups in Third World.
☎ 0191 384 7173

Genesis Screen Prints & Embroidery, 18 Pendre Industrial Estate, Tywyn LL36 9LW
Partner: Mr Michael Stevens. Executive staff 2, Other staff 13. Began 1973; non-denominational. No magazine. Turnover n/a. T-shirts, garments printed, embroidered to any design.
Email: genesis.tshirt@virgin.net
☎ 01654 710 137 Fax 01654 712 461

C Goodliffe Neale Ltd, Arden Forest Industrial Estate, Alcester B49 6ER
Managing Director: Mr R Neale. Executive staff 25. Began 1936; Roman Catholic. No magazine. Turnover £1,000,000–3,000,000 to year end Dec 98. Wholesaling rosaries, statues, books and similar goods.
☎ 01789 763 261 Fax 01789 764 343

Gospel Cards, PO Box 56, Bridgend CF31 2JY
Director: Mr Michael Hart. Executive staff 1, Other staff 1. Began 1982; evangelical. Magazine: *Catalogue* (Circulation n/a half-yearly). Turnover n/a. Producing and selling evangelistic and devotional greetings cards: percentage of sales given to missionary organisations.
☎ 01656 647 551 Fax 01656 647 551

Holy Land Olive Wood, Atlas Developments, Atlas House, Nelson Street, Carlisle CA2 5ND
Director: Mr Dan Russell. Executive staff 2, Other staff 5. Began 1972; ecumenical. No magazine. Turnover £300,000 to year end Apr 94. Importing olive wood items especially nativity sets and crosses from Bethlehem.
☎ 01228 401 018 Fax 01228 401 019

Hughes & Coleman Ltd, Delta Close, Vulcan Road Estate, Norwich NR6 6BG
Managing Director: Mr John Hughes. *Buying Director:* Mrs J Wastell. *Accounts Director:* Mr R Gilbert. Executive staff 3, Other staff 15. Began 1957; evangelical. No magazine. Turnover £1,000,000 to year end Mar 98. Producing and distributing Christian gifts and greetings cards.
☎ 01603 426 159 Fax 01603 486 853

IGWIT, 1 Georges Crescent, Grappenhall, Warrington WA4 2PP
Sole Trader: Claire Hawksworth. No other staff. Began 1998; non-denominational. No magazine. Turnover: first year of operation. IGWIT = In God We Implicitly Trust. Cartoons with Scripture on giftware to gently convey God's word.
Email: claire@igwit.freeserve.co.uk
☎ 01925 269 763 Mobile: 07710 697 608

Impressions, 18 Rosebery Road, Stanwix, Carlisle CA3 9HU
Managing Director: Mr John Smith. Executive staff 2, Other staff 4. Began 1980; non-denominational. No magazine. Turnover n/a. Manufacturing framed texts; wholesale distribution of Christian literature.
☎ 01228 526 310 Mobile: 07798 834 767 Fax 01228 526 310

Israel Bureau (B & TM), 5 Franklin Avenue, Hartley Wintney, Hook RG27 8RB
Director: Mr Ron Bradnam. Executive staff 2. Began 1996; non-denominational. No magazine. Turnover n/a. Marketing technical and gift products from Israel, particularly those produced by Messianic believers.
Web: ourworld.compuserve.com/homepages/ron_bradnam
Email: ronbradnam@ibm.net
☎ 01252 842 108 Fax 01252 843 009

Kenex Bible Citation Markers, 18 Main Street, Kirkby Lonsdale LA6 2AG
Managing Director: Mr Bruce E Woods-Jack. Executive staff 4, Other staff 2. Began 1969; non-denominational. No magazine. Turnover £100,000 to year end Oct 96. Manufacturing and distributing Bible citation clip-on markers.
Email: artstone@easynet.co.uk
☎ 01524 271 603 Fax 01524 271 841
Orders: Autumn House Publishing, Alma House, Grantham NG31 9SL
☎ 01476 590 866

Kingscourt Enterprises, 1 The Courtyard, Leavesden Road, Watford WD2 5ER
Managing Director: Mr Martyn Francis. Executive staff 2. Began 1990; interdenominational. (Previously Top Flight). No magazine. Turnover n/a. Customising T-shirts and other leisurewear, plus a wide range of quality promotional products.
☎ 01923 248 154 Fax 01923 252 563

The Lens Ideas Studio, The Courtyard, Marks Hall Road, Coggeshall, Colchester CO6 1TE
Owner: Mr Leonard Smith. Executive staff 5, Other staff 2. Began 1985; non-denominational. No magazine. Turnover £300,000–500,000 to year end Dec 96. Designing and producing photographic greetings cards; commissioned photography; picture library.
Email: lensideas@easynet.co.uk
☎ 01376 562 727 Fax 01376 563 737

Lifestyle Designs, The Studio, 1 Shaw Street, Gowerton, Swansea SA4 3ER
Proprietor: Mr Carleton D Watts. Executive staff 1, Other staff 1. Began 1989; non-denominational. No magazine. Turnover n/a. Manufacturing Christian T-shirts and sweatshirts and all promotional products.
Email: lifestyledesigns@swig-online.co.uk
☎ 01792 522 319 Fax 01792 534 217

The Lord's Shop Trust, 379 Aspley Lane, Aspley, Nottingham NG8 5RR
Chairman: Mrs Doris A Lilley. Executive staff 1. ***CC*** No.506775. Began 1978; interdenominational. (Previously Green Pastures). No magazine. Turnover n/a. Shop selling greetings cards and good quality second-hand clothing/furniture.
☎ 0115 929 2500

Helen McIldowie-Daltrey, Pilgrims Rest, 34 Guildhall Street, Bury St Edmunds IP33 1QF
Icon Painter / Artist: Mrs Helen McIldowie-Daltrey. No other staff. Began 1994; Roman Catholic. No magazine. Turnover n/a. Icon painting and tuition; religious fine art commissions, gilding, conservation.
☎ 01284 762 076

Herbert Ramsden, 4 Saxony Road, Worthing BN14 7AT
Proprietor: Mr Herbert Ramsden. Other staff 2. Began 1984; interdenominational. No magazine. Turnover n/a. Distributing books, greeting cards, gift items and pictures to Christian bookshops.
☎ 01903 206 039 Mobile: 07976 644 393 Fax 01903 206 039

Rock Cottage Crafts, Cockshades Farm, Stock Lane, Wybunbury, Nantwich CW5 7HA
Partner: Miss Helen Piddock. Executive staff 3. Began 1980; Anglican. No magazine. Turnover n/a. Producing giftware, scriptural texts and verse cards, pictures, tea towels, bookmarks, posters.
☎ 01270 842 030 / 302 Fax 01270 842 030

Stamps Unlimited, The Old Post Office, 8 Swan Street, Kingsclere, Newbury RG20 5TJ
Proprietor: Mr Michael Payne. Full-time staff 2, Part-time staff 2. Began 1986; United Reformed. No magazine. Turnover £50,000 to year end Apr 98. Manufacturing and supplying all types of rubber stamps and marking devices.
☎ 01635 299 110 Mobile: 07785 520 215 🖷 01635 299 295

Steave's Shirts, The Gaines, Whitbourne, Worcester WR6 5RD
Sole Proprietor: Mr Steve Marshall. Executive staff 2, Other staff 2. Began 1982; non-denominational. No magazine. Turnover n/a. Screen printing of T-shirts, sweatshirts, polo shirts, baseball caps, jog pants, scarves, badges; design available.
☎ 01886 821 624 Mobile: 07970 644 994 🖷 01886 821 624

Traidcraft plc, Kingsway, Gateshead NE11 0NE
Managing Director: Mr Philip Angier. Executive staff 4, Other staff 80. Began 1979; non-denominational. Magazine: *Traid Bulletin* (2,500 monthly). Turnover £7,000,000 to year end Mar 98. Promoting fair trade with the Third World.
Web: www.traidcraft.co.uk
Email: comms@traidcraft.co.uk
☎ 0191 491 0591 🖷 0191 482 2690

***Jim Tranter Agencies**, 33 Lower Oxford Road, Newcastle ST5 0PB
Principal: Mr Jim Tranter. Executive staff 1, Other staff 1. Began 1991; non-denominational. No magazine. Turnover £500,000 to year end Dec 98. Supplying bone china beakers, plates, thimbles to clients own design; for special events, fundraising, souvenirs.
☎ 01782 618 115 🖷 01782 634 498

Vision International Products, Old Wheatley Farm, Pocombe Bridge, Exeter EX4 2HA
Partners: Mr & Mrs Paul & Michelle Ablett. Executive staff 2, Other staff 5. Began 1995; non-denominational. No magazine. Turnover n/a. Producing greetings cards, pens, badges to support Christian outlets, supply public with Christian message.
☎ 01392 423 839 🖷 01392 424 262

Mike Williams Publicity and Promotion, Perrowford, Trefusis Road, Redruth TR15 2JN
Sole Trader: Mr Michael Williams. Executive staff 1. Began 1990; non-denominational. No magazine. Turnover £20,000 to year end Mar 98. Promotion and fundraising items; badgemaking, hot foil, letterpress, scan printing, desk-top publishing, transfer printing garments.
Email: mikewilliams@saqnet.co.uk
☎ 01209 213 912

Wirral Textile Motifs, 113 Royden Road, Overchurch, Upton, Wirral CH49 4LX
Partner: Mr Bernard Gallivan. Executive staff 3. Began 1982; non-denominational. No magazine. Turnover n/a. Manufacturing general motifs, embroidered badges and logos for Christian organisations, churches, companies, clubs, schools.
☎ 0151 678 6076 🖷 0151 678 6076

Yaron Morhaim – Gifts from Israel, 54 Cliveden Road, London SW19 3PB
Owner: Mr Y Morhim. Executive staff 5. Began 1986; ecumenical. No magazine. Turnover n/a. Supplying religious giftware from the Holy Land, olive wood nativity sets, jewellery, glassware.
Email: yaron.morhaim@btinternet.com
☎ 020 8540 1647 Mobile: 07802 431 631
🖷 020 8241 0757

DESIGN, LAYOUT & EDITORIAL SERVICES

See also Photographers on Page 320, Marketing & Fundraising Services on Page 434.

***Adept Design**, 15 White Hart Street, Aylsham, Norwich NR11 6HG
Partners: Mr Derek Blois, Mr Geoffrey Clack. Executive staff 2, Other staff 8. Began 1982; non-denominational. No magazine. Turnover £500,000 to year end Apr 98. Artists/graphic designers offering a complete creative service for print, advertising, display, exhibition and the internet.
Web: www.adept.ndirect.co.uk
Email: admin@adept.ndirect.co.uk
☎ 01263 734 198 🖷 01263 734 822

Agapé Press (UK) Ltd, Unit 1D, Kingston Mill, Cobden Street, Pendleton, Salford M6 6WE
Managing Director: Dr Don E Okpalugo. All voluntary staff. ***CC*** No.1059348. Began 1996; non-denominational. Magazine: *Agapé Press Newsletter* (3,500 quarterly). Turnover £10,000 to year end Mar 97. Advancing the Christian faith through creative Christian communication.
☎ 0161 743 1010 🖷 0161 743 9991

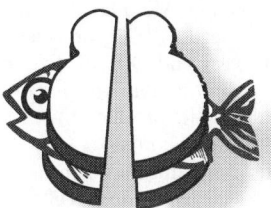

Anno Domini 2000 Designs, Flat 3, 29 Mayfield Road, Moseley, Birmingham B13 9HJ
Proprietor: Adrian P. Miles. Began 1996; non-denominational. No magazine. Turnover n/a. Website design for charities, small businesses, individuals; posters, graphic design.
Web: annodomini.org.uk
Email: anno_domini_2000_designs@btinternet.com
☎ 0121 449 4679

Arcus Design, 22 Mead Lane, Farnham GU9 7DY
Designer: Mr Nick Mills. Other staff 1. Began 1993; ecumenical. No magazine. Turnover n/a. Creative graphic design for print and other media.
☎ 01252 727 470 Fax 01252 727 470

Artlines, 465 West Wycombe Road, High Wycombe HP12 4AQ
Designer: Mr Tom Van Aurich. Executive staff 2, Other staff 1. Began 1985; non-denominational. No magazine. Turnover n/a. Graphic design from briefing to production, stationery and publicity materials, advertising, corporate, handbooks and magazines.
Email: artlines@compuserve.com
☎ 01494 442 988 ISDN: 01494 510 059 Fax 01494 452 949

*__AWM Graphics__, PO Box 4006, Worthing BN13 1AP
Art Director: Mr Richard Lackey. Executive staff 1, Other staff 5. ***CC*** No.214483. Began 1986; interdenominational. No magazine. Turnover £80,000 to year end Dec 97. Producing literature and providing production training for organisations involved in evangelism in the Arab world.
Email: awmginfo@wornet.mhs.compuserve.com
☎ 01903 215 345 Fax 01903 215 456

†**Christian Banners**, 9 Chestnut Court, Chestnut Lane, Amersham HP6 6ED
Administrator: Miss Priscilla Nunnerley. No full-time staff. Began 1982; non-denominational. No magazine. Turnover n/a. Communicating banner-making as a ministry through selling books and correspondence.
☎ 01494 727 528

Christian Computer Art, 33 Bramley Way, Hardwick, Cambridge CB3 7XD
Owner: Mrs Enid Instone-Brewer. Executive staff 1. Began 1992; non-denominational. No magazine. Turnover £20,000 to year end Apr 99. Providing clip art and Bible background pictures on CD/disc for church publicity and teaching.
Web: www.cc-art.com
Email: info@cc-art.com
☎ 01954 210 009 Fax 01954 210 009

Christian Media Centre Magazine Department, 96 Dominion Road, Worthing BN14 8JP
Managing Director: Mr Paul Slide. *Production Director:* Mr Mike Axell. Executive staff 5, Other staff 24. Began 1990; interdenominational. (Previously New Christian Herald Magazine Department). No magazine. Turnover n/a. Magazine editorial, production and distribution sub-contract service using same systems as *New Christian Herald* and *Woman Alive*.
Email: ma@christianmedia.org.uk
☎ 01903 821 082 ISDN: 01903 537 308
Fax 01903 821 081

***Christian Publicity Organisation**, Garcia Estate, Canterbur Road, Worthing BN13 1BW
General Director: Mr Roy P Barbour. *Director of Marketing* Mr Chris Powell. *Design Studio Manager:* Mr Steve Carrol Executive staff 3, Other staff 34. ***CC*** No.221462. Began 195 non-denominational. Magazine: *CPO Catalogue* (25,00 quarterly). Turnover £2,000,000 to year end Apr 9 Supporting the Christian community through design, prir and publishing, in partnership with ministries nationally an internationally.
Email: enquiries@cpo.uk.com
☎ 01903 264 556 ISDN: 01903 830 005 🖷 01903 830 06

D'Art Design, Broadoak House, Horsham Road, Cranleig GU6 8DJ
Designer: Mr Paul Higgins. Executive staff 1, Other staff 1 Began 1989; non-denominational. No magazine. Turnove £62,000 to year end Oct 98. Corporate design, logos, advertis ing campaigns, packaging and print, web site design.
Email: inform@dartdesign.co.uk
☎ 01483 275 054 🖷 01483 268 173

***DM Music for Churches**, Unit 4, Riverside Estate, Coldharbou Lane, Harpenden AL5 4UN
Managing Director: Mr David Moore. Executive staff 2 Other staff 8. Began 1991; non-denominational. Turnove £1,500,000 to year end Dec 98. Experienced in-house desig and advertising service available for brochure, catalogue, lea let, poster and website production.
Web: www.dm-music.co.uk
Email: enquiries@dm-music.co.uk
☎ 01582 761 122 Freephone: 0500 026 930
🖷 01582 768 811

Editorial Services, 163 Clifton Road, Rugby CV21 3QN
Editor: Mr Roger Day. Executive staff 2. Began 199 non-denominational. No magazine. Turnover £12,000 to yea end May 98. Providing a full range of writing, editing and desk top publishing for churches and businesses.
☎ 01788 550 842 Mobile: 07885 823 046 🖷 01788 547 516

Sylvia Evans and Associates, York House, 44 Hawthorn Road Redcar TS10 3PY
Owner: Mrs Sylvia Evans. Executive staff 1, Other staff 1 Began 1972; non-denominational. No magazine. Turnove n/a. Public relations consultancy; television, press, seminars conferences, brochures, publishing, advertising, strategic mar keting.
Email: sylviaevans1@compuserve.uk.co
☎ 01642 473 207 🖷 07070 600 000

Clifford Frost Ltd, Lyon Road, Windsor Avenue, Wimbledon London SW19 2SE
Sales Director: Mr Terry Ingham. Executive staff 10, Othe staff 40. Began 1896; interdenominational. No magazine Turnover £3,000,000 to year end Mar 99. Complete creativ design and printing service.
Email: print@clifford.frost.co.uk
☎ 020 8540 2396 🖷 020 8540 8086

Gazelle Creative Productions Ltd, Concorde House, Grenvill Place, Mill Hill, London NW7 3SA
Managing Director: Mr Nick Jones. Executive staff 2, Othe staff 4. Began 1979; interdenominational. (Previously Nuprin Ltd). No magazine. Turnover n/a. Design, print production publishing and marketing services; books, magazines, cata logues, promotional material and brochures.
Email: gazelle@angushudson.com
☎ 020 8906 9769 Mobile: 07970 883 910 🖷 020 8959 3678

Gillard Brothers Graphics, 24 Mount Pleasant, Biggin Hill, Westerham TN16 3TR
Partners: Mr Geoffrey C Gillard, Mrs Carol A Gillard. Executive staff 2. Began 1973; interdenominational. No magazine. Turnover n/a. Corporate identity, brochure and advertising design, book covers and illustrations, web site design.
☎ 01959 573 710 🖷 01959 573 710

Stephen Goddard Associates, Commercial Business Centre, Victoria Street, Rainhill, Prescot L35 4LP
Principal: Mr Stephen Goddard. Executive staff 1, Other staff 3. Began 1987; interdenominational. No magazine. Turnover n/a. Public relations consultants; product and service launches to Christian and mainstream media; promotional newspaper production.
Email: goddard@asa-net.co.uk
☎ 0151 431 0440 🖷 0151 430 7836

Grax Design Consultants, Sherbourne House, 23 Northolt Road, Harrow HA2 0LH
Design Director: Mrs Heather Knight. *Senior Designer:* Mr Mark Knight. Executive staff 4. Began 1992; non-denominational. No magazine. Turnover £180,000 to year end Nov 98. Designing and producing logos, brochures, reports, exhibition stands, leaflets, websites; design for publishing.
Email: heather@grax.demon.co.uk
☎ 020 8423 8864 🖷 020 8864 8614

Greenleaf Communications Ltd, 12 Montacute Road, Tunbridge Wells TN2 5QR
Chairman: Mr Tony Neeves. *Managing Director:* Mr Roger Hulbert. Executive staff 2, Other staff 2. Began 1979; interdenominational. No magazine. Turnover £475,413 to year end Mar 97. Christian-based design and advertising agency; film and audio-visual producers for major charities and commercial companies.
Web: uk-greenleaf.com
Email: greenleaf@ndirect.co.uk
☎ 01892 512 900 🖷 01892 517 067

H&B Enterprises, 276 South Lambeth Road, London SW8 1UJ
Directors: Rev Haydn & Mrs Beulah Wood. Other staff 2. Began 1990; non-denominational. (Previously Beulah Graphics). No magazine. Turnover n/a. Foreign language desktop publishing; bespoke applications for small businesses.
Email: 100257.165@compuserve.com
☎ 020 7627 4862 🖷 020 7978 2060

Hand of Creation, The Studio, 1 Shaw Street, Gowerton, Swansea SA4 3ER
Studio Manager: Mr Carleton D Watts. Executive staff 2, Other staff 1. Began 1997; non-denominational. (Previously Airbrush Art, Lifestyle Designs). No magazine. Turnover n/a. Corporate promotional products including graphic design and illustration, mugs, mousemats, T-shirts, and full colour printing.
Web: handofcreation.com
Email: sales@handofcreation.com
☎ 01792 522 319 Mobile: 07971 200 401
🖷 01792 534 217

Jill Harris, 54 Ashby House, Essex Road, London N1 3PR
Writer/Editor: Ms Jill Harris. No other staff. Began 1995; non-denominational. No magazine. Turnover n/a. Providing complete editorial and publicity service: copywriting, editing, organising design.
☎ 020 7704 0916 🖷 020 7704 0916

Iden Design Associates, 183 Crescent Drive, Petts Wood, Orpington BR5 1AZ
Director: Mr Ron Iden. Executive staff 1, Other staff 1. Began 1986; non-denominational. (Previously Crescent Graphics). Turnover n/a. Graphic design, copy and print solutions for leaflets, brochures, advertising, packaging and corporate identity.
Email: iden1@compuserve.com
☎ 01689 876 191 🖷 01689 810 091

IKON Productions Ltd, Manor Farm House, Manor Road, Wantage OX12 8NE
Managing Director: Ms Clare Goodrick-Clarke. Executive staff 2. Began 1998; interdenominational. No magazine. Turnover n/a. Publications service (copywriting, editorial, design and print). Fundraising, consultancy to religious/educational institutions, including donor research and strategy.
Email: ikon@globalnet.co.uk
☎ 01235 767 467 🖷 01235 763 211

Image-on Artworks, 37 Hymers Avenue, Hull HU3 1LL
Proprietor: Mr Jonathan Richards. Other staff 1. Began 1994; non-denominational. Turnover £100,000. Graphic design and print to Christian organisations and charities. In-house magazine available.
Email: admin@image-on.demon.co.uk
☎ 01482 445 570 🖷 01482 341 813

Simon Jenkins Associates, 14 Hillcrest Road, Acton, London W3 9RZ
Partner: Mr Simon Jenkins. Admin staff 1. Began 1988; non-denominational. No magazine. Turnover n/a. Creating concepts, copywriting, design for all forms of print media.
Email: simon@west3.demon.co.uk
☎ 020 8993 3936 🖷 020 8752 0949

***Paul Jones Associates**, 98 Eden Way, Beckenham BR3 3DH
Managing Director: Mr Paul Jones. No full-time staff. Began 1979; interdenominational. No magazine. Turnover £50,000–100,000 to year end Dec 98. Designing and printing for Christian organisations; newsletters, magazines, brochures, advertising, catalogues and exhibitions.
Email: pj@pja.u-net.com
☎ 0208 663 3963 Mobile: 07956 383 117 🖷 0208 663 3964

***Just Words**, 7 Blackcroft, Wantage OX12 9EX
Director: Mr David B Hall. No other staff. Began 1986; interdenominational. No magazine. Turnover n/a. Freelance writing of press releases, company features, publicity advice and editorial for fundraising.
Email: davidbhall@compuserve.com
☎ 01235 762 810

King-Fisher Media Services, Charis House, Hardwick Square East, Buxton SK17 6PT
Partner: n/a. Executive staff 2, Other staff 2. Began 1992; interdenominational. (Previously Christian Media Services). Turnover n/a. Website design, electronic media design and production, graphic design, copywriting and editorial services, internet consultants.
Web: www.king-fisher.co.uk
Email: enquiries@king-fisher.co.uk
☎ 01298 258 49 Mobile: 07774 159 157 🖷 01298 270 27

***Lighthouse Graphics**, 122 Glenview, Abbey Wood, London SE2 0SH
Owner Manager: Mr Paul Goodman. Designer 1. Began 1996; Evangelical. No magazine. Turnover n/a. Producing design and layout for print, including press-ads, posters, leaflets, brochures etc.
Email: pgoodman@btinternet.com
☎ 020 8312 1023 🖷 020 8312 1023

M

Stephen Lown, Graphic Designer, Office 3, 23 Gwydir Street, Cambridge CB1 2LG
Graphic Designer: Mr Stephen Lown. No other staff. Began 1991; interdenominational. No magazine. Turnover n/a. Graphic design, artwork and print production for corporate identity, advertising and promotional literature.
Email: slowngd@aol.com
☎ 01223 576 706 Mobile: 07702 346 114 🖷 01223 576 706

Jeremy Mudditt Publishing Services, 3 Longlands, Carlisle CA3 9AD
Partner: Mr Jeremy H L Mudditt. Executive staff 1, Other staff 1. Began 1997; non-denominational. No magazine. Turnover £18,000. Book and magazine project, editorial and production management services for authors and publishers.
Email: jmudditt@aol.com
☎ 01228 547 937

***Elizabeth Nicoll**, 7 Allan Way, Acton, London W3 0PW
Designer: Mrs Elizabeth Nicoll. Executive staff 2. Began 1996; interdenominational. No magazine. Turnover £40,000 to year end Feb 99. Graphic design and print for all sales, marketing and administration purposes.
Email: elizabeth.r.nicoll@btinternet.com
☎ 020 8993 8455 🖷 020 8993 7071

†*Page '90, 31 High Street, Weldon, Corby NN17 3JJ
Proprietor: Mr David Page. Executive staff 1. Began 1990; non-denominational. No magazine. Turnover £20,000 to year end Feb 97. Providing freelance editorial services, consultancy for publishers of books, journals, training material.
☎ 01536 261 647 🖷 01536 409 737

†PBF Marketing Ltd, 3 Bassett Court, Newport Pagnell, Milton Keynes MK16 0JN
Director: Mr Michael Payne. Executive staff 3, Other staff 1. Began 1983; non-denominational. (Previously Partners in Design). No magazine. Turnover £425,000 to year end Dec 94. Design studio.
☎ 01908 616 627 🖷 01908 611 714

***Pertinent PR**, BHCF Buildings, 168 Main Road, Biggin Hill, Westerham TN16 3BA
Consultant: Mrs Cynthia Gibbons-Pert. Other staff 2. Began n/a; Independent. No magazine. Turnover £95,000 to year end Dec 98. Public relations, marketing and business development service to Christian and non-Christian business organisations.
Web: www.pertpr.demon.co.uk
Email: cgp@pertpr.demon.co.uk
☎ 01959 575 276 Mobile: 07889 004 814 🖷 01959 540 965

Pinnacle Creative, 143 The Gardens, Southwick BN42 4AR
Managing Director: Mr Adrian Willard. Executive staff 1, Other staff 7. ***CC*** Began 1980; non-denominational. (Previously Frontiers Publishing International). Turnover n/a. Video production, graphic design and magazine production.
☎ 01273 870 221 🖷 01273 870 229

†Bruce Porteous Design, 13 Charing Cross, Norwich NR2 4AX
Proprietor: Mr Bruce Porteous. Executive staff 1. Began 1986; interdenominational. No magazine. Turnover n/a. Graphic design, including publicity, advertising and book design.
☎ 01603 625 848 🖷 01603 630 159

Profile Design, 12 Northgate, Chichester PO19 1BA
Proprietor: Mr Peter Hamilton. Executive staff 1, Other staff 2. Began 1989; House Church. No magazine. Turnover £260,000 to year end Oct 98. Designing and printing brochures, magazines, stationery, leaflets and reports for the Christian and secular community.
☎ 01243 537 444 🖷 01243 537 440

***Revival digital imaging**, 81 Earles Meadow, Horsham RH12 4HR
Proprietor: Mr Brian Abell. Executive staff 1. Began 1991; non-denominational. Turnover n/a. Providing design and print for Christian, commercial/private requirements; stationery, brochures, magazines, booklets, publicity material.
☎ 01403 251 818 Mobile: 07930 560 423 🖷 01403 251 818

River, The Old Exchange, Fyfield Road, Stapenhill, Burton-on-Trent DE15 9QA
Partners: David Walker, Andy Crockford. Executive staff 4, Other staff 3. Began 1999; interdenominational. (Previously Advent Consulting Ltd). Advent Consulting Ltd and Sprint Origination have joined to form a new partnership. No magazine. Turnover £370,000 to year end Dec 99. Advertising and design: press campaigns, prepress origination, print, exhibition and POS graphics, corporate identities. Website design.
Web: www.river.uk.com
Email: info@river.uk.com
☎ 01283 565 522 🖷 01283 561 177

Russimco Ltd, The Coach House, 21 Broadway, Chilton Polden, Bridgwater TA7 9DR
Director: Mr Simeon Oram. *Business Manager:* Mr Richard Bowman. Exec staff 3, Other staff 10. Began 1993; non-denominational. No magazine. Turnover £450,000 to year end Jun 98. Design and printing services to churches and Christian organisations.
Web: www.russimco.com
Email: printing@russimco.com
☎ 01278 723 450 🖷 01278 723 357

Silver Fish Creative Marketing Ltd, 37 Pottery Lane, Holland Park, London W11 4LY
Managing Director: Mr Stephen Jones. Executive staff 5, Other staff 5. Began 1996; interdenominational. No magazine. Turnover n/a. Providing graphic design, advertising, print management, photography, publishing, public relations.
Email: silver.fish@virgin.net
☎ 020 7727 2871 🖷 020 7727 2875

Sovereign Creative Marketing Ltd, 15 Station Road, Cheadle Hulme, Cheadle SK8 5AF
Managing Director: Mr Nigel Tedford. *Financial Director:* Mrs Dianne Tedford. Executive staff 2, Other staff 4. Began 1984; interdenominational. (Previously Sovereign Advertising & Marketing (CH) Ltd). No magazine. Turnover £500,000–1,000,000 to year end Dec 98. Marketing campaigns, advertisement design and media buying, donor recruitment and development, direct mail, literature design and production.
Web: www.sovereign.uk.com
Email: nigeltedford@sovereign.uk.com
☎ 0161 485 4488 🖷 0161 486 1886

Spirit Design, 143 Leeson Drive, Ferndown BH22 9RE
Partner: Mr Rob Hillman. Executive staff 1, Other staff 2. Began 1996; non-denominational. No magazine. Turnover n/a. Designing stationery, advertising, posters, CD covers; copywriting; desktop publishing.
☎ 01202 890 371 🖷 01202 292 705

Spirit Print, 109 Marmet Avenue, Letchworth SG6 4QF
Proprietor: Mr Brian Evans. No other staff. Began 1992; interdenominational. (Previously Waveney Publishing). No magazine. Turnover n/a. Printing (DTP) services for the smaller church: newsletters, service sheet, notices, campaign handouts etc.
Web: www.marmet.freeserve.co.uk
Email: spirit@marmet.freeserve.co.uk
☎ 01462 681 021 Mobile: 07803 169 204

Stickywicket Design and Print, Great Southsea Street, Southsea PO5 3BY
Partner: Mr Richard P Reilly-Davidson. Full-time staff 9. Began 1993; Elim Pentecostal. Magazine: *Acorn News* (Circulation n/a every two months). Turnover n/a. Supplying initial art work through to design and printing.
Web: www.stickywicket.com
Email: design@stickywicket.com
☎ 023 9273 4201 🖷 023 9273 4020

Teamwork, 44 Rectory Walk, Sompting, Lancing BN15 0DU
Joint Partners: Mr Christopher & Mrs Gail Lawther. Executive staff 2. Began 1985; non-denominational. No magazine. Turnover n/a. Complete design service for books, booklets, periodicals and printed publicity. Publishing service for selected craftbooks.
☎ 01903 750 946

Graham Turner, 39 Honor Oak Road, Forest Hill, London SE23 3SH
Partner: Mr Graham Turner. Other staff n/a. Began 1966; non-denominational. No magazine. Turnover n/a. Designing, typesetting and artwork for print.
Email: 101762.1005@compuserve.com
Email: grahamturner@compuserve.com
☎ 020 8291 1655 🖷 020 8291 6247

Vantage Graphics & Design Ltd, 43 Newton Hall Gardens, Rochford SS4 3EP
Director: Mr Michael D Abbott. Executive staff 1, Other staff 2. Began 1986; non-denominational. (Previously Vantage Advertising and Design Ltd). Turnover £50,000 to year end Dec 98. Creative service in: graphic design and computer graphics for print, multimedia and internet application.
Web: www.vgd.co.uk
Email: mda@vgd.co.uk
☎ 01702 544 604 🖷 01702 544 604

Watermark, Norfolk House, 1 Hamilton Road, Cromer NR27 9HJ
Managing Director: Rev Robert Backhouse. Executive staff 4. Began 1984; non-denominational. No magazine. Turnover n/a. Writing, editing, indexing, typesetting and design.
☎ 01263 515 575

Wingfinger Graphics, 1st floor, 13 Queen Square, Leeds LS2 8AJ
Partners: Mr Bill Phelps, Mr Richard Lether. Executive staff 3. Began 1973; non-denominational. No magazine. Turnover £140,000 to year end Apr 98. Designing and printing magazines, leaflets, publicity, stationery, corporate image; copywriting, editing.
Web: www.wfinger.demon.co.uk
Email: pteri@wfinger.demon.co.uk
☎ 0113 245 0469 🖷 0113 244 4688

Worldwide Christian Communication Network, 54 Edgecoombe, South Croydon CR2 8AB
Director: Rev Remi Caillaux. Executive staff 1. *CC* No.1045313. Began 1995; Pentecostal. Magazine: *Victory* (Circulation n/a every two months). Turnover £90,000 to year end Mar 98. Undertaking creative graphic design, Christian communication for print, other media such as internet.
Web: www.wccn.net
☎ 020 8405 4725 🖷 020 8405 4725

MEDIA PRODUCERS

Abstract Images, 117 Willoughby House, Barbican, London EC2Y 8BL
Managing Director: Mr Howard Ross. Executive staff 1. Began 1990; non-denominational. No magazine. Turnover £300,000 to year end Dec 97. Producing: Television – acts of worship; single documentaries; factual, drama series. Radio – discussion, current/religious affairs.
Email: productions@abstract-images.co.uk
☎ 020 7638 5123 🖷 020 7638 5123

***Alitapes**, 73 Apton Road, Bishop's Stortford CM23 3ST
Proprietor: Ms Alison Burnett. No other staff. Began 1994; non-denominational. No magazine. Turnover £1,000 to year end Nov 98. Helping Christian organisations raise public awareness of their product and message through local radio.
Email: alisonburnett@orangenet.co.uk
☎ 01279 651 195 🖷 01279 651 195

Alpha Recordings Ltd, 1 Abbey Street, Eynsham, Oxford OX8 1HR
Managing Director: Mr H F Mudd. Staff n/a. Began 1964; non-denominational. No magazine. Turnover n/a. Producing and distributing records, church, organ and choral music.
☎ 01865 880 240 🖷 01865 880 240

Anglia Television Ltd, Anglia House, Norwich NR1 3JG
Senior Producer: Mr Mike Talbot. Began 1959; non-denominational. No magazine. Turnover n/a. Producing a diversity of religious programmes for ITV Network and Anglia including weekly magazine 'Sunday Morning'.
Email: sunday.morning@angliatv.co.uk
☎ 01603 615 151 🖷 01603 627 738

M

Anglo-Nordic Productions Trust, 2 Thornton Close, Girton, Cambridge CB3 0NQ
Secretary: Mr Patrick Colquhoun. Executive staff 1. *CC* No.280052. Began 1980; non-denominational. No magazine. Turnover £39,000 to year end Dec 98. Producing and distributing Christian film/video; emphasis on education, churches and Eastern Europe.
Email: 101564.132@compuserve.com
☎ 01223 276 504

Ark Recording Studio, 42 Alexandra Road, Rochford SS4 3HD
Proprietor: Mr John J Staff. No full-time staff. Began 1963; non-denominational. No magazine. Turnover n/a. Small studio with basic facilities; editing and production work accepted.
Email: johnstaff@compuserve.com
☎ 01702 544 881 Mobile: 07778 430 095

Barnard Media Services, 93 Queen Street, Worthing BN14 7BH
Proprietor: Mr Adrian Barnard. Executive staff 1. Began 1995; non-denominational. Turnover £24,000 to year end Jan 99. Producing talking newspapers, audio magazines, prayer tapes; radio production services; scriptwriting; consultancy.
Email: awbarnard@compuserve.com
☎ 01903 233 958 🖷 01903 233 958

BBC School Television: Religious Education and Worship Programmes, White City, 201 Wood Lane, London W12 7TS
Executive Producer: Mr Geoffrey Marshall-Taylor. Executive staff 5, Other staff 2. Began n/a; non-denominational. No magazine. Turnover n/a. Producing TV/Radio programmes, print and on-line resources for schools. Christian and non-Christian faiths.
☎ 020 8752 5252 (Room2236) 🖷 020 8752 4343 (Room2236)

Bethel Communications, PO Box 459, Edinburgh EH12 5TX
Director: Deborah Menelaws. Executive staff 2, Other staff 3. Began 1986; non-denominational. No magazine. Turnover n/a. Media consultancy; video and radio documentaries; ministry on eschatology.
Email: debmen@aol.com
☎ 0131 337 2515 🖷 0131 337 2515

Braeside Recording Studio, Unit 11, The Hatchery Centre, Great North Road, Welwyn Garden City AL8 7SR
Proprietor: Mr Simon George. Executive staff 2. Began 1994; non-denominational. Turnover n/a. Production and recording of music and spoken word; cassette and CD duplication, digital editing.
Web: www.smg.org.uk/braeside
Email: sm.george@virgin.net
☎ 01707 393 477 Mobile: 07711 670069 🖷 01707 393 477

Callister Communications Ltd, 88 Causeway End Road, Lisburn BT28 2ED
Director: Mr John Callister. Executive staff 1, Other staff 2. Began 1990; interdenominational. No magazine. Turnover n/a. Producing 16mm film and video to broadcast standard for Christian organisations and charities.
Email: jcallister@fibus.com
☎ 028 9267 3717 🖷 028 9267 3652

Cambridge Film and Television Productions, Middlewhite Barn, St George's Way, Impington, Cambridge CB4 9AF
Director/Producer: Mr Lester Milbank. *Assistant Producer:* Mrs Jenny Urwin. Admin staff 2, Technical staff 2. Began 1989; Baptist. (Previously Lester Milbank Productions). No magazine. Turnover £320,000 to year end Mar 98. Award winning, compelling and sensitive production of videos for church organisations, charities and broadcasters.
Email: lester@dial.pipex.com
☎ 01223 236 007 🖷 01223 236 555

Catholic Communications Centre, 39 Eccleston Square, London SW1V 1BX
Director: Dr Jim McDonnell. Executive staff 2, Other staff 1. *CC* No.326810. Began 1955; Roman Catholic. No magazine. Turnover n/a. Training and production facilities to enable Catholics and other Christians to communicate effectively through the media.
Web: www.cathcom.com.uk
Email: cathcom@compuserve.com
☎ 020 7233 8196 🖷 020 7931 7497

Christian Channel (Europe) Ltd, Christian Channel Studios, Stonehills, Shields Road, Gateshead NE10 0HW
Chief Executive Office: Mr & Mrs Rory & Wendy Alec. Executive staff 2, Other staff 40. Began 1995; non-denominational. No magazine. Turnover n/a. Producing and distributing Christian television programmes.
Web: www.godnetwork.com
Email: info@godnetwork.com
☎ 0191 495 2244 🖷 0191 495 2266

***Christian Communications Network (Europe) Ltd**, 646 Shore Road, Whiteabbey, Newtownabbey BT37 0PR
President: Dr C Stewart OBE. Executive staff 2, Other staff 2. *CC* Began 1996; interdenominational. No magazine. Turnover n/a. Broadcast quality Christian production centre, producing videos for television and radio stations.
Web: ccneurope.org.uk
Email: ccn@ccneurope.org.uk
☎ 028 9085 3997 🖷 028 9036 5536

Christian Television Association, Wraxall, Bristol BS48 1PG
Executive Director: Mr Malcolm Turner. Other staff 1. ***CC*** No.280329. Began 1978; interdenominational. Magazine: *CTA News* (1,900 every four months). Turnover £100,000 to year end Dec 98. Producing video programmes for sale, on commission and for broadcasting.
Web: www.cta.uk.com
Email: info@cta.uk.com
☎ 01275 851 222 Fax: 01275 851 555

Christian Voice Ltd, PO Box 3040, Ryder Street, West Bromwich B70 0EL
Director: Mr J Peter Wilson. Executive staff 1, Other staff 3. Began 1997; non-denominational. No magazine. Turnover n/a prior to broadcasting. Contemporary Christian music/talk FM Station applying for ILR licence to broadcast to the West Midlands.
Web: www.christianvoice.co.uk
Email: info@christianvoice.co.uk
☎ 0121 224 1678 Fax: 0121 522 6083

Christian World Centre, Grampian House, 144 Deansgate, Manchester M3 3ED
Operations Director: Mr John F Macdonald. Executive staff 1, Other staff 2. ***CC*** Began 1980; interdenominational. (Send the Light Ltd). Magazine: *Christian World News Review* (3,000 monthly). Turnover n/a. Distributing 16mm films; Genesis New Media Bible; computer software & games; CD ROMs.
☎ 0161 834 6060 Fax: 0161 834 6060

Clearwater Communications, 163 Marshall Lake Road, Shirley, Solihull B90 4RB
Director: Mr Don Sanders. Executive staff 1, Other staff 1. Began 1984; interdenominational. No magazine. Turnover £12,000 to year end Aug 98. Producing evangelistic programmes for television, and video materials for churches and schools.
Email: don.sanders@bigfoot.com
☎ 0121 744 3122 Mobile: 07778 502 243 Fax: 0121 624 3866

*__Commission Christian Radio__, Millar Street, Belfast BT6 8JZ
Executive Secretary: Mr Noel Speers. All voluntary staff. ***CC*** Began 1975; non-denominational. Magazine: *Newsletter* (400 quarterly). Turnover £800 to year end June 98. Preparing programmes for missionary, hospital and local radio; assisting in AV and video soundtracks.
☎ 028 9045 3338

*__Cross Rhythms__, PO Box 1110, Stoke-on-Trent ST4 8JR
Chief Executive Officer: Mr Chris Cole. *Co-ordinator:* Mr Jonathan Bellamy. Executive staff 3, Other staff 15. ***CC*** No.1069357. Began 1990; interdenominational. Turnover £100,000 to year end Dec 98. Christian music magazine, festivals and UCB Cross Rhythms national contemporary Christian radio station.
Web: www.crossrhythms.co.uk
Email: admin@crossrhythms.co.uk
☎ 01782 642 444 Fax: 01782 641 121

*__CrossView Audio Visual__, PO Box 22, Felixstowe IP11 9EU
Director: Dr Terry Smith. Executive staff 2, Other staff 1. Began 1993; interdenominational. No magazine. Turnover n/a. Producing top-quality low-budget evangelistic, promotional and teaching videos.
Web: www.crossview.co.uk
Email: crossview@btinternet.com
☎ 01394 270 110 Fax: 01394 270 110

CTVC, Hillside Studios, Merry Hill Road, Bushey, Watford WD2 1DR
Director: Rev Barrie Allcott. Executive staff 6, Other staff 50. ***CC*** No.276286. Began 1959; non-denominational. No magazine. Turnover n/a. Television production and distribution together with some video productions.
Web: www.ctvc.co.uk
Email: hillside@ctvc.co.uk
☎ 020 8950 4426 Fax: 020 8950 1437

*__Cutting Edge Productions__, 39 Rookswood, Alton GU34 2LD
Proprietor: Mr Alan Matthews. Admin staff 3. Began 1994; interdenominational. No magazine. Turnover n/a. Specialising in live multi-camera events, single-camera productions; outside broadcast truck and postproduction facilities.
Web: www.cuttingedgeuk.com
Email: cuttingedgeuk@lineone.net
☎ 01420 544 674 Mobile: 07768 320471
Fax: 01420 544 668

*__CVG Television__, First House, 1 Sutton Street, Birmingham B1 1PE
Director: Mrs Sally Murcott. *Sales Manager:* Mr Andrew Price. Executive staff 2, Other staff 4. ***CC*** No.327352. Began 1983; non-denominational. Magazine: *CVG News* (2,000 quarterly). Turnover £130,000 to year end Dec 96. Producing video and TV specialising in evangelistic, educational and youth programmes for mission and Christian organisations.
Web: www.cvgtv.co.uk
Email: mail@cvgtv.co.uk
☎ 0121 622 1337 Fax: 0121 622 3080

M

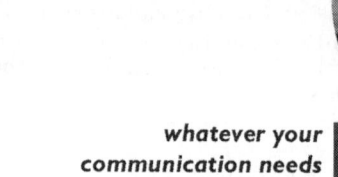

Dales Broadcast Ltd, Nettle Hill, Brinklow Road, Ansty, Coventry CV7 9JL
Managing Director: Mr Julian Boden. *Marketing Director:* Mrs Kate Boden. Executive staff 3, Other staff 2. Began 1984; non-denominational. (Previously Dales Television). No magazine. Turnover £250,000 to year end Mar 98. Producing religious and moral videos and television broadcast programmes.
Web: www.dales-ltd.com
Email: sales@dales-ltd.com
☎ 024 7662 1763 Mobile: 07710 903 730
🖷 024 7660 2732

Dovetail Productions, Dovecote House, Walcot, Sleaford NG34 0SU
Director: Mr Eric Mival. Executive staff 1, Other staff 1. Began 1988. No magazine. Turnover n/a. Producing films, television programmes and videos, special interest in education. Training in basic video skills.
Email: emival@dovetail.nildram.co.uk
☎ 01529 497 081 Mobile: 07770 893 455 🖷 01529 497 081

Evangelical Outreach Ltd, 5 Sperrin Drive, Belfast BT5 7RY
Executive Directors: Donald Preston, Fred Johnston. No full-time staff. ***CC*** No.NI 6596. Began 1966; non-denominational. Magazine: *Newsletter* (Circulation & frequency n/a). Turnover under £10,000 to year end Dec 96. Producing video, evangelistic film festivals/Share Your Faith seminars, video sales and film rentals.
☎ 028 9048 2917 / 9065 5368 🖷 028 9047 3377

***Focus Radio**, 80 Portswood Road, Southampton SO17 2FW
Director: Mr David A Couchman. Executive staff 2, Other staff 3. ***CC*** No.298007. Began 1976; interdenominational. Magazine: *Newsletter* (1,000 quarterly). Turnover £100,000 to year end Mar 98. Making radio programmes for international evangelism and leadership training.
Web: www.focus.org.uk
Email: focus@xc.org
☎ 023 8067 6911 🖷 023 8067 6981

Forward Vision Communications Ltd, 10 Claverdon Close, Solihull B91 1QP
Managing Director: Mr David Furmage. *Co-ordinator:* Mrs Jenny Page. Executive staff 2, Other staff 2. Began 1991; non-denominational. No magazine. Turnover £160,000 to year end Jan 99. Video/broadcast production, music, documentary, conference, promotional, multi-media projects, CD Rom production, packaging design.
Web: www.forwardvision.co.uk
Email: action@forwardvision.co.uk
☎ 0121 711 7500 Mobile: 07050 030 125
🖷 0121 711 7600

***Good News Broadcasting Association (Great Britain) Ltd**, Bawtry Hall, Bawtry, Doncaster DN10 6JH
Chief Executive: Nick Thompson. *Chairman:* Mr Peter Spriggs. Office staff 5. ***CC*** No.275115. Began 1954; non-denominational. (Affiliated to Back to the Bible). Magazine: *Sounding Out* (3,500 monthly). Turnover £470,000 to year end June 98. Producing programmes for national, local and Christian radio; counselling, monthly teaching tape ministry, pulpit supply, internet site.
Web: www.goodnews-uk.u-net.com
Email: info@goodnews-uk.u-net.com
☎ 01302 719 468 / 0500 205 111(radio response line)
Mobile: 07710 463 001 🖷 01302 719 029

Gospel Broadcasting System Ltd (GBS Radio), 14 Grange Road West, Birkenhead CH41 4DA
Director/Secretary: Mr J K Stuffins. All voluntary staff. ***CC*** No.218947. Began 1956; interdenominational. Magazine: *Newsletter* (Circulation n/a quarterly). Turnover £22,000 to year end June 98. Producing Bible teaching and evangelical radio programmes for Africa, India and elsewhere.
Email: info@gbsradio.u-net.com
☎ 0151 639 2450 Fax 0151 639 2450

GRF Christian Radio, GRF Studios, 342 Argyle Street, Glasgow G2 8LY
Programme Controller: Mr Brian W Muir. No full-time staff. ***CC*** Began 1948; non-denominational. No magazine. Turnover £18,000 to year end Mar 99. Producing programmes for worldwide radio networks, BBC radio, British ILR and British Hospital Radio.
Web: www.ed.ac.uk/~gmck/grf.html
Email: grf.radio@scet.com
☎ 0141 221 9447 Fax 0141 332 9187

Hitotsu-Bishi, 22 Hassocks Wood, Stroudley Road, Basingstoke RG24 8UQ
Managing Director: Mr Andrew Earle. *Marketing Director:* Mr Andrew Watkins. Executive staff 2. Began 1986; interdenominational. (Previously Gothic Audio-Visual & Studio 55). No magazine. Turnover £205,000 to year end Nov 98. Preparing training and promotional material utilising film, video, tape-slide & print.
Email: hitbis@aol.com
☎ 01256 471 471 Fax 01256 471 470

Hope FM, Delta House, 56 Westover Road, Bournemouth BH1 2BS
Director: Mr B Crawford. *Chairman:* Mr Derek T Wilkinson. Admin staff 1. ***CC*** No.250619. Began n/a; interdenominational. Turnover £30,000 to year end Dec 98. Community Christian radio serving Bournemouth, Christchurch and Poole. A ministry of Bournemouth YMCA.
Email: bmouthymca@aol.com
☎ 01202 780 396 Fax 01202 317 751

Housetop, 39 Homer Street, London W1H 1HL
Director: Dr John Wijngaards. Executive staff 3, Other staff 4. ***CC*** No.3153215. Began 1982; Roman Catholic. Magazine: *Shout* (Circulation n/a half-yearly). Turnover n/a. Christian communications centre producing Biblical and other videos for the Apostolate.
Web: www.spiritual-wholeness.org
Email: 100114.562@compuserve.com
☎ 020 7402 9679 Fax 020 7723 2668

***International Films**, PO Box 201, West Malling ME19 5RS
Chief Executive Officer: Mr Nigel A M Cooke. Executive staff 2. ***CC*** No.261968. Began 1970; interdenominational. Magazine: *Newsletter* (Circulation n/a periodically). Turnover n/a. Producing own Christian films, videos and television programmes.
Web: members.aol.com/interfilm/home.htm
Email: interfilm@aol.com
☎ 01732 874 784 Mobile: 07768 077 691 Fax 01732 874 785

***Kingsway Music**, Lottbridge Drove, Eastbourne BN23 6NT
Songbooks/Divisional Manager: Mr Stuart Townend. *Recordings:* Mr Les Moir. ***CC*** No.265612. Began n/a; interdenominational. Magazine: *Worship Together* (Circulation n/a every two months). Turnover n/a. Producing worship recordings, songbooks and seminars.
Email: music@kingsway.co.uk
☎ 01323 437 708 Fax 01323 411 970

Lamplight Productions, 30 Horton View, Banbury OX16 9HP
Contact: Mr Mark Howe. Executive staff 2. Began 1987; non-denominational. No magazine. Turnover £100,000 to year end Apr 98. Broadcast quality video production and consultation; also camera crew hire.
Email: lamplight@btinternet.com
☎ 01295 275 708

LangMedia, East Waterside Studios, Upton Marina, Upton-upon-Severn WR8 0PB
Executive Producer: Mr Clive Langmead. Executive staff 2. Began 1988; non-denominational. No magazine. Turnover n/a. Producing radio and TV programmes, audio visuals (Christian and commercial); media training; scriptwriting.
☎ 01684 591 077 Fax 01684 591 077

***Lantern Film & Video Ltd**, 36 High Street, Princes Risborough HP27 0AX
Managing Director: Mr Mike Pritchard. *Director:* Mrs Sally Pritchard. Executive staff 2. Began 1984; non-denominational. (Previously Lantern Productions Ltd). No magazine. Turnover £250,000 to year end Dec 98. Producing corporate and religious training, informational videos and children's drama productions.
Email: 100530.312@compuserve.com
☎ 01844 346 471 Mobile: 07774 459 191 Fax 01844 274 207

Longview Training and Video Services, Longview, 72 Marlow Road, High Wycombe HP11 1TH
Proprietor: Mr Kenneth Acton. Executive staff 2. Began 1983; interdenominational. No magazine. Turnover n/a. Multi-camera video recording; audio conference recording; audio/video duplication; video production.
Email: ltvs@clara.net
☎ 01494 526 930 Fax 01494 526 930

MFJ Productions, PO Box 459, Edinburgh EH12 5TX
Director & Company Secretary: Deborah Menelaws. Executive staff 4. ***CC*** No.SCO 24170. Began 1994; non-denominational. Magazine: *MFJ Newsletter* (300 quarterly). Turnover n/a. Producing and broadcasting radio programmes; working to establish quality full-time Christian radio in Scotland.
Web: members.aol.com/mfjprods/home.html
Email: mfjradio@aol.com
☎ n/a

MRA Productions (The MRA Productions Fund), 12 Palace Street, London SW1E 5JF
Director: Mr David Channer. Executive staff 1, Other staff 3. ***CC*** No.226511. Began 1952; interdenominational. Magazine: *For a Change* (5,000 every two months). Turnover £113,000 to year end Dec 97. Producing films/videos offering a broad perspective on and practical approach to social and moral issues.
Email: 101704.1500@compuserve.com
☎ 020 7828 6591

Multimedia Workstation, Copper Beech, Llandogo, Monmouth NP5 4TL
Proprietor: Mr John Milton Whatmore. Executive staff 1, Other staff 2. Began 1986; non-denominational. (Previously Media Services). No magazine. Turnover n/a. Radio, film and TV production, outside broadcasts, scripts and research.
Email: 106455.1560@compuserve.com
☎ 01594 530 817 Fax 01594 530 817

***Oasis Media**, 115 Southwark Bridge Road, London SE1 0AX
Director: Rev Steve Chalke. Executive staff 4, Other staff 6. Began 1996; non-denominational. No magazine. Turnover £200,000 to year end Dec 98. Television production company and PR consultants.
Email: oasismedia@compuserve.com
☎ 020 7450 9050 Fax 020 7450 9060

M

Pathway Productions, 22 Colinton Road, Edinburgh EH10 5EQ
Director, AV Production: Mr Laurence P Wareing. *Deputy Director:* Mr John Williams. Executive staff 1, Other staff 5. Began 1979; Church of Scotland. No magazine. Turnover £250,000 to year end Dec 98. Video/broadcast programming; religious, educational organisations; production facilities, training courses available; videos for sale/hire.
Web: www.cofs.org.uk/pathway.htm
Email: pathway@dial.pipex.com
☎ 0131 447 3531 Mobile: 07831 618 633 Fax 0131 452 8745

†**Plankton Records**, PO Box 13533, Forest Gate, London E7 0SG
Senior Partner: Rev Simon Law. Executive staff 2, Other staff 1. Began 1977; non-denominational. Magazine: *Sandcastle Productions Catalogue* (1,000 n/a). Turnover £11,791 to year end Dec 96. Record label and music publisher for Christian orientated bands and songwriters.
☎ 020 8534 8500

***Premier Christian Radio 1305*1332*1413MW**, Glen House, Stag Place, London SW1E 5AG
Chairman: Mr David Heron. *Managing Director:* Mr Peter Kerridge. *Finance Director:* Mrs Vicky Fafalios. Executive staff 4, Other staff 25. ***CC*** No.1022073. Began 1991; interdenominational. (Previously Premier Radio). Magazine: *On Air* (Circulation n/a quarterly). Turnover £1,600,000 to year end Sept 98. Christian media centre incorporating MW broadcasting to London and worldwide via www, publishing magazines, helpline.
Web: www.premier.org.uk
Email: premier@premier.org.uk
☎ 020 7316 1300 Fax 020 7233 6706

***Radio Worldwide (WEC International)**, Springhead Park House, Park Lane, Rothwell, Leeds LS26 0ET
Directors: Mr Dick & Mrs Flora Davies. Executive staff 2, Other staff 14. ***CC*** No.237005. Began 1961; interdenominational. Magazine: *Newsletter* (3,000 every four months). Turnover £81,640 to year end Mar 98. Radio programme producers; radio training; oral communication training.
Web: ourworld.compuserve.com/homepages/rw/
Email: rw@compuserve.com
☎ 0113 282 2291 Fax 0113 282 3908

M

Real World Connect, 534 Mumbles Road, Mumbles, Swansea SA3 4DH
Creative Director: Kit Loring. Executive staff 4, Sessional staff 20. Began n/a; non-denominational. No magazine. Turnover n/a. Multi-arts, multi-media presentation in partnership with organisations like Childline, Amnesty, Relate.
Email: kit.loring@virgin.net
☎ 01792 522 342 Mobile: 07711 670 851 Fax 01792 522 342

Revelation Christian Resources (UK) Ltd, 13 King Edward Avenue, Worthing BN14 8DB
Director: Mr John Ray. Executive staff 2. ***CC*** Began 1988; interdenominational. Also known as Sunrise Video Productions. No magazine. Turnover n/a. Promoting, marketing and producing Christian videos.
☎ 01903 205 583

St Paul MultiMedia Productions, Middle Green, Langley, Slough SL3 6BS
Sister-in-Charge: Sister Rina Risitano. Executive staff 1, Other staff 5. ***CC*** No.296042. Began 1987; Roman Catholic. No magazine. Turnover £350,000 to year end Dec 98. Producing and marketing cassettes, videos, posters, stationery and other audio-visual material.
Email: productions@stpaulmultimedia.co.uk
☎ 01753 577 629 Fax 01753 511 809

Scope Productions Ltd, Keppie House, 147 Blythswood Street Glasgow G2 4EN
Head of Programmes: Mr Iain Morris. *Managing Director:* M Malcolm McCalister. *Marketing Director:* Mr Bill Gordon Executive staff 4, Other staff 36. Began 1984; interdenominational. No magazine. Turnover £3,200,000 to year end Dec 98. Producing television resources worldwide.
Email: 106213.755@compuserve.com
☎ 0141 332 7720 Fax 0141 332 1049

***Scripture Union Sound and Vision Unit**, 207 Queensway, Bletchley, Milton Keynes MK2 2EB
Chief Executive: Mr Peter Kimber. Full-time staff 1. ***CC*** No.213422. Began 1964; interdenominational. No magazine. Turnover n/a. Producing video and audio cassettes specialising in group resource material; catalogue and commissioned work.
Web: www.scriptureunion.org.uk
Email: postmaster@scriptureunion.org.uk
☎ 01908 856 000 Fax 01908 856 111

SDA Studio Services, Seventh-day Adventist Church Headquarters, Stanborough Park, Watford WD2 6JP
Communications Director: Pastor John Surridge. Executive staff 1, Other staff 1. Began 1977; Seventh-Day Adventist. (Previously Advent Audio Visuals). No magazine. Turnover n/a. Communication Department in-house audio/video production/post production facility.
Web: www.adventist.org.uk
Email: wnkapon@adventist.org.uk
☎ 01923 672 251 Ext 45 Fax 01923 893 212

Sigma Promotions Ltd, 19 Holly Walk, Harpenden AL5 5RG
Managing Director: Mr Simon George. Executive staff 2. Began 1996; interdenominational. No magazine. All aspects of media production, audio visual, multimedia, internet marketing.
Web: www.smg.org.uk
Email: sigma.media@virgin.net
☎ 01582 765 761 Fax 07070 605 288

Sound Supplement, Thatched Cottage, Otford Hills, Sevenoaks TN15 6XL
Proprietor: Mr Nick Page. No full-time staff. Began 1976; non-denominational. No magazine. Turnover £10,000 to year end Aug 97. Producing and presenting programmes for radio and on cassette; consultancy to Christian organisations.
Email: nickpage@xc.org
☎ 01959 523 740 Fax 01959 525 011

Spark Productions Ltd, Brook Place, Bagshot Road, Chobham, Woking GU24 8SJ
Director: Mr Bart Gavigan. Executive staff 2, Other staff 4. Began 1990; non-denominational. No magazine. Turnover n/a. Freelance commissioned work in radio, television, film; publishing house; editing suite; media seminars.
Email: spark.productions@dial.pipex.com
☎ 01276 855 571 Fax 01276 855 575

STV Videos, PO Box 299, Bromley BR2 9XB
Director: Mr Dave Armstrong. Executive staff 2, Other staff 3. Began 1989; interdenominational. No magazine. Turnover £20,000 to year end Apr 90. Video recording of special events; copying, editing, titles, special effects, large screen; on site duplication.
☎ 020 8464 4287 Fax 020 8464 4287

Tandem TV and Film Ltd, 10 Bargrove Avenue, Hemel Hempstead HP1 1QP
Director: Mr Terry Page. *Producer:* Mrs Barbara Page. Executive staff 2, Other staff 2. Began 1979; non-denominational. Magazine: *Newsletter* (Circulation & frequency n/a). Producing video, film and television for the corporate market as well as Christian organisations.
Web: www.tandem.com
Email: info@tandemtv.com
01442 261 576 — 01442 219 250

Telling Pictures, 6 Waitemeads, Purton, Swindon SN5 9ET
Programmes Director: Mr David Martin. Executive staff 2, Other staff 2. Began 1995; non-denominational. No magazine. Turnover n/a. Producing quality promotional and Christian educational programmes for video distribution and broadcast.
01793 770 171 Mobile: 07836 556 509 — 01278 663 498

Ray Tostevin Media Services, 6 Summerlands, Yeovil BA21 3AL
Broadcast Producer: Mr Ray Tostevin. No other staff. Began 1996; Evangelical. No magazine. Turnover n/a. Television producer and reporter specialising in social justice, environment, current affairs.
Email: rtostevin@aol.com
01935 420 450 Mobile: 07771 710 339
01935 420 450

UCB Europe, Hanchurch Christian Centre, Hanchurch Lane, Stoke-on-Trent ST4 8RY
Managing Director: Mr Gareth Littler. *Station Manager:* Mrs Ann Haccius. *Marketing Manager:* Ms Patricia Hargreaves. Executive staff 7, Other staff 35. ***CC*** No.299128. Began 1986; interdenominational. (Previously United Christian Broadcasters Ltd). Magazine: *The Word for Today* (600,000 quarterly). Turnover £3,000,000 to year end Dec 98. Christian radio, licensed to broadcast by satellite, with music and teaching across UK and Ireland, on 7.56mHz 24hrs.
Web: www.ucb.co.uk
Email: ucb@ucb.co.uk
01782 642 000 — 01782 641 121

***Vision Broadcasting Ministries**, Rochester House, 27 Victoria Road, Swindon SN1 3AW
Chief Executive: Mrs Fran Wildish. Executive staff 1, Other staff 1. ***CC*** Began 1986; non-denominational. Magazine: *Friends of Vision* (400 periodically). Turnover £21,000 to year end Mar 92. Christian TV channel, on cable stations around Britain.
01793 511 244 — 01793 511 244

Vision Net International Ltd, 18 Battlehill Road, Portadown, Craigavon BT62 4ER
Managing Director: Mr David Robinson. Other staff 4. Began 1994; non-denominational. (Previously Vision Network). Magazine: *Newsletter* (1,000 every two months). Turnover n/a. Broadcasting the Gospel of Christ by radio to the nations.
Email: visionetwork@msn.com
028 3835 4503 Mobile: 07050 228 571 — 028 3835 4503

Vision Productions, 111 Ecclesall Road South, Sheffield S11 9PH
Studio Director: Mr Gordon Ramsay. Executive staff 1, Other staff 2. Began 1979; interdenominational. No magazine. Turnover £200,000 to year end Mar 98. Producing films, videos, drama, documentary; training.
Email: visionproductions@easynet.co.uk
0114 262 0700 — 0114 236 3031

Voice in the Dark Production Co Ltd, 534 Mumbles Road, Mumbles, Swansea SA3 4DH
Directors: Mr Kit Loring, Mr David Aldous. Executive staff 2. Began 1994; non-denominational. No magazine. Turnover n/a. Making issue based film and video.
Email: kit.loring@virgin.net
01792 522 342 Mobile: 07711 670 851 — 01792 522 342

***World Wide Films**, The Office London, Victoria House, Victoria Road, Buckhurst Hill IG9 5EX
Team Associate: Mr David Vardy. Executive staff 1, Other staff 1. ***CC*** No.233381. Began 1955; interdenominational. No magazine. Turnover £10,000 to year end Apr 98. Producing and distributing evangelistic films.
020 8559 1180 — 020 8502 9062

MEDIA SERVICES

Acts Sound & Lighting, Riversdene, Howley Lane, Warrington WA1 2DJ
Owner: Mr Martin Naylor. Executive staff 1, Other staff 2. Began 1986; non-denominational. No magazine. Turnover £60,000 to year end Aug 99. Hiring, operating, selling, installing, repairing sound and lighting equipment to churches and others.
☎ 01925 656 469 Mobile: 07711 841 641 🖷 01925 656 469

Alive Church Systems Ltd, Brookhampton, North Cadbury, Yeovil BA22 7DA
Director: Mr Christopher Fone. No other full-time staff. Began 1995; ecumenical. No magazine. Turnover £70,000 to year end Dec 98. Specialising in remote control sound reinforcement systems and concealed loudspeaker design.
☎ 01963 440 808 🖷 01963 440 808

Ambassador Enterprises, Portland Road, London SE25 4PN
Manager: Mr Jack Shellard. Executive staff 2. ***CC*** No.229741. Began 1972; interdenominational. No magazine. Turnover £98,729 to year end Jan 98. Supplying public address systems, overhead and video projectors, musical instruments, communion and most church requirements.
Web: www.victory10.freeserve.co.uk
Email: info@victory10.freeserve.co.uk
☎ 020 8656 2297 🖷 020 8656 2582

***Anchor Recordings Ltd**, 72 The Street, Kennington, Ashford TN24 9HS
Manager: Mr James Harris. Executive staff 3, Other staff 3. ***CC*** No.224579. Began 1973; interdenominational. No magazine. Turnover n/a. Recording and distributing Christian messages; worship and video cassettes.
Web: www.argonet.co.uk/anchor
Email: anchor@argonet.co.uk
☎ 01233 620 958 🖷 01233 620 958

Angel Talk Limited, 9a Shaftesbury Close, Harmans Water, Bracknell RG12 9PX
Managing Director: Mr Malcolm D Powell. Executive staff 2. Began 1981; interdenominational. No magazine. Turnover £8,500 to year end Sept 98. Digital audioediting, audio CD origination, any format CD duplication, audio cassette duplication, blank cassettes, supplies.
Web: www.angeltalk.co.uk
Email: malcolm@angeltalk.co.uk
☎ 01344 425 200 🖷 01344 869 589

Audio and Recording Ministries (ARM), 79 Haycroft Drive, S Leonards Park, Gloucester GL4 6XX
Principal: Mr Anthony N Hubble. Executive staff 3. Began 1986; House Church. No magazine. Turnover £70,000 to yea end Dec 97. Live recording for conferences/special services, PA hire, equipment supply, including loop amplification, church installations.
☎ 01452 418 418 Mobile: 07778 999 900 🖷 01452 418 418

Audio Visual Technology UK Ltd, 2 Riding Lane, Hildenborough, Tonbridge TN11 9HX
Technical Director: Mr Colin Rose. *Sales Manager:* Mr Ian Marchant. Executive staff 2, Other staff 1. Began 1990 non-denominational. (Previously Educomm). No magazine. Turnover £200,000 to year end May 98. Supplying Audio Visual equipment backed by professional advice and service to churches and charities.
Email: avtech@btinternet.com
☎ 01732 832 923/833 688 🖷 01732 833 589

Audioplan, 5 Chaffers Mead, Ashtead KT21 1NA
Proprietor: Mr Geoff Boswell. Executive staff 2, Other staff 1. Began 1985; non-denominational. Turnover n/a. Specifying and installing high quality music and speech sound systems with special emphasis on training.
Web: audioplan.co.uk/audio
Email: sales@audioplan.co.uk
☎ 01372 271 881 Mobile: 07887 554 719
🖷 01372 817 059

The AVC Trust, 16 Dry Hill Road, Tonbridge TN9 1LX
Secretary: n/a. No full-time staff. ***CC*** Began 1985; interdenominational. No magazine. Turnover n/a. Dormant, 1998.
☎ No telephone

B & H Production Services, Unit 1d, Lansbury Estate, Lower Guildford Road, Knaphill GU21 2EP
Managing Director: Mr Andy Callin. Executive staff 2, Other staff 6. Began 1991; interdenominational. No magazine. Turnover n/a. Sound installations hire and design, induction loop specialist.
Web: bhps.com
Email: office@bhps.com
☎ 01483 797 242 🖷 01483 797 256

B & H Sound Services Ltd, The Old School Studio, Crowland Road, Eye, Peterborough PE6 7TN
Managing Director: Mr Brian Hillson. *General Manager:* Mr I B Dunkley. *Recording Services Manager:* Mr M Parking. Executive staff 1, Admin staff 1, Other staff 5. Began 1978; interdenominational. No magazine. Turnover £750,000 to year end Aug 98. Designing and installing sound systems; studio or on-location recording facilities; cassette duplication.
Email: sound@bhsound.co.uk
☎ 01733 223 535 Fax 01733 223 545

BBC Ceefax Religious World, BBC North, Oxford Road, Manchester M60 1SJ
Producer: Ms Anna Cox. Staff n/a. Began n/a; interdenominational. No magazine. Turnover n/a. Providing religious material for BBC Teletext pages.
☎ 0161 955 3695 Fax 0161 955 3680

Bezalel Art Trust, St Luke's Church, Canning Crescent, Oxford OX1 4XB
Chairman: Ernesto Lozada-Uzuriaga. Other staff 1. Began 1994; non-denominational. Magazine: *Quidditas* (1,000 every four months). Turnover n/a. Promoting the relevance of visual arts in the Church by leading art events, workshops, conferences.
Email: philip.clayden@blackfriars.oxford.ac.uk
☎ 01865 251 616

Birmingham Christian Media Services, 1 Hagley Road, Edgbaston, Birmingham B16 8TG
Proprietor: Mr Jon Earnshaw. Executive staff 2, Other staff 6. Began 1994; non-denominational. No magazine. Turnover n/a. Providing services for audio visual media, IT, design and print, conferences, events. Birmingham Christian Directory.
Web: www.bcms.co.uk/
Email: enquiries@charis.net
☎ 0121 248 5800 Fax 0121 248 5810

Roman Catholic Diocesan Press and Information Officers
Arundel and Brighton: Rev Anthony Barry, St Joseph's Hall, Greyfriars Lane, Storrington, Pulborough RH20 4HE
Email: bishop.sec@rcd.ab.btinternet.com
☎ 01903 742 172 Fax 01903 746 336
Birmingham: Rev Paul McNally, Newman College, Genners Lane, Bartley Green, Birmingham B32 3NT
Email: P.C.McNally@newman.ac.uk
☎ 0121 476 1181 ext. 239 Fax 0121 476 4418
Brentwood: Mr Peter Blackman, 62 Hullbridge Road, South Woodham, Ferrers, Chelmsford CM3 5LJ
Email: services@blackman.kemc.co.uk
☎ 01245 322 079 Fax 01245 321 957
Cardiff: Rev John Owen, 62 Park Place, Cardiff CF1 3AS
Email: owenj1@cardiff.ac.uk & r-c-chaplaincy@cardiff.ac.uk
☎ 029 2022 9785 Fax 029 2066 8197
Clifton: Rev Robert D Corrigan, St Ambrose, North Road, Leigh Woods, Bristol BS8 3PW
Email: Robert.Corrigan@btinternet.com
☎ 0117 973 3072 Fax 0117 973 5913
East Anglia: Rev John Warrington, The White House, 21 Upgate, Poringland, Norwich NR14 7SH
Email: office@east-angliadiocese.org.uk
☎ 01508 492 202 Fax 01508 495 358
Hallam: Mrs Sheila Parden, Quarters, Carsick Hill Way, Sheffield S10 3LT
Email: bishopofhallam@btinternet.com
☎ 0114 230 9101 Fax 0114 230 5722
Hexham and Newcastle: Mrs Pat Campbell, Bishop's House, East Denton Hall, 800 West Road, Newcastle upon Tyne NE5 2BJ
☎ 0191 228 0003/0004 Fax 0191 274 0432
Lancaster: Rev Denis Blackledge, Church House, 17 Talbot Road, Blackpool FY1 1LB
Email: denisblackledge@compuserve.com
☎ 01253 297 666 01253 297 888
Leeds: Mr John Grady, 7 St Mark's Avenue, Leeds LS2 9BN
Email: dolpost@aol.com
☎ 0113 244 4788 Fax 0113 244 8084
Liverpool: Mr Peter Heneghan, Curial Offices, 152 Brownlow Hill, Liverpool L3 5TQ
Email: peter.heneghan@ukonline.co.uk
☎ 0151 709 3991 Fax 0151 707 1299
Menevia: Bishop's Secretary, Curial Offices, 27 Convent Street, Swansea SA1 2BX
☎ 01792 644 017 Fax 01792 458 641
Middlesbrough: Mr Jim Whiston, Diocesan Curia, 50a The Avenue, Linthorpe, Middlesbrough TS5 6QT
Email: Jim.Whiston@btinternet.com
☎ 01642 850 505 Fax 01642 851 404
Northampton: Rev David Barrett, St Augustine, 24 Amersham Hill, High Wycombe HP13 6NZ
Email dbbarr@email.msn.com
☎ Fax 01494 523 969
Nottingham: Rev Edward Jarosz, Bishop's House, 27 Cavendish Road East, The Park, Nottingham NG7 1BB
☎ 0115 947 4786 Fax 0115 947 5235
Plymouth: Mr Delian Bower, 18 Devonshire Place, Exeter, Devon EX4 6JA
Email: delian@eclipse.co.uk
☎ Fax 01392 493 334
Portsmouth: Mr Barry Hudd, Night Owls, 100 Enborne Road, Newbury RG14 6AN
Email: bhudd@portsmouth-dio.org.uk
☎ Fax 01635 443 26
Salford: Rev Michael Walsh, St Paul's, 285 Stockport Road, Guide Bridge, Ashton-under-Lyne OL7 0NT
Email: mwalsh1402@aol.com
☎ 0161 330 2777 Fax 0161 343 5595
Shrewsbury: Rev Peter Montgomery, Curial Offices, 2 Park Road South, Birkenhead CH43 4UX
Email: chancellor@dioshr.dircon.co.uk
☎ 0151 652 9855 Fax 0151 653 5172
Southwark: Richard Moth, Archbishop's House, St George's Road, London SE1 6HX
Email: rmoth@rcsouthwark.co.uk
☎ 020 8928 2495 Fax 020 7928 7833
Wrexham: Rev Ian Dalgliesh, St David's, Corbett Avenue, Tywyn LL36 0AH
☎ 01654 710 420

†**Celebration Video**, Trinity Farm, Middleton Quernhow, Ripon HG4 5HX
Director: Mr Peter Snowdon. No full-time staff. Began 1981; non-denominational. No magazine. Turnover £7,000 to year end July 90. Recording live meetings, producing and distributing tapes in UK and beyond.
☎ 01765 640 223

Chapel Lane Ministries/Chapel Lane Studios, Hampton Bishop, Hereford HR1 4JR
Managing Director: Mr Rob Andrews. Executive staff 2, Other staff 1. Began 1976; Pentecostal. No magazine. Turnover n/a. Christian recording studio services; complete productions undertaken.
☎ 01432 870 437

M

***Cheltenham Stage Services**, Unit 31, Ullenwood Court, Ullenwood, Cheltenham GL53 9QS
Proprietor: Mr Peter J Allison. *General Manager:* Mr Stuart Petersen. Executive staff 2, Other staff 4. Began 1981; Anglican. No magazine. Turnover £200,000 to year end July 96. Hiring PA systems to 14kw and stage lighting to 150kw; pull rigging, production facilities, transport.
Email: css@ullenwood.co.uk
☎ 01242 244 978 🖷 01242 250 618

Christian Communications Commission, 91 Hallam Way, West Hallam, Ilkeston DE7 6LP
Co-ordinator: Mr John Q Davis. Executive staff 2. ***CC*** No.1060143. Began n/a; interdenominational. (Previously Christian Broadcasting Campaign). Magazine: *Newsletter* (800 every two months). Turnover £4,068 to year end Mar 98. Co-ordinating Christian and Gospel Broadcasting on the multi-media.
Email: christiancomm@easynet.co.uk
☎ 0115 930 7552 🖷 0115 930 5279

Christian Fabrications Ltd, 5 Chase Side Crescent, Enfield EN2 0JQ
Managing Director: Mr Geoffrey W Yates. *Administrator:* Miss Emma Gooch. Executive staff 1, Other staff 3. Began 1994; non-denominational. (Previously Christian Communication Services Ltd). No magazine. Turnover £350,000 to year end May 96. Designing and installing induction loops for churches, schools, video conversion American / British; supplying audio tape.
☎ 020 8364 6411 Mobile: 07973 734 811 🖷 020 8364 6488

***Christian Resources Project**, 14 Lipson Road, Plymouth PL4 8PW
Administrator: Mr Michael Law. *Centre Manager:* Mrs Audrey Burnham. Executive staff 1, Other staff 2. ***CC*** No.281735. Began 1975; interdenominational. Magazine: *Newsletter* (Circulation n/a Five times a year). Turnover £111,000 to year end Dec 98. Resource centre, video and audio-visual library, video projector, equipment hire, schools work, training, bookselling, missions.
Web: business.thisisplymouth.co.uk/crp
☎ 01752 224 012 🖷 01752 224 012

Church of England Diocesan Communications Officers
Each Diocese has a Communications Officer, who can be contacted via the Diocesan Office. See pages 203–212 in Church Headquarters.

Circle Sound Services, Circle House, 14 Waveney Close, Bicester OX6 8GP
Contact: John Willett. Executive staff 1. Began 1978; non-denominational. No magazine. Turnover £50,000 to year end Dec 98. Location recording unit (digital recording); radio production, editing and recording, sound equipment supply, consultant.
Email: sound@circle.force9.co.uk
☎ 01869 240 051 Mobile: 07973 633 634 🖷 01869 240 051

CN Productions Ltd, 5 Little Way, Moortown, Leeds LS17 6JN
Managing Director: Mr Christopher Norton. Executive staff 1. Began 1982; non-denominational. No magazine. Turnover £350,000 to year end Sept 98. Producing and licensing master tapes internationally; background music for television/film; publishing and music engraving.
Email: cnprod01@aol.com
☎ 0113 269 3930 Mobile: 07802 785 450 🖷 0113 266 2075

Coburn Television Productions, 20 Quantock House, Fore Street North Petherton, Bridgwater TA6 6TN
Manager: Mr Peter Coburn. Other staff 3. Began 1981; interdenominational. No magazine. Turnover n/a. Betacam SP editing and shooting facilities for Christian producers, video production, script to screen service.
Email: pete@coburntv.freeserve.co.uk
☎ 01278 663 498 Mobile: 07775 663 884
🖷 01278 663 498

†***Comtec Services**, Unit 8, Thistle Road, Luton LU1 3XJ
Proprietor: Mr David Hofer. Executive staff 2, Other staff 2 Began 1985; Anglican. No magazine. Turnover n/a. Supplying and installing PA equipment, induction loops, closed circuit television.
☎ 01582 488 856

Cornerstone House, 28 Old Park Road, Peverell, Plymouth PL3 4PY
Sole Proprietor: Mr Chris Cole. *Print Manager:* Mr Peter Nolan. Executive staff 3, Other staff 6. Began 1983; interdenominational. Magazine: *Cross Rhythms* (3,500 every two months). Turnover £200,000 to year end Dec 98. Advertising, print, design. A community of Christians in the marketplace.
Web: www.message.org/cr
Email: crossrhy@cnrstone.avel.co.uk
☎ 01752 225 623 🖷 01752 673 441

†**Creative Audio**, 67 Badshot Park, Badshot Lea, Farnham GU9 9NE
Proprietor: Mr John Ellis. Executive staff 1. Began 1985; interdenominational. No magazine. Turnover n/a. Concert and conference sound; freelance sound engineering; PA system advice, sales and installations.
☎ 01252 318 739 🖷 01252 318 739

***Crystal Clear Audio**, 141 Downham Road, Islington, London N1 3HQ
Partner: Mr Michael Webb. Executive staff 3, Other staff 2. Began 1989; interdenominational. Magazine: *Newsletter* (Circulation & frequency n/a). Turnover £60,000 to year end Dec 98. Supplying PA, recording, video projection, training services for churches/Christian events in London and South-East.
Web: www.cca.ndirect.co.uk
Email: cca@ndirect.co.uk
☎ 01923 445 918 Mobile: 07956 327 664

†**Cunnings Recording Associates**, Brodrick Hall, Brodrick Road, London SW17 7DY
Proprietor: Mr Malcolm J Cunnings. Executive staff 2, Other staff 5. Began 1977; non-denominational. No magazine. Turnover n/a. Supplying and installing sound/PA, loop systems; cassette manufacture and duplication; cassette copiers.
Email: cunnings@compuserve.com
☎ 020 8767 3533 🖷 020 8767 8525

DCM Studio, Dovetales Christian Centre, Gospel Mission, Maygate, Oldham OL9 6TR
Directors: Mr WE & Mrs JA Heap, Marcus Heap. Executive staff 3. Began n/a; interdenominational. No magazine. Turnover n/a. Recording studio available for Christian artistes.
Email: dovetales@globalnet.co.uk
☎ 0161 652 4060 🖷 0161 652 4060

***Day One Projects**, 107 Coniston Road, Palmer's Cross, Tettenhall, Wolverhampton WV6 9DT
Director: Mr J Peter Wilson. Executive staff 1. Began 1998; non-denominational. No magazine. Turnover: first year of operation. Christian music programming, ILR Licence consultant, representing Music 1 radio scheduling software in UK.
Email: dayone@broadcast.net
☎ 01902 829 424 Pager: 07623 120 252 🖷 01902 829 424

Direction Resources Ltd, Oasis Centre, Oxton Road, Wallasey, Wirral CH44 4EH
Editor: Rev Derek J Green. *Advertising Manager:* Mr David Evans. Executive staff 1, Other staff 3. ***CC*** No.251549. Began 1989; Pentecostal. Magazine: *Direction* (22,000 monthly) Turnover n/a. Supplying multimedia, overhead projectors and screens at discount prices to Christian organisations.
Web: www.directionmagazine.com
Email: info@directionmagazine.com
☎ 0151 691 2134 Fax 0151 691 2153

ECHO Recordings & Missionary Technical Services (Evangelical Communications Home and Overseas), 4 Pinery Road, Barnwood, Gloucester GL4 3FL
Director: Mr Don G Feltham. No full-time staff. Began 1965; interdenominational. No magazine. Turnover n/a. Professional recording, cassette duplicating, location recording; PA consultant and supplier.
☎ 01452 613 651 Fax 01452 613 651

Edenfield Communications, 2 South View Place, Midsomer Norton, Bath BA3 2AX
Director: Mr E Michael Jakins. Executive staff 2. Began 1985; non-denominational. No magazine. Turnover n/a. Hiring and installing audio-visual and public address equipment.
Email: michael@downs.telme.com
☎ 01761 414 992 Mobile: 07958 578 417
Fax 01761 411 717

Edvicron Electronic Services, 70 Charlesfield Road, Horley RH6 8BL
Director: Mr Ron Hall. Executive staff 4, Other staff 5. Began 1981; interdenominational. No magazine. Turnover n/a. Designing, supplying and installing sound reinforcement/PA systems for churches. Remote control specialists.
☎ 01293 821 824 Fax 01293 786 215

FCS Cassette Services, Unit 3, Bestwood Works, Drove Road, Portslade, Brighton BN41 2PA
Owner: Mr Steve Priest. *Assistant:* Mr Graham Mairs. Executive staff 1, Other staff 2. Began 1997; non-denominational. No magazine. Turnover £228,000 to year end Jan 99. Selling blank tape; duplicating audio, video tapes; audio presentation cases and conference support services.
Email: steve@fcscassettes.dial.iql.co.uk
☎ 01273 423 440 Mobile: 07711 890 683
Fax 01273 420 544

Film Hire Services, 51 King Ecgbert Road, Totley, Sheffield S17 3QR
Proprietor: Mr Frederick G Cocking. Executive staff 1. Began 1972; House Church. No magazine. Turnover £6,500 to year end Dec 98. Visual aids centre. Hiring equipment, Christian and secular films and VHS videotapes.
☎ 0114 236 6533

The Focus Trust, 25 Spencer Gardens, Shillingstone, Blandford Forum DT11 0TL
Administrator: Mr Tony Tew. No full-time staff. ***CC*** No.282542. Began 1979; non-denominational. No magazine. Turnover n/a. Supporting the professional production of films and videos reflecting and promoting the Christian faith.
Email: tonytew@aol.com
☎ 01258 860 301

FosterFinch Ltd, Registered Office, 3 Lawn Road, Exmouth EX8 1QJ
Director: Mr Tim Finch. Executive staff 2, Other staff 3. Began 1994; interdenominational. Bases in London, Taunton, East Devon & Shropshire. No magazine. Turnover £36,000 to year end Oct 98. Video, music, artistic and IT based media/marketing service – promo videos, leaflets and software. Midi studio.
Web: www.eclipse.co.uk/fosterfinch
Email: timfinch@cix.co.uk
☎ Tim Finch Mobile: 07703 172 994
☎ Bob Foster: 01823 252 522 (Taunton)

Freelance Journalism Workshops, 9 The Lodge, 3 Blackwater Road, Eastbourne BN21 4JF
Trainer: Mrs Wendy Whitehead. No other staff. Began n/a; interdenominational. Turnover n/a. Providing workshops on preparing and submitting church news and information to local and national press.
☎ 01323 638 234

Gospel Sound and Vision Group, 33 Modena Road, Portland Road, Hove BN3 5QF
Director: Mr Bernard H Norris. No full-time staff. Began 1959; non-denominational. No magazine. Turnover £3,000 to year end Apr 98. Selling filmstrips, many with soundtracks on audio cassettes; free advice on projectors; 4-year Bible course.
☎ 01273 772 476

HCVF Television & Video Productions, 67 Kenneth Street, Inverness IV3 5QF
Partner: Mr Jim Eglinton. Executive staff 2, Other staff 4. Began 1981; non-denominational. No magazine. Turnover £250,000 to year end Dec 98. Television and video production, multi-media.
Web: www.hcvf.co.uk
Email: hcvf@aol.com
☎ 01463 224 788 Mobile: 07860 285 872 Fax 01463 711 460

Hitotsu-Bishi, 22 Hassocks Wood, Stroudley Road, Basingstoke RG24 8UQ
Managing Director: Mr Andrew Earle. *Marketing Director:* Mr Andrew Watkins. Executive staff 2. Began 1986; interdenominational. (Previously Gothic Audio-Visual & Studio 55). No magazine. Turnover £205,000 to year end Nov 98. Preparing training and promotional material utilising film, video, tape-slide & print.
Email: hitbis@aol.com
☎ 01256 471 471 Fax 01256 471 470

Hope Press Agency, PO Box 277, Sunderland SR1 1YE
Editor: Mr Peter Wreford. Executive staff 2, Other staff 3. Began 1983; non-denominational. No magazine. Turnover n/a. Providing a Christian news service to the national and regional religious media and beyond.
Email: editor.newlife@ukonline.co.uk
☎ 0191 568 0424 Fax 0191 568 0428

HW Audio Ltd, 174 St George's Road, Bolton BL1 2NZ
Director: Mr Christopher D Harfield. Executive staff 2, Other staff 6. Began 1976; interdenominational. No magazine. Turnover £500,000–1,000,000 to year end Dec 96. Installing PA and audio induction loop equipment.
Email: hwmusic@compuserve.com
☎ 01204 385 199 Mobile: 07000 727 686
Fax 01204 364 057

ICC – International Christian Communications, Silverdale Road, Eastbourne BN20 7AB
Managing Director: Mr Helmut H Kaufmann. Executive staff 2, Other staff 40. Began 1976; interdenominational. No magazine. Turnover n/a. Recording, audio media manufacturing centre. Blank/ duplicated cassettes and videos. CD, CD-ROM, MiniDisc, DVD replication.
Web: www.icc.org.uk
Email: duplication@icc.org.uk
☎ 01323 647 880 Fax 01323 643 095

International Christian Media Commission (ICMC), PO Box 154, Keighley BD20 6UU
Senior UK Associate: Mr Andrew Steele. Executive staff 2. *CC* No.104870. Began 1990; non-denominational. Magazine: *Catalyst* (Circulation n/a quarterly). Turnover n/a. Providing consultancy, training and co-ordination. Association of media professionals from around the world.
Web: www.icmc.org
Email: icmc@xc.org
☎ 01535 612 100 Fax 01535 612 101

***International Media for Ministry**, PO Box 11, Tunbridge Wells TN4 8WZ
General Manager: Mr Gary Preston. Other staff 3. *CC* No.266445. Began 1970; non-denominational. (Previously Christian Hospital Radio, CHR). No magazine. Turnover £20,000 to year end Dec 98. International Curriculum is a Christian video/VCD ministry in over 30 languages for church planting and training.
☎ 01892 549 141 Fax 01892 529 500

ITV Teletext Religious Pages, 14 Oakleigh Park South, London N20 9JU
Editor: Rev Adrian V Benjamin. Executive staff 1. Began 1979; interdenominational. (Previously British Churches Teletext Project). No magazine. Turnover n/a. Providing 5 pages of "Godlines" on ITV Teletext (Channel 4 page 687).
Web: www.allsaints.mcmail.com
Email: allsaints@mcmail.com
☎ 020 8445 4654/8388 Fax 020 8445 6831

KBS Sound, Unit 7, Sandwich Industrial Estate, Sandwich CT13 9LY
Sales & Marketing Director: Mr Bob Forder. Executive staff 2. Other staff 3. Began 1987; non-denominational. No magazine. Turnover n/a. Supplying UK churches with sound and OHP equipment.
☎ 01304 611 158 Fax 01304 611 178

Kings Audio, 15 Oxford Road, Pen Mill Trading Estate, Yeovil BA21 5HR
Proprietor: Rev Mac Kingsbury. *Partner:* Mrs A C Kingsbury. Executive staff 2, Other staff 4. Began 1989; interdenominational. No magazine. Turnover n/a. Distributing and servicing audio cassette copiers; manufacturing and duplicating audio cassettes; on-site recording and duplication.
Email: mac@kingsaudio.co.uk
☎ 01935 411 322 Mobile: 07768 113 258 Fax 01935 706 008

Roy Kirkpatrick Sound Engineering, 29 Burgamot Lane, Comberbach, Northwich CW9 6BU
Proprietor: Mr Roy D Kirkpatrick. Executive staff 1. Began 1976; non-denominational. No magazine. Turnover n/a. Designing, supplying and installing specialised sound systems and magnetic induction loop systems.
☎ 01606 891 939 Mobile: 07831 504 404 Fax 01606 891 939

Let the Bible Speak, 11 Westland Avenue, Ballymoney BT53 6PE
Programme Director: Rev Leslie Curran. Other staff 1. *CC* No.XN48598. Began 1973; Free Presbyterian Church of Ulster. No magazine. Turnover £60,000 to year end Mar 98. Broadcasting the Gospel in USA, Canada, India, Africa, China, Asia and London.
Email: ltbs2@aol.com
☎ 028 7036 62896

***Lighting and Sound Services**, 126 Chester Road, Helsby, Warrington WA6 0QS
Partner: Mr Phil Johnson. Executive staff 2, Other staff 6. Began 1978; non-denominational. No magazine. Turnover n/a. Designing, supplying, hiring and installing PA, lighting, effects, staging and generators.
☎ 01928 723 502 Fax 01928 725 012

Logos Services, 23 Nottingham Road, Stapleford, Nottingham NG9 8AB
Proprietor: Mr John Churchill. Executive staff 1, Other staff 1. Began 1980; non-denominational. (Previously Logos Graphics). No magazine. Turnover n/a. Supplying overhead data/video and slide projectors, screens, accessories, other visual aids, stationery.
Email: jchurchill@fsbdial.co.uk
☎ 0115 939 1711 Fax 0115 939 1711

The Media Suite, St Leonards Road, Amersham HP6 6DR
Managing Director: Mr Chris Doggett. Executive staff 2. Began 1986; interdenominational. (Previously Beta Productions Ltd). No magazine. Turnover £100,000–300,000 to year end Dec 96. Professional recording services, CD production, services to the broadcast media, media training.
Email: mediasuite@cwcom.net
☎ 01494 431 232 Mobile: 07973 182 997 Fax 01494 431 268

***Richard Miller Audio Systems**, 17 Massey Street, Newark NG24 1PE
General Manager: Mr Richard Miller. Executive staff 1, Other staff 2. Began 1992; non-denominational. No magazine. Turnover £90,000 to year end Dec 98. Designing, supplying and installing professional sound reinforcement and induction loop systems (BS 7594) for churches.
Email: datalink@rmaudiosystems.freeserve.co.uk
☎ 01636 613 094 Mobile: 07778 940 868 Fax 01636 683 532

Keith Monks Sound Systems, Brodrick Hall, Brodrick Road, London SW17 7DY
Proprietor: Mr Malcolm J Cunnings. Executive staff 3, Other staff 5. Began 1968; non-denominational. No magazine. Turnover n/a. Manufacturing loudspeakers for churches, supplying and installing sound/PA, loop systems.
Email: 100113.1007@compuserve.com
☎ 020 8682 3456 🖷 020 8767 8525
Also at: Unit 7, Beechnut Industrial Estate, Aldershot GU12 4JA
☎ 01252 334 123 🖷 01252 332 429
And: 29 Tower Park, Fowey PL23 1JD
☎ 01726 833 783 🖷 01726 833 800

Morrison Reprographics, Town Street, Shiptonthorpe, York YO4 3PE
Partner: Mr Malcolm Morrison. Executive staff 2, Other staff 1. Began 1986; non-denominational. No magazine. Turnover £800,000 to year end Dec 98. Supplying low cost overhead and video projectors to Christian organisations and distributing missionary supplies worldwide.
Email: 101632.674@compuserve.com
☎ 01430 872 729 Mobile: 07957 356 086
🖷 01430 871 116

Moving Art, 131 Chilton Street, Bridgwater TA6 3HZ
Director: Mr Geoff Sherring. Executive staff 2, Other staff 3. Began 1968; non-denominational. No magazine. Turnover n/a. Video recording and total production services for events, documentaires, media-100 editing, multi-camera outside broadcasts.
Email: moviart@aol.com
☎ 01278 450 496 Mobile: 07971 356 303 🖷 01823 601 679

MVS Video Productions, Rehoboth, Alkham Valley Road, Folkestone CT18 7EH
Partner: Mr Paul Marshall. Executive staff 2, Other staff 1. Began 1989; interdenominational. No magazine. Turnover £26,000 to year end Oct 96. Video production, filming, editing, duplication services.
Web: www.videoproductions.freeserve.co.uk
Email: mvs@videoproductions.freeserve.co.uk
☎ 01303 891 468 🖷 01303 891 468

New Living Television, PO Box 1908, Finsbury Park, London N4 3NX
Director: Mr Jerry Rosenfield. Executive staff 2, Other staff 4. Began 1986; non-denominational. No magazine. Turnover £14,000 to year end Dec 90. Video production and editing service for conferences, weddings, promotional videos, worldwide cable networks.
☎ 020 8885 5488

PMH Productions, 69 Holyrood Close, Spondon, Derby DE21 7QB
Producer/Director: Mr Philip Holmes. Executive staff 1, Other staff 1. Began 1997; interdenominational. No magazine. Turnover n/a. Producing video and broadcast programmes for a variety of clients using digital broadcast technology.
Email: pmhproductions@hotmail.com
☎ 01332 738 341 Mobile: 07711 259 450 🖷 01332 749 846

Pinnacle Creative, 17 Clarendon Villas, Hove BN3 3RE
Managing Director: Mr Adrian Willard. Executive staff 1, Other staff 7. ***CC*** Began 1980; non-denominational. (Previously Frontiers Publishing International). Turnover n/a. Video production, graphic design and magazine production.
☎ 01273 234 555 🖷 01273 234 556

Psalm 96 Productions Audio & Video, 23 Turle Road, London SW16 5QW
Proprietors: Simon & Marie Yousaf. No other full-time staff. Began 1996; interdenominational. (Previously Sound 96). No magazine. Turnover n/a. Hiring PA for events, concerts, conferences & video production.
☎ 020 8679 8867 Mobile: 07710 020 227

†**Rainbow Sound & Recording**, The Connaught, 131 Lewes Road, Brighton BN2 3LG
Manager: Mr Colin Walker. Executive staff 3, Other staff 1. Began 1991; non-denominational. Magazine: *Newsletter* (Circulation n/a quarterly). Turnover £200,000 to year end July 94. 24-track recording studio, 16-track digital studio; PA system design, installation, hire and sales.
☎ 01273 624 048 🖷 01273 621 119

re:creation sound, 107 Stanstead Road, Forest Hill, London SE23 1HH
Director: Mr Mark Trigg. Other staff 1. Began 1994; non-denominational. (Previously Ichthus Sound Services). No magazine. Turnover £70,000. Public address hire, installation and sales. Event management services.
Email: re_creation_sound@compuserve.com
☎ 020 8699 6000 Mobile: 07973 381 917
🖷 020 8291 6764

*__Reelife Recordings__, Laverick Hall, Halton, Lancaster LA2 6PH
Director: Mr William I Towers, Mr Phil Burt. Executive staff 1, Other staff 5. ***CC*** No.265626. Began 1972; non-denominational. No magazine. Turnover £250,000 to year end Dec 98. Conference recording, PA, audio and video, duplication. High speed copier specialists, 16-track studio and video.
Web: www.reelife.com
Email: reelife@charis.co.uk
☎ 01524 811 282 🖷 01524 811 959

Revival Radio Ltd, PO Box 106, Cumbernauld, Glasgow G67 1JX
Chairman: Ian Dunlop. No full-time staff. ***CC*** No.SCO 24130. Began 1995; interdenominational. Magazine: n/a (Circulation n/a periodically). Turnover £23,500 to year end Oct 98. Developing Christian radio with the aim of securing full-time Christian radio licence in Scotland.
Web: www.christianradio.com/revivalradio
Email: ron.bernard@net.nzl.com
☎ 01236 824 160 📠 01236 725 070

Sain Fflur, Is Y Bryn, Borth Road, Porthmadog LL49 9UP
Director: Rev Aled Davies. No full-time staff. Began 1987; non-denominational. No magazine. Turnover n/a. Hiring PA sound systems.
☎ 01766 512 957 📠 01766 512 957

Sarner International Ltd, 32 Woodstock Grove, Shepherds Bush, London W12 8LE
Sales Manager: Mr David Dempsey. Executive staff 10, Other staff 20. Began 1967; non-denominational. No magazine. Turnover £2,000,000 to year end Oct 98. Audio-visual systems, productions, equipment rental, event staging, hardware sales, museum, heritage and theme presentation.
Web: www.sarner.com
Email: sarner@sarner.com
☎ 020 8743 1288 📠 020 8749 7699

School of Creative Ministries (Kensington Temple), Kensington Park Road, London W11 3BY
Director: Peter Hutchinson. ***CC*** No.251549. Began 1982; Elim Pentecostal. No magazine. Turnover n/a. Providing foundation training in the performing arts: music, dance, technical aspects of TV/video production.
Web: www.ken-temp.org.uk
Email: ibiol@dircon.co.uk
☎ 020 7727 4877 📠 020 7229 7343

Selecta Sound, 5 Margaret Road, Romford RM2 5SH
Proprietor: Mr John Smailes. *Director:* Mrs Carol Smailes. Executive staff 2. Began 1979; non-denominational. No magazine. Turnover n/a. Manufacturing and duplicating audio cassettes, videos and compact discs for studios, churches, businesses and schools.
Email: select@classiques.demon.co.uk
☎ 01708 453 424 Mobile: 07850 582 028 📠 01708 455 565

Shaw Sounds, 5 Douglas Avenue, Harold Wood, Romford RM3 0UT
Sole Proprietor: Mr John L G Shaw. No other staff. Began 1982; interdenominational. No magazine. Turnover £50,000–100,000 to year end Dec 96. Video, television, audio repairs; sales and installation; audio consultancy, public address quotations and supply.
☎ 01708 342 553 Mobile: 07831 359 253/0410 839 853

Sixth Sense Solutions, Unit 31, Ullenwood Court, Ullenwood, Cheltenham GL53 9QS
Partner: Mr Matt McCarty. Executive staff 4. Began 1997; non-denominational. No magazine. Turnover £50,000 to year end Feb 99. Video production for corporate events and touring productions.
Email: sss@ullenwood.co.uk
☎ 01242 529 933 Mobile: 07976 424 437 📠 01242 250 618

†**Sound Systems (SW) Ltd**, Unit 7, Beechnut Industrial Estate Beechnut Road, Aldershot GU12 4JA
Contact: Mr Keith Monks. Executive staff 2, Other staff 4. Began 1968; non-denominational. No magazine. Turnover £462,000 to year end Oct 96. Manufacturing specialised loudspeakers for churches; distributing sound, loops and music systems; exporting.
☎ 01252 334 123 📠 01252 332 429
Also at: 29 Tower Park, Fowey PL23 1JD
☎ 01726 833 783 📠 01726 833 800

*__Sounds Effective__, 22 Duffield Court, Chapel Street, Duffield, Belper DE56 4EQ
Trainer: Miss Wendy Palmer. No other staff. Began 1987; non-denominational. No magazine. Producing materials to enhance individual and church communication skills, including speaking and reading.
☎ 01332 841 832 📠 01332 841 832

Sounds Professional, 4 Goss Barton, Kingsgrove, Nailsea, Bristol BS48 2XD
Director: Mr Mike Bird. Executive staff 1, Other staff 1. Began 1993; non-denominational. No magazine. Turnover £53,000 to year end Apr 98. Freelance sound work. Consultancy, supplying and installing audio, hi-fi and PA equipment.
☎ 01275 858 156 Mobile: 07050 098 093 📠 01275 858 156

Ultrasound, 60 Reynolds Avenue, Chadwell Heath, Romford RM6 4NS
Director: Mr Vince Gray. Executive staff 1. Began 1988; interdenominational. No magazine. Turnover £25,000 to year end Mar 96. Professional audio equipment hire, sale and installation.
☎ 020 8590 2023 📠 020 8590 2023

Vision Screen Services, Bridge Cottage, Church Road, Rawreth, Wickford SS11 8SH
Partner: Mrs Pamela Dent. Executive staff 1. Began 1959; interdenominational. No magazine. Turnover n/a. Special low priced data/video and overhead projectors screen specialists, trollies, flipchart easels, hire facilities.
☎ 01268 765 374 Mobile: 07770 874 431

Vivid Communications, 349 North Circular Road, London N13 5JJ
Partner: Mr David Wisker. Executive staff 2, Admin staff 1. Began n/a; non-denominational. No magazine. Turnover £78,000 to year end Apr 99. Audio visual production, presentation, installation; creative solutions for churches, conferences or events.
Email: davidgwisker@compuserve.com
☎ 020 8889 1288 📠 020 8888 5799

Wigwam Acoustics Ltd, The Courtyard, Green Lane, Heywood OL10 2EX
Managing Director: Mr Michael Roy Spratt. Executive staff 4, Other staff 16. Began 1978; non-denominational. No magazine. Turnover £2,300,000 to year end Feb 96. Supplying, hiring and installing professional audio equipment.
Email: sales@wigwam.co.uk
☎ Sales: 01706 363 400 Hire: 01706 363 800
📠 Sales: 01706 363 410 Hire: 01706 363 810

MUSICAL & THEATRICAL PERFORMERS

ACACIA, BCC, 2 Masons Hill, Bromley BR2 9HA
Singer/Songwriter/Actor: Miss Anna Littler. No other staff. Began 1995; interdenominational. No magazine. Turnover n/a. Original songs and monologues for Christians and non-Christians; worship leader; multi-linguist: overseas missions.
☎ 020 8464 3101 🖷 01942 820 671

Anagram, 534 Mumbles Road, Mumbles, Swansea SA3 4DH
Creative Director: Mr Kit Loring. Executive staff 4, Sessional staff 20. Began 1981; non-denominational. No magazine. Turnover n/a. Music, comedy, theatre, preaching, storytelling for children and young adults; writing commissions.
Email: kit.loring@virgin.net
☎ 01792 522 342 Mobile: 07711 670 851 🖷 01792 522 342

Jerry Arhelger, Meredale, The Dell, Reach Lane, Leighton Buzzard LU7 0AL
Administrator: Mr Paul Davis. No full-time staff. Began 1975; interdenominational. No magazine. Turnover n/a. Singer/songwriter.
☎ 0152 523 7700 🖷 0152 523 7700

Bernie Armstrong, 7 Randle Road, Ham, Richmond TW10 7LT
Musician: Mr Bernie Armstrong. Began 1977; interdenominational. No magazine. Turnover n/a. Worship leader, recording artist and songwriter.
☎ 020 8549 5531

As If, Glebe Farm, Ludgershall, Aylesbury HP18 9PL
Band Leader: Philip Goss. Band members n/a. Began 1994; non-denominational. No magazine. Turnover n/a. Christian rock/dance band playing youth based music for outreach events or churched youth.
☎ 01844 237 916

Rob Ash, 13 Bristol Street, Aberkenfig, Bridgend CF32 9BW
Musician/Evangelist: Mr Robert Ashong. No full-time staff. Began 1982; non-denominational. No magazine. Turnover n/a. Evangelism in schools, churches, concerts.
☎ 01656 722 589

Marilyn Baker Ministries, PO Box 205, Tonbridge TN11 9ZN
Administrator: Mrs Julie Hillary. Other staff 3. ***CC*** No.326553. Began 1984; evangelical. Magazine: *Newsletter* (1,154 quarterly). Turnover n/a. Christian singer/songwriter with particular emphasis in encouraging Christians through live performance and recorded material.
Email: paul@marilynbakerministries.freeserve.co.uk
☎ 01732 852 402

Baly's Cream Jazz, 13 Travers Walk, Bristol BS34 8XW
Band Leader: Mr Paul Baly. Band members n/a. Began n/a; interdenominational. No magazine. Turnover £1,200 to year end Apr 98. Six piece jazz band performing traditional and original music for churches, prisons, private functions.
Email: paul@balys.freeserve.co.uk
☎ 0117 979 9018

*__Cliff and Char Bergdahl__, 105 Victoria Avenue, Hillingdon, Uxbridge UB10 9AJ
Musicians: Rev C Clifford & Mrs Charlotte Bergdahl. No full-time staff. Began 1973; Presbyterian Church, USA. (In association with Youth For Christ). No magazine. Turnover n/a. Christian music ministry, particularly to schools and prisons; Bible teaching.
Email: 106346.3502@compuserve.com
☎ 01895 238 499

Between the Lines Theatre Co, Maybank, 18 Queens Road, Steepleview, Laindon, Basildon SS15 4AN
Creative Directors: Mr David Aldous, Mr Kit Loring. Executive staff 2. Began 1992; non-denominational. No magazine. Turnover n/a. Theatre dealing with real life, challenging issues; commissions for conference work; workshops.
Email: davidaldous@compuserve.com
☎ 01268 459 054 🖷 01268 459 054

The Big Picture, 41 Chatsworth Avenue, Haslemere GU27 1ED
Band Leader: Mr Alvin Allison. Bank members n/a. Began 1990; interdenominational. (Previously The Eden). No magazine. Turnover n/a. Adult-oriented rock band; concerts in churches, town halls, stadiums.
Email: alvin@haslemere41.freeserve.co.uk
☎ No telephone

Blueberry, Event & Management Services, Unit 31, Ullenwood Court, Ullenwood, Cheltenham GL53 9QS
Manager: Mr Alan Wallace. Band members n/a. Began 1997; non-denominational. No magazine. Turnover n/a. Pop band – 90s pop for the Millennium.
Email: emsbands@ullenwood.co.uk
☎ 01242 245 444 Mobile: 07778 532 842 🖷 01242 250 618

†**Caroline Bonnett – The Music Works**, PO Box 1193, Cheddar BS27 3BF
Managers: Derek & Su Elliott. Full-time staff 2. Began 1989; non-denominational. No magazine. Turnover n/a. Songwriter, singer, producer, throughout UK.
Email: 106620.2522@compuserve.com
☎ 01934 741 281 🖷 01934 743 222

The Booley House, Event & Management Services, Unit 31, Ullenwood Court, Ullenwood, Cheltenham GL53 9QS
Agent: Mr Alan Wallace. Band members n/a. Began 1997; non-denominational. No magazine. Turnover n/a. Soulful ballads with Celtic influence.
Email: emsbands@ullenwood.co.uk
☎ 01242 245 444 Mobile: 07778 532 842 🖷 01242 250 618

Cambrensis Ministries, 21 Windsor Road, Porthcawl CF36 3LR
Administrator: Mrs Anne Brown. Other staff 1. ***CC*** No.1026760. Began 1982; interdenominational. No magazine. Turnover £30,000 to year end Mar 93. Choir, youth choir, orchestra, productions company; praise events involving local churches; cassettes, CDs produced regularly.
Email: cambrensis@mizpah.globalnet.co.uk
☎ 01656 784 376 🖷 01656 784 376

Carbon 14, Event & Management Services, Unit 31, Ullenwood Court, Ullenwood, Cheltenham GL53 9QS
Manager: Mr Alan Wallace. Band members n/a. Began 1997; non-denominational. No magazine. Turnover n/a. Rock-Indie band.
Email: emsbands@ullenwood.co.uk
☎ 01242 245 444 Mobile: 07778 532 842 🖷 01242 250 618

Marc Catley, 1 Birch Avenue, Tottington, Bury BL8 3EF
Band Leader: Mr Marc Catley. Executive staff 1. Began 1985; non-denominational. No magazine. Turnover n/a. Singer/songwriter, recording artist, satire, teaching, preaching, composition workshops, guitar tuition.
☎ 01204 885 233

M

†**Cedar Dance**, 42 Gunton Road, London E5 9JS
Artistic Director: Ms Janet Randell. No full-time staff. Began 1974; interdenominational. Magazine: *News Sheet* (250 frequency n/a). Turnover n/a. Professional freelance choreographer and qualified dance teacher; workshops in worship, dance therapy, dance for the disabled.
☎ 020 8806 4609

Christian Arts Promotion Ltd, 20 North Parade, Yate, Bristol BS37 4AN
Secretary/Choir Organiser: Mrs Catherine van Zoen. No paid staff. ***CC*** No.1057199. Began 1993; interdenominational. No magazine. Turnover £25,000 to year end Dec 96. 'Hearts on Fire' choir available (130 singers), HoF festival Glastonbury, contemporary worship, outreach events organised.
Web: home.clara.net/bethany/hof.html
Email: hof@bethany.clara.net
☎ 01454 319 447 Mobile: 07721 637 546 🖷 01454 319 447

Christian Choreographics, Morning Star, 9 Grange Court, Stratton, Cirencester GL7 2JS
Director: Miss Shirley Collins. Staff 4. Began 1998; interdenominational. No magazine. Turnover: first year of operation. Providing set dances for leading worship and performance, through mail order or workshops with choreographers.
Email: shirley.collins@virgin.net
☎ 01285 659 450

CJM Music Ltd, Rolinson Boyce & Stanley, St Mary's House, Coventry Road, Coleshill, Birmingham B46 3ED
Directors: Mr Michael Stanley, Ms Joanne Boyce. Executive staff 3, Other staff 3. Began 1996; Roman Catholic. No magazine. Turnover n/a. Contemporary Christian Musicians; youth ministry, concerts, workshops, publishing, recording.
Web: www.come.to/cjmfirstlight
Email: cjmfirstlight@bigfoot.com
☎ 01675 466 254 Mobile: 07801 375 138
🖷 01675 466 448

Frances Clarke, 274 Harborne Park Road, Harborne, Birmingham B17 0BL
Professional Dancer: Frances Clarke. No other staff. Began n/a; interdenominational. No magazine. Turnover n/a. Professional dancer, choreographer, dance teacher; sharing the Christian faith through dance in worship, evangelism; workshops.
☎ 0121 427 1681 Mobile: 07711 140 104

The Constructive Construction Co (Children's Theatre), 534 Mumbles Road, Mumbles, Swansea SA3 4DH
Creative Director: Mr Kit Loring. Executive staff 4, Sessional staff 20. Began n/a; non-denominational. No magazine. Turnover n/a. Producing children's theatre for primary/secondary schools.
Email: kit.loring@virgin.net
☎ 01792 522 342 Mobile: 07711 670 851
🖷 01792 522 342

Rodney Cordner with Jean-Pierre Rudolph, 21 Tandragee Road, Portadown, Craigavon BT62 3BQ
Singer/Evangelist: Mr Rodney Cordner. No full-time staff. Began 1976; Church of Ireland. No magazine. Turnover n/a. Evangelist and singer using Irish music as vehicle for Gospel; UK, Europe and USA.
Web: www.globalgateway.com/users/rcordner
Email: rodneycordner-david@globalgateway.com
☎ 028 3833 7668

The Covenant Players, Rock Foundation Hall, Little Street Rushden NN10 0LS
National Director: Ms Karen Christie. Executive staff 2, Other staff 20. ***CC*** No.1059359. Began 1972; interdenominational Magazine: *Covenant World* (1,000 quarterly). Turnover £90,000 to year end Dec 97. Communications resource for churches, schools, community; 5 full-time touring drama teams; 1,000 plays; music.
Web: www.covenantplayers.org
Email: cpb10@compuserve.com
☎ 01933 412 553 / 413 830 🖷 01933 412 553

DBA, Event & Management Services, Unit 31, Ullenwood Court, Ullenwood, Cheltenham GL53 2QS
Agent: Mr Alan Wallace. Band members n/a. Began 1997; non-denominational. No magazine. Turnover n/a. Techno dance.
Email: emsbands@ullenwood.co.uk
☎ 01242 245 444 Mobile: 07778 532 842 🖷 01242 250 618

David Daltrey, Pilgrims Rest, 34 Guildhall Street, Bury St Edmunds IP33 1QF
Musician: David Daltrey. No other staff. Began 1967; interdenominational. No magazine. Turnover n/a. Musician; composer; performing guitar, lute, keyboard music; traditional, contemporary, liturgical styles; tuition.
☎ 01284 762 076

Dance for Christ, The Farne House, Marygate, Holy Island, Berwick-upon-Tweed TD15 2SJ
Co-ordinator: Mr Mark Fleeson. No full time staff. Began 1988; non-denominational. Magazine: *Prayer letter* (Circulation n/a occasionally). Collating and providing resources in dance, mime, movement and puppetry.
Web: www.burninglight.co.uk
Email: mark@burninglight.co.uk
☎ 01289 389 247 🖷 01289 389 269

Clive Davenport, 57 Altrincham Road, Gatley, Cheadle SK8 4EG
Musician/Technician/Engineer: Mr Clive Davenport. No other staff. Began 1984; interdenominational. No magazine. Turnover n/a. Worship leading, contemporary concerts, multimedia events. Music technology – recording, technical support, soundtracks, PA, lighting and training.
Web: www.bigfoot.com/~clive.davenport
Email: clive.davenport@bigfoot.com
☎ 0161 718 8596

Norma Davey, 9 Bagnall Close, Norden, Rochdale OL12 7SH
Musician: Ms Norma Davey. No full-time staff. Began n/a; Methodist. No magazine. Turnover n/a. Singer and songwriter ministering God's love for all through song.
☎ 01706 861 758 Mobile: 07703 935 094

***Wes Davis**, Meredale, The Dell, Reach Lane, Leighton Buzzard LU7 0AL
Administrator: Mr Paul Davis. No full-time staff. Began 1975; interdenominational. No magazine. Turnover n/a. Singer/songwriter.
☎ 0152 523 7700 🖷 0152 523 7700

***Daybreak**, 4 Lombard Avenue, Bournemouth BH6 3LY
Treasurer: Mrs Rachel Green. No full-time staff. Began 1984; interdenominational. No magazine. Turnover n/a. Worship evangelism in prisons, churches and other locations, UK and France.
Email: ara-architects@claranet.co.uk
☎ 01202 428 115 🖷 01202 488 522

Diakonos Physical Theatre, PO Box 11073, London SE15 4ZE
Artistic Director: Mr Danny Scott. Executive staff 2, Other staff 3. Began 1996; non-denominational. No magazine. Turnover £20,266 to year end Mar 98. Professional physical theatre company performing/teaching UK/internationally; independent performing arts school, courses, workshops, seminars.
Email: diakonos@compuserve.com
☎ 020 7277 5155 Fax 020 7277 5155

Dominion International Opera, PO Box 62, Woodford Green IG9 5NY
General Director: Mr David Ashmore-Turner. Executive staff 1. *CC* No.1045394. Began 1995; interdenominational. Magazine: *Newsletter*(Circulation & frequency n/a). Turnover n/a. Evangelistic fundraising resource using professional singers performing operatic extracts with gospel message. CD available.
Web: www.dio.org.uk/dio
Email: enquiry@dio.org.uk
☎ 020 8504 6228 Fax 020 8504 6228

Elle M Theatre Company, 10 Inkerman Terrace, Chesham HP5 1QA
Administrator: Ms Emma Govan. Admin staff 1, Other staff 2. Began 1993; non-denominational. No magazine. Turnover n/a. Christian women's theatre company; producing original and challenging work throughout UK; performances and workshops.
Web: ourworld.compuserve.com/homepages/egovan
Email: egovan@compuserve.com
☎ 01494 786 116 Mobile: 07961 966 288

Fellowship of Christian Magicians (Europe), 91 Green Street, Middleton, Manchester M24 2TB
President: Mr Paul Morley. Staff n/a. Began 1987; interdenominational. Magazine: *"Voila!"* (140 quarterly). Turnover £13,018 to year end Nov 98. Proclaiming the Gospel and illustrating Christian truth using sleight of hand, illusion and other visual aids.
☎ 0161 653 6626

David Fitzgerald, 48 Avenue Road, Norwich NR2 3HN
Tutor/Performer: Mr David Fitzgerald. Began 1994; interdenominational. Magazine: *Newsletter* (Circulation n/a quarterly). Turnover £20,000 to year end Dec 98. Musician, teacher, composer, recording artist. Available for concerts, tours, recordings. Woodwinds, reeds, wind synthesis, tuition.
Web: w3.ixs.nl/~jove/
Email: davidftz@aol.com
☎ 01603 632 444 Mobile: 07768 573 284 Fax 01603 632 444

Footprints Trust, St Nicholas Centre, 79 Maid Marian Way, Nottingham NG1 6AE
Company Manager: Miss Mary Richards. Executive staff 2. *CC* No.277884. Began 1978; non-denominational. (Previously Footprints Theatre Company). Magazine: *Sole-Mate News* (200 half-yearly). Turnover n/a. Educational and community work expressing the Christian faith; 'Storymine' Project - storytelling/storymaking workshops/performances.
☎ 0115 958 6554 Fax 0115 952 4624

Freedom Music Ministries, 17 The Quadrant, Romiley, Stockport SK6 2EH
Musicians: Dorike Alli, Scott Fellows. No other staff. Began 1984; interdenominational. No magazine. Turnover n/a. A duo playing wide range of contemporary Christian music in service and outreach situations.
Email: dalli.92147@aol.com
☎ 0161 430 8401

Fresh Claim, 185 Lodge Avenue, Becontree, Dagenham RM8 2HQ
Leader: Rev Simon Law. Executive staff 2, Other staff 2. Began 1986; interdenominational. Magazine: *Newsletter* (250 quarterly). Turnover £4,250. Christian rock band; evangelism through words and music in schools, youth clubs and missions.
☎ 020 8592 5900

***Garden Music Duet**, 10 Mayfield, Welwyn Garden City AL8 7EL
Singer: Mr David Burden. Musicians 2. Began n/a; non-denominational. No magazine. Turnover n/a. Professional musicians communicating the message of Christ through the language of music; christian, classical, contemporary.
Email: garburden@aol.com
☎ 01707 887 393

†Gethsemane Rose – The Music Works, PO Box 1193, Cheddar BS27 3BF
Managers: Derek & Su Elliott. Executive staff 2. Began n/a; non-denominational. Magazine: *Hearsay* (750 quarterly). Turnover n/a. Heavy rock band. Live concerts and media work.
Email: 106620.2522@compuserve.com
☎ 01934 741 281 Fax 01934 743 222

Halycon Days, Event & Management Services, Unit 31, Ullenwood Court, Ullenwood, Cheltenham GL53 2QS
Agent: Mr Alan Wallace. Band members n/a. Began 1997; non-denominational. No magazine. Turnover n/a. Rock band.
Email: emsbands@ullenwood.co.uk
☎ 01242 245 444 Mobile: 07778 532 842 Fax 01242 250 618

***George Hamilton IV**, Meredale, The Dell, Reach Lane, Leighton Buzzard LU7 0AL
Administrator: Mr Paul Davis. No full-time staff. Began 1975; interdenominational. No magazine. Turnover n/a. Singer/songwriter.
☎ 0152 523 7700 Fax 0152 523 7700

Hands Up! Puppet Team, 24 Old Street, Clevedon BS21 6BY
Coordinator: Mrs Zena Butterfield. Puppet team 5. *CC* No.1042944. Began 1993; non-denominational. No magazine. Turnover n/a. Presenting the Gospel with puppets, songs, sketches to schools, fetes, festivals, senior citizen homes.
Web: www.living-waters.org.uk
Email: jap@living-waters.org.uk
☎ 01275 797 999 Fax 01275 797 999

Garth Hewitt, Amos Trust, All Hallows on the Wall, 83 London Wall, London EC2M 5ND
Administrator: Ms Clare Dowding. No full time staff. *CC* No.292592. Began n/a; interdenominational. No magazine. Turnover n/a. Freelance music ministry promoting justice and peace through music and storytelling.
Web: www.onthewall.org
Email: amos_trust@compuserve.com
☎ 020 7588 2661/2638 Fax 020 7588 2663

Paul Heyman, 26 Mavis Court, 4 Raven Close, Colindale, London NW9 5BJ
Proprietor: Mr Paul Heyman. No full-time staff. Began 1989; non-denominational. No magazine. Turnover n/a. Electric violinist; performing messianic Jewish/Christian worship music; 2 albums.
☎ 020 8203 3130

Phil Holburt, 35 Patterdale Avenue, Richmond, Whitehaven CA28 8RX
Singer/songwriter: Mr Phil Holburt. No other staff. Began 1994; interdenominational. Magazine: *Prayer/Newsletter* (Circulation & frequency n/a). Ministering to the church by song and spoken word. Worship leader, available for evangelism.
Email: philholburt@pholburt.freeserve.co.uk
☎ 01946 691 023 Mobile: 07801 424 118

Dave & Lynn Hopwood, Writer & Illustrator, Christ Church, Church Street East, Woking GU21 1YG
Writer: Mr Dave Hopwood. Executive staff 1. Began 1992; non-denominational. Magazine: *Adrenalin* (Circulation n/a quarterly). Turnover £15,000 to year end Dec 94. Fiction, drama & mime material, poetry, screenplays, children's books, greetings cards, collage, pen & watercolour.
☎ 01483 727 496

***In Yer Face Theatre Company**, Mill House, Mill Lane, Cheadle SK8 2NU
Coordinator: Miss Anna Macaulay. Admin staff 1, Other staff 3. *CC* Began 1996; non-denominational. No magazine. Turnover £10,000 to year end Mar 99. Evangelism using theatre as a tool to spread the good news; working mainly in Greater Manchester.
Web: www.domini.org/inyerface
Email: inyerface@domini.org
☎ 0161 491 3090 🖷 0161 491 3090

Iona, P O Box 28, Otley LS21 1XB
Co-ordinator: Debbie Bainbridge. Other staff 2. Began 1989; interdenominational. Magazine: *Friends of Iona* (Circulation n/a quarterly). Turnover n/a. Contemporary folk/rock band.
Web: www.iona.uk.com
☎ 01943 461 689 🖷 01943 461 689

M

†David Isaac, 2 Holme Terrace, Milbourne Street, Carlisle CA2 5XE
Musician: Mr David Isaac. No full-time staff. Began n/a; Elim Pentecostal. No magazine. Turnover £10,000 to year end Mar 95. Singer, songwriter, worship leader; available for concerts, conferences, schools, prisons.
☎ 01228 341 34

***The Island Churches Guernsey Festival Chorus**, Le Campere, Les Villets, Forest, Guernsey GY8 0HP
Musical Director: Mr & Mrs Roy & Maddie Sarre. Admin staff 4. Began 1985; interdenominational. Magazine: *Christian Arts Newsnotes* (50 quarterly). Turnover £10,000 to year end Dec 98. Gospel ministry in Christian arts through media, concerts, classical music, musicals; for all ages.
☎ 01481 650 04

Kato, Event & Management Services, Unit 31, Ullenwood Court, Ullenwood, Cheltenham GL53 2QS
Manager: Mr Alan Wallace. Band members n/a. Began 1997; non-denominational. No magazine. Turnover n/a. Brit pop and rock.
Email: emsbands@ullenwood.co.uk
☎ 01242 245 444 Mobile: 07778 532 842 🖷 01242 250 618

Keep in Step, Reckingdown House, 16 High Street, Weedon, Northampton NN7 4PX
Partners: Mr John & Mrs Sue Ritter. Executive staff 2. Began 1985; interdenominational. No magazine. Turnover £20,000 to year end Dec 96. Youth evangelism and training with a hi-tech musical presentation.
Web: members.aol.com/jsritter
Email: jsritter@aol.com
☎ 01327 341 535 Mobile: 07802 419 815

***Kettle of Fish Theatre**, 92 St Donatts Road, New Cross, London SE14 6NT
Artistic Directors: Mr Marc & Mrs Karen Cavallini. Executive staff 2. *CC* No.1000655. Began 1991; non-denominational. Part of Ichthus Community Projects. Magazine: *Newsletter* (Circulation n/a half-yearly). Turnover £27,000 to year end Aug 98. Providing community and contemporary issues-based theatre; performances, workshops; writing commissions; new theatre forms.
☎ 020 8691 9782 🖷 020 8691 9782

Keynote Trust, Townhaven, Pound Square, Cullompton EX15 1DN
Executive Officer: Mr Andrew Maries. No other staff. *CC* No.1015152. Began 1992; ecumenical. Magazine: *Keynote newsletter* (300 quarterly). Turnover n/a. Musician and worship leader; practical and spiritual consultancy, teaching and training in music and worship.
Email: maries@keynotetrust.freeserve.co.uk
☎ 01884 343 89 🖷 01884 343 89

Langham Arts, St Paul's Church, Robert Adam Street, London W1M 5AH
Administrator: Janet O'Brien. Other staff 2. *CC* No.1059611. Began 1987; non-denominational. Magazine: *Langham Arts News* (7,000 quarterly). Turnover £240,000 to year end June 98. Musical and theatrical performances connected with the arts ministry of All Souls Langham Place.
Web: scotta.demon.co.uk/aso.htm
Email: langhamarts@compuserve.com
☎ 020 7935 7246 🖷 020 7935 7486

***Lantern Arts Centre**, Worple Road, Raynes Park, London SW20 8RA
Artistic Director: Mrs Jacqui Frost. Executive staff 2, Other staff 2. *CC* No.1045719. Began 1995; ecumenical. No magazine. Turnover £20,000 to year end Apr 98. Productions, schools productions, childrens theatre club, arts weekends, arts workshops, café studio, café church.
Web: www.gawayn.demon.co.uk/jdc/nc
Email: rob.frost.team@dial.pipex.com
☎ 020 8944 5794 🖷 020 8947 5152

Alex & Jenny Legg, Event & Management Services, Unit 31, Ullenwood Court, Ullenwood, Cheltenham GL53 9QS
Agent: Mr Alan Wallace. Band members 2. Began 1997; non-denominational. No magazine. Turnover n/a. Acoustic and rock duo.
Email: emsbands@ullenwood.co.uk
☎ 01242 245 444 Mobile: 07778 532 842 🖷 01242 250 618

***Steve Legg – The Breakout Trust**, PO Box 3070, Littlehampton BN17 5AW
Director: Mr Steve Legg. Executive staff 1, Other staff 1. *CC* No.1070960. Began 1989; interdenominational. Magazine: *Breakout Update* (1,000 quarterly). Turnover n/a. Creative evangelism in schools, colleges, universities, prisons and events in UK and abroad.
Web: www.breakout.org.uk
Email: steve@breakout.org.uk
☎ 01903 779 279 🖷 01903 779 280

Peter Lewis (Family Folk), 22 Marlborough Rise, Aston, Sheffield S31 0ET
Singer/Musician: Peter Lewis. No full-time staff. Began 1965; interdenominational. No magazine. Turnover n/a. Sing Life – school assemblies; Sing Love – Family Folk concerts; Sing Jesus – family services, other events.
☎ 0114 287 3087

The London & Home Counties Festivals of Male Voice Praise, 18 Winchelsey Rise, South Croydon CR2 7BN
Secretary: Mr Geoff Forsdyke. No full-time staff. *CC* No.263429. Began 1951; interdenominational. Part of The Festivals of Male Voice Praise. Magazine: *The Christian Choirman* (500 & frequency n/a). Turnover £5,000 to year end July 98. Gospel witness and outreach through singing male voice gospel songs and other Christian musical arrangements.
☎ 020 8688 1346

London Community Gospel Choir (LCGC), 9 Greenwood Drive, Highams Park, London E4 9HL
President: Rev Bazil Meade. Executive staff 1. Began 1982; interdenominational. Magazine: *Focus* (Circulation n/a quarterly). Turnover £58,000 to year end Mar 93. Young people using the ministry of singing and music to reach all people.
Email: grooveking@aol.com
☎ 020 8531 5562 Mobile: 07973 327 955

***London Crusader Chorale**, 48 Beresford Road, Cheam, Sutton SM2 6ER
Leader: Mrs Janis Davidson. No full-time staff. *CC* No.287915. Began 1979; non-denominational. Affiliated to London Festivals of Male Voice Praise. Magazine: *Newsletter* (500 every four months). Turnover n/a. Musical evangelism to prisons, churches, homes for the elderly and disabled.
Email: 106341.1044@compuserve.com or hcc@lineone.net
☎ 020 8770 3896 Mobile: 07775 924 015

London Emmanuel Choir, 2 Buckles Way, Banstead SM7 1HD
President: Mrs Muriel F Shepherd. All voluntary workers. *CC* No.247871. Began 1945; interdenominational. Magazine: *Prayer/Fellowship Letter* (350 every four months). Turnover n/a. Magnifying the name of the Lord Jesus Christ by song and witness; recordings/videos available.
☎ 01737 350 637 Fax: 01737 373 406

Lou Lewis Ministries, Zimrah House, 39 Union Road, Exeter EX4 6HU
Partner: Mr Steve Lewis. Executive staff 2, Other staff 1. Began n/a; interdenominational. No magazine. Turnover n/a. Evangelism, teaching and ministry, particularly in area of 'wholeness' in church or concert situations.
☎ 01392 439 923 Mobile: 07850 618 414

Ally McCrae, Event & Management Services, Unit 31, Ullenwood Court, Ullenwood, Cheltenham GL53 9QS
Manager: Mr Alan Wallace. Singer 1. Began 1997; non-denominational. No magazine. Turnover n/a. Celtic singer / songwriter.
Email: emsbands@ullenwood.co.uk
☎ 01242 245 444 Mobile: 07778 532 842 Fax: 01242 250 618

***Peter McCahon**, Flat 8, 60 St Augustine Avenue, South Croydon CR2 6JJ
Creative Evangelist / Illusionist: Mr Peter McCahon. No other staff. Began 1990; interdenominational. No magazine. Turnover n/a. Presenting the Gospel to all ages in a relevant, creative way using illusion, comedy and escapology.
Email: petermccahon@compuserve.com
☎ 020 8688 3114 Mobile: 07973 135 263

Mid-Scotland Evangelical Choir, 48 Brown Street, Camelon, Falkirk FK1 4QF
Conductor: Mr Alan M McIntyre. No full-time staff. Began 1972; non-denominational with Brethren links. No magazine. Turnover n/a. Evangelical choir involved in Gospel outreach; ministering mainly to residential care homes for the elderly.
☎ 01324 623 933

***Mimeistry UK**, The Coach House, Woodhill, Congresbury BS49 5AF
UK Director: Jacque Hyde. Staff n/a. Began 1982; interdenominational. European contact for Todd Farley. Magazine: *Newsletter* (Circulation n/a half-yearly). Turnover n/a. International performances combining mime, drama, dance; training programme, workshops.
Web: www.mimeistry.org
Email: europe@mimeistry.org
☎ 01934 833 652 Fax: 01934 833 652

†**M-Ocean - The Music Works**, PO Box 1193, Cheddar BS27 3BF
Managers: Derek & Su Elliott. Executive staff 2. Began n/a; non-denominational. Magazine: *Hearsay* (750 quarterly). Turnover n/a. Contemporary worship band for churches, concerts, festivals, seminars.
Email: 106620.2522@compuserve.com
☎ 01934 741 281 Fax: 01934 743 222

More to Life Ministries, 18 Park Court, Bishopbriggs, Glasgow G64 2SQ
Director: Miss Ruth Box. No paid staff. Began 1993; non-denominational. No magazine. Turnover n/a. Easy listening music ministries comprising solo, group and choral performance and worship, itinerant teams.
Email: 101510.1300@compuserve.com
☎ 0141 772 3173 Mobile: 07775 528 947

***David Lyle Morris**, PO Box 46, Beckenham BR3 4YR
Sole Trader: David Lyle Morris. No full-time staff. Began 1988; interdenominational. Magazine: *Tevita Telegraph* (500 quarterly). Turnover n/a. Evangelistic concerts, worship leading, recordings; vocals and acoustic guitar; teaching on worship and vocals.
Email: davidlylemorris@hotmail.com
☎ 020 8658 2152 Mobile: 07623 766 001 🖷 020 8658 0427

†**Never on a Monday**, 1 Camden Road, Blackpool FY3 8HN
Musicians: Mr Michael McVey, Mr Andy Atherton. Executive staff 1. Began 1994; n/a. No magazine. Turnover n/a. Christian Indie (folk) rock band playing to audiences; outreach.
☎ 01253 892 994 🖷 01253 892 994

***New English Orchestra**, 14 Woodbine Road, Barbourne, Worcester WR1 3JB
Artistic/Musical Director: Mr Nigel Swinford. Admin staff 35. Began 1979; interdenominational. Magazine: *NEO Friends* (1,000 half-yearly). Turnover £55,000 to year end Aug 98. Professional orchestra with singers and dancers performing in major venues in the UK and abroad.
☎ 01905 613 771

New Horizons Choir, 16 Braemar Gardens, West Wickham BR4 0JW
Leader: Mr Andrew King. No full-time staff. Began 1983; interdenominational. Magazine: *n/a* (300 half-yearly). Turnover n/a. Encouraging and helping the local church through the ministry of music.
☎ 020 8777 8523

Nia, Nia Management, PO Box HK70, Leeds LS11 6YR
Personal Manager: Mr Kevin D Hoy. Executive staff 3. Began 1987; non-denominational. Magazine: *Newsletter* (2,500 half-yearly). Turnover n/a. International contemporary Christian singer and songwriter.
Web: www.niaconcerts.com
Email: info@niaconcerts.com
☎ 0113 272 1350 🖷 0113 272 1460

NUFFSED, 9 Miles Meadow Close, Willenhall WV12 5YE
Lead singer/ Songwriter: Mr Terence John Mills. No full-time staff. Began 1992; House Church. No magazine. Turnover n/a. Playing and recording Christian roots music; ministering to Christians and non-Christians, leading worship.
☎ 01922 403 033

†**Ben Okafor**, 6 The Manor House, Oakley Road, Brill, Aylesbury HP18 9RS
Musician: Mr Ben Okafor. No other staff. Began n/a; interdenominational. No magazine. Turnover n/a. Performing artist.
☎ No telephone

†**Old Vicarage Ministries**, The Old Vicarage, 77 Addington Village Road, Addington Village, Croydon CR0 5AS
Director: Mr Jeremy Davies. Executive staff 2. ***CC*** No.1014397. Began 1992; non-denominational. No magazine. Turnover n/a. Using creative arts in (all age) worship and mission; children's/youth work, church weekends, evangelism.
☎ 01689 842 952 🖷 01689 800 205

Open Book Storytellers, Hetton Hall, Chatton, Alnwick NE66 5SD
Director: Rev Roy Searle. Executive staff 1, Admin staff 3. Began 1998; interdenominational. Joint project of Northumbria Community and Bible Society. No magazine. Turnover £10,000 to year end Dec 98. Developing a network of Christian storytellers, offering training and resources.
Email: thetellingplace@bigfoot.com
☎ 01289 388 477 🖷 01289 388 477

Ron and Patricia Owens, 27a Grove Road, Redland, Bristol BS6 6UW
UK Representative: Mr Derek Townsend. Executive staff 1, Other staff 1. Began 1981; non-denominational. Magazine: *Newsletter* (Circulation n/a half-yearly). Turnover n/a. Presenting the Gospel in word and song; composing and concerts.
☎ 0117 973 1313 🖷 0117 909 4052

Palaver Productions, 2b Park Road, Monton, Manchester M30 9JJ
Producer: Mr Michael J Austin. Executive staff 2. Began 1994; ecumenical. No magazine. Turnover £15,000 to year end Dec 98. Producing quality new Christian dramas for churches and theatres.
☎ 0161 789 1869 🖷 0161 789 8142

Lance Pierson, 48 Peterborough Road, London SW6 3EB
Performer: Mr Lance Pierson. Executive staff 2. Began 1978; interdenominational. (Previously Freelance Word Wright). No magazine. Turnover £17,000 to year end April 98. One man shows to help Christians enjoy their faith and pass it on.
☎ 020 7731 6544 🖷 020 7731 1858

Powerbulge, Event & Management Services, Unit 31, Ullenwood Court, Ullenwood, Cheltenham GL53 2QS
Agent: Mr Alan Wallace. Band members n/a. Began 1997; non-denominational. No magazine. Turnover n/a. Acid jazz and funk.
Email: emsbands@ullenwood.co.uk
☎ 01242 245 444 Mobile: 07778 532 842 🖷 01242 250 618

Psalmistry, Event & Management Services, Unit 31, Ullenwood Court, Ullenwood, Cheltenham GL53 2QS
Manager: Mr Alan Wallace. Band members n/a. Began 1997; non-denominational. No magazine. Turnover n/a. Techno dance.
Email: emsbands@ullenwood.co.uk
☎ 01242 245 444 Mobile: 07778 532 842 🖷 01242 250 618

Reconcilers Evangelical Ministries (REM), 10 Bury Close, Amos Estate, Rotherhithe, London SE16 1SR
Evangelist: Rev Vincent Onwukanjo. ***CC*** No.1003914. Began 1985; non-denominational. (Previously Reconcilers Gospel Band). Magazine: *REM News* (150 every two months). Turnover £20,000 to year end Dec 98. Preaching, teaching, evangelising the Word. Saturday school, music, dance, drama, serving God with community projects.
Email: remnews@aol.com
☎ 020 7252 2223 Mobile: 07956 651 365

***Resurrection Thatre Co**, 11 Bazley Road, Northenden, Manchester M22 4FL
Chief Executive: Mrs Juliet Muttalib. Executive staff 3, Other staff 4. ***CC*** No.1068645. Began 1994; interdenominational. No magazine. Turnover £10,000 to year end Apr 98. Touring Bible-based theatre; bringing interactive drama workshops to schools, theatres, prisons nationwide.
Web: www.rtc.cwcom.net
Email: rtc@cwcom.net
☎ 0161 945 5486 🖷 0161 945 5486

Revelation Ministries, PO Box 30, North Walsham NR28 0SR
Director: Hamish MacQueen. Staff n/a. Began 1995; Roman Catholic. No magazine. Turnover n/a. Pop/rock bands and solo artists evangelising through music in schools, churches, etc. Recording studio available.
Email: revelation@lineone.net
☎ 01263 834 981 Mobile: 07050 037 162

M

Riverside School of Performing Arts, 21 Alcester Road, Moseley, Birmingham B13 8AR
Course Director: Ms Caroline Turner. Executive staff 1, Other staff 3. *CC* No.1046841. Began 1996; Foursquare Gospel Church. Magazine: *News Update* (200 quarterly). Turnover £28,000 to year end Mar 98. Providing professional training in performing arts and Bible teaching. For young people aged 18 to 25.
Email: rspa@riverside-church.org.uk
☎ 0121 442 4484 🖷 0121 442 4481

Rock Solid Theatre Company, 165 Grove Road, Mitcham CR4 1AF
Manager: Mr Bob Apthorpe. Executive staff 1. *CC* No.1003660. Began 1988; interdenominational. No magazine. Turnover £5,000 to year end Dec 92. Theatre in education, workshops, shows, evangelism, services, preaching and worship.
☎ 020 8646 0310

Rodd & Marco – The Acts Drama Trust, 28 Moray Park, Dalgety Bay KY11 9UN
Directors: Rodd Christensen, Marco Palmer. No other staff. *CC* No.SCO 23654. Began 1995; interdenominational. No magazine. Turnover £28,000 to year end Dec 98. Using comedy, drama and music in ministry in Scotland.
Web: www.rodd&marco.com
Email: marcopalmer@csi.com
☎ 01383 824 533 Mobile: 07785 514 461 🖷 011506 844 642

Salt of the Earth, Event & Management Services, Unit 31, Ullenwood Court, Ullenwood, Cheltenham GL53 2QS
Manager: Mr Alan Wallace. Band members n/a. Began 1997; non-denominational. No magazine. Turnover n/a. Brit pop and rock.
Email: emsbands@ullenwood.co.uk
☎ 01242 245 444 Mobile: 07778 532 842 🖷 01242 250 618

†**Simeon & John – The Music Works**, PO Box 1193, Cheddar BS27 3BF
Managers: Derek & Su Elliott. Executive staff 2. Began 1985; non-denominational. Magazine: *Hearsay* (750 quarterly). Turnover n/a. Professional instrumental duo (flute, panpipes, classical guitar). Available for concert tours and media work.
Email: 106620.2522@compuserve.com
☎ 01934 741 281 🖷 01934 743 222

Adrian Snell, Event & Management Services, Unit 31, Ullenwood Court, Ullenwood, Cheltenham GL53 2QS
Manager: Mr Alan Wallace. Began 1975; non-denominational. No magazine. Turnover n/a. International recording/performing artist, composer and singer, classical and contemporary.
Email: emsbands@ullenwood.co.uk
☎ 01242 254 444 Mobile: 07778 532 842 🖷 01242 250 618

Soft Toy, 19 Pennine Road, Chelmsford CM1 2HG
Manager: Mr Andy Sheldon. Executive staff 1. Began 1994; Evangelical. No magazine. Turnover £500 to year end Jan 99. Christian rock / pop band playing in bars, universities, schools, youth groups, open air.
Email: soft-toy@hotmail.com
☎ 01245 351 683 Mobile: 07050 278 899

Solo Plus Theatre Company, 23 Foley Road, Ward End, Birmingham B8 2JT
Administrator: Miss Linda Mae. Other staff 3. Began 1988; interdenominational. No magazine. Turnover £5,000 to year end Apr 95. Christian and issue-based performances and drama/writing workshops for all ages.
☎ 0121 786 2488

†**Sal Solo – The Music Works**, PO Box 1193, Cheddar BS27 3BF
Managers: Derek & Su Elliott. Full-time staff 2. Began 1993; non-denominational. No magazine. Turnover n/a. Available for evangelism through music at live concerts and media work.
Email: 106620.2522@compuserve.com
☎ 01934 741 281 🖷 01934 743 222

Split Level, Event & Management Services, Unit 31, Ullenwood Court, Ullenwood, Cheltenham GL53 2QS
Manager: Mr Alan Wallace. Band members n/a. Began 1997; non-denominational. No magazine. Turnover n/a. Rock band.
Email: emsbands@ullenwood.co.uk
☎ 01242 245 444 Mobile: 07778 532 842 🖷 01242 250 618

***Springs Dance Company**, 15 Waldegrave Road, Bromley BR1 2JP
Artistic Director: Fru Bird. *CC* No.326521. Began 1979; interdenominational. Magazine: *Regular Newsletters* (Circulation & frequency n/a). Turnover n/a. Christian dance company, highly acclaimed within both Church and secular world.
Email: springsdc@aol.com
☎ 020 8289 8974 Mobile: 07775 628442 🖷 020 8289 8974
Also at: 49 Ellesmere Road, London E3 5QU
☎ 020 8981 5428

Richard Swan, Event & Management Services, Unit 31, Ullenwood Court, Ullenwood, Cheltenham GL53 2QS
Manager: Mr Alan Wallace. Band members n/a. Began 1997; non-denominational. No magazine. Turnover n/a. Acid jazz.
Email: emsbands@ullenwood.co.uk
☎ 01242 245 444 Mobile: 07778 532 842
🖷 01242 250 618

Theatre Roundabout Ltd, 859 Finchley Road, London NW11 8LX
Director: Mr William Fry. Full-time staff 2. *CC* No.234999. Began 1964; Anglican. No magazine. Turnover £19,000 to year end July 98. Professional two-person company presenting Christian plays and parables for today.
☎ 020 8455 4752 Mobile: 07774 638 800

Keith Thompson + Strange Bren, Event & Management Services, Unit 31, Ullenwood Court, Ullenwood, Cheltenham GL53 2QS
Agent: Mr Alan Wallace. Band members n/a. Began 1997; non-denominational. No magazine. Turnover n/a. Blues and rock and roll.
Email: emsbands@ullenwood.co.uk
☎ 01242 245 444 Mobile: 07778 532 842 🖷 01242 250 618

Titanix Theatre (Ken Wylie), 88a De Vere Gardens, Ilford IG1 3EE
Performer: Mr Ken Wylie. Performer 1. Began 1996; interdenominational. (Previously Titanic Brothers). No magazine. Turnover £3,000 to year end Apr 98. Performing mime and physical theatre in churches, halls, schools, inside and outside; workshops all ages.
☎ 020 8554 8765 🖷 020 8554 8765

Valentine International Clown Ministry, 39 Fountain Road, Bridge of Allan, Stirling FK9 4AU
Artistic Director: Mrs Olive M Fleming-Drane. No full time staff. Began 1985; ecumenical. Turnover n/a. Clowning, storytelling, mime for all ages. Evangelism, worship, performance, workshops in churches, schools, prisons, libraries.
Email: johndrane@compuserve.com
☎ 01786 833 028 Mobile: 07711 938 308

Ralph Van Manen, Event & Management Services, Unit 31, Ullenwood Court, Ullenwood, Cheltenham GL53 2QS
Agent: Mr Alan Wallace. Singer 1. Began 1997; non-denominational. No magazine. Turnover n/a. Singer/songwriter.
Email: emsbands@ullenwood.co.uk
☎ 01242 245 444 Mobile: 07778 532 842 🖷 01242 250 618

Marianne Velvárt, 70 Oakley Road, South Norwood, London SE25 4XQ
Singer/Songwriter: Marianne Velvárt. Began 1983; New Church. No magazine. Turnover n/a. Singer, songwriter, poet, outreach, radio work; mostly solo; streetwise, contemporary fusion of styles.
☎ 020 8656 8080

Whiteraven, 48 Silkmore Crescent, Stafford ST17 4JL
Manager: Mr Ian Whyte. No full-time staff. Began n/a; interdenominational. No magazine. Turnover n/a. Contemporary Christian band, ministry of challenge and encouragement mainly to age group 20's to 40's.
☎ 01785 212 115

Why?, Event & Management Services, Unit 31, Ullenwood Court, Ullenwood, Cheltenham GL53 2QS
Manager: Mr Alan Wallace. Band members n/a. Began 1997; non-denominational. No magazine. Turnover n/a. Celtic folk group.
Email: emsbands@ullenwood.co.uk
☎ 01242 245 444 Mobile: 07778 532 842 🖷 01242 250 618

MUSICAL & THEATRICAL SERVICES

Abinger Organs, Little Hoe, Hoe Lane, Abinger Hammer, Dorking RH5 6RH
Partners: Mr Peter Flatau, Mrs Elizabeth Matthews. Executive staff 1, Other staff 2. Began 1983; interdenominational. No magazine. Turnover £140,000 to year end Apr 98. Sales and hire of church organs, keyboards, electric pianos, digital hymn recording and playback units.
Web: www.abinger-organs.co.uk
Email: liz@abinger.globalnet.co.uk
☎ 01306 730 277 Mobile: 07970 950 361
🖷 01306 731 483

M

*__Act for Christ__, Ground Floor Mission House, 34a High Street, Yatton, Bristol BS49 4JA
Director: Mr Michael Saffery. Executive staff 1. *CC* Began 1989; non-denominational. No magazine. Turnover £10,000 to year end Oct 98. Offering evangelism and training using drama in schools, prisons, church missions; UK and overseas.
☎ 01934 835 615

Allen Organs, TRADA Business Campus, Stocking Lane, Hughenden Valley, High Wycombe HP14 4ND
Managing Director: Mr Emyr Davies. *Sales Manager:* Mr David Shepherd. Executive staff 4, Other staff 3. Began 1968; non-denominational. No magazine. Turnover £900,000 to year end Nov 98. Supplying, servicing and hiring of Allen digital computer organs.
Web: allenorgans.co.uk
Email: sales@allenorgans.co.uk
☎ 01494 563 833 🖷 01494 563 546

*__Alliance Music__, Waterside House, Woodley Headland, Peartree Bridge, Milton Keynes MK6 3BY
Managing Director: Mr Ian Hamilton. *Commercial Director:* Mr David Withers. *A & R Director:* Mr David Bruce. Executive staff 3, Other staff 16. Began 1994; non-denominational. No magazine. Turnover £2,500,000 to year end Mar 98. Record company specialising in contemporary, gospel and praise and worship Christian music.
Web: www.alliancemusic.co.uk
Email: music@alliancemusic.co.uk
☎ 01908 677 074 🖷 01908 677 760

Arts in Mission, 24 Yorkshire Place, Warfield Green, Bracknell RG42 3XE
Contact: Elaine & David Chalmers-Brown. Other staff 2. *CC* No.1071313. Began 1996; non-denominational. No magazine. Turnover n/a. Encouraging, enabling and equipping Christian artists, assisting church in mission.
Web: www.wordnet.co.uk/arts
Email: david@chalmers-brown.freeserve.co.uk
☎ 01344 426 286 🖷 01344 426 286

British Association of Christian Bands (Brass), Winyards, Lytton Road, Woking GU22 7BH
Secretary: Mr Norman Gerhold. No full-time staff. Began 1988; inter-denominational. No magazine. Turnover n/a. Offering Christian fellowship to musicians; meetings half-yearly at Welwyn; branches in Andover, Faversham, Nottingham, Teesside.
☎ 01483 760 904

Calamus, 30 North Terrace, Mildenhall, Bury St Edmunds IP28 7AB
Administrators: Mrs Susan Dean, Mr Nicholas Blackford. Executive staff 2, Other staff 2. Began 1991; non-denominational. No magazine. Turnover £100,000 to year end Dec 96. Church music copyright licensing agency.
Web: decanimusic.uk.com
Email: decanimusic@dialdrakken.com
☎ 01638 716 579 Mobile: 07802 736 863 🖷 01638 510 390

CHIME – The Churches' Initiative in Music Education, Sarum College, 19 The Close, Salisbury SP1 2EE
Secretary: Mr Robert Fielding. No full-time staff. *CC* No.1058585. Began 1991; ecumenical. Magazine: *Newsletter* (Circulation n/a half-yearly). Turnover n/a. Providing ecumenical forum for discussion and information about education and training of UK church musicians.
Web: btinternet.com/~chime
Email: chime@sarum.ac.uk
☎ 01722 424 805 Mobile: 07669 031 653 🖷 01722 338 508

Christian Arts Promotions Ltd, Thornfield House, 58 Hill Head Close, Glastonbury BA6 8AL
Chairman: Mr Richard Hillard. No paid staff. *CC* No.1057199. Began 1993; interdenominational. No magazine. Turnover £25,000 to year end Dec 96. Hearts on Fire arts festival in Glastonbury, contemporary worship and outreach events. Choir available for booking.
Web: home.clara.net/bethany/hof.html
Email: hof@bethany.clara.net
☎ 01454 319 447 Mobile: 07721 637 546 Fax 01454 319 447

Christian Copyright Licensing (Europe) Ltd, 26 Gildredge Road, Eastbourne BN21 4SA
Managing Director: Mr Geoff Booker. Executive staff 1, Other staff 17. Began 1991; non-denominational. No magazine. Turnover n/a. Enabling legal reproduction of words and music for a wide range of hymns and worship songs.
Web: www.ccli.com
Email: info@ccli.co.uk
☎ 01323 417 711 Fax 01323 417 722

***Chrysalis Arts Trust**, 78 The Broadway, Chesham HP5 1EG
Chairman: Mr Keith Lawson. Admin staff 2, Other staff 1. *CC* No.1049294. Began 1995; non-denominational. No magazine. Turnover n/a. Resourcing churches to present the gospel relevantly through cabaret-style (outreach) events using the performing arts.
Email: chrysart@aol.com
☎ 01494 581 115 Fax 01494 581 114

†Cobham Agency, PO Box 342, Leeds LS2 9TH
Contact: Mr Tim Cobham. Executive staff 1, Other staff 1. Began 1990; interdenominational. No magazine. Turnover n/a. Music and arts agency; bands and solo performers for missions, concerts, seminars, praise events.
☎ 0113 234 2806 Fax 0113 234 2806

***The Connections Trust**, PO Box 303, Chesham HP5 1RW
Musical Director: Mr Roger Mayor. Executive staff 1. *CC* Began 1992; interdenominational. No magazine. Turnover n/a. Providing music workshops and resources for local churches concerned with adult evangelism events.
☎ 01494 791 876 Fax 01494 791 876

Copeman Hart and Company Ltd, Organ Builders, Finedon Road, Irthlingborough, Wellingborough NN9 5TZ
Managing Director: Mr Ernest C Hart. *General Manager:* Mr Ian Rees. Other staff 10. Began 1960; non-denominational. No magazine. Turnover £400,000 to year end Mar 99. Custom-built pipeless organs for cathedrals, churches and schools.
Web: www.copemanhart.co.uk
Email: info@copemanhart.co.uk
☎ 01933 652 600 Fax 01933 652 288

Crossways Music, 627 London Road, Westcliff-on-Sea SS0 9PE
Manager: Mr Jim McManus. Executive staff 2. Began 1989; interdenominational. (Previously Crossways Records). No magazine. Turnover n/a. Music shop, mail order service and concert organiser; CDs, over 4,000 titles.
☎ 01702 392 222 Fax 01702 390 400

Crystal Sound Gospel Concerts, 13 Oakwood Gardens, Knaphill, Woking GU21 2RX
Director: Mr Gordon Tyerman. Executive staff 1, No other staff. Began 1980; interdenominational. No magazine. Turnover £20,000 to year end Apr 98. Concert promotion, assistance for those planning Gospel concerts; advice and administration planning.
Email: csgc@compuserve.com
☎ 01483 797 906 Fax 01483 832 102

Cutting Edge Productions, 39 Rookswood, Alton GU34 2LD
Proprietor: Mr Alan Matthews. Admin staff 3. Began n/a; interdenominational. Turnover n/a. Specialising in live multi camera events/single camera productions, 6 camera outside broadcast truck available.
Web: www.cuttingedgeuk.com
Email: cuttingedgeuk@lineone.net
☎ 01420 544 674 Mobile: 07768 320 471 Fax 01420 544 668

Cymdeithas Emynau Cymru (Welsh Hymn Society), 21 Heol Abernant, Cwmgors, Ammanford SA18 1RB
Secretary: Rev Richard Jones. No full-time staff. ***CC*** Began 1967; non-denominational. Magazine: *Bulletin Cymdeithas Emynau* (Circulation & frequency n/a). *Cymru* (300 frequency n/a). Turnover £8,000 to year end Apr 98. Furthering the study of Welsh hymnody in its spiritual, cultural and historical context.
☎ 01269 822 723

Stephen Deal, 2 Goodson House, Greenlane, Morden SM4 6SH
Writer: Mr Stephen Deal. Executive staff 1. Began 1984; non-denominational. Turnover n/a. Humorous quick sketch drama, tried and tested by professional actors.
Web: www.deal1.demon.co.uk
Email: stephendeal@deal1.demon.co.uk
☎ 020 8646 1344 Fax 020 8646 1344

Digital Hymnals UK Ltd, 9 South End, Croydon CR0 1BE
Director: Mr Martin Phelps. Executive staff 2, Other staff 4. Began 1996; interdenominational. No magazine. Turnover n/a. Promoting and selling the Gulbransen Digital Hymnal.
Web: www.digital-hymnal.com
Email: 106215.560@compuserve.com
☎ 020 8680 9747 Mobile: 07774 796 251 Fax 020 8680 9471

***DM Music for Churches**, Unit 4, Riverside Estate, Coldharbour Lane, Harpenden AL5 4UN
Managing Director: Mr David Moore. Executive staff 2, Other staff 8. Began 1991; non-denominational. Magazine: Title n/a. (Circulation n/a quarterly). Turnover £1,500,000 to year end Dec 98. Supplying and installing PA equipment and musical instruments to churches and schools; arranging training seminars.
Web: www.dm-music.co.uk
Email: enquiries@dm-music.co.uk
☎ 01582 761 122 Freephone: 0500 026 930
Fax 01582 768 811

M

†Dunamis Enterprises International Ltd, Dunamis House, 398 Barking Road, Plaistow, London E13 8AG
Managing Director: Mr Anthony H Palmer. Executive staff 2, Other staff 2. Began 1993; interdenominational. Turnover £68,000 to year end Dec 96. Promoting events, gospel concerts, shows; wedding services; clothing; accommodation hire; retail marketing.
☎ 020 7511 7798 Fax 020 7511 7799

E-Compile Ltd, 7 Andrews Close, Buckhurst Hill IG9 5BL
Director: Craige Pendleton-Browne. staff 2. Began 1995; non-denominational. No magazine. Turnover n/a. Offering free sample Christian music via the Internet, 100s of tracks – worship & contemporary.
Web: www.ecompile.co.uk
Email: editor@compile.co.uk
☎ 020 8281 1398 Fax 020 8505 1994

***Early Rain Music**, 2 Conifers Close, Alresford, Colchester CO7 8AW
Musician & Singer: Rev John Pantry. No full-time staff. ***CC*** No.291652. Began 1989; Anglican. No magazine. Turnover n/a. Music publishing; administration for John Pantry's missions; concert and seminar bookings.
☎ 01206 824 257 / 020 7316 1377 Fax 01206 824 257

Event & Management Services, Unit 31, Ullenwood Court Ullenwood, Cheltenham GL53 9QS
Partner: Mr Alan Wallace. Executive staff 4. Began 1997 non-denominational. No magazine. Turnover £80,000 to year end Mar 99. Event organisers – conferences, music events, corporate events; Christian music artists.
Email: emx@ullenwood.co.uk
☎ 01242 245 444 Mobile: 07778 532 842 Fax 01242 250 618

Festivals of Christian Music, 57 Ashwell Street, Ashwell, Baldock SG7 5QT
Chairman: Norman J Gurney. Executive staff 1. Began 1989; non-denominational. No magazine. Turnover £3,386 to year end Dec 98. Promoting the Gospel through Christian music in four-part harmony; encouraging the preservation of church choirs.
☎ 01462 742 185

f f g (free for good), Bredon Fields, Eckington Road, Bredon, Tewkesbury GL20 7HE
Partner: Mr David Pick. Executive staff 3. Began 1977; non-denominational. No magazine. Turnover £10,000–50,000 to year end Dec 96. Producing Christian records; 24-track residential recording studio; music for video and broadcasting.
☎ 01684 772 664 Fax 01684 772 902

FosterFinch Ltd, Registered Office, 3 Lawn Road, Exmouth EX8 1QJ
Director: Mr Tim Finch. Executive staff 2, Other staff 3. Began 1994; interdenominational. Bases in London, Taunton, East Devon & Shropshire. No magazine. Turnover £36,000 to year end Oct 98. Offering music theory and practical lessons for wind instruments. Continual assessment music exam certificates Levels 1–8.
Web: www.eclipse.co.uk/fosterfinch
Email: timfinch@cix.co.uk
☎ Tim Finch Mobile: 07703 172 994
☎ Bob Foster: 01823 252 522 (Taunton)

Fountain Publications, 108 Longlands Road, Sidcup DA15 7LF
Editor: Miss Colleen Blake. Executive staff 1, Other staff 1. Began 1988; non-denominational. No magazine. Turnover £10,000–50,000 to year end Dec 96. Christian musical plays, asemblies and song books for schools, churches and youth organisations.
☎ 020 8302 8942 Fax 020 8300 8338

†The Good News Music Company, 32 Windermere Road, Ealing, London W5 4TD
Sole Proprietor: Mr E Richard Bickersteth. Executive staff 3, Other staff 2. Began 1982; non-denominational. No magazine. Turnover £175,000 to year end Sept 93. Promoting musical artists; artist and tour management; record company and merchandising operations.
☎ 020 7567 3355 Fax 020 7932 3978

Gospel Promotions, 29 Orchard Road, Whickham, Newcastle upon Tyne NE16 4TG
Chairman: Mr Doug Forster. All voluntary staff. Began 1985; interdenominational. (Previously Gospel Concert Promotions). Magazine: *Events Diary and Spotlight* (250 every two months). Turnover n/a. Christian artists' resources and publicity of regional events.
☎ 0191 488 2459

Gospel Light Bookshop, 211 Victoria Rise, Clapham, London SW4 0PF
Owner: Mrs Angela Thomas. Admin staff 1. Began 1990; non-denominational. No magazine. Turnover n/a. Specialising in mail order black contemporary Gospel music from around the world, books, church instruments.
☎ 020 7652 3643 Mobile: 07956 276 588
Fax 020 7652 3643

The Gregorian Association, 26 The Grove, Ealing, London W5 5LH
Chairman: Mr A G Ellison-Macartney. All voluntary staff. ***CC*** No.1003775. Began 1870; interdenominational. Magazine: *The Gregorian* (200 occasionally). Turnover n/a. Promoting the study and use of plainsong and its suitability to the English language.
Web: www.beaufort.demon.co.uk/chant.html
☎ 020 8840 5832

The Hymn Society of Great Britain & Ireland, 7 Paganel Road, Minehead TA24 5ET
Secretary: Rev Geoffrey Wrayford. No full-time staff. ***CC*** No.248225. Began 1936; interdenominational. (See also Welsh Hymn Society). Magazine: *The Bulletin* (450 every four months). Turnover £8,500 to year end Dec 98. Studying hymns and encouraging their better use.
☎ 01643 703 530 🖷 01643 703 530

Integrity Music (Europe) Ltd, Berkeley House, 26 Gildredge Road, Eastbourne BN21 4SA
General Manager: Mrs Shirley Ferrier. Executive staff 3, Other staff 9. Began 1986; interdenominational. Magazine: *Newsletter* (Circulation n/a every two months). Turnover n/a. Christian music company creating cassettes, CDs, videos, software.
Email: sferrier@integuk1.mhs.compuserve.com
☎ 01323 430 033 🖷 01323 411 981

Jaw Music Ltd, 3 Tapton House, Sheffield S10 5BY
Production Managers: Ms Ruth Milsom, Ms Bev Ryan, Ms Jackie Williams. Began n/a; interdenominational. No magazine. Turnover n/a. Professional type-setting service, specialising in musical and non-English publications.
Email: jawmusic@aol.com
☎ 0114 267 9988 🖷 0114 267 9989

Jesus People Shop, Nether Heyford, Northampton NN7 3LB
Manager: Peter Taylor. Admin staff 3. Began n/a; Jesus Fellowship. (Previously Jesus Fellowship Resources). No magazine. Turnover £42,000 to year end Dec 98. Books, music tapes and CDs, videos, clothing, other resources by mail order and at conferences.
Web: www.jesus.org.uk/shop
Email: shop@jesus.org.uk
☎ 01327 349 992 🖷 01327 349 997

***Kanlite Stage Lighting**, 4 Tamworth Terrace, Duffield, Derby DE6 4FD
Proprietor: Mr Glyn Owen. Executive staff 1, Other staff 2. Began 1983; non-denominational. No magazine. Turnover n/a. Hiring and selling of stage lighting for all types of Christian events.
☎ 01332 842 391 Mobile: 07836 556 587 🖷 01332 842 391

†**Keystage**, Unit 2, The Courtyard, Ochrelands, Hexham NE46 0AA
Proprietors: Mr Paul & Mr AndrewTorkington. No other staff. Began 1996; non-denominational. No magazine. Turnover n/a. Selling musical instruments and accessories to Christian outlets at discounted prices.
☎ No telephone

King's Trust, 1 Whitehorse Road, Croydon CR0 2JH
Director: Mr Cid Latty. All voluntary staff. ***CC*** No.1032690. Began 1993; non-denominational. Magazine: *News Update* (Circulation n/a n/a). Turnover n/a. Worship leading, teaching worship bands, worship and music training for Oasis Trust and other organisations.
Email: cidlatty@aol.com
☎ 020 8689 8242 Mobile: 07956 258 460 🖷 020 8689 8242

***Kingsway's Thankyou Music**, PO Box 75, Eastbourne BN23 6NW
Song Promoter: Mr Stuart Townend. *Music Copyright:* Mrs Emilie Stokes. Staff n/a. ***CC*** No.265612. Began n/a; interdenominational. No magazine. Turnover n/a. Publishing Christian songs; administration, promotion and issuing of commercial licences.
Email: music@kingsway.co.uk
☎ 01323 437 700 🖷 01323 411 970

The Leaveners, Ground Floor, 1 The Lodge, 1046 Bristol Road, Birmingham B29 6LJ
Co-ordinator: Tina Helfrich. Full-time staff 2, Part-time staff 1. ***CC*** No.292499. Began 1978; Religious Society of Friends. Incorporating Quaker Youth Theatre, Quaker Festival Orchestra and Chorus and Leaveners Theatre Co. Magazine: *Leavenings* (1,000 every four months). Turnover n/a. Training and live arts projects exploring social issues, conflict, non-violence, spirituality, especially with young people.
Email: leavener@globalnet.co.uk
☎ 0121 414 0099 🖷 0121 414 0090

***The Lighthouse Agency**, PO Box 1941, Great Dunmow, Dunmow CM6 1AP
Director: Mr David Bemment. Executive staff 1. Began 1998; interdenominational. No magazine. Turnover n/a. Agency for many leading performers & sportsmen for testimony evenings.
Web: ourworld.compuserve.com/homepages/connectionspm
Email: 106066.327@compuserve.com
☎ 01371 874 544 🖷 01371 874 544

M

Living Music Ltd, 3 Delamere Road, Earley, Reading RG6 1AP
Director: Mr Chris Mitchell. Admin staff 2. Began 1989; non-denominational. No magazine. Turnover n/a. Professional music arranging and typesetting; worship, music and arts training resources.
Email: chris@livmusic.globalnet.co.uk
☎ 0118 926 7754 Mobile: 07973 766 895 🖷 0118 926 7754

Mainstage Management Agency, 40 Skelley Road, Stratford, London E15 4BA
Contact: Mrs Linda Scott. No full-time staff. Began 1991; interdenominational. No magazine. Turnover n/a. Music and arts agency; bands and solo performers for missions, concerts, seminars, praise events.
☎ 020 8555 5510

***Make Way Music Ltd**, PO Box 263, Croydon CR9 5AP
Managing Director: Mr Graham Kendrick. Executive staff 2, Other staff 2. Began 1988; non-denominational. No magazine. Turnover n/a. Publishing and administering the musical ministry of Graham Kendrick.
Web: www.grahamkendrick.co.uk
Email: makewaymusic@compuserve.com
☎ 020 8656 0025 🖷 020 8656 4342

Makin Organs Ltd, Compton House, Franklin Street, Oldham OL1 2DP
Managing Director: Mr David Clegg. *Technical Manager:* Mr David Bostock. Executive staff 5, Other staff 7. Began 1970; non-denominational. Magazine: *Makin News* (5,000 half-yearly). Turnover £800,000 to year end Dec 98. Manufacturing and distributing English and European pipeless classical organs.
Web: www.makinorgans.co.uk
Email: davidc@makinorgans.co.uk
☎ 0161 626 5666 Mobile: 07775 510 968 🖷 0161 665 2284
Also at: 49 High Street, Shoreham, Sevenoaks TN14 7TB
☎ 01959 525 354 🖷 01959 525 554

***Mimeistry UK**, The Coach House, Woodhill, Congresbury BS49 5AF
UK Director: Jacque Hyde. Staff n/a. Began 1982; interdenominational. European contact for Todd Farley. Magazine: *Newsletter* (Circulation n/a half-yearly). Turnover n/a. International performances combining mime, drama, dance; training programme, workshops.
Web: www.mimeistry.org
Email: europe@mimeistry.org
☎ 01934 833 652 🖷 01934 833 652

Mission Through Music, PO Box 6, Prudhoe NE42 6YY
Administrator: Mr Colin Woodcock. No other full-time staff. ***CC*** No.1056502. Began 1994; interdenominational. Magazine: *Newsletter* (Circulation n/a half-yearly). Turnover £11,000 to year end Dec 96. Arranging and organising Christian concerts, conferences and seminars for individuals, churches or organisations.
☎ 01661 831 030 Mobile: 07973 919 477 🖷 01661 831 030

Music and Worship Foundation, 8 Silverdale, Fleet GU13 9TT
Administrator: Mr Granville Lovat. No full-time staff. ***CC*** No.290417. Began 1984; ecumenical. No magazine. Turnover £15,000 to year end Apr 98. Training, resourcing churches in music/worship, local networks, courses up to degree level at London Bible College.
Web: www.btinternet.com/~mwf/
Email: rpeach@btinternet.com
☎ 01252 614 604 Mobile: 07970 829 161

The Music Works, PO Box 1193, Cheddar BS27 3BF
Managers: Derek & Su Elliott. Began 1989; interdenominational. No magazine. Turnover n/a. Artist & Tour Management, representing Sal Solo, Bushbaby.
Email: 106620.2522@compuserve.com
☎ 01934 741 281 🖷 01934 743 222

†**Musicstar**, 29a Hythe Road, Thornton Heath CR7 8QQ
Director: Miss Roney Henderson. Executive staff 1, Other staff 1. Began 1996; New Testament Church of God. No magazine. Turnover n/a. Publicists, promoters and booking agents for USA and UK-based black gospel acts.
☎ 020 7787 2739 🖷 020 7787 6462

The Netherbow Arts Centre, 43 High Street, Edinburgh EH1 1SR
Director: Dr Donald Smith. *General Manager:* Moira Hay. Executive staff 2, Other staff 7. ***CC*** No.SCO 11353. Began 1972; Church of Scotland. No magazine. Turnover £200,000 to year end Dec 96. Full arts centre programme plus mobile workshops in drama, worship and church arts.
☎ 0131 556 9579/2647

***New Music Enterprises**, Meredale, The Dell, Reach Lane, Leighton Buzzard LU7 0AL
Manager: Mr Paul Davis. No full-time staff. Began 1975; interdenominational. No magazine. Turnover n/a. Publishing songs, arranging Gospel concerts, producing Christian recordings.
☎ 01525 237 700 🖷 01525 237 700

New Music Records, Meredale, The Dell, Reach Lane, Leighton Buzzard LU7 0AL
Manager: Mr Paul Davis. No full-time staff. Began 1975; interdenominational. (Previously Eternity Music Sales). No magazine. Turnover n/a. Supplying records, cassettes and CDs.
☎ 01525 237 700 🖷 01525 237 700

***Newby Entertainments**, 100 Fotheringham Road, Enfield EN1 1QE
Managing Director: Mr Dave Newby. Executive staff 1, Other staff 2. Began 1981; non-denominational. No magazine. Turnover £15,000 to year end Apr 95. Children/adults entertainment for Sunday Schools, private parties; Gospel and close-up magic, clowns, puppets, corporate entertainment.
☎ 020 8366 6051

Norwich Organs, Reprographic House, Bidwell Road, Rackheath Industrial Estate, Rackheath, Norwich NR13 6LH
Partners: Mr Muttock, Mr Plummer. Executive staff 2, Other staff 5. Began 1974; non-denominational. No magazine. Turnover n/a. Manufacturing classical electronic organs.
☎ 01603 720 360

On The Spot (Training & Resourcing), 534 Mumbles Road, Mumbles, Swansea SA3 4DH
Creative Director: Mr Kit Loring. Executive staff 4. Began 1997; non-denominational. In association with Reaching the Unreached Network. No magazine. Turnover n/a. Arts and production training, primarily serving seeker services/events.
Email: kit.loring@virgin.net
☎ 01792 522 342 Mobile: 07711 670 851 🖷 01792 522 342

***PEPA Practical, Effective, Performing Arts**, PO Box 1908, London N4 3PY
Staff 20. ***CC*** No.1023328. Began 1991; affiliated to Rainbow Foundation. No magazine. Turnover £65,000 to year end Dec 98. Productions on third world issues and training courses/workshops in the performing arts offered.
Web: easyweb.easynet.co.uk.rain
Email: rain@easynet.co.uk
☎ 020 8885 5488 🖷 020 8885 5007

Phoenix Performing Arts Trust, 26 Manningford Close, Winchester SO23 7EU
Chairman: Mr Sam Wise. No full-time staff. ***CC*** No.803728. Began 1990; interdenominational. No magazine. Turnover £10,000 to year end Dec 98. Development of training in performing arts from a Christian viewpoint, support/encouragement of Christian performers/trainers.
Email: swise10@aol.com
☎ 01962 850 347 📠 01962 850 347

Psalmody International, PO Box 5222, Burton-on-Trent DE14 3WT
UK Directors: Mr Stephen & Mrs Jenny Watson. Other staff 2. ***CC*** No.1042573. Began 1988; interdenominational. Magazine: *The Worshipping Heart* (2,000 frequency n/a). Turnover n/a. Teaching and developing praise and worship as a lifestyle; supplying resources, books, tapes, CDs.
Web: www.psalmody.org
Email: info@psalmody.org
☎ 01283 534 375 Mobile: 07774 938 311 📠 01543 483 383

Radius (The Religious Drama Society of Great Britain), Christ Church and Upton Chapel, 1a Kennington Road, London SE1 7QP
Secretary: Mr Howard Bennett. All voluntary staff. ***CC*** No.214943. Began 1929; ecumenical. Magazine: *Radius* (Circulation n/a quarterly). Turnover £14,000 to year end June 98. Supporting religious drama production for Christian understanding through training, advice, play supplies, lending library.
☎ 020 7401 2422

†RCG Recordings, Freepost, Rayleigh SS6 9BR
Chairman: Mr Martin Johnson. Executive staff 1, Other staff 2. Began 1996; Roman Catholic. No magazine. Turnover £100,000 to year end Mar 97. Mail order of religious music by Catholic artists, religious orders, communities and the priesthood.
☎ 0800 421 220 📠 01268 786 120

Riding Lights Theatre Co Ltd, Marketing House, 8 Bootham Terrace, York YO30 7DH
Artistic Director: Mr Paul Burbridge. *General Manager:* Jonathan Brown. Executive staff 4, Other staff 13. ***CC*** No.1070142. Began 1977; non-denominational. Magazine: *Newsletter* (Circulation n/a quarterly). Turnover £150,000 to year end Mar 96. Professional Christian theatre company; community theatre available to any venue; workshops, books.
Web: www.users.globalnet.co.uk/~rltc/
Email: rltc@globalnet.co.uk
☎ 01904 655 317 📠 01904 651 532

†Rodgers Classical Organs, Atlantic Close, Swansea Enterprise Park, Swansea SA7 9FJ
Divisional Manager: Mr Sean Montgomery. Staff n/a. Began 1989; non-denominational. No magazine. Turnover n/a. Supplying classical electronic musical instruments to churches and schools.
Email: 100067.3415@compuserve.com
☎ 01792 700 139 📠 01792 310 248

Royal School of Church Music, Cleveland Lodge, Westhumble, Dorking RH5 6BW
Director: Prof John Harper. Staff 23. ***CC*** No.312828. Began 1927; interdenominational. Magazine: *Church Music Quarterly* (11,500 quarterly). Turnover £1,600,000 to year end June 98. Teaching and helping, through courses and publications, all those concerned with music in worship.
Web: www.rscm.com
Email: cl@rscm.com
☎ 01306 872 800 📠 01306 887 260

Robin J S Rust, 70 Greenways, Fleet GU13 9XD
Proprietor: Mr Robin J S Rust. Staff 2. Began 1960; non-denominational. No magazine. Turnover £20,000 to year end Apr 98. Pipe organ builders, undertaking tuning, maintenance, cleaning, rebuilds to all types of action.
☎ 01252 617 908 / 372 258 📠 01252 372 258

Shorehill Arts, Thatched Cottage, Otford Hills, Sevenoaks TN15 6XL
Proprietor: Mr Nick Page. No full-time staff. Began 1989; non-denominational. No magazine. Turnover £50,000 to year end Aug 98. Production, presentation and consultancy in public events. Provision of Christian performers.
Email: nickpage@xc.org
☎ 01959 523 740 📠 01959 525 011

Songs of Fellowship Arrangements Service, PO Box 4, Sheffield S1 1DU
Director: Ms Bev Ryan. Executive staff 3, Other staff 2. Began 1982; interdenominational. No magazine. Turnover n/a. Arrangements of Christian songs and hymns for choral and instrumental groups. Catalogues/information packs available.
Email: jawmusic@aol.com
☎ 0114 263 3451 📠 0114 263 3499

Sovereign Music UK, PO Box 356, Leighton Buzzard LU7 8WP
Managing Director: Mr Robert Lamont. Executive staff 2, Other staff 1. Began 1981; interdenominational. No magazine. Turnover n/a. Representing Sovereign Lifestyle Music, Restoration Music, Radical UK Music, Christian Music Ministries.
Email: sovereignm@aol.com
☎ 01525 385 578 📠 01525 372 743

Spirit Enterprises, 161 Sumner Road, London SE15 6JL
Director: Ms Jennifer James. Part-time staff 2. Began 1991; interdenominational. (Previously Spirit). No magazine. Turnover n/a. Distributing Christian music and books.
Email: jjatspirit@aol.com
☎ 020 7277 4777 Mobile: 07930 640 407
📠 020 7703 6978

Spirit Music, 143 Leeson Drive, Ferndown BH22 9RE
Partner: Mr Rob Hillman. Executive staff 2, Other staff 2. Began 1995; non-denominational. No magazine. Turnover £100,000 to year end Dec 98. Record label; distributors of contemporary Christian music, cassettes, CDs, videos.
Email: spiritrhil@aol.com
☎ 01202 890 371 📠 01202 890 422

Talents Music Shop, 9 Brockley Rise, Forest Hill, London SE23 1JG
Senior Partner: Pastor Martin Powell. Full-time staff 3, Part-time staff 20. Began 1989; non-denominational. No magazine. Turnover £250,000 to year end Oct 98. Retailing musical instruments, computers, mobile phones; computer tuition; financial services.
Web: talents.co.uk
Email: sales@talents.co.uk & enquiries@talents.co.uk
☎ 020 8699 4216 📠 020 8699 9149

†Theatre Church, Seymour Road, Bolton BL1 8PU
Administrator: Rev Michael J Austin. Executive staff 1, Other staff 1. ***CC*** Began n/a; Methodist. Magazine: *FRETCH* (Circulation n/a quarterly). Turnover £60,000 to year end Aug 90. Christian performing arts centre with computerised data of performers nationwide.
☎ 01204 543 32

Triple "C", PO Box 199, Horley RH6 9YF
Director: Miss Terry-Anne Preston. Executive staff 1, Other staff 3. Began 1992; non-denominational. No magazine. Turnover n/a. Providing an administration service for Christian and arts organisations.
Email: terry-anne.preston@virgin.net
☎ 01293 824 840 Mobile: 07850 878 814 Fax 01293 824 840

***VM Music**, PO Box 51, East Grinstead RH19 3FQ
General Manager: Mr Geoff Tompkins. Executive staff 2, Admin staff 1. *CC* No.1046242. Began 1998; non-denominational. Turnover n/a. Design, production, marketing, distribution of Christian music in audio / video format. Predominantly that of Vinesong.
Web: www.vmmusic.com
Email: info@vmmusic.com
☎ 01342 410 696 Fax 01342 410 696

Viscount (Church) Organs Ltd, 5 Caxton Way, Watfor[d] WD1 8UA
Managing Director: Mr D A Cuttill. Executive staff 3. Bega[n] 1976; non-denominational. No magazine. Turnover £700,00[0] to year end Sept 98. Supplying 'pipeless'/digital, classicall[y] voiced organs to churches, and instruments for the organist' home.
☎ 01923 247 437 Fax 01923 249 345

Visiting Speakers, 20 Stratford House, Sackville Street, Southse[a] PO5 4BX
Leader: Rev Matt Troke. Executive staff 4. Began 1993; inter denominational. (Previously Him 'N' Us Ministries). No magazine. Turnover n/a. Disco, sound and lighting, Christia[n] engineers.
☎ 023 9273 0250 Mobile: 07958 362 741

NEWSPAPERS AND PERIODICALS

By Circulation and Frequency
Publications which did not supply circulation information are not listed here

Name	Circulation
Weekly	
The Universe	100,000
The War Cry	80,000
Kids Alive!	44,000
Church Times	38,000
Catholic Herald	36,000
Catholic Times	26,500
Methodist Recorder	25,000
Salvationist	23,000
The Tablet	19,500
Christian Herald	18,000
Scottish Catholic Observer	18,000
The Church of England Newspaper	11,000
Baptist Times	10,000
Church of Ireland Gazette	5,000
Fortnightly	
Messenger	9,000
The Briefing	1,500
Y Llan	800
Monthly	
Sign	100,000
Challenge	80,900
Life and Work	58,500
News Special	50,000
The Christian Democrat	45,000
UK Focus	26,000
Direction	22,000
The Christian Outlook	20,000
Welsh Church Life	20,000
The Presbyterian Herald	17,000
The Officer	12,000
Plus/Eagles Wings	12,000
Christianity	11,000
Evangelical Times	11,000
Christian Irishman	10,500
Renewal	10,000
Woman Alive	10,000
Evangelicals Now	7,000
Expository Times	6,000
Joy Magazine	6,000
The Scottish Episcopalian	6,000
The Banner of Truth	5,600
Cheering Words Magazine	5,000
The Little Acorn	5,000
Evangelism	4,000
Priests & People	3,500
Prophetic Witness	3,500
Briefing	3,200
Gospel Standard	2,600
The Instructor	2,300
European Christian Bookstore Journal	2,000
Needed Truth	2,000
The Good News	500
Eleven per year	
Reform	13,000
Grace Magazine	2,000
The Month	2,000
Ten per year	
Third Way	4,000
Nine per year	
Together with Children	3,200
Every two months	
New Life Newspaper	60,000
Prophecy Today	13,000
Church Building	7,500
Wholeness	6,000
Ethos	5,000
The Flame	5,000
The Reformer	5,000
The Upper Room	5,000
Youthwork	5,000
Wake Up!	4,500
Theology	4,200
Goodnews	4,000
Soul Survivor	4,000
Quadrant	3,500
Protestant Truth	3,000
The Ichthus File	2,300
The Evangelical Magazine of Wales	2,000
The Young Reformer	1,600
Gwyliedydd [= Sentinel]	1,000
Orthodox Outlook	1,000
Biblical Archaeology Review	275
Five per year	
Precious Seed Magazine	16,000
Quarterly	
Share It!	55,000
Focus	35,000
Nota Bene	30,000
Maintenance and Equipment News for Churches and Schools	21,500
All the World	18,000
EWCH	11,000
Sword and Trowel	6,500
Worship and Preaching	5,500
Compass Magazine	5,000
The Way	4,000
The Chesterton Review	3,000
Communio	3,000
Epworth Review	2,750
New Testament Studies	2,200
Children's Ministry	2,000
Scottish Journal of Theology	1,750
Transformation	1,400
Christian	1,300
Journal for the Study of the New Testament	1,300
Churchman (Journal of Anglican Theology)	1,000
Y Cylchgrawn Efengylaidd	1,000
Evangelical Quarterly	1,000
The Heythrop Journal	1,000
Review of Theological Literature	1,000
Anvil	850
Kategoria	850
Evangelical Review of Theology	800
British Reformed Journal	300
Christian History Magazine	300
Orthodox England	300
Areopagus	110
Every four months	
Alpha News	200,000
Human Concern	120,000
Look! Hear!	13,500
Country Way	4,000
Church Observer	3,500
The Overcomer	3,500
Ethics and Medicine	1,300
MORIB Update	700
Evangel	600
Feminist Theology	500
Anabaptism Today	300
Christian Correspondence Magazines	200
Half-yearly	
A Bookstalls Newsletter	4,000
Light and Salt	2,200
Science and Christian Belief	2,000
Journal of Theological Studies	1,300
Rutherford Journal of Church and Ministry	1,000
Scottish Bulletin of Evangelical Theology	800
Journal of Education and Christian Belief	600
Studies in Christian Ethics	600
European Journal of Theology	500
Journal of Feminist Studies in Religion	500
Journal of Pentecostal Theology	500
Journal for the Study of the Pseudepigrapha	400
Annually	
Reformed Theological Journal	450
Journal of the European Pentecostal Theological Association	350
Irregularly	
Partnership Publications	450
Symphony	350

NEWSPAPERS & PERIODICALS

All the World, Salvation Army, International Headquarters, 101 Queen Victoria Street, London EC4P 4EP
Editor: Mr Kevin Sims. Executive staff 1. ***CC*** No.2538134. Began 1884; Salvation Army.
Web: www.salvationarmy.org
Email: kevin_sims@salvationarmy.org
Email: allworld@salvationarmy.org
☎ 020 7332 8084 🖷 020 7236 4981

Alpha News, Holy Trinity Church, Brompton Road, London SW7 1JA
Editor: Mark Elsdon Dew. Executive staff 3. ***CC*** Began 1993; interdenominational. Multi-cultural.
Web: dspace.dial.pipex.com/htb.london
Email: htb.london@dial.pipex.com
☎ 020 7581 8255 🖷 020 7589 3390

Anabaptism Today, 14 Shepherds Hill, London N6 5AQ
Editor: Dr Stuart Murray. No full-time staff. ***CC*** No.1021760. Began 1992; non-denominational. Turnover n/a. Providing resources for individuals and churches interested in radical discipleship and Anabaptist history and perspectives.
Email: s.murray@spurgeons.ac.uk
☎ 020 8340 8775 🖷 020 8341 6807

Anvil, 172 Ellerton Road, Surbiton KT6 7UD
Editor: Rev Dr M Gilbertson. No full-time staff. ***CC*** No.1013659. Began 1984; Anglican.
Email: mrgl@netcomuk.co.uk
☎ 020 8399 3636

Areopagus, 101 May Tree Close, Badger Farm, Winchester SO22 4JF
Editor: Mr Julian Barritt. All voluntary staff. Began 1990; interdenominational. Quarterly Christian writers' magazine.
Web: www.churchnet.org.uk/areopagus/index.html
Email: jbarritt@areopagus.freeserve.co.uk
☎ No telephone

The Banner of Truth, The Grey House, 3 Murrayfield Road, Edinburgh EH12 6EL
Editor: Rev Maurice J Roberts. *General Manager:* Mr John Rawlinson. Executive staff 4, Other staff 10. ***CC*** No.235652. Began 1955; non-denominational.
Web: www.banneroftruth.co.uk
☎ 0131 337 7310 🖷 0131 346 7484

Baptist Times, 129 The Broadway, Didcot OX11 8XB
Managing Editor: Mr John Capon. Executive staff 5. Began 1855; owned by Baptist Union but non-denominational.
☎ 01235 517 670 🖷 01235 517 678

Biblical Archaeology Review, Paternoster Periodicals, PO Box 300, Carlisle CA3 0QS
Publisher: Mr Mark Finnie. Staff: See Paternoster Publishing. Began 1975; interdenominational.
www.paternoster-publishing.com
Email: info@paternoster-publishing.com
☎ 01228 512 512 🖷 01228 593 388
Editor: Hershel Shanks, Biblical Archaeology Society, 4710 41st Street NW, Washington DC 20016 USA
Email: basedit@clark.net
☎ 00 1 202 364 2636 🖷 00 1 202 364 3300

Biblicon, Sheffield Academic Press, Mansion House, 19 Kingfield Road, Sheffield S11 9AS
Editor: Alice Bach. Staff n/a. Began 1997; non-denominational.
Web: www.shef-ac-press.co.uk
Email: admin@sheffac.demon.co.uk
☎ 0114 255 4433 🖷 0114 255 4626

Black Theology in Britain, Sheffield Academic Press, Mansion House, 19 Kingfield Road, Sheffield S11 9AS
Editor: Rebecca Cullen. Began n/a; non-denominational.
Web: www.shef-ac-press.co.uk
Email: admin@sheffac.demon.co.uk
☎ 0114 255 4433 🖷 0114 255 4626

A Bookstalls Newsletter, 11 Thorpe Chase, Ripon HG4 1UA
Editor: Mr A Guy Taylor. No full-time staff. Began 1964; non-denominational.
☎ 01765 602 907 🖷 01765 602 907

Briefing, Catholic Media Office, 39 Eccleston Square, London SW1V 1BX
Editor: Rev Kieran Conry. Executive staff 3, Other staff 2. ***CC*** No.257239. Began 1974; Roman Catholic. Turnover n/a. Monthly information and documentation publication of Catholic church in England, Wales and Scotland.
Web: www.tasc.ac.uk/cc/
Email: cathmedia@easynet.co.uk
☎ 020 7828 8709 🖷 020 7931 7678

†***The Briefing**, PO Box 665, London SW20 8RU
UK Publisher: Mr Tim Thornborough. Executive staff 3. Began 1987; non-denominational.
Web: members.australis.net.ou/~xtnnet
Email: 100332.2225@compuserve.com
☎ 020 8947 5686 🖷 020 8944 7091

British Reformed Journal, Fairhaven, Chapel Lane, Walton-by-Kimcote, Lutterworth LE17 5RL
Editor: Mr Hugh Williams. No full-time staff. Began 1993; Presbyterian and Reformed. Propagation of Reformation Protestant faith according to Canons of Dort and Westminster Confession.
Email: hughw@netmatters.co.uk
☎ 01455 554 028

Carer & Counsellor, PO Box 2667, Eastbourne BN21 1RY
Editor: Richard Goodwin. *Publisher:* Catherine Butcher. No full-time staff. Began n/a; interdenominational. Previously published by CWR. Turnover n/a. Promoting meaningful change from a Biblical perspective for Christians involved in pastoral care or counselling.
Email: 113223.3212@compuserve.com
☎ 01323 647 195 🖷 01323 721 549

Catholic Herald, Herald House, Lambs Passage, Bunhill Row, London EC1Y 8TQ
Editor: Dr William Oddie. Executive staff 10, Other staff 24. Began 1885; Roman Catholic.
☎ 020 7588 3101 🖷 020 7256 9728

Catholic Times, St James Court, St James Buildings, Oxford Street, Manchester M1 6FP
Editor: Mr Kevin Flaherty. Executive staff 5. Began 1892; Roman Catholic.
☎ 0161 236 8856 🖷 0161 237 5590

Celebrate, Church of England Newspaper, 10 Little College Street, London SW1P 3SH
Editor: To be appointed. Staff: see Church of England Newspaper. Began 1998; Anglican.
☎ 020 7976 7760 Mobile: 07950 881 655 🖷 020 7976 0783

***Challenge**, PO Box 300, Kingstown Broadway, Carlisle CA3 0QS
Editor: Mr Donald Banks. ***CC*** No.270162. Began 1958; interdenominational.
Web: www.paternoster-publishing.com
Email: challenge@paternoster-publishing.com
☎ 01228 512 512 🖷 01228 593 388
Editorial office: 50 Lexwood Avenue, Worthing BN14 7RA
☎ 01903 824 174 🖷 01903 824 376

Cheering Words Magazine, 22 Victoria Road, Stamford PE9 1HB
Editor & Publisher: Mr D Oldham. Executive staff 1. Began 1851; non-denominational & Reformed. Turnover £11,500 to year end Dec 98. Short articles, topical, historical, poetry, youth page with questions: KJV basis throughout.
☎ 01780 763 780

The Chesterton Review, T & T Clark Ltd, 59 George Street, Edinburgh EH2 2LQ
Editor: Ian Boyd CSB. Staff n/a. Began 1974; non-denominational. Examining important themes in contemporary Christian ethics, with contributions from leading moral theologians.
Web: www.tandtclark.co.uk
Email: mailbox@tandtclark.co.uk
☎ 0131 225 4703 🖷 0131 220 4260

***Children's Ministry**, 26 Lottbridge Drove, Eastbourne BN23 6NT
Executive Editor: Mrs Sue Price. Began n/a; non-denominational. Re-launched 1998. Part of Kingway Communications. Turnover n/a.
Email: churchministries@kingsway.co.uk
☎ 01323 437 722 🖷 01323 411 970

M

Christian, 19 Harvey Road, Guildford GU1 3SE
Editor: Dr Emma Hebblethwaite. All voluntary staff. ***CC*** No.1016104. Began 1991; non-denominational.
Web: www.dcs.ed.ac.uk/~djs/christian/home.html
Email: chaplain@kings.cam.oct.uk
☎ 01223 327 723 🖷 01483 560 775/301 387

†**Christian Correspondence Magazines**, 2 Crombie Avenue, Northenden, Manchester M22 4AG
Editor: Miss Pauline Bower. No full-time staff. Began 1970; interdenominational.
☎ No telephone

†**The Christian Democrat**, PO Box 30, Liverpool L17 8SU
Editors: Mr Tony Lucas, Ms Alison Hull. Executive staff 3. Began 1990; non-denominational.
Email: editor@christian-democrat.co.uk
☎ 0151 727 2712 🖷 0151 728 7175

***Christian Herald**, Christian Media Centre, 96 Dominion Road, Worthing BN14 8JP
Editor: Mr Russ Bravo. *News Editor:* Mrs Karen Carter. *Features Editor:* Miss Jackie Stead. Staff – see Christian Media Centre. Began 1867; interdenominational. (Previously New Christian Herald).
Web: www.christianherald.org.uk
Email: news@christianherald.org.uk
Email: advertising@christianmedia.org.uk
☎ 01903 821 082 ISDN: 01903 537 308
🖷 01903 821 081(general) 537 321 (advertising)

Christian History Magazine, Paternoster Periodicals, PO Box 300, Carlisle CA3 0QS
Publisher: Mr Mark Finnie. See Paternoster Publishing. Began 1970; non-denominational.
Web: www.paternoster-publishing.com
Email: info@paternoster-publishing.com
☎ 01228 512 512 🖷 01228 593 388
Editor: Mark Galli, Christianity Today Inc, 465 Gundersen Drive, Carol Stream IL 60188, USA
Email: chedit@aol.com
☎ 00 1 630 260 6200 🖷 00 1 630 260 0114

†**Christian Irishman**, Irish Mission, Church House, Fisherwick Place, Belfast BT1 6DW
Editor: Rev David J Temple. Executive staff 1, Other staff 4. Began 1710; Presbyterian.
☎ 028 9032 2284 🖷 028 9024 8377

The Christian Outlook, 53 Broad Lane, Tottenham, London N15 4DJ
Editor: Mrs Marjorielyn R Campbell. Executive staff 2, Other staff 3. Began n/a; non-denominational. Turnover n/a. Evangelising non-Christian countries through print media which deliver the message of Jesus Christ.
Web: www.christian-outlook.co.uk
Email: christian.outlook@cableinet.co.uk
☎ 020 8376 7967 🖷 020 8376 7969

***Christianity**, PO Box 17911, London SW1E 5ZR
Editor: Gareth Sturdy. Other staff 4. Began 1996; interdenominational. (Previously Began as Buzz in 1969, subsequently 21 Century Christian and Alpha). Examining real life, real faith – in the real world.
Email: christianity@easynet.co.uk
☎ 020 7316 1450 🖷 020 7316 1453

Christianity and Society, PO Box 2, Taunton TA1 4ZD
Editor: Stephen C Perks. No full-time staff. Began 1990; non-denominational. Applying Christian principles to contemporary society.
Web: www.kuyper.org
Email: c&s@kuyper.org
☎ 01823 665 909 🖷 01823 665 721

Church Building, 1st Floor, St James's Buildings, Oxford Street, Manchester M1 6FP
Editor: Mr Nigel Melhuish. Executive staff 1. Began 1984; non-denominational.
☎ 0161 236 8856 🖷 0161 236 8530

†**Church Observer**, Church Union, Faith House, 7 Tufton Street, London SW1P 3QN
Editor: Mr Geoffrey Wright. No full-time staff. Began 1879; Anglican.
☎ 020 7222 6952 🖷 020 7976 7180

The Church of England Newspaper, 10 Little College Street, London SW1P 3SH
Editor: Mr Colin Blakely. *Advertisement Manager:* Mr Christopher Turner. Other staff 5. Began 1828; Anglican. Incorporating Celebrate.
Web: www.churchnewspaper.com
Email: colin.blakely@parlicom.com
☎ 020 7976 7760 Mobile: 07950 881 655 🖷 020 7976 0783

Church of Ireland Gazette, 36 Bachelor's Walk, Lisburn BT28 1XN
Editor: Rev Canon Cecil W M Cooper. Part-time staff 3. Began 1856; Church of Ireland. Turnover n/a.
Email: coigaz@iol.ie
☎ 028 9267 5743 🖷 028 9267 5743

For additional information see List on Page 310

Church Times, 33 Upper Street, London N1 0PN
Editor: Mr Paul Handley. *Assistant Editor:* Mr Glyn Paflin. *Advertisement Manager:* Mr Stephen Dutton. Executive staff 3, Other staff 15. Began 1863; Anglican. Turnover £1,500,000 to year end Dec 98.
Web: www.churchtimes.co.uk
Email: editor@churchtimes.co.uk
☎ 020 7359 4570 Fax 020 7226 3051/3073

Churchman (Journal of Anglican Theology), Church Society, Dean Wace House, 16 Rosslyn Road, Watford WD1 7EY
Editor: Rev Prof Gerald L Bray. No full-time staff. Began 1878; Anglican. Extensive book reviews.
Web: www.churchsociety.org
Email: churchman@churchsociety.org
☎ 01923 235 111 Fax 01923 800 362

Communio, T & T Clark Ltd, 59 George Street, Edinburgh EH2 2LQ
Editor: Mr David L Schindler. Staff n/a. Began 1972; Roman Catholic. International Catholic journal centred on the theological renewal in 'creative fidelity' to the Church.
Web: www.tandtclark.co.uk
Email: mailbox@tandtclark.co.uk
☎ 0131 225 4703 Fax 0131 220 4260

Compass Magazine, Waverley Abbey House, Waverley Lane, Farnham GU9 8EP
Editor: Mr Gerald Coates. Executive staff 3. *CC* No.327160. Began 1982; New Church. (Previously Pioneer Magazine & Compass Journal). Included in Pioneer Trust.
Web: ds.dial.pipex.com/pioneer_trust
Email: pioneer_trust@dial.pipex.com
☎ 01252 784 733 Fax 01252 784 732

Country Way, Arthur Rank Centre, National Agricultural Centre, Stoneleigh Park, Kenilworth CV8 2LZ
Editor: Mr Jeremy Martineau. No paid staff. *CC* No.209961. Began 1992; ecumenical.
Web: www.rurnet.org.uk/~country_way/
☎ 024 7669 6460 Fax 024 7669 6460

Y Cylchgrawn Efengylaidd, Evangelical Movement of Wales, Bryntirion, Bridgend CF31 4DX
Editor: Robert Rhys. Other staff 2. *CC* No.222407. Began 1948; non-denominational.
☎ 01656 655 886 Fax 01656 656 095

***Direction**, Oasis Centre, Oxton Road, Wallasey, Wirral CH44 4EU
Editor: Rev Derek J Green. *Advertising Manager:* Mr David Evans. Executive staff 1, Other staff 3. *CC* No.251549. Began 1989; Pentecostal.
Web: www.directionmagazine.com
Email: info@directionmagazine.com
☎ 0151 691 2134 Fax 0151 691 2153

Ecotheology, Sheffield Academic Press, Mansion House, 19 Kingfield Road, Sheffield S11 9AS
Editor: Mary Grey. Staff n/a. Began 1978; non-denominational. (Previously Theology in Green). Relaunched 1996.
Web: www.shef-ac-press.co.uk
Email: admin@sheffac.demon.co.uk
☎ 0114 255 4433 Fax 0114 255 4626

English Churchman & St James's Chronicle, 22 Fitch Drive, Brighton BN2 4HX
Hon Editor: Dr Napier Malcolm. Other staff 1. *CC* No.249957. Began 1843; Anglican.
Email: nama@kpws.demon.co.uk
☎ 01273 818 555

Epworth Review, 20 Ivatt Way, Peterborough PE3 7PG
Editor: Dr Richard G Jones. No full-time staff. Began 1973; Methodist.
☎ 01733 332 202 Fax 01733 331 201

Ethics and Medicine, Paternoster Periodicals, PO Box 300, Carlisle CA3 0QS
Publisher: Mr Mark Finnie. Staff: See Paternoster Publishing. Began 1983; interdenominational.
Web: www.paternoster-publishing.com
Email: info@paternoster-publishing.com
☎ 01228 512 512 Fax 01228 593 388
Editor: C Ben Mitchell, Southern Baptist Theological Seminary, 2825 Lexington Road, Louisville KY 40280, USA
Email: c.benmitchell.76041.2412@compuserve.com
☎ 00 1 502 897 4011 Fax 00 1 501 897 4056

Ethos, Ethos Communications Ltd, 13 Norton Folgate, London E1 6DB
Managing Director: Mr Kamal Bengougam. Admin staff 2, Other staff 1. Began 1996; interdenominational.
Web: www.ethosmag.com
Email: ethos@ethosmag.com
☎ 0870 902 5400 Fax 0870 901 5330

For additional information see List on Page 310

European Christian Bookstore Journal (ECBJ), Grampian House, 144 Deansgate, Manchester M3 3ED
Editor: Mr Barry Holmes. Executive staff 1, Other staff 4. Began 1984; interdenominational.
Email: cba.europe@btinternet.com
☎ 0161 833 3003 🖷 0161 835 3000

European Journal of Theology, Paternoster Periodicals, PO Box 300, Carlisle CA3 0QS
Publisher: Mr Mark Finnie. Staff: See Paternoster Publishing. Began 1992; interdenominational.
Web: www.paternoster-publishing.com
Email: info@paternoster-publishing.com
☎ 01228 512 512 🖷 01228 593 388
Editor: J Gordon McConville, Cheltenham & Gloucester College of Higher Education, PO Box 220, Park Campus, Cheltenham GL50 2QF
Email: gmcconville@chelt.ac.uk
☎ 01242 543 483 🖷 01242 532 725

Evangel, Paternoster Periodicals, PO Box 300, Carlisle CA3 0QS
Publisher: Mr Mark Finnie. Staff: See Paternoster Publishing. Began 1982; interdenominational.
Web: www.paternoster-publishing.com
Email: info@paternoster-publishing.com
☎ 01228 512 512 🖷 01228 593 388
Editor: Stephen Dray, Moorlands College, Sopley, Christchurch BH23 7AT
Email: moorlands.college@cin.co.uk
☎ 01425 672 369 🖷 01425 674 162

The Evangelical Magazine of Wales, Evangelical Movement of Wales, Bryntirion, Bridgend CF31 4DX
Chairman of Editorial Board: Rev Stephen Clark. Other staff 1. ***CC*** No.222407. Began 1955; non-denominational.
☎ 01656 655 886 🖷 01656 656 095

M

Evangelical Quarterly, Paternoster Periodicals, PO Box 300, Carlisle CA3 0QS
Publisher: Mr Mark Finnie. Staff: See Paternoster Publishing. Began 1929; interdenominational.
Web: www.paternoster-publishing.com
Email: info@paternoster-publishing.com
☎ 01228 512 512 🖷 01228 593 388
Editor: I Howard Marshall, King's College, Old Aberdeen, Aberdeen AB1 2UB
Email: i.h.marshall@abdnk.ac.uk
☎ 01224 272 388 🖷 01224 273 730

Evangelical Review of Theology, Paternoster Periodicals, PO Box 300, Carlisle CA3 0QS
Publisher: Mr Mark Finnie. Staff: See Paternoster Publishing. Began 1977; interdenominational.
Web: www.paternoster-publishing.com
Email: info@paternoster-publishing.com
☎ 01228 512 512 🖷 01228 593 388
Editor: Bruce J Nicholls, 73 Kohimarama Road, Auckland 1050 New Zealand
Email: k.nicholl@codeworks.gen.nz
☎ 00 64 9 528 6845 🖷 00 64 9 528 6845

Evangelical Times Ltd, Faverdale North Industrial Estate, Darlington DL3 0PH
Business Manager: Mr J H Rubens. *Editor:* Prof E H Andrews. Staff n/a. ***CC*** No.258927. Began 1967; non-denominational. Turnover £125,000.
Web: www.evangelical-times.org
Email: theeditors@evangelical-times.org
☎ 01325 380 232 🖷 01325 466 153

Evangelicals Now, 14 Silverleigh Road, Thornton Heat CR7 6DU
Managing Editor: Dr John E Benton. Executive staff 1, Othe staff 4. ***CC*** No.296794. Began 1986; non-denominational.
Web: www.e-n.org.uk
Email: editor@e-n.org.uk
☎ 020 8689 6252 🖷 020 8665 0994

***Evangelism**, PO Box 1363, Bristol BS99 3DZ
Proprietor: Mr Bill Spencer. Executive staff 2, Other staff 1 Began 1972; non-denominational. (Previously Evangelism Today).
Email: bill.spencer@virgin.net
☎ 0117 904 0548 🖷 0117 904 0548

EWCH, Hafod Lon, 51 Heath Park Avenue, Cardiff CF4 3RF
Editor: Rev Aled Edwards. Executive staff 1. Began 1975 interdenominational. Turnover £1,000 to year end Dec 98 Welsh language mission magazine.
Web: www.users.globalnet.co.uk~aled
Email: aled@globalnet.co.uk
☎ 029 2075 1418

Expository Times, T & T Clark Ltd, 59 George Street, Edinburgh EH2 2LQ
Editor: Rev Dr Cyril S Rodd. Staff n/a. Began 1889; non-denominational. Articles, sermons and book reviews for ministers, scholars and theological students.
Web: www.tandtclark.co.uk
Email: mailbox@tandtclark.co.uk
☎ 0131 225 4703 🖷 0131 220 4260
Editorial address: 61 Warblington Road, Emsworth PO10 7HG
☎ 01243 372 066

Feminist Theology, Sheffield Academic Press, Mansion House, 19 Kingfield Road, Sheffield S11 9AS
Co-editor: Ms Lisa Isherwood. Editors 5. Began 1992; non-denominational.
Web: www.shef-ac-press.co.uk
Email: admin@sheffac.demon.co.uk
☎ 0114 255 4433 🖷 0114 255 4626

The Flame, 14 Milton Road, Weston-super-Mare BS23 2SB
Editor: Major Norman Armistead. Executive staff 3. ***CC*** No.279983. Began 1935; Independent. Turnover n/a.
☎ 01934 636 880

Focus, The Stanborough Press Ltd, Alma Park, Grantham NG31 9SL
Editor: Dr David Marshall. Executive staff 6, Other staff 38. ***CC*** Began 1884; Seventh-Day Adventist.
☎ 01476 591 700 🖷 01476 771 44

The Good News, 63 Durham Street, Hull HU8 8RF
Publisher / Editor: Mr Howard Dobson. No full-time staff. Began 1994; interdenominational. Turnover £500 to year end Dec 98. For Hull and East Yorkshire.
Email: hdobson@jireh.co.uk
☎ 01482 328 280 🖷 01482 328 280

Goodnews, Allen Hall, 28 Beaufort Street, London SW3 5AA
Editor: Miss Kristina Cooper. Other staff 1. ***CC*** No.277425. Began 1979; Roman Catholic/Charismatic. Information, teaching and testimonies about charismatic renewal in the Roman Catholic church.
☎ 020 7352 5298 🖷 020 7351 4486

For additional information see List on Page 310

The Gospel Magazine, Holme Regis, Old School Lane, Stanford, Biggleswade SG18 9JL
Hon Secretary: Mr Peter King. No full-time staff. Began 1766; non-denominational.
Email: gosmag@aol.com
☎ 01462 811 204
Editor: Rev Maurice Handford, 9 Birtlespool Road, Cheadle Hulme, Cheadle SK8 5JZ
☎ 0161 485 3134

Gospel Standard, 12b Roundwood Lane, Harpenden AL5 3DD
Editor: Mr B A Ramsbottom. Executive staff 1, Other staff 1. *CC* No.209373. Began 1835; Strict Baptist.
☎ 01582 765 448 Fax 01582 469 148

Grace Magazine, 72 Crewys Road, London NW2 2AD
Editor: Gary Brady. All voluntary staff. *CC* No.277106. Began 1970; but 1833 as the Gospel Herald; Grace Baptist.
Email: 113051.3017@compuserve.com
☎ 020 8455 2275

Gwyliedydd [= Sentinel], Brion Wylfa, Llanwnda, Caernarfon LL54 5TL
Editor: Mr Aled Morgan. No full-time staff. Began 1809; Methodist.
☎ 01766 831 104

The Heythrop Journal, Heythrop College, Kensington Square, London W8 5HQ
Editor: Rev Dr Thomas J Deidun. No full-time staff. Began 1960; ecumenical.
☎ 020 7795 6600 (Editorial) Fax 020 7795 4200
Publishing: Blackwell Publishers, 108 Cowley Road, Oxford OX4 1JF
☎ 01865 791 100

Home Words, G. J. Palmer & Sons Ltd, St Mary's Works, St Mary's Plain, Norwich NR3 3BH
Editor: Rev John King. *Administrator:* Mr Clive Edwards. Other staff 3. Began 1871; Anglican.
☎ 01603 615 995
Subscriptions Office: G. J. Palmer & Sons Ltd, 16 Blyburgate, Beccles NR34 9TB
☎ 01502 711 231

*__Human Concern__, Society for the Protection of Unborn Children (SPUC), Phyllis Bowman House, 5 St Matthew Street, Westminster, London SW1P 2JT
Editor: Ms Phyllis Bowman. Executive staff 10, Other staff 30. Began 1967; non-denominational. Turnover £1,250,000 to year end Feb 96.
Web: www.spuc.org.uk
Email: sysop@spuc.org.uk
☎ 020 7222 5845 Fax 020 7222 0630

*__The Ichthus File__, PO Box 605, London SW20 8RL
Editor: Mr Al Horn. Executive staff 2, Other staff 1. Began 1995; non-denominational. Turnover £50,000 to year end May 96. Daily Bible Reading resource for young people.
☎ 020 8942 0880 Fax 020 8944 0990

The Instructor, Free Church Manse, Kilberry Road, Tarbert PA29 6XX
Editor: Mrs Irene Howat. No other staff. *CC* No.SCO 12925. Began 1904; Free Church of Scotland. Turnover £587 to year end Dec 98. For primary school aged children.
Email: ihowat@aol.com
☎ 01880 820 134 Fax 01880 820 134

Journal for the Study of the New Testament, Sheffield Academic Press, Mansion House, 19 Kingfield Road, Sheffield S11 9AS
Editor: Stephen Moore. Began 1978; non-denominational.
Web: www.shef-ac-press.co.uk
Email: admin@sheffac.demon.co.uk
☎ 0114 255 4433 Fax 0114 255 4626

Journal for the Study of the Old Testament, Sheffield Academic Press, Mansion House, 19 Kingfield Road, Sheffield S11 9AS
Editors: Prof David J A Clines, Dr Philip R Davies. Began 1976; non-denominational.
Web: www.shef-ac-press.co.uk
Email: admin@sheffac.demon.co.uk
☎ 0114 255 4433 Fax 0114 255 4626

Journal for the Study of the Pseudepigrapha, Sheffield Academic Press, Mansion House, 19 Kingfield Road, Sheffield S11 9AS
Editors: Mr James H Charlesworth, Mr James R Mueller. Executive staff 3. Began 1987; non-denominational.
Web: www.shef-ac-press.co.uk
Email: admin@sheffac.demon.co.uk
☎ 0114 255 4433 Fax 0114 255 4626

Journal of Education and Christian Belief, Paternoster Publishing, PO Box 300, Carlisle CA3 0QS
Publisher: Mr Mark Finnie. Staff: See Paternoster Publishing. Began 1968; interdenominational. (Previously Spectrum).
Web: www.paternoster-publishing.com
Email: info@paternoster-publishing.com
☎ 01228 512 512 Fax 01228 593 388
Editor: John Shortt, Stapleford House Education Centre, Stapleford, Nottingham NG9 8DP
Email: actuk@hway.net
☎ 0115 939 4671 Fax 0115 939 2076

Journal of Feminist Studies in Religion, T & T Clark Ltd, 59 George Street, Edinburgh EH2 2LQ
Editors: Dr Elisabeth Schüssler Fiorenza, Emilie Townes. Staff n/a. Began 1985; n/a. Papers on the academic study of religion from a feminist perspective.
Web: www.tandtclark.co.uk
Email: mailbox@tandtclark.co.uk
☎ 0131 225 4703 Fax 0131 220 4260

Journal of Pentecostal Theology, Sheffield Academic Press, Mansion House, 19 Kingfield Road, Sheffield S11 9AS
Co-editor: Mr Rickie D Moore. Editors 3. Began 1992; Pentecostal.
Web: www.shef-ac-press.co.uk
Email: admin@sheffac.demon.co.uk
☎ 0114 255 4433 Fax 0114 255 4626

Journal of Theological Studies, Oxford University Press, Walton Street, Oxford OX2 6DP
Editors: Dr G Gould, Prof M Hooker. No full-time staff. Began 1899; non-denominational.
☎ 01865 556 767 Fax 01865 556 646

Journal of the European Pentecostal Theological Association, Regents Theological College, London Road, Nantwich CW5 6LW
Editor: Rev Dr Keith Warrington. No other staff. Began 1983; Pentecostal. (Previously Epta Bulletin). Journal with special reference to pentecostal and charismatic issues, though not exclusively.
Email: admin@regentstc.freeserve.co.uk
☎ 01270 610 800 Fax 01270 610 013

M

For additional information see List on Page 310

Joy Magazine, PO Box 277, Sunderland SR1 1YE
Editor: Mr Peter Wreford. Executive staff 3, Other staff 7. ***CC*** Began 1994; Assemblies of God. (Previously Redemption). Turnover n/a.
Email: editor.newlife@ukonline.co.uk
☎ 0191 568 0424 🖷 0191 568 0428

Kategoria, PO Box 665, London SW20 8RU
Editor: Dr Kirsten Birkett. Staff n/a. Began 1996; non-denominational.
Email: massmedia@compuserve.com
☎ 020 8942 0880 🖷 020 8942 0990

Kids Alive!, Salvation Army, UK Territorial Headquarters, 101 Newington Causeway, London SE1 6BN
Editor: Capt Ken Nesbitt. Executive staff 1, Other staff 2. Began 1879; Salvation Army. (Previously YS).
Web: www.salvationarmy.org.uk
Email: kidsalive@salvationarmy.org.uk
☎ 020 7367 4500 🖷 020 7367 4710

Life and Work, 121 George Street, Edinburgh EH2 4YN
Editor: Dr Robin Hill. Executive staff 3, Other staff 2. ***CC*** Began 1879; Church of Scotland.
Email: lifework@dial.pipex.com
☎ 0131 225 5722 🖷 0131 220 3113

Light and Salt, Paternoster Periodicals, PO Box 300, Carlisle CA3 0QS
Publisher: Mr Mark Finnie. Staff: See Paternoster Publishing. Began 1989; interdenominational.
Web: www.paternoster-publishing.com
Email: info@paternoster-publishing.com
☎ 01228 512 512 🖷 01228 593 388
Editors: Nigel Cameron, Kathleen Douthwaite, Care Trust, 53 Romney Street, London SW1P 3RF
Email: enquires@care.org.uk
☎ 020 7233 0455 🖷 020 7233 0983

The Little Acorn, 73 Carlisle Road, Londonderry BT48 6JL
Editor: Mr Kevin Lynch. No other staff. Began 1997; interdenominational. Turnover n/a. Keeping churches in touch with churches and society in touch with God.
Email: tla.mag@breathe.co.uk
☎ 028 7126 1812 🖷 028 7126 1887

Y Llan, 12 Neville Place, Glanyrafon, Cardiff CF1 8EP
Editor: Mr Tim Sanders. Executive staff 1. Began 1881; Church in Wales.
☎ 029 2066 7344 🖷 029 2066 7344
Editor: Education and Communications Centre, Woodland Place, Penarth CF6 2EX
☎ 029 2070 8234

Look! Hear!, c/o 147 Baldwins Lane, Croxley Green, Rickmansworth WD3 3LL
Editor: Mrs R Peedle. No full-time staff. Began 1988; interdenominational.
☎ No telephone

Maintenance and Equipment News for Churches and Schools, PO Box 249, Ascot SL5 0BZ
Editorial: Mrs Christine Stevens. Executive staff 1. Began 1959; non-denominational.
☎ 01344 459 528 🖷 01344 862 569

Maria, Sheffield Academic Press, Mansion House, 19 Kingfield Road, Sheffield S11 9AS
Editors: Sarah Jane Boss, Simon Coleman, Philip Endean, Christopher Maunder. Began 1999; non-denominational. Turnover n/a. Marian studies.
Email: admin@sheffac.demon.co.uk
☎ 0114 255 4433 🖷 0114 255 4626

Messenger, The Stanborough Press Ltd, Alma Park, Grantham NG31 9SL
Editor: Dr David Marshall. Executive staff 6, Other staff 38. ***CC*** No.235245. Began 1884; Seventh-Day Adventist.
☎ 01476 591 700 🖷 01476 771 44

Methodist Recorder, 122 Golden Lane, London EC1Y 0TL
Editor: Ms M Sleight. *General Manager:* Mr B A Slater. *Advertisement Manager:* Mr A Leisinger. Executive staff 2, Other staff 17. Began 1861; Methodist. Turnover £785,000 to year end Dec 98.
Web: www.methodistrecorder.co.uk
Email: editorial@methodistrecorder.co.uk & ads@methodistrecorder.co.uk
☎ 020 7251 8414
🖷 020 7608 3490 🖷 020 7251 8600 (advertising)

The Month, 114 Mount Street, London W1Y 6AH
Editor: Rev Tim Noble. Other staff 1. ***CC*** Began 1864; Roman Catholic [Jesuit].
Email: themonth@dial.pipex.com
☎ 020 7491 7596

MORIB Update, 18 Taylor's Lane, Lindford, Bordon GU35 0SW
Editor: Rev John Hartley. *Secretary:* Mrs Carol Snipe. No full-time staff. Began 1987; Anglican.
☎ 01420 477 508

Needed Truth, Hayes Press, Essex Road, Leicester LE4 9EE
Editor: Mr David Hyland. Executive staff 1, Other staff 5. ***CC*** No.242257. Began 1888; non-denominational.
Email: hayespress@btinternet.com
☎ 0116 2740 204 🖷 0116 274 0200

New Life Newspaper, PO Box 277, Sunderland SR1 1YE
Editor: Mr Peter Wreford. Executive staff 3, Other staff 7. Began 1982; non-denominational. Turnover n/a.
Email: editor.newlife@ukonline.co.uk
☎ 0191 568 0424 🖷 0191 568 0428

New Testament Studies, Theology Faculty Centre, 41 St Giles, Oxford OX1 3LW
Editor: Dr C M Tuckett. No full-time staff. Began 1947; interdenominational.
Email: christopher.tuckett@theology.oxford.ac.uk
☎ 01865 270 791 🖷 01865 270 795
Publishing: Cambridge University Press, The Edinburgh Building, Shaftesbury Road, Cambridge CB2 2RU
☎ 01223 312 393

News Extra, Appleford House, Appleford, Abingdon OX14 4PB
Editor: Mr Gervase Duffield. No other full-time staff. Began 1965; evangelical. Church Magazine Insert.
☎ 01235 848 319

***News Special**, PO Box 300, Kingstown Broadway, Carlisle CA3 0QS
Editor: Mr Donald Banks. ***CC*** No.270162. Began 1968; interdenominational. Outreach newspaper.
Web: www.paternoster-publishing.com
Email: newsspecial@paternoster-publishing.com
☎ 01228 512 512 🖷 01228 593 388

M

For additional information see List on Page 310

'ews Today, Appleford House, Appleford, Abingdon OX14 4PB
Editor: Mr Gervase Duffield. No other full-time staff. Began 1980; evangelical. Church magazine insert.
☎ 01235 848 319

'ota Bene (European Theological Media), Paternoster Periodicals, PO Box 300, Carlisle CA3 0QS
Publisher: Mr Mark Finnie. Staff: See Paternoster Publishing. *CC* No.270162. Began n/a; interdenominational.
Web: www.paternoster-publishing.com
Email: info@paternoster-publishing.com
☎ 01228 512 512 Fax 01228 593 388

'he Officer, The Salvation Army, International Headquarters, 101 Queen Victoria Street, London EC4P 4EP
Editor: Major Peter Farthing. Executive staff 1. Began 1893; Salvation Army.
Web: www.salvationarmy.org.uk
Email: officer@salvationarmy.org
☎ 020 7236 5222 Ext 2279 Fax 020 7329 3268

)rthodox England, Seekings House, 12 Garfield House, Felixstowe IP11 7PU
Editor: Father Andrew Phillips. No other staff. Began 1997; Orthodox. Turnover £2,500 to year end Aug 98. Distributing Orthodox Christian reading, both English and traditional.
☎ No phone

)rthodox Outlook, 42 Withen's Lane, Wallasey CH45 7NN
Editor: Father Pancratios Sanders. Executive staff 3. Began 1986; Orthodox. News, theology and teaching of the Orthodox Church worldwide.
Email: pancratios.outlook@mcmail.com
☎ 0151 639 6509 Mobile: 07850 467 675 Fax 0151 200 6359

The Overcomer, 10 Bydemill Gardens, Highworth, Swindon SN6 7BS
Editor: Michael C Metcalfe. No other staff. *CC* Began 1909; interdenominational.
Email: 106345.3433@compuserve.com
☎ 01793 763 141

Partnership Publications, Paternoster Periodicals, PO Box 300, Carlisle CA3 0QS
Publisher: Mr Mark Finnie. Staff: See Paternoster Publishing. Began 1964; interdenominational.
Web: www.paternoster-publishing.com
Email: info@paternoster-publishing.com
☎ 01228 512 512 Fax 01228 593 388
Editor: Harold Rowden, 45b Haglane Copse, Pennington, Lymington SO4 8DR
☎ 01590 676 407

Playleader, 125 Finchfield Lane, Wolverhampton WV3 8EY
Editor: Mrs Diana Turner. All voluntary staff. Began 1985; interdenominational. Turnover Non-profit making. For Christians involved with pre-school children.
☎ 01902 763 108

***Plus/Eagles Wings**, CPO, Garcia Estate, Canterbury Road, Worthing BN13 1BW
Editor: Mr Donald Banks. *CC* No.267737. Began 1972; interdenominational. Comic for children aged 5 to 12.
Email: Plus@cpo.uk.com
☎ 01903 824 174 ISDN: 01903 830 005 Fax 01903 824 376

Political Theology, Sheffield Academic Press, Mansion House, 19 Kingfield Road, Sheffield S11 9AS
Editors: Graeme Smith, Alison Webster. Began 1999; non-denominational. Turnover n/a.
Email: admin@sheffac.demon.co.uk
☎ 0114 255 4433 Fax 0144 255 4626

Precious Seed Magazine, 5 Turnham Green, Penylan, Cardiff CF23 9DL
Treasurer: Mr Michael Jones. No full-time staff. *CC* No.326157. Began 1945; n/a.
☎ 029 2049 2346

The Presbyterian Herald, Church House, Fisherwick Place, Belfast BT1 6DW
Editor: Rev Arthur Clarke. Executive staff 4. *CC* Began 1943; Presbyterian Church in Ireland.
Web: www.presbyterianireland.org
Email: herald@presbyterianireland.org
☎ 028 9032 2284 Fax 028 9024 8377

Priests & People, Blackfriars, 64 St Giles, Oxford OX1 3LY
Editor: Rev David Sanders. Executive staff 2. Began 1931; Roman Catholic. Journal of pastoral theology for clergy and laity, especially those active in parish and school.
Web: www.thetablet.co.uk/p&p.htm
☎ 01865 514 845 Fax 01865 515 119

Prophecy Today, The Park, Moggerhanger, Bedford MK44 3RW
Managing Editor: To be appointed. *Design/Layout:* Mr Andrew Lewis. Executive staff 1, Other staff 3. *CC* No.326533. Began 1984; interdenominational. Turnover £120,000 to year end Dec 98. Seeking to apply biblical insights to contemporary issues.
Web: www.the-park.u-net.com
Email: pwm@the-park.u-net.com
☎ 01767 641 400 Fax 01767 641 515

Prophetic Witness, Prophetic Witness Movement International, PO Box 109, Leyland, Preston PR5 3GL
Editor: Rev Glyn Taylor. *Director of Ministries:* Rev Alex Passmore. *CC* No.228941. Began 1917; interdenominational. (Previously Your Tomorrow). Proclaiming Christ's return through preaching, regular branch meetings and literature, emphasising evangelism and godly living.
Web: www.pwmi.org
Email: 100067.1226@compuserve.com
☎ 01772 452 846

Protestant Truth, 184 Fleet Street, London EC4A 2HJ
Editor: Rev Samuel R McKay. No full-time staff. *CC* No.248505. Began 1846; interdenominational. (Previously The Churchman's Magazine). Furtherance of Christ's gospel and the promotion of the Protestant Reformed religion and faith.
☎ Subscriptions: 020 8405 4960
Editorial: 104 Hendon Lane, London N3 3SH
☎ No telephone

Quadrant, Christian Research, Vision Building, Footscray Road, Eltham, London SE9 2TZ
Joint Editors: Dr Peter Brierley, Miss Heather Wraight. Executive staff 2, Other staff 4. *CC* No.1017701. Began 1993; interdenominational. (Previously LandMARC). Turnover included in Christian Research.
Web: www.christian-research.org.uk
Email: admin@christian-research.org.uk
☎ 020 8294 1989 Fax 020 8294 0014

Reform, 86 Tavistock Place, London WC1H 9RT
Editor: Rev David Lawrence. Executive staff 1, Other staff 1. Began 1972; United Reformed.
Web: www.urc.org.uk
Email: reform@urc.org.uk
☎ 020 7916 8630(Direct)/7916 2020 Fax 020 7916 2021

M

Reformation and Renaissance Review, Sheffield Academic Press, 19 Kingfield Road, Sheffield S11 9AS
Editor: Paul Ayris. Began 1999; non-denominational. Turnover n/a. Journal of the Society of Reformation Studies.
Email: admin@sheffac.demon.uk
☎ 0114 255 4433 🖷 0114 255 4626

Reformed Theological Journal, 98 Lisburn Road, Belfast BT9 6AG
Joint Editors: Prof Edward Donnelly, Rev C Knox Hyndman, Prof F S Leahy. No full-time staff. Began 1985; Reformed Presbyterian Church of Ireland.
☎ 028 9066 0689

The Reformer, 77 Ampthill Road, Flitwick, Bedford MK45 1BD
General Secretary & Editor: Dr S J Scott-Pearson. Executive staff 2, Other staff 3. ***CC*** Began 1845; interdenominational.
Email: sscottpear@aol.com
☎ 01525 712 348 🖷 01525 712 348

Renewal, Monarch Magazines Ltd, Broadway House, The Broadway, Crowborough TN6 1HQ
Editor: Catherine Butcher. *Executive Editor:* Mr Dave Roberts. Executive staff 2, Other staff 5. Began 1966; interdenominational. Charismatic and evangelical.
Email: monarch@dial.pipex.com
☎ 01892 652 364 🖷 01892 663 329

Review of Theological Literature, T & T Clark Ltd, 59 George Street, Edinburgh EH2 2LQ
Editor: Alexander J M Wedderburn. Staff n/a. Began 1999; non-denominational. English translation of full reviews in theology, biblical studies and religious studies from "Theologische Literaturzeitung".
Web: www.tandtclark.co.uk
Email: mailbox@tandtclark.co.uk
☎ 0131 225 4703 🖷 0131 220 4260

M

Rutherford Journal of Church and Ministry, 17 Claremont Park, Edinburgh EH6 7PJ
Editor: Rev David Searle. Staff n/a. ***CC*** No.SCO 15111. Began 1994; interdenominational.
Web: www.rutherfordhouse.org.uk
Email: searled@rutherfordhouse.org.uk
☎ 0131 554 1206 🖷 0131 555 1002

Salvationist, UK Territorial Headquarters, 101 Newington Causeway, London SE1 6BN
Editor: Capt Charles King. Executive staff 2, Other staff 6. Began n/a; Salvation Army.
Web: www.salvationarmy.org.uk/website/ukpages/salvonli.html
Email: salvationist@salvationarmy.org.uk
☎ 020 7367 4500 🖷 020 7367 4710

Science and Christian Belief, Paternoster Periodicals, PO Box 300, Carlisle CA3 0QS
Publisher: Mr Mark Finnie. Staff: See Paternoster Publishing. Began 1989; interdenominational.
Web: www.paternoster-publishing.com
Email: info@paternoster-publishing.com
☎ 01228 512 512 🖷 01228 593 388
Editor: Denis Alexander, 77 Beaumont Road, Cambridge CB1 4PX
Email: denis.alexander@bbcsrc.ac.uk
☎ 01223 246 696 🖷 01223 246 696

Scottish Bulletin of Evangelical Theology, 17 Claremont Park, Edinburgh EH6 7PJ
Editor: Dr Ken Roxburgh. Staff n/a. Began 1983; interdenominational.
☎ 0131 554 1206 🖷 0131 555 1002

Scottish Catholic Observer, 19 Waterloo Street, Glasgow G2 6B
Editor: Mr E Barnes. Executive staff 1, Other staff 14. Bega 1885; Roman Catholic.
Email: 113061.2520@compuserve.com
☎ 0141 221 4956 🖷 0141 221 4956

†**The Scottish Episcopalian**, 21 Grosvenor Crescent, Edinburg EH12 5EE
Editor: Mrs Nan Macfarlane. No full-time staff. Began n/ Scottish Episcopal.
☎ 0131 225 6357 🖷 0131 346 7247

Scottish Journal of Theology, T & T Clark Ltd, 59 George Stree Edinburgh EH2 2LQ
Editor: Dr I Torrance. Staff n/a. Began 1948; interdenom inational. Historical and systematic theology, including article on biblical and applied theology.
Web: www.tandtclark.co.uk
Email: mailbox@tandtclark.co.uk
☎ 0131 225 4703 🖷 0131 220 4260

***Share It!**, Church Army, Independents Road, Blackheath London SE3 9LG
Director of Marketing: Mr Nigel Edward-Few. *Press & Medi Officer:* Capt Leslie Tennant. *Publications Development Man ager:* Mr Richard Prescott. Staff n/a. ***CC*** No.226226. Bega 1882; Anglican.
Web: churcharmy.org.uk
Email: information@churcharmy.org.uk
☎ 020 8297 6056 🖷 020 8297 6028

Sign, G. J. Palmer & Sons Ltd, St Mary's Works, St Mary's Plain, Norwich NR3 3BH
Editor: Mr Terence Handley-MacMath. *General Manager:* Mr Gordon Knights. Other staff 3. Began 1905; Anglican.
☎ 01603 615 995 🖷 01603 624 483
Subscriptions: G. J. Palmer & Sons Ltd, 16 Blyburgate, Beccles NR34 9TB
☎ 01502 711 231 🖷 01502 711 585

Soul Survivor, Unit 2, Paramount Industrial Estate, Sandown Road, Watford WD2 4XA
Editor: Mr Mike Pilavachi. *Assistant Editor:* Mrs Emma Mitchell. Executive staff 2, Other staff 10. ***CC*** No.1043763. Began 1993; interdenominational. Turnover included in main entry.
Web: www.soulsurvivor.com
Email: magazine@soulsurvivor.com
☎ 01923 333 331 🖷 01923 333 334

Studies in Christian Ethics, T & T Clark Ltd, 59 George Street, Edinburgh EH2 2LQ
Editor: Esther D Reed. Staff n/a. Began 1988; non-denominational. Examining important themes in contemporary Christian ethics, with contributions from leading moral theologians.
Web: www.tandtclark.co.uk
Email: mailbox@tandtclark.co.uk
☎ 0131 225 4703 🖷 0131 220 4260

Sword and Trowel, Metropolitan Tabernacle, Elephant & Castle, London SE1 6SD
Editor: Dr Peter Masters. Other staff 2. ***CC*** Began 1865; non-denominational.
Web: www.metropolitantabernacle.org
Email: swordtrowel@metropolitantabernacle.org
☎ 020 7735 7076

For additional information see List on Page 310

Symphony, Bemerton Press, 9 Hamilton Gardens, London NW8 9PU
Editor: Rev Philip Tait. No full-time staff. Began 1976; non-denominational. Christian poetry.
☎ No telephone

The Tablet, The Tablet Publishing Co Ltd, 1 King Street Cloisters, Clifton Walk, London W6 0QZ
Editor: Mr John Wilkins. *Publisher:* Mr Hugh Kealy. Began 1840; Roman Catholic.
Web: www.thetablet.co.uk
Email: thetablet@compuserve.com
☎ 020 8748 8484 Fax 020 8748 1550

Theology, SPCK, Holy Trinity Church, Marylebone Road, London NW1 4DU
Editor: Dr William Jacob. No full-time staff. ***CC*** No.231144. Began 1920; non-denominational.
Web: www.spck.org.uk
Email: theology@spck.org.uk
☎ 020 7387 5282 Fax 020 7388 2352

Theology and Sexuality, Sheffield Academic Press, Mansion House, 19 Kingfield Road, Sheffield S11 9AS
Co-editor: Ms Elizabeth Stuart. Editors 3. Began 1994; interdenominational.
Web: www.shef-ac-press.co.uk
Email: admin@sheffac.demon.co.uk
☎ 0114 255 4433 Fax 0114 255 4626

Third Way, St Peter's, Sumner Road, Harrow HA1 4BX
Editor: Mr Brian Draper. *Publisher:* Mr Huw Spanner. Executive staff 2. ***CC*** No.327969. Began 1977; non-denominational.
Web: www.thirdway.org.uk
Email: editor@thirdway.org.uk
☎ 020 8423 8494 Fax 020 8423 5367

Together with Children, The National Society, Church House, Great Smith Street, London SW1P 3NZ
Editor: To be appointed. No full-time staff. ***CC*** No.313070. Began 1956; interdenominational. (Previously Together).
Web: www.natsoc.org.uk
☎ 020 7898 1000 Fax 020 7898 1493

Transformation, Paternoster Periodicals, PO Box 300, Carlisle CA3 0QS
Publisher: Mr Mark Finnie. Staff: See Paternoster Publishing. Began 1984; interdenominational.
Web: www.paternoster-publishing.com
Email: info@paternoster-publishing
☎ 01228 512 512 Fax 01228 593 388
Editors: Kwame Bediako, Vinay Samuel, Chris Sugden, Ronald Sider and René Padilla, Oxford Centre for Mission Studies, PO Box 70, Oxford OX2 6HB
Email: 100270.2155@compuserve.com
☎ 01865 556 071 Fax 01865 510 823

UK Focus, Holy Trinity Church, Brompton Road, London SW7 1JA
Editor: Mark Elsdon Dew. Executive staff 3. ***CC*** Began 1993; Anglican.
Web: dspace.dial.pipex.com/htb.london
Email: htb.london@dial.pipex.com
☎ 020 7581 8255 Fax 020 7589 3390

Ulster Christian Magazine, 8 Dufferin Court, Dufferin Avenue, Bangor BT20 3BX
Principal: Mrs Ann King. Executive staff 1, Other staff 12. Began 1995; Conservative Evangelical. Turnover n/a.
Web: www.ucmag.com
Email: editor@ucmag.com
☎ 028 9145 7554 Fax 028 9145 7430

The Universe, Gabriel Communications Ltd, First Floor, St James's Buildings, Oxford Street, Manchester M1 6FP
Editorial Director: Mr Joseph Kelly. Executive staff 4, Other staff 56. Began 1860; Roman Catholic.
Web: www.demon.co.uk/gabcom/
Email: postmaster@gabcom.demon.co.uk
☎ 0161 236 8856 Fax 0161 236 8530

The Upper Room, Methodist Publishing House, 20 Ivatt Way, Peterborough PE3 7PG
Editor: Brian Thornton. No full-time staff. Began 1985; ecumenical. Turnover n/a.
☎ 01733 332 202 Fax 01733 331 201

Wake Up!, 11 Seagate, Irvine KA12 8RH
Editor: Mr Matthew J Browning. Executive staff 1, Admin staff 2. Began 1981; non-denominational. (Previously The Christian Israel Foundation). Published by The Kingdom Foundation. Turnover £20,000 to year end Jun 98.
☎ 01294 275 624 Fax 01294 275 624

The War Cry, Salvation Army, UK Territorial Headquarters, 101 Newington Causeway, London SE1 6BN
Editor: Capt Charles King. Executive staff 2, Other staff 4. Began 1879; Salvation Army.
Web: www.salvationarmy.org.uk/website/ukpages/ewarcry.html
Email: warcry@salvationarmy.org.uk
☎ 020 7367 4500 Fax 020 7367 4710

The Way, Heythrop College, Kensington Square, London W8 5HQ
General Editor: Rev Michael Barnes. Executive staff 3. ***CC*** Began 1961; interdenominational.
Email: the.way@dial.pipex.com
☎ 020 7795 4255 Fax 020 7795 4256
Subscriptions: 114 Mount Street, London W1Y 6AN

Welsh Church Life, Church in Wales Publications, Education Centre, Woodland Place, Penarth CF64 2EX
Editor: To be appointed. No full-time staff. Began 1963; Church in Wales. (Previously Welsh Churchman).
Email: office@mission.churchinwales.org.uk
☎ 029 2070 5278 / 8234 Fax 029 2071 2413

Wholeness, Monarch Magazines Ltd, Broadway House, The Broadway, Crowborough TN6 1HQ
Editor: Mrs Jane Collins. Executive staff 2, Other staff 1. Began 1991; interdenominational. Focusing on healing in widest sense; particularly valuable for pastors and counsellors.
Email: monarch@dial.pipex.com
☎ 01892 652 364 Fax 01892 663 329

*__Woman Alive__, Christian Media Centre, 96 Dominion Road, Worthing BN14 8JP
Editor: Mrs Liz Proctor. Staff – see Christian Media Centre. Began 1982; interdenominational. Incorporating Parentwise.
Email: womanalive@christianmedia.org.uk
Email: advertising@christianmedia.org.uk
☎ 01903 821 082 (general) 602 103 (advertising)
ISDN: 01903 573 308
Fax 01903 821 081 (general) 537 321 (advertising)

Worship and Preaching, Methodist Publishing House, 20 Ivatt Way, Peterborough PE3 7PG
Editor: Rev Peter Barber. No full-time staff. ***CC*** Began 1971; Methodist. Resource for preachers based on the Revised Common Lectionary.
☎ 01733 332 202 Fax 01733 331 201

M

For additional information see List on Page 310

The Young Reformer, 77 Ampthill Road, Flitwick, Bedford MK45 1BD
Editor: Dr S J Scott-Pearson. Executive staff 2, Other staff 3. ***CC*** Began n/a; interdenominational.
Email: sscottpear@aol.com
☎ 01525 712 348 Fax 01525 712 348

Youthwork, PO Box 17911, London SW1E 5ZR
Editor: Mr John Buckeridge. Executive staff 3, Other staff 2. Began 1992; interdenominational. Ideas, resources and guidance for Christians in youth ministry.
Web: www.youthwork.co.uk
Email: youthwork@easynet.co.uk
☎ 020 7316 1450 Fax 020 7316 1453

PHOTOGRAPHERS

Keith Ellis, 10 Forge Close, Holmer Green, High Wycombe HP15 6PY
Photographer: Mr Keith Ellis. No other staff. Began 1964; non-denominational. No magazine. Turnover n/a. General photography; library of b/w and colour photographs relating to the Christian scene including the Holy Land.
☎ 01494 715 735

Jim Loring, 405a Brockley Road, Crofton Park, London SE4 2PH
Photographer: Mr Jim Loring. Executive staff 1. Began 1985; non-denominational. Magazine: *Newsheet* (Circulation n/a occasionally). Turnover n/a. Editorial, documentary, portraits, picture library.
Email: 106704.1424@compuserve.com
☎ 020 8691 4268 Pager: 07881 800 800#857304

***Benedict Parsons**, Priors House, The Court, Croft Lane, Crondall, Farnham GU10 5QF
Photographer: Mr Benedict Parsons. Other staff 1. Began 1994; interdenominational. Turnover n/a. Mission through media photography, press releases to broadsheets, Christian papers; portable studio; function work; large library.
Email: benparsons@aol.com
☎ 01252 851 137/852 205 (direct) Mobile: 07768 105 785
Fax 01252 851 137

†Ian Roberts, 4 Greenway Gardens, Chippenham SN15 1AJ
Photographer: Ian Roberts. No other staff. Began 1996; interdenominational. No magazine. Turnover n/a. Creative photographer specialising in concerts, conferences, events; providing personalised coverage.
☎ 01249 660 907

VIDEO, FILM & CASSETTE LIBRARIES & SUPPLIERS

M

A and C Audio Services, 98 Goremire Road, Carluke ML8 4PF
Partner: Mr Alex Borthwick. Executive staff 2. Began 1990; non-denominational. No magazine. Turnover n/a. Supplying audio equiment and cassette copiers for church cassette ministries. UK and worldwide.
Web: www.aandcaudio.co.uk
Email: enquiries@aandcaudio.co.uk
☎ 01555 772 648 Fax 01555 772 648

L'Abri Cassettes, The Manor House, Greatham, Liss GU33 6HF
Administrator: n/a. Began 1979; non-denominational. No magazine. Turnover £4,000 to year end Dec 98. Distributing talks by Francis Schaeffer and other L'Abri staff; sale or hire; video and cassette.
☎ 01420 538 436 Fax 01420 538 432

***All Souls' Tape Library**, 2 All Souls' Place, London W1N 3DB
Resources Manager: Mrs Sharon Kennedy. No full-time staff. Began 1965; Anglican. No magazine. Turnover £27,000 to year end Dec 98. Distributing worldwide cassettes of teaching and evangelistic sermons preached at All Souls Church.
Email: tape_library@allsouls.org
☎ 020 7580 3522 Fax 020 7436 3019

Bible Scene Multimedia, 26 Home Close, Sharnbrook, Bedford MK44 1PQ
Trustee: Mr Maurice S Thompson. Executive staff 3, Other staff 1. ***CC*** No.327400. Began 1985; interdenominational. (Previously Bible Scene Slide Tours). Magazine: *Update* (150 half-yearly). Turnover n/a. Bible teaching aids. Presentations in schools, prisons, churches; mobile and classroom exhibition; interactive CD-Roms/slides.
Email: howard.roberts@btinternet.com
☎ 01234 781 946 Fax 01234 782 623

***Chichester Christian Fellowship (Tapes)**, 30 Crescent Road, Bognor Regis PO21 1QG
Manager: Mr Ralph Page. Executive staff 1, Other staff 1. ***CC*** No.276242. Began 1970; non-denominational. No magazine. Turnover £22,000 to year end Mar 98. Distributing Christian audio and video Bible study tapes; principally work of the late Roger Price.
Web: www.ccftapes.co.uk
Email: sales@ccftapes.co.uk
☎ 01243 862 621 Fax 01243 862 621

Christian Foundation Publications, 45 Appleton Road, Hale, Altrincham WA15 9LP
Proprietor: Dr Brian J Taylor. No full-time staff. Began 1978; non-denominational. No magazine. Turnover n/a. Producing and distributing literature and cassettes.
☎ 0161 205 1977
Also at: Brunswick Hill, Bradford Road, Manchester M40 7EZ
☎ No telephone Fax 0161 203 4280

***Christian Resources Project**, 14 Lipson Road, Plymouth PL4 8PW
Administrator: Mr Michael Law. *Centre Manager:* Mrs Audrey Burnham. Executive staff 1, Other staff 2. ***CC*** No.281735. Began n/a; interdenominational. Magazine: *Newsletter* (Circulation n/a five times a year). Turnover £111,000 to year end Dec 98. Resource centre, video and audio-visual library, video projector and equipment hire, schools work, training, bookselling, mission.
Web: business.thisisplymouth.co.uk/crp
☎ 01752 224 012 Fax 01752 224 012

cclesia Services, 1 Cranbourne Road, London N10 2BT
Managing Director: Mr Duncan MacDonald. No full-time staff. Began 1986; non-denominational. No magazine. Turnover n/a. Distributing audio cassettes and books by Denis Duncans, William Barclay and J B Phillips.
Email: 106436.550@compuserve.com
☎ 020 8883 1831 🖷 020 8883 8307

ncounter Ministries Trust, PO Box 789, Sutton Coldfield B74 2XJ
Administrator: Mr Philip B South. Other staff 3. ***CC*** No.268110. Began 1973; interdenominational. Magazine: *The Preacher* (300 every four months). Turnover £20,000 to year end Dec 98. Seminars, audio and video cassettes, convention ministry; books by Dr Stephen Olford.
Email: encounter@clara.net
☎ 0121 323 3701 🖷 0121 323 3703

vangelical Films, Danbury Common Old Mission, The Common, Danbury, Chelmsford CM3 4EE
Administrator: Mr Christopher G Bryant. Admin staff 2, Other staff 2. ***CC*** No.270736. Began 1967; interdenominational. No magazine. Turnover n/a. Christian video and 16/35mm film sales, distribution and rental. Video projection equipment and screen sales.
☎ 01245 227 880 / 226 642 Mobile: 07860 340 107
🖷 01245 226 642

GNC Audio, 17 High Cross Street, St Austell PL25 4AN
Director: Rev Don Double. Staff n/a. ***CC*** No.225483. Began n/a; interdenominational. (Previously Good News Crusade Tape Ministry). No magazine. Turnover see Good News Crusade. Supplying 11,000 audio messages from over 80 national and international speakers; Tape of the Month available.
Web: www.gnc.org.uk
Email: info@gnc.org.uk
☎ 01726 813 595

Good News Video Centre, 21 St Leonards Road, Charminster, Bournemouth BH8 8QL
General Manager: Mr & Mrs A Absolom. ***CC*** No.291650. Began 1985; non-denominational. No magazine. Turnover n/a. Video and audio tape library, free loan of tapes – approx 2,000 tapes available.
☎ 01202 515 825

Grace To You, Europe, 2 Caxton House, Wellesley Road, Ashford TN24 8ET
European Director: Mr Anthony Ruston. Executive staff 1, Other staff 5. Began 1990; interdenominational. No magazine. Turnover n/a. Distributing the audio and video teaching materials of Dr John MacArthur; daily radio broadcast.
Web: www.gty.org.uk
Email: gty@ukonline.co.uk
☎ 01233 662 262 🖷 01233 662 262

Hitotsu-Bishi, 22 Hassocks Wood, Stroudley Road, Basingstoke RG24 8UQ
Managing Director: Mr Andrew Earle. *Marketing Director:* Mr Andrew Watkins. Executive staff 2. Began 1986; interdenominational. (Previously Gothic Audio-Visual & Studio 55). No magazine. Turnover £205,000 to year end Nov 98. Preparing training and promotional material utilising film, video, tape-slide & print.
Email: hitbis@aol.com
☎ 01256 471 471 🖷 01256 471 470

Ichthus Media Services Ltd, 107 Stanstead Road, Forest Hill, London SE23 1HH
Director: Mr Michael Borrett. Other staff 4. Began 1989; non-denominational. No magazine. Turnover n/a. Supplying tapes and videos from the ministry of Ichthus Christian Fellowship and others.
Email: media@ichthus.org.uk
☎ 020 8699 4208 🖷 020 8291 6764

Jeremiah Films UK, PO Box 26, Bicester OX6 0GL
Managing Director: Mr Michael J Penfold. Executive staff 1, Other staff 3. Began 1990; non-denominational. No magazine. Turnover n/a. Distributing documentary video films on the cults and the occult.
Email: penfoldbooks@characterlink.net
☎ 01869 249 574 🖷 01869 244 033

Kensington Church Videos, PO Box 8207, London W4 1WQ
Producer: Rev Gerd Swensson. All voluntary staff. ***CC*** No.800574. Began 1987; Anglican. No magazine. Turnover £12,000 to year end Dec 94. Producing and distributing Christian educational videos to churches, schools and others.
🖷 020 8995 8599

Kingdom Power Trust, 37 Quickley Lane, Chorleywood, Rickmansworth WD3 5AE
Director: Rt Rev David Pytches. No full-time staff. ***CC*** No.29618. Began 1987; Anglican. No magazine. Turnover £23,000 to year end Dec 98. Encouraging Christians to minister in the power of the Holy Spirit through conferences and videos.
☎ 01923 447 111 🖷 01923 447 200

Kingdom Video, PO Box 198A, Surbiton KT6 6QF
Director: Mrs Ann Mercer. No full-time staff. Began 1986; interdenominational. No magazine. Turnover £12,000 to year end Mar 98. Mail order sales of videos, audios and books; mail order hire of videos.
☎ 020 8390 6903

The Martyn Lloyd-Jones Recordings Trust, 2 Caxton House, Wellesley Road, Ashford TN24 8ET
Administrator: Mr Anthony M Ruston. Executive staff 2, Voluntary staff 4. ***CC*** No.286003. Began 1982; non-denominational. No magazine. Turnover n/a. Reproducing and distributing the sermons of Martyn Lloyd-Jones; cassette copying service.
Web: web.mlj.org.uk
Email: mlj@ukonline.co.uk
☎ 01233 662 262 Fax: 01233 662 262

***Pinnacle Creative**, 17 Clarendon Villas, Hove BN3 3RE
Managing Director: Mr Adrian Willard. Executive staff 1, Other staff 7. ***CC*** Began 1980; non-denominational. (Previously Frontiers Publishing International). Video production, graphic design and magazine production. No magazine. Turnover n/a.
☎ 01273 234 555 Fax: 01273 234 556

M

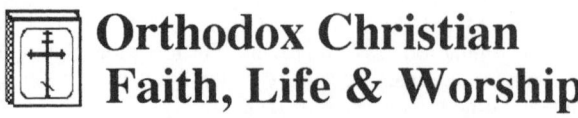

Derek Prince Ministries – UK, PO Box 77, Harpenden AL5 1P
Director: Mr Mark Buchanan. Executive staff 3, Other staff 1 ***CC*** No.327763. Began 1983; interdenominational. Magazin *Newsletter* (Circulation & frequency n/a). Turnover £726,0 to year end Mar 98. International producer/distributor of Bi lical foundational teaching resources (books, audios, video radio and television broadcasting).
Web: www.derekprince.com
Email: enquiries@uk.derekprince.com
☎ 01582 466 200 Fax: 01582 766 777

***Things that Matter**, PO Box 27, Urmston, Manchester M41 6LT
Founder Manager: Mr Alec Brackett. Executive staff 2. C No.1008196. Began 1959; non-denominational. No maga zine. Turnover n/a. Free loan library of audio cassette record ings of Christian teaching; 2,200 titles.
☎ 0161 748 6008

Victory European Ministries, PO Box 204, Southfleet, Graveseno DA13 9LG
Director: Mr Roger Harris. Executive staff 1. Began 1988 non-denominational. No magazine. Turnover n/a. Europea distribution of over 3,000 cassettes by Hobart Freeman Russell Tardo and others.
Email: faith@victoryeuropeanmins.freeserve.co.uk
☎ 01474 833 107 Fax: 01474 833 107

Video Aid, 2 Tuddenham Road, Aylsham, Norwich NR11 6DE
Principal: Mr Richard Allen. Executive staff 1. Began 1986 non-denominational. Magazine: *Video Aid* (Circulation n/a occasionally). Turnover £3,500 to year end May 98. Hiring and supplying Christian videos to churches, youth groups, schools and individuals.
☎ 01263 732 684

***Video Bible Teaching Ministry**, 38 Blackhorse Road, Walthamstow, London E17 7AS
Co-ordinator: Rev George Stirrup. No other staff. Began 1989; interdenominational. No magazine. Turnover n/a. Providing Bible teaching on videotape specifically for homegroups or small churches.
Email: gstirvbt@aol.uk
☎ 020 8521 6853 Mobile: 07885 473 005

The Visual Bible Ltd, PO Box 4593, Kiln Farm, Milton Keynes MK8 0HH
Managing Director: Mr Bob Davis. Executive staff 1, Other staff 2. Began 1996; ecumenical. No magazine. Turnover n/a. Filming the Bible word for word; distributing videos of it to the nations.
Email: bob-davis@lineone.net
☎ 01628 481 425 Fax: 01628 481 426

OVERSEAS

O

EVANGELISTIC AGENCIES (OVERSEAS)

L'Abri Fellowship, The Manor House, Greatham, Liss GU33 6HF
Director: Rev Ranald Macaulay. *Co-ordinator:* Mr Andrew Fellows. Executive staff 10, Other staff 2. ***CC*** No.237618. Began 1971; interdenominational. No magazine. Turnover £120,000 to year end Dec 98. Residential study centres in Europe and USA; emphasising the truthfulness and relevance of Biblical Christianity.
Email: labri_uk@compuserve.com
☎ 01420 538 436 🖷 01420 538 432

Action International Ministries (UK), PO Box 193, Bewdley DY12 2GZ
UK Director: Mr Ingo Abraham. Executive staff 1, Other staff 3. ***CC*** No.1058661. Began 1974; interdenominational. (Previously ACTION UK (Action International Ministries)). Magazine: *Actionpoint* (1,500 quarterly), *Street Children* (1,500 every two months). Turnover £189,000 to year end Mar 98. Reaching urban poor of the world through evangelism, discipleship, social development projects especially amongst street children.
Web: www.actionintl.org
Email: actionuk@btinternet.com
☎ 01299 401 511 🖷 01299 405 273

***AE Evangelistic Enterprise Ltd**, Victoria House, Victoria Road, Buckhurst Hill IG9 5EX
Company Secretary: Miss Jean Wilson. No full-time staff. ***CC*** No.278704. Began 1977; interdenominational. Magazine: *Update* (Circulation n/a quarterly). Turnover £177,000 to year end Dec 97. Supporting evangelistic and relief work in Africa.
Email: 100067.1226@compuserve.com
☎ 020 8559 2422 🖷 020 8502 9062

The Bible Land Mission, PO Box 196, Aberdeen AB15 9HZ
Secretary: Mr George McRobb. No other staff. ***CC*** No.253884. Began 1967; interdenominational. Magazine: *Evangelist* (1,000 quarterly (internationally)). Turnover £20,000 to year end Sept 96. Undertaking church work in Lebanon; orphanage, Bible students, radio and television.
☎ 01224 734 710 Mobile: 07803 296 279
🖷 01224 734 710

O

Biblical Ministries Worldwide, 48 Dell Crescent, Northampton NN3 8SG
Field Leader: Rev James Love. Serving missionaries 18. Began n/a; Evangelical. (Previously Worldwide European Fellowship). No magazine. Turnover n/a. An evangelical church-planting mission society from the USA.
Web: www.biblicalministries.org
Email: JamesLove100545.3077@compuserve.com
☎ 01604 494 778
Also at: *Field Leader:* Rev David Rozelle, The Lothian Bible Mission, 5 Gylers Road, Dirleton, North Berwick EH39 5EZ
☎ 01620 850 245

Blythswood Care, Deephaven, Evanton, Dingwall IV16 9XJ
President: Rev John W Ross. Executive staff 2, Other staff 32. ***CC*** Began 1966; Protestant. Magazine: *News and Prayer Letter* (12,000 seven times a year). Turnover £661,000 to year end Dec 98. Distributing literature and aid, mainly to Eastern Europe and Africa; support for mission work.
Web: www.blythswood.org.uk
Email: info@blythswood.org.uk
☎ 01349 830 777 🖷 01349 830 477

***Café.Net**, Chawn Hill Christian Centre, Chawn Hill, Stourbrid DY9 7JD
Co-Directors: Mr Gerard and Mrs Chrissie Kelly. No oth staff. ***CC*** No.502287. Began 1995; non-denominational. (Pr viously RE:BUILD). No magazine. Turnover £5,000 to ye end Dec 98. A network of Christians active in the future Europe.
Web: www.users.surfaid.org/~cafe
Email: cafe@surfaid.org
☎ 01384 441 471 🖷 01384 441 471

***Christ for All Nations**, Highway House, 250 Coombs Roa Halesowen B62 8AA
UK Administrator: Mr Bernard Jones. Executive staff 3, Othe staff 6. ***CC*** No.327522. Began 1974; interdenominational. U Office opened in 1984, Head office in Frankfurt. Magazin *Revival Report Telegram* (17,500 every two months), *Ministr letters* (17,500 every two weeks). Turnover n/a. Preaching th Gospel in Africa and worldwide; translating and producing lit erature into foreign languages including braille and large print.
Web: www.cfan.org.
Email: info@cfan.org.uk
☎ 0121 602 2000 🖷 0121 559 5042

***Connections Trust**, 71 Hayter Road, Brixton, London SW2 5AD
Director: Mr Philip Mohabir. Admin staff 7. ***CC*** No.1017593 Began n/a; non-denominational. Magazine: *Connectoscop* (1,000 quarterly). Turnover £15,088 to year end Apr 98. Pio neer evangelism, relief, church planting, outreach to Muslim and immigrants, training leaders in underdeveloped nations.
Web: www.connectionsuk.freeserve.co.uk
Email: connuk@aol.com
☎ 020 7924 9700 🖷 020 7924 9800

Dovetales International Trust, 79 Marlborough Road, Royton Oldham OL2 6AU
Trustees: Mr William E & Mrs Janet A Heap. No full-time staff. ***CC*** No.1016673. Began 1993; interdenominational. Nc magazine. Turnover n/a. Taking the Word of God with medical, educational and vocational training to India and worldwide.
Email: dovetale@globalnet.co.uk
☎ 0161 652 4060 🖷 0161 652 4060

Eastern European Outreach, 466 Bordesley Green, Bordesley Green, Birmingham B9 5NS
Administrator: Mrs Sally Hughes. ***CC*** No.290643. Began 1984; interdenominational. Magazine: *Outreach* (2,000 monthly). Turnover £50,000 to year end Dec 98. Evangelism, child sponsorship, children, medical relief, 'hands-on' experience.
☎ 0121 643 8435

***The Ethnos Trust**, PO Box 1744, Poole BH14 9YF
International Director: Mr Terry Johns. Executive staff 4. ***CC*** No.1048798. Began 1994; non-denominational. Magazine: *Taking Possession* (50 quarterly). Turnover £10,000 to year end Dec 98. Training leadership amongst 10/40 Window church planters; emphasis on Fulani and Hausa peoples; development/literacy work.
Web: www.wbtcm.org
Email: church@wbtcm.org
☎ 01202 690 272 Mobile: 07974 055 461
🖷 01202 690 273

urovangelism, PO Box 50, Kingswood, Bristol BS15 1EX
Secretary: Miss Rosemary Boulton. Executive staff 2, Other staff 4. ***CC*** No.247788. Began 1966; interdenominational. Magazine: *Euro News/Eurogram* (4,000 every two months). Turnover £565,000 to year end Mar 98. Missionary service organisation helping Christian nationals in Eastern Europe to be more effective in outreach.
Email: 106020.3202@compuserve.com
☎ 0117 961 5161 🖷 0117 935 2127

urovision Mission to Europe, 41 Healds Road, Dewsbury WF13 4HU
President: Rev David Hathaway. Executive staff 3, Other staff 9. ***CC*** No.1013288. Began 1992; interdenominational. Magazine: *Prophetic Vision* (150,000 quarterly). Turnover £1,000,000 [UK only] to year end Dec 98. Support of churches and evangelists in Siberia, Ukraine and Eastern Europe; TV ministry in Ukraine.
Web: www.propheticvision.org.uk
Email: prophetic@vision139.freeserve.co.uk
☎ 01924 453 693 🖷 01924 465 326

Ghana Christian Support Group, 117 Kingsway, Petts Wood, Orpington BR5 1PP
Trustee: Rev Clive Doubleday. No full-time staff. ***CC*** No.1054905. Began 1994; Baptist. Magazine: *Newsletter* (200 every four months). Turnover £10,000 to year end Dec 96. Supporting Christians in Ghana by prayer, theological training, sponsoring projects; campaigning against child slavery.
Email: clivedoubleday@compuserve.com
☎ 01689 603 680 🖷 01689 603 680

Haggai Institute for Advanced Leadership Training Ltd, 1a Queen Victoria Street, Belfast BT5 5BG
Executive Director: Mr Ron Irvine. Other staff 1. ***CC*** No.327623. Began 1980; interdenominational. Magazine: *Leaders for Today* (Circulation n/a quarterly). Turnover £160,000 to year end Dec 98. Equipping non-western Christian leaders for effective evangelism in their own country and culture.
Email: haggai.uk@aol.com
☎ 028 9045 2022 Mobile: 07885 076 723 🖷 028 9045 2275

Hosanna Family Churches, PO Box 740, Hemel Hempstead HP3 0RH
International Director: Rev David Sullivan. Executive staff 2, Other staff 1. ***CC*** No.1043665. Began 1994; non-denominational. Magazine: *Hosanna* (2,000 every two months). Turnover n/a. Church planting and church development including missions in UK, USA and Europe.
Web: www.geocities.com/athens/1976
Email: international77@hotmail.com
☎ No telephone

The International Messianic Jewish Alliance, PO Box 163, Ramsgate CT11 8GJ
Executive Secretary: Rev Ronald H Lewis. Executive staff 1, Other staff 2. ***CC*** No.231016. Began 1925; interdenominational. Magazine: *Messianic Jewish Life* (5,000 every two months). Turnover n/a. Spiritual and temporal care of Jewish believers in Jesus as Messiah.
Web: www.inja.com
Email: shalom@inja.com
☎ 01843 589 756 🖷 01843 589 756

Irish Evangelistic Band, 30 Cloncarrish Road, The Birches, Craigavon BT62 1RN
Co-ordinator: Miss Vera Smith. Staff 10. ***CC*** Began 1936; interdenominational. Magazine: *Prayer and Praise Circular* (3,000 quarterly). Turnover £60,000 to year end Jan 98. Evangelising Ireland; colportage ministry, youth work, summer teams, bookshops. Missionary emphasis.
Email: aloney@aol.com
☎ 028 3885 1563

***Jesus is the Answer International Mission**, 12 High Street, Camelford PL32 9PQ
President/Administrator: Rev David Flanders. Other staff 2. Began 1981; Assemblies of God. Magazine: *Jam News* (100 every two months). Turnover n/a. Evangelising unreached areas (priority Europe) by crusades, training, printing, church planting, relief, Bible school ministry.
Email: soulsharb@aol.com
☎ 01840 212 620 🖷 01840 212 620

Operation Rescue, 21 Law Cliff Road, Great Barr, Birmingham B42 1LP
Missionary Evangelist: Rev Norman F Smith. Executive staff 2, Other staff 1. Began n/a; interdenominational. No magazine. Turnover n/a. Outreach evangelism to many countries; providing for spiritual and physical needs.
☎ 0121 358 6019

***Reach Out Ministries International**, PO Box 130, Walton-on-Thames KT12 2RU
International Director: Dr Peter J Gammons. Executive staff 6, Other staff 32. ***CC*** No.298954. Began 1976; interdenominational. Magazine: *Breakthrough!* (10,000 every two months). Turnover £142,000 to year end Apr 95. Evangelistic work, leadership training and Gospel radio broadcasting in England and 40 other countries.
Web: www.petergammons.org
Email: info@petergammons.org
☎ 01932 225 549 🖷 01932 242 302

***Romanian Aid Fund**, 2 Torquay Grove, Woodsmoor, Stockport SK2 7BB
Secretary: Mrs Pauline Lucas. No full-time staff. ***CC*** No.285160. Began 1970; interdenominational. Magazine: *Romanian Aid Fund Bulletin* (1,000 quarterly). Turnover £40,000 to year end May 98. Encouraging indigenous evangelical Christian work in Romania by supporting churches, pastors and Christian workers.
Email: romaidfund@aol.com
☎ 0161 612 9013 🖷 0161 612 9015

***Seacare**, PO Box 24224, London SE12 0ZW
Director: Mr Maurice Vitty. Executive staff 2, Other staff 1. ***CC*** No.287071. Began 1981; interdenominational. Magazine: *Prayer Letter* (1,500 every four months). Turnover £30,000 to year end Apr 99. Evangelism, training, UK/overseas, mainly with Mission ship "The Redeemer". Also known as CCP Trust.
Email: vitsea1@aol.com
☎ Admin: 01275 851 773 Director: 020 8851 0443
🖷 Admin: 01275 851 773 Director: 020 8851 0443

***Soapbox Expeditions**, 3 Bank Buildings, 149 High Street, Cranleigh GU6 8BB
National Director: Rev Steve Flashman. Executive staff 1, Other staff 4. ***CC*** Began 1993; interdenominational. Magazine: *On The Box* (1,200 quarterly). Turnover £300,000 to year end Dec 98. Short term projects in developing countries and creative arts mission and evangelism in Western Europe.
Web: website.lineone.net/~soapbox
Email: soapbox@lineone.net
☎ 01483 271 015 Mobile: 07774 672 529

Ukraine Christian Ministries, Heathside, Milland, Liphook GU30 7LU
Director: Rev John David Hendy. Executive staff 2, Other staff 3. *CC* Began 1996; interdenominational. Magazine: *In Touch* (1,000 every four months), *Prayer Diary* (Circulation n/a every two months). Turnover £50,000 to year end Apr 97. Evangelism, church planting, Bible teaching, training, distributing literature and humanitarian aid.
Email: jjhendyucm@aol,com
☎ 01428 741 617 🖷 01428 741 617

Voice of Deliverance, PO Box 61, Gloucester GL4 3AA
Director: Rev Peter Scothern. Executive staff 2, Other staff 8. *CC* Began 1955; interdenominational. Magazine: *Deliverance* (5,000 every two months). Turnover £9,500 to year end De 98. Presenting the Gospel with healing and deliverance; Thir World missionary outreach, Eastern Europe, India, Brazil.
☎ 01452 611 959

*__Voice of Renewal UK__, 28 Cedar Avenue, Nuthall, Nottingha NG16 1AF
Directors: Rev George and Rev Helen Jesze. No full-time staf *CC* Began 1988; interdenominational. Magazine: *Voice c Renewal International* (1,000 quarterly). Turnover n/a. Evan gelism, teaching, cassettes, books; ministering in Europe Russia, Romania, USA.
☎ 0115 927 3816 🖷 0115 913 0080

LITERATURE PRODUCERS & DISTRIBUTORS (OVERSEAS)

Africa Christian Press, 50 Loxwood Avenue, Worthing BN14 7RA
UK Representative: Mr Donald Banks. Other staff 1. *CC* No.243254. Began 1964; interdenominational. No magazine. Turnover n/a. Publishing books mainly by African authors for the African continent.
☎ 01903 232 208 🖷 01903 824 376

*__Bientôt (a WEC International ministry)__, Unit 6, Garcia Trading Estate, Canterbury Road, Worthing BN13 1AL
Editor: Mr Derek Cook. Executive staff 2, Other staff 2. *CC* No.237005. Began 1959; interdenominational. Magazine: *Bientôt (Standard and European Editions)* (450,000 quarterly). Part of Gospel Literature Worldwide. Turnover £14,000 to year end Mar 98. Distributing gospel leaflets in French freely to French-speaking readers worldwide.
Email: bientot@cpo.uk.com
☎ 01903 690 112

O

*__Book AID – mailing address__, 271 Church Road, London SE19 2QQ
Co-ordinator: Mr Bob Hiley. Executive staff 4, Other staff 20. *CC* No.1039484. Began 1987; interdenominational. Magazine: *BOOK AID Update* (5,000 occasional). Turnover £150,000 to year end Dec 98. Sending new and secondhand Christian books and Bibles to book famine areas overseas.
☎ 020 8857 7794 🖷 020 8653 6577
Warehouse and Bookshop (No mail): *Shop Manageress:* Mrs Ada Hiley, Mayeswood Road, Grove Park, London SE12 9RP
Collection Centres: *Manager:* Mr Stephen Green, North Road, Ranskill, Retford DN22 8NL
☎ 01777 817 101 🖷 01777 817 101
And: *Shop Manager:* Mr Maurice Abrahams, 5 Galgate, Barnard Castle DL12 8EQ
☎ 01833 630 209
And: *Shop Manageress:* Mrs Margaret Robertson, 47 Longbrook Street, Exeter EX4 6AW
☎ 0192 213 002
And: *Shop Manager:* Mr Frank Rea, The Haven Christian Centre, 44 Rickamore Road Upper, Templepatrick, Ballyclare BT39 0JE
☎ 028 9443 2061
And: *Shop Manager:* Mr Stephen Green, Bawtry Hall, Bawtrry, Doncaster DN10 6JH
☎ 01777 817 101

*__Christian Publicity Organisation__, Garcia Estate, Canterbur Road, Worthing BN13 1BW
General Director: Mr Roy P Barbour. *Director of Marketing* Mr Chris Powell. *Contract Sales Manager:* Mr Martin Collins Executive staff 3, Other staff 34. *CC* No.221462. Began 1957 non-denominational. Magazine: *CPO Catalogue* (25,000 quarterly). Turnover £2,000,000 to year end Apr 99. High quality design, print and publishing service supporting th international Christian community for 40 years.
Email: enquiries@cpo.uk.com
☎ 01903 264 556 ISDN: 01903 830005 🖷 01903 830 066

*__East European Literature Advisory Committee__, 3 Florence Road Bromley BR1 3NU
General Secretary: Mr Gerry Davey. No other full-time, staff *CC* No.327179. Began 1986; non-denominational. No maga zine. Turnover n/a. Co-operating with East Europeans and former USSR evangelicals to develop indigenous, self supporting publishing houses.
Email: 100117.2360@compuserve.com
☎ 020 8464 0460 🖷 020 8313 1373

East-West Fellowship, PO Box 120, Wigan WN6 0WW
Hon Director: Dr D A Marshall Boxall. No full-time staff. *CC* No.284790. Began 1981; interdenominational. Magazine *East-West Contact* (1,000 quarterly). Turnover £4,259 to year end Dec 98. Providing Bibles, Christian literature; providing support for Christian workers in Central and Eastern Europe.
☎ 01257 400 128

Emmaus Bible School UK, Carlett Boulevard, Eastham, Wirral CH62 8BZ
UK Director: Mr David A Thompson. Other staff 8. *CC* No.267322. Began 1951; interdenominational. Magazine: *By the Way* (2,000 quarterly), *Prayer Letter* (Circulation n/a monthly). Turnover n/a. Offering studies in over 120 languages used by missionaries and missions worldwide. 93 English speaking studies.
Web: kingsnet.org.uk/emmaus
Email: emmaus@kingsnet.org.uk
☎ 0151 327 1172/6153/7373 🖷 0151 327 1592

Evangelical Literature Trust, St Peter's Church Office, Stoke Park Drive, Ipswich IP2 9TH
Director: Dr Andrew Marfleet. No full-time staff. *CC* No.262508. Began 1971; interdenominational. No magazine. Turnover £470,000 to year end Dec 96. Supplying Christian books to theological colleges, students and pastors in Third World and Eastern Europe.
Web: dspace.dial.pipex.com/town/plaza/hrso
Email: a.marfleet@btinternet.com
☎ 01473 687 513 🖷 01473 690 881

very Home Crusade, 2 Clara Street, Belfast BT5 5GB
Founder & Secretary: Mr William E Allen. *Manager:* Mr Samuel Adams. Executive staff 2, Other staff 13. ***CC*** No.XN48143. Began 1960; interdenominational. Magazine: *Good News* (4,000 monthly). Turnover £750,000 to year end Dec 97. Publishing Gospel tracts and booklets in 70 languages sent free to over 110 countries.
Email: 106461.3452@compuserve.com
☎ 028 9045 5026 Fax 028 9045 5026

very Home for Christ, Victoria House, Victoria Road, Buckhurst Hill IG9 5EX
Executive Director (UK): To be appointed. No full time staff. ***CC*** No.286042. Began 1982; interdenominational. Magazine: *Everyhome* (1,800 monthly). Turnover £77,000 to year end Dec 97. Evangelism service organisation specialising in home-to-home distribution methods; leading Schools of Prayer.
Email: 100067.1226@compuserve.com
☎ 020 8559 2806 Fax 020 8502 9062

'eed the Minds, Albany House, 67 Sydenham Road, Guildford GU1 3RY
Director: Dr Alwyn Marriage. Executive staff 2, Other staff 4. ***CC*** No.291333. Began 1963; interdenominational. Magazine: *Feed the Minds News* (5,000 every four months). Turnover £418,601 to year end Mar 98. Supporting indigenous literacy, Christian literature and communication projects in developing countries and Eastern Europe.
Email: feedtheminds@gn.apc.org.uk
☎ 01483 888 580 Fax 01483 888 581
Also at: 41 George IV Bridge, Edinburgh EH1 1EL
☎ 0131 226 5254 Fax 0131 225 8861

'ellowship for the Visually Handicapped, 26 Cross Street, Moretonhampstead, Newton Abbot TQ13 8NL
Director: Mr Lionel G Holmes. *Manager:* Mr Steve W Brown. Executive staff 2, Other staff 5. ***CC*** No.292625. Began 1985; interdenominational. Incorporating Compass Braille and Sightlink. No magazine. Turnover £120,464 to year end Mar 98. Supporting Christian ministry to visually impaired people overseas and producing Christian literature in Asian-language braille.
Web: www.bigfoot.com/~compass_braille
Email: compass_braille@bigfoot.com (Compass Braille)
Email: sightlink@writeme.com (Sightlink)
☎ 01647 440 101 Fax 01647 440 101

Gospel Literature Worldwide (a WEC International ministry), SOON, 44 Twyford Road, Willington, Derby DE65 6BN
Team Leader: Mr Tony Whittaker. Began n/a; interdenominational. Turnover n/a. Direct mail evangelistic papers: SOON (easy-English), BIENTOT (French), CEDO (Portuguese), UPESI (Swahili) also German, Italian, Russian, Shona.
Email: admin@soon.org.uk
☎ 01283 702 334 Fax 01283 702 334

Gospel Printing Mission, 46 Roxy Avenue, Chadwell Heath, Romford RM6 4AY
General Director: Mr David W Cotton. Executive staff 2, Other staff 19. ***CC*** No.267903. Began 1960; non-denominational. Magazine: *GPM Review/Prayer News* (2,000 quarterly). Turnover £30,971 [Donation Income] to year end Dec 98. Publishing and printing tracts and booklets in 44 languages to 100 countries worldwide.
☎ 020 8597 2140

Literature Ministry to Poland, Chapelhouse, 40 Market Street, Southport PR8 1HJ
Administrator: Mr M M Stolarski. No full-time staff. Began 1982; Grace Baptist. Magazine: *News Sheet* (2,000 half-yearly). Turnover £3,000 to year end Dec 98. Helping to provide Bible-based literature in the Polish language.
Email: maciek@gbmlit.mersinet.co.uk
☎ 01704 560 698 Fax 01704 551 226

***No Frontiers (Literature Outreach) Ltd**, PO Box 38, Hastings TN34 3WZ
Manager: Mr Allistair Graham. Executive staff 2, Other staff 1. ***CC*** No.1022425. Began 1992; interdenominational. Magazine: *Update* (2,750 quarterly). Turnover £150,000 to year end Dec 98. Providing foreign language Bibles and Christian literature for international distribution. Over 100 languages.
Web: www.nofrontiers.com
Email: nofrontiers@kingsway.co.uk
☎ 01424 426 768 Fax 01424 202 529

***Open Doors with Brother Andrew**, PO Box 6, Witney OX8 7SP
Regional Director: Mr Peter Cowell. *Development Manager:* Mr Mark Bedford. *Communications Manager:* Ms Elizabeth Philpott. Executive staff 1, Office staff 10. ***CC*** No.260600. Began 1970; interdenominational. Magazine: *Open Doors* (26,000 monthly). Turnover £2,078,000 to year end Dec 98. Bible distribution, encouragement and training for Christians living in countries where they suffer discrimination.
Web: www.od.org/oduk
Email: info@opendoors.uk.com
☎ 01865 300 300 Fax 01865 301 301

Right to Read, 2 Windermere Crescent, Belfast BT8 4XY
Director: Rev Howard Lewis. No full-time staff. ***CC*** Began 1988; interdenominational. No magazine. Turnover £10,000 to year end Dec 98. Facilitating Christian growth and maturity in the developing world by the provision of Christian literature.
☎ 028 9079 9558 Mobile 07887 578 485

***The Rushworth Literature Enterprise Ltd**, 2 Dimple Lane, Crich, Matlock DE4 5BQ
Founder: Rev David Rushworth-Smith. Executive staff 3, Other staff 1. ***CC*** No.241364. Began 1953; non-denominational. Magazine: *Rushworth News* (1,000 seasonally). Turnover £13,000 [excluding second-hand books] to year end Mar 98. Publishing and donating Christian study books to pastors in the Third World.
Web: www.rushworth.lit.virgin.net
Email: rushworth.lit@virgin.net
☎ 01773 857 313 Fax 01773 857 313

***SGM International**, Radstock House, 3 Eccleston Street, London SW1W 9LZ
Executive Director: Mr Bryan Stonehouse. *International Director:* Mr Hugh Davies. *International Publishing Director:* Mr David Atkinson. Executive staff 4, Other staff 36. ***CC*** Began 1888; non-denominational. (Previously Scripture Gift Mission). Magazine: *Interact* (30,000 quarterly). Turnover £2,700,000 to year end Dec 98. Distributing Bible portions in over 400 languages.
Web: members.aol.com/sgmint
Email: lon@sgm.org
☎ 020 7730 2155 Fax 020 7730 0240
Also at: 218 York Street, Belfast BT15 1GY
Email: ire@sgm.org
☎ 028 9074 5551

Society for Promoting Christian Knowledge (SPCK), Holy Trinity Church, Marylebone Road, London NW1 4DU
General Secretary: Mr Paul Chandler. Management staff 6, Other staff 265. *CC* Began 1698; interdenominational but historically Anglican. Magazine: *Theology* (4,000 every two months). Turnover £10,138,000 to year end Apr 98. UK publishers and booksellers making grants and supporting Christian communications worldwide.
Web: www.spck.org.uk
Email: spck@spck.org.uk
☎ 020 7387 5282 🖷 020 7388 2352

***Society for the Protection of Unborn Children (SPUC)**, Phyllis Bowman House, 5 St Matthew Street, Westminster, London SW1P 2JT
National Director: Mr John Smeaton. *Evangelicals Director:* Mr Peter Smith. *Evangelicals Chairman:* Rev Ian Brown. Executive staff 10, Other staff 30. Began 1967; non-denominational. Offices also in Belfast, Cardiff, Glasgow, Preston, Stockton. Magazine: *Human Concern* (120,000 every four months). Turnover £1,250,000 to year end Feb 98. Leading campaigns to tighten abortion law; educating public and parliament about abortion, population control, euthanasia.
Web: www.spuc.org.uk
Email: sysop@spuc.org.uk
☎ 020 7222 5845 🖷 020 7222 0630

***SOON Gospel Literature (a WEC International ministry)**, 44 Twyford Road, Willington, Derby DE65 6BN
Team Leader: Mr Tony Whittaker. Executive staff 11. *CC* No.237005. Began 1962; interdenominational. Part of Gospel Literature Worldwide. Magazine: *SOON* (750,000 quarterly). Turnover £65,000 to year end Mar 98. Distributed by volunteers. Other activities: evangelistic Bible correspondence course, internet outreach, web evangelism training.
Web: www.soon.org.uk
Email: admin@soon.org.uk
☎ 01283 702 334 🖷 01283 702 334

***Sovereign World Trust**, PO Box 777, Tonbridge TN11 OZS
Director: Mrs Jan Mungeam. Part-time staff 3. *C* No.327284. Began 1986; non-denominational. No magazin Turnover £128,000 to year end Sept 98. Sending Christia literature to pastors and leaders in Third World and developir countries.
Email: sovereignworldtrust@compuserve.com
☎ 01732 851 150 🖷 01732 851 077

To Russia – From the Heart, 9 Bullbanks Road, Belvede DA17 6DT
Translator: Mr Alexander Sibilev. No other staff. Began 199 evangelical. No magazine. Turnover n/a. Translating Christia literature for the people of Russia.
☎ 01322 441 399

United Society for Christian Literature, Albany House, 67 Syden ham Road, Guildford GU1 3RY
General Secretary: Dr Alwyn Marriage. No full-time staff. *C* No.226512. Began 1799; interdenominational. In partnershi with Feed The Minds. Magazine: *Annual Report* (Circulatio n/a annually). Turnover £233,650 to year end Mar 98 Supporting Christian literature and theological education i developing countries and Eastern Europe.
Email: feedtheminds@gn.apc.org
☎ 01483 888 580 🖷 01483 888 581

***UPESI Gospel Literature (a WEC International ministry)** Bowstones, Hall Crescent, Gullane EH31 2HA
Editor: Miss Beryl Shannon. *Administrator:* Mr David Eunson Executive staff 1, Other staff 1. *CC* No.237005. Began 1981 interdenominational. Part of Gospel Literature Worldwide Magazine: *Prayer Letter* (85,000 quarterly). Turnover £3,50 to year end Mar 99. Producing and distributing free broadshee in Swahili language to Africa.
Email: bjshannon@soon.org.uk
☎ 01620 842 299 🖷 01620 842 299

O

UK MISSIONARY SOCIETIES AND MISSIONARIES

Information about UK Missionary Societies and Missionaries is contained in the following five lists and two categories. The two categories *Missionary Sending Churches (Direct)* On Page 351 and *Missionary Societies* on Page 352 are preceded by lists showing how many missionaries each society has and where they are working. The list on Page 331 identifies by country and denominational grouping where societies have UK missionaries; in order to save space, abbreviations have been used for society names, and these are given below. The list on Page 346 shows the numbers of staff in each society.

1. ABBREVIATIONS OF SOCIETIES

Missionary Societies (Anglican) = A in list

C	Crosslinks
CMJ	Church's Ministry Among Jewish People
CMS	Church Mission Society
CMSI	Church Missionary Society Ireland (CMS Ireland)
ICS	Intercontinental Church Society
MAM	Mid-Africa Ministry (CMS)
MM	Melanesian Mission
MS	The Missions to Seamen
OXM	Oxford Mission
PNG	Papua New Guinea Church Partnership
RHT	Right Hand Trust
SAMS	South American Mission Society
SSF	Society of St Francis
USPG	United Society for the Propagation of the Gospel

Missionary Sending Churches (Direct) = CH in list

BCC	Basingstoke Community Church
BHCF	Biggin Hill Christian Fellowship
CCF	Coventry Christian Fellowship
EOS	Echoes of Service
HCF	Hollybush Christian Fellowship
ICF	Ichthus Christian Fellowship
KT	Kensington Temple London City Church
LNI	Lifeline Network International

Missionary Societies (Interdenominational) = I in list

A	Agapé
AAM	All India Mission
ACT	Action International Ministries (UK)
AEF	Africa Evangelical Fellowship
AEM	Albanian Evangelical Mission
AGM	Acre Gospel Mission
AIM	Africa Inland Mission International
AM	Antioch Mission UK
AP	Action Partners Ministries
AWM	Arab World Ministries
BCM	BCM International
BEM	Belgian Evangelical Mission
BIS	British & International Sailors' Society
CAI	Christian Associates International
CEF	Child Evangelism Fellowship
CIA	Christians in Action
CLC	Christian Literature Crusade

MA	The Christian and Missionary Alliance
T	Carrot Tops
WI	Christian Witness to Israel
F	Dohnavur Fellowship
AB	Evangelical Action (Brazil)
CM	European Christian Mission (Britain)
I	Emmanuel International
MF	European Missionary Fellowship
MMS	Edinburgh Medical Missionary Society
	Frontiers
EBA	FEBA Radio
MT	France Mission Trust
MSA	Gospel Mission of South America
NF	Gorakhpur Nurseries Fellowship
O	Global Outreach UK
TNM	Go To The Nations Ministry
CJB	HCJB-UK
FES	International Fellowship of Evangelical Students
NF	International Nepal Fellowship
S	INTERSERVE
SI	INTERSERVE Ireland
SS	INTERSERVE Scotland
T	International Teams UK
CL	Japan Christian Link
M	Japan Mission
L	Latin Link UK
M	The Leprosy Mission
MI	The Leprosy Mission (International Office)
MNI	The Leprosy Mission Northern Ireland
MS	The Leprosy Mission Scotland
RI	Language Recordings UK
MAF	Mission Aviation Fellowship
MECO	Middle East Christian Outreach
MEM	Middle East Media
MMG	Mission to Military Garrisons (Inc)
MT	The Messianic Testimony
N	The Navigators
NTM	New Tribes Mission
NTMU	New Testament Missionary Union
NWFF	North West Frontier Fellowship
OM	Operation Mobilisation
OMF	OMF International (UK)
OMS	OMS International
PEI	People International
QIF	Qua Iboe Fellowship
RSMT	Red Sea Mission Team
SAUB	Servants to Asia's Urban Poor
SC	SAO Cambodia
SCFS	Seamen's Christian Friend Society
SCI	Sharing Christ Internationally
SCM	Siloam Christian Ministries
SDM	Sahara Desert Mission
SGM	Spanish Gospel Mission
SIM	SIM UK (Society for International Ministries)
TF	Tearfund
TWR	Trans World Radio
UFM	UFM Worldwide
VMM	Volunteer Missionary Movement
WBT	Wycliffe Bible Translators
WEC	WEC International
WGM	World Gospel Mission
WH	World Horizons (Britain)
WO	World Outreach
YWAM	Youth With A Mission UK
ZMI	Zambesi Mission

Missionary Societies (Other Denominational) = O in list

ACMM	Apostolic Church Missionary Movement
AGWM	Assemblies of God World Ministries
BM	Baptist Missions
BMS	BMS, Baptist Missionary Society
CAM	Central African Missions
CSB	Church of Scotland Board of World Mission
EIM	Elim International Missions
FCS	Free Church of Scotland Foreign Missions Board
FOI	Focus on Israel
FPCS	Free Presbyterian Church of Scotland Mission Committee
FPCU	Free Presbyterian Church of Ulster Mission Board
GBM	Grace Baptist Mission
JGNM	Japan Good News Ministries
MBM	Mennonite Board of Missions
MPM	Maranatha Pentecostal Mission
MCWCO	Methodist Church World Church Office
PCI	Presbyterian Church in Ireland Overseas Board
PCW	Presbyterian Church of Wales Mission Board
SA	Salvation Army
UICR	United Reformed Church International Relations
WAM	World-wide Advent Missions

Missionary Societies (Roman Catholic) = RC in list

Roman Catholics distinguish between Missionary Societies (whose main thrust is directed towards countries overseas) and Mission--Sending Societies (whose activity is mostly in UK, but who either send some personnel overseas or support overseas personnel from their province). The two are integrated in the following lists and the category entries.

The abbreviations are the initials used by the Societies themselves, except where differentiation required additional letters.

Societies in Abbreviation Order

AA	Assumptionists Fathers and Brothers
BS	Sisters of the Good Saviour (Bon Sauveur)
CFC	Congregation of Christian Brothers
CHS	Crusade of the Holy Spirit
CJ	Congregation of Josephites
CLM	Columban Lay Missionaries
CMF	Claretian Missionaries
CMS	Comboni Missionary Sisters (Verona Sisters)
CP	Passionists
CP	Sisters of the Cross and Passion
CSSP	Holy Ghost Fathers
CSSR	Redemptorists
DC	Daughters of Charity of St Vincent de Paul
DHM	Daughters of the Heart of Mary
DHS	Daughters of the Holy Spirit
DJ	Daughters of Jesus
DMJ	Daughters of Mary and Joseph
FCJ	Faithful Companions of Jesus
FD	Fidei Donum Priests
FMA	Salesian Sisters of St John Bosco
FMDM	Franciscan Missionaries of the Divine Motherhood
FMM	Franciscan Missionaries of Mary
FMS	Marist Brothers
FMSA	Franciscan Missionary Sisters for Africa
FMSJ	Franciscan Missionary Sisters of St Joseph
FSC	De La Salle Brothers
FSM	Franciscan Minoresses
FSP	Daughters of St Paul
HFB	Association of the Holy Family of Bordeaux
HHS	Helpers of the Holy Souls
IBVM	Institute of the Blessed Virgin Mary
IC	Institute of Charity (Rosminian Fathers & Brothers)
IMC	Consolata Fathers
JM	Sisters of Charity of Jesus and Mary
JOS	St Joseph's Hospice Association (Jospice International)
LSU	Congregation of La Sainte Union des Sacré-Coeurs
MAFR	Missionaries of Africa (White Fathers)
MC	Consolata Missionary Sisters
MCCJ	Comboni Missionaries
MCH	Missionaries of Charity
MHM	Mill Hill Missionaries
MHM	Associates of Mill Hill Missionaries
MHMJ	St Joseph's Missionary Society, Mill Hill
MMM	Medical Missionaries of Mary
MMS	Medical Mission Sisters (Society of Catholic Medical Missionaries)
MSHR	Missionary Sisters of the Holy Rosary (MSHR)
MSOLA	Missionary Sisters of Our Lady of Africa (White Sisters)
MSSC	Missionary Society of St Columban
MSSPC	Sisters of St Peter Claver
OAR	Augustinian Recollects
OFM	Order of Friars Minor
OFMCap	Capuchin Franciscans (Order of Friars Minor Capuchin)
OFMCon	Franciscan Conventuals
OH	Hospitaller Order of St John of God
OLA	Missionary Sisters of Our Lady of Apostles
OLC	Sisters of Our Lady of Charity
OLF	Sisters of Our Lady of Fidelity
OMI	Oblates of Mary Immaculate
OP	Dominicans
OPC	Dominican Sisters of St Catherine of Siena of Oakford
OPZ	Dominican Sisters of Zimbabwe
OSA	Augustinians
OSB	Grace and Compassion Benedictines

UK Missionary Societies and Missionaries

OSBB	English Benedictine Congregation, Belmont Abbey
OSBW	English Benedictine Congregation, Worth Abbey
OSF/MH	Franciscan Sisters of Mill Hill
OSM	Servite Friars
OSU	Ursulines of the Roman Union
RA	Religious of the Assumption
RGS	Our Lady of Charity of the Good Shepherd
RHF	Sisters of the Holy Family (St Emilie de Rodat)
RJM	Religious of Jesus and Mary
RLR	Sisters of La Retraite
RNDM	Congregation of Our Lady of the Missions
RSCJ	Sacred Hearts Community
RSCJ	Society of the Sacred Heart
RSM	Institute of Our Lady of Mercy
RSMU	Mercy Sisters of the Union of Great Britain
SAC	Pallottine Missionary Sisters
SC	Brothers of the Sacred Heart
SCA	Pallottine Fathers
SCE	Sisters of Charity of Our Lady of Evron
SCI	Sisters of Christian Instruction (St Gildas)
SCJB	Sacred Heart Fathers (Betharram)
SCJD	Sacred Heart Fathers (Dehonians)
SCS	Sisters of Christ
SDB	Salesian Fathers and Brothers
SdeC	Sisters of Charity of St Jeanne Antide Thouret
SDS	Society of the Divine Saviour (Salvatorians)
SHCJ	Society of the Holy Child Jesus
SJ	Society of Jesus
SJA	Sisters of St Joseph of the Apparition
SJC	Sisters of St Joseph of Cluny
SM	Society of Mary
SMA	Society of African Missions
SMM	Montfort Fathers
SMM/SRS	Montfort Sisters, La Sagesse (Daughters of Wisdom)
SMR	Society of Marie Reparatrice
SP	Sisters of Providence, Rosminians
SPC	Sisters of Charity of St Paul
SPS	St Patrick's Missionary Society
SSC	Sisters of St Clare
SSCL	Missionary Sisters of St Columban
SSHJM	Sisters of the Sacred Heart of Jesus and Mary
SSJA	Sisters of St Joseph of Annecy
SSMMP	Sisters of St Marie Madeleine Postel
SSMN	Sisters of St Mary of Namur
SSMND	Sisters of Notre Dame de Namur
SSPS	Missionary Sisters Servants of the Holy Spirit
SVD	Society of the Divine Word
SX	Xaverian Missionary Fathers

Abbreviations in Society Order

AMHM	Associates of Mill Hill Missionaries
HFB	Association of the Holy Family of Bordeaux
AA	Assumptionists Fathers and Brothers
OAR	Augustinian Recollects
OSA	Augustinians
SC	Brothers of the Sacred Heart
OFMCap	Capuchin Franciscans (Order of Friars Minor Capuchin)
CMF	Claretian Missionaries
CLM	Columban Lay Missionaries
MCCJ	Comboni Missionaries
CMS	Comboni Missionary Sisters (Verona Sisters)
CFC	Congregation of Christian Brothers
CJ	Congregation of Josephites
LSU	Congregation of La Sainte Union des Sacré-Coeurs
RNDM	Congregation of Our Lady of the Missions
IMC	Consolata Fathers
MC	Consolata Missionary Sisters
CHS	Crusade of the Holy Spirit
DC	Daughters of Charity of St Vincent de Paul
DJ	Daughters of Jesus
DMJ	Daughters of Mary and Joseph
FSP	Daughters of St Paul
DHM	Daughters of the Heart of Mary
DHS	Daughters of the Holy Spirit
FSC	De La Salle Brothers
OPC	Dominican Sisters of St Catherine of Siena of Oakford
OPZ	Dominican Sisters of Zimbabwe
OP	Dominicans
OSBB	English Benedictine Congregation, Belmont Abbey
OSBW	English Benedictine Congregation, Worth Abbey
FCJ	Faithful Companions of Jesus
FD	Fidei Donum Priests
OFMCon	Franciscan Conventuals
FSM	Franciscan Minoresses
FMM	Franciscan Missionaries of Mary
FMDM	Franciscan Missionaries of the Divine Motherhood
FMSA	Franciscan Missionary Sisters for Africa
FMSJ	Franciscan Missionary Sisters of St Joseph
OSF/MH	Franciscan Sisters of Mill Hill
OSB	Grace and Compassion Benedictines
HHS	Helpers of the Holy Souls
CSSP	Holy Ghost Fathers
OH	Hospitaller Order of St John of God
IC	Institute of Charity (Rosminian Fathers & Brothers)
RSM	Institute of Our Lady of Mercy
IBVM	Institute of the Blessed Virgin Mary
FMS	Marist Brothers
MMS	Medical Mission Sisters (Society of Catholic Medical Missionaries)
MMM	Medical Missionaries of Mary
RSMU	Mercy Sisters of the Union of Great Britain
MHM	Mill Hill Missionaries
MAFR	Missionaries of Africa (White Fathers)
MCH	Missionaries of Charity
MSOLA	Missionary Sisters of Our Lady of Africa (White Sisters)
OLA	Missionary Sisters of Our Lady of Apostles
SSCL	Missionary Sisters of St Columban
MSHR	Missionary Sisters of the Holy Rosary (MSHR)
SSPS	Missionary Sisters Servants of the Holy Spirit
MSSC	Missionary Society of St Columban
SMM	Montfort Fathers
SMM/SRS	Montfort Sisters, La Sagesse (Daughters of Wisdom)
OMI	Oblates of Mary Immaculate
OFM	Order of Friars Minor
RGS	Our Lady of Charity of the Good Shepherd
SCA	Pallottine Fathers
SAC	Pallottine Missionary Sisters
CP	Passionists
CSSR	Redemptorists
RJM	Religious of Jesus and Mary
RA	Religious of the Assumption
SCJB	Sacred Heart Fathers (Betharram)
SCJD	Sacred Heart Fathers (Dehonians)
RSCJ	Sacred Hearts Community
JOS	St Joseph's Hospice Association (Jospice International)
MHMJ	St Joseph's Missionary Society, Mill Hill
SPS	St Patrick's Missionary Society
SDB	Salesian Fathers and Brothers
FMA	Salesian Sisters of St John Bosco
OSM	Servite Friars
JM	Sisters of Charity of Jesus and Mary
SCE	Sisters of Charity of Our Lady of Evron
SdeC	Sisters of Charity of St Jeanne Antide Thouret
SPC	Sisters of Charity of St Paul
SCS	Sisters of Christ
SCI	Sisters of Christian Instruction (St Gildas)
RLR	Sisters of La Retraite
SSMND	Sisters of Notre Dame de Namur
OLC	Sisters of Our Lady of Charity
OLF	Sisters of Our Lady of Fidelity
SSC	Sisters of St Clare
SSJA	Sisters of St Joseph of Annecy
SJC	Sisters of St Joseph of Cluny
SJA	Sisters of St Joseph of the Apparition
SSMMP	Sisters of St Marie Madeleine Postel
SSMN	Sisters of St Mary of Namur
MSSPC	Sisters of St Peter Claver
CP	Sisters of the Cross and Passion
BS	Sisters of the Good Saviour (Bon Sauveur)
RHF	Sisters of the Holy Family (St Emilie de Rodat)
SSHJM	Sisters of the Sacred Heart of Jesus and Mary
SP	Sisters of Providence, Rosminians
SMA	Society of African Missions
SJ	Society of Jesus
SMR	Society of Marie Reparatrice
SM	Society of Mary
SVD	Society of the Divine Word
SHCJ	Society of the Holy Child Jesus
RSCJ	Society of the Sacred Heart
SDS	Society of the Divine Saviour (Salvatorians)
OSU	Ursuline Sisters
SX	Xaverian Missionary Fathers

2. LOCATION OF SERVICE BY COUNTRY

nly those countries in which UK missionaries are specifically known to be working are included in this list. The total number shown for each society orresponds to that shown in brackets after each country in column two of the lists of **Location of Service by Society** on Page 336 and **Sending Churches y Location of Service** on Page 351.

ountry	Denomination	Societies working in country (excluding Associates)	Total personnel	Grand Total (including Associates)
fghanistan	I	PEI(2)	2	**2**
frica	I	A(2)	2	**2**
lbania	CH	EOS(2), ICF(2)	4	**60**
	I	AEM(24), ECM(3), OM(2), WEC(1), YWAM(3)	33	
	O	AGWM(1), BMS(21), EIM(1)	23	
lgeria	RC	MAFR(1)	1	**1**
ngola	CH	EOS(4)	4	**9**
	I	AEF(1), MAF(1)	2	
	O	BMS(2)	2	
	RC	MMM(1)	1	
Antigua & Barbuda	RC	SVD(1)	1	**1**
Argentina	A	SAMS(19), USPG(4)	23	**54**
	CH	EOS(7)	7	
	I	CEF(1), GMSA(1), LL(14)	16	
	O	SA(3)	3	
	RC	CHS(1), FCJ(2), LSU(1), OPC(1)	5	
Armenia	I	IFES(1)	1	**1**
Asia	I	ISI(2)	2	**2**
Australia	A	SSF(4)	4	**55**
	I	CLC(2), CWI(3), NTM(5), WEC(1), YWAM(7)	18	
	O	EIM(2), FPCU(4), SA(5), WAM(2)	13	
	RC	CSSP(1), FMDM(4), FMM(2), MHM(4), MHMJ(3), MSSC(1), SJA(3), SMA(1), SMM(1)	20	
Austria	CH	EOS(1)	1	**30**
	I	ECM(5), IFES(1), IT(5), OM(6)	17	
	O	AGWM(6), GBM(5), SA(1)	12	
Azerbaijan	CH	ICF(5)	5	**6**
	I	IFES(1)	1	
Bahamas	CH	EOS(2)	2	**2**
Bangladesh	A	CMS(1), USPG(5)	6	**26**
	I	IS(5), LM(4), OM(4), SIM(2)	15	
	O	BMS(1), CSB(3), MCWCO(1)	5	
Barbados	RC	OP(3), OSU(1), SJ(1)	5	**5**
Belarus	I	IFES(6)	6	**6**
Belgium	A	ICS(4)	4	**49**
	I	BEM(17), EMF(1), IFES(2), OM(9)	29	
	O	AGWM(2), BMS(2), CSB(2), EIM(7), SA(3)	16	
Belize	A	USPG(4)	4	**4**
Benin	I	SIM(17)	17	**17**
Bermuda	O	CSB(2)	2	**2**
Bolivia	CH	EOS(9)	9	**55**
	A	SAMS(4)	4	
	I	IT(1), LL(19), NTM(2), SIM(10), YWAM(4)	36	
Boliva (contd.)	O	MCWCO(2)	2	
	RC	FD(4)	4	
Botswana	CH	EOS(5), LNI(2)	7	**12**
	O	EIM(1)	1	
	RC	CP(1), CP(3)	4	
Brazil	A	ICS(1), SAMS(8), USPG(2)	11	**180**
	CH	EOS(17)	17	
	I	AGM(8), EAB(4), LL(16), NTM(8), NTMU(1), OMS(2), UFM(28), WBT(13), WEC(5), YWAM(4)	89	
	O	ACMM(2), BMS(40), PCI(3), SA(6)	51	
	RC	AMHM(1), FD(1), MAFR(1), MHM(2), MHMJ(2), MSHR(1), OAR(1), SDB(1), SPS(1), SSMN(1)	12	
Bulgaria	CH	HCF(1), ICF(1)	2	**7**
	I	IFES(5)	5	
Burkina Faso	I	QIF(3), SIM(3), WBT(12), WEC(6), WH(5)	29	**30**
	RC	MAFR(1)	1	
Burundi	A	MAM(1)	1	**5**
	I	TF(4)	4	
Cambodia	I	OMF(9), SAUB(1), SC(11), TF(1), UFM(1), WEC(5), WH(5), YWAM(5)	38	**38**
Cameroon	I	AP(3), UFM(2), WBT(16)	21	**47**
	O	MCWCO(1)	1	
	RC	CSSP(1), FMA(1), FMS(1), LSU(1), MHM(5), MHMJ(5), OSU(1), RLR(1), SCS(4), SDEC(1), SM(1), SSMN(1)	23	
Canada	I	EI(3), IT(1), NTM(4), OM(1), RSMT(1), UFM(2), WBT(1), WEC(2), YWAM(13)	28	**44**
	O	AGWM(2), FPCU(8), SA(6)	16	
Canary Islands	I	AGM(4)	4	**4**
Caribbean	O	MCWCO(7), SA(1)	8	**8**
Cayman Islands	O	UICR(2)	2	**2**
Central African Republic	I	AIM(5)	5	**7**
	O	BMS(2)	2	
Central Asia	A	CMS(7)	7	**43**
	I	F(12), FEBA(4), IS(10), ISS(3), N(2), YWAM(5)	36	
Chad	I	AIM(7), AP(9), MAF(1), WBT(6), WEC(11)	34	**34**
Chile	A	ICS(2), SAMS(16), USPG(3)	21	**45**
	CH	EOS(2)	2	
	I	CLC(2), GMSA(5), SIM(2)	9	
	O	ACMM(2), MCWCO(1), SA(3)	6	

Country	Denomination	Societies working in country (excluding Associates)	Total personnel	Grand Total (including Associates)
Chile (contd.)	RC	CLM(1), DHS(1), DJ(1), FD(1), MSSC(1), RLR(1), SHCJ(1)	7	
China	A	USPG(14)	14	**19**
	CH	BHCF(2)	2	
	I	IS(1)	1	
	O	PCI(2)	2	
Colombia	CH	EOS(2)	2	**32**
	I	CMA(1), IT(1), LL(2), NTM(6), OMS(6), WBT(2), YWAM(8)	26	
	O	GBM(2)	2	
	RC	IMC(1), SX(1)	2	
Comoro Islands	I	AIM(9)	9	**10**
	RC	SDS(1)	1	
Congo (Democratic Republic of)	A	MAM(1)	1	**52**
	CH	EOS(20)	20	
	I	UFM(7), WEC(4)	11	
	O	CAM(14), EIM(3), SA(2)	19	
	RC	MHMJ (1)	1	
Congo (Republic of)	I	WBT(1)	1	**2**
	O	SA(1)	1	
Costa Rica	I	LL(3)	3	**4**
	RC	OAR(1)	1	
Côte d'Ivoire	CH	HCF(1)	1	**62**
	I	NTM(18), UFM(8), WBT(10), WEC(15)	51	
	O	MCWCO(4), WAM(4)	8	
	RC	RSCJ(1), SCE(1)	2	
Croatia	I	IFES(3)	3	**5**
	O	BMS(2)	2	
Cyprus	A	ICS(1), MS(2)	3	**22**
	I	AWM(3), FEBA(4), IS(1), MMG(7), YWAM(4)	19	
Czech Republic	I	IFES(3), OM(2)	5	**13**
	O	PCI(1), SA(7)	8	
Denmark	I	YWAM(6)	6	**8**
	O	SA(2)	2	
Djibouti	I	RSMT(3)	3	**3**
Dominican Republic	I	YWAM(2)	2	**2**
Eastern Europe	CH	EOS(4)	4	**7**
	I	N(3)	3	
Ecuador	CH	EOS(3)	3	**39**
	I	HCJB(9), LL(16), OMS(2)	27	
	RC	FD(5), FMSJ(2), MHMJ(1), OSA(1)	9	
Egypt	A	CMS(3), CMSI(4), USPG(1)	8	**19**
	CH	ICF(2)	2	
	I	AP(2), OM(4)	6	
	O	CSB(1)	1	
	RC	CMS(1), RHF(1)	2	
El Salvador	O	BMS(2)	2	**4**
	RC	SJ(1), SSC(1)	2	
Eritrea	A	CMS(1), USPG(2)	3	**6**
	RC	CMS(2), MCCJ(1)	3	
Ethiopia	A	C(4)	4	**49**
	I	LM(1), MAF(2), N(7), SIM(19), TF(2), WBT(3)	34	
	RC	DC(6), FMA(1), FMSA(2), MCCJ(1), MCH(1)	11	
Europe	I	N(2), WBT(12)	14	**14**
Falkland Islands	A	ICS(1)	1	**9**
	I	MMG(6)	6	
	RC	MHMJ(1), RSMU(1)	2	
Far East	I	WBT(5)	5	**5**
Fiji	RC	MSSC(1)	1	**1**
France	A	C(7), ICS(15), MS(4)	26	**268**
	CH	BCC(0), EOS(71), ICF(16)	87	
	I	AWM(18), CLC(7), CMA(1), ECM(6), EMF(3), FMT(17), IFES(4), MT(2), N(2), OM(7), SIM(2), UFM(1), WEC(10), WH(27), YWAM(11)	118	
	O	BM(3), BMS(14), CSB(2), EIM(2), GBM(3), PCI(4), SA(4), UICR(1)	33	
Gabon	I	SIM(1)	1	**2**
	RC	CSSP(1)	1	
Gambia	A	CMS(1), RHT(5)	6	**21**
	CH	CCF(2)	2	
	I	WEC(8)	8	
	O	MCWCO(2)	1	
	RC	SJC(1), SSJA(2)	3	
Germany	CH	EOS(1)	1	**36**
	I	A(2), OM(19), WEC(1)	22	
	O	FPCU(1), MCWCO(4), SA(7), WAM(1)	13	
Ghana	A	CMS(2)	2	**42**
	I	CEF(1), SIM(2), WBT(13), WEC(2), YWAM(1)	19	
	O	CSB(1), EIM(2), MCWCO(2), SA(7)	12	
	RC	DMJ(1), MAFR(3), SCI(4), SHCJ(1)	9	
Gibraltar	I	WH(4)	4	**7**
	O	AGWM(1), CSB(2)	3	
Greece	A	C(2), ICS(1)	3	**15**
	I	ECM(2), EMF(1), IFES(5), WEC(2), WH(2)	12	
Greenland	CH	EOS(2)	2	**2**
Grenada	I	YWAM(2)	2	**6**
	RC	OP(4)	4	
Guam	RC	RGS(1)	1	**1**
Guatemala	I	YWAM(1)	1	**2**
	RC	SSC(1)	1	
Guinea	A	CMS(4)	4	**8**
	I	LM(2)	2	
	O	BMS(2)	2	
Guinea-Bissau	I	TF(1), WEC(14)	15	**15**
Guyana	A	USPG(1)	1	**10**
	RC	SJ(9)	9	
Haiti	I	EI(1), TF(2)	3	**4**
	RC	LSU(1)	1	
Honduras	I	TF(3)	3	**15**
	O	EIM(7)	7	
	RC	JOS(5)	5	
Hong Kong	A	CMS(1)	1	**27**
	CH	EOS(4), ICF(2)	6	
	I	CEF(1), OMF(3), OMS(1), YWAM(4)	9	
	O	EIM(2), SA(1), WAM(4)	7	
	RC	SDB(2), SSCL(2)	4	

Country	Denomination	Societies working in country (excluding Associates)	Total personnel	Grand Total (including Associates)
Hungary	I	IFES(1), MT(1), OM(2), OMS(1), YWAM(1)	6	**13**
	O	AGWM(2), BMS(2), CSB(2), SA(1)	7	
India	A	C(4), CMS(7), OXM(1), USPG(6)	18	**180**
	CH	BCC(24), EOS(13)	37	
	I	AAM(2), CIA(6), CT(6), DF(1), GNF(3), IS(22), ISI(1), LMS(1), OM(4), OMF(2), SIM(4), WEC(8), YWAM(9)	69	
	O	AGWM(2), BMS(5), CSB(9), GBM(1), MCWCO(2), PCI(7), SA(1), WAM(4)	31	
	RC	FMM(1), FSC(2), IC(2), MAFR(1), MHM(3), MHMJ(2), OFM(1), RGS(2), RNDM(1), RSCJ(5), SCJD(1), SDB(1), SDS(1), SMMSRS(1), SSJA(1)	25	
Indonesia	CH	ICF(2)	2	**33**
	I	LM(1), NTM(2), OMF(14), OMS(1), UFM(1), WBT(7), WEC(2)	28	
	O	PCI(1)	1	
	RC	FCJ(1), SVD(1)	2	
Ireland (Republic of)	CH	EOS(14)	14	**48**
	I	BCM(1), CEF(2), ECM(1), EMF(2), GO(1), SCFS(2), WH(2), YWAM(7)	18	
	O	AGWM(4), BM(8), FPCU(4)	16	
Israel	A	CMJ(23)	23	**60**
	CH	EOS(1)	1	
	I	EMMS(1), MT(2), OM(7)	10	
	O	CSB(12), FOI(4), PCI(3)	19	
	RC	AA(1), DC(1), FMM(1), FSC(1), OFM(2), SJA(1)	7	
Italy	CH	EOS(16)	16	**53**
	I	A(1), BCM(2), CLC(3), ECM(2), EMF(1), IFES(2), OM(2), WEC(1), YWAM(1)	15	
	O	AGWM(3), BMS(6), CSB(2), MCWCO(2), SA(9)	22	
Jamaica	O	AGWM(5), CSB(6), PCI(7)	18	**20**
	RC	DJ(1), OP(1)	2	
Japan	CH	EOS(10)	10	**87**
	A	CMS(3), MS(4), USPG(3)	10	
	I	JCL(4), JM(2), OMF(29), WEC(9), WH(2), YWAM(6)	52	
	O	AGWM(2), JGNM(2), MCWCO(3), SA(2)	9	
	RC	HHS(1), SDB(1), SJ(2), SM(1), SVD(1)	6	
Jordan	A	CMS(1), MS(1)	2	**2**
Kazakhstan	CH	BCC(1)	1	**6**
	I	IFES(1), OM(3), PEI(1)	5	
Kenya	CH	BCC(24), EOS(2)	26	**349**
	A	C(10), CMS(23), CMSI(5), MS(2), RHT(6)	46	
	I	AIM(57), AP(3), MAF(16), N(2), SCM(2), SIM(12), TF(2), VMM(1), WBT(32), WGM(7), YWAM(5)	139	
Kenya (contd.)	O	AGWM(7), CSB(12), FPCS(1), FPCU(4), GBM(6), MCWCO(11), PCI(17), SA(2), WAM(1)	61	
	RC	AMHM(3), CSSP(1), FD(5), FMA(1), FMM(2), FMS(1), FMSA(3), FMSJ(6), IC(1), MAFR(2), MC(1), MHM(12), MHMJ(12), MMM(3), MMS(2), MSOLA(1), OLC(1), OSBB(1), RA(1), RNDM(3), RSCJ(1), RSM(9), SJ(1), SPS(2), SSMND(2)	77	
Korea	A	CMS(1), MS(1)	2	**10**
	I	OMF(5), OMS(1)	6	
	O	AGWM(2)	2	**5**
Kurdistan	I	PEI(1)	1	**1**
Laos	I	LM(2), TF(2)	4	**4**
Latvia	O	GBM(4), SA(2)	6	**6**
Lebanon	A	CMS(6)	6	**28**
	CH	EOS(10), ICF(4)	14	
	I	TF(1)	1	
	O	CSB(5)	5	
	RC	RJM(1), RSMU(1)	2	
Lesotho	CH	BHCF(2), EOS(2)	4	**7**
	O	WAM(2)	2	
	RC	SDB(1)	1	
Liberia	I	TF(3), YWAM(1)	4	**16**
	O	SA(4), WAM(2)	6	
	RC	CFC(1), SDB(3), SMA(2)	6	
Luxembourg	O	AGWM(2)	2	**2**
Macau	RC	SDB(1)	1	**4**
	I	CIA(1), OMF(2)	3	
Macedonia	I	WH(1)	1	**1**
Madagascar	A	USPG(1)	1	**18**
	I	AEF(5), AIM(9)	14	
	O	PCW(1), UICR(1)	2	
	RC	BS(1)	1	
Malawi	A	RHT(4), USPG(6)	10	**70**
	I	AEF(4), N(2), SIM(6), ZMI(4)	16	
	O	ACMM(2), CSB(14), EIM(2), PCI(18), UICR(1)	37	
	RC	MAFR(1), MCH(1), SMM(2), SMMSRS(3)	7	
Malaysia	CH	EOS(1)	1	**16**
	I	OMF(4), WBT(2), WH(3)	9	
	O	MCWCO(2)	2	
	RC	MHM(2), MHMJ(2)	4	
Mali	I	MAF(2), RSMT(2), WBT(12), WEC(2), YWAM(1)	19	**21**
	O	MCWCO(2)	2	
Malta	I	WH(2)	2	**7**
	O	AGWM(4), CSB(1)	5	
Mauritius	RC	FMM(1)	1	**1**
Mercy Ships	I	YWAM(26)	26	**26**
Mexico	CH	BHCF(2), EOS(4)	6	**32**
	I	ACT(7), CIA(1), OMS(3), WBT(3), WEC(3)	17	
	O	SA(4)	4	

UK Missionary Societies and Missionaries

Country	Denomination	Societies working in country (excluding Associates)	Total personnel	Grand Total (including Associates)
Mexico (contd.)	RC	FMM(1), MAFR(1), MCCJ(1), MCCJ(1), SX(1)	5	
Micronesia	I	YWAM(2)	2	**2**
Middle East	CH	EOS(6)	6	**126**
	I	AWM(18), F(2), IS(8), ISI(1), ISS(3), MECO(24), MEM(4), OM(15), WBT(7), WH(36)	118	
	O	GBM(2)	2	
Moldova	I	IFES(3), OM(2)	5	**5**
Monaco	I	TWR(1)	1	**1**
Mongolia	I	IS(4), SCI(2)	6	**6**
Morocco	A	C(1), ICS(1)	2	**2**
Mozambique	CH	LNI(2)	2	**35**
	I	AEF(4), AIM(9), OMS(2), SIM(3), WBT(3), YWAM(1)	22	
	O	ACMM(4), CSB(3), EIM(2), MCWCO(2)	11	
mv Doulos	I	OM(26)	26	**26**
mv Logos	I	OM(18)	18	**18**
Namibia	I	A(2), AEF(5), AIM(6)	13	**15**
	RC	CFC(2)	2	
Near East	I	F(13)	13	**13**
Nepal	A	CMS(14), CMSI(2)	16	**190**
	I	INF(47), IS(30), ISI(5), ISS(9), LM(3), OM(2), TF(4), WEC(4), YWAM(4)	108	
	O	BMS(37), CSB(6), MCWCO(8), PCI(15)	66	
Netherlands	A	ICS(11), MS(4)	15	**44**
	I	CEF(1), OM(2), WEC(3), YWAM(16)	22	
	O	AGWM(2), CSB(4), SA(1)	7	
Netherlands Antilles	CH	EOS(2)	2	**2**
New Caledonia	CH	EOS(2)	2	**2**
New Zealand	A	MS(1)	1	**26**
	I	OM(2), WEC(4), YWAM(2)	8	
	RC	MHM(7), MHMJ(9), SJC(1)	17	
Nicaragua	O	BMS(3)	3	**4**
	RC	FSC(1)	1	
Niger	I	SDM(5), SIM(19), WBT(1), WH(3)	28	**28**
Nigeria	A	CMS(8)	8	**87**
	I	AP(14), LM(2), QIF(14), SIM(8)	38	
	O	AGWM(2), MCWCO(2), WAM(2)	6	
	RC	CSSP(6), DHS(8), FMDM(2), FSC(1), MAFR(1), MMM(3), MSHR(2), OLA(1), OSA(1), SHCJ(1), SMA(1), SSMND(8)	35	
North Africa	A	CMS(4), CMSI(1)	5	**50**
	I	AWM(19), F(9), IS(4), OM(7), TF(6)	45	
Northern Mariana Is	CH	EOS(2)	2	**2**
Norway	CH	EOS(4)	4	**12**
	I	EMF(1), YWAM(2)	3	
	O	SA(5)	5	
Pakistan	A	CMS(18), USPG(1)	19	**111**
	CH	EOS(14)	14	
	I	IS(12), ISI(2), ISS(4), NWFF(2), OM(6), PEI(2), RSMT(1), SIM(10), TF(2)	41	
	O	AGWM(2), CSB(11), SA(2), WAM(4)	19	
	RC	AMHM(1), CLM(1), CSSP(1), DHM(1), FMM(2), HFB(1), MHM(5), MHMJ(4), MSSC(1), RJM(1)	18	
Panama	I	NTM(18)	18	**18**
Papua New Guinea	A	SSF(3)	3	**70**
	I	LM(1), MAF(2), NTM(34), UFM(8), WBT(16)	61	
	O	SA(1)	1	
	RC	CP(1), OFMCAP(1), RNDM(1), SMMSRS(1), SVD(1)	5	
Paraguay	A	SAMS(19)	19	**22**
	I	WH(2), YWAM(1)	3	
Peru	A	C(1), ICS(1), SAMS(1), USPG(2)	5	**104**
	CH	EOS(2)	2	
	I	LL(33), N(4), SIM(13)	50	
	O	AGWM(2), BM(8), FCS(4), GBM(3)	17	
	RC	FD(10), FSC(2), JM(2), MSSC(2), OSBB(3), RSM(4), RSMU(1), SDB(1), SSCL(2), SSMND(3)	30	
Philippines	CH	HCF(2)	2	**120**
	I	ACT(6), FEBA(4), OMF(41), NTM(6), SCM(4), TF(2), WBT(6), WH(1), WO(1), YWAM(8)	79	
	O	AGWM(8), EIM(3), GBM(3), SA(1)	15	
	RC	CLM(3), FCJ(1), FMDM(1), FSC(1), HFB(1), MAFR(1), MCCJ(1), MHM(5), MHMJ(5), RNDM(1), SCJD(1), SSCL(2), SVD(1)	24	
Poland	A	ICS(1)	1	**9**
	I	ECM(2), N(3)	5	
	O	BMS(1), EIM(2)	3	
Portugal	CH	EOS(8)	8	**47**
	I	AGM(6), BCM(2), CAI(1), ECM(6), IFES(4), N(2), SCM(8), WEC(2), YWAM(1)	32	
	O	BMS(4), CSB(2), SA(1)	7	
Romania	CH	HCF(1), ICF(2)	3	**21**
	A	CMS(1)	1	
	I	CLC(1), IFES(1), IT(3), OM(5), WH(3)	13	
	O	CSB(1), PCI(3)	4	
Russia	A	C(2), CMS(5)	7	**41**
	I	A(8), IFES(7), NTM(4), OM(8)	27	
	O	SA(7)	7	

Country	Denomination	Societies working in country (excluding Associates)	Total personnel	Grand Total (including Associates)
Rwanda	A	MAM(5)	5	**9**
	CH	EOS(2)	2	
	RC	SSMN(2)	2	
Samoa	RC	SM(1)	1	**1**
Senegal	CH	CCF(2)	2	**47**
	I	NTM(9), WBT(8), WEC(25)	42	
	O	WAM(2)	2	
	RC	SSJA(1)	1	
Serbia	CH	EOS(2)	2	**2**
Seychelles	I	AIM(2), FEBA(11)	13	**13**
Sierra Leone	A	CMS(4)	4	**18**
	I	UFM(2)	2	
	O	AGWM(2), MPM(2), WAM(2)	6	
	RC	CFC(3), SJC(1), SX(2)	6	
Singapore	A	MS(1)	1	**25**
	I	OMF(16), WH(4), WO(1)	21	
	O	SA(1)	1	
	RC	FMDM(2)	2	
Slovakia	I	IFES(2), OM(1), WH(1)	4	**4**
Slovenia	I	IFES(1)	1	**1**
Solomon Islands	A	MM(1), SSF(1)	2	**3**
	RC	SM(1)	1	
South Africa	A	C(4), CMS(2), USPG(13)	19	**192**
	CH	EOS(16)	16	
	I	AEF(5), FEBA(2), MAF(1), OM(3), SIM(15), WEC(3), YWAM(1)	30	
	O	ACMM(3), AGWM(7), CSB(3), EIM(2), FCS(14), SA(6), WAM(2)	37	
	RC	CSSP(1), CSSR(8), FD(3), FMA(1), FMM(10), FMSA(1), FSM(1), HFB(3), IMC(1), MAFR(1), MCCJ(1), MSHR(4), OFM(15), OMI(2), OP(2), OPC(1), OSA(1), OSFMH(1), OSU(2), RLR(3), SCJD(1), SDB(10), SJ(7), SPC(4), SPS(1), SSMMP(1), SSMND(4)	90	
South Asia	I	F(4), WBT(9)	13	**13**
South East Asia	I	UFM(2)	2	**2**
Spain	A	C(2), ICS(3), SAMS(5)	10	**134**
	CH	BCC(2), EOS(17)	19	
	I	BCM(1), CLC(3), ECM(15), EMF(4), IFES(2), NTMU(1), OM(1), OMS(2), SGM(12), UFM(5), WEC(12), WH(8), YWAM(3)	69	
	O	AGWM(16), EIM(5), FPCU(5), GBM(5), SA(5)	36	
Sri Lanka	A	USPG(1)	1	**17**
	O	BMS(4), CSB(2), MCWCO(3), SA(2), WAM(2)	13	
	RC	FMM(3)	3	
St Helena	A	RHT(4), USPG(2)	6	**8**
	O	SA(2)	2	
Sudan	A	CMS(12)	12	**60**
	I	AIM(3), AP(9), EI(1), LM(1), OM(1), SIM(2), TF(11), WBT(17)	45	
	RC	MCCJ(1), MHM(1), MHMJ(1)	3	
Swaziland	A	RHT(6)	6	**10**
	RC	OSM(2), SDB(2)	4	
Sweden	CH	BCC(24)	24	**34**
	I	OM(2), YWAM(3)	5	
	O	SA(5)	5	
Switzerland	A	ICS(2)	2	**20**
	I	CEF(1), RSMT(1), WEC(1), YWAM(5)	8	
	O	AGWM(2), CSB(4), GBM(2), SA(2)	10	
Syria	A	CMS(1)	1	**3**
	RC	RJM(2)	2	
Taiwan	A	CMS(1)	1	**24**
	I	OMF(16), WEC(1), YWAM(1)	18	
	O	AGWM(3), PCW(1)	4	
	RC	OSU(1)	1	
Tajikistan	I	OM(2), PEI(2)	4	**4**
Tanzania	A	C(39), CMS(7), CMSI(2), MS(1), USPG(5)	54	**150**
	CH	EOS(8)	8	
	I	AEF(2), AIM(19), EI(1), MAF(24), WBT(3), YWAM(1)	50	
	O	EIM(2), SA(2)	4	
	RC	IC(1), LSU(5), MAFR(10), MMM(7), OFM(1), SAC(5), SDS(3), SP(2)	34	
Tatarstan	I	PEI(1)	1	**1**
Thailand	A	MS(1)	1	**75**
	CH	EOS(2)	2	
	I	NTM(10), OMF(25), TF(1), WEC(7), WH(4), YWAM(6)	53	
	O	AGWM(2), BMS(11), CSB(2), EIM(3)	18	
	RC	FSC(1)	1	
Togo & Benin	I	WBT(7)	7	**7**
Tonga	O	MCWCO(2)	2	**3**
	RC	SM(1)	1	
Trinidad & Tobago	CH	EOS(2)	2	**8**
	A	USPG(2)	2	
	O	BMS(4)	4	
Tunisia	A	ICS(1)	1	**2**
	RC	MAFR(1)	1	
Turkey	CH	CCF(6), ICF(4)	10	**27**
	I	EMF(1), OM(7), PEI(8), YWAM(1)	17	
Turkmenistan	I	PEI(4), TF(4)	8	**8**
Uganda	A	C(1), CMS(22), CMSI(8), MAM(29), RHT(12)	72	**146**
	CH	BCC(6), ICF(4)	10	
	I	AAM(2), EI(7), MAF(10), TF(2), WBT(2), YWAM(11)	34	
	O	MCWCO(2)	2	

UK Missionary Societies and Missionaries

Country	Denomination	Societies working in country (excluding Associates)	Total personnel	Grand Total (including Associates)
Uganda (contd.)	RC	CMS(2), FMSA(5), MAFR(3), MCCJ(2), MHM(3), MHMJ(8), MMM(1), MMS(1), OSM(1), SMM(2)	28	
Ukraine	A	ICS(1)	1	**9**
	I	EMF(1), IFES(3), MT(1), OM(1), YWAM(1)	7	
	O	EIM(1)	1	
United Arab Emirates	A	ICS(2), MS(1)	3	**3**
United Kingdom	A	C(8), CMJ(8), CMS(20), MAM(4), MS(17), USPG(1)	58	**1,118**
	CH	HCF(2)	2	
	I	A(3), AP(8), AWM(3), BCM(24), CEF(18), CIA(4), CLC(66), CMA(20), CWI(11), FEBA(2), GO(8), GTNM(20), HCJB(12), IFES(9), IS(37), ISS(2), IT(9), JCL(2), LRI(7), MMG(3), MT(12), N(47), OM(145), OMF(45), RSMT(6), SCFS(18), SIM(38), TWR(5), WBT(2), WEC(131), WGM(4), WH(48), WO(2), YWAM(249)	1,020	
	O	BMS(3), FCS(2), FPCU(16), GBM(11), PCI(4)	36	
	RC	AMHM(2)	2	
Uruguay	A	SAMS(6)	6	**7**
	RC	SDB(1)	1	
USA	A	SSF(2)	2	**112**
	I	CIA(1), N(4), NTM(4), OM(8), OMF(2), TWR(2), UFM(2), WBT(4), WEC(1), WGM(1), WH(1), YWAM(20)	50	
USA (contd.)	O	AGWM(1), FPCU(16), SA(4), WAM(39)	60	
Uzbekistan	I	OM(4), PEI(6)	10	**10**
Vanuatu	RC	SM(1)	1	**1**
Venezuela	A	USPG(2)	2	**7**
	CH	EOS(1)	1	
	I	NTM(3)	3	
	RC	CHS(1)	1	
Windward Islands	A	USPG(1)	1	**1**
Yemen	I	RSMT(6)	6	**6**
Zambia	A	CMSI(3), USPG(6)	9	**151**
	CH	BCC(4), EOS(50), LNI(0)	54	
	I	AEF(18), SIM(20)	38	
	O	AGWM(8), CSB(1), MCWCO(6), SA(5), UICR(1)	21	
	RC	CMS(1), FD(2), FMDM(10), MAFR(4), MSHR(1), OFMCON(2), SSHJM(9)	29	
Zimbabwe	A	C(8), RHT(6), SSF(2), USPG(11)	27	**144**
	CH	BCC(0), EOS(9), LNI(2)	11	
	I	AEF(7), FEBA(8), SIM(6), YWAM(2)	23	
	O	AGWM(7), EIM(2), FPCS(10), MCWCO(4), SA(6)	29	
	RC	CSSR(3), FMDM(9), FMSA(3), IBVM(2), OPZ(4), RSMU(1), SJ(30), SSMND(2)	54	
Other	CH	EOS(26)	26	**93**
	I	F (West Asia 4), ISS (West Asia 9), MAF (West Africa 1), N (West Africa 5), OMF (professional service personnel 41) RSMT(international staff 7)	67	

3. LOCATION OF SERVICE BY SOCIETY

UK missionaries = those serving in cross-culture and own culture mission and on furlough/home leave, but *excluding* associates.
Other countries = countries in which the society is involved but where none of their UK missionaries are currently serving.

Society	Countries with UK Missionaries	UK missionaries	Other Countries	Missionaries Worldwide
Acre Gospel Mission	Brazil(8), Canary Islands(4), Portugal(6)	19	n/a	32
Action International Ministries (UK)	Mexico(7), Philippines(6)	14	Brazil, Colombia, Ecuador, India, Mozambique, Tanzania, Ukraine	155
Action Partners Ministries	Cameroon(3), Chad(9), Egypt(2), Kenya(3), Nigeria(14), Sudan(9), United Kingdom(8)	105	Ghana	51
Africa Inland Mission International	Central African Republic(5), Chad(7), Comoro Islands(9), Kenya(57), Madagascar(9), Mozambique(9), Namibia(6), Seychelles(2), Sudan(3), Tanzania(19)	175	Lesotho, Reunion	176
Agapé	Africa(2), Germany(2), Italy(1), Namibia(2), Russia(8), United Kingdom(3)	73	150 countries worldwide	97
Albanian Evangelical Mission	Albania(24)	26	Kosova, Macedonia	24
All India Mission	India(2), Uganda(2)	6	n/a	90
Antioch Mission UK	n/a	3	Albania, Angola, Italy, Macao, Mozambique, Poland, Portugal, South Africa, Spain, Taiwan, United Kingdom	85
Apostolic Church Missionary Movement	Brazil(2), Chile(2), Malawi(2), Mozambique(4)	20	50 countries worldwide, Angola, Ghana, India, Nigeria, Sierra Leone, South Africa(3), Spain, Sri Lanka, Tanzania	13
Arab World Ministries	Cyprus(3), France(18), Middle East(18), North Africa(19), United Kingdom(3)	63	Canada, Germany, Spain, USA	250

Society	Countries with UK Missionaries	UK missionaries	Other Countries	Missionaries Worldwide
Assemblies of God World Ministries	Albania(1), Austria(6), Belgium(2), Canada(2), Gibraltar(1), Hungary(2), India(2), Ireland (Republic of)(4), Italy(3), Jamaica(5), Japan(2), Kenya(7), Korea(2), Luxembourg(2), Malta(4), Netherlands(2), Nigeria(2), Pakistan(2), Peru(2), Philippines(8), Sierra Leone(2), South Africa(7), Spain(16), Switzerland(2), Taiwan(3), Thailand(2), USA(1), Zambia(8), Zimbabwe(7)	120	Armenia, Bulgaria, Belarus, China, Croatia, Czech Republic, Estonia, France, Germany, Hong Kong, Iraq, Mozambique, Romania, Russia, Serbia, Singapore, Slovakia, Tanzania, Ukraine, Zaire	160
Associates of Mill Hill Missionaries	Brazil(1), Kenya(3), Pakistan(1), United Kingdom(2)	8	Australia, Cameroon, Congo, Ecuador, India, Malaysia, New Zealand, Philippines, Uganda	17
Association of the Holy Family of Bordeaux	Pakistan(1), Philippines(1), South Africa(3)	5	India, Peru	50
Assumptionists Fathers and Brothers	Israel(1)	1	Argentina, Brazil, Chile, Colombia, Congo (Democratic Republic of), Korea, Madagascar, Tanzania, Turkey	n/a
Augustinian Recollects	Brazil(1), Costa Rica(1)	2	n/a	110
Augustinians	Ecuador(1), Nigeria(1), South Africa(1)	3 1	Algeria, Argentina, Bolivia, Brazil, Chile, Colombia, Congo (Democratic Republic of), Cuba, Dominica, India, Indonesia, Japan, Kenya, Korea, Mexico, Panama, Peru, Philippines, Puerto Rico, Tanzania, Tunisia, Uruguay, Venezuela, Vietnam	560
Baptist Missions	France(3), Ireland (Republic of)(8), Peru(8)	20	n/a	19
BCM International	Ireland (Republic of)(1), Italy(2), Portugal(2), Spain(1), United Kingdom(24)	31	45 countries worldwide	700
Belgian Evangelical Mission	Belgium(17)	19	n/a	90
BMS, Baptist Missionary Society	Albania(21), Angola(2), Bangladesh(1), Belgium(2), Brazil(40), Central African Republic(2), Croatia(2), El Salvador(2), France(14), Guinea(2), Hungary(2), India(5), Italy(6), Nepal(37), Nicaragua(3), Poland(1), Portugal(4), Sri Lanka(4), Thailand(11), Trinidad & Tobago(4), United Kingdom(3)	186	China, Indonesia, Jamaica, Middle East, South Central Asia, Zimbabwe	227
British & International Sailors' Society	n/a	19	Australia, Belgium, Bermuda, Brazil, Estonia, Ghana, Indonesia, Jamaica, Madagascar, Netherlands Antilles, New Zealand, Philippines, Russia, South Africa, Ukraine, USA	140
Brothers of the Sacred Heart	n/a	2	Cameroon, Chile, Colombia, Côte d'Ivoire, French Polynesia, Guinea, Haiti, Kenya, Lesotho, Madagascar, Mali, New Caledonia, Peru, Philippines, Senegal, Togo, Uganda, Uruguay, Vanuatu, Wallis and Futuna Is, Zambia, Zimbabwe	5
Capuchin Franciscans (Order of Friars Minor Capuchin)	Papua New Guinea(1)	1	Korea, South Africa, Zambia	2,000
Carrot Tops	India(6)	9	Czech Republic, Israel, Slovakia	8
Central African Missions	Congo (Democratic Republic of)(14)	16	-	14
Child Evangelism Fellowship	Argentina(1), Ghana(1), Hong Kong(1), Ireland (Republic of)(2), Netherlands(1), Switzerland(1), United Kingdom(18)	35	Albania, Bulgaria, Denmark, Finland, France, Germany, Greece, Hungary, Iceland, Italy, Poland, Portugal, Romania, Russia, Sweden	2,000
The Christian and Missionary Alliance	Colombia(1), France(1), United Kingdom(20)	10	Balkans, Poland	22
Christian Associates International	Portugal(1)	3	Croatia, Germany, Ireland (Republic of), Latvia, Netherlands, Russia, Spain, Sweden, Switzerland	75
Christian Literature Crusade	Australia(2), Chile(2), France(7), Italy(3), Romania(1), Spain(3), United Kingdom(66)	85	Angola, Antigua, Austria, Belarus, Bulgaria, Canada, Central Asia, Colombia, Cyprus, French West Africa, Germany, Hong Kong, Hungary, India, Indonesia, Jamaica, Japan, Korea, Myanmar, Netherlands, New Zealand, Pakistan, Panama, Papua New Guinea, Philippines, Poland, Sierra Leone, Sri Lanka, Thailand, Uruguay, USA, Venezuela	710
Christian Witness to Israel	Australia(3), United Kingdom(11)	16	Bulgaria, France, Germany, Hong Kong, India, Israel, New Zealand, USA	35
Christians in Action	India(6), Macau(1), Mexico(1), United Kingdom(4), USA(1)	15	Brazil, Canada, Chile, Colombia, Ecuador, El Salvador, Germany, Ghana, Guatemala, Guinea Bissau, Japan, Korea, Peru, Philippines, Sierra Leone, Taiwan	273
Church Mission Society	Bangladesh(1), Central Asia(7), Egypt(3), Eritrea(1), Ghana(2), Guinea(4), Hong Kong(1), India(7), Japan(3), Jordan(1), Kenya(23), Korea(1), Lebanon(6), Nepal(14), Nigeria(8), North Africa(4), Pakistan(18), Romania(1), Russia(5), Sierra Leone(4), South Africa(2), Sudan(12), Syria(1), Taiwan(1), Tanzania(7), The Gambia(1), Uganda(22), United Kingdom(20)	257	Cyprus, Eastern Europe, Georgia, Malawi, Philippines, Sri Lanka	170
Church Missionary Society Ireland	Egypt(4), Kenya(5), Nepal(2), North Africa(1), Tanzania(2), Uganda(8), Zambia(3)	28	Congo (Democratic Republic of), India, Nigeria, Sudan	28

UK Missionary Societies and Missionaries

Society	Countries with UK Missionaries	UK missionaries	Other Countries	Missionaries Worldwide
Church of Scotland Board of World Mission	Bangladesh(3), Belgium(2), Bermuda(2), Egypt(1), France(2), Ghana(1), Gibraltar(2), Hungary(2), India(9), Israel(12), Italy(2), Jamaica(6), Kenya(12), Lebanon(5), Malawi(14), Malta(1), Mozambique(3), Nepal(6), Netherlands(4), Pakistan(11), Portugal(2), Romania(1), South Africa(3), Sri Lanka(2), Switzerland(4), Thailand(2), Zambia(1)	125	-	88
Church's Ministry Among Jewish People	Israel(23), United Kingdom(8)	44	-	46
Claretian Missionaries	-	0	Argentina, Bolivia, Brazil, Cameroon, Chile, Colombia, Congo (Democratic Republic of), Costa Rica, Cuba, Dominican Republic, Ecuador, El Salvador, Equatorial Guinea, Gabon, Guatemala, Honduras, India, Japan, Mexico, Nicaragua, Nigeria, Panama, Paraguay, Peru, Philippines, Puerto Rica, Uruguay, Venezuela	n/a
Columban Lay Missionaries	Chile(1), Pakistan(1), Philippines(3)	6	Fiji, Ireland, Japan, Taiwan, USA	70
Comboni Missionaries	Eritrea(1), Ethiopia(1), Mexico(1), Philippines(1), South Africa(1), Sudan(1), Uganda(2)	8	Benin, Brazil, Burundi, Central African Republic, Chad, Congo (Democratic Republic of), Costa Rica, Ecuador, Egypt, Ghana, Kenya, Lebanon, Malawi, Mozambique, Peru, Tanzania, Togo, Zambia	1,850
Comboni Missionary (Verona Sisters)	Egypt(1), Eritrea(2), Uganda(2), Zambia(1)	6	Chad, Congo (Democratic Republic of), Congo (People's Republic of), Ecuador, Ethiopia, Israel, Jordan, Kenya, Mexico, Mozambique, Peru, Sudan, Tanzania	57
Congregation of Christian Brothers	Liberia(1), Namibia(2), Sierra Leone(3)	6	Antigua and Barbuda, Argentina, Cook Islands, Côte d'Ivoire, Dominica, Fiji, Gambia, India, Kenya, Papua New Guinea, Paraguay, Peru, South Africa, Sudan, Tanzania, Tonga, Uruguay, Zambia, Zimbabwe	10
Congregation of Josephites	n/a	4	Gabon	n/a
Congregation of La Sainte Union des Sacré-Coeurs	Argentina(1), Cameroon(1), Haiti(1), Tanzania(5)	8	Chile	20
Congregation of Our Lady of the Missions	India(1), Kenya(3), Papua New Guinea(1), Philippines(1)	6	Australia, Bangladesh, Bolivia, Myanmar, New Zealand, Peru, Senegal, Vietnam, Western Samoa	900
Consolata Fathers	Colombia(1), South Africa(1)	1	Argentina, Bolivia, Brazil, Congo (Democratic Republic of), Côte d'Ivoire, Ethiopia, Kenya, Korea (Republic of) Mozambique, Tanzania, Venezuela	n/a
Consolata Missionary Sisters	Kenya(1)	1	Argentina, Bolivia, Brazil, Colombia, Ethiopia, Guinea-Bissau, Liberia, Mozambique, Somalia, Tanzania, Venezuela	12
Crosslinks	Ethiopia(4), France(7), Greece(2), India(4), Kenya(10), Morocco(1), Peru(1), Russia(2), South Africa(4), Spain(2), Tanzania(39), Uganda(1), United Kingdom(8), Zimbabwe(8)	105	Arctic, Austria, Botswana, Portugal	93
Crusade of the Holy Spirit	Argentina(1), Venezuela(1)	2	n/a	350
Daughters of Charity of St Vincent de Paul	Ethiopia(6), Israel(1)	7	Algeria, Argentina, Australia, Bolivia, Brazil, Cameroon, Chile, China, Colombia, Congo (Democratic Republic of), Congo (People's Republic of), Costa Rica, Cuba, Dominican Republic, Ecuador, Egypt, El Salvador, Equatorial Guinea, Fiji, Guatemala, Haiti, Honduras, India, Indonesia, Iran, Japan, Jordan, Korea, Lebanon, Madagascar, Mauritania, Mexico, Morocco, Mozambique, New Zealand, Nicaragua, Nigeria, Panama, Paraguay, Peru, Philippines, Puerto Rico, Rwanda, Sierra Leone, Syria, Taiwan, Tunisia, Uruguay, Venezuela, Vietnam	75
Daughters of Jesus	Chile(1), Jamaica(1)	2	Cameroon, Colombia, Congo (Democratic Republic of), Dominica, Haiti, Honduras	100
Daughters of Mary and Joseph	Ghana(1)	1	Burundi, Cameroon, Uganda	120
Daughters of St Paul	-	0	Argentina, Australia, Bolivia, Brazil, Chile, Colombia, Congo (Democratic Republic of), Côte d'Ivoire, Dominican Republic, Ecuador, Hong Kong, India, Japan, Kenya, Korea, Macao, Madagascar, Malaysia, Mexico, Mozambique, Nigeria, Pakistan, Papua New Guinea, Paraguay, Peru, Philippines, Puerto Rico, Singapore, South Africa, Taiwan, Tanzania, Thailand, Uganda, Uruguay, Venezuela, Zambia	
Daughters of the Heart of Mary	Pakistan(1)	1	Argentina, Brazil, Burkino Faso, Chile, Colombia, Ecuador, Ethiopia, Guatemala, India, Japan, Kenya, Mexico, Peru, Rwanda, Venezuela	2
Daughters of the Holy Spirit	Chile(1), Nigeria(8)	9	Burkina Faso, Cameroon, Peru	82

Society	Countries with UK Missionaries	UK missionaries	Other Countries	Missionaries Worldwide
De La Salle Brothers	India(2), Israel(1), Nicaragua(1), Nigeria(1), Peru(2), Philippines(1), Thailand(1)	9	Argentina, Australia, Benin, Bolivia, Brazil, Burkina Faso, Cameroon, Chad, Chile, Colombia, Congo (Democratic Republic of), Congo (People's Republic of), Costa Rica, Côte d'Ivoire, Cuba, Djibouti, Dominican Republic, Ecuador, Egypt, Equatorial Guinea, Ethiopia, Guatemala, Haiti, Honduras, Hong Kong, Japan, Jordan, Kenya, Libya, Madagascar, Malaysia, Mexico, Mozambique, Myanmar, New Caledonia, New Zealand, Niger, Pakistan, Panama, Papua New Guinea, Puerto Rico, Reunion, Rwanda, Singapore, South Africa, Sri Lanka, St Vincent & the Grenadines, Togo, Venezuela, Vietnam	2000
Dohnavur Fellowship	India(1)	6	-	1
Dominican Sisters of St Catherine of Siena of Oakford	Argentina(1), South Africa(1)	2	n/a	300
Dominican Sisters of Zimbabwe	Zimbabwe(4)	4	Colombia, Zambia	374
Dominicans	Barbados(3), Grenada(4), Jamaica(1), South Africa(2)	10	Algeria, Argentina, Australia, Bolivia, Brazil, Cameroon, Chile, Colombia, Congo (Democratic Republic of), Costa Rica, Côte d'Ivoire, Cuba, Dominican Republic, Ecuador, Egypt (Arab Republic), El Salvador, Guadeloupe, Guatemala, Hong Kong, India, Iran (Islamic republic), Iraq, Israel, Japan, Jordan, Kenya, Lebanon, Lesotho, Mexico, Morocco, Netherlands Antilles, New Zealand, Nicaragua, Nigeria, Pakistan, Panama, Peru, Philippines, Puerto Rico, Rwanda, Senegal, Solomon Islands, Syria (Arab Republic), Taiwan, Trinidad & Tobago, Turkey, Uruguay, Venezuela, Vietnam	7,000
Edinburgh Medical Missionary Society	Israel(1)	4	n/a	14
Elim International Missions	Albania(1), Australia(2), Belgium(7), Botswana(1), Congo (Democratic Republic of)(3), France(2), Ghana(2), Honduras(7), Hong Kong(2), Malawi(2), Mozambique(2), Philippines(3), Poland(2), South Africa(2), Spain(5), Tanzania(2), Thailand(3), Ukraine(1), Zimbabwe(2)	53	Brazil, Burundi, Greece, Guyana, India, Italy, Kenya, Malaysia, Nigeria, Papua New Guinea, Portugal, Rwanda, Uganda, Zambia	67
Emmanuel International	Canada(3), Haiti(1), Sudan(1), Tanzania(1), Uganda(7)	14	Brazil, Malawi, Philippines	38
English Benedictine Congregation, Belmont Abbey	Kenya(1), Peru(3)	4	n/a	n/a
English Benedictine Congregation, Worth Abbey	n/a	1	n/a	n/a
European Christian Mission (Britain)	Albania(3), Austria(5), France(6), Greece(2), Ireland (Republic of)(1), Italy(2), Poland(2), Portugal(6), Spain(15)	45	Croatia, Hungary, Romania, Serbia, Slovenia, Sweden, Ukraine	226
European Missionary Fellowship	Belgium(1), France(3), Greece(1), Ireland (Republic of)(2), Italy(1), Norway(1), Spain(4), Turkey(1), Ukraine(1)	15	Belarus, Germany, Poland, Portugal, Switzerland	80
Evangelical Action (Brazil)	Brazil(4)	4	-	4
Faithful Companions of Jesus	Argentina(2), Indonesia(1), Philippines(1)	4	Bolivia, Sierra Leone	24
FEBA Radio	Central Asia(4), Cyprus(4), Philippines(4), Seychelles(11), South Africa(2), United Kingdom(2), Zimbabwe(8)	41	India, Kenya, Lebanon, Mozambique, Pakistan	37
Fidei Donum Priests	Bolivia(4), Brazil(1), Chile(1), Ecuador(5), Kenya(5), Peru(10), South Africa(3), Zambia(2)	31	n/a	n/a
Focus on Israel	Israel(4)	7	-	2
France Mission Trust	France(17)	21	Madagascar	100
Franciscan Conventuals	Zambia(2)	2	Angola, Argentina, Bolivia, Brazil, China, Colombia, Costa Rica, Ghana, Honduras, India, Indonesia, Japan, Kenya, Korea (Republic of), Mexico, Peru, Philippines, Tanzania, Venezuela	n/a
Franciscan Minoresses	South Africa(1)	1	n/a	n/a
Franciscan Missionaries of Mary	Australia(2), India(1), Israel(1), Kenya(2), Mauritius(1), Mexico(1), Pakistan(2), South Africa(10), Sri Lanka(3)	24	Algeria, Angola, Argentina, Bolivia, Brazil, Burkina Faso, Chile, China, Colombia, Congo (Democratic Republic of), Congo (People's Republic of), Ecuador, Egypt, Ethiopia, Faeroe Islands, French Guyana, Ghana, Guadeloupe, Hong Kong, Indonesia, Japan, Jordan, Korea, Lebanon, Liberia, Libya, Macau, Madagascar, Malaysia, Mauritania, Morocco, Mozambique, Myanmar, Nicaragua, Niger, Papua New Guinea, Paraguay, Peru, Philippines, Reunion, Senegal, Singapore, Syria, Taiwan, Togo, Tunisia, Uruguay, Vietnam	9,000
Franciscan Missionaries of the Divine Motherhood	Australia(4), Nigeria(2), Philippines(1), Singapore(2), Zambia(10), Zimbabwe(9)	28	Jordan, Malaysia, New Zealand	360
Franciscan Missionary Sisters of St Joseph	Ecuador(2), Kenya(6)	8	Chile, Peru	209
Franciscan Sisters of Mill Hill	South Africa(1)	1	Ethiopia, Uganda, Zambia, Zimbabwe	n/a
Free Church of Scotland Foreign Missions Board	Peru(4), South Africa(14), United Kingdom(2)	23	India	20

UK Missionary Societies and Missionaries

Society	Countries with UK Missionaries	UK missionaries	Other Countries	Missionaries Worldwide
Free Presbyterian Church of Scotland Mission Committee	Kenya(1), Zimbabwe(10)	18	Eastern Europe	n/a
Free Presbyterian Church of Ulster Mission Board	Australia(4), Canada(8), Germany(1), Ireland (Republic of)(4), Kenya(4), Spain(5), USA(16), United Kingdom(16)	59	-	60
Frontiers	Central Asia(12), Middle East(2), Near East(13), North Africa(9), South Asia(4), West Asia(4)	56	Albania, Mali, Over 30 countries worldwide	600
Global Outreach UK	Ireland (Republic of)(1), United Kingdom(8)	11	Antigua, Australia, Bangladesh, Belgium, Belize, Bolivia, Brazil, Canada, Colombia, Congo (Democratic Republic of), Denmark, Egypt, France, Gabon, Germany, Ghana, Greece, Guatemala, Haiti, Honduras, Hong Kong, India, Jordan, Kazakhstan, Kenya, Korea, Mexico, Micronesia, Netherlands Antilles, Paraguay, Peru, Philippines, Russia, South Africa, Spain, Sweden, Ukraine, USA, Yugoslavia	436
Go To The Nations Ministry	United Kingdom(20)	22	France, Germany, India, Ireland, Japan, Portugal, Spain	33
Gorakhpur Nurseries Fellowship	India(3)	4	-	4
Gospel Mission of South America	Argentina(1), Chile(5)	7	Uruguay	64
Grace and Compassion Benedictines	-	0	n/a	144
Grace Baptist Mission	Austria(5), Colombia(2), France(3), India(1), Kenya(6), Latvia(4), Middle East(2), Peru(3), Philippines(3), Spain(5), Switzerland(2), United Kingdom(11)	50	-	58
HCJB-UK	Ecuador(9), United Kingdom(12)	22	Gibraltar, North Africa, Spain, Ukraine	600
Helpers of the Holy Souls	Japan(1)	1	Chad, China, Hong Kong, India, Rwanda, Taiwan	n/a
Holy Ghost Fathers	Australia(1), Cameroun(1), Gabon(1), Kenya(1), Nigeria(6), Pakistan(1), South Africa(1)	13	Algeria, Angola, Brazil, Cape Verde, Cayman Islands, Central African Republic, Congo (Democratic Republic of), Congo (People's Republic of), Ethiopia, Gambia, Ghana, Guadeloupe, Guinea-Bissau, Guyana, Haiti, Madagascar, Malawi, Martinique, Mauritania, Mexico, Papua New Guinea, Paraguay, Puerto Rico, Reunion, Senegal, Sierra Leone, Tanzania, Trinidad & Tobago, Zambia, Zimbabwe	3,200
Hospitaller Order of St John of God	-	0	Argentina, Belize, Bolivia, Brazil, Cameroon, Chile, Colombia, Cuba, Ecuador, Ghana, India, Israel, Japan, Korea, Liberia, Malawi, Mauritius, Mexico, Mozambique, Papua New Guinea, Peru, Philippines, Senegal, Sierra Leone, Togo, Venezuela, Vietnam, Zambia	1,200
Institute of Charity (Rosminian Fathers & Brothers)	India(2), Kenya(1), Tanzania(1)	4	Venezuela	n/a
Institute of Our Lady of Mercy	Kenya(9), Peru(4)	14	n/a	n/a
Institute of the Blessed Virgin Mary	Zimbabwe(2)	2	Argentina, Brazil, Chile, India, Korea, Tanzania	n/a
Intercontinental Church Society	Belgium(4), Brazil(1), Chile(2), Cyprus(1), Falkland Islands(1), France(15), Greece(1), Morocco(1), Netherlands(11), Peru(1), Poland(1), Spain(3), Switzerland(2), Tunisia(1), Ukraine(1), United Arab Emirates(2),	56	-	50
International Fellowship of Evangelical Students	Armenia(1), Austria(1), Azerbaijan(1), Belarus(6), Belgium(2), Bulgaria(5), Croatia(3), Czech Republic(3), France(4), Greece(5), Hungary(1), Italy(2), Kazakhstan(1), Moldova(3), Portugal(4), Romania(1), Russia(7), Slovakia(2), Slovenia(1), Spain(2), Ukraine(3), United Kingdom(9)	75	130 countries worldwide, Albania, Bosnia, Denmark, Estonia, Finland, Georgia, Germany, Iceland, Ireland (Republic of), Israel, Kyrgyzstan, Latvia, Lithuania, Macedonia, Netherlands, Norway, Poland, Sweden Switzerland, Uzbekistan, Yugoslavia	180
International Nepal Fellowship	Nepal(47)	48	n/a	160
International Teams UK	Austria(5), Bolivia(1), Canada(1), Colombia(1), Rumania(3), United Kingdom(9)	20	n/a	n/a
INTERSERVE	Bangladesh(5), Central Asia(10), China(1), Cyprus(1), India(22), Middle East(8), Mongolia(4), Nepal(30), North Africa(4), Pakistan(12), United Kingdom(37)	138	n/a	500
INTERSERVE Ireland	Asia(2), India(1), Middle East(1), Nepal(5), Pakistan(2)	12	-	12
INTERSERVE Scotland	Central Asia(3), Middle East(3), Nepal(9), Pakistan(4), United Kingdom(2), West Asia(9)	30	-	30
Japan Christian Link	Japan(4), United Kingdom(2)	10	Japanese communities in Europe	8
Japan Good News Ministries	Japan(2)	3	-	12
Japan Mission	Japan(2)	2	-	40

Society	Countries with UK Missionaries	UK missionaries	Other Countries	Missionaries Worldwide
Language Recordings UK	United Kingdom(7)	8	Australia, Bangladesh, Burkino Faso, Canada, Chad, Germany, Ghana, India, Indonesia, Kenya, Korea, Liberia, Mexico, Nepal, Netherlands, Nigeria, Pakistan, Papua New Guinea, Philippines, Sierra Leone, Switzerland, Togo, USA	20
Latin Link UK	Argentina(14), Bolivia(19), Brazil(16), Colombia(2), Costa Rica(3), Ecuador(16), Peru(33)	107	Cape Verde, Germany, Spain, Sweden, Switzerland	103
The Leprosy Mission	Bangladesh(4), Ethiopia(1), Guinea(2), Indonesia(1), Laos(2), Nepal(3), Nigeria(2), Papua New Guinea(1), Sudan(1)	20	Bhutan, Botswana, Cambodia, Chad, China, Congo (Democratic Republic of), Lesotho, Mozambique, Myanmar, Niger, Singapore, South Africa, Sri Lanka, Swaziland, Thailand, Uganda, Uzbekistan, Zambia, Zimbabwe	66
The Leprosy Mission (International Office)	-	-	Bangladesh, Bhutan, Cambodia, Chad, Ethiopia, Guinea, India, Israel, Laos, Mozambique, Myanmar, Nepal, Niger, Nigeria, Papua New Guinea, South Africa, Sri Lanka, Swaziland, Tanzania, Thailand, Uganda, Uzbekistan, Zambia, Zimbabwe	70
The Leprosy Mission (Northern Ireland)	n/a (2)	2	Ethiopia, Nepal	n/a
The Leprosy Mission (Scotland)	India(1)	6	-	1
Marist Brothers	Cameroon(1), Kenya(1)	2	Ghana	2
Medical Mission Sisters (Society of Catholic Medical Missionaries)	Kenya(2), Uganda(1)	3	Brazil, Ethiopia, Ghana, India, Indonesia, Malawi, Mexico, Nicaragua, Pakistan, Peru, Philippines, Venezuela	21
Medical Missionaries of Mary	Angola(1), Kenya(3), Nigeria(3), Tanzania(7), Uganda(1)	15	Brazil, Ethiopia, Malawi	453
Melanesian Mission	Solomon Islands(1)	2	Vanuatu	1
Mennonite Board of Missions	n/a	5	n/a	129
Mercy Sisters of the Union of Great Britain	Falkland Islands(1), Lebanon(1), Peru(1), Zimbabwe(1)	4	-	4
The Messianic Testimony	France(2), Hungary(1), Israel(2), Ukraine(1), United Kingdom(12)	19	n/a	22
Methodist Church World Church Office	Bangladesh(1), Bolivia(2), Cameroon(1), Caribbean(7), Chile(1), Côte d'Ivoire(4), Germany(4), Ghana(2), India(2), Italy(2), Japan(3), Kenya(11), Malaysia(2), Mali(2), Mozambique(2), Nepal(8), Nigeria(2), Sri Lanka(3), The Gambia(1), Tonga(2), Uganda(2), Zambia(6), Zimbabwe(4)	85	Angola, Argentina, Cuba, East Timor, Equatorial Guinea, Fiji, Guatemala, Hong Kong, Indonesia, Korea, Nicaragua, Pakistan, Panama, Papua New Guinea, Peru, Portugal, Russia, Sierra Leone, Solomon Islands, South Africa	91
Mid-Africa Ministry (CMS)	Burundi(1), Congo (Democratic Republic of)(1), Rwanda(5), Uganda(29), United Kingdom(4)	36	-	32
Middle East Christian Outreach	Middle East(24)	25	Australia	80
Middle East Media	Middle East (incl. N. Africa)(4)	7	Cyprus	16
Mill Hill Missionaries	Australia(4), Brazil(2), Cameroon(5), India(3), Kenya(12), Malaysia(2), New Zealand(7), Pakistan(5), Philippines(5), Sudan(1), Uganda(3)	49	Congo (Democratic Republic of), Ecuador, Falkland Islands, Venezuela	n/a
Mission Aviation Fellowship	Angola(1), Chad(1), Ethiopia(2), Kenya(16), Mali(2), Papua New Guinea(2), South Africa(1), Tanzania(24), Uganda(10), West Africa(1)	80	Bangladesh, Brazil, Central African Republic, Congo (Democratic Republic of), Ecuador, Guatemala, Haiti, Honduras, Indonesia, Lesotho, Mexico, Mozambique, Namibia, Surinam, Venezuala, Zambia, Zimbabwe	1,493
Mission to Military Garrisons (Inc)	Cyprus(7), Falkland Islands(6), United Kingdom(3)	17	-	16
Missionaries of Africa (White Fathers)	Algeria(1), Brazil(1), Burkina Faso(1), Ghana(3), India(1), Kenya(2), Malawi(1), Mexico(1), Nigeria(1), Philippines(1), South Africa(1), Tanzania(10), Tunisia(1), Uganda(3), Zambia(4)	32	Burundi, Chad, Congo (Democratic Republic of) Côte d'Ivoire, Ethiopia, Israel, Lebanon, Mali, Mauritania, Mozambique, Niger, Rwanda, Senegal, Sudan, Zimbabwe	2,048
Missionaries of Charity	Ethiopia(1), Malawi(1)	2	Argentina, Bangladesh, Benin, Bolivia, Brazil, Burundi, Cambodia, Cameroon, Chile, Colombia, Congo (Democratic Republic of), Congo (People's Republic of), Costa Rica, Côte d'Ivoire, Cuba, Ecuador, Egypt, El Salvador, The Gambia, Ghana, Guatemala, Guinea, Guyana, Honduras, Hong Kong, India, Japan, Kenya, Korea, Liberia, Libya, Madagascar, Mauritius, Mexico, Morocco, Mozambique, Nicaragua, Niger, Nigeria, Panama, Paraguay, Peru, Philippines, Rwanda, Seychelles, Sierra Leone, Singapore, Sudan, Taiwan, Tunisia, Uganda, Uruguay, Venezuela, Zambia, Zimbabwe	n/a
Missionary Sisters of Our Lady of Africa (White Sisters)	Kenya(1)	1	Algeria, Burundi, Chad, Congo (Democratic Republic of), Côte d'Ivoire, Ethiopa, Ghana, Malawi, Mali, Mauritania, Mexico, Mozambique, Rwanda, Tanzania, Tunisia, Uganda, Yemen	1,189
Missionary Sisters of Our Lady of Apostles	Nigeria(1)	1	n/a	900
Missionary Sisters of St Columban	Hong Kong(2), Peru(2), Philippines(2)	6	Bolivia, Chile, China, Pakistan	n/a

O

UK Missionary Societies and Missionaries

Society	Countries with UK Missionaries	UK missionaries	Other Countries	Missionaries Worldwide
Missionary Sisters Servants of the Holy Spirit	-	0	Angola, Argentina, Australia, Bangladesh, Bolivia, Botswana, Brazil, Chile, China, Cuba, Ethiopia, Ghana, India, Indonesia, Japan, Kenya, Mexico, Mozambique, Myanmar, Papua New Guinea, Paraguay, Peru, Philippines, Senegal, Taiwan, Togo, Vietnam, Western Samoa	3,600
Missionary Society of St Columban	Australia(1), Chile(1), Fiji(1), Pakistan(1), Peru(2)	6	Belize, Brazil, Jamaica, Japan, Korea, New Zealand, Philippines, Taiwan	785
The Missions to Seamen	Cyprus(2), France(4), Japan(4), Jordan(1), Kenya(2), Korea(1), Netherlands(4), New Zealand(1), Singapore(1), Tanzania(1), Thailand(1), United Arab Emirates(1), United Kingdom(17)	33	Australia, Bahrain, Belgium, Canada, Chile, Fiji, Hong Kong, India, Indonesia, Ireland (Republic of), Mozambique, Namibia, Nigeria, Papua New Guinea, Solomon Islands, South Africa, Sri Lanka, Trinidad, USA	n/a
Montfort Fathers	Australia(1), Malawi(2), Uganda(2)	5	Argentina, Brazil, Colombia, Congo (Democratic Republic of), Ecuador, Haiti, India, Indonesia, Madagascar, Mozambique, Nicaragua, Papua New Guinea, Peru, Philippines	2,000
Montfort Sisters, La Sagesse (Daughters of Wisdom)	India(1), Malawi(3), Papua New Guinea(1)	5	Argentina, Bahamas, Colombia, Congo (Democratic Republic of), Congo (People's Republic of), Ecuador, Haiti, Madagascar, Peru, Philippines	5
The Navigators	Central Asia(2), Eastern Europe(3), Ethiopia(7), Europe(2), France(2), Kenya(2), Malawi(2), Peru(4), Poland(3), Portugal(2), United Kingdom(47), USA(4), West Africa(5)	91	n/a	3,700
New Testament Missionary Union	Brazil(1), Spain(1)	2	n/a	50
New Tribes Mission	Australia(5), Bolivia(2), Brazil(8), Canada(4), Colombia(6), Indonesia(2), Côte d'Ivoire(18), Panama(18), Papua New Guinea(34), Philippines(6), Russia(4), Senegal(9), Thailand(10), USA(4), Venezuela(3)	126	Greenland, Guinea, Mexico, Mongolia, Paraguay	3,514
North West Frontier Fellowship	Pakistan(2)	2	Afghanistan	5
Oblates of Mary Immaculate	South Africa(2)	2	n/a	n/a
OMF International (UK)	Cambodia(9), Hong Kong(3), India(2), Indonesia(14), Japan(29), Korea (South)(5), Macau(2), Malaysia(4), Philippines(41), Singapore(16), Taiwan(16), Thailand(25), United Kingdom(45), USA(2), professional service personnel(41)	266	n/a	1,000
OMS International	Brazil(2), Colombia(6), Ecuador(2), Hong Kong(1), Hungary(1), Indonesia(1), Korea(1), Mexico(3), Mozambique(2), Spain(2)	23	China, Haiti, India, Ireland (Republic of), Japan, Philippines, Russia, Taiwan	450
Operation Mobilisation	Albania(2), Austria(6), Bangladesh(4), Belgium(9), Canada(1), Czech Republic(2), Egypt(4), France(7), Germany(19), Hungary(2), India(4), Israel(7), Italy(2), Kazakhstan(3), Middle East(15), Moldova(2), Nepal(2), Netherlands(2), New Zealand(2), North Africa(7), Pakistan(6), Romania(5), Russia(8), Slovakia(1), South Africa(3), Spain(1), Sudan(1), Sweden(2), Tajikistan(2), Turkey(7), Ukraine(1), United Kingdom(145), USA(8), Uzbekistan(4), mv Doulos(26), mv Logos(18)	366	n/a	2,800
Order of Friars Minor	India(1), Israel(2), South Africa(15), Tanzania(1)	20	n/a	n/a
Our Lady of Charity of the Good Shepherd	Guam(1), India(2)	3	Angola, Argentina, Chile, Colombia, Costa Rica, Ecuador, Egypt, El Salvador, Ethiopia, French Guyana, Guatemala, Guyana, Honduras, Hong Kong, Indonesia, Japan, Kenya, Korea, Macau, Madagascar, Malaysia, Mauritius, Myanmar, Nicaragua, Pakistan, Panama, Paraguay, Peru, Philippines, Puerto Rico, Reunion, Senegal, Singapore, South Africa, Sri Lanka, Sudan, Suriname, Syria, Taiwan, Thailand, Uruguay, Venezuela	n/a
Oxford Mission	India(1)	2	Bangladesh	15
Pallottine Fathers	-	0	Argentina, Australia, Brazil, Cameroon, India, Kenya, Rwanda, South Africa, Tanzania, Uruguay	n/a
Pallottine Missionary Sisters	Tanzania(5)	5	Belize, Brazil, India, Peru, Rwanda, South Africa	n/a
Papua New Guinea Church Partnership	Papua New Guinea(14)	14	-	13
Passionists	Botswana(1)	1	Angola, Argentina, Bolivia, Brazil, Chile, Colombia, Congo (Democratic Republic of), Costa Rica, Cuba, Dominican Republic, Ecuador, El Salvador, Guatemala, Honduras, India, Indonesia, Jamaica, Japan, Kenya, Korea (Republic of), Mexico, Panama, Papua New Guinea, Peru, Philippines, Puerto Rico, South Africa, Tanzania, Uruguay, Venezuela	3,000
People International	Afghanistan(2), Kazakhstan(1), Kurdistan(1), Pakistan(2), Tajikistan(2), Tatarstan(1), Turkey(8), Turkmenistan(4), Uzbekistan(6)	30	Kurgyzia	89

O

Society	Countries with UK Missionaries	UK missionaries	Other Countries	Missionaries Worldwide
Presbyterian Church in Ireland Overseas Board	Brazil(3), China(2), Czech Republic(1), France(4), India(7), Indonesia(1), Israel(3), Jamaica(7), Kenya(17), Malawi(18), Nepal(15), Romania(3), United Kingdom(4)	88	Hungary, Myanmar, Pakistan, Slovakia, Spain, Sudan, Taiwan, Thailand, Togo	54
Presbyterian Church of Wales Mission Board	Madagascar(1), Taiwan(1)	3	n/a	16
Qua Iboe Fellowship	Burkina Faso(3), Nigeria(14)	22	-	17
Red Sea Mission Team	Canada(1), Djibouti(3), Mali(2), Pakistan(1), Switzerland(1), United Kingdom(6), Yemen(6), international staff(7)	21	n/a	75
Redemptorists	South Africa(8), Zimbabwe(3)	11	Argentina, Australia, Bolivia, Brazil, Burkina Faso, Chile, Colombia, Congo (Democratic Republic of), Dominica, Dominican Republic, Ecuador, El Salvador, India, Indonesia, Japan, Lebanon, Mexico, New Zealand, Niger, Peru, Philippines, Puerto Rico, Singapore, Sri Lanka, Thailand, Uruguay, Venezuela, Vietnam	20
Religious of Jesus and Mary	Lebanon(1), Pakistan(1), Syria(2)	4	Argentina, Bolivia, Colombia, Cuba, India, Mexico, Nigeria, Peru	n/a
Religious of the Assumption	Kenya(1)	1	Argentina, Benin, Brazil, Burkino Faso, Cameroon, Côte d'Ivoire, Ecuador, El Salvador, Guatemala, India, Japan, Mexico, Nicaragua, Niger, Philippines, Rwanda, Tanzania, Thailand, Togo	250
Right Hand Trust	Kenya(6), Malawi(4), St Helena(4), Swaziland(6), The Gambia(5), Uganda(12), Zimbabwe(6)	44	Namibia, Windward Islands	43
Sacred Heart Fathers (Betharram)	-	0	Argentina, Brazil, Central African Republic, Côte d'Ivoire, India, Israel, Paraguay, Thailand, Uruguay	n/a
Sacred Heart Fathers (Dehonians)	India(1), Philippines(1), South Africa(1)	1	Argentina, Brazil, Cameroon, Chile, Indonesia, Lesotho, Madagascar, Mexico, Mozambique, Uruguay, Venezuela, Zaire	600
Sacred Hearts Community	-	0	Argentina, Bahamas, Bolivia, Brazil, Chile, Colombia, Congo (Democratic Republic of), Cook Islands, Ecuador, French Polynesia, India, Indonesia, Japan, Mexico, Mozambique, Paraguay, Peru, Puerto Rico, Singapore, Zambia	n/a
Sahara Desert Mission	Niger(5)	5	-	5
St Joseph's Hospice Association (Jospice International)	Honduras(5)	5	n/a	35
St Joseph's Missionary Society, Mill Hill	Australia(3), Brazil(2), Cameroon(5), Congo (Democratic Republic of)(1), Ecuador(1), Falkland Islands(1), India(2), Kenya(12), Malaysia(2), New Zealand(9), Pakistan(4), Philippines(5), Sudan(1), Uganda(8)	56	Venezuela	750
St Patrick's Missionary Society	Brazil(1), Kenya(2), South Africa(1)	4	Cameroon, Malawi, Nigeria, Sudan, Zambia, Zimbabwe	350
Salesian Fathers and Brothers	Brazil(1), Hong Kong(2), India(1), Japan(1), Lesotho(1), Liberia(3), Macao(1), Peru(1), South Africa(10), Swaziland(2), Uruguay(1)	24	Angola, Argentina, Australia, Bahamas, Benin, Bolivia, Burundi, Cameroon, Cape Verde Islands, Central African Republic, Chile, Colombia, Congo (Democratic Republic of), Congo (Republic of), Costa Rica, Côte d'Ivoire, Cuba, Dominican Republic, Ecuador, Egypt, El Salvador, Equatorial Guinea, Ethiopia, Gabon, Guatemala, Guinea, Haiti, Honduras, Indonesia, Iran, Israel, Kenya, Korea, Lebanon, Madagascar, Mali, Mexico, Morocco, Mozambique, Myanmar, Netherlands Antilles, Nicaragua, Nigeria, Panama, Papua New Guinea, Paraguay, Philippines, Puerto Rico, Rwanda, Senegal, Sierra Leone, Sri Lanka, Sudan, Syria, Taiwan, Tanzania, Thailand, Togo, Tunisia, Turkey, Uganda, Venezuela, Vietnam, Western Samoa, Zambia	10,000
Salesian Sisters of St John Bosco	Cameroon(1), Ethiopia(1), Kenya(1), South Africa(1)	4	Zambia	3,500
Salvation Army	Argentina(3), Australia(5), Austria(1), Belgium(3), Brazil(6), Canada(6), Caribbean(1), Chile(3), Congo (Democratic Republic of)(2), Congo (People's Republic of)(1), Czech Republic(7), Denmark(2), France(4), Germany(7), Ghana(7), Hong Kong(1), Hungary(1), India(1), Italy(9), Japan(2), Kenya(2), Latvia(2), Liberia(4), Mexico(4), Netherlands(1), Norway(5), Pakistan(2), Papua New Guinea(1), Philippines(1), Portugal(1), Russia(7), Singapore(1), South Africa(6), Spain(5), Sri Lanka(2), St Helena(2), Sweden(5), Switzerland(2), Tanzania(2), USA(4), Zambia(5), Zimbabwe(6)	135		200
SAO Cambodia	Cambodia(11)	13	-	11
Seamen's Christian Friend Society	Ireland (Republic of)(2), United Kingdom(18)	22	Belgium, Germany, Ghana, Latvia, Netherlands, New Zealand, Philippines, St Lucia	38
Servants to Asia's Urban Poor	Cambodia(1)	11	Cities in S.E. Asian countries, Philippines, Thailand	33
Servite Friars	Swaziland(2), Uganda(1)	3	n/a	300

UK Missionary Societies and Missionaries

Society	Countries with UK Missionaries	UK missionaries	Other Countries	Missionaries Worldwide
Sharing Christ Internationally	Mongolia(2)	5	-	8
Siloam Christian Ministries	Kenya(2), Philippines(4), Portugal(8)	16	Ghana, Uganda, Vietnam	20
SIM UK (Society for International Ministries)	Bangladesh(2), Benin(17), Bolivia(10), Burkina Faso(3), Chile(2), Ethiopia(19), France(2), Gabon(1), Ghana(2), India(4), Kenya(12), Malawi(6), Mozambique(3), Niger(19), Nigeria(8), Pakistan(10), Peru(13), South Africa(15), Sudan(2), United Kingdom(38), Zambia(20), Zimbabwe(6)	228	Angola, Central African Republic, Côte d'Ivoire, Ecuador, Eritrea, Guinea, Liberia, Madagascar, Mauritius, Nepal, Paraguay, Philippines, Reunion, Senegal, Sierra Leone, Somalia, Swaziland, Togo, Uruguay	1,800
Sisters of Charity of Jesus and Mary	Peru(2)	2	-	2
Sisters of Charity of Our Lady of Evron	Côte d'Ivoire(1)	1	n/a	n/a
Sisters of Charity of St Jeanne Antide Thouret	Cameroon(1)	1	-	1
Sisters of Charity of St Paul	South Africa(4)	4	n/a	20
Sisters of Christ	Cameroon(4)	4	Chile, Madagascar	20
Sisters of Christian Instruction (St Gildas)	Ghana(4)	4	Burkina Faso, Mexico	n/a
Sisters of La Retraite	Cameroon(1), Chile(1), South Africa(3)	5	n/a	20
Sisters of Notre Dame de Namur	Kenya(2), Nigeria(8), Peru(3), South Africa(4), Zimbabwe(2)	19	Zambia	120
Sisters of Our Lady of Charity	Kenya(1)	1	n/a	n/a
Sisters of Our Lady of Fidelity	n/a	1	n/a	4
Sisters of St Clare	El Salvador(1), Guatemala(1)	2	n/a	6
Sisters of St Joseph of Annecy	The Gambia(2), India(1), Senegal(1)	5	n/a	36
Sisters of St Joseph of Cluny	The Gambia(1), New Zealand(1), Sierra Leone(1)	3	India, Philippines, South Africa	1,800
Sisters of St Joseph of the Apparition	Australia(3), Israel(1)	4	Argentina, Guatemala, Haiti, India, Jordan, Lebanon, Mauritania, Myanmar, Panama, Peru, Philippines, Syrian Arab Republic, Thailand, Tunisia	400
Sisters of St Marie Madeleine Postel	South Africa(1)	1	n/a	n/a
Sisters of St Mary of Namur	Brazil(1), Cameroon(1), Rwanda(2)	4	Congo (Democratic Republic of), Dominican Republic	n/a
Sisters of St Peter Claver	-	0	Argentina, Australia, Colombia, Lebanon, New Zealand, Uganda, Uruguay	n/a
Sisters of the Cross and Passion	Botswana(3), Papua New Guinea(1)	4	Argentina, Chile, Peru	n/a
Sisters of the Good Saviour (Bon Sauveur)	Madagascar(1)	1	n/a	n/a
Sisters of the Holy Family (St Emilie de Rodat)	Egypt(1)	1	n/a	n/a
Sisters of the Sacred Heart of Jesus and Mary	Zambia(9)	9	Colombia, El Salvador	31
Sisters of Providence, Rosminians	Tanzania(2)	2	n/a	19
Society of African Missions	Australia(1), Liberia(2), Nigeria(1)	4	Argentina, Central African Republic, Congo (Democratic Republic of), Côte d'Ivoire, Egypt (Arab Republic), Ghana, India, Kenya, Morocco, Niger, Philippines, South Africa, Tanzania, Togo, Zambia	45
Society of Jesus	Barbados(1), El Salvador(1), Guyana(9), Japan(2), Kenya(1), South Africa(7), Zimbabwe(30)	51	Algeria, Angola, Argentina, Australia, Bangladesh, Bhutan, Bolivia, Brazil, Burundi, Cameroon, Chad, Chile, China, Colombia, Congo (Democratic Republic of) Congo (People's Republic of), Costa Rica, Côte d'Ivoire, Cuba, Dominican Republic, East Timor, Ecuador, Egypt, Ethiopia, Fiji, Guam, Guatemala, Haiti, Honduras, Hong Kong, India, Indonesia, Israel, Jamaica, Jordan, Korea, Lebanon, Macao, Madagascar, Malawi, Malaysia, Mauritius, Mexico, Micronesia, Morocco, Nepal, New Zealand, Nicaragua, Nigeria, Pakistan, Panama, Papua New Guinea, Paraguay, Peru, Philippines, Puerto Rico, Rwanda, Senegal, Singapore, Sri Lanka, Sudan, Syria, Taiwan, Tanzania, Thailand, Timor East, Uganda, Uruguay, Venezuela, Vietnam, Zambia	69
Society of Marie Reparatrice	n/a	2	Colombia, Guatemala, Kenya, Madagascar, Mauritius, Mexico, Panama, Peru, Puerto Rico, Uganda	n/a
Society of Mary	Cameroon(1), Japan(1), Samoa(1), Solomon Islands(1), Tonga(1), Vanuatu(1)	6	American Samoa, Brazil, Burundi, Fiji, New Caledonia, Papua New Guinea, Peru, Philippines, Senegal, Venezuela, Wallis and Futuna Islands	250
Society of St Francis	Australia(4), Papua New Guinea(3), Solomon Islands(1), USA(2), Zimbabwe(2)	12	n/a	n/a
Society of the Divine Word	Antigua and Barbuda(1), Indonesia(1), Japan(1), Papua New Guinea(1), Philippines(1)	5	Angola, Argentina, Australia, Brazil, Chile, Colombia, Congo (Democratic Republic of), Ecuador, Ghana, Hong Kong, India, Mexico, Panama, Paraguay, Taiwan, Togo	5,700
Society of the Divine Saviour (Salvatorians)	Comoros(1), India(1), Tanzania(3)	5	Australia, Brazil, Colombia, Congo (Democratic Republic of), Philippines, Sri Lanka, Taiwan, Venezuela	5
Society of the Holy Child Jesus	Chile(1), Ghana(1), Nigeria(1)	3	Brazil, Chad, Lesotho	21

O

Society	Countries with UK Missionaries	UK missionaries	Other Countries	Missionaries Worldwide
Society of the Sacred Heart	Côte d'Ivoire(1), India(5), Kenya(1)	6	Argentina, Australia, Brazil, Chad, Chile, Colombia, Congo (Democratic Republic of), Cuba, Egypt, Indonesia, Japan, Korea, Mexico, New Zealand, Nicaragua, Paraguay, Peru, Philippines, Puerto Rico, Taiwan, Uganda, Venezuela	140
South American Mission Society	Argentina(19), Bolivia(4), Brazil(8), Chile(16), Paraguay(19), Peru(1), Spain(5), Uruguay(6)	162	Europe, Portugal	124
Spanish Gospel Mission	Spain(12)	13	-	12
Tearfund	Burundi(4), Cambodia(1), Ethiopia(2), Guinea-Bissau(1), Haiti(2), Honduras(3), Kenya(2), Laos(2), Lebanon(1), Liberia(3), Nepal(4), North Africa(6), Pakistan(2), Philippines(2), Sudan(11), Thailand(1), Turkmenistan(4), Uganda(2)	64	-	74
Trans World Radio	Monaco(1), United Kingdom(5), USA(2)	8	Angola, Argentina, Australia, Austria, Bolivia, Bonaire, Burundi, CIS, Canada, Chile, Côte d'Ivoire, Czech Republic, Denmark, Dominican Republic, Ecuador, Finland, France, Germany, Guam, Hong Kong, Hungary, India, Indonesia, Italy, Japan, Kenya, Korea, Malawi, Mozambique, Myanmar, Netherlands, New Zealand, Norway, Paraguay, Poland, Singapore, Slovak Rep, South Africa, Sri Lanka, Swaziland, Sweden, Switzerland, Taiwan, Uruguay, Venezuala, Zimbabwe	850
UFM Worldwide	Brazil(28), Cambodia(1), Cameroon(2), Canada(2), Congo (Democratic Republic of)(7), Côte d'Ivoire(8), France(1), Indonesia(1), Irian Jaya(1), Papua New Guinea(8), Sierra Leone(2), South East Asia(2), Spain(5), USA(2)	89	Gabon	70
United Reformed Church International Relations	Cayman Islands(2), France(1), Madagascar(1), Malawi(1), Zambia(1)	8	n/a	12
United Society for the Propagation of the Gospel	Argentina(4), Bangladesh(5), Belize(4), Brazil(2), Chile(3), China(14), Egypt(1), Eritrea(2), Guyana(1), India(6), Japan(3), Madagascar(1), Malawi(6), Pakistan(1), Peru(2), South Africa(13), Sri Lanka(1), St Helena(2), Tanzania(5), Trinidad & Tobago(2), United Kingdom(1), Venezuela(2), Windward Islands(1), Zambia(6), Zimbabwe(11)	124	n/a	144
Ursulin Sisters	Barbados(1), Cameroon(1), South Africa(2), Taiwan(1)	5	Botswana, Brazil, Guyana, Hong Kong, Mexico, Peru, Senegal, Venezuela	n/a
Volunteer Missionary Movement	Kenya(1)	4	South America	27
WEC International	Albania(1), Australia(1), Brazil(5), Burkina Faso(6), Cambodia(5), Canada(2), Chad(11), Congo (Democratic Republic of)(4), Côte d'Ivoire(15), France(10), Gambia(8), Germany(1), Ghana(2), Greece(2), Guinea-Bissau(14), India(8), Indonesia(2), Italy(1), Japan(9), Mali(2), Mexico(3), Nepal(4), Netherlands(3), New Zealand(4), Portugal(2), Senegal(25), South Africa(3), Spain(12), Switzerland(1), Taiwan(1), Thailand(7), United Kingdom(131), USA(1)	312	Bulgaria, Equatorial Guinea, Hong Kong, Guinea, Singapore, Venezuala	1,515
World Gospel Mission	Kenya(7), United Kingdom(4), USA(1)	19	Argentina, Bolivia, Brazil, Burundi, Haiti, Honduras, Hungary, India, Japan, Mexico, Paraguay, Taiwan, Tanzania, Uganda	350
World Horizons (Britain)	Burkina Faso(5), Cambodia(5), France(27), Gibraltar(4), Greece(2), Ireland (Republic of)(2), Japan(2), Macedonia(1), Malaysia(3), Malta(2), Middle East(36), Niger(3), Paraguay(2), Philippines(1), Romania(3), Singapore(4), Slovakia(1), Spain(8), Thailand(4), United Kingdom(48), USA(1)	170	Central African Republic, Germany, India, Portugal	450
World Outreach	Philippines(1), Singapore(1), United Kingdom(2)	5	Australia, Bangladesh, Botswana, Canada, Chile, Egypt, Fiji, Hong Kong, India, Indonesia, Japan, Kenya, Korea, Malawi, Malaysia, Netherlands, New Zealand, Papua New Guinea, Russia, South Africa, Thailand, USA, Zimbabwe	96
World-wide Advent Missions	Australia(2), Germany(1), Hong Kong(4), India(4), Côte d'Ivoire(4), Kenya(1), Lesotho(2), Liberia(2), Nigeria(2), Pakistan(4), Senegal(2), Sierra Leone(2), South Africa(2), Sri Lanka(2), USA(39)	105	182 countries worldwide	872

O

UK Missionary Societies and Missionaries

Society	Countries with UK Missionaries	UK missionaries	Other Countries	Missionaries Worldwide
Wycliffe Bible Translators	Brazil(13), Burkina Faso(12), Cameroon(16), Canada(1), Chad(6), Colombia(2), Congo (People's Republic of)(1), Côte d'Ivoire(10), Ethiopia(3), Europe(12), Far East(5), Ghana(13), Indonesia(7), Kenya(32), Malaysia(2), Mali(12), Mexico(3), Middle East(7), Mozambique(3), Niger(1), Papua New Guinea(16), Philippines(6), Senegal(8), South Asia(9), Sudan(17), Tanzania(3), Togo & Benin(7), USA(4), United Kingdom(2), Uganda(2)	255	Australia, Central African Republic, Central America, Congo (Democratic Republic of), New Caledonia, Peru, Solomon Islands, Suriname, Vanuatu	6,000
Xaverian Missionary Fathers	Colombia(1), Mexico(1), Sierra Leone(2)	3	Bangladesh, Brazil, Burundi, Congo (Democratic Republic of), Indonesia, Japan	1,000
Youth With A Mission UK	Albania(3), Australia(7), Bolivia(4), Brazil(4), Cambodia(5), Canada(13), Central Asia(5), Colombia(8), Cyprus(4), Denmark(6), Dominican Republic(2), France(11), Ghana(1), Grenada(2), Guatemala(1), Hong Kong(4), Hungary(1), India(9), Ireland (Republic of)(7), Italy(1), Japan(6), Kenya(5), Liberia(1), Mali(1), Mercy Ships(26), Micronesia(2), Mozambique(1), Nepal(4), Netherlands(16), New Zealand(2), Norway(2), Paraguay(1), Philippines(8), Portugal(1), South Africa(1), Spain(3), Sweden(3), Switzerland(5), Taiwan(1), Tanzania(1), Thailand(6), Turkey(1), Uganda(11), Ukraine(1), United Kingdom(249), USA(20), Zimbabwe(2)	486	Worldwide	10,000
Zambesi Mission	Malawi(4)	5	Mozambique, Zambia, Zimbabwe	4

4. PERSONNEL BY SOCIETY & DENOMINATION

Numbers of personnel were requested as at 1st January 1999 for those working in a cross-cultural and own-cultural context, broken down by career and furlough.

These figures relate to UK personnel only, but as many societies have non-UK members both in the UK and elsewhere, the total given in the final column does not show the total size of a particular society. That may be found in the final column of the lists of *Missionary Sending Churches (Direct)* on Page 351 and *Missionary Societies* on Page 352.

Abbreviations used are as follows:

CCO Cross-culture overseas. No definition was deliberately given for cross-culture or own-culture
OCO Own-culture overseas. The number abroad includes those working in United Missions.
CCU Cross-culture in UK.
OCU Own-culture in UK.
FRL Furlough. The number on furlough or home leave may or may not include those on leave of absence, sick leave, training courses etc.
SEC Secondments, that is missionaries lent to other societies but supported by their primary society. It does not include missionaries seconded from other societies, since these are included in their primary society.
UKE UK Executive staff. Usually those home staff who may be regarded as full mission members.
SUK Total of preceding columns, ie total of Serving UK Missionaries
RCH UK Home staff. Applies only to Roman Catholic societies, who make no distinction between executive staff, office staff, missionaries on home leave etc.
UKO UK Office staff. Mainly clerical staff, some of whom are not strictly full mission members. The distinction between Home staff and Office staff is sometimes not possible.
ASS Associates. Qualification for associate membership varies with societies, and was not defined on the questionnaire. It includes only those working abroad, who are often not financially dependent on the society.
RET Retired personnel. Includes only those who are at least partly financially dependent on the society.
Total UK The total of all UK personnel serving with the society.

A zero in a particular category of personnel for a society usually indicates that the society has no personnel in that category. It may occasionally mean that information was not available.

	CCO	OCO	CCU	OCU	FRL	SEC	UKE	SUK	RCH	UKO	ASS	RET	Total UK
Anglican													
Church Mission Society	171	0	20	0	4	0	62	257	0	42	42	328	669
Church Missionary Society Ireland	25	0	0	0	0	0	3	28	0	2	0	2	32
Church's Ministry Among Jewish People	33	0	0	8	0	0	3	44	0	8	3	6	61
Crosslinks	82	2	8	0	1	0	12	105	0	14	25	50	194

	CCO	OCO	CCU	OCU	FRL	SEC	UKE	SUK	RCH	UKO	ASS	RET	Total UK
Intercontinental Church Society	48	0	0	0	0	0	8	56	0	0	10	2	68
Melanesian Mission	1	0	0	0	0	0	1	2	0	1	0	0	3
Mid-Africa Ministry (CMS)	29	0	0	0	3	0	4	36	0	9	0	3	48
The Missions to Seamen	10	0	17	0	0	0	6	33	0	32	0	5	70
Oxford Mission	1	0	0	0	0	0	1	2	0	1	0	3	6
Papua New Guinea Church Partnership	13	0	0	0	0	0	1	14	0	1	0	0	15
Right Hand Trust	43	0	0	0	0	0	1	44	0	4	15	0	63
Society of St Francis	12	0	0	0	0	0	0	12	0	0	0	0	12
South American Mission Society	70	5	0	0	6	78	3	162	0	4	41	46	253
United Society for the Propagation of the Gospel	95	0	1	0	2	0	26	124	0	29	0	142	295
Apostolic													
Apostolic Church Missionary Movement	13	0	0	0	0	0	7	20	0	4	2	0	26
Assemblies of God													
Assemblies of God World Ministries	102	7	0	0	0	5	6	120	0	1	0	41	162
Baptist													
Baptist Missionary Society, BMS	148	0	3	0	26	5	4	186	0	46	0	146	378
Baptist Missions	19	0	0	0	0	0	1	20	0	2	0	6	28
Church of Scotland													
Church of Scotland Board of World Mission	117	0	0	0	0	0	8	125	0	13	1	260	399
Direct Sending Churches													
Basingstoke Community Church	0	0	10	0	2	0	0	12	0	0	4	0	16
Biggin Hill Christian Fellowship	4	0	0	0	2	0	5	11	0	6	0	0	17
Coventry Christian Fellowship	10	0	0	0	0	0	0	10	0	0	0	0	10
Echoes of Service	354	38	0	0	6	0	2	400	0	9	0	0	409
Hollybush Christian Fellowship	5	0	2	0	6	2	1	16	0	1	0	0	17
Ichthus Christian Fellowship	44	0	0	0	0	8	2	54	0	0	3	0	57
Lifeline Network International	6	0	0	0	0	0	4	10	0	4	0	0	14
Elim Pentecostal													
Elim International Missions	52	0	0	0	0	0	1	53	0	3	0	0	56
Free Church of Scotland													
Free Church of Scotland Foreign Missions Board	18	0	2	0	0	2	1	23	0	1	0	12	36
Free Presbyterian Church of Scotland													
Free Presbyterian Church of Scotland Mission Committee	9	0	0	0	2	0	7	18	0	2	0	1	21
Free Presbyterian Church of Ulster													
Free Presbyterian Church of Ulster Mission Board	42	0	16	0	0	0	1	59	0	0	0	0	59
Full Gospel													
Japan Good News Ministries	2	0	0	0	0	0	1	3	0	1	0	0	4
Grace Baptist													
Grace Baptist Mission	34	2	11	0	0	0	3	50	0	2	0	0	52
Interdenominational/Non-denominational													
Acre Gospel Mission	18	0	0	0	0	0	1	19	0	0	0	3	22
Action International Ministries (UK)	13	0	0	0	0	0	1	14	0	3	0	0	17
Action Partners Ministries	39	0	8	0	2	51	5	105	0	11	2	25	143
Africa Inland Mission International	132	0	0	2	30	2	9	175	0	13	0	3	191
Agapé	13	0	0	55	2	0	3	73	0	17	17	0	107
Albanian Evangelical Mission	21	0	0	0	3	0	2	26	0	3	2	0	31
All India Mission	0	0	0	0	4	0	2	6	0	0	0	0	6
Antioch Mission UK	0	0	0	0	0	0	3	3	0	1	0	0	4
Arab World Ministries	56	0	3	0	2	0	2	63	0	9	0	25	97
BCM International	6	0	0	24	0	0	1	31	0	0	0	2	33
Belgian Evangelical Mission	17	0	0	0	0	0	2	19	0	2	0	0	21
British & International Sailors' Society	0	0	14	0	0	0	5	19	0	114	0	0	133
Carrot Tops	6	0	0	0	0	0	3	9	0	2	0	0	11
Child Evangelism Fellowship	7	0	0	18	0	0	10	35	0	3	0	0	38
The Christian and Missionary Alliance	2	0	1	6	0	0	1	10	0	1	14	0	25
Christian Associates International	1	0	0	0	0	0	2	3	0	0	0	0	3
Christian Literature Crusade	17	0	0	66	1	1	0	85	0	9	0	40	134
Christian Witness to Israel	0	3	0	11	0	0	2	16	0	5	1	20	42

UK Missionary Societies and Missionaries

	CCO	OCO	CCU	OCU	FRL	SEC	UKE	SUK	RCH	UKO	ASS	RET	Total UK
Christians in Action	9	0	0	0	4	0	2	15	0	5	0	0	20
Dohnavur Fellowship	1	0	0	0	0	0	5	6	0	1	0	3	10
Edinburgh Medical Missionary Society	1	0	0	0	0	0	3	4	0	4	0	6	14
Emmanuel International	13	0	0	0	0	0	1	14	0	1	0	0	15
European Christian Mission (Britain)	42	0	0	0	0	0	3	45	0	8	0	16	69
European Missionary Fellowship	14	0	0	0	0	0	1	15	0	5	0	14	34
Evangelical Action (Brazil)	4	0	0	0	0	0	0	4	0	2	0	0	6
FEBA Radio	31	0	0	0	0	2	8	41	0	31	4	3	79
France Mission Trust	17	0	0	0	0	0	4	21	0	2	0	0	23
Frontiers	44	0	0	0	5	2	5	56	0	9	0	0	65
Global Outreach UK	4	0	0	6	0	0	1	11	0	1	12	0	24
Gorakhpur Nurseries Fellowship	2	1	0	0	0	0	1	4	0	0	0	2	6
Gospel Mission of South America	6	0	0	0	0	0	1	7	0	0	0	0	7
Go To The Nations Ministry	0	0	20	0	0	0	2	22	0	3	0	0	25
HCJB-UK	9	0	0	9	0	0	4	22	0	9	3	0	34
International Fellowship of Evangelical Students	51	0	8	6	0	0	10	75	0	4	0	0	79
International Nepal Fellowship	43	0	0	0	4	0	1	48	0	4	0	3	55
International Teams UK	11	0	8	0	1	0	0	20	0	0	0	0	20
INTERSERVE	88	0	37	0	6	2	5	138	0	22	0	6	166
INTERSERVE Ireland	9	0	0	0	2	0	1	12	0	2	0	0	14
INTERSERVE Scotland	28	0	0	0	0	0	2	30	0	1	0	0	31
Japan Christian Link	4	0	2	0	0	2	2	10	0	2	2	3	17
Japan Mission	2	0	0	0	0	0	0	2	0	1	0	0	3
Language Recordings UK	0	0	7	0	0	0	1	8	0	6	0	0	14
Latin Link UK	76	2	0	0	25	0	4	107	0	18	5	23	153
The Leprosy Mission	17	0	0	0	0	0	3	20	0	30	0	0	50
The Leprosy Mission (International Office)	0	0	0	0	0	0	4	4	0	16	0	0	20
The Leprosy Mission (Northern Ireland)	0	0	0	0	0	0	2	2	0	3	0	0	5
The Leprosy Mission (Scotland)	1	0	0	0	0	0	5	6	0	3	0	0	9
The Messianic Testimony	5	0	12	0	1	0	1	19	0	3	0	8	30
Middle East Christian Outreach	24	0	0	0	0	0	1	25	0	3	17	7	52
Middle East Media	4	0	0	0	0	1	2	7	0	4	20	0	31
Mission Aviation Fellowship	60	0	0	0	0	0	20	80	0	38	0	3	121
Mission to Military Garrisons (Inc)	0	13	0	3	0	0	1	17	0	1	0	4	22
The Navigators	36	0	1	46	5	0	3	91	0	5	24	0	120
New Testament Missionary Union	2	0	0	0	0	0	0	2	0	2	0	1	5
New Tribes Mission	120	3	0	0	0	0	3	126	0	22	0	2	150
North West Frontier Fellowship	2	0	0	0	0	0	0	2	0	0	0	1	3
OMF International (UK)	192	0	0	45	17	0	12	266	0	28	0	59	353
OMS International	16	0	0	0	5	0	2	23	0	7	0	7	37
Operation Mobilisation	194	0	4	141	5	10	12	366	0	28	0	0	394
People International	24	0	0	0	3	2	1	30	0	4	0	0	34
Qua Iboe Fellowship	17	0	0	0	0	2	3	22	0	5	0	19	46
Red Sea Mission Team	14	0	6	0	0	0	1	21	0	2	0	5	28
Sahara Desert Mission	4	0	0	0	1	0	0	5	0	2	0	1	8
SAO Cambodia	7	0	0	0	4	0	2	13	0	3	0	0	16
Seamen's Christian Friend Society	2	0	18	0	0	0	2	22	0	3	18	2	45
Servants to Asia's Urban Poor	1	0	0	0	0	9	1	11	0	0	0	0	11
Sharing Christ Internationally	2	0	0	0	0	0	3	5	0	0	0	0	5
Siloam Christian Ministries	14	0	0	0	0	0	2	16	0	2	0	0	18
SIM UK (Society for International Ministries)	151	0	6	32	31	2	6	228	0	31	0	0	259
Spanish Gospel Mission	4	8	0	0	0	0	1	13	0	1	0	1	15
Tearfund	55	0	0	0	0	0	9	64	0	164	1	21	250
Trans World Radio	2	1	0	4	0	0	1	8	0	10	1	1	20
UFM Worldwide	70	0	0	0	0	17	2	89	0	10	0	0	99
Volunteer Missionary Movement	1	0	0	0	0	0	3	4	0	2	0	0	6
WEC International	150	0	0	131	26	0	5	312	0	10	0	63	385
World Gospel Mission	8	0	0	4	0	0	7	19	0	4	0	0	23
World Horizons (Britain)	104	0	2	46	14	0	4	170	0	16	6	0	192
World Outreach	2	0	2	0	0	0	1	5	0	2	0	2	9
Wycliffe Bible Translators	192	4	2	0	39	0	18	255	0	51	0	6	312
Youth With A Mission UK	174	55	2	247	0	0	8	486	0	0	0	0	486
Zambesi Mission	4	0	0	0	0	0	1	5	1	1	0	0	7
Mennonite													
Mennonite Board of Missions	0	0	0	0	0	0	5	5	0	0	0	0	5

	CCO	OCO	CCU	OCU	FRL	SEC	UKE	SUK	RCH	UKO	ASS	RET	Total UK
Methodist													
Methodist Church World Church Office	74	0	0	0	1	0	10	85	0	8	0	160	253
Pentecostal													
Central African Missions	12	0	0	0	2	0	2	16	0	2	0	11	29
Focus on Israel	4	0	0	0	0	0	3	7	0	4	0	0	11
Presbyterian Church in Ireland													
Presbyterian Church in Ireland Overseas Board	70	0	4	0	11	0	3	88	0	6	0	26	120
Presbyterian Church of Wales													
Presbyterian Church of Wales Mission Board	2	0	0	0	0	0	1	3	0	1	0	20	24
Roman Catholic													
Associates of Mill Hill Missionaries	4	0	0	0	3	0	1	8	4	0	0	8	20
Association of the Holy Family of Bordeaux	5	0	0	0	0	0	0	5	0	0	0	0	5
Assumptionists Fathers and Brothers	1	0	0	0	0	0	0	1	0	0	0	0	1
Augustinian Recollects	2	0	0	0	0	0	0	2	0	0	0	0	2
Augustinians	3	0	0	0	0	0	0	3	0	0	0	0	3
Brothers of the Sacred Heart	2	0	0	0	0	0	0	2	0	0	0	0	2
Capuchin Franciscans (Order of Friars Minor Capuchin)	1	0	0	0	0	0	0	1	0	0	0	0	1
Claretian Missionaries	0	0	0	0	0	0	0	0	12	0	0	0	12
Columban Lay Missionaries	5	0	0	0	0	0	1	6	0	2	0	0	8
Comboni Missionaries (Verona Fathers)	8	0	0	0	0	0	0	8	17	0	0	1	26
Comboni Missionary (Verona Sisters)	6	0	0	0	0	0	0	6	9	0	0	2	17
Congregation of Christian Brothers	6	0	0	0	0	0	0	6	0	0	0	0	6
Congregation of Josephites	0	0	0	0	0	0	4	4	2	0	0	1	7
Congregation of La Sainte Union des Sacré-Coeurs	8	0	0	0	0	0	0	8	0	0	0	0	8
Congregation of Our Lady of the Missions	6	0	0	0	0	0	0	6	0	0	0	0	6
Consolata Fathers	1	0	0	0	0	0	0	1	0	0	0	0	1
Consolata Missionary Sisters	1	0	0	0	0	0	0	1	1	0	0	0	2
Crusade of the Holy Spirit	2	0	0	0	0	0	0	2	0	0	0	0	2
Daughters of Charity of St Vincent de Paul	7	0	0	0	0	0	0	7	0	0	0	0	7
Daughters of Jesus	2	0	0	0	0	0	0	2	0	0	0	0	2
Daughters of Mary and Joseph	1	0	0	0	0	0	0	1	0	0	0	0	1
Daughters of St Paul	0	0	0	0	0	0	0	0	0	0	0	0	0
Daughters of the Heart of Mary	1	0	0	0	0	0	0	1	0	0	0	0	1
Daughters of the Holy Spirit	9	0	0	0	0	0	0	9	0	0	0	0	9
De La Salle Brothers	9	0	0	0	0	0	0	9	0	0	0	0	9
Dominican Sisters of St Catherine of Siena of Oakford	2	0	0	0	0	0	0	2	0	0	0	0	2
Dominican Sisters of Zimbabwe	4	0	0	0	0	0	0	4	0	0	0	0	4
Dominicans	10	0	0	0	0	0	0	10	0	0	0	0	10
English Benedictine Congregation, Belmont Abbey	4	0	0	0	0	0	0	4	0	0	0	0	4
English Benedictine Congregation, Worth Abbey	1	0	0	0	0	0	0	1	0	0	0	0	1
Faithful Companions of Jesus	4	0	0	0	0	0	0	4	0	0	0	0	4
Fidei Donum Priests	31	0	0	0	0	0	0	31	0	0	0	0	31
Franciscan Conventuals	2	0	0	0	0	0	0	2	0	0	0	0	2
Franciscan Minoresses	1	0	0	0	0	0	0	1	0	0	0	0	1
Franciscan Missionaries of Mary	24	0	0	0	0	0	0	24	105	0	0	23	152
Franciscan Missionaries of the Divine Motherhood	28	0	0	0	0	0	0	28	72	0	0	11	111
Franciscan Sisters of Mill Hill	1	0	0	0	0	0	0	1	0	0	0	0	1
Franciscan Missionary Sisters of St Joseph	8	0	0	0	0	0	0	8	79	0	0	43	130
Grace and Compassion Benedictines	0	0	0	0	0	0	0	0	0	0	0	0	0
Helpers of the Holy Souls	1	0	0	0	0	0	0	1	0	0	0	0	1
Holy Ghost Fathers	13	0	0	0	0	0	0	13	40	0	0	10	63
Hospitaller Order of St John of God	0	0	0	0	0	0	0	0	0	0	0	0	0
Institute of Charity (Rosminian Fathers & Brothers)	4	0	0	0	0	0	0	4	0	0	0	0	4
Institute of Our Lady of Mercy	14	0	0	0	0	0	0	14	0	0	0	0	14
Institute of the Blessed Virgin Mary	2	0	0	0	0	0	0	2	0	0	0	0	2
Marist Brothers	2	0	0	0	0	0	0	2	0	0	0	0	2
Medical Mission Sisters (Society of Catholic Medical Missionaries)	3	0	0	0	0	0	0	3	11	0	0	0	14

UK Missionary Societies and Missionaries

	CCO	OCO	CCU	OCU	FRL	SEC	UKE	SUK	RCH	UKO	ASS	RET	Total UK
Medical Missionaries of Mary	15	0	0	0	0	0	0	15	16	0	0	1	32
Mercy Sisters of the Union of Great Britain	4	0	0	0	0	0	0	4	0	0	0	190	194
Missionaries of Africa (White Fathers)	32	0	0	0	0	0	0	32	49	0	0	13	94
Missionaries of Charity	2	0	0	0	0	0	0	2	10	0	0	0	12
Missionary Sisters of Our Lady of Africa (White Sisters)	1	0	0	0	0	0	0	1	26	0	0	12	39
Missionary Sisters of Our Lady of Apostles	1	0	0	0	0	0	0	1	4	0	0	4	9
Missionary Sisters of St Columban	6	0	0	0	0	0	0	6	3	0	0	0	9
Missionary Sisters Servants of theHoly Spirit	0	0	0	0	0	0	0	0	6	0	0	0	6
Missionary Society of St Columban	6	0	0	0	0	0	0	6	6	0	0	0	12
Montfort Fathers	5	0	0	0	0	0	0	5	0	0	0	0	5
Montfort Sisters, La Sagesse (Daughters of Wisdom)	5	0	0	0	0	0	0	5	0	0	0	0	5
Oblates of Mary Immaculate	2	0	0	0	0	0	0	2	0	0	0	0	2
Order of Friars Minor	20	0	0	0	0	0	0	20	0	0	0	0	20
Our Lady of Charity of the Good Shepherd	3	0	0	0	0	0	0	3	0	0	0	0	3
Pallottine Fathers	0	0	0	0	0	0	0	0	0	0	0	0	0
Pallottine Missionary Sisters	5	0	0	0	0	0	0	5	0	0	0	0	5
Passionists	1	0	0	0	0	0	0	1	0	0	0	0	1
Redemptorists	11	0	0	0	0	0	0	11	0	0	0	0	11
Religious of Jesus and Mary	4	0	0	0	0	0	0	4	0	0	0	0	4
Religious of the Assumption	1	0	0	0	0	0	0	1	0	0	0	0	1
Sacred Heart Fathers (Betharram)	0	0	0	0	0	0	0	0	0	0	0	0	0
Sacred Heart Fathers (Dehonians)	1	0	0	0	0	0	0	1	0	0	0	0	1
Sacred Hearts Community	0	0	0	0	0	0	0	0	0	0	0	0	0
St Joseph's Hospice Association (Jospice International)	5	0	0	0	0	0	0	5	0	0	0	0	5
St Joseph's Missionary Society, Mill Hill	56	0	0	0	0	0	0	56	93	0	7	20	176
St Patrick's Missionary Society	4	0	0	0	0	0	0	4	1	0	0	0	5
Salesian Fathers and Brothers	24	0	0	0	0	0	0	24	0	0	0	0	24
Salesian Sisters of St John Bosco	4	0	0	0	0	0	0	4	0	0	0	0	4
Servite Friars	3	0	0	0	0	0	0	3	0	0	0	0	3
Sisters of Charity of Jesus and Mary	2	0	0	0	0	0	0	2	0	0	0	46	48
Sisters of Charity of Our Lady of Evron	1	0	0	0	0	0	0	1	0	0	0	0	1
Sisters of Charity of St Jeanne Antide Thouret	1	0	0	0	0	0	0	1	0	0	0	0	1
Sisters of Charity of St Paul	4	0	0	0	0	0	0	4	0	0	0	0	4
Sisters of Christ	4	0	0	0	0	0	0	4	0	0	0	0	4
Sisters of Christian Instruction (St Gildas)	4	0	0	0	0	0	0	4	0	0	0	0	4
Sisters of La Retraite	5	0	0	0	0	0	0	5	0	0	0	0	5
Sisters of Notre Dame de Namur	19	0	0	0	0	0	0	19	0	0	0	0	19
Sisters of Our Lady of Charity	1	0	0	0	0	0	0	1	0	0	0	0	1
Sisters of Our Lady of Fidelity	1	0	0	0	0	0	0	1	0	0	0	0	1
Sisters of Providence, Rosminians	2	0	0	0	0	0	0	2	0	0	0	0	2
Sisters of St Clare	2	0	0	0	0	0	0	2	0	0	0	0	2
Sisters of St Joseph of Annecy	5	0	0	0	0	0	0	5	0	0	0	0	5
Sisters of St Joseph of Cluny	3	0	0	0	0	0	0	3	0	0	0	0	3
Sisters of St Joseph of the Apparition	4	0	0	0	0	0	0	4	17	0	0	13	34
Sisters of St Marie Madeleine Poste	1	1	0	0	0	0	0	0	1	0	0	0	1
Sisters of St Mary of Namur	4	0	0	0	0	0	0	4	0	0	0	0	4
Sisters of St Peter Claver	0	0	0	0	0	0	0	0	0	0	0	0	0
Sisters of the Cross and Passion	4	0	0	0	0	0	0	4	0	0	0	0	4
Sisters of the Good Saviour (Bon Sauveur)	1	0	0	0	0	0	0	1	0	0	0	0	1
Sisters of the Holy Family (St Emilie de Rodat)	1	0	0	0	0	0	0	1	0	0	0	0	1
Sisters of the Sacred Heart of Jesus	9	0	0	0	0	0	0	9	0	0	0	0	9
Society of African Missions and Mary	4	0	0	0	0	0	0	4	14	0	0	2	20
Society of Jesus	51	0	0	0	0	0	0	51	0	0	0	0	51
Society of Marie Reparatrice	2	0	0	0	0	0	0	2	0	0	0	0	2
Society of Mary	6	0	0	0	0	0	0	6	0	0	0	0	6
Society of the Divine Saviour (Salvatorians)	5	0	0	0	0	0	0	5	0	0	0	0	5
Society of the Divine Word	5	0	0	0	0	0	0	5	14	0	0	0	19
Society of the Holy Child Jesus	3	0	0	0	0	0	0	3	0	0	0	0	3
Society of the Sacred Heart	6	0	0	0	0	0	0	6	0	0	0	0	6
Ursulines of the Roman Union	5	0	0	0	0	0	0	5	0	0	0	0	5
Xaverian Missionary Fathers	3	0	0	0	0	0	0	3	9	0	0	0	12
Salvation Army													
Salvation Army	127	4	0	0	0	0	4	135	0	8	0	0	143
Seventh-Day Adventist													
World-wide Advent Missions	73	0	0	0	0	30	2	105	0	6	1	0	112
United Reformed													
United Reformed Church	6	1	0	0	0	0	1	8	0	2	0	0	10

5. SENDING CHURCHES BY LOCATION OF SERVICE

Note: This page excludes a number of New Churches. A research report describing their overseas activity is summarised in *Religious Trends* No 2, Page 3.8

UK missionaries = those serving in cross-culture and own culture mission and on furlough/home leave, but *excluding* associates.
Other countries = countries in which the church is involved but where none of their UK missionaries are currently serving.

Church	Countries with UK Missionaries	UK Missionaries	Other Countries
Basingstoke Community Church	Brazil(2), Hong Kong(2), Spain(2), Uganda(6), Zambia(4)	16	France, India, Kenya, Sweden, Zimbabwe
Biggin Hill Christian Fellowship	China(2), Lesotho(2), Mexico(2)	6	
Coventry Christian Fellowship	Gambia(2), Senegal(2), Turkey(6)	10	
Echoes of Service	Albania(2), Angola(4), Argentina(7), Austria(1), Bahamas(2), Bolivia(9), Botswana(5), Brazil(17), Chile(2), Colombia(2), Congo (Democratic Republic of)(20), Eastern Europe(4), Ecuador(3), France(71), Germany(1), Greenland(2), Hong Kong(4), India(13), Ireland (Republic of)(14), Israel(1), Italy(16), Japan(10), Kenya(2), Lebanon(10), Lesotho(2), Malaysia(1), Mexico(4), Middle East(6), Netherlands Antilles(2), New Caledonia(2), Northern Mariana Is(2), Norway(4), Pakistan(14), Peru(2), Portugal(8), Rwanda(2), Serbia(2), South Africa(16), Spain(17), Tanzania(8), Thailand(2), Trinidad & Tobago(2), Venezuela(1), Zambia(50), Zimbabwe(9), other(26)	404	
Hollybush Christian Fellowship	Côte D'Ivoire(1), Philippines(4), United Kingdom(3)	8	Arctic, Canada
Ichthus Christian Fellowship	Albania(2), Azerbaijan(7), Bulgaria(2), Cyprus (3), Egypt(2), France(8), Hong Kong(2), Indonesia(2), Lebanon(4), Mauritania(1), Pakistan (4) Romania(2), Turkey(11), Uganda(4)	64	
Kensington Temple London City Church	n/a	n/a	
Lifeline Network International	Zimbabwe(2)	2	Caribbean, Latvia, Malawi, Sierra Leone, USA, Zambia

MISSIONARY SENDING CHURCHES (DIRECT)

***Basingstoke Community Church**, The Centre, 18 Winchester Street, Basingstoke RG21 7DY
Senior Pastor: Mr Dave Marchment. *Church Administrator:* Dr Mike Poulton. Serving missionaries 29. ***CC*** No.1067316. Began 1861; re-formed 1978; Salt & Light Ministries. No magazine. Turnover £800,000 to year end Mar 98. Local church with an "Antioch" call to go to the nations.
Email: office@bcc.u-net.com
☎ 01256 461 430 Fax 01256 810 791

***Biggin Hill Christian Fellowship**, Main Road, Biggin Hill, Westerham TN16 3BA
Senior Pastor: Rev Ray Lowe. *Pastor:* Mr Gareth Wales. Serving missionaries 6. ***CC*** No.149022. Began n/a; Baptist/New Frontiers. No magazine. Turnover £160,000 to year end Dec 98.
Email: bhillcf@aol.com
☎ 01959 571 667 Fax 01959 570 215

***Coventry Christian Fellowship**, 70 David Road, Coventry CV1 2BW
Leader: Mr Wesley Longden. Serving missionaries 10. ***CC*** No.510955. Began 1977; non-denominational. No magazine. Turnover n/a.
☎ 024 7622 6309

Echoes of Service, 1 Widcombe Crescent, Bath BA2 6AQ
Managing Editor: John H Burness. *Advisory Editor:* Andrew J Street. Serving missionaries 400. ***CC*** No.234556. Began 1872 first issue of magazine; Christian Brethren. Magazine: *Echoes* (10,000 monthly). Turnover £3,500,000 to year end Dec 98.
Email: echoes_of_service@compuserve.com
☎ 01225 310 893/480 635 Fax 01225 480 134

***Hollybush Christian Fellowship**, Newsham, Thirsk YO7 4DH
Pastor: Mr James Wilkinson. Serving missionaries 8. ***CC*** Began 1967; non-denominational. No magazine. Turnover £100,000 to year end Dec 98.
Email: JuneHollyB@aol.com
☎ 01845 587 386

***Ichthus Christian Fellowship**, 107 Stanstead Road, Forest Hill, London SE23 1HH
Leader: Mr Roger Forster. Serving missionaries 61. ***CC*** No.269575. Began 1974; non-denominational. Magazine: *Celebration Magazine* (5,000 quarterly). Turnover £91,000 to year end Dec 98.
Web: www.ichthus.org.uk
Email: 100074.1000@compuserve.com
☎ 020 8291 4057 Fax 020 8291 6764

Kensington Temple London City Church, PO Box 9161, London W3 6GS
Senior Minister: Rev Colin W Dye. Serving missionaries 14. ***CC*** No.251549. Began n/a; Pentecostal. No magazine. Turnover n/a.
Web: www.ken-temp.org.uk
Email: ken-temp@dircon.co.uk
☎ 020 8752 8600 Fax 020 8229 7343

Lifeline Network International, Lifeline House, Neville Road, Dagenham RM8 3QS
Team Leader: Mr John Singleton. *UK Co-Ordinator:* Miss A McIntyre. Serving missionaries 10. Began 1981; Non-denominational. (Previously Community Resources). Magazine: *Network Facts* (1,000 nine times a year). Turnover n/a.
Email: lifelinenetwork@ndirect.co.uk
☎ 020 8597 2900 Fax 020 8597 1990

MISSIONARY SOCIETIES

Acre Gospel Mission, 33 Ravensdene Park, Belfast BT6 0DA
President: Dr T H Geddis. *Secretary:* Mr Jack Bennett. Executive staff 1, Serving missionaries 19. ***CC*** Began 1937; interdenominational. Magazine: *Missionary News* (6,000 quarterly). Turnover £195,071 to year end Dec 98.
☎ 028 9064 2638 🖷 028 9049 2358

Action International Ministries (UK), PO Box 193, Bewdley DY12 2GZ
UK Director: Mr Ingo Abraham. Executive staff 1, Serving missionaries 13, Other staff 3. ***CC*** No.1058661. Began 1974; interdenominational. (Previously ACTION UK). Magazine: *ACTIONPOINT* (1,500 quarterly), *Street Children* (1,500 every two months). Turnover £189,000 to year end Mar 98. Reaching urban poor of the world through evangelism, discipleship, social development projects especially amongst street children.
Web: www.actionintl.org
Email: actionuk@btinternet.com
☎ 01299 401 511 🖷 01299 405 273

***Action Partners Ministries**, Bawtry Hall, Bawtry, Doncaster DN10 6JH
International Director: Mr Steve Bell. *International Operations Director:* Mr Colin Smith. Executive staff 5, Serving missionaries 105, Other staff 11. ***CC*** No.1037154. Began 1904; interdenominational. Magazine: *Pathways* (5,000 every two months). Turnover £760,000 to year end Dec 98. Working alongside the African church to facilitate holistic mission in Northern Africa.
Web: www.actionpartners.org.uk
Email: info@actionpartners.org.uk
☎ 01302 710 750 🖷 01302 719 399
Also at: 2 West Lynn, Dalry KA24 4LJ
☎ 01294 835 295
And: 95 Dunraven Avenue, Belfast BT5 5JS
☎ 028 9045 9374

***Africa Inland Mission International**, 2 Vorley Road, Archway, London N19 5HE
UK Director: Rev John Brand. *International Director:* Dr Fred Beam. *Overseas Personnel Officer:* Mr Tom Mayo. Executive staff 9, Serving missionaries 175, Other staff 13. ***CC*** No.216355. Began 1895; interdenominational. Magazine: *AIM International* (6,500 quarterly). Turnover £1,619,000 to year end Feb 98. Church planting in unevangelised areas and helping churches grow.
Web: www.aim-eur.org
Email: information@aim-eur.org
☎ 020 7281 1184 🖷 020 7281 4479
Also at: 41 Belhaven Terrace, Wishaw ML2 7AY
☎ 01698 372 549
And: 279 Woodstock Road, Belfast BT6 8PR
☎ 028 9045 3497
And: International Office, 37 Alexandra Park, Bristol BS6 6QB
☎ 0117 942 9771 🖷 0117 944 4134

***Agapé** Fairgate House, Kings Road, Tyseley, Birmingham B11 2AA
National Director: Mr David Wilson. *International President, USA:* Dr William R Bright. Executive staff 3, Serving missionaries 87, Other staff 14. ***CC*** No.258421. Began 1951; interdenominational. Part of Campus Crusade for Christ International. Magazine: *Agapé News* (10,000 every four months). Turnover £1,278,594 to year end Dec 98. Evangelism and discipleship in different segments of society; schools, universities and businesses.
Web: www.agape.org.uk
Email: info@agape.org.uk
☎ 0121 765 4404 🖷 0121 765 4065

Albanian Evangelical Mission, 29 Bridge Street, Penybryn, Wrexham LL13 7HP
Secretary: Mr David M Young. Executive staff 2, Serving missionaries 24. ***CC*** No.1036807. Began 1986; interdenominational. Magazine: *Newsletter* (1,600 five times a year). Turnover £98,000 to year end Mar 98.
Email: dmy@albanianmission.demon.co.uk
☎ 01978 290 138

***All India Mission**, 39 Lees Lane, Northallerton DL7 8DA
Chairman: Mr Steve Cowie. Executive staff 1, Other staff 1. Serving missionaries n/a. ***CC*** No.1042736. Began 1994; non-denominational. Magazine: *All India Mission* (300 occasionally). Turnover £10,000 to year end Dec 98. Mass evangelism, church planting, tribal ministry, medical ministry, Bible School in Bihar, North India.
Email: aimindia@aim.com
☎ 01609 779 285 🖷 01609 777 469
Information from: *Trustee:* Mr David Raine, 2 North Riding Rise, Thornton Le Moor, Northallerton DL7 9EB

***Antioch Mission UK**, 22 Elm Tree Avenue, Frinton-on-Sea CO13 0BE
UK Directors: Pastor Decio & Mrs Azevedo. Executive staff 3, Other staff 1 Currently no UK missionaries serving overseas. ***CC*** Began 1985; interdenominational. Magazine: *Prayer letter* (400 every two months). Turnover £15,000 to year end Mar 99.
☎ 01255 851 372 🖷 01255 679 194

For further information see Lists on Pages 328–350

Apostolic Church Missionary Movement, 24 St Helen's Road, Swansea SA1 1ZH
Chairman, Overseas Board: Rev P Powell. *Adminstrator:* Rev Andrew Saunders. Executive staff 7, Serving missionaries 20. *CC* No.284789. Began 1922; Apostolic. Magazine: *Christian Lifestyle* (1,200 quarterly). Turnover £250,000 to year end Dec 98.
Web:www.apostolic-church.org
Email: admin@apostolic-church.org
☎ 01792 473 992 Fax 01792 474 087

Arab World Ministries, PO Box 51, Loughborough LE11 0ZQ
National Director: To be appointed. *Promotion Manager:* Mr Howard Jones. *Member Care Manager:* Mr Alasdair McLaren. Executive staff 2, Serving missionaries 63, Other staff 12. *CC* No.1059106. Began 1881; interdenominational. Magazine: *Frontline* (7,250 ten times a year). Turnover £900,000 to year end Dec 98.
Web: www.awm.com
Email: 74754.1321@ compuserve.com
☎ 01509 239 525 Fax 01509 264 820
Also at: 3 Crathes Gardens, Livingston EH54 9EN
Email: 101762.70@compuserve.com
☎ 01506 872 900 Fax 01506 872 900
And: 21 Willow Drive, Banbridge BT32 4RF
Email: 101653.1047@compuserve.com
☎ 028 4462 7936
And: International Office, PO Box 4006, Worthing BN13 1AP
Email: recptn@wornet.mhs.compuserve.com
☎ 01903 215 234 Fax 01903 215 456

Assemblies of God World Ministries, Hook Place, Burgess Hill RH15 8RF
General Director: Rev J P Wildrianne. Executive staff 6, Serving missionaries 109, Other staff 6. *CC* Began 1909; Assemblies of God. Magazine: *World Ministries News* (3,500 monthly). Turnover £1,000,000 to year end June 94.
☎ 01444 248 383 Fax 01444 236 038

Associates of Mill Hill Missionaries, St Joseph's College, Lawrence Street, Mill Hill, London NW7 4JX
Coordinator: Ms Alice Keenleyside. Executive staff 1, Serving missionaries 8. *CC* No.220690. Began 1970; Roman Catholic. Mill Hill Society founded 1866. No magazine. Turnover n/a. Taking the Gospel to the marginalised, crossing economic, cultural and religious boundaries.
☎ 020 8959 8254 Ext 175 Fax 020 8959 8493

Association of the Holy Family of Bordeaux, 2 Aberdare Gardens, London NW6 3PX
Provincial Superior: Sister Clare McGrath. Serving missionaries 5. Began 1820; Roman Catholic. No magazine. Turnover n/a.
☎ 020 7624 7573 Fax 020 7625 8984

Assumptionists Fathers and Brothers, 16 Nightingale Road, Hitchin SG5 1QS
Provincial Superior: Rev Robert Henshaw. Serving missionaries 1. *CC* Began n/a; Roman Catholic. Magazine: *Newsletter* (Circulation n/a every four months). Turnover n/a.
☎ 01462 457 673

Augustinian Recollects, 18 Cheniston Gardens, Kensington, London W8 6TQ
Vicar Provincial: Rev Gerald Wilson. *Prior General, Italy:* Rev J Pipaćn. Serving missionaries 2. *CC* Began 1932; Roman Catholic. Magazine: *Friends Letter* (8,000 seven times a year). Turnover n/a.
Web: www.btinternet.com/~augustinian.recollects/
☎ 020 7937 7681 Fax 020 7937 7681

Augustinians, Clare Priory, Ashen Road, Clare, Sudbury CO10 8NX
Provincial Superior: Rev Paul Graham. Serving missionaries 3. *CC* No.233010. Began n/a; Roman Catholic. No magazine. Turnover n/a. Education, secondary and tertiary; pastoral work; spiritual direction; clerical formation.
☎ 01787 278 679 Fax 01787 278 679

†**Baptist Missions**, 117 Lisburn Road, Belfast BT9 7AF
Missions Secretary: Rev Derek Baxter. Executive staff 1, Serving missionaries 19, Other staff 2. *CC* Began 1888; Baptist. Magazine: *Info-Mission* – in The Irish Baptist (3,000 monthly). Turnover £600,000 to year end Jan 97.
☎ 028 9066 3108 Fax 028 9066 3616

***BCM International**, 39a Swiss Road, Weston-super-Mare BS23 3AY
UK Field Director: Rev Bert Weenink. *International Director:* Rev R Evans. Executive staff 1, Serving missionaries 31. *CC* No.1044539. Began 1936; interdenominational. Magazine: *Communicator* (600 quarterly). Turnover £110,000 to year end Dec 98.
Web: www.bcm.org.uk
Email: bcmuk@aol.com
☎ 01934 413 484

***Belgian Evangelical Mission**, PO Box 165, Swindon SN5 6LU
British Co-ordinators: Mr & Mrs Roy & Christine Saint. *President, Belgium:* Rev J Lukasse. Executive staff 2, Serving missionaries 17. *CC* No.247192. Began 1919; interdenominational. Magazine: *Spotlight Belgium* (2,500 quarterly). Turnover £192,000 to year end Jan 98.
☎ 01793 882 368 Fax 01793 882 368

***BMS, Baptist Missionary Society**, PO Box 49, 129 Broadway, Didcot OX11 8XA
General Director: Rev Dr Alistair Brown. *Director for Mission:* Rev David Kerrigan. *Director of Communications:* Mr Richard Wells. Executive staff 12, Serving missionaries 186, Other staff 53. *CC* No.233782. Began 1792; Baptist. Magazine: *BMS Magazine* (18,000 every two months). Turnover £4,807,224 to year end Oct 98. A pioneering mission agency working with Christian partners around the world to reach a needy world.
Web: www.rpc.ox.ac.uk./bms
Email: mail@bms.org.uk
☎ 01235 517 700 Fax 01235 517 601

British & International Sailors' Society, 3a Orchard Place, Southampton SO14 3AT
General Secretary: Mr Graham Chambers. *Principal Chaplain:* Rev James W MacDonald. *Property Manager:* Mr David Hughdie. Executive staff 5, Serving missionaries 33, Other staff 13. *CC* No.237778. Began 1818; interdenominational. Magazine: *Chart and Compass* (60,000 half-yearly). Turnover £3,531,745 to year end Dec 98. Caring for merchant seafarers and their dependants.
Email: chaplains@biss.org.uk
☎ 023 8033 7333 Fax 023 8033 8333

Brothers of the Sacred Heart, Watling House, 8 King Harry Lane, St Albans AL3 4AW
Head Brother: Brother Raymond Reinsant. Serving missionaries 2. Currently no UK missionaries serving overseas. *CC* No.231733. Began 1955; Roman Catholic. No magazine. Turnover n/a.
☎ 01727 861 969

O

Capuchin Franciscans (Order of Friars Minor Capuchin), Provincial Curia, Franciscan Friary, Carlton Road, Erith DA8 1DN
Provincial Minister: Rev John Condon. Serving missionaries 1. ***CC*** No.231143. Began 1873; Roman Catholic. No magazine. Turnover n/a.
Email: jfcapi@cwcominet
☎ 01322 437 281 ☎ 01322 438 361

Carrot Tops, 10 Howard Road, Saffron Walden CB10 2DB
Director: Rev R W Frankland. Executive staff 3, Serving missionaries 9, Other staff 2. ***CC*** No.1016820. Began 1984; interdenominational. (Previously Project India). Magazine: *Carrot Tops* (500 quarterly). Turnover £26,000 to year end Dec 98.
Web: www.buxnet.co.uk/carrot-tops
Email: 106413.2223@compuserve.com
☎ 01799 501 417 ☎ 01799 520 230

Central African Missions, 355 Blackpool Road, Preston PR2 3AB
UK Administrator: Mr Andrew C Ramsey. *UK Director:* Mr David Womersley. Executive staff 2, Serving missionaries 16, Other staff 2. ***CC*** No.1049246. Began 1915; Pentecostal. (Previously Zaire Evangelistic Mission). Magazine: *Contact* (4,000 monthly). Turnover £318,300 to year end Sept 98.
Web: www.centralafricanmissions.org
Email: cam@central-african-missions.org.uk
☎ 01772 717 830 ☎ 01772 719 322

Child Evangelism Fellowship, 64 Osborne Road, Levenshulme, Manchester M19 2DY
National Chairman: Mr Ron McLean. *National Directors:* Mr & Mrs Raymond Barr. Executive staff 4, Serving missionaries 25, Other staff 2. ***CC*** No.235080. Began 1956; interdenominational. Magazine: *Evangelising Today's Child* (30,000 every two months), *Sharing the Vision* (1,200 every four months). Turnover n/a. Working in over 140 countries worldwide.
Web: www.cefinc.org/europe
Email: rmbatcef@aol.com
☎ 0161 224 8023

The Christian and Missionary Alliance, 10 Alpha Avenue, Garsington, Oxford OX44 9BQ
Director: Mr Philip Margesson. Executive staff 1, Serving missionaries 10, Other staff 16. ***CC*** No.802990. Began 1973; interdenominational. No magazine. Turnover £76,692 to year end Jan 98.
Email: 106245.3563@compuserve.com
☎ 01865 711 626 ☎ 01865 711 626
Also at: Box Bush House, Brinkworth, Chippenham SN15 5AJ
Email: philipmargesson@csi.com
☎ 01666 510 416 ☎ 01666 510 416

†**Christian Associates International**, 23 King's Paddock, Hampton TW12 2EF
UK Director: Mr Ron Carlson. Executive staff 2, Serving missionaries 1. Began 1996; interdenominational. Turnover n/a.
Email: 100566.2265@compuserve.com
☎ 020 8979 1213

***Christian Literature Crusade**, Shawton House, 792 Hagley Road West, Oldbury B68 0PJ
British Director: Mr Phil Grant. *International Secretary, UK:* Mr P Horne. Serving missionaries 85. ***CC*** No.1015793. Began 1941; interdenominational. Magazine: *CLC World* (6,000 every two months). Turnover n/a.
Web: www.clc.org.uk
Email: pgrant@clc.org.uk
☎ 0121 422 5755 ☎ 0121 423 2298

Christian Witness to Israel, 166 Main Road, Sundridge, Sevenoaks TN14 6EL
Chief Executive: Rev John S Ross. *General Manager:* Mr Eric Cousins. *Chairman of Council:* Rev Clement Graham. Executive staff 2, Serving missionaries 16, Other staff 6. ***CC*** No.271323. Began 1842; interdenominational. Magazine: *CWI Herald* (13,000 quarterly). Turnover £695,850 to year end Mar 96.
Web: www.cwi.org.uk & www.shalom.org.uk
Email: cwihq@cwi.org.uk
☎ 01959 565 955 ☎ 01959 565 966

***Christians in Action**, 67 Melfort Road, Thornton Heath CR7 7RT
UK Director: Rev Freddie C Roberson Jr. *International President, USA:* Rev Elgin Taylor. Executive staff 2, Serving missionaries 15, Other staff 5. ***CC*** No.257785. Began 1965; interdenominational. No magazine. Turnover £82,000 to year end Mar 98. Discipleship of the nations through practical training and church planting both at home and abroad.
Email: cinalondon@compuserve.com
☎ 020 8684 1603 ☎ 020 8240 1683

***Church Mission Society**, Partnership House, 157 Waterloo Road, London SE1 8UU
General Secretary: Ms Diana Witts. *Regional Secretary, UK:* Rev Mark Oxbrow. Executive staff 62, Serving missionaries 257. ***CC*** No.220297. Began 1799; Anglican. (Previously Church Missionary Society). Magazine: *Yes* (25,000 quarterly). Turnover £6,100,000 to year end Jan 98. Working in partnership with local church in leadership training, community development, health care, teaching.
Web: www/cms-uk.org
Email: info@cms-uk.org
☎ 020 7928 8681 ☎ 020 7401 3215

Church Missionary Society Ireland (CMS Ireland), Church of Ireland House, 61 Donegall Street, Belfast BT1 2QH
General Secretary: Rev Cecil Wilson. *Overseas Personnel Secretary, Republic of Ireland:* Rev Declan Smith. *Mission Development Officer:* Mr Ronnie Briggs. Executive staff 3, Serving missionaries 28, Other staff 2. ***CC*** No.XN 48809. Began 1814; Anglican. Magazine: *TransMission* (5,000 quarterly). Turnover £675,000 to year end Oct 98.
Email: cmsibelfast@ireland.anglican.org
☎ 028 9032 4581 ☎ 028 9032 1756

Church of Scotland Board of World Mission, 121 George Street, Edinburgh EH2 4YN
General Secretary: Rev Prof Kenneth R Ross. *Assistant Secretary (Personnel):* Miss Sheila Ballentyne. Executive staff 8, Serving missionaries 125, Other staff 11. ***CC*** Began 1796; Church of Scotland. No magazine. Turnover £3,078,000 to year end Dec 98.
Web: www.cofs.org.uk
Email: world@cofscotland.org.uk
☎ 0131 225 5722 ☎ 0131 226 6121

***Church's Ministry Among Jewish People**, 30c Clarence Road, St Albans AL1 4JJ
General Director: Rev Tony Higton. *UK Director:* Rev John Lawrence. Executive staff 3, Serving missionaries 44, Other staff 10. ***CC*** No.228519. Began 1809; Anglican. Magazine: *Shalom* (5,000 every four months). Turnover £560,000 to year end Dec 98.
Web: www.cmj.org.uk
Email: cmj_stalbans@compuserve.com
☎ 01727 833 114 ☎ 01727 848 312

For further information see Lists on Pages 328–350

O

Claretian Missionaries, Buckden Towers, Buckden, St Neots, Huntingdon PE18 9TA
Provincial Superior: Rev James Kennedy. *Superior General, Italy:* Rev Aquilino Bocos. Home staff 12. Currently no UK missionaries serving overseas. ***CC*** No.234026. Began 1849; Roman Catholic. Magazine: *New Tidings* (2,000 every four months). Turnover n/a.
Email: claret-centre@cmfbuck.force9.net
☎ 01480 812 980 🖷 01480 812 980

Columban Lay Missionaries, 28 Redington Road, London NW3 7RH
Coordinator: Mr L Poltawski. Executive staff 1, Other staff 2. ***CC*** No.221594. Began 1982; Roman Catholic. Magazine: *Far East* (40,000 worldwide monthly). Turnover £60,000 to year end Mar 99. Pastoral work in Roman Catholic communities in Asia and Latin America.
Web: www.columban.org
Email: imp@laymission.freeserve.co.uk
☎ 020 7435 2299 🖷 020 7794 7074

Comboni Missionaries (Verona Fathers), London Road, Sunningdale, Ascot SL5 01Y
Provincial Superior: Rev Martin Devenish. Serving missionaries 8, Home staff 17. ***CC*** Began 1867; Roman Catholic. Magazine: *Comboni Missions* (12,000 quarterly). Turnover n/a.
Email: verona@globalnet.co.uk
☎ 01344 621 238 🖷 01344 874 175

Comboni Missionary Sisters (Verona Sisters), 26 Blackboy Lane, London N15 3AR
Provincial Superior: Sister Margaret Doyle. Serving missionairies 6, Home staff 9. ***CC*** No.214864. Began 1872; Roman Catholic. No magazine. Turnover n/a.
☎ 020 8809 2893 🖷 020 8809 2893

Congregation of Christian Brothers, Woodeaves, Hale Barns, Altrincham WA15 0HF
Provincial Superior: Rev Brother George Gordon. *Superior General, Italy:* Rev Brother J C Keating. Serving missionaries 6. ***CC*** Began 1822; Roman Catholic. No magazine. Turnover n/a. School education, school for handicapped children.
Email: patrickg.gordon@virgin.net
☎ 0161 904 0786 🖷 0161 903 9182

Congregation of Josephites, St George's College, Weybridge Road, Addlestowe, Weybridge KT15 2QS
Provincial Superior: Rev Paul Connor. Serving missionaries 4. ***CC*** No.312071. Began 1929; Roman Catholic. No magazine. Turnover £100,000 to year end Dec 98.
☎ 01932 839 452/470 🖷 01932 842 268

Congregation of La Sainte Union des Sacré-Coeurs, 53 Croftdown Road, London NW5 1EL
Provincial Superior: Sister Margaret O'Reilly. *Superior General, Italy:* Sister Pauline Cowie. Serving missionaries 8. ***CC*** Began 1859; Roman Catholic. No magazine. Turnover n/a.
☎ 020 7482 7225 🖷 020 7284 4760

Congregation of Our Lady of the Missions, 108 Spencer Road, Wealdstone, Harrow HA3 7AR
Provincial Superior: Sister Anne Collette. *Superior General, Italy:* Sister Claire Himbeault. Serving missionaries 6. ***CC*** Began 1870; Roman Catholic. No magazine. Turnover n/a.
☎ 020 8861 4174 🖷 020 8424 2133

Consolata Fathers, 3 Salisbury Avenue, Finchley, London N3 3AJ
Superior: Rev A Magnante. Serving missionaries 1. Began n/a. Roman Catholic. No magazine. Turnover n/a.
☎ 020 8346 5498 🖷 020 8349 1997

Consolata Missionary Sisters, 13 The Avenue, London E11 2EE
Provincial Superior: Sister Celestia Quaranta. Serving missionaries 1, Home staff 1. ***CC*** No.263229. Began 1960; Roman Catholic. No magazine. Turnover n/a.
☎ 020 8989 6186 🖷 020 7837 2256

*__Crosslinks__, 251 Lewisham Way, London SE4 1XF
General Secretary: Rev Roger Bowen. *President:* Rev Dr Chris Wright. Executive staff 12, Serving missionaries 93, Other staff 39. ***CC*** No.249986. Began 1922; Anglican. Magazine: *The Crosslinks Magazine* (10,000 frequency n/a). Turnover £1,335,000 to year end Dec 95.
Email: crosslinks@crosslinks.org
☎ 020 8691 6111 🖷 020 8694 8023
Also at: 60a Castlereagh Street, Belfast BT5 4NH
Email: james@belfast.region.crosslinks.org
☎ 028 9046 6489 🖷 028 9046 6489

Crusade of the Holy Spirit, 464 Chester Road, Sutton Coldfield B73 5BP
General Director: Rev Bernard Kelly. Serving missionaries 2. ***CC*** No.257147. Began 1970; Roman Catholic. No magazine. Turnover n/a.
☎ 0121 384 4280 🖷 0121 328 8148

Daughters of Charity of St Vincent de Paul, Provincial House, The Ridgeway, Mill Hill, London NW7 1EH
Provincial Superior: Sister Zoe O'Neill. Serving missionaries 7. ***CC*** No.236803. Began 1847; Roman Catholic. No magazine. Turnover n/a. Service/ministry among people suffering from various forms of poverty or handicap; 85 countries worldwide.
☎ 020 8906 3777 🖷 020 8201 0542

Daughters of Jesus, Brook House, 95a Uxbridge Road, Rickmansworth WD3 2DJ
Provincial: Sister Pauline Dinan. Serving missionaries 2. ***CC*** No.234925. Began 1904; Roman Catholic. No magazine. Turnover n/a.
☎ 01923 771 566 🖷 01923 775 048

Daughters of Mary and Joseph, 55 Fitzjames Avenue, Croydon CR0 5DN
Provincial Superior: Sister Sheila Moloney. Serving missionaries 1. ***CC*** No.232421. Began 1869; Roman Catholic. No magazine. Turnover n/a.
☎ 020 8654 8041 🖷 020 8655 4337

Daughters of St Paul, Middle Green, Langley, Slough SL3 6BS
Provincial Superior: Sister Eugene Campara. Currently no UK missionaries serving overseas. ***CC*** No.296042. Began 1955; Roman Catholic. No magazine. Turnover n/a.
Email: productions@stpaulmultimedia.co.uk
☎ 01753 577 629 🖷 01753 511 809

For further information see Lists on Pages 328–350

aughters of the Holy Spirit, 103 Harlestone Road, Northampton NN5 7AQ
Provincial Superior: Sister Ellen Burke. *Superior General, France:* Sister Anne Marie Couloigner. Serving missionaries 9. ***CC*** No.234520. Began 1902; Roman Catholic. No magazine. Turnover n/a.
☎ 01604 587 423 🖷 01604 755 152

e La Salle Brothers, 140 Banbury Road, Oxford OX2 7BP
Provincial Superior: Brother Joseph Hendron. Serving missionaries 9. ***CC*** No.232632. Began 1855; Roman Catholic. No magazine. Turnover n/a.
Web: www.disnet.demon.co.uk
☎ 01865 311 332 🖷 01865 543 56

ohnavur Fellowship, 15 Elm Drive, Harrow HA2 7BS
Secretary for Great Britain: Miss R J van der Flier. *Co-leaders, India:* Miss Nesaruthina Carunia, & Miss Sura Carunia. Serving missionaries 6, Other staff 1. ***CC*** No.232510. Began 1901; interdenominational. Magazine: *Dust of Gold* (2,500 quarterly). Turnover £1,925,850 to year end Apr 98.
☎ 020 8427 2189

ominican Sisters of St Catherine of Siena of Oakford, Dominican Convent, 34 Love Lane, Pinner HA5 3EX
Provincial Superior: Sister Mary O'Rourke. Serving missionaries 2. ***CC*** No.233474. Began n/a; Roman Catholic. No magazine. Turnover n/a. Teaching, nursing and residential homes for elderly, clinics in Africa.
☎ 020 8866 5460/6135 🖷 020 8866 2484

ominican Sisters of Zimbabwe, 38 Hyde Vale, Greenwich, London SE10 8QH
Delegation Superior: Sister Kostka Carew. Serving missionaries 4. ***CC*** No.231237. Began 1890; Roman Catholic. No magazine. Turnover n/a. Teaching, nursing, counselling, parish and social work.
☎ 020 8692 3382

ominicans, St Dominic's Priory, Southampton Road, London NW5 4LB
Prior Provincial: Very Rev Malcolm McMahon. *Master General, Italy:* Rev Timothy Radcliffe. Serving missionaries 10. ***CC*** No.231192. Began 1221; Roman Catholic. Magazine: *New Blackfriars* (Circulation n/a monthly). Turnover n/a. Pastoral work in the West Indies, some teaching in the regional seminary.
Email: 106017.1550@compuserve.com
☎ 020 7485 2760 🖷 020 7485 2760

Edinburgh Medical Missionary Society, 7 Washington Lane, Edinburgh EH11 2HA
Executive Director: Mr Robin G K Arnott. *Projects & PR Manager:* Mrs Dorothy MacKenzie. Executive staff 1, Serving missionaries 4, Other staff 5. ***CC*** No.SCO15000. Began 1841; interdenominational. Magazine: *The Healing Hand* (3,000 every four months). Turnover £325,000 to year end Dec 98.
Email: emms@btinternet.com
☎ 0131 313 3828 🖷 0131 313 4662

Elim International Missions, PO Box 38, Cheltenham GL50 3HN
International Missions Director: Rev Brian G Edwards. Executive staff 1, Serving missionaries 53, Other staff 6. ***CC*** No.251549. Began 1930; Elim Pentecostal. Magazine: *Direction* (24,000 monthly). Turnover £816,000 to year end Dec 98.
Web: www.elim.org.co.uk
Email: kcooper@elimhq.com
☎ 01242 519 904 🖷 01242 542 023

***Emmanuel International**, 29 Harberton Crescent, Chichester PO19 4NY
UK Director: Rev David Bendell. *Manager:* Mr Derek C James. Executive staff 1, Serving missionaries 13, Other staff 1. ***CC*** No.289036. Began 1984; interdenominational. Magazine: *Emmanuel International* (2,000 every four months). Turnover £114,000 to year end June 98.
Web: www.argonet.co.uk/users/emm.int
Email: emm.int@argonet.co.uk
☎ 01243 788 541 🖷 01243 788 541

English Benedictine Congregation, Belmont Abbey, Hereford HR2 9RZ
Abbot: Rt Rev Mark Jabale. Serving missionaries 4. ***CC*** Began n/a; Roman Catholic. No magazine. Turnover n/a.
☎ 01432 277 388 🖷 01432 277 597

English Benedictine Congregation, Worth Abbey, Paddockhurst Road, Crawley RH10 4SB
Abbot: Rt Rev Stephen Ortiger. Currently no UK missionaries overseas. ***CC*** No.233572. Began n/a; Roman Catholic. No magazine. Turnover n/a.
Email: worthabbey@ukonline.co.uk
☎ 01342 710 310 🖷 01342 710 311

***European Christian Mission (Britain)**, 50 Billing Road, Northampton NN1 5DH
Executive Director: Mr David Clark. *British Co-ordinator:* Miss Patricia Briercliffe. *Director for Ireland:* Mr Alan Armstrong. Executive staff 3, Serving missionaries 43, Other staff 8. ***CC*** No.1064037. Began 1904; interdenominational. Magazine: *Europe's Millions* (7,500 quarterly). Turnover £500,000 to year end Dec 98. Planting and developing churches which evangelise and disciple the peoples of Europe.
Web: www.ecmi.org
Email: ecmbritain@ compuserve.com
☎ 01604 621 092 🖷 01604 620 594
Also at: Glenburn House, Glenburn Road South, Dunmurry, Belfast BT17 9JP
☎ 028 9030 1526 🖷 028 9030 1526

European Missionary Fellowship, Guessens, 6 Codicote Road, Welwyn AL6 9NB
Director: Rev Daniel Webber. Executive staff 1, Serving missionaries 17, Other staff 4. ***CC*** No.1071823. Began 1959; interdenominational. Magazine: *Vision of Europe* (10,000 quarterly). Turnover £380,000 to year end Dec 98.
☎ 01438 716 398

Evangelical Action (Brazil), 23 Wellands, Wickham Bishops, Witham CM8 3NF
Secretary/Treasurer: Mrs P White. Serving missionaries 4, Other staff 1. ***CC*** No.277235. Began 1938; interdenominational. (Previously Gospel to Brazil Faith Mission). Magazine: *In Touch* (500 every two months). Turnover £60,000 to year end June 98.
☎ 01621 891 839 🖷 01621 891 839

Faithful Companions of Jesus, 24 Singleton Road, Salford M7 4WL
Provincial Superior: Sister Mary Sykes. Serving missionaries 4. ***CC*** No.239285. Began 1820; Roman Catholic. No magazine. Turnover £1,106,871 to year end Dec 98.
Web: www.fcjsisters.org
Email: mcs003@aol.com
☎ 0161 792 2267 🖷 0161 708 9683

*__FEBA Radio__, Ivy Arch Road, Worthing BN14 8BX
Director for Ministry Support: Mr David Docherty. *Chief Executive, UK:* Mr John Bartlett. *Director for Resources:* Mr Dave Mason. Executive staff 5, Serving missionaries 41, Other staff 38. ***CC*** No.257343. Began 1968; interdenominational. Magazine: *Feba Radio News* (21,000 quarterly). Turnover £2,738,950 to year end Sept 98. Evangelical radio mission broadcasting to over 30 countries.
Web: www.feba.org.uk
Email: reception@feba.org.uk
☎ 01903 237 281 🖷 01903 205 294

Fidei Donum Priests, Saint Margaret Mary, Pilch Lane, Knotty Ash, Liverpool L14 0JG
Contact Person: Rev Gerry Proctor. Serving missionaries 31. Began 1957; Roman Catholic. No magazine. Turnover n/a.
Email: smmp@mersinet.co.uk
☎ 0151 228 1332 🖷 0151 259 6019

Focus on Israel, 29 Clarendon Road, Leytonstone, London E11 1BZ
Chairman: Rev M Tilley. Executive staff 2, Serving missionaries 7. ***CC*** No.803140. Began 1931; Pentecostal. (Previously Pentecostal Jewish Mission). Magazine: *Focus on Israel* (5,000 every two months). Turnover £45,000 to year end Dec 92.
Email: foi@wyrecompute.com
☎ 020 8556 3229 🖷 020 8532 8684

*__France Mission Trust__, The Old Chapel, Chapel Lane, Minchinhampton, Stroud GL6 9DL
British Director: Mr Peter H Farley. *President of French Committee, France:* Mr Gilbert Presle. Executive staff 4, Serving missionaries 17, Other staff 3. ***CC*** No.267979. Began 1974; interdenominational. Magazine: *Action Missionnaire* (8,000 quarterly). Turnover n/a.
Web: www.france-mission.org
Email: fmtrust@france-mission.org
☎ 01453 884 454 🖷 01453 884 454

Franciscan Conventuals, 26 Cornwall Road, Waterloo, London SE1 8TW
Provincial Superior: Rev Philip Doherty. Serving missionaries 2. ***CC*** No.249881. Began 1224; Roman Catholic. Magazine: *Crusader* (15,000 monthly). Turnover n/a.
Email: philipofmconv@compuserve.com
☎ 020 7928 8897 🖷 020 7928 2887

O

Franciscan Minoresses, St Clare's Franciscan Convent, Dalby Road, Melton Mowbray LE13 0BP
Provincial Superior: Sister Columba Redmond. Serving missionaries 1. ***CC*** No.232532. Began n/a; Roman Catholic. No magazine. Turnover n/a.
☎ 01664 624 22

Franciscan Missionaries of Mary, 5 Vaughan Avenue, London W6 0XS
Provincial: Sister Philomena Wright. *Superior General, Italy:* Sister Maura O'Connor. Serving missionaries 24, Home staff 105. ***CC*** Began 1901; Roman Catholic. No magazine. Turnover n/a. Pastoral work, care of the sick and elderly, retreats, counselling, school governers.
Email: provsecuk@aol.com
☎ 020 8748 4077 🖷 020 8741 9618

Franciscan Missionaries of the Divine Motherhood (FMDM), Ladywell Convent, Ashtead Lane, Godalming GU7 1ST
Superior General: Sister Ann Keily. Serving missionaries 28, Home staff 72. ***CC*** No.232098. Began 1887; Roman Catholic. Magazine: *The Voice* (2,000 half-yearly). Turnover n/a. Health care and pastoral care, especially of the poor and deprived.
☎ 01483 425 775 🖷 01483 426 244

Franciscan Missionary Sisters of St Joseph, St Joseph's Conver
Greenleach Lane, Worsley, Manchester M28 2TS
Superior General: Sister Theadora Slot. Serving missionaries
Home staff 79. ***CC*** No.232533. Began 1883; Roman Catholi
No magazine. Turnover n/a. Building up communities throu
medical, social, educational and pastoral work among the po
and marginalised.
☎ 0161 794 1062 🖷 0161 794 6420

Franciscan Sisters of Mill Hill, St Francis Cottage, The Ridgewa
Mill Hill, London NW7 4HX
Superior General: Sister Margaret McElroy. Serving missiona
ies 1. ***CC*** No.232494. Began 1868; Roman Catholic. No mag
zine. Turnover n/a.
☎ 020 8959 4854 🖷 020 8906 9370

†*__Free Church of Scotland Foreign Missions Board__, 5 Kilmardimr
Drive, Bearsden, Glasgow G61 3PD
Secretary: Mr Peter Morrison. *General Treasurer:* Mr Iain Gi
Executive staff 1, Serving missionaries 20, Other staff 3. *C*
No.SCO 12925. Began 1843; Free Church of Scotland. Mag
zine: *Monthly Record* (7,000 monthly), *Missionary Magazi*
(5,000 annually). Turnover £350,000 to year end Dec 96.
☎ 0141 943 1701 🖷 0141 943 1701

Free Presbyterian Church of Scotland Mission Committee, Fre
Presbyterian Manse, Raasay, Kyle IV40 8PB
Clerk to Committee: Rev James R Tallach. *Clerk of Synod:* Re
John MacLeod. Executive staff 5, Serving missionaries 14. *C*
No.SCO 03545. Began n/a; Free Presbyterian Church of Sco
land. No magazine. Turnover £500,000 to year end Dec 98
Preaching the gospel with medical (hospital) and educationa
(secondary school) work as handmaids.
Web: www.fpchurch.org.uk
Email: jmac1265@aol.com
☎ 01478 660 216

Free Presbyterian Church of Ulster Mission Board, Carginag
Road, Kilkeel, Newry BT34 4NE
Chairman: Rev David McIlveen. *Secretary:* Rev Ro
Johnston. Executive staff 1, Serving missionaries 59. Bega
1978; Free Presbyterian Church of Ulster. Magazine: *Mission ary Newsletter* (4,500 every four months). Turnover n/a.
Email: fpcmisson@aol.com
☎ 028 4176 5574 🖷 028 4176 5574

*__Frontiers__, PO Box 7, Northampton NN1 5AF
British Director: Dr Peter Hopkins. *General Director, UK:* D
Greg Livingstone. Executive staff 5, Serving missionaries 56,
Other staff 3. ***CC*** No.1012566. Began 1991; interdenominational. Magazine: *Team News* (3,400 quarterly). Turnove
£370,000 to year end Dec 98.
Web: www.frontiers.org
Email: info@uk.frontiers.org
☎ 01604 233 535 🖷 01604 250 053
Also at: International Office, PO Box 4, High Wycombe HP14 3YX
☎ 01494 484 391 🖷 01494 485 917

*__Global Outreach UK__, 108 Sweetbriar Lane, Exeter EX1 3AR
UK Secretary: Rev David T Cole. *President, USA:* Dr James O Blackwood. Executive staff 1, Serving missionaries 9. ***CC*** No.281583. Began 1980; interdenominational. Magazine: *Global Times* (10,000 every two months). Turnover £4,336 to year end Aug 98.
Email: davecgom@aol.com
☎ 01392 259 673 🖷 01392 491 176

For further information see Lists on Pages 328–350

o To The Nations Ministry, 2 Southern Road, Sale M33 6HQ
European Coordinator: Mr Cesar Pereira. Executive staff 2, Other staff 1, Currently no serving UK missionaries. ***CC*** No.1062124. Began 1993; interdenominational. Magazine: *What's Going On?* (1,000 quarterly). Turnover £40,000 to year end Dec 98. Bringing Brazilian missionaries to live and work in partnership with local churches throughout Europe.
Web: www.gonations.org
Email: info@gonations.org
☎ 0161 962 0770 🖷 0161 962 0770

Gorakhpur Nurseries Fellowship, 37 Thetford Road, New Malden KT3 3AP
Hon Secretary: Mrs Joy Devis. *Leader, India:* Dr Rosemary Page. Serving missionaries 4. Began 1908; interdenominational. Magazine: *Newsletter* (1,000 every four months). Turnover £1,200 to year end Apr 94. Children's home.
☎ 020 8942 0270

Gospel Mission of South America, Woodlands, 43 Beach Road, Fleetwood FY7 8PS
General Secretary: Ms Pauline English. *International Director USA:* Rev Terry Thompson. Executive staff 1, Serving missionaries 6. ***CC*** No.260812. Began n/a; interdenominational. Magazine: *Southern Sentinel* (700 quarterly). Turnover £26,000 to year end Dec 96.
☎ 01253 874 349 🖷 01253 874 349

Grace and Compassion Benedictines, St Benedict's, 1 Manor Road, Kemp Town, Brighton BN2 5EA
Prioress General: Mother Mary Garson. Currently no UK missionaries. ***CC*** No.1056064. Began 1954; Roman Catholic. Magazine: *Our Lady's Newsletter* (6,000 quarterly). Turnover n/a. Caring for the frail, elderly in England and the sick, all ages, in Third World.
Web: max.roehampton.ac.uk/link/aandb.gcb.htm
Email: generalate@graceandcompassion.co.uk
☎ 01273 680 720 🖷 01273 680 527

Grace Baptist Mission, 12 Abbey Close, Abingdon OX14 3JD
General Secretary: Mr J Chris Richards. *Church Relations Secretary:* Mr D Higham. *Financial Secretary:* Mr A Sadler. Executive staff 2, Serving missionaries 50, Other staff 4. ***CC*** No.263133. Began 1861; Grace Baptist. Magazine: *The Herald* (6,500 quarterly). Turnover £551,000 to year end June 98.
Email: 101715.43@compuserve.com
☎ 01235 520 147 🖷 01235 559 796

HCJB-UK, 131 Grattan Road, Bradford BD1 2HS
Executive Director, UK: Ray Thurgood. *President, Ecuador:* Rev Ronald A Cline. Executive staff 4, Serving missionaries 22, Other staff 3. ***CC*** No.263449. Began 1931; interdenominational. Magazine: *Wave-length* (3,000 every four months), *Prayer Guide Lines* (Circulation n/a monthly). Turnover £280,113 to year end Aug 97. Radio, medical and training ministries.
Web: www.hcjb.org
Email: airwave@uk.hcjb.org
☎ 01274 721 810 🖷 01274 741 302

Helpers of the Holy Souls, 60 St Mary's Road, Liverpool L36 5ST
Provincial Superior: Sister Maryrose Fitzsimmons. Serving missionaries 1. ***CC*** No.240876. Began 1873; Roman Catholic. No magazine. Turnover n/a.
☎ 0151 489 0220 🖷 0151 481 0072

Holy Ghost Fathers, 26 Eastbury Avenue, Northwood HA6 3LN
Provincial Superior: Rev Peter Ward. Serving missionaries 13, Home staff 40. ***CC*** No.227350. Began 1703; Roman Catholic. Magazine: *Missionwide* (10,500 quarterly). Turnover n/a.
Email: cssp@mdx.ac.uk
☎ 01923 829 655 🖷 01923 836 975

Hospitaller Order of St John of God, Monksgarth, Scorton, Richmond DL10 6EB
Provincial Superior: Brother Robert Moore. Currently no UK serving missionaries. ***CC*** Began 1572; Roman Catholic. No magazine. Turnover £7,000,000 to year end Mar 98.
☎ 01748 811 535 🖷 01748 818 194

Institute of Charity (Rosminian Fathers & Brothers), 383 Fosse Way, Ratcliffe on the Wreake, Leicester LE7 4SJ
Provincial Superior: Rev Anthony Meredith. Serving missionaries 4. ***CC*** Began 1828; Roman Catholic. No magazine. Turnover n/a. Formation, mission station orphanage and leprosy colony work.
Email: anthony.ic@btinternet.com
☎ 01509 817 048 🖷 01509 817 048

Institute of Our Lady of Mercy, Convent of Mercy, Cemetry Road, Yeadon, Leeds LS19 7UR
Superior General: Sister Noreen Cullen. Serving missionaries 14. ***CC*** Began 1839; Roman Catholic. No magazine. Turnover n/a.
Email: ilom@zetnet.co.uk
☎ 0113 250 0253 🖷 0113 250 0241

Institute of the Blessed Virgin Mary, 23 Blossom Street, York YO2 2AQ
Provincial Superior: Sister Cecila Goodman. Serving missionaries 2. ***CC*** Began 1609; Roman Catholic. No magazine. Turnover n/a.
☎ 01904 622 902 🖷 01904 622 926

Intercontinental Church Society, 1 Athena Drive, Tachbrook Park, Warwick CV34 6NL
International Director: Rev Canon John Moore. *Communications Manager:* Mr David Healey. Executive staff 8, Serving missionaries 71, Other staff 16. ***CC*** No.1072584. Began 1823; Anglican. Magazine: *Going Places* (3,000 quarterly), *English Speaking Churches Abroad* (2,000 half-yearly). Turnover £538,000 to year end Dec 98. Also sending clergy on short term assignments within Europe and Mediterranean and chaplaincies.
☎ 01926 430 347 🖷 01926 330 238

***International Fellowship of Evangelical Students (IFES Trust International Office)**, 55 Palmerston Road, Wealdstone, Harrow HA3 7RR
General Secretary: Mr Lindsay Brown. Executive staff 11, other staff 48. ***CC*** No.247919. Began 1947; interdenominational. IFES Europe and CIS. Magazine: *Special Reports* (15,000 every four months), *Praise & Prayer* (9,000 ten times a year). Turnover £2,400,000 to year end Dec 98. Partnering student witness in over 140 countries involving more than 300,000 students world-wide.
Web: www.ifesworld.org
Email: ifes@xc.org
☎ 020 8863 8688 🖷 020 8863 8229
European & CIS Office: Kennett House, 108 London Road, Headington, Oxford OX3 9AW
Regional Secretary: Mr Jonathan Lamb. *Associate Regional Secretary for CIS:* Mr Barrett Horne, *Coordinator for SE Europe:* Rev Dan Denk, IFES Europe.
Executive staff 10, Other Staff 4, Serving missionaries 173. Turnover £2,600,000 to year end Dec 98.
Email: ifeseurope@ibm.net
☎ 01865 308 801 🖷 01865 308 802

For further information see Lists on Pages 328–350

***International Nepal Fellowship**, 69 Wentworth Road, Harborne, Birmingham B17 9SS
UK Director: John Reynolds. *International Director, Nepal:* Asbjorn Voreland. *Chairman:* John Bradley. Executive staff 1, Serving missionaries 48, Other staff 4. ***CC*** No.1047178. Began 1940; interdenominational. Magazine: *Today in Nepal* (1,800 quarterly). Turnover £781,727 to year end July 98.
Web: www.inf.org.uk
Email: ukoffice@inf.org.uk
☎ 0121 427 8833 🖷 0121 428 3110

***International Teams UK**, PO Box 11, Brecon LD3 9WJ
Director: Mr Chris Jones. Other staff 5, Serving missionaries 20. ***CC*** No.1047932. Began 1960; interdenominational. Turnover £134,000 to year end Dec 98. Magazine: Title n/a (Circulation n/a quarterly).
Web: www.iteams.org
Email: 100623.1241@ compuserve.com
☎ 01874 611 995 🖷 01874 611 799

***INTERSERVE**, 325 Kennington Road, London SE11 4QH
National Director: Mr Richard Clark. *International Director, Cyprus:* Mr James A Tebbe. *Personnel Director:* Miss Ruth Millson. Executive staff 5, Serving missionaries 138, Other staff 17. ***CC*** No.1020758. Began 1852; interdenominational. Magazine: *GO* (11,000 quarterly). Turnover £1,886,000 to year end Dec 97.
Web: www.interserve.org
Email: isewi@isewi.globalnet.co.uk
☎ 020 7735 8227 🖷 020 7587 5362
Ireland, 14 Glencregagh Court, Belfast BT6 0PA
National Director: Mr Tony McGall. *Chairman of Council:* Rev A Dunlop. Executive staff 1, Serving missionaries 12, Other staff 2. ***CC*** No.16632. Began 1852; interdenominational. Magazine: *Irish Info* (900 quarterly), *GO* (900 quarterly). Turnover n/a.
Web: www.interserve.org
Email: 100517.3155@compuserve.com
☎ 028 9040 2211 🖷 028 9040 1298
Scotland, 12 Elm Avenue, Lenzie, Glasgow G66 4HJ
National Director: Mr John Jackson. Executive staff 2, Serving missionaries 30, Other staff 3. ***CC*** No.SCO 05316. Began 1852; interdenominational. Magazine: *INTERVIEW* (2,500 quarterly). Turnover £250,000 to year end Dec 98.
Web: www.interserve.org
Email: info@isscot.prestel.co.uk
☎ 0141 578 0207 🖷 0141 578 0207

***Japan Christian Link**, 275 London Road, North End, Portsmouth PO2 9HE
Director: Mr J N Cloake. Executive staff 2, Serving missionaries 8, Other staff 2. ***CC*** No.213834. Began 1903; interdenominational. (Previously Japan Evangelistic Band). Magazine: *Japan News* (1,600 quarterly). Turnover £80,990 to year end Dec 98.
Email: jcl@jebuk.globalnet.co.uk
☎ 023 9266 6151 🖷 023 9266 6151

Japan Good News Ministries, 36 Suffolk Road, North Harrow, Harrow HA2 7QQ
Treasurer (UK): Mr George Smith. *President, Japan:* Rev Lionel H Thomson. Executive staff 1, Serving missionaries 3, Other staff 1. Began 1970; Full Gospel. Magazine: *Hour of Evangelism* (Circulation n/a quarterly). Turnover £7,680 to year end Dec 98.
Email: pacifics@sainet.or.jp
☎ 020 8427 0131 🖷 020 8861 3137

Japan Mission, 7 Westbourne House, Farcroft Avenu Handsworth, Birmingham B21 8AE
Secretary: Miss Mabel Maddock. *Co-founder (with his wife Japan:* Mr N Verwey. Serving missionaries 2, Other staff 1. ***C*** No.252768. Began 1957; interdenominational. Magazin *Prayer Letter* (1,320 every two months). Turnover £30,379 t year end Mar 98.
☎ 0121 523 7897

***Language Recordings UK**, PO Box 197, High Wycomb HP14 3YY
Director: Mr Jim McKechnie. Executive staff 2, Serving Mi sionaries 8. ***CC*** No.266476. Began 1955; interdenomina tional. Magazine: *The Messenger* (1,200 every two months Turnover £64,178 to year end June 97. Producing culturall relevant gospel messages on cassette in story-telling form in th mother tongue.
Web: www.gospelrecordings.com
Email: lr_uk@compuserve.com
☎ 01494 485 414 🖷 01494 485 414

***Latin Link UK**, 175 Tower Bridge Road, London SE1 2AB
International Director: Mr John Chapman. *UK Team Leader* Mr Alan Tower. Executive staff 4, Serving missionaries 107 Other staff 18. ***CC*** No.1020826. Began 1908; interdenom inational. Magazine: *Newsfile* (7,500 quarterly). Turnove £1,600,000 to year end Mar 98.
Email: ukoffice@latinlink.org
☎ 020 7939 9000 🖷 020 7939 9015

***The Leprosy Mission**, England and Wales Office, Goldhay Way Orton Goldhay, Peterborough PE2 5GZ
Executive Director: Rev Dr Tony Lloyd. *Director of Financ and Information:* Mr Keith Nicholson. *Director of Fundraising and Publicity:* Mr Nigel Slater. Executive staff 3, Serving missionaries 20, Other staff 30. ***CC*** No.1050327. Began 1874 interdenominational. Magazine: *New Day* (165,000 half yearly). Turnover £3,921,805 to year end Dec 97.
Web: www.leprosymission.org/
Email: post@tlmew.org.uk
☎ 01733 370 505 🖷 01733 370 960
International Office, 80 Windmill Road, Brentford TW8 0QH
General Director: Mr Trevor Durston. *International Chairman* Mr Stewart Smith. *Honorary Treasurer:* Miss Christine Osman Executive staff 4, Other staff 17. CC No.211432. Began 1874 interdenominational. Turnover n/a. Working in over 3(counties.
Web: www.leprosymission.org
Email: friends@tlmint.org
☎ 020 8569 7292 🖷 020 8569 7808
Northern Ireland, Leprosy House, 44 Ulsterville Avenue, Belfast BT9 7AQ
Director: Mr Colin Ferguson. *Finance/Promotion Officer:* Rev Tom Robinson. Executive staff 2. ***CC*** No.XR 11501. Began n/a; interdenominational. Magazine: *New Day* (6,500 half-yearly). Turnover £480,000 to year end Dec 97.
Email: 106125.167compuserve.com
☎ 028 9038 1937 🖷 028 9038 1842
Scotland, 89 Barnton Street, Stirling FK8 1HJ
Executive Director: Mr Anthony R N Black. Executive staff 5, Serving missionaries 1, Other staff 3. Began n/a; interdenominational. Magazine: *New Day* (19,000 half-yearly). Turnover £444,083 to year end Dec 94.
☎ 01786 449 266

Marist Brothers, Kinharvie House, New Abbey, Dumfries DG2 8DZ
Provincial: Rev Brother Ronald McEwan. Serving missionaries 2. ***CC*** No.SCO 18168. Began 1852; Roman Catholic. No magazine. Turnover n/a.
Email: armce@msn.com
☎ 01387 850 433 🖷 01387 850 414

For further information see Lists on Pages 328–350

Medical Mission Sisters (Society of Catholic Medical Missionaries), 36 Valmer Road, Ealing, London SE5 9NG
District Co-ordinator: Sister Barbara Terlau. Serving missionaries 3, Home staff 11. *CC* No.232742. Began 1925; Roman Catholic. Magazine: *Medical Missionary News* (1,000 every four months). Turnover £118,574 to year end Jan 92.
Email: medmisister@qn.apc.org
☎ 020 7738 4754

Medical Missionaries of Mary, 66 Newland Street, Silvertown, London E16 2HN
Regional Representative: Sister Mary Canty. Serving missionaries 15, Home staff 16. *CC* No.293494. Began n/a; Roman Catholic. No magazine. Turnover n/a. Offering a healing service to people on the margins of life, especially mother and child.
☎ 020 7366 1462

Melanesian Mission, The Rectory, 2 Harpsden Way, Henley-on-Thames RG9 1NL
General Secretary: Rev Peter Fox. Executive staff 1, Serving missionaries 2. *CC* No.205800. Began 1848; Anglican. Magazine: *Melanesian News* (1,200 every four months). Turnover £77,000 to year end Mar 98. Liaison with church of Melanesia, care of visiting Melanesians, encouraging links financially, prayerfully and administratively.
Email: cmelanesuk@aol.com
☎ 01491 573 401 Fax 01491 579 871

***Mennonite Board of Missions**, London Mennonite Centre, 14 Shepherds Hill, Highgate, London N6 5AQ
Contact: Mark Nation. Executive staff 5. Currently no UK missionaries serving overseas. Began n/a; Mennonite. No magazine. Turnover n/a.
Email: 100127.1371@ compuserve.com
☎ 020 8340 8775 Fax 020 8341 6807

Mercy Sisters of the Union of Great Britain, Mercy Union Generalate, St Edwards Convent, 11 Harewood Avenue, London NW1 6LD
Superior General: Sister Mary Dominic Timmins. Serving missionaries 4. *CC* No.288158. Began 1846; Roman Catholic. No magazine. Turnover n/a.
Email: rsmgeneral@aol.com
☎ 020 7402 7785 Fax 020 7224 8551

***The Messianic Testimony**, 93 Axe Street, Barking IG11 7LZ
Director: Mr Anthony M Pearce. *Chairman of Council:* Mr H G Gamston. Executive staff 2, Serving missionaries 19, Other staff 2. *CC* No.274750. Began 1973; interdenominational. Merger of The Mildmay Mission to the Jews and The Hebrew Testimony to Israel. Magazine: *The Messianic Testimony* (7,000 quarterly). Turnover £425,894 to year end Dec 98. Sharing the gospel with Jewish people, teaching God's purposes for Israel to the church.
Web: www.charitynet.org/~messianic
Email: tmt@mcmail.com
☎ 020 8594 3072 Fax 020 8220 0150

Methodist Church World Church Office, 25 Marylebone Road, London NW1 5JR
Team Leader: Rev Winston Graham. Executive staff 10, Serving mission partners 85, Office staff 8. *CC* Began 1786; Methodist. (Previously Methodist Church Overseas Division). Magazine: *Facets* (35,000 quarterly). Turnover £4,536,094 to year end Aug 99.
☎ 020 7486 5502 Fax 020 7935 1507

***Mid-Africa Ministry (CMS)**, 157 Waterloo Road, London SE1 8UU
General Secretary: Rev Robert de Berry. *Personnel Secretary:* Mr Chris Hindley. Executive staff 4, Serving missionaries 36, Other staff 9. *CC* No.220297. Began 1921; Anglican. Magazine: *MAM News* (7,000 every two months). Turnover £800,000 to year end Jan 99. Serving Jesus in partnership with African churches through medical, theological and educational needs and sponsorship.
Email: mid_africa_ministry@compuserve.com
☎ 020 7261 1370 Fax 020 7401 2910
Also at: 44 Ulsterville Avenue, Belfast BT9 7AQ
Email: mam.ireland'dnet.co.uk
☎ 028 9068 3238 Fax 028 9066 8636

***Middle East Christian Outreach**, 22 Culverden Park Road, Tunbridge Wells TN4 9RA
UK Director: Rev John Carrick. *International Director, Cyprus:* Mr David Judson. Executive staff 1, Serving missionaries 25, Other staff 3. *CC* No.272327. Began 1976; interdenominational. Magazine: *Crossroads* (5,500 quarterly). Turnover £340,076 to year end Mar 98.
Web: www.gospelcom.net/meco
Email: 100704.3646@compuserve.com
☎ 01892 521 541 Fax 01892 549 745

***Middle East Media**, PO Box 118, London SE9 2UB
UK Director: Mr Michael Thomas. *International Director, Cyprus:* Mr Mark Marlowe. Executive staff 1, Serving missionaries 7. *CC* No.271373. Began 1975; interdenominational. Magazine: *Memo* (3,000 every two months). Turnover £314,353 to year end Dec 96.
Email: mem@memuk.freeserve.co.uk
☎ 020 8859 4035 Fax 020 8859 4035

For further information see Lists on Pages 328–350

Mill Hill Missionaries, St Michael's, 40 George Leigh Street, Ancoats, Manchester M4 5DG
Superior: Rev Liam Armour MHM. *Regional Superior, Dublin:* Very Rev Jim O'Connell. Staff n/a. ***CC*** No.220690. Began n/a; Roman Catholic. Turnover n/a.
Web: www.millhillmissionaries.org
☎ 0161 950 8697 🖷 0161 950 8697

***Mission Aviation Fellowship**, Castle Hill Avenue, Folkestone CT20 2TN
Chief Executive, MAF UK: Mr Keith Jones. *Chief Executive, MAF Europe:* Mr Bill Harding. *Deputy Chief Executive MAF UK:* Mr David Marfleet. Executive staff 20, Serving missionaries 80, Other staff 38. ***CC*** No.1064598. Began 1945; interdenominational. Magazine: *MAF News* (47,000 quarterly). Turnover £7,100,035 to year end Sep 97.
Web: www.maf-uk.org
Email: maf-uk-hq@maf.org
☎ 01303 850 950 🖷 01303 852 800

Mission to Military Garrisons (Inc), Challenge House, 29 Canal Street, Glasgow G4 0AD
Secretary & Treasurer: Mr Ian Yule. Executive staff 1, Serving missionaries 20, Other staff 1. ***CC*** No.SCO 05038. Began 1883; interdenominational. Magazine: *MMG News* (1,500 quarterly). Turnover £500,000 to year end Jan 99.
Email: mmg@hqglasgow.freeserve.co.uk
☎ 0141 333 0703 🖷 0141 331 0563

Missionaries of Africa (White Fathers), 42 Stormont Road, London N6 4NP
Provincial Superior: Rev John Gould. *Superior General, Italy:* Rev Francois Richard. Serving missionaries 32, Home staff 49. ***CC*** No.233302. Began 1868; Roman Catholic. Magazine: *White Fathers/ White Sisters* (37,500 every two months). Turnover n/a. Liberation and emancipation of African peoples wherever they are.
Web: www.users.skynet.be/lavigerie
Email: missionaries@africamail.com
☎ 020 8348 7799/8340 5036 🖷 020 8347 8147

Missionaries of Charity, 177 Bravington Road, London W9 3AR
Provincial Superior: Sister Tanya. Serving missionaries 2, Home staff 10. ***CC*** No.262578. Began n/a; Roman Catholic. No magazine. Turnover n/a.
☎ 020 8960 2644

Missionary Sisters of Our Lady of Africa (White Sisters), 25 Waldemar Avenue, West Ealing, London W13 9PZ
Provincial Superior: Sister Marion Carabott. *Superior General, Italy:* Sister Marie Macdonald. Serving missionaries 1, Other staff 26. ***CC*** No.228983. Began 1869; Roman Catholic. Magazine: *White Fathers/White Sisters* (37,500 every two months). Turnover £254,000 to year end Dec 92.
☎ 020 8567 6980 🖷 020 8579 7822

Missionary Sisters of Our Lady of Apostles, 10 Vincent Road, London N15 3QH
Provincial Superior: To be appointed. Serving missionaries 1, Home staff 4. Began n/a; Roman Catholic. No magazine. Turnover n/a.
☎ 020 8888 9036

Missionary Sisters of St Columban, 53 Thornhill Road, Birmingham B21 9BT
Regional Superior: Sister Mary Nolan. Serving missionaries 6, Home staff 3. Began n/a; Roman Catholic. No magazine. Turnover n/a.
☎ 0121 515 2043 🖷 0121 551 2896

Missionary Sisters Servants of the Holy Spirit, Convent of th Holy Spirit, The Pitchens, Wroughton, Swindon SN4 0RU
Provincial Superior: Sister Carmen Lee. *Superior General, Ital* Sister Agada Brand. Home staff 6. Currently no UK missiona ies serving overseas. ***CC*** Began 1889; Roman Catholic. Maga zine: *Newsletter* (400 regularly). Turnover n/a.
☎ 01793 812 211 🖷 01793 845 531

Missionary Society of St Columban, Widney Manor Road Knowle, Solihull B93 9AB
Regional Director: Rev Bernard McDermott. *Superior Genera Republic of Ireland:* Rev Nicholas Murray. Serving missionar ies 6, Home staff 6. ***CC*** No.221594. Began 1935; Roman Cath olic. Magazine: *The Far East* (69,000 nine times a year) Turnover n/a. Working worldwide in pastoral, education and health projects.
Email: colsol@btinternet.com
☎ 01564 772 096 🖷 01564 770 500

The Missions to Seamen, St Michael Paternoster Royal, College Hill, London EC4R 2RL
Secretary General: Rev Canon Glyn Jones. *Ministry Secretary:* Rev Canon Bill Christianson. *Justice & Welfare Secretary:* Rev Canon Ken Peters. Executive staff 7, Serving missionaries 40, Other staff 32. ***CC*** No.212432. Began 1856; Anglican. Magazine: *Flying Angel News* (16,000 quarterly), *The Sea* (21,000 every two months). Turnover £3,133,000 to year end Dec 97. Locally based missions in many countries.
Web: www.missionstoseamen.org
Email: general@missionstoseamen.org
☎ 020 7248 5202 🖷 020 7248 4761

Montfort Fathers, 28 Burbo Bank Road, Blundellsands, Liverpool L23 TH
Provincial Superior: Rev Robert Douglas. Serving missionaries 5. ***CC*** No.241963. Began 1712; Roman Catholic. No magazine. Turnover n/a.
Email: smml@nildram.co.uk
☎ 0151 287 6862 🖷 0151 287 0410

Montfort Sisters, La Sagesse (Daughters of Wisdom), 10 The Abbey, Romsey SO51 8EL
Provincial Superior: Sister Maureen Seddon. Serving missionaries 5. ***CC*** No.234184. Began 1891; Roman Catholic. No magazine. Turnover n/a.
☎ 01794 516 129 🖷 01794 518 702

***The Navigators**, Adyar House, 32 Carlton Crescent, Southampton SO15 2EW
National Director: Mr Martin Cooper. *National Administrator:* Mr Simon Wroe. *General Director, USA:* Dr Jerry White. Executive staff 3, Serving missionaries 91, Other staff 8. ***CC*** No.215277. Began 1955; interdenominational. Magazine: *Harvest* (3,000 monthly). Turnover £1,124,258 to year end Aug 98.
Web: www.navigators.co.uk
Email: info@navigators.co.uk
☎ 023 8022 3743 🖷 023 8023 7548

New Testament Missionary Union, 32 Downham Road North, Heswall, Wirral CH61 6UN
Secretary & Treasurer: Mr Albert S Robinson. Serving missionaries 2, Other staff 2. ***CC*** No.282565. Began 1902; interdenominational. Magazine: *Pressing On* (1,000 quarterly). Turnover £51,000 to year end Dec 97. Missionaries concentrate on evangelism and church planting to follow the New Testament pattern.
☎ 0151 342 4237

For further information see Lists on Pages 328–350

New Tribes Mission, North Cotes, Grimsby DN36 5XU
UK Co-ordinator: Edward Hinds. *Missionary Training & Candidate Co-ordinator:* Joseph Bailie. *Short Term Missions Co-ordinator:* Geoff McGrath. Other staff n/a, Serving missionaries 126. ***CC*** No.278627. Began 1979; non-denominational. Magazine: *Brown Gold (International)* (3,000 in UK, monthly), *News & Views (within Europe)* (Circulation n/a quarterly). Turnover £1,600,000 to year end Dec 98. Evangelism, Bible translation and church planting amongst unreached ethnic groups.
Web: www.ntm.org.uk
Email: ntm@ntm.org.uk
☎ 01472 389 379 🖷 01472 389 099

North West Frontier Fellowship, 26 Wigmore Avenue, Swindon SN3 1ET
Chairman, Executive Council: Dr Steven Ringer. Serving missionaries 2. ***CC*** Began 1944; interdenominational. Magazine: *NWFF Prayer Bulletin* (1,200 quarterly). Turnover £60,000 to year end Aug 96.
☎ 01793 487 676 🖷 01793 487 676

Oblates of Mary Immaculate, St Teresa's Presbytery, Sedgemoor Road, Norris Green, Liverpool L11 3BW
Provincial: Very Rev Michael Ryan. Serving missionaries 2. Began 1816; Roman Catholic. No magazine. Turnover n/a.
☎ 0151 226 1354

OMF International (UK), Station Approach, Borough Green, Sevenoaks TN15 8BG
National Director: Mr Chris Wigram. *General Director, Singapore:* Mr David Pickard. *Director of Public Ministries:* Mr Guido Brashi. Executive staff 12, Serving missionaries 266, Other staff 28. ***CC*** No.226168. Began 1865; interdenominational. Magazine: *East Asia's Millions* (13,500 quarterly). Turnover £4,567,000 to year end Dec 98.
Web: www.omf.org.uk
Email: omf@omf.org.uk
☎ 01732 887 299 🖷 01732 887 224
East/South East England Regional Office: *Regional Director:* Ray Porter, Danehurst, The Avenue, Bushey, Watford WD2 2LL
Email: erd@omf.org.uk
☎ 01923 247 382 🖷 01923 247 382
West England & South Wales Office: *Regional Director:* John Aitken, 174 Redland Road, Bristol BS6 6YG
Email: wrd@omf.org.uk
☎ 0117 973 7490 🖷 0117 973 7490
North England & North Wales Office: *Regional Director:* Keith Wood, 440 Parrs Wood Road, Didsbury, Manchester M20 5GP
Email: nrd@omf.org.uk
☎ 0161 434 3883 🖷 0161 434 3883
Ireland Regional Office: *Regional Director:* Hugh Meekin, 53 Wellington Park, Belfast BT9 6DP
Email: ird@omf.org.uk
☎ 028 9038 1995 🖷 028 9068 3472
Scotland Regional Office: *Regional Director:* John Rushton, Lechler House, 25 Abbey Drive, Jordanhill, Glasgow G14 9JP
Email: srd@omf.org.uk
☎ 0141 959 4180 🖷 0141 959 4180

***OMS International**, 1 Sandileigh Avenue, Didsbury, Manchester M20 3LN
Executive Director: Mr Bill Burnett. *International President, USA:* Dr J B Crouse, Jnr. Executive staff 2, Serving missionaries 23, Other staff 10. ***CC*** No.245145. Began 1901; interdenominational. Magazine: *OMS Outreach* (2,500 quarterly). Turnover £464,000 to year end Sept 98.
Web: www.omsinternational.org
Email: omsuk@compuserve.com
☎ 0161 283 7992 🖷 0161 283 8981

***Operation Mobilisation**, The Quinta, Weston Rhyn, Oswestry SY10 7LT
UK Director: Mr Peter Nicoll. *Associate UK Director:* Mr Gary Sloan. *UK Head of Financial Services:* Dr Mike Clark. Executive staff 12, Serving missionaries 366, Other staff 28. ***CC*** No.1008196. Began 1962; interdenominational. Magazine: *International Monthly* (26,000 monthly). Turnover £6,000,000 to year end Dec 98.
Web: www.uk.om.org
Email: info@uk.om.org
☎ 01691 773 388 🖷 01691 778 378
Also at: International Office, PO Box 27, Carlisle CA1 2HG
☎ 01228 615 100

Order of Friars Minor, 56 St Antony's Road, Forest Gate, London E7 9QB
Minister Provincial: Rev Austin McCormack. Serving missionaries 24. ***CC*** No.232177. Began 1224; Roman Catholic. Magazine: *Troubador* (Circulation n/a quarterly). Turnover n/a.
Email: friarsminor@btinternet.com
☎ 020 8472 6012 🖷 020 8503 5797

Our Lady of Charity of the Good Shepherd, Good Shepherd Provincialate, 61 East End Road, London N2 0SF
Provincial Superior: Sister Lucina Wogan. *Superior General, Italy:* Sister M G Cadena. Serving members 3. ***CC*** No.234880. Began 1835; Roman Catholic. No magazine. Turnover n/a.
Email: rgslondon@aol.com
☎ 020 8346 8100 🖷 020 8343 0970

For further information see Lists on Pages 328–350

Oxford Mission, PO Box 86, Romsey SO51 8YD
General Secretary: Mrs Mary K Marsh. Executive staff 1, Serving missionaries 2, Other staff 1. *CC* No.211618. Began 1880; Anglican. Magazine: *Oxford Mission News* (2,000 half-yearly). Turnover £230,122 to year end Dec 97.
☎ 01794 515 004 🖷 01794 515 004

†**Pallottine Fathers**, 358 Greenford Road, Greenford UB6 9AN
Provincial Superior: Rev George Ranahan. Currently no UK missionaries serving overseas. Began n/a; Roman Catholic. No magazine. Turnover n/a.
☎ 020 8578 1363 🖷 020 8813 2238

Pallottine Missionary Sisters, 52 Park Mount Drive, Macclesfield SK11 8NT
Provincial Superior: Sister Marie Keegan. Serving missionaries 5. *CC* No.234185. Began 1909; Roman Catholic. No magazine. Turnover n/a.
☎ 01625 616 459 🖷 01625 869 080

Papua New Guinea Church Partnership, Partnership House, 157 Waterloo Road, London SE1 8XA
General Secretary: Mrs Chris Luxton. *Chairman:* Dr James Harper. Executive staff 1, Serving missionaries 13, Other staff 1. *CC* No.249446. Began 1901; Anglican. Magazine: *PNGCP Newsletter* (600 occasionary), *Family Magazine* (200 every four months). Turnover £102,000 to year end Dec 97. Supporting the Anglican church of Papua New Guinea.
Email: pngcp@uspg.org.uk
☎ 020 7928 8681 🖷 020 7928 2371

Passionists, 143 Granby Street, Liverpool L8 2UR
Provincial Superior: Rev Nicholas Postlethwaite. Serving missionaries 1. *CC* Began 1720; Roman Catholic. No magazine. Turnover n/a.
☎ 0151 727 2024 🖷 0151 726 9459

***People International**, PO Box 310, Tunbridge Wells TN4 8ZJ
UK Director: Mr Philip Grubb. *International Director, UK:* Mr Clive Pritchard. Executive staff 1, Serving missionaries 30, Other staff 4. *CC* No.280036. Began 1979; interdenominational. Magazine: *SCAN* (6,500 half-yearly), *People International News* (4,000 every two months). Turnover £203,154 to year end Dec 98.
Web: members.aol.com/peopleintl
Email: peopleuk@aol.com
☎ 01892 545 509 Mobile: 07775 855 343
🖷 01892 545 520

***Presbyterian Church in Ireland Overseas Board**, Church House, Fisherwick Place, Belfast BT1 6DW
Executive Officer & Secretary of Overseas Board: Rev R J T McMullan. *Associate Secretary:* Miss Elizabeth Brian. *Education for Mission Secretary:* Mr Nigel Eves. Executive staff 3, Serving missionaries 88, Other staff 3. *CC* No.XN 45376. Began 1840; Presbyterian. Magazine: *Wider World* (28,000 quarterly). Turnover £1,117,000 to year end Dec 97.
Web: www.presbyterianireland.org
Email: overseas@presbyterianireland.org
☎ 028 9032 2284 🖷 028 9023 6605

Presbyterian Church of Wales Mission Board, 53 Richmond Road, Cardiff CF2 3UP
Mission Secretary: Rev D A Jones. Executive staff 1, Serving missionaries 2, Other staff 1. *CC* Began 1840; Presbyterian. Magazine: *Treasury* (1,200 monthly), *Y Goleuad* (1,800 weekly). Turnover £300,000 to year end Dec 92.
☎ 029 2049 4913 Mobile: 07711 490 310

***Qua Iboe Fellowship**, 14 Glencregagh Court, Belfast BT6 0PA
General Secretary: Rev John P Cardoo. Executive staff 3, Serving missionaries 20, Other staff 11. *CC* No.XN 45493. Began 1887; interdenominational. Magazine: *Dispatch* (3,700 every four months). Turnover £240,000 to year end Dec 98.
Web: web.ukonline.co.uk/qua.iboe
Email: jcardoo.qif@ukonline.co.uk
☎ 028 9040 2850 🖷 028 9079 9190
Also at: 44 Quarry Drive, Kilmacolm PA13 4OA
☎ 01505 873 731

***Red Sea Mission Team**, PO Box 19929, London N3 1WW
UK Home Director: Rev Neil Pheasant. *International Team Leader, UK:* Rev Dr Robert Smith. Executive staff 1, Serving missionaries 21, Other staff 2. *CC* No.232703. Began 195[illegible] interdenominational. Magazine: *Islam Shall Hear* (1,300 n/a). Turnover £143,000 to year end Mar 98.
Web: www.rsmt.u-net.com
Email: postbox@rsmt.u-net.com
☎ 020 8346 1222 🖷 020 8346 9782

Redemptorists, St Mary's Church, Clapham, London SW4 7AP
Provincial Superior: Rev John Trenchard. *Superior General, Italy:* Rev Juan M Lasso de la Vega. Serving missionaries 1[illegible] *CC* No.1062084. Began 1732; Roman Catholic. No magazine. Turnover n/a.
☎ 020 7622 2793 🖷 020 7627 3153

Religious of Jesus and Mary, 58 Wrentham Avenue, London NW10 3HG
Provincial Superior: Sister Genevieve Devereux. Serving missionaries 4. Began n/a; Roman Catholic. No magazine. Turnover n/a.
☎ 020 8960 7128 🖷 020 8964 8377

Religious of the Assumption, 23 Kensington Square, London W8 5HN
Provincial Superior: Sister Jessica Gatty. *Superior General, France:* Sister Cristina, Gonzalez. Serving missionaries 1. *CC* Began 1839; Roman Catholic. No magazine. Turnover n/a.
☎ 020 7937 6112 🖷 020 7938 1621

Right Hand Trust, Gelligason, Llanfair Caereinion, Welshpool SY21 9HE
Director: Mr Mark Wright. Executive staff 1, Admin staff 4, Serving missionaries 44. *CC* No.1014934. Began 1991; Anglican. Magazine: *Bush Telegraph* (1,000 every two months). Turnover £115,327 to year end Jun 98. Sending young people to live as guests of the church in remote rural African communities.
Web: www.ourworld.compuserve.com/homepages/righthandtrust
Email: righthandtrust@compuserve.com
☎ 01938 810 215 🖷 01938 810 215

†**Sacred Heart Fathers (Betharram)**, St Joseph's, Mather Lane, Leigh WN7 2PR
Provincial Superior: Rev Austin Hughes. Currently no UK missionaries serving overseas. Began n/a; Roman Catholic. No magazine. Turnover n/a.
☎ 01942 677 718 🖷 01942 269 094

Sacred Heart Fathers (Dehonians), St Joseph's, Malpas SY14 7DD
Provincial Superior: Rev Hugh Hanley. *General Superior, Italy:* Rev Antonio Panteghini. Serving missionaries 1. *CC* Began 1936; Roman Catholic. Magazine: *Contact* (5,000 every four months). Turnover n/a.
☎ 01948 860 416 🖷 01948 860 619

For further information see Lists on Pages 328–350

Sacred Hearts Community, 372 Uxbridge Road, Ealing, London W5 3LH
Provincial: Very Rev Patrick Lynch. Currently no UK missionaries serving overseas. *CC* Began 1954; Roman Catholic. No magazine. Turnover n/a.
☎ 020 8992 5941

Sahara Desert Mission, 36 Chestnut Way, Godalming GU7 1TS
Hon Secretary: Mr R W Ellement. *Superintendent, Niger:* Rev F Baggott. Serving missionaries 5, Other staff 2. Began 1953; interdenominational. Magazine: *Streams in The Desert* (1,000 every four months). Turnover £50,000 to year end Feb 98.
☎ 01483 416 501

St Joseph's Hospice Association (Jospice International), St Joseph's Hospice, Ince Road, Liverpool L23 4UE
Director: Rev Father Francis O'Leary. Serving missionaries 5. *CC* No.250778. Began 1966; Roman Catholic. Magazine: *Newsletter* (8,000 quarterly). Turnover n/a. Caring for terminal and chronic sick without charge.
Web: www.garrick.co.uk/stjoseph.html
☎ 0151 924 3812/7871 🖷 0151 931 5757

St Joseph's Missionary Society, Mill Hill, St Joseph's College, Lawrence Street, Mill Hill, London NW7 4JX
Superior General: Rev Maurice McGill. Serving missionaries 56, Home staff 93. *CC* Began 1866; Roman Catholic. Magazine: *Missions and Missionaries* (200,000 every two months). Turnover n/a.
☎ 020 8959 3222 🖷 020 8959 8493

St Patrick's Missionary Society, 50 Eton Road, Datchet, Slough SL3 9AY
Superior: Rev Brian Cunningham. *Superior General Republic of Ireland:* Rev Kieran Birmingham. Serving missionaries 4, Home staff 1. *CC* No.269640. Began 1970; Roman Catholic. Magazine: *Africa* (17,000 nine times a year). Turnover n/a.
Email: spsuk@aol.com
☎ 01753 581 009 🖷 01753 593 608

Salesian Fathers and Brothers, 266 Wellington Road North, Stockport SK4 2QR
Provincial Superior: Rev Francis Preston. *Rector Major, Italy:* Rev Egidio Vigano. Serving missionaries 24. *CC* Began 1887; Roman Catholic. Magazine: *Salesian Bulletin* (10,000 quarterly). Turnover n/a.
Web: www.salesians.org.uk
Email: gbrsdb1@msn.com
☎ 0161 431 6633 🖷 0161 443 2378

Salesian Sisters of St John Bosco, Provincial Office, 13 Streatham Common North, London SW16 3HG
Provincial Superior: Sister Margaret Cahill. Serving missionaries 4. *CC* No.250888. Began 1872; Roman Catholic. Magazine: *Da Mihi Animas* (Circulation n/a monthly). Turnover n/a. Youth work: schools, clubs, volunteering, scholastic/social recuperation, catechis, parish work, overseas missions.
Email: provincialoffice.fma@ukonline.co.uk
☎ 020 8677 4573 🖷 020 8677 4523

Salvation Army, 101 Queen Victoria Street, London EC4P 4EP
International Leader: General John Gowans. *Chief of Staff:* Commissioner John Larsson. *Territorial Commander, UK Territory:* Commissioner Alex Hughes. Executive staff 4, Serving missionaries 135, Other staff 8. *CC* No.214779. Began 1865; Salvation Army. Turnover £78,819,000 to year end Dec 98. 90 countries worldwide.
☎ 020 7332 8002 🖷 020 7236 6272

***SAO Cambodia**, Bawtry Hall, Bawtry, Doncaster DN10 6JH
Business Manager: Mr Ivor Greer. *International Director, UK:* Mr John M Heard. *Executive Director, Cambodia:* Mr Nigel Goddard. Executive staff 2, Serving missionaries 11, Other staff 1. *CC* No.293382. Began 1973; interdenominational. (Previously Southeast Asian Outreach). Magazine: *Vision* (800 quarterly). Turnover £301,000 to year end Mar 98. Promoting the Christian faith and relieving the poverty and distress among Cambodian people.
Email: saouk@gn.apc.org
☎ 01302 714 004 🖷 01302 710 027

***Seamen's Christian Friend Society**, 48 South Street, Alderley Edge SK9 7ES
Director: Mr Michael J Wilson. *Administrator:* Mr J C Gordon Pickering. Executive staff 2, Serving missionaries 22, Other staff 1. *CC* No.209133. Began 1846; interdenominational. Magazine: *The Helmsman* (10,000 quarterly). Turnover £200,000 to year end Dec 98.
Email: scfs_hq@compuserve.com
☎ 01625 590 010 🖷 01625 585 442

***Servants to Asia's Urban Poor**, 34 Downend Park Road, Downend, Bristol BS16 5SZ
UK Co-ordinator: Mrs Helen Sidebotham. No full time staff, Serving missionaries 11. *CC* No.1031973. Began 1992; interdenominational. Magazine: *Servants UK Newsletter* (170 quarterly). Turnover £9,500 to year end Dec 98. Living and participating with the poor in evangelism and community development in Asia's urban slums.
Web: www.zeta.org.au/~servants/
Email: info@servants.u-net.com
☎ 0117 957 2471

Servite Friars, St Philip's Priory, Begbroke, Oxford OX5 1RX
Prior Provincial: Rev Bernard Barlow. Serving missionaries 3. *CC* Began 1864; Roman Catholic. Magazine: *Servite Missions* (10,000 annually). Turnover n/a.
☎ 01865 372 149 🖷 01865 370 394

Sharing Christ Internationally, PO Box 351, London W10 5GB
Contact Point: Mr Duncan McPhee. *Field Director, Mongolia:* Mr John Gibbens. Executive staff 3, Serving missionaries 2. *CC* No.328110. Began 1986; interdenominational. Magazine: *Focus on Mongolia* (1,300 quarterly). Turnover £15,682 to year end May 94.
Email: 106375.2655@compuserve.com
☎ 020 8969 6744 🖷 020 8969 6744

Siloam Christian Ministries, 5 Clarendon Place, Leamington Spa CV32 5QL
Director: Mr Richard Norton. Executive staff 2, Serving missionaries 16, Other staff 2. *CC* No.327396. Began 1982; interdenominational. Magazine: *Love in Action* (12,000 monthly). Turnover £1,089,500 to year end Dec 98.
☎ 01926 335 037 🖷 01926 431 193

***SIM UK (Society for International Ministries)**, Wetheringsett Manor, Wetheringsett, Stowmarket IP14 5QX
Director, UK & North Europe: Mr Malcolm McGregor. Executive staff 6, Serving missionaries 228, Other staff 31. *CC* No.219763. Began 1889; interdenominational. Now incorporates the work of Africa Evangelical Fellowship. Magazine: *Mission Together* (10,000 quarterly). Turnover £3,031,494 to year end Sept 98.
Web: www.sim.org
Email: postmast@sim.co.uk
☎ 01449 766 464 🖷 01449 767 148
Also at: 285a Woodstock Road, Belfast BT6 8PR
☎ 028 9045 1451
And: 47 Ryde Road, Wishaw ML2 7DX
☎ 01698 359 067

Sisters of Charity of Jesus and Mary, Provincial House, 108 Spring Road, Letchworth SG6 3SL
Provincial Superior: Sister Mary-Anna Lonergan. Members 5, Serving missionaries 2. *CC* No.251262. Began 1802. Roman Catholic. No magazine. Turnover n/a. Educational, pastoral, medical care.
☎ 01462 675 694 🖷 01462 682 153

Sisters of Charity of Our Lady of Evron, Emmaus, Sudell Street, Collyhurst, Manchester M4 4JG
Provincial Superior: Sister Mary Linnane. Serving missionaries 1. Began n/a; Roman Catholic. No magazine. Turnover n/a.
☎ 0161 832 6954 🖷 0161 833 3674

Sisters of Charity of St Jeanne Antide Thouret, 53 Bethune Road, Stoke Newington, London N16 5EE
Regional Superior: Sister Mary Bernadette Hunston. Serving missionaries 1. *CC* No.246712. Began 1903; Roman Catholic. No magazine. Turnover n/a.
☎ 020 8802 3430 🖷 020 8800 5182

Sisters of Charity of St Paul, 94 Selly Park, Birmingham B29 7LL
Superior General: Sister Mary Lyons. Serving missionaries 4. *CC* No.211200. Began 1847; Roman Catholic. No magazine. Turnover n/a.
Web: easyweb.easynet.co.uk/~stpaul/
Email: stpaul@easynet.co.uk
☎ 0121 415 6100 🖷 0121 414 1063

Sisters of Christ, 9 Lower Road, Bedhampton, Havant PO9 3LH
Sister Superior: Sister Joyce Bone. Serving missionaries 4. *CC* No.294746. Began n/a; Roman Catholic. No magazine. Turnover n/a.
☎ 023 9247 5112 🖷 023 9248 1556

Sisters of Christian Instruction (St Gildas), 26 Briston Grove, Crouch Hill, London N8 9EX
Regional Superior: Sister Anne Hogan. Serving missionaries 4. *CC* No.265715. Began 1903; Roman Catholic. No magazine. Turnover n/a.
☎ 020 8340 3925 🖷 020 8341 1670

Sisters of La Retraite, 8 Thirlmere Road, Streatham, London SW6 1QW
Provincial: Sister Hilary White. Serving missionaries 5. *CC* No.266160. Began 1880; Roman Catholic. No magazine. Turnover n/a.
☎ 020 8769 2134 🖷 020 8769 6535

Sisters of Notre Dame de Namur, Speke Road, Liverpool L25 7TL
Provincial Moderator: Sister Helen Darragh. Serving missionaries 19. *CC* No.232411. Began 1804; Roman Catholic. No magazine. Turnover n/a.
Email: ukprov@aol.com
☎ 0151 421 0302 🖷 0151 428 2067

†**Sisters of Our Lady of Charity**, Fairlight, The Avenue, North Ascot, Ascot SL5 7LY
Provincial Superior: Sister Kay Finnegan. Serving missionaries 1. *CC* Began 1641; Roman Catholic. No magazine. Turnover n/a.
☎ 01344 266 22 🖷 01344 291 063

Sisters of Our Lady of Fidelity, Virgo Fidelis Convent, Central Hill, Upper Norwood, London SE19 1RS
Mother Superior: Sister Betty-Mary Hampson. Serving missionaries 1. *CC* No.245644. Began 1841; Roman Catholic. (Previously Society of the Faithful Virgin). No magazine. Turnover n/a. Clinic, nutritional centre and training.
☎ 020 8670 2506 🖷 020 8761 7459

Sisters of St Clare, St Clare's Convent, Clevis Hill, Porthcaw CF36 5NR
Regional Superior: Sister Catherine Ryan. Serving missionaries 2. *CC* No.247380. Began 1212; Roman Catholic. No magazine. Turnover n/a.
☎ 01656 784 553 🖷 01656 773 144

Sisters of St Joseph of Annecy, St Joseph's House, Llantarnam Abbey, Cwmbran NP44 2YJ
Provincial Superior: Sister Alice Mary Brennar. Serving missionaries 5. *CC* No.232835. Began 1650; Roman Catholic. No magazine. Turnover n/a.
☎ 01633 867 317 🖷 01633 867 317

Sisters of St Joseph of Cluny, St Joseph's Convent, Lichfield Road, Stafford ST17 4LG
Superior: Sister Teresa Cunniffe. Serving missionaries 3. *CC* No.237340. Began 1903; Roman Catholic. No magazine. Turnover n/a.
☎ 01785 515 77 🖷 01785 223 836

Sisters of St Joseph of the Apparition, Provincial House, Ryleys Lane, Alderley Edge SK9 7UU
Provincial Superior: Sister Moira Worth. *General Superior, France:* Sister Cecilia Schembri. Serving missionaries 4, Home staff 17. *CC* No.225671. Began 1904; Roman Catholic. No magazine. Turnover n/a.
☎ 01625 585 655 🖷 01625 585 655

Sisters of St Marie Madeleine Postel, 236 Alcester Road South, Kings Heath, Birmingham B14 6DR
Provincial Superior: Sister Frances Ryan. Serving missionaries 1. *CC* No.264529. Began 1894. Roman Catholic. No magazine. Turnover n/a. Education, nursing, pastoral ministry and evangelisation.
☎ 0121 444 7463

Sisters of St Mary of Namur, 47 Cornwall Crescent, London W11 1PG
Provincial Superior: Sister Louise Swanston. Serving missionaries 4. *CC* No.232842. Began 1896; Roman Catholic. No magazine. Turnover n/a.
Email: louise@ssmnbrit.demon.co.uk
☎ 020 7221 4160 🖷 020 7221 3382

†**Sisters of St Peter Claver**, 70 The Avenue, Beckenham BR3 2EX
Provincial Superior: Sister Regina Zalasek. Currently no UK missionaries serving overseas. Began n/a; Roman Catholic. No magazine. Turnover n/a.
☎ 01753 523 241

Sisters of the Cross and Passion, Cross and Passion Convent, Boarshaw Road, Middleton, Manchester M24 2PF
Provincial Superior: Sister Moya Cleary. Serving missionaries 4. Began 1852; Roman Catholic. No magazine. Turnover n/a.
☎ 0161 655 3184 🖷 0161 653 3666

Sisters of the Good Saviour (Bon Sauveur), Brynhyfryd, Longford Road, Holyhead LL65 1TR
Superior: Sister Miranda Richards. Serving missionaries 1. *CC* No.225925. Began 1907; Roman Catholic. No magazine. Turnover n/a.
☎ 01407 762 084

Sisters of the Holy Family (St Emilie de Rodat), 36 Albert Square, South Lambeth, London SW8 1BZ
Provincial Superior: Sister Marion Daly. *Superior General, France:* Sister Marie K Nichaud. Serving missionaries 1. *CC* Began 1904; Roman Catholic. No magazine. Turnover n/a.
☎ 020 7735 4751 🖷 020 7735 6568

For further information see Lists on Pages 328–350

Sisters of the Sacred Heart of Jesus and Mary, 803 Chigwell Road, Woodford Green IG8 8AX
Superior General: Sister John Vincent MacDonald. Serving missionaries 9. ***CC*** No.287232. Began 1903; Roman Catholic. No magazine. Turnover n/a.
Email: sshjmmarie@aol.com
☎ 020 8504 1624 📠 020 8559 2149

Sisters of Providence, Rosminians, The Convent, Park Road, Loughborough LE11 2EF
Councillor: Sister M Angela Bennett. Serving missionaries 2. ***CC*** No.229120. Began 1843; Roman Catholic. No magazine. Turnover n/a.
☎ 01509 212 054 📠 01509 269 451

Society of African Missions, 378 Upper Brook Street, Manchester M13 0EP
Provincial Superior: Rev Tom Ryan. *Superior General, Italy:* Very Rev P Harrington. Serving missionaries 4, Home staff 14. ***CC*** No.232541. Began 1923; Roman Catholic. Magazine: *Mission News* (5,000 quarterly). Turnover n/a.
Email: thomasjryan@compuserve.com
☎ 0161 224 4949 📠 0161 248 0241

Society of Jesus, 114 Mount Street, London W1Y 6AH
Provincial Superior: Rev James Crampsey. *Superior General, Italy:* Rev Peter H Kolvenbach. Serving missionaries 51. ***CC*** No.230165. Began 1540; Roman Catholic. Magazine: *Jesuits & Friends* (12,000 every four months). Turnover n/a.
Web: www.jesuit.co.uk
Email: gbprov@polenco.qn.apc.org
☎ 020 7499 0285 📠 020 7499 0549

Society of Marie Reparatrice, 115 The Ridgway, Wimbledon, London SW19 4RB
Provincial Superior: Sister Maureen Peart. Serving missionaries 2. Began n/a; Roman Catholic. No magazine. Turnover n/a.
☎ 020 8947 9820 📠 020 8947 9820

Society of Mary, Provincial House, 3 Hamilton Road, Sidcup DA15 7HB
Provincial Superior: Rev Clive Birch. Serving missionaries 6. ***CC*** No.235412. Began 1836; Roman Catholic. No magazine. Turnover n/a.
Web: freespace.virgin.net/marist.sidcup
Email: cbirch@compuserve.com
☎ 020 8300 5339 📠 020 8300 9733

†**Society of St Francis**, St Francis House, Normanby Road, Scunthorpe DN15 6AR
Minister, European Province: Brother Damian Kirkpatrick. Serving missionaries 12. ***CC*** Began 1921; Anglican. No magazine. Turnover n/a.
☎ 01724 853 899 📠 01724 853 899

Society of the Divine Word, Divine Word Missionaries, Hadzor, Droitwich WR9 7DS
Provincial: Rev Michael McPake. Serving missionaries 5, Home staff 14. ***CC*** No.276345. Began 1931; Roman Catholic. Also known as Divine Word Missionaries. Magazine: *The Word* (Circulation n/a monthly). Turnover n/a.
☎ 01905 772 117

Society of the Holy Child Jesus, 10 Holland Villas Road, London W14 8BU
Provincial Superior: Sister Mary Lalor. Serving missionaries 2. ***CC*** No.223035. Began 1846; Roman Catholic. No magazine. Turnover n/a.
Web: www.shcj.org
Email: shcjeuropeanoffice@compuserve.com
☎ 020 7603 2133 📠 020 7602 7304

Society of the Sacred Heart, 3 Bute Gardens, London W6 7DG
Provincial Superior: Sister Barbara Sweeney. *Superior General, Italy:* Mother Helen McLaughlin. Serving missionaries 6. ***CC*** No.227848. Began 1842; Roman Catholic. No magazine. Turnover n/a.
Email: sshprovincial@email.msn.com
☎ 020 8748 9353 📠 020 8748 6814

Society of the Divine Saviour (Salvatorians), 129 Spencer Road, Harrow Weald, Harrow HA3 7BJ
Provincial: Rev Desmond Cantwell. Serving missionaries 5. ***CC*** No.231410. Began 1901; Roman Catholic. No magazine. Turnover n/a.
Email: glprove@aol.com
☎ 020 8861 6544 📠 020 8427 6924

***South American Mission Society**, Allen Gardiner House, 12 Fox Hill, Birmingham B29 4AG
General Secretary: Rt Rev David Evans. *Personnel & Assistant General Secretary:* Rev Canon John Sutton. *Financial & Administrative Secretary:* Mr Philip Tadman. Executive staff 7, Serving missionaries 162, Associates 46. ***CC*** No.221328. Began 1844; Anglican. Magazine: *Share* (12,000 quarterly). Turnover £1,353,000 to year end Dec 97.
Web: www.demon.co.uk/charities/sams
Email: samsgb@compuserve.com
☎ General Secretary 0121 472 2616 📠 0121 472 7977
☎ Personnel Secretary 020 8502 3504 📠 020 8502 3504
☎ Financial Secretary 01892 538 647 📠 01892 525 797
Registered Office: Allen Gardiner House, Pembury Road, Tunbridge Wells TN2 3QU

Spanish Gospel Mission, 286 North Wingfield Road, Grassmoor, Chesterfield S42 5EP
Home Secretary: Rev Matthew W Hill. *Secretary of Field Council Spain:* Sr Fran Ruiz Caraballo. Executive staff 1, Serving missionaries 13. ***CC*** No.1017224. Began 1913; interdenominational. Magazine: *Spotlight on Spain* (3,000 half-yearly). Turnover £117,000 to year end Dec 97.
Web: members.aol.com/spngospel
Email: spngospel@aol.com
☎ 01246 854 254 📠 01246 854 254

***Tearfund**, 100 Church Road, Teddington TW11 8QE
General Director: Mr Doug Balfour. Executive staff 11, Serving missionaries 51, Other staff 205. ***CC*** No.265464. Began 1968; interdenominational. Magazine: *Tear Times* (145,000 quarterly). Turnover £23,800,000 to year end Mar 98.
Web: www.tearfund.org.uk
Email: enquiry@tearfund.dircon.co.uk
☎ 020 8977 9144 📠 020 8943 3594
Ireland Co-ordinator: Mr Alan McIlhenny, 23 University Street, Belfast BT7 1FY
Email: E-@tearfund.dircon.co.uk
☎ 028 9032 4940 📠 028 9023 6930
Scotland Co-ordinator: Mr Peter Chirnside, Challenge House, 29 Canal Street, Glasgow G4 0AD
☎ 0141 332 3621 📠 0141 332 3621

***Trans World Radio**, PO Box 1020, Bristol BS99 1XS
Director: Mr David Tucker. *President, USA:* Dr Tom Lowell. Executive staff 1, Serving missionaries 8, Other staff 10. ***CC*** No.233363. Began 1954; interdenominational. Magazine: *Listening World* (24,000 quarterly). Turnover £1,126,000 to year end Dec 98.
Web: www.twr.org
Email: info@uk.twr.org
☎ 0117 925 1775 📠 0117 925 1454

For further information see Lists on Pages 328–350

***UFM Worldwide**, 47a Fleet Street, Swindon SN1 1RE
Director: Rev Peter Milson. Executive staff 2, Serving missionaries 89, Other staff 10. *CC* No.219946. Began 1931; interdenominational. Magazine: *Light and Life* (9,000 every four months). Turnover n/a.
Web: www.ufm.org.uk
Email: swindon@ufm.org.uk
☎ 01793 610 515 Fax 01793 432 255
Also at: Howard Buildings, 26 Howard Street, Belfast BT1 6PD
Email: belfast@ufm.org.uk
☎ 028 9023 2404
And: 11 Newton Place, Glasgow G3 7PR
Email: glasgow@ufm.org.uk
☎ 0141 353 0666

United Reformed Church International Relations, 86 Tavistock Place, London WC1H 9RT
Secretary: Rev Philip Woods. Executive staff 1, Serving missionaries 8, Other staff 2. *CC* Began 1795; United Reformed. Magazine: *Reform* (16,000 monthly). Turnover £739,000 to year end Dec 97.
Web: www.urc.co.uk
Email: international@urc.co.uk
☎ 020 7916 8654 Fax 020 7916 2021

United Society for the Propagation of the Gospel, Partnership House, 157 Waterloo Road, London SE1 8XA
General Secretary: Rt Rev Mano Rumalshah. Executive staff 26, Serving missionaries 163, Other staff 29. *CC* No.234518. Began 1701; Anglican. Magazine: *TransMission* (25,000 quarterly). Turnover £5,856,000 to year end Dec 97. Working with churches worldwide exchanging people, resources and training for mission.
Email: enquiries@uspg.org.uk
☎ 020 7928 8681 Fax 020 7928 2371

Ursuline Sisters, 28 Mansel Road, Wimbledon, London SW19 4AA
Provincial: Sister Anne Benyon. Serving missionaries 5. *CC* No.245661. Began 1862; Roman Catholic. No magazine. Turnover n/a.
Email: ursprov@aol.com
☎ 020 8946 8191 Fax 020 8946 4569

Volunteer Missionary Movement, 1 Stockwell Green, London SW9 9JF
General Co-ordinator: Dr Vincent Kenny. Executive staff 1, Serving missionaries 4, Other staff 2. *CC* No.314104. Began 1969; interdenominational. Magazine: *VMM Newsletter* (2,000 every four months). Turnover £130,000 to year end Dec 97. Working in partnership with local communities to address the causes and symptoms of hunger, poverty, disease and injustice.
Email: vmmuk@surfaid.org
☎ 020 7737 3678 Fax 020 7346 5955
Also at: PO Box 2225, Glasgow G33 2YB
☎ 0141 770 5090 Fax 0141 770 5090

***WEC International**, Bulstrode, Oxford Road, Gerrards Cross SL9 8SZ
UK Director: Mr Stewart Moulds. *Deputy UK Director:* Mr Norman Cuthbert. *International Director, UK:* Mr Evan Davies. Serving missionaries 312, Other staff 22. *CC* No.237005. Began 1913; interdenominational. Magazine: *Worldwide* (6,500 every two months). Turnover £1,106,445 [excluding designated donations] to year end Mar 98.
Web: www.wec-int.org
Email: 100546.1550@compuserve.com
☎ 01753 884 631 Fax 01753 882 470

Scottish Headquarters, 16 Holmwood Avenue, Uddingston Glasgow G71 7AJ
☎ 01698 810 452
Ireland Headquarters, 35 Seagoe Road, Portadown, Craigavon BT63 5HW
Email: 106321.346@compuserve.com
☎ 028 3833 9759

†*World Gospel Mission, 2 Blundell Drive, Birkdale, Southport PR8 4RG
UK Director: Rev Ronald W Storey. *President, USA:* Dr Thomas H Hermiz. Executive staff 7, Serving missionaries 12, Other staff 4. *CC* No.274142. Began 1910; interdenominational. Magazine: *Call To Prayer* (800 every two months). Turnover n/a.
Email: 100701.123@compuserve.com
☎ 01704 566 551 Fax 01704 566 551

***World Horizons (Britain)**, Centre for the Nations, North Dock, Llanelli SA15 2LF
International Director, UK: Mr Tim Morris. *Team Leaders:* Mr Graham Davies, Mr Mike Adams. Executive staff 4, Serving missionaries 170, Other staff 25. *CC* No.513524. Began 1976; interdenominational. No magazine. Turnover £750,000 to year end Jan 96.
Web: www.whorizons.org
Email: ndock@whorizons.org
☎ 01554 750 005 Fax 01554 773 304

World Outreach, 28 Trinity Street, Dorchester DT1 1EH
British Director: Mr David Greening. *International Director, Singapore:* Rev John Elliott. Executive staff 1, Serving missionaries 4, Other staff 2. *CC* No.258378. Began 1960; interdenominational. Magazine: *New Evidence* (11,000 quarterly). Turnover £260,650 to year end Dec 96.
Email: 101673.1470.compuserve.com
☎ 01305 263 791 Fax 01305 250 958

World-wide Advent Missions, Stanborough Park, Watford WD2 6JP
Director: Pastor Cecil R Perry. Executive staff 2, Serving missionaries 73, Other staff 37. *CC* Began 1913; Seventh-Day Adventist. No magazine. Turnover £467,606 to year end Dec 98.
Email: wwam.adventist.org.uk
☎ 01923 672 251 Fax 01923 893 212

***Wycliffe Bible Translators**, Horsleys Green, High Wycombe HP14 3XL
Executive Officer: Mr Geoff Knott. *International Executive Director, UK:* Dr John Watters. *International President, UK:* Dr John Bendor-Samuel. Executive staff 18, Serving missionaries 255, Other staff 110. *CC* No.251233. Began 1954; interdenominational. Magazine: *Take My Word* (11,300 quarterly). Turnover £3,141,229 to year end Sept 98. Translation and distribution of the Scriptures in minority languages with related literacy and language development.
Web: www.wycliffe.org.uk
Email: general_uk_delivery@wycliffe.org
☎ 01494 482 521 Fax 01494 483 297
Also at: 2 Oxgangs Path, Edinburgh EH13 9LX
☎ 0131 445 2000 Fax 0131 445 4100
And: 5 Glenkeen Avenue, Newtownabbey BT37 0PH
☎ 028 9086 6649 Fax 028 9085 2988

Xaverian Missionary Fathers, 130 Holden Road, London N12 7EA
Provincial Superior: Rev Tom Welsh. Serving missionaries 3, Home staff 9. *CC* No.35191. Began 1895; Roman Catholic. Magazine: *Xaverian Report* (3,500 quarterly). Turnover n/a.
Email: london@xaverians.freeserve.co.uk
☎ 020 8445 6430 Fax 020 8492 0127

For further information see Lists on Pages 328–350

outh With A Mission UK, Stanely House, 14 Stanely Crescent, Paisley PA2 9LF
UK & Ireland Director: Mr Stephen Mayers. *Europe, Middle East & Africa Director:* Mr Lynn Green. *England Director:* Mr Laurence Singlehurst. Executive staff 8, Serving missionaries 478. *CC* No.264078. Began 1972; interdenominational. Magazine: *Advance* (5,800 quarterly), *Scotland Commission* (2,500 quarterly). Turnover £2,684,000 to year end Aug 98.
Email: 106616.3706@compuserve.com
☎ 0141 884 8844 🖷 0141 884 3868
YWAM England National Office, Highfield Oval, Ambrose Lane, Harpenden AL5 4BX
Email: 100126.1261@compuserve.com
☎ 01582 463 300 🖷 01582 463 300
YWAM Scotland National Office: *Director Scotland:* Mr Ian Peters, Seamill Training Centre, Glenbryde Road, West Kilbride KA23 9NJ
Email: 100566.60@compuserve.com
☎ 01294 829 400 🖷 01294 829 312
YWAM Wales National Office *Director Wales:* Mr Martin Abel, PO Box 37, Pontyclun CF72 9XX
Email: postmaster@ywam.co.uk
☎ 01443 681 149
YWAM Ireland National Office: *Director Republic of Ireland:* Mr Rob Clarke, High Park, Grace Park Road, Drumcondra, Republic of Ireland
Email: 101354.2702@compuserve.com
☎ 00 353 183 74676 🖷 00 353 183 67044
YWAM Northern Ireland: *Director Northern Ireland:* Mr Mike Oman, 19 Ashgrove Avenue, Banbridge BT32 3RG
Email: 100071.1477@compuserve.com
☎ 028 4462 7927 🖷 028 4466 2936

***Zambesi Mission**, 38 East Road, Isleham, Ely CB7 5SN
Administrator: Mr Colin Cresswell. *Honorary Treasurer:* Mr David Faulkner. Executive staff 1, Serving missionaries 5. *CC* No.259348. Began 1892; interdenominational. Magazine: *In Prayer* (1,100 quarterly), *Malawi Update* (1,100 quarterly). Turnover £134,503 to year end Dec 98.
Email: zm@cresswell38.freeserve.co.uk
☎ 01638 780 537 🖷 01638 780 537

MISSIONARY SUPPORT ORGANISATIONS

AD2000 and Beyond Movement: Missions Mobilisation Network, c/o Operation Mobilisation, International Co-ordinating Team, PO Box 660, Forest Hill, London SE23 3ST
International Co-ordinator: Mr Chacko Thomas. Executive staff 1, Other staff 3. Began 1993; interdenominational. (Previously AD2000 Mobilizing New Missionaries Network). No magazine. Turnover n/a. Resourcing mission mobilisers to significantly increase the missionary workforce worldwide, especially among unreached peoples.
Email: chacko.thomas@l.ict.om.org
☎ 020 8699 6077 🖷 020 8699 7160

African Pastors Fellowship, 2 Binley Avenue, Binley, Coventry CV3 2EE
Director: Rev Ralph Hanger. *Administrator:* Mr S Giles Wakeling. Executive staff 1, Other staff 2. *CC* No.287756. Began 1974; interdenominational. Magazine: *Information Sheet* (1,500 every two months). Turnover £120,000 to year end Dec 97. Providing training and practical support for church leaders and their dependants in Africa.
Web: www.worldpeople.org
Email: apf@compuserve.com
☎ 024 7644 8068 🖷 024 7644 8068

Aid to Russia and the Republics, PO Box 200, Bromley BR1 1QF
Manager: Miss Anna Littler. *Aid Projects Co-ordinator:* Miss Helen Comber. Other staff 2. *CC* No.281099. Began 1973; interdenominational. (Previously Aid to Russian Christians). Magazine: *ARC Newsletter* (5,000 every two months), *ARRC Cards and Gifts* (8,500 annually). Turnover £180,000 to year end Mar 99. Church and humanitarian initiatives, development work, Christian literature, serving communities of former USSR.
Web: www.vois.org.uk/arc
Email: 106226.363@compuserve.com
☎ 020 8460 6046 🖷 020 8466 1244

Aid to the Church in Need, 1 Times Square, Sutton SM1 1LF
National Director: Mr Neville Kyrke-Smith. Executive staff 4, Other staff 8. *CC* No.265582. Began 1972; Roman Catholic. Magazine: *Mirror* (26,000 every six weeks). Turnover £2,157,000 to year end Dec 97. Pastoral aid agency for the Roman Catholic church wherever she is in need.
Web: www.kirche-in-not.org
Email: acnuk@msn.com
☎ 020 8642 8668 🖷 020 8661 6293

***Anvil Trust**, 104 Townend Road, Deepcar, Sheffield S36 2TS
Programme Coordinator: Mr Noel Moules. Executive staff 3. *CC* No.1010354. Began 1983; interdenominational. Magazine: *Anvil News* (3,500 half-yearly). Turnover £151,244 to year end Aug 98. Courses: Workshop (0114 288 8816), Praxis (020 7350 1386), Firebrand (01902 310 360). See also Supplyline.
Web: dialspace.dial.pipex.com/anvil
Email: anvil@dial.pipex.com
☎ 0114 288 8816 🖷 0114 288 8817

The Arctic Fellowship, 81 Kerrysdale Avenue, Leicester LE4 7GN
Secretary/Treasurer: Miss Mavis Dean. No full-time staff. *CC* No.248371. Began n/a; Anglican. Magazine: *The Arctic News* (Circulation n/a half-yearly). Turnover £10,000 to year end Jan 95. Supporting the work of the Diocese of the Arctic, Canada by prayer and giving.
☎ 0116 266 8664/281 2517

***Asia Link**, 2 Kingswood Close, Lytham St Annes FY8 4RE
Honorary President: Rev Norman Dudgeon. Executive staff 2, Other staff 4. *CC* No.327165. Began 1982; interdenominational. (Previously Asian Outreach UK). No magazine. Turnover n/a. Working with the church in Asia to reach the unreached people groups of Asia.
Email: asialink@btinternet.com
☎ 01253 733 801 🖷 01253 733 770

The Asian Christian Development Programme, 18 Woodville Road, Brierfield, Nelson BB9 5RW
Trustee/International Director: Rev David L White. Executive staff 4. Began 1990; interdenominational. No magazine. Turnover £9,000 to year end Dec 98. Supporting Christian workers, developing the Christian community and Church in Pakistan and Asia.
Email: wwhite@provider.co.uk
☎ 01282 613 094 🖷 01282 613 094

***Assist Europe**, PO Box 789, Sutton Coldfield B74 2XJ
Executive Director: Mr Philip B South. Executive staff 2. *CC* No.328309. Began 1989; interdenominational. No magazine. Turnover £10,000 to year end Sept 98.
Email: 100537.367@compuserve.com
☎ 0121 323 3701 🖷 0121 323 3703

O

Association for Christian Conferences Teaching and Service, Havelock House, Barrack Road, Aldershot GU11 3NP
Executive Director: Mr Geoffrey Skippage. Executive staff 2. ***CC*** No.284203. Began 1974; interdenominational. Also known as (ACCTS). Magazine: *Newsletter* (500 quarterly). Turnover £100,000 to year end Apr 98. Evangelism, support and encouragement of indigenous armed service people of Europe, Africa, Indian sub-continent and Eastern Europe.
Email: 100023.1460@compuserve.com
☎ 01252 311 222 🖷 01252 350 722

Austrian Bible Mission, 22 Five Acres, Danbury, Chelmsford CM3 4NB
General Secretary: Pastor A E Pokorny. *Chairman of Trustees:* Raymond M Dew. Admin staff 2. ***CC*** No.238905. Began 1948; interdenominational. Magazine: *ABM Newsletter* (5,000 half-yearly). Turnover £121,090 to year end Mar 98. Distributing Scriptures in schools, prisons, hospitals, refugee camps in 95 languages; also Scripture diaries.
☎ 01245 225 983

Banner Financial Services Group Ltd, Banner House, Church Road, Copthorne, Crawley RH10 3RA
Directors: Mr John R Jones, Lord Alton of Liverpool, Mr Howard Tingley. Executive staff 2, Other staff 3. Began 1990; interdenominational. No magazine. Turnover £450,000 to year end Dec 98. Providing medical travel insurance for overseas personnel to EMA and other missionary organisations.
Email: info@bannergroup.com
☎ 01342 717 917 🖷 01342 712 534

***Bethany Ministries**, 64 London Road, Coalville LE67 3JA
Chairman: Rev Robert W A Wildgoose. No full-time staff. ***CC*** No.701425. Began 1984; interdenominational. Magazine: *Contempo* (1,000 half-yearly). Turnover £17,825 to year end Apr 98. Organising itineraries of visiting overseas ministries, support of UK missionaries abroad and musical events.
☎ 01530 835 743 Mobile: 07970 147 207 🖷 01530 831 885

BibleLands, PO Box 50, High Wycombe HP15 7QU
Chief Executive: Mr Andrew Jong. *Head of Development & Fundraising:* Mr Julian Burtt. Executive staff 3, Other staff 10. ***CC*** No.226093. Began 1854; non-denominational. (Previously The Bible Lands Society). Magazine: *The Star in the East* (69,000 every four months). Turnover £3,539,000 [16 months to Apr 98]. Supporting Christians in Bible lands: health, education, welfare of children, especially the blind or disabled.
☎ 01494 521 351 🖷 01494 462 171

***Bible Society (The British and Foreign Bible Society)**, Stonehill Green, Westlea, Swindon SN5 7DG
Executive Director: Mr Neil Crosbie. *Director of Mission and Theology:* Rev Dr Martin Robinson. *Commercial Director:* Dr Ashley Scott. Executive staff 8, Other staff 97. ***CC*** No.232759. Began 1804; interdenominational. Magazine: *Word in Action* (165,000 every four months). Turnover £10,140,000 [Voluntary income: £7,370,000, Sales: 2,770,000] to year end Dec 98. Making the Bible available where it is needed and challenging indifference to the Bible wherever it exists.
Web: www.biblesociety.org.uk
Email: info@bfbs.org.uk
☎ 01793 418 100 🖷 01793 418 118

Board of Mission (General Synod), Church House, Great Smith Street, Westminster, London SW1P 3NZ
Secretary: Rev Canon Philip King. *Adminstrator:* Mr Alan Tuddenham. Executive staff 11, Other staff 7. ***CC*** Began 1972; Anglican. Magazine: *Ambassador* (550 every four months), *Good News* (650 every two months). Turnover n/a. Promoting evangelisation of England; world mission through Anglican agencies; ecumenical inter-faith work; rural affairs marking the Millennium.
Email: bom@c-of-e.org.uk
☎ 020 7898 1000 🖷 020 7898 1431

***Capernwray Missionary Fellowship of Torchbearers**, Capernwra Hall, Carnforth LA6 1AG
Managing Director: Rev Mark Thomas. *Company Secretar* Mr David Bell. Executive staff 8, Other staff 25. *C* No.1073139. Began 1948; interdenominational. Magazin *Torchbearing* (6,000 half-yearly). Turnover £1,000,000 to yea end Apr 98. International centre-based ministry of residenti Bible teaching, evangelism, missions, conferences,holidays an camps.
Web: www.capernwray.co.uk
Email: info@capernwray.co.uk
☎ 01524 733 908 🖷 01524 736 681

***Care for Mission**, Elphinstone Wing, Carberry, Musselburg EH21 8PW
Directors: Dr Michael & Mrs Elizabeth Jones. Executive sta 3, Other staff 2. ***CC*** No.SCO 00948. Began 1983; interdenom inational. Magazine: *Newsletter* (200 n/a). Turnover £97,14 to year end Apr 98. Residential and out-patient medical care rest, debriefing assessment and counselling for missionarie and UK Christian workers.
Email: 100633.2065@compuserve.com
☎ 0131 653 6767 Mobile: 07710 276 208 🖷 0131 653 3646

Roman Catholic Bishops' Conference Department for Mission an Unity, 39 Eccleston Square, London SW1V 1BX
Chairman: Rt Rev Cormac Murphy O'Connor. Executive staf 2. ***CC*** No.257239. Began 1984; Roman Catholic. No magazine. Turnover n/a. Encouraging Christian unity, relationships with other faiths, home and overseas mission.
☎ 020 7834 5612

Catholic Missionary Union of England and Wales, Holcombe House, The Ridgeway, London NW7 4HY
General Secretary: Rev Joe Brankin. Executive staff 2, Other staff 1. ***CC*** No.257239. Began 1971; Roman Catholic. (Previously National Missionary Council of England and Wales). Magazine: *Focus* (750 five times a year). Turnover n/a. Forum where all missionary activity and interests come together.
Email: camec@compuserve.com
☎ 0121 329 2058 Mobile: 0780 807 8714 🖷 0121 378 4761

***CEDARS (Charity Equipment for Development & Relief Services)**, Bulstrode, Oxford Road, Gerrards Cross SL9 8SZ
Director: Mrs Brenda Chudley. Executive staff 2, Other staff 4. ***CC*** No.326101. Began 1982; interdenominational. No magazine. Turnover n/a. Freight forwarding for Christians overseas; funding for aid equipment for missions.
Email: unimatco@compuserve.com
☎ 01753 886 738 🖷 01753 889 378

Morris Cerullo World Evangelism Society of Great Britain, PO Box 277, Hemel Hempstead HP2 7DH
European Director: Mr Julian Richards. Executive staff 3, No other staff. ***CC*** Began 1961; interdenominational. No magazine. Turnover n/a. Evangelising and training nationals worldwide.
Web: www.mcwe.com
Email: enoffice@mcwe.com
☎ 01442 232 432 🖷 01442 692 404

†***Children's Evangelism Ministry International**, European & English Headquarters, 6 Dock Offices, Surrey Quays Road, London SE16 2XU
Director: Mr C A Anierebi. Executive staff 3, Other staff 25. ***CC*** No.1015515. Began 1990; interdenominational. Magazine: *Newsletter & Bulletin* (1,500 every two months). Turnover £27,000 to year end Dec 96. Evangelism, training, seminars, conferences, children's clubs, holiday schools, children's library and schools.
☎ 020 7394 1677/7237 0404 🖷 020 7394 1677

hinese Church Support Ministries, Silver Street Chambers, 12 Silver Street, Bury BL9 0EX
UK Director: Mr Ian Robertson. Executive staff 2, Other staff 5. ***CC*** No.327709. Began 1987; interdenominational. Magazine: *China Challenge* (1,000 monthly). Turnover £220,000 to year end Apr 94. China ministries; radio, literature, tapes, sending of professionals, mission outreach to students.
Email: 101642.1423@compuserve.com
☎ 0161 763 1500 Fax: 0161 763 1555

he Christian Distributors' & Shippers' Association (CDSA), 1 Civic Square, Tilbury RM18 8AA
Managing Director: Mr Mark Waller. *Tilbury Office Operations Manager:* Mr Rod Bartlett. Executive staff 4, Other staff 12. Began 1994; Anglican. No magazine. Turnover £2,500,000 to year end Mar 98. Assisting Christian organisations in the international movement of goods worldwide, including books and supplies.
Email: waller_mark@hotmail.com
☎ 01375 840 371 Mobile: 07957 446 182 Fax: 01375 840 012
Sales and Marketing
☎ 01277 636 122 Fax: 01277 636 122

hristian International Relief Mission (CIRM), 1 Malham Road, Stourport-on-Severn DY13 8NN
Director: Mr Stephen Methuen. Executive staff 2, Other staff 2. ***CC*** No.1044410. Began 1958; interdenominational. Magazine: *CIRM News* (2,000 quarterly). Turnover £75,000 to year end Dec 98. Promoting church planting, evangelism, discipleship and social projects/programmes worldwide.
Email: 100606.3160@compuserve.com
☎ 01299 825 710 Mobile: 07710 543 777 Fax: 01299 825 710

***Christian Solidarity Worldwide**, PO Box 99, New Malden KT3 3YF
National Director: Rev Stuart Windsor. *President:* Baroness Caroline Cox. *Chairman:* Mr Mervyn Thomas. Executive staff 5, Other staff 10. ***CC*** No.281836. Began 1979; interdenominational. Magazine: *Response* (22,000 every two months), *Action Info* (6,500 every two months). Turnover £632,000 to year end Dec 97. Religious liberty organisation helping persecuted Christians by prayer, campaigns and material aid throughout the world.
Web: www.csw.org.uk
Email: csw@clara.net
☎ 020 8942 8810 Mobile: 07770 755 660
Fax: 020 8942 8821

***Christian Vision**, Ryder Street, West Bromwich B70 0EJ
Regional Manager, Europe: Mr Andrew James. Executive staff 4, Other staff 5. ***CC*** No.1031031. Began 1988; interdenominational. No magazine. Turnover n/a. Supporting evangelism, leadership training, church planting programmes through nationals and media.
Web: www.christianvision.org
Email: 100131.3711@compuserve.com
☎ 0121 522 2000/6087 Fax: 0121 522 6083

Christian Visual Aids Team, 68 Church Crescent, Muswell Hill Road, London N10 3NE
Hon Organising Secretary: Mr K E E Ponder. All voluntary staff. Began 1952; interdenominational. No magazine. Turnover n/a. Missionary and church support ministry for film and filmstrip loan/hire; projector service.
☎ 020 8883 4590

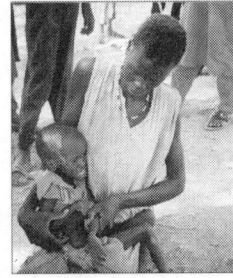

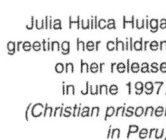

Christians Aware, 124 New Walk, Leicester LE1 7JA
Executive Secretary: Mrs Barbara Butler. Executive staff 1. ***CC*** No.328322. Began 1977; ecumenical. Magazine: *Ecumenical Magazine* (1,200 quarterly). Turnover £101,516 to year end Sept 98. Developing international multi-cultural understanding, friendship and encounter.
Web: www.christiansaware.co.uk
Email: bjb@overtown.free-online.co.uk
☎ 0116 254 0770 Fax 0116 254 0770

Christians in Health Care, 11 Grove Road, Northwood HA6 2AP
Director: Mr Howard Lyons. No full-time staff. ***CC*** No.328018. Began 1989; interdenominational. Magazine: *Among All Nations (published with MMA)* (5,000 quarterly). Turnover £5–10,000 to year end Dec 98. Specialist management consultants for medical-oriented missions; resource for missions and individuals in overseas health care.
Web: www.christian-healthcare.org.uk
Email: howardlyons@msn.com
☎ 01923 825 634 Mobile: 07979 811 140
Fax 01923 840 562

Churches Commission on Mission, Inter-Church House, 35 Lower Marsh, London SE1 7RL
Commission Secretary: Rev Donald W Elliott. *Associate Commission Secretary:* Mr Simon Barrow. Executive staff 3, Other staff 3. ***CC*** Began 1990; interdenominational. Magazine: *Connections* (500 every four months). Turnover £200,000 to year end Dec 98. Relating the churches' commitments to mission in Britain and Ireland with those in the wider world.
Email: donx@cix.compulink.co.uk
☎ 020 7523 2126 Fax 020 7928 0010

Churches International, 1 Avondale Close, Lingwood, Burlingham, Norwich NR13 4BG
Missions Director: Mr L John Rose. Executive staff 2. ***CC*** No.1010130. Began 1991; interdenominational. Magazine: *Two Forty-Four* (Circulation n/a occasionally). Turnover £850 to year end Apr 98. Bible studies for overseas churches so as to promote spiritual growth and development.
☎ 01603 716 691

Contact International Christian Fellowship, PO Box 50, Burntwood WS7 8WL
Director: Mr Stephen Allport. Executive staff 2, Other staff 7. ***CC*** No.1013648. Began 1992; interdenominational. Magazine: *Contact* (1,500 every two months). Turnover £12,000 to year end Mar 98. Giving practical aid and support to church work and social care projects in Eastern Europe.
Web: www.c-i-c-f.dircon.co.uk
Email: c-i-c-f@dircon.co.uk
☎ 01543 682 565 Fax 01543 682 565

Council for World Mission, 32 Great Peter Street, London SW1P 2DB
General Secretary: Dr D Preman Niles. *Secretary for Personnel Sharing:* Rev Andrew Prasad. *Director for Communications:* Dr Andrew Morton. Executive staff 6, Other staff 14. ***CC*** No.232868. Began 1795; reformed 1977 as an international and ecumenical body. Magazine: *Inside Out* (4,000 every two months). Turnover £5,000,000+ to year end Apr 97. Co-ordinating missionary activity of 32 churches worldwide, assisting them in sending and receiving personnel.
Web: www.cwmission.org.uk
Email: council@cwmission.org.uk
☎ 020 7222 4214 Fax 020 7233 1747

The David House Fellowship, 78 Woodville Road, Card
CF2 4ED
Director: Mr Kenneth J Price. Other staff 2. ***CC*** No.26707 Began 1974; interdenominational. Magazine: *The Vineya* (24,000 monthly). Turnover £100,000 to year end Jan 9 Establishing and advancing the Christian gospel of Jesus Chri among Jews.
☎ 029 2039 9119 Fax 029 2064 5027

***East African Ministries Trust**, 50 Zetland Street, Poplar, Londo E14 6RB
UK Co-ordinator: Mr Peter Nickerson. No other UK staff. ***C*** No.1038998. Began 1994; non-denominational. Turnov £8,000 to year end May 96. Supporting African Pastors an workers in ministry, evangelism, child care, youth trainin education. Mainly Uganda.
☎ 020 7515 2617 Fax 020 7515 2617

East European Ministries, 117 Kingsway, Petts Wood, Orpingto BR5 1PP
Director: Rev Clive Doubleday. No full-time staff. Bega 1989; Baptist. No magazine. Turnover n/a. Supporting th Christian church in Eastern Europe through aid, praye finance, mission and publicity.
Email: clivedoubleday@compuserve.com
☎ 01689 603 680 Fax 01689 603 680

†***East West Ministries**, Elmdene, Nascot Place, Watford WD1 3Q
Director: Mr Ron Hibbert. Executive staff 4, Other staff 1 Began 1985; interdenominational. No magazine. Turnove £200,000 to year end Apr 94. Eastern Europe suppor programme involving Bible training and literature.
☎ 01923 232 620

L'Eau Vive UK Trust, 172 Weir Road, London SW12 0NP
Chairman: Mr David Woods. No full-time staff. ***CC*** Begar 1980; interdenominational. Magazine: *Newsletter* (500 half-yearly). Turnover n/a. Supporting Christian outreach and training in France, especially among young people, and church planting.
☎ 020 8675 2943

ECHO International Health Services Ltd, Ullswater Crescent, Coulsdon CR5 2HR
Chief Executive: Mr Mark Radford. Executive staff 6, Other staff 44. ***CC*** Began 1966; non-denominational. Magazine: *ECHO Around the World* (5,000 half-yearly). Turnover £4,500,000 to year end Dec 98. Supplying medical equipment and drugs for health work in developing countries and needy areas overseas.
Email: cs@echohealth.org.uk
☎ 020 8660 2220 Fax 020 8668 0751

Echoes of Service, 1 Widcombe Crescent, Bath BA2 6AQ
Executive staff 3, Other staff 9. ***CC*** Began 1872; Christian Brethren. Magazine: *Echoes of Service* (10,000 monthly). Turnover £2,400,000 to year end Dec 94. Missionary support group for Assembly missionaries; publishing news, forwarding gifts, caring for missionaries.
Email: echoes_of_service@compuserve.com
☎ 01225 310 893/480 635 Fax 01225 480 134

Egypt Diocesan Association, 26 Bickerton Road, Headington, Oxford OX3 7LS
Secretary: Lady Ghislaine Morris. Staff n/a. Began n/a; Anglican. No magazine. Turnover n/a. Support group for the Anglican Diocese of Egypt.
☎ 01865 761 461

O

Europe Now, PO Box 248, Guildford GU2 6WY
UK Director: Mr Paul Hazelden. Executive staff 2, Other staff 1. *CC* No.1051283. Began 1995; non-denominational. Magazine: *Borderlines* (1,700 every three to four months). Turnover £40,000 to year end Dec 98. Equipping the church to proclaim the gospel in mainland Europe.
Web: www.oaci.org
Email: en@oaci.org
☎ 01483 579 955 Fax 01483 579 955

Evangelical Missionary Alliance, Whitefield House, 186 Kennington Park Road, London SE11 4BT
Executive Director: Rev Stanley L Davies. *Associate Director:* Rev Richard Tiplady. Other staff 4. *CC* No.274521. Began 1958; interdenominational. Trading as Global Connections. Magazine: *Global Connections* (850 quarterly), *World Prayer News* (1,600 every two months). Turnover £209,400 to year end Dec 97. Providing global connections by networking, resourcing and representing world mission in the UK.
Email: sdavies@ema.co.uk
☎ 020 7207 2156 Fax 020 7207 2159

Experience Exchange and Root Group International Programmes, United College of the Ascension, Weoley Park Road, Selly Oak, Birmingham B29 6RD
RGI Development Officer: Mandy Quayle. Other staff 4. *CC* No.234518. Began 1978; Anglican and Methodist. (Previously Short Term Experience Programmes). Joint programmes of USPG – Anglican and Methodist Church. No magazine. Turnover £100,000 to year end Dec 98. Providing opportunities to work in mission situations overseas (6–12 months) or in community in Britain/Ireland (12 months).
Email: uca@sellyoak.ac.uk
☎ 0121 472 1667 Fax 0121 472 4320

Fellowship of Faith for the Muslims (FFM), PO Box 5864, Basildon SS13 3FF
Chairman: Mr Malcolm Steer. No full-time staff. *CC* No.77687. Began 1915; interdenominational. Magazine: *Prayer Bulletin* (800 ten times a year). Turnover £16,000 to year end Dec 98. Challenging the church to join in prayer for the Muslim world; literature work. Inter-mission fellowship.
Email: 113421.2717@compuserve.com
☎ No telephone
Administration Address: *Bulletin Editor:* Dr Paul Shepherd, FFM, PO Box 58, Wakefield WF2 9YD

†**Flying Doctor Development Service Ltd**, 57 Coopers Lane, Leyton, London E10 5DG
Hon General Secretary: Rev Ian Duncan. No full-time staff. *CC* Began 1960; interdenominational. No magazine. Turnover £10,000 to year end Mar 93. Promoting two-way radio communications to assist health and other rural development services.
☎ 020 8539 5933

Friends of Ludhiana, 157 Waterloo Road, London SE1 8UU
Executive Officer: Miss Heather Smith. Executive staff 1. *CC* No.314148. Began 1894; interdenominational. Magazine: *Ludhiana* (4,000 occasionally). Turnover £80,500 to year end Dec 97. Supporting the work of the Christian Medical College and Hospital in Ludhiana, Punjab, North India.
Email: foluk@charis.co.uk
☎ 020 7928 1173 Fax 020 7620 1070

Friends of Mengo Hospital, 45 Tunwells Lane, Great Shelford, Cambridge CB2 5LJ
Members Secretary: Mrs Oliver. All voluntary staff. *CC* No.289737. Began 1960; Church of Uganda [Anglican]. Magazine: *Mengo Notes* (750 half-yearly). Turnover £50,000 to year end Dec 98. Supporting Mengo hospital in Uganda by prayer, interest and giving.
☎ 01223 842 919

Friends of Padhar Hospital, 38 Stoke Lane, Westbury-on-Trym, Bristol BS9 3DN
Secretary: Mr Jim Knowles. No full-time staff. *CC* No.271362. Began 1976; interdenominational. Magazine: *Newsletter* (Circulation n/a occasionally). Turnover £20,000 to year end Dec 98. Supporting and promoting the evangelistic activities of an indigenous Church in Central India.
☎ 00 46 573 33016 (Sweden)
Fax 00 46 573 33016 (Sweden)

Friends of the Church in China, 49 Pages Lane, Muswell Hill, London N10 1QB
Chairman: Dr Martin Conway. No full time staff. *CC* No.1004221. Began 1984; ecumenical. Magazine: *Newsletter* (550 every four months). Turnover £18,000 to year end Sep 98. Promoting contact, friendship, encouragement and understanding between Christians in Britain and Ireland and China.
☎ 020 8883 2350

Friends of the Church in India, 12 Bedgbury Close, Rochester ME1 2UT
Secretary: Rev Barrie Scopes. No full-time staff. *CC* No.1042850. Began 1992; interdenominational. Magazine: *Pilgrim* (700 half-yearly). Turnover £4,650 to year end Mar 96. Encouraging prayerful interest in the life, work and mission of the united churches in India.
☎ 01634 288 491

***Friends of Turkey**, PO Box 10, Nottingham NG11 8BE
Hon Secretary: D. J. R. All voluntary staff. *CC* No.1060199. Began 1973; non-denominational. Magazine: *Call to Prayer* (500 every two months). Turnover £4,550 to year end Feb 98. Informing and encouraging prayer and other support for Christian work in Turkey and Turkic world.
☎ 0115 921 7886 Fax 0115 921 7886

Friends of Vellore, PO Box 25122, London SW1V 3WD
Director: Mrs E C Howes. Executive staff 2. ***CC*** No.209168. Began 1940; interdenominational. Magazine: *Vellore Newsletter* (2,000 half-yearly). Turnover £100,000 to year end Dec 96. Supporting medical work in Vellore, South India through a Christian medical college and hospital and outreach.
☎ 020 7828 9920 🖷 020 7821 5813

Garden Tomb (Jerusalem) Association, South Hall, Merrow Grange, Horseshoe Lane East, Guildford GU1 2QW
General Secretary: Mr Peter G L Wells. Executive staff 1. ***CC*** No.1004062. Began 1893; interdenominational. No magazine. Turnover n/a. Maintaining the tomb and garden believed to be the garden of Joseph of Arimathea.
Web: www.gardentomb.com
Email: mail@gardentomb.com
☎ 01483 505 464 🖷 01483 450 689

The Girls' Brigade International, The Old Bridewell, 3 Burgh Road, Aylsham, Norwich NR11 6AJ
Vice President: Miss Sheena MacFarlane. Executive staff 1, Other staff 2. ***CC*** Began 1893; interdenominational. No magazine. Turnover £100,000 to year end Dec 98. Youth service movement operating in over 60 countries.
☎ 01263 734 917 🖷 01263 734 917

***Helps International Ministries**, 44 Nickey Lane, Mellor, Blackburn BB2 7HF
European & Middle East Director: Mr Malcolm H Jones. Executive staff 2, Other staff 14. ***CC*** No.1002336. Began n/a; interdenominational. Turnover £10,000 to year end Jun 96. Assisting missions with renovation and building maintenance.
☎ 01254 812 816 🖷 01254 813 092

Hope in Action / Gobaith mewn Gweithrediad, 32 Garth Drive, Liverpool L18 6HW
Founders: Rev Dr D Ben Rees, Ms Hefin E Rees. No full-time staff. ***CC*** Began 1987; interdenominational. (Previously Faith in Action). Magazine: *Hope* (Circulation n/a Annually). Turnover £1,500 to year end Dec 98. Assisting African countries in education and propagating the Gospel, especially Kenya.
☎ 0151 724 1989 🖷 0151 724 5691

Horizons International, 13 Victory Grove, Audenshaw, Manchester M34 5XA
Executive Director: Rev Colin Carson. Executive staff 2, Admin staff 1. ***CC*** Began 1998; interdenominational. No magazine. Turnover: first year of operation. Working with national leaders in Eastern / Central Europe, providing training, relief, literature, support.
Email: ccarson129@aol.com
☎ 0161 301 1162 🖷 0161 370 2494

ICCOWE (International Charismatic Consultation on World Evangelisation), PO Box 2000, Haywards Heath RH16 3YB
Chairman: Father Michael Harper. Other staff 1. ***CC*** No.1003378. Began 1989; interdenominational. Magazine: *LINK* (1,000 annually). Turnover £12,000 to year end Dec 98. Furthering spiritual renewal, unity in Christ and evangelisation through international meetings and conferences.
Email: iccowe@compuserve.com
☎ 01444 413 321 🖷 01444 417 871

***Ichthus Motor Mission Ltd**, Grove Close, Forest Hill, London SE23 1AS
Chairman: Mr L R Carne. All voluntary staff. ***CC*** No.1028735. Began 1981; non-denominational. No magazine. Turnover £150,000 to year end Dec 95. Supplying motor vehicles to missionaries home on furlough or deputation.
Email: 106454.2000@compuserve.com
☎ 020 8291 5144 🖷 020 8291 1652

IDWAL (Inter-Diocesan West Africa Link), The Church Office, Portsmouth Road, Liphook GU30 7DJ
Secretary: Mrs Brenda Halsey. All voluntary staff. Began 1964; Anglican. No magazine. Turnover n/a. Anglican friendship link between Dioceses of Guildford, Chichester and Portsmouth, and Provinces of Nigeria and West Africa.
☎ 01428 725 390 🖷 01428 725 390

India Link Ministries, PO Box 5884, Basildon SS13 3AJ
Administrator: Mr Paul Barnes. No full time staff. ***CC*** No.1063882. Began 1996; interdenominational. No magazine. Turnover £13,000 to year end Dec 98. Assisting full-time Christian workers in India by partnership, practical aid, literature and Bible teaching/training.
Web: www.grace.org.uk/orgs/ilm.htm/
Email: pb_ilm@compuserve.com
☎ 01268 552 895 🖷 01268 463 049

Indian Evangelical Team, 7 Castle Street, Rugby CV21 2TP
Leading Elder: Rev John Saunders. Executive staff 1. Began 1976; Charismatic. Magazine: *Faith Today* (10,000 monthly worldwide). Turnover £10,000 to year end Mar 99. Representing Indian Evangelical Teams in the UK; collecting funds, deputation work.
Web: ourworld.compuserve.com/homepages/rugby_fellowship/
Email: rugby_fellowship@compuserve.com
☎ 01788 542 852

***Interdev UK**, PO Box 210, West Drayton UB7 8NN
UK Director: Mrs Derath Nicklas-Carter. Executive staff 3, Admin staff 7, Other staff 8. ***CC*** No.327997. Began 1988; interdenominational. Magazine: *60 Day Update* (Circulation n/a every two months). Turnover £383,000 to year end Jun 98. Providing consultancy and training service for the development and operation of international partnerships for evangelism.
Email: interdev-uk@ xc.org
☎ 01895 438 321 Mobile: 07889 426 631 🖷 01895 438 323

***INTERHEALTH**, Partnership House, 157 Waterloo Road, London SE1 8US
Director: Dr Ted Lankester. *Director of Resources:* Peter J Chapman. Medical staff 12, Admin staff 7, Volunteers 2. ***CC*** No.801475. Began 1989; interdenominational. Magazine: *Newsletter* (Circulation & frequency n/a). Turnover £573,000 to year end Sep 98. Providing comprehensive healthcare services for missions, aid agencies, volunteers, acting as medical advisor to many Christian organisations.
Email: interhealth@compuserve.com
☎ 020 7902 9000 🖷 020 7928 0927

***Interlinks**, PO Box 210, West Drayton UB7 8NN
Programme Coordinator: Mrs Kathryn Rogers. Admin staff 1. ***CC*** No.327997. Began 1998; interdenominational. A ministry of Interdev. No magazine. Turnover: first year of operation. Linking mission agencies with UK churches who wish to adopt an unreached people group.
Email: jkathrynrogers@xc.org
☎ 01895 438 321 🖷 01895 438 323

***International Needs (UK)**, 9 Station Approach, Sanderstead Road, South Croydon CR2 0PL
National Director: Mr Peter Staley. Part time staff 3. ***CC*** No.1010597. Began 1976; non-denominational. Magazine: *UK Update* (500 quarterly). Turnover £90,000 to year end Dec 97. Supporting national workers worldwide; orphan sponsorship, relief, social projects; training centres, evangelism, missions.
Email: inuk@international-needs.org
☎ 020 8651 3100 🖷 020 8651 3100

The Jerusalem and the Middle East Church Association, 1 Hart House, The Hart, Farnham GU9 7HA
Secretary: Mrs Vanessa Wells. Executive staff 1. *CC* No.248799. Began 1887; Anglican. Magazine: *Bible Lands* (3,500 half-yearly). Turnover n/a. Enabling organisation serving the Anglican province of the Episcopal Church in Jerusalem and Middle East.
☎ 01252 726 994 🖷 01252 735 558

Jesuit Missions, 11 Edge Hill, Wimbledon, London SW19 4LR
Director: Mr Anthony E Montfort. *Assistant Director:* Mr Alan Fernandes. Executive staff 1, Other staff 2. *CC* No.230165. Began 1896; Roman Catholic. Magazine: *Jesuits and Friends* (28,000 every four months). Turnover £1,000,000 to year end Sept 98. Supporting Jesuits working in Guyana, Zimbabwe and South Africa.
Email: jesuitmissions@compuserve.com
☎ 020 8946 0466 🖷 020 8946 2292

Kenya Church Association, 35 Parliament Hill, Hampstead, London NW3 2TA
Hon Secretary: Jean Breckenridge. No full-time staff. *CC* Began 1920; interdenominational. Magazine: *KCA Bulletin* (400 half-yearly). Turnover £5,000 to year end Dec 98. Uniting Christians formerly working and living in Kenya to maintain contact with and support for the Kenyan church.
☎ 020 7794 7557 🖷 020 7435 8704

Keston Institute, 4 Park Town, Oxford OX2 6SH
Director: Lawrence Uzzell. *Research Director:* Dr Philip Walters. Executive staff 3, Other staff 6. *CC* No.314103. Began 1970; interdenominational. Publications: *Religion, State and Society* (circulation n/a, quarterly, academic journal), *Frontier* (circulation n/a every two months), *Keston New Service* (300 weekly, e-mail news bulletin). Turnover £309,596 to year end Mar 98. Monitors freedom of religion and researches religious affairs in Communist and post-Communist countries.
Web: www.keston.org
Email: keston.institute@keston.org
☎ 01865 311 022 🖷 01865 311 280

Liberty Ministries, 257 Green Lane, Norbury, London SW16 3LY
Founders: Rev Donald Attenborough, Mr Ken Dyer. Began 1993; Baptist. Magazine: *Newsletter* (Circulation n/a Occasionally). Turnover £1,500 to year end Dec 94. Providing resources for Christians in Estonia, Uganda, India, Serbia and Malawi.
Email: dta@cwcom.net
☎ 020 8764 6093 Mobile: 07801843378 🖷 020 8239 9320

Life Changing Ministries International, Bemersley House, Gitana Street, Hanley, Stoke-on-Trent ST1 1DY
Director: Rev David P Griffiths. Executive staff 1. *CC* No.1065192. Began 1996; non-denominational. No magazine. Turnover £16,707 to year end Apr 98. Sending UK-based missionaries on short-term equipping trips to Asia to equip nationals to evangelise.
Email: dave4219@aol.com
☎ 01270 582 080 🖷 01270 582 080

Link & Learn, CHIME Worldwide, 11a Upper Teddington Road, Hampton Wick, Kingston upon Thames KT1 4DL
Directors: Miss Sandra Kimber, Mrs Cath Dunlop. *CC* No.1823. Began 1907; Anglican. Previously linked to the Intercontinental Church Society, now operated by CHIME Worldwide. Magazine: *Newsletter* (Circulation n/a quarterly). Turnover n/a. Writing and sending monthly packs of Sunday school lessons to English-speaking children living abroad.
☎ 020 8977 5809 🖷 020 8977 5899

***Links International**, Oasis House, Essex Road, Chadwell Heath, Romford RM6 4JA
Director: Mr Norman Barnes. Executive staff 1, Other staff 2. *CC* No.327000. Began 1982; in association with Pioneer. Magazine: *Nexus* (2,500 frequency n/a). Turnover £170,000 to year end Dec 98. Joining together to serve the church around the world.
Email: 106301.3546@compuserve.com
☎ 020 8598 9507 🖷 020 8983 8139

Logos Ministries, 147 Albertbridge Road, Belfast BT5 4PS
Director: Rev Thomas McClean. Executive staff 2, Other staff 8. *CC* No.NI 46135. Began 1977; interdenominational. (Previously Youth Evangelical Missionary Trust). Magazine: *Edge* (1,500 quarterly). Turnover £98,000 to year end Dec 98. Motivating people into mission; providing information on missions and job opportunities both home and overseas.
Web: www.charis.co.uk/logos.ministries
Email: logos.ministries@charis.co.uk
☎ 028 9045 8362 🖷 028 9045 8362

Manna Ministries, West House Cottage, 21 Broadway, Chilton Polden, Bridgwater TA7 9DR
Chief Executive: Rev David E J Oram. Executive staff 1. Began 1997; non-denominational. Magazine: *Macedonian Quarterly* (400 quarterly). Turnover £11,000 to year end Aug 98. Raising support for workers and Bible teaching in Eastern Europe through ministry and electronic media.
☎ 01278 722 310 🖷 01278 723 357

*__Henry Martyn Trust,__ Henry Martyn Hall, 24 Market Street, Cambridge CB2 3NZ
World Mission Advisor: Mrs Sue Anderson. Other staff 4. ***CC*** No.266612. Began 1887; Anglican. No magazine. Turnover n/a. Promoting world missionary concern and offering vocational advice.
☎ 01223 355 397

MasterServe, Thames House, 63 Kingston Road, New Malden KT3 3PB
Director: Mr Gordon Miller. No other staff. ***CC*** No.1050931. Began 1997; non-denominational. Linked to MasterSki. No magazine. Turnover included in MasterSki. Supporting churches and missionary work in tourist areas.
Email: mplan1uk@aol.com
☎ 020 8942 9442 Fax 020 8949 4398

*__Medical Missionary Association__, Partnership House, 157 Waterloo Road, London SE1 8XN
Secretary: Dr David Clegg. Part time staff 3. ***CC*** No.224636. Began 1878; interdenominational. Work alongside Christian Medical Fellowship & Christians in Healthcare. Magazine: *Saving Health* (Circulation & frequency n/a), *Among All Nations* (5,000 quarterly). Turnover £70,000 to year end Dec 98. Stimulating interest in world mission; providing resources for Christian health professionals working overseas.
Web: www.healthserve.org
Email: 106333.673@compuserve.com
☎ 020 7928 4694 Fax 020 7620 2453

*__Medical Service Ministries__, PO Box 35, Hailsham BN27 3XW
Candidates Secretary: Mrs Jean Hayward-Lynch. ***CC*** No.234037. Began 1903; interdenominational. (Previously Missionary School of Medicine). No magazine. Turnover £28,000 to year end Sept 98. Personal and community health care training for Christian workers.
☎ 01323 849 047 Fax 01323 849 047

Mildmay International, 1 Nelson Mews, Southend-on-Sea SS1 1AL
Chief Executive: Mrs Ruth Sims. *Group Director of Finance and Business Development:* Mr David Rouse. Other staff 60. ***CC*** No.292058. Began 1996; interdenominational. No magazine. Turnover £985,000 to year end Mar 2000. Consultancy and training in palliative HIV/AIDS care worldwide.
Web: www.mildmay.org.uk
Email: mildint@globalnet.co.uk
☎ 01702 394 450 Fax 01702 394 454

†**Mission 10/40**, 4 School Road, Tilehurst, Reading RG31 5AL
Co-ordinator: Mr Bob Smart. All voluntary staff. Began n/a; non-denominational. Magazine: (Circulation n/a quarterly). Turnover n/a. Planting churches in the 10/40 window; mission partnership with Latin American churches.
☎ No Telephone Fax 01734 412 953

*__Mission Supplies Ltd__, Dawson House, 128 Carshalton Road, Sutton SM1 4TW
Managing Director: Mr Gerald Slessenger. *Finance Officer:* Mr Carl Biggs. *Medical Director:* Mrs Janet Slessenger. Executive staff 5, Other staff 6. Began 1982; interdenominational. (also International Supplies). No magazine. Turnover £1,250,000 to year end Dec 98. Supplying/packing/freighting everything required by relief agencies, missionary societies, missionaries overseas; VAT free sales.
Web: www.mission-supplies.co.uk
Email: mission_supplies@compuserve.com
☎ 020 8643 0205/1126 Fax 020 8643 3937
Also at: Mission Supplies Ireland Ltd, 13 Hulls Lane, Lisburn BT28 2SR
Director: Mr John Rodgers. Executive staff 2, Admin staff 7.
Web: www.tricord.co.uk
Email: msi@tricord.co.uk
☎ 028 9260 6950 Fax 028 9260 6951

Missionaries' Children's Fund, PO Box 133, Bath BA1 2YU
Administrator: Stewards Company Ltd. No full-time staff. ***C*** No.220204. Began 1966; Christian Brethren. No magazin Turnover £26,000 to year end Jan 98. Supporting missionar families with educational expenses of children (those com mended by UK Assemblies).
☎ 01225 310 893 Fax 01225 480 134

*__Missionary Mart__, 99 Woodmansterne Road, Carshalto SM5 4EG
Company Secretary: Mr Brian E Chapman. Other staff 3. ***C*** No.289030. Began 1965; non-denominational. Trading arm of Wallington Missionary Mart and Auctions. No magazine Turnover £315,011 to year end Dec 96. Warehouse selling donated furniture and other items daily to raise funds fo missionary work overseas.
☎ 020 8643 3616
Warehouse: 105 Stafford Road, Wallington SM6 9AP
☎ 020 8669 3495

The Missionary Training Service, Flat 5, 40 Buckingham Gate, London SW1E 6BS
Co-ordinator: Rev Ian E Benson. Other staff 1. ***CC*** No.1073046. Began 1993; non-denominational. Magazine: *Newsletter* (300 every four months). Turnover £7,143 to year end Dec 97. Organising missionary training, providing teaching and materials for church multiplication among unreached people groups.
Web: www.btinternet.com/~ajg/mtshome.htm
Email: coordmts@xc.org
☎ 020 7932 0728 Fax 020 7932 0728

Missionary Ventures Europe, 82 St Andrews Road South, Lytham St Annes FY8 1PS
Director: Rev Luther L Meier. Executive staff 4, Other staff 3. ***CC*** No.1067612. Began 1995; non-denominational. Magazine: *MVE Update* (200 quarterly). Turnover £45,000 to year end Dec 98. Facilitating indigenous pastors through sponsorship and short term evangelistic, medical, construction, teaching teams; Bible schools.
Web: www.missionaryventures.org
Email: mveurope@compuserve.com
☎ 01253 727 927 Fax 01253 727 927

Moravian Missions (London Association in Aid of Moravian Missions), Moravian Church House, 5 Muswell Hill, London N10 3TJ
Secretary: Jackie Morten. No full-time staff. ***CC*** Began 1817; interdenominational. Magazine: *News and Views* (400 annually). Turnover £30,000 to year end Apr 98. Supporting British Moravian Church in its partnership with Moravian Church overseas, especially in Tanzania, India, Labrador, Jamaica.
Email: moravianchurchhouse@btinternet.com
☎ 020 8883 3409 Fax 020 8365 3371

The North Eastern Caribbean and Aruba Association, 77 Hangleton Way, Hove BN3 8AF
Chairman: Rev Canon Robert Eke. All voluntary staff. ***CC*** Began 1906; Anglican. Magazine: *Newsletter* (Circulation n/a occasionally). Turnover £2,703 to year end Dec 95. Supporting the work of NECA diocese.
☎ 01273 421 443

Northwood Missionary Auctions, Freepost, Northwood HA6 1BR
Chairman: Mr Leslie Munns. No full-time staff. ***CC*** Began 1969; interdenominational. No magazine. Turnover £43,000 to year end Aug 98. Sale of items donated for the benefit of Christian charities.
Web: www.nmauctions.org.uk
☎ 01923 836 634

Novi Most International, Bushell House, 118 Broad Street, Chesham HP5 1ED
Director: Mr Paul H Brooks. *Bosnia Field Director:* Rev Nikola Skrinjaric. Executive staff 4, Other staff 20. *CC* No.1043501. Began 1993; non-denominational. Magazine: *New Bridge* (Circulation n/a quarterly). Turnover £277,725 to year end Sep 98. Evangelism, church planting, relief, development in Bosnia-Herzegovina; ministry to traumatised young people.
Web: www.novimost.org
Email: chesham@novimost.org
☎ 01494 793 242 Fax 01494 793 771

Partnership for World Mission (Part of Board of Mission, Archbishops' Council), Partnership House, 157 Waterloo Road, London SE1 8XA
Secretary: Mr John Clark. Executive staff 1, Other staff 1. Began 1978; Anglican. No magazine. Turnover n/a. Co-ordinating body for world mission work of mission agencies and Archbishops' Council of Church of England.
Email: john_clark@ecunet.org
☎ 020 7928 8681 Fax 020 7633 0185

Pocket Testament League, Clarence Court D, Rushmore Hill, Orpington BR6 7LZ
General Director: Mr Donald Ford. *Assistant Director:* Mr Peter J Honour. Executive staff 2, Other staff 3. *CC* No.281910. Began 1908; interdenominational. Magazine: *Newsdesk* (5,000 every four months). Turnover £156,236 to year end June 98. Evangelism and scripture distribution in UK. Support in Brazil, India, Pakistan, Portugal, Spain and Yugoslavia.
Web: www.ptl.org.uk
Email: ptl@zetnet.co.uk
☎ 01689 858 066 Fax 01689 853 353

Pontifical Missionary Societies, 23 Eccleston Square, London SW1V 1NU
National Director: Rev John Corcoran. Executive staff 1, Other staff 10. *CC* No.1056651. Began 1833; Roman Catholic. Incorporating Association for the Propagation of the Faith, Missionary Union, Society of St Peter the Apostle, Society of the Holy Childhood. Magazine: *Mission Outlook* (2,300 quarterly), *Mission Together* (90,000 quarterly), *Mission Today* (206,000 quarterly). Turnover £3,296,274 to year end Dec 98. Raising funds to support the Catholic Church in mission territories and mission education.
Email: mission@netcomuk.co.uk
☎ 020 7821 9755 / 7834 5680

Portable Recording Ministries, Newton Lodge, Cynwyl Elfed, Carmarthen SA33 6SP
Hon Treasurer: Mr Alan Lansdown. No full-time staff. Began 1983; interdenominational. No magazine. Turnover £2,000 to year end Mar 98. Teaching the use of cassette communication for church planting and growth.
☎ 01267 281 252 Fax 01267 281 252

***Radstock Ministries**, 2a Argyle Street, Mexborough S64 9BW
Co-ordinator: David L Mills. Executive staff 6, Other staff 13. *CC* No.326879. Began 1984; non-denominational. Magazine: *Rapport* (5,000 every two months). Turnover £150,000 to year end Dec 98. Helping churches in the UK, Ireland and the former Soviet Union to make mission their priority.
Email: 100540.1645@compuserve.com
☎ 01709 582 345 Fax 01709 583 202

Redbourn Missionary Trust, 35 Lemsford Road, St Albans AL1 3PP
Hon Secretary: Mrs Carol Evershed. No full-time staff. *CC* No.251960. Began 1968; evangelical. Magazine: *Newsletter* (500 half-yearly). Turnover £20,000 to year end Sept 92. Four houses and a flat for missionaries on furlough; four retirement flats for retired missionaries.
☎ 01727 852 019

***Release International**, PO Box 19, Bromley BR2 9TZ
General Director: Mr Brian D Loader. Executive staff 1, Other staff 11. *CC* No.280577. Began 1968; interdenominational. (Previously Christian Mission to the Communist World). Magazine: *Release in Action* (17,000 every two months). Turnover £380,000 to year end Dec 92. Evangelism and support in Eastern Europe and ministry to the persecuted church worldwide.
Email: releaseint@aol.com
☎ 020 8460 9319 Fax 020 8290 4585
Scotland Release International Dykeside, Robieston, Huntly AB54 4SJ
☎ 01466 792 740

***Romanian Missionary Society**, PO Box 51, Torquay TQ2 6HN
British Director: Mr Les Tidball. Executive staff 1, Other staff 1. *CC* No.327724. Began 1987; interdenominational. Magazine: *RMS Review* (800 quarterly). Turnover £100,000 to year end Dec 92. Teaching Romanians to a high level of theological education.
Email: lestidball@tidfam.freeserve.co.uk
☎ 01803 323 225 Fax 01803 315 031

RURCON (Rural Development Counsellors For Christian Churches in Africa), Communications Unit, Alsace, 48 High Park Road, Ryde PO33 1BX
Communications Unit Coordinator: Dr E John Wibberley. Executive staff 5, Other staff 12. *CC* No.275581. Began 1971; interdenominational. Magazine: *RURCON Newsletter:* (2,500 quarterly), *Friends of RURCON* (300 quarterly). Turnover £65,000 to year end Dec 97. Africa-controlled team of rural development counsellors visiting and training Christians throughout Africa.
Email: 101511.1120@compuserve.com
☎ 01983 566 770 Fax 01983 566 770

Russian Ministries (Peter Deyneka), 24 Birchgrove, Cobham, Woking KT11 2HR
Chairman, British Advisory Council: Mr Ian S Bull. Admin staff 1. Began 1998; interdenominational. Magazine: *Network* (8,000 worldwide quarterly). Turnover n/a. Evangelism and church planting in the former USSR through strategic ministry development, global Christian partnerships.
Web: www.russianministries.org
☎ 01932 867 086

St Francis Leprosy Guild, 26 Inglis Road, London W5 3RL
Hon Secretary: Sister Eleanor Marshall. *President:* Mrs Gwen Sankey. Executive staff 2. *CC* No.208741. Began 1895; Roman Catholic. Magazine: *Yearbook* (8,000 annually). Turnover £300,000 to year end Dec 98. Collecting funds to help care for leprosy sufferers abroad.
☎ 020 8992 0799 Fax 020 8752 0119

SAT-7 Trust, PO Box 1214, Bristol BS99 2RS
Development Director: Mr David Radford. Other staff 2. *CC* No.1060612. Began 1997; interdenominational. Magazine: *Uplink* (2,000 quarterly). Turnover £233,000 to year end Dec 98. Supporting all Christians of the Middle East in their discipleship, through satellite television broadcasts.
Web: www.sat7.org
Email: bristol@sat7.org
☎ 0117 905 5003 Fax 0117 905 5093

Scottish Episcopal Church Mission Association (Links), 21 Grosvenor Crescent, Edinburgh EH12 5EE
Provincial Secretary: Mrs Margaret A Deas. No full-time staff. *CC* No.SCO 23290. Began 1875; Scottish Episcopal Church. (Previously Church Womens' Missionary Association). Magazine: *Links* (3,000 half-yearly). Turnover £20,000 to year end Dec 97. Supporting mission outreach overseas and raising awareness at home.
☎ 0131 225 6357

***Scripture Union International Office**, 207 Queensway, Bletchley, Milton Keynes MK2 2EB
International Secretary: Mr Emmanuel Oladipo. Executive staff 2, Other staff 3. *CC* No.213422. Began 1867; interdenominational. Magazine: *Catalyst* (5,000 half-yearly). Turnover n/a. Representing the eight regions of Scripture Union work worldwide.
Web: www.scriptureunion.org.uk
Email: 100536.1331@compuserve.com
☎ 01908 856 188 🖷 01908 856 111

Sedgley International Christian Ministries, PO Box 1216, Dudley DY3 1GW
Director: Rev Stewart R Bloor. Executive staff 3, Other staff 9. *CC* No.1057488. Began 1992; interdenominational. Magazine: *Newsletter* (500 quarterly). Turnover £38,000 to year end Feb 98. Home and overseas missions opportunities, evangelism training, resourcing third-world church leaders, working in over 20 nations.
Email: sicm@wfcsmail.com
☎ 01902 883 221 Mobile: 07956 444 628 🖷 01902 883 221

Seed, Bible Mission International, PO Box 100, Middlesbrough TS6 0XZ
Executive Director: Mr Tony John. Executive staff 3. *CC* No.1068968. Began 1985; non-denominational. Magazine: *New Update* (5,000 every two months). Turnover £60,000 to year end Aug 98. Supplying Scripture and aid to Christians in closed countries.
Web: www.bethany.co.uk/bmi
Email: bmi@seed.org.uk
☎ 01642 454 433 🖷 01642 469 992

SEN UK, 3 Springfield Road, Hinckley LE10 1AN
Executive Officer: Mrs Judi Oglesby. *Director:* Mr Marsh Moyle. No other UK staff. *CC* No.327237. Began 1984; non-denominational. (Previously Central European Missionary Fellowship, Central European Foundation). Magazine: *The City Gate* (3,000 every four months). Turnover £150,000 to year end Dec 98. Demonstrating historic Biblical Christianity in Central European cultures; study centre, research for missions, publishing, evangelism.
Web: www.citygate.org
Email: senuk@citygate.org
☎ 01455 446 899 🖷 01455 446 898

***Servants Fellowship International**, The Old Rectory, River Street, Pewsey SN9 5DB
Director: Dr Patrick Sookhdeo. Executive staff 2, Other staff 7. *CC* No.280859. Began 1975; interdenominational. (Previously In Contact Ministries). Magazine: *SFI News and Prayer Update* (2,200 every two months). Turnover n/a. Cross-cultural urban mission; training.
Email: 101376.2103@compuserve.com
☎ 01672 564 938 🖷 01672 564 939

***Share Trust**, 58 Slimmons Drive, St Albans AL4 9AP
Director: Mr John Barron. Executive staff 2. *CC* No.801625. Began 1989; interdenominational. No magazine. Turnover n/a. Encouraging new Christian initiatives in Africa.
Email: 100537.3365@compuserve.com
☎ 01727 862 935 🖷 01727 862 935

Shunem Trust, 4 Tinkers Drive, Winslow, Buckingham MK18 3RD
Administrator: Mr Philip King. No full-time staff. *CC* No.276109. Began 1978; interdenominational. No magazine. Turnover £5,000 to year end Mar 94. Providing accommodation for needy missionaries and other Christian workers on home leave.
☎ 01296 715 341

***Sierra Leone Mission**, 31 John Amner Close, Ely CB6 1DT
Contact Person: Mr Douglas Staplehurst. No full time staff. *CC* No.232674. Began 1841; Countess of Huntingdon's Connexion. Magazine: *Voice* (750 quarterly). Turnover £80,000 to year end June 98. Providing spiritual, financial and material support for ministers, evangelists, teachers, churches, schools in Sierra Leone.
☎ 01353 669 393

Siloam Christian Ministries, 5 Clarendon Place, Leamington Spa CV32 5QL
Director: Mr Richard Norton. Executive staff 2, Other staff 2. *CC* No.327396. Began 1982; interdenominational. Magazine: *Love in Action* (12,000 monthly). Turnover £1,089,500 to year end Dec 98. Transporting aid to Eastern Europe in trucks or containers overseas.
☎ 01926 335 037 🖷 01926 431 193

Slav Lands Christian Fellowship, 28 Hayesford Park Drive, Bromley BR2 9DB
Secretary: Mr R J Weil. Executive staff 1. *CC* No.1037023. Began 1959; interdenominational. Magazine: *Slavonia* (1,000 annually). Turnover £20,000 to year end Apr 98. Support and encouragement of Christian work in E. Europe and Russia.
☎ 020 8402 0695

***Slavic Gospel Association (British Section) Ltd**, 37a The Goffs, Eastbourne BN21 1HF
General Director: Mr Trevor Harris. *Director of Home Ministries (UK):* Mr Tony Crosbie. Executive staff 7, Office staff 3. *CC* No.258253. Began 1934; interdenominational. Magazine: *Breakthrough* (12,000 five times a year). Turnover £475,000 to year end Dec 98. Bible teaching, training, support, funding for literature projects in Central/Eastern Europe and CIS.
Email: sga@jireh.co.uk
☎ 01323 725 583 🖷 01323 739 724

Society of St John the Divine (Natal) English Association, 7 Hewgate Court, Henley-on-Thames RG9 1BD
Joint Secretaries: Mr & Mrs J E Coffee. No full-time staff. Began 1911; Anglican. Magazine: *Newsletter* (75 half-yearly). Turnover n/a. Supporting sisters in South African convent.
☎ 01491 578 885

SOMA (Sharing of Ministries Abroad), PO Box 6002, Health and Reach, Leighton Buzzard LU7 0ZA
National Director: Rev Don Brewin. Executive staff 1, Other staff 3. *CC* No.279759. Began 1979; Anglican. Magazine: *Sharing* (3,000 n/a). Turnover £70,000 to year end Dec 97. Sharing charismatic renewal with countries overseas by short term visits, conferences for mutual encouragement.
Email: somauk@compuserve.com
☎ 01525 237 953 📠 01525 237 954

SPCK Worldwide (Society for Promoting Christian Knowledge), Holy Trinity Church, Marylebone Road, London NW1 4DU
Director: Ms Sue Parks. Executive staff 1, Other staff 3. *CC* Began 1698; interdenominational but historically Anglican. No magazine. Turnover n/a. Grants to support Christian literature communication work in over 75 countries each year.
Email: spckww@spck.co.uk
☎ 020 7387 5282 📠 020 7388 2352

Spatial Post, 5 West End, Long Whatton, Loughborough LE12 5DW
Postal Manager: Mr Ron O'Meara. Other staff 80. Began 1984; non-denominational. Turnover n/a. International and UK mailing company.
Email: post@the-spatial-group.com
☎ 01509 646 811 📠 01509 646 805

The Spring Project, 8 Badgers Green, Morpeth NE61 3RU
Trustee: Mr Richard Hubbard. No other staff. *CC* No.1067992. Began 1997; non-denominational. No magazine. Turnover £6,000 to year end Mar 98. Making Baygen clockwork radios available to churches and missionaries in remote areas of the world.
Email: rhubbard1@csi.com
☎ 01670 510 725 📠 01661 868 488

Stamps for Christian Missions, 40 Montgomery Crescent, Bolbeck Park, Milton Keynes MK15 8PR
Chief Executive: Rev Arthur Rowley. Executive staff 2. Began 1987; interdenominational. No magazine. Turnover n/a. Collecting used postage stamps for sale to stamp dealers.
☎ 01908 605 659

***Stamps for Evangelism**, 11 St John's Drive, Chaddesden, Derby DE21 6SD
Secretary: Mr Peter Bysh. No full-time staff. Began 1966; non-denominational. Magazine: *Annual Report* (1,500 annually). Turnover £18,134 to year end Dec 98. Making gifts of money to those engaged in evangelism from selling used postage stamps.
☎ 01332 663 270 📠 01332 663 270

STUDYLINK-EFAC International Training Partnership, 8 Brook Cottage, Corston, Bath BA2 9BA
Secretary: Mr Peter LeRoy. No full time staff. *CC* No.1073169. Began 1965; Anglican. Turnover £55,000 to year end Aug 98. Bursary scheme training potential Third World Church leaders in UK evangelical colleges and parishes.
Email: a.leroy@clara.net
☎ 01225 873 023 📠 01225 873 871

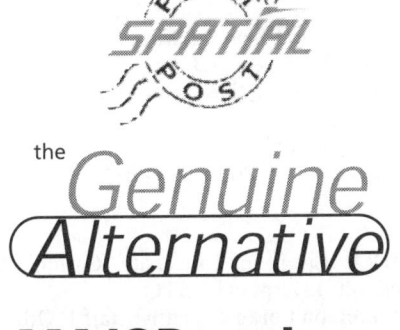

***Supplyline**, 13 Paget Road, Wolverhampton WV6 0DS
Director: Mr Jamie Handscomb. Executive staff 1. *CC* No.1010354. Began 1965, Anvil Trust, 1999; interdenominational. Magazine: *Supplyline News* (250 three times a year). Turnover £10,000 to year end Apr 98. Christian partnership with West Africa linking those who have with those who have not.
Email: anvil@dial.pipex.com
☎ 01902 686 643 🖷 0114 288 8817

Survive – MIVA, Liverpool University, Catholic Chaplaincy, Mount Pleasant, Liverpool L3 5TQ
Director: Mr Simon Foran. Executive staff 1, Other staff 3. *CC* No.268745. Began 1974; Roman Catholic. Magazine: *Awareness* (9,600 half-yearly). Turnover £526,224 to year end Dec 99. Providing essential transport to missionaries working in the developing world.
Web: www.survive-miva.org
Email: info@survive-miva.org
☎ 0151 708 7250 🖷 0151 708 9253

***Tearcraft (Tearfund Trading)**, 100 Church Road, Teddington TW11 8QE
General Director: Mr Doug Balfour. Other staff 8. *CC* No.265464. Began 1975; interdenominational. No magazine. Turnover £1,100,000 to year end Dec 98. Providing Third World craft producers with a livelihood by importing and marketing their goods.
Web: www.tearfund.org.uk
Email: enquiry@tearfund.dircon.co.uk
☎ 020 8977 9144 🖷 020 8943 3594

***Titus Ministries Worldwide**, 7 Grange Drive, Ossett WF5 0SH
Director: Mr John Farrant. Executive staff 2, Other staff 7. *C* No.1049749. Began 1995; non-denominational. Magazine *Seedtime and Harvest* (100 half-yearly). Turnover £11,000 t year end Mar 98. Helping the developing world church fulfil it vision.
☎ 01924 261 771 🖷 01924 261 771

†*Tools With a Mission, Unit 3 Perry Barn, Burstall Lane Sproughton, Ipswich IP8 3DJ
Administrative Secretary: Mr E Tallant. Executive staff 3 Other staff 15. *CC* No.250334. Began 1983; Baptist. Magazine: *Tools With a Mission* (Circulation & frequency n/a). Turnover £10,000 to year end Oct 96. Supplying basic tools and equipment to mission-based vocational training in the Third World.
☎ 01473 652 029 🖷 01473 652 029

***The Toybox Charity**, PO Box 660, Amersham HP6 6EA
Director: Mr Duncan Dyason. *Administrator:* Mrs Margaret Byatt. Full-time staff 1. *CC* No.1015945. Began 1991; non-denominational. Magazine: *Toybox Newsletter* (5,000 every two months). Turnover £400,000 to year end Dec 98. Promoting the plight of street children in Latin America and helping in practical ways.
Web: www.toybox.org
Email: toybox@toybox.org
☎ 01494 432 591 🖷 01494 432 593

Unimatco Mission Aid Ltd, Bulstrode, Oxford Road, Gerrards Cross SL9 8SZ
Director: Mr John Chudley. Executive staff 1, Other staff 1. Began 1976; interdenominational. No magazine. Turnover n/a. Land Rover export specialist.
Email: unimatco@cin.co.uk
☎ 01753 886 105 / 880 230 🖷 01753 889 378

***Vision International Healthcare Ltd**, PO Box 248, Tunbridge Wells TN2 5BZ
Director: Mr H F Harper. *Administrator:* Mr C R Webb. Executive staff 1, Other staff 1. *CC* No.1012920. Began 1990; interdenominational. No magazine. Turnover £247,000 to year end May 96. Building eye clinics in Central Asia, public health, training the blind.
Email: 100142.3521@compuserve.com
☎ 01892 518 358 🖷 01892 518 381

***Viva Network**, PO Box 633, Oxford OX2 0XZ
Director: Mr Patrick McDonald. Other staff 16. *CC* No.1053389. Began 1994; non-denominational. Magazine: *Connect* (1,000 quarterly). Turnover £90,000 to year end Dec 98. Helping children at risk by linking and enhancing the Christian response.
Web: www.viva.org
Email: helpdesk@viva.org
☎ 01865 450 800 🖷 01865 203 567

Waldensian Church Missions, 21 de Freville Avenue, Cambridge CB4 1HW
Executive Secretary: Mrs Erica Scroppo-Newbury. No full-time staff. *CC* Began 1825; non-denominational. Magazine: *Waldensian Review* (900 half-yearly). Turnover £9,687 to year end Dec 98. Supporting Waldensian work in Italy; encouraging interest in UK through tours, meetings and literature.
Email: richardnewbury@msn.com
☎ 01223 315 753 🖷 01223 562 2605

***Wallington Missionary Mart and Auctions**, 20 Dalmeny Road, Carshalton SM5 4PP
Chairman: Mr Vernon W W Hedderly OBE. Paid Staff 5, Volunteers 80. *CC* No.1797729. Began 1974; non-denominational. No magazine. Turnover £300,000 to year end Dec 98. Organising auctions of antiques, jewellery, silver, pictures & selling household goods. Proceeds donated to missionary work by donors.
☎ 020 8647 8437

MA-UK, PO Box 436, Reading RG1 1FW
Executive Director: Rev Glenn Schwartz. Executive staff 1, Other staff 1. ***CC*** No.1029198. Began 1993; interdenominational. Magazine: *WMA Perspectives* (1,500 quarterly), *Transition notes* (1,500 quarterly). Turnover £20,000 to year end Dec 96. Conducting seminars and consultations primarily in Africa on dependancy and self-reliance for mission-established institutions.
Web: www.wmausa.org
Email: glennschwartz@msn.com
☎ 01491 680 288

Workaid, Unit 2b, St Georges Industrial Estate, White Lion Road, Amersham HP7 9JQ
Chairman: Mr John Geraghty. Full-time staff 1, Other staff volunteers. ***CC*** No.1041574. Began 1986; interdenominational. Magazine: *Workaid World* (5,000 every four months). Turnover n/a. Collecting and refurbishing tools and sewing machines to send to training centres around the world.
Web: www.btinternet.com/~workaid
Email: workaid@btinternet.com
☎ 01494 765 506 🖷 01494 765 507

World Association for Christian Communication, 357 Kennington Lane, London SE11 5QY
General Secretary: Rev Carlos A Valle. *President:* Rev Dr Albert van den Heuvel. Executive staff 9, Other staff 13. ***CC*** No.296073. Began 1975; interdenominational. Magazine: *Action Newsletter* (2,400 ten times a year), *Media Development* (1,700 quarterly). Turnover £2,116,000 to year end Jan 96. Working in 60 countries to promote communication for human dignity.
Web: www.wacc.org.uk
Email: wacc@wacc.org.uk
☎ 020 7582 9139 🖷 020 7735 0340

World Christian Ministries, 148 Duchy Drive, Paignton TQ3 1EW
Director: Rev Roy David. Executive staff 5. ***CC*** No.1001691. Began 1988; Assemblies of God. No magazine. Turnover £158,000 to year end Aug 98. Working with churches in Asia, Africa, Europe; raising sponsorship for students, widows, orphans, day care centres.
Email: wcmin@iname.com
☎ 01803 663 681/523 317 🖷 01803 665 166

World Evangelical Fellowship, Les Emrais de Bas, Castel, Guernsey GY5 7YF
International Treasurer: Mr John E Langlois. *International Director:* Dr Agustin Vencer. Executive staff 9, Other staff 10. ***CC*** No.273042. Began 1846; non-denominational. Magazine: *Theological News* (Circulation n/a quarterly), *Evangelical Review of Theology* (Circulation n/a quarterly), *Evangelical World* (Circulation n/a quarterly). Turnover £150,000 [UK only] to year end June 98. Worldwide association of national evangelical alliances and fellowships.
Web: www.worldevangelical.org
Email: johnlanglois@xc.org
Email: johnlanglois@compuserve.com
☎ 01481 544 71 Mobile: 07887 681 426
🖷 01481 557 34

***World in Need**, Mill Crescent, Park Road, Crowborough TN6 2QU
International Director: Mr Ron George. Admin staff 5, Other staff 30. ***CC*** No.800940. Began 1991; interdenominational. Magazine: *WIN News* (Circulation & frequency n/a). Turnover n/a. Changing attitudes through aid and education, training and sending workers into Muslim lands.
Email: win@pavilion.co.uk
☎ 01892 669 834 🖷 01892 669 894

***WorldShare**, Bawtry Hall, Bawtry, Doncaster DN10 6JH
Chief Executive: Mr John Rose. *Public Relations Manager:* Mr Peter Roberson. Executive staff 1, Other staff 8. ***CC*** No.803575. Began 1943; interdenominational. (Previously Christian Nationals). Magazine: *Christian Nationals News* (5,500 quarterly). Turnover £375,000 to year end June 98. Assisting evangelism, Bible training and child education by national Christians.
Web: www.worldshare.org.uk
Email: 1000657.147@compuserve.com
☎ 01302 710 273 🖷 01302 710 027

***Wycliffe Associates (UK)**, 7 Conwy Street, Rhyl LL18 3ET
National Co-ordinators: David & Rachel Landin. Staff. ***CC*** No.1007772. Began 1989; interdenominational. Magazine: *Help!* (1,200 every four months). Turnover £15,000 to year end Aug 97. Using people's gifts at home to serve overseas missionaries – Wycliffe Bible Translators and other missions.
Web: www.globalnet.co.uk/~wa_uk
Email: wycliffeassociates@iname.com
☎ 01745 343 300

***Youth Ministries International**, PO Box 1317, Bedworth CV12 9ZS
Executive Director: Rev Ian Green. *Field Director:* Mr John Smith. Executive staff 4, Other staff 15. ***CC*** No.1034023. Began 1991; interdenominational. No magazine. Turnover £250,000 to year end Dec 98. Church planting and leadership training in Eastern Europe; short-term missions in UK and Eastern Europe.
Web: www/ymieurope.com
Email: info@ymieurope.com
☎ 024 7664 3415 🖷 024 7664 3503

RELIEF & DEVELOPMENT AGENCIES

Across UK, Bawtry Hall, Bawtry, Doncaster DN10 6JH
Chairman: Mr Steve Bell. No other UK staff. ***CC*** No.1069973. Began 1998; interdenominational. No magazine. Facilitating relief of poverty and the advancement of Christianity in Sudan and Kenya.
☎ 01302 710 750 🖷 01302 719 399

Action Around Bethlehem Children with Disability (ABCD), Wapping, Long Crendon, Aylesbury HP18 9AL
Founder/Trustee: Mrs Val Jourdan. *Director:* Georgina Mortimer. All voluntary staff. ***CC*** No.327327. Began 1986; interdenominational. Magazine: *ABCD Newsletter* (4,000 annually). Turnover £124,000 to year end Mar 96. Providing training courses and relief programmes to aid disabled people in West Bank and Gaza Strip.
Email: mortimer@btinternet.com
☎ 020 8343 4246 🖷 020 8343 4048

Action by Christians Against Torture, Quex Road, Methodist Church, Kilburn, London NW6 4PR
Director: Miss Lois Stamelis. No full-time staff. Began 1984; interdenominational. Magazine: *Newsletter* (500 every two months). Turnover n/a. Campaigning, information and prayer for victims of torture; prisoners support scheme.
☎ 020 7372 7347 🖷 01752 849 821

Action International Ministries (UK), PO Box 193, Bewdley DY12 2GZ
UK Director: Mr Ingo Abraham. Executive staff 1, Other staff 3. ***CC*** No.1058661. Began 1988; interdenominational. (Previously ACTION UK). Magazine: *Actionpoint* (1,500 quarterly), *Street Children* (1,500 every two months). Turnover £189,000 to year end Mar 98. Reaching urban poor of the world through evangelism, discipleship, social development projects especially amongst street children.
Web: www.actionintl.org
Email: actionuk@btinternet.com
☎ 01299 401 511 🖷 01299 405 273

***Adopt-A-Child**, PO Box 5589, Inverness IV1 1ZL
UK & Ireland Director: Mr Paul Cocking. *Admin office Manager:* Miss Jenny Dougal. Executive staff 1, Other staff plus associates 4. ***CC*** No.SCO 10326. Began 1993; interdenominational. No magazine. Turnover £200,000 to year end Mar 99. Sharing the whole Gospel with children in need through sponsored feeding programmes and other integrated ministries.
Web: www.foreserve.co.uk/aoc.htm
Email: adopt_a_child@compuserve.com
☎ 01463 711 926 🖷 01463 711 926

Adventist Development and Relief Agency (ADRA-UK), Stanborough Park, Watford WD2 6JP
Director: Mr D J Sinclair. Other staff 1. Began 1980; Seventh-Day Adventist. Magazine: *ADRA Today* (Circulation n/a quarterly). Turnover £1,018,400 to year end Dec 96. Providing assistance for disaster relief and humanitarian work in the developing countries.
Email: adra@adventist.org.uk
☎ 01923 681 723 🖷 01923 681 723

†***Aid to Romania**, PO Box 453, Bedford MK45 3ZL
UK Operations Manager: Mrs Hazel Snowball. Executive staff 5. ***CC*** No.1020084. Began 1991; non-denominational. Magazine: *Newsletter* (Circulation & frequency n/a). Turnover n/a. Medical relief, two mobile clinics, orphanage team, evangelism.
☎ 01234 743 421 🖷 01234 350 544

Amos Trust, All Hallows on the Wall, 83 London Wall, London EC2M 5ND
Director: Rev Garth Hewitt. *Projects Co-ordinator:* Ms Beki Bateson. Other staff 2. ***CC*** No.292592. Began 1986; interdenominational. No magazine. Turnover £135,000 to year end Apr 98. Promoting justice and development through music, education and projects worldwide; also supporting Garth Hewitt's ministry.
Web: www.onthewall.org
Email: amos_trust@compuserve.com
☎ 020 7588 2661/2638 🖷 020 7588 2663

†**Asian Aid**, 81 Norwood Road, Southall UB2 4EA
Chairman: Rev D Burgess. Other staff. ***CC*** No.1048373. Began n/a; interdenominational. Turnover £20,000 to year end Mar 96. Providing eductional, medical, clothing aid in Indian subcontinent. Charity shop.
☎ No telephone

***Barnabas Fund**, The Old Rectory, River Street, Pewsey SN9 5D
Director: Dr Patrick Sookhdeo. Executive staff 2, Other st 10. ***CC*** No.271602. Began 1993; interdenominational. Ma zine: *Barnabas* (13,000 quarterly). Turnover n/a. Providi financial assistance and prayer information to suffering Chr tians in the Muslim world.
Web: www.barnabasfund.org
Email: 101376.2103@compuserve.com
☎ 01672 564 938 🖷 01672 564 939

Breadline, 60 Green Lane, Purley CR8 3PJ
Director: Mr Michael Kirkwood. No paid staff. ***C*** No.1060661. Began 1995; interdenominational. Magazin *Breadline Update* (1,000 half-yearly). Turnover £40,000 year end Dec 98. Relieving poverty, development, evangelis in Eastern Europe, through local Christian partners.
Email: 101623.2255@compuserve.com
☎ 020 8668 2816 🖷 020 8668 2816

British Eastern Aid Doorways, 15 Willow Park, Minsterle Shrewsbury SY5 0EH
Secretary: Mr James A Baker. Executive Staff 3. ***C*** No.1064603. Began 1997; interdenominational. Magazin *Breadlines* (450 quarterly). Turnover £15,000 to year end De 98. Assisting local churches in the former Soviet Union to hel needy people in their areas.
Email: breadtrust@aol.com
☎ 01743 791 919 🖷 01743 792 625

***Care & Compassion**, 23 Glen Crescent, Darvel KA17 0BG
Secretary: Mrs Ann Da Silva. Executive staff 2, Other staff 22 ***CC*** No.SCO 18368. Began 1988; interdenominational. (Previously PAM Mission). Magazine: *Newsletter* (1,000 monthly) Turnover £50,000. Providing homes to care for street childre in Brazil and to bring them to Christ.
☎ 01560 323 206 🖷 01560 322 727

Catholic Fund for Overseas Development (CAFOD), Romero Close, Stockwell Road, London SW9 9TY
Director: Mr Julian Filochowski. Executive staff 8, Other staff 110. ***CC*** No.285776. Began 1962; Roman Catholic. Magazine: *CAFOD Magazine* (250,000 every four months). Turnover £14,000,000 to year end Dec 98. Official overseas development aid agency of Roman Catholic Church in England and Wales.
Web: www.cafod.org.uk
Email: hq@cafod.org.uk
☎ 020 7733 7900 🖷 020 7274 9630

Catholic Institute for International Relations, Unit 3, Canonbury Yard, 190a New North Road, London N1 7BJ
Executive Director: Dr Ian Linden. Executive staff 4, Other staff 43. ***CC*** No.294329. Began 1940; Roman Catholic. Magazine: *CIIR Newsletter* (Circulation n/a 4–5 times a year). Turnover £4,400,000 to year end Apr 98. Promoting justice and development in the Third World; sending skilled workers overseas; publishing, analysis, advocacy.
Web: www.ciir.org
Email: ciir@ciir.org
☎ 020 7354 0883 🖷 020 7359 0017

Children in Distress, Unit 2/1 Thirsk Industrial Estate, York Road, Thirsk YO7 3BX
Director: Rev Dr John W Walmsley. Executive staff 3, Other staff 4. ***CC*** No.1001327. Began 1990; interdenominational. Magazine: *Vision* (50,000 every four months). Turnover £750,000 to year end Sept 92. Providing hospice care for children in Eastern Europe.
Email: info@children-in-distress.org
☎ 01044 559 9300 🖷 01044 559 9950

hildren of Romania and Eastern Europe, 1 Western Terrace, Chiswick Mall, London W6 9TX
Trustee: Mrs Carolyn Green. All voluntary staff. *CC* No.1015557. Began 1991; interdenominational. No magazine. Providing food, medical aid, practical assistance; assisting Romanian projects working with local churches in outreach.
Email: carolyn@thefree.net
☎ 020 8746 3141

hildren's Aid Direct, 12 Portman Road, Reading RG30 1EA
Executive Director: Mr David Grubb. Executive staff 2, Other staff 80. *CC* No.803236. Began 1990; non-denominational. (Previously Feed the Children). No magazine. Turnover n/a. Improving the lives of children and carers who are affected by conflict, poverty and disaster.
Web: www.cad.org.uk
Email: enquiries%cad@notesgw.compuserve.com
☎ 0118 958 4000 🖷 0118 958 8988

hristian Aid, PO Box 100, London SE1 7RT
Director: Daleep Mukarji. Other staff 320. *CC* No.258003. Began 1945; interdenominational. Magazine: *Christian Aid News* (230,000 every four months). Turnover £37,928,000 to year end Mar 98. Operating in most Third World countries often through national councils of churches and their members.
Web: www.christian-aid.org.uk
Email: info@christian-aid.org
☎ 020 7620 4444 🖷 020 7620 0719

Christian Blind Mission, Winship Road, Milton, Cambridge CB4 6BQ
UK National Director: Dr William McAllister. *Administration Manager:* Mr Martin Carter. Executive staff 2, Other staff 4. *CC* No.1058162. Began 1996; ecumenical. Magazine: *Light* (Circulation n/a every two months). Turnover £1,062,498 to year end Dec 98. Showing Christ's love by preventing and curing blindness in the developing world.
Email: cbm@cbmuk.org.uk
☎ 01223 426 161 🖷 01223 425 455

The Christian Children's Fund of Great Britain, 4 Bath Place, Rivington Street, London EC2A 3DR
National Director: Mr Robert J H Edwards. *Director Fundraising:* Miss Louisa Phillips. *Director Finance and IT:* Mr Robert Namey. UK Executive staff 10, Other staff 17. *CC* No.287545. Began 1983; non-denominational. Magazine: *Childworld GB* (19,000 quarterly). Turnover £4,270,000 to year end June 98. Assisting needy children in developing countries and Eastern Europe, mainly through one-to-one sponsorship.
Web: www.ccfgb.org.uk
Email: gen@ccfgb.org.uk
☎ 020 7729 8191 🖷 020 7729 8339

Christian Community Ministries, 97 Runcorn Road, Barnton, Northwich CW8 4EX
Chairman & Overseas Mission Director: Mr Maxwell Keelty. Executive staff 1. *CC* No.1020071. Began 1992; interdenominational. Magazine: *Newsletter* (2,000 every two months). Turnover n/a. Providing aid to Eastern European children's home; facilitating Christians overseas to minister within their local community.
Web: homepages.tesco.net/~ccminternational
Email: maxkeelty.ccm@tesco.net
☎ 01606 782 244 🖷 01606 782 244

Christian Engineers in Development, The Byre, 15 Catrail Road, Galashiels TD1 1NW
Secretary: Mr Gareth Cozens. No UK full-time staff, Overseas staff 3. *CC* No.293734. Began 1985; interdenominational. Magazine: *CED Newsletter* (150 quarterly). Turnover £115,000 to year end Mar 98. Professional engineering services in partnership with churches and community groups in developing countries.
Email: ced@netcomuk.co.uk
☎ 01896 755 498 🖷 01896 757 891

***Church Relief International**, OCC Area Centre, 53 West Way, Oxford OX2 0JE
Director: Rev Stephen P Thomas. No full-time staff. *CC* No.1071600. Began 1986; Salt and Light Ministries. Magazine: *Update* (Circulation & frequency n/a). Turnover £52,000 to year end July 96. Relief projects in Third World; medical, educational, orphanages.
☎ 01865 793 239 🖷 01865 248 044

***CORD (Christian Outreach – Relief and Development)**, 1 New Street, Leamington Spa CV31 1HP
Director: Mr Martin Lee. *Personnel Officer:* Mrs Kay Bugg. Executive staff 2, Other UK staff 12. *CC* No.1070684. Began 1967; non-denominational. (Previously Christian Outreach). Magazine: *Compassion in Action* (6,000 every two months). Turnover £1,928,000 to year end Dec 97. Healthcare development work among refugees and destitute children in the developing world, especially in areas of conflict.
Web: ourworld.compuserve.com/homepager/cord_uk
Email: cord.uk@compuserve.com
☎ 01926 315 301 🖷 01926 885 786

Dentaid, The Old Bakery, Mount Road, Llanfair Caereinion, Welshpool SY21 0AT
Executive Director: Mr Peter Gardner. Executive staff 1, Other staff 2. *CC* No.1058519. Began 1996; evangelical. Magazine: *Dentaid Update* (2,500 monthly). Turnover £76,000 to year end Mar 98. Providing dental equipment to dentists in Third World and Eastern Europe. Placing volunteers overseas.
Web: www.derweb.ac.uk/dentaid
Email: info@dentaid.freeserve.co.uk
☎ 01938 811 017 🖷 01938 811 107

***Elam Ministries**, Grenville, Grenville Road, Shackleford, Godalming GU8 6AX
Executive Director: Rev Samuel Yeghnazar. Executive staff 14, Other staff 7. *CC* No.281457. Began 1988; non-denominational. Magazine: *Elam News* (Circulation n/a quarterly). Turnover n/a. Relieving poverty; advancing education; furtherance of the Christian faith.
Email: 101553.2044@compuserve.com
☎ 01483 427 778 🖷 01483 427 707

Eurovision Aid Ltd, Eden Lodge, St Crispins Hospital, Northampton NN4 5UN
President: Rev David Hathaway. Executive staff 4, Other UK staff 4. *CC* No.1013288. Began 1992; interdenominational. Aid division of Eurovision Mission to Europe. Magazine: *Prophetic Vision* (150,000 quarterly). Turnover n/a. Humanitarian Aid to Ukraine, Siberia and Eastern Europe.
Email: eurovisionaid@compuserve.com
☎ 01604 590 460 🖷 01604 590 466

Father Marek Sujkowski Children's Aid to Ukraine, Romania and Poland, 38 Gunton Road, London E5 9JS
Director: Rt Rev Fr Abbot Marek Sujkowski. Staff n/a. *CC* No.1031451. Began 1994; ecumenical. (Previously Children's Aid to Ukraine, Romania and Poland). No magazine. Turnover £1,887 to year end Dec 96. Preserving good health and relieving sickness and need amongst the children of the world.
☎ 0780 113 8117

***Food for the Hungry**, 44 Copperfield Road, Bassett, Southampton SO16 3NX
Executive Officer: Mr Doug Wakeling. *Chairman:* John Perowne. Executive staff 1, Other staff 1. *CC* No.328273. Began 1989; interdenominational. Magazine: *Food for the Hungy UK Newsletter* (300 half-yearly). Turnover £162,442 to year end Dec 97. Facilitating emergency relief and sustainable development, motivated by Christ's love.
Email: uk@fhi.net
☎ 023 8090 2327 🖷 023 8090 2327

O

Friends of Ibtida, The Vicarage, School Lane, Shurdington, Gloucester GL51 5TQ
Chair: Rev David Primrose. No full-time staff. Began 1987; ecumenical. No magazine. Turnover £250 to year end Dec 98. UK support for ministry amongst drug addicts in Diocese of Karachi, Pakistan.
Email: primrose@cableinet.co.uk
☎ 01242 862 241 Fax 01242 701 662

***Global Care**, Global Care House, 2 Dugdale Road, Coventry CV6 1PB
Chief Executive: Mr Ron Newby. Other staff 8. *CC* No.1054008. Began 1983; interdenominational. Magazine: *News-Update* (6,000 quarterly). Turnover £450,000 to year end Dec 98. Working internationally for needy children, through relief, development, education and childcare programmes.
Web: www.globalcare.org.uk
Email: hq@globalcare.org.uk
☎ 024 7660 1800 Fax 024 7660 1800

Hawkesley Christian Romania Trust, PO Box 2368, King's Norton, Birmingham B38 8RZ
Administrator: Miss Sylvia Fox. Other staff 1. *CC* No.1002326. Began 1990; ecumenical. Magazine: *Newsletter* (300 quarterly). Turnover £47,000 to year end Mar 98. Setting up and networking of health promotion and related projects; ecumenical centre for reconciliation.
Email: hcrt@charis.co.uk
☎ No telephone

Help International, Nettle Hill, Brinklow Road, Anstey, Coventry CV7 9JL
UK Co-ordinating Director: Mr George Jarvis. *Regional Representative:* Mr Bob Hamer. Executive staff 2, Other staff 3. *CC* No.327645. Began 1986; Covenant Ministries. Magazine: *Newsletter* (15,000 every two months). Turnover £300,000 to year end Dec 98. Assisting mission and providing relief and development in more impoverished countries worldwide.
Web: www.oneworld.org/helpinternational
Email: hlpinternational@dial.pipex.com
☎ 024 7661 1244 Fax 024 7660 2992

O

***Holy Ground Mission in Faith**, 1 Farrow Close, Dodworth, Barnsley SY5 3TE
Mission Directors: Jacqueline & Paul Ryalls. Executive staff 5, Other staff 13. *CC* No.327329. Began 1992; interdenominational. Turnover £50,000 to year end Dec 98. Furthering the Christian gospel; providing medical/hospice care; distributing humanitarian aid to poor in Bosnia.
☎ 01226 200 133 Mobile: 07970 387 184 Fax 01226 203 291

The HoverAid Trust, 101a High Street, Gosport PO12 1DS
Chairman: Mr Nigel Pool. Staff n/a. *CC* No.1005977. Began 1991; interdenominational. No magazine. Turnover £20,000 to year end Mar 99. Developing appropriate technology hovercraft for use by missions and relief agencies in developing countries.
Web: www.hoverlifeline.com
Email: ha@hoverlifeline.com
☎ 023 9251 0593 Fax 023 9250 2302

Incare, 16 Bridgford Road, West Bridgford, Nottingham NG2 6AF
Director: Rev John P Wildrianne. Other staff 1. Began 1984; Assemblies of God. No magazine. Turnover £70,000. International care, relief and social concern department of Assemblies of God.
☎ 0115 981 1188 Fax 0115 981 3377
National Care Co-ordinator: Mr Harry Wake, 31 Ryeburn Way, Wellingborough NN8 3AH
☎ 01933 229 598

India Ministries Fellowship, 14 McLuckie Drive, Kilwinni[ng] KA13 6DL
Chairman: Rev Malcolm Duff. No full-time staff. *CC* No.SC 19558. Began 1984; interdenominational. Magazine: *Prayer Newsletter* (250 quarterly). Turnover £20,000 to year end D[ec] 98. Working in partnership with Indian Christians to provi[de] care, education and training for destitute children.
Email: grahamdickson@compuserve.com
☎ 01294 551 565

International Care and Relief (ICR), 27 Church Road, Tunbrid[ge] Wells TN1 1HT
Chief Executive: Mr Adrian Hatch. Executive staff 1, Oth[er] staff 10. *CC* No.298316. Began 1978; interdenominationa[l]. (Previously International Christian Relief). Magazine: *IC[R] News* (13,000 quarterly). Turnover n/a. Encouraging Thir[d] World development through medical, agricultural and educa[-]tional projects.
Email: icr@centrenet.co.uk
☎ 01892 519 619 Fax 01892 529 029

International China Concern, 8 Badgers Green, Morpet[h] NE61 3RU
Chairman of Trustees: Mr Richard Hubbard. Admin staff 1. *CC* No.1068349. Began 1998; non-denominational. No mag[-]azine. Turnover £27,000 to year end Mar 98. Bringing hope t[o] Chinese orphanages through demonstrating the Gospel i[n] direct practical ways.
Email: rhubbard1@csi.com
☎ 01670 510 725 Fax 01661 868 488

International Christian Service for Africa, 10 Ederline Avenue, Norbury, London SW16 4RY
General Director: Mr Walter Pollyn. No full-time staff. *CC* No.801269. Began 1986; interdenominational. Magazine: *ICSA Newsletter* (150 quarterly). Turnover £460 to year end Sept 98. Helping Africans to make the best use of their resources through indigenous leadership.
☎ 020 8679 3238

International Fellowship for the Handicapped, 11 Coastguard Square, Eastbourne BN22 7EE
Secretary: Mr Martyn J Relf. No full-time staff. Began 1989; non-denominational. Turnover n/a. Encouraging evangelisation and integration of people with handicaps which cause them to be socially excluded; worldwide.
☎ 01323 638 744 Fax 01323 638 744
Administrator: Mrs Sylvia Cronin, 16 Beacon Hill, Bexhill-on-Sea TN39 5DF
☎ 01424 219 425 Fax 01424 219 425

Jubilee 2000 Coalition, PO Box 100, London SE1 7RT
Co-ordinator: Ms Ann Pettifor. Executive staff 8. *CC* No.1055675. Began 1996; non-denominational. Magazine: *Jubilee 2000 News & Action* (10,000 quarterly). Turnover n/a. Calling for cancellation of unpayable debt owed by world's poorest countries, by the year 2000.
Web: www.jubileee2000uk.org
Email: mail@jubilee2000uk.org
☎ 020 7401 9999 Fax 020 7401 3999

***Jubilee Action**, St Johns, Cranleigh Road, Wonersh, Guildford GU5 0QX
Director: Mr Danny Smith. Executive staff 2, Other staff 2. *CC* No.1013587. Began 1986; non-denominational. (Previously Jubilee Campaign). Magazine: *Newsletter* (12,500 quarterly). Turnover n/a. Action on children's rights issues, religious liberty and supporting long-term aid and awareness programmes.
Email: info@jubileecampaign.demon.co.uk
☎ 01483 894 787 Fax 01483 894 797

ingscare, The King's Centre, High Street, Aldershot GU11 1DJ
Director: Mr George Dowdell. *Chairman of Trustees:* Mr Derek Brown. Other staff 1. ***CC*** No.1072613. Began 1988; non-denominational. Turnover £165,900 to year end Dec 98. Showing the love of God in a practical and caring way in developing countries.
Web: ourworld.compuserve.com/homepages/kingscare
Email: kingscare@compuserve.com
☎ 01252 333 233 Fax 01252 310 814

IFE Centre of Croatia, No address
UK Hon Representative: Mr Antony Miles. No full-time staff. Began 1991; non-denominational. (Previously Croatian Appeal). No magazine. Turnover n/a. Co-ordinating aid via Christian workers for refugees in former Yugoslavia; volunteer programme.
Email: milesphoto@aol.com
☎ 01323 720 113

ink Romania, Link House, 59 Lyndhurst Road, Tarring, Worthing BN11 2DB
Director: Mr Mark Shipperlee. *Administrator:* Mrs Mandy Halloway. Executive staff 2, Other staff 5. ***CC*** No.1011065. Began 1990; interdenominational. Magazine: *Newslink* (4,000 quarterly). Turnover £1,000,000 to year end Apr 98. Providing aid to needy communities in Romania; agricultural and medical development, transport service; street children, charity development.
Web: www.wordnet.co.uk/linkro.html
Email: linkrom@linkrom.org
☎ 01903 529 333 Fax 01903 529 007

)avid Livingstone International, 9a Woodside Terrace, Glasgow G3 7UY
Executive Director: Mr Robert S Boyd. Executive staff 1, Other staff 2. ***CC*** No.53789. Began 1974; non-denominational. Magazine: *International Newsletter* (30,000 quarterly). Turnover n/a. Emergency food/medical shipments and operating orphanages, hospitals, schools.
Web: www.livingstone.com
Email: livingstone@compuserve.com
☎ 0141 332 9423 Fax 0141 331 1321

Love Russia, 28a Park Street, Bordon GU35 0EB
Director: Mr Alex Cooke. Admin staff 2. ***CC*** No.1024901. Began 1993; non-denominational. Magazine: *News Digest* (3,500 quarterly). Turnover £193,000 to year end June 98. Providing spiritual and humanitarian aid to orphans and others in need in Russia.
Email: love.russia@ukonline.co.uk
☎ 01420 477 668 Fax 01420 477 668

Medair UK, PO Box 25, Harpenden AL5 4BY
Directors: Mr Andrew Tanswell, Mr Warren Lancaster. Executive staff 4, Other staff 10. ***CC*** No.1056731. Began 1996; non-denominational. Magazine: *Mediar News* (2,500 every two months). Turnover £186,000 to year end Dec 97. Responding to communities facing humanitarian crisis by providing a Christian presence and qualified technical assistance.
Web: www.medair.org
Email: 106345.1370@compuserve.com
☎ 01582 765 532 Fax 01582 765 632

Methodist Relief and Development Fund, 1 Central Buildings, Westminster, London SW1H 9NH
Team Leader: Mr Martin Watson. *Development Education Officer:* Ms Caro Ayres. Other staff 3. ***CC*** No.291691. Began 1946; Methodist. Magazine: *Funds in Focus* (10,000 quarterly). Turnover £1,000,000 to year end Aug 98. Relief and development overseas through Methodist, ecumenical and secular channels; development education in UK.
Email: ayres@mrdf.demon.co.uk
☎ 020 7222 8010 Fax 020 7799 2153

***Mission to Eastern Europe**, 109 Albert Road, Widnes WA8 6LB
Mission Director: Mr John Rushworth. Admin staff 2, Other staff 6. ***CC*** No.1048423. Began 1990; interdenominational. No magazine. Turnover £25,000 to year end Dec 97. Providing aid and Christian literature to Romania; building work in churches, hospitals, orphanages.
Web: www.wolfsbane.demon.co.uk\romania
Email: john@mteeromania.swinternet.co.uk
☎ 0151 423 5782 Mobile: 08778 888 853

Mission Without Borders (UK) Ltd, Lakeside Pavilion, Chaucer Business Park, Kemsing, Sevenoaks TN15 6QY
National Director UK & Ireland: Mr E Colin Stewart. *UK Co-ordinator:* Mr Jon Stewart. Executive staff 5. ***CC*** No.270659. Began 1960; interdenominational. Incorporating Child Rescue International. Magazine: *Mission Without Borders* (8,500 monthly). Turnover £1,062,393 to year end Dec 97. Providing material and spiritual aid to Christians in Eastern Europe and China.
Web: www.mwbi.org
Email: mwb@zoo.co.uk
☎ 01732 765 200 Fax 01732 765 208

Nepal Leprosy Trust, 15 Duncan Road, Richmond TW9 2JD
General Administrator: Mr James Lowther. *Administrative Assistant:* Mr Ronald Roberts. Executive staff 2. ***CC*** Began 1972; interdenominational. Magazine: *NLT News* (700 quarterly). Turnover £220,000 to year end Dec 98. Income-generation, social welfare, and health care projects in Nepal.
Email: nlt@dial.pipex.com
☎ 020 8332 9023 Fax 020 8948 2703

Opportunity International UK, Freepost (OF1552), Oxford OX1 4YZ
Director: Mr Neil Cuthbert. *Head of Programmes:* Mr Robert John. *Marketing Manager:* Mr Dave Mann. Other staff 6. ***CC*** No.1008372. Began 1992; interdenominational. (Previously Opportunity Trust). No magazine. Turnover £1,300,000 to year end Dec 98. Business development and job creation through micro-credit to the poor in Africa, Asia, Latin America and Eastern Europe.
Web: www.opportunity.org.uk
Email: impact@opportunity.uk.org.uk
Email: impact@opportuk.demon.co.uk
☎ 01865 794 411 Fax 01865 295 161/791 343

Rom-Aid, 4 St Helier's Road, Cleethorpes DN35 7LQ
Chairman: Rev Frederick Grossmith. Executive staff 3, Other staff 12. Began 1991; interdenominational. Magazine: *Rom-Aid News* (3,000 every four months). Turnover £20,000 to year end Dec 96. Relief to Romania, working with Romanian Evangelical Alliance and Nazarene Compassionate Ministries.
☎ 01472 603 258 Fax 01472 697 526

Romania Concern, Barnes Close, Malthouse Lane, Chadwich, Bromsgrove B61 0RA
Contact: Rev John Johansen-Berg. Executive staff 2, Other staff 4. ***CC*** No.295113. Began 1984; ecumenical. Linked to Community for Reconciliation. No magazine. Turnover n/a. Ecumenical network providing aid for projects, courses on reconciliation, twinning and exchanges.
Web: ourworld.compuserve.com/homepages/communityforreconciliation
Email: johnjoberg@aol.com
☎ 01562 710 231 Fax 01562 710 278

***Samaritan's Purse International**, Victoria House, Victoria Road, Buckhurst Hill IG9 5EX
UK Director: Rev David Applin. No full-time staff. ***CC*** No.1001349. Began 1989; interdenominational. No magazine. Turnover n/a. Worldwide Christian service agency.
Email: 100067.1226@compuserve.com
☎ 020 8559 2044 Fax 020 8502 9062

O

Scottish Catholic International Aid Fund (SCIAF), 5 Oswald Street, Glasgow G1 4QR
Executive Director: Mr Paul Chitnis. *President:* Rt Rev John Mone. Other staff 17. ***CC*** No.SCO 12302. Began 1965; Roman Catholic. No magazine. Turnover £3,200,000 to year end Dec 98. Supporting relief and development projects in the Third World; development education in Scotland.
Email: sciaf@medc.org.uk
☎ 0141 221 4447 🖷 0141 221 2373

Send A Cow, Unit 4, Priston Mill, Priston, Bath BA2 9EQ
UK Operations Manager: Mrs Ann Hallett. *UK Coordinator:* Mr Kevin Gullick. Executive staff 1, Other staff 1. ***CC*** No.299717. Began 1988; non-denominational. Magazine: *Lifeline* (5,000 quarterly). Turnover £206,000 to year end Mar 97. Operating self help programmes for needy families in East Africa in eliminating malnutrition and poverty.
Web: web.ukonline.co.uk/members/send.a.cow/
Email: send.a.cow@ukonline.co.uk
☎ 01225 447 041 🖷 01225 317 627

***Servants to Asia's Urban Poor**, 34 Downend Park Road, Downend, Bristol BS16 5SZ
UK Co-ordinator: Mrs Helen Sidebotham. No full-time staff. ***CC*** No.1031973. Began 1992; interdenominational. Magazine: *Servants UK Newsletter* (170 quarterly). Turnover £9,500 to year end Dec 98. Working with local churches in evangelism and community development in Asia's urban slums.
Web: www.zeta.org.au/~servants/
Email: info@servants.u-net.com
☎ 0117 957 2471

†SPICMA Church Supplies, Bluecoats, 127 Fore Street, Hertford SG14 1AX
Director: Mr Patrick J Phelan. Executive staff 1, No other paid staff. ***CC*** No.270794. Began 1987; ecumenical. No magazine. Turnover £280,000 to year end July 94. Providing development and medical aid to Uganda, India, Romania, Tanzania.
☎ 01992 303 452 🖷 01992 303 452

Streams in the Desert, Hamble Lodge, 20 Hamble Lane, Burlesdon, Southampton SO31 8BR
Coordinator: Miss Helen J Mears. All voluntary staff. ***CC*** No.1043034. Began 1994; non-denominational. Magazine: *Streams Update* (Circulation n/a quarterly). Turnover n/a. Providing housing for elderly new immigrants in Israel; teaching Biblical basis of work.
☎ 023 8040 6385 🖷 023 8040 6385

***Teachers for China**, The Longcroft, Storeton Lane, Barnston, Heswall, Wirral CH61 1BU
Director: Mr Cyril Thomas. Executive staff 2, Admin staff 7. ***CC*** No.1007284. Began 1991; non-denominational. Incorporating Caring for China's Children. No magazine. Turnover £91,000 to year end Oct 98. Placing and supporting Christians teaching English in Chinese colleges and running several model childcare centres.
Email: lynda@leelyn.freeserve.co.uk
☎ 0151 648 2042 🖷 0151 648 0157

Teso Development Trust, 18 Duke Street, Wednesfie[ld,] Wolverhampton WV11 1TH
Administrative Secretary: Mr Roger Stevens. Executive staff ***CC*** No.1005139. Began 1989; non-denominational. Mag[a]zine: *Teso Newsletter* (500 half-yearly). Turnover £45,000 year end Mar 98. Assisting with rehabilitation and develo[p]ment in Teso in Uganda cooperating with church and oth[er] organisations.
Email: rogandmarg@aol.com
☎ 01902 733 501 🖷 01902 739 500

UNAFRAID (United Africa Aid), Barnes Close, Malthouse Lan[e,] Chadwich, Bromsgrove B61 0RA
Contact: Rev John Johansen-Berg. No other UK staff. ***C[C]*** No.295113. Began 1984; ecumenical. Linked to Communi[ty] for Reconciliation. Turnover n/a. Conflict resolution an[d] peacebuilding courses (biblical and practical) mainly E Afric[a;] project support; partnership with African organisations.
Web: ourworld.compuserve.com/homepages/communityforreconciliatio[n]
Email: johnjoberg@aol.com
☎ 01562 710 231 🖷 01562 710 278

***World Emergency Relief**, The Barley Mow Centre, 10 Barley Mo[w] Passage, Chiswick, London W4 4PH
Director of Operations: Miss Estelle Fleming. *Chief Executiv[e] Officer:* Rev Joel MacCollam. Executive staff 2, Admin statt 2 ***CC*** No.1045672. Began 1994; interdenominational. No magazine. Turnover £4,914,880 to year end Mar 98. Linking wit[h] local charities, churches overseas to identify relief needs an[d] deliver aid cost effectively.
Web: www.wer-uk.org
Email: 100700.1554@compuserve.com
☎ 020 8994 6477 🖷 020 8742 3405

***World Vision UK**, World Vision House, 599 Avebury Boulevard Milton Keynes MK9 3PG
Executive Director: Mr Charles Clayton. *Church Relations Manager:* Mr Peter Scott. *Human Resources Director:* Mrs Jennifer York. Executive staff 5, Other staff 77. ***CC*** No.285908. Began 1979; interdenominational. Magazine: *World Vision Magazine* (75,000 every four months). Turnover £17,862,000 to year end Sept 98. Serving the poor and needy in over 40 countries.
Web: www.worldvision.org.uk
Email: united_kingdom@wvi.org
☎ 01908 841 002 🖷 01908 841 001

SERVICES

ADDICTIONS & REHABILITATION CENTRES

See also Residential Homes for Disadvantaged People on Page 104,
Social Service & Welfare Organisations on Page 463.

***Adullam Homes Housing Association**, Gordana House, The Mount, Shelton, Shrewsbury SY3 8BH
Senior Drugs Adviser: Trevor Baker. Other staff 5. ***CC*** No.326743. Began 1970; interdenominational. (The Mount Project). Magazine: *Lifebuilder* (4,000 half-yearly). Turnover £200,000 to year end Apr 94. Drug and alcohol dependency treatment centre for 28 people.
☎ 01743 365 050 🖷 01743 365 070

***The Arbour**, 16 The Chase, Clapham, London SW4 0NH
Chief Operating Officer: Mr Wendell Smith. Executive staff 2, Other staff 6. Began 1991; non-denominational. No magazine. Turnover £100,000 to year end Dec 98. Residential rehabilitation for drug/alcohol addictions and other life controlling problems through Christian discipleship programme.
Email: thearbour@aol.com
☎ 020 7498 2423 🖷 020 7498 2423

***Beechwood House**, 69 Old Perth Road, Inverness IV1 3JH
Unit Manager: Ms Lorna Gunn. Admin staff 1, Other staff 19. ***CC*** No.SCO 24366. Began 1991; Church of Scotland. No magazine. Turnover n/a. Residential accommodation: 15 rehabilitation beds, 4 support beds, 4 designated places.
☎ 01463 711355 🖷 01463 711 544

***BETEL of Britain**, Windmill House, Weatheroak Hill, Alvechurch, Birmingham B48 7EA
Directors: Kent and Mary Alice Martin. ***CC*** No.1047909. Began 1945; interdenominational. (Previously Windmill House (Birmingham Association of Youth Clubs)). A ministry of WEC International. No magazine. Turnover n/a. Free Christian residence, helping restore the lives of alcoholics, drug addicts, the homeless and desperately needy (30 places).
Email: info@betel.charis.co.uk
☎ 01564 822 356 🖷 01564 824 929

Castle Craig Clinic, Castle Craig, Blyth Bridge, West Linton EH46 7DH
Medical Director: Dr Margaret McCann. Executive staff 4, Other staff 26. Began 1988; non-denominational. No magazine. Turnover £2,000,000 to year end Sept 98. Residential treatment for alcoholism and other addictions; detoxification and emergency care; specialist medical supervision. 77 beds.
☎ 01721 752 625 🖷 01721 752 662

Coke Hole Bridge, Town Mills House, 20a Bridge Street, Andover SP10 1BL
Administrive Office: Mrs Laura Ivey. Executive staff 4, Other staff 18. ***CC*** No.1042688. Began 1987; non-denominational. (Previously Clouds House (Life Anew Trust), Coke Hole Trust). No magazine. Turnover £300,000 to year end Mar 98. Residential treatment programmes for men and women with substance misuse problems. 14 men's beds, 16 women & children in residential treatment centre.
☎ 01264 361 745

***Crisis Centre Ministries**, 12 City Road, St Pauls, Bristol BS2 8TP
Director: Rev Derek W Groves. Executive staff 3, Other staff 15. ***CC*** No.298528. Began 1986; non-denominational. No magazine. Turnover £109,000 to year end Jan 98. Serving young people with life-controlling problems: addictions, homelessness, unemployment.
Web: www.crisis-centre.org.uk
Email: dgroves106@aol.com
☎ 0117 942 3088 Mobile: 07887 521 233 🖷 0117 924 0799

***Deeford Centre**, 59 Riverside Drive, Aberdeen AB10 7LE
Unit Manager: Mr Thomas H G Fraser. Other staff 7. ***C***
No.SCO 24366. Began 1978; Church of Scotland. Magazin
Circle of Care (Circulation n/a quarterly). Turnover n/a. Res
dential centre for adults over 20 with alcohol and/or dru
addiction.
☎ 01224 585 453

***Evangelical Coalition on Drugs (ECOD)**, Whitefield House, 18
Kennington Park Road, London SE11 4BT
Chairman: Ruth Valerio. No full-time staff. ***CC*** No.21232
Began 1987; interdenominational. An Evangelical Allianc
Network. No magazine. Turnover: finance included with Evan
gelical Alliance. Network providing support, advice, informa
tion exchange in the field of drug and alcohol misuse.
Email: rvalerio@eauk.org
☎ 020 7207 2100 🖷 020 7207 2150

Fewster House Alcoholism Rehabilitation Unit, 10 Terrace Road
Greenock PA15 1DJ
Officers-in-Charge: Captains Dean & Alison Logan. Executiv
staff 3. ***CC*** Began n/a; Salvation Army. No magazine. Turnove
n/a. Care for 4 men.
☎ 01475 721 572

Gloucester House, 6 High Street, Highworth, Swindon SN6 7AG
Unit Manager: Mr David Read. Executive staff 1, Other staff 9
CC Began 1959; Salvation Army. No magazine. Turnover n/a
Unregistered residential rehabilitation centre for 9 men and
women. Mainly alcohol. Also day programme.
☎ 01793 762 365
Halfway House: Accommodation for 3 men, 214 Windrush
Highworth, Swindon SN6 6HX

***Greig House**, 20 Garford Street, West India Dock Road, London
E14 8JG
Officer-in-Charge: To be appointed. Admin staff 5, Other staff 7. ***CC*** No.215174. Began 1959; Salvation Army. No magazine. Turnover n/a. Residential alcohol detoxification unit for 13 men and women.
☎ 020 7987 5658 🖷 020 7536 1601

***The Hebron Trust**, Hebron House, 12 Stanley Avenue, Norwich NR7 0BE
Director: Andrew Bevan. *Administrator:* Ms Philippa Morris. Executive staff 1, Other staff 8. ***CC*** No.1020095. Began 1993; interdenominational. No magazine. Turnover £265,000 to year end Mar 98. Residential treatment and care for women with serious drug or alcohol problems and their children.
☎ 01603 439 905 🖷 01603 700 799

Helping Hand, 45 Rossall Road, Ansdell, Lytham St Annes FY8 4ES
Director: Mr Dave Linington. Executive staff 1, Other staff 2. ***CC*** Began 1997; interdenominational. No magazine. Turnover £13,800 to year end Mar 98. Meeting the physical, psychological, spiritual and social needs of those addicted to drugs or alcohol.
Email: 101457.2223@compuserve.com
☎ 01253 733 955 Mobile: 07956 846 905
🖷 01253 735 796

ope House Project, Stoneham Housing Association, 36 Moor Street, Luton LU1 1HA
Project Leader: Mr Paddy Bannon. Executive staff 1, Full-time staff 2, Part-time staff 2. *CC* Began 1979; non-denominational. No magazine. Turnover n/a. For 14 men and women with substance abuse problems.
☎ 01582 722 673 🖷 01582 488 240

en Manor, Cranbrook Road, Staplehurst, Tonbridge TN12 0ER
Director: Sr Rosemary Kean. Executive staff 3, Other staff 40. *CC* No.234880. Began 1934; Roman Catholic, but open to all. (Administered by the Good Shepherd Sisters). No magazine. Turnover n/a. Registered Nursing Home and Primary Treatment Centre for 27 women suffering from addictions.
☎ 01580 891 261 🖷 01580 893 323

aleidoscope Project, 40 Cromwell Road, Kingston upon Thames KT2 6RE
Director: Rev Martin Blakebrough. Executive staff 4, Other staff 30. *CC* Began 1968; Baptist. Magazine: *The Scope* (Circulation & frequency n/a). Turnover £814,000 to year end Dec 98. Counselling, accommodation, medical and specialist drug help, educational/social facilities for young people in need.
☎ 020 8549 2681 🖷 020 8547 0228

enward Trust, Kenward House, Yalding, Maidstone ME18 6AH
Director: Mr Godfrey Featherstone. *Deputy Director:* Mrs Jean Park. *Administrator:* Mr Peter Brook. Executive staff 6, Other staff 30. *CC* No.265394. Began 1968; interdenominational. Magazine: *Prayer Letter* (500 quarterly). Turnover £764,000 to year end Mar 98. Communities for the care of men and women with alcohol and other drug problems.
☎ 01622 814 187 🖷 01622 815 805

The Kestrel Trust, PO Box 2742, Reading RG4 6FN
Chairman of Trustees: Mr Benedict Hawkins. No full-time staff. *CC* No.1014426. Began 1986; non-denominational. Magazine: *Free Indeed* (1,500 half-yearly). Turnover £6,566 to year end 97. Supporting Christian people recovering or recovered from dependence on drugs and/or alcohol.
☎ 0118 947 8353

The Langley House Trust, PO Box 181, Witney OX8 6WD
Chief Executive: Mr John Adams. *Promotions Officer:* Mr Paul Langley. Executive staff 8, Other staff 90. *CC* No.290059. Began 1958; interdenominational. Magazine: *Newsletter* (3,500 every four months). Turnover £2,338,858 to year end Mar 98. Providing residential care and rehabilitation for ex-offenders in a Christian environment: 20 projects.
Email: langley_house@cin.co.uk
☎ 01993 774 075 🖷 01993 772 425

***Life For The World Trust**, Wakefield Building, Gomm Road, High Wycombe HP13 7DJ
General Director: Mr Patrick D Prosser. Executive staff 5, Other staff 12. *CC* No.1038410. Began 1967; non-denominational. Magazine: *Release* (2,000 quarterly). Turnover £233,800 to year end May 98. Rehabilitating drug/alcohol misusers; equipping the church in drug issues; operating in UK, Poland and Ukraine.
Web: www.doveuk.com/lfw
Email: lfw@cwcom.net
☎ 01494 462 008 🖷 01494 446 268
Also at: *Manager:* Miss Maggie Heddon, Caleb House, 21 Victoria Road, Clevedon BS21 7RU
☎ 01275 341 112 🖷 01275 341 112

***Lydia House Trust**, 29 West Cliff, Preston PR1 8HX
House Leaders: Mr Stu & Mrs Anne Beaumont. *CC* Began 1990; interdenominational. Part of Mission Vision. No magazine. Turnover n/a.
☎ 01772 884 458

***Malta House**, 1 Malta Terrace, Edinburgh EH4 1HR
Unit Manager: Mr Stan Smith. Admin staff 1. Other staff 11. *CC* No.SCO 24366. Began n/a; Church of Scotland. No magazine. Turnover n/a. Seven-month rehabilitation programme for those with alcohol or drug dependency.
☎ 0131 332 3217 🖷 0131 315 2313

***The Matthew Project**, 24 Pottergate, Norwich NR2 1DX
Director: Mr Peter Farley. *Assistant Director – Operations:* Mr Andrew Gathercole. Executive staff 1, Other staff 9. *CC* No.285256. Began 1982; non-denominational. Magazine: *Report* (600 annually). Turnover £190,000 to year end Mar 99. Counselling, advice, information and support for drug-users, their families or friends. Education and prevention.
Web: www.gurney.co.uk/watton/social/matthew
Email: thematthewproject@btinternet.com
☎ 01603 626 123 / 01603 764 754 (24hr helpline)

Newmills Christian Centre, Burnthill, Lochwinnoch PA12 4JR
Director: Mr David Leishman. Executive staff 3, Other staff 2. *CC* Began 1986; Baptist. No magazine. Turnover £75,000 to year end June 98. Working with alcoholics in Scotland and providing residential care for 12 people.
☎ 01505 842 527

Peniel Christian Centre, Halterburn, Kirk Yetholm, Kelso TD5 8PP
Centre Leaders: Mr Brian & Mrs Iris Wilkinson. Executive staff 1, Other staff 2. *CC* No.SCO 26038. Began 1969; interdenominational. No magazine. Turnover n/a. Providing residential rehabilitation for 13 people.
☎ 01573 420 639

***Rainbow House**, 1 Belhaven Terrace, Glasgow G12 0TF
Unit Manager: Miss Nancy H Geddes. Other staff 8. *CC* No.SCO 24366. Began n/a; Church of Scotland. No magazine. Turnover n/a. Providing residential drug rehabilitation for 14 people.
☎ 0141 339 2691

***Rankeillor Project**, 11 Rankeillor Street, Edinburgh EH8 9JA
Unit Manager: Mr David Flett. Admin staff 1, Other staff 3. *CC* No.SCO 24366. Began n/a; Church of Scotland. No magazine. Turnover n/a. Supported accommodation and home support service for adults with addiction problems.
☎ 0131 662 0322

Remar Association UK, PO Box 82, Sheffield S1 2XT
Director and Trustee: Mr Victor Coutinho. All voluntary staff 30. *CC* No.1010448. Began 1992; non-denominational. Magazine: *Newsletter* (Circulation n/a quarterly). Turnover £50,000 to year end Mar 98. Rehabilitating drug addicts, alcoholics and people on the margin of society.
Web: www.remar.org www.tverbo.org
Email: remar-uk@infotrade.co.uk &
Email: D2273789@infotrade.co.uk
☎ 0114 273 0443 🖷 0114 273 0443

Rhoserchan, Capel Seion, Aberystwyth SY23 4ED
Manager: Mrs Virginia Lowe. Executive staff 3, Counsellors 5. *CC* No.1015750. Began 1984; non-denominational. No magazine. Turnover £210,756 to year end Mar 98. Providing residential rehabilitation for people with an addictive illness.
☎ 01970 611 127 🖷 01970 625 447

***Ronachan House**, Clachan, Tarbert PA29 6XW
Unit manager: Ms Cathie Cairns. Other staff 8. ***CC*** No.SCO 24366. Began n/a; Church of Scotland. No magazine. Turnover n/a. Providing residential alcohol and drug rehabilitation for 20 people.
☎ 01880 740 252

St Joseph's Centre for Addiction, Holy Cross Hospital, Hindhead Road, Haslemere GU27 1NQ
Director: Mrs Lindi Kornblum. Executive staff 14. ***CC*** No.1068661. Began 1986; Roman Catholic. No magazine. Turnover £250,000 to year end Mar 92. Providing residential drug and alcohol detoxification rehabilitation for 14 people.
Web: www.holycross.org.uk
Email: sjc@holycross.org.uk
☎ 01428 656 517

St Thomas Fund for the Homeless, 9 Churchill Court, The Street, Rustington, Littlehampton BN16 3DJ
Project Manager: Janice Horsman. *Co-ordinating Secretary:* David Royce. Other staff 10. ***CC*** No.1057037. Began 1981; ecumenical. Turnover £300,000 to year end Mar 98. Providing accommodation, care and building self esteem, to 14 homeless alcohol or drug dependant people.
☎ 01903 859 400 Fax 01903 850 448

***Spitalfields Crypt Trust**, 22a Hanbury Street, London E1 6QR
Director: Mr Graham P Marshall. Executive staff 1, Other staff 10. ***CC*** No.247252. Began 1965; Anglican. Magazine: *Crypt Newsletter* (1,100 half-yearly). Turnover £250,000 to year end Apr 96. Rehabilitating homeless alcoholics and contact point for homeless people; operating 4 charity shops.
☎ 020 7247 7766

Sunnybrae Christian Trust, Sunnybrae Christian Centre, Woodhead, Fyvie, Turriff AB53 8LS
Manager: Mr Norman A Ogston. *Chairman of Management Committee:* John S Strachan. Executive staff 4. ***CC*** No.SCO 04829. Began 1982; interdenominational. No magazine. Turnover £150,000 to year end May 98. Rehabilitation of men with alcohol dependency, offering hope of renewal for whole person, mental, physical, spiritual.
Email: keithhepbuan@msn.com
☎ 01651 891 627

†***Teen Challenge UK**, 52 Penygroes Road, Gorslas, Llane SA14 7LA
National Director: Rev John E J Macey. Executive staff Other staff 24. ***CC*** Began 1958; non-denominational. No ma azine. Turnover n/a. Evangelism outreach on streets, schools, churches; 19 residential centres for people with addi tion problems.
☎ 01269 842 718 Fax 01269 845 313

Tower Hamlets Mission, 31 Mile End Road, London E1 4TP
Director: Mr Andrew Bannell. Executive staff 2, Other staff 1 ***CC*** No.259534/259535. Began 1870; non-denominationa (The F N Charrington Tower Hamlets Mission). Magazin *The Record* (500 every four months). Turnover £322,339 t year end Mar 98. Residential alcohol/drug therapy unit fc homeless men (Charis), final stage rehabilitation project (Th Terrace).
Email: charis@thmission.force9.co.uk
☎ 020 7790 3040

***Victoria View**, 21 Westlands Drive, Glasgow G14 9NY
Unit Manager: Ms Jacqui Bicknell. Full-time staff 7. ***C*** No.SCO 24366. Began n/a; Church of Scotland. No magazine Turnover n/a. Alcohol and drug rehabilitation centre; 1 places.
☎ 0141 959 1679

†**The White Ribbon Association Inc**, Rosalind Carlisle House 23 Dawson Place, London W2 4TH
General Secretary: Mrs C Scroggie. All voluntary staff. ***CC*** Began 1876; interdenominational. Magazine: *The White Ribbon* (1,000 quarterly). Turnover n/a. All women's grou campaigning for total abstinence.
☎ 020 7229 0804

Willowdene Farm Drug Rehabilitation Centre, Willowdene Farm Chorley, Bridgnorth WV16 6PP
Director: Mr John Home. Executive staff 2, Other staff 3 Began 1988; interdenominational. No magazine. Turnove £250,000 to year end Dec 98. Providing drug rehabilitation fo 13 men.
☎ 01746 718 658 Fax 01746 718 658

***Yeldall Christian Centres**, Yeldall Manor, Hare Hatch, Reading RG10 9XR
Director, Yeldall Manor: Mr Ken Wiltshire. *Director, Yeldal Homeless Projects:* Rev Graham Duncan. Executive staff 2, Other staff 27. ***CC*** No.1000038. Began 1977; non-denominational. Magazine: *Newsletter* (3,750 every four months). Turnover £688,954 to year end Mar 98. Drug/alcohol rehabilitation through Christian discipleship; training for churches; single homeless projects; back-to-work project.
Email: ycc@patrol.i-way.co.uk
☎ 0118 940 1093 Fax 0118 940 4852

S

ANIMAL WELFARE AGENCIES

Anglican Society for the Welfare of Animals, Old Toll Gate, Hound Green, Hook RG27 8LQ
Organising Secretary: Mrs Samantha Chandler. No full-time staff. Began 1972; Anglican. Magazine: *The Bulletin* (600 half-yearly). Turnover n/a. Prayer, study and action on behalf of animals.
☎ 0118 932 6586

Animal Christian Concern, PO Box 70, Horsforth, Leeds LS18 5UX
Co-ordinator: Mrs May Tripp. All voluntary staff. Began 1985; non-denominational. Magazine: *ACC News* (650 half-yearly). Turnover £3,000 to year end Feb 92. Recognising Christ Jesus as Lord of all creation; seeking justice for all His creatures.
☎ 0113 258 3517

The Catholic Study Circle for Animal Welfare, 39 Onslow Gardens, South Woodford, London E18 1ND
Development Officer: Miss Deborah Jones. Executive staff 1, All other staff voluntary. ***CC*** No.231022. Began 1929; interdenominational. Magazine: *The Ark* (2,500 every four months). Turnover £10,000 to year end May 98. Promoting better treatment of all animals through prayer, propaganda and example.
☎ 020 8989 0478 Fax 020 8989 0478

Christian Animal Rights Education (CARE), PO Box 407, Sheffield S1 1ED
Organiser: Mr White. Executive staff 1. Began 1987; non-denominational. No magazine. Turnover £80 to year end Dec 98. Campaigning against vivisection, factory farming and all cruelty, through prayer, videos, books, demonstrations.
☎ No telephone

Fellowship of Life, 43 Braichmelyn, Bethesda, Bangor LL57 3RD
Hon Secretary: Mrs Claire Harral. No full-time staff. Began 1973; ecumenical. Magazine: *Newsletter* (800 annually). Turnover £450 to year end Jan 99. Establishing cruelty-free, green living as a Christian way of life, through the publication of literature.
☎ No telephone

Quaker Concern for Animals, 10 Whitefield Court, Mayland Green, Mayland, Chelmsford CM3 6BN
Hon Secretary: Sylvia Izzard. No full-time staff. Began 1891; Religious Society of Friends. Magazine: *Newsletter* (600 half-yearly). Turnover £4,000 to year end Dec 92. Encouraging the ideal of living without cruelty.
☎ No telephone

BENEVOLENT ORGANISATIONS

Additional Curates Society, Gordon Browning House, 8 Spitfire Road, Birmingham B24 9PB
Secretary: Rev Stephen Leach. Executive staff 1, Other staff 3. *CC* No.209448. Began 1837; Anglican. Magazine: *Good News* (13,000 half-yearly). Turnover n/a. Giving grants to parishes to help pay costs of curates and encouraging vocations.
☎ 0121 382 5533 🖷 0121 382 6999

All Saints' Educational Trust, St Katharine Cree Church, 86 Leadenhall Street, London EC3A 3DH
Secretary: Mr Alfred W Bush. No full-time staff. *CC* Began 1979; Anglican. No magazine. Turnover £600,000 to year end July 98. Supporting teachers/intending teachers/dietitians to obtain/further their qualifications; corporate awards for educational projects. ?
☎ 020 7283 4485 🖷 020 7283 2929

Frances Ashton's Charity, Charities Aid Foundation, Kings Hill, West Malling ME19 4TA
Receiver: Mrs Barbara Davis. Executive staff 2. *CC* No.200162. Began 1747; Anglican. No magazine. Turnover £55,000 to year end Dec 98. Giving annual grants to Church of England clergy and widows in need.
☎ 01732 520 081

The Auxiliary Fund of the Methodist Church, 1 Central Buildings, Westminster, London SW1H 9NH
Secretary: Mrs Jane Thomas. *Treasurer:* Mr Philip Bedford-Smith. No full-time staff. Began n/a; Methodist. No magazine. Turnover £600,000 to year end Aug 98. Giving grants to retired Methodist ministers and their widows/ widowers.
☎ 020 7222 8010 🖷 020 7930 5355

Gordon Barclay Vietnam Fund, 77 Maze Hill, Greenwich, London SE10 8XQ
Hon Secretary: Dr Gordon Barclay. No full-time staff. *CC* No.261702. Began 1968; Religious Society of Friends. No magazine. Turnover £5,000 to year end Dec 98. Fund for South East Asians especially children deaf or blind and medical/ educational care.
Email: barcviet@aol.com
☎ 020 8858 4968 🖷 020 8333 5183

Mrs Becker's Charity for Clergy, 71 Eastfield Avenue, Weston, Bath BA1 4HH
Secretary: Mr A P Newman. No full-time staff. *CC* No.230673. Began 1855; Anglican. (Previously Mrs Becker's Bounty). No magazine. Turnover £4,152 to year end Dec 96. Giving grants to clergy retired from the ministry either through sickness or age.
☎ 01225 424 229

Catenian Association, 8 Chesham Place, London SW1X 8HP
Grand Secretary: Mr Terence McManus. Executive staff 1, Other staff 4. *CC* Began 1908; Roman Catholic. Magazine: *Catena* (11,500 monthly). Turnover n/a. Social and benevolent association for professional people and businessmen.
Email: catena@dial.pipex.com
☎ 020 7235 6671 🖷 020 7235 9344 (?)

Catholic Clothing Guild, Orchard House, High Street Green, Sible Hedingham, Halstead CO9 3LG
Hon Secretary: Mrs F Ripper. All voluntary staff. *CC* No.277952. Began 1886; Roman Catholic but ecumenical. n/a. Magazine: *CNG Annual Report* (500 annually). Supplying new, useful and warm clothing to those in real need.
☎ 01787 460 234

Catholic Council for Polish Welfare, 240 King Street, London W6 0RF
Hon Secretary: Mr Olgierd M Stepan KCSG. All voluntary staff. *CC* Began 1942; Roman Catholic but ecumenical. No magazine. Turnover £5,500 to year end June 98. Assisting people of Polish origin not covered by other welfare bodies.
☎ 020 8992 3328

Christian Workers Relief Fund, Silver Birch Barn, Leamington Hall Farm, Fosse Way, Chesterton, Leamington Spa CV33 9JP
Treasurer: Mr John McEwen. No full-time staff. *CC* No.234676. Began 1961; Christian Brethren. (Previously Home Workers Fund). No magazine. Turnover £8,800 to year end Dec 98. Providing support for retired, infirm and needy evangelists and Bible teachers from the Christian Brethren.
Email: john.mcewen@lineone.net
☎ 01926 339 328

Church and Community Trust, Napier Hall, Hide Place, Westminster, London SW1P 4NJ
Co-ordinator: Mrs Pam Nicholls. Executive staff 1. *CC* No.269319. Began 1975; interdenominational. Magazine: *Living Stones* (5,000 Annually). Turnover £98,000 to year end Apr 98. Advising churches in total stewardship of buildings and resources for effective outreach and community caring.
☎ 020 7976 6347 🖷 020 7976 6347

Church Commissioners, 1 Millbank, London SW1P 3JZ
First Church Estates Commissioner: Sir Michael Colman Bt. *Secretary:* Mr Howell Harris Hughes. Full-time staff 257. *CC* Began 1948; Anglican. No magazine. Turnover £135,300,000 to year end Dec 97. Principally management of funds to provide for pay, pensions and housing of clergy of the Church of England.
☎ 020 7898 1000 🖷 020 7898 1131

Church Housing Trust, Sutherland House, 70 West Hendon Broadway, London NW9 7BT
Chief Executive: Jan Bunstead. *Trust Manager:* Sally Isaacs. Staff 6. *CC* No.802801. Began 1984; Anglican. Magazine: *Newsletter* (15,000 half-yearly). Turnover £500,000 to year end Mar 98. Charitable support for people in housing need through English Churches Housing group.
Web: www.charitynet.org/~cht
Email: cht@dial.pipex.com [X]
☎ 020 8202 3458 🖷 020 8202 1440

S

Church Schoolmasters' and Schoolmistresses' Benevolent Institution, Glen Arun, 9 Athelstan Way, Horsham RH13 6HA
Administrator: Mr D J F Godfrey. Executive staff 1, Other staff 1. ***CC*** No.207236. Began 1857; Anglican. No magazine. Turnover n/a. Nursing and residential accommodation; grants for retired Anglican teachers, widows, orphans and dependents.
☎ 01403 253 881

Church Urban Fund, 2 Great Peter Street, London SW1P 3LX
Chief Executive: Ms Angela Sarkis. *Grants Manager:* Mrs Mandy J Ala. *Director of Fund-raising:* Mr Stuart Willson. Executive staff 5, Other staff 11. ***CC*** No.297483. Began 1987; Anglican. Magazine: *City Lights* (23,000 every four months). Turnover £3,700,000 to year end Dec 98. Furthering urban regeneration in England's inner cities and outer estates, channeling resources to locally organised projects.
Web: www.cuf.org.uk
☎ 020 7898 1000 🖷 020 7898 1601

Corporation of the Sons of the Clergy, 1 Dean Trench Street, Westminster, London SW1P 3HB
Registrar: Mr R C F Leach. Executive staff 2, Other staff 6. ***CC*** Began 1655; Anglican. Magazine: *Annual Report* (1,500 annually). Turnover £1,700,000 to year end Dec 94. Assisting Anglican clergy, their widows and dependent children who are in need.
☎ 020 7222 5887/7799 3696 🖷 020 7233 1913

The Ecumenical Preceptory of the Holy Trinity, 151 Gloucester Place, London NW1 6DX
Trustee: Dr F M S Muller. Other staff 1. ***CC*** No.801437. Began 1989; ecumenical. No magazine. Turnover £10,000 to year end Sept 98. Providing and maintaining, by endowments, ecumenical churches and chapels, libraries and educational facilities.
☎ 020 7706 2812

Edith M Ellis 1985 Charitable Trust, 41 Vine Street, London EC3N 2AA
Trustee: Samantha McCoy. No full-time staff. ***CC*** Began 1953; Religious Society of Friends. No magazine. Turnover £39,930 to year end Apr 92. Financial assistance to religious, social and international work (not for individual study).
☎ 020 7481 4841 🖷 020 7488 0084

The Epiphany Trust, 13 Winwick Lane, Lowton, Warrington WA3 1LR
Director: Mr Bill Hampson. Executive staff 3. ***CC*** No.1006653. Began 1990; interdenominational. (Previously Movement for Christian Democracy Trust). No magazine. Turnover £80,000 to year end June 98. Education, specifically political; relief and aid work for children in Eastern Europe and Asia.
Email: epiphany@pamh.globalnet.co.uk
☎ 01942 671 581 🖷 01942 261 249

Friends of Friendless Churches, St Ann's Vestry Hall, 2 Church Entry, London EC4V 5HB
Hon Director: Mr Matthew Saunders. No full-time staff. ***CC*** No.209456. Began 1957; non-denominational. Magazine: *Newsletter* (2,000 every four months). Turnover £80,000 to year end Mar 98. Conservation of beautiful and historic places of worship once they have closed.
☎ 020 7236 3934

The Friends of the Clergy Corporation, 27 Medway Street, London SW1P 2BD
Secretary: Mrs Alison M Jones. Executive staff 2, Other staff 3. ***CC*** No.264724. Began 1849; Anglican. No magazine. Turnover £937,912 to year end Jan 96. Providing financial help, retirement accommodation for clergy of Anglican communion and dependants.
Email: focc@btinternet.com
☎ 020 7222 2288 🖷 020 7233 1244

GOD Christian Channel, Christian Channel Studios, Stonehill Shield Road, Gateshead NE10 0HW
Co-Founder and Chairman: Mr Rory Alec. ***CC*** No.102028 Began 1995; non-denominational. The Angel Christian Telev sion Trust is the official charity of the Christian Channe Magazine: *Angel* (7,500 quarterly). Turnover n/a. Cros denominational television channel providing Christians i the UK and Europe with Bible-based, family oriente programming.
Web: www.godnetwork.com
Email: info@godnetwork.com
☎ 0191 495 2244 🖷 0191 495 2266

Group of Scriptural Protestant Evangelical Labourers (GOSPEL) 85 Brixey Road, Parkstone, Poole BH12 3EY
Secretary: Mr Michael F Rabjohns. No full-time staff. ***CC*** Began 1988; interdenominational. Member of the Unite Protestant Council. Magazine: *Newsletter* (170 quarterly) Turnover £6,000 to year end Dec 97. Providing literature sup port to individuals and groups and encouraging Christianity i education, where Protestant based.
Web: www.gospelorg.freeserve.co.uk
Email: michaelrabjohns@gospelorg.freeserve.co.uk
☎ 01202 733 238

Guild of Servants of the Sanctuary, 20 Doe Bank Road, Tiptor DY4 0ES
Secretary-General: Mr R S T Cresswell. Executive staff 1. ***CC*** Began 1898; Anglican. Magazine: *The Server* (2,200 quarterly). Turnover n/a. Church guild for servers; grants to ordination candidates.
☎ 0121 556 2257

Haddon House Trust, 46 Prince of Wales Road, Westbourne, Bournemouth BH4 9HF
Director: Mrs Honor Beesley. No full-time staff. ***CC*** Began 1976; interdenominational. No magazine. Turnover n/a. Supporting financially the Evangelical Movement and those churches and people working in it.
☎ 01202 762 848

***The Harvesters Trust**, 20 Oxford Street, Chorley, Preston PR7 2BB
Chairman: Mr Michael Wood. No full-time staff. ***CC*** No.1031741. Began 1993; non-denominational. Turnover £7,000 to year end Apr 98. Grant-making trust to advance the Christian religion and relieve persons in distress worldwide.
Web: wkweb.cableinet.co.uk/harvesters
Email: harvesters@cableinet.co.uk
☎ 01257 277 141

HCPT The Pilgrimage Trust, 100a High Street, Banstead SM7 2RB
Chief Executive: Mr R A Mills. Executive staff 9, Other staff 2. ***CC*** No.281074. Began n/a; HCPT (1956) and HH Trust (1971) merged in 1980; interdenominational. (Previously Handicapped Children's Pilgrimage Trust & Hosanna House Trust). Magazine: *Trust News* (Circulation n/a quarterly). Turnover £3,065,098 to year end Oct 98. Taking children and adults with disabilities on holiday/pilgrimage to Lourdes.
Web: www.hcpt.org.uk
Email: hq@hcpt.org.uk
☎ 01737 353 311 🖷 01737 353 008

Historic Churches Preservation Trust, Fulham Palace, London SW6 6EA
Secretary: Wing Cdr Michael Tippen. Executive staff 2, Other staff 2. ***CC*** No.207402. Began 1952; non-denominational. Magazine: *Annual Report* (4,500 annually). Turnover £1,000,000 to year end Sept 96. Assisting eligible churches of all recognised Christian denominations with essential fabric repairs.
☎ 020 7736 3054

Rebecca Hussey's Book Charity, 21 Erleigh Road, Reading RG1 5LR
Clerk to the Trustees: Mrs C A Butters. No full-time staff. ***CC*** No.207101. Began 1862; non-denominational. No magazine. Turnover £6,500 to year end Dec 98. Giving grants to certain institutions for purchase of Christian books.
☎ 0118 987 1845

The Keswick Hall Trustees, School of Education, University of East Anglia, Norwich NR4 7TJ
Executive Secretary: Mrs Helen Herrington. Other staff 2. ***CC*** No.311246. Began 1981; Anglican. No magazine. Turnover £132,000 to year end Mar 98. Giving grants to support Religious Education in schools through teachers' initial and in-service training and research.
☎ 01603 505 975

King Edward Orthodox Trust Company Ltd, St Edward Brotherhood, St Cyprian's Avenue, Brookwood, Woking GU24 0BL
Chairman: Very Rev Archmandrite Alexis. No full-time staff. ***CC*** Began 1981; Orthodox. (Previously Orthodox Trust Company Ltd). Affiliatied with K.E.O.T. No magazine. Turnover n/a. Providing properties to further the mission of Orthodox Christians.
☎ 01483 487 763

The Graham Leavers Memorial Trust, 1 Hall Close, Henham, Bishop's Stortford CM22 6AU
Secretary: Mrs Linda Peake. All voluntary staff. ***CC*** No.279885. Began 1979; Baptist, but open to all. No magazine. Turnover n/a. Giving small grants to enable individuals from deprived home situations to attend a Christian activity centre or camp, UK only – no overseas.
☎ 01279 850 374

Methodist Local Preachers Mutual Aid Association, 89 High Street, Rickmansworth WD3 1EF
General Secretary: Mr Godfrey Talford. Executive staff 1, Other staff 98. ***CC*** No.213001. Began 1849; Methodist. Magazine: *Local Preachers' Magazine* (23,000 quarterly). Turnover £2,335,740 to year end Aug 98. Financial assistance to necessitous local preachers and their widow(er)s; providing suitable housing for elderly/infirm preachers.
Email: headoffice@lpma.demon.co.uk
☎ 01923 775 856

National Society for Promoting Religious Education, Church House, Great Smith Street, London SW1P 3NZ
General Secretary: Rev Canon John Hall. *Deputy Secretaries:* Mr David Lankshear, Mr Alan Brown. Executive staff 7, Other staff 7. ***CC*** No.313070. Began 1811; Anglican. Magazine: *Together with Children* (3,000 nine times a year), *NS News* (5,000 every four months). Turnover £867,000 to year end Dec 97. Supporting church schools, RE and parish education, publishing resources, training courses, and archives.
Web: www.natsoc.org.uk
☎ 020 7898 1000 Fax 020 7898 1493
Also at: National Society RE Centre, 36 Causton Street, London SW1P 4AU
☎ 020 7932 1190
And: RE Centre, The College, Lord Mayor's Walk, York YO3 7EX
☎ 01904 616 858

The Ouseley Trust, 127 Coleherne Court, London SW5 0EB
Clerk to the Trustees: Mr Martin Williams. No full-time staff. ***CC*** No.252716. Began 1989; Church of England, Church in Wales, Church of Ireland. No magazine. Turnover £160,000 to year end Dec 98. Making grants to promote and maintain a high standard of choral service.
Email: 106200.1023@compuserve.com
Fax 020 7341 0043

Partis College, Newbridge Hill, Bath BA1 3QD
Bursar: Major M J Young. Executive staff 1, Other staff 11. ***CC*** No.200606. Began 1825; Anglican. No magazine. Turnover £120,000 to year end Dec 92. Providing a home for retired Anglican ladies of good social background.
☎ 01225 421 532

The Payne Charitable Trust, 1st Floor, Copthorne House, The Broadway, Abergele LL22 7DD
Secretary: Mr John Payne. Executive staff 1, Other staff 1. ***CC*** No.241816. Began n/a; non-denominational. No magazine. Turnover £45,000 to year end Apr 97. Giving grants for the furtherance of the Gospel.
☎ 01745 825 779 Fax 01745 833 161

***Quantock Christian Trust**, 9 Rosary Drive, Bridgwater TA6 7JS
Administrator: Mr John Elford. Executive staff 1, Other staff 1. ***CC*** Began 1985; non-denominational. No magazine. Turnover £180,000 to year end Mar 94. Christian trust for evangelical purposes; Bible teaching ministry, counselling, bookshop, aid agency for Eastern Europe.
☎ 01278 455 596

S

Queen Victoria Clergy Fund, Church House, Dean's Yard, London SW1P 3NZ
Secretary: Mr Colin Menzies. No full-time staff. ***CC*** No.213258. Began 1897; Anglican. No magazine. Turnover £132,000 [Grants] to year end June 98. Assisting (through the Dioceses) Church of England clergy in financial need.
☎ 020 7222 5261 🖷 020 7799 2301

Queen's Hall Help, Wigan, 160 Gidlow Lane, Wigan WN6 7EA
Administrator: Mrs Patrica Rudd. Executive staff 1. ***CC*** No.506518. Began 1970; Methodist. (Previously Wigan Help Committee, Queen's Hall). No magazine. Turnover n/a. Investigating areas of need; initiating ways of meeting the need.
☎ 01942 324 883

Dr George Richards' Charity, 51 Pole Barn Lane, Frinton-on-Sea CO13 9NQ
Secretary: Mr David J Newman. No full-time staff. ***CC*** No.246965. Began 1837; Anglican. No magazine. Turnover £23,879 to year end Dec 98. Financial assistance for Anglican clergymen retired early through ill health; also widows and dependants.
☎ 01255 676 509

***Scriptural Knowledge Institution**, Müller House, 7 Cotham Park, Bristol BS6 6DA
Chief Executive: Mr Julian Marsh. Executive staff 1, Other staff 2. ***CC*** No.202652. Began 1834; interdenominational. Part of the George Müller Foundation. Magazine: *Annual Report* (4,000 annually). Turnover £450,000 to year end Feb 98. Providing prayer and facilities for passing on financial gifts to missionaries working at home and abroad.
☎ 0117 924 5001 🖷 0117 924 4855

Shared Interest, 25 Collingwood, Newcastle upon Tyne NE1 1JE
Managing Director: Ms Stephanie Sturrock. *Operations Director:* Mr Colin Crawford. *Promotion Officer:* Ms Allison Barrett. Executive staff 5, Other staff 5. Began 1990; ecumenical. Magazine: *Quarterly Return* (14,000 quarterly). Turnover £17,200,000 to year end Sept 98. Social investment society; people investing in fair trade with the people of the Third World.
Web: www.oneworld.org/shared_int.
Email: post@shared-interest.com
☎ 0191 233 9100 🖷 0191 233 9110

Society for Relief of Poor Clergymen, CPAS, Athena Drive, Tachbrook Park, Warwick CV34 6NG
Hon Chairman: Rev David Bubbers. *Secretary:* Mrs Irene Wilde. ***CC*** No.232634. Began 1788; Anglican. No magazine. Turnover £20,000 to year end Dec 98. Helping evangelical Anglican clergy in times of financial need, caused by illness, bereavement, removal.
☎ 01926 458 458 🖷 01926 458 459

The Society of St Vincent de Paul, 546 Sauchiehall Stree[t] Glasgow G2 3NG
National Executive Secretary (Scotland): Ms Kathlee[n] Gorman. Staff n/a. ***CC*** Began n/a; National 1845; International 1833; Roman Catholic. Magazine: *Scottish Ozanam News* (1,750 quarterly). Turnover n/a. Alleviating all forms of poverty through personal contact, financial and other assistance.
☎ 0141 332 7752 🖷 0141 332 6775
Also at: *National Executive Secretary (England & Wales):* M[r] Alban W Dunn, 14 Blandford Street, London N1H 4DP
Email: svpuk@btconnect.com
☎ 020 7935 9126 🖷 020 7935 9136

†**Strict Baptist Pension Fund**, 9 Hamilton Gardens, St John's Wood, London NW8 9PU
Secretary: Rev Philip Tait. No full-time staff. ***CC*** No.250195. Began 1931; Grace Baptist. No magazine. Turnover £8,453 to year end Dec 96. Giving grants to retired pastors.
☎ 020 7286 3875

†**Strict Baptist Trust**, 9 Hamilton Gardens, St John's Wood, London NW8 9PU
Secretary: Rev Philip Tait. No full-time staff. ***CC*** No.250485. Began 1930; Grace Baptist. No magazine. Turnover £6,052 to year end Dec 96. Augmenting stipends of pastors in small churches.
☎ 020 7286 3875

STUDYLINK-EFAC International Training Partnership, 8 Brook Cottage, Corston, Bath BA2 9BA
Secretary: Mr Peter LeRoy. No full-time staff. ***CC*** No.1073169. Began 1965; Anglican. (Previously EFAC Bursary Scheme). No magazine. Turnover £55,000 to year end Aug 98. Providing bursaries for clergy from the developing world to study for further theological degrees.
Email: a.leroy@clara.net
☎ 01225 873 023 🖷 01225 873 871

Tentmakers Ltd, Burstead Cottages, Little Hallingbury, Bishop's Stortford CM22 7QU
Managing Director: Mr Robin Horton. Executive staff 2. Began 1996. No magazine. Turnover n/a. Giving 80% of the distributable profit from purchases to chosen charity/mission of purchaser.
Web: www.tentmaker.co.uk
Email: sales@tentmakers.co.uk
☎ 01279 726 798 🖷 01279 723 344

†**Westminster Abbey Trust**, 20 Dean's Yard, Westminster, London SW1P 3PA
Secretary: Rear Admiral K A Snow. Other staff 1. ***CC*** Began 1973; non-denominational. No magazine. Turnover £1,536,470 to year end Apr 94. Funding the most massive restoration that Westminster Abbey has had in its long history.
☎ 020 7222 5752

BLIND ORGANISATIONS

See Disabilities, Organisations for People with on Page 410.

BUILDINGS & CHURCH DESIGN

See also Furnishing, Fabric & Church Interiors on Page 424.

for Architect, 33 Fairlands Avenue, Thornton Heath CR7 6HD
Partner: Mr John Eynon. Executive staff 2. Began 1991; non-denominational. No magazine. Turnover n/a. Consultancy offering advice on all aspects of design and buildings for churches; initial free consultation.
Email: aforarchitect@btinternet.com
☎ 020 8665 9871 Mobile: 07956 640 328 📠 020 8665 9871

yrom Clark Roberts Ltd, Main Office, 117 Portland Street, Manchester M1 6EH
Executive Directors: Mr Andrew W Hawksworth, Mr D Andrew Gooud, Mr Alex E H Roberts. Other Directors 4, Other staff 65. Began 1925; non-denominational. Magazine: *BCR Matters* (Circulation n/a quarterly). Turnover £2,000,000 to year end June 98. Providing architectural, building surveying, structural and civil engineering, project management services for all building types.
Web: www.byromclarkroberts.ltd.uk
Email: bcrmcr@byromclarkroberts.ltd.uk
☎ 0161 236 9601 📠 0161 236 5074
Sheffield Office: Jubilee House, West Bar Green, Sheffield S1 2BT
☎ 0114 275 7879 📠 0114 272 8954

he Cathedrals Fabric Commission for England, Fielden House, Little College Street, London SW1P 3SH
Secretary: Dr Richard Gem. Executive staff 2, Other staff 1. *CC* Began 1991; Anglican. (Previously Cathedrals Advisory Commission for England). No magazine. Turnover n/a. Statutory body controlling and advising on alterations to cathedral churches, contents and precincts.
☎ 020 7222 3793 📠 020 7222 3794

hurch Projects Ltd, 33 Darley Road, Eastbourne BN20 7UT
Managing Director: Mr Derek Kemp. Executive staff 3. Began 1990; non-denominational. No magazine. Turnover n/a. Architects and church redevelopment consultants.
☎ 01323 416 900 📠 01323 416 378

Craig Hall & Rutley, 2 John Street, London WC1N 2HJ
Partner: Mr Barry Wilmshurst. Executive staff 6, Other staff 2. Began 1963; interdenominational. No magazine. Turnover £250,000 to year end Apr 94. Providing architecture, surveying and planning supervisor services.
☎ 020 7831 7575 📠 020 7430 1113

D G J Flett Chartered Architect, Ardcraig, Bankhead Grove, Dalmeny, South Queensferry EH30 9JZ
Architect/Principal: Mr Douglas G J Flett. Executive staff 1, Other staff 1. Began 1981; non-denominational. No magazine. Turnover n/a. Architect to churches and community groups; church consultant on vision, structure and development.
Email: dgj.flett@uk.iccc.net
☎ 0131 331 3310

Historic Chapels Trust, 29 Thurloe Street, London SW7 2LQ
Director: Dr Jennifer Freeman. *Chairman:* Sir Hugh Rossi. Executive staff 1, Other staff 5. *CC* No.1017321. Began 1993; non-denominational. Magazine: *Newsletter* (500 half-yearly). Turnover £500,000 to year end Dec 98. Acquisition and repair of redundant Grade I and II* listed places of worship. Eleven chapels open to public.
☎ 020 7584 6072 📠 020 7225 0607

Glyn Leaman Architects, 11 Beaconsfield Road, Clifton, Bristol BS8 2TR
Principal: Mr Glyn Leaman. Other staff 2. Began 1983; non-denominational. No magazine. Turnover n/a. Quinquennial inspections, repairs, re-ordering, new buildings, landscape design.
☎ 0117 923 8617 📠 0117 974 2781

Bob Massey Associates (Consulting Engineers), 9 Worral Avenue, Arnold, Nottingham NG5 7GN
Principal Consulting Engineer: Mr Bob Massey. Executive staff 2, Other staff 5. Began 1989; interdenominational. No magazine. Turnover n/a. Consulting engineer for large or small theatre/visual arts projects: for architects, consultants (including for churches).
Email: masseybob@netscape.net
☎ 0115 967 3969 📠 0115 967 3969

†**Mayfair (UK) Ltd**, 384 Green Lane, London SE9 3TQ
Managing Director: Mr D Hussey. Staff n/a. Began n/a; non-denominational. No magazine. Turnover n/a. Restoring churches; specialists in roofing, decoration, stone restoration, masonry and cleaning.
☎ 020 8851 3980 📠 020 8857 8908

***New Wineskins**, 16a Belmont Hill, Lewisham, London SE13 5BD
Chairman of Trustees: Mr Raymond Hall. Staff n/a. ***CC*** No.1013750. Began 1973; non-denominational. No magazine. Turnover n/a. Helping the Church to shine through building design and development.
Email: 106673.3107@compuserve.com
☎ 020 8318 9233 Fax 020 8463 0634

People and Places Cost Management, 2 Parish Lane, London SE20 7LH
Director: Mr Martyn Tickner. Executive staff 1. Began 1989; non-denominational. No magazine. Turnover £7,000 to year end Nov 98. Building cost control, quantity surveying, planning supervision and project co-ordination for churches and charities.
☎ 020 8776 7997 Fax 020 8776 7220

People and Places International: Architects and Development Surveyors, 16 Belmont Hill, Lewisham, London SE13 5BD
Director: Mr Raymond Hall. Began 1973; non-denominational. No magazine. Turnover n/a. Design and development; architecture, planning, interiors, landscape, cost control, surveying, property and development.
Email: 106673.3107@compuserve.com
☎ 020 8318 9233 Fax 020 8463 0634
Also at: *Director:* Mr Henry Clarke, 17 Queen Anne's Gate, London SW1H 9BU
☎ 020 7799 2986 Fax 020 7799 3068

Christopher Rayner & Associates, Apple Cross House, 52 The Rise, Sevenoaks TN13 1RN
Principal: Mr Christopher Rayner. Executive staff 1, Other staff 3. Began 1991; Anglican. No magazine. Turnover £40,000 to year end Dec 98. Architects working with churches and religious bodies, guided by Christian belief.
☎ 01732 461 806 Fax 01732 461 806

SDA Architects Ltd, The Courtyard, Swillington Lan Hollinthorpe, Leeds LS26 8BZ
Directors: Mr Martin Fryer, Mr B C Foxley, Mr G P Ford an Mr C R Pearson. Other staff 30. Began 1955; non denominational. (Previously Stocks Design Build Ltd). N magazine. Turnover £1,800,000 to year end June 98. Special ising in design and build, traditional procurement. Interio design. Nationwide service.
Email: main@sdadesign.co.uk
☎ 0113 232 0222 Fax 0113 232 0777

KC White Partnership, 10 Duke Street, Chelmsford CM1 1HL
Partners: Mr Anthony Hall, Mr Richard J Naylor. Executive staff 6, Other staff 2. Began 1963; interdenominational. No magazine. Turnover £163,000 to year end Apr 98. Designing and maintaining churches, schools, community facilities, including working with historic buildings.
Email: kcwhite@aol.com
☎ 01245 359 022 Fax 01245 493 096

Whitechapel Bell Foundry, 34 Whitechapel Road, London E1 1DY
Directors: Mr & Mrs Alan & Kathryn Hughes. Other staff 35. Began 1420; non-denominational. No magazine. Turnover n/a. Bell founders, bell hangers, musical handbells, handbell music and accessories, clock bells.
Web: www.whitechapelbellfoundry.co.uk
Email: bells@whitechapelbellfoundry.co.uk
☎ 020 7247 2599 Fax 020 7375 1979

CHILDREN'S CARE & ADOPTION SOCIETIES

***The Agapé Trust**, 118 Hastings Road, Battle TN33 0TQ
Project Managers: Dr Peter Frost, Rev Kenneth Baird. Executive staff 1, Other staff 2. ***CC*** No.1011416. Began 1992; non-denominational. Magazine: *Newsletter* (1,000 quarterly). Turnover £800,000 to year end Apr 99. Offering lifecare and short stay respite/shared care to young people with profound learning disabilities/complex needs.
Email: agapetrust@hastingsproject.freeserve.com.uk
☎ 01424 775 042 Fax 01424 775 042
Barcombe and Lewis Project: *Development Officer:* Dr Peter Frost, Oakfield, Cooks Bridge Road, Barcombe, Lewis BN8 5TJ
☎ 01273 400 979

Blackburn Diocesan Adoption Agency, St Mary's House, Cathedral Close, Blackburn BB1 5AA
Principal Social Worker: Mr Brian Williams. Executive staff 5, Other staff 2. ***CC*** No.1033041. Began 1948; Anglican. No magazine. Turnover £190,000 to year end Dec 98. Providing a comprehensive adoption service for all parties involved in all aspects of adoption.
☎ 01254 577 59 Fax 01254 670 810

Catholic Care (Diocese of Leeds), 31 Moor Road, Headingley, Leeds LS6 4BG
Director: Mr Stuart W Hanlon. *Assistant Director:* Mr Stephen Hargrave. *Residential Services Manager:* Sister Margaret Bannerton. Staff 140. ***CC*** No.513063. Began 1944; Roman Catholic. No magazine. Turnover £1,399,939 to year end Mar 96. Social work service to children/families; adoption, fostering; residential care and supported housing projects.
Email: catholiccare@compuserve.com
☎ 0113 278 7500 Fax 0113 278 9089

Catholic Caring Services (Diocese of Lancaster), 218 Tulketh Road, Preston PR2 1ES
Director: Mr James Cullen. Other staff 43. ***CC*** Began 1936; Roman Catholic. No magazine. Turnover n/a. Caring for children in need, service to deaf and people with learning disabilities; adoption, fostering.
☎ 01772 732 313 Fax 01772 768 726

Catholic Children and Family Care Society – Wales, Bishop Brown House, Durham Street, Grangetown, Cardiff CF1 7PB
Administrator: Mr W Morris. Executive staff 7, Other staff 6. ***CC*** No.509163. Began n/a; Roman Catholic. No magazine. Turnover n/a. Adoption, fostering and pastoral care in schools; care of unmarried mothers and the mentally handicapped.
☎ 029 2066 7007 Fax 029 2039 4344

atholic Children's Rescue Society (Diocese of Salford), 390 Parrs Wood Road, Didsbury, Manchester M20 5NA
Secretary: Rev Bernard Wilson. *Director of Social Work:* Mr Michael J Turner. *Assistant Director of Social Work:* Mrs Susan Bunch. Executive staff 6, Other staff 150. ***CC*** No.239172. Began 1886; Roman Catholic. No magazine. Turnover £2,700,000 to year end Mar 98. Residential care of children, young pregnant homeless women and young men; preventative social work, adoption, fostering. Also centres in Rochdale, Blackburn and Bolton.
☎ 0161 445 7741

Catholic Children's Society (Dioceses of Arundel and Brighton, Portsmouth and Southwark), 49 Russell Hill Road, Purley CR8 2XB
Director: Mr T Connor. Executive staff 5, Other staff 170. ***CC*** Began 1887; Roman Catholic. Magazine: *Child* (42,000 half-yearly). Turnover £3,236,000 to year end Mar 96. Child care including 'special needs' children, adoption, counselling and community projects.
☎ 020 8668 2181 🖷 020 8763 2274

Catholic Children's Society (Diocese of Brentwood), 5 Security House, Ongar Road, Brentwood CM15 9AT
Director: Mr Frank Maguire. *Chair of Trustees:* Mr Harry Kerr. Admin staff 2, Other staff 5, Volunteers 3. ***CC*** No.1000661. Began 1984; Roman Catholic. Magazine: *Newsletter* (1,500 quarterly). Turnover £180,000 to year end Mar 98. Working with children and families who turn to us for care and support irrespective of race or religion.
☎ 01277 229 550 🖷 01277 229 551

Catholic Children's Society (Diocese of Clifton), 58 Alma Road, Bristol BS8 2DQ
Director: Ms J Ball. Social Workers 5, Admin Staff 3. ***CC*** No.286814. Began 1904; Roman Catholic but interdenominational. Magazine: *Annual Report* (Circulation n/a). Turnover £290,000 to year end Mar 98. Adoption agency; social work support to families; adoption counselling and parenting project.
☎ 0117 973 4253 🖷 0117 923 8651

Catholic Children's Society (Diocese of Nottingham), 7 Colwick Road, West Bridgford, Nottingham NG2 5FR
Director: Canon Christopher Fisher. *Assistant Director:* Ms Margaret Dight. Total Staff 15. ***CC*** No.213692. Began 1946; Roman Catholic. Magazine: *Connections* (Circulation n/a half-yearly). Turnover £460,347 to year end Mar 98. Registered adoption agency (Notts, Derbys, Leics, Lincs).
Web: www.ccsnotts.co.uk
Email: enquiries@ccsnotts.co.uk
☎ 0115 955 8811 🖷 0115 955 8822

Catholic Children's Society (Diocese of Shrewsbury), St Paul's House, Farm Field Drive, Beechwood, Birkenhead CH43 7ZT
Director: Mr Ged Edwards. Executive staff 1, Other staff 8. ***CC*** No.509793. Began 1889; Roman Catholic. Turnover £133,000 to year end Mar 96. Social and community work agency for disadvantaged children and families. Support for local initiatives.
Email: ccs@childsoc.freeserve.co.uk
☎ 0151 652 1281 🖷 0151 652 5002

Catholic Children's Society (Diocese of Westminster), 73 St Charles Square, London W10 6EJ
Director: Mr Jim Richards. *Deputy Director:* Ms Rosemary Keenon. *Appeals Manager:* Ms Patricia Hatton. Executive staff 5, Admin staff 10, Social work staff 37. ***CC*** No.210920. Began 1859; Roman Catholic. (Previously Crusade of Rescue). Magazine: *Network* (4,000 half-yearly). Turnover £966,563 to year end Dec 96. Helping children and families through counselling, family centres, fostering, adoption, psychotherapy, irrespective of race or creed.
Email: rosemaryk@cathchild.org.uk
☎ 020 8969 5305 🖷 020 8960 1464

Childlink Adoption Society, 10 Lion Yard, Tremadoc Road, London SW4 7NQ
Director: Ms Caroline Hesslegrave. Other staff 12. ***CC*** Began 1913; non-denominational. (Previously The Church Adoption Society). Magazine: *Annual Report* (600 annually). Turnover n/a. Finding homes for babies and children with special needs; counselling services and inter-country adoption.
☎ 020 7498 1933 🖷 020 7498 1791

The Children's Society, Edward Rudolf House, 69 Margery Street, London WC1X 0JL
Chief Executive: Mr Ian Sparks OBE. Executive staff 5, Other staff 1200. ***CC*** No.221124. Began 1881; Anglican. Magazine: *Children in Focus* (340,000 every four months). Turnover £26,000,000 to year end Dec 97. Working with children, young people and families under pressure; 90 projects throughout England and Wales.
☎ 020 7837 4299 🖷 020 7837 0211
Also at: *Divisional Social Work Manager:* Mr Keith Drinkwater, Midlands Group, Unit 4, Mitre Court, Lichfield Road, Sutton Coldfield B74 2LZ
☎ 0121 354 2266
And: *Divisional Social Work Manager:* Ms Celia Burn, Northern Group, 131 Neville Road, Kersal, Salford M7 3PP
☎ 0161 792 8885
And: *Divisional Social Work Manager:* Mr Michael Sherriff, South & East Group, 33 Upper George Street, Luton LU1 2RD
☎ 01582 421 932
And: *Divisional Social Work Manager:* Mr John Denne, West & Wales Group, Brook House, Pennywell Road, Bristol BS5 0TX
☎ 0117 941 4333

***Churches' Child Protection Advisory Service**, PO Box 133, Swanley BR8 7UQ
Director: Mr David Pearson. *Social Work Adviser:* Mr Simon Bass. Executive staff 3, Other staff 8. ***CC*** No.1004490. Began 1977; non-denominational. Part of PCCA Christian Child Care. Magazine: *Caring* (5,000 half-yearly), *PCCA Bulletin* (12,000 quarterly). Turnover £234,400 to year end Mar 98. Child protection advice, training, policy implementation. Crisis management in cases of abuse; follow-up support.
Web: www.doveuk.com/pcca
Email: pcca_galro@msn.com
☎ 01322 667 207/660 011
Mobile: 07836 376 803/07958 362 290
🖷 01322 614 788

Father Hudson's Society (Archdiocese of Birmingham), Coventry Road, Coleshill, Birmingham B46 3ED
Director: Mr Kevin P Caffrey. *Finance Manager:* Mr Tim Bradford. *Fieldwork Manager:* Ms Felicity Aitken. Executive staff 4, Admin staff 12, Other staff 50. ***CC*** No.512992. Began 1902; Roman Catholic, but serving all. (Previously Father Hudson's Homes). Magazine: *Reaching Out* (15,000 quarterly). Turnover £3,456,980 to year end Mar 98. Offering services and support, including adoption, to children and families.
☎ 01675 463 187 🖷 01675 466 607

S

***Fegans**, 160 St James Road, Tunbridge Wells TN1 2HE
Director: Mr Ken Holland. *Senior Social Worker:* Mr Alan Vincent. Executive staff 2, Other staff 32. ***CC*** No.209930. Began 1870; interdenominational. Magazine: *Focus* (4,000 half-yearly). Turnover £367,000 to year end Dec 97. Residential family centre; pre-school day care provision; visiting, counselling and support of needy families.
☎ 01892 538 288
Also at: Little Dumpton, 1 Seacroft Road, Broadstairs CT10 1TL
☎ 01843 863 043
And: 10 High Street, Heathfield TN21 8LS
☎ 01435 866 122

The Haven Community Home, Springfield Road, Sydenham, London SE26 6HG
Officer-in-Charge: Captain Mary Bullock. Admin staff 3. ***CC*** Began n/a; Salvation Army. No magazine. Turnover n/a. Accommodating 24 children.
☎ 020 8659 4033/4

Marshfield Community Home, 79 Albert Road, Southport PR9 9LN
Deputy Officer-in-Charge: Captain Emily Oliver. Staff n/a. ***CC*** Began n/a; Salvation Army. No magazine. Turnover n/a. Accommodating 22 children and a day nursery for 15.
☎ 01704 538 643 Mobile: 07711 799 778 (Duty Officer)
🖷 01704 542 030

***Mill Grove**, 10 Crescent Road, South Woodford, Londo E18 1JB
Director: Mr Keith White. *Assistant Director:* Mrs Ruth White Executive staff 2, Other staff 8. ***CC*** No.211119. Began 1899 non-denominational. Magazine: *Links* (2,500 annually). Turn over £134,000 to year end Dec 97. Supporting, caring for chil dren and families through Christian extended family network rooted in family home.
Email: millgrove@btinternet.com
☎ 020 8504 2702

NCH Action for Children, 85 Highbury Park, London N5 1UD
Chief Executive: Mr Deryk Mead. *Pastoral Director:* Rev W M Lynn. Other staff 3000. ***CC*** No.215301. Began 1869; Methodist. No magazine. Turnover £37,600,000. Over 320 projects helping more than 3000 children, young people and their families in the UK.
Web: www.nchafc.org.uk
☎ 020 7226 2033 Mobile: 07802 610 860 🖷 020 7226 2537
Also at: London Region, 22 Lucerne Road, London N5 1TZ
☎ 020 7704 7070 🖷 020 7704 7080
And: Midlands Region, Princess Alice Drive, Chester Road North, Sutton Coldfield B73 6RD
☎ 0121 355 4615 🖷 0121 354 4717
And: North East Region, 12 Granby Road, Harrogate HG1 4ST
☎ 01423 524 286 🖷 01423 501 987
And: North West Region, 39 Wilson Patten Street, Warrington WA1 1PG
☎ 01925 445 453 🖷 01925 231 271
And: NCH Scotland, 17 Newton Place, Glasgow G3 7PY
☎ 0141 332 4041 🖷 0141 332 7002
And: South East Region, 158 Crawley Road, Roffey, Horsham RH12 4EU
☎ 01403 225 900 🖷 01403 225 911
And: South West Region, Horner Court, 637 Gloucester Road, Horfield, Bristol BS7 0BJ
☎ 0117 935 4440 🖷 0117 951 2470
And: Thames Anglia Region, Chesham House, Church Lane, Berkhamsted HP4 2AX
☎ 01442 877 999 🖷 01442 877 677
And: Wales Region, Saint David's Court, 68a Cowbridge Road East, Cardiff CF1 9DN
☎ 029 2022 2127 🖷 029 2022 9952

The Orange Grove Foster Care Agency, 203 West Malvern Road, West Malvern WR14 4BB
Executive Director: Mr Granville Orange. Other staff n/a. ***CC*** Began 1945; non-denominational. (Previously Children's Family Trust). Applications from Christian foster carers welcomed. Magazine: *Children's Newsletter* (3,000 half-yearly). Turnover £950,000. Independent foster care agency providing short and long-term foster care with experienced foster carers.
Email: theorangegrove@compuserve.com
☎ 01684 567 724 Mobile: 07770 584 358 🖷 01684 568 190

***PCCA Christian Child Care**, PO Box 133, Swanley BR8 7UQ
Director: Mr David Pearson. *Treasurer:* Mr John Perkins. Executive staff 3, Other staff 8. ***CC*** No.1004490. Began 1977; non-denominational. (Previously Pentecostal Child Care Association). Magazine: *Caring* (5,000 half-yearly), *PCCA Bulletin* (12,000 quarterly). Turnover £234,400 to year end Mar 98. Supporting churches, leaders, carers nationwide; child care/protection issues. Respite care for children, West Midlands.
Web: www.doveuk.com/pcca
Email: pcca_galro@msn.com
☎ 01322 667 207/660 011 Mobile: 07836 376 803
🖷 01322 614 788

t Francis Children's Society (Diocese of Northampton), 20a Park Avenue North, Northampton NN3 2HS
Director: Mr Alf Harrison. Executive staff 2, Other staff 7. ***CC*** Began 1869; Roman Catholic. No magazine. Turnover £260,000 to year end Mar 98. Registered adoption and fostering agency for Catholic diocese of Northampton.
☎ 01604 715 202
Also at: 64 Gardenia Avenue, Luton LU3 2NS
☎ 01582 492 277 📠 01582 560 585

Strawberry Field Community Home, Beaconsfield Road, Woolton, Liverpool L25 6LJ
Officer-in-Charge: Mr Stephen Sabourin. Admin staff 3. ***CC*** Began n/a; Salvation Army. No magazine. Turnover n/a. Accommodation for 20 children.
☎ 0151 428 1647 📠 0151 421 0520

COMPUTER & BUSINESS SERVICES

See also Design, Layout & Editorial Services on Page 278, Marketing & Fundraising Services on Page 434.

AFD Computers/AFD Software Ltd, Management Centre, Old Post Office Lane, West Quay, Ramsey IM8 1RF
Senior Partner/Managing Director: Mr David Dorricott. *Technical Services Director:* Mr John Dolman. *Secretary:* Mrs Ann Dorricot. Executive staff 20, Other staff 5. Began 1983; non-denominational. Magazine: *Postcode News* (8,000 quarterly). Turnover £2,000,000 to year end June 98. Supplying address list management and postcoding software, computer systems and supplies.
Web: www.afd.co.uk
Email: postcode@afd.co.uk
☎ 01624 811 711 📠 01624 817 695

AMS (Administration Management Services), 38 Firbeck, Skelmersdale WN8 6PW
Principal: Mr Tim Baxter. Executive staff 1. Began 1987; non-denominational. No magazine. Turnover £15,000 to year end Apr 97. Providing computer consultancy, programming and services for fundraising, finance and administration.
Email: timb@synergy.org.uk
☎ 01695 51970 Mobile: 07768 114 135 📠 01695 724 292

***Brian Clews Services (BCS)**, PO Box 680, Maidenhead SL6 9ST
Director: Mr Brian Clews. Executive staff 2. Began 1992; non-denominational. No magazine. Turnover £25,000 to year end June 98. Project co-ordination, administration services, merchandise handling facility.
Email: brian.clews@dial.pipex.com
☎ 01628 525 314 Mobile: 07860 290 115

Bristol Christian Resource Centre, 4 Greenlands Way, Henbury, Bristol BS10 7PR
Trustee: Mr Michael P J Simmons. Executive staff 4, Other staff 8. ***CC*** No.1011132. Began 1983; non-denominational. No magazine. Turnover £16,202 to year end Mar 98. Resource centre and mailing service to 24,000 church leaders in England and Wales.
☎ 0117 950 7355

Britannia Systems Ltd, Brittania House, Albion Street, Clifford, Wetherby LS23 6HY
Managing Director: Dr David Barrow. Executive staff 4, Other staff 1. Began 1991; non-denominational. No magazine. Turnover £75,000 to year end May 97. Supplying computer systems and software to support churches, charities, other Christian organisations.
Email: britannia.systems@virgin.net
☎ 01937 840 440 📠 01937 840 441

Business & Technology Management, 5 Franklin Avenue, Hartley Wintney, Hook RG27 8RB
Director: Mr Ronald Bradnam. Executive staff 2. Began 1979; non-denominational. No magazine. Turnover n/a. Bespoke Biblically based administration and growth support services for churches, church plants and church centres.
Web: ourworld.compuserve.com/homepages/ron_bradnam
Email: ronbradnam@ibm.net
☎ 01252 842 108 📠 01252 843 009

Capstone Systems Ltd, 48 Woodpond Avenue, Hockley SS5 4PX
Director: Mr D C Godfrey. Admin staff 2. Began 1986; non-denominational. No magazine. Turnover n/a. Supplying computer software (ReadyRiter) for hospices, ministries, charities, churches; accounting, administration and fundraising. Patient records.
Email: capstonesystems@compuserve.com
☎ 01702 207 742 📠 01702 200 286

CdotC Technologies, 25 Colenso Road, Ilford IG2 7AH
Proprietor: Mr Paul G J Cienciala. Executive staff 1, Other staff 1. Began 1999; non-denominational. No magazine. Turnover n/a. Serving the Christian and wider business community by providing an internet presence development service.
Web: www.cdotc.com
Email: info@cdotc.com
☎ 020 8597 9400 📠 020 8597 9409

Charis Internet Services Ltd, 1 Hagley Road, Edgbaston, Birmingham B16 8TG
Managing Director: Mr Jon Earnshaw. *Finance Director:* Mr John Ellison. Executive staff 3, Other staff 8. Began 1996; non-denominational. No magazine. Turnover n/a. Providing internet access and comprehensive web services to individuals, businesses and Christian organisations nationwide.
Web: www.charis.co.uk
Email: enquiries@charis.co.uk
☎ 0121 248 5800 🖷 0121 248 5810

Christian Duplicating Service, 3 Castle Road, Nottingham NG1 6AA
Proprietor: Mr Trevor Smith. Executive staff 2, Other staff 1. Began 1966; non-denominational. No magazine. Turnover £50,000-100,000 to year end Dec 96. Offset duplicating, copying and print finishing services.
☎ 0115 947 5311

†**Christian Information Network**, 5 Norham Gardens, Oxford OX2 6PS
Proprietor: Mr Darren Grant. Other staff 1. Began 1994; non-denominational. (Previously Seeds). No magazine. Providing internet services including e-mail and web hosting, supplying Christian software for most systems.
Web: www.cin.co.uk
Email: admin@cin.co.uk
☎ 01865 559 986 🖷 01865 559 986

Christian Media, PO Box 525, Newcastle ST5 0QJ
Director: Jon L Love. Executive staff 2, Other staff 4. Began 1996; interdenominational. No magazine. Turnover n/a. Internet applications and sales.
Web: www.christianmedia.co.uk
Email: info@christianmedia.co.uk
☎ Mobile: 07071 881 196 🖷 07071 881 195

Church Computer Users Group, 76 Merrybent, Darlington DL2 2LE
Chairman of Executive: Rev Stoker Wilson. No full-time staff. ***CC*** No.327530. Began 1982; non-denominational. Magazine: *Church Computer* (1,500 every four months), *Church Computer Directory* (1,500 annually). Turnover £14,000 to year end Dec 98. Supporting all in the churches who are using computers and their associated technologies.
Web: www.churchcomputer.org.uk
Email: stoker@cix.co.uk
☎ 01325 374 510

***Anthony Collins Solicitors**, St Philip's Gate, 5 Waterloo Street, Birmingham B2 5PG
Senior Partner: Mr Anthony Collins. Executive staff 60, Other staff 60. Began 1973; non-denominational. No magazine. Turnover n/a. Providing a wide range of private and corporate legal services, especially to charities and churches.
☎ 0121 200 3242 🖷 0121 212 7442

Computers for Charities, 106 London Road, Hailsham BN27 3AL
Principal: Mr Simon Rooksby. No paid staff. ***CC*** No.1070286. Began 1994; interdenominational. No magazine. Turnover £18,000 to year end June 99. Charity providing loan of recycled computers, UK and overseas. Project provides advice on related matters.
Email: c.f.c@btinternet.com
☎ 01323 840 641

Covenant Technology, 11 Brownings Road, Canningto
Bridgwater TA5 2RH
Proprietor: Rev Christopher Brown. Executive staff 1, Othe staff 1. Began 1998; non-denominational. No magazine. Turr over n/a. Supplying computers, software, web site desig upgrades, repairs, consultancy.
Web: www.covenant.ndirect.co.uk
Email: info@covenant.ndirect.co.uk
☎ 01278 653 706 🖷 01278 653 706

Data Developments, Wolverhampton Science Park, Staffor Road, Wolverhampton WV10 9RU
Partner: Mr Alan Redmond. Executive staff 2, Other staff 4 Began 1985; non-denominational. No magazine. Turnove n/a. Supplying computers, specialist programs consultancy training, installation, software to churches and charities.
Web: data-developments.co.uk
Email: sales@data-developments.co.uk
☎ 01902 824 044 🖷 01902 824 046

***Daystar Computing Solutions**, Daystar House, Burnage Lane, Manchester M19 2NG
Partners: Mr Stephen & Mrs Heather Noller. Other staff 1. Began 1991; non-denominational. No magazine. Turnover £100,000 to year end Dec 97. Advice, installation and support of Microsoft and Novell servers, printers and internet connectivity.
Web: www.daystar.co.uk
Email: snoller@daystar.co.uk
☎ 0161 248 8088 🖷 0161 224 2522

†**Dean Computer Consultants**, 14 Brownleaf Road, Brighton BN2 6LB
Director: Mr J Dean. No other staff. Began 1993; evangelical. No magazine. Turnover n/a. Income processing and fundraising software.
☎ 01273 302 545 🖷 01273 302 545

Dove Marketing & Dove UK, Meadow View, Stratford Drive, Wooburn Green, High Wycombe HP10 0QH
Director: Barry Croall. Staff n/a. Began 1996; non-denominational. No magazine. Turnover £40,000 to year end Dec 98. Free web sites for Christian-based or charitable organisations; marketing, mailing, database and training services.
Web: www.doveuk.com
Email: info@doveuk.com
☎ Mobile: 07000 368 385 🖷 01494 512 442

Downs Associates, 2 South View Place, Midsomer Norton, Bath BA3 2AX
Partner: Mr E Michael Jakins. Executive staff 1, Other staff 1. Began 1984; non-denominational. No magazine. Turnover n/a. Consultancy, training and supplying computer systems for administration and finance.
Email: michael@downs.telme.com
☎ 01761 411 805 Mobile: 07958 578 417 🖷 01761 411 717

Ellis-Fermor & Negus, Market Place, Ripley DE5 3BS
Senior Partner: Mr David P Negus. *Partner:* Mr David R Wells. *Practice Manager:* Mr Michael E Amos. Executive staff 17, Other staff 43. Began 1893; non-denominational. Magazine: *Newsletter* (Circulation n/a quarterly). Turnover £1,400,000 to year end Apr 98. Solicitors.
Email: ripley@ellis-fermor.co.uk
☎ 01773 744 744 🖷 01773 570 047
Also at: 35 Derby Road, Long Eaton, Nottingham NG10 1LU
Email: longeaton@ellis-fermor.co.uk
☎ 0115 972 5222 🖷 0115 946 1152
And: 2 Devonshire Avenue, Beeston, Nottingham NG9 1BS
Email: beeston@ellis-fermor.co.uk
☎ 0115 922 1591 🖷 0115 925 9341

***Elsdon Mailing**, Unit 16, Nonsuch Industrial Estate, Epsom KT17 1EG
Partner: Mrs Elsie Boorer. Staff n/a. Began 1974; Methodist. No magazine. Turnover n/a. Mailing house for quantity direct mail.
☎ 01372 720 613 🖷 01372 720 613

Evangelsoft Ltd, PO Box 224, Kingston upon Thames KT1 2NX
Director: Dr Ken Dean. All voluntary staff. *CC* No.298489. Began 1986; interdenominational. (Owned by Evangeltrust). No magazine. Turnover n/a. Producing Bible-based computer programs, CD clip art and OHP acetates.
☎ 020 8549 2280

Exousia Ltd, 53 Hindes Road, Harrow HA1 1SQ
Computer Consultant: Mr Savash Munir. Executive staff 1, Other staff 3. Began 1992; non-denominational. (Previously Exousia Computer Consultancy). No magazine. Turnover £85,000 to year end Dec 98. Providing computer consultancy, network support, web design; publishing and distributing Christian software.
Web: www.exousia.uk.com
Email: sales@exousia.uk.com
☎ 020 8424 0900 Mobile: 07956 591 064
🖷 020 8424 0901

Explan Computers Ltd, PO Box 32, Tavistock PL19 8YU
Director: Mr Paul Richardson. Executive staff 2, Other staff 2. Began 1994; non-denominational. (Previously Explan). No magazine. Turnover £80,000 to year end Nov 96. Bible software publishers. Multimedia multi-ligual software for Risc OS computers in churches and schools.
Web: www.explan.demon.co.uk
Email: explan@explan.demon.co.uk
☎ 01822 613 868 🖷 01822 610 868

Footprints Christian Bookshop, 130a Newgate Street, Bishop Auckland DL14 7EM
Partner: Mr John Gaines. Executive staff 2. Began 1992. (Previously Footprints). No magazine. Turnover £60,000 to year end June 98. Retailing computers, software, peripherals; Acorn dealers.
☎ 01388 602 657 🖷 01388 661 999

FosterFinch Ltd, Registered Office, 3 Lawn Road, Exmouth EX8 1QJ
Director: Mr Tim Finch. Executive staff 2, Other staff 3. Began 1994; interdenominational. No magazine. Turnover £36,000 to year end Oct 98. IT Consultancy: Database and bespoke software development. IT Training: Desktop PC computer training. Also media and music services. Bases in London, Taunton, East Devon & Shropshire.
Web: www.eclipse.co.uk/fosterfinch
Email: timfinch@cix.co.uk
☎ Mobile: 07703 172 994
Also at: Mr Bob Foster, 14 Trendle Road, Taunton TA1 4DN
☎ 01823 252 522

Galena Business Computer Solutions, Rick Barton House, Chideock, Bridport DT6 6JW
Deputy Manager: Mrs Janice Collins. Executive staff 2, Other staff 2. Began 1985; non-denominational. No magazine. Turnover n/a. Supplying computer systems for the booktrade; distribution of Bible and worship software, multimedia applications.
Email: sales@houghtonsbooks.com/galena
☎ 01297 489 276 🖷 01297 489 868

Independent Examiners Ltd, 3 West Close, Felpham, Bognor Regis PO22 7LQ
Director: Mr D F Martin. Executive staff 1, Admin staff 1. Began 1997; interdenominational. Magazine: *The Examiner* (3,000 half-yearly). Turnover £40,000 to year end Dec 98. Offering comprehensive range of services to charities including account preparation and examination, charity set-up, advice.
Email: estoril@zoo.co.uk
☎ 01243 584 917 🖷 01243 584 917
Also at: *Independent Examiner:* Mr Peter Saltiel, 41 Oak Road, Caterham CR3 5TT
Email: 113666.181@compuserve.com
☎ 01883 341 186

Jireh.co.uk, 18 Park Lane, Cottingham HU16 5RD
Owner: Mr Andrew John Bruce. No paid staff. Began 1997; interdenominational. No magazine. Turnover n/a. Providing a cost effective internet service. Specialists in name registration and web hosting.
Web: www.jireh.co.uk
Email: ajb@jireh.co.uk
☎ 01482 875 532 Mobile: 07966 400 323 🖷 01482 875 132

***JPR Consultancy Ltd**, 16 Welland Road, Keynsham, Bristol BS31 1PB
Director: Mr Jean-Paul Raby. *Company Secretary:* Mrs Ruth Raby. Executive staff 2. Began 1995; non-denominational. (Previously Jean-Paul Raby Consultancy Services). No magazine. Turnover £170,000 to year end Sep 96. IT Service Management, IT Project Management, IT Training, IT Process Business Improvements.
Web: www.jprc.co.uk
Email: jp.raby@jprc.co.uk
☎ 0117 986 1848 Mobile: 07885 825 409
🖷 0117 986 1848

Marcus Systems Ltd, 16 Orchard Grove, Chalfont St Peter, Gerrards Cross SL9 9EY
Consultant: Mr John Marcus. No other staff. Began 1982; non-denominational. No magazine. Turnover £70,000 to year end Mar 99. Supplying and installing PC hardware, networks and accounting and other software to charities.
Email: john.marcus@btinternet.com
☎ 01753 886 882 Mobile: 07702 307 132

Mission Computers, Manor Farm, 14 Alms Hill, Bourn, Cambridge CB3 7SH
Partner: Mr Paul Gildersleve. Executive staff 2, Other staff 1. Began 1987; non-denominational. Magazines: '*Who? What? Where?*' Church resources (Circulation & frequency n/a), '*The Book*' Schools resources (Circulation & frequency n/a). Turnover n/a. Desktop publishing, database and mailing service, publishers of resource directories for churches and schools.
Email: miscom@compuserve.com
☎ 01954 718 076 Fax 01954 719 703

NCA Practical Business Support, 67 Glendon Drive, Sherwood, Nottingham NG5 IFN
Proprietor: Mrs Nicky Webb. Executive staff 1, Self-employed staff 3. Began 1994; ecumenical. No magazine. Turnover n/a. Working with businesses where people matter, with marketing, research, managing projects, business development, managing change.
☎ 0115 929 1024 Mobile: 07809 042 706
Fax 0115 929 1024

Gerald E Newns, 191 Station Road, West Drayton UB7 7NQ
Unix Consultant: Mr Gerald E Newns. Executive staff 1. Began 1990; non-denominational. No magazine. Turnover £60,000 to year end Jul 98. Unix system administration and www author.
Web: www.newns.com
Email: gerald@newns.com
☎ 01895 431 614 Fax 01895 422 565

No Problem Computing, 19 Regent Square, Belvedere DA17 6EP
Consultant: Mr Neil Gowers. No full-time staff. Began 1997; non-denominational. No magazine. Turnover n/a. Specialist in custom-made PCs, upgrades, repairs; web site design, implementation for Christian organisations.
Email: neilg@netcomuk.co.uk
☎ 01322 431 054 Mobile: 07050 104 403 Fax 01322 431 054

Oak Mailing, 41 Oak Road, Caterham CR3 5TT
Proprietor: Mr Peter Saltiel. No full-time staff. Began 1991; non-denominational. Magazine: *Mini Mentions* (3,000 quarterly). Turnover n/a. Mailing Christian literature to evangelical churches and fellowships.
Email: 113666.131@compuserve.com
☎ 01883 341 186

The Office London Ltd, Victoria House, Victoria Road, Buckhurst Hill IG9 5EX
Director: Miss Jean Wilson. Executive staff 2, Other staff 4. Began 1959; interdenominational. No magazine. Turnover £300,000 to year end Dec 98. Administration services.
Email: 100067.1226@compuserve.com
☎ 020 8559 1180 Fax 020 8502 9062

Online Bible Foundation, 12 Birkfield Place, Carluke ML8 4PZ
Director: Mr James G Black. Executive staff 1, Admin staff 1. *CC* No.SCO 023693. Began 1990; non-denominational. Turnover £35,000 to year end Mar 97. Distributing computer software.
Email: 100674.2270@compuserve.com
☎ 01555 752 943 Fax 01555 752 943

P & W Enterprises, 21 Gallows Hill, Kings Langley WD4 8PG
Owner: Mr Paul Vernon. Executive staff 2, Other staff 5. Bega n/a; non-denominational. No magazine. Turnover £100,000 t year end Apr 98. Producing Alpha & Omega church compute system.
Email: pandwe@aol.com
☎ 01923 266 964 Mobile: 07802 486 100
Fax 01923 443 607

Graham Pearce & Company (Solicitors), Centre Court, 130 Stratford Road, Hall Green, Birmingham B28 9HH
Senior Partner: Mr Graham Pearce. Began 1981; non denominational. No magazine. Turnover n/a. Solicitors dealing with private clients and business and charitable organisations.
Email: grahampearce.co.uk
☎ 0121 711 1999 Fax 0121 711 1083

Professional Office Software Training Ltd, 3 Vicarage Road, Leyton, London E10 5EF
Director: Mr Graham Yetton. Executive staff 2. Began 1997; non-denominational. No magazine. Turnover £60,000 to year end Apr 98. Training and advising Christians how to make the best out of their investment in computers.
Email: gyetton@netcomuk.co.uk
☎ 020 8928 0368 Fax 020 8928 0368

Professional Resource Development, 7 Church Road, Battisford, Stowmarket IP14 2HQ
Director: Mr Bryan C Hilton. Executive staff 1, Other staff 2. Began 1986; interdenominational. No magazine. Turnover n/a. Business development; marketing; training in business skills.
Email: bryanhilton@compuserve.com
☎ 01449 721 112 Mobile: 07711 000 050 Fax 01449 722 290

***Reprotec Office Solutions Ltd**, Reprotec House, 7 Churchill Park, Colwick, Nottingham NG4 2HF
Managing Director: Mr Michael Williamson. Executive staff 3, Other staff 20. Began 1981; interdenominational. (Previously Reprotec (Business Services) Ltd). No magazine. Turnover £1,400,000 to year end Dec 98. Supplying photocopiers, digital scancopy printers, fax to churches, businesses, Christian organisations throughout UK.
Email: user@reprotec-o-s.demon.co.uk
☎ 0115 940 0900 Fax 0115 940 4101

Maurice Rowlandson Consultancy, The Round House, 7 Cliff Way, Frinton-on-Sea CO13 9NL
Principal: Mr Maurice L Rowlandson. Executive staff 1, Other staff 2. Began 1987; interdenominational. No magazine. Turnover £25,000 to year end Mar 96. Consultant on administration to Christian organisations and charities.
Web: ourworld.compuserve.com/homepages/mau
Email: 101625.2744@compuserve.com
☎ 01255 676 617 Mobile: 07860 300 174 Fax 01255 673 122

Saltshakers Ltd, 4 St Andrews Road, London E13 8QD
Manager: Mr Steve Maltz. Executive staff 1, Other staff 3. Began 1990; non-denominational. (Previously Shards Software). No magazine. Turnover n/a. Design and programming of Christian software and web sites. Multimedia and education experts.
Web: www.saltshakers.com/software/home.htm
Email: steve@saltshakers.com
☎ 020 7476 4832 Mobile: 07785 941 848 Fax 020 7476 4832

S

Shanway Computing, 328 Antrim Road, Belfast BT15 5AB
Director: Mr Charles O'Neill. Executive staff 4, Other staff 2. Began 1988; interdenominational. No magazine. Turnover £30,000 to year end May 92. Supplying computer software and hardware; training and development work.
☎ 028 9077 7979 📠 028 9077 4392

Sunrise Software, PO Box 300, Kingstown Broadway, Carlisle CA3 0QS
Manager: Mr Barry C Heaton. Executive staff 3. Began 1990; non-denominational. A Division of Send The Light Ltd. No magazine. Turnover n/a. Distributing/producing Christian software, multimedia and electronic publishing: Bible study, graphics, church administration, interactive learning.
Web: www.sunrise-software.com
E Email: sales@sunrise-software.com
☎ 01228 512 512 📠 01228 514 949

Timperley Evangelical Trust, 183 Wythenshawe Road, Northern Moor, Wythenshawe, Manchester M23 0AD
Hon Secretary: Mr Roydon C Bolton. No other staff. ***CC*** No.273710. Began 1977; non-denominational. No magazine. Turnover £30,000 to year end Mar 97. Online Bible, Bible study CDs and computers. Encouraging Holy Spirit empowered study of the word of God.
Web: www.users.globalnet.co.uk/~tetrcb
E Email: tetrcb@globalnet.co.uk
☎ 0161 374 1089

The TriCord Partnership, Trinity House, Lisburn BT28 2YY
Partner: Mr John Rodgers. Executive staff 2, Admin staff 7. Began 1995; non-denominational. No magazine. Turnover £200,000 to year end Apr 98. Developers of the Omega System for church membership administration, includes income recording and covenants.
Web: www.tricord.co.uk
E Email: omega@tricord.co.uk
☎ 028 9260 6966 📠 028 9260 6965

Trinity Online Information Services, 18 Sylvan Road, Pennsylvania, Exeter EX4 6EW
Director: Mr John M Burden. Executive staff 1, Other staff 1. Began 1987; non-denominational. No magazine. Turnover n/a. Online information and electronic mail services; library of software; mailing list administration.
E Email: john.burden@trinity.dircon.co.uk
☎ 01392 412 270 📠 01392 412 370

Triptych Systems Ltd, Buckingham House, Station Road, Gerrards Cross SL9 8EL
Managing Director: Miss Alison Patriarca. *Sales Manager:* Mr Stewart Hodges. Staff 18. Began 1983; non-denominational. No magazine. Turnover £1,800,000 to year end Dec 98. Supplying and developing computer systems for Christian Bookshops and developing Internet sites.
Web: www.triptych.co.uk
E Email: info@triptych.co.uk
☎ 01753 889 988 📠 01753 880 060

Truedata Computer Services, 23 Park Road, Ilkeston DE7 5DA
Chairman/Administrator: Mr John R Moorley. Executive staff 2. Began 1983; interdenominational. No magazine. Turnover n/a. Mailing list services, subscription handling, typesetting, data storage and retrieval for Christian organisations.
Web: ourworld.compuserve.com/homepages/truedata
E Email: truedata@compuserve.com
☎ 0115 932 0643

John Truscott, 69 Sandridge Road, St Albans AL1 4AG
Church Consultant & Trainer: Mr John Truscott. No other staff. Began 1999; interdenominational. No magazine. Turnover: first year of operation. Consultancy and training on organisation and communication for churches, ministers and mission agencies.
Web: john-truscott.co.uk
E Email: get-help@john-truscott.co.uk
☎ 01727 832 176 📠 01727 832 176

UK-Church.net (1st-Web), 37 Thisselt Road, Canvey Island SS8 9BP
Director: Mr Ian C Walmsley. Executive staff 1, Other staff 4. Began 1997; ecumenical. No magazine. Turnover £30,000 to year end Dec 98. Internet services to UK Christians, including the uk-church.net database listing UK churches from all denominations.
Web: www.1st-web.co.uk
E Email: admin@uk-church.net / admin@1st-web.co.uk
☎ 01268 692 982 Mobile: 07860 692 982 📠 01268 510 100

Unigraph (UK) Ltd, Unigraph House, Pitsmoor Road, Sheffield S3 9AS
Managing Director: Mr Stephen Hunter. *Sales Director:* Mr S Ellis. *Company Accountant:* Mr P J Homewood. Executive staff 5, Other staff 25. Began 1966; interdenominational. No magazine. Turnover £4,000,000 to year end July 96. Supplying stationery, duplicating, copying and OHP products; print contractors; operators of national church copier scheme.
Web: www.unigraph.uk.com
☎ 0114 275 2801 📠 0114 275 9769

***World Action Ministries**, PO Box 789, Sutton Coldfield B74 2XJ
Executive Director: Mr Philip B South. Executive staff 2. ***CC*** No.295793. Began 1986; non-denominational. No magazine. Turnover £60,000 to year end Mar 98. Servicing Christian organisations including CHIEF, Lifestyle Ministries, In Touch Ministries and Encounter Ministries.
☎ 0121 323 3701 📠 0121 323 3703

Worldwide Christian Communication Network, 54 Edgecoombe, South Croydon CR2 8AB
Director: Rev Remi Caillaux. Executive staff 1. ***CC*** No.1045313. Began 1995; Pentecostal. Magazine: *Victory* (Circulation n/a UK and France every two months). Turnover £90,000 to year end Mar 98. Providing internet services including web hosting, authoring, design, adverts; programming; multimedia; training.
Web: www.wccn.net
☎ 020 8405 4725 📠 020 8405 4725

COUNSELLING ORGANISATIONS

See also Information and Telephone Organisations on Page 431.
For career counselling see Personnel Consultancy and Placement on Page 439.
For marriage counselling see Marriage Ministries on Page 437.

Acorn Pregnancy Counselling Centre, Oasis Centre, 19a Broadwater Road, Worthing BN14 8AD
Chair: Mrs Mary Harman. All voluntary staff 19. ***CC*** No.1061813. Began 1995; interdenominational. No magazine. Turnover £2,200 to year end Feb 99. Offering free pregnancy testing; pregnancy and post-abortion counselling.
Email: ministries@gracemin.globalnet.co.uk
☎ 01903 823 893 📠 01903 521 462

Tom Allan Centre, 23 Elmbank Street, Glasgow G2 4PB
Leader: Mrs Dorothy Smith. Executive staff 3. Began 1962; Church of Scotland. No magazine. Turnover n/a. Counselling personal, emotional, marital and family problems; training in related subjects.
☎ 0141 221 1535

Alternatives Pregnancy Counselling Centre, City Gate Centre, 84 London Road, Brighton BN1 4JF
Administrator: Mrs Sue Lyndon. Volunteer 8, counsellors. ***CC*** Began 1991; evangelical. No magazine. Turnover £6,000 to year end Dec 98. Providing free, confidential counselling to enable women to make informed decisions about their pregnancy; practical support.
☎ 01273 687 687

Association of Christian Counsellors, 173a Wokingham Road, Reading RG6 1LT
Chair: Mrs J Muir. *General Secretary:* Chris Thacker. Other staff 3. ***CC*** No.1018559. Began 1991; interdenominational. Magazine: *Accord* (2,000 quarterly). Turnover £98,344 to year end Dec 98. Running an accreditation system for Christian counsellors; recognition of Christian counselling training courses.
Web: www.doveuk.com/acc
Email: christian.counsel@zetnet.co.uk
☎ 0118 966 2207 📠 0118 926 9635

†**Beacon Foundation**, 3 Grosvenor Avenue, Rhyl LL18 4HA
Director: Mrs Maureen Davies. Executive staff 2. Began 1991; interdenominational. No magazine. Turnover £8,000 to year end Dec 94. Counselling, training and supervising those who have suffered sexual/sadistic abuse; training and supervising counsellors.
☎ 01745 343 600 📠 01745 345 090

Bodey House Counselling Centre, Stock Road, Stock CM4 9DH
Director: Mrs Sue Clements-Jewery. *Deputy Director:* Rev Vernon Muller. Counselling staff 20, Other staff 4. ***CC*** No.249768. Began 1983; Ecumenical. Accredited with British Association of Sexual and Marital Therapists. No magazine. Turnover £113,000 to year end Mar 99. Providing professional counselling in a Christian context to individuals, couples, families. Branches in Essex and E.London.
☎ 01277 840 668

CaPA, St Andrew's Centre, St Andrew's Road, London E133 8QD
Counsultant Psychiatrist: Dr Chris Andrew. Executive staff 2, Admin staff 1. Began 1994; interdenominational. No magazine. Turnover £20,000 to year end Dec 98. Christian counselling for individuals and groups; training in deep release, communication skills, group work.
Email: capa@compuserve.com
☎ 020 7511 6011 Mobile: 07767 426 119 📠 020 7511 6011

Cardiff Concern Christian Counselling Service, Regal House, Gelligaer Lane, Cathays, Cardiff CF4 3JS
Co-ordinator: Mrs Margaret Elwood. Voluntary staff. ***CC*** No.1007504. Began 1990; interdenominational. No magazine. Turnover £12,000 to year end Dec 98. Providing a counselling service to the community around Cardiff and Glamorgan and training in Christian counselling.
☎ 029 2066 4410

***Care for Mission**, Elphinstone Wing, Carberry, Musselburgh EH21 8PW
Directors: Dr Michael & Mrs Elizabeth Jones. Executive staff 3, Other staff 2. ***CC*** No.SCO 00948. Began 1983; interdenominational. Magazine: *Newsletter* (200 n/a). Turnover £97,140 to year end Apr 98. Residential and out-patient medical care debriefing assessment, counselling and retreat for missionaries and UK Christian workers.
Email: 100633.2065@compuserve.com
☎ 0131 653 6767 Mobile: 07710 276 208 📠 0131 653 3646

***Care in Crisis**, 39 Union Street, Lurgan BT66 8DY
Director: Dr Richard Barr. Executive staff 1, Admin staff 2. ***CC*** No.XR 1098. Began 1994; interdenominational. Turnover £82,000 to year end Mar 98. Crisis counselling: pregnancy, miscarriage, bereavement, relationships, post-abortion; abstinence centred sex education programme for schools.
☎ 028 3832 9900 📠 028 3832 9602

Career Focus, Crossways, 2a Court Lane, Dulwich, London SE21 7DR
Principal: Mr Rodney Radcliffe. Executive staff 1. Began 1977; non-denominational. (Previously New Life Career and Development Services). No magazine. Turnover £8,000 to year end Apr 98. Providing career review and development consultancy services.
☎ 020 8693 1670 📠 020 8693 4845

†**CARIS**, Telephone contact only, Cambridge
CC Began 1994; interdenominational. (Previously Christian Caring). No magazine. Turnover n/a. Network of independent Christian counsellors providing professional therapy service for Christians and non-Christians.
☎ 01223 368 264

Centre for Health and Pastoral Care, Holy Rood House, 10 Sowerby Road, Sowerby, Thirsk YO7 1HX
Directors: Rev Stanley & Rev Elizabeth Baxter. Executive staff 4, Other staff 6. ***CC*** No.511151. Began 1974; ecumenical. Magazine: *Newsletter* (1,000 quarterly). Turnover £100,000 to year end Dec 96. Therapeutic community and team affiliated to BAC. Creative arts, massage, counselling, and retreat training.
☎ 01845 522 580 📠 01845 527 300

Cephas, 75 High Street, Amblecote, Stourbridge DY8 4LY
Pastoral Director: Pastor Jim Wilson. No full-time staff. ***CC*** No.1009248. Began 1991; interdenominational. No magazine. Turnover £7,874 to year end Mar 96. Restoring and rebuilding broken lives through encouragement, healing, teaching.
☎ 01384 444 459 / 896 741

Christian Counselling Service, 4 Liverpool Terrace, Corwen LL21 0DU
Chief Executive: Ms Esther Wintringham. Executive staff 2, Other staff 2. Began 1993; Free evangelical. Magazine: *Forerunner* (Circulation & frequency n/a). Turnover n/a. Offering foundational, Scriptural teaching. Courses available.
☎ 01490 412 480

hristian Fellowship Ministry, The Lighthouse Centre, 34 Yarm Road, Stockton-on-Tees TS18 3NG
Hon Director: Mr Gordon Clarke. All voluntary staff. ***CC*** No.328335. Began 1983; ecumenical. No magazine. Turnover £10,000 to year end Apr 98. Counselling, training, and outreach ministry (including international), community and pastoral emphasis. ACC recognised.
Email: Lighthouse@cfmstocktonfreeserve.co.uk
☎ 01642 611 497

:hristian Guidelines, 7 Queen Street, Belfast BT1 6EA
Director: Mr Michael Perrott. Full-time staff 1, Voluntary counsellors 24, Part-time staff 4. ***CC*** No.XR 2927. Began 1994; interdenominational. Magazine: *Guide to Guidelines* (2,000 annually). Turnover £90,000 to year end May 98. Christian counselling, teaching on the family, church based evangelism.
☎ 028 9023 0005 🖷 028 9031 2098

The Claybury Trust, PO Box 108, Edgware HA8 0YR
Director: Rev Colin D Buckland. Executive staff 2. ***CC*** No.1072978. Began 1993; non-denominational. No magazine. Turnover n/a. Serving the church, offering encouragement, healing, resources to benefit leaders in their lives and relationships.
Web: www.claybury.org
Email: info@claybury.com
☎ 020 8906 2737 🖷 020 8381 2124

The Cog Wheel Trust, The Stoneyard Centre, 41b St Andrews Street, Cambridge CB2 3AR
Director: Mr Ben Palmer. Full time staff 2, Counsellors 10. ***CC*** Began 1988; non-denominational. Magazine: *Cognews Letter* (Circulation n/a every four months). Turnover £100,000 to year end Dec 98. Providing counselling and therapy to individuals, families, couples, marriage preparation. Disability issues.
☎ 01223 464 385

Compass (Counselling on Merseyside Pastoral and Supporting Service), 25 Hope Street, Liverpool L1 9BQ
Director: Esther Langrish. *Assistant Director:* Ms Brenda Hodgson. Paid staff 9, Volunteer counsellors 70. ***CC*** Began 1978; interdenominational. No magazine. Turnover £120,000 to year end Dec 98. Counselling for those with emotional problems and training in counselling. Supervision for clergy in pastoral work.
☎ 0151 708 6688 🖷 0151 707 8728

Connect Christian Counselling Service, 8 Portesbery Road, Camberley GU15 3TA
Director: Rev Christine Simons. Executive staff 1, Other staff 3. ***CC*** No.1042852. Began 1994; ecumenical. (Previously Camberley Christian Counselling Service). Magazine: *Connect News* (2,000 every four months), *Connections* (2,000 half-yearly). Turnover £100,000 to year end Mar 99. Providing professional counselling in a Christian context, providing training at Introductory Level and in Pastoral Care and Counselling.
☎ 01276 242 10 🖷 01276 223 11

***Contact for Christ**, Selsdon House, 212 Addington Road, South Croydon CR2 8LD
Administrator: Mr Andrew Taylor. Executive staff 1, Other staff 2. ***CC*** No.243305. Began 1975; non-denominational. Magazine: *Newsletter* (7,500 annually). Turnover n/a. Personal contact and follow-up service throughout UK; publishers of outreach material.
Email: cfc@deo-gloria.co.uk
☎ 020 8651 6246 🖷 020 8651 6429

***Cormack Consultancies**, King's Gate, St Mary's Tower, Birnam, Dunkeld PH8 0BJ
Director of Counselling: Mrs Edith Cormack. Executive staff 2, Other staff 3. Began 1985; non-denominational. No magazine. Turnover £150,000. Counselling training within a Christian context, nationally recognised accreditation; professional counselling to individuals, families, organisations.
☎ 01350 728 715 🖷 01350 728 716

Cornerstone, 1 Daniel House, 45 Rickmansworth Road, Pinner HA5 3TJ
Co-ordinator: Mr Stewart Wilson. No full-time staff. Began 1990; interdenominational. No magazine. Turnover n/a. Network of Christian counsellors and psychotherapists working in the London area, professional fees apply.
☎ 020 8429 4086

Counsel For Life (Personal Wholeness Trust), 10 The Broadway, Woodford Green IG8 0HL
Executive Director: Rev David Blackledge. Other staff 10. ***CC*** No.1000837. Began 1989; non-denominational. No magazine. Turnover £80,000 to year end Mar 98. Professional care and counselling for individuals and couples, based on Christian beliefs and values.
Email: cflpwt@aol.com
☎ 020 8491 0222 🖷 020 8505 8426

***Counselling & Prayer Trust**, 138 Greyhound Road, London W6 8NS
Principal: Rev Agnes Sullivan. Counsellors 3. ***CC*** No.1027526. Began 1993; non-denominational. No magazine. Turnover £35,000 to year end Dec 99. Professional counselling training; individual counselling including specific work with couples, men, women, psychotherapy groups.
Web: counsellingpray.org
Email: counselling@pray.org
☎ 020 7386 9998 🖷 020 7386 7663

Counselling Service, 21 Rutland Square, Edinburgh EH1 2BB
Manager: Mr Jonathan Wood. Executive staff 2, Admin staff 2. ***CC*** No.SCO 11353. Began n/a; Church of Scotland. (Previously Simpson House). No magazine. Turnover n/a. Counselling service for general public, with a small children's service and an art therapy department.
☎ 0131 221 9377 🖷 0131 221 9399

***Courage**, PO Box 338, Watford WD1 5HZ
Director: Mr Jeremy Marks. Executive staff 2, Other staff 2. ***CC*** No.328730. Began 1988; interdenominational. Magazine: *Newsletter* (1,150 quarterly). Turnover £70,000 to year end Aug 98. Discipleship groups with regular teaching to help people overcome homosexuality.
Web: www.courage.org.uk
Email: courage@btinternet.com
☎ 020 8420 1066 🖷 020 8421 1692

***Credit Action**, 6 Regent Terrace, Cambridge CB2 1AA
Director: Mr Keith Tondeur. Executive staff 1, Other staff 3. ***CC*** No.1035783. Began 1987; non-denominational. No magazine. Turnover n/a. Helping people with money problems, through written materials, seminars and freephone helpline.
Email: credit.action@dial.pipex.com
☎ 01223 324 034 🖷 01223 324 034

Crossline Christian Centre, 5 Heavitree Road, Exeter EX1 2LD
Secretary: Mr Brian Warren. All voluntary staff. ***CC*** No.281168. Began 1977; non-denominational. No magazine. Turnover n/a. 24-hour counselling service; day-centre for ex-offenders and down-and-outs.
☎ 01392 433 333

Crossline Coventry, Crossline-CCM, PO Box 40, Coventry CV6 2PR
Co-ordinator: Dr John Pither. Voluntary staff 26. ***CC*** No.519000. Began 1992; non-denominational. No magazine. Turnover n/a. Providing confidential Christian staffed telephone helpline for the general public and provision for counselling.
Web: www.users.zetnet.co.uk/covcitymission
Email: covcitymission@zetnet.co.uk
☎ 024 7661 5931 Helpline: 024 7660 3603

Crossline Edinburgh, 9 Pilrig Street, Edinburgh EH6 5AH
Administrator: Mrs Anne D MacLeen. Executive staff 2. ***CC*** No.SCO 12385. Began 1990; interdenominational. No magazine. Turnover £5,741 to year end Dec 96. Providing Christian-run telephone helpline and counselling agency.
☎ 0131 555 3333

***Crossline (Plymouth City Mission)**, 37 Grenville Road, Plymouth PL4 9PY
Director: Rev Jon Bush. No other staff. ***CC*** No.251197. Began n/a; interdenominational. Please address mail to co-ordinator. No magazine. Turnover £8,000 to year end Dec 98. Providing 24-hour helpline; counselling; training.
☎ 01752 664 243 24hr Helpline: 01752 666 777

Crossline Shrewsbury, Claremont Baptist Church, Claremont Street, Shrewsbury SY1 1QG
Counselling Co-ordinator: Mrs Nina Lucas. All voluntary staff. Began 1986; interdenominational. No magazine. Turnover £2,400 to year end Sept 94. Telephone listening service and face-to-face counselling by appointment serving Christians and non-Christians.
☎ 01743 236 424

***Crossroads Christian Counselling Service**, Victoria Park Baptist Church, Grove Road, Bow, London E3 5TG
Project Co-ordinator: Miss Kim Gooding. Executive staff 1, Admin staff 1. Counsellors 6. ***CC*** No.1043304. Began 1994; evangelical. No magazine. Turnover £30,000 to year end Apr 98. Counselling for individuals aged over 16, resident in Tower Hamlets.
☎ 020 8981 8388

CURA, Colmcille House, 1a Miller Street, Londonderry BT48 6SU
Hon Secretary: Ms Ann O'Hagan. All voluntary staff. ***CC*** Began 1977; Roman Catholic. No magazine. Turnover £40,000 to year end Dec 93. Confidential telephone information, counselling and referral service for pregnant women.
☎ 028 7126 8467 🖷 028 7126 8467

S

***CWR (Crusade for World Revival)**, Waverley Abbey House, Waverley Lane, Farnham GU9 8EP
Chief Executive: Mr John Muys. *General Manager Ministry:* Mr Sean Gubb. *Counselling Course Director:* Mr Paul Grant. Executive staff 3, Other staff 43. ***CC*** No.294387. Began 1987; interdenominational. (Previously Waverley Christian Centre). No magazine. Turnover £2,500,000 to year end Dec 98. Providing training in pastoral care and Christian counselling; counselling referrals.
Web: www.cwr.org.uk
Email: training@cwr.org.uk
☎ 01252 784 731 🖷 01252 784 734

†**DialogCentre UK**, BM DialogCentre, London WC1N 3XX
National Director: Mr Christian Szurko. All voluntary staff. Began 1985; interdenominational. No magazine. Turnover n/a. Research, re-evaluation and rehabilitation counselling, public information and counsellor-training re new religions.
☎ 01235 200 404

***Family Life Foundation**, 3 Queen Street, Carrickfergus BT38 8A[illegible]
Director: Rev Roy Kerr. Executive staff 1, Other paid staff [illegible] Volunteers 40. ***CC*** No.XR 16542. Began 1995; interdenom[illegible]national. No magazine. Turnover £35,000 to year end Apr 9[illegible] Caring for families through Christian Caring Initiativ[illegible] programme, counselling, training, Family Care-in-Canc[illegible] project.
Web: www.flfc.freeserve.co.uk
Email: roykerr@familylife.freeserve.co.uk
☎ 028 9336 8899 Mobile: 07889 519 953 🖷 028 9336 880[illegible]

The Five Gables Trust, 66 Lottbridge Drive, Hampden Par[illegible] Eastbourne BN22 9PB
Administrator: Mrs R Heptinstall. Admin staff 1. ***C[illegible]*** No.1059421. Began 1985; interdenominational. No maga[illegible]zine. Turnover £20,000 to year end Dec 98. Providing counsel[illegible]ling, training, supervision, parenting courses.
☎ 01323 509 002 🖷 01323 509 002

Foundation Ministries, 7a Russell Street, Armagh BT60 9AA
Director: Dr Eleanor Burton. *Counsellor:* Mr W A McGilto[illegible] Executive staff 1. ***CC*** No.45237 A. Began 1979; interdenom[illegible]inational. Magazine: *Prayer Letter* (500 n/a). Turnove[illegible] £24,500 to year end Dec 99. Ministry of counselling[illegible] evangelism offering help to the anxious, suicidal, guilty, lonely[illegible] fearful, etc.
☎ 028 3752 5282

Freshfields Charitable Trust, 1 Forest Drive East, Leytonstone[illegible] London E11 1JX
Trustee: Mr Harry Johnson. Executive staff 2, Other staff 7[illegible] ***CC*** No.1015521. Began 1992; Anglican. No magazine. Turnover £38,000 to year end Dec 98. Prayer counselling and healing ministry; training for that ministry.
☎ 020 8539 8002

Grace Ministries, PO Box 1500, Fifth Avenue, Lancing BN15 0ZQ
Principals: Mr & Mrs Ron & Dorothy Dennis. Executive staff 2. Began 1991; interdenominational. No magazine. Turnover n/a. Counselling supervision and resources; Christian counsellor's directory; healthcare and energy conservation.
Web: www.users.globalnet.co.uk/~gracemin/
Email: gracemin@globalnet.co.uk
☎ 01903 761 818 🖷 01903 521 462

***Growing Through**, 3 Grange Road, Erdington, Birmingham B24 0DG
National Director: Mr Dale Erickson. Executive staff 2, Other staff 4. ***CC*** No.1059743. Began 1995; interdenominational. No magazine. Turnover £8,474 to year end Dec 98. Community outreach through divorce recovery, single parenting and redundancy workshops, stress management and communication courses.
Email: dalericks@aol.com
☎ 0121 681 6855

Help Counselling Service, Bridge House, Stallard Street, Trowbridge SN15 3DZ
Service Manager: Mr David Thompson. Executive staff 1, Other staff 2. ***CC*** No.297034. Began 1983; interdenominational. (Previously Help Trowbridge Project). No magazine. Turnover £42,000 to year end Mar 99. Free confidential counselling for anyone in West Wiltshire with any personal or family problems.
☎ 01225 767 459

†***HOPE Christian Counsellors**, 3rd Floor, 2 Princes Buildings, George Street, Bath BA1 2ED
Director: Mrs Karen Noad. Executive staff 1, Other staff 2. ***CC*** No.800831. Began 1987; interdenominational. No magazine. Turnover £12,800 to year end Feb 95. Offering professional accredited Christian counselling, the supervision of accredited Christian counsellors.
☎ 01225 312 085

stitute of Counselling, 6 Dixon Street, Glasgow G1 4AX
Principal of College of Counselling: Rev Neil Morrison. Executive staff 12, Other staff 45. Began 1985; interdenominational. Magazine: *The Living Document* (600 every four months). Turnover £400,000 to year end Jan 98. Diploma in clinical and pastoral counselling skills, home study training; mail order books. University accredited.
Web: www.collegeofcounsel.com
Email: iofcounsel@aol.com
☎ 0141 204 2230 🖷 0141 221 2841

nverness Crisis Pregnancy Centre, 48 Huntly Street, Inverness IV3 5HR
Administrator: Mrs Catherine MacInnes. Admin staff 1, Volunteers 17. ***CC*** No.SCO 20756. Began 1992; interdenominational. Magazine: *Life Issues* (3,000 every two months). Turnover £8,000 to year end Jul 98. Providing free advice and counselling, talking to senior pupils in schools, practical help.
☎ 01463 713 999 🖷 01463 223 983

ainos Trust For Eating Disorders, Lower George House, High Street, Newnham GL14 1BS
Director: Miss Helena Wilkinson. Executive staff 1, Admin staff 2. ***CC*** No.1058040. Began 1995; interdenominational. Magazine: *Kainos News* (500 quarterly). Turnover £82,500 to year end Mar 98. Helping eating disorder sufferers to reach and maintain full recovery through teaching and counselling.
☎ 01594 516 284 🖷 01594 516 284

Key Counselling Services Limited, 12 Davies Close, Rainham RM13 9LJ
Administrator: Mr David Fowler. Executive staff 2, Other staff 3. ***CC*** No.1069652. Began 1997; non-denominational. No magazine. Turnover £2,000 to year end Jul 98. Caring, confidential counselling provided by professionally trained counsellors.
Email: keycounselling@fowler16.freeserve.co.uk
☎ 01708 522 293

Kings Communications, Meadow View, Stratford Drive, Wooburn Green, High Wycombe HP10 0QH
Directors: Mr Andy & Mrs Dot Croall. Other staff 8. Began 1988; non-denominational. No magazine. Turnover £45,000 to year end July 98. Professional Christian counselling; training programmes for organisations and individuals.
Web: www.doveuk.com/kings
Email: kings@doveuk.com
☎ 01494 512 441 🖷 01494 512 442
Also at: First Floor, Wakefield Building, Gomm Road, High Wycombe HP13 7DJ

The Light House Christian Care Ministry, 1a Argyll Street, Coventry CV2 4FJ
General Manager: Mr David Depledge. Other staff 8. ***CC*** No.1064132. Began 1986; interdenominational. No magazine. Turnover £103,000 to year end Mar 98. General Christian counselling service; training courses in Christian counselling; ACC affiliated.
Email: christian.counsel@zetnet.co.uk
☎ 024 7644 0095

***Lighthouse Family Trust**, 72 Longacre, Chelmsford CM1 3BJ
Chairman: Mrs Alison Macklin. Executive staff 1. ***CC*** No.803069. Began 1989; interdenominational. No magazine. Turnover £12,000 to year end Sept 98. Pregnancy, post-abortion and miscarriage counselling; free pregnancy testing; practical help. ACC, Care for Life & BAC affiliated.
☎ 01245 494 838 🖷 01245 495 427

Listening Post (Christian Counselling Service), YMCA Building, Sebert Street, Gloucester GL1 3BS
Director: Mr David H Walker. Other staff 2. ***CC*** No.1013442. Began 1991; ecumenical. No magazine. Turnover £50,000 to year end Mar 98. Counselling Christians and non-Christians; training Christians to ACC standards.
☎ 01452 383 820
Also at: YMCA Building, Vittoria Walk, Cheltenham GL50 1TP
☎ 01242 256 060
And: 20 John Street, Stroud GL5 2HA
☎ 01453 750 123

Littledale Trust, Littledale Hall, Lancaster LA2 9EY
Directors: Mr Stuart & Mrs Wendy Rushton. Executive staff 2, Other staff 7. ***CC*** No.328268. Began 1989; interdenominational. No magazine. Turnover £92,000 to year end Nov 98. Bringing wholeness and rest to leaders, individuals, family groups, retreats, counselling service, training programmes.
Web: www.doveuk.com/littledale
Email: littledale@compuserve.com
☎ 01524 770 266 🖷 01524 771 553

***Living Springs**, 105 High Street, Stourbridge DY8 1EE
Directors: Mr Robert Chapman, Mr Roger Eames. Executive staff 3, Other staff 7. ***CC*** No.701674. Began 1989; interdenominational. No magazine. Turnover n/a. Counselling centre and pregnancy crisis service; bookshop; coffee shop.
Email: roger@livingsprings.prestel.co.uk
☎ 01384 443 636 Mobile: 07801 255 175
🖷 01384 443 636

S

***Living Waters Discipleship & Healing Trust**, PO Box 1530, London SW1W 9WL
Director: Rev Christopher Guinness. Executive staff 2, Admin staff 1. ***CC*** No.1056150. Began 1991; interdenominational. No magazine. Turnover £80,000 to year end Aug 98. Healing and discipleship church-based programmes and conferences for Christians struggling with gender and relationship issues.
Email: lwluk@aol.com
☎ 020 7730 8611 🖷 020 7730 8611

***Manna Counselling Service**, 2 Prentis Road, London SW16 1XU
Counselling Coordinator: Mrs J Kendall. Other staff 1. Began 1981; interdenominational. Part of Streatham Baptist Church. No magazine. Turnover n/a. Counselling service mainly for individuals; information service; training for local churches.
Email: mannacouns@aol.com
☎ 020 8769 1718

Manna House Counselling Service, The Manna House, St Giles Street, Northampton NN1 1JW
Director: Mr John Nightingale. Other staff 4. ***CC*** No.286358. Began 1985; interdenominational. No magazine. Turnover £70,000 to year end Dec 98. Providing Christian counselling to the community; offering training courses locally, nationally and internationally; ACC accredited staff.
☎ 01604 633 304 🖷 01604 635 498

Kay Marion Memorial Foundation, PO Box 2156, West Bromwich B70 6HA
Director: Rev David R Marsh. Executive staff 1, Other staff 3. Began 1995; non-denominational. No magazine. Turnover n/a. Providing support to the families and friends of murder and manslaughter victims; counselling; training; resources.
Email: kmmf@centrepointchurch.freeserve.co.uk
☎ 0121 531 0110 🖷 0121 531 0110

Network Counselling and Training, 10 Cotham Park, Cotham, Bristol BS6 6BU
Director: Rev T J Marks. *Administrator:* Mrs O A Marks. Other staff 2, Volunteer counsellors 86. ***CC*** No.292801. Began 1986; non-denominational. Magazine: *Support* (2,500 half-yearly), *Broadsheet* (Circulation n/a half-yearly). Turnover £150,000 to year end June 98. Providing a counselling service in Bristol and surrounding areas; training in Christian counselling.
Web: www.network.org.uk
Email: info@network.org.uk
☎ 0117 942 0066 🖷 0117 942 8806

New Beginnings, 20 Stratford House, Sackville Street, Southsea PO5 4BX
Founder: Mrs Becky Troke. Executive staff 5. Began 1988; interdenominational. No magazine. Turnover £1,500 to year end Apr 94. Counselling adult survivors of child abuse; support for families; seminars.
☎ 023 9273 0250 Mobile 07930 676 056

New Door: Christian Care and Support, Oliver Bird Hall (Rear of), Church Hill Road, Solihull B91 1AE
Chairman: Mrs Wendy Carter. Began 1987; interdenominational. No magazine. Turnover n/a. Christian care and support through drop-in sessions staffed by Christian listeners. Counselling available by appointment.
☎ 0121 704 2355

Nicholaston House, Penmaen, Gower, Swansea SA3 2HL
Resident Managers: Mr & Mrs Derek & Anne Styants. Admin staff 2. ***CC*** No.700248. Began 1988; interdenominational. No magazine. Turnover £22,000 to year end Dec 97. Small retreat centre offering residential safe house facilities for those needing counselling and ministry.
☎ 01793 371 318

Orpington Christian Counselling Service, 9 Birchwood Road, Pe Wood, Orpington BR5 1NX
Director: Ms Jill Dare. All voluntary staff. ***CC*** No.104268 Began 1986; interdenominational. No magazine. Turnov n/a. Providing counselling through varying circumstanc training in counselling skills, supervision offered.
☎ 01689 827 019

The Oxford Christian Institute for Counselling (OCIC), Oxfo Healthy Living Centre, Oxford Road, Temple Cowley, Oxfor OX4 2ES
Director: Mr Charles Hampton. Executive staff 1, Other sta 2. ***CC*** No.291819. Began 1985; ecumenical. No magazin Turnover £50,000 to year end June 98. Providing counsellin supervision, mediation training and consultation.
☎ 01865 777 755

***Pilgrims Hall**, Ongar Road, Brentwood CM15 9SA
Leader: Mr Peter F Garratt. Admin staff 2, Other staff 8. *C* No.257216. Began 1968; non-denominational. Turnove £70,000 to year end July 98. Conferences, teaching, trainin retreats, counselling.
☎ 01277 372 206 🖷 01277 375 590

Professional Counselling Services, 163 Clifton Road, Rugb CV21 3QN
Counselling Co-ordinator: Mr Roger Day. Executive staff 2 Began 1995; non-denominational. No magazine. Turnove £12,000 to year end May 98. Professional counselling and psychotherapy for individuals and families; training in counsellin skills and coping strategies.
☎ 01788 550 842 Mobile: 07885 823 046 🖷 01788 547 516

***REACH Merseyside**, 85a Allerton Road, Liverpool L18 2DA
Co-ordinator: Andy Bond. Executive staff 1, Other staff 2. ***CC*** No.701330. Began 1986; interdenominational. Magazine *REACH Newsletter* (2,500 half-yearly). Turnover £34,501 to year end Sept 98. Meeting people at their point of need through counselling and training across the North West.
☎ 0151 737 2121 🖷 0151 737 2185

St Marylebone Centre for Healing Counselling, St Marylebone Church, 17 Marylebone Road, London NW1 5LT
Director: Rev Dr Julian Davies. Executive staff 3, Other staff 5. ***CC*** Began 1987; non-denominational. No magazine. Turnover n/a. General counselling, crisis listening, befriending, spiritual direction.
☎ 020 7935 6374 🖷 020 7935 6374

***Salt Centre**, 24 Old Street, Clevedon BS21 6BY
Administrator: Mr Julian Perkins. Admin staff 1. ***CC*** No.1042944. Began 1998; non-denominational. No magazine. Turnover Nil to year end Sep 98. Family crisis and counselling service.
Web: www.living-waters.org.uk
Email: jap@living-waters.org.uk
☎ 01275 797 999 🖷 01275 797 999

***Sanctuary Counselling and Training**, 6 Bankside Walk, Stakeford, Choppington NE62 5BL
Director: Mr David Merritt. Other staff n/a. ***CC*** No.326950. Began 1998; non-denominational. (Previously The Bud Christian Trust, The Bud Counselling and Training Agency). No magazine. Turnover £4,000 to year end Dec 98. Relational and personal counselling. Team building and life skills training. ACC member.
☎ 01670 819 056

Sevenoaks Christian Counselling Service, The Bridge, Littlecourt Road, Sevenoaks TN13 2JG
Senior Counsellor: Maureen King. Executive staff 1. ***CC*** No.288191. Began 1983; interdenominational. No magazine. Turnover n/a. Counselling is offered to all irrespective of religious or sexual orientation. Training is also available.
☎ 01732 450 118

Skills For Living, Littledale Hall, Littledale, Lancaster LA2 9EY
Co-Founder: Mr Walter Acuff. Executive staff 2. Began 1994; non-denominational. No magazine. Turnover £19,000 to year end Dec 98. Retreats; training for group leaders; workshops for personal relationship and marriage issues including abuse.
Web: www.skills.org
📧 Email: littledale@compuserve.com
☎ 01524 770 266 📠 01524 771 553

Skylight – Pregnancy Counselling Centre, PO Box 40, Coventry CV6 2PR
Project Coordinator: Dr John Pither. All voluntary staff. ***CC*** No.519000. Began 1998; non-denominational. No magazine. Turnover n/a. Providing confidential counselling service to women and partners facing a crisis because of unexpected pregnancy.
☎ 024 7661 5931 Helpline: 024 7660 3444

Sozo Ministries International, PO Box 29, Romsey SO51 0YU
Director: Mrs Marion Daniel. Executive staff 6, Other staff 2. ***CC*** No.1042420. Began 1983; non-denominational. Magazine: *Newsletter* (300 every three weeks). Turnover n/a. Christian counselling, healing and deliverance through public meetings, conferences and private counselling.
📧 Email: sozomin@msn.com
☎ 01794 323 516 📠 01794 322 167

Stockport Christian Counselling, Admin. Office, Stockport Baptist Church, Thomson Street, Stockport SK3 0TS
All voluntary staff. ***CC*** No.1025437. Began 1991; interdenominational. No magazine. Turnover £3,800 to year end July 98. Providing counselling service to the churches and the community.
☎ 0161 474 1090 (ansaphone) 0161 439 0070 (counselling)

Stroud Pregnancy Crisis Centre, Top Flat, 52 London Road, Stroud GL5 2AD
Coordinator: Mrs Rachel Coysh. No other staff. ***CC*** No.1039328. Began 1987; non-denominational. No magazine. Turnover £6,000 to year end Mar 98. Providing counselling, support and information about crisis pregnancies and abortion; resources for schools and churches.
☎ 01453 757 643

Support Group & Counselling Service, PO Box 30, Potters Bar EN6 3JD
Manager: Mr Daniel Lim. No full-time paid staff. Began 1992; interdenominational. No magazine. Turnover n/a. Counselling people with stress and other mental problems.
☎ 01707 659 996 Mobile: 07710 782 008

Sycamore Education & Training, Friars House, 6 Parkway, Chelmsford CM2 0NF
Director: Linda Hopper. Tutors 2. ***CC*** No.249768. Began 1995; Baptist. No magazine. Turnover £61,000 to year end Apr 97. Providing courses in counselling, mental health; counselling for children.
📧 Email: sycamore@prontomail.com
☎ 01277 841 773 📠 01245 359 101

***Touchstones (London & South East)**, 22 Sandringham Road, Bromley BR1 5AS
Chairman: Mr Malcolm Green. All voluntary staff. ***CC*** No.1054292. Began 1993; interdenominational. No magazine. Turnover £400 to year end Dec 98. Counselling for people with mental health problems, providing education and training to the church.
📧 Email: touchstones@cwcom.net
☎ 020 8402 1427 Mobile: 07958 592 708
📠 020 8402 8629

***True Freedom Trust**, PO Box 3, Upton, Wirral CH49 6NY
Director: Mr Martin Hallett. Executive staff 2, Other staff 1. ***CC*** No.513863. Began 1977; interdenominational. (Merged with Turnabout 1991). Magazine: *TFT Newsletter* (1,200 quarterly). Turnover £70,000 to year end Apr 98. Christian counselling, support and teaching on homosexuality and related issues.
Web: www.tftrust.u-net.com
📧 Email: martin@tftrust.u-net.com
☎ 0151 653 0773 📠 0151 653 7036

***U-Turn Anglia Trust**, PO Box 138, Witnesham, Ipswich IP6 9EP
Director: Rev George A Harvey. Executive staff 3. ***CC*** No.1004424. Began 1987; interdenominational. Magazine: *U-Turn Anglia Newsletter* (300 every four months). Turnover n/a. Christian counselling ministry to homosexual men and women seeking healing; assisting church understanding; ACC accredited.
☎ 01473 785 129

†**United Churches Healing Ministry Trust**, St James Parish Church, Station Road, Slaithwaite, Huddersfield HD7 4AW
Director: Mrs Helga Taylor. Executive staff 1, Other staff 3. ***CC*** Began 1992; interdenominational. (Previously Scapegoat Hill Baptist Church Counselling Ministry). Magazine: *Healing Leaves* (Circulation n/a quarterly). Turnover £7,000 to year end Apr 94. Counselling; counselling training; seminars in ordinary Christian life.
☎ 01484 847 152

***Wellspring Christian Trust**, 9 Church Street, Frodsham, Warrington WA6 7DN
Trustee: Dr Andrew Faraday. Admin staff 2, Voluntary staff 20. ***CC*** No.1035086. Began 1992; ecumenical. Turnover n/a. Sharing the love of God through Christian listening ear service, coffee shop, bookshop.
☎ 01928 735 589

Whitchester Christian Guest House and Retreat Centre, Borthaugh, Hawick TD9 7LN
Administrators: John & Dinah Rogers, Richard & Nanette Gee. Other staff 4. ***CC*** Began 1984; interdenominational. No magazine. Turnover n/a. Spiritual guidance, prayer ministry and counselling; training conferences and small groups facilitated. Affiliated to ACC.
☎ 01450 377 477 📠 01450 371 080

CREATION MOVEMENTS

See also Environmental Movements on Page 413

Answers in Genesis, PO Box 5262, Leicester LE2 3XU
Chief Executive: Mr Graham Scott. Other staff 4. ***CC*** No.1024543. Began 1991; non-denominational. (Previously Creation Science Foundation UK). Magazine: *Creation Ex Nihilo* (2,500 quarterly). Turnover n/a. Promoting belief in Biblical creation through seminars, magazine, books, videos.
Web: answersingenesis.org
☎ 0116 270 8400 🖷 0116 270 0110

The Biblical Creation Society, PO Box 22, Rugby CV22 7SY
Administrators: Mr Brian Watt, Mrs Elizabeth Reeves. No full-time staff. ***CC*** No.42386. Began 1976; interdenominational. Magazine: *Origins* (800 half-yearly). Turnover £16,000. Spreading Biblical and scientific opposition to the theory of evolution especially among Christians.
Web: www.pages.org/bcs/index.html
☎ 01788 810 633

***Creation Resources Trust**, Mead Farm, Downhead, West Camel, Yeovil BA22 7RQ
Director: Mr Geoff Chapman. Executive staff 1. ***CC*** No.1016666. Began 1981; non-denominational. Magazine: *Creation Update* (1,000 quarterly), *Our World (for children)* (4,000 quarterly), *Original View (for teenagers)* (2,000 every four months). Turnover £25,000 to year end Dec 98. Sharing the evidence for Biblical creation: literature, books, visual aids, seminars and all-age 'creation discovery days'.
Web: ourworld.compuserve.com/homepages/creationresources
Email: creationresources@compuserve.com
☎ 01935 850 569

***Creation Science Movement**, PO Box 888, Portsmouth PO6 2YD
Hon Secretary & Treasurer: Mrs Joan Rosevear. Executive sta 5, Other staff 3. ***CC*** No.801745. Began 1932; no denominational. Magazine: *Creation* (2,100 every tw months). Turnover £100,000 to year end Aug 98. Publishin distributing literature; lecturing on doctrine of creation a opposed to secular evolution; exhibiting.
Web: www.csm.org.uk
☎ 023 9229 3988 🖷 023 9229 3988
Bookshop at: 17 The Hard, Portsmouth PO1 3DT

Daylight Origins Society, 19 Francis Avenue, St Albans AL3 6BL
Editor & Secretary: Mr Anthony Nevard. No paid staff. Bega 1991; Roman Catholic. (Previously CESHE-UK). Magazine *Daylight* (250 quarterly). Turnover £2,000 to year end Dec 98 Organising meetings and distributing literature and audio visuals to inform Catholics on creation science.
☎ 01727 868 427

DISABILITIES, ORGANISATIONS FOR PEOPLE WITH

Relevant entries previously in Blind Organisations, Social Associations or Social Services & Welfare Organisations

Archbishop's Council – Committee for Ministry among Deaf People, Church House, Great Smith Street, London SW1P 3NZ
Secretary: Rev Canon H James Clarke. Executive staff 1. ***CC*** Began 1929; Anglican. (Previously ABM Committe for Ministry among Deaf People). No magazine. Turnover n/a. Pastoral and spiritual care of deaf people; training for deaf people and those working with them.
☎ 020 7233 1153 Text No: 020 7898 1429
🖷 020 7898 1421

Association of Blind Catholics, 58 Oakwood Road, Horley RH6 7BU
Hon Secretary: Mr Paul Questier. All voluntary staff. ***CC*** No.259343. Began 1961; Roman Catholic. Magazine: *Catholic Talking Newspaper* (400 monthly (cassette)). Turnover n/a. Assisting blind Roman Catholics to take a fuller part in the life of the Church.
☎ 01293 772 104

Catholic Handicapped Fellowship, 15 Woodlands Park Drive, Blaydon-on-Tyne NE21 5PQ
National Secretary: Mr John Mair. Executive staff 2. ***CC*** No.208717. Began 1957; Roman Catholic, but open to all. No magazine. Turnover £5,000 to year end Mar 96. Providing a forum where leaders of Diocesan Handicapped Groups meet to discuss items of mutual interest.
☎ 0191 414 3221

***Christian Deaf Link UK**, Westminster Chapel, Buckingham Gate, London SW1E 6BS
Chairman of Trustees: Mr John Delve. No full time staff. ***CC*** No.1071830. Began 1998; non-denominational. (Previously London Christian Deaf Link). Magazine: *Deaflink Magazine* (500 quarterly). Turnover £20,359 to year end Mar 99. Developing innovative Christian work, meeting the spiritual needs of deaf people through "Grace" programme.
Email: deaflink01@aol.com.uk
☎ No telephone 🖷 01277 632 558

Christian Outreach to the Handicapped, 95 Genesta Road, London SE18 3EX
Principal: Mr Edwin Cross. Executive staff 1, Other staff 2. Began 1978; Christian Brethren. No magazine. Turnover £275,000 to year end Dec 98. Propagating the Gospel among the disabled. Worldwide outreach.
☎ 020 8316 5389

†**Church Action on Disability**, 50 Scrutton Street, London EC2A 4PH
Co-ordinator: Mr Martyn Pope. No full-time staff. ***CC*** No.1003716. Began 1987; interdenominational. Magazine: *All People* (1,100 quarterly). Turnover £21,000 to year end Mar 96. Ecumenical, educational campaign addressing attitudes to all forms of disability in the churches.
☎ 020 7452 2085 🖷 020 7452 2001

ompassionate Response, 44 Queen Street, Lydney GL15 5LY
Coordinator: Mr David Middleton. Executive staff 2, No other paid staff. Began 1994; interdenominational. (Previously Handi *Vangelism UK). No magazine. Turnover n/a. Providing practical/teaching programmes for people with life long or long term hurts and disabilities.
Email: david-cr@cwcom.net
☎ 01594 843 711 🖷 01594 843 711

eaf Christian Network (Hands Together), PO Box 212, Doncaster DN2 5XA
Administrator: Mr Kenneth R Nuttall. Other staff 1. ***CC*** No.253131. Began 1990; interdenominational. (Previously Reachout to the Deaf). Magazine: *Newsletter* (Circulation n/a quarterly). Turnover n/a. National resource centre, providing literature, newsletters, ministry videos in sign language for the deaf.
Web: www.deafcn.dircon.co.uk
Email: deafcn@dircon.co.uk
☎ 01302 369 684

Disability Network, Whitefield House, 186 Kennington Park Road, London SE11 4BT
Chair: Ruth Valerio. No full-time staff. ***CC*** No.123448. Began n/a; interdenominational. (Previously Disability Forum). An Evangelical Alliance Network. No magazine. Turnover: finance included with Evangelical Alliance. Working with Christian disability organisations to be an effective force for change in church and society.
Web: www.eauk.org
Email: rvalerio@eauk.org
☎ 020 7207 2100 🖷 020 7207 2130

***Disabled Christians Fellowship**, 213 Wick Road, Brislington, Bristol BS4 4HP
General Secretary: Miss Jenny Edwards. Full-time staff 8, Voluntary staff. ***CC*** No.1059250. Began 1959; interdenominational. Magazine: *Vital Link* (6,000 monthly). Turnover £58,000 to year end Dec 96. Providing Day Centre and holidays for handicapped Christians; local groups.
Email: jennywheel@aol.com.
☎ 0117 983 0388 🖷 0117 914 8910

***Evangelical Concern for People with Disabilities**, 48 Peel Close, Chingford, London E4 6XU
Administrator: Miss Elizabeth McMillan. ***CC*** No.1056174. Began 1994; interdenominational. No magazine. Turnover n/a. Counselling, prayer, integration into a church; educating churches and caring; distributing Bibles and cassettes.
☎ 020 8281 9682 Mobile: 07956 651 940

***Field Lane Foundation**, 16 Vine Hill, London EC1R 5EA
Director: Mr Jeremy Lamb. *Director of Fundraising and PR:* Mr Peter Rosenvinge. Executive staff 12, Other staff 296. ***CC*** No.207493. Began 1841; non-denominational. Magazine: *Inside Lane Newsletter* (Circulation & frequency n/a). Turnover £3,087,008 to year end Mar 98. Nursing/residential homes for elderly and disabled people; day centres for elderly, disabled and homeless families.
☎ 020 7837 0412

***John Grooms**, 50 Scrutton Street, London EC2A 4XQ
Executive Director: Rev Michael Shaw. *Head of Communications:* Miss Karin Weighton. Executive staff 5, Other staff 490. ***CC*** No.212463. Began 1866; interdenominational. Magazine: *Grooms News* (50,000 half-yearly). Turnover £8,000,000 to year end Mar 98. Providing care and housing for people with physical disabilities including holidays, rehabilitation and residential care.
Web: www.johngrooms.org.uk
Email: charity@johngrooms.org.uk
☎ 020 7452 2000 🖷 020 7452 2001

***Hard of Hearing Christian Fellowship**, PO Box 91, Reading RG1 5YR
Administrator: Mr G Naish. Part-time staff 1. ***CC*** No.284487. Began 1974; interdenominational. Magazine: *Hearing Eye* (300 quarterly). Turnover £12,000 to year end Dec 98. Additional fellowship and support for hearing-impaired Christians. Conferences, advising churches on pastoral care and loops/equipment.
Email: graeme_naish@compuserve.com
☎ 0118 987 2166

†Lightwing Projects, 91 Fairlee Road, Newport PO30 2EL
Chairman: Mr Peter Le Brocq. No full-time staff. ***CC*** No.1016529. Began 1987; non-denominational. Magazine: *Newsletter* (150 quarterly). Turnover £3,000 to year end Dec 96. Producing Christian books and magazines in Braille by computer.
Web: www.argonet.co.uk/users/flintdes/lwing.html
Email: le_brocq@msn.com
☎ 01983 523 784

***Logres Trust**, Forest Dene, Christchurch Hospital, Christchurch BH23 2JX
General Manager: Mr R A Gregory. Executive staff 1, Other staff 10. ***CC*** No.298189. Began 1989; non-denominational. No magazine. Turnover £35,000 to year end Dec 96. Assisting arthritic and disabled people in the community.
☎ 01202 486 361 Ext 5349

***Michael Roberts Charitable Trust (MRCT)**, 8 Chapel Fields, Harlow CM17 9EG
Director/Trustee: Mr Gary Knott. Executive staff 1. ***CC*** No.1065006. Began 1991; non-denominational. Magazine: *Capstone* (400 every four months). Turnover £20,000 to year end Mar 98. Enabling people with learning/physical disabilities to develop work and social opportunities, meeting Christian needs.
Web: www.mrct.freeserve.co.uk
Email: garyknott@mrct.freeserve.co.uk
☎ 01279 301 893 Fax 01279 301 893

†Mission to Deaf People, 5 College Square North, Belfast BT1 6AR
Chaplain: Rev William A Murphy. Executive staff 1. ***CC*** Began 1888; Church of Ireland. No magazine. Turnover n/a. Providing pastoral care for deaf people in Northern Ireland.
☎ 028 9032 1733 Fax 028 9023 3868

***PROSPECTS for People with Learning Disabilities**, PO Box 351, Reading RG1 7AL
Chief Executive: Mr Peter Levell. *Director of Living PROSPECTS:* Miss Maureen Wise. *Director of Causeway PROSPECTS:* Mr Tony Phelps-Jones. Executive staff 4, Other staff 186. ***CC*** No.1060571. Began 1976; interdenominational. (Previously A Cause for Concern). (See also Causeway PROSPECTS). Magazine: *Better Prospects* (10,000 half-yearly). Turnover £3,500,000 to year end Mar 99. Providing residential support, day services, development opportunities and spiritual ministry for people with learning disabilities.
Email: info@prospects.org.uk
☎ 0118 950 8781 Fax 0118 939 1683

The Royal Association in Aid of Deaf People (RAD), Walsingham Road, Colchester CO2 7BP
Chief Executive: Mr Tom Fenton. Executive staff 8, Other staff 40. ***CC*** No.207358. Began 1841; Anglican. No magazine. Turnover £1,500,000 to year end Dec 98. Promoting the spiritual, social and general welfare of deaf people.
Web: www.royaldeafuk
Email: info@royaldeaf.org.uk
☎ 01206 509 509 Text: 01206 577 090 Fax 01206 769 755

Through The Roof, PO Box 178, Cobham KT11 1YN
Director: Mr Paul Dicken. Executive staff 1, Other staff 3. ***CC*** No.1061010. Began 1997; non-denominational. UK ministry of Joni Eareckson Tada. Magazine: *Through The Roof News* (1,900 every four months). Turnover £75,000 to year end Dec 98. Raising awareness of disability among Christians, empowering disabled people. Equipping and advising churches.
Web: www.throughtheroof.org
Email: info@throughtheroof.org
☎ 01932 866 333 Fax 01932 866 333

orch Trust for the Blind, Torch House, Hallaton, Market Harborough LE16 8UJ
Administrator: Mr Michael Stafford. *Technical Director:* Dr M Townsend. Executive staff 6, Other staff 52. *CC* No.208678. Began 1959; interdenominational. Magazine: *Torch Family News* (8,000 frequency n/a). Turnover £485,195 to year end Sept 97. Providing Christian literature in Braille, giant print and cassettes. Fellowship and holidays for the visually impaired.
Email: torchtrust@dial.pipex.com
☎ 01858 555 301 🖷 01858 555 371

***The Woodhill Project**, Moelfre, Llansilin, Oswestry SY10 7QX
Chairman: Ms Janet Randell. Admin staff 1, Other staff 1. *CC* No.1050270. Began 1995; interdenominational. No magazine. Turnover n/a. Serving disadvantaged people through therapeutic, environmental and rural amenities including wheelchair access, workshops and retreat.
☎ 01691 791 486 🖷 01691 791 486

ENVIRONMENTAL MOVEMENTS

See also Creation Movements on Page 410.

Christian Ecology Link, 20 Carlton Road, Harrogate HG2 8DD
Correspondent/Information Officer: Mr George E Dent. No full-time staff. *CC* No.328744. Began 1981; interdenominational. Magazine: *Green Christians* (700 quarterly). Turnover n/a. Creating awareness of ecological problems and suggesting responses; promoting Christian understanding within the Green movement.
Web: www.christian-ecology.org.uk
Email: info@christian-ecology.org.uk
☎ 01423 871 616

Evangelical Environment Network, Institute for Contemporary Christianity, St Peter's Church, Vere Street, London W1M 9HP
Director: Dr Bob Carling. No full-time staff. Began 1994; non-denominational. No magazine. Turnover £200 to year end Dec 98. Acting as a liaison organization linking together Christians with environmental concerns.
Web: homepages.tcp.co.uk/~carling/eenhome.html
Email: carling@tcp.co.uk
☎ 023 8077 8830 / 8334 2838 🖷 023 8034 2838

Quaker Green Concern, The Folly, Yarpole Lane, Luston HR6 0BX
Secretary: Anne Adams. No full-time staff. *CC* Began 1986; Religious Society of Friends. Magazine: *Earth Quaker* (200 quarterly). Turnover £1,500 to year end Nov 98. Supporting each other in changing lifestyles and influencing the Religious Society of Friends.
☎ 01568 780 886

REEP (Religious Education and Environment Programme) and Planet Pledge Network (PPN), 8th Floor, Rodwell House, 100 Middlesex Street, London E1 7HJ
Programme Director: Fr Vincent Rossi. Full-time staff 1. *CC* No.1000998. Began 1994; ecumenical. *Reep News* (Circulation & frequency n/a). Turnover £16,000 to year end Dec 98. In-service training of teachers. Handbook, events/PPN showing environmental relevance of religious practice.
Web: www.users.globalnet.co.uk/~reep
Email: reep@globalnet.co.uk
☎ 020 7377 1077 / 0604 🖷 020 7247 2144

***A Rocha Trust**, 3 Hooper Street, Cambridge CB1 2NZ
UK Administrator: Mrs Barbara Mearns. *International Co-ordinators:* Peter and Miranda Harris. UK Staff 1, Overseas Staff 10. *CC* No.288634. Began 1983; non-denominational. Magazine: *A Rocha News* (1,700 quarterly). Turnover £200,000 to year end Dec 98. Christian international conservation organisation campaigning and working practically to care for God's creation.
Web: www.arocha.org/
Email: a_rocha@compuserve.com
☎ 01387 710 286 🖷 01387 710 286

ETHNIC MINORITY ASSOCIATIONS

For overseas national church congregations see Church Headquarters on Page 195.

Africa Christian Fellowship UK and Eire, United Reformed Church Hall, 86 Tavistock Place, Regent Square, London WC1H 9RT
President: Dr Abbey Adeyema. No full-time staff. *CC* Began 1969; interdenominational. Magazine: *ACF Magazine* (500 quarterly). Turnover £10,000 to year end Sept 90. Uniting and encouraging African Christians and friends of Africa in the faith.
☎ 020 7278 8284 / 01322 438 331

***African and Caribbean Evangelical Alliance**, Whitefield House, 186 Kennington Park Road, London SE11 4BT
Director: Mr Mark Sturge. Other staff 3, Voluntary staff 60. *CC* No.802887. Began 1984; interdenominational. In partnership with Evangelical Alliance. Magazine: *Focus* (3,000 five times a year). Turnover £62,000 to year end Mar 98. Representing and promoting black Christian faith in UK; promoting reconciliation across cultures and ethnic groups.
Email: acea@eauk.org
☎ 020 7735 7373 🖷 020 7735 7275

†***African Brethren Connect (ABC)**, 30 Snowfields, London SE1 3SU
Co-ordinator: Rev Abraham Oshuntola. Other staff 2. *CC* Began 1990; interdenominational. Magazine: *African Brethren Connect* (Circulation n/a quarterly). Turnover n/a. Organising and co-ordinating African church events.
☎ 020 7403 9718

†***Alliance of Asian Christians**, Carrs Lane Church Centre, Carrs Lane, Birmingham B4 7SX
Executive Secretary: Mr Pradip Sudra. Executive staff 1, Other staff 3. *CC* No.1020767. Began 1989; non-denominational. In partnership with Evangelical Alliance. Magazine: *Aaeki Haae* (2,000 half-yearly). Turnover £75,000 to year end Jun 96. Support and representative organisation for Asian individuals and churches.
☎ 0121 633 4533 🖷 01902 620 811

S

***Anglo-Japanese Christian Ministries (AJCM)**, 9 Beaminster Avenue, Stockport SK4 3HU
Ministry Directors: Mr Trevor & Mrs Cheryl Howard. Executive staff 2. *CC* No.1008099. Began 1991; interdenominational. No magazine. Turnover £21,000 to year end Apr 98. Evangelistic and pastoral work amongst Japanese in Greater Manchester; encouraging evangelism of Japanese in UK.
Email: thowand@ajcm.u-net.com
☎ 0161 442 4282 🖷 0161 442 4282

Asian Christian Fellowship, 26 Lyndhurst Road, Penn Fields, Wolverhampton WV3 0AA
Leader: Mr Marlin Summers. Executive staff 3. Began 1973; non-denominational. No magazine. Turnover £30,000 to year end Dec 98. Church building through evangelism by literature, visitation and other forms of outreach.
☎ 01902 341 089

Asian Concern, PO Box 613, Edinburgh EH15 2LY
Honorary Field Workers: Mr Shamaun & Mrs Mhairi Tufail. No other full-time staff. *CC* No.SCO 20697. Began 1989; interdenominational. Magazine: *Newsletter* (150 quarterly). Turnover £1,300 to year end Mar 99. Sharing God's love with Asians; evangelism by literature, visitation, teaching, hospitality, practical help.
Email: afanderson@compuserve.com
☎ 0131 665 9708 🖷 0131 665 9708

†**Association of Nigerian Catholics**, 8a Battersea Park Road, Battersea, London SW8 4BH
Chaplain: Rev F E Chukwu. Executive staff 1, Admin staff 1. Began 1990; Roman Catholic. Magazine: *Nigerian Catholic Community Newsletter* (2,500 quarterly). Turnover n/a. Providing welfare, chaplaincy, consultancy services; pilgrimages, retreats.
☎ 020 8317 8364 🖷 020 7498 7848

Austrian Catholic Centre, 29 Brook Green, London W6 7BL
Social workers in charge: Miss Helga Berchtel, Miss Anne Ringler. Executive staff 2. *CC* No.240896. Began 1955; Roman Catholic. No magazine. Turnover £85,000-90,000 to year end Dec 95. Hostel, social centre and welfare work for Austrians.
☎ 020 7603 2697 🖷 020 7603 2697

The British Messianic Jewish Alliance, PO Box 607, Harrow HA2 9TF
Office Secretary: Mrs D Rodgers. No full-time staff. Began 1866; interdenominational. (Previously The Hebrew Christian Alliance of Great Britain). Magazine: *Chai* (Circulation n/a quarterly). Turnover n/a. Spiritual/temporal care of Jewish people who believe in Jesus the Messiah and those who wish to stand alongside them.
Email: debbie@bmja.freeserve.co.uk
☎ 020 8204 7592

Care Community Centre, c/o 24 Windsor Close, Hemel Hempstead HP2 4JU
Elder: Mr Ric Munro. No full-time staff. Began 1996; non-denominational. No magazine. Turnover £4,000 to year end Dec 98. Serving Turkish speakers with practical help, advice, Bible teaching, weekly Bible meeting.
Email: tulin.munro@dial.pipex.com
☎ 07970 494 039 🖷 01442 213 459

Chinese Overseas Christian Mission, 4 Earlsfield Road, Lond SW18 3DW
Director: Miss Mary Wang. *Field Director:* Rev David Cheun *Council Chairman:* Prof Michael Chan. Executive staff 2, Oth staff 40. *CC* No.232651. Began 1950; interdenominationa Magazine: *COCM Link* (5,000 quarterly), *Living Wat* (12,000 every two months), *Prayer News* (5,000 monthly Turnover £670,000 to year end Dec 98. Evangelism, churc planting, literature, bookroom, students, restaurant worker scholars and British-born Chinese ministries.
Web: www.glink.net.hk/~cocmhk
Email: cocm@compuserve.com
☎ 020 8870 2251 🖷 020 8877 1357

Derby Asian Christian Ministry Partnership, St Augustine Church Office, Upper Dale Road, Derby DE23 8BP
Minister: Rev Basil Scott. Executive staff 2. Began 1978; Loca ecumenical partnership. Magazine: *Derby Dost* (Circulation & frequency n/a). Turnover £40,000 to year end Dec 98. Pro moting ecumenical and multi-cultural Christian ministrie among Asian communities in Derby.
Email: 100600.233@compuserve.com
☎ 01332 772 360/270 837

Ethiopian Christian Fellowship Church in the UK, 105 Foundlin Court, Brunswick Centre, London WC1N 1AN
Co-ordinator: n/a. No full-time staff. *CC* Began 1981; Pente costal. Magazine: *Kebron* (500 quarterly). Turnover n/a Bringing the Gospel of Jesus Christ to Ethiopians living in the United Kingdom and Europe.
☎ 020 7833 3309

German Catholic Mission (Wynfrid House), 20 Mulberry Street, London E1 1EH
Priest-in-Charge: Father H Medoch. *Administrator:* Mrs A E Greaves. Other staff (part-time) 3. Began 1861; Roman Catholic. No magazine. Turnover n/a. Caring for all German Catholics in the UK; providing temporary accommodation, mainly for youth groups.
☎ 020 7247 6110/5773 🖷 020 7247 0552

German Young Men's Christian Association, 35 Craven Terrace, Lancaster Gate, London W2 3EL
General Secretary: Mr Bernd Hildebrandt. Executive staff 3. *CC* No.250118. Began 1860; interdenominational. No magazine. Turnover £333,500 to year end Dec 98. Community centre, programme of cultural and social activities.
☎ 020 7723 9276 🖷 020 7706 2870

The Great Commission Evangelical Fellowship, PO Box 3805, London SW17 9XE
General Secretary: Pastor Isaac William. Executive staff 1, Other staff 20. Began 1991; interdenominational. (Previously Eastern-Asian Outreach). No magazine. Turnover n/a. Evangelism and outreach among the Asian community; peace research project; seminars, leadership and training.
☎ 020 8672 9034 🖷 020 8672 9034

***Interserve – MAB**, Fourth floor, Cornerstone House, 5 Ethel Street, Birmingham B2 4BG
Team Leader: Rev David Corfe. Executive staff 2, Other staff 40. *CC* No.1020758. Began 1984; interdenominational. (Previously Ministry among Asians in Britain). Magazine: *The Church & Asians in Britain* (1,500 half-yearly). Turnover £310,000 to year end Dec 98. Evangelism and church education in cross cultural ministry; encouragement of ethnic minority Christians.
Email: davidcorfe@mabham.globalnet.co.uk
☎ 0121 643 7771 🖷 0121 643 7772

Japanese Christian Fellowship (UK), 10 Lancing Close, Reading RG30 2UQ
Representative: Rev Susumu Morinaga. ***CC*** Began n/a; interdenominational. Magazine: *Newsletter* (300 monthly). Turnover £30,000 to year end Mar 99. Providing cultural outreach to local Japanese mothers.
☎ 020 8876 4493

Jericho Community Project, Church of God of Prophecy, 47 George Street, Balsall Heath, Birmingham B12 9RG
Project Manager: Mr Trevor Minto. Executive staff 1. ***CC*** No.1037084. Began 1988; interdenominational. No magazine. Turnover n/a. African Caribbean mental health service providing counselling, carers, educational support, training, spiritual support.
☎ 0121 440 7548 Helpline (24 hours): 0800 389 3349
🖷 0121 440 7548

Overseas Fellowship of Nigerian Christians, National Office, 142 Dantzic Street, Manchester M4 4DN
Chairman: Dr Olusola Osundeko. No full-time staff. ***CC*** Began 1974; interdenominational. Magazine: *Arise* (Circulation n/a quarterly). Turnover £30,000 to year end Aug 94. Encouraging Christian love, fellowship and service among Nigerians in UK.
☎ 0161 834 2499

Polish Institute of Catholic Action, 240 King Street, London W6 0RF
General Secretary: Mr Olgierd Stepan KCSG. All voluntary staff. Began 1948; Roman Catholic. Magazine: *Czyn Katolicki-Wiadomosci* (900 quarterly). Turnover £8,500 to year end Mar 98. Lay apostolate among people of Polish origin; representation in international Catholic organisations.
☎ 020 8563 0206 🖷 020 8563 0206

The Serve China Trust, 12 Brookside Avenue, Wollaton, Nottingham NG8 2RD
Adminstrator: Mrs Kum Kew Wells. No full-time staff. ***CC*** No.1001001. Began 1990; interdenominational. No magazine. Turnover £3,942 to year end Feb 98. Providing Scriptures, literature and tapes for Mandarin speaking Chinese in Britain.
☎ 0115 928 3290

***South Asian Concern**, PO Box 43, Sutton SM2 5WL
Chairman: Mr Ram Gidoomal. Admin staff 5. ***CC*** No.1002270. Began 1989; interdenominational. Magazine: *Concern* (2,000 quarterly). Turnover £90,000 to year end Mar 98. Enabling Asian and other Christians to be more effective in leadership and outreach among South Asians.
Email: 100126.3641@compuserve.com
☎ 020 8770 9717 🖷 020 8770 9747

***South West London Asian Outreach**, 22 Lewin Road, Streatham, London SW16 6JD
Pastoral Leader: Pastor Akhtar Samuel. Admin staff 1, Other staff 3. ***CC*** No.249703. Began 1992; interdenominational. No magazine. Turnover n/a. Outreach to those of other faiths, discipling Asian Christians, bridge-building between Church and Asians.
☎ 020 8769 1515 🖷 020 8677 3486

***Southampton Asian Christian Outreach**, 114 St Mary Street, Southampton SO14 1PF
Senior full-time worker: Mr K S Rajo. Executive staff 2. ***CC*** No.290183. Began 1984; interdenominational. No magazine. Turnover n/a. Evangelising Asians through Hampshire Asian Christian Fellowship; outreach centre/craft shop.
Web: www.saco.freeserve.co.uk
Email: clive.thorne@saco.freeserve.co.uk
☎ 023 8043 5455

Turkish Christian Fellowship, Downs Baptist Church, Downs Road, London E5 8DS
Contact Person: Mr T R Spring. No full-time staff. Began 1992; Baptist. No magazine. Turnover n/a. Offering a translation into Turkish of services at Downs Baptist Church; contact for Turkish-speaking Christians.
Email: tim.spring@ukonline.co.uk
☎ 020 8985 2958

FINANCIAL SERVICES

See also Computer & Business Services on Page 399.

Allchurches Investment Ltd Management Services, Beaufort House, Brunswick Road, Gloucester GL1 1JZ
Director: Mr George Prescott. Executive staff 7. Began 1988; non-denominational. No magazine. Turnover £4,000,000 to year end Dec 98. The Amity Fund is a unit trust which avoids investment in areas such as armaments and tobacco.
☎ 01452 305 958 🖷 01452 311 690

Anchorline & Co, Lake House, 47 The Common, Earlswood, Solihull B94 5SJ
Principal: Mrs Aileen Swain. Executive staff 1. Began 1995; Free Church. No magazine. Turnover n/a. Chartered accountants, registered auditors; offering services relating to accountancy, tax, financial advice.
Web: ourworld.compuserve.com/homepages/anchorline/
☎ 01564 702 007

The Anglican Stewardship Association, 71 Dee Banks, Chester CH3 5UX
General Secretary: Mrs Carol Sims. ***CC*** No.235081. Began 1964; Anglican. Magazine: *Link* (Circulation n/a every four months). Turnover n/a. Promoting generous proportionate giving, responsible ownership, lay ministry and pastoral care amongst Christians.
Email: peter@patent.u-net.com
☎ 01244 341 996 🖷 01244 400 338
Also at: 1 Maer Road, Exmouth EX8 2DA
☎ 01395 272 227
And: 22 Westfield Street, Scalford, Melton Mowbray LE14 4DW
☎ 01664 444 239

Ansvar Insurance Company Ltd, Ansvar House, 31 St Leonards Road, Eastbourne BN21 3UR
Managing Director: Mr Geoffrey Williams. Executive staff 8, Other staff 43. Began 1959; non-denominational. No magazine. Turnover £8,000,000 to year end Dec 98. Providing insurance for churches, Christian organisations and charities; Personal Lines insurance for non-drinkers.
☎ 01323 737 541 🖷 01323 430 977

Association of Christian Independent Financial Advisers, c/o Quest Financial, Bank Chambers, Market Place, Chipping Norton OX7 5NA
Chairman: Mr Mark W Roach. No full-time staff. Began 1988; interdenominational. Magazine: *Newsletter* (Circulation & frequency n/a). Turnover n/a. Providing sound and biblical financial advice to individuals and businesses.
Web: www.questfs.co.uk/acifa
Email: acifa@questfs.co.uk
☎ 0800 783 7951 Fax 01608 641 698

Banner Financial Services Group Ltd, Banner House, Church Road, Copthorne, Crawley RH10 3RA
Senior Partner: Mr Howard Tingley. *Partner:* Mr John R Jones. Executive staff 2, Other staff 3. Began 1987; interdenominational. No magazine. Turnover £150,000 to year end Dec 98. Independent financial adviser, ethical investment pensions specialist.
Email: info@bannergroup.com
☎ 01342 717 917 Fax 01342 712 534

Baptist Insurance Company plc, 19 Billiter Street, London EC3M 2RY
General Manager: Mr Terence Mattholie. *Assistant General Manager:* Mr A J Green. *Accountant:* Mr P J Mitchell. Executive staff 2, Other staff 8. Began 1905; Baptist. No magazine. Turnover £1,800,000 to year end Dec 98. Denominational insurer of Baptist churches and members.
☎ 020 7481 8072 Fax 020 7702 9214

Baptist Union Corporation Ltd, Baptist House, 129 Broadwa Didcot OX11 8RT
Manager: Mr Peter Price. Executive staff 2, Other staff 5. C No.249635. Began 1890; Baptist. No magazine. Turnov £1,444,000 to year end Dec 98. Accepting trusteeships of Ba tist properties, administering the Baptist Union Loan Fund an covenant scheme.
Web: www.baptist.org.uk
Email: buc.corp@baptist.org.uk
☎ 01235 517 700 Fax 01235 517 715

Barchester Green Investment, Barchester House, 45 Catherin Street, Salisbury SP1 2DH
Principal: Mr Geoffrey W Griffiths. *General Manager:* M Rodney Palmer. Executive staff 6, Other staff 10. Began 1985 non-denominational. Magazine: *Barchester Chronicle* (Circu lation n/a annually). Turnover £13,800,000 to year end Ap 97. Advising on ethical implications of investment.
Web: www.barchestergreen/ethical
Email: info@barchestergreen.co.uk
☎ 01722 331 241 Fax 01722 414 191

***A T Bell Insurance Brokers Ltd**, 40 Croydon Road, West Wickham BR4 9HT
Director: Mr Peter Bell. Executive staff 2, Admin staff 9. Began 1970; non-denominational. No magazine. Turnover £1,240,000 to year end Mar 98. General insurance broking, but specialising in church related risks.
☎ 020 8462 0769 Fax 020 8462 0773

A J Bennewith & Co, Hitherbury House, 97 Portsmouth Road, Guildford GU2 5DL
Principal: Mr Tony Bennewith. *Trainee:* Mrs Heather Cheesman. Executive staff 5, Admin staff 1. Began 1986; non-denominational. No magazine. Turnover £300,000 to year end Sep 98. Christian chartered accountancy practice offering audit and independent examination services. Charitable Trust available for fees.
Email: abennewith@aol.com
☎ 01483 539 777 Fax 01483 576 235

Ronald Blue & Co (UK) PLC, PO Box 163, Leeds LS17 8BF
Directors: Mr David S Flowers, Mr Richard Child, Mr Barry Horner. Executive staff 6, Other staff 20. Began 1989; interdenominational. (Previously The Investment Practice). No magazine. Turnover £1,400,000 to year end Dec 98. Fee only financial planning and asset management from a biblically based perspective. PIA regulated. Other branches London and Bristol.
Email: davidf@tip.uk.com
☎ 0113 237 1979 Mobile: 07976 432 381
Fax 0113 237 1118

***Caladine Stevens**, 1 The Avenue, Eastbourne BN21 3YA
Principal: Mr John Caladine. *Office Manager:* Mrs Lesley Downes. Executive staff 3, Admin staff 5. Began 1989; interdenominational. Turnover £170,000 to year end Mar 99. Chartered certified accountants: church and charity accounts, minister's tax returns, trust charity formations compliance.
Email: calster@mistrel.co.uk
☎ 01323 644 579 Fax 01323 417 643

Cansdale & Co., Bourbon Court, Nightingales Corner, Little Chalfont, Amersham HP7 9QS
Senior Partner: Mr Michael Hardman. *Partners:* Mr David Stephenson, Mr Nick Evans. Executive staff 4, Other staff 25. Began 1935; non-denominational. Magazine: *Spotlight Newsletter* (3,000 occasionally). Turnover £1,000,000 to year end Apr 98. Chartered accountants, registered auditor, independent financial adviser serving charities, churches, businesses of all sizes.
Email: davids@cansdales.co.uk
☎ 01494 765 428 📠 01494 763 911

CCLA Investment Management Ltd, St Alphage House, 2 Fore Street, London EC2Y 5AQ
Managing Director: Mr Andrew Gibbs. Executive staff 26, Other staff 42. Began 1988; Anglican. (Previously Central Board of Finance of Church of England Investment Office). Regulated by IMRO in the conduct of investment business. No magazine. Turnover n/a. Providing investment services for churches and charities; common investment funds and cash management.
☎ 020 7588 1815 📠 020 7588 6291

The Central Board of Finance of the Church of England, Church House, Great Smith Street, Westminster, London SW1P 3NZ
Secretary: Mr D M Williams. Executive staff 26, Other staff 26. *CC* Began 1914; Anglican. Magazine: *Annual report* (Circulation n/a annually). Turnover n/a. Financial executive to General Synod of Church of England; Church of England's financial advisory body.
☎ 020 7898 1000 📠 020 7588 6291
Investment Office: See previous entry

Central Finance Board of the Methodist Church, 4th Floor, Friendly House, 52 Tabernacle Street, London EC2A 4NJ
Secretary: Mr Peter Forward. Executive staff 2, Other staff 14. *CC* Began 1960; Methodist. No magazine. Turnover n/a. Established under the Methodist Church Funds Act 1960 as investment body of the Methodist Church.
E Email: cfbmc@netcomuk.co.uk
☎ 020 7251 5060 📠 020 7251 4914

Christian Ethical Investment Group, Postal enquiries to: Miss Patricia Raikes, CEIG Enquiries, 2a New High Street, Headington, Oxford 0X3 7AQ
Secretary: Mr Tony Weekes. No full-time staff. Began 1988; ecumenical. Magazine: *Newsletter* (Circulation n/a occasionally). Turnover £6,700 to year end Dec 98. Promoting seminars, meetings and research on ethical investment for Christian churches, institutions and laity.
Email: tony.weekes@cwcom.net
☎ No telephone

***Christian Insurance Services**, 28 Sutton Street, Durham DH1 4DA
Senior Partner: Mr David McHarry. *Partner:* Mrs Julie Wilson. *Office Manager:* Mr Kevin Wilson. Executive staff 2, Admin staff 5. Began 1994; non-denominational. No magazine. Turnover £1,600,000 to year end Jun 98. Providing home, motor, personal, travel, commercial insurance for individuals, churches and Christian businesses.
Web: www.christian-insurance.co.uk
Email: sales@christian-insurance.co.uk
☎ 0191 384 0934 📠 0191 386 8858

S

ıurch of England Pensions Board, 7 Little College Street, Westminster, London SW1P 3SF
Secretary: Mr Roger Radford. Head Office staff 54, Other staff (homes) 129. ***CC*** No.236627. Began 1926; Anglican. No magazine. Turnover n/a. Pensions and retirement housing for those in the Church's Ministry; pension schemes for layworkers; residential & nursing homes.
☎ 020 7898 1800 🖷 020 7898 1801

hurch of Scotland Board of Stewardship and Finance, 121 George Street, Edinburgh EH2 4YN
Secretary: Mr William Farrell. No full-time staff. Began 1959; Church of Scotland. Magazine: *Life and Work* (125,000 monthly). Turnover £90,000,000 to year end Dec 98. Promoting Christian stewardship and financial management throughout the Church of Scotland.
☎ 0131 225 5722

:hurch of Scotland General Trustees, 121 George Street, Edinburgh EH2 4YR
Secretary and Clerk: Mr Alan Cowe. Executive staff 4, Admin staff 10. ***CC*** No.SCO 14574. Began 1921; Church of Scotland. Magazine: *Life and Work* (125,000 monthly). Turnover £14,000,000 to year end Dec 99. Statutory corporation administering trust propery and funds, with ancillary duties as directed by General Assembly.
☎ 0131 225 5722 🖷 0131 220 3113

:ongregational and General Insurance plc, Currer House, Currer Street, Bradford BD1 5BA
Chief Executive: Mr David J Collett. Executive staff 4, Other staff 58. Began 1891; United Reformed/Congregational. No magazine. Turnover £10,700,000 to year end Mar 98. General insurance for churches, private houses (including manses) and commercial risks.
Email: cgi@congregational.co.uk
☎ 01274 700 700 🖷 01274 370 754

Courtiers Financial Services Ltd, 18a Hart Street, Henley-on-Thames RG9 2AU
Director: Mr Philip Manning. Executive staff 2, Other staff 20. Began 1982; non-denominational. Regulated by the Personal Investment Authority. Magazine: *Courtiers Financial Review* (5,500 quarterly). Turnover £1,000,000 to year end Mar 99. Pensions, investment, ISAs, life assurance, mortgage advice to companies, individuals and charities.
Email: philipmanning@courtiers.co.uk
☎ 01491 578 368 🖷 01491 572 294

Courtiers Investment Services Ltd, 18a Hart Street, Henley-on-Thames RG9 2AU
Director: Mr Philip Manning. Executive staff 2, Other staff 20. Began 1982; non-denominational. Regulated by the Personal Investment Authority. Magazine: *Courtiers Financial Review* (5,500 quarterly). Turnover £1,000,000 to year end Mar 99. Discretionary management, pensions administration, ethical investments.
Email: philipmanning@courtiers.co.uk
☎ 01491 578 368 🖷 01491 572 294

***Credit Action**, 6 Regent Terrace, Cambridge CB2 1AA
Director: Mr Keith Tondeur. Executive staff 1, Other staff 3. ***CC*** No.1035783. Began 1988; non-denominational. No magazine. Turnover n/a. Aiming to prevent personal debt through educational and counselling programme; publishing materials on money management.
Email: credit.action@dial.pipex.com
☎ 01223 324 034 🖷 01223 324 034

Crusade Services (Insurance Brokers) Ltd, 31 St Leonards Road, Eastbourne BN21 3UU
Manager: Mrs Cottrell. Executive staff 1, Other staff 3. Began 1976; non-denominational. Subsidiary of Ansvar Insurance Co. Ltd. No magazine. Turnover £60,000 to year end Dec 98. Specialising in motor, home, church and church-related organisations; insurances.
☎ 01323 638 393 🖷 01323 430 969

Debt Solutions, Havering Grange Centre, Havering Road, Romford RM1 4HR
Insolvency Practitioner: Mr Mike Reeves. Executive staff 1, Other staff 2. Began 1989; non-denominational. No magazine. Turnover n/a. Debt and insolvency advice and assistance.
☎ 01708 750 093 🖷 01708 736 292

Ecclesiastical Insurance Group plc, Beaufort House, Brunswick Road, Gloucester GL1 1JZ
Managing Director: Mr Bernard V Day. Executive staff 7, Other staff 720. Began 1887; non-denominational. Magazine: *Policy Profile* (Circulation n/a half-yearly). Turnover £191,399,000 to year end Dec 98. Property insurance, life assurance, pensions and unit trusts for churches, charities, commerce and individuals.
Web: eigonline.co.uk
Email: gbeigmkg@ibmmail.com
☎ 01452 528 533 🖷 01452 423 557
Also at: Belfast, Birmingham, Bristol, Cambridge, Cardiff, East Grinstead, Edinburgh, Harrogate, London, Manchester and Southampton

Ethical Financial Ltd, 7 Tyverlon Business Park, Barry CF6 3BE
Chairman: Mr Brian Spence. *Managing Director:* Ken Walters. Executive staff 2, Other staff 26. Began 1989; interdenominational. Magazine: *Ethical Investor* (Circulation n/a occasionally). Turnover £5,000,000 to year end Oct 94. Providing the Christian community with ethically-related financial advice.
Web: www.ethical-financial.co.uk
Email: ethical@ethical-financial.co.uk
☎ 01446 421 123 Mobile: 07831 400 972 🖷 01446 421 478
Regional Offices: Dyfed, Middlesex, Midlands, North East England, Powys, Suffolk

Fidelity Trust Ltd, Keeley House, 22 Keeley Road, Croydon CR0 1TE
Director: Mr Bernard Moss. No full-time staff. ***CC*** Began 1909; Anglican. No magazine. Turnover n/a. Trustees of the property and investments of Church societies and communities; private wills and settlements.
☎ 020 8661 6081 🖷 020 8661 6081

Finnan & Company, 40 West Street, Bognor Regis PO21 1XE
Financial adviser: Mr Keith Henderson. Other staff 3. Began 1992; non-denominational. PIA regulated, a member of the Burns-Anderson Independent Network Plc. No magazine. Turnover £96,000 to year end Mar 98. Helping people with investments, life insurance, pensions and mortgages as an independent financial adviser.
☎ 01243 841 535 🖷 01243 841 257

***Forerunner Charitable Trust**, 110 London Street, Reading RG1 4SJ
Trustee: Mr Brian Mills. Executive staff 1. ***CC*** Began 1988; non-denominational. Turnover £22,000 to year end Dec 98. Charitable trust providing seed corn resources for church initiatives.
Email: 106206.1226@compuserve.com
☎ 0118 926 4523 Mobile 07885 600 903
🖷 0118 926 4523

S

S

uentin Foulkes Financial Services Ltd, Andola House, 3 Old Market Place, Harleston IP20 9BE
Director: Mr Martin Roden. Other staff 10. Began 1975; non-denominational. No magazine. Turnover n/a. Independent financial advice from committed Christians about investments, pensions, life assurance, mortgage, finance.
Email: qfoulkes@dial.pipex.com
☎ 01379 854 858 📠 01379 854 856

uentin Foulkes Insurance Services, Andola House, 3 Old Market Place, Harleston IP20 9BE
Partner: Mr Quentin Foulkes. Other staff 10. Began 1975; non-denominational. No magazine. Turnover n/a. Providing and advising on motor, household, commercial liability, travel and health insurance.
Email: qfoulkes@dial.pipex.com
☎ 01379 854 858 📠 01379 854 856

unding Through Fellowship, Office 11, 42 Bridge Street, Hereford HR4 9DG
Christian Funding Consultant: Mr Peter F Garner. Executive staff 1. Began 1989; interdenominational. No magazine. Turnover n/a. Enabling churches and Christian groups to mobilize their full financial strength for mutually agreed projects.
☎ 01432 342 218

The Derek Gardiner Partnership, 21 Rockingham Avenue, Hornchurch RM11 1HH
Senior Partner: Mr Derek Gardiner. Executive staff 3, Other staff 3. Began 1968; Anglican. No magazine. Turnover £230,000 to year end Feb 99. Independent financial advisors; pensions, life assurance, inheritance tax, ethical unit trusts, investments. PIA regulated.
☎ 01708 476 351 📠 01708 448 833

David Gee and Company Financial Services, 3 Rockleaze Road, Sneyd Park, Bristol BS9 1NF
Partners: Mr David & Mrs Lynne Gee. Other staff 3. Began 1974; non-denominational. Member of Countrywide Independent Advisers Ltd. No magazine. Turnover £250,000 to year end Nov 98. Independent advice on investment and retirement planning; specialist advisors to clergy.
Email: d_a_gee@email.infrotrade.co.uk
☎ 0117 962 6278 📠 0117 962 6276

Griffin Stone, Moscrop & Co, 41 Welbeck Street, London W1M 8HD
Senior Partner: Mr Geoffrey Hill. Partners 4, Other staff 24. Began 1920; interdenominational. Magazine: *Business Update* (700 quarterly). Turnover n/a. Chartered accountants and registered auditors providing a comprehensive service to businesses, charities, trusts, individuals.
Email: gsmoscrop@aol.com
☎ 020 7935 3793 📠 020 7486 8705

Guardsman Underwriting Agencies Ltd, 18a High Street, Maidstone ME14 1HT
Underwriting Director: Mr Howard Cooke. Executive staff 1, Other staff 1. Began 1997; non-denominational. Associate of Williams & Whybrow Ltd. No magazine. Turnover n/a. Specialising in issue of exclusive high-value general property insurance.
☎ 01622 674 956 📠 01622 690 242
Registered Office: Buckingham House (East), The Broadway, Stanmore HA7 4YS

Alan Hiscox Financial Services Partnership, 263 Mitcham Lane, London SW16 6QB
Partners: Mr Alan Hiscox, Mr Richard Hiscox. Executive staff 4, Other staff 3. Began 1982; Christian Brethren. No magazine. Turnover £400,000 to year end May 98. Life assurance pensions, domestic and commercial mortgages and general insurance, full Christian financial planning.
Web: www.lendex.co.uk/hiscox
Email: onestop@compuserve.com
☎ 020 8677 7177 📠 020 8677 7177

***Impact Giving UK Trust**, M Tatton & Co, Chartered Accountants, 18 Tunstall Road, Biddulph, Stoke-on-Trent ST8 6HH
Director: Mr Ken Greenwood. Other staff 1. *CC* No.296834. Began 1986; non-denominational. No magazine. Turnover £800,000 to year end Sept 98. Helping individuals to maximise their giving via covenants and gift aid.
☎ 01782 522 000

Jacob, Cavenagh & Skeet, 6 Tudor Court, Brighton Road, Sutton SM2 5AE
Managing Partner: Mr Andrew Hazael. Executive staff 2, Other staff 40. Began 1927; non-denominational. Magazine: *Journal* (Circulation n/a monthly). Turnover £1,700,000 to year end Apr 98. Assisting family companies and Christian charities with audit, accountancy and taxation matters.
Web: www.btinternet.com/~jcssutton
Email: jcssutton@btinternet.com
☎ 020 8643 1166 📠 020 8643 3467

Kingsworld Walder Ltd, Royal London House, Lansdowne, Bournemouth BH1 3LT
Managing Director: Mr Robert Banks. Executive staff 4, Other staff 10. Began 1979; non-denominational. No magazine. Turnover n/a. Helping Christians be good stewards; financial, investment, pensions and tax advice; schemes for Christian organisations.
Email: kingsworldwalder@compuserve.com
☎ 01202 467 700 📠 01202 467 736

The Kubernesis Partnership, 36 Acomb Wood Drive, York YO24 2XN
Chief Executive: Dr Gareth G Morgan. Executive staff 3, Other staff 2. Began 1979; interdenominational. Magazine: *Kubernesis News* (Circulation n/a half-yearly). Turnover n/a. Training and consultancy in charity finance, fundraising and strategy; software for membership, accounts, covenants, giving.
Email: kubernesis@cix.co.uk
☎ 01904 788 885 📠 01904 339 117

S

***Macedonian (Evangelical) Trust**, 6 Eastmead Close, Bickley, Bromley BR1 2JG
Secretary: Mr Ian Morrison. *Secretary's Personal Assistant:* Mrs Betty Morrison. *Administrative Assistant:* Miss Karen Morrison. Executive staff 1, Other staff 2. *CC* No.1063466. Began 1967; non-denominational. No magazine. Turnover £3,000,000 to year end Apr 98. Providing a covenanting and tax recovery service and distributing gifts requested by covenantors.
☎ 020 8285 0058

***Maxco Trust**, 57 Beacon Way, Rickmansworth WD3 2PB
Director: Dr P B Cockburn. No full-time staff. *CC* No.261238. Began 1970; interdenominational. No magazine. Turnover £2,719,277 to year end Dec 97. Service for Christians to maximise use of tax concessions in giving from capital by gifts, loans, legacies.
☎ 01923 350 221

Methodist Insurance plc, Brazennose House, Brazennose Street, Manchester M2 5AS
General Manager: David A Blanks. *Financial Controller and Secretary:* Grayham Simpson. *Underwriting Manager:* Ronald W Barnet. Executive staff 4, Other staff 34. Began 1872; Methodist. No magazine. Turnover £7,300,000 to year end June 98. Insurers of churches, charities, schools, colleges, hotels, houses, shops, weddings, hostels, residential homes.
☎ 0161 833 9696 🖷 0161 833 1287

MMY Accountancy Services, Clarence House, 35 Clarence Street, Market Harborough LE16 7NE
Principal: Mr Mans Yousuf. Executive staff 3, Admin staff 1. Began 1977; evangelical. No magazine. Turnover n/a. Public accountants and taxation advisers serving small/medium sized businesses: accounts, VAT, PAYE, bookkeeping.
☎ 01858 432 006 Mobile: 07850 868 833 🖷 01858 462 006

The Moss Charitable Trust, 7 Church Road, Parkstone, Poole BH14 8UF
Correspondent: Mr Peter D Malpas. Executive staff 1. ***CC*** No.258031. Began 1965; non-denominational. No magazine. Turnover £302,558 to year end Apr 98. Receiving covenant and gift aid income and legacies and distributing to contributors' requests.
☎ 01202 730 002

†M Pringle Ltd, 5 Goresbrook Road, Dagenham RM9 6UX
Director: Mr Malcolm MacDavid. Executive staff 1, Other staff 3. Began 1991; non-denominational. No magazine. Turnover £220,000 to year end Dec 92. Registered general insurance brokers.
☎ 01708 733 593 🖷 01708 733 677

Rechabite Friendly Society, Rechabite House, 14 Byrom Stre
Manchester M3 4RB
Managing Director: Mr William Turnbull. Executive staff Admin staff 10. Began 1835; interdenominational. (Previous Independent Order of Rechabites). Magazine: *Rechabite Ne* (5,000 quarterly). Turnover £180,000 to year end Dec 98. Te totallers Friendly Society; life and general insurance.
☎ 0161 832 4821 🖷 0161 839 1725

Reliance Bank Ltd, 101 Queen Victoria Street, London EC4P 4E
Managing Director: Mr Gerald Birkett. *Banking Manage* Mr Michael Meads. *Head of Customer Services:* M Lloyd Watkins. Executive staff 15. Began 1891; no denominational. No magazine. Turnover £1,700,000 [taxab profit] to year end Mar 97. Commercial Bank providing fu range of services; profits to parent, Salvation Army.
☎ 020 7248 4128 🖷 020 7248 4714

Ross & Co, 14 Ludlow Drive, Thame OX9 3XS
Partner: Mary Ross. Executive staff 2, Other staff 3. Bega 1978; interdenominational. No magazine. Turnover n/a. A general insurances; household, church, office, motor, trave etc.
Web: www.cin.co.uk/ross/
Email: ossie_ross@csi.com
☎ 01844 261 400 🖷 01844 261 345

***Sovereign Giving**, 6 Heatherwood Close, Thorpe End, Norwic NR13 5BN
Treasurer: Mr Malcolm Jackson. Executive staff 1, Other staf 4. ***CC*** No.242773. Began 1960; interdenominational. Registered as North Staffordshire Evangelical Trust. No magazine Turnover £3,000,000 to year end Apr 98. Covenanting and ta recovery service, gifts distributed for covenantors; gift aid service/charity donation card available.
Web: www.sovereign-giving.org.uk
Email: mjackson@sovereign-giving.org.uk
☎ 01603 700 174 🖷 01603 434 344

***Stewardship Services (United Kingdom Evangelization Trust Inc-UKET)**, PO Box 99, Loughton IG10 3QJ
Manager: Mr Anthony E Wakeling. *Manager Legal Services:* Mr David Jones. *Manager Accountancy Services:* Mr Kevin Russell. Executive staff 4, Other staff 14. ***CC*** No.234714. Began 1906; non-denominational. (Previously United Kingdom Evangelization Trust Inc (UKET)). Magazine: *Stewardship* (18,000 half-yearly). Turnover £11,900,000 to year end Apr 98. Covenant, gift aid, capital / property administration; church loans, insurance, accounts examinations, charity formations, helpline, seminars.
Web: www.stewardship.co.uk
Email: stewardship@compuserve.com
☎ 020 8502 5600 🖷 020 8502 5333

Trustees for Methodist Church Purposes, Central Buildings, Oldham Street, Manchester M1 1JQ
Secretary: Rev Kenneth E Street. Executive staff 1, Other staff 3. ***CC*** Began 1866; Methodist. No magazine. Custodian trustee of Methodist real property and investments.
☎ 0161 236 5194

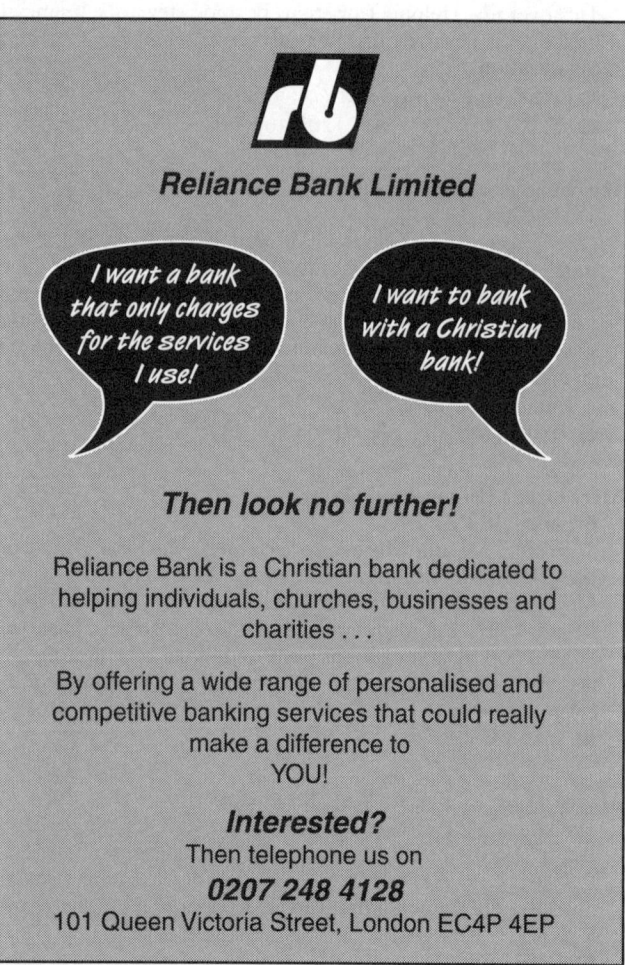

Watchman Underwriting Agencies Ltd, 18a High Street, Maidstone ME14 1HT
Underwriting Director: Mr Howard Cooke. Other staff 2. Began 1993; non-denominational. No magazine. Turnover n/a. Providing specialist cover for unoccupied properties and a wide range of property-based general insurance contracts.
☎ 01622 674 957 🖷 01622 690 242
Registered Office: Buckingham House (East), The Broadway, Stanmore HA7 4YS

Max Willey & Co, 71 Ridgway, Wimbledon, London SW19 4SS
Proprietor: Mr Max Willey. Other staff 2. Began 1993; non-denominational. No magazine. Turnover n/a. Solicitors dealing with charity law (including for churches), conveyancing, wills, probate, personal tax.
☎ 020 8944 6633 🖷 020 8947 0262

Williams and Whybrow Ltd, 18a High Street, Maidstone ME14 1HT
Agency and Schemes Director: Mr Howard Cooke. UK Directors 8, Other staff 38. Began 1948/1975; non-denominational. amalgamated 1994. No magazine. Turnover n/a. Registered Insurance Brokers, Independent Financial Advisers (IBRC No 5014405).
☎ 01622 674 955 🖷 01622 690 242
Registered Office: Buckingham House (East), The Broadway, Stanmore HA7 4YS

M Wood Insurance Services Ltd, 68 Llandaff Road, Canto
Cardiff CF1 9NL
Senior Partner: Mr Michael Wood. Other staff 28. Began 198
non-denominational. (Previously Wood Insurance Group). N
magazine. Turnover £5,000,000 to year end Dec 97. All typ
of insurance excluding life and investments.
☎ 029 2023 0636 🖷 029 2034 0546
Also at: 115 Oxford Street, Pontycymmer, Bridgen
CF32 8DE
☎ 01656 873 100

FURNISHINGS, FABRIC & CHURCH DESIGN

See also Buildings & Church Design on Page 395.

Architectural Metal Furnishings, Hill End Lane, Hainsworth Moor, Queensbury, Bradford BD13 2LY
Ecclesiastical Sales Manager: Mr Melvyn Hills. Executive staff 6, Other staff 42. Began 1964; non-denominational. No magazine. Turnover £1,800,000 to year end Mar 96. Manufacturing quality contract furnishings for churches, community centres and all leisure facilities.
Web: www.amf-uk.co.uk
Email: sales@amf-uk.co.uk
☎ 01274 882 506 🖷 01274 817 982

Art Glass Stained Glass Studio, Great James Street, Londonderry BT48 7DF
Designer: Mrs Sinead Mallon. Other staff 10. Began 1982; non-denominational. No magazine. Turnover n/a. Design, restoration, manufacture, installation and stormglazing of stained glass for churches, hospitals, convents and schools.
☎ 028 7126 9369 🖷 028 7127 1127

Avon Silversmiths Ltd, 10 Avenue Road, Bishop's Stortford CM23 5NU
Chairman: Mr Michael McCarthy. Executive staff 1, Other staff 5. Began 1994; interdenominational. No magazine. Turnover n/a. Manufacturing church silver plate and giftware, new millennium products.
Web: www.church-silver.co.uk
Email: mike@church-silver.co.uk
☎ 01279 508 084 🖷 01279 831 828

Big Tops Ltd, 400 Derby Road, Nottingham NG7 2GQ
Director: Mr John Rodmell. Executive staff 1, Other staff 3. Began 1984; non-denominational. (Previously Equipment Outreach). No magazine. Turnover £250,000 to year end Dec 98. Marquees, big tops, chairs, stage, lights, tables for outreach.
☎ 0115 924 9216 🖷 0115 924 9218

Bolsius (UK) Ltd, Isle Port Business Park, Highbridge TA9 4JR
Managing Director: Mr Tony Ellson. Executive staff 6, Other staff 70. Began 1984; non-denominational. No magazine. Turnover £7,000,000 to year end Dec 98. Manufacturing and supplying candles of various types.
Email: uk@uk.bolsius.com
☎ 01278 772 900 🖷 01278 772 901

Budget Direct, Global House, 38 High Street, West Wickhan
BR4 0NE
Sales Director: Mr David Janes. Executive staff 3, Other staf
18. Began 1974; non-denominational. Magazine: *Budge
Direct* (Circulation n/a n/a). Turnover £5,000,000 to year enc
Dec 98. Supplying quality church, school and nursery furniture.
Web: www.budgetdirect.co.uk
Email: sales.budget@dial.pipex.com
☎ 020 8777 0099 🖷 020 8777 9355

Chancellor's Church Furnishings, Rivernook Farm, Sunnyside, Walton-on-Thames KT12 8ET
Proprietors: Mr Lawrence Skilling, Mr S Williams. Executive staff 1, Other staff 5. Began 1989; interdenominational. No magazine. Turnover £250,000 to year end Dec 98. Buying and supplying pre-1950 church furniture, fixtures and fittings, from pews to pulpits.
Email: antchurch@aol.com
☎ 01932 252 736 Mobile: 07973 139 308 🖷 01932 252 736

James Chase & Son (Furnishings) Ltd, 191 Thornton Road, Bradford BD1 2JT
Managing Director: Mr David Cleaver. Executive staff 2, Other staff 1. Began 1931; non-denominational. Magazine: *Church Furnishings* (10,000 half-yearly). Turnover £800,000 to year end June 98. Supplying all types of church furniture.
Email: sales@james-chase.co.uk
☎ 01274 738 282 🖷 01274 737 836

Christians in Carpets, 9 St John's Street, Wirksworth, Matlock DE4 4DR
Contact: Mr Steve Slater. Executive staff 3, Other staff 3. Began 1987; interdenominational. No magazine. Turnover £300–500,000 to year end Dec 96. Retailing and fitting carpet, smooth flooring, curtains and blinds, including for churches.
☎ 01629 824 815 🖷 01629 825 748

The Churches Purchasing Scheme Ltd, Beaufort House, Brunswick Road, Gloucester GL1 1JZ
Director: Mr F Holland. *Manager:* Mr Ron Carter. *Sales Administration Supervisor:* Mr Paul Playford. Other staff 3. Began 1984; interdenominational. No magazine. Turnover £1,400,000 to year end Dec 98. Providing goods and services at discounted prices for churches, charities and educational establishments.
Web: www.cpsonline.co.uk
Email: sales@cpsonline.co.uk
☎ 01452 383 080 🖷 01452 383 621

lear Text Design, Unit 1, Cheyney Crescent, Heacham, King's Lynn PE31 7BT
Owner: Angus Henderson. No other staff. Began n/a; non-denominational. Turnover n/a. Engraving all types of glass and crystal.
Email: anghendy@saqnet.co.uk
☎ 01485 571 633 Fax 01485 571 633

he Contract Furniture Specialists, Carrington Building, 1 Colonial Drive, Bollo Lane, Chiswick, London W4 5NU
Sales and Marketing Director: Mr David Moss. Executive staff 3, Admin staff 8. Began 1996; non-denominational. No magazine. Turnover £1,000,000 to year end Apr 98. Designing, supplying, installing church furniture and furnishings and other general furniture projects.
Web: www.tcfs-london.demon.co.uk
Email: sales@tcfs-london.demon.co.uk
☎ 020 8932 6292 Mobile 07767 407 743
Fax 020 8932 6299

Duncans of Ironbridge Ltd, Duncan House, 1 Madeley Road, Ironbridge, Telford TF8 7PP
Managing Director: Mr Morley. Other staff 3. Began n/a; non-denominational. No magazine. Turnover n/a. Designing and manufacturing civic, ecclesiastical and university robes and vestments.
Web: www.duncanhouse.co.uk
☎ 01952 433 861 Fax 01952 433 293

Dunphy Ecclesiastical Heating, Unit SE, Princess Street, Rochdale OL12 0HA
Managing Director: Mr Christopher Dunphy. *Company Secretary:* Mr Vincent Hughes. Other staff n/a. Began 1972; interdenominational. (Previously Christopher M Dunphy & Co). No magazine. Turnover £750,000 to year end Aug 98. Designing, installing, maintaining, repairing, heating systems specifically for churches.
☎ 01706 522 702 Fax 01706 354 815

ECL Ltd, Albion House, Albion Park, Warrington Road, Glazebury, Warrington WA3 5PG
Partner: Mr Robert O F Harper. Other staff 35. Began 1981; non-denominational. (Previously Harper Metalcraft). No magazine. Turnover £2,250,000 to year end Apr 98. Specially commissioned church furnishings and artefacts in various metals. Exhibition stands.
Web: ecl-ltd.co.uk
Email: darren@ecl-ltd.co.uk
☎ 01925 767 373 Fax 01925 767 374

A Edward-Jones Ltd, St Dunstan Works, 27 Pemberton Street, Warstone Lane, Birmingham B18 6NY
Managing Director: Mr Nigel R Burton. Executive staff 4, Other staff 13. Began 1902; interdenominational. No magazine. Turnover £450,000 to year end June 92. Manufacturing silversmiths specialising in ecclesiastical metalwork.
Web: www.a-edward-jones.co.uk
☎ 0121 236 3293 Fax 0121 212 1775

Ethos Candles Ltd, Quarry Fields Industrial Estate, Mere, Warminster BA12 6LA
Director: Mr M Keene. Executive staff 2, Other staff 18. Began 1970; non-denominational. No magazine. Turnover n/a. Manufacturing church candles; distributing candles and all sacristy supplies through Christian bookshops.
Web: www.ethos-candles.co.uk/candlelight
Email: sales@ethos-candles.co.uk
☎ 01747 860 960 Fax 01747 860 934

Charles Farris Ltd, 110 York Road, Battersea, London SW11 3RU
Sales Manager: Mr Alan Matthews. Executive staff 1, Other staff 6. Began 1845; non-denominational. No magazine. Turnover n/a. Supplying candles and requisites for the Church.
☎ 020 7924 7544 Fax 020 7738 0197

Galgorm Chemicals, 7 Corbally Road, Ballymena BT42 1JQ
Sales Manager: Mr Brian Mewha. Staff n/a. Began n/a; non-denominational. No magazine. Turnover n/a. Agents for Gopack Ltd manufacturers of church furniture.
☎ 028 2548 521 Fax 028 2547 614

Goddard & Gibbs Studios Ltd, 41 Kingsland Road, Shoreditch, London E2 8AD
Managing Director: Mr Neil Maurer. *Glass Conservator:* Mr Drew Anderson. Executive staff 5, Other staff 22. Began 1868; non-denominational. No magazine. Turnover £1,300,000 to year end Dec 98. Design and manufacture of stained and decorative glass including conservation accredited grade five.
Email: sales@goddard.co.uk
☎ 020 7739 6563 Fax 020 7739 1979

John Hardman Studios, Lightwoods House, Lightwoods Park, Hagley Road West, Warley B67 5DP
Manager: Mr David P Williams. Executive staff 8. Began 1838; non-denominational. No magazine. Turnover n/a. Restoring and conserving stained glass windows and interior church decoration, designing and making new windows.
Web: members.aol.com/hdmnstudio
Email: jhardman@netcomuk.co.uk
☎ 0121 429 7609 Fax 0121 420 2316

Hayes & Finch Ltd, Hanson Road, Aintree, Liverpool L9 7BP
Managing Director: Mr Simon T J Finch. Executive staff 4, Other staff 120. Began 1882; non-denominational. No magazine. Turnover n/a. Manufacturing candles; church furnishers and altar wine shippers.
Web: www.hayes-and-finch-ltd.co.uk
Email: sales@hayes-and-finch-ltd.co.uk
☎ 0151 523 6303 Fax 0151 525 1246
Also at: 17 Lower Trinity Street, Deritend, Birmingham B9 4AG
☎ 0121 773 9213 Fax 0121 753 0022
And: Front Street, Kibblesworth, Gateshead NE11 0XB
☎ 0191 410 2129 Fax 0191 492 1091
And: Branch Street, Paddock, Huddersfield HD1 4JL
☎ 01484 532 778 Fax 01484 432 854
And: 41 Parkhouse Street, Camberwell, London SE5 7TU
☎ 020 7701 4186 Fax 020 7252 5806
And: Palace Craig Street, Whifflet, Coatbridge ML5 4RY
☎ 01236 431 116 Fax 01236 431 3202

Juliet Hemingray Church Textiles, The Derwent Business, Centre, Clarke Street, Derby DE1 2BU
Director: Mrs Juliet Hemingray. Executive staff 1, Other staff 9. Began 1980; interdenominational. No magazine. Turnover n/a. Custom made altar frontals, banners, vestments and general church furnishings.
Web: www.griffin.co.uk/users/church-textiles
Email: church-textiles@griffin.co.uk
☎ 01332 366 740 Fax 01332 292 817

Henwood Decorative Metal Studios Ltd, The Bayle, Folkestone CT20 1SQ
Managing Director: Mr P J Rose. Executive staff 1, Other staff 10. Began 1921; interdenominational. No magazine. Turnover n/a. Manufacturing, repairing, supplying church silver, brassware, oil-filled candles, vestments, linens, wafers, wine.
Email: henwood.churchsupplies@virgin net
☎ 01303 250 911 Fax 01303 850 224

Hilltop Banners, Hilltop House, 54 Elizabeth Way, Stowmarket IP14 5AX
Owner: Mrs Patricia Eastwell. No other staff. Began n/a; non-denominational. No magazine. Turnover n/a. Supplying textile wall hangings on commission for churches; smaller hangings for gifts or domestic use.
☎ 01449 674 730

HW Audio Ltd, 174 St George's Road, Bolton BL1 2NZ
Director: Mr Christopher D Harfield. Executive staff 2, Other staff 6. Began 1976; interdenominational. No magazine. Turnover £500,000-1,000,000 to year end Dec 96. Installing PA and audio induction loop equipment.
Email: hwmusic@compuserve.com
☎ 01204 385 199 Mobile: 07000 727 686
🖷 01204 364 057

Bob Jackson Glasscraft, 2 Robinson Road, High Wycombe HP13 7BL
Partner: Mr Bob Jackson. Other staff 2. Began 1983; non-denominational. No magazine. Turnover n/a. Stained glass and leaded window makers. Restoration and repairs.
Email: bob.jackson@rni.co.uk
☎ 01494 813 220 Mobile: 07770 0370 982 483
🖷 01494 814 364

Kevin Kearney Church Supplies, 7 Skerriffe Road, Cullyhanna, Newry BT35 0JG
Owner: Mr Kevin Kearney. Executive staff 3. Began 1944; non-denominational. No magazine. Turnover n/a. Religious wholesalers, manufacturers, importers and distributors.
☎ 028 3086 1522 🖷 028 3086 8352

Graham Laird Fine Furniture, 4 The Hilders, Ashtead KT21 1LS
Proprietor: Mr Graham Laird. Admin staff 1, Other staff Began n/a; non-denominational. No magazine. Turnov £40,000 to year end Apr 98. Designing and making furniture the highest quality from English timbers, particularly f churches.
Email: glaird@compuserve.com
☎ 01372 275 683 🖷 01372 271 719

Makin Organs Ltd, Compton House, Franklin Street, Oldha OL1 2DP
Director & General Manager: Mr David Clegg. Executive sta 5, Other staff 7. Began 1970; non-denominational. Magazin *Makin News* (5,000 half-yearly). Turnover £600,000 to yea end Mar 99. Manufacturers and distributors of English an European pipeless classical organs.
Web: www.makinorgans.co.uk
Email: sales@makinorgans.co.uk
☎ 0161 626 5666 🖷 0161 665 2284
Also at: 49 High Street, Shoreham, Sevenoaks TN14 7TB
Email: makin.shoreham@which.net
☎ 01959 525 354 🖷 01959 525 554

J and M Mitchell Church Supplies, 3 Crownest Lane, Bingley BD16 4HN
Manager & Owner: Mr John Mitchell. Other staff 3. Began 1979; non-denominational. No magazine. Turnover n/a Manufacturer/importer of over 5,000 church items trade/retail. Silverware, brassware, furniture, vestments, linen etc.
Web: www.churchsupplies.force9.co.uk
Email: john@churchsupplies.force9.co.uk
☎ 01274 786 828 🖷 01274 409 188

Ollerton Hall Decor Services, Ollerton Hall, Knutsford WA16 8SF
Manager: Mrs Suzanne Merrells. Other staff 7. Began 1969; interdenominational. No magazine. Turnover n/a. Supplying and delivering nationwide Wilton-type carpets, matching hassocks and pew runners.
Web: www.i-i.ollertonhall
☎ 01565 650 222 🖷 01565 634 455

Pendle Stained Glass, 39 Burnley Road, Padiham, Burnley BB12 8BY
Proprietor: Mr David Moore. Other staff 10. Began 1989; non-denominational. No magazine. Turnover £150,000 to year end Sep 98. Specialising in design, manufacture, restoration, protection of stained glass and leaded lights.
☎ 01282 772 449 🖷 01282 774 775

Pendleburys Church Candles, Church House, Portland Avenue, Stamford Hill, London N16 6HJ
Proprietor: Mr John Pendlebury. Executive staff 1, Admin staff 1. Began n/a; non-denominational. No magazine. Supplying church candles and requisites.
Web: www.clique.co.uk/pendleburys
Email: books@pendleburys.demon.co.uk
☎ 020 8809 4922 🖷 020 8809 4922

Richard & Co – Carrodelta Ltd, Unit 405, Commercial Centre, Andover SP11 6RU
Director: Miss Terri A Dandy. *Administrator:* Mr Paul Jones. Executive staff 2. Began 1956; Anglican. No magazine. Turnover £360,000 to year end Sept 98. Contract furniture for churches, offices, restaurants, study bedrooms.
☎ 01264 339 944 🖷 01264 336 225

sehill Contract Furnishing, Fernbank House, Tuytherington Business Park, Macclesfield SK10 2XA
Sales Director: Mr Mark McKenzie. Executive staff 6, Other staff 44. Began 1976; interdenominational. No magazine. Turnover £1,600,000 to year end Mar 94. Manufacturing multi-functional seating for Churches, public areas, crematoria, village halls, hospitals and education.
Email: sales@rosehill.co.uk
☎ 01625 502 834 🖷 01625 502 552

Martin Vestment Ltd, Lutton, Spalding PE12 9LR
Proprietor: Rev David Hill. Executive staff 1, Other staff 6. Began 1973; non-denominational. No magazine. Turnover £80,000 to year end May 98. Producing church robes, banners, altar frontals for all denominations.
Web: jcb@johnsplace.force9.co.uk
☎ 01406 362 386

PICMA Church Supplies, Bluecoats, 127 Fore Street, Hertford SG14 1AX
Managing Director: Mr Patrick Phelan. Staff n/a. *CC* No.270794. Began 1990; interdenominational. (Previously SPICMA Trading). Trading arm of SPICMA (Special Projects in Christian Missionary Areas). No magazine. Turnover £60,000 to year end Apr 94. Supplying church candles, incense, altar breads, communion wine.
☎ 01992 303 452 🖷 01992 552 052

ummit Furniture Ltd, Unit 3, Aber Park Industrial Estate, Flint CH6 5EX
Sales Director: David H Gorton. Staff n/a. Began n/a; non-denominational. No magazine. Turnover n/a. Manufacturing and supplying furniture for offices, churches and on contract.
☎ 01352 730 731 🖷 01352 730 812

anpoulles Ltd, 1 Old Lodge Lane, Purley CR8 4DG
Accounts Director: Mr Peter Appleton. *Sales Director:* Mr Andrew Appleton. Executive staff 3, Other staff 11. Began 1908; non-denominational. No magazine. Turnover £1,500,000 to year end Dec 94. Supplying all church furnishings including textiles, silver, brassware, statuary, furniture, candles.
Web: www.vanpoulles.co.uk
Email: sales@vanpoulles.co.uk
☎ 020 8668 6266 🖷 020 8668 1033
Also at: 1 Chalice Close, Lavender Vale, Wallington SM6 9QS
☎ 020 8669 3121

Andrew Ward – Bespoke Furniture, The Danor Works, 39 Southgate Road, London N1 3LA
Managing Director: Mr Andrew Ward. Executive staff 1, Other staff 1. Began 1996; non-denominational. Turnover n/a. Producing interior refurbishments and storage solutions for offices, churches, charities and private households.
☎ 020 8442 1931 Mobile: 07958 794 543
🖷 020 8442 1931

Webbcraft Specialist Weaver, Unit HB, Mill 3, Pleasley Ball Business Park, Pleasely, Mansfield NG19 8RL
Proprietor: Mr Nigel R Webb. Executive staff 1, Other staff 2. Began 1991; ecumenical. Turnover n/a. Weaving individually crafted hangings, carpeting, soft furnishings, vestments and other commissions to design.
☎ 01629 582 581 Mobile 07809 042 706
🖷 0115 929 1024

Whytock & Reid, Sunbury House, Belford Mews, Edinburgh EH4 3DN
Manager, Church Department: Mrs Isobel Reid. Executive staff 3, Other staff 24. Began 1807; Protestant. No magazine. Turnover n/a. Cabinet makers, upholsterers, interior design and furnishers supplying church furniture and requisites.
☎ 0131 226 4911 🖷 0131 226 4595

***Frank Wright Mundy & Co Ltd**, Copthorne House, The Broadway, Abergele LL22 7DD
Managing Director: Mr John Payne. Executive staff 3, Other staff 1. Began 1858; non-denominational. No magazine. Turnover n/a. Producing and supplying non-alcoholic communion wine and communion equipment.
Email: comwine@aol.com
☎ 01745 827 451 🖷 01745 833 161

S

HEALTH & HEALING ORGANISATIONS

See also Hospices on Page 89, Counselling Organisations on Page 404.

***ACET – AIDS Care Education and Training**, PO Box 3693, London SW15 2TG
Executive staff 3, Other staff 50. ***CC*** No.299293. Began 1988; non-denominational. Magazine: *ACET Newsletter* (Circulation n/a every four months). Turnover £1,300,000 to year end Mar 98. Providing practical community care for people ill with HIV / AIDS; schools education programme; UK and overseas.
Email: acet@acetuk.org
☎ 020 8780 0400 📠 020 8780 0450

***Acorn Christian Healing Trust**, Whitehill Chase, High Street, Bordon GU35 0AP
Director: Rev Russ Parker. *Warden:* Rev Denis Brazell. Executive staff 8, Other staff 11. ***CC*** No.326373. Began 1983; interdenominational. Magazine: *Acorn* (2,100 every four months). Turnover £320,000 to year end May 98. Resourcing the church in its practice of Christian healing and care.
Web: www.acorncht.force9.co.uk
Email: acorn@acorncht.force9.co.uk
☎ 01420 478 121 📠 01420 478 122

***Anorexia and Bulimia Care**, 15 Fernhurst Gate, Aughton, Ormskirk L39 5ED
Directors: Mrs Doreen Williams, Maureen Morris. Executive staff 2. ***CC*** No.1004468. Began 1989; non-denominational. Magazine: *Lifeline* (Circulation n/a quarterly), *Careline* (Circulation n/a quarterly). Turnover £8,000 to year end Dec 98. Giving support to sufferers of eating disorders and their carers; resources and education.
Email: doreenabc@compuserve.com
☎ 01695 422 479

***The Bethany Trust**, Bethany House, Histon, Cambridge CB4 9HG
Director: Dr Peter Curtis-Prior. Executive staff 1, Other staff 2. ***CC*** No.1000586. Began 1990; interdenominational. No magazine. Turnover n/a. Supporting the medical research of the Cambridge Research Institute regarding new therapeutic proposals from academics.
Email: curtisprior@bridge.anglia.ac.uk
☎ 01223 233 053 📠 01223 233 053

Braehead House Christian Healing Centre, Braidwood Road, Crossford, Carluke ML8 5NQ
Resident Chaplain: Rev George Fox. Executive staff 3. ***CC*** No.SCO12091. Began 1972; interdenominational. No magazine. Turnover £17,000 to year end Dec 92. Divine healing through public services, conferences and retreats, private counselling, prayer ministry, private appointments available.
☎ 01555 867 16

Breath Ministries, incorporating PACT (Positive Approach to Complementary Therapies), Weald House, 10a High Street, Tunbridge Wells TN1 1UX
Joint Leaders: Rev John & Mrs Christine Huggett. Executive staff 2. ***CC*** No.1010802. Began 1979; interdenominational. No magazine. Turnover £20,000 to year end Dec 98. Promoting the spread of wholeness in Christ through teaching and training; encouraging Christian healing.
☎ 01892 514 112 📠 01892 533 211

***Burrswood Christian Centre for Healthcare and Ministr**
Burrswood, Groombridge, Tunbridge Wells TN3 9PY
Director: Dr Gareth Tuckwell. *Senior Chaplain:* R Michael Fulljames. Executive staff 10, Other staff 120, Volu teers 130. ***CC*** No.229261. Began 1948; Anglican. (The Dor thy Kerin Trust). Magazine: *Burrswood Newsletter* (2,5C quarterly). Turnover £2,327,207 to year end Dec 97. Providir care for short stay admissions, post-operative, palliativ respite and terminal care. Hydrotherapy, physiotherap counselling.
Web: www.burrswood.org.uk
Email: admin@burrswood.org.uk
☎ 01892 863 637 📠 01892 863 623

***Care for Mission**, Elphinstone Wing, Carberry, Musselburg EH21 8PW
Directors: Dr Michael & Mrs Elizabeth Jones. Executive sta 3, Other staff 4. ***CC*** No.SCO 00948. Began 1983; interdenom inational. Magazine: *Newsletter* (200 frequency n/a). Turnove £97,140 to year end Apr 98. Residential and out-patient med cal care, debriefing assessment, counselling, retreat for mission aries and UK Christian workers.
Email: 100633.2065@compuserve.com
☎ 0131 653 6767 Mobile: 07710 276 208 📠 0131 653 3646

Catholic AIDS Link (CAL), PO Box 201, Winchester SO23 9XA
Chair: Father Anthony Hamson. No staff. ***CC*** No.1024865. Began 1988; Roman Catholic. Magazine: *Newsletter* (2,00(quarterly). Turnover n/a. National organisation offerin non-judgmental, spiritual, emotional, practical, financial sup port to those affected by HIV/AIDS.
☎ 01962 627 494 📠 01962 627 494

The Cautley Trust, 95 Seabrook Road, Seabrook, Hythe CT21 5QY
Director: Rev Patrick Jones. Other staff 3. ***CC*** No.802861. Began 1990; Anglican. Magazine: *Newsletters* (Circulation n/a n/a). Turnover n/a. Christian centre for healing and wholeness in Canterbury diocese; accommodation, day visitors.
Email: cautleyhouse@compuserve.com
☎ 01303 230 762

Centre for Health and Pastoral Care, Holy Rood House, 10 Sowerby Road, Sowerby, Thirsk YO7 1HX
Directors: Rev Stanley & Rev Elizabeth Baxter. Executive staff 2, Other staff 6. ***CC*** No.511151. Began 1974; ecumenical. Magazine: *Newsletter* (1,000 quarterly). Turnover £100,000 to year end Dec 96. Residential therapeutic centre for spiritual direction, Christian healing, professional counselling and pastoral care.
☎ 01845 522 580

The Christian Fellowship of Healing (Scotland), 6 Morningside Road, Edinburgh EH10 4DD
Chaplain: Rev Jenny Williams. Executive staff 1, Other staff 1. ***CC*** No.SCO 17129. Began 1952; interdenominational. Magazine: *Newsletter* (250 every four months). Turnover £43,000 to year end Dec 98. Restoring healing ministry to the church, fostering links with the medical profession.
☎ 0131 228 6553

Christian Healing Mission, 8 Cambridge Court, 210 Shepherds Bush Road, London W6 7NJ
Director: Rev John Ryeland. Executive Staff 1, Other staff 2, Part time staff 1. ***CC*** No.211713. Began 1948; interdenominational. (Previously London Healing Mission). Turnover n/a. Working alongside local churches in the ministry of healing and praying with individuals for healing.
Email: healingmission@compuserve.com
☎ 020 7603 8118

Clerkenwell and Islington Medical Mission, Woodbridge Chapel, Woodbridge Street, Clerkenwell, London EC1R 0EX
Superintendent: Rev James Thomas. Executive staff 1, Other staff 5. ***CC*** No.210271. Began 1889; interdenominational. Magazine: *News and Prayer Letter* (300 half-yearly). Turnover £41,700 to year end Mar 98. Healing the sick, preaching the Gospel, succouring the lonely.
☎ 020 7253 1506

Crocus Ministries, 6 Moorcroft, Colton, Rugeley WS15 3ND
Director: Mrs Norma Heasman. Admin staff 2. ***CC*** No.1046184. Began 1995; interdenominational. Turnover n/a. Providing rest, training, listening ears, intercession for leaders in Christian ministry. Accommodation for 12 people at 3 centres.
Web: home.clara.net/crocus/
Email: crocus@clara.co.uk
☎ 01889 582 650

Crowhurst Christian Healing Centre, The Old Rectory, Crowhurst, Battle TN33 9AD
Director: Rev Trevor Blackshaw. Executive staff 5, Other staff 19. ***CC*** No.208738. Began 1928; Anglican but ecumenical. Magazine: (Circulation n/a quarterly). Turnover £341,640 to year end Mar 98. Offering the healing ministry of Jesus, healing and creative courses also available in the context of daily worship.
☎ 01424 830 204 Fax 01424 830 053

Deep End Ministries, 12 Cox Lane, Chessington KT9 1DE
Coordinator: Mr Dave Pistol. Executive staff 1, No other staff. Began 1999; non-denominational. Turnover: first year of operation. Healing through the Word, faith building, teaching others to heal.
Email: pistol@deepend.freeserve.co.uk
☎ 020 8255 6786

Doncaster Canaan Trust, The Manor House, Old Hexthorpe, Doncaster DN4 0HY
Hon Director: Mrs Ruth Bennett. Executive staff 2, Other staff 3. ***CC*** No.515927. Began 1984; interdenominational. Magazine: *Newsletter* (500 occasionally). Turnover n/a. Pastoral care, referrals by clergy/medical agencies; retreats; small conferences, disabled facilities, eventual respite care.
☎ 01302 818 184

***Ellel Ministries**, Ellel Grange, Ellel, Lancaster LA2 0HN
International Director: Mr Peter Horrobin. Executive staff 9, Other staff 140. ***CC*** No.1041237. Began 1986; non-denominational. Magazine: *Newsletter* (16,000 frequency n/a). Turnover £1,450,000 to year end Dec 97. Centres for training and ministry in Christian healing and discipleship (conferences, schools, courses, retreats, resources).
Web: www.ellelministries.org
Email: info@grange.ellel.org.uk
☎ 01524 751 651 Fax 01524 751 738
Also at: Glyndley Manor, Stone Cross, Pevensey BN24 5BS
Email: info@glyndley.ellel.org.uk
☎ 01323 440 440 Fax 01323 440 877
And: Ellel Pierrepont, Frensham, Farnham GU10 3DL
Email: info@pierrepont.ellel.org.uk
☎ 01252 794 060 Fax 01252 794 039

Ellenor Foundation, Livingstone Community Hospital, East Hill, Dartford DA1 1SA
Appeals Director: Dr Ross White. *Director:* Mrs Carol Stone. *Medical Director:* Dr Mary Baines. Executive staff 3, Other staff 24. ***CC*** No.291870. Began 1985; non-denominational. Magazine: *Ellenor Newsletter* (6,000 quarterly). Turnover £1,200,000 to year end Dec 98. Hospice home care in Bexley, North West Kent and Brason, Romania.
Email: ellenor@talk21.com
☎ 01322 221 315 Fax 01322 626 503

Friends Fellowship of Healing, Claridge House Retreat Centre for Healing, Dormansland, Lingfield RH7 6QH
Warden: To be appointed. Staff 6. ***CC*** No.228102. Began 1953; Religious Society of Friends. No magazine. Turnover £97,000 to year end Dec 98. Centre for healing for bringing into balance and harmony the mind, body, spirit and emotion.
☎ 01342 832 150 Fax 01342 836 730

Green Pastures Christian Centre of Healing, 17 Burton Road, Branksome Park, Poole BH13 6DT
Director/Chaplain: Rev J G Petrie. Executive staff 1, Other staff 10. ***CC*** No.209083. Began 1955; interdenominational. Magazine: *Update* (1,500 every four months). Turnover £200,000 to year end Dec 98. Providing short-term residential centre with a counselling and healing ministry; Free Church bias.
Email: green-pastures@dial.pipex.com
☎ 01202 764 776 Fax 01202 768 144

Guideposts Trust Ltd, Two Rivers, Station Lane, Witney OX8 6BH
Director: Mr Clifford L Upex. *General Manager:* Mr Stephen Paine. Executive staff 5, Other staff 34. ***CC*** No.272619. Began 1972; interdenominational. No magazine. Turnover £895,271 to year end Dec 98. Providing care through day services centres, outreach projects, establishing a teaching nursing home.
☎ 01993 772 886 Fax 01993 778 160

The Guild of Health Ltd, Edward Wilson House, 26 Queen Anne Street, London W1M 9LB
General Secretary: Rev Antonia Lynn. Executive staff 1. ***CC*** Began 1904; interdenominational. Magazine: *Way of Life* (1,200 quarterly). Turnover n/a. Helping people to experience within the fellowship of God's family, freedom and life through prayer and sacraments.
☎ 020 7580 2492

†The Guild of St Raphael, The Vicarage, Skirwith, Penrith CA10 1RQ
General Secretary: Rev Michael Burden. *Editor:* Rt Rev George Hacker. Other staff 1. ***CC*** No.210258. Began 1915; Anglican. Magazine: *Chrism* (1,500 quarterly). Turnover n/a. Ministry of healing by prayer, sacraments and co-operation with medical profession.
☎ 01768 886 63

Harnhill Centre of Christian Healing, Harnhill Manor, Cirencester GL7 5PX
Warden/Chaplain: Rev Paul & Mrs Bryony Springate. Executive staff 6, Other staff 5. ***CC*** No.292173. Began 1986; Anglican Foundation. No magazine. Turnover £178,000 to year end June 98. Resource centre for Christian healing offering residential stays, counselling facilities, training courses and healing services.
Web: www.btinternet.com/~harnhill
Email: harnhill@btinternet.com
☎ 01285 850 283 Fax 01285 850 519

Holton Lee, East Holton, Holton Heath, Poole BH16 6JN
Director: Mr Tony Heaton. Executive staff 1, Other staff 8. ***CC*** No.1011867. Began n/a; non-denominational. Magazine: *Holton Lee Newsletter* (2,000 quarterly). Turnover £150,000 to year end Mar 99. Respite accommodation primarily for disabled and carers; opportunities for counselling therapy, art, retreats.
Web: www.lds.co.uk/holtonlee
Email: holton@lds.co.uk
☎ 01202 625 562 Fax 01202 632 632

***InterHealth**, Partnership House, 157 Waterloo Road, London SE1 8US
Director: Dr Ted Lankester. *Director of Resources:* Peter J Chapman. Medical staff 12, Admin staff 7, Volunteers 2. ***CC*** No.801475. Began 1989; interdenominational. Magazine: *Newsletter* (Circulation & frequency n/a). Turnover £573,000 to year end Sep 98. Provides detailed medical / lifestyle reviews for those in Christian ministry.
Email: interhealth@compuserve.com
☎ 020 7902 9000 Fax 020 7928 0927

The Linacre Centre for Health Care Ethics, 60 Grove End Road, St John's Wood, London NW8 9NH
Director: Mr Luke Gormally. *Research Fellow:* Dr Helen Watt. Executive staff 3, Other staff 2. ***CC*** No.274327. Began 1977; Roman Catholic. Magazine: *Newsletter* (Circulation n/a half-yearly). Turnover £171,000 to year end Dec 97. Defence and development, through education/research, of traditional medical ethic informed by Catholic teaching. Largest bioethics library in UK.
Web: www.linacre.org
Email: admin@linacre.org
☎ 020 7289 3625 Fax 020 7266 5424

The Maranatha Community, 102 Irlam Road, Flixton, Manche-ter M41 6JT
Community Leader: Mr Dennis Wrigley. Paid Staff 3, Volu-tary Staff 100. ***CC*** No.327627. Began 1981; ecumenica Magazine: *Maranatha Newsletter* (6,000 every two months Turnover £96,000 to year end Dec 96. Dispersed interdenom national community committed to Christian unity, healing an renewal.
Email: office@maranthacommunity.freeserve.co.uk
☎ 0161 748 4858 Fax 0161 747 7379

The Matthew Trust, PO Box 604, London SW6 3AG
Director: Mr Peter Thompson. Executive staff 3, Other staff 2 ***CC*** No.294966. Began 1977; non-denominational. No maga-zine. Turnover £134,955 to year end Mar 98. Christian menta health reform and caring agency for those in prison and victim of aggression.
Web: www.activ-8.com/matthew-trust
Email: matthew-trust@dial.pipex.com
☎ 020 7736 5976 Fax 020 7731 6961

***Mission Care**, 5 Oaklands Road, Bromley BR1 3SJ
Director: Mr Gerry Armstrong. *Groupcare Manager:* M Malcolm Green. *Chairman:* Mr Roy Wisdom. Executive staf 5, Other staff 375. ***CC*** No.284967. Began n/a; Bermondsey 1904; Brook Lane 1937; interdenominational. (Previously Bermondsey and Brook Lane Medical Mission). Magazine *Christmas Letter* (1,200 annually). Turnover £5,500,000 to year end Mar 98. Eight nursing homes and residential care homes, NVQ Assessment Centre.
☎ 020 8289 7925 Fax 020 8402 8629

***Nissi in Health**, 43 Harold Road, Upper Norwood, London SE19 3PL
Medical Director: Dr Naomi Bankole. Executive staff 1, Other staff 1. ***CC*** No.299242. Began 1987; interdenominational. (Previously Nissi, Caring for Life). No magazine. Turnover £5,600 to year end June 98. Christian health initiatives.
☎ 020 8771 3328 Mobile: 07957 398 333

***Northumbrian Centre of Prayer for Healing**, Beggars Roost, 26 Painshawfield Road, Stocksfield NE43 7PF
Director: Rev Vickers. No full-time staff. ***CC*** No.1064164. Began 1991; interdenominational. No magazine. Turnover £6,000 to year end Aug 99. Promoting through ministry and teaching the healing ministry of Jesus for the Body of Christ.
Web: www.northheal.freeserve.co.uk
Email: healingcentre@northheal.freeserve.co.uk
☎ 01661 842 364 Fax 01661 842 364

Omega – Winford Manor, Winford, Bristol BS40 8DW
Prior: Rev Canon Peter Spink. *Administrator:* Mr James Fahey. Admin staff 3, Other staff 3. ***CC*** No.280512. Began 1980; Anglican/Roman Catholic. Magazine: *Omega News* (2,500 every four months). Turnover £196,000 to year end Mar 97. Contemplative community of men/women. Retreats, seminars, individual spiritual direction, arts, healing, conferences, residential home.
Web: members.aol.com/omegatrust/omega/omega.html
Email: omegatrust@aol.com
☎ 01275 472 262 Fax 01275 472 065

***Pennefather Christian Medical Community Trust**, 22a Hanbury Street, London E1 6QR
President: Miss Edna Cox. No full-time staff. ***CC*** Began 1948; interdenominational. (Previously League of Friends of Mildmay Mission Hospital). Magazine: *Bulletin* (700 half-yearly). Turnover £30,000 to year end Dec 98. Supporting Christian medical projects in Tower Hamlets and London's East End.
☎ 020 7247 0912

uaker Medical Society, 77 Maze Hill, Greenwich, London SE10 8XQ
Chairman: Dr Gordon A Barclay. No full-time staff. ***CC*** Began 1930; Religious Society of Friends. Magazine: *Newsletter* (Circulation n/a occasionally). Turnover £50 to year end Dec 94. For members of the healing professions to discuss Quakerism and relevant subjects.
Email: barcviet@aol.com
☎ 020 8858 4968

t Luke's Hospital for the Clergy, 14 Fitzroy Square, London W1P 6AH
General Secretary: Rev Canon Paul Thomas. *Director of Finance:* Mr Peter Rogers. *Director of Nursing:* Ms Ann Hales. Executive staff 5, Other staff 40. ***CC*** No.209236. Began 1892; Anglican. Magazine: *Annual Handbook* (12,000 annually). Turnover £961,000 to year end Dec 98. Treating and healing Church of England ministering personnel; 22 beds mainly for surgical cases.
☎ 020 7388 4954 Fax 020 7383 4812

ozo Ministries International, PO Box 29, Romsey SO51 0YU
Director: Mrs Marion Daniel. Executive staff 6, Other staff 2. ***CC*** No.1042420. Began 1983; non-denominational. Magazine: *Newsletter* (300 every three weeks). Turnover n/a. Salvation, healing and deliverance through public meetings and conferences.
Email: sozomin@msn.com
☎ 01794 323 516 Fax 01794 322 167

***Trinity Care plc**, 15 Musters Road, West Bridgford, Nottingham NG2 7PP
Chief Executive: Mr David G Henderson. *Director of Care:* Dr Mervyn Suffield. Executive staff 5, Other staff 1500. Began 1987; non-denominational. Magazine: *Trinity Times* (Circulation & frequency n/a). Turnover £13,814,000 to year end Mar 98. Developing/managing nursing homes and apartments for elderly people, bungalows for people with learning disabilities.
Email: enquiry@trinitycare.co.uk
☎ 0115 945 5485 Fax 0115 982 1919

***Wellsprings**, Bawtry Hall, Bawtry, Doncaster DN10 6JH
Co-ordinator: Miss Marjorie Salmon MBE. No other staff. ***CC*** No.280638. Began 1997; interdenominational. No magazine. Turnover n/a. An active service trust providing rest and renewal for Christian workers.
☎ 01302 710 020 Fax 01302 710 027

INFORMATION & TELEPHONE ORGANISATIONS

See also Counselling Organisations on Page 404, Help Lines on Page 529.

CACLB – Churches Advisory Council for Local Broadcasting, PO Box 124, Westcliff-on-Sea SS0 0QU
General Secretary: Mr Jeff Bonser. Executive staff 1. ***CC*** No.297766. Began 1967; interdenominational. (Previously Churches Advisory Council for Local Broadcasting (CACLB)). Magazine: *Crosstalk* (1,000 quarterly). Turnover £76,000 to year end Dec 98. Ecumenical body for the advancement of Christian religion through radio/television broadcasting; annual awards, conference.
Web: www.caclb.org.uk
Email: office@caclb.org.uk
☎ 01702 348 369 Fax 01702 305 121

Catholic Enquiry Office, The Chase Centre, 114 West Heath Road, London NW3 7TX
Director: Rev P Billington. Executive staff 4, Other staff 4. ***CC*** No.233699. Began 1954; Roman Catholic. Magazine: *Catholic Gazette* (3,500 monthly). Turnover n/a. Advertising through the press and the distribution of free literature for evangelisation.
Web: www.opinet.co.uk/go/ceo/
Email: catholic.enquiry.office@cms.org.uk
☎ 020 8458 3316 Fax 020 8905 5780

Catholic Media Office, 39 Eccleston Square, London SW1V 1BX
Director: Mgr Kieran Conry. Executive staff 3, Other staff 2. ***CC*** No.257239. Began 1968; Roman Catholic. Magazine: *Briefing* (3,200 monthly), *Signum* (1,900 monthly). Turnover £100,000 to year end Dec 90. Press and information office for Catholic church in England and Wales.
Web: www.tasc.ac.uk/cc/
Email: cathmedia@easynet.co.uk
☎ 020 7828 8709 Fax 020 7931 7678

Catholic Press and Media Office, 5 St Vincent Place, Glasgow G1 2DH
Director: Rev Tom Connelly. Executive staff 1, Other staff 2. Began 1968; Roman Catholic. No magazine. Turnover n/a. Ensuring a good relationship between church and the media and supplying information/news.
Web: www.stac.ac.uk/cmo/
Email: scotbishopsconference@compuserve.com
☎ 0141 221 1168

Christian Enquiry Agency, Inter-Church House, 35 Lower Marsh, London SE1 7RL
Director: Rev Dr Philip Clements-Jewery. Executive staff 1. ***CC*** No.297393. Began 1985; interdenominational. Magazine: *Newsletter* (1,500 half-yearly). Turnover £30,000 to year end Dec 95. Dealing with enquiries on the Christian faith resulting from advertising in the media and elsewhere.
Web: www.christianity.org.uk
Email: enquiry@christianity.org.uk
☎ 020 7523 2123 (Direct) 020 7620 0718 (24hr ansaphone)
Fax 020 7928 0010

†Christian Resources Centre (Christians in Business Association), 46 Ringwood Road, Eastney, Portsmouth PO4 9JL
Directors: Mr Graham Keeping, Mr Steve Oliver. No full-time staff. Began 1990; interdenominational. Magazine: *Acorn News* (4,000 monthly). Turnover n/a. Giving help, advice, practical assistance, clearing house for information, ideas, dates.
☎ 023 9273 8862 Fax 023 9287 3351

S

Christian Voice, PO Box 62, Royston SG8 7UL
National Director: Stephen Green. All voluntary staff. Began 1994; non-denominational. Magazine: *Christian Voice* (Circulation n/a ten times a year). Turnover £28,000 to year end Dec 98. Upholding the Christian constitution of the United Kingdom through prayer and action informed by Scripture.
Email: tele-sense@roysil.freeserve.co.uk
☎ 01763 241 726 Fax 01763 231 980

Christian World Centre, Grampian House, 144 Deansgate, Manchester M3 3ED
Operations Director: Mr John F Macdonald. Executive staff 1, Other staff 12. *CC* Began 1980; interdenominational. No magazine. Turnover n/a. Information, advice and counselling bureau; 90-seat studio and exhibition theatre; 100-seat restaurant and coffee lounge.
☎ 0161 834 6060 Fax 0161 834 6060

Church in History Information Centre, 21 Elm Road North, Birkenhead CH42 9PB
Director: Mr Dennis Barton. No other staff. Began 1985; Roman Catholic. No magazine. Turnover n/a. Making available information regarding the involvement of the church in history.
☎ 0151 608 3952

Church News Service, PO Box 77, Gosport PO12 2YT
Managing Editor: Mr Andy Patterson. Executive staff 1, Other staff 1. Began 1967; interdenominational. No magazine. Turnover £100,000 to year end Dec 98. Providing monthly service of articles, news, quotes, cartoons, and illustrations for 5,000 local church magazines.
Web: ourworld.compuserve.com/homepages/aphenna
☎ No telephone

Church of Scotland London Advisory Service (COSLAS), 42 Gro venor Gardens, London SW1W 0EB
Administrator: Ms Siobhan Hogan. *Director:* Mr Steph Convill. Executive staff 5. *CC* No.208437. Began 188 Church of Scotland. No magazine. Turnover n/a. Assistir homeless Scots in London.
☎ 020 7881 9242 Fax 020 7881 9241

Churches Information for Mission, Inter-Church House, 35 Lowe Marsh, Waterloo, London SE1 7RL
Deputy Secretary: Rev Dr Philip Clements-Jewery. Executiv staff 1. *CC* Began 1997; interdenominational. No magazin Turnover £30,000 to year end Dec 97. Maintaining database c information gathered by churches and agencies, making available for mission.
Email: clements-jewery@cim.org.uk
☎ 020 7620 4444 Fax 01268 284 479

Communications Department, Church House, Church House Great Smith Street, London SW1P 3NZ
Director of Communication: Rev Dr William Beaver. Executiv staff 4, Other staff 3. *CC* Began n/a; Anglican. No magazine Turnover n/a. Promoting the work of the Church of England i proclaiming the Gospel.
Email: sarah_williams@c-of-e.org.uk
☎ 020 7898 1000 Fax 020 7898 1461

†**Copyright Advisory Service**, 42 Evesham Road, Cookhill, Alceste B49 5LJ
Proprietor: Dr Eric Thorn. No full-time staff. Began 1985 non-denominational. No magazine. Turnover n/a. Advising churches and Christian organisations on all matters pertaining to copyright legislation.
☎ No telephone

†**Council for the Care of Churches (General Synod)**, Fielden House, Little College Street, London SW1P 3SH
Secretary: Dr Thomas H Cocke. Executive staff 6, Other staff 5. *CC* Began 1921; Anglican. Magazine: *Churchscape* (1,500 annually). Turnover n/a. Advising on care of churches and their furnishings; co-ordinating Diocesan Advisory committees; has statutory responsibilities.
☎ 020 7222 3793 Fax 020 7222 3794

*__Deo Gloria Outreach__, Selsdon House, 212 Addington Road, South Croydon CR2 8LD
Co-ordinator: Miss Joy Caton. Executive staff 1. *CC* No.243305. Began 1965; non-denominational. Magazine: *Newsletter* (7,500 annually). Turnover n/a. Supplying information and advice on new religious movements.
Email: dgo@deo-gloria.co.uk
☎ 020 8651 6430 Fax 020 8651 6429

Dial-A-Bible-Message Ministry, 74 Scrub Rise, Billericay CM12 9PE
Teachers: Mr Trevor Argent, Mr Stan Portch. No full-time staff. Began 1981; interdenominational. No magazine. Turnover n/a. Recorded Bible Teaching Ministry, 24 hours a day on 01277 654 455.
☎ 01277 626 309

Enquiry Centre, Church House, Church House, Great Smith Street, London SW1P 3NZ
Enquiry Centre Officer: Mr Stephen Empson. No other staff. Began 1963; Anglican. No magazine. Turnover n/a. Answering enquiries on matters relating to the Church of England.
☎ 020 7898 1000 Fax 020 7898 1461

Evangelical Missionary Alliance, Whitefield House, 186 Kennington Park Road, London SE11 4BT
Executive Director: Rev Stanley L Davies. *Associate Director:* Rev Richard Tiplady. Other staff 4. *CC* No.274521. Began 1958; interdenominational. Trading as Global Connections. Magazine: *Global Connections* (850 quarterly), *World Prayer News* (1,600 every two months). Turnover £209,400 to year end Dec 97. Providing global connections by networking, resourcing and representing world mission in the UK.
Email: sdavies@ema.co.uk
☎ 020 7207 2156 Fax 020 7207 2159

Farmers' Christian Information Centre, 4 Homend Walk, Ledbury HR8 1BX
Organiser: Mrs Irene D Clegg. No full-time staff. Began 1962; interdenominational. (Previously Sunday School by Post, Rural Christian Information Centre). See also Farmers Christian Postal Service. Magazine: *Prayer Bulletin* (Circulation n/a every two months). Turnover n/a. Reaching rural families nationwide by post and telephone; also Christian Information Service.
☎ 01531 634 113 Fax 01531 634 113

Fellowship of St Alban & St Sergius, 1 Canterbury Road, Oxford OX2 6LU
General Secretary: Rev Stephen Platt. Executive staff 1, Other staff 2. *CC* No.245112. Began 1928; interdenominational. (Incorporating Eastern Churches Review). Magazine: *Sobornost* (1,300 half-yearly). Turnover £40,000 to year end Mar 94. Aiding theological understanding between Eastern & Western Christians.
Web: www.btinternet.com/~sobornost.albanandsergius
Email: stephen.platt-albanandsergius@btinternet.com
☎ 01865 552 991 Fax 01865 316 700

***Incest Help Line and Support Group**, PO Box 42, Grantham NG31 6AA
Secretary: Mrs Judy McGibbon. Other staff 4. *CC* No.250068. Began 1985; interdenominational. No magazine. Turnover £1,000 to year end Apr 96. Telephone helpline, correspondence and face-to-face counselling for survivors of incest and sexual abuse.
☎ 01476 591 807

Lord's Day Fellowship in Wales/Cymdeithas Dydd yr Arglwydd yng Nghymru, 32 Garth Drive, Liverpool L18 6HW
Hon Secretary: Rev Dr D Ben Rees. Other staff 1. Began 1937; interdenominational. Magazine: *Inheritance/Etifeddiaeth* (1,500 half-yearly). Turnover £2,300 to year end Dec 98. Safeguarding Sunday.
☎ 0151 724 1989 Fax 0151 724 5691

Message: The Christian Telephone Service, 46 Gurney Road, New Costessy, Norwich NR5 0HJ
Chairman: Mr Michael Graves. All voluntary staff. *CC* No.297409. Began 1969; interdenominational. Magazine: *Ring Round* (1,500 half-yearly). Turnover £2,000 to year end Mar 98. Recorded telephone ministry with call-back; providing 24-hour outreach and teaching Christians to witness.
Web: www.jbaassoc.demon.co.uk/message
Email: message@jbaassoc.demon.co.uk
☎ 01603 746 859 Fax 0870 055 3907

Methodist Church Press Service, 1 Central Buildings, Westminster, London SW1H 9NH
Press Officer: Ms Geraldine Ranson. Executive staff 1, Other staff 1. Began n/a; Methodist. No magazine. Turnover n/a. Informing all media concerning Methodist work, news and views throughout Britain.
Web: www.methodist.org.uk
Email: press.office@methodist.btinternet.com
☎ 020 7222 8010 Fax 020 7799 2152

National Christian Helpline, Folly Croft, Melmerby, Penrith CA10 1HE
National Promotions Director: Rev Nigel D Holme. Executive staff 3. Began 1996; non-denominational. No magazine. Turnover n/a. National Christian helpline: 0345 056 064. Church registration system.
☎ 0768 881 966 Fax 01768 881 966
Helpline: 0845 300 528

†National Council for Christian Standards, 65 Warwick Square, London SW1V 2AL
Chairman: Lady Watherstone. Executive staff 1. *CC* Began 1986; non-denominational. Magazine: *News Bulletin* (30,000 half-yearly). Turnover n/a. Seeking to re-establish Biblical Christian Gospel teaching in the nation, through parliament and the media.
☎ 020 7630 6162 Fax 020 7828 3442

The Oriental Orthodox News Service (OONS), 10 Heathwood Gardens, Charlton, London SE7 8EP
Director: Father Sergius Scott. Other staff n/a. Began n/a; Orthodox. Magazine: *Ex Oriente Lux* (Circulation n/a electronic, monthly). Turnover n/a. A monthly electronic news bulletin on behalf of the Oriental Orthodox Churches.
Email: oons-request@uk-christian.net
☎ 020 8854 3090 Fax 020 8244 7888

***Premier Lifeline**, PO Box 13000, London SW1E 5PP
Manager: Jonathan Clark. All voluntary staff. *CC* No.1022073. Began 1995; interdenominational. An activity of Premier Radio. No magazine. Turnover n/a. Confidential telephone helpline offering prayer, listening ear, advice, information.
Web: www.premier.org.uk
Email: lifeline@premier.org.uk
☎ 020 7316 0808 Fax 020 7233 6706

St George Orthodox Information Service, The White House, Mettingham, Bungay NR35 1TP
General Secretary: Mr Andrew Bond. Executive staff 2, Other staff 2. Began 1969; pan-Orthodox. Magazine: *Orthodox News* (3,000 quarterly). Turnover n/a. Serving the Orthodox Church as public relations office, bookstore and church supplies company.
☎ 01986 896 708 Fax 01986 896 708

†SOS Prayer Line, Address: n/a
No full-time staff. *CC* Began 1988; Roman Catholic. No magazine. Turnover £30,000 to year end Mar 93. Listening, prayer service for those in any kind of need.
☎ 01243 377 331

***Spotlight Wales**, PO Box 9, Blackwood NP2 2PY
Staff: all Voluntary. Began 1990; interdenominational. Magazine: *Spotlight* (1,000 monthly). Turnover n/a. Keeping Christians in Wales informed of events and resources in Wales.
☎ 01495 225 305

†UK and Ireland Revival Network, 188 Main Street, Callander, Stirling FK17 8BG
Executive Director: Mr Tony Black. No other staff. Began 1996; interdenominational. No magazine. Turnover n/a. Catalyst for unity and the sharing of resources as part of a global information network.
Web: www.grm-uk.org/ukirn
Email: tony@grm-uk.org
☎ 01877 331 736 Fax 01877 331 736

MARKETING & FUNDRAISING SERVICES

See also Design, Layout & Editorial Services on Page 278, Computer & Business Services on Page 399.

Action Planning, Mid-Day Court, 30 Brighton Road, Sutton SM2 5BN
Principal: Mr David Saint. *Senior consultant:* Mr Sam McGuire. Executive staff 2, Other staff 3. Began 1990; non-denominational. Magazine: *Actionlink* (4,000 every four months). Turnover £381,000 to year end Mar 98. Fundraising and management services to voluntary organisations and charities; Christian organisations a speciality.
Web: www.actionplanning.co.uk
Email: info@actionplanning.co.uk
☎ 020 8642 4122 Fax 020 8770 2090

Brawn Marketing and Fundraising, 7a Matham Road, East Molesey KT8 0SX
Managing Director: Mr Tim Brawn. Executive staff 2, Other staff 1. Began 1993; non-denominational. No magazine. Turnover n/a. Marketing, direct mail and fundraising consultancy for Christian organisations.
Email: TimBrawn@aol.com
☎ 020 8941 8789 Fax 020 8941 7303

Capstone Systems Ltd, 48 Woodpond Avenue, Hockley SS5 4PX
Director: Mr D C Godfrey. Admin staff 2. Began 1986; non-denominational. No magazine. Turnover n/a. Supplying computer software (ReadyRiter) for hospices, ministries, charities, churches; accounting, administration and fundraising. Patient records.
Email: capstonesystems@compuserve.com
☎ 01702 207 742 Fax 01702 200 286

†**Charity Support Services**, 49 Oakhurst, Lichfield WS14 9AL
Director: Mr John Wilson. Executive staff 1, Other staff 5. Began 1991; non-denominational. No magazine. Turnover £40,000 to year end Jan 96. Funding campaigns; business planning; PR; marketing events; presentations; newsletters; training; computer services; direct mail.
Email: charityss@aol.com
☎ 01543 268 678 Fax 01543 411 685

Churches' Advertising Network, Baptist House, 129 Broadway, Didcot OX11 8RT
Chairman: Jackie Sheppard. No full-time staff. Began 1992; ecumenical. No magazine. Turnover £25,000 to year end Dec 94. Co-ordinating major advertising initiatives between denominations and regions, and advising churches on religious advertising.
Email: jsheppard@baptist.org.uk
☎ 01235 517 700 Fax 01235 517 715

The Churches' Media Trust, Church House, North Hinksey, Oxford OX2 0NB
Chairman: Rev Richard Thomas. Executive staff 1. *CC* Began 1991; interdenominational. Magazine: *Another Voice* (1,000 occasionally). Turnover £20,000 to year end Dec 94. Co-ordinating funding, providing new vision for the churches' work with all areas of the media.
☎ 01865 244 566 Fax 01865 790 470

The Domain Group, 80 St Martin's Lane, London WC2N 4AA
UK Partner: Mr Stephen Butler. Executive staff 6, Admin staff 6. Began 1994; non-denominational. No magazine. Turnover n/a. Fundraising and advertising for Christian and charity organisations.
Email: shbutler@thedomaingroup.com
☎ 020 7836 3700 Fax 020 7836 3701

DRM Consulting, PO Box 5905, London W13 8ZR
Director: Mr David Ryde. Executive staff 1. Began 1994; non denominational. No magazine. Turnover n/a. Helping organisations achieve business and communications goals: strategic planning, marketing, business development.
☎ 020 8810 7495 Mobile: 07956 946 926
Fax 020 8991 0008

Eleventh Hour, The Rural Business Centre, Winterbourne Whitechurch, Blandford Forum DT11 9AW
Contact: Mr Graham Burton. Executive staff 2, Other staff 1. Began 1990; Anglican. No magazine. Turnover £100,000 to year end Apr 98. Professional and economical approach for educational, environmental or cultural biased products or services, various marketing disciplines.
Web: www.homepages.nildram.co.uk/~euros/
Email: euros@nildram.co.uk
☎ 01258 880 050 Fax 01258 881 448
Also at: The Green Office, Park Farm, Milton Abbas, Blandford Forum DT11 0AX
☎ 01258 881 448

Erne Agency International, Inis Ceithleann House, Lower Celtic Park, Enniskillen BT74 6HP
Director: Mr Bill Thompson. Executive staff 4, Other staff 2. Began 1985; non-denominational. No magazine. Turnover n/a. Marketing, advertising, direct mail, promotions, incentives, public relations for churches, charities and voluntary organisations.
☎ 028 6632 3387 Fax 028 6632 3387

Hitotsu-Bishi, 22 Hassocks Wood, Stroudley Road, Basingstoke RG24 8UQ
Managing Director: Mr Andrew Earle. *Marketing Director:* Mr Andrew Watkins. Executive staff 2. Began 1986; interdenominational. (Previously Gothic Audio-Visual & Studio 55). No magazine. Turnover £205,000 to year end Nov 98. Preparing training and promotional material utilising film, video, tape-slide & print.
Email: hitbis@aol.com
☎ 01256 471 471 Fax 01256 471 470

***Jerry Marshall Associates**, 7 Hodgetts Lane, Burton Green, Kenilworth CV8 1PH
Director: Mr Jerry Marshall. Executive staff 1, Other staff 1. Began 1987; non-denominational. Magazine: *JMA Update* (Circulation & frequency n/a). Turnover n/a. Marketing consultancy producing practical, researched marketing plans and feasibility studies, international business development and training.
Email: jerry.marshall@akma.com
☎ 0247 642 2544 Fax 0247 642 2544

Stephen Maxted and Associates Ltd, 12 Cranston Road, Forest Hill, London SE23 2HB
Director: Mr Stephen Maxted. Executive staff 1, Other staff 1. Began 1987; non-denominational. No magazine. Turnover n/a. Marketing, advertising and fundraising consultancy.
Email: maxted@dircon.co.uk
☎ 020 8699 2265 Fax 020 8244 7387

S

Oulton-Lee Marketing Services Ltd, 40 Fairmount Drive, Loughborough LE11 3JR
Managing Director: Mrs Sue Garner. Executive staff 1, Other staff 1. Began 1991; non-denominational. No magazine. Turnover n/a. Strategic marketing planning; research, both questionnaires and groups; statistical analyses of numerical trends, eg donations.
Email: oulton_lee@compuserve.com
☎ 01509 264 141 Mobile: 07721 992 405 🖷 01509 264 141

†**PRP Marketing Ltd**, Redcroft House, 521 Waterside, Chesham HP5 1QF
Director: Mr David C Bennett. *Secretary:* Mrs Sue M Bennett. Executive staff 2, Other staff 6. Began 1991; non-denominational. No magazine. Turnover £105,000 to year end Sept 96. Promoting Christian businesses in the marketplace; helping other Christian organisations to communicate their message effectively.
☎ 01494 792 525 🖷 01494 783 570

***Ian M Pryce & Associates**, 24 Medway Avenue, Oakley, Basingstoke RG23 7DP
Partner: Mr Ian Pryce. Executive staff 2. Began 1994; non-denominational. No magazine. Turnover £120,000 to year end Sept 98. Marketing and market research in Christian, charity and social marketing environment; IT training package development.
Email: pryce1@aol.com
☎ 01256 782 188 🖷 01256 782 188

Richard Felton Fundraising and Appeals Consultant, 22 New Road, Reepham, Norwich NR10 4ND
Proprietor: Mr Richard Felton. No other staff. Began 1995; non-denominational. No magazine. Turnover £25,000 to year end Dec 96. Freelance fundraiser to Christian organisations and charities, offering research, designs.
Email: rfelton@compuserve.com
☎ 01603 872 194 Mobile: 07885 067 087 🖷 01603 872 194

Sovereign Creative Marketing Ltd, 15 Station Road, Cheadle Hulme, Cheadle SK8 5AF
Managing Director: Mr Nigel Tedford. *Financial Director:* Mrs Dianne Tedford. Executive staff 2, Other staff 4. Began 1984; interdenominational. (Previously Sovereign Advertising & Marketing (CH) Ltd). No magazine. Turnover £500,000–1,000,000 to year end Dec 98. Marketing campaigns, advertisement design and media buying, donor recruitment and development, direct mail, literature design and production.
Web: www.sovereign.uk.com
Email: nigeltedford@sovereign.uk.com
☎ 0161 485 4488 🖷 0161 486 1886

Support Team Building, MAF Services Ltd, 2 Valley Road, Sandgate, Folkestone CT20 3BT
Consultant: Mr David Longley. No full-time staff. Began 1985; interdenominational. No magazine. Turnover n/a. Helping Christian organisations build strong teams of supporters; copywriting services; address list management consultancy.
Email: david.longley@maf-uk.org
☎ 01303 852 807 🖷 01303 852 800

Wilkinson Associates, Westmorland Business Centre, Unit 3, Yard 2, Stricklandgate, Kendal LA9 4ND
Owner: Adrian Wilkinson. Executive staff 1, Other staff 3. Began 1995; interdenominational. No magazine. Turnover £61,000 to year end Nov 98. Supplying church administrative, marketing and public relations service; church resource material.
Email: adrianw@dircon.co.uk
☎ 01539 736 076 Mobile: 07831 393 699
🖷 01539 736 076

MARRIAGE MINISTRIES

See also Counselling Organisations on Page 404.

Association for Marriage Enrichment, Westminster Pastoral Foundation, 23 Kensington Square, London W8 5HN
Chaircouple: Dr Ron & Mrs Rosemary Foyle. No full-time staff. *CC* No.327606. Began 1979; non-denominational. Magazine: *Newsletter* (350 every four months). Turnover £8,000 to year end Dec 96. Enabling couples to communicate more effectively, understand each other better and cope with conflict.
Web: www.amefocus.demon.co.uk
Email: david@amefocus.demon.co.uk
☎ 01932 862 090

Broken Rites, 114 Brown Edge Road, Buxton SK17 7AB
National Secretary: Ms Christine McMullen. All voluntary staff. Began n/a; Anglican and interdenominational. Magazine: *Rite Lines* (300 quarterly). Turnover £2,000 to year end Apr 95. Independent support and action group concerned with the breakdown of clergy marriages.
Email: christin@noc6.u-net.com
☎ 01298 739 97

Catholic Centre for Healing in Marriage, Oasis of Peace, Penamser Road, Porthmadog LL49 9NY
Coordinator: Mr Antony P Dady. Executive staff 2, Admin staff 3. Began 1992; Roman Catholic. No magazine. Turnover £20,000 to year end Dec 98.
☎ 01766 514 300 Fax 01766 515 227

Concern For Family and Womanhood, Springfield House, Chedworth, Cheltenham GL54 4AH
Chairman: Mr David W Stayt. Staff n/a. *CC* No.291323. Began 1985; interdenominational. No magazine. Turnover £49,000 to year end Apr 98. Preserving the value of different sex roles and marriage in accordance with the Bible.
Web: www.mackey.demon.co.uk/cfw
Email: cfwsec@mackey.demon.co.uk
☎ 01285 720 454

Couples for Christ, South East London Community, 53 St Johns Park, Blackheath, London SE3 7JW
Co-ordinator: Mr Louis Alexander. Other staff 3. *CC* No.1024147. Began 1988; interdenominational. Magazine: *CFC Newsletter* (500 monthly). Turnover £15,000 to year end Dec 98. Helping families live Christ-centred lives, through teaching, prayer and fellowship.
Email: keyskills@mcmail.com
☎ 020 8853 1719/8305 1027 Fax 020 8305 1027

***Family Alive!**, 1668 High Street, Knowle, Solihull B93 0LY
Co-ordinator: Mr Roger Vann. Executive staff 1, Other staff 2. *CC* No.258421. Began 1967; interdenominational. (A ministry of Agapé). No magazine. Turnover n/a. Residential weekends and local church seminars for couples, strengthening communication and intimacy in marriage.
Web: www.webcom.com/agape
Email: 100604.343@compuserve.com
☎ 01564 776 133 Fax 01564 776 133

FLAME – Family Life And Marriage Education, Robert Runcie House, 60 Marsham Street, Maidstone ME14 1EW
Chairman: Rev Canon David Grimwood. No full-time staff. *CC* No.1001753. Began 1989; Anglican. Magazine: *Newsline* (Circulation & frequency n/a). Turnover £2,000 to year end Dec 90. Strengthening family life and marriage education; exchanging information and expertise between dioceses.
Web: welcome.to/familylife
Email: ann@csr.org.uk
☎ 01622 755 014 Fax 01622 693 531

The Marriage Agenda, 10 Dukes Close, Cranleigh GU6 7JU
Directors: Pastor David & Mrs Maureen Brown. Executive staff 2. *CC* No.281184. Began 1989; Free Church. No magazine. Turnover £12,000 to year end Dec 98. Marriage enhancing weekends, preparation courses, day seminars, church training programmes on marriage and family.
Email: dandmbrown@compuserve.com
☎ 01483 272 016 Fax 01483 272 016
Also at: The Marriage Agenda (Scotland), 1 Moubray, Naemoor Road, Crook of Devon, Kinross KY13 7UH
☎ 01577 840 561

Marriage Care, Clitherow House, 1 Blythe Mews, Blythe Road, London W14 0NW
Chief Executive: Mrs Mary Corbett. Other staff n/a. *CC* No.218159. Began 1946; Roman Catholic. (Previously Catholic Marriage Advisory Council). Magazine: *Marriage Care Bulletin* (3,000 quarterly). Turnover n/a. Providing counselling for individuals/couples; marriage preparation courses; natural family planning and fertility awareness service.
Web: www.fertilityuk.org
Email: marriagecare@btinternet.com
☎ 020 7371 1341 Helpline: 0345 573 921 Fax 020 7371 4921

Marriage Encounter – Anglican Expression, 5 Hillside Way, Welwyn AL6 0TY
Lay Executives: Mr & Mrs Peter & Janet Cox. No full-time staff. *CC* No.292594. Began 1978; Anglican. No magazine. Turnover £70,000 to year end June 98. Providing weekends for married couples aimed at deepening their relationship through improved communications. Also Engaged Encounter.
Web: www.marriageencounter.freeserve.co.uk
Email: peter_janet_cox@hotmail.com
☎ 01438 715 337 Fax 01438 715 337

***Marriage Encounter – Baptist Expression**, 26 Bellingdon Road, Chesham HP5 2HA
Secretary: Bill & Brenda Reynolds. No full-time staff. Began 1981; Baptist. Magazine: *News Sheet* (400 every four months). Turnover n/a. Encouraging married couples to strengthen and deepen their relationship with each other.
☎ 01494 782 466

Marriage Refreshment, Banks Farm, Barcombe, Lewes BN8 5DY
Leaders: Mr Michael & Mrs Gillian Warren. No full-time staff. Began 1984; Anglican. No magazine. Turnover £3,000 to year end n/a. Residential marriage weekends for Christian couples, to strengthen and encourage.
☎ 01273 400 205

***Marriage Resource**, 24 West Street, Wimborne BH21 1JS
UK Director: Mr Richard Kane. Other staff 2. *CC* No.1034114. Began 1994; evangelical. No magazine. Turnover £114,542 to year end Dec 98. Setting up and developing local church based marriage support groups; nationwide information regarding marriage support services.
Web: www.marriageresource.org.uk
Email: marriage@netcomuk.co.uk
☎ 01202 849 000 Mobile: 07702 426 500 Fax 01202 849 934

***Marriage Review**, 9 Grovesnor Gardens, Upminster RM14 1DL
Administrator: Mr Derek J Saunders. No full-time staff. *CC* No.1002002. Began 1975; non-denominational. No magazine. Turnover £19,000 to year end Mar 98. Mainly weekend courses of marriage enrichment and renewal for married couples; follow-up; training programme.
☎ 01708 225 344 Fax 01708 225 344

***Mission to Marriage**, Forge Cottage, Fishery Road, Boxmoor, Hemel Hempstead HP1 1NA
Director: Dr Tony Hobbs. Executive staff 3. ***CC*** No.273658. Began 1977; non-denominational. Magazine: *Newsletter* (1,600 quarterly). Turnover n/a. Public marriage enrichment seminars, marriage events for churches and organisations, publication of resources concerning marriage.
Email: drahobbs@aol.com
☎ 01442 215 414 Fax 01442 403 062

***National Marriage Week**, 24 West Street, Wimborne BH21 1JS
Director: Mr Richard Kane. Other staff 2. ***CC*** No.1034114. Began 1994; evangelical. No magazine. Turnover £18,430 to year end Dec 98. Annual church based and media event designed to promote and support marriage.
Web: www.marriageresource.org.uk
Email: marriage@netcomuk.co.uk
☎ 01202 849 000 Mobile: 07702 426 500
Fax 01202 849 934

Partners for Life, Welford Hill Farm, Welford on Avon, Stratford-upon-Avon CV37 8AE
Leader: Dr David Stanley. Executive staff 2. Began 1993; non-denominational. No magazine. Turnover £10,000 to year end Dec 98. Running residential marriage enrichment weekends for churches and other groups.
Web: www.wwww.uk.com
Email: wel@welford.co.uk
☎ 01789 750 565 Fax 01789 751 901

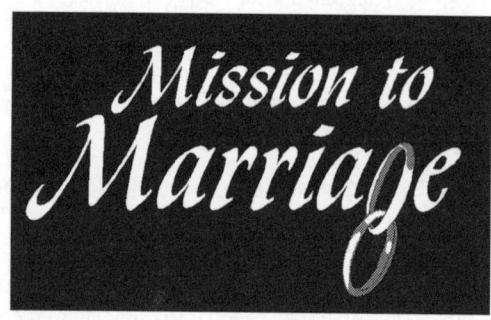

***Radiant Life Ministries**, 47 Gloucester Road, Alkrington, Middleton, Manchester M24 1HT
Directors: Rev W & Mrs L Crick. No other staff. ***CC*** No.1004581. Began 1991; interdenominational. Magazine: *Newsletter* (Circulation & frequency n/a). Turnover £4,000 to year end Mar 98. Enriching marriage through a unique range of seminars and training events for the local church.
Web: cw.orangenet.co.uk/~radiant
Email: radiantlife@orangenet.co.uk
☎ 0161 653 3040

***Rapport**, National Family Centre, Leon Avenue, Cardiff CF4 7RG
Director: Mr Peter Reynolds. Executive staff 2, Other staff 2. ***CC*** No.288485. Began 1991; interdenominational. (Previously Marriage and Family Foundation). No magazine. Turnover See Care for the family (merged 1998). Courses on communication in marriage, communication workshops, parenting workshops; focus on non Christian community.
Web: www.care-for-the-family.org.uk
Email: care.for.the.family@dial.pipex.com
☎ 029 2081 1733 Fax 029 2081 4089

Scottish Marriage Care, 50 Greenock Road, Paisley PA3 2LE
Chief Executive: Mrs Mary Toner. Other staff 1. Began 1967; Roman Catholic. (Previously Catholic Marriage Advisory Council Scotland). No magazine. Turnover £37,000 to year end Dec 96. Providing counselling to people with marriage and relationship difficulties; helping couples prepare for marriage.
☎ 0141 849 6183

Skills For Living, Littledale Hall, Littledale, Lancaster LA2 9EY
Co-Founder: Mr Walter Acuff. Executive staff 2. Began 1994; non-denominational. No magazine. Turnover £19,000 to year end Dec 98. Retreats; training for group leaders; workshops for personal relationship and marriage issues including abuse.
Web: www.skills.org
Email: littledale@compuserve.com
☎ 01524 770 266 Fax 01524 771 553

***Treasures in Heaven Trust**, PO Box 26, Sevenoaks TN15 0ZP
Director: Mr Max Sinclair. Executive staff 2, Admin staff 1. ***CC*** No.1073068. Began 1998; interdenominational. Turnover: first year of operation. Offering cringe-free evangelism, training, Bible teaching, church weekends, to enrich marriage and family life.
Email: maxsinclair@cvm.telme.com
☎ 01732 834 297 Fax 01732 834 298

United Marriage Encounter, 211 Mottram Road, Stalybridge SK15 2QX
Secretaries: Mr & Mrs Graham & Lee Leech. No full-time staff. ***CC*** No.1065937. Began 1994; interdenominational. Magazine: *Quest* (170 quarterly). Turnover £25,000 to year end Dec 98. Weekend residential programme offering encouragement, hope and help to strengthen marriages.
Web: www.muscanet.com/~ume
Email: gpl@maunsell.co.uk
☎ 0161 338 3035 Fax 0161 236 0694

Worldwide Marriage Encounter, 55 Bramcote Drive, Beeston, Nottingham NG9 1HR
Leaders: Mr & Mrs Jeremy & Glenys Moore, Fr Pat Heekin. No full-time staff. ***CC*** No.272318. Began 1972; Roman Catholic. Magazine: *Spirit* (400 quarterly). Turnover n/a. Enriching the sacrament of matrimony for couples and the sacrament of holy orders for priests.
☎ 01159 174 584 Fax 01159 174 584

PERSONNEL COUNSULTANCY & PLACEMENT

See also Counselling Organisations on Page 404.

Career Plan Ltd, 33 John's Mews, London WC1N 2NS
Director: Sir Timothy Hoare OBE. Executive staff 4, Other staff 2. Began 1970; non-denominational. No magazine. Turnover n/a. Personnel consultants; staff assessment and recruitment, executive search, redundancy and pre-retirement counselling, vocational guidance.
Email: careerplan@btinternet.com
☎ 020 7242 5775 🖷 020 7831 7623

Careforce, 35 Elm Road, New Malden KT3 3HB
Director: Rev Ian R L Prior. Executive staff 5. *CC* No.279443. Began 1980; interdenominational. Magazine: *Annual Magazine* (8,000 annually). Turnover £189,500 to year end Mar 98. Serving evangelical churches and caring organisations by recruiting volunteers (aged 18 to 25) to serve for a year.
Web: careforce.co.uk
Email: enquiry@careforce.co.uk
☎ 020 8942 3331 🖷 020 8942 3331

Christian Contact / Mallon De Theological College, 11a Methley Grove, Leeds LS7 3PA
Organiser: Rev Steve H Hakes. Executive staff 1. Began 1975; interdenominational. No magazine. Turnover n/a. Providing monthly lists and compatibility scheme with marriage and/or friendship in view for those aged over 18.
Web: www.detc.freeserve.co.uk
Email: mallon.detc@bigfoot.com
☎ No telephone

***Christian Friendship Fellowship**, Bawtry Hall Christian Centre, Bawtry, Doncaster DN10 6JH
Chief Executive Officer: Mr Bryan Conway. Executive staff 1, Other staff 7. *CC* No.327940. Began 1976; interdenominational. Magazine: *News & Views* (3,500 quarterly). Turnover £50,000 to year end Sept 98. Ministry for nationwide unattached Christians; fellowship groups, social events, holidays, penfriends, music groups, international section.
Email: cffbawtry@yahoo.com
☎ 01302 711 007 🖷 01302 710 027

***Christian Vocations (CV)**, Holloway Street West, Lower Gornal, Dudley DY3 2DZ
Centre Director: Mr Paul Lindsay. *Services Co-ordinator:* Rev Geoff Thompson. Executive staff 1, Other staff 5. *CC* No.801806. Began 1985; interdenominational. (Previously Christian Service Centre). Magazine: *In Service* (3,000 every four months), *STS Directory* (4,500 annually), *Jobs Abroad Directory* (3,000 annually). Turnover £115,000 to year end Dec 98. Releasing God's people into God's work through vocational guidance, teaching and listings of current opportunities.
Email: info@christianvocations.org
☎ 01902 882 836 🖷 01902 881 099

Christians Abroad, 1 Stockwell Green, London SW9 9HP
General Secretary: Mr Colin South. *Information Officer:* Mr Kevin Cusack. Executive staff 1, Other staff 4. *CC* No.265867. Began 1973; non-denominational. Magazine: *Opportunities Abroad* (1,000 monthly), *WSE Guide* (25,000 annually). Turnover £130,000 to year end Dec 94. Providing information and advice about work abroad; project management and recruitment for overseas projects.
Web: wse.org.uk or cabroad.org.uk
Email: wse@cabroad.org.uk
☎ 020 7346 5950 🖷 020 7346 5955

Creative Mentors Ltd, 9 Timothy Close, Norwich NR1 4AG
Managing Director: Dr John Clements. Executive staff 2. Began 1986; non-denominational. (Previously John Clements Associates). No magazine. Turnover n/a. Providing coaching/mentoring in personal effectiveness, servant leadership and character development; training in presentation skills.
Web: www.creativementors.com
Email: john@creativementors.com
☎ 01603 436 658 🖷 01603 700 734

New Day Personnel, 15 Greave Close, Rawtenstall BB4 8JT
Partner: Mrs Susan Saxon. Executive staff 2, Admin staff 3. Began 1997; interdenominational. (Previously New Day Recruitment Consultants). No magazine. Turnover n/a. Placing people in employment nationwide specialising in direct sales and financial sales/financial advisors.
Web: www.churchnet.org.uk/churchnet/new_day
Email: suenewda@aol.com
☎ 01706 224 049

***Partnership Link-up Service**, 15 Barncroft, Berkhamsted HP4 3NL
Administrator/Secretary: Mr Alan J Batchelor. No other staff. Began 1991; Christian Brethren. No magazine. Turnover £1,500 to year end Dec 98. Linking independent evangelical churches with those seeking full-time paid appointments.
☎ 01442 864 281

SLB Management & Design, Redland House, 1 Redland Way, Aylesbury HP21 9RJ
Consultant: Mr Simon Baker. Executive staff 2, Admin staff 1. Began 1997; interdenominational. No magazine. Turnover n/a. Managing human resource needs, developing people for the future.
Email: slb@slbmandes.nildram.co.uk
☎ 01296 334 424 🖷 01296 434 143

***Senior Volunteer Network**, 30 Silverwood Avenue, Ravenshead, Nottingham NG15 9BU
Director: Mr John Hallett. Executive staff 1. *CC* No.1068049. Began 1996; non-denominational. No magazine. Turnover £2,000 to year end Mar 98. Linking retired Christian teachers with UK and overseas organisations that need their skill and experience.
Email: calebsnet@aol.com
☎ 01623 793 863 🖷 01623 490 724

SIMA (UK) Ltd Management Consultancy, Clockhouse Barn, Sugworth Lane, Radley, Oxford OX14 2HX
Managing Director: Dr Nick Isbister. Executive staff 3, Other staff 2. Began 1985; non-denominational. No magazine. Turnover £205,000 to year end Mar 98. Helping organisations and companies make more productive use of their people and strengths.
Email: simauk@patrol.i-way.co.uk
☎ 01865 321 123 🖷 01865 326 611

Andrew Stanton Associates, 157 Hoo Road, Kidderminster DY10 1LP
Director: Mr Andrew Stanton. Executive staff 1, Other staff 1. Began 1987; non-denominational. (Previously ASA Consultants). No magazine. Turnover £25,000 to year end Dec 98. Helping organisations develop people through management training, team building, personal counselling, "Investors in People" consultancy.
☎ 01562 755 338

Personnel Consultancy & Placement

Welford Enterprises Ltd, Welford Hill Farm, Welford on Avon, Stratford-upon-Avon CV37 8AE
Managing Director: Dr David Stanley. Executive staff 2, No other full time staff. Began 1991; non-denominational. No magazine. Turnover £150,000 to year end Mar 98. Mentoring senior managers; change management consultancy based on Christian values.
Web: www.wwww.uk.com
Email: wel@welford.co.uk
☎ 01789 751 900 Fax 01789 751 901

Workfinders, The Mega Centre, Sheffield S2 5BQ
Director: Mr Chris Rawson. *Development Manager:* Mr Ian Cambe. Executive staff 5. Began n/a; non-denominational. No magazine. Turnover £500,000 to year end Jun 99. A practical Christian initiative operating as a not-for-profit employment agency and driving school.
Email: ian@visions.freeserve.co.uk
☎ 0114 272 7271 Fax 0114 272 7237

Peter Young Consulting and Training, 4 Whitehouse Road, Oxford OX1 4NA
Management Consultant: Mr Peter Young. Executive staff 1. Began 1998; non-denominational. No magazine. Turnover n/a. Helping organisations to realize their vision by developing robust strategies and effective people/leaders.
Email: pete.y@virgin.net
☎ 01865 725 195

PRAYER FELLOWSHIPS

†Apostleship of Prayer, 114 Mount Street, London W1Y 6AH
National Secretary: Rev M Beattie. No full-time staff. Began 1869; Roman Catholic. Magazine: *Messenger of the Sacred Heart* (Circulation n/a (Irish magazine) monthly). Turnover £24,000 to year end Dec 90. A union effected by prayer for Christ's desires and the consecration of daily life.
☎ No telephone

Christian Road Safety Association, 7 Goldstone Close, Hove BN3 7PD
Hon Organising Secretary: Rev Eric Thorn. Executive staff 1, Other staff 4. ***CC*** No.258938. Began 1937; interdenominational. Magazine: *Christian Road Safety Journal* (2,500 annually). Turnover n/a. Teaching the Christian concepts of behaviour to all road users through care and prayer.
☎ 01273 554 598 Fax 01273 554 598

†Concern for Scotland, 70 Saughtonhall Drive, Edinburgh EH12 5TL
Co-ordinator: Mr Stephen Anderson. No full-time staff. Began 1981; interdenominational. Magazine: *Prayer Bulletin* (800 every two months). Turnover £1,200 to year end Dec 94. Providing a national bulletin for prayer and information.
☎ No telephone

Divine Healing Ministries, 32 Townsend Street, Belfast BT13 2ES
Pastoral Director: Rev Brother David Jardine. Executive staff 2. ***CC*** No.XN 91984. Began 1993; interdenominational. No magazine. Turnover £20,489 to year end Sep 96. Prayer with laying on of hands, intercession for the sick, prayer for our land.
☎ 028 9031 1532

Fellowship for Revival, 295 Milton Road East, Edinburgh EH15 2LA
Secretary: Rev J P Wood. No full-time staff. Began 1938; evangelical. Magazine: *Revival Digest* (1,000 half-yearly). Turnover n/a. Prayer fellowship for revival.
☎ 0131 669 1124

The Fellowship of Contemplative Prayer, 202 Ralph Road, Shirley, Solihull B90 3LE
General Secretary: Rev Canon Martin W Tunnicliffe. All voluntary staff. ***CC*** No.298850. Began 1949; interdenominational. Magazine: *Come* (2,000 annually), *Living Word* (1,000 occasional). Turnover £6,000 to year end Apr 99. Encouraging and promoting contemplative prayer by teaching, organising prayer groups, quiet days and retreats.
Web: www.zyworld.com/fcp
Email: fcp@202rr.freeserve.co.uk
☎ 0121 745 6522

The Fellowship of Meditation, Marian Dunlop House, 8 Prince of Wales Road, Dorchester DT1 1PW
Company Secretary: Dr Jeremy Harvey. Other staff 2. ***CC*** No.213323. Began 1952; non-denominational. No magazine. Turnover £22,000 to year end Dec 98. Teaching and practice of Christian contemplative meditation to grow nearer to the likeness of Christ.
☎ 01305 251 396

Fellowship of Prayer for Unity, 29 Ramley Road, Pennington, Lymington SO41 8LH
Hon Chaplain: Rev Paul Renyard. All voluntary staff. ***CC*** No.254142. Began 1963; ecumenical. Magazine: *Fellowship News & Meditation* (Circulation n/a every four months). Turnover n/a. Working and praying for unity at local and national level.
☎ 01590 672 646

Guild of St Leonard, HMP Moorland, Bawtry Road, Hatfield Woodhouse, Doncaster DN7 6EE
Warden: Bishop Leslie Lloyd-Rees. *Chaplain & Secretary:* Rev Peter J Walker. Executive staff 2, Other staff 1. Began 1900; interdenominational. Magazine: *Intercession Paper* (750 quarterly). Turnover n/a. Supporting by prayer those in prison and for all prison and related Home Office staff.
☎ 01302 351 500 Fax 01302 350 896

The Guild of the Holy Ghost The Comforter, 2 Norris Gardens, Warblington, Havant PO9 2TT
Secretary: Mr B. Dev Hardcastle. No full-time staff. Began 1893; Anglican. Magazine: *Prayer Leaflet* (150 every two months). Turnover n/a. Bringing to bear the influence of the Holy Spirit on the church and nations of the world.
☎ 023 9248 2922

S

ıter Prayer, 69 Lakeside, Earley, Reading RG6 7PG
Director: Mr Brian Mills. Executive staff 3, Other staff 4. Began 1997; non-denominational. Magazine: *Interprayer News* (500 quarterly). Turnover £16,000 to year end Apr 98. Building partnerships together in prayer across the nations, emphasising reconciliation, revival, church planting and the harvest.
Email: 106206.1226@compuserve.com
☎ 0118 926 4523 Mobile: 07885 600 903 Fax 0118 926 4523

ıtercessors for Britain, 14 Orchard Road, Moreton, Wirral CH46 8TS
Director: Mr Raymond Borlase. Other staff 3. *CC* No.290664. Began 1969; interdenominational. Magazine: *Prayer Letter* (3,500 every two months), *Watchman* (Circulation n/a every four months). Turnover n/a. Promoting regular and disciplined intercession for the nation.
☎ 0151 677 6767 Fax 0151 604 0072

The Julian Meetings, 5 Fernbrook Drive, Harrow HA2 7EE
National Convener: Yvonne Walker. No full-time staff. Began 1973; non-denominational. Magazine: *Julian Meetings Magazine* (Circulation n/a quarterly), *JM Newsletter* (Circulation n/a quarterly). Turnover £4,000 to year end Dec 96. Fostering the teaching and practice of contemplative prayer and Christian meditation.
☎ No telephone

The League of Prayer, 69 Fitzwalter Road, Sheffield S2 2SJ
General Director: Rev Leslie Evans. Executive staff 1. *CC* No.1040100. Began 1891; interdenominational. Magazine: *Newsletter* (1,000 every two months). Turnover £25,000 to year end Dec 94. Promoting prayer and holiness.
☎ 0114 272 6788

Lydia Fellowship International, PO Box 85, Waterlooville, Portsmouth PO7 7QU
UK and European Leader: Mrs Molly Osborne. All voluntary staff. Began 1970; non-denominational. Magazine: *Newsletter* (Circulation n/a quarterly). Turnover n/a. Prayer fellowship primarily for women.
☎ 023 9226 7684 Fax 023 9226 7684

The Magdalene Fellowship, The Vicarage, 1 Gelli Crescent, Risca, Newport NP1 6QG
Joint Guardians: Rev & Mrs David Norwood. No full-time staff. *CC* No.1011604. Began 1986; interdenominational. Magazine: *Newsletter* (Circulation n/a monthly). Turnover £5,040 to year end Aug 98. National fellowship with rule of life and intercession particularly for divorced and separated Christians.
☎ 01633 612 307

Ministry of Christian Communication Prayer Fellowships (MCCPF), 35 Four Acres, Saffron Walden CB11 3JD
General Secretary: Mr John E Maddams. No paid staff. Began 1956; interdenominational. Magazine: *MCCPF Prayer News* (100 quarterly). Turnover £2,000 to year end Jun 98. Intercession, pen friend outreach, distributing literature and cassettes, UK and overseas.
☎ No telephone

Pray for Denmark, Ivy Cottage, 6 The Paddocks, Aylsham, Norwich NR11 6LH
Co-ordinator: Mr Bruce Porteous. No full time staff. Began 1997; interdenominational. Linked with Bønnepartnere for Danmark. No magazine. Turnover n/a. Network linking those praying for revival in Denmark.
Email: prayfordk@iname.com
☎ 01263 734 472

***Pray for Revival**, Cornerstone House, 5 Ethel Street, Birmingham B2 4BG
Co-ordinator: Mr Ian Cole. No other full-time staff. *CC* No.328403. Began 1988; interdenominational. No magazine. Turnover £103,456 to year end Sept 94. Encouraging Christians to pray for revival in UK and around the world.
Email: pfr@charis.co.uk
☎ 0121 643 5611

Prayer at Twelve Fellowship, 17 Villers Road, Woodthorpe, Nottingham NG5 4FB
Leader: Rev David Monkton. No full-time staff. Began 1975; non-denominational. Magazine: *Twelve* (400 occasionally). Turnover n/a. Midday prayer fellowship/support movement for those who are ill or in special need.
Web: www.users.surfaid.org/~monkton
Email: monkton@surfaid.org
☎ 01159 622 599

***Prayer Fellowship for South Asia**, PO Box 43, Sutton SM2 5WL
Chairman: Mr Robin Thomson. No full-time staff. Began 1940; interdenominational. Magazine: *Prayer Notes* (200 every two months). Turnover £4,000 to year end Dec 98. Prayer fellowship for the peoples of South Asia, both in the Indian sub-continent and elsewhere.
Email: 100126.3641@compuserve.com
☎ 020 8770 9717 Fax 020 8770 9747

†***Prayer for the Nations**, PO Box 15027, London SE5 9ZU
Administrator: Mr Peter C Wilks. Other staff 2. *CC* No.326994. Began 1992; interdenominational. Magazine: *Prayer sheets* (Circulation n/a occasionally). Turnover £23,000 to year end Dec 95. Training school of prayer and intercession; city (UK) wide prayer events; prayer for the nation.
Email: 100534.1117@compuserve.com
Email: lbtc@compuserve.com
☎ 020 7708 5294

Prayer Network for Revival, 1 St Teiling, Lanark ML11 7HY
Administrator: Mr David C Black. No full-time staff. Began 1988; non-denominational. No magazine. Turnover n/a. Prayer network in Scotland organising conferences, leaders days, seminars on revival.
Web: www.scotland2000.freeserve.co.uk
☎ 01555 664 883

The Quiet Garden Trust, Stoke Park Farm, Park Road, Stoke Poges, Slough SL2 4PG
Director: Rev Philip D Roderick. Executive staff 2, Other staff 2. *CC* No.1038528. Began 1992; ecumenical. Magazine: *Quiet Places* (Circulation n/a n/a). Turnover n/a. Encouraging ministry of hospitality and prayer on an occasional basis in local homes, gardens, other centres.
Web: web.ukonline.co.uk/members/
Email: quiet.garden@ukonline.co.uk
☎ 01753 643 050 Fax 01753 643 081

Scottish Prayer Centre, 26 St Leonards Street, Lanark ML11 7AB
Administrator: Rev David Black. Staff 2. Began 1998; non-denominational. (Previously Prayer Network for Revival). Turnover £5,000 to year end Dec 98. Prayer centre for revival in Scotland; prayer shield for leaders; prayer school national calls.
Email: pray@scotland2000.freeserve.co.uk
☎ No telephone

Servants of Christ the King, Well Cottage, The Street, Kilmington, Axminster EX13 7RW
Enquirers' Correspondent: Mrs Sylvia Wilsdon. No full-time staff. *CC* No.249609. Began 1942; interdenominational. Magazine: *SCK Newsletter* (500 quarterly). Turnover £5,000 to year end Dec 98. Companies waiting upon God in silence followed by controlled discussion leading to corporate action.
☎ 01297 341 42

***Telephone Prayer Chain Ministry**, Challenge House, 29 Canal Street, Glasgow G4 0AD
UK Leader: Mrs Jessie McFarlane. All voluntary staff. *CC* No.SCO 20478. Began 1981; interdenominational. Magazine: *Chain Link* (1,000 quarterly). Turnover £6,000 to year end Aug 96. Nationwide prayer by telephone available Monday 10.00am-4.00pm, Wednesday 11.00am-3.00pm.
✉ Email: 101373.3661@compuserve.com
☎ 0141 332 6382/5152 Mobile: 07979 206 843
🖷 0141 332 8500

***There is Hope**, 24 Clement Rise, Livingston EH54 6JY
Director: Mr David Hill. Other staff 3. *CC* No.100511. Began 1985; interdenominational. Magazine: *Hopeline* (500 monthly). Turnover £45,000 to year end June 98. Providing an opportunity for prayer for revival and for churches to work together in evangelism.
Web: www.there-is-hope.com
✉ Email: info@there-is-hope.com
☎ 01506 495 576 🖷 01506 495 576

Trumpet Call, 30 Tyler Way, Thrapston, Kettering NN14 4UE
Chairman: Rev Graham Timson. No paid staff. Began 1996; non-denominational. Magazine: *Trumpet Call* (300 quarterly). Turnover £760 to year end Nov 98. Gathering, encouraging, teaching intercessors of every denomination across the region to pray for revival.
✉ Email: ggtimson@hotmail.com
☎ 01832 734 991 🖷 01832 734 880

Wholeness Through Christ, WTC Office, Waggon Roa[d,] Brightons, Falkirk FK2 0EL
Executive staff 2. *CC* No.327055. Began 1971; interdenom[in]inational. No magazine. Turnover n/a. Enabling people to li[ve] in a life transforming relationship with Jesus Christ.
☎ 01324 714 946 🖷 01324 714 946

†**Women Take Five Ministries International**, 7 Glazebrook Clos[e,] Heywood OL10 3EA
Administrator: Mrs Marion Needham. Executive staff 3. *C*[*C*] Began 1992; interdenominational. No magazine. Turnove[r] n/a. Encouraging women to spend five minutes in daily praye[r] for revival throughout our land.
☎ 01706 622 848

Women's World Day of Prayer, Commercial Road, Tunbridg[e] Wells TN1 2RR
Admin Secretary: Mrs Lynda Lynam. Executive staff 1, Othe[r] staff 2. *CC* No.233242. Began 1932; interdenominational. Magazine: *Together in Prayer* (13,500 annually). Turnove[r] £258,000 to year end Dec 98. Organising and training for th[e] Day of Prayer.
☎ 01892 541 411 🖷 01892 541 411

World Day of Prayer – Scottish Committee, St Columba's Manse Kilbirnie KA25 7JU
Secretary: Mrs Margaret A Broster. No full-time staff. *CC* No.SCO 20446. Began 1930; interdenominational. No magazine. Turnover £48,172 to year end Apr 98. Preparing and distributing worship materials, organising and training for the Day of Prayer.
Web: davbros.demon.co.uk
✉ Email: wdp@davbros.demon.co.uk
☎ 01505 683 342 🖷 01505 684 024

PRINTERS

Agapé Press (UK) Ltd, Unit 1D, Kingston Mill, Cobden Street, Pendleton, Salford M6 6WE
Managing Director: Dr Don E Okpalugo. All voluntary staff. *CC* No.1059348. Began 1996; non-denominational. Magazine: *Agap, Press Newsletter* (3,500 quarterly). Turnover £10,000 to year end Mar 97. Designing and printing outreach leaflets and booklets for churches, charities and other businesses.
☎ 0161 743 1010 🖷 0161 743 9991

Bookprint Creative Services, PO Box 827, Eastbourne BN21 3YJ
Senior Partner: Mr David Nickalls. Executive staff 2, Other staff 3. Began 1993; non-denominational. Turnover n/a. Book production and design for publishers, Christian organisations and authors, paperbacks, hardbacks, music books, Bibles.
✉ Email: bcs@bookprint.co.uk
☎ 01323 411 315 🖷 01323 410 461

Campsie Litho Ltd, 51 French Street, Glasgow G40 4EH
Managing Director: Mr Ronald McNeish. Executive staff 52. Began 1979; non-denominational. Turnover £2,600,000 to year end Feb 98. Graphic designers and litho printers.
☎ 0141 554 5225 🖷 0141 556 3457

Christian Mission Press, 62 Whitby Road, Ruislip HA4 9DP
Master Printer: Mr Colin Drake. Executive staff 2. Began 1987; non-denominational. Turnover n/a. Wide range of printing services including full colour for Christian organisations, churches and individuals.
☎ 01895 672 161 🖷 01895 672 161

Christian Printing Services, 54 Roseford Road, Cambridge CB4 2HD
Proprietor: Mr Trevor Hames. Executive staff 2, Other staff 1. *CC* No.255001. Began 1992; interdenominational. No magazine. Turnover £70,000 to year end Apr 98. Printing all types of material from copying to four-colour.
Web: dspace.dial.pipex.com/christian.books.direct
✉ Email: cps@christianbooksdirect.co.uk
☎ 01223 322 277 🖷 01223 322 277

hristian Publicity Organisation, Garcia Estate, Canterbury Road, Worthing BN13 1BW
General Director: Mr Roy P Barbour. *Creative Director:* Mr Gerald Palframan. *Editor:* Mr Andrew Halloway. Executive staff 4, Other staff 33. ***CC*** No.221462. Began 1957; non-denominational. Turnover £1,450,000 to year end Apr 97. Supporting the Christian community through design, print and publishing, in partnership with ministries nationally and internationally.
Web: www.cpo.uk.com
Email: enquiries@cpo.uk.com
☎ 01903 264 556 ISDN: 01903 830 005
Fax: 01903 830 066

:M Print, 61 Station Road, Portslade, Brighton BN41 1DF
Partner: Mr Alan Jarred. Executive staff 2, Other staff 8. Began 1985; non-denominational. Turnover £400,000 to year end Dec 96. Printing for churches, businesses and personal requirements.
☎ 01273 420 983 Fax: 01273 415 013

Effective Services, 58 St Wulstan Way, Southam, Leamington Spa CV33 0TU
General Manager: Mr C Pratt. Executive staff 1, Other staff 1. Began 1991; interdenominational. Turnover n/a. Printing, publishing, organising seminars and exhibitions.
☎ 01926 812 110 Fax: 01926 812 110

Emprint, 9 Harbour Street, Whitstable CT5 1AG
Proprietor: Mr Kingsley B Empett. Executive staff 2. Began 1971; non-denominational. Turnover n/a. General printers specialising in Christian work including magazines and books.
☎ 01227 274 952/360 603

Goldprint, 1a Belvedere Grove, Bridlington YO15 3LY
Partners: Joyce & Derrick Bates. Executive staff 2, Other staff 1. Began 1986; non-denominational. Turnover n/a. Printing in gold, silver, white, colours and rainbow; fundraisers, business cards, stationery, Scripture text items.
☎ 01262 678 425 Fax: 01262 678 425

Stanley L Hunt (Printers) Ltd, Midland Road, Rushden NN10 9UA
Managing Director: Mr Andrew M Hunt. Executive staff 6, Other staff 45. Began 1920; non-denominational. Turnover n/a. General printers, major suppliers to Christian organisations and institutions for over 70 years.
☎ 01933 356 226 Fax: 01933 356 613

Imprint, 187 Lynchford Road, Farnborough GU14 6HD
Proprietor: Mr John Reading. Executive staff 2, Other staff 2. Began 1983; non-denominational. Turnover n/a. Printing, artwork and design for church magazines, newsletters, leaflets, brochures, letterheads, calling cards.
Email: imprint187@aol.com
☎ 01252 547 023 Fax: 01252 376 004

Kingsley (Litho) Printers, The Old Blacksmiths, 52 High Street, Ilfracombe EX34 9QB
Mr David Lane. *Partners:* Mr Peter Marnell. Executive staff 2, Other staff 5. Began 1954; Anglican. Turnover £240,000 to year end Jan 99. General printers.
☎ 01271 863 131 Fax: 01271 866 646

Palmers Print & Design Ltd, Unit 2, Birch Walk, Fraser Road, Erith DA8 1QX
Managing Director: Mr Martin Palmer. Executive staff 4, Other staff 8. Began 1981; non-denominational. Turnover n/a. Printers to Christian organisations; one-colour leaflets to four-colour magazines.
☎ 01322 441 741 Fax: 01322 441 717

†Penderel Press Ltd, Faraday House, Gladstone Road, Croydon CR0 2BQ
Managing Director: Mr David Burr. Executive staff 3, Other staff 11. Began 1977; non-denominational. Turnover £660,000 to year end June 92. Designers, colour and commercial printers; consultancy for all aspects of printing from Christian viewpoint.
☎ 020 8683 1953 Fax: 020 8689 2213

Wright's (Sandbach) Ltd, 9 Old Middlewich Road, Sandbach CW11 1DP
Directors: Mr G F Galway, Mr D A Sahne. Executive staff 2, Other staff 23. Began 1896; interdenominational. Turnover £1,500,000 to year end May 98. Graphic design, commercial and Christian printing.
☎ 01270 762 416 Fax: 01270 760 278

PROFESSIONAL CHRISTIAN GROUPS

ACB – Association of Christians in Broadcasting, PO Box 124, Westcliff-on-Sea SS0 0QU
Secretary: Mr Jeff Bonser. Executive staff 1. ***CC*** No.297766. Began 1980; interdenominational. (Previously Association of Christians in Local Broadcasting). (Under the aegis of Churches Advisory Council for Local Broadcasting). Magazine: *Crosstalk* (1,000 frequency n/a). Turnover £7,000 to year end Dec 98. Support, help, advice for Christians interested or involved in broadcasting; prayer scheme; annual conference.
Web: www.caclb.org.uk
Email: acb@caclb.org.uk
☎ 01702 348 369 🖷 01702 305 121

Actors' Church Union, St Paul's Church, Bedford Street, Covent Garden, London WC2E 9ED
Senior Chaplain: Rev Canon Bill Hall. No full-time staff. ***CC*** No.207315. Began 1899; Anglican. Magazine: *Newsletter* (Circulation n/a half-yearly). Turnover £23,531 to year end Mar 98. Serving the theatrical profession through members and 200 chaplains to theatres, studios and drama schools.
☎ 020 7836 5221

**ACUTE – Alliance Commission on Unity & Truth among Evangelicals*, Whitefield House, 186 Kennington Park Road, London SE11 4BT
Chair: Rev David Hilborn. No full-time staff. ***CC*** No.123448. Began n/a; interdenominational. An Evangelical Alliance Partnership for Change. No magazine. Turnover: finance included with Evangelical Alliance. Working for agreed Biblical concensus and united evangelical response on theological and other public issues.
Web: www.eauk.org
Email: acute@eauk.org
☎ 020 7207 2114 🖷 020 7207 2130

Agricultural Christian Fellowship, 38 De Montfort Street, Leicester LE1 7GP
Chairman: Rev Terry Brinkley. No full-time staff. ***CC*** Began 1964; interdenominational. Magazine: *ACF Bulletin* (200 half-yearly). Turnover n/a. Encouraging practical Christian living and developing informed Christian understanding amongst Christians in agriculture. A UCCF group.
Email: acf@uccf.org.uk
☎ 0116 255 1700 🖷 0116 255 5672

Airline, Aviation and Aerospace Christian Fellowships, 103 Ambleside Road, Lightwater GU18 5UJ
General Secretary: Mr John Brown. Staff 5. ***CC*** No.277929. Began 1971; interdenominational. Magazine: *Crossway Outreach Magazine* (20,000 frequency n/a), *Newsline* (2,000 every four months), *Aviation News (Fairford)* (16,000 annually). Turnover n/a. Evangelistic outreach in the aviation professions throughout the world.
☎ 01276 472 724 🖷 01276 472 724

***Arts Centre Group**, The Courtyard, 59a Portobello Road, London W11 3DB
Administrator: Ms Carla Moss. Executive staff 1. ***CC*** No.289763. Began 1971; interdenominational. Magazine: *Artyfact* (1,000 every two months), *Articulate* (1,200 annually). Turnover £50,000 to year end Mar 98. Supporting Christians working professionally in the arts, media and entertainment.
Web: dspace.dial.pipex.com/acg
Email: acg@dial.pipex.com
☎ 020 7243 4550 🖷 020 7221 7689

***Association of Bible College Principals**, Birmingham Bible Institute, 5 Pakenham Road, Edgbaston, Birmingham B15 2NN
Secretary: Dr Richard Massey. No full-time staff. Began 197[illegible]; interdenominational. No magazine. Turnover £1,000 to year end Mar 97. Association of 25 Bible/Theological colleges. Encouraging fellowship and support between Bible colleges.
☎ 0121 440 4016 🖷 0121 440 3175

The Association of British Christian Outdoor Centres, CCI (UK), PO Box 169, Coventry CV1 4PW
Secretary: n/a. No full-time staff. Began 1982; non-denominational. No magazine. Turnover n/a. Fraternity of Christian centres which offer structured outdoor activities led by qualified staff.
Email: cciinuk@aol.com
☎ 024 7655 9099 🖷 024 7655 9099

Association of Christian Law Firms, 1 Bulstrode Way, Gerrards Cross SL9 7QT
Hon Secretary: Mr Nigel Spoor. No full-time staff. Began 1990; non-denominational. No magazine. Turnover n/a. Encouraging and training for Christian law firms and support of Christian work.
Email: aclf@fairchilds.co.uk
☎ 01753 883 127

***Association of Christian Teachers**, 94a London Road, St Albans AL1 1NX
General Secretary: Mr Richard L Wilkins. Executive staff 2, Other staff 3. ***CC*** No.2056400. Began 1971; interdenominational. Magazine: *Act Now* (5,000 every four months), *Digest* (1,000 every four months). Turnover £125,000 to year end Aug 96. Servicing and supporting Christians working at all phases of education.
Web: www.christian-teachers.org
Email: actoffice@christian-teachers.org
☎ 01727 840 298 🖷 01727 848 966

Association of Christian Teachers of Wales, 17 Brynmawr Place, Maesteg, Bridgend CF34 9PB
Hon Secretary: Miss J A Miller. No full-time staff. ***CC*** No.505329. Began 1974; non-denominational. Magazine: *ACTW News* (250 frequency n/a). Turnover £7,000 to year end Aug 98. Upholding Christian ideals and values in education today.
☎ 01656 734 118

***Association of Christian Teachers (Scotland)**, Rutherford House, 17 Claremont Park, Edinburgh EH6 7PJ
Chairman: Miss Kirsti Paterson. Part time staff 2. ***CC*** No.09798. Began 1971; interdenominational. Magazine: *Interact* (550 every four months). Turnover £15,612 to year end May 98. Support, resources and prayer for Christian teachers; Christian voice on educational issues in consultations and media.
☎ 0131 554 1206 🖷 0131 555 1002

†**Association of Christian Writers**, 74 Longleaze, Wootton Bassett, Swindon SN4 8AS
Contact Person: Mrs Juliet Hughes. No full-time staff. Began 1969; interdenominational. (Previously Fellowship of Chrisian Writers). Magazine: *Writers Newsletter* (400 quarterly). Turnover n/a. Providing encouragement, advice, workshops and forums for Christian writers from beginner to professional.
☎ 01792 852 296

Association of Christians in Higher Education (ACHE), 38 De Montfort Street, Leicester LE1 7GP
Secretary: Dr Gwynne Davies. No full-time staff. *CC* Began 1987; interdenominational. Magazine: *Forum for the Association of* (250 annually). Turnover n/a. Fellowship for academic and administrative staff applying Christian thought to higher education. A UCCF group.
Email: ache@uccf.org.uk
☎ 0116 255 1700 📠 0116 255 5672

Association of Christians in Planning and Architecture (ACPA), 38 De Montfort Street, Leicester LE1 7GP
Professional Groups Secretary UCCF: n/a. No full-time staff. Began 1983; non-denominational. Magazine: *ACPA Newsletter* (250 annually). Turnover n/a. Developing thought on architectural and planning theory from a Biblical basis. A UCCF group.
Email: acpa@uccf.org.uk
☎ 0116 255 1700 📠 0116 255 5672

***At Work Together**, 14 Horsted Square, Uckfield TN22 1QQ
Executive Director: Mr Alan Johnson. Executive staff 5, Admin staff 27. *CC* No.1014540. Began 1998; non-denominational. Part of Spring Harvest. No magazine. Turnover: finance included in Spring Harvest. Providing conferences and resources for leaders from all walks of life, including workplace and church.
Web: www.springh.org
Email: leaders@springh.org
☎ 01825 769 111 📠 01825 769 141

Baptist Ministers' Fellowship, 11 Barns Close, Kirby Muxloe, Leicester LE9 2BA
Secretary: Rev Bob Almond. No full-time staff. Began 1939; Baptist. Magazine: *The Baptist Ministers' Journal* (1,800 four times a year). Turnover n/a. Promoting fellowship among Baptist ministers in various parts of the world and furthering their interests.
Web: www.bmf.ukweb.nu
Email: bmf@revbob.globalnet.co.uk
☎ 0116 239 2731 📠 0116 239 5222

†**BBC Christian Fellowship**, Room 5152, BBC White City, 201 Wood Lane, London W12 7TS
Secretary: Mrs Eilidh Young. No full-time staff. Began 1949; non-denominational. Magazine: *Cross Talk* (Circulation n/a occasionally). Turnover n/a. Fellowship and support for Christians working in the media, especially the BBC.
Email: eilidh.young@bbc.co.uk
☎ 020 8752 5562 📠 020 8752 5055

Business Men's Fellowship, National Service Centre, 454 Crow Road, Glasgow G11 7DR
Service Centre Co-ordinator: Mr Andrew Greenwood. No other staff. *CC* No.SCO 25720. Began n/a. Magazine: *Answer* (6,000 quarterly). Turnover n/a. Evangelical, interdenominational, full gospel laymen's ministry.
Email: agreenwood@bmf-uk.com
☎ Mobile: 07703 597 311

***Business Study Group**, 38 De Montfort Street, Leicester LE1 7GP
Chairman: Mr David Parish. No full-time staff. *CC* Began 1965; non-denominational. No magazine. Turnover n/a. Exploring and applying Biblical principles in the business and working world. A UCCF group.
Email: bsg@uccf.org.uk
☎ 0116 255 1700 📠 0116 255 5672

***CARE for Education**, 53 Romney Street, London SW1P 3RF
Director: Mrs Ann Holt. Executive staff 1, Other staff 3. *CC* No.288485. Began 1986; interdenominational. (Previously Christians in Education). Magazine: *CARE magazine supplement* (8,000 half-yearly). Turnover £100,000 to year end Dec 98. Equipping parents, governers, teachers and churches to be prayerfully and effectively involved in education.
Web: www.care.org.uk
Email: cfe@care.org.uk
☎ 020 7233 0455 📠 020 7233 0983

Catholic Association of Teachers, Schools and Colleges, 4 The Avenue, Moulton, Northampton NN3 1TL
Professional Development Officer: Mr John Shoreland. No full-time staff. Began 1996 from Catholic Teachers Federation (1907) and Association of Catholic Schools and Colleges (1993/1896); Roman Catholic. (Previously Catholic Teachers' Federation). Magazine: *Newsletter* (Circulation n/a every two months). Turnover £40,000 to year end Dec 98. Providing support for Catholic teachers and schools.
☎ 01352 732 788 📠 01352 735 983

Catholic Police Guild, 42 Francis Street, London SW1P 1QW
Secretary: Mr Brendan McWilliams. No full-time staff. Began 1914; Roman Catholic. Magazine: *The Catholic Constable* (400 quarterly). Turnover n/a. Providing a fraternal organisation of Catholic policemen and women.
☎ 020 8647 0195

Professional Christian Groups

Choir Schools Association, Minster School, Deangate, York YO1 7JA
Adminstrator: Mrs Wendy Jackson. No other staff. Began 1921; Anglican and Roman Catholic. Affiliated with the Choir Schools Bursary Trust. Magazine: *Choir Schools Today* (5,000 annually). Turnover n/a. Publicising the life and educational opportunities of Cathedral and Collegiate choirs.
☎ 01904 624 900 🖷 01904 632 418

Christian Booksellers Association Ltd, Grampian House, 144 Deansgate, Manchester M3 3ED
Executive Vice-Chairman: Mr John F Macdonald. *General Secretary:* Mr Ian Matthews. Executive staff 3, Other staff 2. Began 1984; interdenominational. Magazine: *European Christian Bookstore Journal* (2,000 monthly). Turnover £100,000 to year end Dec 98. International trade association for booksellers, publishers, distributors, libraries, church and school bookstalls.
Email: cba.europe@btinternet.com
☎ 0161 833 3003 🖷 0161 835 3000

Christian Booksellers Convention Ltd, Victoria House, Victoria Road, Buckhurst Hill IG9 5EX
Director: Miss Jean S Wilson. No full-time staff. Began 1975; non-denominational. No magazine. Turnover £200,000 to year end June 98. Arranging annual event for booksellers and publishers in Great Britain; exhibitions/seminars.
Email: 100067.1226@compuserve.com
☎ 020 8559 2975 🖷 020 8502 9062

Christian Booksellers Group, Booksellers Association of Great Britain and Ireland, Minster House, 272 Vauxhall Bridge Road, London SW1V 1BA
Chairman: Mr Geoff Wallace. *Secretary:* Mr John Parke. Began n/a; non-denominational. No magazine. Turnover n/a. Seeking solutions to the problems and fighting for the interests of its members.
☎ 020 7834 5477 🖷 020 7834 8812

***Christian Business Alliance**, Carey House, The Pickenham Centre, North Pickenham, Swaffham PE37 8LG
Director: Mr Peter Gillett. Executive staff 2, Other staff 1. Began 1989; interdenominational. Magazine: *Internet Newsletter* (500 quarterly). Turnover n/a. Fellowship and encouragement, teaching, prayer and intercession; Internet newsletters, articles, trade directory, links, business opportunities.
Web: www.pickenham.clara.net
Email: pickenham@clara.co.uk
☎ 01760 440 561 🖷 01760 440 561

Christian Dance Fellowship of Britain, 25 Scardale Crescent, Scarborough YO12 6LA
National Co-ordinators: Angela Courtney, Candy Hadler. No other staff. *CC* No.1040446. Began 1990; interdenominational. Magazine: *Tent of David* (650 half-yearly). Turnover £6,000 to year end Mar 98. Networking Christian dancers irrespective of denomination, and teaching/training of all abilities and styles.
Email: angela.cdfb@lineone.net
☎ 01723 500031 Mobile: 07711 948940 🖷 01723 503 399

Christian Dental Fellowship, 44 Pool Road, Hartley Wintney, Hook RG27 8RD
Secretary: n/a. No full-time staff. *CC* No.261350. Began 1955; interdenominational. Magazine: *Newsround* (425 every four months). Turnover £30,000 to year end Sept 96. Fellowship of Christians in the dental profession; supporting dental missionary work. (No advice given).
Web: www.users.globalnet.co.uk/~rmje
Email: 101547.1774@compuserve.com
☎ No telephone 🖷 01252 844 018

Christian Engineers Association, 38 De Montfort Street, Leicest LE1 7GP
Chairman: Mr John Baden Fuller. No full-time staff. *CC* Beg 1981; interdenominational. Magazine: *CEA Newsletter* (1 half-yearly). Turnover n/a. Study and fellowship group for pr fessional engineers. A UCCF group.
Email: cea@uccf.org.uk
☎ 0116 255 1700 🖷 0116 255 5672

***Christian Medical Fellowship**, 157 Waterloo Road, Lond SE1 8XN
General Secretary: Dr D Andrew N Fergusson. Executive sta 7, Other staff 8. *CC* No.1039823. Began 1949; interdenom inational. Magazine: *Triple Helix – Christian dimensions Healthcare* (7,000 frequency n/a). Turnover £500,000 to ye end Dec 98. Fellowship of doctors; evangelism, Christian et ics, literature, student and mission support; international links
Web: www.cmf.org.uk
Email: 106173.327@compuserve.com
☎ 020 7928 4694 🖷 020 7620 2453

***Christian Police Association**, John Williamson House, 40 Uppingham Road, Leicester LE5 2DP
Executive Director: Mr Harry Spain. Executive staff 2, Othe staff 1. *CC* No.220482. Began 1883; interdenominationa Magazine: *On & Off Duty* (2,000 quarterly). Turnover £50,00 to year end Dec 98. Spiritual welfare of police officers and evan gelistic outreach to members of the Police Service.
Web: members.aol.com/cpauk
Email: cpahq@cix.co.uk
☎ 0116 241 2416 🖷 0116 241 9207

Christians At Work, 148 Railway Terrace, Rugby CV21 3HN
General Secretary: Mr T. Mark McConnell. Executive staff 1 *CC* No.254887. Began 1942; non-denominational. Magazine *Work & Witness* (7,800 every two months). Turnover £40,00 to year end Mar 98. Encouraging, supporting and equippin Christian witness in the workplace.
☎ 01788 579 738

***Christians in Caring Professions**, King's House, 175 Wokingham Road, Reading RG6 1LT
Director: n/a. Staff 3. *CC* No.288888. Began 1968 non-denominational. Magazine: *CiCP Newsletter* (1,80 monthly). Turnover £116,000 to year end July 97. Equipping and encouraging Christians to live for Christ in their professional lives.
Web: www.cicp.org.uk/cicp
Email: office@cicp.org.uk
☎ 0118 966 0515 🖷 0118 926 3663

***Christians in Entertainment**, PO Box 17205, London SE26 4ZL
Director: Mr Christopher Gidney. Other staff 2. *CC* No.801327. Began 1988; interdenominational. Magazine: *Newsletter* (Circulation n/a quarterly). Turnover £30,000 to year end Dec 96. Spiritual and emotional support for professionals in the entertainment business.
Web: ourworld.compuserve.com/homepages/chrisgidney
Email: chrisgidney@compuserve.com
☎ 01757 550 375

Christians in Finance, St Margarets Church, Lothbury, London EC2R 7HH
Chairman: Mr Gerard Long. No full-time staff. *CC* No.268974. Began 1875; interdenominational. (Previously London Banks' Christian Union). Magazine: *Newsletter* (300 quarterly). Turnover £5,000 to year end Dec 98. Evangelism, fellowship and support of missionaries in the London financial centre; weekly meetings.
☎ 020 7606 8330

hristians in Pharmacy, 202 Reading Road, Wokingham RG41 1LH
Administrator: Mr Ralph H Higson. No other staff. Began 1993; non-denominational. Magazine: *Fly in the Ointment* (150 half-yearly). Turnover n/a. Distributing Christian literature to Christians working in the UK pharmaceutical service.
☎ 01189 775 036

hristians in Property, Church Commissioners, 1 Millbank, London SW1Y 3JZ
Secretary: Mr Andrew Brown. No full-time staff. Began 1953; interdenominational. Magazine: *Newsletter* (400 every four months). Turnover n/a. Encouraging and providing fellowship and witness among surveyors, quantity surveyors, estate agents and architects.
☎ 020 7222 7010

:hristians in Public Life, Westhill College, Selly Oak, Birmingham B29 6LL
Co-ordinator: Rev Dr David Clark. No full-time staff. ***CC*** Began 1992; interdenominational. Magazine: *Newsletter* (800 every four months). Turnover £10,000 to year end Mar 97. Enabling Christians in public life to co-operate in addressing issues of fundamental concern for society.
Web: www.doncaster.org/workout/cipl/
Email: cipl@westhill.ac.uk
☎ 0121 472 7245 Fax 0121 415 5399

:hristians in Science, 88 Sylvandale, Welwyn Garden City AL7 2HT
Membership Secretary: Mrs Pauline Williams. No full-time staff. Began 1943; interdenominational. UCCF affiliated. Magazine: *Science and Christian Belief* (800 half-yearly). Turnover £17,000 to year end Dec 98. Exploring God's work in creation; encouraging environmental concern; applying biblical principles to science and technology.
Web: www.cis.org.uk
Email: 106446.423@compuserve.com
☎ 01707 390 448

Christians in Science Education, 5 Longcrofte Road, Edgware HA8 6RR
Secretary: Mr John Bausor. No full-time staff. Began 1989; interdenominational. Magazine: *CISE Newsletter* (300 half-yearly). Turnover £1,000 to year end Jan 99. Helping science educators through discussion, support and information on aspects of science and faith.
Web: www.cis.org.uk/cise/java
Email: cise@bausor.clara.net
☎ 020 8952 5349 Fax 020 8930 1160

·Christians in Shell Centre, CMKCB/9, Shell Centre, London SE1 7PG
Contact: Mrs Anne Strobel. No full-time staff. Began 1948; interdenominational. No magazine. Turnover n/a. Christian fellowship of Shell employees.
☎ 020 7934 6036

***Christians in Sport**, PO Box 93, Oxford OX2 7YP
Directors: Rev Andrew Wingfield Digby, Mr Stuart Weir. Executive staff 5, Other staff 2. ***CC*** No.281110. Began 1976; interdenominational. Magazine: *n/a* (10,000 quarterly). Turnover £300,000 to year end Oct 98. Reaching the world of sport for Christ.
Web: www.way.co.uk/~christians_sport
Email: stuart@christiansinsport.org.uk
☎ 01865 311 211 Fax 01865 311 334

***Christians in the City**, Office 11, 41 Bridge Street, Hereford HR4 9DG
Co-ordinator: Mr Peter Garner. Executive staff 1. Began 1986; interdenominational. No magazine. Turnover n/a. Fellowship of Christians working out together the Christian response to workplace issues.
☎ 01432 342 218

Christians in Road Transport, PO Box 5729, Corby NN17 2ZQ
Chairman: Mr John Milne. No full time staff. Began 1997; non-denominational. Magazine: *Talking Diesel* (100 every two months). Turnover £1,000 to year end Nov 98. Providing Christian fellowship and encouragement for people in the road transport industry. Evangelism amongst drivers.
Web: www.northchurch.com/cirt
Email: cirt@milne3951.freeserve.co.uk
☎ 01442 392 225

Church of England Guild of Vergers, 14 Pennington Court, 245 Rotherhithe Street, London SE16 1FT
General Secretary: Mr Ian M Griffiths. No full-time staff. Began 1932; Anglican. Magazine: *The Verger* (900 every two months). Turnover £11,500 to year end Dec 98. International fellowship offering training to vergers.
Web: www.societies.anglican.org/guild-of-vergers
Email: iangensec@btinternet.com
☎ 020 7231 6888

Churches National Housing Coalition, Central Buildings, Oldham Street, Manchester M1 1JT
National Director: Brendan Bowles. *Administrator:* J Lazarus. Other staff 3. ***CC*** No.1050288. Began 1991; interdenominational. Magazine: *Just Housing* (1,100 quarterly). Turnover £160,000 to year end Mar 97. Mobilising Christian action on homelessness and poor housing.
Email: mail@cnhc.cablenet.co.uk
☎ 0161 236 9321 Fax 0161 237 5359

Civil Service Christian Union, 48 Blakes Lane, New Malden KT3 6NR
Hon Secretary: Rev Anthony Hardy. No full-time staff. ***CC*** No.299187. Began 1872; non-denominational. No magazine. Turnover £2,300 to year end Dec 98. Promoting Christian fellowship and witness among Government servants mainly through a contact list.
☎ 020 8949 0703

Clergy Against Nuclear Arms, The Rectory, 20 Church Path, Emsworth PO10 7DP
Chairman: Rev David Partridge. No full-time staff. Began 1982; interdenominational. Magazine: *Peace Maker* (500 every four months). Turnover £2,000 to year end Dec 98. Nuclear pacifist resource, education and support group for Christians and other enquirers.
☎ 01243 372 428

College of Health Care Chaplains, 2 Edwards College, South Cerney, Cirencester GL7 5TR
Registrar: Mr Chris Webber. Part-time staff 2. Began 1991; interdenominational. Magazine: *Journal of Health Care Chaplaincy* (850 quarterly). Turnover £75,000 to year end Dec 96. Providing professional support to health care chaplains and those who work with them.
Web: www.msf.org.uk
Email: cjw@dialin.net
☎ 01285 861 312 Mobile: 07771 723 060

Conference of Religious (COR), 114 Mount Street, London W1Y 6DQ
General Secretary: Sister Lorna Brockett. Executive staff 1, Other staff 3. ***CC*** No.277024. Began 1985; Roman Catholic. No magazine. Turnover n/a. Promoting the welfare of Apostolic Institutes of men and women Religious in England and Wales.
Email: confrelig@aol.com
☎ 020 7493 1817 🖷 020 7409 2321

Conference of Religious in Scotland, 15d Hill Street, Glasgow G3 6RN
General Secretary: Sister Winifred Connolly. No full-time staff. Began 1971; Roman Catholic. Magazine: *ROC News* (300 quarterly). Turnover n/a. Circulating information among Roman Catholic Religious Orders and sharing experiences.
☎ 0141 332 3094

English Clergy Association, The Old School, Norton Hawkfield, Pensford, Bristol BS39 4HB
Chairman: Rev J W Masding. No full-time staff. ***CC*** No.258559. Began 1938; Anglican. Magazine: *Parson and Parish* (600 half-yearly). Turnover £24,000 to year end Dec 95. Upholding the ministry of parish, diocesan, and cathedral clergy within the Established Church; holiday grants.
Email: masding@breathe.co.uk
☎ 01275 830 017 🖷 01275 830 017

†**European Christian Publishers Conference Ltd**, Scripture Union, 207 Queensway, Bletchley, Milton Keynes MK2 2EB
Secretary: Mr David Rosser. No other staff. Began 1977; interdenominational. No magazine. Turnover n/a. Providing three-yearly conference for Christian publishers.
Email: davidr@scriptureunion.org.uk
☎ 01908 856 000 🖷 01908 856 111

***Evangelical Alliance Coalition on the Occult and New Spiritualities (EACONS)**, Whitefield House, 186 Kennington Park Road, London SE11 4BT
Co-Chairs: Rev Paul Harris, Mr Doug Harris. No full-time staff. ***CC*** No.123448. Began n/a; interdenominational. An Evangelical Alliance Partnership for Change. No magazine. Turnover: finance included with Evangelical Alliance. Providing a forum concerning cults, the occult and new spiritualities; counselling, information, campaigning.
Web: www.eauk.org
Email: members@eauk.org
☎ 020 7207 2100 🖷 020 7207 2150

S

Federation of Catholic Priests, The Vicarage, Palace Place, Paignton TQ3 3AQ
Secretary General: Rev Preb Brian Tubbs. No full-time staff. ***CC*** Began n/a; Anglican. Magazine: *ACTA* (Circulation n/a annually). Turnover n/a. Mutual support in propagating, maintaining and defending catholic doctrine and practice.
Email: father_tubbs@compuserve.com
☎ 01803 559 059

Fellowship of European Broadcasters, 23 The Service Road, Potters Bar EN6 1QA
Chairman: Mr Harvey Thomas. No full-time staff. Began 1991; interdenominational. Magazine: *European Update* (5,200 every four months). Turnover n/a. Fellowship of European Christians involved with broadcasting.
☎ 01707 649 910 🖷 01707 662 653

***Fellowship of European Evangelical Theologians**, 16 Manor Cou[rt], Pinehurst, Grange Road, Cambridge CB3 9BE
Secretary: Dr GL Bray. *Chair:* Professor I Howard Marsha[ll]. No full-time staff. ***CC*** No.SCO 22952. Began 1976; no[n-]denominational. Magazine: *European Journal of Theology* (5[0]C half-yearly). Turnover Nil. Promoting evangelical theologic[al] research, supporting theologians in Europe by conferences a[nd] other contacts.
Email: glbray@samford.edu
☎ 01223 311 804

Glasgow Theological Forum, 20 Westgate, North Berwic[k] EH39 4AF
Chairman: Rev Dr David J Graham. No full-time staff. Bega[n] 1989; interdenominational. Magazine: *Vision* (200 quarterly). Turnover £350 to year end Dec 98. Stimulating thought an[d] writing in theology and other areas of Christian concern.
☎ 0141 334 9849 🖷 0141 334 0012

God's Squad Christian Motorcycle Club (UK Chapter), PO Bo[x] 437, Reading RG30 3DF
President: Sean Stillman. No staff. Began 1994; non[-]denominational. Associated with Care and Communicatio[n] Concern, Australia. Magazine: *Squad Supporter*(Circulation & frequency n/a). Turnover n/a. Operating in an evangelistic an[d] chaplaincy capacity among 'outlaw' motorcycle fraternity an[d] associated fringe groups.
☎ 01792 480 391 🖷 01792 480 391

The Good Gardeners Association, Pinetum Lodge, Churcham, Gloucester GL2 8AD
Secretary: Mr John D Wilkin. Executive staff 2, Other staff 2. ***CC*** Began 1966; Anglican. Magazine: *Newsletter* (500 quarterly). Turnover £15,000 to year end Dec 98. Promoting an[d] researching natural growing methods of healthy food. Healt[h] and ecology.
☎ 01452 750 554 🖷 01452 750 402

Guild of Catholic Doctors, 60 Grove End Road, London NW8 9NH
Hon Secretary: Dr Michael Jarmulowicz. No full-time staff. ***CC*** No.1002374. Began 1911; Roman Catholic. Magazine: *Catholic Medical Quarterly* (1,500 quarterly). Turnover £40,000 to year end Oct 98. Providing facilities to members for prayer and study and upholding Christian moral principles in the practice of medicine.
Web: www.catholicdoctors.org.uk
☎ 020 7266 4246 🖷 020 7266 4813

***Healthcare Christian Fellowship International**, 349 Beersbridge Road, Belfast BT5 5DS
British Isles Promoter: Mrs Ann Silvester. *Secretary, Ireland:* Miss Irene Montgomery. Executive staff 4. ***CC*** Began 1964; non-denominational. (Previously Hospital Christian Fellowship International). Magazine: Title n/a (2,000 annually). Turnover n/a. Bringing Christians into fellowship and equipping them to be effective witnesses to staff and patients.
☎ 028 9045 3595
Also at: *Secretary, Scotland:* Mrs Ann Jack, 49 Priestfield Crescent, Edinburgh EH16 5JH
☎ 0131 667 4494
And: *Secretary, Wales:* Mr Jeff Dyas, 26 Wenvoe Terrace, Barry CF6 8EF
☎ 01446 421 674
And: *Secretary, England:* Miss Brenda Alexander, 86 Uxbridge Road, Hanworth, Feltham TW13 5EH
☎ 020 8894 9710
And: *Secretary, Channel Islands:* Mrs Liz Reed, La Conchee, Les Rues, St Saviours, Guernsey GY7 9FN
☎ 01481 643 19

ıdependent Schools Christian Alliance (TISCA), 29 Stumperlowe Park Road, Fulwood, Sheffield S10 3QP
General Secretary: Rev Michael Hepworth. No full-time staff. *CC* No.1047025. Began 1995; interdenominational. (Previously Wadhurst Fellowship). Magazine: *TISCA News* (250 Termly). Turnover £10,000 to year end Oct 98. Promoting and defending a Biblical Christian faith, applying it to educational issues.
Email: tisca@orangenet.co.uk
☎ 0114 263 0714 🖷 0114 263 0714

dustrial Christian Fellowship, St Matthews House, 100 George Street, Croydon CR0 1PE
Information: Capt T Drummond. No other staff. *CC* Began 1877; ecumenical. (Previously Industry Churches Forum (ICF)). Magazine: *Faith in Business Journal* published in association with Ridley Hall, Cambridge (Circulation & frequency n/a). Turnover £37,000 to year end Mar 99. Strengthening the relationship between the Christian faith and daily work.
Email: yro86@dialpipex.com
☎ 020 8656 1644 🖷 020 8656 1644

ıstitute for British Liberation Theology, 178 Abbeyfield Road, Sheffield S4 7AY
Director: Rev Dr John Vincent. No full time staff. Began 1991; ecumenical. Incorporating Urban Theologians International and International Urban Ministry Network. No magazine. Turnover n/a. Arranging conferences and research for practitioners in British Liberation Theology and publishing their results.
☎ 0114 243 6688 🖷 0114 243 6688

ıternational Christian Chamber of Commerce (AISBL), Grovelands House, Woodlands, Bradley Stoke, Bristol BS32 4JT
Secretary: Mr Tim Simpson. Part-time staff 1. *CC* Began 1987; interdenominational. (Registered in UK as Council of Christians in Commerce Ltd). Magazine: *The Market Calling* (Circulation n/a every four months), *The National Standard* (Circulation & frequency n/a). Turnover n/a. Encouraging/equipping Christians in the marketplace to come into a new dimension of faith required for work.
Web: www.uk.iccc.net
Email: office@uk.iccc.net
☎ 01454 626 119 🖷 01454 626 129

Lawyers Christian Fellowship, 20 Waterside Drive, Newton Mearns, Glasgow G77 6TL
Secretary: Mrs Joyce Holloway. Executive staff 2, Other staff 2. *CC* No.1017695. Began 1852; interdenominational. Magazine: *FuLCrum* (1,900 every four months). Turnover £89,349 to year end Dec 97. Encouraging, educating and equipping Christian lawyers/law students in fellowship, prayer, service, witness and evangelism.
Web: www.lawcf.org
Email: lcfadmin@compuserve.com
☎ 0141 616 0522 🖷 0141 616 0522

'Leadership Development, Whitefield House, 186 Kennington Park Road, London SE11 4BT
Chair: Duncan Banks. No full-time staff. *CC* No.123448. Began n/a; interdenominational. (Previously Younger Leaders). An Evangelical Alliance Partnership for Change. No magazine. Turnover: finance included with Evangelical Alliance. Seeking to equip existing leaders to train and empower new generations of leaders.
Web: www.eauk.org
Email: members@eauk.org
☎ 020 7207 2114 🖷 020 7207 2130

***Librarians Christian Fellowship**, 34 Thurlestone Avenue, Seven Kings, Ilford IG3 9DU
Hon Secretary: Mr Graham Hedges. No full-time staff. Began 1973; non-denominational. Magazine: *LCF Newsletter* (500 every four months), *Christian Librarian* (500 annually). Turnover £6,000 to year end Dec 98. Organising events and publications helping Christian librarians to relate their faith to their work.
Web: churchnet.ucsm.ac.uk/lcf/lcfhome.htm
Email: fm128@viscount.org.uk
☎ 020 8599 1310 / 8708 3100

Literary Studies Group, 38 De Montfort Street, Leicester LE1 7GP
Secretary: Dr Roger Kojecky. No full-time staff. *CC* Began 1983; interdenominational. Magazine: *The Glass* (60 periodically). Turnover n/a. Discussing Christian approaches to literature for those with a professional interest in literary criticism. A UCCF group.
Email: lsg@uccf.org.uk
☎ 0116 255 1700 🖷 0116 255 5672

***London Leaders Consultations (Evangelical Alliance)**, Whitefield House, 186 Kennington Park Road, London SE11 4BT
Contact: Rev Joel Edwards. No full-time staff. Began n/a; interdenominational. An Evangelical Alliance Partnership for Change. No magazine. Turnover: finance included with Evangelical Alliance. Drawing together evangelical leaders in London across the denominations.
Web: www.eauk.org
Email: london@eauk.org
☎ 020 7207 2100 🖷 020 7207 2150

***Merchant Navy Christian Fellowship**, 48 South Street, Alderley Edge SK9 7ES
Director: Mr Michael J Wilson. Executive staff 1, Other staff 2. *CC* No.209133. Began 1958; interdenominational. No magazine. Turnover £10,000 to year end Dec 98. Providing pastoral ministry to Christian seafarers worldwide; international network to provide hospitality.
Email: scfs_hq@compuserve.com
☎ 01625 590 010 🖷 01625 585 442

Midweek in Mayfair, 26 Binney Street, London W1Y 1YN
Director of Pastoral Care: Mr Chris Dindsale. Executive staff 2. *CC* No.1048051. Began 1987; non-denominational. Magazine: *Midweek Marketplace* (300 every two months). Turnover £54,000 to year end Dec 97. Resourcing people in London's West End workplace through Biblical teaching and pastoral care.
Web: www.doveuk.com/midweek
Email: midweek@doveuk.com
☎ 020 7629 2348 🖷 020 7629 6480

Movement of Christian Workers, MCW Headquarters, St Joseph's, Watford Way, London NW4 4TY
Chair: Mr Paul Edwards. Admin staff 1. *CC* No.1023531. Began 1991; ecumenical. Magazine: *MCW Review* (500 quarterly). Turnover £25,000 to year end Dec 97. Promoting justice based on the values of equality, social justice and solidarity.
Email: mcworkers@aol.com
☎ 020 8203 6290 🖷 020 8203 6291

†National Conference of Priests, St Mary's, Ford Green Road, Norton-Le-Moors, Stoke-on-Trent ST6 8LT
Executive Secretary: Rev Mervyn Smith. No full-time staff. *CC* Began 1970; Roman Catholic. Magazine: *Newsletter* (5,000 half-yearly). Turnover n/a. Co-ordinating pastoral work of priests; forum for discussion of faith, church and ministry.
☎ 01782 535 404

Naval Christian Fellowship, 2b South Street, Gosport PO12 1ES
General Secretary: Cdr J Christopher Mather. Executive staff 1, Other staff 3. ***CC*** No.256726. Began 1948; interdenominational. Magazine: *Newsletter* (1,000 monthly). Turnover £58,000 to year end Mar 98. Evangelical fellowship linking Christians in the Royal Navy, European and other navies.
Web: dspace.dial.pipex.com/ncf
Email: ncf@dial.pipex.com
☎ 023 9258 3878 📠 023 9258 0058

Network of Christians in Psychology (NeCIP), c/o Psychology Department, University of East London, London E15 4LZ
Hon Secretary: Mr Martyn Baker. No full-time staff. Began 1989; interdenominational. Magazine: *The Christian Psychologist* (170 half-yearly). Turnover £3,500 to year end Dec 98. Supporting network for Christian psychologists with regional groups and annual conference.
Email: m.c.baker@uel.ac.uk
☎ 020 8590 7000 Ext: 4562

Nurses Christian Fellowship International, 18 Buckland Road, Maidstone ME16 0SL
General Director: Mr Harry Louden. Executive staff 1, Other staff 3. ***CC*** No.258936. Began 1959; interdenominational. Magazine: *Christian Nurse International* (3,000 quarterly). Turnover £80,000 to year end Dec 96. Developing Christian beliefs and values in personal and professional life, through teaching and consultancy.
Web: welcome.to/ncfi
Email: ncfi@compuserve.com
☎ 01622 753 111 Mobile: 07798 676 403 📠 01622 754 111

Officers Christian Union, Havelock House, Barrack Road, Aldershot GU11 3NP
General Secretary: Sqn Leader M Warwood RAF (Rtd). Executive staff 2, Other staff 3. ***CC*** No.249636. Began 1851; interdenominational. Magazine: *Contact* (3,000 quarterly). Turnover £225,000 to year end Dec 97. Christian work among officers in HM Armed Forces.
Web: ourworld.compuserve.com/homepages/ocu
Email: ocuoffice@aol.com
☎ 01252 311 221 📠 01252 350 722

Optical Christian Fellowship, 1 Carisbrooke Drive, Charlton Kings, Cheltenham GL52 6YA
Chairman: Mr Keith Holland. No full-time staff. Began 1960; interdenominational. No magazine. Turnover n/a. Providing Christian fellowship within optical professions; advice and support to students; optical missionary support.
Email: 72132.1135@compuserve.com
☎ 01242 233 500 📠 01242 227 666

The Oriental Orthodox Mailing List, 10 Heathwood Gardens, Charlton, London SE7 8EP
Director: Father Sergious Scott. Other staff n/a. Began n/a; Orthodox. Magazine: *via email.* Turnover n/a. Friendly and scholarly electronic discussion and exchanges for those interested in canonical Oriental Orthodox Churches.
Email: orthodox@uk-christian.net
☎ 020 8854 3090 📠 020 8244 7444

The People and Work Programme, Parish Resource Centre, Peterborough House, 90 Harlestone Road, Northampton NN5 7AG
Director: Mr John Raymond. No other staff. Began 1991; Anglican. Magazine: *Newsletter* (1,800 half-yearly). Turnover n/a. Encouraging and equipping all Christians to live out their faith at and through work.
Web: www.users.2etnet.co.uk/peopleandwork
& www.online.freeserve.co.uk
Email: parish@resources53.freeserve.co.uk
☎ 01604 751 907 📠 01604 580 301

***The Post Office and Telecommunications Christian Associati (Christians in Communications)**, 2 Ashbourne Place, Yc YO24 2UJ
General Secretary: Mr John W Hield. Executive staff 1, Otl staff 1. ***CC*** No.238329. Began 1887; non-denomination Magazine: *The 'Mail'* (1,200 every four months). Turnov £16,000 to year end Apr 98. Fellowship of Christians in t Communications industries.
Web: www.christiancomm.org.uk
Email: john.hield@cwcom.net
☎ 01904 784 167 📠 01904 784 167

***Probation Service Christian Fellowship**, Lismore Hous Heathside Road, Woking GU22 7HT
Chair: Mr Michael Rees. All voluntary staff. ***CC*** No.105905 Began 1954; non-denominational. Magazine: *Probation Se vice Christian Fellowship Newsletter* (Circulation n/a every fo months). Turnover £5,912 to year end Dec 98. Fellowship criminal/ civil justice workers, to stimulate Christian perspe tives and action in social work.
Email: francis@prittie48.freeserve.co.uk
☎ 01483 776 262 📠 01483 727 244

Religious & Theological Studies Fellowship (RTSF), 38 D Montfort Street, Leicester LE1 7GP
Secretary: Dr Tony Gray. No full-time staff. ***CC*** Began 193 non-denominational. Magazine: *RTSF News & Prayer Lette* (Circulation n/a every four months), *Themelios* (2,500 ever four months). Turnover n/a. Helping students of Theology an Religious Studies in their biblical understanding and trainin for future services. A UCCF group.
Web: www.uccf.org.uk/rtsf
Email: rtsf@uccf.org.uk
☎ 0116 255 1700 📠 0116 255 5672

Religious Education Council of England & Wales, c/o CEM, Roya Buildings, Victoria Street, Derby DE1 1GW
Hon Secretary: Dr Stephen Orchard. No full-time staff. Bega 1973; non-denominational. Magazine: *Reports* (2,000 occasionally). Turnover £4,000. Providing a forum for the professional and religious institutions concerned with religiou education in schools.
☎ 01332 296 655 📠 01322 432 53

Schools Ministry Network, 207 Queensway, Bletchley, Milton Keynes MK2 2EB
Administrator: Mrs Ruth Thomas. No full-time staff. Began 1993; interdenominational. Magazine: *Newsletter* (300 half-yearly). Turnover £7,500. Bringing together organisations and individuals committed to maintaining high standards of schools ministry.
Web: www.scriptureunion.org.uk
Email: rutht@scriptureunion.org.uk
☎ 01908 856 000 📠 01908 856 111

Science and Religion Forum, 17 Trafford Road, Alderley Edge SK9 7NN
Secretary: Dr John Kempster. No full-time staff. ***CC*** No.1034657. Began 1971; interdenominational. Magazine: *Reviews* (300 frequency n/a). Turnover £7,000 to year end Dec 96. Enabling scientific knowledge to be related to religious faith and practice; sharing interests and information.
Web: www.srforum.org
Email: info@srforum.org
☎ 01625 584 223 📠 01625 584 223

Scottish Evangelical Theology Society, Bel Abri, Leadgate, Alston CA9 3EL
Secretary: Rev Canon Peter Cook. No full-time staff. Began n/a; non-denominational. Magazine: *Scottish Bulletin of Evangelical Theology* (700 half-yearly). Turnover n/a. Fellowship of those concerned to advance the cause of evangelical theology; annual theological conference.
☎ 01434 381 873

Secretaries and Administrators Christian Fellowship, c/o ICSA, 16 Park Crescent, London W1N 4AH
Chairman: Mr Alan King. No full-time staff. *CC* No.278183. Began 1959; interdenominational. Magazine: *Intercom* (Circulation n/a quarterly). Turnover £750 to year end Dec 96. Promoting Christian fellowship for students/members of the Institute of Chartered Secretaries and Administrators.
☎ 020 7580 4741

Social Workers Christian Fellowship, c/o Truedata Subscriptions, 23 Park Road, Ilkeston DE7 5DA
Membership Secretary: Ms Grace Gunnell. No full-time staff. *CC* Began 1964; interdenominational. Magazine: *The Extra Mile* (Circulation n/a every four months). Turnover n/a. Providing professional, intellectual, spiritual and social support to Christians in social work, care and action.
☎ 01383 731 720

Society of Catholic Artists, 19 Cranford Close, West Wimbledon, London SW20 0DP
President: Rt Rev Patrick O'Donoghue. All voluntary staff. Began 1929; Roman Catholic. Magazine: *SCA Bulletin* (150 annually). Turnover £2,000 to year end Dec 98. Providing mutual support for Catholic artists and information for those commissioning work for churches.
☎ 020 8947 6476

The Study Group on Christianity and History, 38 De Montfort Street, Leicester LE1 7GP
Chairman: Dr John Wolffe. No full-time staff. *CC* Began 1988; interdenominational. Magazine: *Christianity and History Newsletter* (150 frequency n/a). Turnover n/a. Promoting Christian thinking and discussion on all areas of history. A UCCF group.
Email: sgch@uccf.org.uk
☎ 0116 255 1700 Fax 0116 255 5672

Therapy Students Christian Fellowship (TSCF), 38 De Montfort Street, Leicester LE1 7GP
Secretary: Gail Tyson. No full-time staff. *CC* Began 1952; non-denominational. (Previously Paramedical Students Christian Fellowship). Magazine: *TSCF Magazine* (Circulation n/a termly). Turnover n/a. Helping therapy students in witness, ethical understanding and other issues related to their studies. A UCCF group.
Web: www.uccf.org.uk/cus/course/tscf
Email: tscf@uccf.org.uk
☎ 0116 255 1700 Fax 0116 255 5672

Tyndale Fellowship for Biblical and Theological Research, Tyndale House, 36 Selwyn Gardens, Cambridge CB3 9BA
Secretary: Dr Kevin Ellis. Other full-time staff 1. *CC* No.273458. Began 1944; non-denominational. Magazine: *Tyndale Bulletin* (1,100 annually). Turnover n/a. Fellowship of Christians in biblical and theological research; promoting the faith through careful, scholarly study.
Web: www.tyndale.cam.ac.uk/
Email: dj208@cam.ac.uk
☎ 01223 566 601 Fax 01223 566 608

S

Professional Christian Groups

Victoria Institute (Philosophical Society of Great Britain), 41 Marne Avenue, Welling DA16 2EY
Secretary: Mr Brian H T Weller. No full-time staff. ***CC*** No.285871. Began 1865; non-denominational. Magazine: *Faith and Thought Bulletin* (400 half-yearly), *Science & Christian Belief* (400 half-yearly). Turnover £7,000 to year end Dec 97. Helping the non-specialist relate Christian thought to advancing knowledge and specialisation.
☎ 020 8303 0465 🖷 020 8303 0465

West Midlands Vision 1986, 14 Elmdon Road, Selly Park, Birmingham B29 7LF
Consultant: Mr George J N Tuck. Staff n/a. ***CC*** Began 1986; non-denominational. No magazine. Turnover £10,000 to year end Jan 98. Networking Christians in leadership to make a corporate impact upon the business and civic community.
☎ 0121 472 1431 🖷 0121 472 1431

The WorkNet Partnership, 56 Baldry Gardens, Lond SW16 3DJ
Director: Geoff Shattock. Staff n/a. ***CC*** No.1069411. Beg 1997; non-denominational. Magazine: *Briefing* (Circulati n/a quarterly). Turnover n/a. Connecting, equippi resourcing Christians in the workplace; churches, str training for companies, partnership schemes.
Web: www.worknetpartnership.org.uk
Email: training@worknetpartnership.org.uk
☎ 020 8764 8080 🖷 020 8764 3030

PRO-LIFE ORGANISATIONS

***CARE for LIFE (A department of CARE)**, 1 Winton Square, Basingstoke RG21 8EN
National Co-ordinator: Mrs Joanna Thompson. Executive staff 1, Other staff 3. Began 1989; interdenominational. Magazine: *CARE Magazine* (1,200 half-yearly). Turnover £100,000 to year end Dec 98. Networking Christian Pregnancy Crisis Centres; helping establish new centres; encouraging Christians to compassionate action.
Web: www.care.org.uk
Email: cfl@care.org.uk
☎ 01256 477 300

Evangelicals for LIFE, LIFE House, Newbold Terrace, Leamington Spa CV32 4EA
Organiser: Dr John R Ling. No full-time staff. Began 1982; interdenominational. Turnover n/a. Presenting the Biblical case against abortion and encouraging evangelicals to work within the LIFE organisation.
Web: www.lifeuk.org
☎ 01970 880 416 🖷 01926 336 497

Human Rights Society, Mariners Hard, Cley, Holt NR25 7RX
Secretary: Mrs Jennifer J Murray. Executive staff 1. Began 1969; non-denominational. Magazine: *Newsletter* (Circulation n/a annually). Turnover n/a. Opposing the legalisation of euthanasia; providing education material; information about hospices and pain relief.
☎ 01263 740 990 🖷 01263 740 990

***IMAGE**, PO Box 51, Hyde SK14 1PY
Co-ordinator: Mrs Christine Fidler. No full-time staff. Bega 1990; non-denominational. Magazine: *Image News* (950 ever two months). Turnover n/a. Organising prayer; providin information, literature, training, encouragement to Christian and churches in pro-life activity.
Email: chris.image@mcrl.poptel.org.uk
Email: chrisfidler.im@mcrl.poptel.org.uk
☎ 0161 368 8875

***Society for the Protection of Unborn Children (SPUC)**, Phylli Bowman House, 5 St Matthew Street, Westminster, Londo SW1P 2JT
National Director: Mr John Smeaton. *Evangelicals Director* Mr Peter Smith. *Evangelicals Chairman:* Rev Ian Brown. Exec utive staff 10, Other staff 30. Began 1967; non denominational. Offices also in Belfast, Cardiff, Glasgow Preston, Stockton. Magazine: *Human Concern* (120,000 every four months). Turnover £1,250,000 to year end Feb 98 Leading campaigns to tighten abortion law; educating public and parliament about abortion, population control euthanasia.
Web: www.spuc.org.uk
Email: sysop@spuc.org.uk
☎ 020 7222 5845 🖷 020 7222 0630

RECONCILIATION GROUPS

Anglican Pacifist Fellowship, 11 Weavers End, Hanslope, Milton Keynes MK19 7PA
Hon Secretary: Dr Tony Kempster. No full-time staff. ***CC*** No.209610. Began 1937; Anglican. Magazine: *Challenge* (1,500 every two months). Turnover £19,000 to year end Apr 96. Witnessing to the pacifist understanding of the Christian faith within the Anglican Communion.
Email: kempster@compuserve.com
☎ 01908 510 642

Association of Interchurch Families, Inter-Church House, 35 Lower Marsh, London SE1 7RL
Honorary Secretary: Dr Ruth Reardon. Other staff 2, Voluntary staff. ***CC*** No.283811. Began 1968; interdenominational. Magazine: *Interchurch Families* (1,000 half-yearly). Turnover £40,000 to year end Aug 98. Support network and voice for interchurch families (usually Roman Catholic and another Christian communion).
Email: aife@msn.com
☎ 020 7523 2152 🖷 020 7928 0010

ptist Peace Fellowship, 21 Cuckoo Hill Road, Pinner HA5 1AS
Hon Secretary: Prof Norman Kember. No full-time staff. Began 1932; Baptist. Affiliated to the Fellowship of Reconciliation. Magazine: *Newsletter* (Circulation n/a annually). Turnover n/a. Keeping issues of peace and justice before the Baptist churches and denomination.
Web: traffard1.demon.co.uk
Email: bathtub@surfaid.org
☎ 020 8866 0068

atholic Association for Racial Justice (CARJ), 9 Henry Road, Manor House, London N4 2LH
Director: Mr Stephen Corriette. *CC* No.291601. Began 1984; Roman Catholic. Membership organisation. No magazine. Turnover £80,000 to year end Mar 99. Black and white Catholics promoting awareness, understanding and action on issues of racial justice in church and society.
Email: stephen@carj.freeserve.co.uk
☎ 020 8802 8080 Fax 020 8211 0808

atholic Peace Action, 7 Putney Bridge Road, London SW18 1HX
Secretary: To be appointed. No full-time staff. Began 1982; Roman Catholic foundation; ecumenical. Magazine: *Newsletter* (Circulation n/a regularly). Turnover n/a. Peace work involving communication with the Ministry of Defence and resistance to nuclear war preparations.
☎ 020 8871 3436

entre for the Advancement of Responsive Travel (CART), 70 Dry Hill Park Road, Tonbridge TN10 3BX
Director: Dr Roger N Millman. No full-time staff. Began 1988; interdenominational. No magazine. Turnover n/a. Pursuing fairer, enriching relations between tourists and hosts through travel in spirit of Biblical pilgrimage.
Email: rmillman@dial.pipex.com
☎ 01732 352 757 Fax 01732 352 757

Christian Campaign for Nuclear Disarmament, 162 Holloway Road, London N7 8DQ
National Co-ordinator: n/a. No full-time staff. Began 1960; non-denominational. Magazine: *Ploughshare* (1,000 quarterly). Turnover £11,000 to year end Mar 98. Building Christian witness against weapons of mass destruction and militarism, for global peace and justice.
Web: www.gn.apc.org/ccnd
Email: ccnd@gn.apc.org
☎ 020 7700 4200 Fax 020 7700 2357

Christian International Peace Service (CHIPS), Bix-Bottom Farm, Henley-on-Thames RG9 6BH
Director: Mr R Calvocoressi. Executive staff 2. *CC* No.267140. Began 1974; non-denominational. Magazine: *Newsletter* (650 half-yearly). Turnover £100,000 to year end Apr 98. Developing the Christian contribution to peacemaking and running practical projects in areas of tension.
☎ 01491 577 745 / 416 616

Christian Mediation & Arbitration Service, PO Box 78, Greenford UB6 0JR
General Secretary: Mr Christopher Hutson. No full-time staff. Began 1990; interdenominational. No magazine. Turnover £1,275 to year end Dec 90. Reconciliation and dispute resolution by mediation and arbitration, particularly for business and other substantial disputes.
☎ 020 8993 6886 Fax 020 8992 1164

Christian Renewal Centre, 44 Shore Road, Rostrevor, Newry BT34 3ET
Leader: Rev Cecil Kerr. *Leader/Prayer Co-ordinator:* Mr Harry Smith. Community 14. Began 1974; interdenominational. Magazine: *Prayer Diary* (700 monthly), *Newsletter* (3,313 half-yearly). Turnover £138,000 to year end Apr 98. A community committed to prayer, reconciliation and renewal for the Church in Ireland.
☎ 028 3073 8492 Fax 028 3073 8996

Christians for Social Justice, 31 Prince of Wales Lane, Yardley Wood, Birmingham B14 4LB
Director: Dr Christine Parkinson. All voluntary staff. Began 1988; interdenominational. Magazine: *Newsletter* (175 half-yearly). Turnover £300 to year end Dec 98. A membership organisation which raises awareness amongst Christians about issues on the socio-political agenda.
☎ 0121 430 8980

Churches Commission for Racial Justice, Inter-Church House, 35 Lower Marsh, London SE1 7RL
Moderator: Rev Theo Samuel. *Secretary:* Rev Arlington Trotman. Executive staff 2, Other staff 2. *CC* No.259688. Began 1992; ecumenical. Magazine: *Church + Race* (15,000 every four months). Turnover £300,000 to year end Dec 98. Co-ordinating work of churches across Britian and Ireland on racial justice issues.
Email: ccrj@ctbi.org.uk
☎ 020 7620 4444 Fax 020 7928 0010

Co-operation Ireland, 7 Botanic Avenue, Belfast BT7 1JG
Chief Executive: Mr Tony Kennedy. Other staff 38. Began 1979; non-denominational. (Previously Co-operation North). Magazine: *Co-operation Ireland News* (2,500 quarterly). Turnover £1,000,000 to year end Dec 96. Advancing mutual understanding and respect by promoting practical co-operation between the peoples of Ireland.
Email: info@co-operation-n.ireland.com
☎ 028 9032 1462 Fax 028 9024 7522

Columbanus Community of Reconciliation, 683 Antrim Road, Belfast BT15 4EG
Community Leader: Sister Roisin Hannaway. Other staff 2. *CC* No.XN 67880A. Began 1983; interdenominational. Magazine: *Light* (1,600 half-yearly). Turnover £80,000 to year end Dec 97. Residential interchurch community, centre for reconciliation, educational programmes, worship, library, forum for dialogue, accommodation avaliable.
Email: columbanus@btinternet.com
☎ 028 9077 8009 Fax 028 9077 8009

Cornerstone Community, 445 Springfield Road, Belfast BT12 7DL
Director: Mr Tom Hannon. Executive staff 3. *CC* No.NI 20406. Began 1982; ecumenical. Magazine: *Newsletter* (1,000 every four months). Turnover £90,000 to year end Dec 98. Reconciliation, peace work, prayer groups, social action; community building.
Web: www.d-n-a.net-users-cornerstone
Email: cornerstone@d.net.co.uk
☎ 028 9032 1649 Fax 028 9032 7323

Corrymeela, 8 Upper Crescent, Belfast BT7 1NT
Leader: Rev Trevor Williams. Full-time staff 31, Other staff 8. *CC* No.XN 48052A. Began 1965; interdenominational. Magazine: *Connection* (2,300 quarterly). Turnover £900,000 to year end Mar 98. Dispersed Christian community of reconciliation in Northern Ireland; resource centre, residential centre.
Web: www.corrymeela.org.uk
Email: belfast@corrymeela.org.uk
☎ 028 9032 5008 / 028 9076 2626
Fax 028 9031 5385 / 028 9076 2770

S

Reconciliation Groups

Corrymeela Link, PO Box 4829, Earley, Reading RG6 1XX
Co-ordinator: n/a. Staff n/a. ***CC*** Began 1976; ecumenical. Magazine: *Corrymeela Connection* (6,000 half-yearly). Turnover £50-100,000 to year end Dec 98. Stimulating spiritual and financial support throughout Britain for the Corrymeela Community of reconciliation in Northern Ireland.
☎ 0118 926 1062

Council of Christians and Jews, Drayton House, 30 Gordon Street, London WC1H 0AN
Director: Sister Margaret Shepherd. ***CC*** No.238005. Began 1942. Magazine: *Common Ground* (5,500 every four months). Turnover £165,000 to year end Mar 98. Helping Christians and Jews appreciate their distinctive beliefs and practices, recognise common ground, and fight prejudice.
Web: www.ccj.org.uk
Email: ccjuk@aol.com
☎ 020 7388 3322 Fax 020 7388 3305

The Council on Christian Approaches to Defence and Disarmament, St Bride Foundation Institute, Bride Lane, London EC4Y 8EQ
Adminstrative Secretary: Miss Liza Hamilton. No full-time staff. ***CC*** No.245130. Began 1963; non-denominational. No magazine. Turnover £15,000 to year end Mar 92. Studying problems relating to defence and disarmament within a Christian context.
☎ 020 7583 4145

Cross Group, 6a Cumberland Park, Dundonald, Belfast BT16 0AY
Founder: Ms Maura Kiely. No full-time staff. Began n/a; non-denominational. No magazine. Turnover n/a. Providing social support group for those bereaved through violence in Northern Ireland.
☎ 028 9048 3952

Cymdeithas Y Cymod Yng Nghymru (Fellowship of Reconciliation, Wales), Ty Hen Gapel John Hughes, Pont Robert, Meifod SY22 6JA
General Secretary: Miss Nia Rhosier. No full-time staff. ***CC*** No.700609. Began 1914; non-denominational. Magazine: *Cymod* (Circulation n/a annually), *Peacelinks* (Circulation n/a every two months). Turnover £8,000 to year end Dec 98. Renunciation of war; peacebuilding, reconciliation by practice of love taught by Jesus Christ.
☎ 01938 500 631 Fax 01938 500 631

***Evangelical Contribution on Northern Ireland (ECONI)**, Howard House, 1 Brunswick Street, Belfast BT2 7GE
Director: Mr David W Porter. *Development Officer:* Mr Derek Poole. Executive staff 3, Other staff 4. ***CC*** No.XR8080. Began 1988; non-denominational. Magazine: *Lion & Lamb* (3,000 quarterly). Thinking biblically, building peace, programme for Christian peacebuilding and for biblical research on conflict/culture in Ireland.
Web: www.econi.org
Email: admin@econi.org
☎ 028 9032 5258 Mobile: 07801 017 420
Fax 028 9043 4156

†*Evangelical Peacemakers, Mulberry Court, Stockton-on-Teme, Worcester WR6 6UT
Administrator: Rev Chris Walton. No full-time staff. Began 1983; non-denominational. Magazine: *Newsletter* (500 half-yearly). Turnover £5,000 to year end Sept 94. Network advocating the Gospel of peace; training for practical peacemaking and mediation; challenging warmaking.
☎ 01584 881 607

Fellowship of Reconciliation, England, The Eirene Centre, The C School, Clopton, Kettering NN14 3DZ
Co-ordinator: Mr Robert Drost. *Administrator:* Mr Bri Harder. Executive staff 1, Admin staff 1. ***CC*** No.20782 Began 1914; interdenominational. Magazine: *Reconciliati Quarterly* (800 quarterly), *Peacelinks* (1,500 every t months). Turnover £112,052 to year end Dec 96. Promoti spiritual development, witness and service; reconciling people with God and with each other.
Web: www.gn.apc.org/fore
Email: fellowship@gn.apc.org
☎ 01832 720 257 Fax 01832 720 557

The Human City Institute, Westhill College, Selly Oak, Birmin ham B24 6LL
Co-ordinator: Rev Dr David Clark. Executive staff 1, Oth staff 1. ***CC*** No.1073215. Began 1997; ecumenical. Magazin *Human City Bulletin* (2,500 quarterly). Turnover £20,000 year end Dec 98. Bringing religious and secular bodies togeth to enable Birmingham to become a human city.
Web: www.humancity.org
Email: hci@westhill.ac.uk
☎ 0121 472 7245 Fax 0121 415 5399

International Centre for Reconciliation, Coventry Cathedral, Priory Row, Coventry CV1 5ES
Director of International Ministry: Rev Canon Andrew P White. *Research Assistant:* Mrs Lynne Griffiths-Fulton. Sta 2. Began 1974; interdenominational. (Previously Communit of the Cross of Nails). Magazine: *Network* (100,000 frequenc n/a), *International Briefing Papers* (Circulation & frequenc n/a). Turnover n/a. Support Cross of Nails Centres, a networ of individuals/groups working for peace/reconciliation world wide.
Web: www.coventrycathedral.org
Email: sfirem1@globalnet.co.uk
☎ 024 7655 2654 Fax 024 7655 2654

Iona Community, Community House, Pearce Institute, 84(Govan Road, Glasgow G51 3UU
Community Leader: Rev Norman Shanks. *Support Service Manager:* Mr Graham Boyle. *Warden, Iona Abbey:* Rev Brian Woodcock. ***CC*** No.SCO 03794. Began 1938; ecumenical, Church of Scotland based. Magazine: *The Coracle* (3,100 every two months). Turnover £897,000 to year end Dec 97. Seeking new ways to live the Gospel in today's world.
Web: www.iona.org.uk
Email: ionacomm@iona.org.uk
☎ 0141 445 4561 Fax 0141 445 4295
Also At: Iona Abbey, Isle of Iona PA76 6SN
☎ 01681 700 404 Fax 01681 700 460
And: Camas Centre, Bunessan, Isle of Mull PA67 6DX
☎ 01681 700 367

Justice and Peace Scotland, 65 Bath Street, Glasgow G2 2BX
National Secretary: Mrs Maryanne Ure. Other staff 3. Began 1979; Roman Catholic. Magazine: *Justice & Peace Magazine* (860 monthly). Turnover n/a. Advising the Scottish Bishops Conference regarding social justice, international peace, human rights and world development.
Email: justicepeace@virgin.net
☎ 0141 333 0238 Fax 0141 333 0238

ethodist Peace Fellowship, The Eirene Centre, Old School House, Clopton, Kettering NN14 3DZ
No full-time staff. *CC* Began 1934; Methodist. An integral part of Fellowship Of Reconciliation, England. No magazine. Turnover n/a. Pacifist witness; sponsorship of young people taking part in peace projects at home and overseas.
Secretary: Rev Maurice H Wright, 84 Station Road, Wem, Shrewsbury SY4 5BL
☎ 01939 232 404

ational Justice & Peace Network, 38 Eccleston Square, London SW1V 1BX
Secretary: Mrs Maureen Matthews. No other full-time staff. *CC* No.257239. Began 1987; Roman Catholic. (Previously National Liaison Committee of Diocesan Justice & Peace Groups). Magazine: *NJPN Newsletter* (8,500 every four months). Turnover £18,000 to year end Dec 98. Networking between Diocesan Justice and Peace groups, religious congregations and Christian agencies; annual conference.
☎ 020 7834 8550 🖷 020 7630 5166

ax Christi (British Section), St Joseph's, Watford Way, Hendon, London NW4 4TY
General Secretary: Ms Patricia Gaffney. Executive staff 1. Began 1970; Roman Catholic. Magazine: *Just Peace* (2,000 six times a year). Turnover £79,900 to year end Dec 98. Promoting peace education and non-violence; campaigning on arms trade, nuclear proliferation.
Email: paxchristi@gn.apc.org
☎ 020 8203 4884 🖷 020 8203 5234

eace Care, 39 Halsdon Road, Exmouth EX8 1SR
Co-ordinator: Rev David J Harding. Other staff 3. Began 1987; ecumenical. No magazine. Turnover n/a. Supporting and developing the understanding and practice of Christian non-violence in social and political life.
☎ 01395 268 060

he Pilgrims of St Francis, 2 Margaret Street, Derby DE1 3FE
National Guardian: Rev Canon Sheana Barby. All voluntary staff. Began 1969; ecumenical. Magazine: *The Way* (100 quarterly). Turnover n/a. International pilgrim movement for peace, social justice and Christian unity amongst the nations.
☎ 01332 383 301

Quaker Peace & Service, Friends House, Euston Road, London NW1 2BJ
Joint Operations Manager: Anne Benett. Executive staff 15, Other staff 18. Began 1978; Religious Society of Friends. Magazine: *Quaker News* (15,000 quarterly), *Opportunities for Action* (5,000 every four months). Peace work in Britain and overseas; service projects overseas; international reconciliation.
Email: vivf@quaker.org.uk
☎ 020 7663 1048 🖷 020 7663 1001

Reconciliation International, PO Box 3590, Christchurch BH23 3XS
Chief Executive: Mr Tony Black. Executive staff 2, Other staff 14. *CC* No.SCO 26256. Began 1997; interdenominational. Magazine: *The Joseph and Maranatha Projects* (6,000 quarterly). Turnover n/a. Providing Christian support for all the peoples of Israel.
Web: www.revivalnet.net/joseph
Email: joseph@revivalnet.net
☎ 01202 483 453 🖷 01202 481 581

Sisters of Our Lady of Sion, 34 Chepstow Villas, Notting Hill, London W11 2QZ
Provincial: Sister Margaret Macdonald. Community 78. *CC* Began 1858; Roman Catholic. Magazine: *Sidic* (1,000 every four months). Turnover n/a. Promoting relations between Christians and Jews.
☎ 020 7229 4464 🖷 020 7221 1556

***Youth Action for Peace**, Methold House, North Street, Worthing BN11 1DU
Co-ordinator: Teresa García-Roberts. Other staff 1. Began 1961; interdenominational. (Previously Christian Movement for Peace). Magazine: *Newsletter* (200 quarterly). Turnover £6,000 to year end Dec 94. Co-ordinating exchange of volunteers on medium-term placements UK and abroad; British summer projects.
☎ 01903 528 619 🖷 01903 528 611

RESEARCH & DEVELOPMENT ORGANISATIONS

Barley Research, The Vicarage, Dunsford, Exeter EX6 7AA
Principal: Rev Lynda Barley. Executive staff 1. Began 1987; interdenominational. No magazine. Turnover n/a. Qualitative and quantitative market research, statistical consultancy and interpretation, for management of Christian organisations.
Email: lmb24@tutor.open.ac.uk
☎ 01647 253 296 🖷 01647 253 296

Board for Social Responsibility (Archbishops' Council), Church House, Great Smith Street, Westminster, London SW1P 3NZ
General Secretary: Mr David Skidmore. Executive staff 6, Other staff 4. Began 1958; Anglican. Magazine: *Crucible* (800 quarterly). Turnover n/a. Promoting and co-ordinating the thought and action of the Church in matters affecting the lives of all in society.
☎ 020 7898 1000 🖷 020 7898 1536

Christendom Trust, 24 Westbourne Road, Lancaster LA1 5DB
Hon Secretary: Angela Cunningham. No full-time staff. *CC* No.262394. Began 1970; non-denominational. No magazine. Turnover £39,000 to year end Nov 98. Support of non-degree related research and the application of research into Christian social thought.
Web: www.christendomtrust.demon.co.uk
☎ No telephone

The Christian Institute, 26 Jesmond Road, Newcastle upon Tyne NE2 4PQ
Director: Mr Colin J Hart. Other staff 5. *CC* No.1004774. Began 1991; non-denominational. Incorporating CATS Trust (Christians and Tyneside Schools). Magazine: *News Digest* (Circulation & frequency n/a), *News Update* (Circulation & frequency n/a). Turnover £200,000 to year end Dec 98. Equipping Christians for action through research, conferences and publications.
Web: www.christian.org.uk
Email: info@christian.org.uk
☎ 0191 281 5664 🖷 0191 281 4272

*__Christian Research__, Vision Building, 4 Footscray Road, Eltham, London SE9 2TZ
Executive Director: Dr Peter Brierley. *Research Assistant:* Mrs Georgina Sanger. Executive staff 2, Other staff 5. ***CC*** No.1017701. Began 1993; interdenominational. (Previously MARC Europe). Magazine: *Quadrant* (3,500 every two months). Turnover £271,600 to year end Dec 98. Resource centre for Christian leaders, specialising in research, information dissemination, consultancy and quantitative church data.
Web: www.christian-research.org.uk
Email: admin@christian-research.org.uk
☎ 020 8294 1989 🖷 020 8294 0014

Christian Research Network, PO Box 5058, Great Bromley, Colchester CO7 7JY
Directors: Peter Glover, Chris Hand, Alan Howe. No other staff. Began 1997; non-denominational. Magazine: *CRN Journal* (1,000 5 times a year), *3 Newsletters* (Circulation & frequency n/a). Turnover £15,000 to year end Dec 98. Researching news, beliefs and practices in the contemporary church, publications and book sales.
Web: web.ukonline.co.uk/crn
Email: crn@ukonline.co.uk
☎ 01206 252 062

City Vision Ministries, 12a Moorland Road, Burslem, Stoke-on-Trent ST6 1DW
Director: Mr Robert J Mountford. Executive staff 1, Admin staff 2. Began 1994; interdenominational. Magazine: *Newsletter* (200 every two months). Turnover n/a. Researching past and present to facilitate planning and fuel prayer towards a better future.
Web: lineone.net/~city_vision
Email: city_vision@lineone.net
☎ 01782 832 563 🖷 01782 811 938

Credo, Mayflower Family Centre, Vincent Street, Canning Town, London E16 1LZ
Research Consultant: Greg Smith. Executive staff 1, Other staff 3. ***CC*** Began n/a; non-denominational. No magazine. Turnover £50,000 to year end Dec 98. Community research development empowering organisation.
Web: www.newtel.org/orgs/credo/credo.html
Email: gregs@xena.uel-ac.uk
☎ 020 7474 2255

S

Culham College Institute, The Malthouse, 60 East St Helen Street, Abingdon OX14 5EB
Director: Rev Dr John Gay. Executive staff 5. ***CC*** No.309671. Began 1980; Anglican. No magazine. Turnover n/a. Research, development and information agency in the fields of Church schools, colleges and Religious Education.
Web: www.culham.ac.uk
Email: enquiries@culham.ac.uk
☎ 01235 520 458 🖷 01235 535 421

Ecumenical Council for Corporate Responsibility (ECCR), PO Box 4317, Bishop's Stortford CM22 7GZ
Co-ordinator: Rev Crispin White. No full-time staff. Began 1989; ecumenical. Magazine: *ECCR Bulletin* (200 quarterly). Turnover n/a. Research, education and campaigning arising from the social responsibility of companies and churches.
Email: eccr@geo2.poptel.org.uk
☎ 01279 718 274 🖷 01279 718 097

Farmington Institute for Christian Studies, Harris Manches College, Mansfield Road, Oxford OX1 3TD
Director: Mr Martin Rogers. ***CC*** Began 1965; interdeno inational. No magazine. Turnover n/a. Support for Christi education; fellowships and bursaries for teachers; publishi papers, arranging seminars and conferences.
Web: info.ac.uk/~manc0039/farn.html
Email: martin.rogers@hmc.oxford.ac.uk
☎ 01865 271 965 🖷 01865 271 969

Globalbridge, 2 Great Quarry, Guildford GU1 3XN
Senior Consultant: Mr David Falkus. Consultants 6. Beg 1989; non-denominational. (Previously Spacebridge comm nications). No magazine. Turnover n/a. Network of speciali consultants; research, writing technical articles; advising inter-active distance learning and multimedia.
Email: david.falkus@mcmail.com
☎ 01483 504 539 Mobile: 07802 832 712 🖷 01483 505 59

The Grubb Institute of Behavioural Studies, Cloudesley Stree London N1 0HU
Directors: Mr Colin Quine, Mr John Bazalgette, Miss Jea Hutton. Executive staff 4, Other staff 5. ***CC*** No.313460. Bega 1969; non-denominational. No magazine. Turnover n/ Advice and research in organisational behaviour, managemer of cultural and organisational change; commitment to religiou bodies.
Email: grubuk@aol.com
☎ 020 7278 8061 🖷 020 7278 0728

*__Institute for the Study of Islam and Christianity__, PO Box 154 Pewsey SN9 5QW
Director: Dr Patrick Sookhdeo. Other staff 4. ***CC*** No.280859 Began 1989; interdenominational. Magazine: *Religious Freedom Today* (1,000 monthly). Turnover n/a. Research, training conferences, advocacy, publicity and promoting prayer for suffering Christians in the Muslim world.
Web: www.rftoday.org
Email: 101376.2103@compuserve.com
☎ 01672 564 938 🖷 01672 564 939

*__International Research Office (WEC International)__, Bulstrode Oxford Road, Gerrards Cross SL9 8SZ
Director: Mr Patrick Johnstone. Executive staff 2, Other staff 4. ***CC*** No.237005. Began 1982; interdenominational. No magazine. Turnover n/a. Holding extensive information regarding worldwide evangelisation, electronic information, overheads, maps, people profiles and more.
Web: www.wec_int.org
Email: 100433.1301@compuserve.com
☎ 01753 890 828 🖷 01753 882 470

*__The Jubilee Centre__, Jubilee House, 3 Hooper Street, Cambridge CB1 2NZ
Director: Dr Michael Schluter. *Deputy Director:* Bryan Johnston. Executive staff 3, Other staff 5. ***CC*** No.288783. Began 1983; non-denominational. Magazine: *Jubilee News* (5,000 quarterly). Turnover £150,000 to year end Aug 97. Applying biblical research to public policy and supporting the work of the Relationships Foundation.
Email: jubilee.centre@clara.net
☎ 01223 566 319 🖷 01223 566 359

Kingdom Trust, 30a Musters Road, West Bridgford, Nottingham NG2 7PL
Director: Mr Roy McCloughry. Executive staff 1. ***CC*** No.326924. Began 1984; non-denominational. Magazine: *Prayer news leaflet* (Circulation & frequency n/a). Turnover n/a. Research and consultancy on the relationship between Christianity and culture; ethical approaches to policy making.
Email: roy@kingdom.demon.co.uk
☎ 0115 945 5542 Mobile: 07971 249 302 🖷 0115 969 6304

S

The Kuyper Foundation, PO Box 2, Taunton TA1 4ZD
Director: Stephen C Perks. No full-time staff. ***CC*** No.327537. Began 1987; non-denominational. Magazine: *Christianity and Society* (Circulation n/a quarterly). Turnover n/a. Promoting the renaissance of Christian culture.
Web: www.kuyper.org
Email: kuyper@kuyper.org
☎ 01823 665 909 Fax 01823 665 721

Latimer House (Oxford Evangelical Research Trust), 131 Banbury Road, Oxford OX2 7AJ
Chairman of Council: Rev Dr Mark Burkill. Executive staff 2. ***CC*** Began 1960; Anglican. Magazine: *Latimer Studies* (1,000 every four months). Turnover n/a. Theological research and writing institution for evangelicals in the Church of England.
☎ 01865 513 879 Fax 01865 566 706

***Men, Women and God**, St Peter's Church, Vere Street, London W1M 9HP
No full-time staff. ***CC*** No.294993. Began 1986; interdenominational. Magazine: *Double Image* (300 every four months). Turnover £2,000 to year end Dec 98. Activating and encouraging good practice re gender justice, bulletin issued to share practice and stimulate.
☎ No telephone

MODEM (Managerial & Organisational Disciplines for the Enhancement of Ministry), Carselands, Woodmancote, Henfield BN5 9SS
Treasurer: Peter J Bates. No full-time staff. ***CC*** No.1048772. Began 1993; non-denominational. Magazine: *MODEM Matters* (600 quarterly). Turnover £5,500 to year end Dec 98. Facilitating and developing the exchange of management and organisational skills between churches and the workplace.
Web: churchnet.ucsm.ac.uk/modem/modem.htm
Email: peter@bateshouse.freeserve.co.uk
☎ 01273 493 172 Fax 01273 493 172

Oulton-Lee Marketing Services, 40 Fairmount Drive, Loughborough LE11 3JR
Managing Director: Mrs Sue Garner. Executive staff 1, Other staff 1. Began 1991; non-denominational. No magazine. Turnover n/a. Strategic marketing planning; research, both questionnaires and groups; statistical analyses of numerical trends, eg donations.
Email: oulton-lee@compuserve.com
☎ 01509 264 141 Mobile: 07721 992 405 Fax 01509 264 141

Religious Experience Research Centre, Westminster College, Oxford OX2 9AT
Director: Peggy Morgan. Executive staff 2. ***CC*** No.286682. Began 1969; non-denominational. (Previously AH Religious Experience Research Centre). Magazine: *De Numine* (750 occasionally). Turnover £35,000 to year end June 94. Scientific studies of the nature and functions of religious and spiritual experiences.
Web: www.charitynet.org~rerc
☎ 01865 247 644 Ext 5292 Fax 01865 201 197

Rutherford House, 17 Claremont Park, Edinburgh EH6 7PJ
Warden: Rev David Searle. *House Manager:* Miss Edna Morrow. Executive staff 3, other staff 3. ***CC*** No.SCO 15111. Began 1983; non-denominational. Magazine: *Scottish Bulletin of Evangelical Theology* (800 half-yearly), *Rutherford Journal of Church & Ministry* (700 half-yearly). Turnover £130,000 to year end Dec 98. Training ministers and elders in pastoralia, leadership, preaching. Publishing study aids. Residential facilities, theological library.
Web: www.rutherfordhouse.org.uk
Email: info@rutherfordhouse.org.uk
☎ 0131 554 1206 Fax 0131 555 1002

Teilhard Centre, Plas Maelog, Beaumaris LL58 8BH
Chairman: Mr Siøn Cowell. No full-time staff. ***CC*** No.31368[illegible]. Began 1965; non-denominational. No magazine. Turnov[illegible] £9,500 to year end Dec 98. Study and development of Teilha[illegible] de Chardin's evolutionary vision culminating in the Cosm[illegible] Christ.
Email: sioncowell@bt.internet.com
☎ 01248 810 402 Fax 01248 810 936

William Temple Foundation, Manchester Business School, Boo[illegible] Street West, Manchester M15 6PB
Executive Secretary: Rev Malcolm Brown. Executive sta[illegible] 2, Other staff 3. ***CC*** No.528790. Began 1947; no[illegible] denominational. Magazine: *Foundations* (1,000 quarterly[illegible] *Occasional Papers* (250 frequency n/a). Turnover £100,000 t[illegible] year end Dec 98. Action-research and training in urban indu[illegible] trial mission and community action in Britain and Europe.
Email: ecg-wen@mcr1.poptel.org.uk
☎ 0161 275 6534 Fax 0161 272 8663

The Traidcraft Exchange, Kingsway, Team Valley Trading Estate Gateshead NE11 0NE
General Director: Mr Graham Young. Executive staff 5, Othe[illegible] staff 32. ***CC*** No.1048752. Began 1981; non-denominational Magazine: *Annual report* (15,000 annually). Turnove[illegible] £1,349,365 to year end Mar 98. Business assistance to commu[illegible] nity enterprises in developing countries; promoting fair trad[illegible] and ethical business awareness in the UK.
Web: www.traidcraft.co.uk
Email: comms@traidcraft.co.uk
☎ 0191 491 0591 Fax 0191 482 2690

†**University of Stirling Centre for the Study of Christianity & Contemporary Society**, University of Stirling, Stirling FK9 4LA
Director: To be appointed. Executive staff 1, Other staff 4. Began 1992; ecumenical. No magazine. Turnover n/a. Research into Christianity and society/culture, teaching; short courses, consultancy.
Email: jwdl@stir.ac.uk
☎ 01786 467 594 Fax 01786 451 335

University of the Holy Land, Tangnefedd, Windmill Road, Weald, Sevenoaks TN14 6PJ
UK Director: Mr Ian Mitchell Lambert. Executive staff 1, Other staff 2. Began 1988; interdenominational. (Previously Centre for the Study of Early Christianity). Magazine: *Newsletter* (500 occasionally). Turnover £500 to year end Aug 96. Academic research; full-time higher education courses in Israel; study tours of Israel; information resource.
Web: www.uhl.u-k.ac
Email: uhl@u-k.ac
☎ 01732 463 460 Fax 01732 741 475

World Development Action Fund, 1 Central Buildings, Westminster, London SW1H 9NH
Funds Administrator: Miss Carolyn Maynard. No full-time staff. Began 1981; Methodist. Magazine: *Funds in Focus* (5,000 every two months). Turnover £10,000 to year end Aug 98. Campaign (includes small grant giving) on policies affecting world's poorest people.
☎ 020 7222 8010 Fax 020 7799 2153

S

:H Hotels & Conference Centres – UK, 56 The Drive, Northampton NN1 4SJ
General Secretary: Mr Alan Brett. Executive staff 2. Began 1996; interdenominational. Turnover n/a. Providing free information on Christian hotels and conference centres in UK and Europe.
Web: www.ach.co.uk
Email: alan.w.brett@epworth.co.uk
☎ 01604 714 265 Fax 01604 458 702

he Antioch Community, 31 Linton Road, London W3 9HL
Senior Leaders: Mr Michael Shaughnessy. Executive staff 1, Other staff 3. ***CC*** No.282690. Began 1979; interdenominational. Magazine: *Antioch Newsletter* (120 fortnightly). Turnover £100,000 to year end Mar 98. Non-residential charismatic lay community living out Christian unity in covenant together, doing evangelism.
Email: 106275.163@compuserve.com
☎ 020 8896 3387 Fax 020 8896 3387

shram Community, 239 Abbeyfield Road, Sheffield S4 74T
Leader: Rev Dr John J Vincent. No full-time staff. ***CC*** No.290459. Began 1967; ecumenical. Magazine: *ACT* (500 annually). Turnover n/a. Voluntary association of 100 radical Christians, mainly working in deprived urban areas.
☎ 0114 243 2572
Also at: New Roots Shop, 347 Glossop Road, Sheffield S10 2HP
☎ 0114 270 61
And: Community House, 75 Rock Street, Sheffield S3 9JB
☎ 0114 276 1319
And: Community House, 77 Rock Street, Sheffield S3 9JB
☎ 0114 272 7144
And: Community House, 10 Edale Way, Fairfield Estate, Buxton SK17 7YB
☎ 01298 700 49

Baptist Caravan Fellowship, 96c Greenvale Road, Eltham, London SE9 1PF
Administrative Secretary: Mrs Betty Fuller. No full-time staff. Began 1968; Baptist. Magazine: *Highway* (160 quarterly). Turnover £6,400 to year end Sep 98. Holding weekend rallies throughout the country fostering fellowship among caravanning Christians and supporting small churches.
☎ 020 8859 5336

Boaters Christian Fellowship, Pondside Barn, Canal Road, Thrupp, Kidlington OX5 1JQ
Secretary: Not supplied. All voluntary staff. Began 1995; interdenominational. Magazine: *The Word* (160 quarterly). Turnover n/a. Christian fellowship, worship and witness on the inland waterways.
Web: www.blacksheep.org/canals/orgs/bcf/html
Email: david@pondside.freeserve.co.uk
☎ 01865 841 114 Fax 01865 841 114

Caravanners and Campers Christian Fellowship, Jads House, 27 Charlton Road, Weston-super-Mare BS23 4HG
National Director: Mr Alex Harries. All voluntary staff. ***CC*** No.281757. Began 1969; interdenominational. Magazine: *Newsline* (800 every two months). Turnover £55,000 to year end Sep 98. Evangelical Christian holiday fellowship; various weekend and holiday rallies, annual national rally, winter day rallies.
Web: www.cccf.freeserve.co.uk
Email: e.m.cccf@alexharries.clara.net
☎ 01934 412 902 Mobile: 07831 810 391 Fax 01934 412 902

Cathedral & Church Shops Association, St Alban's Cathedral, St Albans AL1 1BY
Chairman: Mr John Simmons. No paid staff. Began 1988; interdenominational. No magazine. Turnover n/a. Association supporting Cathedral and Church shops in the UK; annual Trade Fair; conference, meetings.
☎ 01727 864 738 Fax 01727 850 944

Catholic Students Society, Canmore, 24 The Scores, St Andrews KY16 9AS
President: Mr John Page. No full-time staff. Began 1971; Roman Catholic. (Previously Canmore Society). No magazine. Turnover £200 to year end Mar 98. Social and religious society for Catholic students and others interested.
☎ 01334 472 179

†**Catholic Youth Hostellers**, 85 Spur Road, Orpington BR6 0QP
Representative: Mr Michael J Riley. No full-time staff. Began 1984; Roman Catholic. No magazine. Turnover n/a. Helping the Church on YHA matters and vice versa.
☎ 01689 832 012

Central Council of Church Bell Ringers, 50 Cramhurst Lane, Witley, Godalming GU8 5QZ
Hon Secretary: Mr C H Rogers. All voluntary staff. ***CC*** No.270036. Began 1890; non-denominational. Magazine: *The Ringing World* (4,300 weekly). Turnover £30,000 to year end Dec 98. Promoting the ringing of church bells; advising on changing ringing standards.
☎ 01428 682 790

*__Christian Camping International (UK)__, PO Box 169, Coventry CV1 4PW
National Co-ordinator: Mr Leigh N Belcham. No full-time staff. ***CC*** No.326637. Began 1983; non-denominational. Magazine: *Update* (400 quarterly). Turnover £39,000 to year end Dec 97. Resource, training and support association for all in Christian conference, holiday and outdoor centre ministries.
Email: cciinuk@aol.com
☎ 024 7655 9099 Fax 024 7655 9099

The Christian Conference Trust, The Hayes Conference Centre, Swanwick, Alfreton DE55 1AU
Director: Mr Brian Cupples. ***CC*** No.1056604. Began 1911; non-denominational. Magazine: *CCT News* (Circulation n/a half-yearly). Turnover n/a. Providing facilities for conferences, retreats, meetings at The Hayes and High Leigh Conference Centres.
☎ 01773 602 482/3 Fax 01773 540 841

Christian Guild Holidays, Derwent House, Cromford, Matlock DE4 5JG
General Manager: Mr Geoff Griffiths. Began 1910; ecumenical. (Previously Methodist Guild Holidays Ltd). No magazine. Turnover n/a. Hotels/conference centres in Derbyshire Dales, Grange-over-Sands, St Ives (Cornwall), Sidmouth, Whitby, Wye Valley.
Web: www.cgholidays.co.uk
Email: cgholidays@aol.com
☎ 01629 580 550 Fax 01629 580 025

***Christian Link Association of Single Parents (CLASP)**, Linden, Shorter Avenue, Shenfield, Brentwood CM15 8RE
Executive Director: Mrs Christine Tufnell. All voluntary staff. ***CC*** No.326731. Began 1982; interdenominational. Magazine: *Clasp Together* (1,000 every four months). Turnover £12,000 to year end Dec 98. Enabling Christian single parents to support each other and share together nationally and locally.
☎ 01277 233 848

***Christian Motorcyclists Association UK**, PO Box 113, Wokingham RG11 5UB
National Administrator: Dr Paul Mitchell. No full-time staff. Began 1979; non-denominational. Magazine: *Chainlink* (350 quarterly). Turnover £6,000 to year end May 98. Witnessing, promoting a wholesome lifestyle to motorcyclists in general; providing fellowship to Christian motorcyclists.
Web: bike.org.uk/cma
Email: cma-admin@bike.org.uk
☎ 0870 606 3610

Christian Prison Ministries, PO Box 8806, Carluke ML8 4RJ
Director: Rev Colin Cuthbert. No full-time staff. ***CC*** No.SCO 27020. Began 1988; non-denominational. (Previously Prayer Network for Revival). Magazine: *Newsletter* (Circulation & frequency n/a). Turnover £18,000 to year end Dec 98. Involved in prison ministry, primarily evangelism & addictions, also aftercare of ex-prisoners.
Web: www.scotland2000.freeserve.co.uk
☎ 01555 771 157 📠 01555 771 157

Christian Rambling Club, 5 Marigold Walk, Ashton, Bristol BS3 2PD
Membership Secretary: Miss Julie Excell. No full-time staff. Began 1981; interdenominational. Magazine: *Newsletter* (500 quarterly). Turnover £5,000 to year end Dec 96. Rambling, hill and fell walking, mountaineering with Christian fellowship and witness.
☎ 0117 963 8710

Christian Social Order, 157 Vicarage Road, London E10 5DU
Secretary: Mr Ronald King. Began 1965; Roman Catholic. Magazine: *Keys of Peter* (Circulation & frequency n/a). Turnover n/a. Promoting Christian social endeavours throughout Europe.
Email: king@petrine.freeserve.co.uk
☎ 020 8539 3876

Christian Socialist Movement, 1st Floor, Bradley Close, White Lion Street, London N1 9PF
Director: Mr Graham Dale. Executive staff 2. Began 1960; non-denominational. Magazine: *The Christian Socialist* (5,000 quarterly), *CSM Pamphlet* (5,000 half-yearly). Turnover £80,000. Christian Socialists active in politics to secure change for common good. Affiliated to the Labour Party.
Web: members.aol.com/csmnet/
Email: csmoffice@aol.com
☎ 020 7833 0666 Mobile 07623 182 694
📠 020 7833 4102

Christianity and the Future of Europe (CAFE), Lincoln Theological Institute, 36 Wilkinson Street, University of Sheffield, Sheffield S10 2GB
Director: To be appointed. Executive staff 2. ***CC*** No.1024822. Began 1989; ecumenical. Turnover £20,000 to year end Apr 96. Making a British contribution to public Euro-values; studying the impact of EU on British church.
☎ 0114 276 3973 📠 0114 222 6399

Church of Scotland Total Abstainers' Association, McOmish Hart & Co, 5 St Vincent Place, Glasgow G1 2HT
Hon Treasurer: Mr R J M Hart. No full-time staff. Began 1948; Church of Scotland. No magazine. Turnover £1,850 to year end Dec 98. Encouraging total abstinence among chur members.
☎ 0141 248 6820 📠 0141 248 6820

Clergy Correspondence Chess Club, St Nicolas Vicarag Hedworth Lane, Boldon Colliery NE35 9JA
Secretary: Rev W P Bruce Carlin. No full-time staff. Beg 1967; interdenominational. Magazine: *Chess Minister* (6 every four months). Turnover n/a. Enabling clergy to play che by correspondence or phone.
Email: brucecarlin@msn.com
☎ 0191 536 7552 📠 0191 537 4409

Conservative Christian Fellowship, PO Box 25158, Westminste London SW1P 4JL
Director: Mr Tim Montgomery. Exec staff 3. Began 199 interdenominational. Magazine: *The Wilberforce Revie* (2,000 every two months). Turnover £60,000 to year end De 98. Developing Christian contribution to the Conservativ Party's life and thinking.
Web: www.tory.org.uk/ccf
Email: tory.christians@lineone.net
☎ 020 7896 4245 Mobile: 07973 614 276 📠 020 7896 424

The Evangelical Fellowship for Lesbian & Gay Christians, Lanza Portesbery Road, Camberley GU15 3TD
Convenor: Ms Brenda Harrison. No full-time staff. Began 1979; interdenominational. (Previously The Evangelica Fellowship within the Lesbian & Gay Christian Movement) Magazine: *EF News* (100 quarterly). Turnover n/a. Offering affirming support and fellowship to evangelical lesbian and gay Christians through conferences and publications.
Web: www.users.zetnet.co.uk/pcgardner/eflgc
Email: ef.lgc@virgin.net
☎ 01276 248 93

Families for Discipline, 173 Frinton Road, Kirby Cross, Frinton-on-Sea CO13 0PD
Spokeswoman: Mrs Anne Davis. All voluntary staff. Began 1992; non-denominational. Magazine: *Families for Discipline* (1,500 occasionally). Turnover n/a. Upholding the responsibility of parents to reasonably decide how to discipline their children.
☎ 01255 671 616 📠 01255 671 616

Fellowship of Christian Motorcyclists, 6 St Anne's Close, Formby, Liverpool L37 7AX
Chairman: Mr Philip Crow. No full-time staff. Began 1976; non-denominational. Magazine: *Trans-mission* (100 monthly). Turnover £1,500 to year end Dec 98. Combining motorcycling activities with Christian fellowship and social events, so witnessing to non-Christians.
Web: homepages.which.net/~richard.hopwood/
☎ No telephone

Integrity, PO Box 27328 London E15 4UZ
Project Development Worker: Mr Tony Green. Executive staff 1. Began 1994; interdenominational. Magazine: *Integrity News* (100 monthly). Turnover £1,000 to year end Dec 98. Offering evangelical-friendly safe space for lesbian, gay and bisexual christians.
Web: www.integrityuk.org
Email: info@integrityuk.org
☎ 0845 673 6736

Interlinks Home and Overseas Friendship Group, 45 Bromwich Road, Sheffield S8 0GG
International Organiser: Mrs Betty Rae. No full-time staff. Began 1971; interdenominational. Magazine: *Newsletter* (1,000 quarterly). Turnover n/a. Putting people in touch internationally as penfriends.
☎ No telephone

S

ternational Association for Reformed Faith and Action, Outwood House, Outwood Lane, Horsforth, Leeds LS18 4HR
Hon General Secretary: Mr David R Hanson. No full-time staff. *CC* No.612513. Began 1958; non-denominational. No magazine. Turnover n/a. Promoting reformed spirituality and biblical insights into contemporary and historical reality.
☎ 0113 258 9300

he Keep Sunday Special Campaign, Jubilee House, 3 Hooper Street, Cambridge CB1 2NZ
Director: Dr Michael Schluter. Executive staff 2, Other staff 2. Began 1984; non-denominational. Linked to the Jubilee Centre. Magazine: *Jubilee News* (5,000 quarterly). Turnover £150,000 to year end Aug 97. Working to restore the special character of Sunday for rest, family activities and worship.
Email: jubilee.centre@clara.net
☎ 01223 566 319 📠 01223 566 359

esbian and Gay Christian Movement (LGCM), Oxford House, Derbyshire Street, London E2 6HG
General Secretary: Rev Richard Kirker. Executive staff 1. *CC* No.1048842. Began 1976; non-denominational. Magazine: *Lesbian & Gay Christian* (2,000 every four months). Turnover £90,000 to year end Dec 98. Offering gay liberation to the churches and Christ to the gay community. Counselling helpline.
Web: members.aol.com/lgcm
Email: lgcm@aol.com
☎ 020 7739 1249 Helpline: 020 7739 8134
📠 020 7739 1249

Liberal Democrat Christian Forum, Millbrooke, Goodacres Lane, Lacey Green, Princes Risborough HP27 0QD
Chairman: Counsellor Jean Gabbitas. No full-time staff. Began 1988; non-denominational. Magazine: *Christian Focus* (250 quarterly). Turnover £2,000 to year end Sept 96. Relating prayer and worship to political action; providing fellowship and debate for Christian Liberal Democrats.
☎ 01844 346 469

Living Stones, St Mary's University College, Strawberry Hill, Twickenham TW1 4SX
Director: Rev Duncan Macpherson. No full-time staff. Began 1986; ecumenical. Magazine: *Living Stones* (600 every two months). Turnover £10,000 to year end Mar 97. Promoting contacts between Christians in Britain and the Holy Land through pilgrimages, conferences and publications.
Email: cabu@arab-british-u-net.com
☎ 020 8240 4197 / 020 7373 8414
📠 020 8240 4255 / 020 7835 2088

Methodist Holiday Hotels Ltd, trading as Epworth Hotels, PO Box 176, Scarborough YO11 2YF
Managing Director: Mr Roderick E Rodgers. *Marketing Director:* Mr Alan W Brett. Executive staff 18, Other staff 102. Began 1922; non-denominational. No magazine. Turnover £2,110,108 to year end Feb 98. Five holiday hotels with a Christian ethos, catering for all denominations.
Web: www.email-it.co.uk/epworth/
Email: alan.w.brett@epworth.co.uk
☎ 01723 361 144 📠 01723 361 155

S

Movement for Christian Democracy, Mayflower Centre, Vincent Street, Canning Town, London E16 1LZ
General Secretary: Mr Jonathan Bartley. Executive staff 6. *CC* No.1006653. Began 1990; interdenominational. Magazine: *Integrity* (20,000 quarterly). Turnover £110,000 to year end Dec 96. All-party, non-denominational group devoted to promoting Christian inspired values in politics.
Web: www.mcdpolitics.org
Email: mcdwest@globalnet.co.uk
☎ 020 7474 1142 🖷 020 7474 6045

National Retreat Association, The Central Hall, 256 Bermondsey Street, London SE1 3UJ
Executive Officer: Mrs Paddy Lane. Executive staff 1, Other staff 3. *CC* No.328746. Began 1989; interdenominational. Comprising Anglican, Baptist, Methodist, Quakers, Roman Catholic, United Reformed retreat groups. Magazine: *Retreats* (14,500 annually). Turnover £60,000 to year end Mar 98. Providing information and resources in connection with retreats and spiritual direction.
Web: www.retreats.org.uk
☎ 020 7357 7736 🖷 020 7357 7724

National Viewers and Listeners Association, All Saints House, High Street, Colchester CO1 1UG
Director: Mr John Beyer. Executive staff 2. Began 1965; non-denominational. Magazine: *The Viewer and Listener* (10,000 every four months). Turnover n/a. Encouraging active involvement/discussion about the effect of broadcasting on the individual/family/society.
Email: info@nvala.org
☎ 01206 561 155 🖷 01206 766 175

The Network, PO Box 20, Braunton EX33 2YX
Proprietors: Mr David & Mrs Gill Ruffle. Executive staff 2. Began 1988; non-denominational. (Previously Christian Computer-Link). Magazine: *Christian Single* (1,300 quarterly). Turnover n/a. Promoting holidays and friendship for Christians who are unattached.
Email: ccl@enterprise.net
☎ 01271 817 093

New Day Introductions, 15 Greave Close, Rawtenstall, Rossendale BB4 8JT
Proprietor: Mrs Susan Saxon. Executive staff 2. Began 1990; interdenominational. No magazine. Turnover n/a. Arranging professional marriage introductions for single, widowed and divorced Christians. Nationwide.
Web: www.churchnet.org.uk/churchnet/new_day
Email: suenewda@aol.com
☎ 01706 224 049

Olive Grove Introductions, 68 High Street, Benwick, March PE15 0XA
Director: Ms Marie Cadier. No full-time staff. Began 1983; interdenominational. (Previously Agapé Introductions). No magazine. Turnover n/a. Introducing unattached Christian professionals; advertisments by photograph. Special niche for clerics. Send stamps for details.
☎ No telephone

†**One for Christian Renewal**, 67 Beverley Road, Ruislip HA4 9AN
Membership Secretary: Mr Roger Malbby. No full-time staff. *CC* Began 1961; interdenominational. Magazine: *One for Christian Renewal* (350 every four months). Turnover £4,000 to year end Dec 94. Support network and forum for people seeking a radical form of Christian discipleship.
☎ No telephone

†**Quest**, BM Box 2585, London WC1N 3XX
Chair: Mr J Donnelly. All voluntary staff. *CC* Began 1973; Roman Catholic. Magazine: *Quest Chronicle* (550 quarterly), *Quest Bulletin* (350 quarterly). Turnover £18,000 to year end Mar 94. Increasing the spiritual and social well-being of gay and lesbian Christians in Britain.
Web: www.users.dircon.co.uk/~quest/
Email: quest@dircon.co.uk
☎ 020 7792 0234/01419480397

RTA (Rural Theology Association), Brecklands Cottage, Brecklands Green, North Pickenham, Swaffham PE37 8LG
Hon Secretary: Rev Geoff Platt. No full-time staff. *CC* No.327029. Began 1981; non-denominational. Magazine: *A Better Country* (500 every four months). Turnover £8,300 to year end Dec 95. Encouraging discussions and practical responses to rural Christianity.
Email: geoff@brecklands.demon.co.uk
☎ 01760 441 581

The St Barnabas Society, 4 First Turn, Wolvercote, Oxford OX2 8AH
Secretary: Mr Keith C Jarrett. Executive staff 2, Other staff 4. *CC* No.1009910. Began 1992; Roman Catholic. Magazine: *Annual Report* (Circulation n/a annually). Turnover £495,000 to year end May 98. Assisting clergy and religious who have been received into the Catholic church.
Email: stbarnabas@charity.vfree.com
☎ 01865 513 377 🖷 01865 516 542

†**Study Centre for Christian-Jewish Relations**, 17 Chepstow Villas, London W11 3DZ
Contact: Sister Clare Jardine. No paid staff. *CC* No.248747. Began 1963; Roman Catholic. Magazine: *Several publications* (Circulation n/a occasionally). Turnover n/a. Understanding and fostering the Church's relationship with the Jewish people.
☎ 020 7727 3597

Teetotallers Nationwide Publicity Register, 9 The Lodge, 3 Blackwater Road, Eastbourne BN21 4JF
Register Compiler: Mrs Wendy Whitehead. Executive staff 1. Began 1986; interdenominational. No magazine. Turnover n/a. Focus on education, prayer and prevention of disease; grassroots discussions as guided by TT network.
☎ 01323 638 234

Toc H, 1 Forest Close, Wendover, Aylesbury HP22 6BT
Director: Mr Mike Lyddiard. *Chairman:* Mr Peter Ellis. Executive staff 2, Other staff 51. *CC* No.211042. Began 1915; ecumenical. Magazine: *Point Three* (5,000 monthly). Turnover £2,310,250 to year end Mar 96. Christian voluntary movement providing opportunities for discovering spiritual values through friendship and work in the community.
Web: www.toch.org.uk
Email: info@toch.org.uk
☎ 01296 623 911 🖷 01296 696 137

***Twenty Thirty**, PO Box 266, Staines TW18 4GP
Group Co-ordinator: Mr Barry Mockford. Admin staff 2. *CC* No.1031597. Began 1992; interdenominational. No magazine. Turnover £30,000 to year end Dec 96. Serving local churches by providing well organised events for twenties and thirties age range.
Web: www.20-30.org.uk
Email: tt2030@aol.com
☎ 01784 462 219 Mobile: 07976 877 790
🖷 01784 490 031

nited Evangelical Project, 29 Trinity Road, Aston, Birmingham B6 6AJ
Director: Rev James Herbert. *Chairman:* Rev L George. Staff 20. ***CC*** No.284543. Began 1976; interdenominational. (Previously Prison Link – United Evangelical Project). A Community Care umbrella project. Magazine: *Newsletter* (Circulation n/a every two months). Turnover £300,000. Providing support and advice to Black and Asian prisoners and their families from Birmingham area.
☎ 0121 551 1207 🖷 0121 554 4894
Aston Legal Centre *Contact:* Mr G Morris
☎ 0121 523 0965
Community Education Programme *Director:* Rev James Herbert
☎ 0121 551 1207
Prison Link *Contact:* Mr C Chambers
☎ 0121 551 1207
Pulse Magazine *Contact:* Mr V Graham
☎ 0121 551 1207
Volunteer Programme *Contact:* Miss L Lewis
☎ 0121 551 1207
Youth Accommodation Project *Contact:* Miss E Burke
☎ 0121 554 0689

SOCIAL SERVICE & WELFARE ORGANISATIONS

The 174 Trust, The Old Manse, Duncairn Avenue, Belfast BT14 6BP
Director: William Shaw. *Chairperson:* Pastor George Crory. Executive staff 6, Other staff 30. ***CC*** No.XN62669. Began 1983; non-denominational. Magazine: *Trust Times* (500 quarterly). Turnover £500,000 to year end Sept 96. Caring Christian witness, community development, practical service to the people of North Belfast.
Email: 174trust@dial.pipex.com
☎ 028 9074 7114 🖷 028 9074 9299

Action Workwise, The Old Barn, Watton Road, Ashill, Thetford IP25 7AQ
Co-ordinator: Mr James Walker. Executive staff 1, Admin staff 1. ***CC*** No.1014280. Began 1991; non-denominational. No magazine. Turnover £16,000 to year end Dec 95. Supporting and advising people who are unemployed or facing redundancy, and their families.
☎ 01760 441 177

Ambless Society, Shalom House, Lower Celtic Park, Enniskillen BT74 6HP
Director: Mr John Wood. Executive staff 2, Other staff 4. Began 1984; non-denominational. Magazine: *Our Companion Newsletter* (3,500 quarterly). Turnover n/a. Christian medical charity offering compassion and care to the terminally ill, the lonely and the bereaved.
☎ 028 6632 0320 Mobile: 07767 272 127 🖷 028 6632 0320

†**Apostleship of the Sea**, Stella Maris Atlantic House, New Strand, Bootle L20 4TQ
Port Chaplain: Rev Patrick Harnett. Executive staff 1, Other staff 12. ***CC*** Began 1920; Roman Catholic. Magazine: *The Anchor* (Circulation n/a quarterly). Turnover n/a. Promoting the spiritual and social welfare of all seafarers.
☎ 0151 922 6161

Apostleship of the Sea (Scotland), Stella Maris Seamen's Centre, 937 Dumbarton Road, Glasgow G14 9UF
National Director: Mr Leo Gilbert. Executive staff 3. ***CC*** No.SCO 18200. Began 1923; Roman Catholic. Magazine: *Tidelines* (Circulation n/a quarterly). Turnover £85,000 to year end Dec 94. Providing pastoral care of seafarers, migrant oil workers, tourists and others on the move.
☎ 0141 339 6657 🖷 0141 334 7463

†**Barnabus Project**, 102 Irlam Road, Flixton, Manchester M41 6JT
Leader: Mr Peter Green. All voluntary staff. ***CC*** Began 1994; interdenominational. (Affiliated to the Maranatha Community). Turnover n/a. Christian street work with the homeless, prostitutes and drug addicts; mobile surgery.
☎ 0161 748 4858 🖷 0161 747 7379

***Bethany Christian Trust**, Bethany Hall, 18 Jane Street, Edinburgh EH6 5HD
Director: Rev Alan Berry. Other staff 85. ***CC*** No.SCO 03783. Began 1983; interdenominational. Magazine: *Bethany Newsletter* (4,000 quarterly). Turnover £1,600,000 to year end Apr 98. Holistic care for homeless people including streetwork, housing, addiction care, employment training and charity shops.
Email: bethany@ccis.org.uk
☎ 0131 467 3030 🖷 0131 467 3030

The Bourne Trust, Lincoln House, 1 Brixton Road, London SW9 6DE
Director: Myra Fulford. *Administrator:* Mr D Kelly. Executive staff 2, Other staff 10. ***CC*** No.219278. Began 1898; Roman Catholic but open to all. Qualified counsellors. Not a grant giving trust. Magazine: *Fresh Start* (3,000 half-yearly). Turnover £193,000 to year end Aug 98. Qualified counsellor visiting family members of prisoners/ prisoners on remand; creche/visitor centres Wormwood Scrubs, Belmarsh.
☎ 020 7582 6699 🖷 020 7735 6077

Canehill Christian Foundation Ltd, PO Box 892, Coulsdon CR5 3AW
Director: Rev Howard Curtis. Executive staff 4, Other staff 4. Began 1990; interdenominational. No magazine. Turnover £8,600 to year end Apr 92. Community care development, transforming redundant sites for the benefit of local communities.
☎ 020 8645 9586 🖷 020 8645 0412

***CARE Campaigns (A department of CARE)**, 53 Romney Street, London SW1P 3RF
Head of Public Policy: Mr Charlie Colchester. ***CC*** No.288485. Began 1983; interdenominational. Magazine: *Parliamentary Update* (2,500 five times a year). Turnover £78,000 to year end Dec 97. Campaigning for public policy in harmony with Christian principles in Westminster, Brussels, devolved parliaments/assemblies.
Web: www.care.org.uk
Email: publicpolicy@care.org.uk
☎ 020 7233 0455 🖷 020 7233 0983

***The Care Centre**, 97 Monkstown Road, Newtownabbey BT37 0LG
Vice Chair: Mr Alan Taylor. Executive staff 1, Other staff 2. ***CC*** No.XR 29636. Began 1994; interdenominational. No magazine. Turnover £96,000 to year end Mar 98. All age social provision, providing facilities and opportunities for volunteering among local churches.
☎ 028 9086 8055

S

***Care for the Family**, Garth House, Leon Avenue, Cardiff CF4 7RG
Director: Rev Jonathan Booth. Executive staff 11, Other staff 37. *CC* No.1066905. Began 1988; interdenominational. Magazine: *CARE for the Family* (55,000 every four months). Turnover n/a. Providing family support nationally through seminars, workshops, resources, special events, media work and advice.
Web: www.care-for-the-family.org.uk
Email: care.for.the.family@dial.pipex.com
☎ 029 2081 0800 Fax 029 2081 4089

Carers Christian Fellowship, 14 Yealand Drive, Ulverston LA12 9JB
Secretary: Mrs Brenda Baalham. All voluntary staff. *CC* No.1063112. Began 1994; interdenominational. Magazine: *Newsletter* (420 quarterly). Turnover £2,000 to year end Dec 96. Providing spiritual support and fellowship to Christians caring at home for sick and disabled relatives.
☎ 01229 585 974

Caris, London Diocesan House, 36 Causton Street, London SW1P 4AU
Director: Rev Chris Brice. *Principal Community Ministry Adviser:* Ms Ann Morisy. Full-time staff 4. *CC* No.277173. Began 1889; Anglican. Magazine: *Network* (Circulation n/a quarterly). Turnover £220,000 to year end Dec 96. Providing advice and development resource on social policy and London-wide issues; community ministry.
Email: chrisbrice@dlondon.org.uk
☎ 020 7932 1100 Fax 020 7932 1112

Catholic Housing Aid Society, 209 Old Marylebone Road, London NW1 5QT
Director: Ms Robina Rafferty. Executive staff 2, Other staff 14. *CC* No.294666. Began 1956; Roman Catholic based, but non-denominational. Magazine: *Housing Plus – Newsletter* (2,000 every four months). Turnover £613,196 to year end Sept 97. Housing advice and policy, education and community work to help homeless and badly housed people.
Web: www.chasnat.demon.co.uk
☎ 020 7723 7273 Fax 020 7723 5943
Also at: CHAS Birmingham, The Tower Room, St Catherine's, Bristol Street, Birmingham B5 7BE
☎ 0121 622 1581
And: CHAS Bradford, St Patrick's Centre, Sedgfield Terrace, Bradford BD1 2RU
☎ 01274 726 790
And: CHAS Bristol, 86 Stokes Croft, Bristol BS1 3RH
☎ 0117 942 6247
And: CHAS Croydon/Sutton, 10a Station Road, Croydon CR0 2RB
☎ 020 8688 7900
And: CHAS Dewsbury, 8 Empire House, Wakefield Old Road, Dewsbury WF12 8DJ
☎ 01924 324 990
And: CHAS Kirklees, Standard House, 1st Floor, Half Moon, Huddersfield HD1 2JF
☎ 01484 223 922
And: CHAS Leeds, Harehills Housing Aid, 188 Roundhay Road, Leeds LS8 5PL
☎ 0113 249 2484
And: CHAS Palace, PO Box 524, Croydon CR9 2QR
☎ 020 8667 1377
And: CHAS York, 57 Micklegate, York YO1 1LJ
☎ 01904 651 570

Christ Church Community Services Ltd, Parish Office, Wycliffe Lane, Bridlington, North Humberside YO15 2AU
Chief Executive: n/a. Full time staff 3, Volunteers 80. *CC* Began 1993; Anglican. No magazine. Turnover £20,000 to year end Dec 96. Providing day and domiciliary care services and facilities to people in Bridlington area.
☎ 01262 401 902

***Christian Au Pairs**, 106 Grattons Drive, Pound Hill, Crawley RH10 3JP
Directors: Mr & Mrs Mark & Diana Jeffery. Other staff 2. Began 1991; interdenominational. No magazine. Turnover £30,000 to year end Mar 98. Providing opportunities for Christian young adults to improve English working as au pairs in Christian families.
Web: www.christianaupairs.com
Email: au.pairs@virgin.net
☎ 01293 882 200 Fax 01293 414 488

***Christian Concern**, St Paul's Centre, Hightown, Crewe CW1 3BY
Director: Rev Rob Wykes. *Trust Administrator:* Mrs Joy Keegan. Full-time staff 6, Voluntary staff 14, Part-time staff 4. *CC* No.1001566. Began 1987; non-denominational. (Previously 3C Teamwork). No magazine. Turnover £154,554 to year end Apr 98. Providing a range of services for people in need.
Email: christianconcern.freeserve.co.uk
☎ 01270 586 186 Mobile: 07957 871 723 Fax 01270 250 683

***Christian Council on Ageing**, Epworth House, Stuart Street, Derby DE1 2EQ
Chairman: Rev Roy Allison. Part-time staff 1, Other staff voluntary. *CC* No.289463. Began 1982; interdenominational. Magazine: *Plus* (800 quarterly). Turnover n/a. National voluntary organisation for the spiritual needs and potential of elderly people.
Email: 106232.1524@compuserve.com
☎ 01858 431 227 Fax 01803 722 415

Christian Family Concern, 42 South Park Hill Road, South Croydon CR2 7YB
Chief Executive: Hazel Taylor. Executive staff 1, Other staff 30. *CC* No.279962. Began 1893; interdenominational. Magazine: *Newsletter* (4,000 half-yearly). Turnover £488,000 to year end Mar 97. Day nursery bedsit scheme for lone parents with young children; bedsit scheme for young people; drop-in; after school club.
☎ 020 8688 0251 Fax 020 8688 7114

Christian Funeral Service Ltd, 41 Ingleborough Way, Leyland PR5 2ZS
Director: Rev Michael Wilson. No other staff. Began 1993; non-denominational. Conducting a Christian funeral service for people who do not belong to a church.
☎ 01772 436 817 Mobile: 07889 380 398

***Christian Victory Group – I Care Project**, 3rd Floor, 445 Hackney Road, London E2 9DZ
Administrator: Rev Adegboyega Omooba. Executive staff 3, Other staff 2. *CC* No.1012692. Began 1992; interdenominational. Magazine: *News of Victory* (500 quarterly). Turnover n/a. Providing and promoting community projects to show the love of Christ through practical care.
Web: www.elusion.co.uk/icave.htm
☎ 020 7377 8689 Fax 020 7377 8689

Church Action on Poverty, Central Buildings, Oldham Street, Manchester M1 1JT
National Co-ordinator: Mr Niall Cooper. *Chairperson:* Mr Erik Cramb. Other staff 9. *CC* No.328614. Began 1982; non-denominational. Incorporating Church Action with the Unemployed. Magazine: *Poverty Network* (1,500 quarterly). Turnover £275,000 to year end Mar 99. Ecumenically-supported national campaign, tackling poverty in the UK; organising Unemployment Sunday.
☎ 0161 236 9321 Fax 0161 237 5359

S

hurch of Scotland Board of Social Responsibility, Charis House, 47 Milton Road East, Edinburgh EH15 2SR
Director of Social Work: Mr Ian D Baillie CBE. Admin staff 64, Other staff 1,600. *CC* No.SCO 24366. Began 1869; Church of Scotland. Magazine: *Circle of Care* (45,000 every four months). Turnover £33,700,000 to year end Mar 98. Voluntary social work agency; residential and day care for elderly people; centres for dependency problems; counselling services.
Email: info@charis.org.uk
☎ 0131 657 2000 🖷 0131 657 5000

hurch Welfare Association, 15 Marina Court, Alfred Street, Bow, London E3 2BH
Secretary: Mr D J Boddington. No full-time staff. *CC* No.209992. Began 1851; Anglican. (Previously Church Moral Aid Association). No magazine. Turnover n/a. Assisting single mothers and their children, through Christian social work organisations.
☎ No telephone

hurches Community Work Alliance, 36 Sandygate, Wath upon Dearne, Rotherham S63 7LW
Resource & Development Officer: Rev Brian Ruddock. Executive staff 1. *CC* No.1004053. Began 1990; interdenominational. Magazine: *Newsletter* (3,600 every two months). Turnover £54,000 to year end Mar 99. Networking with other community work organisations, workers and projects.
Email: ccwa@btinternet.com
☎ 01709 873 254 🖷 01709 873 254

Churches Together for Families, 27 Tavistock Square, London WC1H 9HH
Secretary: Ms Pauline Butcher. No full-time staff. *CC* No.293389. Began 1981; ecumenical. (Previously Family Life Education Ecumenical Project). No magazine. Turnover n/a. Encouraging development of family life education programmes ecumenically and within member denominations.
☎ 020 7387 8413 🖷 020 7383 0150

*__Daventry Contact__, Unit 2 South March, Long March Industrial Estate, Daventry NN11 4PH
Chairman: Mr A W McFeat. Executive staff 1, Other staff 21. *CC* No.1002659. Began 1991; ecumenical. Magazine: *Keeping in Contact* (200 every four months). Turnover: non-profit making. Providing training for people with mental illness, furniture collected and delivered.
☎ No phone

Lena Fox House, Crimscott Street, London SE1 5TE
Homeless Services Team Manager: Carrie Sommerton. Admin staff 3, Other staff 20. *CC* No.221948. Began 1991; interdenominational. (Shaftesbury Society). No magazine. Turnover n/a. Enabling homeless young people aged 16 to 26 to find longer term accommodation.
☎ 020 7237 1286 🖷 020 7231 8713
Also at John Kirk Centre, Thompsons Avenue, Camberwell, London SE5 0YG
☎ 020 7703 6787

*__Grandma's__, PO Box 1392, London SW6 4EJ
Director: Miss Amanda Williams. *Family Work Manager:* Cathy Johnson. Other staff 9. *CC* No.800941. Began 1990; non-denominational. Magazine: *Newsletter* (750 quarterly). Turnover £125,000 to year end Dec 98. Community-based practical support for HIV infected and affected children, their families and carers.
Email: grandmas@btinternet.com
☎ 020 7610 3904

*__Help the Aged__, St James Walk, Clerkenwell Green, London EC1R 0BE
Director General: Mr Michael Lake CBE. *Deputy Director General:* Mrs Janet South. *President:* Mr Peter Bowring CBE. HQ staff 250, Regional staff 1,000. *CC* No.272786. Began 1962; interdenominational. (Previously Voluntary Christian Service). Magazine: *Help the Aged News* (6,000 every four months), *Adopt a Granny News* (16,000 every four months), *Church Friend Briefing* (3,500 Advent and Pentecost). Turnover £60,000,000 to year end Apr 98. Improving the quality of life of older people in the UK and internationally.
Web: www.helptheaged.org.uk
Email: hta@pipex.dial.com.uk
☎ 020 7253 0253 🖷 020 7895 1407

Father Hudson's Society (Archdiocese of Birmingham), Coventry Road, Coleshill, Birmingham B46 3ED
Director: Mr Kevin P Caffrey. *Finance Manager:* Mr Tim Bradford. *Fieldwork Manager:* Ms Felicity Aitken. Executive staff 4, Admin staff 12, Other staff 50. *CC* No.512992. Began 1902; Roman Catholic, but serving all. (Previously Father Hudson's Homes). Magazine: *Reaching Out* (15,000 quarterly). Turnover £3,443,538 to year end Mar 96. Improving the quality of life for children, families and adults.
☎ 01675 463 187 🖷 01675 466 607

*__Interlink Haven (Northampton Rotate)__, 35 Holly Road, Northampton NN1 4QL
Director: Mr Steve Pollock. Executive staff 1, No other paid staff. *CC* No.1017379. Began 1985; non-denominational. No magazine. Turnover £51,000 to year end Mar 98. Christian charity distributing donated second-hand furniture and household goods to people in need.
☎ 01604 602 162

International Christian Maritime Association, 2 Orchard Place, Southampton SO14 3BR
General Secretary: Rev Jacques Harel. Executive staff 1. *CC* No.1003211. Began 1969; interdenominational. Magazine: *ICMA News* (Circulation n/a half-yearly). Turnover n/a. Voluntary association of Christian organisations promoting the welfare of seafarers and their families.
Web: dspace.dial.pipex.com/icma/
Email: icma@dial.pipex.com
☎ 023 8033 6111 🖷 023 8033 3567

Jericho Community Business Project, 196 Edward Road, Balsall Heath, Birmingham B29 9LX
Project Manager: Rev C J Blom. Executive staff 2, Other staff 6. *CC* Began 1998; interdenominational. No magazine. Turnover £22,000 to year end Dec 98. Not-for-profit community business providing paid work for long term unemployed socially-excluded people.
☎ 0121 440 7919 🖷 0121 440 7919

Jesuit Volunteer Community: Britain, St Wilfrid's Enterprise Centre, Royce Road, Hulme, Manchester M15 5BJ
Staff: Mr Chris Hogg, Kate Goodrich. Other staff n/a. *CC* No.230165. Began 1987; Roman Catholic. Magazine: *JVC Newsletter* (550 every four months). Turnover £220,000 to year end Dec 98. Offering year of voluntary work, community living and reflective development programme for adults aged 18 to 35.
Email: staff@jvc.u-net.com
☎ 0161 226 6717 🖷 0161 226 7808

S

L'Arche, 10 Briggate, Silsden, Keighley BD20 9JT
General Secretary: Mr John Peet. *Regional Co-ordinators:* Ms Shirley Locite, Mr John Renn. Executive staff 5, Other staff 204. ***CC*** No.264166. Began 1974; interdenominational. Magazine: *Newsletter (UK)* (2,000 annually), *Letters of L'Arche* (1,000 quarterly). Turnover £3,470,376 to year end July 98. Creating communities where people with learning disabilities and their assistants can live and work together.
Web: web.ukonline.co.uk.larche
Email: larche@ukonline.co.uk
☎ 01535 656 186 🖷 01535 656 426
Also at: Bognor Regis Community, 51a Aldwick Road, Bognor Regis PO21 2NJ
☎ 01243 863 426
And: Brecon Community, Bugeildy, 1 Lion Street, Brecon LD3 7AU
☎ 01874 624 483
And: Edinburgh Community, 132 Constitution Street, Leith, Edinburgh EH6 6AJ
☎ 0131 553 3478
And: Inverness Community, 13 Drummond Crescent, Inverness IV2 4QR
☎ 01463 239 615
And: Kent Community, Little Ewell, Barfrestone, Dover CT15 7JJ
☎ 01304 830 930
And: Lambeth Community, 15 Norwood High Street, London SE27 9JU
☎ 020 8670 6714
And: Liverpool Community, The Ark, Lockerby Road, Liverpool L7 0HG
☎ 0151 260 0422
And: Preston Community, 3 Moor Park Avenue, Preston PR1 6AS
☎ 01772 251 113

The Langley House Trust, PO Box 181, Witney OX8 6WD
Chief Executive: Mr John Adams. *Promotions Officer:* Mr Paul Langley. Executive staff 8, Other staff 90. ***CC*** No.290059. Began 1958; interdenominational. Magazine: *Newsletter* (3,500 every four months). Turnover £2,338,858 to year end Mar 98. Providing residential care and rehabilitation for ex-offenders in a Christian environment: 20 projects.
Email: langley_house@cin.co.uk
☎ 01993 774 075 🖷 01993 772 425

London Churches Employment Development Unit, Unit 5, 1st Floor, Lafone House, 11 Leathermarket Street, London SE1 3HN
Coordinator and Company Secretary: Ms Anne Kelso. Executive staff 5, Admin staff 2. ***CC*** No.1043528. Began 1987; ecumenical. Magazine: *LCEDU News* (1,500 quarterly). Turnover £62,000 to year end Mar 98. Advisory body to churches establishing employment projects: development, fund raising, budgets, legal-structures, feasibility studies.
☎ 020 7378 7188 🖷 020 7357 8821

London Irish Centre Charity, 52 Camden Square, London NW1 9XB
Director: Rev Jerry Kivlehan. Executive staff 2, Other staff 10. ***CC*** No.221172. Began 1952; interdenominational. No magazine. Turnover £352,000 to year end Mar 98. Welfare advice, referral training and cultural outreach counselling services.
Email: irishcen@hostels.org.uk
☎ 020 7916 2222 🖷 020 7916 2638

The Martha Trust, Sandwich Road, Hacklinge, Deal CT14 0A
Director: Graham Simmons. Other staff 40. ***CC*** No.106788 Began 1982; interdenominational. Magazine: *Newslett* (3,000 half-yearly). Turnover n/a. Providing residential ca and therapy facilities for children and adults with severe lear ing disabilities
☎ 01304 615 223 🖷 01304 615 462

The Mersey Mission to Seamen, Colonsay House, 20 Crosb Road South, Liverpool L22 1RQ
Chaplain: Rev G John Simmons. Executive staff 4, Other sta 9. ***CC*** No.220793. Began 1855; Anglican. Magazine: *News sheet* (550 quarterly). Turnover n/a. Caring for seafarers retired and serving, and their families.
Web: netministries.org/see/charmin/cm01395
Email: liverangel@aol.com
☎ 0151 920 3253 🖷 0151 928 0244

***The Müller Homes for Children**, 7 Cotham Park, Bristol BS6 6DA
Chief Executive: Mr J P Marsh. Executive staff 1, Other staf 35. ***CC*** No.1066832. Began 1836; interdenominational. Part of the George Müller Foundation. Magazine: *Report on the work* (4,000 annually). Turnover £630,000 to year end Feb 98. Day care and family care centres, educational care, schools work, community care and evangelism.
☎ 0117 924 5001 🖷 0117 924 4855

***The Nehemiah Project**, PO Box 12828, London SW4 0ZN
Chief Operating Officer: Mr Wendell Smith. Executive staff 4, Other staff 13. ***CC*** No.1058536. Began 1997; non-denominational. Magazine: *Newsletter* (1,000 quarterly). Turnover £300,000 to year end Dec 98. Providing accommodation for homeless, vulnerable; rehabilitation for addicts; move-on accommodation for those leaving care.
☎ 020 7498 7755 🖷 020 7498 2423

Network Crafts, 18 Lambert Gardens, Shurdington, Cheltenham GL51 5SW
Chairman: Mr T A Thomson. No full-time staff. ***CC*** No.1023011. Began 1983; interdenominational. (Previously Network). No magazine. Turnover n/a. Helping unwaged, unemployed, retired, single parents by providing workshop with DIY facilities and expert advice.
Email: alexcraft@aol.com
☎ 01242 862 600

New Assembly of Churches, 15 Oldridge Road, Balham, London SW12 8PL
Chief Executive: Rev Carmel Jones. Executive staff 1, Other staff 5. ***CC*** No.298841. Began 1985; Pentecostal Church of God. No magazine. Turnover £41,000 to year end Sept 90. Rehabilitating of young offenders, ex-offenders, those at risk of offending; support for their families.
☎ 020 8673 0595 🖷 020 8675 8768

Newham Community Renewal Programme Ltd, 170 Harold Road, Plaistow, London E13 0SE
Chief Executive Officer: Rev Mother Ann Easter. Executive staff 12, Other staff 36. ***CC*** No.275796. Began 1971; interdenominational. Magazine: *News for Newham* (300 monthly). Turnover £950,000 to year end Mar 98. Community development in urban areas, including projects for the homeless, unemployed.
☎ 020 8472 2785 🖷 020 8472 2805

ugent Care Society, 150 Brownlow Hill, Liverpool L3 5RF
Director: Mr John Kennedy. *Assistant Director (Support Services):* Mr J A Fallon. *Assistant Director (Operational Services):* Appointment awaited. Executive staff 5. *CC* No.222930. Began 1881; Roman Catholic. Magazine: *Caring* (4,000 half-yearly), *Special schools edition* (95,000 annually). Turnover £14,171,759 to year end Mar 98. Providing residential care for 440 adults, 210 children; community social welfare services; registered adoption agency.
Email: btnugent@globalnet.co.uk
☎ 0151 708 0566 🖷 0151 709 0695

)rder of Christian Unity/Christian projects, 58 Hanover Gardens, London SE11 5TN
Administrator: Mr Antony Porter. Other staff 1. *CC* No.266183. Began 1955; ecumenical. Magazine: *Focus* (1,000 every four months). Turnover £29,000 to year end June 96. Promoting Christian values in the areas of family life, education, medical ethics, the media.
☎ 020 7735 6210 🖷 020 7582 1174

Pecan Ltd, 1 Atwell Road, London SE15 4TW
Managing Director: Mr Simon Pellew. *Operations Manager:* Mr Ian Stedman. Staff 43. *CC* No.801819. Began 1989; non-denominational. Magazine: *Newsletter* (800 quarterly). Turnover £600,000 to year end June 97. Training long-term unemployed in job search, ESOL, literacy, IT; fundraising and project development training for organisations.
Web: www.pecan.org.uk
Email: welcome@pecan.globalnet.co.uk
☎ 020 7740 9200 🖷 020 7525 9201

Pentecostal Youth & Adult Welfare Association, 220 Ellison Road, Streatham, London SW16 5DJ
General Secretary: Mrs Norma Howard. All voluntary staff. *CC* No.287223. Began 1979; interdenominational. No magazine. Turnover n/a. Providing advice, representation, information, training and counselling.
☎ 020 8679 7573

Pilgrim Homes, Nasmith House, 175 Tower Bridge Road, London SE1 2AL
Chief Executive: Mr P A Tervet. Executive staff 10, Other staff 202. *CC* No.242266. Began 1807; non-denominational. (Previously Aged Pilgrims' Friend Society). Magazine: *Quarterly* (5,000 quarterly), *Annual Report* (3,000 annually). Turnover £3,800,000 to year end Dec 98. Providing sheltered housing, residential care and nursing for 372 elderly Protestant Christians in 12 locations.
Email: pilgrimhomes@compuserve.com
☎ 020 7407 5466 🖷 020 7403 5433

Prama-Care, 1551 Wimborne Road, Kinson, Bournemouth BH10 7AZ
General Manager: Mr Roger A Gregory. *Office Manager:* Mrs Joy Farmer. *Chairman:* Dr Chris Moran. Executive staff 3, Other staff 200. *CC* No.801967. Began 1982; interdenominational. Not a grant making trust. Magazine: *Newsletter* (Circulation & frequency n/a). Turnover £750,000 to year end Dec 97. Home assistance organisation undertaking the work that a caring relative would do; operating in South-East Dorset.
Web: www.users.globalnet.co.uk/~prama
Email: prama@globalnet.co.uk
☎ 01202 599 199

***Prison Fellowship England and Wales**, PO Box 945, Maldon CM9 4EW
Executive Director: Mr Peter A Walker. *Training Director:* Miss Helen Durant. Executive staff 6, Other staff 4. *CC* No.279446. Began 1979; non-denominational. Magazine: *Prison Fellowship News* (8,000 every four months). Turnover £318,000 to year end Mar 98. Enabling and equipping volunteers in ministry to prisoners, ex-prisoners and their families. 160 local groups.
Email: fi34@dial.pipex.com
☎ 01621 843 232 🖷 01621 843 303

Prison Fellowship Northern Ireland, 39 University Street, Belfast BT7 1FY
Executive Director: Mr Robin Scott. Executive staff 1, Other staff 4. *CC* No.XN 45576. Began 1981; non-denominational. Magazine: *Newletter* (600 every four months). Turnover £91,600 to year end Mar 98. Responding to spiritual, emotional, social and physical needs of prisoners, exprisoners and their families.
Email: rscott@pfni.thegap.com
☎ 028 9024 3691 🖷 028 9024 3691

***Prison Fellowship Scotland**, 101 Ellesmere Street, Glasgow G22 5QS
Director: Mr Allan Grant. *Chairman:* Mr Derek Watt. Other staff 3. *CC* No.SCO 02222. Began 1981; interdenominational. Magazine: *Jubilee* (2,000 quarterly). Turnover £117,000 to year end July 98. Supporting work of church and chaplains in serving the needs of prisoners, ex-prisoners and their families.
Web: users.colloquium.co.uk/~pfscotland/
Email: pfscotland@cqm.co.uk
☎ 0141 332 8870 🖷 0141 332 8870

Quaker Social Responsibility and Education, Friends House, Euston Road, London NW1 2BJ
Joint Operations Manager: Anne Bennett. Executive staff 1, Other staff 7. *CC* No.237698. Began 1978; Religious Society of Friends. Magazine: *Quaker News* (15,000 quarterly). Turnover n/a. Furthering Friends' concerns in the field of social responsibility and education.
☎ 020 7663 1037 🖷 020 7663 1001

Queen Victoria Seamen's Rest (Seamen's Mission of the Methodist Church), 121 East India Dock Road, London E14 6DF
General Secretary: Mr Terence J Simco. Executive staff 4, Other staff 37. *CC* No.225967. Began 1843; Methodist. Magazine: *Annual Report* (3,000 annually). Turnover n/a. Ministering to the spiritual needs of seamen; promoting their social and moral welfare.
☎ 020 7987 5466/4622 🖷 020 7537 0665

Ragamuffin: Creative-Interactive, 534 Mumbles Road, Mumbles, Swansea SA3 4DH
Creative Director: Kit Loring. Executive staff 4, Sessional staff 20. Began 1999; non-denominational. No magazine. Turnover: first year of operation. Interactive arts with children/young adults in crisis; schools, young offender units, special needs, referral units.
Email: ragamuffin@net.ntl.com
☎ 01792 522 342 🖷 01792 522 342

Royal National Mission to Deep Sea Fishermen, 43 Nottingham Place, London W1M 4BX
Mission Secretary: Mr Paul Jarrett MBE. Executive staff 3, Other staff 130. *CC* No.232822. Began 1881; interdenominational. Magazine: *Network* (30,000 half-yearly). Turnover £2,500,000 to year end Oct 98. Ministering nationwide to fishermen and their families spiritually, materially, physically.
Email: rnmdsf@msn.com
☎ 020 7487 5101 🖷 020 7224 5240

***RSR (Royal Sailors' Rests)**, 5 St George's Business Centre, St George's Square, Portsmouth PO1 3EY
Executive Director: Rev Jonathan Martin. *Head of Administration:* Mr Brian Deverson. Other staff 17. *CC* No.238748. Began 1876; interdenominational. Magazine: *Ashore and Afloat (free)* (7,200 quarterly). Turnover £631,000 to year end Mar 97. Evangelism through spiritual, moral and physical care of members of the Royal Navy and their families.
Web: www.rsr.org.uk
Email: aggies@globalnet.co.uk
☎ 023 9229 6096 🖷 023 9229 5824
Also centres in: Helensburgh, Plymouth and Gosport

St Cuthbert's Care, St Cuthberts House, West Road, Newcastle upon Tyne NE15 7PY
Director: Mr Austin Donahoe. *Deputy Director:* Mr Steve Hunter. *Marketing Manager:* Ms Denise Farrar. Staff 250. *CC* No.512912. Began 1946; Roman Catholic. (Previously Catholic Care North East). Magazine: *Vision* (10,000 annually), *School Vision* (10,000 annually), *Annual Report* (6,000 annually). Turnover £5,000,000 to year end Dec 98. Services for children, families in crisis, children/adults with learning disabilities, fostering, post-adoption counselling/family tracing.
☎ 0191 228 0111 🖷 0191 228 0177
Also at: 40a Coniscliffe Road, Darlington DL3 7RG
☎ 01325 463 914
And: St Aidan's Presbytery, Station Road, Ashington NE63 8AD
☎ 01670 521 496

†St George's Crypt at Salem, 43 Hunslet Road, Leeds LS10 1JW
Senior Social Worker: Mr Peter Sanders. *Administrator:* Mr Tony Beswick. Executive staff 5, Other staff 29. *CC* No.250016. Began 1930; Anglican. Magazine: *Prayer Diary* (Circulation n/a quarterly). Turnover £450,000 to year end Dec 96. Providing night centre, family centre, 3 hostels.
☎ 0113 245 9061 🖷 0113 244 3646

St Hilda's East Community Centre, 18 Club Row, London E2 7EY
Chair: Ms Sarah Hutchinson. Staff 40. *CC* No.212208. Began 1889; non-denominational. Magazine: *Annual Report* (1,000 annually). Turnover £500,000 to year end Mar 99. Providing advice, social and educational facilities for ethnic groups, the young and the elderly.
☎ 020 7739 8066 🖷 020 7729 5172

Salvation Army Social Services, 101 Newington Causeway, London SE1 6BN
Social Services Secretary: Col Derek Elvin. Executive staff 20, Other staff 2437. *CC* Began 1884; Salvation Army. No magazine. Turnover £34,000,000 to year end Mar 98. Meeting human need through professional caring services.
☎ 020 7367 4500 🖷 020 7367 4712

***Salvation Army Social Services, Ireland**, 12 Station Mews, Sydenham, Belfast BT4 1TL
Divisional Commander: Major Geoff Blurton. Executive staff 6, Other staff 13. *CC* No.214779. Began 1880. Salvation Army. No magazine. Turnover n/a. Providing Christian-based residential and Day Centre facilities.
☎ 028 9067 5000 🖷 028 9067 5011
Also at: 114 Marlborough Street, Dublin 1, Republic of Ireland
☎ 00 353 1874 0987 🖷 00 353 1874 7478

Scottish Churches Housing Agency, Walpole Hall, Manor Plac[e] Edinburgh EH3 7EB
Co-ordinator: Mr Alastair Cameron. No full-time staff. *C[C]* No.SCO 22214. Began 1993; interdenominational. Magazin[e:] *Our Homeless Neighbour* (1,000 quarterly). Turnover £62,00[0] to year end Mar 98. Motivating Scotland's churches in workin[g] towards the elimination of homelessness, through national an[d] local action.
Email: scotchho@ednet.co.uk
☎ 0131 226 2080 🖷 0131 226 2190

Secretariat for Migrant Workers and Tourists, Stella Maris Seaman's Centre, 937 Dumbarton Road, Glasgow G14 9UF
Secretary: Mr Leo Gilbert. Executive staff 1. Began 198[0;] Roman Catholic. No magazine. Turnover n/a. Fostering interest in pastoral care of seamen, migrant oil workers, and tourists.
☎ 0141 339 6657 🖷 0141 334 7463

Seed, Vickers House, Priestley Road, Basingstoke RG24 9RA
Executive Manager: Mr Peter Hawkins. Executive staff 1. Other staff n/a. *CC* No.1045718. Began 1993; non-denominational. Magazine: *Seed in Action* (500 quarterly). Turnover £53,000 to year end Mar 98. Helping Christians become more involved in practical social action with the needy in their communities.
Web: www.users.globalnet.co.uk/~payne/seed.html
Email: pghawkin@aol.com
☎ 01256 363 447 🖷 01256 810 889

Set Free, PO Box 62, Kendal LA9 4GF
Coordinator: Rosemary Campbell. Voluntary staff 4. Began 1996; non-denominational. No magazine. Turnover £300 to year end Apr 99. Raising awareness about domestic abuse; providing educational resources; supporting and empowering those affected.
☎ 01539 624 837 🖷 01539 624 837

***The Shaftesbury Society**, 16 Kingston Road, London SW19 1JZ
Chief Executive: Ms Fran Beckett. Executive staff 7, Other staff 1600. *CC* No.221948. Began 1844; interdenominational. Magazine: *Shaftesbury People* (Circulation n/a every four months). Turnover £19,548,000 to year end Mar 98. Helping people with a disability, people on low incomes, the homeless and older people.
☎ 020 8239 5555 🖷 020 8239 5580
London Region: *Regional Manager:* David Eldridge, Suite 8, 37 Western Road, Mitcham CR4 3ED
☎ 020 8646 7555
North and East Region: *Regional Manager:* Ken Tucker, Graphic House, Ferrars Road, Huntingdon PE18 6EE
☎ 01480 453 333
South and West Region: *Regional Manager:* Judith Westcott, Crown Chambers, South Street, Andover SP10 2BN
☎ 01264 361 135

Simon Community, PO Box 1187, London NW5 4HW
Leader: n/a. No full-time staff. *CC* Began 1963; non-denominational. Magazine: *Simon Star* (6,000 quarterly). Turnover £250,000 to year end Mar 98. Living and working with London's long-term rough sleepers; nightshelter, residential houses, tea runs.
☎ 020 7485 6639 🖷 020 7482 6305

Society of Mary and Martha, The Sheldon Centre, Dunsford, Exeter EX6 7LE
Warden: Mr Carl A Lee. Executive staff 3, Other staff 6. *CC* No.327394. Began 1987; interdenominational. No magazine. Turnover n/a. Practical (not financial) support for people in Christian ministry at times of stress or crisis.
☎ 01647 252 752

he Sons of Divine Providence, 25 Lower Teddington Road, Kingston upon Thames KT1 4HB
Senior Administrator: Mr Michael Healy. Executive staff 2, Other staff 150. ***CC*** No.220608. Began 1952; Roman Catholic. Magazine: *The Bridge* (6,000 quarterly). Turnover n/a. Running daycare facilities and 7 residential homes for the elderly and those with learning disabilities.
Email: london.divineprovidence@btinternet.com.uk
☎ 020 8977 5130/3434 Fax 020 8977 0105

purgeon's Child Care, 74 Wellingborough Road, Rushden NN10 9TY
Chief Executive: Mr David Culwick. Executive staff 3, Other staff 189. ***CC*** No.307560. Began 1867; interdenominational. Magazine: *Open House* (22,000 every four months). Turnover £2,333,800 to year end Mar 98. Supporting children, young people, families, through local authority and church-based partnerships, international locations.
Web: www.garrick.co.uk/spurgeon.html
☎ 01933 412 412 Fax 01933 412 010

he Stepping Stones Trust, PO Box 344, Richmond TW9 1GQ
Director: Mr Bob Kimmerling. Wardens 3. ***CC*** No.288542. Began 1985; interdenominational. Magazine: *Newsletter* (1,200 quarterly). Turnover £140,000 to year end Dec 98. Providing accommodation and support for Christian ex-offenders.
Web: www.geocities.com/heartland/1737
Email: stepsto@aol.com
☎ 020 8287 5524

Teen Challenge UK, 52 Penygroes Road, Gorslas, Llanelli SA14 7LA
National Director: Rev John E J Macey. Executive staff 5, Other staff 30. ***CC*** Began 1968; non-denominational. No magazine. Turnover n/a. Evangelism, outreach on streets, in schools and churches; residential programmes for men and women. 19 centres.
☎ 01269 842 718 Fax 01269 845 313

Third Wave Group of Companies, Third Wave Centre, Bakewell Street, Derby DE22 3SB
Group Director: Mr Carl Taylor. *Finance Director:* Mr Philip Sharples. Executive staff 13, Other staff 12. Began 1988; interdenominational. No magazine. Turnover £450,000 to year end Mar 98. Providing social welfare services, sustainable jobs, advice, training, building services, housing support, project development.
Email: j.p.s@btinternet.com
☎ 01332 344 260 Fax 01332 294 018

Turnabout Trust, Winters, Shopland Road, Rochford SS4 1LH
Managing Director: Mr Tom Tyer. No other full-time staff. ***CC*** No.1062599. Began 1997; non-denominational. Magazine: *Turnabout News* (Circulation n/a occasionally). Turnover n/a. Helping unemployed and disadvantaged people through training, social and spiritual initiatives.
Email: turntyer@fon.co.uk
☎ 01702 542 564

Voice of the People Trust, 277 Reddings Lane, Tyseley, Birmingham B11 3DD
Projects Manager: Rev Philip Evens. All voluntary staff. ***CC*** No.1000508. Began 1985; evangelical. No magazine. Turnover £8,000 to year end Dec 94. Ministering among disaffected youth, the socially excluded.
☎ 0121 777 2433

***Watford New Hope Project**, 87 Queens Road, Watford WD1 2QN
Director: Mr Basil Lazenby. Other staff n/a. ***CC*** No.1004276. Began 1990; interdenominational. Magazine: *Report* (8,000 annually). Turnover £466,166 to year end Mar 98. Day centre, night shelter, hostel, community home, charity shop serving homeless and disadvantaged people.
☎ 01923 210 680 Fax 01923 235 329

The Wayside Club for Homeless & Hostel People, PO Box 140, 32 Midland Street, Glasgow G1 4PR
President: Mr L McGarry. Executive staff 13, Other staff 7. ***CC*** Began 1932; Roman Catholic. No magazine. Turnover n/a. Meeting place and relief centre for hostel and homeless men; free advice centre.
☎ 0141 221 0169 Fax 0141 248 1245

***YMCA, City of Belfast**, 12 Wellington Place, Belfast BT1 6GE
General Secretary: Mr Ivor Mitchell. *Operations Director:* Mrs June Spindler. *Programme Director:* Mr Colin Taylor. Executive staff 3, Other staff 45. ***CC*** Began 1850; interdenominational. Magazine: *YMCA* (3,000 half-yearly). Turnover £975,827 to year end Mar 97. Caring for young people, both practically and spiritually; striving for reconciliation in the community.
Email: admin@ymca-bfs.dnet.co.uk
☎ 028 9032 7231 Fax 028 9023 5826

TRAVEL: AGENTS, SERVICES & TOUR OPERATORS

Autosave (UK) Ltd, Ivy House, The Dale, Sheffield S8 OPS
Managing Director: Mrs Jane E Newett. Other staff 36. Began 1983; non-denominational. No magazine. Turnover £10,800,000 to year end Mar 98. Supplying new and used vehicles to churches, clergy, charities at discounted prices.
Web: www.autosave.co.uk
Email: helpline@autosave.co.uk
☎ 0114 255 4040 Fax 0114 255 4949

Baptist Holiday Fellowship Ltd, 1 The Esplanade, Minehead TA24 5BE
General Manager: Mrs Christine Lawrence. Executive staff 1, Other staff 2. ***CC*** No.270618. Began 1907; Baptist. No magazine. Turnover n/a. Operating 7 self-catering flats; tours, UK and overseas.
☎ 01643 703 473 Fax 01643 703 473

C-L Tours, 29 Ramsdell, Stevenage SG1 1QY
Director: Mr Chris Hill. Executive staff 1, Admin staff 3. Began 1990; non-denominational. Turnover n/a. Israel Tours with Chris Hill, bringing the Bible to life.
Email: barrywbrown@compuserve.com
☎ 01473 311 128

Centre Travel (Centre for Service Ltd), Christian Centre, High Road, Gorefield, Wisbech PE13 4NZ
Company Secretary: Rev L Warren. Other staff 3. Began 1993; interdenominational. No magazine. Turnover £180,000 to year end Aug 98. Christian mission travel consultants specialising in low cost flights worldwide.
Web: www.netcomuk.co.uk/~fgospelf/fgfmain.htm
Email: centre@netcomuk.co.uk
☎ 01945 870 149 Fax 01945 870 867

Christian Endeavour Coach Holidays Ltd, 16 Tinkerfield, Fulwood, Preston PR2 9RT
Contact: Mr S McKinnell. Staff n/a. *CC* No.1039170. Began n/a; interdenominational. No magazine. Coach holidays to all CE Holiday/ Conference centres.
☎ 01772 466 322

Christian Holidays Ltd, Lasada House, 10 Lewes Road, Brighton BN2 3HP
Manager: Mrs Heather Coltart. Executive staff 4, Other staff 1. Began 1995; interdenominational. Turnover n/a. Offering holidays for Christians in South of France and supporting local missionary work.
☎ No telephone

Christian House Exchange Fellowship (CHEF), Karakorum, Sunnyfield Lane, Up Hatherley, Cheltenham GL51 6JE
National Organiser: Mr Peter Worsley. No full-time staff. Began 1976; interdenominational. No magazine. Turnover £3,000 to year end Dec 98. Making possible cheap holidays for Christian families by exchanging their homes by mutual arrangement.
Email: peterchef@aol.com
☎ 01242 521 886

Christian Tours (UK) Ltd, Lombard House, 12 Upper Bridge Street, Canterbury CT1 2NF
General Manager: Mr James Murray. *Operations Executive:* Mr Milford Lingard. *Development Executive:* Ms Lara Kennett. Executive staff 4, Other staff 3. Began 1995; interdenominational. No magazine. Turnover £10,000,000 to year end Dec 98. Group tours and pilgrimages to the Bible lands, Oberammergau and world-wide.
Email: 106147.342@compuserve.com
☎ 01227 760 133 🖷 01227 451 278

Christian Travel International Ltd, PO Box 802, London SE25 6RS
Director: Mrs Christine Wheeler. Executive staff 2, Other staff 2. Began 1972; interdenominational. (Also called Living Water Fellowship). Magazine: *Newsletter* (2,000 half-yearly). Turnover £50,000 to year end Mar 98. Travel service aimed at saving money for missions, charities and all involved in the Lord's work.
Email: awheeler@mail.bogo.co.uk
☎ 020 8771 5141 🖷 020 8771 5142

***Christian Travel Services**, Andola House, 3 Old Market Place, Harleston IP20 9BE
Manager: Mr John Burton. Staff n/a. Began 1988; non-denominational. No magazine. Turnover n/a. Publishers of Christian Holiday Handbook.
Web: uk-christiantravel.co.uk
Email: uk-christiantravel@dial.pipex.com
☎ 01379 854 857 🖷 01379 854 856

Mike Coles World-Wide Travel, 29 Sydney Road, Exeter EX2 9AH
Senior Partner: Mr Mike Coles. Executive staff 2, Other staff 4. Began 1982; interdenominational. No magazine. Turnover £1,500,000 to year end June 96. Specialising in low cost flights for missionaries and other Christian workers worldwide; also for students.
Web: www.mike-coles-travel.co.uk
Email: 100045.1764@compuserve.com & sales@mike-coles-travel.co.uk
☎ 01392 219 499/422 090 🖷 01392 752 96

Raymond Cook Christian Tours, 136 London Road, Leicester LE2 1EN
Managing Director: Mr Michael Fossey. Executive staff 3, Other staff 10. Began 1935; interdenominational. A division of Page & Moy. No magazine. Turnover n/a. Arranging Holy Land pilgrimages for group and independent travellers.
Email: hem@page-moy.co.uk
☎ 0116 250 7670 🖷 0116 250 7462

ETS Tours for Churches, 19 Heron Gardens, Portishead, Bristol BS20 7DH
Manager: Mr John Hadler. *Managing Director:* Mr Mark Sanders. *General Manager:* Mrs Carole Kelly. Executive staff 4, Admin staff 24. Began n/a; non-denominational. No magazine. Turnover £10,000,000 to year end Dec 98. Advising, designing and organising tours for church groups; Israel and other Biblical and pilgrimage destinations.
Email: churchea@etstravel.co.uk
☎ 01275 844 889 🖷 01275 814 160
Head Office: ETS Travel, 65 London Road, Stapleford CB2 5DG
Email: ets@etstravel.co.uk
☎ 01223 723 456 🖷 01223 723 459

†**Fellowship Tours**, PO Box 29, Chard TA20 2YY
Managing Director: Mr Paul Matherick. *Chairman:* Mr Vince Matherick. Full-time staff 7. Began 1974; interdenominational. (Previously F T Tours Ltd). No magazine. Turnover £1,200,000 to year end Feb 97. Christian holidays to Holy Land, Greece, Cyprus, Austria, Jordan, Turkey, Egypt, Switzerland; groups or individuals.
Email: fellowship.tours@dial.pipex.com
☎ 01460 220 540 🖷 01460 221 406

The Flight Bureau, Flight House, 139 Newington Road, Edinburgh EH9 1QW
Partner: Mr Alan Scobie. Executive staff 4, Other staff 14. Began 1990; non-denominational. No magazine. Turnover £2,500,000 to year end Mar 98. Supplying discounted worldwide air tickets and travel insurance.
Web: www.flightbureau.com
Email: flight@flightbureau.com
☎ 0131 477 7777 🖷 0131 477 7888

Gold Hill Holidays, Hobbit Hollow, Bull Lane, Gerrards Cross SL9 8RZ
Partner: Mr Clive Beattie. Executive staff 1, Other staff 2. Began 1986; non-denominational. No magazine. Turnover £300,000 to year end Apr 96. Providing outdoor activity holidays; skiing, walking and multi-activities, with Christian teaching.
☎ 01753 880 753 🖷 01753 880 754

Good News Travel Ltd, 65 Moorfield Road, Salford M6 7EY
Director: Mr John D Ogden. Executive staff 2. Began 1984; non-denominational. No magazine. Turnover £600,000 to year end Dec 98. Flight consultants with a ministry of arranging flight itineraries.
Email: jdogden@compuserve.com
☎ 0161 736 5769 🖷 0161 736 1561

Highway Journeys, 3 Winchester Street, Whitchurch RG28 7AH
Manager: Mr John Pickett. Admin staff 1. *CC* No.244075. Began 1963; interdenominational. (Previously Highway Holidays). No magazine. Turnover n/a. Arranging journeys to the Bible Lands and other countries, encouraging contact with the 'Living Stones'.
☎ 01256 895 966 🖷 01256 896 144

Holy Land Travel, 10 Keswick Road, Boscombe Manor, Bournemouth BH5 1LP
Owner: Mrs Elaine Applegate. No other full-time staff. Began 1971; evangelical. No magazine. Turnover n/a. Arranging Pilgrimage/Bible tours to the Holy Land.
☎ 01202 395 698 🖷 01202 394 397

Ichthus Motor Services, Grove Close, Forest Hill, London SE23 1AS
Proprietor: Dr L R Carne. Executive staff 2, Other staff 8. Began 1979; non-denominational. No magazine. Turnover n/a. Carrying out mechanical and body repairs; car sales, MOTs.
E Email: 106454.2000@compuserve.com
☎ 020 8291 1652 🖷 020 8291 1652

S

Inter-Church Travel Ltd, Middelburg Square, Folkestone CT20 1AZ
General Manager: Mr Karl Watson. Other staff 6. Began 1954; interdenominational. No magazine. Turnover n/a. Arranging group and individual travel; pilgrimages, religious/cultural tours and retreats; specialist in tailor-made itineraries.
☎ 01303 771 535 🖷 01303 771 100

Israel Travel Service, 427 Royal Exchange, Old Bank Street, Manchester M2 7EP
Managing Director: Mr Adrian J Cohen. *Director of Operations:* Mrs Hilary Sheldon. *Director of Finance:* Mr David Clayton. Executive staff 4, Other staff 5. Began 1991; non-denominational. No magazine. Turnover £1,800,000 to year end Sept 98. Pilgrimage tour operator offering tailor-made itineries to suit every group including; to Israel and Middle East.
E Email: all@its-travel.u-net.com
☎ 0161 839 1111/2222 Freephone: 0800 0181 839
🖷 0161 839 0000

***Key Services**, Trust Cottage, 27a Grove Road, Redland, Bristol BS6 6UW
Owner: Mr Derek Townsend. Executive staff 2, Other staff 10. Began 1985; non-denominational. (Previously Trust Voyageur). No magazine. Turnover n/a. ABTA (Grosvenor Travel) travel service for group travel worldwide and conference and event management.
☎ 0117 973 1313 🖷 0117 909 4052

Key Travel, 92 Eversholt Street, London NW1 1BP
Sales Manager: Mr Peter Bush. Executive staff 6, Other staff 34. Began 1981; non-denominational. No magazine. Turnover £13,500,000 to year end Sept 96. Arranging low-cost airfares for churches, missionary societies, charities, educational establishments and independent travellers.
☎ 020 7387 4933 🖷 020 7387 1090

***Lawrence Tours of Jerusalem**, 27a Grove Road, Redland, Bristol BS6 6UW
UK Representative: Mr Derek Townsend. Staff n/a. Began 1984; non-denominational. No magazine. Turnover n/a. Special travel service for groups to the Holy Land, Jordan and Egypt for touring and conventions.
☎ 0117 973 1313 🖷 0117 909 4052

McCabe Pilgrimages, 53 Balham Hill, London SW12 9DR
Managing Director: Mr Alistair McCabe. *Directors:* Mr Robert Trimble, Miss Rosemary Nutt. Executive staff 5, Other staff 8. Began 1982; non-denominational. Magazine: *MET Agenda* (Circulation & frequency n/a). Turnover £4,064,000 to year end Oct 98. Christian tour operator specialising in Holy Land, Turkey and other Bible lands.
Web: www.mccabe.u-net.com
E Email: info@mccabe-travel.co.uk
☎ 020 8675 6828 🖷 020 8673 1204

S

Maranatha Tours (Euro) Ltd, Trafalgar House, Horton, Slough SL3 9NU
Director: Mr Michael F Hodgson. Executive staff 3, Other staff 5. Began 1978; non-denominational. No magazine. Turnover £1,800,000 to year end Dec 92. Specialising in group tours to the lands of the Bible.
Web: www.maranatha.co.uk
Email: mail@maranatha.uk
☎ 01753 689 568 🖷 01753 689 768

***MasterSki**, Thames House, 63 Kingston Road, New Malden KT3 3PB
Managing Director: Mr Bob Fleming. *Directors:* Mrs Jill Fleming, Mr Gordon Miller. Office staff 25, Resort staff 19. Began 1984; non-denominational. Magazine: *Unwind* (60,000 quarterly). Turnover £5,000,000 to year end Sep 98. Arranging Christian ski holidays by air in Europe; hotels and chalets.
Web: www.itsnet.co.uk.mastersun
Email: mplan1uk@aol.com
☎ 020 8942 9442 🖷 020 8949 4396

***MasterSun**, Thames House, 63 Kingston Road, New Malden KT3 3PB
Managing Director: Mr Bob Fleming. *Directors:* Mrs Jill Fleming, Mr Gordon Miller. Office staff 25, Resort staff 140. Began 1988; non-denominational. Magazine: *Unwind* (60,000 quarterly). Turnover: finance included in MasterSki. Arranging Christian holiday programme using hotels in Greece, Italy, Turkey, France, Israel, cruises to Bible lands.
Web: www.itsnet.co.uk.mastersun
Email: mplan1uk@aol.com
☎ 020 8942 9442 🖷 020 8949 4396

North South Travel, Moulsham Mill Centre, Parkway, Chelmsford CM2 7PX
Manager: Ms Brenda Skinner. Executive staff 3. Began 1982; non-denominational. No magazine. Turnover n/a. Offering discount fares to church groups. Profits go to projects in the developing world.
Email: brenda@nstravel.demon.co.uk
☎ 01245 492 882 🖷 01245 356 612

Oak Hall Expeditions and Skiing, Otford Manor, Otford, Sevenoaks TN15 6XF
Director: Mr Ian Mayo. Staff n/a. Began 1966; non-denominational. No magazine. Turnover n/a. Arranging worldwide summer holidays and winter skiing; Bible teaching given by Christian team.
Web: www.oakhall.clara.net
Email: oakhall@clara.net
☎ 01732 763 131 🖷 01732 763 136

Orientours Pilgrimages, 2nd Floor, Sovereign House, 11 Ballards Lane, London N3 1UX
Managing Director: Mr Stuart Lewis. Staff n/a. Began 1959; interdenominational. (A division of Peltours). No magazine. Turnover n/a. Organising pilgrim tours to the Holy Land and other religious sites for all denominations.
Web: www.peltours.com
Email: sales@peltours.com
☎ 020 8346 1515 🖷 020 8340 0579

Pact Activity Holidays, 72 Greenway, Berkhamsted HP4 3LF
Administrator: Mr J Beavis. No full-time staff. *CC* Began 1956; non-denominational. No magazine. Turnover £30,000 to year end Dec 92. Summer ventures for youth and families combining an enjoyable holiday with the presentation of the Christian message.
Email: pact@dial.pipex.com
☎ 01442 870 877 🖷 01277 263 948

Pax Travel Ltd, 152 Kentish Town Road, London NW1 9QB
Managing Director: Mr Philip Dean. Executive staff 3. Bega 1978; non-denominational. No magazine. Turnover n/ Organising pilgrimage tours.
Email: paxtravel@aol.com
☎ 020 7485 3003 🖷 020 7485 3006

Pilgrim Adventure, 120 Bromley Heath Road, Downend, Bristc BS16 6JJ
Co-ordinator: Mr David Gleed. Other staff 2. Began 1987; ecu menical. Magazine: *Shoreline* (Circulation n/a half-yearly Turnover n/a. Pilgrim journeys for people who like to travel o the beaten track.
☎ 0117 957 3997 🖷 0117 952 1180

Purpose Holidays, Worthy Park Grove, Abbots Worthy, Win chester SO21 1AN
Director: Rev David Steele. Executive staff 1, Other staff 1. *CC* No.326081. Began 1974; interdenominational. No magazine Turnover n/a. Evangelism among British holidaymakers i Spain, France, Italy, Greece and Croatia; training give beforehand.
☎ 01962 882 082

Reliance World Travel Ltd, 101 Queen Victoria Street, London EC4P 4EP
Manager/Director & Company Secretary: Major Anthony Smyth. *Senior Travel Consultant:* Mr Mark Edwards. *Travel Consultant:* Major Rosemary Dickens. Executive staff 2, Other staff 2. Began 1982; Salvation Army. No magazine. Turnover £882,000 to year end Mar 98. Christian travel agents and tour operators; low cost missionary/clergy travel.
Email: rwt@salvationarmy.org
& anthonysmyth@salvationarmy.org
☎ 020 7489 0571 🖷 020 7489 8861

Rivers Travel, PO Box 54, Barnstaple EX32 9YR
Proprietor: Mr Alan Butler. Executive staff 1, Admin staff 1. Began 1997; non-denominational. Magazine: *Christian Traveller* (email only) (500 quarterly). Turnover £250,000 to year end Mar 99. Discount flights for groups or individuals on ministry or business, insurance and car-hire.
Web: www.rivers.co.uk
Email: travel@rivers.co.uk
☎ 01271 327 447 🖷 01271 327 447

St Paul Tours, 38 Victoria Street, Felixstowe IP11 7EW
Managing Director: Mr Stephen J Page. Executive staff 2. Began 1989; interdenominational. No magazine. Turnover n/a. Specialising in tailor-made tours for groups to the six countries associated with St Paul.
☎ 01394 282 198 🖷 01394 275 034

Shoresh Study Tours, 30c Clarence Road, St Albans AL1 4JJ
Administrator: Miss Helen Chilton. Admin staff 1. *CC* No.228519. Began 1986; interdenominational. No magazine. Turnover £404,000 to year end Dec 97. Tours and sabbaticals to Israel looking at the Hebraic roots of the Christian faith.
Web: www.cmj.org.uk
Email: shoreshuk@compuserve.com
☎ 01727 810 817 🖷 01727 848 312

Special Pilgrimages, 55 Queen's Road, Southend-on-Sea SS1 1LT
Managing Director: Mr Issa K Tahhan. Other staff 8. Began 1983; interdenominational. No magazine. Turnover £500,000 to year end Dec 92. Arranging pilgrimages to Holy Land, Italy, Spain, Mexico, Egypt and Turkey.
☎ 01702 394 000 🖷 01702 395 000

urecar Consultants, 171 Broad Lane, Coventry CV5 7AP
Senior Partner: Mr Stephen Crowter. Executive staff 2. Began 1991; interdenominational. No magazine. Turnover £2,100,000 to year end Dec 98. Supplying new and used discount cars to order; most models available.
☎ 024 7667 3971 Mobile: 07973 914 269
🖷 024 7671 5619

'imeline Heritage Tours, 5 Laggotts Close, Hinton Waldrist, Faringdon SN7 8RY
Proprietor & Tour Leader: Mr Graham E Hall. Executive staff 2. Began 1994; non-denominational. No magazine. Turnover £60,000 to year end Dec 98. Increasing awareness of Britain's Christian heritage through tours, themed excursions, church-based Christian history seminars.
Web: www.oxlink.co.uk/business/timeline.html
Email: timelineheritage@msn.com
☎ 01865 821 084 Mobile: 07971 692 642
🖷 01865 821 084

Travel Friends International, Saint Clare, The Street, Pakenham, Bury St Edmunds IP31 2JU
Honorary Director: Rev Canon Edward Finch. Executive staff 1, Admin staff 2. Began 1995; ecumenical. Turnover n/a. Promoting ecumenical and inter-country people-to-people, creative, sustainable tourism.
Email: brenda@nstravel.demon.co.uk
☎ 01359 232 385 🖷 01359 232 385

Trust Vehicle Services, Whatley's Garage, High Street, Horam, Heathfield TN21 0EL
Owner: Mr Michael Wilding. Executive staff 2, Other staff 1. Began 1985; non-denominational. No magazine. Turnover £230,000 to year end Mar 96. Supplying used and new cars, vans and minibuses; car hire, speciality long-term for missionaries.
☎ 01435 812 995 🖷 01435 813 337

Venture Abroad, Arc House, 1 Coal Hill Lane, Farsley, Leeds LS28 5NA
Directors: Mr David Humphreys, Mr Graham Harvey. Executive staff 2, Other staff 10. Began 1972; interdenominational. Magazine: *Newsletter* (Circulation & frequency n/a). Turnover n/a. Specialising in European/worldwide holidays for youth and church groups.
Email: ventureabroad.demon.co.uk
☎ 0113 256 1444 🖷 0113 204 0234

Wind, Sand & Stars Ltd, 2 Arkwright Road, London NW3 6AD
Director: Miss Emma Loveridge. Executive staff 2, Other staff 2. Began 1991; non-denominational. No magazine. Turnover n/a. Arranging pilgrimages and desert journeys to the Sinai including St Catherine's sixth century monastery and Mount Sinai.
Web: www.windsandstars.co.uk
Email: office@windsandstars.co.uk
☎ 020 7433 3684 🖷 020 7431 3247

Worldwide Group, 36 Coldharbour Road, Redland, Bristol BS6 7NA
Managing Director: Rev Cyril A Hadler. *Directors:* Mr Stuart Hadler, Mr Ron & Mrs Jocelyn Pimm. Executive staff 3, Other staff 2. Began 1967; interdenominational. No magazine. Turnover £2,000,000 to year end Dec 98. Providing group holidays for churches, conferences; group air ticketing for missionaries, ministers and Christian workers.
Web: www.hadlertours.ltd.uk
Email: info@hadlertours.ltd.uk
☎ 0117 973 1840 🖷 0117 973 2434

Young Life Holidays, Spring Cottage, Spring Road, Leeds LS6 1AD
Secretary: Mrs Joanna Jones. No full-time staff. ***CC*** No.207899. Began 1911; interdenominational. (Part of Young Life). No magazine. Turnover £18,000 to year end Dec 96. Evangelistic programme of holidays for young people; promoting Christian discipleship.
Web: younglife.org.uk
Email: ylhq@younglife.org.uk
☎ 0113 275 3565 🖷 0113 230 4363

YOUTH ORGANISATIONS

See also Children's Care & Adoption Societies on Page 396.

All Souls Clubhouse, 141 Cleveland Street, London W1P 5PH
Clubhouse Vicar: Rev Andy Rider. *Centre Co-ordinator:* Mr Keith Dally. Executive staff 4, Other full time staff 4. ***CC*** No.303292. Began 1958; Anglican. No magazine. Turnover £180,000 to year end Dec 96. Community centre and church serving the locality, also youth work, provision for those aged over 60.
Email: club-house@compuserve.com
☎ 020 7387 1360 🖷 020 7387 2593

Back 2 School Ministries, 155 Hart Road, Thundersley, Benfleet SS7 3QP
Schools workers: Mr Chris & Mrs Sue Govus. Executive staff 2. ***CC*** No.1005205. Began 1991; interdenominational. Magazine: *Back 2 School News* (250 quarterly). Turnover £18,000 to year end Dec 98. Schools work; children's evangelism; holiday clubs and family outreach missions; training in children's work; preaching.
☎ 01268 743 404

†**Baptist Union Youth Office**, Baptist House, PO Box 44, 129 Broadway, Didcot OX11 8RT
Youth adviser: Mr Iain Hoskins. Executive staff 1. ***CC*** Began n/a; Baptist. Magazine: *Perspectives* (Circulation n/a quarterly). Turnover £55,000 to year end Dec 96. Providing spiritual and professional support to young people and those who work with them.
Email: 100442.1750@compuserve.com
☎ 01235 512 077 🖷 01235 811 537

Baptist Youth (Baptist Union of Ireland), 117 Lisburn Road, Belfast BT9 7AF
Baptist Youth Secretary: Mr Jackie Whyte. Executive staff 1, Other staff 1. ***CC*** No.XN45793A. Began 1977; Baptist. No magazine. Turnover £80,000 to year end Dec 98. Promoting all aspects of youth and children's work, leadership training and evangelistic outreach.
Email: buofi@aol.com
☎ 028 9066 3108 🖷 028 9066 3616

S

***Bar-N-Bus Trust**, 360 London Road, Hadleigh, Benfleet SS7 2DD
Project Coordinator: Mr Rod Maycock. Staff 3. ***CC*** No.1055210. Began 1992; interdenominational. No magazine. Turnover £60,000 to year end Dec 98. Reaching out to young people in south-east Essex.
Email: barnbus01@aol.com
☎ 01702 551 881 🖷 01702 551 880

***Barnabas Trust Ltd**, Carroty Wood, Higham Lane, Tonbridge TN11 9QX
Chief Executive: Mr G Carruthers. *Marketing Manager:* Mr Mark Dullaway. Other staff 12. ***CC*** No.276346. Began 1978; interdenominational. Magazine: *Barnabas News* (Circulation & frequency n/a). Turnover £463,000 to year end Mar 98. Operating 5 holiday and conference centres located in Littlehampton, the Scottish Borders, Northamptonshire, Sevenoaks and Tonbridge.
Email: headoffice@barnabas.org.uk
☎ 01732 366 766 🖷 01732 360 429

***Boys' Brigade**, Felden Lodge, Hemel Hempstead HP3 0BL
Brigade Secretary: Mr Sydney Jones OBE. Executive staff 6, Office staff 34. ***CC*** No.305969. Began 1883; interdenominational. Magazine: *Boys' Brigade Gazette* (12,000 every two months). Turnover £2,742,000 to year end Mar 98. Christian uniformed organisation for boys aged 6 to 18.
Web: www.boys-brigade.org.uk
Email: felden@boys-brigade.org.uk
☎ 01442 231 681 🖷 01422 235 391
Also at: 80 Woodville Road, Cathays, Cardiff CF2 4ED
☎ 029 2023 2052
And: Mr Ian McLaughlan, Carronvale House, Carronvale, Larbert FK5 3LH
☎ 01324 562 008 🖷 01324 552 323
And: Mr Alec Hunter MBE, Rathmore House, 126 Glenarm Road, Larne BT40 1DZ
☎ 028 2827 2794 🖷 028 2827 5150

***Campaigners**, Campaigner House, St Mark's Close, Colney Heath, St Albans AL4 0NQ
Director General: Rev Kenneth Argent. Executive staff 4, Other staff 6. ***CC*** No.283171. Began 1922; interdenominational. Magazine: *Clan Life* (4,500 quarterly). Turnover £308,000 to year end Dec 98. Church-based, evangelistic uniformed children's and youth ministry.
Web: www.charity.net.org/~campaigners
☎ 01727 824 065 🖷 01727 825 049

Glen Cartwright, Freelance Youth Consultant, 64 Adamton Roa North, Prestwick KA9 2ES
Freelance Youth Consultant: Glen Cartwright. Executive staf 1. Began 1998; interdenominational. Turnover n/a. Loca church based ministry in the area of developing young anc emerging leaders.
☎ 01292 477 136 🖷 01292 477 136

†Catholic Scout Advisory Council, 44 Darwin Avenue, Chesterfiel S40 4RU
Secretary: Miss Mary Platts. All voluntary staff. Began 1925; Roman Catholic. Magazine: *The Link* (6,000 every four months). Turnover n/a. Supporting Catholics in Scouting; providing support material for religious and spiritual aspects of Scout programme.
☎ 01246 276 202

Catholic Youth Services, 39 Eccleston Square, London SW1V 1BX
Director: M A Connolly. Executive staff 3, Other staff 1. ***CC*** No.305981. Began 1962; Roman Catholic. Magazine: *CYS News* (Circulation n/a quarterly). Turnover n/a. Youth work agency of the Bishop's Conference attached to the Department for Catholic Education and Formation.
Email: cys@btinternet.com
☎ 020 7834 1175 🖷 020 7834 0098
Diocesan Youth Officers:
Arundel and Brighton: Mr Peter Fraher and Mr Ray Mooney, Christian Education Centre, 4 Southgate Drive, Crawley RH10 6RP
☎ 01293 612 299 🖷 01293 616 945
Birmingham: Rev Eamonn Corduff, St Joan's House, Coventry Road, Coleshill, Birmingham B46 3ED
☎ 01675 466 912 🖷 01675 466 909
Brentwood: Mr Nick Rowlett, Cathedral House, 28 Ingrave Road, Brentwood CM15 8AT
☎ 01277 232 021 🖷 01277 214 060
Clifton: Miss Mary McGinty, Clifton Diocesan Offices, St Nicholas House, Lawford's Gate, Bristol BS5 0RE
☎ 0117 983 3904 🖷 0117 983 3933
East Anglia: Rev John Warrington, The White House, 21 Upgate, Poringland, Norwich NR14 7SH
☎ 01508 492 202/493 956 🖷 01508 495 358
Email: office@east-angliadiocese.org.uk
Hallam: Rev Kevan Grady, Hallam Diocesan Pastoral Centre, St Charles Street, Attercliffe, Sheffield S9 3WU
☎ 0114 256 2246 🖷 0114 256 2673
Email: youthservice@diocese_of_hallam.demon.co.uk
Hexam and Newcastle: Rev Dermott Donnelly, 16 Arthur Street, Blyth NE24 1EA
☎ 01670 351 703 🖷 01670 364 873

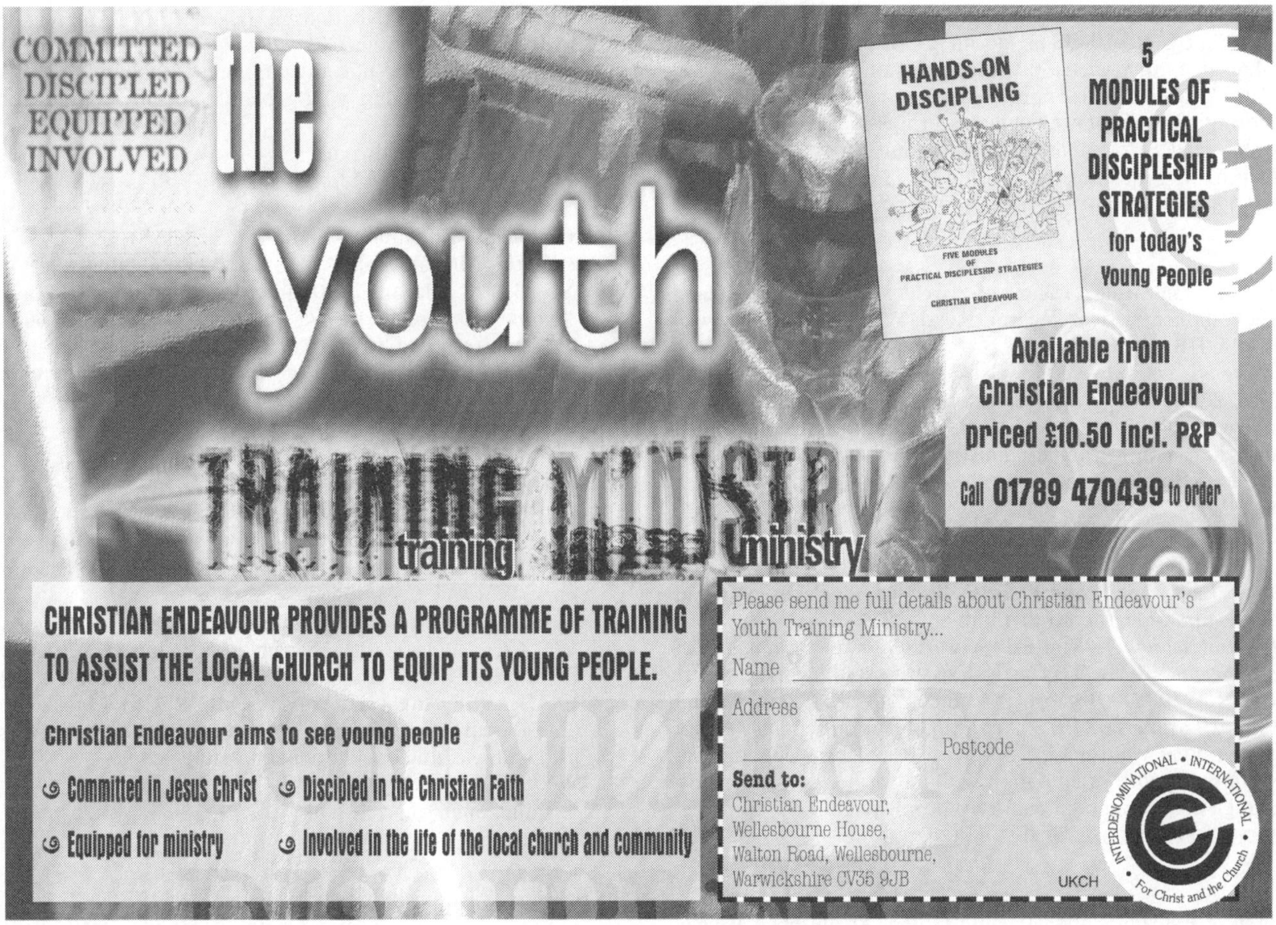

Lancaster: Miss Anne Kennedy, Education Centre, Balmoral Road, Lancaster LA1 3BT
☎ 01524 846 259 🖷 01524 846 258
Leeds: Rev Nick Farrell, 5 St Mark's Avenue, Leeds, LS2 9BN
☎ 0113 245 2091 🖷 0113 245 2091
Liverpool: None
Menevia: None
Middlesbrough: Rev Paul Farrer, The Curial Offices, 50a The Avenue, Linthorpe, Middlesbrough TS5 6QT
☎ 01642 850 505 🖷 01642 851 404
Northampton: Mr Brin Dunsire, 29 Desborough House, Amersham Hill, High Wycombe HP13 6HH
☎ 01494 539 112
Email: brin@ntondys.force.co.uk
Nottingham: Rev Gregory Tobin, The Briars Residential Youth Centre, Crich Common, Crich, Matlock DE4 5BW
☎ 01773 852 044 🖷 01773 852 968
Plymouth: None
Portsmouth: Miss Julie Meads, Park Place Pastoral Centre, Winchester Road, Wickham, Fareham PO17 5HA
☎ 01392 834 677 🖷 01329 833 452
Email: youth@portsmouth-dio.org.uk
Salford: Miss Theresa Davies, 5 Gerald Road, Pendleton, Salford M6 6DL
☎ 0161 736 1421 🖷 0161 745 9708
Shrewsbury: Rev Anthony Leonard, St Peter's, St Joseph's Catholic Youth Centre, North Road, Birkenhead CH42 7JY
☎ 0151 652 2835 🖷 0151 652 2835
Email: youth@youth_centre.demon.co.uk
Southwark: Rev John Considine, 135 Nightingale Lane, London SW12 8NE
☎ 020 8673 4422 🖷 020 8673 2288
Email: swkcys@col.com
Westminster: Rev Valdimir Felzmann, All Saints Pastoral Centre, Shenley Lane, London Colney, St Albans AL2 1AF
☎ 01727 822 010 🖷 01727 822 927
Wrexham: None

***Children Worldwide**, Dalesdown, Honeybridge Lane, Dial Post, Horsham RH13 8NX
President: Mr David Iliffe. Executive staff 18, Other staff 22. ***CC*** No.1072626. Began 1975; interdenominational. Magazine: *Children Worldwide News* (650 every four months). Turnover n/a. Evangelising children and families, training events, producing and retailing resources.
Email: chwwide_fft_dalesdown@compuserve.com
☎ 01403 710 712 🖷 01403 710 716

†***Children's Evangelism Ministry International**, European & English Headquarters, 6 Dock Offices, Surrey Quays Road, London SE16 2XU
Director: Mr C A Aniereobi. Executive staff 3, Other staff 25. ***CC*** No.1015515. Began 1990; interdenominational. Magazine: *Newsletter & Bulletin* (1,500 every two months). Turnover £27,000 to year end Dec 96. Evangelism, training, seminars, conferences, children's clubs, holiday schools, children's library and schools.
☎ 020 7394 1677 / 7237 0404 🖷 020 7394 1677

CHIME Worldwide (Children In Mission and Evangelism), 11a Upper Teddington Road, Kingston upon Thames KT1 4DL
Directors: Miss Sandra Kimber, Mrs Cath Dunlop. Executive staff 2. *CC* No.1043543. Began 1994; interdenominational. Magazine: *Stopwatch* (500 every two months), *CHIME Times* (1,000 quarterly). Turnover £7,500 to year end Dec 97. Promoting participation by children in mission; resourcing children's leaders to communicate world mission.
Email: s.kimber@chimeworldwide.clara.co.uk
☎ 020 8977 5899 🖷 020 8977 5899

***Christian Endeavour Union of Great Britain and Ireland**, Wellesbourne House, Walton Road, Wellesbourne, Warwick CV35 9JB
National Organiser: Mr George Campbell. Staff 2. *CC* No.228608. Began 1896; interdenominational. Magazine: *Focus* (1,200 quarterly), *Junior Focus* (500 quarterly). Turnover n/a. Youth training ministry, training young people for service within their local church.
☎ 01789 470 439

Church Lads' and Church Girls' Brigade, 2 Barnsley Road, Wath-upon-Dearne, Rotherham S63 6PY
General Secretary: Wing Cdr Stewart Cresswell. *Assistant General Secretary:* Mr D B Harris. Executive staff 6, Office staff 1. *CC* No.276821. Began n/a; Church Lads 1893 and Church Girls 1923 merged 1978; Anglican. Magazine: *Report* (1,000 annually). Turnover £150,000 to year end June 96. Anglican voluntary youth organisation with uniformed sector for boys and girls, accommodation for 40 people.
☎ 01709 876 535 🖷 01709 878 089

Church of England National Youth Office (Archbishop's Council Board of Education), Church House, Great Smith Street, London SW1P 3NZ
National Youth Officers: Mr P Ball, Ms M Green. Executive staff 2, Admin staff 2. *CC* Began 1970; Anglican. (Previously Church of England Youth Services (General Synod)). Magazine: *Newsboard* (600 monthly). Turnover n/a. Advising dioceses and General Synod; taking action in the field of youth and community work.
Email: peter.ball@c-of-e.org.uk
☎ 020 7898 1508 🖷 020 7898 1493
Diocesan Youth Advisers: Youth advisers in each diocese can be contacted via the Diocesan Office. See Pages 203–212.

Church of Ireland Youth Council, 217 Holywood Road, Belfast BT4 2DH
Youth Officer: Mrs Arlene Kee. Other staff 4. *CC* No.XR 18583. Began 1971; Anglican. Magazine: *Linx* (3,000 half-yearly). Turnover n/a. Providing training, resource material, support and advice for youth leaders, young people, clergy.
☎ 028 9047 2744 🖷 028 9065 8768

Cliff Centre, School Lane, Harmston, Lincoln LN5 9SP
Diocesan Youth Work Adviser: Mr Dave Rose. No full-time staff. *CC* No.1048459. Began 1989; Anglican. Turnover n/a. Self catering accommodation for youth groups.
Web: www.lincoln.anglican.org
Email: lincoln@claranet.co.uk
☎ No telephone
Bookings: The Forum Office, Church House, Old Palace, Lincoln LN2 1PU
☎ 01522 528 886 🖷 01522 512 717

Congregational Federation Youth (CF Youth), 4 Castle Ga[te,] Nottingham NG1 7AS
National Youth Coordinator: Mrs Janice Carrington. N[o] full-time staff. *CC* No.264839. Began 1972; Congregation[al] Federation. Magazine: *Youth Outlook* (500 every fo[ur] months). Turnover n/a. Encouraging Christian commitme[nt] and growth amoung young people within Congregation[al] Churches.
Email: ramble@dwp.net
☎ 0115 941 3801 Mobile: 07788 581 502

***Covenanters**, Mill House, Mill Lane, Cheadle SK8 2NU
Director: Mr Paul Wilcox. Executive staff 4, Other staff 4. *C[C]* No.282122. Began 1930; interdenominational. Magazin[e:] *Youthwork* (Circulation n/a quarterly), *Upbeat!* (Circulatio[n] n/a quarterly), *CONTACT* (4,000 quarterly). Turnove[r] £220,000 to year end Mar 98. Evangelical Bible and churc[h] based organisation supporting children's and youth wor[k.] Non-uniformed and flexible.
Web: www.coviesholidays.org.uk
Email: covies@dial.pipex.com
☎ 0161 428 5566 🖷 0161 428 2299

***CPAS (Youth and Children Division)**, Athena Drive, Tachbroo[k] Park, Warwick CV34 6NG
Head of Division: Mrs P Frank. Executive staff 5, Other sta[f]f 10. *CC* No.1007820. Began 1983; but CYFA 1931 Pathfinders 1935; Explorers, Climbers, Scramblers 1967 FAUF 1984; Anglican. (Previously CYPECS). Magazine: *C[Y]* (5,000 quarterly). Turnover n/a. Aiding the Church in evange[-]lism and teaching of children and young people.
Web: www.cpas.org.uk
Email: mail@cpas.org.uk
☎ 01926 458 440 🖷 01926 458 459

***Crusaders**, 2 Romeland Hill, St Albans AL3 4ET
General Director: Dr John Coatman. *Holidays Manager:* Mr Roger Stacey. *Business and Finance Manager:* Mr Ray Allison. Executive staff 10, Other staff 40. *CC* No.223798. Began 1906; interdenominational. Magazine: *Link* (11,000 every four months), *Link Update* (3,000 every four months). Turnover £1,900,000 to year end Dec 97. Youth groups for Christian outreach, supported by training, teaching materials, holidays, centres and specialised resources.
Web: www.crusaders.org.uk
Email: email@crusaders.org.uk
☎ 01727 855 422 🖷 01727 848 518

***CYFA Pathfinder Ventures Ltd**, CPAS, Athena Drive, Tachbrook Park, Warwick CV34 6NG
Head of Ventures: Geoff Mason. Executive staff 5. *CC* No.271391. Began 1974; Anglican. Magazine: *Ventures Brochure* (35,000 frequency n/a). Turnover £1,226,000 to year end Dec 97. Running residential activities for Explorer, Pathfinder, CYFA group members; Falcon camps for children from disadvantaged areas.
Web: www.cpas.org.uk/ventures/
Email: ventures@cpas.org.uk
☎ 01926 458 456 🖷 01926 458 459

Down and Connor Pioneer Association, Pioneer Information Centre, 511 Ormeau Road, Belfast BT7 3GS
Diocesan President: Mrs Siobhan Walker. Executive staff 2. *CC* No.XR4449. Began 1982; Roman Catholic. Magazine: *DCPA News* (1,000 quarterly), *Pioneer Press* (2,000 quarterly). Turnover £15,000 to year end Apr 98. Educating and supporting young people who wish to live without alcohol or drugs.
Web: www.dcpa.net
Email: mjmagill@awol.com
☎ 028 9049 2424 🖷 028 9049 2424

S

[Ev]angelical Alliance Youth & Children's Unit, Whitefield House, 186 Kennington Park Road, London SE11 4BT
Chair: Rev John S Smith. No full-time staff. *CC* Began 1987; interdenominational. An Evangelical Alliance Partnership for Change. No magazine. Turnover: finance included in Evangelical Alliance. Addressing declining Christian values, low family commitment, broken families, young people's future.
Web: www.eauk.org
Email: jsmith@eauk.org
☎ 020 7207 2131 🖷 020 7207 2150

[T]he Family Trust, St Luke's House, St Luke's Road, Maidstone ME14 5AW
Children's Worker: Mr Richard Blackaby. Executive staff 3, Other staff 1. *CC* Began 1988; non-denominational. No magazine. Turnover £35,000 to year end Dec 96. Children's evangelism, primary school assemblies and children's clubs, camps, holiday Bible clubs, training, all-age worship.
Email: familytrust@bigfoot.com
☎ 01622 687 074

[F]ellowship Finders, PO Box 35, Haslemere GU26 6XJ
Director: Mr Roderic Nelson. Other staff 2. *CC* No.278027. Began 1979; interdenominational. (Previously Christian Youth Contact Service). Sponsored by The Christian Youth Challenge Trust. No magazine. Turnover £12,000 to year end Mar 98. Helping Christian young people to find a local church and Christian fellowship.
Web: www.finders.easynet.co.uk
Email: finders@easynet.co.uk
☎ 01428 606 500 🖷 01428 606 500

The Fellowship of St Nicholas, 10 Carisbrooke Road, St Leonards-on-Sea TN38 0JS
Director: Mr Anthony M Cox. *Chairman:* Mrs Mollie Green. Full time staff 5, Part time staff 26. *CC* No.208446. Began 1939; Anglican. No magazine. Turnover £150,000 to year end Mar 98. Daycare services for children. Playbus after school and holiday playschemes. Children's centre.
☎ 01424 423 683

Fellowship of United Reformed Youth (FURY), 86 Tavistock Place, London WC1H 9RT
Secretary for Youth Work: Ms Lesley Anne Di Marco. Began 1972; United Reformed. Magazine: *FURY National* (2,000 frequency n/a). Turnover n/a. Promoting work amongst young people in local churches; nationally and ecumenically; helping informed choice about the Christian way.
Email: youth@urc.cix.co.uk
☎ 020 7916 2020 🖷 020 7916 2021

***Frontier Youth Trust**, 70 City Road, 4th Floor, London EC1Y 2BT
Secretary & Development Officer: Mr David Wiles. *Executive Officer:* Mr Martin Hardwidge. Executive staff 2, Other staff 9. *CC* No.1059328. Began 1964; interdenominational. Magazine: *FYT Update* (800 every four months), *News Special* (3,000 every four months). Turnover £200,000 to year end Mar 90. Associating, servicing and training Christians working with disadvantaged young people mainly in urban/industrial areas.
Web: www.fyt.org.uk
Email: frontier@fyt.org.uk
☎ 020 7336 7744 🖷 020 7324 9900
And: FYT East, 48 Harriet Martineau Close, Thetford IP24 1UB
☎ 01842 764 540
And: FYT Midlands, 7 Herbert Close, Whetstone, Leicester LE8 3NS
☎ 0116 286 5186
And: FYT North East, 3 Wesley Terrace, Chester-le-Street DH3 3EJ
☎ 0191 388 2995
Also at: FYT Northern Ireland, 157 Albertbridge Road, Belfast BT5 4PS
☎ 028 9045 4806
And: FYT Scotland, Anderston Kelvingrove, Church, 759b Argyle Street, Glasgow G3 8DS
☎ 0141 204 4800
And: FYT South & West, City Road Baptist Church, City Road, Bristol BS2 8TP
☎ 0117 924 3353

***Fusion**, PO Box 58, Chichester PO19 2UD
Chairman: Roger Ellis. Full time staff 2, Part time staff 2. Began 1996; interdenominational. No magazine. Turnover £57,000 to year end Dec 98. Resourcing Christian students in Further and Higher Education.
Web: www.fusion.uk.com
Email: admin@fusion-uk.org.uk
☎ 01243 531 898 🖷 01243 531 959

GCU (Girl Crusaders' Union), 31 Catherine Place, Westminster, London SW1E 6EJ
Director: Miss Eunice Bolton. Executive staff 5. *CC* No.226487. Began 1915; interdenominational. No magazine. Turnover n/a. Running Bible groups and holidays for schoolgirls.
Email: gcu@dial.pipex.com
☎ 020 7834 4085 🖷 020 7630 1126

GFS Platform for Young Women, Townsend House, 126 Queen's Gate, London SW7 5LQ
Chief Executive: Mrs H G Crompton. *Support Services Manager:* Mr Richard Luker. *Central President:* Miss Pauline Searle. Executive staff 6, Other staff 40. *CC* No.1054310. Began 1875; Anglican. (Previously Girls' Friendly Society). Magazine: *Newsletter* (2,000 half-yearly). Turnover £916,276 to year end Sept 98. Working with young women where they are in housing, communities and local parishes.
Web: www.tabor.co.uk/gfs/
Email: platform@gfs.u-net.com
☎ 020 7589 9628 🖷 020 7225 1458

***The Girls' Brigade England and Wales**, Girls' Brigade House, Foxhall Road, Didcot OX11 7BQ
National Secretary: Ruth Gilson. Executive staff 5, Other staff 16. *CC* No.206655. Began 1893; interdenominational. Magazine: *The View* (5,000 every two months). Turnover n/a. Varied outreach activities amongst girls and young women leading to evangelism, nurture and Christian discipleship.
Web: www.girlsbrigadeew.org.uk
Email: girlsbrigade@ew.org.uk
☎ 01235 510 425 🖷 01235 510 429

The Girls' Brigade in Scotland, Boys' Brigade House, 168 Bath Street, Glasgow G2 4TQ
Brigade Secretary: Mrs Ann Webster. Executive staff 2, Other staff 9. *CC* No.SCO 10980. Began 1893; interdenominational. Turnover n/a. Offering enjoyable learning opportunities for girls and leaders; personal and social development of all members.
Web: www.girls-brigade-sco.org.uk
Email: hg@girlsbrigade-scotland.org.uk
☎ 0141 332 1765 🖷 0141 331 2681

Grove House Centre, 37b Blythewood Park, Bromley BR1 3TN
Leader: Mr William Riley. Other staff 1. Began 1967; interdenominational. No magazine. Turnover n/a. Providing all-round ministry to young people.
☎ 020 8460 1470

Hertford Youth Together, 52 Cowper Crescent, Bengeo, Hertford SG14 3DZ
Chairperson: Miss Sarah Davies. No full-time staff. Began 1992; ecumenical. Magazine: *Rhythm* (200 quarterly). Turnover £3,000 to year end Mar 97. Providing support, advice, teaching, prayer, finance for Christian youth work in and around Hertford.
☎ 01992 583 920 🖷 020 7217 4567

*__Hi, Kids!__, PO Box 13100, London W14 9FL
National Coordinator: Mrs Lynn Murdoch. No full-time staff. *CC* No.1059759. Began 1996; interdenominational. No magazine. Turnover £17,000 to year end Oct 98. Providing weekly Christian stories on the telephone; free club literature for children.
Web: www.hikids.inuk.com
Email: hikids.inuk.com
☎ 020 7386 8638 Storyline: 0870 600 6026
🖷 020 7386 8638

International Catholic Society for Girls (ACISJF), 21a Soho Square, London W1V 6NR
Welfare Officer: Sister Sheelah Clarke. Executive staff 1, Other staff 2. *CC* No.278468. Began 1924; Roman Catholic. Turnover £4,000 to year end Dec 96. Advisory group, au pair welfare, UK and continent placement.
☎ 020 7734 2156 🖷 020 7287 6282

*__Ipswich Christian Youth Ministries__, 6 Great Colman Street, Ipswich IP4 2AD
Administrator: Mr Ian France. *Director:* Mr David Pepper. Executive staff 4, Voluntary staff 10. *CC* No.288789. Began 1983; interdenominational. Magazine: *CYM Bulletin* (3,500 termly). Turnover £110,000 to year end Mar 98. Conducting children's and young people's work through schools, houseparties, listening, training, teaching.
Email: ian@cym.keme.co.uk
☎ 01473 216 712 🖷 01473 216 712

*__Kingdom Creative__, Elim Centre, 45 Rowlands Road, Worthing BN11 3JN
Director: Rev Jim Bailey. Executive staff 1, Other staff 3. Began 1989; non-denominational. (Previously Kingdom Kids). No magazine. Turnover n/a. Children's and all age performing arts, evangelism, training workers, providing all-age worship.
Web: kingdomc.cwcom.net
Email: jimbailey@cwcom.net
☎ 01903 523 171 🖷 01903 601 922

Kingswell Centre, Arthur Street, Oswestry SY11 1JN
Centre Manager: Mr Tudor Humphreys. Executive staff 2, Other staff 2. *CC* No.512756. Began 1984; interdenominational. In partnership with Spurgeon's Child Care. No magazine. Turnover £64,000 to year end Feb 98. Developmental youth work; work with young offenders; family support; neighbourhood project.
☎ 01691 655 126 🖷 01691 654 064

*__Link Up Holidays__, 112 Carlton Road, Rugby CV22 7PE
Chairman: Dr Mark Richmond. No full-time staff. *CC* No.1020197. Began 1986; interdenominational. No magazine. Turnover £10,000 to year end Dec 98. Christian activity holidays for young people aged 15 to 18. Outward bound activities, truth taught challengingly.
Web: www.linkupholidays.freeserve.co.uk
Email: info@linkupholidays.freeserve.co.uk
☎ 01788 813 455

Logos Ministries, 147 Albertbridge Road, Belfast BT5 4PS
Director: Rev Thomas McClean. Executive staff 2, Other sta 8. *CC* No.NI 46135. Began 1977; interdenominational. (Previously Youth Evangelical Missionary Fellowship). Magazine: *Edge* (1,500 quarterly). Turnover £90,000 to year end Dec 9 Reaching young people with the claims and challenges of Jesus; extensive schools ministry throughout UK.
Web: www.charis.co.uk/logos.ministries
Email: logos.ministries@charis.co.uk
☎ 02890 458 362 🖷 02890 458 362

MAYC (Methodist Association of Youth Clubs), Methodist Church House, 25 Marylebone Road, London NW1 5JR
National Secretary: Rev Mark H Wakelin. Executive staff , Other staff 6. Began 1945; Methodist. Magazine: *Share* (4,00 every four months). Turnover n/a. Expressing the church responsibility to young people everywhere – the Methodist church serving young people.
Web: www.pinicle.demon.co.uk/maycweb/
☎ 020 7486 5502 🖷 020 7486 7792

Methodist Church Children's Work, Methodist Church House, 2 Marylebone Road, London NW1 5JR
Coordinating Secretary for Children's Work: Mrs Judy Jarvis. Began 1932; Methodist. No magazine. Turnover n/a. Coordinating Methodist Church work with children and supporting workers with children in their local churches.
Email: co-ordsec@methodistchurch.org.uk
☎ 020 7486 5502 🖷 020 7486 7792

Methodist Church in Ireland Department of Youth and Children's Work, Aldersgate House, University Road, Belfast BT7 1NA
General Secretary: Rev David Neilands. Executive staff 2 Other staff 5. *CC* Began 1965; Methodist Church in Ireland Magazine: *Equip* (700 every four months). Turnover n/a Developing work among young people and children.
Web: www.iol.ie\~dycw
Email: dywcmci@aol.com
☎ 028 9032 7191 🖷 028 9024 1322

*__Midlands Centre for Youth Ministry__, St John's College, Bramcote, Beeston, Nottingham NG9 3DS
Director: Ms Sally Nash. *CC* No.1026706. Began 1998; interdenominational. No magazine. Turnover: first year of operation. Offering BA in Youth and Community Work and Applied Theology, jointly with Youth for Christ.
Email: youth@stjohns-nottm.ac.uk
☎ 0115 922 1322 🖷 0115 943 6438

†**The National Council of YMCAs of Ireland**, St George's Buildings, 37 High Street, Belfast BT1 2AB
National General Secretary: Mr J Stephen Turner. Executive staff 20, Other staff 50. *CC* No.XN 45820. Began 1844; interdenominational. Magazine: *Hope in Action* (200 quarterly). Turnover £800,000 to year end Mar 95. Assisting young people in physical, mental and spiritual development, bringing them to wholeness in Christ.
Web: niweb.com/org/ymca
Email: sturner@ymca-ire.dnet.co.uk
☎ 028 9032 7757 🖷 028 9043 8809

*__Northamptonshire Association of Youth Clubs__, Kings Park, Kings Park Road, Moulton Park, Northampton NN3 6LL
Chief Executive: Mr John M Whittaker. Executive staff 4, Other staff 3. *CC* No.803431. Began 1961; interdenominational. Turnover n/a. Providing support services to 250 youth clubs; 'Octopus' after school project; 4 conference/activity centres.
☎ 01604 499 699 🖷 01604 499 656

asis No. 15 (Shalom), PO Box 9550, London SW17 8ZE
Coordinator: Mr Paul Hine. Other staff 2. ***CC*** No.1026487. Began 1983; interdenominational. (Previously Shalom Community Youth Ministries). No magazine. Turnover £50,000 to year end Mar 98. Hostel offering supportive accommodaton to 6 young people from in and around Wandsworth referred by social workers.
☎ 020 8673 4111

xford Kilburn Club, Christian Holt House, 45 Denmark Road, London NW6 5BP
Chairman: Mr John Kinder. Executive staff 6, Other staff 3. ***CC*** No.306108. Began 1960; non-denominational. Magazine: *Prayer Letter* (350 quarterly). Turnover £59,000 to year end Aug 94. Working with young people aged 7 to 20 and their families. Accommodation for 12 young people.
Email: ox-club@compuserve.com
☎ 020 7624 6292

xford Youth Works, Old Mission Hall, 57b St Clements, Oxford OX4 1AG
Director: Mrs Sam Richards. *Project Leader:* Mr Ian Watkins. Other staff 8. ***CC*** No.299754. Began 1988; interdenominational. Magazine: *Initiative* (750 every four months). Turnover £200,000 to year end Sept 98. 3 year degree course, Theology and Christian youth.
Email: oxfordyouthwork@cw.com.net
☎ 01865 438 383 Fax 01865 438 383

athfinder Fellowship, Bickersteth House, 25 Sheffield Terrace, London W8 7NQ
Warden & Secretary: Mrs Mary M Mason. Executive staff 1. ***CC*** No.222612. Began 1922; Anglican. No magazine. Turnover £51,000 to year end Dec 98. Christian education for young people by means of study meetings, prayer and community life.
Email: mary@bickerstethhouse.demon.co.uk
☎ 020 7727 5586

ilots, United Reformed Church, 86 Tavistock Place, London WC1H 9RT
Master Pilot: n/a. No full-time staff. Began 1936; United Reformed and Congregational. Magazine: *The Bridge* (Circulation n/a every four months). Turnover n/a. Christian, non-uniformed ecumenical organisation, for children and young people, with emphasis on the world church.
Email: pilots@urc.org.uk
☎ 020 7916 2020 Fax 020 7916 2021

Powerpack (Heather Thompson), 21a Mountside, Guildford GU2 5JD
Director: Miss Heather Thompson. ***CC*** No.1050323. Began 1984; Independent. No magazine. Turnover £12,000 to year end Apr 96. Training and resourcing children's leaders and churches; leading children's meetings and family services; nationwide and abroad.
Email: heather@powerpack.force9.co.uk
☎ 01483 576 447

Presbyterian Church of Wales Youth & Children's Centre, Coleg y Bala, Ffrydan Road, Bala LL23 7RY
Director of Youth & Children's Work: Rev W Bryn Williams. Executive staff 7, Other staff 5. ***CC*** Began 1967; Presbyterian Church of Wales. No magazine. Turnover £100,000 to year end Dec 94. To encourage a personal faith in Jesus Christ through various outdoor activities.
Web: www.ebcpcw.org.uk
Email: wbwcyb@aol.com
☎ 01678 520 565 Mobile: 07710 406 908
Fax 01678 520 849

***Presbyterian Youth Board**, Church House, Fisherwick Place, Belfast BT1 6DW
Youth Officer: Miss Roz Stirling. Executive staff 1, Other staff 9. ***CC*** Began 1840; Presbyterian Church in Ireland. Magazine: *Youth in Focus* (2,500 quarterly). Turnover n/a. Facilitating local congregations in carrying out youth work.
Web: www.presbyterianireland.org
Email: youth@presbyterianireland.org
☎ 028 9032 2284 Fax 028 9023 6605

Salesian Volunteers, Salesian Youth Office, 60 Orbel Street, Battersea, London SW11 3NY
Director: Tom Williams. Centre staff 3. ***CC*** No.233779. Began 1980; Roman Catholic. Magazine: *Salesian Bulletin* (10,000 quarterly), *Network* (700 frequency n/a). Turnover n/a. Working from small youth based communities in the service of young people at risk.
Web: www.roehampton.ac.uk/linkdonbosco_uk/don_bosco_uk.html
Email: youthoffice@msn.com
☎ 020 7924 3252 Fax 020 7801 9306

***The Salmon Youth Centre in Bermondsey**, 43 Old Jamaica Road, London SE16 4TE
Executive Director: Mr Mark Blundell. *Administration Manager:* Mr Jim Guild. Executive staff 2, Other staff 10. ***CC*** No.278979. Began 1906; non-denominational. Magazine: *Newsletter* (600 quarterly). Turnover £220,000 to year end Mar 98. Evangelism within youthwork in Bermondsey, South East London; residential Christian community.
Web: www.salmoncentre.co.uk
Email: info@salmoncentre.co.uk
☎ 020 7237 3788 Mobile: 07767 623 701 Fax 020 7252 0285

***Salvation Army Youth Department**, UK Territorial Headquarters, 101 Newington Causeway, London SE1 6BN
Territorial Youth Secretary: Major Joy Paxton. Executive staff 3, Other staff 74. ***CC*** Began 1865; Salvation Army. Magazine: *Forum (YP/Youth workers)* (1,600 quarterly), *Grapevine (Students)* (1,400 frequency n/a), *Kids Alive (Children's Paper)* (41,000 frequency n/a). Turnover £225,941 to year end Mar 97. Supporting, developing and encouraging work among youth and young people.
☎ 020 7367 4500 Fax 020 7367 4711

***Scottish Crusaders**, Challenge House, 29 Canal Street, Glasgow G4 0AD
Scottish Director: Mr Kevin Simpson. Office staff 2. ***CC*** No.SCO 008518. Began 1927; interdenominational. Magazine: *Newsletter* (Circulation n/a monthly). Turnover £90,000 to year end Dec 98. Youth groups for unchurched young people aged 8 to 18 years old.
Web: www.charitynet.org/~scotcrus
Email: 106424.2300@compuserve.com
☎ 0141 331 2400

***Scripture Union in Schools**, 207 Queensway, Bletchley, Milton Keynes MK2 2EB
Team Leaders: Mr Emlyn Williams, Rev Tim Sterry. Other staff 27. ***CC*** Began 1947; interdenominational. Magazine: *On Track* (300 termly), *Open Lines* (300 termly). Turnover n/a. Christian work in schools; voluntary groups, residential activities, support and training of local associate workers.
Web: www.scriptureunion.org.uk
☎ 01908 856 000 Fax 01908 856 111

Sea Houses Hostel, The Vicarage, North Sunderland, Seahouses NE68 7TU
Warden: Rev David Rogerson. No full-time staff. ***CC*** No.1059550. Began 1963; Anglican. No magazine. Turnover £9,000 to year end Dec 98. Developing the churches' work with young people.
☎ 01665 720 202

S

Seventh-Day Adventist Pathfinder Club, Stanborough Park, Watford WD2 6JP
Director: Pastor Paul Tompkins. Executive staff 1, Other staff 1. *CC* No.1044071. Began 1950; Seventh-Day Adventist. (Previously Pathfinder Club). No magazine. Turnover n/a. Promoting all aspects of youth work (for those aged 10 to 16) with emphasis on outdoor pursuits.
Web: www.youthpages.org
Email: ptompkins@adventist.org.uk
☎ 01923 672 251 Fax 01923 893 212

Seventh-Day Adventist Youth Society, Stanborough Park, Watford WD2 6JP
Youth Ministries Director: Pastor Paul Tompkins. Executive staff 1, Other staff 1. *CC* No.1044071. Began 1907; Seventh-Day Adventist. Advent Youth Society. Magazine: *Encounter* (4,500 quarterly). Turnover n/a. Promoting all aspects of youth work including summer camps.
Web: www.youthpages.org
Email: ptompkins@adventist.org.uk
☎ 01923 672 251 Fax 01923 893 212

Soli House, Mill Lane, Stratford-upon-Avon CV37 6BJ
Director: Rev John Seeney. *Administrator:* Mrs M Welch. Executive staff 3, Other staff 3. *CC* No.234216. Began 1950; Roman Catholic. No magazine. Turnover £150,000 to year end Dec 98. Youth retreat centre also available for self catering groups and adult retreats.
☎ 01789 267 011

Soul Survivor, Unit 2, Paramount Industrial Estate, Sandown Road, Watford WD2 4XA
Director: Mr Mike Pilavachi. *Co-Director:* Ms Liz Biddulph. Executive staff 2, Other staff 13. *CC* No.1043763. Began 1993; interdenominational. Magazine: *Soul Survivor* (4,000 every two months). Turnover £700,000 to year end Dec 98. Youth festivals – attendance 16,500, conferences, roadshows, youth leaders support programme, residential discipleship training courses, schools work.
Web: www.soulsurvivor.com
Email: info@soulsurvivor.com
☎ 01923 333 331 Fax 01923 333 334

Teens in Crisis, Unit 6/13, The Mews, Brook Street, Mitcheldean GL17 0SL
Chief Executive: Mr Nathan TA Jones. Executive staff 9, Other staff 25. *CC* No.1045429. Began 1993; non-denominational. Magazine: *Focus* (2,000 quarterly). Crisis prevention intervention and care through schools and youth work; advice, information and counselling services.
Web: www.users.globalnet.co.uk/~tic
Email: tic@globalnet.co.uk
☎ 01594 544 281 Fax 01594 544 281

S

***The Time For God Scheme**, 2 Chester House, Pages Lane, Muswell Hill, London N10 1PR
Director: Mr Roger Taylor. *Deputy Director:* Ms Tracy Phillips. Executive staff 7. *CC* No.286163. Began 1965; interdenominational. No magazine. Turnover £200,000 to year end Mar 98. Providing full-time voluntary service, training, support for young Christians in churches and other organisations, also overseas.
Web: ourworld.compuserve.com/homepages/time_for_god/
Email: time_for_god@compuserve.com
☎ 020 8883 1504 Fax 020 8365 2471

***The Turnpike Trust**, Long Cottage, Norwich Road, Stonh[a]m Parva, Stowmarket IP14 5JT
Chairman of Trustees: Pastor Neville W Rule. Admin staff [...] *CC* No.1058744. Began 1997; non-denominational. No ma[g]azine. Turnover £12,000 to year end Dec 98. Community pr[o]ject providing youth activities, bookshop, refreshmen[ts], counselling etc.
☎ 01449 711 488

Venturers Norfolk Broads Cruise, 5 Raymond Avenue, Lond[on] E18 2HF
Hon Secretary: Mr T J Smith. No full-time staff. *C[C]* No.262348. Began 1946; interdenominational. Magazine: *T[he] Venturers News Letter* (200 half-yearly). Turnover £8,000 [to] year end May 92. Operating Christian sail-training holid[ay] scheme for boys and girls.
☎ 020 8989 6153

Winchester Diocesan Youth and Children, Faith Developme[nt] Department, Church House, 9 The Close, Winchest[er] SO23 9LS
Field Officers: Nigel Argall, Mel McPherson, Diana Lester. *C[C]* No.249276. Began n/a; Anglican. Magazine: *Youth Ne[ws]* (Circulation n/a quarterly). Turnover n/a. Training, resourcin[g] and supporting parishes in delivering youth and children's ministry.
Web: win.diocese.org.uk
Email: nigel.argall@dial.pipex.com
☎ 01962 844 644 Ext 233 Fax 01962 841 815

Word of Life Ministries (UK) Ltd, 8 Beech Crescent, Larbe[rt] FK5 3EY
Director: Rev David Kelso. Executive staff 1, Other staff 6. *C[C]* No.283041. Began 1980; interdenominational. No magazin[e]. Turnover n/a. Serving local churches through children's work, youth evangelism and discipleship, camps and open a[ir] evangelism.
Web: www.woluk.org
Email: kelsowoluk@mcmail.com
☎ 01324 558 535 Fax 01324 551 442
English Office, Mr Dave Knight, 150 Manor Lane, Charfield, Wotton-under-Edge GL12 8TW
☎ 01454 260 458
Camps Office, Mrs Rosemary Carter, 72 Pound Road, Kingswood, Bristol BS15 4QU
North East Office, Mr & Mrs Alec & Timea Kelly, The Manse, Derwentwater Road, Gateshead NE8 2XX
☎ 0191 478 6972

The World Conference, 17a East King Street, Helensburgh G84 7QQ
Executive Secretary: Mr Eric Woodburn. *Administrative Assistant:* Miss Caroline Goodfellow. Other staff 2. *CC* No.275036. Began 1963; ecumenical. Magazine: *World News* (10,000 half-yearly), *On-line* (1,000 half-yearly). Turnover £130,000. Promoting Christian youth work; liaison and support through autonomous member organisations.
Email: theworldconference@compuserve.com
☎ 01436 678 087 Fax 01436 678 087

YMCA, England, 640 Forest Road, London E17 3DZ
National Secretary: Mr Eddie Thomas. Staff 800. *CC* No.212810. Began 1844; non-denominational. (Previously National Council of YMCAs). Supports 160 autonomous local YMCAs. No magazine. Turnover £25,500,000 to year end Mar 98. Helping young people grow in body, mind and spirit; housing, training, personal/social development, youth work, sport.
Web: www.ymca.org.uk
☎ 020 8520 5599 Fax 020 8509 3190

MCA, Hove, 17 Marmion Road, Hove BN3 5FS
Chief Executive: Mr David Standing. *Assistant Chief Executive:* Miss Janet Rix. *Chair:* Mr Gareth Stacey. Executive staff 6, Other staff 20. ***CC*** No.305261. Began 1919; non-denominational. No magazine. Turnover £641,000 to year end Mar 98. Youth and community work with a focus on the homeless and excluded young people.
Email: centre@hove.ymca.org.uk
☎ 01273 731 724 Fax 01273 885 565

MCA, Lisburn, 28 Market Square, Lisburn BT28 1AG
General Secretary: Mr Peter Crory. *Projects Manager:* Mr Shane Magee. Executive staff 5, Other staff 8. ***CC*** No.NI 15660. Began 1988; non-denominational. Magazine: *In Touch* (Circulation n/a quarterly). Turnover £220,000 to year end Apr 97. Providing youth clubs, sports and community activities. Six homes for teenagers in crisis.
Email: pcrory@ymca-lis.dnet.co.uk
☎ 028 9267 0918 Fax 028 9266 7573

MCA Scotland, 11 Rutland Street, Edinburgh EH1 2AE
National General Secretary: Rev John Knox. Executive staff 10, Other staff 48. ***CC*** No.SCO 13792. Began 1844; interdenominational. Magazine: *Newsletter* (500 quarterly). Turnover £1,200,000 to year end Mar 98. Providing programmes and services, especially for young people, to enable growth, development and maturity in Christ.
☎ 0131 228 1464 Fax 0131 228 5462

'ou What, 86 Petersfield Road, Staines TW18 1DL
Leader: Mr Simon Taylor. No full-time staff. Began 1996; interdenominational. No magazine. Turnover n/a. Supporting, resourcing, organising and assisting local youth leaderships.
☎ 01784 454 243

'oung Adult Network (YAN), National Youth Office, Church House, Great Smith Street, London SW1P 3NZ
Coordinator: Stuart Emmason. Staff n/a. Began n/a; Anglican. No magazine. Turnover n/a. Encouraging young adults to participate fully in all areas in the Anglican Church.
☎ 020 7898 1508

Young Christian Workers, National HQ, St Joseph's, Watford Way, London NW4 4TY
Administrator: Mr David Stretton. *National President:* Suzanne Mannion. Executive staff 1, Other staff 7. ***CC*** No.306149. Began 1937; interdenominational. Magazine: *New Life* (500 every four months). Turnover £150,000 to year end Mar 98. Helping young working people develop their Christian faith and play an active part in society.
Email: ycworkers@aol.com
☎ 020 8203 6290 Fax 020 8203 6291

Young Friends General Meeting, 1046 Bristol Road, Selly Oak, Birmingham B29 6LJ
Administrator: To be appointed. No full-time staff. ***CC*** No.1064763. Began 1911; Religious Society of Friends. (Previously Young Friends Central Committee). Magazine: *Young Quaker* (350 monthly). Turnover £27,200 to year end Dec 97. Linking Quakers and enquirers aged 18 to 30 in a supportive network, a forum for their varied concerns.
Email: yfgm@quaker.org.uk
☎ 0121 472 1998 Fax 0121 472 1998

Young Life, Spring Cottage, Spring Road, Leeds LS6 1AD
Director: Mr Steve Wright. Executive staff 2, Other staff 1. ***CC*** No.207899. Began 1911; interdenominational. Magazine: *Young Life* (3,000 every two months). Turnover n/a. Undertaking youth evangelism, teaching, in-service training and resources through local branches countrywide.
Web: younglife.org.uk
Email: office@younglife.org.uk
☎ 0113 275 3565 Fax 0113 230 4363
Also at: 511 Scottish Provident Buildings, 7 Donegall Square West, Belfast BT1 6JG
☎ 028 9023 1133

†**Youth Alive Ministries**, PO Box 43, Newtown SY16 1WB
Director: Mr Peter Goulding. Executive staff 2, Other staff 2. ***CC*** Began 1958; Assemblies of God. No magazine. Turnover n/a. Mobilising young people to mission, training youth workers, summer youth and children's camps, school ministries.
☎ 01686 623 291
Missions Department Dagenham
☎ 020 8595 9457
Schools Department Manchester
☎ 0161 682 4646

Youth Connection, PO Box 266, Staines TW18 4GP
Director: Mr Barry Mockford. No full-time staff. ***CC*** No.1031597. Began 1997; interdenominational. (Previously Barry Mockford). No magazine. Turnover n/a. Designed to inform youth leaders of what is happening locally, nationally, and when.
Web: www.youth-connect.org.uk
Email: fcwbsm@aol.com
☎ 01784 462 219 Mobile: 07976 877 790
Fax 01784 490 031

S

Youth Organisations

***Youth For Christ Northern Ireland**, 3 Fitzwilliam Street, Belfast BT9 6AW
National Director: Mr John Duncan. *Deputy National Director:* Mr Stuart Hamilton. Executive staff 14, Other staff 10. ***CC*** No.XN 48776. Began 1947; interdenominational. Magazine: *YFC News* (2,500 quarterly). Turnover £404,000 to year end Mar 97. Evangelising, discipling and mobilising young people through missions, local centres, mobile youth clubs, street work.
Web: www.yfc-ireland.com
Email: 100734.3634@compuserve.com
☎ 028 9033 2277 Mobile: 07710 029 976 Fax 028 9023 0024

Youth Link, 143a University Street, Belfast BT7 1HP
Training & Development Officer: Miss Ann Dickson. Executive staff 3, Other staff 2. ***CC*** Began 1943; interdenominational. (Previously The Churches Youth Service Council). No magazine. Turnover n/a. Inter-church training and service agency for youth leaders and young people.
☎ 028 9032 3217

***Youth With A Mission UK (YWAM)**, Stanely House, 14 Stanely Crescent, Paisley PA2 9LF
Director, UK & Ireland: Mr Stephen C Mayers. Executive staff 8. ***CC*** No.264078. Began 1972; interdenominational. 33 locations for training and ministry. Magazine: *Advance (England)* (6,000 n/a), *Commission (Scotland)* (3,000 n/a). Turnover £2,508,000 to year end Aug 98. Mobilising youth to fulfil the Great Commission through evangelism, training and mercy ministries.
Email: 106616.3706@compuserve.com
☎ 0141 884 8844 Fax 0141 884 3868

YWAM England National Office: *Director Europe, Middle East & Africa:* Mr Lynn Green. *Director England:* Mr Laurence Singlehurst, Highfield Oval, Ambrose Lane, Harpenden AL5 4BX
Email: 100126.1261@compuserve.com
☎ 01582 463 300 Fax 01582 463 305

YWAM Ireland National Office: *Director Republic of Ireland:* Mr Rob Clarke, High Park, Grace Park Road, Drumcondra, Dublin 9, Republic of Ireland
Email: 101354.2702@compuserve.com
☎ 00 353 183 74676 Fax 00 353 183 67044

YWAM Northern Ireland *Director Northern Ireland:* Mr M Oman, 19 Ashgrove Avenue, Banbridge, BT32 3RG
Email: 100071.1477@compuserve.com
☎ 028 4062 7927 Fax 028 4066 2936

YWAM Scotland National Office: *Director Scotland:* Mr I Peters, Seamill Training Centre, Glenbryde Road, W Kilbride KA23 9NJ
Email: 100566.60@compuserve.com
☎ 01294 829 400 Fax 01294 829 312

YWAM Wales National Office: *Director Wales:* Mr Mar Abel, PO Box 37, Pontyclun CF72 9XX
Email: postmaster@ywam.co.uk
☎ 01443 681 149

Yregin Newydd Education/Children (Youth Dept), Ty Ilston (Ilst House), 94 Mansel Street, Swansea SA1 5TZ
General Secretary: Rev Peter D Richards. Executive staff 3. ***C*** Began 1930; Welsh Baptist. (Previously Urdd Y Seren Fo (Welsh Baptist Children's Movement)). Magazine: *Newsle ter* (Circulation n/a occasionally). Turnover n/a. Worki amongst children in Welsh-speaking churches; youth camp weekends, Sunday School material.
☎ 01792 554 68

***YWCA of Great Britain**, Clarendon House, 52 Cornmark Street, Oxford OX1 3EJ
Chief Executive: Ms Gillian Tishler. *President:* Mrs Shei Brain. Staff 800. ***CC*** Began 1855; interdenominational. Turr over £18,000,000 to year end Mar 96. Providing supporte accommodation and welfare services for young women.
☎ 01865 304 200 Fax 01865 204 805

London and Southern England, Regional Office, 16 Grea Russell Street, London WC1B 3LR
☎ 020 7580 4827

North East Regional Office, Jesmond House, Clayton Road Jesmond, Newcastle upon Tyne NE2 1UJ
☎ 0191 281 1233

Scottish Council Headquarters, 7 Randolph Crescen Edinburgh EH3 7TH
☎ 0131 225 7592

Welsh Council Office, 87 Minion Road, Cardiff CF2 3ET
☎ 029 2048 0738

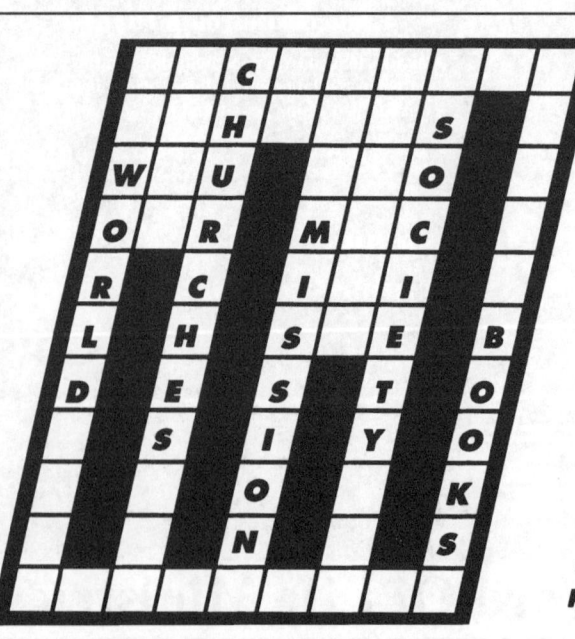

TRAINING

T

BIBLE STUDY AGENCIES

Action Bookshare, PO Box 694, Rhyl LL18 1JU
UK Director: Mr Ingo Abraham. Executive staff 1, Other staff 2. ***CC*** No.1058661. Began 1959; interdenominational. (Previously Fishers Fellowship). Magazine: *Prayer Newsletter* (1,500 every two months). Turnover £27,000 to year end June 96. Training in personal evangelism and effective follow-up to produce mature believers through Bible study.
Web: www.actionintl.org
Email: actionuk@btinternet.com
☎ 01299 401 511 🖷 01299 405 273

Bible Fellowship Union, 4 Manor Gardens, Barnstone, Nottingham NG13 9JL
Editor: Mr Derrick Nadal. No full-time staff. ***CC*** No.1064607. Began 1946; non-denominational. Magazine: *Bible Study Monthly* (Circulation n/a every two months). Turnover n/a. Publishing scriptural literature.
☎ 01949 860 416

Bible Reading Fellowship, Peter's Way, Sandy Lane West, Oxford OX4 5HG
Chief Executive Officer: Mr Richard Fisher. Executive staff 1, Other staff 8. ***CC*** No.233280. Began 1922; interdenominational. Magazine: *Day by Day with God* (95,000 every four months). Turnover n/a. Helping people of all ages to encounter the living God through Bible reading and prayer.
Web: www.brf.org.uk
Email: enquiries@brf.org.uk
☎ 01865 748 227 🖷 01865 773 150

Catholic Biblical Association, PO Box 6201, Edgbaston, Birmingham B16 9LB
Hon Secretary: Sr M T Roberts MMM. No full-time staff. ***CC*** No.215454. Began 1940; Roman Catholic. Magazine: *Scripture Bulletin* (Circulation n/a half-yearly). Turnover £2,000 to year end Dec 98. Promoting knowledge, use and love of the Bible.
☎ 0121 472 3040

***Christian Women Communicating International in UK**, Autumn's Grace, Wildwood Close, Cranleigh GU6 7LP
Office Administrator: Mrs June Dodson. Other staff 1. ***CC*** No.1002596. Began 1978; interdenominational. Magazine: *Newslink* (3,500 half-yearly). Turnover £10,500 to year end June 94. Bible teaching ministry for women.
Email: cwci@dial.pipex.com
☎ 01483 274 101

***Community Bible Study**, 7 Lords Close, Bolsover, Chesterfi S44 6UT
National Director: Mrs Joyce Bromley. No full-time staff. No.1044255. Began 1980; non-denominational. In partn ship with Community Bible Study International, USA. Ma zine: *Newsletter* (550 half-yearly). Turnover £20,000 to ye end Aug 98. Local classes offering CBS home study materia group discussion and teaching; with leadership training a support.
☎ 01246 283 448

***CWR (Crusade for World Revival)**, Waverley Abbey Hou Waverley Lane, Farnham GU9 8EP
Chief Executive: Mr John Muys. *General Manager Minist* Mr Sean Gubb. *General Manager Business:* Miss Lor Browne. Executive staff 3, Other staff 43. ***CC*** No.29438 Began 1965; interdenominational. Magazine: *Every Day w Jesus* (Circulation n/a every two months), *YP's, Topz* (Circul tion n/a every two months). Turnover £2,500,000 to year e Dec 98. Publishing Bible reading notes and other resources help people read and understand the Bible. Distribution to 1 countries.
Web: www.cwr.org.uk
Email: mail@cwr.org.uk
☎ 01252 784 700 🖷 01252 784 734

***ICI Bible Study (International Correspondence Institute)**, Regen Park, London Road, Nantwich CW5 6LW
National Director: Mr Tony Coles. Executive staff 1, Oth staff 4. ***CC*** No.295124. Began 1976; interdenominational. N magazine. Turnover £86,000 to year end Dec 98. Providin group study materials; distance learning - four levels, 100 title college curriculum materials.
Web: www.ici.edu
Email: icibible@netcentral.co.uk
☎ 01270 624 123 🖷 01270 610 020

International Bible Reading Association, 1020 Bristol Road, Sell Oak, Birmingham B29 6LB
General Manager: Sheila Sharman. Executive staff 4, Othe staff 10. ***CC*** No.211542. Began 1882; non-denominationa Turnover £300,000 to year end Feb 92. Publishing seve different Bible reading notes, 135,000 annually, distributed i approximately 90 countries.
Web: www.ncec.org.uk
Email: ncec@ncec.org.uk
☎ 0121 472 4242 🖷 0121 472 7575

gos Ministries, 147 Albertbridge Road, Belfast BT5 4PS
Director: Rev Thomas McClean. Executive staff 2, Other staff 8. *CC* No.NI 46135. Began 1977; interdenominational. (Previously Youth Evangelical Missionary Fellowship). Magazine: *Edge* (1,500 quarterly). Turnover £98,000 to year end Dec 98. Bible teaching worldwide; training Christians around the world to be leaders in tomorrow's church.
Web: www.charis.co.uk/logos.ministries
Email: logos.ministries@charis.co.uk
☎ 028 9045 8362 Fax 028 9045 8362

he Open Bible Trust, Bethany, Tresta, Shetland ZE2 9LT
Administrator: Mr Duncan McGregor. Executive staff 1. *CC* No.326717. Began 1984; non-denominational. Magazine: *Search* (600 every two months). Turnover £21,000 to year end Aug 98. Aiding understanding of Scripture by publishing Bible study resources, commentaries, tapes and computer disks.
Email: openbible.trust@zetnet.co.uk
☎ 01595 810 434 Fax 01595 810 434

erek Prince Ministries – UK, PO Box 77, Harpenden AL5 1PJ
Director: Mr Mark Buchanan. Executive staff 3, Other staff 10. *CC* No.327763. Began 1983; interdenominational. Magazine: *Newsletter* (Circulation & frequency n/a). Turnover £726,000 to year end Mar 98. International producer/distributor of Biblical foundational teaching resources (books, audios, videos, broadcasting). Correspondence course.
Web: www.derekprince.com
Email: enquiries@uk.derekprince.com
☎ 01582 466 200 Fax 01582 766 777

rophetic Word Ministries Trust, The Park, Moggerhanger, Bedford MK44 3RW
Director: Rev Dr Clifford Hill. Executive staff 3, Other staff 5. *CC* No.326533. Began 1984; interdenominational. Magazine: *Prophecy Today* (10,700 every two months). Turnover £200,600 to year end Dec 98. Biblically-based teaching/publishing ministry; Hebraic Study Centre offering sabbaticals, courses, distance learning; residential conference facilities.
Email: pwm@the-park.u-net.com
☎ 01767 641 400 Fax 01767 641 515

Purley & Andover Christian Trust, 4 Humberstone Road, Andover SP10 2EJ
Director: Rev Frank Cooke. Executive staff 1. *CC* No.272729. Began 1977; interdenominational. Magazine: *Newsletter* (450 quarterly). Turnover £14,000 to year end Aug 96. Making the Bible plain by all and every means possible, at home and abroad.
Web: freespace.virgin.net/frank.cooke.pact
Email: frank.cooke.pact@virgin.net
☎ 01264 352 587

Radio Bible Class (Europe) Trust, PO Box 1, Carnforth LA5 9ES
European Director: Mr Billy Strachan. Executive staff 1, Other staff 7. *CC* No.327384. Began 1964; interdenominational. Magazine: *Our Daily Bread* (50,000 quarterly). Turnover n/a. Distributing free Biblical study resources, booklets, video library, audio tapes.
Email: 100723.1177@compuserve.com
☎ 01524 733 166

Small Group Resources, 1 Hilton Place, Harehills, Leeds LS8 4HE
Partners: Mr Chris Powell, Mr Pete Richardson. No full-time staff. Began 1985; interdenominational. No magazine. Turnover n/a. Writing and publishing materials and training leaders for small group learning, growth and Bible exploration.
Email: sgr@sparkmail.force9.co.uk
☎ 0113 237 4974 Fax 0113 237 4964

***The WORDplus**, Fishergate Christian Centre, Fishergate, Norwich NR3 1SE
Lead Elder: Goff Hope. Staff n/a. *CC* No.801693. Began 1995; interdenominational. No magazine. Turnover n/a. A modular training scheme covering basic systematic theology, designed for use in churches and regions.
Email: wordplus@btinternet.com
☎ 01603 765 795 Fax 01603 761 222

Walk Thru the Bible Ministries, Tendring Road, Thorpe-le-Soken, Clacton-on-Sea CO16 0AA
Director: Cliff Keeys. Executive staff 1, Other staff 7. *CC* No.299722. Began 1984; interdenominational. Magazine: *Newsletter* (Circulation n/a quarterly). Turnover £100,000 to year end June 98. Refreshing approach to the Bible for all ages enabling understanding of the storyline and geography.
Web: www.bible.org.uk
Email: walkthru@bible.org.uk
☎ 01255 861 868 Fax 01255 861 869

***Word of Life**, PO Box 14, Oldham OL1 3WW
Extension Secretary: Mr Kenneth Stocks. Executive staff 1. *CC* No.328492. Began 1988; interdenominational. Magazine: *Najat* (500 quarterly). Turnover £19,108 to year end Dec 98. Publishing and distributing Bible courses and materials to evangelise Muslims, particularly in the UK.
Web: www.domini.org
Email: word_of_life@domini.org
☎ 0161 628 4051 Fax 0161 628 4051

***The Word Worldwide (a WEC International Ministry)**, National Headquarters, 74 Fford Aneurin, Pontyberem, Llanelli SA15 5DE
Ministry Leaders: Mr Kip & Mrs Doreen Wear. Executive staff 14. *CC* No.237005. Began 1913; interdenominational. (A department of WEC International). Magazine: *Worldwide* (Circulation 6,500 every two months). Turnover £12,000 to year end Mar 97. Producing evangelistic Bible study aids for individuals, neighbourhood and church groups and giving personal encouragement.
☎ 01269 870 842 Fax 01269 861 699

CONVENTIONS, BIBLE WEEKS, EXHIBITIONS & FESTIVALS

T

Alpha Conferences, Holy Trinity Church, Brompton Road, London SW7 1JA
Alpha/Events Director: Miss Tricia Neill. Executive staff 3. *CC* Began 1992; Anglican. (Previously Focus Holiday Week). No magazine. Turnover n/a. Two day training conferences for church leaders and their teams.
Email: alpha@htb.org.uk
☎ 020 7581 8255 Fax 020 7584 8536

The Apostolic Church International Convention, 24 St Helen's Road, Swansea SA1 1ZH
Administrative Secretary: Mr Andrew Saunders. Staff n/a. *CC* No.284789. Began n/a; Apostolic Church. No magazine. Turnover £40,000 to year end Aug 98. Annual convention held in Penygroes, Carmarthenshire in August for the deepening of spiritual life.
Web: www.apostolic-church.org
Email: admin@apostolic-church.org
☎ 01792 473 992

***Bournemouth & Poole Bible Convention**, c/o Ropewind, Snails Lane, Ringwood BH24 3PG
Secretary: Mr John Trapnell. No paid staff. Began 1950; interdenominational. No magazine. Turnover £1,300 to year end Dec 98. Annual Bible Convention, four nights in June.
☎ 01425 478 899

Carey Conference, 22 Leith Road, Darlington DL3 8BG
Organising Secretary: Mr John Rubens. No full-time staff. Began 1970; non-denominational. No magazine. Turnover n/a. Annual national conferences for Reformed Baptist ministers and their families.
Email: rubens.ep@btinternet.com
☎ 01325 353 634

Catholic People's Week, 89 Marlborough Park Avenue, Sidcup DA15 9DY
Hon Secretary: Mr Ted Monks. No full-time staff. ***CC*** No.241556. Began 1945; Roman Catholic. Magazine: *Newsletter* (700 every four months). Turnover n/a. Organising holiday family study weeks in all parts of the country.
☎ 020 8300 4432

***Celebration Camp**, PO Box 130, Walton-on-Thames KT12 2RU
International Director: Dr Peter J Gammons. *Administrator:* Mrs Dorothy Wigley. Executive staff 6, Other staff 32. ***CC*** No.298954. Began 1990; interdenominational. Part of Reach Out Ministries. Magazine: *Breakthrough!* (10,000 every two months). Turnover £120,000 to year end Apr 97. Annual summer camp and convention.
Email: info@petergammons.org
☎ 01932 225 549 Fax 01487 710 311

***Christian Resources Exhibitions Ltd**, 2 Forge House, Summerleys Road, Princes Risborough HP27 9DT
Chairman: Mr Gospatric Home. *Marketing Director:* Joy Bussell. *Exhibition Organiser:* Mr Tony Kerwood. Executive staff 15. Began 1985; interdenominational. Magazine: *Exhibition Handbooks* (10,000 half-yearly). Turnover £730,000 to year end May 99. Exhibitions of caring, educational, practical resources for churches and Christians in Esher, Manchester, Birmingham and Glasgow.
Web: www.resourcex.co.uk
Email: cre@resourcex.co.uk
☎ 01844 342 894 Fax 01844 344 988

†**Creative Worship**, Woodspring Church, 109 High Street, Worle, Weston-super-Mare BS22 0HA
UK National Co-ordinator: Mr David Taylor. No full-time staff. Began 1994; interdenominational. (Previously Worship Symposium). No magazine. Turnover n/a. Annual weekend of practical Arts in the Church teaching and creative worship.
☎ 01934 522 772

Days of Destiny, 18 Winchester Street, Basingstoke RG21 7DY
Event Co-ordinator: Mr Michael Poulton. Administrative staff 1. ***CC*** No.3603373. Began n/a; non-denominational. Turnover n/a. Annual Bible week in Harrogate, Yorkshire to refresh and equip Christians of all ages.
Web: www.saltandlight.u-net.com/destiny
Email: destiny@saltandlight.u-net.com
☎ 01256 461 430 Fax 01256 810 791

***Good News Crusade**, 17 High Cross Street, St Austell PL25 4AN
Director: Rev Don Double. *Conference Secretary:* Mrs Anne Double. ***CC*** No.225483. Began 1960; interdenominational. Magazine: *Frontline Connections* (10,000 quarterly), *Frontline News* (2,500 quarterly). Turnover: see Good News Crusade. Family camp, teaching the importance of the Christian family.
Web: www.gnc.org.uk
Email: info@gnc.org.uk
☎ 01726 722 82 Fax 01726 698 53

***Grapevine**, 257 Freeman Street, Grimsby DN32 9DW
Director: Mr Dave Kitchen. Executive staff 1, Admin staff ***CC*** No.1001599. Began 1982; interdenominational. Part Ground Level. No magazine. Turnover £180,000 to year e Dec 98. Family celebration camp, August Bank Holiday wee end, offering worship, teaching, ministry for all ages.
Web: www.groundlevel.org.uk
Email: grapevine@groundlevel.org.uk
☎ 01472 313 388 / 240 871 Mobile: 07768 757 406
Fax 01472 346 186

Greenbelt Festivals, The Greenhouse, St Luke's Churc Hillmarton Road, London N7 9JE
Festival Manager: Mr Andy Thornton. Executive staff 2, Oth staff 4. ***CC*** No.289372. Began 1974; non-denominational. N magazine. Turnover £644,000 to year end Sept 92. Annu Christian arts festival held in the last weekend in July; assoc ated events throughout the year.
Web: www.greenbelt.org.uk
☎ 020 7700 6585 Fax 020 7700 5765

***Hearts on Fire**, Christian Arts Promotions Ltd, Thornfield Hous 58 Hill Head Close, Glastonbury BA6 8AL
Chairman: Mr Richard Hillard. No paid staff. ***C*** No.1057199. Began 1993; interdenominational. No maga zine. Turnover £25,000 to year end Dec 98. Promotion of th Gospel through Christian artists, worship leaders and the arts.
Web: home.clara.net/bethany/cap.html
Email: cap@bethany.clara.net & hof@bethany.clara.net
☎ 01454 319 447 Fax 01454 319 447

***Hollybush Christian Fellowship and Convention Centre**, Hollybus Farm, Newsham, Thirsk YO7 4DH
Administrator: Mrs June Brown. Other staff 1. Began 1968 interdenominational. (Previously Hollybush Bible Week) Magazine: *Newsletter* (Circulation n/a monthly). Turnove £100 to year end Apr 98. Providing refreshment and teaching for Christians. Resourcing the Church through outreach and mission; hire of facilities.
Email: junehollyb@aol.com
☎ 01845 587 386 Fax 01845 587 103

***The Keswick Convention**, Keswick Convention Centre, Skiddaw Street, Keswick CA12 4BY
Chairman: Mr Jonathan Lamb. *Convention Secretary:* Mr Mark Smith. Admin staff 6, Other staff 1. ***CC*** No.225557. Began 1875; interdenominational. Magazine: *Newsletter* (6,000 half-yearly). Turnover £306,000 to year end Aug 97. Bible convention with emphasis on practical, biblical holiness; 2 weeks at end of July.
Web: www.sovereign.uk.com/keswick
Email: kesconv@aol.com
☎ 01768 772 589 Fax 01768 775 276

Keswick-in-Wales Convention, Carneddau, Highbury Field, Llanyre, Llandrindod Wells LD1 6NF
Hon Secretary: Mr John W Mitson. No full-time staff. Began 1903; interdenominational. No magazine. Turnover £5,300 to year end Oct 97. Week in Llandrindod Wells (includes first Monday in August), for deepening spiritual life.
☎ 01597 822 700

Kingdom Faith Bible Week, Roffey Place Christian Training Centre, Faygate, Horsham RH12 4SA
Director: Rev Colin Urquhart. Staff n/a. ***CC*** Began 1978; non-denominational. Magazine: *Impact* (Circulation n/a quarterly). Turnover n/a. Proclaiming the Gospel, renewal and revival; held at the East of England Showground, Peterborough.
Web: www.kingdomfaith.com
Email: info@kingdomfaith.com
☎ 01293 851 543 Fax 01293 851 330

T

Living Water, The Old Barn, Watton Road, Ashill, Thetford IP25 7AQ
Trust Administrator: Rev Stephen Mawditt. Executive staff 1. ***CC*** No.1037997. Began 1994; interdenominational. No magazine. Turnover £100,000 to year end Jun 96. Annual event May Day Bank Holiday; events, conferences to encourage renewal in churches, Christian life.
Web: www.btinternet.com/~living.water
Email: living.water@btinternet.com
☎ 01760 441 441

Movement for World Evangelization, Victoria House, Victoria Road, Buckhurst Hill IG9 5EX
Honorary Secretary: Miss Jean Wilson. No full-time staff. ***CC*** No.230959. Began 1931; interdenominational. Turnover n/a. Annual residential conference, Autumn Praise.
☎ 020 8559 1180 Fax 020 8502 9062

New Horizon, 12 Killyvally Road, Garvagh BT51 5JZ
Chairman: Mr Derek Hunter. Admin staff 1. ***CC*** Began n/a; interdenominational. No magazine. Turnover £75,000 to year end Dec 98. Week of Christian teaching, worship and fellowship for all ages.
Web: www.newhorizon.org.uk
Email: office@newhorizon.org.uk
☎ 028 2555 7157 Fax 028 2557 7157

New Wine, 4a Ridley Road, Ealing, London W13 9XW
Leaders: Rt Rev David Pytches, Rev John Cole. *Networks Overseer:* Rev Bruce Collins. Other staff 6. ***CC*** No.1043763. Began 1989; interdenominational. No magazine. Turnover £750,000 to year end Dec 98. National and regional family and church leaders gatherings, training retreats, network publishing magazine.
Web: www.new-wine.org
Email: info@new-wine.org
☎ 020 8567 6717
Also at: Unit 2, Paramount Industrial Estate, Sandown Road, Watford WD2 4XA
☎ 01923 333 331

North London Bible Convention, Christ Church Vicarage, Chalk Lane, Cockfosters, Barnet EN4 9JQ
Chairman: Rev Anthony Rees. No full-time staff. Began 1955; interdenominational. No magazine. Turnover n/a. Annual Christian convention for the deepening of spiritual life, last week in June.
☎ 020 8441 1230

***Peniel Pentecostal Church Conferences**, 49 Coxtie Green Road, Pilgrims Hatch, Brentwood CM14 5PS
Principal: Rev Dr Michael S B Reid. Executive staff 5, Administrative staff 10. Began 1977; Pentecostal. Magazine: *Trumpet Call Newspaper* (120,000 frequency n/a). Turnover n/a. Conferences held over Easter and August Bank Holidays, accommodation provided.
Web: www.peniel.org
Email: msbr@peniel.org
☎ 01277 372 996 Fax 01277 375 046

†Restoration Bible Week, Covenant Ministries, Nettle Hill, Brinklow Road, Ansty, Coventry CV7 9JL
Administrator: Mr Ron Tempest. Executive staff 1, Other staff 1. Began 1983; Covenant Ministries. No magazine. Turnover n/a. Conference to experience God's presence and power and to hear His Word.
☎ 024 7660 2777 Fax 024 7660 2992

Martin Rowley Associates, 8 Duke Street, Princes Risborough HP27 0AT
Principal Associate: Rev Martin Rowley. Executive staff 1, Other staff 2. Began 1997; interdenominational. Magazine: *Exhibition handbook* (5,000 annually). Turnover n/a. Exhibition, Conference and Display consultants.
Email: mrowley@elim.org.uk
☎ 01844 275 888 Fax 01844 275 822

Soul Survivor, Unit 2, Paramount Industrial Estate, Sandown Road, Watford WD2 4XA
Director: Mr Mike Pilavachi. *Co-Director:* Ms Liz Biddulph. Executive staff 2, Other staff 13. ***CC*** No.1043763. Began 1993; interdenominational. Magazine: *Soul Survivor* (4,000 every two months). Turnover £700,000 to year end Dec 98. Youth festivals – attendance 16,500, conferences, roadshows, youth leaders support programme, residential discipleship training courses, schools work.
Web: www.soulsurvivor.com
Email: info@soulsurvivor.com
☎ 01923 333 331 Fax 01923 333 334

***Southport Methodist Holiness Convention**, 2 Crown Drive, Inverness IV2 3NL
Trustees' Secretary: Rev John M Haley. No full time staff. ***CC*** Began 1885; Methodist and interdenominational. No magazine. Turnover n/a. Annual Summer Fire celebration week, Southport, early August; teaching scriptural holiness.
Web: dunnwilson.future.easyspace.com
Email: johnmhaley@aol.com
☎ 01463 231 170

T

***Spring Harvest**, 14 Horsted Square, Uckfield TN22 1QL
Executive Director: Mr Alan D Johnson. Executive staff 5, Other staff 27. ***CC*** No.1014540. Began 1979; interdenominational. No magazine. Turnover n/a. Annual event including teaching, worship, relaxation, equipping family and Church to serve the nation.
Web: www.springh.org
Email: info@springh.org
☎ 01825 769 111 🖷 01825 769 141

Stoneleigh Bible Week, 17 Clarendon Villas, Hove BN3 3RE
Administrator: Mr Nigel Ring. Other staff 5. ***CC*** Began n/a. New Frontiers. No magazine. Turnover n/a. Providing worship, fellowship and teaching to encourage the growth of individuals and churches.
Web: www.n-f-i.org
☎ 01273 234 555 🖷 01273 234 556

***Swanwick Ladies' Conference**, 289 Lordswood Road, Birmingham B17 8PR
Hostess: Mrs Pat Wearn. No full-time staff. Began 1967; interdenominational. No magazine. Turnover £17,000 to year end Dec 97. Annual conference second weekend September; practical Bible teaching with nationally-known speakers.
☎ 0121 429 3273

***Worldwide Missionary Convention**, 15 Ranfurly Avenue, Bangor BT20 3SN
Hon Secretary: Mr Raymond J Pitt. No full-time staff. Began 1937; non-denominational. No magazine. Turnover £140,000 to year end Dec 98. Annual convention held in Bangor during last week in August.
☎ 028 9146 0868

EDUCATIONAL AGENCIES

***Amethyst Centre for Alcohol Concern**, 57 London Street, Reading RG1 4PS
Director: Mr Kevin Woods. Executive staff 1, Other staff 2. ***CC*** No.235564. Began 1832; interdenominational. Magazine: *Contact* (2,000 every four months). Turnover £90,000 to year end Dec 98. Offering alcohol and drug education through speakers, literature distribution, multi-media presentations. Alcohol free drinks.
Email: kevinwoods@amethyst.unet
☎ 0118 958 9400 🖷 0118 958 9400

Anglican Group Educational Trust, Liturgical Office, The Chapter House, St Paul's Churchyard, London EC4M 8AD
Hon Secretary: Rev Lucy Winkett. No full-time staff. ***CC*** No.265221. Began 1973; Anglican. No magazine. Turnover £9,199 to year end Dec 97. Assisting Anglican women clergy engaged in theological study overseas (Roxburgh Scholarship) only.
☎ 020 7246 8323 🖷 020 7246 8336

The Archbishops Examination in Theology (Lambeth Diploma), 3 The College, Durham DH1 3EQ
Hon Secretary: Canon Martin Kitchen. No full-time staff. Began 1906; Anglican, but open to all. No magazine. Turnover n/a. Providing opportunity for theological study by examination syllabus or thesis (STh and MA).
☎ 0191 384 2415 🖷 0191 386 4267

Association of Centres of Adult Theological Education, The Old Deanery, Wells BA5 2UG
Hon Secretary: Ms Helen Stanton. No full-time staff. Began 1981; interdenominational. Magazine: *British Journal of Theological Education* (450 every four months). Turnover £9,500 to year end Dec 98. Linking centres of theological education, supporting working groups on issues, conferences and consultations, occasional publications.
☎ 01749 670 777 🖷 01749 674 240

Association of Laity Centres, Scottish Churches House, Kirk Street, Dunblane FK15 0AJ
Hon Secretary: Brian Baker. No full-time staff. Began 1965; non-denominational. Magazine: *Newsletter* (35 every four months). Turnover £700 to year end Mar 98. Ecumenical association of centres for Christian education, renewal and social concern.
Email: schse@dial.pipex.com
☎ 01786 823 588 🖷 01786 825 844

***Beehive School & Nursery**, PO Box 1908, London N4 3PY
Principle: n/a. Staff 15. ***CC*** No.1023328. Began 1991; affiliated to Rainbow Foundation. No magazine. Turnover £65,000 to year end Dec 98. For children aged 5 to 16, nursery for children aged 2½ to 5 years.
Web: easyweb.easynet.co.uk/rain
Email: rain@easynet.co.uk
☎ 020 8885 5488 🖷 020 8885 5007

Bible Scene Multimedia, 26 Home Close, Sharnbrook, Bedford MK44 1PQ
Trustee: Mr Maurice S Thompson. Executive staff 3, Other staff 1. ***CC*** No.327400. Began 1985; interdenominational. (Previously Bible Scene Slide Tours). Magazine: *Update* (150 half-yearly). Turnover n/a. Bible teaching aids. Presentations in schools, prisons, churches; mobile and classroom exhibition; interactive CD-Roms/slides.
Email: howard.roberts@btinternet.com
☎ 01234 781 946 🖷 01234 782 623

Bibles for Children, 11 Southlands Drive, Timsbury, Bath BA3 1HB
Founder: Mr Ted Hudson. No paid staff. ***CC*** No.1063200. Began 1997; interdenominational. No magazine. Turnover £351,000 to year end Dec 98. Providing Bibles and Bible related materials to Primary School children and their schools.
☎ 01761 471 169

Board of Education (Church of England), Church House, Great Smith Street, London SW1P 3NZ
General Secretary: Rev Canon John Hall. *PA to General Secretary:* Mrs Liz Carter. Executive staff 10, Other staff 9. Began 1970; Anglican. Magazine: *Newsboard* (400 ten times a year). Turnover n/a. Advising dioceses and the General Synod; taking action in the field of education.
Email: john.hall@c-of-e.org.uk
☎ 020 7898 1500 🖷 020 7898 1520

Bridgebuilders International Charitable Trust, 30 Farley Copse, Binfield, Bracknell RG42 1PF
Director: Mr Richard Emery. No other staff. ***CC*** No.1043086. Began 1995; interdenominational. No magazine. Turnover n/a. Teaching and encouraging the application of Biblical principals in work and business throughout developing nations.
Email: 100525.3553@compuserve.com
☎ 01344 484 235 🖷 01344 484 219

T

British and Irish Association for Mission Studies, Henry Martyn Centre, Westminster College, Cambridge CB3 0AA
Secretary: Ms Kirsteen Kim. No full-time staff. Began 1990; interdenominational. Magazine: *Newsletter* (200 half-yearly). Turnover n/a. Promoting study of the history, theology and practice of Christian mission.
Email: kjk25@cam.ac.uk
☎ 01223 741 088 🖷 01223 741 052

British Israel Bible Truth Fellowship, Manor Barn, Horsington, Templecombe BA8 0ET
General Secretary: Mr Paul Boyd-Lee. Staff n/a. *CC* No.272447. Began 1974; interdenominational. Magazine: *Bible Truth* (1,000 every two months). Turnover £10,000 to year end Dec 96. Advancing Christian religion by proclaiming Anglo-Saxon Celtic people descend from Biblical Israel and Judah.
Email: paul.a0017516@infotrade.co.uk
☎ 01963 371 137

The British Israel World Federation, 8 Blades Court, Deodar Road, London SW15 2NU
Secretary: Mr Alan E Gibb. Executive staff 2. *CC* No.208079. Began 1919; non-denominational. Magazine: *B.I.W.F* (Circulation n/a quarterly). Turnover £130,000 to year end Mar 98. Studying the Biblical prophecies concerning the descendants of the House of Israel.
Web: www.britishisrael.co.uk
Email: janice1@easynet.co.uk
☎ 020 8877 9010 🖷 020 8871 4770

Cardiff Adult Christian Education Centre, City Church, Windsor Place, Cardiff CF1 3BZ
Administrator: Mr Norman Preston. No full-time staff. *CC* No.1019934. Began 1961; interdenominational. Magazine: *Programme of Courses* (6,000 annually). Turnover £10,000 to year end Dec 98. Ecumenical study centre for adults.
☎ 029 2022 5190 🖷 029 2022 5190

***CARE (Christian Action Research and Education)**, 53 Romney Street, London SW1P 3RF
Executive Chairman: Rev Lyndon Bowring. *Executive Director:* Mr Charlie Colchester. Executive staff 4, Other staff 40. *CC* Began 1983; interdenominational. Magazine: *CARE Prayer Guide* (50,000 quarterly), *CARE Magazine* (50,000 half-yearly). Turnover £1,725,000 to year end Dec 97. Equipping individual Christians and local churches to care and campaign; representing Christians through parliamentary lobbying.
Web: www.care.org.uk
Email: enquiries@care.org.uk
☎ 020 7233 0455 🖷 020 7233 0983
Also Offices in, Belfast, Cardiff, Glasgow, Brussels

Roman Catholic Bishops' Conference Department for Catholic Education & Formation, 39 Eccleston Square, London SW1V 1BX
Chairman: Rt Rev Vincent Nichols. Other staff 2. *CC* No.313147. Began 1984; Roman Catholic. No magazine. Turnover n/a. Concerned with theology, Christian and ministerial formation, young people and education.
☎ 020 7630 5101 🖷 020 7630 5166

Catholic Education Service, 39 Eccleston Square, Lond SW1V 1BX
Director: Mrs Margaret Smart OBE. Executive staff 4, Oth staff 5. *CC* No.313147. Began 1905; Roman Catholic. N magazine. Turnover £500,000. Promoting and representi Catholic education in England and Wales.
Email: cesew.demon.co.uk
☎ 020 7828 7604 🖷 020 7233 9802

Catholic Missionary Education Centre, Holcombe House, Th Ridgeway, London NW7 4HY
General Secretary: Rev Joe Brankin. Executive staff 2. *C* No.257239. Began 1973; Roman Catholic. No magazin Turnover n/a. Information and resource centre on oversea Catholic missionary activity for purposes of mission educatio at home.
Email: camec@compuserve.com
☎ 0121 329 2058 Mobile: 07808 078 714
🖷 0121 378 4761

†**Centre for Adult Religious Education (CARE)**, St Mary's University College, Strawberry Hill, Twickenham TW1 4SX
Director: Dr Tony McCaffry. No full-time staff. Began 1983 non-denominational. No magazine. Turnover £10,000 to yea end Aug 96. Training, research and development in adult religious education.
☎ 020 8240 4196 🖷 020 8240 4255

†**The CHREST Foundation**, 45 Barnhorn Road, Little Common, Bexhill-on-Sea TN39 4QB
Director: Mr Walter de M Seaman. Executive staff 1. *CC* No.269114. Began 1970; non-denominational. No magazine. Turnover n/a. Promoting the historical and fundamental tenets of the Christian Faith through videos and tours.
☎ 01424 844 241

†**Christian Council for the Schools of Wales**, Calon Y Dderwen, 27 Queen Street, Pontrhydyfen, Port Talbot SA12 9TF
Schools Worker: Mr Alan Rees. Executive staff 1. *CC* Began 1981; non-denominational. Magazine: *Wales News* (300 termly). Turnover £17,000 to year end Mar 92. Supporting, co-ordinating and furthering Christian work in schools of Wales; helping Christian Unions, teachers.
☎ 01639 897 637

***Christian Education Europe**, PO Box 770, Highworth, Swindon SN6 7TU
Executive Director: Mr Arthur Roderick. Executive staff 3, Other staff 4. Began 1990; interdenominational. (Associated with The School of Tomorrow). Magazine: *Accelerator* (1,000 n/a). Turnover n/a. Starting, supporting and supplying Christian schools and home education with Bible-based curriculum and creationist literature.
Web: www.christian-education.org
Email: christianeducationeurope@compuserve.com
☎ 01793 783 783 🖷 01793 783 783

Christian Education Movement, Royal Buildings, Victoria Street, Derby DE1 1GW
General Secretary: Rev Dr Stephen Orchard. *Director of Publications:* Rev Colin Johnson. *Director of Professional Services:* Mrs Pamela Draycott. Executive staff 9, Other staff 9. *CC* No.241509. Began 1965; ecumenical. Magazine: *RE Today* (11,500 every four months), *British Journal of Religious Education* (2,500 every four months). Turnover £773,000 to year end May 98. Developing and improving Religious Education in schools and encouraging Christian reflection about education.
Email: cem@cem.org.uk
☎ 01332 296 655 🖷 01332 432 53

ıristian Educator Network, 45 Trafalgar Road, Moseley, Birmingham B13 8BJ
Director: Mr David Isgrove. No other staff. Began 1999; ecumenical. No magazine. Turnover n/a. Enabling Christian training organisations to gain secular accreditation and further education links; consultancy and networking.
Email: david@isgroves.freeserve.co.uk
☎ 0121 449 3156 🖷 0121 449 3156

hristian Friends of Israel UK, PO Box 2687, Eastbourne BN22 7LZ
Director: Mr Derek White. Executive staff 1, Other staff 4. ***CC*** No.1051316. Began 1985; interdenominational. Magazine: *Newsletter* (3,500 every two months), *Prayer letter* (3,000 monthly). Turnover £235,000 to year end Dec 98. Educating Christians about Israel's situation; encouraging prayer; teaching about the Jewish roots of the Christian faith.
Email: info@cfi.org.uk
☎ 01323 410 810 🖷 01323 410 211

Christian Meditation Centre, 29 Campden Hill Road, London W8 7DX
Director: Sister Eileen Byrne. All voluntary staff. ***CC*** Began 1986; interdenominational. Magazine: *Newsletter* (2,000 quarterly). Turnover n/a. Teaching the tradition of Christian meditation.
☎ 020 7912 1371

Christian Rural Concern, 36 The Windings, Sanderstead, South Croydon CR2 0HU
Course Director: Rev John Whitehead. No full-time staff. ***CC*** No.328204. Began 1989; interdenominational. Magazine: *Newsletter* (200 annually). Turnover £2,500 to year end June 98. Correspondence courses and local groups addressing rural church and environmental issues from a Christian standpoint.
☎ 020 8657 0831

The Christian Schools' Trust, Havering Grange Centre, Havering Road, Romford RM1 4HR
Chair: Mrs Hilary Reeves. Other staff 1. ***CC*** No.293315. Began 1989; non-denominational. Magazine: *Christian Schools Newsletter* (500 every four months). Turnover £18,000 to year end Dec 95. Supporting, encouraging and strengthening independent Christian schools in the UK; developing and promoting Christian education.
Email: cst@netcomuk.co.uk
☎ 01708 733 339 🖷 01708 733 339

Christians Aware, 124 New Walk, Leicester LE1 7JA
Executive Secretary: Mrs Barbara Butler. Executive staff 1. ***CC*** No.2417029. Began 1977; ecumenical. Magazine: *Ecumenical Magazine* (1,200 quarterly). Turnover £101,516 to year end Sept 98. Developing international multi-cultural understanding, friendship and encounter.
Web: www.christiansaware.co.uk
Email: bjb@overtown.free-online.co.uk
☎ 0116 254 0770 🖷 0116 254 0770

Christians in Britain, Grampian House, 144 Deansgate, Manchester M3 3ED
Senior UK Executive: Mr John F Macdonald. Executive staff 1. ***CC*** Began 1986; interdenominational. Magazine: *Christian World* (3,000 monthly). Turnover n/a. Organising national campaign to restore Christian belief, culture and education in society.
☎ 0161 835 2000 🖷 0161 835 3000

Church of Scotland Board of Parish Education, Annie Small House, 18 Inverleith Terrace, Edinburgh EH3 5NS
General Secretary: Mr Iain W White. Executive staff 1, Other staff 15. Began 1993; Church of Scotland. No magazine. Turnover £600,000 to year end Dec 92. Providing Christian education resources; production and training at national presbytery and congregation levels.
☎ 0131 332 0343 🖷 0131 315 2161

Church of Scotland Department of Education, 121 George Street, Edinburgh EH2 4YN
General Secretary: Rev John Stevenson. Executive staff 1, Admin staff 1. ***CC*** No.SCO 11353. Began 1827; Church of Scotland. Magazine: *School Chaplaincy Bulletin* (6,500 every two years). Turnover £67,098 to year end Dec 98. Church response to government legislation affecting state education; training school chaplains; religious education in schools.
Web: www.cofs.org.uk
Email: amullen@cofs.org.uk
☎ 0131 225 5722 🖷 0131 220 3113

Clinical Theology Association, Queen's College, Somerset Road, Edgbaston, Birmingham B15 2QH
Executive Director: Rev Alister Ross. Executive staff 2, Other staff 3. ***CC*** No.296816. Began 1962; ecumenical. Magazine: *Lingdale Papers* (750 half-yearly), *Contact: Interdisciplinary Journal of Pastoral Studies* (3,000 every four months). Turnover £80,000 to year end Dec 98. Training in Christian pastoral care and pastoral counselling.
☎ 0121 454 1527 🖷 0121 454 8171

College of Preachers, 10a North Street, Bourne PE10 9AB
Director: Rev Dr Stephen I Wright. *Administrator:* Mrs Karen Atkin. Other staff 2. ***CC*** No.220764. Began 1960; ecumenical. Magazine: *The Journal* (2,000 half-yearly). Turnover £98,059 to year end Dec 97. Organising training courses to help, encourage and stimulate those engaged in the ministry of preaching.
Web: www3.mistral.co.uk/collpreach
Email: collpreach@mistral.co.uk
☎ 01778 422 929 🖷 01778 422 929

The Concordant Bible Society of Great Britain, 7 Fern Lawn, Abbeydale, Gloucester GL4 5XS
Hon Secretary: Mr David Osgood. No full-time staff. ***CC*** No.281860. Began 1975; interdenominational. No magazine. Turnover £5,300 to year end Nov 98. Restoring the original meaning of the Divine Word by the concordant method of translation.
☎ 01452 421 224

†**The Council for Sunday Schools and Christian Education in Wales**, Awelon, Morfa Nefyn, Pwllheli LL53 6BL
Secretary: Mrs Helen Oswy Roberts. Executive staff 2, Other staff 1. ***CC*** Began 1965; interdenominational. No magazine. Turnover n/a. Establishing and supporting Sunday Schools; producing syllabus and resources; publishing co-editions in the Welsh language.
☎ 01286 672 593

Croydon Religious Education Resource Centre, The Crescent, Croydon CR0 2HN
Resources Officer: Lyn Stone. Executive staff 1. ***CC*** No.1038238. Began 1980; ecumenical. Magazine: *CRERC News* (Circulation n/a every four months). Turnover n/a. LEA/religious community partnership servicing the RE needs of churches and schools locally.
☎ 020 8689 5343

Ecumenical Olympus Network (EON), The Vicarage, Epping Green, Epping CM16 6PN
Company Secretary: Rev Chris Bard. All voluntary staff. ***CC*** No.803448. Began 1989; ecumenical. No magazine. Turnover n/a. Advancing ecumenical education through the use of communications satellites and advanced communications technology.
☎ 01992 572 949 🖷 01992 578 892

T

Ecumenical Order of Ministry, Barnes Close, Malthouse Lane, Chadwich, Bromsgrove B61 0RA
Company Secretary: Rev John Johansen-Berg. Executive staff 2, Other staff 4. ***CC*** No.295111. Began 1990; ecumenical. Administered by Community for Reconciliation. Magazine: *Newslink* (450 quarterly). Turnover n/a. Mutual recognition of ministry; fellowship, united service and witness in Christ's name, shared proclamation of faith, symbol of unity.
Web: ourworld.compuserve.com/homepages/communityforreconciliation
Email: johnjoberg@aol.com
☎ 01562 710 231 📠 01562 710 278

The European Academy for Christian Homeschooling, PO Box 770, Highworth, Swindon SN6 7TU
Principal: Mr Arthur Roderick. *Pastoral Director:* Mr Neville Downs. Executive staff 2, Other staff 1. Began 1996; non-denominational. (Previously National Christian College for Home Education). Associated with Maranatha Foundation. Magazine: *TEACH* (1,000 frequency n/a). Turnover £100,000 to year end Dec 98. Supporting home education families in the UK and missionary families abroad.
Web: www.christian-education.org
☎ 01793 783 775 📠 01793 783 775

*Evangelical Coalition on Educational Issues, Whitefield House, 186 Kennington Park Road, London SE11 4BT
Chairman: Mr John Hallett. No full-time staff. ***CC*** Began 1987; interdenominational. An Evangelical Alliance Partnership for Change. No magazine. Turnover: finance included in Evangelical Alliance. Meeting of organisations concerned with education: cooperation, information exchange, joint action.
Web: www.eauk.org
Email: members@eauk.org
☎ 020 7207 2100 📠 020 7207 2150

***Growing Families International**, PO Box 770, Highworth, Swindon SN6 7TU
Director: Mr Arthur Roderick. Executive staff 2, Admin staff 2. Began 1997; interdenominational. Supported by Maranatha Foundation. No magazine. Turnover n/a. Distributing books, audio and video training courses on Biblical parenting; establishing local church groups interdenominationally.
Email: christianeducationeurope@compuserve.com
☎ 01793 783 455 📠 01793 783 783

Hockerill Educational Foundation, 16 Hagsdell Road, Hertford SG13 8AG
Secretary: Mr Colin Broomfield. Executive staff 1. ***CC*** No.2151348. Began 1977; Anglican. Magazine: *Hockerill Lecture* (2,000 annually). Turnover £215,353 to year end June 98. Awards to teachers or intending teachers especially of religious education in UK schools.
☎ 01992 303 053 📠 01992 303 053

Home Service, The Hawthorns, 48 Heaton Moor Road, Heaton Moor, Stockport SK4 4NX
Secretary: Mrs Ruth Slack. No full-time staff. Began 1992; non-denominational. Magazine: *Home Time* (350 every four months). Turnover £4,000 to year end Dec 98. National Centre for encouragement and support of Christian Home Education; conferences, contact list, advice, resources.
Web: www.alphainfo.co.uk/homeservice
☎ 0161 432 3782

The Institute for the Study of Christianity and Sexuality, Oxford House, Derbyshire Street, London E2 6HG
Secretary: Rev Richard Kirker. Executive staff 1. ***CC*** No.327822. Began 1989; interdenominational. No magazine. Turnover £2,000 to year end Dec 98. Promoting debate within the churches on human sexuality.
Email: lgcm@aol.com
☎ 020 7739 1249 📠 020 7739 1249

Institute of Christian Political Thought, PO Box 2, Taunt
TA1 4ZD
Director: Stephen C Perks. No full time staff. Began 199 non-denominational. No magazine. Turnover n/a. Think tar dedicated to developing and articulating a distinctively Chri tian political theory and ethics.
Web: www.kuyper.org
Email: icpt@kuyper.org
☎ 01823 665 909 📠 01823 665 721

International Ecumenical Fellowship, Dryfe View, Borelan Lockerbie DG11 2LH
Hon Secretary: Miss June Foster. All voluntary staff. ***C*** No.272271. Began 1967; interdenominational. Magazine: *IE Newsletter* (250 quarterly). Turnover £3,500 to year end De 98. International ecumenical encounters at the grassroot especially through eucharistic worship, fellowship, study an conferences.
☎ 01576 610 341

Jewish Education Bureau, 8 Westcombe Avenue, Leeds LS8 2B
Director: Rabbi Douglas S Charing. Other staff n/a. Bega 1974; non-denominational. No magazine. Turnover £30,00 to year end Mar 98. Teaching Judaism in religious educatio and to Christians, providing books, videos, posters, CD-Roms.
☎ 0870 7300 532 Mobile: 07971 867 512
📠 0113 293 3533

***Joshua Generation**, The Church, Worple Road, Wimbledon, London SW19 4SZ
Director: Mr Matt Bird. Executive staff 2, Admin staff 1. ***CC*** No.1059592. Began 1996; interdenominational. No magazine. Turnover £21,000 to year end Nov 98. Training and mentoring emerging generations of leaders in the workplace and church.
Web: www.users.globalnet.co.uk/~joshgen
Email: joshgen@globalnet.co.uk
☎ 020 8947 1313 📠 020 8947 9414

†Edward King Institute for Ministry Development, Church House, Churchyard, Hitchin SG5 1HP
Secretary: Mrs Vivien Tyler. No full-time staff. ***CC*** No.327223. Began 1985; interdenominational. Magazine: *Ministry Journal* (500 every four months). Turnover n/a. Providing a service for professional development in Christian churches of all denominations.
☎ 01406 330 392

***Maranatha Foundation**, PO Box 770, Highworth, Swindon SN6 7TU
Chairman: Mr Arthur Roderick. Executive staff 2, Other staff 1. ***CC*** No.1045685. Began 1996; interdenominational. Associated with The European Academy for Christian Homeschooling. Magazine: *Accelerator* (1,000 frequency n/a), *T.E.A.C.H.* (1,000 n/a). Turnover £200,000. Starting, supporting and advising Christian schools and parents educating their children at home.
Web: www.christian-education.org
Email: christianeducationeurope@compuserve.com
☎ 01793 783 783 📠 01793 783 783

***Henry Martyn Centre**, Henry Martyn Hall, Westminster College, Cambridge CB3 0AA
Henry Martyn Lecturer in Missiology: Rev Canon Graham Kings. Other staff 3. ***CC*** No.266612. Began 1995; ecumenical. Supported by the Henry Martyn Trust. No magazine. Turnover n/a. Promoting the academic study of mission and world Christianity.
Web: www.martynmission.cam.ac.uk
Email: grk1001@cam.ac.uk
☎ 01223 741 088/089 📠 01223 741 052

ational Christian Education Council (NCEC), 1020 Bristol Road, Sellyoak, Birmingham B29 6LB
Co-ordinator: Miss Elizabeth Bruce. No full-time staff. *CC* No.211542. Began 1973; ecumenical. Magazine: *Viewpoints* (Circulation n/a every four months). Turnover n/a. Network for all involved in adult religious education and training; incorporating Adult Network.
Web: www.ncec.org.uk
Email: ncec@ncec.org.uk
☎ 0121 472 4242 🖷 0121 472 4242

ational Family Trust, 101 Queen Victoria Street, London EC4P 4EP
Chairman: Mr Bill Halson. Staff n/a. *CC* No.297783. Began 1987; non-denominational. No magazine. Turnover £20,000 to year end Mar 92. Promoting the family by education and social policies which enrich marriage, child welfare, family relationships.
Email: jan.owen@btinternet.com
☎ 01242 251 583 🖷 01242 251 583

Network for the Study of Implicit Religion, 95 High Street, Winterbourne, Bristol BS36 1RD
Administrator: Mrs Diane Rix. No full-time staff. *CC* No.326876. Began 1978; non-denominational. No magazine. Turnover £5,000 to year end June 98. Stimulating study of overall individual and social commitments, in the light of study of religion.
Email: eibailey@csircs.freeserve.co.uk
☎ Office: 01454 776 518/01454 775 224

'The Oakbeams' Education Support Network, 15 Coulsdon Road, Coulsdon CR5 2LJ
Co-ordinator: Miss Patricia Dorbin. No other full-time, staff. Began 1990; non-denominational. (Previously Education Support Network). No magazine. Turnover £2,000 to year end Apr 94. Promoting physical, mental and spiritual health education of children, parents/carers, teachers and community members.
☎ 020 8763 0070 🖷 020 8763 0070

***Overseas Council for Theological Education & Mission**, 52 High Street, Thornbury, Bristol BS35 2AN
Executive Director: Mr Herbert L Cann. Staff 3. *CC* No.327569. Began 1986; non-denominational. Magazine: *The Newsletter* (2,500 half-yearly). Turnover n/a. Helping leadership training by scholarship support; library; campus development.
☎ 01454 281 288 🖷 01454 281 880

***Passion**, PO Box 16180, Camden Town, London NW1 9ZG
Facilitators: Mr Roger & Mrs Sue Mitchell. Executive staff 4, Other staff 3. *CC* No.1069653. Began 1997; non-denominational. No magazine. Turnover £100,000 to year end Mar 99. Servant team providing training and people resources for tomorrow's church, particularly by facilitating leaders.
Web: www.passion.org.uk
Email: admin@passion.org.uk
☎ 020 7586 3044 🖷 020 7586 3050

***Peniel Academy**, Brizes Park, Ongar Road, Kelvedon Hatch, Brentwood CM15 0DG
Principal: Rev Dr Michael S B Reid. Other staff 44. Began 1982; Pentecostal. No magazine. Turnover n/a. Comprehensive school for 150 pupils, preschool to A-level.
Web: www.peniel.org
Email: penielacademy@peniel.org
☎ 01277 374 123 🖷 01277 373 596

Pilgrim Adventure, 120 Bromley Heath Road, Downend, Bristol BS16 6JJ
Co-ordinator: Mr David Gleed. Staff n/a. Began 1987; ecumenical. Magazine: *Shoreline* (Circulation n/a half-yearly). Turnover n/a. Discovery and development through pilgrimage; offering tailor-made programmes for schools, youth groups, those exploring vocation.
☎ 0117 957 3997 🖷 0117 952 1180

Preachers' Help, PO Box 34, Welwyn Garden City AL7 3BW
Director: Rev Geoffrey Stonier. Staff 2. *CC* No.1071608. Began 1995; interdenominational. Magazine: *Bulletin* (Circulation n/a quarterly). Turnover £3,000 to year end 1998. Helping preachers to increase the Biblical content of gospel ministry through distance-learning courses.
Web: www.digibank.demon.co.uk/preacher/
Email: preacher@digibank.demon.co.uk
🖷 01707 390 410

Rechabite Friendly Society, Rechabite House, 14 Byrom Street, Manchester M3 4RB
Managing Director: Mr William Turnbull. *Youth Education Coordinator:* Mrs Jane Ronson. Executive staff 2, Admin staff 10. Began 1835; interdenominational. (Previously Independent Order of Rechabites). Magazine: *Rechabite News* (5,000 quarterly). Turnover £180,000 to year end Dec 98. Teetotallers Friendly Society; alcohol and drug re-education.
☎ 0161 832 4821 🖷 0161 839 1725

St Luke's College Foundation, Heathayne, Colyton EX24 6RS
Director: Prof Michael Bond. Executive staff 2. *CC* No.306606. Began 1978; Anglican. No magazine. Turnover £153,000 to year end July 97. Advancing higher and further education in theology and religious education only.
☎ 01297 552 281

†**St Vincent's School for the Deaf and Blind**, 30 Fullarton Avenue, Tollcross, Glasgow G32 8NJ
Head Teacher: Mrs Alicia A Crilly. Executive staff 2, Other staff 14. Began 1911; Roman Catholic. No magazine. Turnover n/a. Education and Communication Departments.
☎ 0141 778 2254

Schools Outreach, 10 High Street, Bromsgrove B61 8HQ
Chief Executive: Mr Gordon Bailey. Executive staff 3, Other staff 15. *CC* No.516184. Began 1973; non-denominational. Turnover £294,134 to year end Mar 98. Recruiting, training, employing school-based pastoral care workers; training days for churches; training for individuals.
Email: schools.outreach@mcmail.com
☎ 01527 574 404

Scottish Joint Committee on Religious and Moral Education, Educational Institute of Scotland, 46 Moray Place, Edinburgh EH3 6BH
Joint Secretaries: Mr Frederick L Forrester, Rev John Stevenson. No full-time staff. Began n/a; interdenominational. No magazine. Turnover n/a. Representing teacher organisations, churches, minority faith bodies; developing policy on religious and moral education in Scotland.
☎ 0131 225 6244 🖷 0131 220 3151

The Scottish Reformation Society, The Magdalen Chapel, 41 Cowgate, Edinburgh EH1 1JR
Secretary: Rev A Sinclair Horne. Executive staff 1, Other staff 2. *CC* No.SCO 07756. Began 1850; interdenominational. Magazine: *The Bulwark* (4,200 every two months). Turnover £26,000 to year end Dec 92. Witnessing to the Reformed Faith through publications, lectures, videos, holiday tours; open to visitors.
☎ 0131 220 1450

T

***South Bristol Christian Centre**, Churchlands Road, Bedminster, Bristol BS3 3PW
Manager: Mr Les Potter. Other staff 8. ***CC*** No.1026672. Began 1993; interdenominational. Magazine: *Centre Calling* (500 quarterly). Turnover £2,875 to year end Mar 96. Serving the local churches and community through fellowship, training and social programmes.
☎ 0117 963 6329 🖷 0117 963 6329

***The Stapleford Centre**, Stapleford House, Wesley Place, Stapleford, Nottingham NG9 8DP
Head of Teacher Education & Training: Dr Trevor Cooling. *Head of Curriculum Resources:* Mrs Alison Farnell. Executive staff 3, Other staff 10. ***CC*** No.1063856. Began 1980; interdenominational. Magazine: *Journal of Education & Christian Belief* (Circulation & frequency n/a). Turnover: £271,591 [for nine months to end August 98]. Promoting development in education from a Christian perspective, curriculum resources, training courses and educational research.
Web: www.stapleford-centre.org
Email: admin@stapleford-centre.org
☎ 0115 939 6270/939 4671 🖷 0115 939 2076

Student Christian Movement, Westhill College, 14 Weoley Park Road, Selly Oak, Birmingham B29 6LL
Coordinator: Carolyn Styles. Other staff 3. ***CC*** No.241896. Began 1889; ecumenical. Magazine: *Movement* (1,000 every four months). Turnover £75,000 to year end Aug 98. Promoting exploration of faith and its relevance to the contemporary world through groups, conferences, publications.
Email: scm@charis.co.uk
☎ 0121 471 2404 🖷 0121 414 1251

Sunday Schools Council for Wales, School of Education, University of North Wales, Normal Site, Holyhead Road, Bangor LL57 2PX
General Secretary: Rev Aled Davies. Executive staff 2, Other staff 4. ***CC*** No.525766. Began 1966; interdenominational. Magazine: *Cysylltiad* (2,000 quarterly). Turnover £150,000 to year end Dec 98. Developing work of Sunday School and Christian Education in Wales, through the Welsh language.
Web: www.bangor.ac.uk
Email: edsooe@bangor.ac.uk
☎ 01248 382 947 🖷 01248 383 954

Sutherland Education and Training Agency, Old Fallings Hall, O Fallings Lane, Wolverhampton WV10 8BL
Education Adviser: Mr Neal Lawrence. No full-time sta Began 1998; non-denominational. No magazine. Turnov n/a. Christian approaches to education, organisation, heal through training, consulting, various media to impro performance.
Email: sutherland@cablenet.co.uk
☎ 01902 558 371 🖷 01902 558 294

Theology Through the Arts, Ridley Hall, Cambridge CB3 9HG
Director: Rev Dr Jeremy Begbie. Executive staff 1, Admin sta 1. ***CC*** Began 1997; non-denominational. Magazine: *Theolog Through the Arts – update* (500 half-yearly). Turnover n/a Cambridge University project exploring how different ar forms generate new models for doing Christian theology.
Web: www.divinity.cam.ac.uk/carts/tta.html
Email: jb215@cam.ac.uk
☎ 01223 741 078 🖷 01223 741 079

The Welsh National Centre for Religious Education, UWB, Schoo of Education, Normal Site, Holyhead Road, Bangor LL57 2PX
Director: Mr Rheinallt A Thomas. Executive staff 1, Other staff 7. Began 1979; non-denominational. Magazine: *RE News/ Newyddion A G* (3,500 termly). Turnover £170,500 to year end July 98. Religious and world education work; resources for schools and churches throughout Wales; bookshop.
Web: weblife.bangor.ac.uk/addysg/wncre/home.htm
Email: edsood@bangor.ac.uk
☎ 01248 382 956 🖷 01248 383 954

WYSOCS (West Yorkshire School of Christian Studies), Outwood House, Outwood Lane, Leeds LS18 4HR
Hon Secretary: Mrs Ruth Hanson. All voluntary staff. Began 1985; non-denominational. No magazine. Turnover £3,000 to year end Mar 98. Organising study events with the aim of applying the Christian faith to many callings.
☎ 0113 258 9300 🖷 0113 258 1309

Zion Teaching Ministries, Jacobs Well, 78 Curbar Road, Great Barr, Birmingham B42 2AU
Director: Rev Richard Hey-Smith. Executive staff 2, Other staff 2. Began 1982; interdenominational. No magazine. Turnover n/a. Bible teaching/preaching: seminars, schools, video, audio, radio.
Email: 106606.2066@compuserve.com
☎ 0121 605 0353

EDUCATIONAL RESOURCE CENTRES

Archdiocese of Southwark Christian Education Centre, 21 Tooting Bec Road, London SW17 8BS
Director: Rev Nicholas Hudson. Executive staff 6, Other staff 4. ***CC*** Began 1967; Roman Catholic. Magazine: *BEC News* (1,100 half-yearly). Turnover n/a. Servicing Christian education and formation of adults and children in parishes and schools.
Email: office@cectootingbec.org.uk
Email: bookshop@cectootingbec.org.uk
☎ 020 8672 7684/2422 🖷 020 8672 8894

Bath and Wells Diocesan Education Resource Centre, The Old Deanery, Wells BA5 2UG
Director of Education: Mr M Evans. Executive staff 7, Other staff 7. ***CC*** No.249398. Began 1981; Anglican. No magazine. Turnover £140,000 to year end Dec 98. Providing resources and support for religious education and worship for churches and schools.
Web: www.bathwells.anglican.org
Email: education@bathwells.anglican.org
☎ 01749 670 777 🖷 01749 674 240

irmingham Council of Christian Education, Carrs Lane Church Centre, Birmingham B4 7SX
Hon Secretary: Philip Longman. Executive staff 2, Other staff 14. ***CC*** No.502831. Began 1842; ecumenical. Interim period for re-structuring. Magazine: (Circulation n/a quarterly). Turnover n/a. Promoting Christian education, particular reference to training children's and young people's workers in churches.
☎ 0121 643 6603 🖷 0121 632 5320

radford Diocesan Resource Centre, Diocesan Office, Cathedral Hall, Stott Hill, Bradford BD1 4ET
Administrator: To be appointed. Executive staff 1, Other staff 1. ***CC*** Began n/a; Anglican. No magazine. Turnover n/a. Supplying Christian resources to parishes, schools and the public; equipment hire.
☎ 01274 725 958 🖷 01274 726 343

arlisle Diocesan Religious Education Resource Centre, West Walls, Carlisle CA3 8UE
Adviser in Religious Education: Rev B J Thomas. Executive staff 1. ***CC*** No.251977. Began 1975; Anglican. Magazine: *Title n/a* (Circulation n/a every four months). Turnover £25,000 to year end Dec 96. Lending/selling resources for RE and Christian formation to schools, church groups and voluntary organisations.
☎ 01228 538 086 🖷 01228 815 409

Chelmsford Diocesan Resources Centre, 53 New Street, Chelmsford CM1 1AT
Resource Centre Manager: Mr Brian Beattie. Executive staff 1, Admin staff 1. ***CC*** Began n/a; Anglican. No magazine. Turnover £90,000 to year end Dec 98. Providing books on loan for all ages; general sales; support of Diocesan staff, parishes, schools.
Email: bbeattie@chelmsford.anglican.org
☎ 01245 294 400 🖷 01245 294 477

Christians Involved In Derbyshire Schools (CIDS), 2 Dale Road, Matlock DE4 3LT
Executive Director: Mrs Dorothy Whitaker. Other staff 1. ***CC*** No.1003799. Began 1988; interdenominational. Magazine: *Newsletter* (Circulation n/a termly). Turnover n/a. Association of Christians with concern for schools in Derbyshire; Christian Schools Resources Centre.
☎ 01629 565 63 🖷 01629 565 63

Gloucester Diocesan Religious Education Resource Centre, 9 College Green, Gloucester GL1 2LX
Warden: Mrs Gillian Calvert. Executive staff 1. ***CC*** No.251234. Began 1971; Anglican. No magazine. Turnover n/a. Providing resources for religious education for churches and schools.
☎ 01452 385 217 🖷 01452 308 324

Guildford Diocesan Education Centre, The Education Centre, The Cathedral, Stag Hill, Guildford GU2 5UP
Director of Education: Rev Canon A R Chanter. Executive staff 6, Other staff 5. ***CC*** Began n/a; Anglican. No magazine. Turnover n/a. Supporting parishes and schools by providing consultancy, courses and loaning resource materials.
☎ 01483 450 423 🖷 01483 450 424

***Hope UK**, 25(f) Copperfield Street, London SE1 0EN
Executive Director: Mr George Ruston. *National Education Co-ordinator:* Mr Martin Perry. *Training Co-ordinator:* Ms Sarah Brighton. Executive staff 5, Other staff 10. ***CC*** No.1044475. Began 1855; interdenominational. Magazine: *ACTION* (5,000 half-yearly). Turnover £450,000 to year end Dec 97. Preventing drug-related harm and promoting drug-free lifestyles with literature, speakers and training.
Email: enquiries@hopeuk.org
☎ 020 7928 0848 (24 hours) 🖷 020 7401 3477

***Independent Methodist Resource Centre**, Fleet Street, Pemberton, Wigan WN5 0DS
Manager: Mr Andrew M Rigby. Executive staff 1, Other staff 2. ***CC*** No.248813. Began 1805; Independent Methodist. Magazine: *Connexion* (2,500 monthly). Turnover n/a. Administration, supplies, resources. Independent Methodist Church's archives.
Email: 106570.2444@compuserve.com
☎ 01942 223 526 🖷 01942 227 768

***London Mennonite Centre**, 14 Shepherds Hill, Highgate, London N6 5AQ
Administrator: Mr W H Newcomb. *Director:* Mr Mark Thiessen Nation. Executive staff 3, Other staff 4. ***CC*** No.227410. Began 1954; Mennonite. No magazine. Turnover £140,000 to year end Dec 97. Christian resource centre with seminar programme, library, book service and church conflict and mediation service.
Web: www.btinternet.com/~lmc
Email: menno@compuserve.com
☎ 020 8340 8775 🖷 020 8341 6807

***The Mothers' Union Media Awareness Project (MAP)**, The Mother's Union Action and Outreach Unit, 24 Tufton Street, London SW1P 3RB
Project Officer: Jane Groves. Executive staff 1, Other staff 1. ***CC*** Began 1988. (Previously Media Awareness Project). Magazine: *MAP Bulletin* (4,000 every four months). Turnover n/a. Promoting media awareness through resource materials, programmes and consultancy.
Web: themothersunion.org
Email: action@themothersunion.org
☎ 020 7222 5533 🖷 020 7222 1591

National Christian Education Council (NCEC), 1020 Bristol Road, Selly Oak, Birmingham B29 6LB
Marketing Coordinator: Mr B Morgan. *Training/Publishing Manager:* Rev Martin Lambourne. Executive staff 3, Other staff 12. ***CC*** No.211542. Began 1803; non-denominational. Magazine: *Sparks* (Circulation n/a every four months). Turnover £500,000 to year end Feb 96. Developing Christian education in the Church through consultations, training and publications.
Web: www.ncec.org.uk
Email: ncec@ncec.org.uk
☎ 0121 472 4242 🖷 0121 472 7575

North East London Religious Education Centre, Marshall Hall, Eric Road, Chadwell Heath, Romford RM6 6JH
Administrator: Mrs Carolyn Marriott. Other staff 1. ***CC*** No.271981. Began 1975; interdenominational. No magazine. Turnover £26,000 to year end May 96. Book and other resource centre.
☎ 020 8590 5331 🖷 020 8503 8982

North East Religious Learning Resources Centre Ltd, Carter House, Pelaw Leazes Lane, Durham DH1 1TB
Director: Ms K Passmore. Executive staff 5. ***CC*** No.1055285. Began 1975; ecumenical. (Previously Durham Religious Education Resources Centre). Magazine: (Circulation n/a annually). Turnover £95,000 to year end Dec 98. Resources training information and support for schools and parishes in the North East.
☎ 0191 375 0586 🖷 0191 384 7529
Also at: Denewood, Clayton Road, Newcastle upon Tyne NE2 1TL
☎ 0191 281 1636

North Wales Gospel Outreach (NOWGO), The Oasis Christian Centre, Ysguborwen Road, Dwygyfylchi, Penmaenmawr LL34 6PS
Director: Rev Bob Searle. Executive staff 6, Admin staff 4. ***CC*** No.1048524. Began 1994; non-denominational. No magazine. Turnover n/a. Centre for worship, prayer, teaching, mission teams, Christian literature sales and distribution, conventions, retreats, seminars.
Web: www.churches.net/userpages/oasisdwygyfylchi.html
Email: oasis@oasisdwygyfylchi.freeserve.co.uk
☎ 01492 623 229 Fax 01492 623 222

The Olive Branch Christian Resource Centre, 5 Cleveland Rise, East Ogwell, Newton Abbot TQ12 6FF
Partner: Mr Michael R Cullen. Executive staff 1. Began 1986; interdenominational. No magazine. Turnover n/a. Free loan of video and audio tapes, audio-visuals, children/youth teaching materials, book library.
☎ 01626 331 436 Fax 01626 331 436

Prophetic Word Ministries Trust, The Park, Moggerhanger, Bedford MK44 3RW
Director: Rev Dr Clifford Hill. Executive staff 3, Other staff 5. ***CC*** No.326533. Began 1984; interdenominational. Magazine: *Prophecy Today* (10,700 every two months). Turnover £200,600 to year end Dec 98. Biblically-based teaching/publishing ministry; Hebraic Study Centre offering sabbaticals, courses, distance learning; residential conference facilities.
Email: pwm@the-park.u-net.com
☎ 01767 641 400 Fax 01767 641 515

St Albans Diocesan Education Centre, Hall Grove, Welwyn Garden City AL7 4PJ
Director of Education: Rev Canon Jim Birtwhistle. Executive staff 7, Other staff 4. Began 1973; Anglican. No magazine. Turnover £55,000 to year end Dec 98. Bringing together resources to support statutory and voluntary work with young people throughout the diocese.
Email: stalbansdys@enterprise.net
☎ 01707 332 321 Fax 01707 373 089

St Asaph Diocesan Resource Centre, 20 Rhosnesni Lane, Wrexham LL12 7LY
Administrator: Mrs P Williams. Executive staff 2, Other staff 2. Began 1978; Anglican. No magazine. Turnover n/a. Offering RE resources, photocopying facilities, conference rooms, bookshop.
☎ 01978 265 967/357 713 Fax 01978 290 454

Sheffield Christian Education Council, Montgomery Hall, Surr
Street, Sheffield S1 2LG
Administrator: Mrs Carole Darlow. Other staff 5. C
No.229564. Began 1812; interdenominational. Magazin
Spotlight (1,200 every two months). Turnover n/a. Resourc
centre for churches and Sunday Schools.
☎ 0114 272 0455

***Society for the Protection of Unborn Children (SPUC)**, Phylli
Bowman House, 5 St Matthew Street, Westminster, Londo
SW1P 2JT
National Director: Mr John Smeaton. *Evangelicals Director*
Mr Peter Smith. *Evangelicals Chairman:* Rev Ian Brown
Executive staff 10, Other staff 30. Began 1967; non
denominational. Magazine: *Human Concern* (120,000 every
four months). Turnover £1,250,000 to year end Feb 98
Educating public and parliament about abortion, populatio
control, euthanasia and human embryo experimentation.
Web: www.spuc.org.uk
Email: sysop@spuc.org.uk
☎ 020 7222 5845 Fax 020 7222 0630
Also offices in Belfast, Cardiff, Glasgow, Preston, Stockton.

Training Image Resource, Mill House, Church Road, Bickerstaffe, Ormskirk L39 0EB
Director: Mr Ian Stewart. Executive staff 2. Began 1973; independent. (Previously Recording Ministries). No magazine. Turnover £12,000 to year end Apr 96. Providing support and training to meet needs in the Church; video, audio and publication.
☎ 01695 724 035

York Religious Education Centre, University College of Ripon & York St John, Lord Mayor's Walk, York YO3 7EX
Head of Centre: Ms Eileen Bellett. Other staff 3. Began 1976; n/a. No magazine. Turnover £20,000 to year end Apr 98. Promoting RE in schools, churches and colleges; courses, resources, loans, consultancy.
Email: l.alexander@ucrysj.ac.uk
Email: c.mercier@ucrysj.ac.uk
☎ 01904 656 771 Fax 01904 612 512

TEACHING ENGLISH AS A FOREIGN LANGUAGE SCHOOLS

***The Abbey Christian School for the English Language Ltd**, 16a Abbey Road, London NW8 9BD
Principal: Rev Hugh Bishop. *Bursar/Company Secretary:* Mr David Warner. Executive staff 3, Other staff 9. ***CC*** No.281940. Began 1963; interdenominational. No magazine. Turnover £254,603 to year end June 98. Teaching the English language to Christians and others from overseas, some intending to be missionaries.
Web: www.abbeyschool.com
Email: abbeycs@prestel.co.uk
☎ 020 7289 0706 Fax 020 7266 2628

***Christian English Language Centre**, Exchange Buildings, Upper Hinton Road, Bournemouth BH1 2EE
Directors: Mr Derek & Mrs Jackie White. Executive staff 3, Other staff 8. Began 1977; interdenominational. No magazine. Turnover n/a. Teaching English to foreign Christians and missionary candidates and equipping them spiritually.
Web: homepages.tcp.co.uk/~celc/
Email: celc@tcp.co.uk
☎ 01202 518 492/297 729 Fax 01202 518 492

nctional English, 5 Chubb Hill Road, Whitby YO21 1JU
Principal: Mr Neil McKelvie. *Chaplain:* Mr Philip Smith. *Director of Studies:* Mr Lindsay Barber. Executive staff 4, Other staff 25. Began 1972; interdenominational. No magazine. Turnover £440,000 to year end Dec 97. Providing English language courses for 75 foreign adults, beginners to advanced. Recognised by the British Council.
Web: www.functional.co.uk
Email: funenglish@easynet.co.uk
☎ 01947 603 933 🖷 01947 820 703

ternational School of Languages (Kensington Temple), PO Box 9161, London W3 6GS
Director: Will Napier. Executive staff 1, Other staff 7. *CC* No.251549. Began 1995; Elim Pentecostal but open to all. No magazine. Turnover n/a. Providing English courses full-time, beginners to advanced; Cambridge exams; English for missionaries.
Web: www.ken-temp.org.uk/index.htm
Email: ibiol@dircon.co.uk
☎ 020 8752 8600 🖷 020 8896 2628

nternational Training Network, Exchange Buildings, Upper Hinton Road, Bournemouth BH1 2HH
Executive Director: Mr Len Grates. *Director of Studies:* Mr Dick Dendle. Executive staff 3, Other staff 4. *CC* No.1048521. Began 1994; interdenominational. No magazine. Turnover £110,000. Training teachers of English as a Foreign Language for TESOL; focus on evangelism/mission abroad.
Web: www.users.globalnet.co.uk/~itnet
Email: itnet@globalnet.co.uk
☎ 01202 789 089 🖷 01202 789 089

Logos Linguistics, 2 Beaconsfield Road, Canterbury CT2 7HF
Director: Mr Peter Dufort. Executive staff 2. Began 1992; non-denominational. No magazine. Turnover n/a. Family-based English language school; outreach; preparing Christians for Bible College/Christian work.
☎ 01227 766 663 🖷 01227 766 663

Olivet English Language School, 50 Norfolk Square, Brighton BN1 2PA
Director: Angela Starnes. Executive staff 1, Other staff 5. Began 1977; interdenominational. No magazine. Turnover £165,000 to year end Dec 97. Teaching English to non-English speakers and training teachers in TESOL.
Web: www.edunet.com/olivet
Email: olivetschl@aol.com
☎ 01273 325 839 🖷 01273 325 839

***Operation Mobilisation Language School**, Conwy House Training Centre, 115 Russell Road, Rhyl LL18 3NR
Head of Centre: Mr Ian Orton. *Language School Director:* Mrs Ann Atkin. Executive staff 4, Other staff 20. *CC* No.1008196. Began 1987; interdenominational. Magazine: *Focus* (12,000 quarterly). Turnover £360,000 to year end Dec 98. Teaching English as a foreign language, plus personal development courses for current and potential missionaries.
Email: postmaster@rhyl.om.org
☎ 01745 343 085 🖷 01745 330 790

Regents English Language Centre, London Road, Nantwich CW5 6LW
Director: Mrs Margaret Ward. Executive staff 3, Other staff 5. *CC* No.251549. Began 1981; interdenominational. No magazine. Turnover £102,000 to year end Dec 98. Providing courses in English as a foreign language for those aged 15 upwards. Beginners to advanced.
Web: regents.ac.uk
Email: admin@regentstc.freeserve.co.uk
☎ 01270 610 800 🖷 01270 610 013

Siloam Christian Ministries, 5 Clarendon Place, Leamington Spa CV32 5QL
Director: Mr Richard Norton. Executive staff 2, Other staff 2. *CC* No.327396. Began 1982; interdenominational. Magazine: *Love in Action* (12,000 monthly). Turnover £1,089,500 to year end Dec 98. Offering accommodation to female overseas English language students attending Warwickshire college in Leamington Spa.
☎ 01926 335 037 🖷 01926 431 193

***Southall School of Languages and Missionary Orientation**, Western Road, Southall UB2 5DS
Director: Pastor Boyd Williams. *Secretary:* Mrs Christine Streets. Executive staff 4, Other staff 12. *CC* Began 1989; Baptist. No magazine. Turnover £250,000 to year end Dec 96. English teaching and missionary orientation; concern to help students from newer sending countries.
Email: 106766.1364@compuserve.com
☎ 020 8574 4456 🖷 020 8606 9699

T

***Trinity English Language Centre**, Trinity College, Stoke Hill, Stoke Bishop, Bristol BS9 1JP
Principal: Rev Canon David Gillett. Began 1995; interdenominational. Turnover n/a. Academic or general English courses from 4 weeks to full year. IELTS, Cambridge, Pitmans exams.
Web: www.trinity-bris.ac.uk/elc
Email: elc@trinity-bris.ac.uk
☎ 0117 968 2803 🖷 0117 968 7470

THEOLOGICAL COLLEGES & BIBLE SCHOOLS (RESIDENTIAL)

By Denomination
Colleges which did not supply any of this information are not listed here
Fees are per annum unless otherwise stated

Name	Places				Students		Course Details	Fees		
	Resident			Non-						
	M	W	M/W	Res	M	W		Tuition	Combined	Acco
Anglican										
Church Army, Wilson Carlile College of Evangelism	-	-	35	n/a	29	6	3 years Diploma in evangelism studies	£4,380		£1,8
College of the Resurrection	35	0	-	3	n/a	0	3 years undergraduate 1 to 3 years postgraduate	£2,006		
Crowther Hall	-	-	36	0	n/a	n/a	1, 2 or 3 terms £2,490 per term	n/a		
Oak Hill Theological College	-	-	80	60	n/a	n/a	2 or 3 years undergraduate, postgraduate	£3,419		£2,8
Ridley Hall	25	25	-	0	25	27	2 to 3 years, undergraduate and postgraduate	£4,400		£2,4
Ripon College	-	-	70	0	n/a	n/a	2 or 3 years	n/a		
St Chad's College	-	-	310	0	168	142	Undergraduate, postgraduate, PhD	£1,000		£2,1
St John's College, Durham with Cranmer Hall	65	65	-	n/a	46	9	2 or 3 years undergraduate	£4,374		£2,1
St John's College, Nottingham	-	-	80	60	46	9	1 to 3 years undergraduate/postgraduate, research		£7,320	
St Michael and All Angels' Theological College	n/a	n/a	-	n/a	n/a	n/a	3 terms	£4,300		£2,6
St Stephen's House	-	-	50	0	40	10	2/3 years undergraduate, postgraduate, diploma, certificate.		Vary according to course	
Simon of Cyrene Theological Institute	n/a	n/a	n/a	n/a	n/a	n/a	1 year	n/a		
Trinity Theological College	-	-	120	20	90	30	1 to 3 years, Cert, Diplomas, BA, MA, M.Phil, M.Litt, PhD,	£2,120		£2,6
Westcott House	–	–	58	58	n/a	n/a	2 or 3 years undergraduate, 58 students – M & W	n/a		
Wycliffe Hall	87	87	-	90	65	22	1, 2 or 3 years undergraduate, various postgraduate	£2,200		£4,3
Anglican/Methodist										
United College of the Ascension	n/a	n/a	-	-	27	13	Undergraduate Health and Mission, 1 year postgraduate Church management and Women's leadership	n/a		
The Apostolic Church										
The Apostolic Church Training School	12	12	-	0	n/a	n/a	1 to 3 years n/a	n/a		
Assemblies of God										
Mattersey Hall	108	52	-	0	108	52	1 to 3 years, certificates/diplomas/BA/MA	£2,500		£1,9
Baptist										
Bristol Baptist College	-	-	16	34	n/a	n/a	3 years		£7,600	
Northern Baptist College	-	-	30	50	n/a	n/a	1 to 6 years, full and part-time, undergraduate (certificate, diploma, BA), postgraduate (MA, MPhil, PhD)		£5,435	
Regent's Park College	-	-	40	40	n/a	n/a	3 years		£6,900 (home & EEC) £9,713 (other overseas)	
South Wales Baptist College	-	-	-	28	n/a	n/a	3 years undergraduate 1 year postgraduate		£1,950	
Spurgeon's College	75	75	-	150	n/a	n/a	1,2 or 3 years full and part-time and open learning undergraduate, postgraduate	£4,250		£1,9
Baptist, Congregational, Presbyterian, United Reformed										
St Andrew's Hall Missionary College	n/a	n/a	-	n/a	n/a	n/a	1 year		£6,996	
Roman Catholic										
Allen Hall	40	0	-	10	30	0	6 years	n/a		r
Margaret Beaufort Institute of Theology	0	6	-	0	0	5	2 to 4 years undergraduate BTh, CTM / MA		£2,600	
Campion House	50	0	-	0	25	0	Half year pre-seminary courses	n/a		r
Franciscan Ecumenical Study Centre	40	20	-	20	30	20	1 to 6 years		£2,850	
Institute of St Anselm	65	65	-	0	65	65	6 weeks–6 years. Diploma, accreditation, summer courses.		£6,000	
St John's Roman Catholic Seminary	80	0	-	60	64	0	3 to 6 years, diploma in theology, undergraduate (Bth) and postgraduate (MTh)		£8,300	
St Mary's, Strawberry Hill	-	-	300	n/a	n/a	n/a	Undergraduate and postgraduate degrees in Theology and Religious Studies. Management Studies with business ethics	n/a		r
St Mary's Seminary	90	0	-	0	n/a	0	6 years		£5,040	
Scotus College	28	0	-	0	n/a	0	6 years		£2,500	
Ushaw College	72	0	-	0	n/a	0	3 or 6 years	n/a		r
Roman Catholic foundation, but open to all										
Heythrop College (University of London)	n/a	n/a	-	-	n/a	n/a	3 years undergraduate, 1–3 years postgraduate	n/a		n
Church of Christ										
Springdale College	25	25	-	0	15	15	1 to 3 years CTS, Dip TS		£2,000	
Church of Scotland										
Christ's College, Aberdeen	n/a	n/a	-	100	n/a	n/a	3 or 4 years Tuition as University of Aberdeen fees	n/a		n
Parish Education Centre and College	–	–	34	0	n/a	n/a	2 years	£2,410		n
Church of the Nazarene										
Nazarene Theological College	10	10	-	181	10	10	1 to 4 years, BA Hons Theology, MA/PhD	£2,550		£1,9
Elim Pentecostal										
Regents Theological College	-	-	100	80	71	30	1 to 3 years full / part-time, undergraduate / postgraduate	£2,340		£2,1
Free Presbyterian										
Whitefield College of the Bible and Theological Hall of the Free Presbyterian Church of Ulster	35	8	-	12	17	1	2 to 4 years, undergraduate	£909		£1,0

T

ame	Places				Students		Course Details	Fees		
	Resident			Non-				Tuition		Accom.
	M	W	M/W	Res	M	W			Combined	
terdenominational / Ecumenical / Non-denominational										
Adelaide College	20	10	-	0	20	10	3 years			
All Nations Christian College	-	-	180	0	72	108	Certificate, Diploma, BA, MA, PhD	£3,276	£5,943	£2,667
Belfast Bible College	-	-	40	86	63	63	3 months to 3 years	£1,945		£1,575
Bible College of Wales	20	15	-	4	10	8	2 years college diploma		£2,250	
Birmingham Bible Institute	30	30	-	0	30	30	1 to 3 years BA, MA	£760		£640
Capernwray Bible School	85	115	-	0	85	115	8 months college diploma	£648		£2,507
Christ for the Nations UK	40	40	-	40	9	12	2 years undergraduate	£1,640		£1,640
Christian Workers Programme	6	6	-	0	4	5	One year diploma	£500		£700
Covenant College	-	-	-	25	n/a	n/a	1 or 2 years certificate/diploma	£2,775		£2,800
Ellel Ministries	-	-	250	0	n/a	n/a	1 year		£6,000	
The Evangelical Theological College of Wales	90	30	-	0	92	13	3 years undergraduate 2/3 years postgraduate, distance learning	£2,660		£1,340
Faith Mission Bible College	20	20	-	0	20	20	2 year diploma, 3 year degree	£1,995		£1,995
International Christian College, Glasgow	-	-	-	140	81	52	Foundation, undergraduate and postgraduate. Full time (1 to 4 years), part time (up to 9 years)	£3,486		£1,575
Kensit Memorial Bible College	18	0	-	0	18	0	2 years, preparation for the Christian ministry	n/a		n/a
King's Bible College	-	-	40	0	n/a	n/a	10 months, diploma	£1,395		£3,600
King's College, London, Department of Theology and Religious Studies	150	150	-	n/a	n/a	n/a		n/a		n/a
Kingdom Faith Bible College	n/a	n/a	-	n/a	n/a	n/a	1 to 2 year courses	n/a		n/a
Kingdom Faith Church, Lamplugh House	25	0	-	10	n/a	0	10 weeks		£800 per team	
London Bible College	55	58	-	200	200	116	1 to 3 years, certificates HE to PhD	n/a		n/a
London Theological Seminary	n/a	0	-	20	26	0	2 years preparation for Christian ministry	£2,115		£1,395
Moorlands College	80	80	-	0	68	65	1 to 3 years BA, DipHE, Access	£3,160		£1,710
Nehemiah Bible Training Centre	-	-	-	n/a	n/a	n/a	Correspondance course		£160 per course	
New Hope Bible College	-	-	120	0	n/a	n/a	3 months to 4 years		£3,344	
Queen's, Birmingham, The Ecumenical Foundation for Theological Education	40	40	-	0	n/a	n/a	1 to 4 years certificate, diploma, BA, MA	£4,749		£1,557
Redcliffe College	n/a	n/a	-	0	24	42	1 to 3 years, cert (HE), dip (HE), BA (Hons)	n/a		n/a
Selly Oak Colleges	363	362	-	1,275	n/a	n/a	n/a	n/a		n/a
Tilsley College (Gospel Literature Outeach)	8	8	-	0	7	5	1 year		£2,380	
University of Aberdeen, Department of Divinity with Religious Studies	35	35	-	100	n/a	n/a	3 or 4 years	n/a		n/a
University of Edinburgh, Centre for the Study of Christianity in the non-Western World	-	-	n/a	n/a	30	10	Various lengths of postgraduate course	n/a		n/a
University of Edinburgh, Faculty of Divinity	-	-	470	n/a	235	235	4 years	£750		n/a
University of Glasgow, Faculty of Divinity	-	-	220	n/a	110	110	3 or 4 years, undergraduate, postgraduate	n/a		n/a
University of St Andrews, School of Divinity	115	115	-	n/a	111	114	3 or 4 years undergraduate, postgraduate	£750		£2,500
Word of Life International	50	50	-	0	n/a	n/a	9 months to 3 years ministry training	£585		£2,016
Lutheran										
Westfield House	-	-	12	12	n/a	n/a	5 years		£2,950	
Methodist										
Cliff College	-	-	80	85	33	32	1 or 2 years, under or post graduate	£2,270		£1,945
Edgehill Theological College	-	-	60	60	n/a	n/a	3 years 2 years postgraduate	£750		n/a
Hartley Victoria College		-	25	30	n/a	n/a	2 or 3 years undergraduate or postgraduate. BA, MA, MPhil, PhD	n/a		n/a
Wesley House, Cambridge	-	-	n/a	n/a	n/a	n/a	3 years	n/a		n/a
Wesley College	-	-	-	70	n/a	n/a	2 or 3 years, BA (Theology), MA,	£4,480		£1,530
New Testament Church of God										
Overstone College	-	-	100	n/a	n/a	n/a	3 years		£1,917	
Pentecostal										
Centre for International Christian Ministries	34	34	-	0	n/a	n/a	2 years		£1,200	
International Bible Training Institute	30	20	-	0	25	17	2 years basic Variable postgraduate	£1,900		£2,000
Presbyterian Church of Wales										
The United Theological College	30	28	-	0	n/a	n/a	3 years BD, BTh	£1,300		£1,750
Presbyterian										
Union Theological College	70	30	-	100	30	2	3 years undergraduate	£1,855		£1,400
Religious Society of Friends										
Woodbrooke Quaker Study Centre	35	35	-	0	n/a	n/a	2 days to 1 year adult education, research	£900		£1,400
Salvation Army										
William Booth Memorial Training College	10	14	44	2	34	38	2 years undergraduate	£2,020		£3,166
Scottish Episcopal Church										
Theological Institute of the Scottish Episcopal Church	-	-	-	24	n/a	n/a	Full time 2 or 3 years, part time 3 years	n/a		n/a
Seventh-Day Adventist										
Newbold College	166	117	-	90	162	117	3 to 4 years undergraduate, 1 to 2 years postgraduate	£3,360		£2,865
United Reformed										
Westminster College, Cambridge	-	-	60	n/a	n/a	n/a	4 years	n/a		n/a
United Reformed and Congregational										
Northern College	-	-	-	40	n/a	n/a	3 or 4 years undergraduate		£6,500	
Mansfield College	-	-	30	0	n/a	n/a	4 years		£4,600	

T

THEOLOGICAL COLLEGES & BIBLE SCHOOLS (RESIDENTIAL)

Note: University Colleges and other similar academic institutions which offer tertiary level courses are included here eve
if they are entirely non-residential, because of the nature of the courses offered.

***Adelaide College**, 3 Nineyard Street, Saltcoats KA21 5HS
Principal: Rev Dennis Paterson. Lecturers 9, Admin staff 12, Other staff 6. ***CC*** No.240168. Began 1964; interdenominational. Turnover £18,250 to year end Dec 95.
Web: www.comebacktogod.org
Email: campaign@comebacktogod.org
☎ 01294 463 911 Fax 01294 463 366

***All Nations Christian College**, Easneye, Ware SG12 8LX
Principal: Rev Dr Chris Wright MA, PhD. *Vice Prinicipal:* Rev Bob Hunt. *Bursar:* Mr Peter Norman. Lecturers 17, Other staff 20. ***CC*** No.311028. Began 1971; interdenominational. Turnover £1,300,000 to year end Dec 98. Providing residential courses in biblical, missionary and related studies.
Web: www.allnations.ac.uk
Email: mailbox@allnations.ac.uk
☎ 01920 461 243 Fax 01920 462 997

Allen Hall, 28 Beaufort Street, Chelsea, London SW3 5AA
Rector: Fr James Overton MA, STL, BD. Lecturers 19, Other staff 9. ***CC*** No.233699. Began 1568; Roman Catholic. Part of Westminster Roman Catholic Diocese Trustee. Turnover n/a. Training men for ordination to Roman Catholic priesthood.
Email: secretary@allenhall.co.uk
☎ 020 7351 1296 Fax 020 7349 5601

The Apostolic Church Training School, Caerbryn Roa
Penygroes, Llanelli SA14 7PH
Principal: Rev Eric Horley. Lecturers 10, Other staff 4. Bega n/a; Apostolic. Turnover n/a.
Email: ehwacts@aol.com
☎ 01269 832 069 Fax 01269 842 299

Margaret Beaufort Institute of Theology, Wesley House, Jesu Lane, Cambridge CB5 8BQ
Principal: Sr Bridget Tighe FMDM, MA, MSc. Other staff 3 ***CC*** No.1041031. Began 1993; Roman Catholic. Member o the Cambridge Theological Federation. Turnover n/a.
Email: btt20@cam.ac.uk
☎ 01223 741 039 Fax 01223 741 054

***Belfast Bible College**, Glenburn House, Glenburn Road South Dunmurry, Belfast BT17 9JP
Principal: Rev Graham Cheesman BD, MPhil, ALBC. Lecturers 7, Other staff 7. ***CC*** No.XN 47242A. Began 1943; interdenominational. Turnover n/a. Training men and women fo Christian service, helping them to grow academically, practically and spiritually.
Email: staff@bbc.dnet.co.uk
☎ 028 9030 1551 Fax 028 9043 1758

***Bible College of Wales**, Derwen Fawr Road, Sketty, Swansea SA2 8EB
Hon Director: Rev Samuel R Howells MA(Oxon). Visiting lecturers 4, Resident lecturers 6, Other staff 10. ***CC*** No.212216. Began 1924; interdenominational. Turnover n/a.
☎ 01792 203 463

***Birmingham Bible Institute**, 5 Pakenham Road, Edgbaston, Birmingham B15 2NN
Principal: Rev Dr Richard D Massey, MA, BD, PhD, ALBC. Lecturers 8, Other staff 10. ***CC*** No.1002205. Began 1953; interdenominational. Turnover £230,000. Training full and part-time for pastoral, evangelistic and cross-cultural mission.
Web: www.charis.co.uk/bbi/
Email: bbi@charis.co.uk
☎ 0121 440 4016

***William Booth Memorial Training College**, Champion Park, Denmark Hill, London SE5 8Q
Principal: Lt Col Robert Street. Lecturers 24, Other staff 31. ***CC*** No.214779. Began 1929; Salvation Army. Turnover n/a.
☎ 020 7733 1191

Bristol Baptist College, The Promenade, Clifton Down, Clifton, Bristol BS8 3NJ
Principal: Rev Dr Brian Haymes MA, PhD. Lecturers 5, Other staff 3. ***CC*** No.311778. Began 1679; Baptist. Offering training for Baptist ministry and youth leaders under Centre for Youth Ministry.
Email: admin@bristol-baptist.ac.uk
☎ 0117 946 7050 Fax 0117 946 7787

Campion House, 112 Thornbury Road, Osterley, Isleworth TW7 4NN
Principal: Rev Michael Barrow SJ. Lecturers 4, Other staff 7. ***CC*** No.230165. Began 1919; Roman Catholic. Turnover n/a. Preparing men for the Roman Catholic priesthood.
Email: campionhouseosterley@compuserve.com
☎ 020 8560 1924 Fax 020 8569 9645

For additional information see List on Pages 500, 501

apernwray Bible School, Capernwray Hall, Carnforth LA6 1AG
Principal: Mr Charles Price. Lecturers 8, Other staff 28. Began 1949; interdenominational. Turnover n/a.
Web: www.capernwray.co.uk
Email: registrar@capernwray.co.uk
☎ 01524 733 908 📠 01524 736 681

entre for International Christian Ministries, 98 Covelees Wall, Beckton, London E6 4WS
Director: To be appointed. Lecturers 15, Other staff 5. ***CC*** Began 1980; Pentecostal Holiness. Turnover n/a.
☎ 020 8800 9763 📠 020 8880 2038

hrist for the Nations UK, Dodsley Lane, Easebourne, Midhurst GU29 0AD
Director: Rev K J Swadling. *Dean:* Dr Jonathan Newell. Lecturers 8, Other staff 10. ***CC*** No.1064962. Began 1995; interdenominational. Turnover £140,000 to year end Dec 98.
Web: christforthenationsuk.org
Email: cfnuk@aol.com
☎ 01730 817 775 📠 01730 817 992

hrist's College, Aberdeen, 25 High Street, Aberdeen AB24 3EE
Master: Rev Dr Prof Alan Main TD, MA, BD, STM, PhD. Lecturers 14. ***CC*** Began 1843; Church of Scotland. Turnover n/a.
☎ 01224 272 138 📠 01224 273 750

hristian Workers Programme, 70 Raglan Road, Smethwick, Warley B66 3ND
Principal: Derrick Harrison. Lecturers 2, Visiting Lecturers 10. ***CC*** No.1020504. Began 1993; interdenominational. Turnover £10,000 to year end Dec 96. To equip men and women to serve the church.
Web: www.raglanroad.mcmail.com/cwp
Email: christian.w.prog@mcmail.com
☎ 0121 555 5891 📠 0121 555 5891

Church Army, Wilson Carlile College of Evangelism, 50 Cavendish Street, Sheffield S3 7RZ
Principal: Rev David Jeans MA. Lecturers 6, Other staff 8. ***CC*** Began 1882; Anglican. Turnover n/a. Training of evangelists principally for ministry with church army.
Email: training@sheffieldcentre.org.uk
☎ 0114 278 7020 📠 0114 279 5863

***Cliff College**, Calver, Hope Valley S32 3XG
Principal: Rev G Howard Mellor MA, BD. *Administrative officer:* Mr Maurice Houghton. *Senior Tutor:* Rev Paul Ashby. Lecturers 6, Other staff 25. ***CC*** No.529386. Began 1883; Methodist. Turnover £1,006,345 to year end Dec 98. Evangelism training, missions, research, conferences.
Email: prin.see@cliff.shef.ac.uk
☎ 01246 582 321 📠 01246 583 739

College of the Resurrection, Mirfield WF14 0BW
Principal: Rev Christopher Irvine. Lecturers 6. ***CC*** Began 1902; Anglican. Turnover n/a.
☎ 01924 490 441 📠 01924 492 738

†**Covenant College**, Nettle Hill, Brinklow Road, Ansty, Coventry CV7 9JL
Principal: Mr Roger Aubrey DipTh. Lecturers 20, Other staff 1. Began 1980; non-denominational. Turnover n/a.
Email: convenant.college@dial.pipex.com
☎ 024 7660 2700 📠 024 7660 2992

***Crowther Hall**, Weoley Park Road, Selly Oak, Birmingham B29 6QT
Principal: Rev George I Kovoor. Lecturers 5. ***CC*** No.220297. Began 1969; Anglican. Turnover n/a.
Email: crowtherhall@sellyoak.ac.uk
☎ 0121 472 4228 📠 0121 471 2662

Edgehill Theological College, 9 Lennoxvale, Malone Road, Belfast BT9 5BY
Principal: Rev Dr W Dennis D Cooke BA, BD, MTh, PhD. *Senior Tutor:* Rev Donald P Ker. Lecturers 4, Other staff 2. Began 1926; Methodist. Turnover £130,000 to year end Dec 98. Encouraging others to prepare for Christian ministry, especially reconciliation.
Email: office.edgehill@netmatters.co.uk
☎ 028 9066 5870

***Ellel Ministries**, Ellel Pierrepont, Frensham, Farnham GU10 3DL
Principal: Mr Peter Horrobin. Lecturers 20, Other staff 50. ***CC*** No.1041237. Began 1986; non-denominational. Turnover n/a. Centre for training and ministry in Christian healing and discipleship.
Web: ellelministries.org
Email: info@pierrepont.ellel.org.uk
☎ 01252 794 060 📠 01252 794 039

T

***The Evangelical Theological College of Wales**, Bryntirion House, Bridgend CF31 4DX
Principal: Rev Dr D Eryl Davies BA, BD, MA, PhD. *Lecturer:* Rev Stuart Olyott. Lecturers 14, Other staff 6. *CC* No.517324. Began 1985; interdenominational. (incorporating South Wales Bible College). Turnover £438,000 to year end Dec 98. Training men for preaching/pastoral ministry, men and women for Christian service. Full/part-time.
Web: www.etcw.ac.uk
Email: secretary@etcw.ac.uk
☎ 01656 645 411 🖷 01656 668 709

***Faith Mission Bible College**, 2 Drum Street, Gilmerton, Edinburgh EH17 8QG
Principal: Rev Dr Alexander Roger. Lecturers 3, Part-time lecturers 5. *CC* No.SCO 05119. Began 1886; interdenominational. Turnover n/a.
Web: www.faithmission.org
Email: college@faithmission.org
☎ 0131 664 4336 🖷 0131 672 1322

Franciscan Ecumenical Study Centre, Giles Lane, Canterbury CT2 7NA
Principal: Rev Jarlath M McDonagh, OFM BPh, STL. Lecturers 11, Other staff 7. *CC* Began 1973; Roman Catholic.
☎ 01227 769 349 🖷 01227 786 648

Hartley Victoria College, Luther King House, Brighton Grove, Rusholme, Manchester M14 5JP
Principal: Rev Dr John A Harrod BSc, MA, PhD. *Tutor:* Rev Dr Keith Davie. Lecturers 3. *CC* Began 1881; Methodist but open to all. Within the Partnership for Theological Education, Manchester. Turnover £150,000 to year end Dec 98. Ordination and lay education validated by Manchester University.
☎ 0161 224 2215

Heythrop College (University of London), Kensington Square, London W8 5HQ
Principal: Rev Dr John McDade SJ, BD, MA, PhD. *Vice-Principal:* To be appointed. *Secretary and Registrar:* Ms Annabel Clarkson. Lecturers 30, Other staff 9. *CC* No.312923. Began 1614; Roman Catholic foundation, but open to all. Turnover n/a.
Web: www.heythrop.ac.uk
Email: heythrop@heythrop.ac.uk
☎ 020 7795 6600 🖷 020 7795 4200

Institute of St Anselm, Edgar Road, Cliftonville, Margate CT9 2EU
Director: Rev Father L Kofler MHM. *Administrator:* Miss Thalia Slinn. *Senior Clerk:* Mrs L McAuliffe. Lecturers 10, Institute staff 24, Community 120. *CC* No.294625. Began 1986; Roman Catholic. Magazine: *Growth* (2,000 quarterly). Turnover £654,015 to year end Jun 96. Deepening spirituality using psychology to become fully alive and to facilitate others on this path.
Email: stanselm@adept.co.uk
☎ 01843 221 865 🖷 01843 226 629

International Bible Training Institute, Hook Place, Cuckfield Road, Burgess Hill RH15 8RF
Directors: Rev J P & Mrs Doreen H Wildrianne, Rev J J Zbinden. Lecturers 7, Other staff 5. *CC* Began 1947; Independent Pentecostal. Turnover n/a.
☎ 01444 233 173 🖷 01444 236 038

***International Christian College, Glasgow**, 110 St James Roa
Glasgow G4 0PS
Principal: Rev Dr Tony Sargent. *Vice Principal:* Dr T
Herbert. Lecturers 9, Other staff 8. *CC* No.SCO 28032. Bega
1892; interdenominational. Formed by merger of Glasgo
Bible College and Northumbria Bible College, Sept 199
Turnover £470,000 to year end Dec 98. Biblical, spiritua
practical, academic training for Christian service to undergra
uate and post-graduate level.
Web: www.icc.clara.co.uk
Email: college@icc.clara.co.uk
☎ 0141 334 9849 🖷 0141 334 0012

Kensit Memorial Bible College, 104 Hendon Lane, Finchle
London N3 3SQ
Principal: Rev Philip H Eveson BA, MA, MTh. Lecturers
Other staff 3. *CC* No.248506. Began 1905, reconstitute
1968; interdenominational. Turnover n/a.
☎ 020 8349 9408

***King's Bible College**, Whitchester House, Duns TD11 3SF
Principal: Mr Tony R Gray BA. Lecturers 20, Other staff 7. *CC*
No.1071600. Began 1983; interdenominational. Turnove
£140,000 to year end Dec 98. Training to handle the Bible wit
integrity and communicate truth with conviction and clarity.
Web: www.saltandlight.u-net.com/kbc/
Email: kbc@saltandlight.u-net.com
☎ 01361 890 271 🖷 01361 890 393

King's College, London, Department of Theology and Religious Studies, Strand, London WC2R 2LS
Head of Department: Prof Michael Knibb. Lecturers 21. Began
1829; interdenominational. Turnover n/a.
Web: www/kcl.ac.uk/theorelig
☎ 020 7873 2339 🖷 020 7873 2255

Kingdom Faith Bible College, Roffey Place Christian Training Centre, Faygate, Horsham RH12 4SA
Principal: Rev Michael Barling. Lecturers 5, Other staff 10. *CC* Began 1984; interdenominational. (Previously Roffey Place Christian Training Centre). Turnover n/a.
Web: www.kingdomfaith.com
Email: info@kingdomfaith.com
☎ 01293 851 543 🖷 01293 851 330

Kingdom Faith Church, Lamplugh House, Thwing, Driffield YO25 0DY
Principal: Rev John McKay. *Pastor:* Mr Gary Rumbold. Lecturers 3, Other staff 8. *CC* Began 1991; interdenominational. Turnover £50,000 to year end Dec 98. Church and The Way of the Spirit Training Centre.
☎ 01262 470 282 🖷 01262 470 536

***London Bible College**, Green Lane, Northwood HA6 2UW
Principal: Rev Dr Derek Tidball BA, BD, PhD. Lecturers 25, Other staff 40. *CC* No.312778. Began 1943; interdenominational. Associated College of Brunel University. Turnover n/a.
Web: www.londonbiblecollege.ac.uk
Email: mailbox@londonbiblecollege.ac.uk
☎ 01923 456 000 🖷 01923 456 001

London Theological Seminary, 104 Hendon Lane, Finchley, London N3 3SQ
Principal: Rev Philip H Eveson BA, MA, MTh. Lecturers 4, Other staff 1. *CC* No.281464. Began 1977; Evangelical Protestant. Turnover n/a.
Web: www.lts.u-net.com
Email: principal@lts.u-net.com
☎ 020 8346 7587 🖷 020 8371 8783

For additional information see List on Pages 500, 501

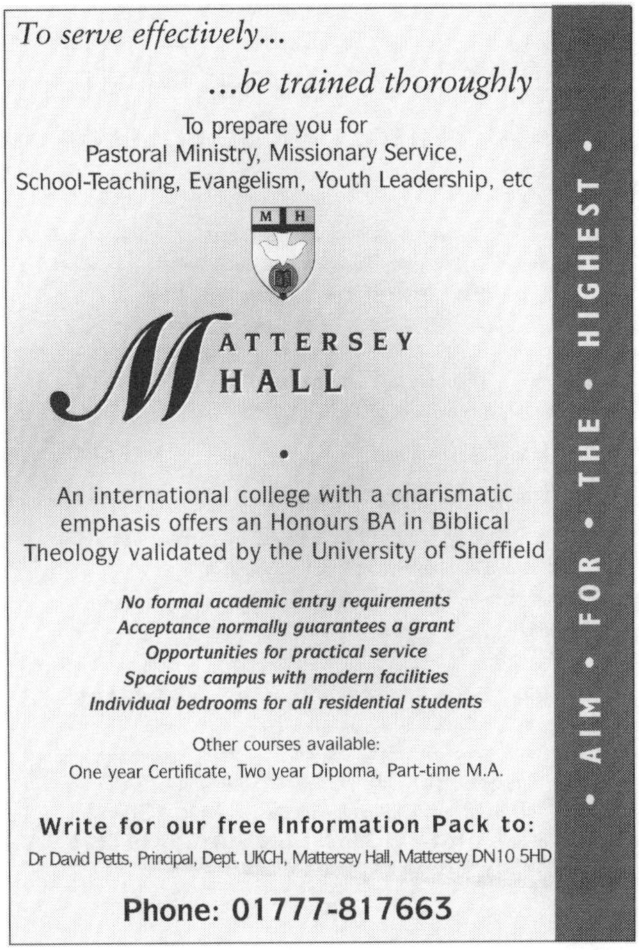

Mansfield College, Mansfield Road, Oxford OX1 3TF
Director of Ministerial Training: Rev Dr Catherine Middleton. Lecturers 5, Other staff 15. *CC* Began 1886; United Reformed, Congregational Federation. Turnover n/a.
Email: catherine.middleton@mansfield.ox.ac.uk
☎ 01865 270 999 Fax 01865 270 970

***Mattersey Hall**, Mattersey, Doncaster DN10 5HD
Principal: Rev Dr David Petts MA, MTh, PhD. Lecturers 6, Other staff 12. *CC* Began 1919; Assemblies of God but open to all. Turnover n/a.
☎ 01777 817 663 Fax 01777 816 195

***Moorlands College**, Sopley, Christchurch BH23 7AT
Principal: Rev Dr Steve Brady. *Registrar:* Miss Sharon Prior. *Bursar:* Mr Mike Coulson. Lecturers 10, Other staff 17. *CC* No.286334. Began 1948; interdenominational. Turnover n/a.
Web: www.moorlands.u-net.com
Email: enquiries@moorlands.ac.uk
☎ 01425 672 369 Fax 01425 674 162

***Nazarene Theological College**, Dene Road, Didsbury, Manchester M20 2GU
Principal: Rev Dr Herbert McGonigle BD, MA, PhD, DD. Lecturers 12, Other staff 8. *CC* No.526675. Began 1943; Church of the Nazarene. Incorporating Emmanuel Bible College. Turnover n/a. Integrating academic excellence and professional ministry skills training within a context of broadly Wesleyan-Holiness spirituality.
Web: www.nazarene.moose.co.uk/ntc/
Email: enquiries@nazarene.ac.uk
☎ 0161 445 3063 Fax 0161 448 0275

Nehemiah Bible Training Centre, Nehemiah House, Yr Erw, Brynmor Road, Penmaenmawr LL34 6AN
Principal: Rev J M Levy. Other staff n/a. *CC* No.252872. Began n/a; interdenominational. Turnover n/a. Correspondence course.
☎ 01492 622 800 / 623 229

***New Hope Bible College**, Faith Acres, Peterhead AB42 3DQ
Principal: Rev Dr Simon Cameron DD. Lecturers 9, Other staff 15. *CC* Began 1974; interdenominational, Full Gospel. Turnover n/a.
Email: info@newhopetrust.com
☎ 01779 838 251 Fax 01779 838 549

Newbold College, St Marks Road, Binfield, Bracknell RG42 4AN
Principal: Dr Andrea Luxton, BA, MA, PhD. *Head, Department of Theological Studies:* Dr Laurence Turner. *Vice Principal:* Dr Michael D Pearson. Lecturers 33, Other staff 32. *CC* No.1052494. Began 1901; Seventh-Day Adventist. Turnover £2,700,000.
Web: www.newbold.ac.uk
Email: admissions@newbold.ac.uk
☎ 01344 454 607 Fax 01344 861 692

Northern Baptist College, Luther King House, Brighton Grove, Rusholme, Manchester M14 5JP
Principal: Rev Dr Richard Kidd. *Dean of Studies:* Rev Dr Martin Scott. Lecturers 5, Other staff 5. *CC* No.526653. Began 1964; ecumenical. Turnover £300,000.
Email: richard.kidd@mcc.ac.uk
☎ 0161 224 2214 Fax 0161 248 9201

T

For additional information see List on Pages 500, 501

Northern College, Luther King House, Brighton Grove, Rusholme, Manchester M14 5JP
Principal: Rev Dr David R Peel BSc, BD, STM, PhD. Lecturers 5. ***CC*** No.529253. Began 1843; United Reformed and Congregational. Turnover n/a.
☎ 0161 224 4381 🖷 0161 248 9201

***Oak Hill Theological College**, Chase Side, Southgate, London N14 4PS
Principal: Rev Dr David Peterson MA, BD, PhD. *Vice Principal:* Rev Paul Weston. Lecturers 11, Other staff 16. ***CC*** No.310031. Began 1932; Anglican. Turnover n/a. Biblical training for contemporary ministry including pastor-teachers, evangelists, youth workers and other roles in today's world.
Web: www.oakhill.ac.uk
Email: clareo@oakhill.ac.uk
☎ 020 8449 0467/0041 🖷 020 8441 5996

†***Overstone College**, The Main House, Overstone, Northampton NN6 0AD
Principal: Dr C L Ryan. Lecturers 6, Other staff 9. Began 1963 as Ebenezer College, 1982 as Overstone. New Testament Church of God. Turnover n/a.
☎ 01604 491 242

Parish Education Centre and College, Annie Small House, 18 Inverleith House, Edinburgh EH3 5NS
General Secretary: Mr Iain Whyte BA, DCE. Lecturers 11, Other staff 14. ***CC*** Began 1887; Church of Scotland but open to all. (Previously Saint Colm's Education Centre). Turnover n/a.
☎ 0131 332 0343 🖷 0131 315 2161

Queen's, Birmingham, The Ecumenical Foundation for Theologic Education, Somerset Road, Edgbaston, Birmingham B15 2Q
Principal: Rev Peter Fisher MA. *Director of Research:* Rev I Kenneth Wilson. Lecturers 10, Other staff 4. ***CC*** No.52898 Began 1828; ecumenical. Turnover n/a.
Email: queens_college@compuserve.com
☎ 0121 454 1527 🖷 0121 454 8171

***Redcliffe College**, Wotton House, Horton Road, Gloucest GL1 3PT
Principal: Rev Simon Steer, BA, DipTh, MDiv, PGC Lecturers 6, Other staff 7. ***CC*** No.1054907. Began 1892; inte denominational. Turnover £400,000 to year end Dec 98. Spe cialist mission training.
Web: www.redcliffe.org
Email: admin@redcliffe.org
☎ 01452 308 097 Mobile: 0958 800 131 🖷 01452 503 94

Regent's Park College, Pusey Street, Oxford OX1 2LB
Principal: Rev Dr Paul S Fiddes MA, DPhil. Lecturers 5, Othe staff 6. ***CC*** No.309710. Began 1810; Baptist. Turnove £900,000 to year end Dec 98.
Web: www.rpc.ox.ac.uk
Email: postmaster@regents.ox.ac.uk
☎ 01865 288 120 🖷 01865 288 121

***Regents Theological College**, London Road, Nantwich CW5 6BR
Principal: Rev Dr William P Atkinson. Lecturers 13, Othe staff 55. ***CC*** No.251549. Began 1925; Elim Pentecostal bu open to all. (Previously Elim Bible College). Turnover n/a.
Web: regents-tc.ac.uk
Email: regentstc@aol.com
☎ 01270 610 800 🖷 01270 610 013

***Ridley Hall**, Ridley Hall Road, Cambridge CB3 9HG
Principal: Rev Graham Cray BA. Lecturers 7, Other staff 3. ***CC*** No.311456. Began 1880; Anglican. Turnover n/a.
☎ 01223 741 080 🖷 01223 741 081

Ripon College, Cuddesdon, Oxford OX44 9EX
Principal: Rev John Clarke, MA, BD. Lecturers 7, Other staff 9. ***CC*** No.309714. Began 1854; Anglican. Turnover n/a.
☎ 01865 874 595 🖷 01865 875 431

St Andrew's Hall Missionary College, Weoley Park Road, Selly Oak, Birmingham B29 6QX
Principal: To be appointed. Lecturers 3, Other staff 12. ***CC*** Began 1966; Baptist.
☎ 0121 472 6144 🖷 0121 472 8852

St Chad's College, 18 North Bailey, Durham DH1 3RH
Principal: Rev Dr Joseph Cassidy. *Chaplain, Admissions Tutor:* Rev Dominic Barrington. *Senior Tutor:* Dr Alan Klottrup. Lecturers 15, Other staff 20. ***CC*** No.109442. Began 1904; Anglican. Magazine: *The Chadsian* (2,000 half-yearly). Turnover £1,100,000 to year end Jul 98. University College committed to Christian values and strong personal support.
Web: www.dur.ac.uk\stchads
Email: j.p.cassidy@durham.ac.uk
☎ 0191 374 3364 🖷 0191 386 3422

***St John's College, Durham with Cranmer Hall**, 3 South Bailey, Durham DH1 3RJ
Principal: Rt Rev Stephen Sykes. *Warden:* Rev Dr Steven J L Croft. Lecturers 9, Other staff 38. ***CC*** No.113496. Began 1909; Anglican (Methodists, Independents also registered). Turnover n/a.
Email: david.day@durham.ac.uk
☎ 0191 374 3561 🖷 0191 374 3573

For additional information see List on Pages 500, 501

St John's College, Nottingham, Chilwell Lane, Bramcote, Beeston, Nottingham NG9 3DS
Principal: Canon Dr Christina Baxter BA, PhD. *Vice Principal:* Dr Stephen Travis. Lecturers 9, Other staff 15. ***CC*** No.1026706. Began 1863; as the London College of Divinity; Anglican. Turnover £660,000 to year end Aug 98.
Web: www.stjohns-nottm.ac.uk
Email: college@stjohns-nottm.ac.uk
☎ 0115 925 1114 🖷 0115 943 6438

St John's Roman Catholic Seminary, Wonersh, Guildford GU5 0QX
Rector: Rev K Haggerty MA, STL, PhD. Lecturers 21. ***CC*** No.251342. Began 1891; Roman Catholic. Turnover n/a.
Web: dspace.dial.pipex.com/town/avenue/aba24/contents.shtml
Email: wonersh@dial.pipex.com
☎ 01483 892 217 🖷 01483 894 531

St Mary's, Strawberry Hill, Department of Theology and Religious Studies, Waldegrave Road, Twickenham TW1 4SX
Head of Department: Dr James Byrne STB, STL, PhD. Lecturers 9, Other staff 2. Began n/a; Roman Catholic. (Previously University of Surrey, St Mary's College). Turnover n/a.
Web: www.smuc.ac.uk/dept/trs/index.htm
Email: trs@smuc.ac.uk
☎ 020 8240 4198 🖷 020 8240 4255

St Mary's Seminary, Oscott College, Sutton Coldfield B73 5AA
Rector: Rt Rev Mgr Kevin McDonald. Lecturers 12, Other staff 4. ***CC*** Began 1794; Roman Catholic. Turnover n/a.
☎ 0121 354 2490

St Michael and All Angels' Theological College, Llandaff, Cardiff CF5 2YJ
Warden: Rev J I Holdsworth BA, BD, MTh, PhD. Lecturers-full-time 4, Lecturers-part-time 2. ***CC*** No.634466. Began 1892; Anglican. Turnover n/a.
Email: stmichaels@nildram.co.uk
☎ 029 2056 3379 🖷 029 2057 6377

St Stephen's House, 16 Marston Street, Oxford OX4 1JX
Principal: Rev Jeremy Sheehy MA, DPhil. Lecturers 5, Other staff 7. ***CC*** No.309693. Began 1876; Anglican. Turnover £600,000 to year end Dec 98. Training of men and women for ordained and other ministries.
☎ 01865 247 874 🖷 01865 794 338

School of Mission and World Christianity, Selly Oak Colleges, Birmingham B29 6LQ
Head and Dean: Rev J Andrew Kirk. *Director: Centre for the Study of New Religious Movements:* Dr Allan Anderson. Lecturers 18. ***CC*** No.1056401. Began 1973; interdenominational. Magazine: *Encounters* (500 half-yearly). Turnover £280,000 to year end Jul 99. Courses for mission candidates going overseas, postgraduate studies, short courses.
Web: www.sellyoak.ac.uk/mission.htm
Email: mission@sellyoak.ac.uk
☎ 0121 415 2268/2282 🖷 0121 472 8852

Scotus College, 2 Chesters Road, Bearsden, Glasgow G61 4AG
Rector: Rev Neil Donnachie. Lecturers 7, Other staff 10. Began 1985; Roman Catholic. Turnover n/a.
☎ 0141 942 8384 🖷 0141 943 1767

T

For additional information see List on Pages 500, 501

Selly Oak Colleges, Central House, Birmingham B29 6LQ
President: Rev Dr Michael Taylor. *Vice-President:* Bishop Joe Aldred. *Dean of Mission:* Rev Andrew Kirk. Lecturers 118, Other staff 99. ***CC*** No.3213954. Began 1922; interdenominational. Turnover n/a.
Web: www.sellyoak.ac.uk/sellyoak
☎ 0121 472 4231 🖷 0121 472 8852

†**Simon of Cyrene Theological Institute**, 2 St Ann's Crescent, Wandsworth, London SW18 2LR
Principal: To be appointed. Lecturers 4, Other staff 2. ***CC*** Began 1989; Anglican. Turnover n/a.
☎ 020 8874 1353

South Wales Baptist College, 54 Richmond Road, Cardiff CF2 3UR
Principal: Rev D Hugh Matthews MA, BD, MPhil. Lecturers 3, Other staff 5. ***CC*** No.525777. Began 1807; Baptist. Turnover n/a.
Web: www.cf.ac.uk/uwc/relig/swbc_e.html
Email: swbc@cardiff.ac.uk
☎ 029 2025 6066

***Springdale College**, 54 Weoley Park Road, Selly Oak, Birmingham B29 6RB
Principal: Dr Dennis R Lindsay MA, BA. Lecturers 6, Other staff 3. ***CC*** No.515928. Began 1980; Church of Christ. Turnover n/a.
Email: springdale@sellyoak.ac.uk
☎ 0121 472 0726 🖷 0121 472 0726

***Spurgeon's College**, 189 South Norwood Hill, London SE25 6DJ
Principal: Rev Michael Quicke MA. *Deputy Principal:* Dr Martin Selman. *Academic Dean:* Rev Dr John Colwell. Lecturers 10, Other staff 21. ***CC*** No.299148. Began 1856; Baptist but open to all. Turnover n/a. Equipping Christians to lead the people of God in mission and ministry in the contemporary world.
Web: www.spurgeons.ac.uk
Email: enquiries@spurgeons.ac.uk
☎ 020 8653 0850 🖷 020 8771 0959

Theological Institute of the Scottish Episcopal Church, Old Coates House, 32 Manor Place, Edinburgh EH3 7EB
Principal: Rev Canon R A Nixon BD, MA, MTh. Lecturers 22, Other staff 2. Began 1810; Scottish Episcopal Church. Turnover n/a. Initial ministerial education.
Email: tisec@scotland.anglican.org
☎ 0131 220 2272 🖷 0131 220 2294

***Tilsley College (Gospel Literature Outeach)**, 78 Muir Street, Motherwell ML1 1BN
Principal: Mr David Clarkson. Lecturers 3, Other staff 1. ***CC*** No.CR 41802. Began 1975; non-denominational. (Previously Gospel Literature Outreach Training for Service). Turnover n/a. Training, service, mission.
Email: glotrain@aol.com
☎ 01698 266 776 🖷 01698 275 418

Trinity College Carmarthen, Carmarthen SA31 3EP
Principal: Mr D Clive Jones-Davies MA, MPhil, FRSA. Lecturers 105, Other staff 74. ***CC*** Began 1848; Anglican. Turnover n/a.
☎ 01267 237 971 🖷 01237 230 933

***Trinity Theological College**, Stoke Hill, Stoke Bishop, Brist BS9 1JP
Principal: Dr Francis Bridger, BA, MA, PhD. *Vice Princip* Rev Howard Peskett. *Director of Pastoral Studies and Evang lism:* Rev David Runcorn. Lecturers 12, Other staff 40. ***C*** No.311793. Began 1972; Anglican but open to all. Turnov £1,100,000 to year end Dec 98. Training God's people for bo ordained and lay ministry and mission.
Web: www.trinity-bris.ac.uk
Email: admissions@trinity-bris.ac.uk
☎ 0117 968 2803 🖷 0117 968 7470

Union Theological College, 108 Botanic Avenue, Belfast BT7 1J
Principal: Rev Professor J C McCullough BA, BD, PhD. Lecturers 6, Other staff 11. Began 1853; Presbyterian but open t all. Affiliated to Queen's University. Turnover n/a.
Web: www.union.org.uk
Email: j.mccullough@union.org.uk
☎ 028 9020 5080 🖷 028 9031 6839

United College of the Ascension, Weoley Park Road, Selly Oak Birmingham B29 6RD
Principal: Rev Canon Dr Andrew Wingate MA, MPhi DipTh. *Director of mission studies in the Methodist church tutor:* Rev Dr Emmanuel Jacob. Lecturers 6, Other staff 21. ***CC*** No.234518. Began 1923; Anglican/Methodist. (Previousl College of the Ascension). Turnover £540,000 to year end De 98. Mission training for the world church and the church i Britain and Ireland.
Email: uca@sellyoak.ac.uk
☎ 0121 472 1667 🖷 0121 472 4320

The United Theological College, Aberystwyth SY23 2LT
Principle: Rev Dr John Tudno Williams MA, PhD. *Academic Secretary:* Mrs Susan Lloyd. Lecturers 3, Other staff 3. Began 1906; Presbyterian Church of Wales but open to all. Turnover n/a.
Email: esl998@aber.ac.uk
☎ 01970 624 574 🖷 01970 626 350

University of Aberdeen, Department of Divinity with Religious Studies, Aberdeen AB24 3UB
Head of Department: Prof William Johnstone BD, MA, DLitt. Lecturers 15, Other staff 3. Began 1495; interdenominational. Turnover n/a.
Web: www.abdn.ac.uk/divinity/
Email: divinity@abdn.ac.uk
☎ 01224 272 380 🖷 01224 273 750

University of Edinburgh, Centre for the Study of Christianity in the non-Western World, New College, Mound Place, Edinburgh EH1 2LX
Director: Professor David Kerr, BA, MA, DPhil. Lecturers 5, Other staff 4. ***CC*** Began 1982; non-denominational. Magazine: *Bulletin of the Scottish Institute of Missionary Studies* (Circulation n/a annually), *Non-Western Christianity* (Circulation n/a annually). Turnover n/a.
Email: fernona@srvo.div.ed.ac.uk.
☎ 0131 650 8952 🖷 0131 650 7972

University of Edinburgh, Faculty of Divinity, New College, Mound Place, Edinburgh EH1 2LX
Dean: Rev Professor Duncan B Forrester MA, BD, DPhil, Theo.D. Lecturers 27, Other staff 15. Began 1584; non-denominational, 1846 as Church of Scotland. Turnover n/a.
☎ 0131 650 8900 🖷 0131 650 6579

University of Glasgow, Faculty of Divinity, Trinity College, Glasgow G12 8QQ
Dean: Rev Prof David Jasper. Lecturers 15, Other staff 2. Began 1452; non-denominational. Turnover n/a.
Web: www.religious.divinity.gla.ac.uk
Email: d.jasper@arts.gla.ac.uk
☎ 0141 339 8855 Ext 5297

For additional information see List on Pages 500, 501

iversity of St Andrews, School of Divinity, St Mary's College, South Street, St Andrews KY16 9JU
Principal of College: Dr R A Piper BA, BD, PhD. Lecturers 14, Other staff 3. ***CC*** No.SCO 13532. Began 1410; College 1539 interdenominational. Turnover n/a.
Web: www.st-andrews.ac.uk/~www-sd/home.html
Email: rap@st-andrews.ac.uk
☎ 01334 462 851 🖷 01334 462 852

shaw College, Durham DH7 9RH
President: Rev J O'Keefe. Lecturers 16, Other staff 5. ***CC*** Began 1808; Roman Catholic. Turnover n/a.
☎ 0191 373 1366 🖷 0191 373 7009

Vesley College, College Park Drive, Henbury Road, Bristol BS10 7QD
Principal: Rev Dr Neil Richardson. Lecturers 5, Other staff 4. ***CC*** Began 1842; Methodist but open to all. Turnover n/a.
Email: wescoll@demon.co.uk
☎ 0117 950 1608 🖷 0117 950 1277

Vesley House, Cambridge, Jesus Lane, Cambridge CB5 8BJ
Principal: Rev Dr Philip Luscombe. Lecturers 2. ***CC*** No.311446. Began n/a; Methodist. Turnover n/a. For the training of men and women in the Methodist ministry.
Web: www.wesley.org.uk
Email: bursar@wesley.org.uk
☎ 020 7639 3052 🖷 01223 321 177

Westcott House, Jesus Lane, Cambridge CB5 8BP
Principal: Rev Michael Roberts MA MDiv. Lecturers 5, Other staff 8. ***CC*** No.311445. Began 1881; Anglican. Turnover n/a.
Web: www.ely.anglican.org/westcott/
☎ 01223 741 000 🖷 01223 741 002

Westfield House, 30 Huntingdon Road, Cambridge CB3 0HH
Preceptor: Rev Reginald C Quirk BA BD MPhil (Cantab). Lecturers 3, Other staff 1. ***CC*** No.220466. Began 1962; Lutheran. Turnover £100,000 to year end Dec 98. Teaching theology within a confessional Lutheran framework, including preparation for ordination.
Email: rcq@compuserve.com
☎ 01223 354 331 🖷 01223 355 265

Westminster College, Cambridge, Madingley Road, Cambridge CB3 0AA
Principal: Rev Dr David Cornick MA, BD, PhD. Lecturers 5, Other staff 10. ***CC*** Began 1899; United Reformed. Turnover n/a.
☎ 01223 741 084 🖷 01223 300 765

Whitefield College of the Bible and Theological Hall of the Free Presbyterian Church of Ulster, 117 Banbridge Road, Gilford, Craigavon BT63 6DL
Principal: Dr John Douglas. Lecturers 13, Other staff 4. ***CC*** No.XN 59402. Began 1979; Free Presbyterian. Turnover n/a.
Email: whitefd@globalnet.co.uk
☎ 0182 06 62232 🖷 0182 06 62232

Woodbrooke Quaker Study Centre, 1046 Bristol Road, Selly Oak, Birmingham B29 6LJ
Principal: Jennifer Barraclough MA. *Head of Community:* Helen Rowlands. *Bursar:* Howard Saunders. Lecturers 4, Other staff 19. ***CC*** No.313816. Began 1903; Religious Society of Friends. Turnover n/a. Adult religious education for Quakers and others.
Web: www.woodbrooke.org.uk/woodbrooke/
Email: enquiries@woodbrooke.org.uk
☎ 0121 472 5171 🖷 0121 472 5173

Word of Life International, Summerhill Court, Lang Stracht, Aberdeen AB15 6TW
Director: Pastor Jim Addison. Executive staff 2, Other staff 8. ***CC*** No.SCO 22163. Began 1978; interdenominational. Turnover n/a.
Email: church@wordoflife.co.uk
☎ 01224 326 622 🖷 01224 312 727

Wycliffe Hall, 54 Banbury Road, Oxford OX2 6PW
Principal: Rev Dr Alister McGrath BD, MA, DPhil. *Development Officer:* Rev Dr Peter Walker. *Director of Evangelism:* Rev Dr Graham Tomlin. Lecturers 9, Other staff 5. ***CC*** No.309703. Began 1877; Anglican. Turnover £600,000 to year end Dec 96.
Web: www.wycliffe.ox.ac.uk
Email: enquiries@wycliffe.ox.ac.uk
☎ 01865 274 200 🖷 01865 274 215

THEOLOGICAL COLLEGES & BIBLE SCHOOLS (NON-RESIDENTIAL)

Tuition fees per annum unless stated otherwise
Colleges which did not supply any of this information are not listed here.

Name	Students	Course details	Fees
Anglican			
Lincoln Theological Institute for the Study of Religion and Society	n/a	Postgraduate research, MA	n/a
Oak Hill Open Learning Centre	n/a	Courses for personal or group study, lay or ordained	n/a
St Albans and Oxford Ministry Course	130	3 years. Ministerial and lay training.	£3,069, £575 (associate student)
St John's Extension Studies	2,000	Biblical and theological studies, religious education, pastoral counselling, crosscultural mission	n/a
Anglican, Methodist, United Reformed			
Carlisle and Blackburn Diocesan Training Institute	n/a	3 years. For ordinands and lay people	£1,956
The North East Oecumenical Course (NEOC)	36	3 years for ordinands and lay people	£2,040
North Thames Ministerial Training Course	Unlimited	For ordinands and lay ministry	n/a
South East Institute for Theological Education (SEITE)	n/a	3 years. Ministerial and lay training	£2,115
South West Ministry Training Course	Unlimited	Part-time, for ordinands	n/a
West Midlands Ministerial Training Course	60	For ordinands and lay people	£5,708

Theological Colleges & Bible Schools (Non-Residential)

Name	Students	Course details	F
Apostolic Episcopal Free Church			
Anglian Ecclesiastical and Theological Seminary	n/a	Ministerial training; spiritual healing, counselling	
Baptist			
Y Coleg Gwyn (North Wales Baptist College)	n/a	3 years. Pastoral and ministerial training, theology.	As univers
Irish Baptist College	50	1 to 3 years. For pastors and overseas missionaries.	Varia
Scottish Baptist College	25	4 years. Ministerial training	£1,3
Roman Catholic			
Catholic Bible School	20	Bible study, counselling, spiritual direction	n
Missionary Institute London	n/a	6 years Bachelor of Theology; 1 to 3 years diploma, missionary training, pastoral course	£1,400, £12 p d
Church in Wales			
Monmouth Ordination Course (NSM)	6	For non-stipendiary ministers	n
Free Church of Scotland			
Free Church College	30	3 or 4 years	£1,3
Interdenominational / Ecumenical / Non-denominational			
Central School of Religion	n/a	1 to 5 years. For ministers, graduates, church musicians, lay preachers.	Variab
Christian Life Bible College	n/a	2 years	£1,08 Part-time £64
Cornhill Training Course	60	1 year. Bible training for ministry	n.
Covenant Bible College	n/a	2 years part-time or full-time. Biblical theology, diploma of biblical studies or Christian ministries	n/
East Anglian Ministerial Training Course	80	Full- and part-time. For ordinands and lay	n/
The East Midlands Ministry Training Course	n/a	Part-time MA/Diploma/Certificate Courses; theological & pastoral studies	n/
East Midlands School of Christian Ministry	120	1 or 2 years. Theology; correspondences course in Greek, Hebrew	£7
Edinburgh Bible College	n/a	Applied contemporary theology, for lay people	n/
Emmaus Bible School UK	n/a	Studies in over 120 languages. For missionaries and missions	n/
Greenwich School of Theology	n/a	2 or 3 years. Theology by distance learning at undergraduate and postgraduate level.	£85
Hampstead Bible College	100	NVQs in Biblical studies, City and Guilds Further Education Teacher's training, Information Technology	n/
Highland Theological College	Unlimited	Up to 3 years	n/
ICI Bible Study (International Correspondence Institute)	n/a	Distance learning at 4 levels	n/
The Independent Theological Academy	15	For ministers, missionaries, church workers	n/
Institute for Community and Development Studies	Unlimited	1 to 4 years, from certificate to MA in community development	n/
Mallon De Theological College	n/a	Open, distance learning in theology	n/
Manchester Christian College/Training Centre	50	3 years	£96
Manchester Christian Institute	n/a	BA (Hons) in Theology; part-time; for ordinands and lay people	n/
Metropolitan College of Ministry	n/a	Training for ministry	n/
Midlands Bible College	52	2 year Diploma undergraduate level, short courses	n/
New Life School of Ministries	30	1 year Bible school with practical training	n/a
Northern Federation for Training in Ministry	n/a	Ministerial and lay training	n/
Northern Ordination Course	n/a	Ministerial training	n/
The Open Theological College	n/a	6 years part-time distance learning, Honours degree in theology	n/a
Oxford Centre for Mission Studies	150	Guided research and Masters courses	n/a
Sarum College	n/a	Short courses in theological education and training	n/a
S.E.A.N. International (UK)	n/a	Theological Education by Extension, basic level students, local churches, group study	n/a
STETS Southern Theological Education and Training Scheme	100	Ministerial and lay training	n/a
Theological Training Course	n/a	4 years, for preaching and pastoral ministry. 2 residential weeks per year	£191
West of England Ministerial Training Course	100	For ordinands and readers	n/a
Methodist			
Edgehill Christian Education Centre	250	Part-time/correspondence. Theological access course	n/a
Westminster College School of Humanities	150 full-time 600 part-time	Theology and Religious Studies, certificate, diploma, undergraduate, postgraduate. Research.	n/a
Pentecostal			
Christ the Redeemer Bible College	47	Varying length, for ministers	n/a
El Shaddai Bible College of Advanced Ministry (UK)	n/a	Training leaders and lay for ministry	n/a
International Bible Institute of London (Kensington Temple)	170 full-time 150 part-time	1 or 2 year Diplomas	n/a
The Maria Morley Crawcrook Pentecostal College	n/a	1 year part-time/correspondence; for potential church leaders and groups	n/a
New Life Bible School	n/a	1 or 2 years, for lay people	n/a
Peniel Bible College	145	2 or 3 years, degree and diploma	n/a
Reformed and Congregational			
Cranmer Memorial and Reformation Theology College	n/a	1 to 3 years. Theology: diploma, general ordination, licentiate, fellowship courses	n/a
Reformed Presbyterian Church of Ireland			
Reformed Theological College	15	3 years. For men, for ministry and missionaries	£800

T

THEOLOGICAL COLLEGES & BIBLE SCHOOLS (NON-RESIDENTIAL)

Note: University Colleges and other similar academic institutions which offer tertiary level courses are included in the Redidential category even if they are entirely Non-Residential, because of the nature of the courses offered.

nglian Ecclesiastical and Theological Seminary, Flat 5, 3 Canfield Gardens, London NW6 3JR
Principal: Most Rev Dr Bruno Von Ehrenberg MD, D.Hom, DD, OSC. Lecturers 3. Began 1995; Apostolic Episcopal Free Churches. No magazine. Turnover n/a. Ordination training for the Apostolic Episcopal Free Churches Alliance; courses in spiritual healing, counselling.
☎ 020 7328 0162

ambridge Theological Federation, Wesley House, Jesus Lane, Cambridge CB5 8BQ
Executive Officer: Mr Chris Wright. Other staff 3. Began 1972; ecumenical. (Previously Cambridge Federation of Theological Colleges). No magazine. Turnover £90,000 to year end Aug 97. Co-ordinating all that is done together by the member bodies of the Federation.
Web: www.ely.anglican.org.westcott
Email: cpww2@cam.ac.uk
☎ 01223 741 047   🖷 01223 741 055

'arlisle and Blackburn Diocesan Training Institute, Church House, West Walls, Carlisle CA3 8UE
Principal: Rev Canon Tim Herbert, BA, MPhil. Lecturers 1. Began 1978; Anglican, Methodist and United Reformed. (Previously Carlisle Diocesan Training Institute). Associated with the University College of St Martin, Lancaster. No magazine. Turnover n/a. Training for all categories of ordained ministry; Anglican, Methodist, and others.
☎ 01228 522 573   🖷 01228 815 400

Catholic Bible School, Nutbourne House, Farm Lane, Nutbourne, Chichester PO18 8SD
Director: Mrs Joan Le Morvan DipEd. Staff n/a. *CC* Began 1988; Roman Catholic. No magazine. Turnover n/a. Bible Study courses, correspondence courses, counselling training for 20 students, spiritual direction training, hope alive therapy.
Web: www.tregalic.co.uk/catholic/bibleschool/
Email: bibleschool@tregalic.co.uk
☎ 01243 371 766   🖷 01243 371 459

Central School of Religion, 49 Upper Tooting Park, London SW17 7SN
Director of Studies: J Pinnington MA, DPhil, DD. No full-time staff. Began 1896; non-denominational. No magazine. Turnover n/a. Part-time tutorial/correspondence courses for ministers/graduates, church musicians; training courses for lay preachers.
☎ 020 8675 0180   🖷 020 8675 0180

Chinese Overseas Christian Mission, 4 Earlsfield Road, London SW18 3DW
Director: Miss Mary Wang. *Field Director:* Rev David Cheung. *Council Chairman:* Prof Michael Chan. Executive staff 2, Other staff 40. *CC* No.232651. Began n/a; interdenominational. No magazine. Turnover £670,000 to year end Dec 98.
Web: www.-glink.net.hk/cocmhk
Email: cocm@compuserve.com
☎ 020 8870 2251   🖷 020 8877 1357

***Christ the Redeemer Bible College**, Unit B1, North Acton Business Park, Victoria Road, London W3 6UL
Principal: Pastor Daniel Akhazemea. Executive staff 1, Admin staff 1. *CC* No.803698. Began 1998; Pentecostal. Magazine: *CRBC News* (3,000 quarterly). Turnover £50,000 to year end Jun 99. Training religious ministers.
Web: www.rccg.org
Email: crbcrccg@aol.com
☎ 020 8896 0280   🖷 020 8896 0286

†***Christian Life Bible College**, The City Temple, 49 Shoe Lane, London EC4A 3BL
Principal: Rev Christopher Hill. Lecturers 12, Other staff 4. *CC* Began 1969; interdenominational. Incorporating Christian Life Ministries. No magazine. Turnover n/a. 2 year course.
☎ 020 7583 6324

Cornhill Training Course, Willcox House, 140 Borough High Street, London SE1 1LB
Director: Rev David J Jackman MA, DipTh. Lecturers 3, Other staff 1. *CC* Began 1991; interdenominational. No magazine. Turnover n/a. One-year training course in understanding and teaching the Bible for full-time ministry.
Email: ctc@proctrust.org.uk
☎ 020 7407 0562   🖷 020 7407 0569

***Covenant Bible College**, 214 Elephant and Castle Shopping Centre, London SE1 6TE
Director: Rev Paul Jinadu. *Provost:* Rev Gbenro Adewunmi. *CC* No.1004343. Began 1988; interdenominational. Part of New Covenant Church. Magazine: *U-turn* (2,000 quarterly). Turnover n/a.
Email: covbible.co@aol.com
☎ 020 7701 9959 / 7277 0272

Cranmer Memorial and Reformation Theology College, PO Box 20, Bexhill-on-Sea TN40 2ZH
Principle: Rev P J Gadsden FTh PhD. Lecturers 4. Began 1936; Reformed and Congregational. (Amalgamated with Institute of Evangelical Protestant Research and Development). No magazine. Turnover n/a. Correspondence course in theology, including diploma, general ordination, licentiate and fellowship courses.
☎ 01424 734 345

East Anglian Ministerial Training Course, 5 Pound Hill, Cambridge CB3 0AE
Principal: To be appointed. *Vice-Principal:* Rev Andrew Todd. Lecturers 3. Began 1977; interdenominational. No magazine. Turnover n/a. Full and part-time theological education for ordinands or lay people.
Email: admin@eamtc.org.uk
☎ 01223 741 026   🖷 01223 741 027

The East Midlands Ministry Training Course, Block D, Cherry Tree Buildings, University Park, Nottingham NG7 2RD
Principal: Rev Michael J Taylor MA, STB,PhL. Lecturers 3, Other staff 2. *CC* No.512143. Began 1973; interdenominational. No magazine. Turnover n/a. Part-time diploma course in theological and pastoral studies for students remaining in regular work.
Web: www.nottingham.ac.uk/cont-ed/emmtc.htm
Email: emmtc@nottingham.ac.uk
☎ 0115 951 4854   🖷 0115 951 4817

East Midlands School of Christian Ministry, Elim Church Centre, Ashby Road, Loughborough LE11 3AF
Principal: Mr Richard Lee. Part-time lecturers 13, Other staff 5. *CC* No.251549. Began 1995; non-denominational. No magazine. Turnover £3,800 to year end Jun 98. Providing training for busy people, including Christian theology and correspondence course, Greek, Hebrew.
Web: www.geocities.com/athens/8530/
Email: scm-richard@geocities.com
☎ 01509 234 306

T

Edgehill Christian Education Centre, 9 Lennoxvale, Malone Road, Belfast BT9 5BY
Administrator: Mrs Elaine Barnett. Lecturers 2, Other staff 4. Began 1984; Methodist but open to all. No magazine. Turnover £20,000 to year end Dec 98. Lay training centre for 250 students: theological access course (accredited), part-time classes, correspondence courses.
Web: welcome.to/edgehill
Email: elaine.edgehill@netmatters.co.uk
☎ 028 9066 5870 Answerphone: 028 9068 2153

†**Edinburgh Bible College**, PO Box 19001, Edinburgh EH6 5YL
Principal: Rev Dr Campbell Campbell-Jack BD MTh PhD. Lecturers 5. *CC* No.SCO 26255. Began 1997; interdenominational. No magazine. Turnover n/a. Teaching nationally recognised courses in applied contemporary theology to lay people.
☎ No telephone

El Shaddai Bible College of Advanced Ministry (UK), Top Chapel, Elliott Street, Tyldesley, Manchester M29 8DR
Principal: Rev Keith Graves BMin. Lecturers 7. *CC* No.1052741. Began 1992; Elim Independent. No magazine. Turnover n/a. Training leaders and lay persons for the ministry to which God has called them.
Email: topchapel@mcmail.com
☎ 01942 875 973 Fax 01942 877 990

Emmaus Bible School UK, Carlett Boulevard, Eastham, Wirral, Merseyside CH62 8BZ
UK Director: Mr David A Thompson. Other staff 8. *CC* Began 1951; interdenominational. Magazine: *By the Way* (2,000 Frequency n/a). *Prayer Letter* (Circulation & Frequency n/a). Turnover n/a. Offering studies in over 120 languages used by missionaries and missions worldwide. 93 English speaking studies.
Web: www.kingsnet.org.uk/emmaus
Email: emmaus@kingsnet.org.uk
☎ 0151 327 1172 / 6153 / 7373 Fax 0151 327 1592

Free Church College, 15 North Bank Street, The Mound, Edinburgh EH1 2LS
Principal: Rev Archibald C Boyd MA, BD. Lecturers 5, Other staff 1. *CC* No.SCO 12925. Began 1843; Free Church of Scotland. No magazine. Turnover n/a.
Web: www.freechurch.org
Email: secretary@freescotcoll.ac.uk
☎ 0131 226 4978 Fax 0131 220 0597

Greenwich School of Theology, 9 Wolversdene Gardens, Andover SP10 2BB
Registrar: Dr C Killacky TD, MA, BSc. Tutors 64, Other staff 4. Began 1964; interdenominational. Magazine: *Bulletin* (Circulation n/a annually). Turnover £50,000 to year end Dec 98. Teaching theology at a distance, Bachelor, Master and Doctoral levels through programme of individually-guided study.
Email: ckillacky@aol.com
☎ 01264 358 512 Fax 01264 358 512

For additional information see List on Pages 509, 510

mpstead Bible College, 224 Walworth Road, London SE17 1JE
Principal: Rev Jan Owbridge. Lecturers 12, Other staff 5. *CC* No.1050760. Began 1983; non-denominational. (Previously Hampstead Bible School). No magazine. Turnover n/a. NVQ levels 2 & 3 in Biblical studies. Full and part time, day and evening courses.
Email: janhbc@aol.com
☎ 020 7708 2185 Mobile: 07957 113 975
Fax: 020 7708 2206

ghland Theological College, High Street, Dingwall IV15 9HA
Principal: Rev Dr A T McGowan BD. STM, PhD. Full-time lecturers 5, Part-time lecturers 7, Other staff 4. *CC* No.SCO 22838. Began 1994; interdenominational. No magazine. Turnover n/a. Various courses up to 3 years. No limit on student numbers.
Email: hti@fc.uhi.ac.uk
☎ 01349 867 600 Fax: 01349 867 555

I Bible Study (International Correspondence Institute), Regents Park, London Road, Nantwich CW5 6LW
National Director: Mr Tony Coles BA. Other staff 5. *CC* No.295124. Began 1976; interdenominational. No magazine. Turnover £86,000 to year end Dec 98. Distance learning courses at four levels; college and group study materials; theological books by mail order.
Web: www.ici.edu
Email: icibible@netcentral.co.uk
☎ 01270 624 123 Fax: 01270 610 020

he Independent Theological Academy, Westbury Chapel, Broad Street, Wolverhampton WV1 1JD
Principal: To be appointed. Executive staff 1, Other staff (part-time) 10. Began 1993; interdenominational. No magazine. Turnover n/a. Training ministers, missionaries and church workers.
☎ 01902 424 811 Fax: 01902 424 811

nstitute for Community and Development Studies, Greatfields Hall, King Edward's Road, Barking IG11 7TR
Director: Rt Rev Henry Kontor. All voluntary staff. *CC* No.1022993. Began 1991; interdenominational. Magazine: *Newsletter* (Circulation n/a every four months). Turnover n/a. Promoting church-involved Community Development practice. MA accredited course.
Email: icds@aol.com
☎ 020 8507 2603 Mobile: 07711 855 373
Fax: 020 8507 2603

International Bible Institute of London (Kensington Temple), PO Box 9161, London W3 6GS
President: Rev Colin W Dye BD. *Principle:* Will Napier. Lecturers 9, Other staff 3. *CC* No.251549. Began 1985; Elim Pentecostal but open to all. Incorporating School of Creative Ministries. No magazine. Turnover n/a. 1 or 2 year Diplomas with simultaneous translation into Portuguese.
Web: www.ken-temp.org.uk
Email: ibiol@dircon.co.uk
☎ 020 8896 3736 Fax: 020 8896 2628

Irish Baptist College, 67 Sandown Road, Belfast BT5 6GU
Principal: Dr Hamilton Moore BD, MTh, PhD. Lecturers 9, Other staff 2. Began 1892; Baptist. No magazine. Turnover n/a. Traingin for pastoral and overseas missionary work.
Email: ibcollege@aol.com
☎ 028 9047 1908 Fax: 028 9047 1363

Lincoln Theological Institute for the Study of Religion and Society, Sheffield University, 36 Wilkinson Street, Sheffield S10 2GB
Director: Rev Canon Dr Martyn Percy MA PhD. *Administrator/Librarian:* Miss Caroline Dicker. Staff 4. *CC* No.527278. Began 1997; Anglican but open to all. Magazine: *Annual Report* (Circulation n/a annually). Turnover £100,000 to year end Dec 98. Postgraduate students. Research projects including public health, Europe, jubilee issues, culture, the Bible and society.
Web: www.shef.ac.uk/~lti
Email: lincoln@sheffield.ac.uk
☎ 0114 222 6399 Fax: 0114 276 3973

***Mallon De Theological College**, 11a Methley Grove, Leeds LS7 3PA
Principal: Rev Steve Hakes. Lecturers 2, Other staff 1. Began 1989; ecumenical. (Previously Ekklesia). No magazine. Turnover n/a. Providing Open Distance Learning theological courses.
Web: www.detc.freeserve.co.uk
Email: mallon.detc@bigfoot.com
☎ No telephone

***Manchester Christian College/Training Centre**, Chippenham Road, Ancoats, Manchester M4 6FF
Principal: Rev C Andrews BBS. Lecturers 6. *CC* Began 1978; interdenominational. No magazine. Turnover £55,000 to year end Dec 98. 3 year degree programme, affiliated to Logos Bible Institute.
Email: mca.uk@virgin.net
☎ 0161 203 5242 Fax: 0161 203 5778

†**Manchester Christian Institute**, Luther King House, Brighton Grove, Rusholme, Manchester M14 5JP
Director: Rev Dr J M Sutcliffe MA. Other staff 2. *CC* No.515358. Began 1977; ecumenical. Magazine: *Opportunity* (2,800 every four months). Turnover £70,000 to year end Aug 96. Providing a part-time BA(Hons) in Theology for lay people and ordinands.
Email: john.sutcliffe@mcc.ac.uk
☎ 0161 225 4372

The Maria Morley Crawcrook Pentecostal College, 8 Kepier Chare, Ryton NE40 4TS
Administrators: Rev Audrey Graham, Rev Judith Gray, Rev Linda Butler. Lecturers 4, Other staff 6. Began 1979; Pentecostal but open to all . (Previously The Maria Morley Bible College & Crawcrook Pentecostal Ecumenical Bible College). No magazine. Turnover n/a. Training for those who wish to lead Pentecostal churches or groups & personal education. Part-time and correspondence courses.
Web: members.aol.com/mmorleyspc/college.htm
Email: mmorleyspc@aol.com
☎ 0191 413 3221 Fax: 0191 413 9535

†***Metropolitan College of Ministry**, 13a Leonard Street, London EC2A 4QS
Principal: Rev Dr Peter Rowe BMin, MTh, PhD. Executive staff 1, Other staff 9. *CC* Began 1993; interdenominational. No magazine. Turnover n/a. Ministry training college.
☎ 020 7739 7770 Fax: 020 7739 7771

Midlands Bible College, St John's Cloisters, St John's Square, Wolverhampton WV2 4AT
Principal: Rev Calvin Smith. Lecturers 5, Other staff 3. *CC* Began 1990; interdenominational. Magazine: *The Reviewer* (250 quarterly). Turnover n/a. For full-time and lay ministry, also correspondence course.
Web: www.btinternet.com/~midlandsbiblecollege
Email: midlandsbiblecollege@btinternet.com
☎ 01902 423 320

T

For additional information see List on Pages 509, 510

Missionary Institute London, Holcombe House, The Ridgeway, Mill Hill, London NW7 4HY
President: Rev Dr Lawrence Nemer BA, LMiss, MA, PhD. Lecturers 30, Other staff 6. *CC* No.269713. Began 1967; Roman Catholic. (Affiliated to Leuven University, Belgium and Middlesex University). Magazine: *MIL Record* (Circulation n/a annually). Turnover n/a. Bachelors of Theology, 1 or 3 year diploma courses, missionary training courses, pastoral studies course.
Email: mil@mdx.ac.uk
☎ 020 8906 1893

Monmouth Ordination Course (NSM), The Rectory, 19 Main Road, Portskewett, Newport NP6 4SG
Director: Canon Terry Palmer. Other staff 4. Began 1970; Church in Wales. (Previously Monmouth School of Ministry (NSM)). No magazine. Turnover n/a. Training course for non-stipendiary ministers for the Church in Wales.
☎ 01291 420 313

†**New Life Bible School**, 207b East Lane, Wembley HA0 3NG
Principal: Rev Ian Christensen. Other staff 3. *CC* Began 1991; Assemblies of God. No magazine. Turnover n/a. Teaching and training Christians to be more effective in their ministries; 1 or 2 year course.
☎ 020 8908 5652 Fax 020 8908 5652

***New Life School of Ministries**, Cairo New Road, Croydon CR0 1XP
Director: Mr Arthur Hibbert. Lecturers 13. *CC* No.1003768. Began 1993; non-denominational. (Previously New Life Christian Centre Bible School). No magazine. Turnover n/a. 1-year Bible school course with practical training opportunities. Limited accommodation available.
Email: arthur_hibbert@yahoo.com
☎ 020 8680 7671 Fax 020 8686 7692

The North East Oecumenical Course (NEOC), Ushaw College, Durham DH7 9RH
Principal: Rev Canon Trevor Pitt BA, MA, STM, Prof Dip Post Comp Ed. *Director of Practical Theology:* Rev Rhona Jones. Lecturer 1, Other staff 2. Began 1976; Anglican/United Reformed/Methodist. (Previously The North East Ordination Course). No magazine. Turnover £150,000 to year end Sept 98. Training course for ordination and lay candidates.
Email: neocoffice@aol.com
☎ 0191 373 7600 Fax 0191 373 7601

North Thames Ministerial Training Course, Chase Side, Southgate, London N14 4PS
Principal: Rev David Sceats MA. Other staff 6. *CC* Began 1994; Anglican. (Previously Oak Hill Ministerial Training Course). No magazine. Turnover n/a. Part-time course for Anglican, Methodist and United Reformed ordinands, and for lay ministry trainees.
☎ 020 8364 9442 Fax 020 8364 8889

Northern Federation for Training in Ministry, Luther King House, Brighton Grove, Rusholme, Manchester M14 5JP
President: Rev Dr Richard Kidd. *General Manager:* Mr Keith Baby. *CC* No.517496. Began 1984; interdenominational. Home to the Partnership for Theological Education, Manchester. No magazine. Turnover £260,000. Interdenominational ministerial and lay training. Conference/residential facilities available and overnight or short stay accommodation.
☎ 0161 224 6404 Fax 0161 248 9201

Northern Ordination Course, Luther King House, Brigh[ton] Grove, Rusholme, Manchester M14 5JP
Principal: Rev Canon Michael J Williams BA, BD, *from* [...] *2000:* Rev Dr Christopher Burdon. Lecturers 5. [...] No.1067982. Began 1970; interdenominational. No magazine. Turnover n/a. Ordination training, mainly for Angli[can] and Methodist ministries.
Email: office@noc1.u-net.com
☎ 0161 225 6668 Fax 0161 248 9201

***Oak Hill Open Learning Centre**, Chase Side, Southgate, Lond[on] N14 4PS
Manager: Mr Peter Wood BA, DipM. Other staff 1. [...] No.310031. Began 1986; Anglican but open to all. (Previou[sly] Oak Hill Extension College). Part of Oak Hill Theologi[cal] College. No magazine. Turnover n/a. Conferences, courses a[nd] resources for ministers and Christians wishing to dig deeper [in] their faith.
Web: www.oakhill.ac.uk
Email: peterw@oakhill.ac.uk
☎ 020 8449 0467 Fax 020 8441 5996

The Open Theological College, PO Box 220, The Park Camp[us,] The Park, Cheltenham GL50 2QF
Director: Mr Keith J Hacking. Full-time staff 5. *C*[*C*] No.1016819. Began 1992; interdenominational. No magazine. Turnover n/a. 6-year part-time distance learning honou[rs] degree in theology.
Web: www.chelt.ac.uk/cwis/otc.htm
Email: otc@chelt.ac.uk
☎ 01242 532 837 Fax 01242 532 801

***Oxford Centre for Mission Studies**, St Philip and St James Churc[h,] PO Box 70, Woodstock Road, Oxford OX2 6HB
Executive Director: Rev Canon Dr Vinay Samuel Bsc, B[...] MLitt, DD. *Director of Academic Affairs:* Rev Dr Christoph[er] Sugden MA, MPhil, PhD. Academic staff 5, Admin staff 1[...] *CC* No.290112. Began 1984; non-denominational. See als[o] Regnum Books. Magazine: *Transformation* (2,500 quarterly[).] Turnover £375,000 to year end Dec 97. Research and resourc[e] centre of the International Fellowship of Evangelical Missio[n] Theologians.
Web: www.icmc.org/ocms
Email: ocms@ocms.ac.uk
☎ 01865 556 071 Fax 01865 510 823

***Peniel Bible College**, 49 Coxtie Green Road, Pilgrims Hatch[,] Brentwood CM14 5PS
Principal: Rev Dr Michael S B Reid ThD, DD, MA. Lecturer[s] 10. Began 1982; Free Pentecostal. No magazine. Turnover n/a[.] Courses are part-time or correspondence; degree and diploma courses available.
Web: www.peniel.org
☎ 01277 372 996 Fax 01277 375 332

Reformed Theological College, 98 Lisburn Road, Belfas[t] BT9 6AG
Principal: Rev Frederick Leahy MTh. Lecturers 5. *CC* Began 1854; Reformed Presbyterian Church of Ireland. No magazine. Turnover £16,000 to year end Dec 96. Training men for the Gospel ministry and for missionary service; small classes.
☎ 028 9066 0689

St Albans and Oxford Ministry Course, Church House, North Hinksey, Oxford OX2 0NB
Principal: Rev Dr Mike Butterworth. *Vice Principal:* Dr Steve Moyise. Other staff 6. *CC* No.1041832. Began 1972; Anglican but open to all. No magazine. Turnover £350,000 to year end Aug 98. Ordination training part-time for Anglican, Methodist and United Reformed Churches.
Email: mikebutterworth@compuserve.com
☎ 01865 208 260 Fax 01865 790 470

T

For additional information see List on Pages 509, 510

John's Extension Studies, Chilwell Lane, Bramcote, Nottingham NG9 3RL
Director of Extension Studies: Rev David Muir MA, DPS. *Business Manager:* Mr David Payne. Other staff 3. ***CC*** No.1026706. Began 1978; Anglican. Magazine: *Extension News* (1,900 every four months). Turnover £326,000 to year end Aug 98. Resourcing Christians in practical and theological skills for ministry, through distance learning courses and publications.
Web: www.stjohns-nottm.ac.uk
Email: ext.studies@stjohns-nottm.ac.uk
☎ 0115 925 1117 🖷 0115 943 6438

rum College, 19 The Close, Salisbury SP1 2EE
Principal: Rev Canon Bruce Duncan. *Vice-Principal:* Professor Philip Sheldrake. *College Secretary:* Mrs Linda Cooper. Lecturers 9, Other staff 21. ***CC*** No.309501. Began 1864; ecumenical. (Previously Salisbury and Wells Theological College). Magazine: *Sarum College Newsletter* (2,000 half-yearly). Turnover £714,000 to year end Jun 98. Providing short courses in theological education and training for adults of all denominations.
Web: www.sarum.ac.uk
Email: admin@sarum.ac.uk
☎ 01722 424 800 🖷 01722 338 508

cottish Baptist College, 12 Aytoun Road, Glasgow G41 5RN
Principal: Rev Dr Kenneth B E Roxburgh BA, MTh, PhD. Lecturers 2, Other staff 8. ***CC*** Began 1894; Baptist. Magazine: *In Touch Magazine* (Circulation n/a annually). Turnover £80,000 to year end May 96. Training for ministry in Baptist churches.
Email: ken@baptist.demon.co.uk
☎ 0141 424 0747 Mobile: 07711 968 649

.E.A.N. International (UK), Park House, 191 Stafford Road, Wallington SM6 9BT
Administration & Development Manager: Derek Birmingham. Other staff 9. ***CC*** No.286965. Began 1976; interdenominational. Magazine: *Newsletter* (Circulation n/a quarterly). Turnover £50-100,000 to year end Dec 96. Theological Education by Extension for basic level students or local church, area or regional study groups.
Web: ourworld.compuserve.com/homepages/sean_uk
Email: sean_uk@compuserve.com
☎ 020 8773 3948 🖷 020 8773 4199

South East Institute for Theological Education (SEITE), SEITE Office, Deanery Gate, The Precinct, Rochester ME1 1SJ
Principal: Rev Alan Le Grys. ***CC*** No.288011. Began n/a; Anglican, Methodist, United Reformed. No magazine. Turnover n/a. Training for ministers, part-time courses for lay people: three centres in the south-east.
Email: seite@easynet.co.uk
☎ 01634 846 683 🖷 01634 819 347
Also at: 48 Union Street, London SE1 1TD
☎ 020 7378 7880 🖷 020 7378 7882
And: University of Kent, Darwin College, Canterbury CT2 7NY
☎ 01227 764 000 🖷 01227 475 470
And: Chatham Maritime Centre. Contact SEITE Office

South West Ministry Training Course, North Petherwin, Launceston PL15 8LW
Principal: Rev Dr David Hewlett. Other staff 2. ***CC*** No.1056606. Began 1981; Anglican, Methodist, United Reformed. No magazine. Turnover n/a. Part-time training Anglican, Methodist and United Reformed ordinands.
Email: swmtc@surfaid.org
☎ 01566 785 545 🖷 01566 785 749

STETS Southern Theological Education and Training Scheme, 19 The Close, Salisbury SP1 2EE
Director: Rev Dr Christopher Cocksworth. Training staff 5, Admin staff 5. ***CC*** No.1059977. Began 1997; ecumenical. (Previously Southern Dioceses Ministerial Training Scheme). No magazine. Turnover £341,793 to year end Aug 98. Preparing Anglican, Methodist, United Reformed ordinands; developing education and training for all God's people.
Email: dgollop@stets.ac.uk
☎ 01722 412 996 🖷 01722 338 508

Theological Training Course, Evangelical Movement of Wales, Bryntirion, Bridgend CF31 4DX
Principal: Rev Graham S Harrison BA, MA, BLitt. No full-time staff. ***CC*** No.222407. Began 1972; non-denominational. No magazine. Turnover n/a. Preparation for preaching and pastoral ministry; 4-year course including 2 residential weeks per annum.
☎ 01656 655 886 🖷 01656 656 095

West Midlands Ministerial Training Course, Queen's Birmingham, The Ecumenical Foundation for Theological Education, Somerset Road, Edgbaston, Birmingham B15 2QH
Director: Rev Dr Dennis L Stamps MDiv, MA, PhD. Lecturers 2, Other staff 1. ***CC*** No.528989. Began 1973; Anglican, Methodist, United Reformed. No magazine. Turnover £100,000 to year end Aug 96. Training for Anglican, Methodist and United Reformed ordinands and lay people.
Email: queens-college@compuserve.com
☎ 0121 454 8597 🖷 0121 454 8171

West of England Ministerial Training Course, 7c College Green, Gloucester GL1 2LX
Principal: Rev Dr Richard Clutterbuck. *Vice Principal:* Rev Keith Crouch. Part-time lecturers 20. Began 1964; ecumenical. No magazine. Turnover £120,000 to year end Aug 98. Training candidates for ordained and reader ministry in Gloucester, Bristol and Ludlow.
Web: www.wcmtc.freeserve.co.uk
Email: wcmtc.freeserve.co.uk
☎ 01452 300 494 🖷 01452 300 494

Westminster College School of Humanities, Westminster College, Oxford OX2 9AT
Principal: Rev Dr Richard G Ralph. Full-time lecturers 16, Part-time lecturers 40. ***CC*** No.309672. Began 1851; Methodist but open to all. Magazine: *De Numine* (750 occasionally). Turnover n/a.
Web: www.ox-west.ac.uk/
Email: theology@ox-west.ac.uk
☎ 01865 247 644 🖷 01865 201 197

Y Coleg Gwyn (North Wales Baptist College), Ffriddoedd Road, Bangor LL57 2EH
Warden: Rev Dr D Densil Morgan. Lecturers 1. ***CC*** Began 1862; Baptist. (Coleg Y Bedyddwyr). No magazine. Turnover n/a. Pastoral courses and ministerial training, also theological courses in conjunction with Bangor University.
Web: www.bangor.ac.uk/rs/cglc.htm
Email: rs013@bangor.ac.uk
☎ 01248 382 079 🖷 01248 353 759

T

TRAINING CENTRES & SERVICES

The 222 Trust, 24 Old Street, Clevedon BS21 6BY
Executive Officer: Mr Charles Sibthorpe. Executive staff 3, Other staff 3. ***CC*** No.327866. Began 1987; interdenominational. Magazine: *On Eagles Wings* (2,000 quarterly). Turnover £75,000 to year end Mar 98. Charles and Joyce Sibthorpe's teaching and preaching ministry based on 2 Timothy 2:2.
Web: living-waters.org.uk
Email: charles@living-waters.org.uk
☎ 01275 797 999 Fax 01275 797 999

†**4:12 Ministries**, Flaxley House, Broadwater Road, Holme-next-the-Sea, Hunstanton PE36 6LQ
Directors: Mr Bryan & Mrs Judith Spence. Lecturers 4, Other staff 3. ***CC*** No.1058105. Began 1992; interdenominational. Magazine: *Newsletter* (Circulation & frequency n/a). Turnover £39,000 to year end Dec 98. Discipleship training courses of one day to four weeks. Leadership days maximum of fifty people.
Email: equip@globalnet.co.uk
☎ 01485 525 297 Fax 01485 525 668

***Abernethy Trust Ardeonaig**, Killin FK21 8SY
Centre Director: Mr Philip A Simpson. *Deputy Centre Director:* Mrs Rosemary K Simpson. Executive staff 1, Other staff 15. ***CC*** No.SCO 06270. Began 1984; non-denominational. (Previously Ardeonaig Outdoor Centre). No magazine. Turnover £212,000 to year end Oct 98. Fully-staffed residential centre offering courses for groups to develop leadership and team skills.
Web: www.abernethytrust.org.uk
Email: abernethytrustardeonaig@compuserve.com
☎ 01567 820 523 Fax 01567 820 955

***Administry**, PO Box 57, St Albans AL1 3DT
Executive Director: Mr Rob Norman. Other staff 2. ***CC*** No.289211. Began 1982; non-denominational. Magazine: *Administry Update* (4,000 every two months). Turnover £314,693 to year end Dec 98. Helping churches to co-ordinate their activities by training events, publications and consultancy.
Web: www.stalbansdc.gov.uk/stalbans/external/adminis.html
Email: administry@ibm.net
☎ 01727 856 370 Fax 01727 843 765

Adventist Discovery Centre, Stanborough Park, Garston, Watford WD2 6JU
Principal: Pastor Mike Stickland. Other staff 4. ***CC*** No.1044071. Began 1947; Seventh-Day Adventist. (Previously Voice of Prophecy Correspondence School). Magazine: *Newletter* (Circulation n/a quarterly). Turnover n/a. Offering free correspondence courses on the Bible, Family and Health for the general public.
Email: discovery@adventist.org.uk
☎ 01923 672 606 Fax 01923 894 835

Agapé Press (UK) Ltd, Unit 1D, Kingston Mill, Cobden Street, Pendleton, Salford M6 6WE
Managing Director: Dr Don E Okpalugo. All voluntary staff. ***CC*** No.1059348. Began 1996; non-denominational. Magazine: *Agapé Press Newsletter* (3,500 quarterly). Turnover £10,000 to year end Mar 97. Advancing the Christian faith through creative Christian communication.
☎ 0161 743 1010 Fax 0161 743 9991

All Souls' Training, All Souls Church Complex, 2 All Souls Pla London W1N 3DB
Director of Training: Rev Dr Paul Blackham. No other sta ***CC*** Began 1976; Anglican. No magazine. Turnover n Training courses and materials to prepare members for serv in their churches.
Email: vestry@allsouls.org
☎ 020 7935 9811 / 7580 3522 Fax 020 7436 3019

Alpha Course, Holy Trinity Church, Brompton Road, Lond SW7 1JA
Events Director: Miss Tricia Neill. Executive staff 6. ***CC*** Beg 1977; interdenominational. Magazine: *Alpha News* (200,0 every four months). Turnover n/a. A 15 session, 10 we practical introduction to the Christian faith, primarily f non-church goers. Multicultural.
Email: alpha@htb.org.uk
☎ 020 7581 8255 / 7590 6267 Fax 020 7584 8536

***Anvil Trust**, 104 Townend Road, Deepcar, Sheffield S36 2TS
Programme Coordinator: Mr Noel Moules. Executive staff ***CC*** No.1010354. Began 1983; interdenominational. Mag zine: *Anvil News* (3,500 half-yearly). Turnover £151,244 t year end Aug 98. Initiatives: Workshop, Praxis, The Art Facilitation, Firebrand. See also Supplyine.
Web: dialspace.dial.pipex.com/anvil
Email: anvil@dial.pipex.com
☎ 0114 288 8816 Mobile: 07768 761 217
Fax 0114 288 8817

Articles of Faith Ltd, Resource House, Kay Street, Bury BL9 6BU
Managing Director: Ms Christine Howard. *Director:* Mr Lesli Howard. Executive staff 2, Other staff 10. Began 1991; non denominational. No magazine. Turnover £600,000 to year en Jul 98. Supplying artefacts, books and resources for religiou education to schools and colleges by mail order.
☎ 0161 763 6232 Fax 0161 763 5366

Audio Visual Ministries, PO Box 1, Newcastle BT33 0EP
Principal: Mr K Gerner BA. ***CC*** No.XN 88288. Began 1969 interdenominational. No magazine. Turnover n/a. Teaching by audio and video tape, Biblesoft computer programmes for IBM PCs and free video.
Web: www.audio-visual.org
Email: 100543.3150@compuserve.com
& avmuk@aol.com
☎ 028 4476 8007 Mobile: 07801 474 630

AVEC Resources, 125 Waxwell Lane, Pinner HA5 3ER
Secretary: Ms Catherine Widdicombe. Staff n/a. ***CC*** No.226023. Began 1994; ecumenical. (Previously AVEC (A Service Agency for Church and Community Work)). No magazine. Turnover £4,000 to year end Sept 98. Books on group skills; work and vocational consultancy; applied theology.
☎ 020 8866 2195 Fax 020 8866 1408

Barnabas Training Consortium Ltd, Pilgrims Hall, Ongar Road, Brentwood CM15 9SA
Director: Mr Peter Garratt. Executive staff 6. Began 1993; non-denominational. No magazine. Turnover £66,000 to year end Nov 97. Offering professional courses in pastoral care and counselling.
☎ 01277 375 590 Fax 01277 375 590

T

chard Baxter Institute for Ministry, Baptist Church, Victoria Road South, Chelmsford CM1 1LN
Chairman: Rev Dr Paul Beasley-Murray. No full-time staff. ***CC*** No.1050561. Began 1994; interdenominational. Magazine: *Ministry Today* (500 every four months). Turnover n/a. Promoting excellence in the practice of ministry.
Web: www.rbim.freeserve.co.uk
Email: beasleymurray@compuserve.com
☎ 01245 347 095 🖷 01245 347 016

aconlight Trust, 150 High Street, Banstead SM7 2NZ
Chairman: Rev Dr Paul Adams. Executive staff 1, Other staff 2. ***CC*** No.1047046. Began 1995; non-denominational. No magazine. Turnover £29,000 to year end Jun 98. Providing training courses and counselling to promote Biblical Christian faith and lifestyle.
Email: ashhouse@globalnet.co.uk
☎ 01737 361 313 🖷 01737 814 100

erea Bible College, St Mary's House, Ocklynge Road, Eastbourne BN21 1PL
Principal: Rev Phil Stanton. Executive staff 1, No other staff. Began 1993; non-denominational. No magazine. Turnover n/a. Teaching the Word of God to all, including Hebrew and Greek studies.
Web: philstanton.freeserve.co.uk
Email: berea@philstanton.freeserve.co.uk
☎ 01323 728 187

ibleworld & Mobile Bibleworld, Bible House, 7 Hampton Terrace, Edinburgh EH12 5XU
Educational Exhibition Co-ordinators: Mr David Cochrane, Mrs Sheila Fraser. Staff n/a. ***CC*** Began 1861; interdenominational. (The National Bible Society of Scotland). No magazine. Turnover n/a. Hi-tech exhibition experience for late primary/early secondary school children in Edinburgh/Scotland (and mobile).
Web: www.nat-bible-society.org
Email: Bibleworld@nat-bible-society.org
☎ 0131 337 9701 🖷 0131 337 0641

Brainstormers, 115 Southwark Bridge Road, London SE1 0AX
Conference Organiser: Ms Tina Vygus. *Chair:* Mr Jonny Baker. No other staff. ***CC*** No.1054065. Began 1986; interdenominational. No magazine. Turnover £100,000 to year end Mar 99. Resourcing Christians in youth work.
Email: bstormers1@aol.com
☎ 020 7450 9090 🖷 020 7450 9001

Bristol School of Evangelism, St Philip and St Jacob Church, Tower Hill, Old Market, Bristol BS2 0ET
Administrator: Mr John Riley. No full-time staff. Began 1988; interdenominational. No magazine. Turnover n/a. Training for 35 men and women.
Email: jr.at.pipnjay@ukonline.co.uk
☎ 0117 929 3386 🖷 0117 929 3386

***CWR (Crusade for World Revival)**, Waverley Abbey House, Waverley Lane, Farnham GU9 8EP
Chief Executive: Mr John Muys. *General Manager Ministry:* Mr Sean Gubb. *Counselling Course Director:* Mr Paul Grant. Executive staff 3, Other staff 43. ***CC*** No.294387. Began 1987; interdenominational. (Previously Waverley Christian Centre). No magazine. Turnover £2,500,000 to year end Dec 98. Pastoral care and counselling, Biblical Studies and a wide range of residential and non-residential courses.
Web: www.cwr.org.uk
Email: training@cwr.org.uk
☎ 01252 784 731 🖷 01252 784 734

Carberry, Musselburgh EH21 8PY
Warden: Mr Bill Alcorn. Executive staff 3, Other staff 19. ***CC*** No.SCO 24381. Began, 1961, 1996 as an Independent Trust; interdenominational. (Previously Carberry Tower). Magazine: *Carberry News* (1,500 half-yearly). Turnover £350,000 to year end Dec 98. Providing courses and conference facilities.
Web: dspace.dial.pipex.com/carberry
Email: carberry@dial.pipex.com
☎ 0131 665 3135/3488 🖷 0131 653 2930

***Centre for Black and White Christian Partnership**, Selly Oak Colleges, Bristol Road, Birmingham B29 6LQ
Director: Bishop Joe Aldred. Executive staff 2. ***CC*** No.326998. Began 1978; non-denominational. Magazine: *Newsletter* (1,000 quarterly), *Journal* (Circulation n/a annually). Turnover £92,000 to year end Aug 98. Encouraging partnership between black and white Christians through education, inter-church relations, information, research, international links.
Email: cbwcp@sellyoak.ac.uk
☎ 0121 472 7952 🖷 0121 415 2400

Centre for Contemporary Ministry, The Park, Moggerhanger, Bedford MK44 3RW
Joint Directors: Rev Dr Clifford & Mrs Monica Hill. Executive staff 1, Other staff 1. ***CC*** No.1022698. Began 1992; interdenominational. No magazine. Turnover £30,000 to year end Dec 98. Providing in-service training courses and sabbaticals for ministers of all denominations; leadership consultations; resource centre.
Web: www.the-park.u-net.com
Email: ccm@the-park.u-net.com
☎ 01767 641 007 🖷 01767 641 515

Centre for International Briefing, The Castle, Farnham GU9 0AG
Director: Mr David Ellison. Executive staff 3, Other staff 47. ***CC*** No.313648. Began 1953; non-denominational. No magazine. Turnover £1,500,000 to year end Sept 96. Briefing programmes, intensive language tuition for people going to live and work abroad; residential conferences.
Web: www.cibfarnham.com
Email: dellison@cibfarnham.com
☎ 01252 721 194 🖷 01252 711 283

Centre for International Christian Ministries, PO Box 16262, London N4 2WN
Director: Rev Steve Cofer. Executive staff 2, Other staff 4. ***CC*** Began 1980; Pentecostal Holiness. Magazine: *Worldorama* (Circulation n/a quarterly). Turnover £60,000 to year end Dec 94. Advanced training in urban church planting for missionaries, national, Third World leaders; full-time two-year Bible College.
Email: 103145.764@compuserve.com
☎ 020 7473 4405 🖷 020 7473 4409

***Centre for Islamic Studies and Muslim-Christian Relations**, London Bible College, Green Lane, Northwood HA6 2UW
Director: Dr P Riddell. Teaching staff 2. ***CC*** No.312778. Began 1985; interdenominational. (Previously Carey Institute for Islamic Studies). Magazine: *CIS Newsletter* (Circulation & frequency n/a). Turnover n/a. Providing undergraduate and postgraduate training, seminars and consultancy services to facilitate Christian-Muslim relations.
Email: mailbox@londonbiblecollege.ac.uk
☎ 01923 826 061

Centre for the Study of Implicit Religion & Contemporary Spirituality, Middlesex University, White Hart Lane, London N17 8HR
Founding Director: Professor Edward Bailey. Executive staff 1, Lecturers 1. ***CC*** No.1047179. Began 1995; non-denominational. Magazine: *Implicit Religion* (Circulation n/a half-yearly). Turnover £1,000 to year end Jun 98. Focussing research, teaching and communication regarding religiosity inherent in secular life.
Email: e.i.bailey@mdx.ac.uk
☎ 020 8362 6220

Centre for Youth Ministry, PO Box 442, Swindon SN5 7JH
Project Leader: Rev David Howell. Executive staff 1, No other full time staff. ***CC*** No.299754. Began 1996; interdenominational. No magazine. Turnover n/a. Partnership of key Christian youth agencies to create and provide Christian youth work training, resources.
Email: 100451.255@compuserve.com
☎ 01793 418 336 🖷 01793 418 118

Chiltern Christian Training Programme, 175 Dashwood Avenue, High Wycombe HP12 3DB
Director: Rev Peter Ballentine. Executive staff 2. Began 1980; interdenominational. No magazine. Turnover £22,000 to year end Dec 98. Providing Christian courses on practical, scriptural and theological themes, training Readers and enabling leadership.
☎ 01494 474 788 🖷 01494 474 788

Christian Centre for Buddhist Studies, PO Box 74, Loughbrough LE11 3ZF
Co-ordinator: Mr Robin Evans. Executive staff 1, Other staff 2. Began 1995; non-denominational. Magazine: *Update* (250 every two months). Turnover £5,000 to year end Sep 96. Raising awareness of Buddhism, providing and co-ordinating resources, encouraging prayer for Buddhist people.
Web: www.dcs.shef.ac.uk/~paulw/update.htm
Email: 101647.3715@compuserve.com
☎ 01509 234 982 🖷 01509 234 982

†**Christian Conventions**, Admatha, 18 Smith Hill, Rochdale OL16 3ER
Overseer: Mr Peter Keefe. Executive staff 3, Other staff 40. Began 1904; Exclusive Brethren. No magazine. Turnover n/a. Monitoring cults; organising seminars and providing support to those exiting cults.
☎ 01378 147 468

†**The Christian Education & Training Consultancy**, 169 St. Annes Road, Fordhouses, Wolverhampton WV10 6SL
Director: Mr Neal Lawrence. Executive staff 1. Began 1997; non-denominational. Magazine: *The Face of Learning* (100 quarterly). Turnover n/a. Promoting the practice of Christ-centred approaches to education, training and organisation in contemporary contexts.
☎ No telephone

***Christian Research**, Vision Building, 4 Footscray Road, Eltham, London SE9 2TZ
Executive Director: Dr Peter Brierley. *Assistant Director:* Heather Wraight. Executive staff 2, Other staff 5. ***CC*** No.1017701. Began 1993; interdenominational. (Previously MARC Europe). Magazine: *Quadrant* (3,500 every two months). Turnover £271,600 to year end Dec 98. Offering day and residential briefings and management seminars for Christian leaders based on Biblical principles; consultancy.
Web: www.christian-research.org.uk
Email: admin@christian-research.org.uk
☎ 020 8294 1989 🖷 020 8294 0014

Christian Resources International, 4 Liverpool Terrace, Corw LL21 0DU
Secretary: Ms Esther Wintringham. Executive staff 2, Otl staff 2. Began 1993; Free evangelical. No magazine. Offeri foundation Scriptural teaching courses.
☎ 01490 412 480 🖷 01490 412 480

Christian Training Centre, Magee House, 7 Rugby Road, Belfa BT7 1PS
Director: Rev Dr A H Graham. Executive staff 1, Other staff Began 1980; Presbyterian Church in Ireland. No magazin Turnover £60,000 to year end Dec 94. Training courses f ministers and lay leaders.
Web: www.btinternet.com/~ctc.pcl/
Email: ctc@presbyterianireland.org
☎ 028 9024 8424 🖷 028 9031 3212

***Cormack Consultancies**, King's Gate, St Mary's Tower, Birnar Dunkeld PH8 0BJ
Managing Director: Dr David Cormack. *Director of Cou selling:* Mrs Edith Cormack. Executive staff 2, Other staff Began 1985; non-denominational. No magazine. Turnov £150,000 to year end Mar 97. Strategic consulting and trainin to church, mission, business worldwide; counselling trainin within a Christian context.
☎ 01350 728 715 🖷 01350 728 716

Crossline Scotland, 2 Glasgow Road, Camelon, Falkirk FK1 4H
Chairman: Mr Norman Aitken. No full-time staff. ***CC*** No.SC 22489. Began 1993; interdenominational. No magazine. Turn over n/a. Providing training in Christian counselling and pasto ral care, in pastoral and community settings.
☎ 01324 630 643

***Crusaders Training**, 2 Romeland Hill, St Albans AL3 4ET
Training Director: Mr Brian Spurling. Staff n/a. ***CC*** No.223798. Began 1906; interdenominational. No magazine Turnover n/a. Offering youth leadership courses for potential new, established youth leaders; workshops, seminars weekends.
Email: email@crusaders.org.uk
☎ 01727 847 332 🖷 01727 848 518

†**The Damaris Project**, 52 Portswood Road, Southampton SO15 7PB
Director: Mr Nick Pollard. Executive staff 2. Began 1996; non-denominational. No magazine. Turnover n/a. Equipping Christians involved in evangelism with tools for understanding, evaluating and responding to contemporary culture.
☎ 01703 574 174

***Darash Trust**, Darash Centre, Ashwells Road, Brentwood CM15 9SE
Chairman: Rev David Matthews. Executive staff 1. ***CC*** No.1008795. Began 1991; interdenominational. No magazine. Turnover £56,500 to year end Sep 98. Forwarding the Christian faith through conferences, seminars, training and missions.
☎ 01277 374 844 🖷 01277 374 881

***DCI Trust**, 4 Home Farm Lane, Colton Bassett, Nottingham NG12 3FQ
Director: Dr Les Norman. *Webmaster:* Dr Graham Crosbie. Other staff 4. ***CC*** No.1001236. Began 1987; non-denominational. Magazine: *e-mail.* Turnover £250,000 to year end Nov 98. Training and equipping leaders and churches for mission, social action and commerce for local funding.
Web: www.worldchristians.org
Email: lesnorman@csi.com
☎ 01949 811 909 / 653 236 🖷 01949 81 116

eedline Ltd, 1 Gorse Close, Rugby CV33 6SH
Director: Mr David Shepherd. Executive staff 1. Began 1994; non-denominational. No magazine. Turnover £10,000 to year end Feb 95. Training, vocational guidance, selection, career development, outplacement and psychometric testing for individuals and companies.
☎ 01788 578 868 🖷 01788 578 868

isciple Course, Disciple Office, 20 Ivatt Way, Peterborough PE3 7PG
Chief Executive: Mr Brian Thornton. Executive staff 1. Began 1996; ecumenical. No magazine. Turnover n/a. Bible study programme taking participants through the Bible in 34 weeks.
Email: chief.exec@mph.org.uk
☎ 0800 801 017 🖷 01733 331 201

llel Ministries, Ellel Grange, Ellel, Lancaster LA2 0HN
Director: Mr Peter Horrobin. Executive staff 9, Other staff 140. ***CC*** No.1041237. Began 1986; non-denominational. Magazine: *Newsletter* (16,000 n/a). Turnover £1,450,000 to year end Dec 97. Centres for training and ministry in Christian healing and discipleship (conferences, schools, courses, retreats, resources).
Web: www.ellelministries.org
Email: info@grange.ellel.org.uk
☎ 01524 751 651 🖷 01524 751 738
Also at: Glyndley Manor, Stone Cross, Pevensey BN24 5BS
Email: info@glyndley.ellel.org.uk
☎ 01323 440 440 🖷 01323 440 877
And: Pierrepoint, Churt Road, Frensham, Farnham GU10 3DL
Email: info@pierrepoint.ellel.org.uk
☎ 01252 794 060 🖷 01252 794 039

Equip, Bawtry Hall, Bawtry, Doncaster DN10 6JH
Manager: Mr Tony Horsfall. Other staff 1. ***CC*** No.225364. Began 1989; interdenominational. No magazine. Turnover £76,500 to year end Dec 98. Providing training for Christians in intercultural ministry and local church leadership.
Email: bawtry-hall@compuserve.com
☎ 01302 710 020 🖷 01302 710 027

Europe Now, PO Box 248, Guildford GU2 6WY
UK Director: Mr Paul Hazelden. Executive staff 2, Other staff 1. ***CC*** No.1051283. Began 1995; non-denominational. Magazine: *Borderlines* (1,700 every four months). Turnover £40,000 to year end Dec 98. An intensive, varied, practical one-year training course for evangelists in the UK or France.
Web: www.oaci.org
Email: en@oaci.org
☎ 01483 579 955 🖷 01483 579 955

Evangelical Urban Training Project, 336a City Road, Sheffield S2 1GA
National Co-ordinator: Jenny Richardson. Other staff 3. ***CC*** No.313454. Began 1974; interdenominational. No magazine. Turnover £48,000 to year end Dec 98. Working with the urban marginalised; supporting the local church through resource materials, workshop events, consultation.
☎ 0114 276 2038 (training) 0114 276 2035 (admin)
🖷 0114 276 2035

***Evangelism Training Centre (Good News Crusade)**, 17 High Cross Street, St Austell PL25 4AN
Director: Rev Don Double. *Director of Studies:* Mr Tim Jones. Lecturers 9. ***CC*** No.225483. Began 1994; interdenominational. No magazine. Turnover: see main Good News Crusade listing. Training Centre for 15 people.
Web: www.gnc.org.uk
Email: info@gnc.org.uk
☎ 01726 722 82 🖷 01726 698 53

***Family Foundations Trust Ltd**, Dalesdown, Honeybridge Lane, Dial Post, Horsham RH13 8NX
Manager: Mr Alex Parsons. Executive staff 1. ***CC*** No.284006. Began 1987; non-denominational. No magazine. Turnover n/a. Providing teaching and training for youth and families using seminars, camps and family activities.
☎ 01403 710 712 🖷 01403 710 716

Ghetto Blasters, 73 Apton Road, Bishop's Stortford CM23 3ST
Producer: Ms Alison Burnett. No other staff. Began 1989; non-denominational. No magazine. Turnover £300 to year end Nov 98. Using the media to discover how churches can be a presence in local radio/newspapers.
Email: alisonburnett@orangenet.co.uk
☎ 01279 651 195 🖷 01279 651 195

†**Gilead Counselling & Training Services**, 11 University Road, Belfast BT7 1NA
Director: Rev David McLoughlin-Tasker. Lecturers 3, Other staff 1. ***CC*** Began 1993; interdenominational. (Previously Mourne Christian Ministries Training Centre). Magazine: *Pastoral Counselling Today* (1,000 quarterly). Turnover n/a. Offering courses from 1 day to 3 years; operating the Gilead Centre counselling service.
Email: gileadcmt@aol.com
☎ 028 9029 3434 🖷 028 9029 3333

Hawkstone Hall Pastoral Centre, Marchamley, Shrewsbury SY4 5LG
Rector: Very Rev D McBride. *Secretary:* Mrs Julia Kerr. Executive staff 3, Other staff 22. ***CC*** No.252041. Began 1973; Roman Catholic. No magazine. Turnover £425,000 to year end Mar 96. International renewal course for people in ministry.
Web: www.hawkstone-hall.com
Email: hawkhall@aol.com
☎ 01630 685 242 🖷 01630 685 565

Bryn Hughes Training and Consultancy, 3 Pound Bank Close, West Kingsdown, Sevenoaks TN15 6UA
Director: Mr Bryn Hughes. Executive staff 2. Began 1992; non-denominational. No magazine. Turnover n/a. Training and consultancy, especially to churches, missionary societies, charitable organisations.
☎ 01474 854 774 🖷 01474 854 774

†**Ichthus Christian Fellowship Training Courses**, 107 Stanstead Road, Forest Hill, London SE23 1HH
Training Co-ordinator: Mr Mike Pears. Executive staff 3, Other staff 4. ***CC*** Began 1975; non-denominational. Magazine: *Celebration* (Circulation & frequency n/a). Turnover n/a. Courses in evangelism (including short-term summer course); church planting/ leadership training with specialist streams (one year).
Email: 100074.1000@compuserve.com
☎ 020 8291 4057 🖷 020 8291 6764

***Institute for Community and Development Studies**, Greatfields Hall, King Edward's Road, Barking IG11 7TR
Director: Rt Rev Henry Kontor. Executive staff 1, Other staff 4. ***CC*** No.1022993. Began 1991; interdenominational. (Sponsored by The Riches of Grace Community Ministry). Magazine: *Neighbourhood Redevelopment* (500 quarterly). Turnover £70,000. Training Christians to work as community development facilitators and leaders; initiating community development projects.
Email: icds@aol.com
☎ 020 8507 2600 Mobile 07711 855 373
🖷 020 8507 2603

T

***Institute for Contemporary Christianity**, St Peter's Church, Vere Street, London W1M 9HP
Director: Mr Mark Greene. *Manager:* Mrs Kirstie Goddard. Executive staff 2, Other staff 2. ***CC*** No.286102. Began 1982; non-denominational. (Previously Christian Impact). Merged in 1988 with Shaftesbury Project. No magazine. Turnover £259,821 to year end Mar 98. Seminars, courses, resources and research helping Christians engage biblically with issues faced in today's world.
Email: contemporary_christianity_edu@msn.com
☎ 020 7629 3615 🖷 020 7629 1284

†***Inter-cultural Mission Training and English Language Teaching**, Southall Evangelical Church, 9 Norwood Road, Southall UB2 4AE
Director: Rev David Burgess. ***CC*** Began 1997; interdenominational. (Previously Inter-cultural Bible Study Centre). No magazine. Turnover n/a. Expository Biblical and English language teaching, particularly in an inter-ethnic context.
Email: 106575.2657@compuserve.com
☎ 01784 248 973 🖷 01784 248 973

***The Joshua Project**, Joshua House, 27 Crestbrooke, Northallerton DL7 8YP
Principal: Rev Kingsley N Armstrong. No other staff. Began 1996; interdenominational. Magazine: *Regular Newsletter* (Circulation & frequency n/a). Turnover n/a. Offering 3 week residential course in practical evangelism, also on location in churches.
☎ 01609 771 027

***Lindisfarne Mustard Seed Project**, Retreat Cottage, Maryga Holy Island, Berwick-upon-Tweed TD15 2SD
Founder: Rev Ray Simpson. No other full-time staff. C No.1054649. Began 1996; interdenominational. Magazir *LMSP Newsletter* (340 quarterly). Turnover £13,000 to ye end Dec 98. Supporting the community of Aidan and Hilda Lindisfarne. Retreats, consultations, soul-friending; cel Christian roots.
Web: www.ndirecto.co.uk/~raysimpson
Email: raysimpson@ndirect.com.uk
☎ 01289 389 249 🖷 01289 389 249

†***Lindley Educational Trust Ltd**, Hollowford Centre, Back Stree Castleton, Hope Valley S30 2WB
Managing Director: Mr Derek Handforth. Executive staff Other staff 45. ***CC*** Began 1969; interdenominational. No ma azine. Development training of young people, supervisors an managers for industry, commerce and church.
☎ 01433 621 341 🖷 01433 620 622

McCabe Educational Trust, 53 Balham Hill, London SW12 9DR
Chairman: Rev Iain Paton. Executive staff 4, Trustees 4. C Began 1990; interdenominational. Magazine: *Newsletter* (Ci culation n/a annually). Turnover £20,000 to year end Nov 9 Advancing knowledge and understanding of Bible lands; pro jects assisting Christians in Holy lands.
Email: trust@mccabe-travel.co.uk
☎ 020 8675 9189 🖷 020 8673 1204

†**Mainstream**, 101 Heathdene Drive, Belvedere DA17 6HY
Secretary: Mr Paul Winslow. No full-time staff. Began 1986 interdenominational. Magazine: *Newsletter* (300 quarterly) Turnover £1,000 to year end Dec 94. Promoting qualified ca noeing expertise to meet the requirements of Christian centre and camps.
☎ 01322 434 995

***Media Associates International**, European Office, Concord House, Grenville Place, Mill Hill, London NW7 3SA
Hon Chairman of Trustees: Mr Nicholas Gray. Executive staf 2, Other staff 4. ***CC*** No.328568. Began 1985; interdenom inational. Magazine: *Profile* (3,300 quarterly). Turnover n/a Training for indigenous Christian writing, literature and pub lishing; Africa, Asia, Latin America and Central Europe.
Email: rods@angushudson.com
☎ 020 8906 9768 🖷 020 8959 3678

***Medical Service Ministries**, PO Box 35, Hailsham BN27 3XW
Candidates Secretary: Mrs Jean Hayward-Lynch. ***CC*** No.234037. Began 1903; interdenominational. (Previously Missionary School of Medicine). No magazine. Turnover £28,000 to year end Sept 98. Personal and community health care training for Christian workers.
☎ 01323 849 047 🖷 01323 849 047

***Moorlands College**, Sopley, Christchurch BH23 7AT
Principal: Rev Dr Steve Brady. Executive staff 12. ***CC*** No.286334. Began 1948; interdenominational. Magazine: *Moorings* (Circulation & frequency n/a). Turnover n/a. Providing Partnership in Action, one-year training courses based in local churches; college two days weekly.
Web: www.moorlands.u-net.com
Email: enquiries@moorlands.ac.uk
☎ 01425 672 369 🖷 01425 674 162

ational Bible Society of Scotland, Bible Use Department, Bible House, 7 Hampton Terrace, Edinburgh EH12 5XU
Staff n/a. *CC* Began 1861; interdenominational. Magazine: *Word at Work* (70,000 every four months). Turnover n/a. Training courses and programmes enabling church leaders and members to use the Bible more effectively.
Web: www.nat-bible-society.org
Email: nbss@nat-bible-society.org
☎ 0131 337 9701 Fax 0131 337 0641

he Newman Association, 73 St Charles Square, London W10 6EJ
Secretary: Mrs Maureen Thomas. No full-time staff. *CC* No.1006769. Began 1942; Roman Catholic. Member of the Catholic international intellectual movement Pax Romana. Magazine: *The Newman Journal* (1,000 every four months). Turnover n/a. Promoting adult religious formation for Catholic laity through conferences, lecture programmes, journal.
Web: www.cablenet/~newman/
Email: info@newman.cablenet.co.uk
☎ No telephone

North of England Institute for Christian Education, Carter House, Pelaw Leazes Lane, Durham DH1 1TB
Director: Rev Prof Jeff Astley. Executive staff 2. *CC* No.513106. Began 1981; interdenominational. No magazine. Turnover n/a. Providing theoretical and empirical research in Christian education; theology study days, publications and educational support.
Email: jeff.astley@durham.ac.uk
☎ 0191 384 1034 Fax 0191 384 7529

Open Learning Centre, 25 Marylebone Road, London NW1 5JR
Secretary: Rev Roger L Walton. Other staff 3. *CC* Began 1928; Methodist. (Previously Methodist Church Open Learning Centre). Magazine: *Newsletter* (Circulation & frequency n/a). Turnover n/a. Correspondence, distance and open learning courses; small group study materials.
Web: www.base25.co.uk/olc
☎ 020 7467 5174 Fax 020 7935 2104

PACT Community Projects, Brighthelm, North Road, Brighton BN1 1YD
General Manager: Mr David Nicholls. Executive staff 6, Other staff 44. *CC* Began 1978; interdenominational. (Previously People and Churches Together (PACT) Ltd). Magazine: *Impact* (2,000 quarterly). Turnover £650,000 to year end Mar 94. Community development, training, management and marketing for projects in East and West Sussex.
☎ 01273 821 914 Fax 01273 747 313

***Pioneer DNA**, PO Box 58, Chichester PO19 2UD
National Administrator: Mr Tim Raynes. *Team Leader:* Mr Pete Gilbert. Executive staff 4. *CC* No.327160. Began 1982; Pioneer. (Previously TiE Teams). Magazine: *Pioneer Update* (1,000 monthly). Turnover £144,000 to year end Sept 99. Training in personal discipleship, leadership, evangelism and church planting; supporting local churches as they grow.
Web: freespace.virgin.net/pioneer.dna/
Email: pioneer.dna@virgin.net
☎ 01243 531 898 Fax 01243 531 959

Post Green Community Trust, East Holton Farm House, Holton Heath, Poole BH16 6JN
Chairman: Sir Thomas Lees. Executive staff 1, No other staff. *CC* No.231175. Began 1975; interdenominational. Associated with East Holton Charity. Magazine: *Newsletter* (500 every two months). Turnover £30,000 to year end Mar 99. Promoting the gospel, unity and community; helping people with mental/physical disability; annual teaching event.
Email: 100275.373@compuserve.com
☎ 01202 622 317 Fax 01202 632 632

Prepared for Service, Lapithos, 1 Bower Road, Queens Park, Bournemouth BH8 9HQ
Administrator/Co-ordinator: Mr David W Matson. No other full-time staff. *CC* No.263354. Began 1994; FIEC. No magazine. Turnover n/a. Two-year training and placement programme working in partnership with evangelical churches.
Email: dave@lapithos.freeserve.co.uk
☎ 01202 303 263 Fax 01202 303 263
Also at: 3 Church Road, Croydon CR0 1SG
☎ 020 8681 7422 Fax 020 8760 5067

***Proclaimers International**, Drayton Hall, Hall Lane, Drayton, Norwich NR8 6DP
Director: Rev David Tinnion. *School Director:* Mr Richard Chamberlain. Staff members 30. *CC* No.280469. Began 1980; non-denominational. (Previously Kerygma International Christian Ministries). No magazine. Turnover £269,000. Spirit & Word School; full/part time or correspondence training programme in Christian ministry, discipleship, leadership.
Web: www.proclaim.org.uk
Email: school@proclaim.org.uk
☎ 01603 260 222 Fax 01603 261 222

The Proclamation Trust, 140 Borough High Street, London SE1 1LB
Chairman: Rev R C Lucas. Executive staff 2, Other staff 3. *CC* No.293976. Began 1986; non-denominational. No magazine. Turnover n/a. Encouragement and training in expository preaching.
Email: pt@proctrust.org.uk
☎ 020 7407 0561 Fax 020 7407 0569

***The Psychology Shop**, 79 Harman Road, Enfield EN1 1LA
Counsellor: Mr Craig Ward. Executive staff 1, Other staff 1. Began 1995; Anglican. No magazine. Turnover n/a. Providing information, talks and short courses on psychology, mental health issues and counselling.
☎ 020 8364 4829

Purpose Ministries, Worthy Park Grove, Abbots Worthy, Winchester SO21 1AN
Director: Rev David Steele. Executive staff 1, Other staff 1. *CC* No.326081. Began 1982; interdenominational. No magazine. Turnover n/a. Training courses in person-to-person evangelism and in leading Bible discussion groups.
☎ 01962 882 082

***Radio Worldwide (WEC International)**, Springhead Park House, Park Lane, Rothwell, Leeds LS26 0ET
Directors: Mr Dick & Mrs Flora Davies. Executive staff 2, Other staff 14. *CC* No.237005. Began 1961; interdenominational. Magazine: *Newsletter* (3,000 every four months). Turnover £81,640 to year end Mar 98. Radio programme producers; radio training (UK and overseas); oral communication training.
Web: ourworld.compuserve.com/homepages/rw/
Email: rw@compuserve.com
☎ 0113 282 2291 Fax 0113 282 3908

Arthur Rank Centre, National Agricultural Centre, Stoneleigh Park, Kenilworth CV8 2LZ
Director: Rev John Clarke. Executive staff 6, Other staff 6. Began 1972; ecumenical. Magazine: *Country Way* (4,000 every four months). Turnover n/a. Focus for the rural church: mission, ministry, agricultural chaplaincy, conservation, ethics, rural community issues.
Web: freespace.virgin.net/arthur_rank.centre
Email: arthur.rank.centre@virgin.net
☎ 024 7669 6969 Ext 216 Fax 024 7641 4808

T

Rapha Ministries Ltd, Waterfront, Kingsdown Road, Walmer CT14 7LL
Director: Miss Susan Williams. Executive staff 2, Admin staff 4. Began 1993; non-denominational. No magazine. Turnover £45,000 to year end Sep 99. Training based on Biblical principles, promoting spiritual maturity through wholeness and discipleship.
Email: waterfront@btinternet.com
☎ 01304 239 621 Fax 01304 239 621

***Ridley Hall Foundation**, Ridley Hall, Cambridge CB3 9HG
Director: Dr Richard Higginson. No other full-time staff. ***CC*** No.311456. Began 1989; non-denominational. Magazine: *Faith in Business* produced jointly with Industrial Christian Fellowship (Circulation n/a quarterly). Turnover n/a. Relating Christian faith to business; seminars at Ridley Hall and nationwide; regular publications.
☎ 01223 741 080 Fax 01223 741 081

Royal School of Church Music, Cleveland Lodge, Westhumble, Dorking RH5 6BW
Director: Prof John Harper. Staff 23. ***CC*** No.312828. Began 1927; interdenominational. Magazine: *Church Music Quarterly* (11,500 quarterly). Turnover £1,600,000 to year end June 98. Teaching and generally helping, through courses and publications, all those concerned with music in worship.
Web: www.rscm.com
Email: cl@rscm.com
☎ 01306 872 800 Fax 01306 887 260

St George's College Jerusalem, 12 Hatchgate Gardens, Burnham, Slough SL1 8DD
UK Secretary: Rev Malcolm White. No other UK staff. Began 1975; Anglican but open to all. Magazine: *British Friends' News* (250 annually), *St George's Update* (200 annually). Turnover £2,061 to year end Dec 97. Residential centre in the Holy Land for field work, study and reflection.
Email: malcolm@sleepy-hollow.freeserve.co.uk
☎ 01628 662 739 Fax 01628 662 739

St George's House, Windsor Castle, Windsor Castle, Windsor SL4 1NJ
Warden: Professor Alfred P Smyth. *Director of Studies:* Mr Ian Madelin. Executive staff 3, Other staff 4. ***CC*** No.251946. Began 1966; ecumenical. Magazine: *Annual Review* (2,200 annually). Turnover £400,000 to year end Aug 98. Residential study/conference centre for internal and external events dealing with a wide range of issues.
☎ 01753 861 341 Fax 01753 832 115

***St Mark's College**, Audley End, Saffron Walden CB11 4JD
Warden: Jonathan Wayper. Executive staff 2, Other staff 3. ***CC*** No.1031174. Began 1993; Anglican. Magazine: *Newsletter* (Circulation n/a annually). Turnover n/a. Residential youth and conference centre, 38 beds. Volunteer opportunities.
☎ 01799 522 006 Fax 01799 520 326

St Ninian's Training and Resource Centre, Comrie Road, Crieff PH7 4BG
Director: Dr Adrian Varwell. Executive staff 3, Other staff 11. ***CC*** No.SCO 14279. Began 1958; Church of Scotland but open to all. Magazine: *Crieff Comment* (800 every four months). Turnover £213,425 to year end Dec 98. Encouraging and resourcing mission and renewal; training and conferences; mission projects; research and development.
Email: stninians@dial.pipex.com
☎ 01764 653 766 Fax 01764 655 824

Satya Bhavan (South Asian Concern), PO Box 43, Sutt[...] SM2 5WL
Director: Mr Robin Thomson. Other staff 1. ***CC*** Began 199[...] interdenominational. No magazine. Turnover n/a. Trainin[g] research and outreach among South Asians in the UK, Sou[th] Asia and the Diaspora.
Email: 100126.3641@compuserve.com
☎ 020 8770 9717 Fax 020 8770 9747

Scottish Churches Open College, Annie Small House, 18 Inverleit[h] Terrace, Edinburgh EH3 5NS
Principal: Rev Jane Scott. *President:* Very Rev Prof Rober[t] Davidson. Full-time staff 11. Began 1990; interdenominational. No magazine. Turnover £178,000 to year end Fe[b] 99. Consortium of churches and agencies providing and supporting Christian adult education across Scotland.
☎ 0131 311 4713 Fax 0131 315 2161

Seeds, 30 Grasvenor Road, Barnet EN5 2BZ
Chairperson: Mr Chris Norris. No full-time staff. ***CC*** Began 1982; interdenominational. No magazine. Turnover £25,00[0] to year end Apr 94. Encouraging creative, artistic skills and discussion of contemporary issues in schools and churches.
Email: seeds30@aol.com
☎ 020 8364 9652 Mobile: 07971 332 267

Sion Catholic Community for Evangelism, Sawyers Hall Lane, Brentwood CM15 9BX
Training Director: Mrs Michelle Moran. *President:* Rev Pat Lynch. Community 28, Other staff 5. ***CC*** No.327967. Began 1985; Roman Catholic. Magazine: *New Century* (2,000 periodically). Turnover £150,000 to year end Apr 98. Evangelising in parishes, schools, towns; training and equipping people for evangelism; conference centre for 42 people.
Web: www.btinternet.com/-sioncommunity
Email: sioncommunity@btinternet.com
☎ 01277 215 011 Mobile: 07860 621 794 Fax 01277 234 401

***Southampton Action for Employment (SAFE)**, 170 Northam Road, Northam, Southampton SO14 0QF
Project Coordinator: Mr Andy Foreman. Executive staff 3, Other staff 2. ***CC*** No.1057784. Began 1994; non-denominational. No magazine. Turnover £65,000 to year end Mar 99. Pre-employment training/confidence – building programme for long-term unemployed; providing effective church involvement.
Web: www.safe.org.uk
Email: info@safe.org.uk
☎ 023 8034 5777 Fax 023 8034 5777

†**Standard Ministries Trust**, 23 Faskally Avenue, Bishopbriggs, Glasgow G64 3PJ
General Secretary: Mr S Bruce Thomson. No paid staff. ***CC*** No.SCO 25029. Began 1996; interdenominational. No magazine. Turnover n/a. Providing training in church growth theory to ministers and senior lay leadership.
☎ 0141 772 1244 Fax 0141 772 1244

***Stepping Stones Christian Training Project**, 14 Lant Close, Duggins Lane, Tile Hill, Coventry CV4 9TG
Director: Mr John Rogers. No full-time staff. Began 1991; interdenominational. No magazine. Turnover £5,000 to year end Dec 98. Offering training and experience to established Christians in evangelical churches, for mutual benefit.
Web: www.steppingstones.org.uk
Email: sstonesctp@aol.com
☎ 024 7647 1991 Fax 024 7647 1991

T

r Halley Stewart Age Awareness Project, Methodist Homes, Epworth House, Stuart Street, Derby DE1 2EQ
Project Administrator: Rev Albert Jewell. No full-time staff. Began 1995; ecumenical. No magazine. Turnover £15,000 to year end Dec 98. Distributing resources and leading seminars on the spiritual needs of older people.
☎ 01332 296 200 🖷 01332 296 925

rategic Prayer School, Prayer for the Nations, PO Box 15027, London SE5 9ZU
Principal: Rev Rod Anderson. Lecturers 20, Other staff: part-time 1, Volunteers 12. ***CC*** No.326994. Began 1983; interdenominational. (Previously Liberty Bible Training Centre). Magazine: *Watchman's Journal* (Circulation & frequency n/a). Turnover £130,000 to year end July 98. Leadership and Bible training; correspondence and individual spiritual growth courses available.
Email: pfn@dial.pipex.com
☎ 0171 708 5294 🖷 0171 708 5294
Also At: Emmanuel Centre, 9 Marsham Street, London SW1P 3DW

Stress and Life Trust (SALT), The Istana, Freezeland Lane, Bexhill-on-Sea TN39 5JD
Chief Executive: Dr Bill Munro. Executive staff 3, Other staff 2. Began 1989; interdenominational. No magazine. Turnover £23,705 to year end June 96. Stress prevention/management, seminars, resources on successful living for organisations secular and Christian, churches, consultancy, counselling.
Email: saltmunro@compuserve.com
☎ 01424 219 133 🖷 01424 219 133

Summer Crusades, 21 Elm Grove, Aldbrough, Hull HU11 4RQ
Leader: Rev Arthur Dean. Executive staff 1, Other staff 3. ***CC*** Began 1969; interdenominational. Magazine: *Wentworth Ministries* (700 quarterly). Turnover n/a. Training and prison ministry, UK and international.
☎ 01964 527 743 Mobile: 07971 720 927

Summer Institute of Linguistics (British School), Horsleys Green, High Wycombe HP14 3XL
Director: Tony Canvin. Executive staff 5, Other staff 12. ***CC*** No.313854. Began 1953; non-denominational. No magazine. Turnover n/a. Intensive courses in language learning, linguistic analysis, literacy, anthropology and translation for those going overseas.
Web: www.sil.org/schools/
Email: british_school_uk@sil.org
☎ 01494 482 521 🖷 01494 483 297

***TASK (Training and Advice for Service in the Kingdom)**, 13 School Road, Bradenham, Thetford IP25 7QU
Director: Mr Roger G Wells. No other staff. ***CC*** No.1068212. Began 1994; interdenominational. Magazine: *Newsletter* (250 quarterly). Turnover £7,000 to year end Oct 98. Advising and training Christians to work effectively in secular and cross-cultural positions overseas.
Email: roger@taskgb.freeserve.co.uk
☎ 01760 440 200

The Teal Trust, 11 Lincoln Road, Northburn Green, Cramlington NE23 9XT
Director: Dr John Preston. Executive staff 1. ***CC*** No.1063395. Began 1997; interdenominational. No magazine. Turnover £7,500 to year end Feb 99. Encouraging Christian leadership through training, prayer support and consultancy.
Web: www.teal.org.uk
Email: teal@clara.net
☎ 01670 717 452

†***Time Ministries International**, Emmanuel Church, Main Road, Hawkwell, Hockley SS5 4NR
Directors: Rev Tony & Mrs Patricia Higton. Other staff 1. ***CC*** No.1047110. Began 1991; interdenominational. Magazine: *Time Now* (5,000 annually). Turnover £10,000 to year end Dec 96. Providing courses, conferences, tapes on development of the local church, eschatology, Jesus the only Saviour.
Email: 101343.164@compuserve.com
☎ 01702 543 514 🖷 01702 543 554

TnT Ministries, 29 Buxton Gardens, Acton, London W3 9LE
Director: Mr Trevor Blundell. Executive staff 2. ***CC*** No.294775. Began 1993; non-denominational. No magazine. Turnover n/a. Non-denominational. Teaching and training people to teach the Bible to children. Sunday school materials available.
☎ 020 8992 0450

John Truscott, 69 Sandridge Road, St Albans AL1 4AG
Church Consultant & Trainer: Mr John Truscott. No other staff. Began 1999; interdenominational. No magazine. Turnover: first year of operation. Consultancy and training on organisation and communication for churches, ministers and mission agencies.
Web: www.john-truscott.co.uk
Email: get-help@john-truscott.co.uk
☎ 01727 832 176 🖷 01727 832 176

***Tynddol Challenge Centre**, Cwmystwyth, Aberystwyth SY23 4AG
Director: Mr Robin Morris. Admin staff 3, Other staff 6. ***CC*** No.1019827. Began 1986; interdenominational. No magazine. Turnover n/a. Providing practical Christian training for young people considering service at home and abroad.
Email: tynddolcc@aol.com
☎ 01974 282 618

Upside Down Trust, Mere View, Church Road, Great Livermere, Bury St Edmunds IP31 2JR
Team Co-ordinator: Mr Jim Hartley. Executive staff 3, Admin staff 3. ***CC*** Began 1997; interdenominational. (Previously Scripture Union Training & Development Unit). No magazine. Turnover £99,000 to year end Dec 98. Providing tailored training, facilitation and consultation (group or individual) to church and voluntary groups.
☎ 01359 268 120 🖷 01359 268 120

Urban Presence, 17 Upper West Grove, Chorlton-on-Medlock, Manchester M13 0BB
Chair of Trustees: Dr Caesar Merrifield. Executive staff 2. ***CC*** No.1069404. Began 1992; non-denominational. Magazine: *Newsletter* (400 quarterly). Turnover £2,000 to year end Apr 99. Offering consultancy, training, liaison for urban churches and organisations; mainly in Greater Manchester area.
Web: www.urbanpresence.freeserve.co.uk
Email: paul@urbanpresence.freeserve.co.uk
☎ 0161 273 7900

Urban Theology Unit, Pitsmoor Study House, 210 Abbeyfield Road, Sheffield S4 7AZ
Director: Rev Inderjit Bhogal. *Director of Studies:* Rev Christine Jones. Executive staff 2, Other staff 2. ***CC*** No.505334. Began 1969; ecumenical. Magazine: *New City* (2,000 n/a), *UTU News* (2,000 every four months), *New City Specials* (2,000 n/a), *People's Bible Studies* (2,000 periodically). Turnover £139,000 to year end Dec 98. Training ministers and lay people for urban work, new styles of church work, theology.
☎ 0114 243 5342 🖷 0114 243 5342

Vacation Term for Biblical Study (Oxford), 13 Oxford Road, Dewsbury WF13 4LN
Chairman: Dr Barbara Spensley. No full-time staff. ***CC*** Began 1903; interdenominational. No magazine. Turnover £8,000 to year end Sept 98. Two week residential course for 100 people (July and August annually).
☎ 01924 467 319

The Veritas Trust, 37 Balmoral Crescent, Dronfield Woodhouse, Dronfield S18 8ZY
Director: Mr Steve Richards. No full-time staff. ***CC*** Began 1989; non-denominational. No magazine. Turnover £8,000 to year end May 93. Supporting the teaching ministry of local churches.
Email: steve.richards@zetnet.co.uk
☎ 01246 410 122 🖷 01246 410 122

***The Wayside Training Centre**, 77 Broadway, Sandown PO36 9AQ
Director: Rev Nigel Cox. Executive staff 2, Other staff 6. ***CC*** No.1036560. Began 1994; interdenominational. No magazine. Turnover £10,000 to year end Apr 96. Equipping people through teaching, training, support, to use the Bible confidently for discipling and teaching.
☎ 01983 407 808

Wesley & Methodist Studies Centre (WMSC), Westmins College, Oxford OX2 9AT
Director of WMSC: Rev Tim Macquiban. Teaching staff Admin staff 2. Began 1993; Methodist. Magazine: *WMS Newsletter* (500 quarterly). Turnover £60,000 to year end J 99. Research and development of ministries within Metho ism, through courses, publications, conferences, teaching.
Web: www.ox-west.ac.uk/wmsc/
Email: t.macquiban@ox-west.ac.uk
☎ 01865 253 359 🖷 01865 253 417

The Whitefield Institute, Frewin Court, Oxford OX1 3HZ
Director: Dr E David Cook. *Co-Director:* Rev Dr David Smit Executive staff 2, Other staff 2. ***CC*** No.273458. Began 198 non-denominational. Magazine: *Newsletter* (250 every fou months), *Whitefield Briefings* (200 every two months). Turn over £160,000 to year end Apr 98. Institute for research an writing in theology, ethics and education. An activity of UCCF
Email: admin@whitefield.nildram.co.uk
☎ 01865 202 838 🖷 01865 247 198

The WorkNet Partnership, 56 Baldry Gardens, Londo SW16 3DJ
Director: Geoff Shattock. Staff n/a. ***CC*** No.1069411. Bega 1997; non-denominational. Magazine: *Briefing* (Circulatio n/a quarterly). Turnover n/a. Offering a unique combination o faith to work resourcing, metaskills training, and a partnershi scheme.
Web: www.worknetpartnership.org.uk
Email: training@worknetpartnership.org.uk
☎ 020 8764 8080 🖷 020 8764 3030

Worth Abbey Lay Community, Worth Abbey, Turners Hill, Crawley RH10 4SB
Co-ordinator: Fr James Catto. Admin staff 2. ***CC*** No.23572 Began 1970; Roman Catholic. No magazine. Turnover £82,000 to year end Aug 98. For young lay people. Benedictine.
Web: ukonline.co.uk/worth.abbey.homepages.htm
Email: worthabbeylc@ukonline.co.uk
☎ 01342 710 300

YMCA, Dunford House, Midhurst GU29 0DG
General Manager: Mrs Pauline Dey. Admin staff 2, Other staff 12. ***CC*** No.212810. Began 1951; non-denominational. No magazine. Turnover £270,000 to year end Mar 96. Conference and training centre venue, residential facilities, historic house set in 60 acres of grounds.
☎ 01730 812 381 🖷 01730 817 042

†YMCA, George Williams College, 199 Freemasons Road, Canning Town, London E16 3PY
Principal: Mr Chandu Christian. Academic staff 7, Admin staff 10. ***CC*** No.1044624. Began 1970; interdenominational. No magazine. Turnover n/a. Voluntary-aided higher education college offering courses in informal education and management.
☎ 020 7540 4900 MiniCom 01715114901
🖷 020 7511 4900

***Youth With A Mission (Education and Training)**, Highfield Oval, Ambrose Lane, Harpenden AL5 4BX
Director of Training: Mr Grahame Fawcett. Lecturers 35, Other staff 100. ***CC*** Began 1973; interdenominational. Magazine: *UKI Training Brochure* (10,000 frequency n/a). Turnover n/a. Training in missions and ministry, 15 locations in UK and Ireland.
Email: 100425.1002@compuserve.com
☎ 01582 463 300 🖷 01582 463 305

EXTRA INFORMATION

X

OTHER CHURCHES & RELIGIOUS HEADQUARTERS, MULTI-FAITH ORGANISATIONS

Note: The Handbook essentially lists organisations in the UK which would ascribe to the Trinitarian position described c Page 4. The groups included here do not satisfy the Trinitarian criterion for inclusion. These entries were previously ar appendix of the Church Headquarters category, but have been moved to this Section, all of which (except the Late Entries) are non-Trinitarian organisations which are included for information purposes

3HO (Healthy, Happy, Holy), The Lotus Healing Centre, 7 New Court Street, St John's Wood, London NW8 7AA
Teacher: Yogi Bhajan. No full-time staff. Began 1975. No magazine.
☎ 020 7722 5797 🖷 020 7722 5751

The Aetherius Society, 757 Fulham Road, London SW6 5UU
Founder President: Sir George King. No other staff. Began 1955. Magazine: *Cosmic Voice* (Circulation n/a periodically), *Newsletter* (Circulation n/a periodically).
Web: www.inpotential.org
☎ 020 7736 4187/7731 1094 🖷 020 7731 1067
Also at: The Inner Potential Centre, 36 Kelvedon Road, London SW6 5BW
☎ 020 7736 4187

Brahma Kumaris, Global Co-operation House, 65 Pound Lane, London NW10 2HH
UK Director: Sister Jayanti. *Programme Co-ordinator:* Sister Maureen. Voluntary staff 20. ***CC*** No.269971. Began 1937. Magazine: *Retreat* (3,500 half-yearly). Turnover £100,000 + Dec 96.
Web: www.bkwsu.com
Email: bk@bkwsugch.demon.co.uk
☎ 020 8727 3350 🖷 020 8727 3351

The Buddhist Society, 58 Eccleston Square, London SW1V 1PH
General Secretary: Mr Ronald C Maddox. Admin staff 3. ***CC*** No.208677. Began 1924. Magazine: *The Middle Way* (3,000 quarterly).
Web: www.buddsoc.org.uk
☎ 020 7834 5858 🖷 020 7976 5238

†**Cherubim and Seraphim Church Council**, 175 Earlham Grove, Forest Gate, London E7 9AP
Church General Secretary: Evangelist K Sonuga Davies. Executive staff 4. ***CC*** Began 1965. Magazine: *The Light* (Circulation n/a quarterly).
☎ 020 8534 0378

†**Christadelphians**, 404 Shaftmoor Lane, Hall Green, Birmingham B28 8SZ
Editor: Mr Michael Ashton. Executive staff 2, Other staff 9. ***CC*** No.240090. Began 1864. Magazine: *The Christadelphian Magazine* (Circulation n/a monthly).
☎ 0121 777 6328 🖷 0121 778 5024

Christadelphian Publications, 66 Carlton Road, Nottingham NG3 2AP
Manager: Mr A Cave. No full-time staff. ***CC*** Began 1948. Magazine: *The Dawn Ecclesial* (850 monthly).
☎ 0115 958 7208

The Church of Christ, Scientist (Christian Science Church), 2 Elysium Gate, 126 New Kings Road, London SW6 4LZ
District Manager, Publications Comm: Mrs Hazel Joynes. Other staff 5. ***CC*** Began 1879. Magazine: *Christian Science Journal* (Circulation n/a monthly), *Christian Science Sentinel* (Circulation n/a weekly), *Christian Science Monitor* (Circulation n/a daily).
Web: www.tfccs.com
Email: chancep@compub.org
☎ 020 7371 0600 🖷 020 7371 9204

The Church of Jesus Christ of Latter-day Saints (Mormons), Publ Affairs, Church Offices, 751 Warwick Road, Solihu B91 3DQ
Area President: Elder Spencer J Condie. Executive staff Admin staff 95. ***CC*** Began 1837. Magazine: *The Ensign* (7,00 monthly).
☎ 0121 712 1202 🖷 0121 709 0180

The Church of Scientology, Office of Special Affairs, Saint Hi Manor, East Grinstead RH19 4JY
Public Affairs Director: Mr G Wilson. Serving ministers 15(Other staff 68. Began 1952. Magazine: *Freedom* (40,000 quar terly), *Auditor* (100,000 monthly), *Advance* (100,000 ever two months).
Web: www.scientology.org
☎ 01342 318 229 🖷 01342 325 474

Creme: Maitreya, Share International, Tara Press, PO Box 3677 London NW5 1RU
Author & Editor: Mr Benjamin Creme. No full-time staff Began 1974. Magazine: *Share International* (Circulation n/a periodically).
Web: www.shareintl.org
☎ 020 7482 1113 🖷 020 7267 2881

†**Da Free John**, Da Avatara Ashram, Barefoot Adidam, Tasburgh Hall, Lower Tasburgh, Norwich NR15 1LT
The Bright Leader: Da Avabhasa. *Mission Manager:* Colin Bright. Other staff n/a. Began 1984. Magazine: *Open Eyes* (5,000 quarterly).
☎ 01508 471 402 🖷 01509 471 401

†**Eckankar**, Eck Information Centre, PO Box 695, Sheffield S8 8QZ
Leader: Mr Harold Klemp. No full-time staff. ***CC*** Began 1965. Magazine: *The Golden Vessel* (Circulation n/a periodically).
☎ No telephone

†**Federation of Jain Organisations in the UK**, 11 Lindsay Drive, Harrow HA3 0TA
Co-ordinator: Mr Vinod Kapashi. Began n/a. No magazine.
☎ 020 8204 2871

Friends of the Western Buddhist Order (FWBO), Madhyamaloka, 30 Chantry Road, Moseley, Birmingham B13 8HD
Leader: Ven Sangharakshita Padmaloka. Members of the order 790. ***CC*** Began 1968. Magazine: *Dharma Life* (3,000 every four months), *Lotus Realm* (Circulation n/a every four months).
☎ 0121 449 3700 🖷 0121 449 3780
Information office London Buddhist Centre, 51 Roman Road, London E2 0HU
☎ 020 8981 1225
Press office 12 Park Road, Moseley, Birmingham B13 8AB
☎ 0121 449 8272

neral Assembly of Unitarian and Free Christian Churches, Essex Hall, 1 Essex Street, Strand, London WC2R 3HY
General Secretary: Mr Jeffrey J Teagle. *Deputy General Secretary:* Rev John Clifford. Executive staff 6, Other staff 4, Serving ministers 64. ***CC*** No.250788. Began 1928. Magazine: *The Inquirer* (2,300 fortnightly), *The Unitarian* (2,000 monthly).
Web: www.unitarian.org.uk
Email: ga@unitarian.org.uk
☎ 020 7240 2384 Fax 020 7240 3089

e General Conference of the New Church, 11 Seaview Road, Brightlingsea, Colchester CO7 0PP
Secretary of Conference: Mr Gordon S Kuphal. *President:* Rev John M Sutton. Executive staff 3, Admin staff 2, Serving ministers 14. ***CC*** No.253206. Began 1787; incorporated 1872. Magazine: *New Church Magazine* (Circulation n/a every four months), *Lifeline* (400 ten times a year), *Outlook* (2,000 quarterly).
☎ 01206 302 932 Fax 01206 302 932
Also at: 20 Bloomsbury Way, London WC1A 2TH
☎ 020 7229 9340
And: New Church College, 25 Radcliffe New Road, Radcliffe, Manchester M26 1LE
☎ 0161 766 2521 Fax 0161 796 1142

he Greater World Christian Spiritualist Association, 3 Conway Street, Fitzrovia, London W1P 5HA
General Manager: Ray Robinson. Executive staff 6. Began 1921. Magazine: *The Greater World* (Circulation & frequency n/a), *Newsletter* (8,000 quarterly).
Email: www.greaterworld.com
☎ 020 7436 7555 Fax 020 7580 3485

Hindu Centre, 39 Grafton Terrace, London NW5 4JA
General Secretary: Prof Dharadwaj. Executive staff 14, Other staff 7. ***CC*** Began 1935. Magazine: *Sruti* (1,000 monthly).
☎ 020 7485 8200 Fax 020 8200 0931

International Churches of Christ, 25 Euston Road, King's Cross, London NW1 2SD
Administrator: Mr Neville Lee. Staff n/a. Began 1982. (Previously London Church of Christ (LCC)). Magazine: *A Light to London* (Circulation n/a quarterly).
Web: www.icoc.org.uk/london
Email: icoc.uk.force9.net
☎ 020 7713 6028 Fax 020 7278 3644
Also at: Birmingham Church of Christ, 33 Reservoir Road, Ladywood, Edgbaston, Birmingham B16 9EL
☎ 0121 454 2576
And: Manchester Christian Church, 118 Cringle Road, Levenshulme, Manchester M19 2RT
☎ 0161 432 0782

International Society for Krishna Consciousness, Bhaktivedanta Manor, Hilfield Lane, Aldenham, Watford WD2 8EZ
Governing Body Commissioner: Shiva Rama Swami. *President:* Mr Vipramukhya Swami. Executive staff 40, Other staff 450. ***CC*** No.259649. Began 1969. Magazine: *Back to Godhead* (150,000 every two months).
Email: bhaktivedanta.manor@com.bbt.se
☎ 01923 857 244 Fax 01923 852 896

Islamic Cultural Centre & London Central Mosque, 146 Park Road, London NW8 7RG
Director General: Dr Hamad Al-Majed. Other staff n/a. Began 1944. Magazine: *Islamic Quarterly* (1,200 quarterly).
☎ 020 7724 3363 Fax 020 7724 0493

Islamic Foundation, Markfield Conference Centre, Ralby Lane, Markfield, Leicester LE67 9SY
Director General: Dr Muhammad M Ahsan. Admin staff 30. ***CC*** Began 1973. Magazine: *Muslim World Book* (Circulation & frequency n/a), *Review* (2,000 quarterly), *Encounters* (1,000 half-yearly).
Web: www.islamic-foundation.org.uk
Email: i-foundation@islamic-foundation.org.uk
☎ 01530 244 944 Fax 01530 244 946

Jehovah's Witnesses, Watch Tower House, The Ridgeway, London NW7 1RN
Admin staff 30. Began 1900. Magazine: *The Watchtower* (606,000 fortnightly), *Awake!* (556,500 fortnightly).
☎ 020 8906 2211 Fax 020 8906 3938
Ireland: Watch Tower House, 291 Jamestown Road, Finglas, Dublin 11, Republic of Ireland

Jewish Communities in the United Kingdom, Board of Deputies of British Jews, Commonwealth House, 1 New Oxford Street, London WC1A 1NF
Chief Executive: Mr Neville Nagler. Staff n/a. Began 1760. Magazine: *The Jewish Chronicle* (Circulation n/a weekly). Turnover n/a.
Email: info@bod.org.uk
☎ 020 7543 5400

Mahikari, Sukio Mahikari, Suffolk Road, South Norwood, London SE25 6ES
Leader: Seishu Okada. Staff n/a. ***CC*** Began 1983 in the UK. No magazine.
☎ 020 8771 4449

Musama Disco Christo Church, 40 Brailsford Road, Tulse Hill, London SW2 2TE
Superintendent Minister (UK): Rev Jerisdan H Jehu-Appiah. Executive staff 3. ***CC*** No.328063. Began 1978. Magazine: *The Gospel Ministry* (250 quarterly). Counselling; conferences, workshops in: Theology, African Christianity, pastoral studies, mental health, race relations.
Email: hartna@computers.co.uk
☎ 020 8671 5099

The Muslim Educational Trust, 130 Stroud Green Road, London N4 3RZ
Director: Mr Ghulam Sarwar. Executive staff 3, Other staff 2. ***CC*** No.313192. Began 1966. Magazine: *Reflect* (Circulation n/a every four months).
☎ 020 7272 8502 Fax 020 7281 3457

National Spiritual Assembly of the Bahá'is of the United Kingdom, 27 Rutland Gate, London SW7 1PD
Secretary-General: Hon Barnabas Leith. Staff n/a. ***CC*** Began n/a. No magazine.
Email: secretariat@bahai.org.uk
☎ 020 7584 2566 Fax 020 7584 9402

The Pagan Federation, BM Box 7097, London WC1N 3XX
President: Mr P Jennings. Voluntary staff 400. Began 1971. Magazine: *Pagan Dawn* (6,600 quarterly).
Web: www.paganfed.demon.co.uk
Email: secretary@paganfed.demon.co.uk
☎ 01928 770 909 Mobile: 07778 366 469 Fax 01928 770 910

†The Raelian Movement, BCM Minstrel, London WC1N 3XX
National Guide: Dr Marcus Wenner. No full-time staff. Began 1975. Magazine: *Apocalypse Magazine* (Circulation n/a quarterly).
☎ 0117 923 7447

†Reorganized Church of Jesus Christ of Latter Day Saints, British Isles Region, Headquarters, 769 Yardley Wood Road, Billesley, Birmingham B13 0PT
Region Administrator: Rev Alan Riley. Executive staff 2, Admin staff 4, Serving ministers 2. ***CC*** No.255657. Began 1863. Magazine: *Region Courier* (450 five times a year).
Web: www.rlds.org
☎ 0121 444 5243 🖷 0121 444 5243

†Sahaja Yoga, Life Eternal Trust, 44 Chelsham Raod, Clapham, London SW4 6NP
UK Leader: Ms Hester Spiro. Staff n/a. ***CC*** Began 1972. No magazine.
☎ No telephone

†Solara, Star-Borne Unlimited, Holistic Centre, Unit N & M, Royal Albert Walk, Albert Road, Southsea PO4 0JT
Leader: Solara. No full-time staff. Began 1986. Magazine: *The Starry Messenger* (800 frequency n/a).
☎ 023 9229 3668

The Spiritualist Association of Great Britain, 33 Belgrave Square, London SW1X 8QB
President: Mrs S Blair. Other staff 4. ***CC*** Began 1872. Magazine: *Service* (3,500 every four months).
☎ 020 7235 3351 🖷 020 7245 9706

The Theosophical Society in England, 50 Gloucester Place, London W1H 4EA
National President: Mr Peter Barton. Executive staff 3, Other staff 5. ***CC*** Began 1888. Magazine: *Insight* (2,500 every two months).
☎ 020 7935 9261 🖷 020 7935 9543

Unification Church (Holy Spirit Association for the Unification of World Christianity), 44 Lancaster Gate, London W2 3NA
General Secretary: Mr D Franklin. Other staff 200, Serving ministers 53. ***CC*** No.256598. Began 1968. Magazine: *One World* (10,000 quarterly).
☎ 020 7723 0721 🖷 020 7724 2262

United Lodge of Theosophists, 62 Queen's Gardens, London W2 3AL
Leader: n/a. Admin staff 2. Began 1925. Magazine: *Theosophy and The Theosophical Movement* (Circulation & frequency n/a).
☎ 020 7723 0688 / 262 8639

The World Sikh Foundation (Sikh Cultural Society of Great Britain), 33 Wargrave Road, Harrow HA2 8LL
General Secretary: Mr Amar Singh Chhatwal. Staff n/a. ***CC*** No.1054913. Began 1960. (Previously Sikh Cultural Society of Great Britain). Magazine: *The Sikh Courier International* (3,000 quarterly).
☎ 020 8864 9228

†World Zoroastrian Organisation, 135 Tennyson Road, South Norwood, London SE25 5NF
Director: n/a. Staff n/a. Began n/a. No magazine.
☎ No telephone

MULTI-FAITH ORGANISATIONS

The Association for Pastoral Care and Counselling, British Asso ation for Counselling, 1 Regent Place, Rugby CV21 2PJ
Chair: Rev Michael Wright. No full-time staff. ***CC*** No.2983 Began 1973. Magazine: *Contact* (600 every four month Turnover £8,000 to year end Dec 96. Advancing and develo ing nationwide the theory and practice of pastoral care a counselling.
Web: www.counselling.co.uk
Email: bac@bac.co.uk
☎ 01788 550 899 🖷 01788 562 189

Inner Cities Religious Council, Department of the Environme Transport and the Regions, 4/K/10, Eland House, Bressend Place, London SW1E 5DU
Secretary: Rev David Rayner. Executive staff 5. Began 199 Magazine: *General Profile* (Circulation & frequency n/a), *Cha lenging Religious Discrimination* (Circulation & frequency n A Guide for Faith Communities). Turnover n/a. Forum f Faith Communities and Government with an emphasis o regeneration.
☎ 020 7890 3703 🖷 020 7890 3709

The Inter Faith Network for the United Kingdom, 5 Tavistoc Place, London WC1H 9SN
Director: Mr Brian Pearce. Full time staff 4. ***CC*** No.106893 Began 1987. Magazine: *Newsletter* (Circulation n/a every fou months). Turnover £137,000 to year end Dec 98. Links over 8 member organisations and works with them to promote mutua respect and understanding between the different faith commu nities in the UK.
Email: ifnet.uk@btinternet.com
☎ 020 7388 0008 🖷 020 7387 7968

Monastery of St Francis & Gorton Trust Ltd, Gorton Monastery Gorton Lane, Manchester M18 8BT
Chairman: Mrs Elaine Griffiths. ***CC*** No.1061457. Began 1996; ecumenical. Magazine: *Update* (Circulation n/a quarterly). Turnover n/a. Developing a national visitor centre, museum, education centre in Manchester for major faiths in the UK.
Web: www.mancat.u-net.com/monastery
Email: elaine.griffiths@virgin.net
☎ 01565 723 838 Mobile: 07831 397 222 🖷 01565 723 845

†Prayer for Peace, 70 Weymouth Road, Frome BA11 1HJ
Co-ordinator: Mrs Ingrid Schultz. All voluntary staff. Began 1981. No magazine. Turnover n/a. Arranging worldwide daily inter-faith noon prayer vigil focusing on peace, environment; mail order materials.
☎ 01373 471 317

World Congress of Faiths, 2 Market Street, Oxford OX1 3EF
Executive Secretary: Diana Hanmer. Executive staff 1, Other staff 1. ***CC*** Began 1936. Magazine: *World Faiths Encounter* (800 every four months). Turnover n/a. Encouraging interfaith understanding and co-operation.
☎ 01865 202 751 🖷 01865 202 746

X

ORGANISATIONS & AGENCIES

HELP LINES

Al Anon
☎ 020 7403 0888

Alcoholics Anonymous Helpline
☎ 020 7352 3001

Childline
☎ 0800 1111 (24 hours)

Cot Death Helpline
☎ 020 7235 1721 (24 hours)

Cruse Bereavement Line
☎ 020 8332 7227

Eating Disorders Association
☎ 01603 621 414

LIFE National Hotline
☎ 01926 311 511

Marriage Care
☎ 0345 573 921 (Mon-Thur from 3pm–9pm)

National Aids Helpline
☎ 0800 567 123 (Freephone; 24 hours)

National Drugs Helpline
☎ 0800 776 600 (Freephone; 24 hours)

National Missing Persons Helpline
☎ For Help and Advice (Freephone; 24 hours): 0500 700 700
To leave a message for family and friends: Call Free: 0500 700740
To register a missing person; 020 8392 2000

National Volunteering Helpline
☎ 0345 221 133 (local rate)

NSPCC Child Protection Helpline
☎ 0800 800 500 (Freephone; 24 hours)

The Salvation Army Family Tracing Service
☎ 020 7383 2772

Samaritans
☎ 0345 909 090 (local rate; 24 hours)

Saneline
☎ 0345 678 000 (local rate)

Scope – Cerebral Palsy Helpline
☎ 0800 626 216 (Freephone)

Shelter
☎ 0808 800 4444

Womens Aid Federation England (WAFE)
☎ 0345 023 468

ORGANISATIONS AND AGENCIES

ACAS, Advisory, Conciliation and Arbitration Service, Brandon House, 180 Borough High Street, London SE1 1LW
☎ 020 7210 3000 🖷 020 7210 3708

ACENVO (Association of Chief Executives of National Voluntary Organisations), 130 College Road, Harrow HA1 1BQ
Email: acenvo@dircon.co.uk
☎ 020 8424 2334 🖷 020 8426 0055

ACTIONAID, Hamlyn House, MacDonald Road, London N19 5PG
☎ No telephone

Age Concern England, Astral House, 1268 London Road, London SW16 4ER
Web: www.ace.org.uk
☎ 020 8679 8000 🖷 020 8765 7211

Air Training Corps, Headquarters, RAF College, Cranwell, Sleaford NG34 8HB
☎ No telephone

Alcoholics Anonymous, PO Box 1, Stonebow House, Stonebow, York YO1 7NJ
☎ 01904 644 026 🖷 01904 629 091

Amnesty International, International Secretariat, 1 Easton Street, London WC1X 8DJ
☎ 020 7413 5500 🖷 020 7956 1157

ARCISS, Association of Research Centres in Social Sciences, c/o National Institute of Economic and Social Research, 2 Dean Trench Street, Smith Square, London SW1P 3HE
Email: jkirkland@niesr.ac.uk
☎ 020 7654 1920 🖷 020 7654 1900

†**Army Cadet Force**, 15 Co. Royal Green Jackets ACF, Hamilton Road, London E15 3AE
☎ 020 7474 9584

Arts Council of England, 14 Great Peter Street, London SW1P 3NQ
☎ 020 7333 0100

ASA (Advertising Standards Authority Ltd), Brook House, 2 Torrington Place, London WC1E 7HW
Web: www.asa.org.uk
☎ 020 7580 5555 🖷 020 7631 3051

Automobile Association, Head Office, Norfolk House, Priestley Road, Basingstoke RG24 9NY
Web: www.theaa.co.uk/theaa
☎ 0990 444 444

Barnardos, Tanners Lane, Ilford IG6 1QG
☎ 020 8550 8822 🖷 020 8551 6870

Board of Inland Revenue, Somerset House, The Strand, London WC2R 1LB
☎ 020 7438 6622

The Booksellers Association of Great Britain and Ireland, Minster House, 272 Vauxhall Bridge Road, London SW1V 1BB
☎ 020 7834 5477 🖷 020 7834 8812

The British Computer Society, 1 Sanford Street, Swindon SN1 1HJ
Web: www.bcs.org.uk\par
Email: bcshq@bcs.org.uk
☎ 01793 417 417 🖷 01793 480 270

The British Council, 10 Spring Gardens, London SW1A 2BN
☎ 020 7930 8466 🖷 020 7839 6347

British Film Institute, 21 Stephen Street, London W1P 2LN
☎ 020 7255 1444 🖷 020 7436 7950

British Institute of Management, Management House, Cottingham Road, Corby NN17 1TT
Web: www.mic.inst.mgp.org.uk
Email: mic@inst-mgp.org.uk
☎ 01536 204 222 🖷 01536 201 651
Also at: 3rd Floor, 2 Savoy Court, London WC2 0EZ
☎ 020 7497 0580 🖷 020 7497 0463

British Library, 96 Euston Road, London NW1 2DB
☎ 020 7412 7000 🖷 020 7412 7268

British Museum, Great Russell Street, London WC1B 3DG
☎ 020 7636 1555 🖷 020 7323 8118

British Red Cross, Tuition House, 516 Francis Grove, Wimbledon, London SW19 4DT
☎ 020 8944 8909 🖷 020 8944 8785

Broadcasting Standards Commission, 7 The Sanctuary, London SW1P 3JS
☎ 020 7233 0544 🖷 020 7233 0397

Cabinet Office, 70 Whitehall, London SW1A 2AS
☎ 020 7270 1234

Cancer Research Campaign, 6 Cambridge Terrace, London NW1 4JL
Web: www.crc.org.uk
Email: toastmastercrc.org.uk
☎ 020 7224 1333 🖷 020 7487 4310

CARE (Cooperative for American Relief to Everywhere, Inc), 36 Southampton Street, London WC2E 7AF
☎ No telephone

Carers National Association, 1st Floor, 20 Glasshouse Yard, London EC1A 4JS
☎ 020 7490 8898

CBI (Confederation of British Industry), Centre Point, New Oxford Street, London WC1A 1DU
Web: www.cbi.org.uk
☎ 020 7379 7400 🖷 020 7240 1578

Central Office of Information, Hercules Road, London SE1 7DU
☎ 020 7928 2345
see also: Office for National Statistics

†**Charinco/Charishare**, Mercury Asset Management plc, 33 King William Street, London EC4R 9AS
☎ 020 7280 2800 🖷 020 7280 2820

Charities Advisory Trust, Radius Works, Back Lane, Hampstead, London NW3 1HL
Web: webb.ukonline.co.uk/charities.advisory.trust/
☎ 020 7794 9835 🖷 020 7431 3739

Charities Aid Foundation, Kings Hill, West Malling ME19 4TA
CC No.268369.
Web: www.charitynet.org
Email: enquiries@caf.charitynet.org
☎ 01732 520 000 🖷 01732 520 001

The Charity Commission, Harmsworth House, 13 Bouverie Street, London EC4Y 8DP
☎ 020 7674 2333 (Press Office)

†**The Charity Forum,** 60 Laurel Avenue, Potters Bar EN6 2AB
☎ 01707 662 448 🖷 01707 664 350

Child Poverty Action Group, 4th Floor, 1 Bath Street, London EC1V 9PY
☎ No telephone

Child Support Commissioners, Office of the Social Security & Child Support Commissioners, 5th Floor, Newspaper House, 8 Great New Street, London EC4A 3BN
☎ 020 7353 5245 🖷 020 7936 2171

Childline, Freepost 1111, London N1 0BR
Administration: 2nd Floor, Royal Mail Building, Studd Street, London N1 0QW
Web: www.childline.org.uk
☎ 020 7239 1000 🖷 020 7239 1001

Commission for Racial Equality, Elliot House, 10 Allington Street, London SW1E 5EH
☎ 020 7828 7022 🖷 020 7630 7605

Commonwealth War Graves Commission, 2 Marlow Road, Maidenhead SL6 7DX
Email: cwgc@dial.pipex.com
☎ 01628 634 221 🖷 01628 771 208

Community Service Volunteers (CSV), 237 Pentonville Road, London N1 9NJ
☎ 020 7278 6601

Computing Services and Software Association, 20 Red Lion Street, London WC1R 4QN
Web: www.cssa.co.uk
Email: cssa@cssa.co.uk
☎ 020 7395 6700 Fax 020 7404 4119

Conservative & Unionist Central Office, 32 Smith Square, London SW1P 3HH
Web: www.tory.org.uk
Email: ccoffice@conservative-party.org.uk
☎ 020 7222 9000 Fax 020 7222 1135

Countryside Agency, John Dower House, Crescent Place, Cheltenham GL50 3RA
☎ 01242 521 381 Fax 01242 584 270

Cruse-Bereavement Care, Cruse House, 126 Sheen Road, Richmond TW9 1UR
☎ 020 8940 4818 Fax 020 8940 7638

Cult Information Centre, BCM CULTS, London WC1N 3XX
☎ 01689 833 800 Mobile: 07589 168 610

HM Customs and Excise, New King's Beam House, 22 Upper Ground, London SE1 9PJ
☎ 020 7629 1313 Fax 020 7865 5005

Data Protection Commissioner, Wycliffe House, Water Lane, Wilmslow SK9 5AF
Web: www.open.gov.uk/dpr/dprhome.htm
Email: data@wycliffe.demon.co.uk
☎ 01625 545 745 Fax 01625 524 510

Department for Culture, Media & Sport, 2 Cockspur Street, London SW1Y 5DH
☎ 020 7211 6200 Fax 020 7211 6210

Department for Education and Employment, Sanctuary Buildings, Great Smith Street, London SW1P 3BT
☎ Information Office: 020 7925 5555

Department for International Development, 94 Victoria Street, London SW1E 5JL
Web: www.oneworld.org/dfid
Email: library@dfid.gtnet.gov.uk
☎ 020 7917 7000

Department of Health, Richmond House, 79 Whitehall, London SW1A 2NS
☎ 020 7210 3000

Department of Social Security, Richmond House, 79 Whitehall, London SW1A 2NS
☎ 020 7238 3000

Department of Trade & Industry, 1 Victoria Street, London SW1H 0ET
Web: www.dti.gov.uk
Email: dti.enquiries@imsv.dti.gov.uk
☎ 020 7215 5000 Fax 020 7222 2629

Department of the Environment, Transport & the Regions, Eland House, Brassenden Place, London SW1E 5DU
Web: www.detr.gov.uk
☎ 020 7890 3000

Design Council, 34 Bow Street, London WC2 7AT
Web: www.design_council.org.uk
☎ 020 7420 5200 Fax 020 7420 5300

Direct Mail Advertising, Marketing & Mail Services, 64 Priory Crescent, London SE19 3EE
☎ 020 7437 1067 Fax 01293 562 996

Duke of Edinburgh's Award, Award House, 7 St Matthew Street, London SW1P 2JT
☎ 020 7222 4111 Fax 020 7222 4112

English Heritage, 23 Saville Row, London W1X 1AB
Web: www.english-heritage.co.uk
☎ 020 7973 3000 Fax 020 7973 3001

English Nature (Nature Conservancy Council for England), Northminster House, Peterborough PE1 1UA
☎ 01733 455 000 Fax 01733 568 834

English Sports Council, 16 Upper Woburn Place, London WC1H 0QP
☎ 020 7273 1500

English Tourist Board, Thames Tower, Black's Road, London W6 9EL
☎ 020 8846 9000 Fax 020 8563 0302

Environment Agency, Rio House, Waterside Drive, Aztec West, Almondsbury, Bristol BS12 4UD
Email: @environment-agency.gov.uk
Fax 01454 624 409

Equal Opportunities Commission, Overseas House, Quay Street, Manchester M3 3HN
☎ 0161 833 9244

Eurostat, Unit A2, Rue Alcide de Gasperie, JMO B3/099A, L-2920 Luxembourg
☎ 00 352 4301 32048
Fax 00 352 4301 32594

FAIR (Family Action Information and Resource), BCM Box 3535, PO Box 12, London WC1N 3XX
☎ 01642 898 412 Fax 01642 898 412

Family Policy Studies Centre, 9 Tavistock Place, London WC1H 9SN
Web: www.vois.org.u/fpsc
Email: fpsc@mailbox.ulcc.ac.uk
☎ 020 7388 5900 Fax 020 7388 5600

Foreign & Commonwealth Office, Downing Street, London SW1A 2AL
☎ 020 7270 3000

Forestry Commission, 231 Corstorphine Road, Edinburgh EH12 7AT
☎ 0131 334 0303 Fax 0131 334 3047

Friends of the Earth, 26 Underwood Street, London N1 7JQ
Web: www.foe.co.uk
Email: info@ssoe.co.uk
☎ 020 7490 1555 Fax 020 7490 0881

†**Gamblers Anonymous**, 6 Hurlingham Business Park, Sullivan Road, London SW6 3DU
☎ 020 7384 3040

Gestetner, 24a Burryport Road, Brackmills, Northampton NN4 7BB
☎ 01604 766 111 Fax 01604 391 44

Gingerbread, 16 Clerkenwell Close, London EC1R 0AA
☎ 020 7336 8183

Government Office for the Eastern Region, Building A, Westbrook Centre, Milton Road, Cambridge CB4 1YG
☎ Enquiries: 01223 346 766
Fax 01223 319 051

Government Office for the East Midlands, The Belgrave Centre, Stanley Place, Talbot Street, Nottingham NG1 5GG
☎ Enquiries: 0115 971 2750
Fax 0115 971 2404

Government Office for London, Riverwalk House, 157 Millbank, London SW1P 4RR
☎ 020 7217 3456 Fax 020 7217 3450

Government Office for Merseyside, Cunar Building, Water Street, Liverpool L3 1QB
☎ Enquiries: 0151 224 6302
Fax 0151 224 6470

Government Office for the North East, Stanegat House, 2 Groat Market, Newcastle upo Tyne NE1 1YN
☎ Enquiries: 0191 201 3300

Government Office for the North West, Sunle Tower, Picadilly Plaza, Manchester M1 4BA
☎ Enquiries: 0161 952 4000

Government Office for the South East, Bridg House, 1 Walnut Tree Close, Guildforc GU1 4GA
☎ Enquiries: 01483 882 255

Government Office for the South West, The Pithay, Bristol BS1 2PB
Web: www.gosw.gov.uk/gosw
Email: goswbrus@online.rednet.co.uk
☎ Enquiries: 0117 900 7000
Fax 0117 900 1900

Government Office for the West Midlands, 77 Paradise Circus, Queensway, Birmingham B1 2DT
☎ 0121 212 5050 Fax 0121 212 1010

Government Office for Yorkshire & the Humber, PO Box 213, City House, New Station Street, Leeds LS1 4US
☎ 0113 280 0600 Fax 0113 283 6394

Greenpeace Ltd, Canonbury Villas, London N1 2PN
☎ 020 7865 8100 Fax 020 7865 8200

The Guide Association, Commonwealth Headquarters, 17 Buckingham Palace Road, London SW1W 0PT
Web: www.guides.org.uk
Email: chq@guides.org.uk
☎ 020 7834 6242 Fax 020 7828 8317

The Guide Dogs for the Blind Association, Hillfields, Burghfield Common, Reading RG7 3YG
☎ 0118 983 5555

Guinness Publishing, 338 Euston Road, Regent's Place, London NW1 3BD
Email: gworlds@itl.net
☎ 020 8891 4567 Fax 020 7891 4501

Help the Aged, St James Walk, Clerkenwell Green, London EC1R 0BE
Web: www.helptheaged.org.uk
Email: hta@pipex.dial.com.uk
☎ 020 7253 0253 Fax 020 7895 1407

The Henley Centre, 9 Bridewell Place, London EC4V 6AY
Web: www.henleyventre.com
Email: future@henleycentre.com
☎ 020 7955 1800 Fax 020 7353 2899

Henley Management College, Greenlands, Henley-on-Thames RG9 3AU
Web: www.henleymc.ac.uk
☎ 01491 571 454 Fax 01491 571 635

Home Office, 50 Queen Anne's Gate, London SW1H 9AT
☎ 020 7273 4000

Hunger Project, 11 Carteret Street, London SW1H 9DL
☎ No telephone

Imperial Cancer Research Fund, 44 Lincoln Inn Fields, London WC2 3PX
Web: www.icnet.uk
☎ 020 7242 0200 Fax 020 7269 3100

INFORM (Information Network Focus On Religious Movements), Houghton Street, London WC2A 2AE
Email: inform@lse.ac.uk
☎ 020 7955 7654 Fax 020 7955 7679

Institute of Business Ethics, 24 Greencoat Place, London SW1
☎ 020 7931 0495

Institute of Charity Fundraising Managers, Market Towers, Nine Elms Lane, London SW8 5NQ
☎ 020 7627 3436 Fax 020 7627 3508

Institute of Directors, 116 Pall Mall, London SW1Y 5ED
Web: www.id.co.uk
☎ 020 7839 1233 Fax 020 7930 1949

Institute of Economic Affairs, 2 Lord North Street, Westminster, London SW1P 3LB
☎ 020 7799 3745

Labour Party Head Office, 150 Walworth Street, London SE17 1JT
☎ 020 7701 1234 Fax 020 7234 3300

HM Land Registry, Lincoln's Inn Fields, London WC2A 3PH
☎ 020 7917 8888 Fax 020 7955 0110

Liberal Democrats, Head Office, 4 Cowley Street, London SW1P 3NB
Web: www.libdems.org.uk
Email: libdems@cix.co.uk
☎ 020 7222 2999 Fax 020 7799 2170

Library Association, 7 Ridgemount Street, London WC1E 7AE
Web: www.la-hq.org.uk
Email: info@la-hq.org.uk
☎ 020 7636 7543 Fax 020 7436 7218

LIFE – Save The Unborn Child, Life House, 1a Newbold Terrace, Leamington Spa CV32 4EA
☎ 01926 421 587 Fax 01926 336 497
London Region: 83 Margaret Street, London W1N 7HB
☎ No telephone

Lord Chancellor's Department, Selborne House, 54 Victoria Street, London SW1E 6QW
☎ Enquiries: 020 7210 8500

Macmillan Cancer Relief, 15 Britten Street, London SW3 3TZ
Web: www.mcmillan.org.uk
☎ 020 7351 7811 Fax 020 7376 8098

Market Research Society, 15 Northburgh Street, London EC1 0JR
Web: www.mrs.org.uk
☎ 020 7490 4911 Fax 020 7490 0608

Mechanical Copyright Protection Society Ltd (MCPS), Elga House, 41 Streatham High Road, London SW16 1ER
☎ 020 8769 4400 Fax 020 8769 8792

MENCAP, 123 Golden Lane, London EC1Y 0RX
☎ 020 7454 0454 Fax 020 7608 3254

Mental Health Foundation, 20 Cornwall Terrace, London NW1 4QL
Web: www.mentalhealth.org.uk
Email: mhf@mentalhealth.org.uk
☎ 020 7535 7400 Fax 020 7535 7474

MIND (National Association for Mental Health), 15 Broadway, London E15 4BQ
☎ 020 8519 2122
Information line: 0345 660 163

Ministry of Agriculture, Fisheries and Food (MAFF), Nobel House, 17 Smith Street, London SW1P 3JR
☎ Public enquiries: 01645 335 577
Fax 020 7270 8125

Ministry of Defence, Main Building, Horseguards Avenue, London SW1A 2HB
☎ 020 7218 9000

Monopolies and Mergers Commission, New Court, 48 Carey Street, London WC2A 2JT
Web: www.open.gov.uk/mmc
Email: mmc@gtnet.gov.uk
☎ 020 7324 1467 Fax 020 7324 1400

National Association of Citizens Advice Bureaux, Myddleton House, 115 Pentonville Road, London N1 9LZ
Web: www.nacab.org.uk
Email: consortancy@nacab.org.uk
☎ 020 7833 2181 Fax 020 7833 4371

National Centre for Social Research, 35 Northampton Square, London ECIV 0AX
Web: www.natcen.ac.uk
Email: info@natcen.ac.uk
☎ 020 7250 1866 Fax 020 7250 1524

National Children's Bureau, 8 Wakley Street, London EC1V 7QE
☎ 020 7843 6000

National Council for One-Parent Families, 255 Kentish Town Road, London NW5 2LX
☎ 020 7428 5400 Fax 020 7482 4851

National Council of Voluntary Organisations (NCVO), Regent's Wharf, 8 All Saints Street, London N1 9RL
☎ 020 7713 6161 Fax 020 7713 6300

National Federation of Young Farmers Club, YFC Centre, National Agriculture Centre, Stoneleigh Park, Coventry CV8 2LG
Web: www.yfc-web.org.uk
Email: post@nfyfc.org.uk
☎ 024 7685 7200 Fax 024 7685 7229

National Trust Head Office, 36 Queen Anne's Gate, London SW1H 9AS
☎ 020 7222 9251 Fax 020 7222 5097

Newspaper Publishers Association, 34 Southwark Bridge Road, London SE1 9EU
☎ 020 7928 6928 Fax 020 7928 6928

The Newspaper Society, Bloomsbury House, 74 Great Russell Street, London WC1B 3DA
Web: www.newspapersoc.org.uk
☎ 020 7636 7014 Fax 020 7631 5119

Northern Ireland Office, 11 Millbank, London SW1P 4QE
☎ 020 7210 3000
And at Stormont House, Belfast BT4 3ST
☎ 028 9052 0700

NSPCC (National Society for the Prevention of Cruelty to Children), 42 Curtain Road, London EC2A 3NH
☎ 020 7825 2500

Office for National Statistics, 1 Drummond Gate, London SW1V 0EZ
Web: www.ons.gov.uk
☎ 020 7533 6363 Fax 020 7533 5863

Office of Electricity Regulation (OFFER), Hagley House, Hagley Road, Birmingham B16 8QG
☎ 0121 456 2100 Fax 0121 456 4664

Office of Fair Trading, Field House, Breams Building, London EC4A 1PR
☎ 020 7211 8000 Fax 020 7211 8800

Office of Gas Supply (OFGAS), Stockley House, 130 Wilton Road, London SW1V 1LQ
☎ 020 7828 0898 Fax 020 7932 1600

Office of Water Services (OFWAT), Centre City Tower, 7 Hill Street, Birmingham B5 4UA
☎ 0121 625 1300 Fax 0121 625 1400

Office of the National Lottery (OFLOT), 2 Monck Street, London SW1P 2BQ
☎ 020 7227 2000 Fax 020 7227 2005

Office of the Rail Regulator, 1 Waterhouse Square, 138 Holborn, London EC1N 2ST
Web: www.rail-reg.gov.uk
Email: orr@dial.pipex.com
☎ 020 7282 2000 Fax 020 7282 2040

Ordnance Survey, Romsey Road, Southampton SO16 4GU
Web: www.ordsvy.gov.uk
Email: custinfo@ordsvy.gov.uk
☎ 0345 330 011 Fax 023 8079 2452

OXFAM, 274 Banbury Road, Oxford OX2 7DZ
Web: www.oxfam.org.uk
Email: oxfam@oxfam.org.uk
☎ 01865 311 311 Fax 01865 312 600

Pensions Ombudsman, 11 Belgrave Road, London SW1V 1RB
☎ 020 7834 9144 Fax 020 7821 0065

Performing Rights Society, 29 Berners Street, London W1P 4AA
Web: www.prs.co.uk
Email: (persons initials)@prs.co.uk
☎ 020 7580 5544 Fax 020 7306 4455

The Periodical Publishers Association, Queen's House, 28 Kingsway, London WC2B 6JR
Web: www.ppa.co.uk
☎ 020 7404 4166 Fax 020 7404 4167

Police Complaints Authority, 10 Great George Street, London SW1P 3AE
☎ 020 7273 6450 Fax 020 7273 6401

The Prince's Trust, 18 Park Square East, London NW1 4LH
☎ 020 7543 1234

Public Records Office, Kew, Richmond TW9 4DU
☎ 020 8876 3444 Fax 020 8878 8905

Publishers Association, 1 Kingsway, London WC2B 6XF
Email: www.publishers.org.uk
☎ 020 7565 7474 Fax 020 7836 4543

RSPCA, Causeway, Horsham RH9 8JB
☎ 01403 223 284

RAC, 89 Pall Mall, London SW1Y 5HS
☎ 020 7930 2345 Fax 020 7976 1086

RADAR (Royal Association for Disability and Rehabilitation), Unit 12, City Forum, 250 City Road, London EC1V 8AF
Web: www.radar.org.uk
Email: radar@radar.org.uk
☎ 020 7250 3222 Fax 020 7250 0212

Relate Marriage Guidance, National Headquarters, Herbert Gray College, Little Church Street, Rugby CV21 3AP
Web: www.relate.org.uk
☎ 01788 573 241 Fax 01788 535 007

Research Exhibitions, St Giles House, 50 Poland Street, London W1V 4AX
☎ 020 7970 4000 Fax 020 7970 4696

Retail Price Index, Consumer Prices General Inflation, Floor D2/16, 1 Drummond Gate, London SW1V 2QQ
Web: www.ons.gulf.org.uk
☎ 020 7533 5874 📠 020 7533 5863

Rights of Women, 52 Featherstone Street, London EC1Y 8RT
🖂 Email: info@row.org.uk
☎ 020 7251 6577 📠 020 7608 0928

Royal National Institute for Deaf People, Speedfix House, 19 Featherstone Street, London EC1Y 8SL
☎ 020 7296 8199
Helpline: 0870 605 0123
Textphone: 020 7296 8001

Royal National Institute for the Blind, 224 Great Portland Street, London W1N 5HG
☎ 020 7388 1266

Royal National Lifeboat Institute (RNLI), Head Office: West Quay Road, Poole BH15 1HZ
☎ 01202 663 000
Fundraising, 20 Buckingham Street, London WC2N 6EF
☎ 020 7839 3369 📠 020 7839 3369

RSPB (Royal Society for the Protection of Birds), The Lodge, Potton Road, Sandy SG19 2DL
Web: www.rspb.org.uk
🖂 Email: bird@rspb.demon.co.uk
☎ 01767 680 551 📠 01767 692 365

St John Ambulance Brigade, 1 Grosvenor Crescent, London SW1X 7EF
☎ 020 7235 5231

The Samaritans, 10 The Grove, Slough SL1 1QP
☎ 01753 216 500 (Administration, not advice)
📠 01753 819 004

SANDS (Stillbirth and Neonatal Death Society), 28 Portland Place, London W1N 4DE
☎ 020 7436 7940

The Save The Children Fund, 17 Grove Lane, Camberwell, London SE5 8RD
☎ 020 7703 5400 📠 020 7703 2278

Scope
PO Box 833, Milton Keynes MK12 5NY
☎ 0800 626 216

The Scottish Office, Dover House, Whitehall, London SW1A 2AU
☎ 020 7270 3000
And at St Andrew's House, Edinburgh EH1 3DG
☎ 0131 556 8400

The Scout Association, Programme and Development Department, Gilwell Park, Bury Road, Chingford, London E4 7QW
☎ 020 8524 5246 📠 020 8498 5329

†**The Sea Cadet Corps**, 202 Lambeth Road, London SE1 7JF
☎ 020 7928 8914

Shelter, 88 Old Street, London EC1V 9HU
☎ 020 7505 2000 📠 020 7505 2169

Shelter London, Kingsbourne House, 229 High Holborn, London WC1V 7DA
☎ 020 7404 7447 📠 020 7404 7771

Survival International, 11 Emerald Street, London WC1N 3QL
☎ No telephone

HM Treasury, Allington Towers, Allington Street, London SW1E 5EB
☎ 020 7270 4870

TUC (Trades Union Congress), Congress House, 23 Great Russell Street, London WC1B 3LS
☎ 020 7636 4030 📠 020 7636 0632

The UK Direct Marketing Association, Haymarket House, 1 Oxendon Street, London SW1Y 4EE
Web: www.dma.org.uk
🖂 Email: dma@dma.org.uk
☎ 020 7321 2525 📠 020 7321 0191

United Nations Library, Millbank Towe
Millbank, London SW1 4QH
Web: www.un.org
🖂 Email: info@uniclondon.org
☎ 020 7630 1981 📠 020 7976 6478

Victim Support, Cranmer House, 39 Brixto
Road, London SW9 6DZ
☎ 020 7735 9166

†**The Voluntary Agencies Directory**, Bedfor
Square Press, 26 Bedford Square, Londo
WC1B 3HU
☎ 020 7636 4066

Voluntary Service Overseas, 317 Putney Bridg
Road, London SW15 2PN
☎ 020 8780 7200 📠 020 8780 7376

Voluntary Service, Women's Royal, 234 Stock
well Road, London SW9 9SP
☎ No telephone

Welsh Office, Gwydyr House, Whitehall
London SW1A 2ER
☎ 020 7270 3000
And at Cathays Park, Cardiff CF1 3NQ
☎ 029 2082 5111

J Whitaker & Sons Ltd (The Bookseller) London
(Books in Print), Whitaker Information
Services, Woolmead House West, Bear
Lane, Farnham GU9 7LG
Web: www.whitaker.uk
☎ 01252 742 500 📠 01252 742 501

Women's Aid Federation England (WAFE), PO Box 391, Bristol BS99 7WS
☎ 0117 944 4411

World Development Movement, 25 Beehive Place, London SW9 7QR
Web: www.wdm.org.uk
🖂 Email: wdm@wdm.org.uk
☎ 020 7737 6215 📠 020 7274 8232

World Wide Fund for Nature, Panda House, Weyside Park, Godalming GU7 1XR
☎ 01483 426 444

WRVS (Women's Royal Voluntary Service), Milton Hill House, Milton Hill, Abingdon OX13 6AF
☎ 01235 442 900 📠 01235 861 166

RADIO & TELEVISION BBC

Corporate Headquarters & National Radio Stations Radio 1, Radio 2, Radio 3, Radio 4, BBC Broadcasting House, Portland Place, London W1A 1AA
☎ 020 7580 4468

Television, Radio 5 Live, Television Centre, Wood Lane, London W12 7RJ
☎ 020 8743 8000

REGIONAL OFFICES

English Regions, Pebble Mill, Pebble Mill Road, Birmingham B5 7QQ
☎ 0121 432 8888

Scotland, Broadcasting House, Queen Margaret Drive, Glasgow G12 8DG
☎ 0141 338 2000

Wales, Broadcasting House, Llantrisant Road, Llandaff, Cardiff CF5 2YQ
☎ 029 2032 2000

Northern Ireland, Broadcasting House, 25 Ormeau Avenue, Belfast BT2 8HQ
☎ 028 9033 8000

HEADS OF RELIGIOUS DEPARTMENTS

Religious Programmes (Radio and Television), New Broadcasting House, PO Box 27, Oxford Road, Manchester M60 1SJ
Head of Religious Programmes: Rev Ernest Rea.
☎ 0161 200 2020

BBC Radio News, Television Centre, Wood Lane, London W12 7RJ
Religious Correspondent: Emily Buchanan.
☎ 020 7743 8000

BBC Regions, New Broadcasting House, Oxford Road, Manchester M60 1SJ
Religious Correspondent: Richard Staples.
☎ 0161 200 2020

BBC World Service, PO Box 76, Bush House, Strand, London WC2B 4PN
Head of Religion: Alison Hilliard.
☎ 020 7240 3456

BBC LOCAL RADIO STATIONS

Asian Network, Epic House, Charles Street, Leicester LE1 3SH
Religious Producer: Ishsaq Ahmed.
☎ 0116 251 6688 📠 0116 251 1463

Coventry and Warwickshire, Holt Court, 1 Greyfriars Road, Coventry CV1 2WR
Religious Producer: Steve Woodall. (Previously Radio Coventry and Warwickshire).
☎ 024 7686 0086 📠 024 7657 0100

Essex, 198 New London Road, Chelmsford CM2 9AB
Religious Producer: Chris Bard. (Previously Radio Essex).
☎ 01245 262 393 📠 01245 490 703

GLR, 35c Marylebone High Street, London W1A 4LG
Religious Producer: Jumoké Fashola.
☎ 020 7224 2424 📠 020 7935 3535

MR, PO Box 951, Oxford Road, Manchester M60 1SD
Religious Producer: Richard Jones. (Previously GMR Talk).
☎ 0161 200 2000 🖷 0161 236 5804

ereford & Worcester, Hylton Road, Worcester WR2 5WW
Religious Producer: Phil Simpson.
☎ 01905 748 485 🖷 01905 748 321

adio Bristol/Somerset Sound, PO Box 194, Bristol BS99 7QT
Religious Producer: Alan Bain.
☎ 0117 974 1111 🖷 0117 923 8323

adio Cambridgeshire, Broadcasting House, 104 Hills Road, Cambridge CB2 1LD
Religious Producer: Pat Heap.
☎ 01223 259 696 🖷 01223 460 832

adio Cleveland, PO Box 95FM, Newport Road, Middlesbrough TS1 5DG
Religious Producer: Alex Strangwayes-Booth.
☎ 01642 225 211 🖷 01642 211 356

adio Cornwall, Phoenix Wharf, Truro TR1 1UA
Religious Producer: Nina Davey.
☎ 01872 275 421 🖷 01872 240 679

adio Cumbria, Annetwell Street, Carlisle CA3 8BB
Religious Producer: Richard Corrie.
☎ 01228 592 444 🖷 01228 511 195

Radio Derby, PO Box 269, Derby DE1 3HL
Religious Producer: Donald MacDonald.
☎ 01332 361 111 🖷 01332 290 794

Radio Devon, PO Box 5, Broadcasting House, Seymour Road, Mannamead, Plymouth PL3 5YQ
Religious Producer: Damian Davies.
☎ 01752 260 323 🖷 01752 234 599

Radio Gloucestershire, London Road, Gloucester GL1 1SW
Religious Producer: Geoff Crago.
☎ 01452 308 585 🖷 01452 309 491

Radio Guernsey, Commerce House, Les Banques, St Peter Port, Guernsey GY1 2HS
Religious Producer: Colin Le Ray.
☎ 01481 728 977 🖷 01481 713 557

Radio Humberside, 9 Chapel Street, Hull HU1 3NU
Religious Producer: Mike Morris.
☎ 01482 323 232 🖷 01482 326 038

Radio Jersey, 18 Parade Road, St Helier, Jersey JE2 3PL
Religious Producer: Tracey Benn.
☎ 01534 870 000 🖷 01534 325 69

Radio Kent, Sun Pier, Chatham ME4 4EZ
Religious Producer: Colin Johnson.
☎ 01634 830 505 🖷 01634 830 053

Radio Lancashire, 26 Darwen Street, Blackburn BB2 2EA
Religious Producer: Joe Wilson.
☎ 01254 262 411 🖷 01254 841 043

Radio Leeds, Broadcasting House, Woodhouse Lane, Leeds LS2 9PN
Religious Producer: Jackie Cox.
☎ 0113 244 2131 🖷 0113 242 0652

Radio Leicester, Epic House, Charles Street, Leicester LE1 3SH
Religious Producer: Sandra Herbert.
☎ 0116 251 6688 🖷 0116 251 1463

Radio Lincolnshire, Radio Buildings, Newport, Lincoln LN1 3XY
Religious Producer: Adrienne Jones.
☎ 01522 511 411 🖷 01522 511 058

Radio Merseyside, 55 Paradise Street, Liverpool L1 3BP
Religious Producer: Steve Williams.
☎ 0151 708 5500 🖷 0151 794 0988

Radio Newcastle, Broadcasting Centre, Barrack Road, Newcastle upon Tyne NE99 1RN
Religious Producer: Francis Wood.
☎ 0191 232 4141 🖷 0191 261 8907

Radio Norfolk, Norfolk Tower, Surrey Street, Norwich NR1 3PA
Religious Producer: Ivan Bailey.
☎ 01603 617 411 🖷 01603 633 692

Radio Northampton, Broadcasting House, Abington Street, Northampton NN1 2BH
Religious Producer: Paul Needle.
☎ 01604 239 100 🖷 01604 233 027

Radio Nottingham, London Road, Nottingham NG2 4UU
Religious Producer: Andrew David.
☎ 0115 955 0500 🖷 0115 902 1985

Radio Sheffield, Ashdell Grove, 60 Westbourne Road, Sheffield S10 2QU
Religious Producer: Jack Shaw.
☎ 0114 268 6185 🖷 0114 266 5102

Radio Shropshire, 2–4 Boscobel Drive, Shrewsbury SY1 3TT
Religious Producer: Anni Holden.
☎ 01743 248 484 🖷 01743 271 702

Radio Solent, Broadcasting House, Havelock Road, Southampton SO14 7PW
Religious Producer: Georgina Windsor. (Previously Solent /Dorset FM).
☎ 023 8063 1311 🖷 023 8033 9648

Radio Stoke, Cheapside, Hanley, Stoke-on-Trent ST1 1JJ
Religious Producer: Ben Cohen.
☎ 01782 208 080 🖷 01782 289 115

Radio Suffolk, Broadcasting House, St Matthew's Street, Ipswich IP1 3EP
Religious Producer: Maureen Garratt.
☎ 01473 250 000 🖷 01473 210 767

Radio WM, Pebble Mill Road, Birmingham B5 7SD
Religious Producer: Michael Blood.
☎ 0121 432 9000 🖷 0121 432 9939

Radio York, 20 Bootham Row, York YO3 7BR
Religious Producer: Simon Stanley.
☎ 01904 641 351 🖷 01904 613 108

Southern Counties Radio, Broadcasting Centre, Guildford GU2 5AP
Religious Producer: Mark Norman.
☎ 01483 306 306 🖷 01483 304 952

Thames Valley, 269 Banbury Road, Summertown, Oxford OX2 7DW
Religious Producer: Hedley Feast. (Previously Radio Thames Valley FM).
☎ 01865 311 444 🖷 0645 311 555

Three Counties Radio, PO Box 3CR, Luton LU1 5XL
Religious Producer: Barry Amis.
☎ 01582 441 000 🖷 01582 401 467

Wiltshire Sound, Broadcasting House, Prospect Place, Swindon SN1 3RW
Religious Producer: Emma Cooper.
☎ 01793 513 626 🖷 01793 513 650

RADIO & TELEVISION – INDEPENDENT

Independent Television Commission, 33 Foley Street, London W1P 7LB
Religious Broadcasting Officer: Rachel Viney.
☎ 020 7255 3000 🖷 020 7306 7800

INDEPENDENT NATIONAL TELEVISION COMPANIES

Channel 4, 124 Horseferry Road, London SW1P 2TX
Commissioning Editor for Religion: Gill Brown.
☎ 020 7396 4444 🖷 020 7306 8366

Channel 5, 22 Long Acre, London WC2E 9LY
Programme Controller – Religion: Nick Wilson.
☎ 020 7550 5555 🖷 020 7550 5554

INDEPENDENT REGIONAL TELEVISION COMPANIES (CHANNEL 3)

Anglia Television Ltd, Anglia House, Norwich NR1 3JG
☎ 01603 615 151 🖷 01603 631 032

Border Television plc, The Broadcasting Centre, Durranhill, Carlisle CA1 3NT
☎ 01228 251 101 🖷 01228 541 384

Carlton Broadcasting Ltd, 101 St Martin's Lane, London WC2N 4AZ
☎ 020 7240 4000 🖷 020 7240 4171

Central Broadcasting Ltd, Central Court, Gas Street, Birmingham B1 2JT
☎ 0121 643 9898 🖷 0121 634 4740

Channel Television Ltd, The Television Centre, St Helier, Jersey JE1 3ZD
☎ 01534 816 816 🖷 01534 816 817

GMTV Ltd, London Television Centre, Upper Ground, London SE1 9TT
☎ 020 7827 7000 🖷 020 7827 7001

Grampian Television plc, Queen's Cross, Aberdeen AB15 2XJ
☎ 01224 846 846 🖷 01224 846 800

Granada Television Ltd, Granada Television Centre, Manchester M60 9EA
☎ 0161 832 7211 🖷 0161 827 2180

HTV Group plc Cymru (Wales), Television Centre, Culverhouse Cross, Cardiff CF5 6XJ
☎ 029 2059 0590 🖷 029 2059 7183

HTV Group plc West, Television Centre, Bath Road, Bristol BS4 3HG
☎ 0117 972 2722 🖷 0117 972 2400

LWT (Holdings) Ltd – London Weekend Television, London Television Centre, Upper Ground, London SE1 9LT
☎ 020 7620 1620 🖷 020 7261 1290

Meridian Broadcasting Ltd, The Television Centre, Southampton SO14 0PZ
☎ 023 8022 2555 🖷 023 8033 5050

Scottish Television plc, Cowcaddens, Glasgow G2 3PR
☎ 0141 300 3000 🖷 0141 300 3030

Tyne Tees Television Ltd, The Television Centre, City Road, Newcastle upon Tyne NE1 2AL
☎ 0191 261 0181 🖷 0191 261 2302

Ulster Television plc, Havelock House, Ormeau Road, Belfast BT7 1EB
☎ 028 9032 8122 🖷 028 9024 6695

Westcountry Television Ltd, Western Wood Way, Langage Science Park, Plymouth PL7 5BG
☎ 01752 333 333 🖷 01752 333 030

Yorkshire Television Ltd, The Television Centre, Leeds LS3 1JS
☎ 0113 243 8283 🖷 0113 244 5107

INDEPENDENT NATIONAL RADIO STATIONS

Atlantic 252, 74 Newman Street, London W1P 3LA
☎ 020 7637 5252 🖷 020 7436 4015

Classic FM, 7 Swallow Place, London W1R 7AA
☎ 020 7343 9000 🖷 020 7344 2700

Talk Radio UK, 76 Oxford Street, London W1N 0TR
☎ 020 7636 1089 🖷 020 7636 1053

Virgin Radio, 1 Golden Square, London W1R 4DJ
☎ 020 7434 1215 🖷 020 7434 1197

INDEPENDENT LOCAL RADIO STATIONS

2CR FM, 5 Southcote Road, Bournemouth BH1 3LR
☎ 01202 259 259 🖷 01202 255 244

2 TEN FM, PO Box 2020, Reading RG31 7FG
Associated with Classic Gold 1431.
☎ 0118 945 4400 🖷 0118 928 8456

95.8 Capital FM, 29 Leicester Square, London WC2H 7LA
(Previously Capital FM) Associated with Capital Gold.
☎ 020 7766 6000 🖷 020 7766 6100

96 Trent, 29 Castle Gate, Nottingham NG1 7AP
(Previously Trent FM) Associated with Classic Gold Gem
☎ 0115 952 7000 🖷 0115 912 9333

96.3 Aire FM, PO Box 2000, Leeds LS3 1LR
Associated with Magic 828.
☎ 0113 283 5500 🖷 0113 283 5501

96.3 QFM, 26 Lady Lane, Paisley PA1 2LG
Religious Producer: George Martin.
☎ 0141 887 9630 🖷 0141 887 0963

96.4 FM BRMB, Radio House, Aston Road North, Birmingham B6 4BX
(Previously BRMB-FM). Associated with Capital Gold (1152).
☎ 0121 359 4481 🖷 0121 359 1117

96.4 The Eagle, Dolphin House, North Street, Guildford GU1 4AA
Religious Producer: Steve Flashman. Associated with County Sound Radio 1476.
☎ 01483 300 964 🖷 01483 531 612

96.6 Oasis FM, 9 Christopher Place, St Albans AL3 5DQ
(Previously 96.6 FM Classic Hits).
☎ 01727 831 966 🖷 01727 834 456

96.9 Viking FM, Commercial Road, Hull HU1 2SG
(Previously Viking FM).
☎ 01482 325 141 🖷 01482 587 067

97.2 Stray FM, Stray Studios, PO Box 972, Station Parade, Harrogate HG1 5YF
Religious Producer: Les Gunn. (Previously Stray FM).
☎ 01423 522 972 🖷 01423 522 922

97.4 Vale FM, Longmead, Shaftesbury SP7 8QQ
Religious Producer: Cameron Smith. (Previously Gold Radio).
☎ 01747 855 711 🖷 01747 855 722

97.6 Chiltern FM, Broadcast Centre, Chiltern Road, Dunstable LU6 1HQ
(Previously Chiltern FM). Associated with Classic Gold 729 / 828.
☎ 01582 676 200 🖷 01582 676 201

100.7 Heart FM, PO Box 1007, 1 The Square, 111 Broad Street, Edgbaston, Birmingham B15 1AS
☎ 0121 626 1007 🖷 0121 696 1007

103.4 The Beach, PO Box 103.4, Lowestoft NR32 2TL
(Previously The Beach).
☎ 07000 001 035 🖷 07000 001 036

106 CTFM Radio, 16 Lower Bridge Street, Canterbury CT1 2HQ
☎ 01227 789 106 🖷 01227 785 106

107.2 Wire FM, Warrington Business Park, Long Lane, Warrington WA2 8TX
☎ 01925 445 545 🖷 01925 657 705

107.5 Cat FM, Regent Arcade, Cheltenham GL50 1JZ
(Previously Cheltenham Radio).
☎ 01242 699 555 🖷 01242 261 666

107.6 Kestrel FM, 2nd Floor, Paddington House, Walks Shopping Centre, Basingstoke RG21 7LJ
Religious Producer: Gordon Hunter.
☎ 01256 694 000 🖷 01256 694 111

107.7 Chelmer FM, Cater House, High Street, Chelmsford CM1 1AL
Religious Producer: Martin Lawford.
☎ 01245 259 400 🖷 01902 259 558

107.7 The Wolf, 10th Floor, Mander House, Wolverhampton WV1 3NB
☎ 01902 571 070 🖷 01902 571 079

107.8 Arrow FM, Priory Meadow Centre, Hastings TN34 1PJ
☎ 01424 461 177 🖷 01424 422 662

107.8 Thames FM, 45c High Street, Hampt
Wick, Kingston upon Thames KT1 4DG
Religious Producer: Jenny Costello. (Pre
ously Thames FM).
☎ 020 288 1300 🖷 020 288 1312

Active 107.5, 7 Western Road, Romfo
RM1 3LD
☎ 01708 731 643 🖷 01708 730 383

Alpha 103.2, 11 Woodland Road, Darlingt
DL3 7BJ
☎ 01325 255 552 🖷 01325 255 551

Asian Sound Radio, Globe House, Southa
Street, Manchester M3 1LG
☎ 0161 288 1000 🖷 0161 288 9000

B97 Chiltern FM, Broadcast Centr
Goldington Road, Bedford MK40 3LT
☎ 01234 272 400 🖷 01234 218 580

The Bay, PO Box 969, St George's Qua
Lancaster LA1 3LD
☎ 01524 848 747 🖷 01524 848 787

Beacon FM, 267 Tettenhall Road
Wolverhampton WV6 0DQ
(Previously Beacon Radio). Associated wit
Classic Gold WABC.
☎ 01902 838 383 🖷 01902 838 266

The Breeze, Radio House, Clifftown Road
Southend-on-Sea SS1 1SX
☎ 01702 333 711 🖷 01702 345 224

Broadland 102, St George's Plain, 47 Colegate
Norwich NR3 1DB
Religious Producer: Andrew Hopley. Associated with Classic Gold Amber.
☎ 01603 630 621 🖷 01603 666 252

The Buzz 97.1, Media House, Claughton Road,
Birkenhead CH45 6EY
☎ 0151 650 1700 🖷 0151 647 5427

Cambridge Red 107.9, PO Box 492, Cambridge
CB1 2UW
☎ 01223 722 300 🖷 01223 577 686

Capital Gold, 29 Leicester Square, London WC2H 3DR
Associated with 95.8 Capital FM
☎ 020 7766 6000 🖷 020 7766 6100

Capital Gold 1152, Radio House, Aston Road North, Birmingham B6 4BX
(Previously Xtra AM). Associated with BRMB.
☎ 0121 359 4481 🖷 0121 359 1117

Capital Gold 1170 & 1557, Radio House, Whittle Avenue, Segensworth West, Fareham PO15 5SH
(Previously South Coast Radio).
☎ 01489 589 911 🖷 01489 589 453

Capital Gold 1242 & 603, Radio House, John Wilson Business Park, Whitstable CT5 3QX
Associated with Invicta FM
☎ 01227 772 004 🖷 01277 771 558

Capital Gold 1323 & 945, Radio House, PO Box 2000, Brighton BN41 2SS
☎ 01273 430 111 🖷 01273 430 098

Central FM, 201 High Street, Falkirk FK1 1DU
Religious Producer: Douglas Aitken.
☎ 01786 451 188 🖷 01786 461 883

Centre FM, 5 Aldergate, Tamworth B79 7DJ
☎ 01827 318 000 🖷 01827 318 002

X

ntury 105, Century House, Waterfront Quay, Salford Quays, Manchester M5 2XW
☎ 0161 400 0105 🖷 0161 400 1105

ntury 106, City Link, Nottingham NG2 4NG
(Previously Radio 106 FM).
☎ 0115 910 6100 🖷 0115 910 6107

ntury Radio, PO Box 100, Gateshead NE8 2YX
☎ 0191 477 6666 🖷 0191 477 1771

'M, PO Box 964, Carlisle CA1 3NG
☎ 01228 818 964 🖷 01228 819 444

iampion FM, Parc Menai, Bangor LL57 4BN
☎ 01248 671 888 🖷 01248 671 971

iannel 103 FM, 6 Tunnell Street, St Helier, Jersey JE2 4LU
☎ 01534 888 103 🖷 01534 887 799

hannel Travel Radio, Main Control Building, Eurotunnel UK Terminal, PO Box 2000, Folkestone CT18 8XY
☎ 01303 283 873 🖷 01303 283 874

hoice FM (Brixton), 291 Borough High Street, London SE1 1JG
Religious Producer: Dave P
☎ 020 7378 3969 🖷 020 7378 3936

ity Beat 96.7 FM, Lamont Buildings, Stranmills Embankment, Belfast BT9 5FM
Religious Producer: Gail Hunter.
☎ 028 9020 5967 🖷 028 9020 0023

lassic Gold 774, 155 Bridge Street, Eastgate Centre, Gloucester GL1 1SS
Religious Producer: Peter Jackson. Associated with Severn Sound FM.
☎ 01452 423 791 🖷 01452 529 446

lassic Gold 792 / 828, Broadcast Centre, Chiltern Road, Dunstable LU6 1HQ
Associated with 97.6 Chiltern FM.
☎ 01582 676 200 🖷 01582 676 231

lassic Gold 936/1161 AM, PO Box 2000, Swindon SN4 7EX
(Previously Brunel Classic Gold, Swindon).
☎ 01793 842 600 🖷 01793 842 602

Classic Gold 1260, PO Box 2020, Bristol BS99 7SN
Religious Producer: Liz Black. (Previously Brunel Classic Gold).
☎ 0117 984 3200 🖷 0117 984 3202

Classic Gold 1332, Queensgate Centre, Peterborough PE1 1XJ
Associated with Hereward FM 102.7.
☎ 01733 460 460 🖷 01733 281 445

Classic Gold 1359, Hertford Place, Coventry CV1 3TT
Religious Producer: Gavin Coxhead. Associated with Mercia FM.
☎ 024 7686 8200 🖷 024 7686 8202

Classic Gold 1431, PO Box 2020, Reading RG31 7FG
Associated with 2 TEN FM.
☎ 0118 945 4400 🖷 0118 928 8456

Classic Gold 1557, 19 St Edmund's Road, Northampton NN1 5DY
Associated with Northants 96.
☎ 01604 792 411 🖷 01604 721 934

Classic Gold Amber (Norfolk), St George's Plain, 47 Colegate, Norwich NR3 1DB
Religious Producer: Andrew Hopley. (Previously Amber Radio, Norfolk). Associated with Broadland 102.
☎ 01603 630 621 🖷 01603 666 252

Classic Gold Amber (Suffolk), Radio House, Alpha Business Park, Ipswich IP1 5LT
(Previously Amber Radio, Bury St Edmunds).
☎ 01473 461 000 🖷 01473 741 200

Classic Gold Gem, 29 Castle Gate, Nottingham NG1 7AP
(Previously Trent FM).
☎ 0115 952 7000 🖷 0015 912 9333

Classic Gold WABC, 267 Tettenhall Road, Wolverhampton WV6 0DQ
(Previously WABC). Associated with Beacon FM.
☎ 01902 838 383 🖷 01902 838 266

Classic Gold – West Yorkshire, Forster Square, Bradford BD1 5NE
Religious Producer: Colin Lowther.
☎ 01274 203 040 🖷 01274 203 130

Clyde 1 and
Clyde 2, Clydebank Business Park, Clydebank, Glasgow G81 2RX
Religious Producer: Alan Sorensen.
☎ 0141 565 2200 🖷 0141 565 2265

Coast FM, 41 Conwy Road, Colwyn Bay LL28 5AB
Religious Producer: Simon Ferrer.
☎ 01492 534 555 🖷 01492 535 248

Connect FM, Church Street, Wellingborough NN8 4XX
Religious Produer: Rob Quicke.
☎ 01933 224 972 🖷 01933 442 333

Cool FM, PO Box 974, Belfast BT1 1RT
☎ 028 9181 7181 🖷 028 9181 4974

Country 1035, PO Box 1035, London W1A 2ZT
☎ 020 7546 1010 🖷 020 7546 1020

County Sound Radio, Dolphin House, North Street, Guildford GU1 4AA
Religious Producer: Steve Flashman. Associated with 96.4 The Eagle.
☎ 01483 300 964 🖷 01483 531 612

Crash FM, 27 Fleet Street, Liverpool L1 4AR
Religious Producer: Kenny Murray.
☎ 0151 707 3107 🖷 0151 707 3109

Delta 97.1 FM, 65 Weyhill, Haslemere GU27 1HN
(Previously Delta Radio).
☎ 01428 651 971 🖷 01428 658 971

Delta FM 102, Prospect Place, Mill Lane, Alton GU23 2SY
Religious Producer: Greg Williams. (Previously Wey Valley Radio).
☎ 01420 544 444 🖷 01420 544 044

Downtown Radio, Kiltonga Industrial Estate, Belfast Road, Newtownards BT23 4ES
Religious Producer: Colm Flanagan.
☎ 028 9181 5555 🖷 028 9181 8913

Dream 100 FM, Northgate House, St Peter's Street, Colchester CO1 1HT
(Previously Mellow 1557).
☎ 01206 764 466 🖷 01206 764 672

Dune FM, The Power Station, Victoria Way, Southport PR8 1RR
Religious Producer: David Raynor.
☎ 01704 502 500 🖷 01704 502 540

Eleven Seventy AM, PO Box 1170, High Wycombe HP13 6YT
☎ 01494 446 611 🖷 01494 445 400

Essex FM, Radio House, Clifftown Road, Southend-on-Sea SS1 1SX
☎ 01702 333 711 🖷 01702 345 224

Fame 1521, The Stanley Centre, Kelvin Way, Crawley RH10 2SE
☎ 01293 519 161 🖷 01293 565 663

FLR 107.3, PO Box 1073, London SE8 4WU
Religious Producer: Producer of The Gospel Show.
☎ 020 8691 9202 🖷 020 8691 9193

FM 102 The Bear, The Guardhouse Studios, Banbury Road, Stratford upon Avon CV37 7HX
Religious Producer: Julien Hicks.
☎ 01789 262 636 🖷 01789 263 102

FM107 The Falcon, Unit 2, Brunel Mall, Stroud GL5 2BP
☎ 01453 767 369 🖷 01453 757 107

Forth FM and
Forth AM, Forth House, Forth Street, Edinburgh EH1 3LF
Religious Producer: Andrew Monaghan.
☎ 0131 556 9255 🖷 0131 558 3277

Fosseway Radio, PO Box 107, Hinckley, Leicester LE10 1WR
Religious Producer: Daniel Bruce.
☎ 01456 614 151 🖷 01456 616 888

Fox FM, Brush House, Pony Road, Oxford OX4 2XR
☎ 01865 871 000 🖷 01865 871 036

Galaxy 101, Millennium House, 26 Baldwin Street, Bristol BS1 1SE
(Previously Galaxy Radio).
☎ 0117 901 0101 🖷 0117 901 4666

Galaxy 102, 127 Portland Street, Manchester M1 6ED
(Previously Kiss 102)
☎ 0161 228 0102 🖷 0161 228 1020

Galaxy 102.2, 95 Broad Street, Birmingham B15 1AU
Religious Producer: Nicky Tapper. (Previously Choice FM (Birmingham)).
☎ 0121 616 1000 🖷 0121 616 1011

Galaxy 105, 2A Joseph's Well, Park Lane, Leeds LS3 1AB
(Previously Kiss 105)
☎ 0113 213 0105 🖷 0113 213 1055

Gemini FM, Hawthorne House, Exeter Business Park, Exeter EX1 3QS
Associated with Westward Radio
☎ 01392 444 444 🖷 01392 444 433

GWR FM, PO Box 2000, Swindon SN4 7EX
☎ 01793 842 600 🖷 01793 842 602

Hallam FM, Radio House, 900 Herries Road, Hillsborough, Sheffield S6 1RH
☎ 0114 285 3333 🖷 0114 285 3159

Heart 106.2, The Chrysalis Building, Bramley Road, London W10 6SP
☎ 020 7468 1062 🖷 020 7470 1062

Heartland FM, Lower Oakfield, Pitlochry PH16 5HQ
Religious Producer: Dorothy Morrison.
☎ 01796 474 040 🖷 01796 474 007

Hereward FM 102.7, Queensgate Centre, Peterborough PE1 1XJ
Associated with Classic Gold 1332.
☎ 01733 460 460 🖷 01733 281 445

Horizon FM 103, Broadcast Centre, Crownhill, Milton Keynes MK8 0AB
☎ 01908 269 111 🖷 01908 564 063

Huddersfield FM, The Old Stable Block, Brewery Drive, Lockwood Park, Huddersfield HD1 3UR
Religious Producer: Dave Rhodes.
☎ 01484 321 107 🖷 01484 311 107

Invicta FM, Radio House, John Wilson Business Park, Whitstable CT5 3QX
☎ 01227 772 004 🖷 01277 771 558

Island FM, 12 Westerbrook, St Sampsons, Guernsey GY2 4QQ
☎ 01481 420 00 🖷 01481 496 76

Isle of Wight Radio, Dodnor Parl, Newport PO30 5XE
☎ 01983 822 557 🖷 01983 822 109

Isles FM, PO Box 333, Stornoway HS1 2PU
Religious Producer: Stanley Bennie.
☎ 01851 703 333 🖷 01851 703 322

Jazz FM 100.4, The World Trade Centre, Exchange Quays, Manchester M5 3EJ
☎ 0161 877 1004 🖷 0161 877 1005

Jazz FM 102.2, The Jazz House, 26 Castlereagh Street, London W1H 6DJ
☎ 020 7706 4100 🖷 020 7723 9742

KCBC, Broadcast Centre, Unit 1, Centre 2000, Robinson Close, Telford Way Industrial Estate, Kettering NN16 8PU
(Previously KCBC 1584 AM).
☎ 07000 1074 🖷 01536 517 390

Key 103 FM, Castle Quay, Castlefield, Manchester M15 4PR
Associated with Piccadilly 1152.
☎ 0161 288 5000 🖷 0161 288 5001

KFM, 1 East Street, Tonbridge TN9 1AR
Religious Producer: Alan Jenkins.
☎ 01732 369 200 🖷 01732 369 201

Kingdom FM, Haig House, Haig Business Park, Markinch KY7 6AQ
☎ 01592 753 753 🖷 01592 757 788

Kiss 100 FM, Kiss House, 80 Holloway Road, London N7 8JG
☎ 020 7700 6100 🖷 020 7700 3979

Kix 96, St Mark's Church Annexe, Bird Street, Coventry CV1 4FH
☎ 024 7652 5656 🖷 024 7655 1744

KL.FM 96.7, 18 Blackfriars Street, King's Lynn PE30 1NN
☎ 01553 772 777 🖷 01553 766 453

Lantern FM, The Light House, 17 Market Place, Bideford EX39 2DR
Religious Producer: Adrian Philpott.
☎ 01237 424 444 🖷 01237 423 333

LBC 1152, 200 Grays Inn Road, London WC1X 8XZ
Associated with News Direct 97.3 FM
☎ 020 7973 1152 🖷 020 7973 8833

Leicester Sound, Granville House, Granville Road, Leicester LE1 7RW
Religious Producer: Andrew Fewster.
☎ 0116 256 1300 🖷 0116 256 1303

Liberty Radio 963/972, 100 Brompton Road, London SW3 1ER
☎ 020 7893 8966 🖷 020 7893 8965

Lincs FM, Witham Park, Waterside South, Lincoln LN5 7JN
Religious Producer: Sean Dunderdale.
☎ 01522 549 900 🖷 01522 549 911

Lite AM 1458, PO Box 1458, Quay West, Trafford Park, Manchester M17 1FL
☎ 0161 872 1458 🖷 0161 872 0206

Lochbroom FM, Mill Street Industrial Estate, Ullapool IV26 2UN
☎ 01854 613 131 🖷 01854 613 132

London Greek Radio, Florentia Village, Vale Road, London N4 1TD
☎ 020 8800 8001 🖷 020 8800 8005

London Turkish Radio, 185b High Road, Wood Green, London N22 6BA
☎ 020 8881 0606 🖷 020 8881 5151

Magic 105.4, 97 Tottenham Court Road, London W1P 9HF
(Previously Melody FM).
☎ 020 7504 7000 🖷 020 7504 7001

Magic 828, PO Box 2000, Leeds LS3 1LR
Associated with 96.3 Aire FM
☎ 0113 283 5500 🖷 0113 283 5501

Magic 1152, Newcastle upon Tyne NE99 1BB
(Previously Great North Radio).
☎ 0191 420 3040 🖷 0191 488 9222

Magic 1161 AM, Commercial Road, Hull HU1 2SG
☎ 01482 325 141 🖷 01482 587 067

Magic 1170, Radio House, Yale Crescent, Thornaby, Stockton-on-Tees TS17 6AA
☎ 01642 888 222 🖷 01642 868 288

Magic 1548 AM, 8 Stanley Street, Liverpool L1 6AF
Associated with Radio City 96.7
☎ 0151 227 5100 🖷 0151 471 0330

Magic 999, PO Box 974, St Paul's Square, Preston PR1 1XR
(Previously Red Rose Gold)
☎ 01772 556 301 🖷 01772 201 917

Magic AM, Radio House, 900 Herries Road, Sheffield S6 1RH
☎ 0114 285 2121 🖷 0114 285 3159

Mansfield 103.2 FM, The Media Suite, Brunts Business Centre, Samuel Brunts Way, Mansfield NG18 2AH
☎ 01623 646 666 🖷 01623 660 606

Manx Radio, PO Box 1368, Broadcasting House, Douglas IM99 1SW
Religious Producer: David Guest.
☎ 01624 661 066 🖷 01624 682 604

Marcher Gold, The Studios, Mold Road, Wrexham LL11 4AF
Religious Producer: Simon Ferrer. Associated with MFM.
☎ 01978 752 202 🖷 01978 759 701

Medway FM, Berkeley House, 186 High Street, Rochester ME1 1EY
☎ 01634 841 111 🖷 01634 841 122

Mercia FM, Hertford Place, Coventry CV1 3TT
Religious Producer: Gavin Coxhead. Associated with Classic Gold 1359.
☎ 024 7686 8200 🖷 024 7686 8202

Mercury FM, The Stanley Centre, Kelvin Way, Crawley RH10 2SE
Associated with Fame 1521
☎ 01293 519 161 🖷 01293 565 663

Metro FM, PO Box 9, Newcastle Upon Tyne NE99 1BB
☎ 0191 420 0971 🖷 0191 488 9222

MFM 103.4, The Studios, Mold Road, Wrexham LL11 4AF
Religious Producer: Simon Ferrer. Associated with Marcher Gold.
☎ 01978 752 202 🖷 01978 759 701

Millennium Radio, Harrow Manor W
Thamesmead, London SE2 9XH
Religious Producer: Wendy Saunders.
☎ 020 8311 3112 🖷 020 8312 1930

Minster FM, PO Box 123, Dunnington, Yo
YO1 5ZX
☎ 01904 488 888 🖷 01904 481 088

Mix 96, Friars Square Studios, 11 Bourb
Street, Aylesbury HP20 2PZ
Religious Producer: John Hanson.
☎ 01296 399 396 🖷 01296 398 988

Moray Firth Radio, PO Box 271, Inverne
IV3 8SF
Religious Producer: Len Black.
☎ 01463 224 433 🖷 01463 243 224

NECR, Town House, Kintore, Inverur
AB51 0US
(Previously North East Community Radio
☎ 01467 632 878 🖷 01467 632 969

Neptune Radio, PO Box 1068, Dov
CT16 1GB
Religious Producer: Mark Browning.
☎ 01304 202 505 🖷 01304 212 717

Nevis Radio, Inverlochy, Fort Willia
PH33 6LU
Religious Producer: Geoff Wright.
☎ 01397 700 007 🖷 01397 701 007

News Direct 97.3 FM, 200 Grays Inn Roa
London WC1X 8XZ
Associated with LBC 1152
☎ 020 7973 1152 🖷 020 7312 8565

NorthSound One & Two, 45 King's Gat
Aberdeen AB2 6EL
Religious Producer: David Haggart. (Previously NorthSound Radio).
☎ 01224 337 000 🖷 01224 637 289

Northants 96, 19 St Edmund's Road
Northampton NN1 5DY
(Previously Northants Radio). Associate
with Classic Gold 1557.
☎ 01604 795 600 🖷 01604 795 601

Oak FM, 18 Jubilee Drive, Loughborough
LE11 5TQ
Religious Producer: Steve Merike.
☎ 01509 211 711 🖷 01509 264 104

Oban FM, McLeod Units, Lochavullin Estate, Oban PA34 0AA
Religious Producer: George Verry.
☎ 01631 570 057 🖷 01631 570 057

Ocean FM, Radio House, Whittle Avenue, Segensworth West, Fareham PO15 5SH
☎ 01489 589 911 🖷 01489 589 453

Orchard FM, Haygrove House, Taunton TA3 7BT
☎ 01823 338 448 🖷 01823 320 444

Oxygen FM, Suite 41, The Westgate Centre, Oxford OX1 1PD
(Previously Oxygen 107.9 FM).
☎ 01865 724 442 🖷 01865 726 161

Peak 107 FM, Radio House, Foxwood Road, Chesterfield S41 9RF
Religious Producer: Dave Kilner.
☎ 01246 269 107 🖷 01246 269 933

Piccadilly 1152, Castle Quay, Castlefield, Manchester M15 4PR
Associated with Key 103 FM.
☎ 0161 288 5000 🖷 0161 288 5001

Pirate FM 102, Carn Brea Studios, Wilson Way, Redruth TR15 3XX
Religious Producer: John Butt.
☎ 01209 314 400 🖷 01209 314 345

mouth Sound, Earl's Acre, Plymouth PL3 4HX
Religious Producer: Chris Cole.
☎ 01752 227 272 🖷 01752 670 730

wer FM, Radio House, Whittle Avenue, Segensworth, West Fareham PO15 5SH
Associated with Ocean FM.
☎ 01489 589 911 🖷 01489 589 453

emier Radio, PO Box 13000, London SW1E 5PP
Station Director: Peter Kerridge.
☎ 020 7316 1300 🖷 020 7233 6706

he Pulse, PO Box 3000, Bradford BD1 5NE
☎ 01274 203 040 🖷 01274 203 130

102.9, The Old Waterside Railway Station, Duke Street, Waterside, Londonderry BT47 1DH
☎ 028 7134 4449 🖷 028 7131 1177

103 FM, The Vision Park, Chivers Way, Histon, Cambridge CB4 9WW
☎ 01223 235 255 🖷 01223 235 161

uay West Radio, Harbour Studios, The Esplanade, Watchet TA23 0AJ
Religious Producer: Roy Fernihough.
☎ 01984 634 900 🖷 01984 634 811

adio Borders, Tweedside Park, Galashiels TD1 3TD
Religious Producer: Steve Clipston.
☎ 01896 759 444 🖷 01896 759 494

adio Ceredigion, Yr Hen Ysgol Gymraeg, Ffordd Alexandra, Aberystwyth SY23 1PE
Religious Producer: Peter Thomas.
☎ 01970 627 999 🖷 01970 627 206

adio City 96.7, 8 Stanley Street, Liverpool L1 6AF
(Previously City FM and Radio City 1548 AM). Associated with Magic 1548 FM.
☎ 0151 227 5100 🖷 0151 471 0330

Radio Maldwyn, The Studios, The Park, Newtown SY16 2NZ
Religious Producer: Kenn Morris.
☎ 01686 623 555 🖷 01686 623 666

Radio Tay AM, 6 North Isla Street, Dundee DD3 7JQ
Religious Producer: Lorraine Stevenson. Associated with Tay FM.
☎ 01382 200 800 🖷 01382 593 252

Radio XL 1296 AM, KMS House, Bradford Street, Birmingham B12 0JD
☎ 0121 753 5353 🖷 0121 753 3111

Ram FM, The Market Place, Derby DE1 3AA
☎ 01332 292 945 🖷 01332 292 229

Red Dragon FM, West Canal Wharf, Cardiff CF1 5XL
Associated with Touch Radio.
☎ 029 2038 4041 🖷 029 2038 4014

RNA FM, Arbroath Infirmary, Rosemount Road, Arbroath DD11 2AT
☎ 01241 879 660 🖷 01241 439 664

Rock FM, PO Box 974, St Paul's Square, Preston PR1 1XR
Associated with Magic 999.
☎ 01772 556 301 🖷 01772 201 917

Rutland Radio, 40 Melton Road, Oakham LE15 6AY
Religious Producer: Keith Briggs.
☎ 01572 757 868 🖷 01572 757 744

Sabras Sound, Radio House, 63 Melton Road, Leicester LE4 6PN
☎ 0116 261 0666 🖷 0116 266 7776

Scot FM, No 1 Shed, Albert Quay, Leith, Edinburgh EH6 7DN
☎ 0131 554 6677 🖷 0131 554 2266

Severn Sound FM, Bridge Street Studios, Eastgate Centre, Gloucester GL1 1SS
Religious Producer: Peter Jackson. Associated with Classic Gold 774.
☎ 01452 313 200 🖷 01452 313 213

SGR-FM, Radio House, Alpha Business Park, Ipswich IP1 5LT
Associated with Classic Gold Amber (Suffolk).
☎ 01473 461 000 🖷 01473 741 200

SGR Colchester, Abbeygate Two, 9 Whitewell Road, Colchester CO2 7DE
☎ 01206 575 859 🖷 01206 561 199

SIBC, Market Street, Lerwick ZE1 0JN
☎ 01595 695 299 🖷 01595 695 696

Signal FM, Regent House, Heaton Lane, Stockport SK4 1BX
(Previously Signal Cheshire).
☎ 0161 285 4545 🖷 0161 285 1050

Signal One and
Signal Two, Stoke Road, Stoke-on-Trent ST4 2SR
☎ 01782 747 047 🖷 01782 744 110

Silk FM, Radio House, Bridge Street, Macclesfield SK11 6DJ
Religious Producer: Jeff Cooper.
☎ 01625 268 000 🖷 01625 269 010

South West Sound, Cambell House, Bankend Road, Dumfries DG1 4TH
☎ 01387 250 999 🖷 01387 265 629

Southern FM, Radio House, PO Box 2000, Brighton BN41 2SS
☎ 01273 430 111 🖷 01273 430 098

Sovereign Radio, 14 St Mary's Walk, Hailsham BN27 1AF
Religious Producer: Paul Martin.
☎ 01323 442 700 🖷 01323 440 643

Spectrum International Radio, 204 Queenstown Road, London SW8 3NR
☎ 020 7627 4433 🖷 020 7627 3409

Spire FM, City Hall Studios, Malthouse Lane, Salisbury SP2 7QQ
☎ 01722 416 644 🖷 01722 416 688

Spirit FM, Dukes Court, Bognor Road, Chichester PO19 2FX
Religious Producer: Bernard Allen.
☎ 01243 773 600 🖷 01243 786 464

Star FM, Tristar Broadcasting Ltd, The Observatory Shopping Centre, Slough SL1 1LH
☎ 01753 551 066 🖷 01753 512 277

Sun FM, PO Box 1034, Sunderland SR5 2YL
(Previously SunCity 103.4).
☎ 0191 548 1034 🖷 0191 548 7171

Sunrise FM, Sunrise House, 30 Chapel Street, Little Germany, Bradford BD1 5DN
☎ 01274 735 043 🖷 01274 728 534

Sunrise Radio, Sunrise House, Sunrise Road, Southall UB2 4AU
☎ 020 8574 6666 🖷 020 8813 9800

Sunshine 855, Sunshine House, Waterside, Ludlow SY8 1GS
Religious Producer: Bob Horsfield.
☎ 01584 873 795 🖷 01584 875 900

Surf 107, PO Box 107, Brighton BN1 1QS
☎ 01273 386 107 🖷 01273 273 107

Swansea Sound, Victoria Road, Gowerton, Swansea SA4 3AB
Religious Producer: Kevin Johns. Associated with The Wave 96.4 FM.
☎ 01792 511 170 🖷 01792 511 171

Tay FM, 6 North Isla Street, Dundee DD3 7JQ
Religious Producer: Lorraine Stevenson. Associated with Radio Tay AM.
☎ 01382 200 800 🖷 01382 593 252

Telford FM, PO Box 1074, Mercury House, Stafford Park, Telford TF3 3WG
☎ 01952 280 011 🖷 01952 280 010

Ten 17, Latton Bush Centre, Southern Way, Harlow CM18 7BU
Religious Producer: James Cassidy.
☎ 01279 432 415 🖷 01279 445 289

TFM Radio, Radio House, Yale Crescent, Thornaby, Stockton-on-Tees TS17 6AA
☎ 01642 888 222 🖷 01642 868 288

Thanet Local Radio, Imperial House, 2 High Street, Margate CT9 1DH
☎ 01843 220 222 🖷 01843 299 666

Touch Radio, West Canal Wharf, Cardiff CF1 5XL
Associated with Red Dragon FM.
☎ 029 2023 7878 🖷 029 2038 4014

Tower FM, The Mill, Browlow Way, Bolton BL1 2RA
☎ 01204 387 000 🖷 01204 534 065

Trax FM, White Hart Yard, Bridge Street, Worksop S80 1HR
Religious Producer: Paul Chivers.
☎ 01909 500 611 🖷 01909 500 445

Valleys Radio, PO Box 1116, Ebbw Vale NP3 6XW
Religious Producer: John Curtis.
☎ 01495 301 116 🖷 01495 300 710

Vibe FM, Reflection House, The Anderson Centre, Olding Road, Bury St Edmunds IP33 3TA
☎ 01284 718 800 🖷 01284 718 839

Virgin Radio – London, 1 Golden Square, London W1R 4DJ
☎ 020 7434 1215 🖷 020 7434 1197

Wave 105 FM, 5 Manor Court, Barnes Wallis Road, Segensworth East, Fareham PO15 5TH
Religious Producer: Blair Crawford.
☎ 01489 481 050 🖷 01489 481 060

The Wave 96.4 FM, Victoria Road, Gowerton, Swansea SA4 3AB
(Previously Soundwave). Associated with Swansea Sound.
☎ 01792 511 964 🖷 01792 511 965

The Wave 96.5, 965 Mowbray Drive, Blackpool FY3 7JR
Religious Producer: Simon Tate. (Previously RadioWave).
☎ 01253 304 965 🖷 01253 301 965

Waves Radio Peterhead, Unit 2, Blackhouse Industrial Estate, Peterhead AB42 1BW
Religious Producer: Ken Cowe.
☎ 01779 491 012 🖷 01779 490 802

Wessex FM, Radio House, Trinity Street, Dorchester DT1 1DJ
☎ 01305 250 333 🖷 01305 250 052

West Sound Radio, Radio House, Holmston Road, Ayr KA7 3BE
Religious Producer: Gordon McArthur.
☎ 01292 283 662 🖷 01929 283 665

Westward Radio, Hawthorne House, Exeter Business Park, Exeter EX1 3QS
Religious Producer: Shirley Ann Williams. Associated with Gemini FM.
☎ 01392 444 444 🖷 01392 444 433

Wish 102.4, Orrell Lodge, Orrell, Wigan WN5 8HJ
☎ 01942 761 024 🖷 01942 777 694

Wyvern FM, Barbourne Terrace, Worcester WR1 3JZ
(Previously Radio Wyvern).
☎ 01905 612 212 🖷 01905 215 80

XFM, 30 Leicester Square, London WC2H 7LA
☎ 020 7766 6600 🖷 020 7766 6601

Yorkshire Coast Radio, PO Box 9
Scarborough YO12 5YX
Religious Producer: Chris Sigsworth.
☎ 01723 500 962 🖷 01723 501 050

Yorkshire Dales Radio, Gargrave Ro
Skipton BD23 1YD
Religious Producer: Ron Nicholson.
☎ 01756 799 991 🖷 01756 799 771

LOCAL RADIO STATIONS BY COUNTY

BBC stations are listed first, Independent stations follow.

REGIONAL STATIONS

North East
Century Radio, Galaxy 105

North West
Century 105, Jazz FM 100.4

Yorkshire
Galaxy 105

East Midlands
Century 106

West Midlands
100.7 Heart FM

Eastern England
Vibe FM

South West England & South Wales
Galaxy 101

Solent
Wave 105 FM

Northern Ireland
BBC Radio Ulster
Cool FM, Downtown Radio

Scotland
BBC Radio Scotland, Radio Nan Gaidheal

Central Scotland
Scot FM

Wales
BBC Radio Wales, Radio Cymru

ENGLAND

Avon
BBC Radio Bristol
Classic Gold 1260, GWR FM

Bedfordshire
BBC Three Counties Radio
97.6 Chiltern FM, B 97Chiltern FM, Classic Gold 729/828

Berkshire
BBC Thames Valley
2 TEN FM, Classic Gold 1431, Star FM

Buckinghamshire
BBC Three Counties Radio
Eleven Seventy AM, Horizon FM 103, Mix 96

Cambridgeshire
BBC Radio Cambridgeshire
Cambridge Red 107.9, Classic Gold 1332, Hereward FM 102.7, Q103 FM

Cheshire
BBC Radio Stoke, BBC Radio Merseyside
Marcher Gold, MFM, Signal FM, Signal One, Signal Two, Silk FM

Cleveland
BBC Radio Cleveland
Alpha 103.2, Magic 1170, TFM Radio

Cornwall
BBC Radio Cornwall
Pirate FM 102

Cumbria
BBC Radio Cumbria
CFM

Derbyshire
BBC Radio Derby
Classic Gold Gem, Peak 107 FM, Ram FM

Devon
BBC Radio Devon
Gemini FM, Lantern FM, Plymouth Sound AM/FM, Westward Radio

Dorset
BBC Radio Solent, 2CR FM, 97.4 Vale FM, Classic Gold 828, Wessex FM

Co Durham
BBC Radio Cleveland, BBC Radio Newcastle
Alpha 103.2, Magic 1170

East Sussex
BBC Southern Counties Radio
107.8 Arrow FM, Capital Gold 1323 & 945, Southern FM, Sovereign Radio

Essex
BBC Essex
107.7 Chelmer FM, Active 107.5, The Breeze, Dream 100 FM, Essex FM, SGR (Colchester), Ten 17

Gloucestershire
BBC Radio Gloucestershire
107.5 CAT FM, Classic Gold 774, FM 107 The Falcon, Severn Sound FM

Greater Manchester
BBC GMR
Galaxy 102, Jazz FM 100.4, Key 103 FM, Lite AM 1458, Picadilly 1152, Tower FM

Hampshire
BBC Radio Solent
107.6 Kestrel FM, Capital Gold 1170 & 1557, Delta FM, Ocean FM, Power FM

Hereford
BBC Hereford & Worcester
Wyvern FM

Hertfordshire
BBC Three Counties Radio
96.6 Oasis FM, Classic Gold 792/828

Humberside
BBC Radio Humberside
Magic 1161 AM, Viking FM

Isle of Wight
BBC Radio Solent
Isle of Wight Radio

Kent
BBC Radio Kent
106 CTFM Radio, Capital Gold 1242 & 603, Channel Travel Radio, Invicta FM, Medwa FM, Neptune Radio, Thanet Local Radio

Lancashire
BBC Radio Lancashire
Asian Sound Radio, The Bay, Dune FM, Magi 999, Rock FM, The Wave 96.5, Wish 102.4 FM

Leicestershire
BBC Radio Leicester
Fosseway Radio, Leicester Sound, Oak FM Sabras Sound

Lincolnshire
BBC Radio Lincolnshire
Lincs FM

London
BBC GLR
Capital FM, Capital Gold 1548, Choice FM (Brixton), Country 1035, FLR 107.3, Heart 106.2, Jazz FM 102.2, Kiss 100 FM, LBC 1152, Liberty Radio 963/972, London Greek Radio, London Turkish Radio, Magic 105.4, Millennium Radio, News Direct 97.3 FM, Premier Radio, Spectrum International Radio, Sunrise Radio, Thames FM, Virgin FM, Xfm

Merseyside
BBC Radio Merseyside
107.2 Wire FM, The Buzz 97.1, Crash FM, Magic 1549 AM, Radio City 96.7

Norfolk
BBC Radio Norfolk
103.4 The Beach, Broadland 102, Classic Gold Amber, KL.FM 96.7

North Yorkshire
BBC Radio York
Minster FM, Stray FM, Yorkshire Coast Radio, Yorkshire Dales Radio

Northamptonshire
BBC Radio Northampton
Classic Gold 1557, Connect FM, KCBC, Northants 96

rthumberland
C Radio Newcastle
agic, Metro FM

ttinghamshire
C Radio Nottingham
Trent FM, Classic Gold Gem, Mansfield 103.2, Trax FM

xfordshire
3C Thames Valley
x FM, Oxygen FM

utland
BC Radio Leicester
utland Radio

hropshire
BC Radio Shropshire
lassic Gold WABC, Beacon FM, Sunshine 855, Telford FM

omerset
BC Radio Bristol / Somerset Sound
rchard FM, Quay West Radio

outh Yorkshire
BC Radio Sheffield
Iallam FM, Magic AM

Staffordshire
BBC Radio Stoke
Centre FM, Signal One, Signal Two

Suffolk
BBC Radio Suffolk
03,4 The Beach, Classic Gold Amber (Suffolk), SGR FM

Surrey
BBC Southern Counties Radio
96.4 The Eagle, Country Sound, Radio Delta 97.1

Tyne & Wear
BBC Radio Newcastle
Century Radio, Magic 1152, Metro FM, Sun FM

Warwickshire
BBC Coventry and Warwickshire
FM 102 The Bear, Classic Gold 1359, Kix 96, Mercia FM

West Midlands
BBC Radio WM
96.4 FM BRMB, 107.7 FM The Wolf, Beacon FM, Capital Gold 1152, Classic Gold WABC, Galaxy 102.2, Radio XL 1296 AM

West Sussex
BBC Southern Counties Radio
Capital Gold (1323 & 945), Fame 1521, Mercury FM, Southern FM, Spirit FM, Surf 107

West Yorkshire
BBC Radio Leeds
96.3 Aire FM, Classic Gold – West Yorks, Huddersfield FM, Magic 828, The Pulse, Sunrise FM

Wiltshire
BBC Wiltshire Sound
97.4 Vale FM, Classic Gold 936/1161 AM, GWR FM, Spire FM

Worcestershire
BBC Hereford & Worcestr
Wyvern FM

CHANNEL ISLANDS

Guernsey
BBC Radio Guernsey
Island FM

Jersey
BBC Radio Jersey
Channel 103 FM

ISLE OF MAN

Manx Radio (Independent)

NORTHERN IRELAND

Belfast
City Beat 96.7 FM (Independent)

Co Londonderry
BBC Radio Foyle
Q102.9 FM

SCOTLAND (ALL INDEPENDENT)

Aberdeenshire
NECR, North Sound One & Two, Waves Radio Peterhead

Angus
Radio Tay AM, RNA FM, Tay FM

Argyll & Bute
Oban FM

Ayrshire
West Sound Radio

Central
Central FM

Dumfries & Galloway
South West Sound

Edinburgh
Forth AM, Forth FM

Fife
Kingdom FM

Glasgow
Clyde 1, Clyde 2

Inverness-shire
Moray Firth Radio, Nevis Radio

Isle of Lewis
Isles FM

Perthshire
Heartland FM

Renfrewshire
96.3 QFM

Ross-shire
Lochbroom FM

Selkirshire
Radio Borders

Shetland
SIBC

WALES (ALL INDEPENDENT)

Clwyd
Coast FM, Marcher Gold, MFM

Dyfed
Radio Ceredigion

Gwent
Red Dragon FM, Touch AM, Valleys Radio

Gwynedd
Champion FM

Powys
Radio Maldwyn

South Glamorgan
Red Dragon FM, Touch AM

West Glamorgan
Swansea Sound, The Wave 96.4 FM

Information about radio stations supplied by CACLB – Churches Advisory Council for Local Broadcasting ☎ 01702 348 369 🖷 01702 305 121

NATIONAL PRESS RELIGIOUS CORRESPONDENTS

The Daily Express, 245 Blackfriars Road, London SE1 9UX
Religious Correspondent: Lisa Reynolds.
☎ 020 7928 8000 🖷 020 7620 1654

The Daily Telegraph, 1 Canada Square, Canary Wharf, London E14 5DT
Religious Correspondent: Victoria Combe.
☎ 020 7538 5000 🖷 020 7538 6242

The Guardian, 119 Farringdon Road, London EC1R 3ER
Religious Correspondent: James Meike.
☎ 020 7278 2332 🖷 020 7239 9787

The Independent, 1 Canada Square, Canary Wharf, London E14 5DT
Religious Correspondent: Clare Garner.
☎ 020 7293 2682 🖷 020 7293 2435

The Independent on Sunday, 1 Canada Square, Canary Wharf, London E14 5DT
Religious Correspondent: Clare Garner.
☎ 020 7292 2682 🖷 020 7293 2047

The Observer, 119 Farringdon Road, London EC1R 3ER
Religious Correspondent: To be appointed.
☎ 020 7278 2332 🖷 020 7713 4250

Press Association Ltd, 292 Vauxhall Bridge Road, London SW1V 1AE
Religious Correspondent: n/a.
☎ 020 7963 7000 🖷 020 7963 7192

The Sunday Telegraph, 1 Canada Square, Canary Wharf, London E14 5DT
Religious Correspondent: Jonathon Petre.
☎ 020 7538 5000 🖷 020 7538 6242

The Sunday Times, 1 Pennington Street, London E1 9XN
Religious Correspondent: Christopher Morgan.
☎ 020 7782 5000 🖷 020 7782 5988

The Times, 1 Pennington Street, London E1 9XN
Religious Correspondent: Ruth Gledhill.
Email: ruth.gledhill@dial.pipex.com
☎ 020 7782 5001 🖷 020 7782 5988

WEB SITE ADDRESSES

Organisations with an entry in the *Handbook*
(For page number of entry see Main Index)

The 222 Trust
living-waters.org.uk
The 40:3 Trust
ourworld.compuserve.com/homepages/40-3-trust
A and C Audio Service
www.aandcaudio.co.uk
The Abbey Christian School for the English Language Ltd
www.abbeyschool.com
The Abbey of Our Lady Help of Christians
web.ukonline.co.uk/worth.abbey/homepage.htm
Abernethy Trust Ardgour
www.abernethytrust.org.uk
Abernethy Trust Ardeonaig
www.abernethytrust.org.uk
Abernethy Trust Nethy Bridge
www.abernethytrust.org.uk
Abinger Organs
www.abinger-organs.co.uk
Abundant Life Ministries
www.alcentre.force9.co.uk
ACB – Association of Christians in Broadcasting
www.caclb.org.uk
ACH Hotels & Conference Centres – UK
www.ach.co.uk
Acorn Christian Bookshop
www.acorndirect.co.uk & www.christian.music.co.uk
Acorn Christian Healing Trust
www.acorncht.force9.co.uk
Action International Ministries (UK)
www.actionintl.org
Action Partners Ministries
www.actionpartners.org.uk
Action Planning
www.actionplanning.co.uk
Adelaide College
www.comebacktogod.org
Adept Design
www.adept.ndirect.co.uk
Administry
www.stalbansdc.gov.uk/stalbans/external/adminis.html
Adullam Homes Housing Association Ltd
adullum.org.uk
The Aetherius Society
www.inpotential.org
AFD Computers/AFD Software Ltd
www.afd.co.uk
Africa Inland Mission International
www.aim-eur.org
African Pastors Fellowship
www.worldpeople.org
Agapé
www.agape.org.uk
Age Concern England
www.ace.org.uk
Aid to Russia and the Republics
www.vois.org.uk/arc
Aid to the Church in Need
www.kirche-in-not.org
Alban Books Ltd
www.albanbooks.com
ALIVE UK
www.peniel.org
All Nations Christian College
www.allnations.ac.uk
All the World
www.salvationarmy.org
Allen Organs
allenorgans.co.uk
Alliance Music
www.alliancemusic.co.uk
Alpha News
dspace.dial.pipex.com/htb.london
Alpha Supplies
alpha-furnishing.co.uk
Ambassador Enterprises
www.victory10.freeserve.co.uk
The Ammerdown Centre
www.midsomernorton.co.uk/smallpages/ammerdown.htm
Amos Trust
www.onthewall.org
Anchor Recordings Ltd
www.argonet.co.uk/anchor
Anchorline & Co
ourworld.compuserve.com/homepages/anchorline/
The Andipa Gallery
www.andipa.com
Angel Talk Limited
www.angeltalk.freeserve.co.uk
Anglican Renewal Ministries
members.aol.com/armderby
Anno Domini 2000 Designs
annodomini.org.uk
Hugo & Sharon Anson
www.grassroots.org.uk
Answers in Genesis
answersingenesis.org
Anvil Trust
dialspace.dial.pipex.com/anvil
Apologia Publications
www.apologia.free-online.co.uk
The Apostolic Church Headquarters, International Convention, Missionary Movement
www.apostolic-church.org
Arab World Ministries
www.awm.com
Archbishop's Officer for the Millennium
www.2000ad.org
Architectural Metal Furnishings
www.amf-uk.co.uk
Areopagus
www.churchnet.org.uk/areopagus
Army of Ants
www.armyofants.org
Arts Centre Group
dspace.dial.pipex.com/acg
Arts in Mission
www.wordnet.co.uk/arts
ASA (Advertising Standards Authority Ltd)
www.asa.org.uk
Ashburnham Christian Trust, Bookshop and Prayer Centre
www.ashburnham.org.uk
Association for Marriage Enrichment
www.amefocus.demon.co.uk
The Association for Pastoral Care and Counselling
www.counselling.co.uk
Association of Christian Counsellors
www.doveuk.com/acc
Association of Christian Independent Financial Advisers
www.questfs.co.uk/acifa
Association of Christian Teachers
www.actengland.co.uk

ssociation of Vineyaed Churches
www.vineyard.uk
Work Together
www.springh.org
udio Visual Ministries
www.audio-visual.org
udioplan
audioplan.co.uk/audio
ugustinian Recollects
www.btinternet.com/~augustinian.recollects/
utomobile Association
www.theaa.co.uk/theaa
utosave (UK) Ltd
www.autosave.co.uk
von Silversmiths Ltd
www.church-silver.co.uk

& H Production Services
bhps.com
adger House
www.charitynet.org/~cornelius
he Banner of Truth Trust
www.banneroftruth.co.uk
aptist Peace Fellowship
traffard1.demon.co.uk
aptist Union Headquarters and all Departments
www.baptist.org.uk
aptist Union of Great Britain: Metropolitan Area
ourworld.compuserve.com/homepages/cphicks/lbahome.htm
Baptist Union of Scotland
www.scottishbaptist.org.uk
Barchester Green Investment
www.barchestergreen/ethical
The Barn Christian Association for Youth
www.cnet.clara.net/barn/
Barnabas Fund
www.barnabasfund.org
Barratt Ministries
www.members.aol.com/bminmcr/bm.htm
Bath and Wells Diocesan Education Resource Centre
www.bathwells.anglican.org
Bath Christian Trust
www.bathcitychurch.org.uk
Bawtry Hall
ourworld.compuserve.com/homepages/bawtry_hall
Richard Baxter Institute for Ministry
www.rbim.freeserve.co.uk
BCM International
www.bcm.org.uk
Beechwood Court (CE Holiday/Conference Centre Ltd)
www.marketsite.co.uk/beechwd
Beehive School & Nursery
easyweb.easynet.co.uk/rain
Belfast Central Mission
www.geocities.com/heartland/meadows/3315
Ben Doran Guest House
www.asper.co.uk/bendoran.html
Berea Bible College
philstanton.freeserve.co.uk
Berean Publishing Trust
ourworld.compuserve.com/homepages/bptsales/homepage.htm
Bible Reading Fellowship
www.brf.org.uk
The Bible Shop
www.castledouglas.net/thebibleshop
Bible Society (The British and Foreign Bible Society)
www.biblesociety.org.uk
Biblical Archaeology Review
www.paternoster-publishing.com
The Biblical Creation Society
www.pages.org/bcs/index.html
Biblical Ministries Worldwide
www.biblicalministries.org
Biblicon
www.shef-ac-press.co.uk
Jacquie Binns
ourworld.compuserve.com/homepages/churchtextiles_jacquiebinns
Birmingham Bible Institute
www.charis.co.uk/bbi/
Birmingham Christian Media Services
www.bcms.co.uk/
Birmingham Churches Together
ourworld.compuserve.com/homepages/revmark/
Birmingham City Mission and Bookshop/Video Library
www.internet-pilots.com/city_missions
Black Theology in Britain
www.shef-ac-press.co.uk
B H Blackwell Ltd (Religion Dept)
www.bookshop.blackwell.co.uk
The Blue Idol/Thakeham Friends Meeting House
ourworld.compuserve.com/homepages/spencer_the_blue_idol
Blythswood Care and Bookshop
www.blythswood.org.uk
BMS, Baptist Missionary Society
www.rpc.ox.ac.uk./bms
Boaters Christian Fellowship
www.blacksheep.org/canals/orgs/bcf/html
Books in Print
www.rkmcevoy.clara.net
Don Bosco Publications
www.salesians.org.uk
Boys' Brigade
www.boys-brigade.org.uk
Braeside Recording Studio
www.smg.org.uk/braeside
Brahma Kumaris
www.bkwsu.com
Bray Libraries Worldwide
www.spck.org.uk
Briefing
www.tasc.ac.uk/cc/
The Briefing
members.australis.net.ou/~xtnnet
Bristol Cathedral
www.cliftoncathedral.org.uk
Bristol International Students Centre
come.to/bisc
British Antiochian Orthodox Deanery
www.antiochian-orthodox.co.uk
British Church Growth Association
www.u-net.com/~the-park
The British Computer Society
www.bcs.org.uk\par
British Institute of Management
www.mic.inst.mgp.org.uk
The British Israel World Federation
www.britishisrael.co.uk
The British Orthodox Church of the British Isles
www.uk-christian.net/boc
Christopher Brown
www.covenant.ndirect.co.uk
Bruderhof Communities in the UK
www.bruderhof.org
Brunel Manor
www.brunel-manor.org.uk
The Buddhist Society
www.buddsoc.org.uk
Budget Direct
www.budgetdirect.co.uk
The Burning Light
www.burninglight.co.uk
Burrswood Christian Centre for Healthcare and Ministry
www.burrswood.org.uk

X

Business & Technology Management
ourworld.compuserve.com/homepages/ron_bradnam
Byrom Clark Roberts Ltd
www.byromclarkroberts.ltd.uk

C.net
c.net.hants.org.uk
CACLB – Churches Advisory Council for Local Broadcasting
www.caclb.org.uk
Café.Net
www.users.surfaid.org/~cafe
Calamus
decanimusic.uk.com
Camas Adventure Camp (Iona Community)
www.iona.org.uk
Cambridge Theological Federation
www.ely.anglican.org.westcott
Cambridge University Press
www.cup.cam.ac.uk
Campaign Christian Books
www.comebacktogod.org
Cancer Research Campaign
www.crc.org.uk
Capernwray Bible School, Bookshop and Missionary Fellowship of Torchbearers
www.capernwray.co.uk
Caravanners and Campers Christian Fellowship
www.cccf.freeserve.co.uk
Carberry
dspace.dial.pipex.com/carberry
CARE (Christian Action Research and Education), CARE Campaigns, CARE for Education and CARE for LIFE
www.care.org.uk
Care for the Family
www.care-for-the-family.org.uk
Careforce
careforce.co.uk
Carlisle Diocesan Youth Centre
www.btinternet.com/~cdyc
Carmelite Friars and Book Service
www.carmelite.org
Carrot Tops
www.buxnet.co.uk/carrot-tops
The Cathedral Shop, Southwark
www.dswark.org
Catholic Bible School and Bookshop
www.tregalic.co.uk/catholic/bibleschool/
Roman Catholic Bishops' Conference Department for Christian Life & Worship
www.liturgy.demon.co.uk
Catholic Child Welfare Council
www.vois.org.uk/cathchild
Catholic Children's Society (Diocese of Nottingham)
www.ccsnotts.co.uk
Catholic Communications Centre
www.cathcom.com.uk
Roman Catholic Dioceses
Clifton
www.btinternet.com/~Diocese.Clifton
Lancaster
www.churchnet.ucsm.ac.uk/lancs_rc
Northampton
www.cableol.co.uk/diocese/
Paisley
ourworld.compuserve.com/homepages/dioceseofpaisley
Salford
www.wardleyhall.org.uk
Catholic Enquiry Office
www.opinet.co.uk/go/ceo/
Catholic Fund for Overseas Development (CAFOD)
www.cafod.org.uk
Catholic Housing Aid Society
www.chasnat.demon.co.uk
Catholic Institute for International Relations
www.ciir.org
Catholic Media Office
www.tasc.ac.uk/cc/
Catholic Press and Media Office
www.stac.ac.uk/cmo/
Catholic Record Society
www.catholic-history.org.uk/crs
Catholics for a Changing Church
www.c-c-c.freeserve.co.uk
CBI (Confederation of British Industry)
www.cbi.org.uk
CCBI Publications
www.ccbi.org.uk
CdotC Technologies
www.cdotc.com
Cefn Lea Park Midwales Christian Holiday and Conference Complex
www.cefnlea.wyrecompute.com
Celebration 2000
www.merseyworld.com/faith/html_file/octhead.htm
Celtic Orthodox Church: British Eparchy
www.stanne.dircon.co.uk
Central African Missions
www.centralafricanmissions.org
Centre for Christian Communication
www.xiancomm.org
Centre for Contemporary Ministry
www.the-park.u-net.com
Centre for International Briefing
www.cibfarnham.com
Centre Travel (Centre for Service Ltd)
www.netcomuk.co.uk/~fgospelf/fgfmain.htm
Morris Cerullo World Evangelism Society of Great Britain
www.mcwe.com
Challenge
www.paternoster-publishing.com
Chapel Lodge Ministries (Go Evangelise Mission)
www.netcomuk.co.uk/~fgospelf/fgfmain.htm
Chapter & Verse
www.chapterandverse.co.uk
Chapter Two (Publishing Division)
www.chaptertwo.org
Charis Internet Services Ltd
www.charis.co.uk
Charities Advisory Trust
webb.ukonline.co.uk/charities.advisory.trust/
Charities Aid Foundation
www.charitynet.org
Charney Manor
www.quaker.org.uk/charney.html
Chester Cathedral and Shop
www.chestercathedral.org.uk
The Chesterton Review
www.tandtclark.co.uk
Chichester Christian Fellowship (Tapes)
www.ccftapes.co.uk
Chichester Institute of Higher Education
www.chihe.ac.uk
Child Evangelism Fellowship
www.cefinc.org/europe
A Child Is Born Charitable Trust
www.achildisborn.org.uk
Children's Aid Direct
www.cad.org.uk
CHIME – The Churches' Initiative in Music Education
btinternet.com/~chime
Chinese Church in London
www.ccil.u-net.com

hinese Overseas Christian Mission
www.glink.net.hk/~cocmhk
hrist for All Nations
www.cfan.org.
hrist for the Nations UK
christforthenationsuk.org
hrist the Redeemer Bible College
www.rccg.org
hristendom Trust
www.christendomtrust.demon.co.uk
hristian
www.dcs.ed.ac.uk/~djs/christian/home.html
hristian Aid
www.christian-aid.org.uk
he Christian Alliance Housing Association Hostel, London (Waterloo)
www.dircon.co.uk/~genesis/CACW/
hristian Arts Promotions Ltd
home.clara.net/bethany/hof.html
hristian Au Pairs
www.christianaupairs.com
hristian Book Centre
www.icbc.co.uk
hristian Book Promotion Trust
dspace.dial.pipex.com/christian.books.direct
hristian Books & Music, Kensington Temple
www.ukbusiness.com/christianbooksmusic
hristian Books Direct
dspace.dial.pipex.com/christian.books.direct
Christian Bookshop, Aberystwyth
www.aber.ac.uk/~emk/ap/
Christian Business Alliance
www.pickenham.clara.net
Christian Business Pages
www.cbpages.co.uk
Christian Campaign for Nuclear Disarmament
www.gn.apc.org/ccnd
Christian Centre for Buddhist Studies
www.dcs.shef.ac.uk/~paulw/update.htm
Christian Channel (Europe) Ltd
www.godnetwork.com
The Christian Children's Fund of Great Britain
www.ccfgb.org.uk
Christian Communications Network (Europe) Ltd
ccneurope.org.uk
Christian Communications Partnership Ltd
www.youthwork.co.uk
Christian Community Ministries
homepages.tesco.net/~ccminternational
Christian Computer Art
www.cc-art.com
Christian Contact / Mallon De Theological College
www.detc.freeserve.co.uk
Christian Copyright Licensing (Europe) Ltd
www.ccli.com
Christian Dental Fellowship
www.users.globalnet.co.uk/~rmje
Christian Ecology Link
www.christian-ecology.org.uk
Christian Education Europe
www.christian-education.org
Christian English Language Centre
homepages.tcp.co.uk/~celc/
Christian Enquiry Agency
www.christianity.org.uk
Christian Focus Publications
www.christianfocus.com
Christian Friends of Israel
cfi.org.uk
Christian Guild Holidays
www.cgholidays.co.uk
Christian Herald
www.christianherald.org.uk
Christian History Magazine
www.paternoster-publishing.com
Christian Information Network
www.cin.co.uk
The Christian Institute
www.christian.org.uk
Christian Insurance Services
www.christian-insurance.co.uk
Christian Literature Centre
www.adlib.co.uk/sbt
Christian Literature Crusade
www.clc.org.uk
Christian Media
www.christianmedia.co.uk
Christian Media Centre
www.christianherald.org.uk
Christian Medical Fellowship
www.cmf.org.uk
Christian Motorcyclists Association UK
bike.org.uk/cma
Christian Music Ministries
www.cmm.org.uk
The Christian Outlook
www.christian-outlook.co.uk
Christian Pages
www.cbd.org.uk
Christian Peoples Alliance
www.cpalliance.net
Christian Police Association
members.aol.com/cpauk
Christian Printing Services
dspace.dial.pipex.com/christian.books.direct
Christian Prison Ministries
www.scotland2000.freeserve.co.uk
Christian Publicity Organisation
www.cpo.uk.com
Christian Research, Christian World Library, Quadrant
www.christian-research.org.uk
Christian Research Network
web.ukonline.co.uk/crn
Christian Resources Exhibitions Ltd
www.resourcex.co.uk
Christian Resources Project
business.thisisplymouth.co.uk/crp
Christian Socialist Movement
members.aol.com/csmnet/
Christian Solidarity Worldwide
www.csw.org.uk
Christian Student Action (Part of Agapé)
www.agape.org.uk
Christian Television Association
www.cta-jesus.uk.com
Christian Training Centre
www.btinternet.com/~ctc.pcl/
Christian Travel Services
uk-christiantravel.co.uk
Christian Victory Group – I Care Project
www.elusion.co.uk/icave.htm
Christian Viewpoint for Men
www.domini.org/cum
Christian Vision
www.christianvision.org
Christian Voice Ltd
www.christianvoice.co.uk
Christian Witness Ministries
www.cwm.org.uk
Christian Witness to Israel
www.cwi.org.uk & www.shalom.org.uk
Christian Workers Programme
www.raglanroad.mcmail.com/cwp
Christian Youth Enterprises Sailing Centre
ourworld.compuserve.com/homepages/cye

Christianity and Society
www.kuyper.org
Christians Abroad
wse.org.uk & cabroad.org.uk
Christians Aware
www.christiansaware.co.uk
Christians in Caring Professions
www.cicp.org.uk/cicp
Christians in Entertainment
ourworld.compuserve.com/homepages/chrisgidney
Christians in Health Care
www.christian-healthcare.org.uk
Christians in Public Life
www.doncaster.org/workout/cipl/
Christians in Road Transport
www.northchurch.com/cirt
Christians in Science
www.cis.org.uk
Christians in Science Education
www.cis.org.uk/cise/java
Christians in Sport
www.iway.co.uk/~christians_sport
Church Army
churcharmy.org.uk
Church Computer Users Group
www.churchcomputer.org.uk
Church House Publishing and Bookshop
www.chpublishing.co.uk
Church Housing Trust
www.charitynet.org/~CHT
Church Mission Society
www/cms-uk.org
Church News Service
ourworld.compuserve.com/homepages/aphenna
The Church of Christ, Scientist (Christian Science Church)
www.tfccs.com
Church of England Dioceses
Europe
www.europe.anglican.org
Bath and Wells
www.bathwells.anglican.org
Blackburn
web.ukonline.co.uk/anchorsholme/
Durham
www.durham.anglican.org
Gloucester
www.doma.demon.co.uk/glosdioc.htm
Leicester
www.leicester.anglican.org
Oxford
www.oxford.anglican.org
Rochester
www.anglican.org.uk/rochester/
St Albans
www.stalbans.gov.uk/diocese
St Edmundsbury and Ipswich
www.stedmundsbury.anglican.org
Salisbury
www.eluk.co.uk/spireweb
Sheffield
web.ukonline.co.uk/members/trafic
Truro
www.truro.anglican.org
Wakefield
www.wakefield.anglican.org
Church of England Guild of Vergers
www.societies.anglican.org/guild-of-vergers
The Church of England Newspaper
www.churchnewspaper.com
The Church of Scientology
www.scientology.org
Church of Scotland Board of World Mission
www.cofs.org.uk
Church of Scotland Department of Education
www.cofs.org.uk
Church Pastoral Aid Society
www.cpas.org.uk
Church Society
www.churchsociety.org
Church Times
www.churchtimes.co.uk
Church Urban Fund
www.cuf.org.uk
Church's Ministry Among Jewish People
www.cmj.org.uk
Churches of God, UK
www.cgom.org & www.abcog.org
The Churches Purchasing Scheme Ltd
www.cpsonline.co.uk
Churches Together in Britain and Ireland
www.ccbi.org.uk
Churches Together in Dorset
home.clara.net/ctdorset
Churches Together in All Lincolnshire
www.ctal.org.uk
Churches' Child Protection Advisory Service
www.doveuk.com/pcca
Churchman (Journal of Anglican Theology)
www.churchsociety.org
Chyvounder Consolidated Publishing
www.indirect.co.uk/~chyvounder
City Vision Ministries
www.lineone.net/~city_vision
CJM Music Ltd, Rolinson Boyce & Stanley
www.come.to/cjmfirstlight
T & T Clark
www.tandtclark.co.uk
James Clarke and Co Ltd
www.jamesclarke.co.uk
The Claybury Trust
www.claybury.org
Cliff Centre
www.lincoln.anglican.org
Coastline Christian Resources
www.btinternet.com/~coastline
Coed-y-Go Farm Holiday Centre
ourworld.compuserve.com/homepages/davidarnott1
Coleg Trefeca
ebcpcw.org.uk/pcwtrefeca.html
Mike Coles World-Wide Travel
www.mike-coles-travel.co.uk
College of Health Care Chaplains
www.msf.org.uk
College of Preachers
www3.mistral.co.uk/collpreach
The College, Millport (Argyll Diocesan Conference Centre)
www.sol.co.uk/s/sedati/millport.htm
Columban Lay Missionaries
www.columban.org
Come Back to God Campaign
www.comebacktogod.org
Communio
www.tandtclark.co.uk
Community for Reconciliation
ourworld.compuserve.com/homepages/communityforreconciliation
Community of Aidan & Hilda
www.john316.com/~aidan
Compass Magazine
ds.dial.pipex.com/pioneer_trust
Computing Services and Software Association
www.cssa.co.uk
Concern For Family and Womanhood
www.mackey.demon.co.uk/cfw

nnections Trust
www.connectionsuk.freeserve.co.uk
nnexion
visitweb.com/connexion
nservative & Unionist Central Office
www.tory.org.uk
nservative Christian Fellowship
www.tory.org.uk/ccf
ntact International Christian Fellowship
www.c-i-c-f.dircon.co.uk
e Contract Furniture Specialists
www.tcfs-london.demon.co.uk
peman Hart and Company Ltd, Organ Builders
www.copemanhart.co.uk
ORD (Christian Outreach – Relief and Development)
ourworld.compuserve.com/homepager/cord_uk
odney Cordner with Jean-Pierre Rudolph
www.globalgateway.com/users/rcordner
ornerstone
www.merseyworld.com/cornerstone/
ornerstone Community
www.d-n-a.net-users-cornerstone
ornerstone House
www.message.org/cr
orrymeela
www.corrymeela.org.uk
ouncil for World Mission
www.cwmission.org.uk
ouncil of Christians and Jews
www.ccj.org.uk
ounselling & Prayer Trust
counsellingpray.org
ounties
members.aol.com/counties30
ountry Way
www.rurnet.org.uk/~country_way/
ourage
www.courage.org.uk
he Covenant Players
www.covenantplayers.org
ovenant Publishing Co Ltd
www.britishisrael.co.uk
ovenant Technology
www.covenant.ndirect.co.uk
ovenanters
www.coviesholidays.org.uk
Coventry Cathedral and Bookshop
www.coventrycathedral.org
Coventry City Mission
www.users.zetnet.co.uk/covcitymission
CPAS (Youth and Children Division)
www.cpas.org.uk
CPAS Sales
www.christianbookshop.com
Craig Lodge
www.craiglodge.org
Cranmer Memorial Bible Society
www.bt.internet.com/~gadsden/pt1/pt1
Creation Resources Trust
ourworld.compuserve.com/homepages/creationresources
Creation Science Movement
www.csm.org.uk
Creative Mentors Ltd
www.creativementors.com
Credo
www.newtel.org/orgs/credo/credo.html
Creme: Maitreya
www.shareintl.org
Crisis Centre Ministries
www.crisis-centre.org.uk
Crocus Ministries
home.clara.net/crocus/
Croft Farm Celtic Cottages
www.webscape.co.uk/farmaccom/wales/pembrokeshire/croft-farm/
Cross Rhythms
www.crossrhythms.co.uk
Crossfire Trust
www.btinternet.com/~crossfire.trust/
Crossline Coventry
www.users.zetnet.co.uk/covcitymission
CrossView Audio Visual
www.crossview.co.uk
Crosswinds Prayers Trust
crosswindsprayer.com
Crusader Centre, Westbrook
web.ukonline.co.uk/members/crusaders/
Crusaders
www.crusaders.org.uk
Crystal Clear Audio
www.cca.ndirect.co.uk
CTVC
www.ctvc.co.uk
Culham College Institute
www.culham.ac.uk
Cutting Edge Productions
www.cuttingedgeuk.com
CVG Television
www.cvgtv.co.uk
CWR (Crusade for World Revival)
www.cwr.org.uk
CYFA Pathfinder Ventures Ltd
www.cpas.org.uk/ventures/
Cyhoeddiadau'r Gair
www.bangor.ac.uk
CYTUN: Churches Together in Wales
www.cytun.freeserve.co.uk/

Dales Broadcast Ltd
www.dales-ltd.com
Dance for Christ
www.burninglight.co.uk
Data Developments
data-developments.co.uk
Data Protection Commissioner
www.open.gov.uk/dpc/dpchome.htm
Clive Davenport
www.bigfoot.com/~clive.davenport
Day of Salvation Ministries
www.dofs.mcmail.com
Day One Publications
www.dayone.co.uk
Days of Destiny
www.saltandlight.u-net.com/destiny
Daystar Computing Solutions
www.daystar.co.uk
DCI Trust
www.worldchristians.org
De La Salle Brothers
www.disnet.demon.co.uk
Deaf Christian Network (Hands Together)
www.deafcn.dircon.co.uk
Stephen Deal
www.deal1.demon.co.uk
Decani Music
decanimusic.uk.com
Dentaid
www.derweb.ac.uk/dentaid
Department for International Development
www.oneworld.org/dfid
Department of the Environment, Transport & the Regions
www.detr.gov.uk
Department of Trade & Industry
www.dti.gov.uk
Design Council
www.design_council.org.uk

Diaconal Association of the Church of England
societies.anglican.org/dace
Digital Hymnals UK Ltd
www.digital-hymnal.com
Direction and Direction Resources Ltd
www.directionmagazine.com
Discovery (Part of Agapé)
www.agape.org.uk
Discovery Cruising
www.discoverycruising.co.uk
DM Music for Churches
www.dm-music.co.uk
Dominion International Opera
www.dio.org.uk/dio
Dove Marketing & Dove UK
www.doveuk.com
Down and Connor Pioneer Association
www.dcpa.net
Duncans of Ironbridge Ltd
www.duncanhouse.co.uk
Durham Cathedral
www.btinternet.com/~durhamcathedral/
Dutch Church
www.dutchchurch.org.uk

E-Compile Ltd
www.ecompile.co.uk
Ealing Abbey
members.aol.com/ealingmonk/
The East Midlands Ministry Training Course
www.nottingham.ac.uk/cont-ed/emmtc.htm
East Midlands School of Christian Ministry
www.geocities.com/athens/8530/
East to West
www.e2w.dircon.co.uk
ECL Ltd
ecl-ltd.co.uk
Ecotheology
www.shef-ac-press.co.uk
Ecumenical Order of Ministry
ourworld.compuserve.com/homepages/communityforreconciliation
Edgehill Christian Education Centre
welcome.to/edgehill
Edward King House
www.lincoln.anglican.org/ekh/
A Edward-Jones Ltd
www.a-edward-jones.co.uk
Eleventh Hour
www.homepages.nildram.co.uk/~euros/
Elim International Missions
www.elim.org.co.uk
Elle M Theatre Company
ourworld.compuserve.com/homepages/egovan
Ellel Ministries
www.ellelministries.org
Elmham House (Pilgrim Bureau)
www.walsingham.org.uk
Emmaus Bible School
www.kingsnet.org.uk/emmaus
Emmanuel International
www.argonet.co.uk/users/emm.int
English Heritage
www.english-heritage.co.uk
Ethical Financial Ltd
www.ethical-financial.co.uk
Ethics and Medicine
www.paternoster-publishing.com
The Ethnos Trust
www.wbtcm.org
Ethos
www.ethosmag.com

Ethos Candles Ltd
www.ethos-candles.co.uk/candlelight
Europe Now
www.oaci.org
The European Academy for Christian Homeschooling
www.christian-education.org
European Christian Mission (Britain)
www.ecmi.org
European Institute of Protestant Studies
www.ianpaisley.org
European Journal of Theology
www.paternoster-publishing.com
Eurovision Mission to Europe
www.propheticvision.org.uk
Evangel
www.paternoster-publishing.com
Evangel Christian Shop and Resource Centre
www.evangeluk.com
Evangelical Alliance, all Departments, Coalitions, Partnerships e
www.eauk.org
Evangelical Contribution on Northern Ireland (ECONI)
www.econi.org
Evangelical Environment Network
homepages.tcp.co.uk/~carling/eenhome.html
The Evangelical Fellowship for Lesbian & Gay Christians
www.users.zetnet.co.uk/pcgardner/eflgc
Evangelical Fellowship of Congregational Churches
www.compulink.co.uk/~digby/efccpub.html
Evangelical Literature Trust
dspace.dial.pipex.com/town/plaza/hrso
Evangelical Presbyterian Church in England and Wales
www.epcew.org.uk
Evangelical Presbyterian Church in Ireland
web.ukonline.co.uk/epc
Evangelical Press
www.evangelical-press.org
Evangelical Quarterly
www.paternoster-publishing.com
Evangelical Review of Theology
www.paternoster-publishing.com
The Evangelical Theological College of Wales
www.etcw.ac.uk
Evangelical Times Ltd
www.evangelical-times.org
Evangelical Tract Society
www.grace.org.uk/mission/ets/
Evangelical (Youth Movement) Ministries
www.emins.com
Evangelicals for LIFE
www.lifeuk.org
Evangelicals Now
www.e-n.org.uk
The Evangelism Fellowship
www.buxnet.co.uk/evangelism
Evangelism Training Centre (Good News Crusade)
www.gnc.org.uk
EWCH
www.users.globalnet.co.uk~aled
Exousia Ltd
www.exousia.uk.com
Explan Computers Ltd
www.explan.demon.co.uk
Expository Times
www.tandtclark.co.uk

Faith Builders
www.faith-builders.co.uk
The Faith Mission
www.faithmission.org
Faith Mission Bible College
www.faithmission.org

ithful Companions of Jesus
www.fcjsisters.org
lkirk Christian Centre
www.yell.co.uk/sites/falkirk-christianctr/
lmouth Beach Resort Hotel and Conference Centre
members.aol.com/falbeach
mily Alive!
www.webcom.com/agape
mily Life Foundation
www.flfc.freeserve.co.uk
mily Policy Studies Centre
www.vois.org.u/fpsc
rmington Institute for Christian Studies
info.ac.uk/~ma0039/farn.html
ather Books
www.feather-books.com
EBA Radio
www.feba.org.uk
ellowship Afloat Charitable Trust
www.mccom.co.uk.fact/
ellowship Finders
www.finders.easynet.co.uk
ellowship for Evangelising Britain's Villages
website.lineone.net/~febv
ellowship of Christian Motorcyclists
hompages.whichnet/~richard.hopwood/
ellowship of Churches of Christ
www.charis.co.uk/coc-erdington/
he Fellowship of Contemplative Prayer
www.zyworld.com/fcp
ellowship of Independent Evangelical Churches
www.fiec.co.uk
ellowship of Reconciliation, England
www.gn.apc.org/fore
ellowship of St Alban & St Sergius
www.btinternet.com/~sobornost.albanandsergius
ellowship of Word and Spirit
www.stjames.org.uk/fws/home.htm
eminist Theology
www.shef-ac-press.co.uk
avid Fitzgerald
w3.ixs.nl/~jove/
FLAME – Family Life And Marriage Education
welcome.to/familylife
The Flight Bureau
www.flightbureau.com
Focus Radio
www.focus.org.uk
Forward Vision Communications Ltd
www.forwardvision.co.uk
Foster Finch Ltd
www.eclipse.co.uk/fosterfinch
France Mission Trust
www.france-mission.org
Free Church College
www.freechurch.org
Free Presbyterian Church of Scotland Headquarters, Bookroom, Mission Committee and Publications
www.fpchurch.org.uk
Friends Book Centre
www.quaker.org.uk
Friends of the Earth
www.foe.co.uk
Frontier Youth Trust
www.fyt.org.uk
Frontiers
www.frontiers.org
Rob Frost Team
www.ncl.ac.uk/~ndjs/robfrost
Full Gospel Business Men's Fellowship International
dialspace.dial.pipex.com/town/lane/kbw15
Functional English
www.funenglish.co.uk
Fusion
www.fusion.uk.com

Gage Postal Books
home.clara.net/gagebooks
Garden Tomb (Jerusalem) Association
www.gardentomb.com
Gartmore House Conference and Activity Centre
www.gartmore.uk.com
GEM Books
www.netcomuk.co.uk/~fgospelf/fgfmain.htm
General Assembly of Unitarian and Free Christian Churches
www.unitarian.org.uk
GFS Platform for Young Women
www.tabor.co.uk/gfs/
The Gideons International in the British Isles
www.gideons.org.uk
The Girls' Brigade England and Wales
www.girlsbrigadeew.org.uk
The Girls' Brigade in Scotland
www.girls-brigade-sco.org.uk
Glenada Holiday and Conference Centre
www.glenada.org.uk
GLO Bookshop
members.aol.com:/gloadmin/glo.htm
Global Care
www.globalcare.org.uk
Global March for Jesus
www.newns.com/gmfj/
GNC Audio
www.gnc.org.uk
Go To The Nations Ministry
www.gonations.org
GOD Christian Channel
www.godnetwork.com
Going Public
www.company-net.co.uk/~going public
Good Books
www.houghtonsbooks.com/goodbooks
Good News Broadcasting Association (Great Britain) Ltd
www.goodnews-uk.u-net.com
Good News Crusade and Bookshop
www.gnc.org.uk
Good News Family Care (Homes) Ltd.
www.king-fisher.co.uk/familycare
Gospel Literature Outreach
members.aol.com/gloadmin/GLO.htm
Government Office for the South West
www.gosw.gov.uk/gosw
Grace and Compassion Benedictines
max.roehampton.ac.uk/link/aandb/gcb.htm
Grace Ministries
www.users.globalnet.co.uk/~gracemin/
Grace To You, Europe
www.gty.org.uk
Grapevine
www.groundlevel.org.uk
Grassroots
www.grassroots.org.uk
Greenbelt Festivals
www.greenbelt.org.uk
Greenleaf Communications Ltd
uk-greenleaf.com
The Gregorian Association
www.beaufort.demon.co.uk/chant.html
GRF Christian Radio
www.ed.ac.uk/~gmck/grf.html
John Grooms
www.johngrooms.org.uk
John Grooms Housing Association
www.johngrooms.org.uk

Ground Level Ministry Team
www.groundlevel.org.uk
Group for Evangelism and Renewal
www.gearpub.freeserve.co.uk
Group of Scriptural Protestant Evangelical Labourers (GOSPEL)
www.gospelorg.freeserve.co.uk
The Guide Association
www.guides.org.uk
Guild of Catholic Doctors
www.catholicdoctors.org.uk

The Guild of St Helena
www.army.mod.uk/army/press
Habitat for Humanity Great Britain
www.habitat.org
Hand of Creation
handofcreation.com
Hands Up! Puppet Team
www.living-waters.org.uk
John Hardman Studios
members.aol.com/hdmnstudio
Harnhill Centre of Christian Healing
www.btinternet.com/~harnhill
HarperCollins*Religious*
www.christian-publishing.com
The Harvesters Trust
wkwe5.cableinet.co.uk/harvesters
Haven Christian Holiday Centre
www.havencentre.freeserve.co.uk
Hawkstone Hall Pastoral Centre
www.hawkstone-hall.com
Hayes & Finch Ltd
www.hayes-and-finch-ltd.co.uk
The Hayes Conference Centre
www.cct.org.uk
Hayes Press
www.tripod.hayes-press.com
HCJB-UK
www.hcjb.org
HCPT The Pilgrimage Trust
www.hcpt.org.uk
HCVF Television & Video Productions
www.hcvf.co.uk
Headway
www.soft.net.uk/greenhill/index
Hearts on Fire
home.clara.net/bethany/cap.html
Heath Christian Bookshop Charitable Trust
www.christian-bookshop.co.uk
Help International
www.oneworld.org/helpinternational
Help the Aged
www.helptheaged.org.uk
Juliet Hemingray Church Textiles
www.griffin.co.uk/users/church-textiles
Hengrave Hall Centre
www.hengravehallcentre.org.uk
The Henley Centre
www.henleyventre.com
Henley Management College
www.henleymc.ac.uk
Henwood Decorative Metal Studios Ltd
www.henwoodchurchsupplies.co.uk
Garth Hewitt
www.onthewall.org
Heythrop College (University of London)
www.heythrop.ac.uk
Hi, Kids!
www.hikids.inuk.com
High Adventure Ministries
www.highadventure.org
High Leigh Conference Centre
www.cct.org.uk
Highlands Hotel Ltd
www.hlands.dircon.co.uk
His Paper
www.influenceuk.com,
Alan Hiscox Financial Services Partnership
www.lendex.co.uk/hiscox
Holland House
www.users.surfaid.org/~laycentre
Holton Lee
www.lds.co.uk/holtonlee
Holy Trinity Brompton Bookshop
dspace.dial.pipex.com/htb.london
Home Service
www.alphainfo.co.uk/homeservice
Hope Now Ltd
www.hopenow.org.uk
Hoplon Plastic Cards
ourworld.compuserve.com/homepages/plasticcards
The Horstead Centre
www.zoo.co.uk/~horstead.centre
Hosanna Books & Music Ltd
www.hosanna.co.uk
Hosanna Family Churches
www.geocities.com/athens/1976
Hothorpe Hall Christian Conference Centre
www.hothorpe.co.uk
Housetop
www.spiritual-wholeness.org
The HoverAid Trust
www.hoverlifeline.com
Hull International House
www.methodist.org.uk/hih
The Human City Institute
www.humancity.org
Human Concern
www.spuc.org.uk
Humber Books
www.netguides.co.uk/ukhumber.html

ICC – International Christian Communications
www.icc.org.uk
Ichthus Christian Fellowship
www.ichthus.org.uk
Ichthus Team Ministries
www.ichthus.org.uk
ICI Bible Study (International Correspondence Institute)
www.ici.edu
Impart Books
www.press.mid-wales.net
Imperial Cancer Research Fund
www.icnet.uk
In Yer Face Theatre Company
www.domini.org/inyerface
India Link Ministries
www.grace.org.uk/orgs/ilm.htm/
Indian Evangelical Team
ourworld.compuserve.com/homepages/rugby_fellowship/
Inn Christian Ministries
www.inn.org.uk
Institute for the Study of Islam and Christianity
www.rftoday.org
Institute of Christian Political Thought
www.kuyper.org
Institute of Counselling
www.collegeofcounsel.com
Institute of Directors
www.id.co.uk
Integrity
www.geocities.com/westhollywood/9380

er-Church Relations Board
www.presbyterianireland.org
ernational Bible Institute of London (Kensington Temple)
www.ken-temp.org.uk
ernational Bible Reading Association
www.ncec.org.uk
ernational Bible Society (UK)
www.gospelcom.net/ibs/
ternational Centre for Reconciliation
www.coventrycathedral.org
ternational Christian Chamber of Commerce (AISBL)
www.uk.iccc.net
ternational Christian College, Glasgow
www.icc.clara.co.uk
ternational Christian Maritime Association
dspace.dial.pipex.com/icma/
ternational Christian Media Commission (ICMC)
www.icmc.org
ternational Churches of Christ
www.icoc.org.uk/london
ternational Fellowship of Evangelical Students (IFES Trust [UK])
www.ifesworld.org
ternational Films
members.aol.com/interfilm/home.htm
ternational Gospel Outreach
www.churches.net/userpages/oasisdwygyfylchi.htm/
ternational Lutheran Student Centre
www.lutheran.org.uk
he International Messianic Jewish Alliance
www.INJA.com
nternational Nepal Fellowship
www.inf.org.uk
nternational Research Office (WEC International)
www.wec_int.org
nternational School of Languages (Kensington Temple)
www.ken-temp.org.uk/index.htm
nternational Student Christian Services
www.ics.org.uk
nternational Teams UK
www.iteams.org
nternational Training Network
www.users.globalnet.co.uk/~itnet
NTERSERVE
www.interserve.org
nto The Light
www.itl.org.uk
ona, Iona Community, Macleod Centre and Iona Abbey
www.iona.org.uk
rish Council of Churches
www.unite.co.uk/customers/icpep
slamic Foundation
www.islamic-foundation.org.uk
srael Bureau (B & TM)
ourworld.compuserve.com/homepages/ron_bradnam
It's About Time
www.lite.co.uk/its-about-time
ITV Teletext Religious Pages
www.allsaints.mcmail.com
IVP Bookstall Service
www.ivpbooks.com

Jacob, Cavenagh & Skeet
www.btinternet.com/~jcssutton
The James Begg Society
easyweb.easynet.co.uk/~jbeggsoc/jbshome.html
Janus Publishing Company
www.januspublishing.co.uk
Jarom Books
homepages.tesco.net/~jacquesmore/book_cover.htm
Jay Books
www.houghtonbooks.com
JC2000 – The Millennium Arts Festival for Schools
www.jc2000.org
Jentech Computers Ltd
www.jentech.co.uk
Jesus Day
www.gmfi.org
Jesus Fellowship, Jesus Army and Jesus People Shop
www.jesus.org.uk
Jesus is Alive! Ministries
www.gocin.com/jesusisalive
Jesus the Christ
www.armyofants.org
Jews for Jesus
www.jews-for-jesus.org
Jireh.co.uk
www.jireh.co.uk
The Jonas Trust
www.users.globalnet.co.uk/~jonas
Keith Jones Christian Bookshop
www.keithjones.co.uk
Joshua Generation
www.users.globalnet.co.uk/~joshgen
Journal for the Study of the New Testament
Journal for the Study of the Old Testament
Journal for the Study of the Pseudepigrapha
Journal of Pentecostal Theology
www.shef-ac-press.co.uk
Journal of Education and Christian Belief
www.paternoster-publishing.com
Journal of Feminist Studies in Religion
www.tandtclark.co.uk
JPR Consultancy Ltd
www.jprc.co.uk
Jubilee 2000 Coalition
www.jubileee2000uk.org

Kairos Centre
www.kairoscentre.demon.co.uk
Keep in Step
members.aol.com/jsritter
Kensington Temple London City Church
www.ken-temp.org.uk
Kepplewray Centre
www.kepplewray.org.uk
Keston Institute
www.keston.org
Kestrel Lodge Residential Centre
www.kestrel98.freeserve.co.uk
KeyChange
www.keychange.org.uk
Kids Alive!
www.salvationarmy.org.uk
King's Bible College
www.saltandlight.u-net.com/kbc/
King's College, London, Department of Theology and Religious Studies
www/kcl.ac.uk/theorelig
King-Fisher Media Services
www.king-fisher.co.uk
Kingdom Creative
kingdomc.cwcom.net
Kingdom Faith Church Headquarters, Bible College and Bible Week
www.kingdomfaith.com
Kingham Hill School
www.kingham-hill.oxon.sch.uk
Kings
www.kings-books.com
Kings Communications
www.doveuk.com/kings
Kingscare
ourworld.compuserve.com/homepages/kingscare

The Kingsway Adventure Centre
www.bigfoot.com/~kingsway
The Kuyper Foundation
www.kuyper.org

L'Arche
web.ukonline.co.uk.larche
Langham Arts
scotta.demon.co.uk/aso.htm
Language Recordings UK
www.gospelrecordings.com
Lantern Arts Centre
www.gawayn.demon.co.uk/jdc/nc
Latin Mass Society
www.sonnco.uk/credo.ims.htm
Launde Abbey
webleicester.co.uk/customer/laundeabbey/welcome.htm
Lawyers Christian Fellowship
www.lawcf.org
Leadership Bookclub
www.ivpbooks.com
Lee Abbey Fellowship
www.leeabbey.org.uk
Lee Abbey International Students' Club
www.leeabbeylondon.freeserve.co.uk
Lee Bay Hotel
manorgroup.uk
Steve Legg – The Breakout Trust
www.v-ocean.co.uk
Legge House
www.legge-house.demon.co.uk
The Leprosy Mission
www.leprosymission.org
Lesbian and Gay Christian Movement (LGCM)
members.aol.com/lgcm
Liberal Democrats
www.libdems.org.uk
Librarians Christian Fellowship
churchnet.ucsm.ac.uk/lcf/lcfhome.htm
Library Association
www.la-hq.org.uk
Lichfield Cathedral
www.lichfield-cathedral.org
Life Changing Ministries
www.lcm.clara.net
Life For The World Trust
www.doveuk.com/lfw
Light and Salt
www.paternoster-publishing.com
Light for the Last Days
www.charitynet.org/~messianic
The Lighthouse Agency
ourworld.compuserve.com/homepages/connectionspm
Lightwing Projects
www.argonet.co.uk/users/flintdes/lwing.html
The Linacre Centre for Health Care Ethics
www.linacre.org
Lincoln Theological Institute for the Study of Religion and Society
www.shef.ac.uk/~lti
Lindisfarne Mustard Seed Project
www.ndirecto.co.uk/~raysimpson
Link Romania
www.wordnet.co.uk/linkro.html
Link Up Holidays
www.linkupholidays.freeserve.co.uk
Lion Publishing plc
www.lion-publishing.co.uk
Littledale Trust
www.doveuk.com/littledale
Living Water
www.btinternet.com/~living.water

David Livingstone International
www.livingstone.com
The Martyn Lloyd-Jones Recordings Trust
web.mlj.org.uk
The Lodge on the Loch Hotel
www.freedomglen.co.uk
Logos Ministries
www.charis.co.uk/logos.ministries
London Bible College
www.londonbiblecollege.ac.uk
Kensington Temple London City Church
www.ken-temp.org.uk
London Mennonite Centre and Trust
www.btinternet.com/~lmc
London Theological Seminary
www.lts.u-net.com
Look and Listen Ministries
www.broch.com/llm
Lord's Day Observance Society (Day One Publications)
www.lordsday.co.uk
Loyola Hall – Jesuit Spirituality Centre
home.clara.net/loyola
LUKE (Love UK Evangelism)
www.om.org
Lutheran Council of Great Britain
www.lutheran.org.uk
Lutterworth Press
www.lutterworth.com

McCabe Pilgramages
www.mccabe.u-net.com
Macmillan Cancer Relief
www.mcmillan.org.uk
Make Way Music Ltd
www.grahamkendrick.co.uk
Makin Organs Ltd
www.makinorgans.co.uk
Manchester Network Evangelical Fellowship
www.users.zetnet.co.uk/urbanpresence/network.html
Manna Ministries International
www.heartbeat-music.com/manna
Maranatha Christian Bookshop
www.maranathabookshop.co.uk
Maranatha Foundation
www.christian-education.org
Maranatha Tours (Euro) Ltd
www.maranatha.co.uk
March for Jesus
www.gmfi.org
The Maria Morley Crawcrook Pentecostal College
members.aol.com/mmorleyspc/college.htm
Market Research Society
www.mrs.org.uk
Marriage Care
www.fertilityuk.org
Marriage Encounter, Anglican Expression
www.marriageencounter.freeserve.co.uk
Marriage Resource
www.marriageresource.org.uk
Henry Martyn Centre
www.martynmission.cam.ac.uk
Marygate House
www.lindisfarne.org.uk/marygate/
MasterSki and MasterSun
www.itsnet.co.uk.mastersun
The Matthew Project
www.gurney.co.uk/watton/social/matthew
The Matthew Trust
www.activ-8.com/matthew-trust
MAYC (Methodist Association of Youth Clubs)
www.pinicle.demon.co.uk/maycweb/

vin Mayhew
www.kevinmayhewltd.com
edair UK
www.medair.org
edical Missionary Association
www.healthserve.org
edina Valley Centre for Outdoor Education
www.medinavalleycentre.org.uk
ie Mega Mondo Trust
members.aol.com/megamondo/mmt
iental Health Foundation
www.mentalhealth.org.uk
lercer House
freespace.virgin.net/graeme_james.williams/mercer.htm
ie Mersey Mission to Seamen
netministries.org/see/charmin/cm01395
lessage to Schools Trust
www.message.org.uk
lessage: The Christian Telephone Service
www.jbaassoc.demon.co.uk/message
he Messianic Testimony
www.charitynet.org/~messianic
letanoia Book Service
www.btinternet.com/~lmc
lethodist Church Headquarters and Press Service
www.methodist.org.uk
lethodist Church: Cymru District
www.westwales.co.uk/methodism
lethodist Church: Sheffield District
members.aol.com/sheffmeth/
lethodist Church in Ireland Department of Youth and Children's Work
www.iol.ie\~dycw
lethodist Holiday Hotels Ltd, trading as Epworth Hotels
www.email-it.co.uk/epworth/
lethodist Publishing House
www.mph.org.uk
lethodist Recorder
www.methodistrecorder.co.uk
IFJ Productions
members.aol.com/mfjprods/home.html
Michael Roberts Charitable Trust (MRCT)
www.mrct.freeserve.co.uk
Middle East Christian Outreach
www.gospelcom.net/meco
Middleton Christian Bookshop
www.teesdalecomputers.co.uk
Middlewich Narrowboats
www.middlewichboats.co.uk
Midlands Bible College
www.btinternet.com/~midlandsbiblecollege
Midweek in Mayfair
www.doveuk.com/midweek
Mildmay International and Mildmay Hospital UK
www.mildmay.org.uk
Mill Hill Missionaries
www.millhillmissionaries.org
Mimeistry UK
www.mimeistry.org
Mission Aviation Fellowship
www.maf.org
Mission for Christ (Rural Evangelism)
www.surfaid.org/~mfcrural
Mission Supplies Ireland Ltd
www.tricord.co.uk
Mission Supplies Ltd
www.mission-supplies.co.uk
Mission to Eastern Europe
www.wolfsbane.demon.co.uk
Mission Without Borders (UK) Ltd
www.mwbi.org
Missionaries of Africa (White Fathers)
www.users.skynet.be/lavigerie
The Missionary Training Service
www.btinternet.com/~ajg/mtshome.htm
Missionary Ventures Europe
www.missionaryventures.org
The Missions to Seamen
www.missionstoseamen.org
J and M Mitchell Church Supplies
www.churchsupplies.force9.co.uk
MODEM
churchnet.ucsm.ac.uk/modem/modem.htm
The Modern Churchpeople's Union
www.mcm.co.uk/modchurchunion
Monastery of St Francis & Gorton Trust Ltd
www.mancat.u-net.com/monastery
Monopolies and Mergers Commission
www.open.gov.uk/mmc
Moorlands College
www.moorlands.u-net.com
Moravian Church in Great Britain and Ireland
www.moravian.org.uk
Morley Retreat and Conference House
www.btinternet.com/~treasure/aml/morley/
The Mothers' Union and Media Awareness Project
www.themothersunion.org
Movement for Christian Democracy
www.mcdpolitics.org
Multiply Christian Network
www.multiply.org.uk
Multiply Publications
www.jesus.org.uk/multiply/publications
Music and Worship Foundation
www.btinternet.com/~mwf/
MVS Video Productions
www.videoproductions.freeserve.co.uk

National Association of Citizens Advice Bureaux
www.nacab.org.uk
National Bible Society of Scotland, all Departments
www.nat-bible-society.org
National Centre for Social Researcch
www.natcen.ac.uk
National Christian Education Council (NCEC) and Book Sales
www.ncec.org.uk
The National Council of YMCAs of Ireland
niweb.com/org/ymca
National Federation of Young Farmers Club
www.yfc-web.org.uk
National Marriage Week
www.marriageresource.org.uk
National Retreat Association
www.retreats.org.uk
National Society for Promoting Religious Education
www.natsoc.org.uk
Naval Christian Fellowship
dspace.dial.pipex.com/ncf
The Navigators
www.navigators.co.uk
Nazarene Theological College
www.nazarene.moose.co.uk/ntc/
NCEC/IBRA
www.ncec.org.uk
NCH Action for Children
www.nchafc.org.uk
Network Christian Trust
members.aol.com/kingch/kings
Network Counselling and Training
www.network.org.uk
New Creation Christian Community
www.jesus.org.uk/nccc
New Dawn Books and Bookshop and Connection Coffee House
www.struthers-church.org

New Day Introductions and Personnal
www.churchnet.org.uk/churchnet/new_day
New Frontiers International
home.ml.org/nfi
New Hope Publications
www.newhopetrust.org
New Horizon
www.newhorizon.org.uk
New Life Radio
www.mike-coles-travel.co.uk_newliferadio
New Tribes Mission
www.ntm.org.uk
New Wine
www.new-wine.org
Newbold College
www.newbold.ac.uk
Newcastle Cathedral
www.hexham-newcastle-diocese.org.uk/stmaryscathedral
Newington Court
www.goodnews.co.uk/newcourt
The Newman Association
www.cablenet/~newman/
Gerald E Newns
www.newns.com
News Special
www.paternoster-publishing.com
The Newspaper Society
www.newspapersoc.org.uk
NGM
www.ngm-uk.org
Nia
www.niaconcerts.com
No Frontiers (Literature Outreach) Ltd
www.nofrontiers.com
North Wales Gospel Outreach (NOWGO)
www.churches.net/userpages/oasisdwygyfylchi.html
Northern Light
www.users.zetnet.co.uk/stmarks
Northumbrian Centre of Prayer for Healing
www.northheal.freeserve.co.uk
Northwood Missionary Auctions
www.nmauctions.org.uk
Norwegian Church and Seamen's Mission
dspace.dial.pipex.com/londonkirken/
Not Yet
www.notyet.org
Nota Bene (European Theological Media)
www.paternoster-publishing.com
Novi Most International
www.novimost.org
Nurses Christian Fellowship International
welcome.to/ncfi

Oak Hall Expeditions and Skiing
www.oakhall.clara.net
Oak Hill Theological College and **Open Learning Centre**
www.oakhill.ac.uk
Oasis Trust
www.u-net.com/oasis
The Oast Houses
easyweb.easynet.co.uk/oast.houses/
Office for National Statistics
www.ons.gov.uk
Office of the Rail Regulator
www.rail-reg.gov.uk
The Officer
www.salvationarmy.org.uk
Officers Christian Union
ourworld.compuserve.com/homepages/ocu
Olivet English Language School
www.edunet.com/olivet
Ollerton Hall Decor Services
www.i-i.ollertonhall
Omega – Winford Manor
members.aol.com/omegatrust/omega/omega.html
OMF International (UK)
www.omf.org.uk
OMS International
www.omsinternational.org
Open Air Campaigners
web.ukonline.co.uk/oacministries
Open Air Mission
www.btinternet.com oamission
The Open Churches Trust
ww.merseyworld.com/faithful/html_file/octhead.htm
Open Doors with Brother Andrew
www.od.org/oduk
Open Learning Centre
www.base25.co.uk/olc
The Open Theological College
www.chelt.ac.uk/cwis/otc.htm
Operation Mobilisation
www.uk.om.org
Opportunity International UK
www.opportunity.org.uk
Ordnance Survey
www.ordsvy.gov.uk
Orientours Pilgrimages
www.peltours.com
Antiochian Orthodox Cathedral
www.antiochian-orthodox.co.uk
Orthodox Fellowship of St John the Baptist
www.ofsjb.org
OXFAM
www.oxfam.org.uk
Oxford Centre for Mission Studies
www.icmc.org/ocms
Oxford University Press Bible Department
www.oup.co.uk/
Oxfordshire Community Churches
www.oxcc.u-net.com

The Pagan Federation
www.paganfed.demon.co.uk
Pamela House Women's Hostel (Birmingham City Mission)
www.internet-pilots.com/city_missions/
Parish Pump
www.parishpump.co.uk
Partners for Life
www.wwww.uk.com
Partnership Publications
www.paternoster-publishing.com
Passion
www.passion.org.uk
Paternoster Publishing
www.paternoster-periodicals.com
Pathway Productions
www.cofs.org.uk/pathway.htm
PCCA Christian Child Care
www.doveuk.com/pcca
Pecan Ltd
www.pecan.org.uk
Pendlebury's and Pendleburys Church Candles
www.clique.co.uk/pendleburys
Peniel Pentecostal Church and Academy, Bible College, Conferences
www.peniel.org
Peniel Bookshop
www.aliveuk.com
The People and Work Programme
www.users.2etnet.co.uk/peopleandwork
& www.online.freeserve.co.uk
People International
members.aol.com/peopleintl

:PA Practical, Effective, Performing Arts
easyweb.easynet.co.uk/rain
rforming Rights Society
www.prs.co.uk
e Periodical Publishers Association
www.ppa.co.uk
rtinent PR
www.pertpr.demon.co.uk
wsey Christian Bookshop
www.campuscc.org/sfi
e Philo Trust
www.philo.ndirect.co.uk
oneer
www.pioneer.org.uk
ioneer DNA
freespace.virgin.net/pioneer.dna/
ough Publishing House of the Bruderhof Communities in the UK
www.bruderhof.org
lumbline Ministries
www.plumbline.org.uk
luscarden Abbey Bookshop
www.celide.ndirect.co.uk/pluscarden
ocket Testament League
www.ptl.org.uk
he Post Office and Telecommunications Christian Association
www.christiancomm.org.uk
rama-Care
www.users.globalnet.co.uk/~prama
rayer at Twelve Fellowship
www.users.surfaid.org/~monkton
rayer Network for Revival
www.scotland2000.freeserve.co.uk
reachers' Help
www.digibank.demon.co.uk/preacher/
remier Christian Radio 1305*1332*1413MW and **Premier Lifeline**
www.premier.org.uk
The Presbyterian Church in Ireland Headquarters and Overseas Board, Presbyterian Herald, Youth Board
www.presbyterianireland.org
Presbyterian Church of Wales Headquarters and Youth & Children's Centre
www.ebcpcw.org.uk
Presentation Sisters
www.pbvmepro.clara.net
Priests & People
www.thetablet.co.uk/p&p.htm
Derek Prince Ministries – UK
www.derekprince.com
Prinknash Abbey
www.brunel.co.uk//davidw//.prinknash.html#1
Prinknash Benedictines
web.ukonline.co.uk/david.w34/davidw/_prinknash.html
Prison Fellowship Scotland
users.colloquium.co.uk/~pfscotland/
Proclaimers International
www.proclaim.org.uk
Project Evangelism
www.jbu.edu/projev
Prophecy Today
www.the-park.u-net.com
Prophetic Witness Movement International
www.pwmi.org
Psalmody International
www.psalmody.org
Rosemary Pugh Second Hand Books
www.freenet.co.uk/homepages/rosemarypugh/home.html
Purley & Andover Christian Trust
freespace.virgin.net/frank.cooke.pact

Qua Iboe Fellowship
web.ukonline.co.uk/qua.iboe
Quest
www.users.dircon.co.uk/~quest/
The Quiet Garden Trust
web.ukonline.co.uk/members/
Quinta Press
www.cix.co.uk/~digby/qp.html

RADAR (Royal Association for Disability and Rehabilitation)
www.radar.org.uk
Radiant Life Ministries
cw.orangenet.co.uk/~radiant
Radio Worldwide
ourworld.compuserve.com/homepages/rw/
The Railway Mission
www.page-net.co.uk/web_sites/rmission
Rainbow Churches
easyweb.easynet.co.uk/rain
The Ranch Outdoor Discovery Centre
members.xoom.com/the_ranch
Arthur Rank Centre
freespace.virgin.net/arthur_rank.centre
Rapport
www.care-for-the-family.org.uk
Rapport Trust (Servants of God Trust)
www.rapport.org/rap
The John Ray Initiative
www.jri.org.uk
RE Bookshop/Llyfrfa AG
weblife.bangor.ac.uk/addysg/wncre/home.htm
Reach Out Ministries International
www.petergammons.org
Reachout Trust
www.reachouttrust.org
Reconciliation International
www.revivalnet.net/joseph
Red Sea Mission Team
www.rsmt.u-net.com
Redcliffe College
www.redcliffe.org
Redemptorist Publications
www.redempt.org
REEP (Religious Education and Environment Programme) and Planet Pledge Network (PPN)
www.users.globalnet.co.uk/~reep
Reform
www.urc.org.uk
Reformed Presbyterian Church of Ireland
www.rpc.org
Regent's Park College
www.rpc.ox.ac.uk
Regents Theological College and Conference Centre, English Language Centre
regents.ac.uk
Relate Marriage Guidance
www.relate.org.uk
Release Foundation
www.releasefoundation.com
Religious & Theological Studies Fellowship (RTSF)
www.uccf.org.uk/rtsf
Religious Experience Research Centre
www.charitynet.org~rerc
Religious Society of Friends (Quakers) in Britain
www.quaker.org.uk
Remar Association UK
www.remar.org www.tverbo.org
Renewal Servicing
www.renewal-servicing.freeserve.co.uk/
Reorganized Church of Jesus Christ of Latter Day Saints
www.rlds.org
Resurrection Theatre Co
www.rtc.cwcom.net

X

Retail Price Index
www.ons.gulf.org.uk
Review of Theological Literature
www.tandtclark.co.uk
Revival (Hour of Revival Association)
www.wornet.co.uk/revival.htm
Revival Radio Ltd
www.christianradio.com/revivalradio
Riding Lights Theatre Co Ltd
www.users.globalnet.co.uk/~rltc/
Right Hand Trust
www.ourworld.compuserve.com/homepages/righthandtrust
Ripon Cathedral
www.riponcathedral.org.uk
River
www.river.uk.com
Rivers Travel
www.rivers.co.uk
A Rocha Trust
www.arocha.org/
Rodd & Marco – The Acts Drama Trust
www.rodd&marco.com
Romania Concern
ourworld.compuserve.com/homepages/communityforreconciliation
Ross & Co
www.cin.co.uk/ross/
Maurice Rowlandson Consultancy
ourworld.compuserve.com/homepages/mau
Royal Association in Aid of Deaf People (RAD)
www.royaldeaf.uk
Royal School of Church Music
www.rscm.com
RSPB (Royal Society for the Protection of Birds)
www.rspb.org.uk
RSR (Royal Sailors' Rests)
www.rsr.org.uk
Rural Evangelism Network
www.users.zetnet.co.uk/bosborne/fre.html
The Rushworth Literature Enterprise Ltd
www.rushworth.lit.virgin.net
Russian Ministries (Peter Deyneka)
www.russianministries.org
Russian Orthodox Bookshop
home.clara.net/sourozh
Russimco Ltd
www.russimco.com
Rutherford House
www.rutherfordhouse.org.uk
Rutherford Journal of Church and Ministry
www.rutherfordhouse.org.uk
Rydal Hall (Carlisle Diocesan Conference and Retreat House)
users.aol.com/rydalhall

St Albans Cathedral
www.stalbansdioc.org.uk/cathedral/
St Beuno's
home.aol.com/stbeunos
St Chad's College
www.dur.ac.uk\stchads
St Christopher's Fellowship
www.users.dircon.co.uk/~st-chris
St Clements Retreat House
www.reds-belfast.com
St Columba's Horton Outreach
www.bradford.anglican.org/bfd/col
St Deiniol's Residential Library
st-deiniols.chester.ac.uk
St John's College, Nottingham and St John's Extension Studies
www.stjohns-nottm.ac.uk
St John's Roman Catholic Seminary
dspace.dial.pipex.com/town/avenue/aba24/contents.shtml

St Joseph's Centre for Addiction
www.holycross.org.uk
St Joseph's Hospice Association (Jospice International)
www.garrick.co.uk/stjoseph.html
St Martin Vestment Ltd
jcb@johnsplace.force9.co.uk
St Mary's, Strawberry Hill
www.smuc.ac.uk/dept/trs/index.htm
St Matthew Publishing Ltd
www.phar.cam.ac.uk/stmatts/
St Michael's Bookshop
www.stmikes.clara.net
St Pauls bookshop (Westminster Cathedral)
stpauls.ie
St Paul's Cathedral
stpauls.london.anglican.org
St Peter's Grange, Prinknash Abbey
www.brunel.co.uk//davidw//-prinknash.html#1
St Stephen's Press
www.sourozh.clara.net
Salem Court
salemcourt.co.uk
Salesian Fathers and Brothers
www.salesians.org.uk
Salesian Volunteers
www.roehampton.ac.uk/linkdonbosco_uk/don_bosco_uk.htm
The Salmon Youth Centre in Bermondsey
www.salmoncentre.co.uk
Salt Centre
www.living-waters.org.uk
Saltbox Christian Centre
www.fenetre.co.uk/~cvm/saltbox.htm
Saltmine Trust
www.saltmine.org
Saltshakers Ltd
www.saltshakers.com
The Salvation Army, UK Territorial Commander
www.salvationarmy.org.uk
Salvation Army Housing Association
www.saha.org.uk
Salvationist
www.salvationarmy.org.uk/website/ukpages/salvonli.html
Sarner International Ltd
www.sarner.com
Sarum College
www.sarum.ac.uk
SAT-7 Trust
www.sat7.org
Scargill House Ltd
ds.dial.pipex.com/scargill.house/
School of Creative Ministries (Kensington Temple)
www.ken-temp.org.uk
School of Mission and World Christianity
www.sellyoak.ac.uk/mission.htm
Schools Ministry Network
www.scriptureunion.org.uk
Science and Christian Belief
www.paternoster-publishing.com
Science and Religion Forum
www.srforum.org
Scottish Crusaders
www.charitynet.org/~scotcrus
Scottish Episcopal Church: Diocese of Argyll and the Isles
www.argyll.anglican.org
Scottish Journal of Theology
www.tandtclark.co.uk
Scripture Truth Publications
www.morpethnet.co.uk/scripturetruth/
Scripture Union, all Departments
www.scripture.org.uk
Scripture Union Resource Centre
www.suni.co.uk

X

ripture Union Scotland
www.scriptureunionscotland.org.uk
)A Studio Services
www.adventist.org.uk
E.A.N. International (UK)
ourworld.compuserve.com/homepages/sean_uk
:ed
www.users.globalnet.co.uk/~payne/seed.html
:ed, Bible Mission International
www.bethany.co.uk/bmi
:lly Oak Colleges
www.sellyoak.ac.uk/sellyoak
EN UK
www.citygate.org
end A Cow
web.ukonline.co.uk/members/send.a.cow/
ervants to Asia's Urban Poor
www.zeta.org.au/~servants/
essions of York, The Ebor Press
www.sessionsofyork.co.uk
:eventh-Day Adventist Church
www.adventist.org.uk
:eventh-Day Adventist Pathfinder Club and Youth Society
www.youthpages.org
;GM International
members.aol.com/sgmint
;hare It!
churcharmy.org.uk
;hared Interest
www.oneworld.org/shared_int.
;heffield Academic Press
www.shef-ac-press.co.uk
Sheffield Cathedral
www.sheff.ac.uk/uni/projects/sheffcath
Ship of Fools
ship-of-fools.com
Shoresh Study Tours
www.cmj.org.uk
Sigma Promotions Ltd
www.smg.org.uk
SIM UK (Society for International Ministries)
www.sim.org
Sion Catholic Community for Evangelism
www.btinternet.com/-sioncommunity
Sisters of Charity of St Paul
easyweb.easynet.co.uk/~stpaul/
Sisters of Our Lady
www.snd1.org
Skills For Living
www.skills.org
Soapbox Communications and Expeditions
www.lineone.net/~soapbox
Society for Promoting Christian Knowledge (SPCK) Head Office and Bookshops Head Office
www.spck.org.uk
Society for the Protection of Unborn Children (SPUC)
www.spuc.org.uk
Society of Jesus
www.jesuit.co..uk
Society of Mary
freespace.virgin.net/marist.sidcup
Society of the Holy Child Jesus
www.shcj.org
The Soldier's and Airmen's Scripture Readers Association (SASRA)
www.sasra.org.uk
Solent Christian Trust
www.sct.org.uk
SOON
www.soon.org.uk
Soul Survivor
www.soulsurvivor.com
South American Mission Society
www.demon.co.uk/charities/sams
South Wales Baptist College
www.cf.ac.uk/uwc/relig/swbc_e.html
Southampton Action of Employment (SAFE)
www.safe.org.uk
Southampton Asian Christian Outreach
www.saco.freeserve.co.uk
Southport Methodist Holiness Convention
dunnwilson.future.easyspace.com
Southwark Cathedral
www.dswark.org
Sovereign Creative Marketing Ltd
www.sovereign.uk.com
Sovereign Giving
www.sovereign-giving.org.uk
Sovereign Publications
ourworld.compuserve.com/homepages/bowdenmalcolm
Spanish Gospel Mission
members.aol.com/spngospel
Spear Trust
domini.org/spear
Spirit Print
www.marmet.freeserve.co.uk
Spring Harvest
www.springh.org
Spurgeon's Child Care
www.garrick.co.uk/spurgeon.html
Spurgeon's College
www.spurgeons.ac.uk
Stainer & Bell Ltd
www.stainer.co.uk
The Stapleford Centre
www.stapleford-centre.org
Star Tours and Holidays
www.travelink.uk.com/startours.htm
Stepping Stones Christian Training Project
www.steppingstones.org.uk
The Stepping Stones Trust
www.geocities.com/heartland/1737
Stewardship Services (United Kingdom Evangelization Trust Inc-UKET)
www.stewardship.co.uk
Stickywicket Design and Print
www.stickywicket.com
Stoneleigh Bible Week
www.n-f-i.org
Struthers Memorial Churches
www.struthers-church.org
Studies in Christian Ethics
www.tandtclark.co.uk
Summer Institute of Linguistics (British School)
www.sil.org/schools/
Summit Publishing Ltd
www.summitpublishing.co.uk
Sunday Schools Council for Wales
www.bangor.ac.uk
Sunrise Software International Ltd
www.sunrise-software.com
Survive – MIVA
www.survive-miva.org
Swedish Church (Lutheran)
www.swednet.org.uk/swedish-church
Sword and Trowel
www.metropolitantabernacle.org

Tabernacle Bookshop
www.metropolitantabernacle.org
The Tablet
www.thetablet.co.uk
Talents Music Shop
talents.co.uk

Tandem TV and Film Ltd
www.tandem.com
Tarbat Free Church Caravan Site
www.highlander.zetnet.co.uk/tfc/caravan
The Teal Trust
www.teal.org.uk
Tear Fund and Tearcraft
www.tearfund.org.uk
Teens in Crisis
www.users.globalnet.co.uk/~tic
TELit
www.users.globalnet.co.uk/~telit/
Tentmakers Ltd
www.tentmaker.co.uk
Teresian Press
www.carmelite.org.uk
TES (The Evangelization Society)
ourworld.compuserve.com/homepages/theevangelizationsociety
Theology
www.spck.org.uk
Theology and Sexuality
www.shef-ac-press.co.uk
Theology Through the Arts
www.divinity.cam.ac.uk/carts/tta.html
Therapy Students Christian Fellowship (TSCF)
www.uccf.org.uk/cus/course/tscf
There is Hope
www.there-is-hope.com
Third Way
www.thirdway.org.uk
Stanley Thornes (Publishers) Ltd
www.thornes.co.uk
Through Faith Missions
www.btinternet.com/~walk1000
Through The Roof
www.throughtheroof.org
The Time For God Scheme
ourworld.compuserve.com/homepages/time_for_god/
Timeline Heritage Tours
www.oxlink.co.uk/business/timeline.html
Timperley Evangelical Trust
www.users.globalnet.co.uk/~tetrcb
Toc H
www.toch.org.uk
Together with Children
www.natsoc.org.uk
Top Ten Travel
www.hadlertours.ltd.uk
Touchstone Centre
www.methodist.org.uk/touchstone
The Toybox Charity
www.toybox.org
The Traidcraft Exchange
www.traidcraft.co.uk
Traidcraft plc
www.traidcraft.co.uk
Trans World Radio
www.twr.org
Transformation
www.paternoster-publishing.com
The TriCord Partnership
www.tricord.co.uk
Trimstone Manor Hotel
manorgroup.uk
Trinitarian Bible Society
biz.ukonline.co.uk/trinitarian.bible.society/contents.htm
Trinity English Language Centre
www.trinity-bris.ac.uk/elc
Trinity Hospice, Clapham
www.trinityhospice.org.uk
Trinity Theological College and Conference Centre
www.trinity-bris.ac.uk

Triptych Systems Ltd
www.triptych.co.uk
True Freedom Trust
www.tftrust.u-net.com
Truedata Computer Services
ourworld.compuserve.com/homepages/truedata
Twenty Thirty
www.20-30.org.uk
Tyndale House and Fellowship for Biblical and Theologic Research
www.tyndale.cam.ac.uk

UCB Europe
www.ucb.co.uk
UFM Worldwide
www.ufm.org.uk
UK and Ireland Revival Network
www.grm-uk.org/ukirn
The UK Direct Marketing Association
www.dma.org.uk
UK Focus
dspace.dial.pipex.com/htb.london
UK-Church.net (1st Web)
www.1st-web.co.uk
Ulster Christian Magazine
www.ucmag.com
UNAFRAID (United Africa Aid)
ourworld.compuserve.com/homepages/communityforreconciliation
Unigraph (UK) Ltd
www.unigraph.uk.com
Union Theological College
www.union.org.uk
United Beach Missions
home.aol.com/ubmhq
United Bible Societies, World Service Centre
www.biblesociety.org
United Free Church of Scotland
www.ufcos.org.uk
United Marriage Encounter
www.muscanet.com/~ume
United Nations Library
www.un.org
United Reformed Church in the United Kingdom
www.compulink.co.uk/~urc/urc_home.html
International Relations
www.urc.co.uk
Eastern Province
members.aol.com/urc7/welcome.htm
Thames North Synod
ourworld.compuserve.com/homepages/thamesnorthurc
Wales Province
www.urcwalesprovince.uk
Yorkshire Province
dspace.dial.pipex.com/urc.yorkshire
Universal Church of the Kingdom of God
www.universalchurch.org
The Universe
www.demon.co.uk/gabcom/
Universities and Colleges Christian Fellowship (UCCF)
www.uccf.org.uk
University of Aberdeen, Department of Divinity with Religious Studies
www.abdn.ac.uk/divinity/
University of Glasgow, Faculty of Divinity
www.religious.divinity.gla.ac.uk
University of St Andrews, School of Divinity
www.st-andrews.ac.uk/~www-sd/home.html
University of the Holy Land
www.uhl.u-k.ac
Urban Presence
www.urbanpresence.freeserve.co.uk

X

anpoulles Ltd
www.vanpoulles.co.uk
antage Graphics & Design Ltd
www.vgd.co.uk
ictory Tracts and Posters
www.victory10.freeserve.co.uk
iva Network
www.viva.org
M Music
www.vmmusic.com

'alk of 1000 Men
www.btinternet.com/~walk1000/
/alk Thru the Bible Ministries
www.bible.org.uk
he War Cry
www.salvationarmy.org.uk/website/ukpages/ewarcry.html
/ATCH National (Women and the Church)
www.watchwomen.com
/CA-UK (Willow Creek Association – UK)
www.willowcreek.org
/EC International
www.wec-int.org
/elford Enterprises Ltd and Welford Hill Farm
www.wwww.uk.com
'he Welsh National Centre for Religious Education
weblife.bangor.ac.uk/addysg/wncre/home.htm
/esley & Methodist Studies Centre (WMSC)
www.ox-west.ac.uk/wmsc/
/esley House, Cambridge
www.wesley.org.uk
Wesley Owen Books and Music
www.wesleyowen.com
West End Outdoor Centre
www.yorkshiremet.co.uk/accgde.westend
West London Mission
www.methodist.org.uk/west.london.mission
West of England Ministerial Training Course
www.wcmtc.freeserve.co.uk
Westcott House
www.ely.anglican.org/westcott/
Westminster Abbey Library
www.westminster-abbey.org
Westminster Cathedral
www.westminstercathedral.org.uk
Westminster College School of Humanities
www.ox-west.ac.uk/
Westminster John Knox Press (UK Office)
www.wjk.org
J Whitaker & Sons Ltd (The Bookseller) London
www.whitaker.uk
Ian White
members.aol.com/sheffmeth/
Whitechapel Bell Foundry
www.whitechapelbellfoundry.co.uk
Whitechapel Mission
www.whitechapel.uk
Wild Goose Publications (The Iona Community)
www.iona.org.uk
Winchester Diocesan Youth and Children
win.diocese.org.uk
Wind, Sand & Stars Ltd
www.windsandstars.co.uk
Windmill Christian Centre
www.netlink.co.uk/users/dk/arbroath/windmill/
Wingfinger Graphics
www.wfinger.demon.co.uk
WMA-UK
www.wmausa.org
Woodbrooke Quaker Study Centre
www.woodbrooke.org.uk/woodbrooke/
The Word for Life Trust
www.doveuk.com/wflt
Word Music and Publishing
www.premieronline.co.uk
Word of Life
www.domini.org
Word of Life Ministries (UK) Ltd
www.woluk.org
Workaid
www.btinternet.com/~workaid
The WorkNet Partnership
www.worknetpartnership.org.uk
World Association for Christian Communication
www.wacc.org.uk
World Day of Prayer – Scottish Committee
davbros.demon.co.uk
World Development Movement
www.wdm.org.uk
World Emergency Relief
www.wer-uk.org
World Evangelical Fellowship
www.worldevangelical.org
World Horizons (Britain)
www.whorizons.org
World Outreach
www.harpbbt.com.au/comm/outreach
World Vision UK
www.worldvision.org.uk
WorldShare
www.worldshare.org.uk
Worldwide Christian Communication Network
www.wccn.net
Worldwide Christian Travel Ltd
www.hadlertours.ltd.uk
The Worldwide Church of God (UK)
www.wcg.org/pt/uk/index.html
Worldwide Harvest Ministries
www.worldwideharvest.org
Worth Abbey Lay Community
ukonline.co.uk/worth.abbey/homepages.htm
Wycliffe Associates (UK)
www.globalnet.co.uk/~wa_uk
Wycliffe Bible Translators
www.wycliffe.org.uk
Wycliffe Hall
www.wycliffe.ox.ac.uk

Y 2000
www.y-2000.com
Y Coleg Gwyn (North Wales Baptist College)
www.bangor.ac.uk/rs/cglc.htm
YMCA
England
www.ymca.org.uk
Birkenhead
www.btinternet.com/~s.larmour
Cambridge
www.pcug.co.uk/ymca/regions/central/project/cam0.html
Cheltenham
www.cheltenhamymca.org.uk
Crewe
ymca-crewe.demon.co.uk
Lincoln
www.ymca.org.uk
London, Ealing & District
www.ymca.org.uk/
London, Waltham Forest
wforest.ymca.org.uk
Londonderry
niweb.com/org/ymca
Penzance
www.cornwall.co.uk/ymcapenzance
Welwyn/Hatfield
www.intecc.co.uk/ymca

Young Life and **Young Life Holidays**
younglife.org.uk
Youth Connection
www.youth-connect.org.uk
Youth for Christ
www.yfc.co.uk
Youth For Christ Northern Ireland
www.yfc-ireland.com
Youth Ministries International
www/ymieurope.com
Youthwork
www.youthwork.co.uk

The Zacharias Trust
www.rzim.com

OTHER WEB SITE ADDRESSES

Notes:

1. Organisations with an entry in the *UK Christian Handbook* and which have a Web site are given in the list on Page 000.
2. In the occasional case where the web site address is too long for one line, it should be treated as one continuous address.
2. All addresses should be preceded by http:// This is normally supplied automatically by Web Browers, and is thus not included here.

INTRODUCTION

The following list has been complied by Vernon Blackmore of Write Connection (www.writeconnection.co.uk).

The aim was to provide starting points for access to information which is either specifically Christian, or of use to Christians. It is nc restricted to UK-based sites because geographical boundaries are irrelevant on the Internet.

Sites have been listed in a number of broad categories, and these are in alphabetical order. All these addresses were correct as of May 199 but users should be aware that the Internet is a dynamic medium which is constantly growing and changing. The statement on Page 00 regarding other entries in this *Handbook* also applies here: "While every effort has been made to be comprehensive, and to include organisa tions relevant to this publication, no responsibility can be taken by the Editors for the omission of an organisation. The inclusion of a organisation does not necessarily imply agreement by the Editors with its work."

BIBLE, BIBLE STUDY AND THEOLOGY

APS Research Guide—Theology
www.utoronto.ca/stmikes/theobook.htm
BBC Education Webguide: Religion
db.bbc.co.uk/education-webguide/pkg_main.p_results?in_cat=557
Bible Commentaries
www.cyberhighway.net/~cochac/library.htm
Bible-Links Page
www1.uni-bremen.de/~wie/bibel.html
Bibles: Public Domain Reference
www.bible.org/docs/public/readme.htm
Christian History
www.christianity.net/christianhistory/
Fides Quaerens Internetum – Christian Theology
www.bu.edu/people/bpstone/theology/theology.html
Guide to Early Church Documents
www.iclnet.org/pub/resources/christian-history.html
Mark Goodacre's Web Resources
www.bham.ac.uk/theology/goodacre/links.htm
On-line Bibles
www.geocities.com/Heartland/Acres/3964/bibles/
RE-XS for Schools
re-xs.ucsm.ac.uk
Religious Studies Resources on the Internet
fn2.freenet.edmonton.ab.ca/~cstier/religion/toc.htm
Resource Pages for Biblical Studies
www.hivolda.no/asf/kkf/rel-stud.html
Sacred Scriptures Resources
www.vocations.org/library/linkss.htm
Virtual Religion Index
religion.rutgers.edu/links/vrindex.html

BOOKS ON-LINE

Alex Catalogue of Electronic Texts
sunsite.berkeley.edu/alex/
Books On-line
www-cgi.cs.cmu.edu/cgi-bin/book/subjectstart?BR-BX
Christian Classics Ethereal Library
ccel.wheaton.edu
Electric Library
www.elibrary.com
The English Server
eserver.org
Guide to Christian Literature on the Internet
www.iclnet.org/pub/resources/christian-books3.html
The Internet Public Library
ipl.sils.umich.edu
IPL On-line Texts on Religion
readroom.ipl.org/bin/ipl/ipl.books-idx.pl?type=deweystem&q1=20C
New Advent
www.sni.net/advent/

CHURCHES—NATIONAL/INTERNATIONAL/ SOCIETIES

Anglican Communion
www.anglicancommunion.org
Anglican Communion Virtual Tour
www.anglicancommunion.org/virtualtour
Anglicans Online
www.anglican.org/online/
Anglocatholicism
www.btinternet.com/~i.am/main.htm
Assemblies of God
www.ag.org
Baptist
www.baptist.org
Baptist Union of Great Britain
www.baptist.org.uk
Baptist World Alliance
www.bwanet.org
Catholic Information Center
www.catholic.net
Catholic Online
www.catholic.org
Catholic Resources on the Net
www.cs.cmu.edu/People/spok/catholic.html
Cell Church
www.cellchurch.co.uk
Christian Brethren
www.brethren.org
The Church in Wales
www.churchinwales.org.uk
Church of England
www.church-of-england.org
Church of England Yellow Pages
web.ukonline.co.uk/Members/anchorsholme/yellow_pages/

X

urch of Scotland
www.cofs.org.uk
urch of the Brethren Network
www.cob-net.org
urch of the Nazarene
www.nazarene.org
ongregational Federation
www.users.zetnet.co.uk/bosborne/cong.htm
cumenical Links
www.geocities.com/Heartland/Ranch/9925/ecumenical.html
piscopal Church (Unofficial)
www.mit.edu/~tb/anglican/
vangelical Alliance
www.eauk.org
ree Church of Scotland
www.freechurch.org
oly See, Vatican City Roman Catholic Church
www.vatican.va
esus Army (Jesus Fellowship Church)
www.jesus.org.uk
utheran World Federation
lutheranworld.org
utherans.Net
www.lutherans.net
he Methodist Church of Great Britain
www.methodist.org.uk
ethodist World
welcome.to/methodist.world/
n-line Research and Resource Library
www.vocations.org/library/linkhome.htm
Pentecostal World Conference
www.pentecostalworldconf.org
Pioneer
www.pioneer.org.uk
Quakers
www.quaker.org
Reformed Ecumenical Council
www.gospelcom.net/rec/
Reformed Episcopal Church
www.recus.org
Salvation Army (UK)
www.salvationarmy.org.uk
Seventh-Day Adventists
www.adventist.org
United Reformed Church: UK
www.urc.org.uk
World Council of Churches
www.wcc-coe.org
World Evangelical Fellowship
www.worldevangelical.org

GRAPHICS

AltaVista Photo Finder
image.altavista.com
Art Today
www.arttoday.com
Christian Graphics Gallery
www.webauthors.org/gallery/chrgraph.shtml
Cross Search clipart
www.crosssearch.com/Art/Clip_Art/
The Free Site: graphics
www.thefreesite.com/freegraphics.htm
Lycos Picture Search
www.lycos.com/lycosmedia.html
NEC USA
www.nec.com

INTERNET CHAT

Best of the Christian Web
www.botcw.com
Best of the Christian Web—Chat
www.botcw.com/search/Chat_Rooms/
Christian Chat Network
www.cchat.net
Christian Cyberspace
www.chrsites.com/chat.htm
CircaNet—Christian IRC Network
www.circanet.org
In the Beginning
www.serve.com/larryi/begin.htm
Wilibrord's Christian Chat Sites
members.tripod.com/~Erala/chat.html

INTERNET INFORMATION

COIN
www.coin.org.uk
Computers Don't Bite
www.bbc.co.uk/education/cdb/
CyberAtlas
cyberatlas.internet.com
The Directory of Internet Service Providers
www.thedirectory.org
InetUK—UK and Irish Internet Company Directory
www.limitless.co.uk/inetuk/
The Gallup Organization
www.gallup.com
Learn the Net
www.learnthenet.com/english/
The List
thelist.internet.com
NOP
www.maires.co.uk
Rough Guide to the Internet
www.roughguides.com
Search Engine Watch: child safety
searchenginewatch.com/facts/kids.html
W3C—The World Wide Web Consortium
www.w3.org
Web Novice
www.webnovice.com
What is?
whatis.com

INTERNET NEWSGROUPS

Deja News
www.dejanews.com
Liszt
www.liszt.com
Miami Christian University Virtual Library
mcu.edu/library/
Newsgroups
alt.bible.prophecy
alt.christnet
alt.christnet.atheism
alt.christnet.bible
alt.christnet.christianlife
alt.christnet.ethics
alt.christnet.evangelical
alt.christnet.hypocrisy
alt.christnet.philosophy
alt.christnet.public
alt.christnet.religion
alt.christnet.second-coming.real-soon-now
alt.christnet.theology
alt.messianic
alt.religion.christian
alt.support.ex-cult
bit.listserv.christia
rec.music.christian
soc.religion.christian
soc.religion.christian.bible-study
soc.religion.christian.youth-work
uk.religion.christian
Publicly Accessible Mailing Lists
www.neosoft.com/internet/paml/

INTERNET SEARCHING—CHRISTIAN DIRECTORIES

711.Net Christian Internet Assistance
www.711.net
About.com
about.com/culture/religion/
All In One Christian Index
www.allinone.org
Anointed Christian Links
members.tripod.com/~cockatoo/links.html
Aussie Christian Search Engine
www.crosscape.com.au/search/
Australian Christian Web Index
www.sevenlights.ironbark.id.au/WebGuide/
Australian Churches
www.vision.net.au/~kevin_keep/churches.htm
Awesome Christian Sites
www.awesome-sites.com
Best of the Christian Web
www.botcw.com
Christian Topics
www.christiantopics.com
Christianity Today
www.christianity.net
Christianity.Net
www3.christianity.net/search/
ChristianLife Menu Page
www.mindspring.com/~mamcgee/christianlife.html
Christianlinks
www.christianlinks.com
Church Net UK
www.churchnet.org.uk
Church of England Yellow Pages
web.ukonline.co.uk/Members/anchorsholme/yellow_pages/
ChurchSurf Christian Directory
www.churchsurf.com
Crosssearch
www.crosssearch.com
Crosswalk
omnilist.crosswalk.com
Down Under Christian Directory
www.ozemail.com.au/~phopwood/
Find Directory at Guideposts
www.guideposts.org/gp2/gmail/gmail_find.shtml#directory
Fish Net
www.fni.com/xstart/
GCN Search
www.gcnhome.com/asp/search.asp
God on the Net
www.godonthenet.com
GOSHEN
www.goshen.net
Gospel Communicators Network
www.gospelcom.net
Guideposts
www.guideposts.org
HIS-Net Christian Network
www.his-net.com
Houses of Worship
www.housesofworship.net
In the Beginning
www.serve.com/larryi/begin.htm
Internet Christian Library
www.iclnet.org
Miami Christian University Virtual Library
mcu.edu/library/
Net Ministries
netministries.org
Not Just Bibles
www.iclnet.org/pub/resources/christian-resources.html
On-line Research and Resource Library
www.vocations.org/library/linkhome.htm
OurChurch.com
www.ourchurch.com
Prayer Net
www.churchnet.org.uk/prayer
Theology Library
www.mcgill.pvt.k12.al.us/jerryd/cathmob.htm
UK Christian Net
www.uk-christian.net
UK-Church.Net
uk-church.net/uk-listings.htm
Webway
www.saltshakers.co.uk/webway/
World Council of Churches
www.wcc-coe.org
YouthPastor.Com
youthpastor.com

INTERNET SEARCHING—GENERAL

About.com
www.about.com
AltaVista
altavista.digital.com
AOL NetFind
www.aol.com/netfind/
The Argus Clearinghouse
www.clearinghouse.net
Ask Jeeves
www.askjeeves.com
Ask Jeeves for Kids
www.ajkids.com/index.asp
Big Book
www.bigbook.com
Big Yellow
www.bigyellow.com
Bigfoot in the UK
www.bigfoot.co.uk
Charities Direct
www.caritasdata.co.uk
Charity Commission
www.charity-commission.gov.uk
Charity Net Links
www.charitynet.org/resources/charitylinks/
Deja News
www.dejanews.com
DirectHit
www.directhit.com
Electronic Yellow Pages
www.eyp.co.uk
EuroSeek
www.euroseek.net
Excite
www.excite.com
Excite—UK
www.excite.co.uk
FeMiNa
www.femina.com
Go
go.com
HotBot
www.hotbot.com
InfoSeek
www.infoseek.com
Internet Sleuth
www.isleuth.com
Lifestyle UK
www.lifestyle.co.uk
Liszt
www.liszt.com
LookSmart
www.looksmart.com
LookSmart—UK
www.looksmart.co.uk

ycos
www.lycos.com
agellan
www.mckinley.com
EC USA
www.nec.com
orthern Light
www.northernlight.com
ublicly Accessible Mailing Lists
www.neosoft.com/internet/paml/
ough Guide to the Internet
www.roughguides.com
avvySearch
www.savvysearch.com
urf Searcher
www.melt.co.uk/surfsearcher/index2.html
witchboard
www.switchboard.com
JK Index
www.ukindex.co.uk
JKMax
www.ukmax.com
Yahoo
www.yahoo.com
Yahoo – UK
www.yahoo.co.uk
Yahooligans
www.yahooligans.com
Yell
www.yell.co.uk

MISSION AND MISSION ORGANIZATIONS

Mission agencies listed in the *Handbook* and which have Web sites are included in the list on Page 540. In addition, the following may be useful.

Adherents.com
www.adherents.com
Agape Europe
www.webcom.com/~nlnnet/agape.html
Billy Graham Online
www.billygraham.org
Brigada
www.brigada.org
Global Consultation On World Evangelization
www.ad2000.org/gcowe95/
International Bible Society
www.gospelcom.net/ibs/
Jesus Film Project
www.jesusfilm.org
Lausanne Committee for World Evangelism
www.lausanne.org
Luis Palau Evangelistic Association
www.gospelcom.net/lpea/

MUSIC

All Music Guide
www.allmusic.com/index.html
Anglican Church Music
www.churchmusic.org.uk
Choral Directory
members.tripod.com/~choral/
Christian Midi Files
www.filecity.com/midi/christian/
Christian Music Online
www.cmo.com
Christian Music
christianmusic.about.com
The Cyber Hymnal
tch.simplenet.com
English Cathedral Music
www.cathmus.ndirect.co.uk
Hymnsite.com
www.hymnsite.com
Lycos MP3 Search
mp3.lycos.com
MP3.com
www.mp3.com
The Ultimate Band List
www.ubl.com

NEWS—CHRISTIAN

Anglican Communion News Service (UK)
www.anglicancommunion.org/acns/
Anglicans Online
www.anglican.org/online/
Catholic News Service (USA)
www.catholicnews.com
Christian Daily News
www.christiandailynews.org
Christian Radio
www.christianradio.com
Christian Spotlight on the Movies
www.christiananswers.net/spotlight/
Church Net UK News Service
www.churchnet.org.uk/news/
Church Times
www.churchtimes.co.uk
Ecumenical News International
www.eni.ch
Fides Quaerens Internetum – Journals
www.bu.edu/people/bpstone/theology/journals.html
Methodist Recorder
www.methodistrecorder.co.uk
New Christian Herald
www.newchristianherald.org
The Tablet
www.thetablet.co.uk
The Universe
www.the-universe.net
Worldwide Faith News
www.wfn.org

NEWS—GENERAL

Electronic News Stand
enews.com
Magazine Rack
www.magazine-rack.com
MediaInfo
www.mediainfo.com/edpub/
PA NewsCentre
www.pa.press.net
The Paperboy
www.thepaperboy.com
Pathfinder
www.pathfinder.com
Reuters
www.reuters.com

OTHER BELIEFS

A—Z of Cults
www.guardian.co.uk/observer/cults/a-z-cults/
Academic Info: Religion
www.academicinfo.net/religindex.html
Comparative Religion
weber.u.washington.edu/~madin/
Cult Awareness & Information Centre
student.uq.edu.au/~py101663/zentry1.htm
RE-XS for Schools
re-xs.ucsm.ac.uk
Religious Studies Page
www.clas.ufl.edu/users/gthursby/rel/
Religious Studies Resources on the Internet
fn2.freenet.edmonton.ab.ca/~cstier/religion/toc.htm

Web Addresses

Yahoo: Religions
www.yahoo.com/society_and_culture/religion/

REFERENCE

A Web of On-line Dictionaries
www.facstaff.bucknell.edu/rbeard/diction.html
Bartlett's Quotations
www.columbia.edu/acis/bartleby/bartlett/
British Library
portico.bl.uk
Chambers Electronic Encyclopedia
www.encyclopedia.com
Christian Quotation of the Day
www.gospelcom.net/cqod/
CIA's World Factbook
www.odci.gov/cia/publications/factbook/
COPAC: University Research Library Catalogue
copac.ac.uk/copac/
English Server—Reference Links
eng.hss.cmu.edu/reference/
The Gallup Organization
www.gallup.com
History Index
kuhttp.cc.ukans.edu/history/
Library of Congress
lcweb.loc.gov/homepage/lchp.html
Libweb—Librarywww Servers
sunsite.berkeley.edu/Libweb/
National Map Centre
www.mapsworld.com
One Look
www.onelook.com
The Quotations Archive
www.aphids.com/quotes/index.shtml
United Nations Population Information Network
www.undp.org/popin/
UpMyStreet
www.upmystreet.com

SOFTWARE

Angelfire Communications
www.angelfire.com/ca/cvanbeek7/
Completely Free Software
www.completelyfreesoftware.com
Download.com
www.download.com
FilePile
filepile.com
GOSHEN—Christian Software
www.christianshareware.net
InfoMac HyperArchive
hyperarchive.lcs.mit.edu/HyperArchive/
Jumbo Shareware
www.jumbo.com
Shareware.com
www.shareware.com
TUCOWS
www.tucows.com
Useful Free Stuff on the Web
members.tripod.com/~castlemarketing/Freestuf.htm
The Well Connected Mac
www.macfaq.com

YOUTH AND CHILDREN

Ask Jeeves for Kids
www.ajkids.com/index.asp
Berit's Best Sites for Children
db.cochran.com/li_toc:theoPage.db
EduWeb
www.eduweb.co.uk
Gospel.com youth links
www.gospelcom.net/ys/central/
Internet Public Library: Youth Division
www.ipl.org/youth/
The Schools Register
www.schools-register.co.uk
Search Engine Watch: child safety
searchenginewatch.com/facts/kids.html
The Site
www.thesite.org.uk
Yahooligans
www.yahooligans.com
YouthPastor.Com
youthpastor.com
YouthSearch
www.christianteens.net/search/

LATE ENTRIES

Alpha Supplies, 64 London End, Beaconsfield HP9 2JD
Senior Partner: Mr Phil MacInnes. Executive staff 1, Other staff 2. Began 1997; interdenominational. No magazine. Turnover £400,000 to year end Mar 99. Retailing quality furniture for churches, schools etc; offering reliable service.
Web: alpha-furnishing.co.uk
Email: info@alpha-furnishing.co.uk
☎ 01494 670 060 Fax 01494 678 181

Diana Bailey Associates, 10 Epping Close, Reading RG1 7YD
Managing Director: Miss Diana Bailey. Executive staff 1, Admin staff 1. Began 1999; interdenominational. No magazine. Turnover: first year of operation. Supporting churches and charities with management/training resources; courses for organisational, church, personal development.
Email: dmbailey@globalnet.co.uk
☎ 0118 939 4900 Mobile: 07971 419 919 Fax 0118 939 4900

Heather Bilbey Calligraphy, 15 Faustin Hill, Wetheral, Carlisle CA4 8JZ
Scribe: Heather Bilbey. No full-time staff. Began 1999; interdenominational. No magazine. Turnover: first year of operation. Creative calligraphy, commissions: greetings cards, posters, texts illuminated in various styles and languages.
☎ 01228 561 844 Fax 01228 561 844

***Black Christian Civic Forum, UK**, Mile End New Testament Church of God, Bow, London E3 5AT
Executive Director: Dr David Muir. Executive staff 1. *CC* Began 1999; interdenominational. No magazine. Turnover: first year of operation. Promoting citizenship, political education and civic participation in church and community.
Email: rakeshra@aol.com
☎ 020 8473 6771 Fax 020 8480 7914

Centre for Marketplace Theology, PO Box 18175, London EC1M 6AU
Director: Rev David Prior. No full-time staff. *CC* No.1062076. Began 1987; interdenominational. Turnover n/a. Independent support and teaching group for Christians working in the financial market.
Email: dprior.cmt@city.co.uk
☎ 020 8942 9128 Fax 020 8361 7598

***Centre for Christian Communication**, Cross Gate Centre, Alexandra Crescent, Durham DH1 4HF
Director: Mr Geoffrey Stevenson. Executive staff 1, Other staff 1. Began 1996; non-denominational. Linked to St John's College, Durham. No magazine. Turnover n/a. Training, education and research in communication and preaching in contemporary culture.
Web: xiancomm.org Email: dir@xiancomm.org
☎ 0191 374 4405 Fax 0191 374 4401

X

Christfirst Ltd, 28a Beulah Road, Thornton Heath CR7 8JG
Managing Director: Mr Anthony Martin. Executive staff 2, Other staff 2. Began 1997; interdenominational. No magazine. Turnover n/a. Manufacturing and supplying transparent acrylic furnishings for churches, schools, halls and meeting rooms.
Email: anthony@christfirst.org.uk
020 8771 2388 Mobile: 07778 804 809 020 8406 8285

Christian Action Networks (CANs), Evangelical Alliance, Whitefield House, 186 Kennington Park Road, London SE11 4BT
Development Manager: Mr Mannie Stewart. Executive staff 2. *CC* No.212325. Began n/a; interdenominational. An Evangelical Alliance initiative. Turnover n/a. Facilitating local forums concerning Christian social action and community development in UK's urban centres.
Email: cans@eauk.org
020 8207 2152 020 7207 2150

Christian Peoples Alliance, PO Box 932, Sutton SM1 1HQ
Chair: Mr David Campanale. Executive staff 1. Began 1999; interdenominational. Turnover: first year of operation. Political party in the Christian Democratic tradition; running candidates for public office.
Web: www.cpalliance.net
Email: info@cpalliance.net
020 8274 9043

Christians in Media, Maiden Outdoor Advertising, 24 Buckingham Palace Road, London SW1W 0QP
Coordinator: Francis Goodman. No full-time staff. Began n/a; non-denominational. No magazine. Turnover n/a. Association of professionals in advertising who produce campaigns for Christians.
Email: taryn.collins@maidenoutdoor.co.uk
020 7838 4000 020 7838 4002

***Crosswinds Prayer Trust**, PO Box 1041, Nailsea, Bristol BS48 4SD
National Director: Preb John Simons. Executive staff 2. *CC* No.1031629. Began 1994; interdenominational. Turnover £7,500 to year end Apr 98. Mobilising interdenominational prayer weeks within UK's 120 postcode areas, and global intercession via the internet.
Web: crosswindsprayer.com
Email: crosswinds@btinternet.com
01275 852 700 01275 794 952

***Dorcas Project**, 116 Bramley Road, London W10 6SU
Pastor: Rev Candido Giraldo. Executive staff 2, Admin staff 2. *CC* No.280694. Began 1960; interdenominational. No magazine. Turnover £25,000 to year end Mar 99. Advice centre for the welfare of the Hispanic community in London.
Email: dorcaspro@aol.com
020 8960 5634 / 964 1520 020 8960 5468

Emmaus House, 115 Valley Drive, Harrogate HG2 0JS
Matron/Manager: Mrs Christine Hornby. Other staff n/a. *CC* No.519535. Began 1987; interdenominational. Turnover n/a. Residential home for elderly Christians. Beds: 18 single, 8 double.
01423 565 932

***The Evangelical Alliance Conference Centre**, Whitefield House, 186 Kennington Park Road, London SE11 4BT
Conference Centre Administrator: Margaret Jones. No other staff. *CC* No.123448. Began n/a; interdenominational. Turnover: included in Evangelical Alliance. Non-residential conference centre with 3 conference rooms; catering available.
Email: mjones@eauk.org
020 7207 2100 020 7207 2100

Faith to Faith, Carrs Lane Church Centre, Carrs Lane, Birmingham B4 7SX
Director: Dr Ida Glaser. Executive staff 1. *CC* No.1070878. Began 1998; non-denominational. Magazine: *Faith to Faith* (1,500 every four months). Turnover £15,000 to year end Dec 98. Helping churches relate to and communicate with people of other faiths, through consultancy, training, research.
Email: i.glaser.crowther@sellyoak.ac.uk
0121 415 2313 0121 471 2662

Peter Foster Design, 23 Poplar Road, Bath BA2 2AJ
Proprietor: Mr Peter Foster. Executive staff 1, Admin staff 1. Began 1992; non-denominational. No magazine. Turnover £50,000 to year end Mar 99. Producing flags, banners, promotional support materials, graphic design and print.
01225 830 060 01225 830 060

Global Missions and Bible Training Institute, 281 Rye Lane, Peckham, London SE15 4UA
President/Founder: Bishop Paul Hackman Dip. Biblical Studies, ThD. Executive staff 3, Admin staff 2. *CC* No.1028128. Began 1994; Pentecostal. (Previously Global Missions Bible Institute). Magazine: *Global Missions News* (200 every four months). Turnover £22,000 to year end Mar 99. Offering 2-year diploma. Number of places: 16 male, 19 female; number of students: 16 male, 17 female. Tuition fee £1,500 pa.
Email: globalmiss@aol.com
020 7639 8619 Mobile: 07808 868 194 020 7639 8619

His Paper 'On the Internet', PO Box 15, Southwold IP18 6JX
Executive Editor & Proprietor: Mr Vic Ramsey. Executive staff 2, Other staff 2. Began 1972; non-denominational. Relaunched as web-zine, 1992. Turnover n/a.
Web: www.influenceuk.com
Email: hispaper@influenceuk.com
01502 725 069 01502 725 482

***Hospitable House**, 13 Kirchen Road, West Ealing, London W13 0TY
Pastor: Rev Candido Giraldo. Executive staff 2, Admin staff 2. *CC* No.280694. Began 1960; interdenominational. No magazine. Turnover £12,000 to year end Mar 99. Hostel for Spanish speaking girls aged 18 to 35 offering evangelism and practical help. 10 spaces.
Email: cevangelic@aol.com
020 8566 3458

***idea**, Evangelical Alliance, Whitefield House, 186 Kennington Park Road, London SE11 4BT
Editor: Phil Seager. *Advertisements:* Jack Merrifield. Other staff n/a. *CC* No.123448. Began n/a; interdenominational. Turnover: included in Evangelical Alliance. For EA members and others. Circulation 40,000 frequency five times a year.
Web: www.eauk.org
Email: info@eauk.org
020 7207 2100 020 7207 2150

Jentech Computers Ltd, Smithfield Christian Centre, Whitburn Street, Bridgnorth WV16 4QP
Managing Director: Mr A S Vincent. *Administrator:* Natalie Fisher. Executive staff 4, Admin staff 1. Began n/a; non-denominational. No magazine. Turnover £250,000 to year end Jan 99. Specialists in computer systems, supply, maintenance, support, accounts, office automation, internet, intranet, network installations.
Web: www.jentech.co.uk
Email: alan@jentech.co.uk
01746 761 458 01746 766 869

Jian Hua Foundation, 77 Southcliffe Road, Carlton, Nottingham NG4 1ES
Co-ordinator for Europe: Doug Plummer. Exec staff 1, No other full-time staff. *CC* No.327925. Began 1982; interdenominational. No magazine. Turnover n/a. Placing Christian professionals in China.
Email: dougplummer@compuserve.com
☎ 0115 911 0103 Fax 0115 911 1990

Kingham Hill School, Kingham, Chipping Norton OX7 6TH
Headmaster: Mr Michael Payne. Staff n/a. *CC* No.310031. Began 1886; interdenominational. Magazine: *The Hill* (2,000 every four months). Turnover n/a. Christian independent boarding and day school for 230 boys/girls aged 11 to 18. Also vacation camping/accommodation.
Web: www.kingham-hill.oxon.sch.uk
Email: admissions@kingham-hill.oxon.sch.uk
☎ 01608 658 999 Fax 01608 658 658

Latin Mass Society, 11 Macklin Street, London WC2B 5NH
Secretary: Mr David Lloyd. Admin staff 1. *CC* No.248388. Began 1965; Roman Catholic. No magazine. Turnover £72,000 to year end Mar 99. Promoting Catholic liturgy according to the Roman missal of 1962.
Web: www.sonnco.uk/credo/ims.htm
☎ 020 7404 7284 Fax 020 7831 5585

Liberal Catholic Church (Grail Community), Bishop's House and Oratory of Our Lady, Chalice House, Torridge Hill, Bideford EX39 2AZ
Bishop-in-Charge: Rt Rev Roy Bannister. Staff n/a, Serving ministers n/a. Began 1991. No magazine. Turnover n/a.
☎ 01237 424 737

Look & Listen Ministries, 20 Manor Road, Ruislip HA4 7LB
Director: Mr Bill Upchurch. Executive staff 1. Began 1994; non-denominational. No magazine. Turnover £35,000 to year end Mar 98. Facilitating visual media (videos, libraries) for churches/small organisations; specialising in video/data projectors.
Web: www.broch.com/llm
Email: llm@broch.com
☎ 08456 624 774 (local call) Fax 08456 624 775

March Christian Bookshop, 19a Station Road, March PE15 8LE
Manageress: n/a. Executive Staff 1, Other staff 2. Began 1992; non-denominational. Turnover n/a. Coffee shop. 2,300 Christian titles, 500 sq.ft.
☎ No telephone

Middleton Christian Bookshop, 6a Chapel Row, Middleton-in-Teesdale, Barnard Castle DL12 0SN
Co Director: Mr David Moore. Executive staff 1, Admin staff 2. Began 1999; non-denominational. Turnover: first year of operation. Christian gifts, cards and books. Titles stocked: 2,000 (all Christian); second hand titles: 20 (Christian), 200 sq.ft.
Web: www.teesdalecomputers.co.uk
Email: enquiries@teesdalecomputers.co.uk
☎ 01833 640 001 Fax 01833 840 414

***Derek Moon**, c/o Frinton Free Church, Connaught Avenue, Frinton-on-Sea CO13 9PW
Evangelist: Rev Derek J Moon. No full-time staff. Began n/a; interdenominational. No magazine. Turnover n/a. Evangelism through organ concerts with personal testimony.
Email: derek.moon@virgin.net
☎ 01255 679 585

New Life Radio, 29 Sydney Road, Exeter EX2 9AH
Director of Operations: Mr Mike Coles. Executive staff 2, Oth staff 1. Began 1998; interdenominational. No magazine. Tur over n/a. RSL Licensed radio station broadcasting gospel mi istry teaching on VHF FM. Two weeks annually, south Devor
Web: www.mike-coles-travel.co.uk-newliferadio
Email: nlr@mike-coles-travel.co.uk
☎ 01392 219 499 Fax 01392 275 296

Nimbus Press, 18 Guildford Road, Leicester LE2 2RB
Managing Editor: Clifford Sharp. Executive staff 2. Bega 1991; non-denominational. Turnover n/a. Fostering th writing of new plays on Christian themes, publishing dram humour, short books.
Email: sales@nimbuspress.demon.co.uk
☎ 0116 270 6318 Fax 0116 270 6318

Northern Light, 64 Greenhead Road, Utley, Keighley BD20 6ED
Administrator: Karl Jones. No full-time staff. Began 1997 interdenominational. No magazine. Turnover n/a. Family holi day conference week held annually, mid August in Nort Yorkshire.
Web: www.users.zetnet.co.uk/stmarks
Email: stmarks@zetnet.co.uk
☎ 01535 607 003 Fax 01535 611 353

The Open Churches Trust, 22 Tower Street, London WC2H 9NS
Administrator: Brigadier Adam Gurdon. Executive staff 1, Admin staff 1. *CC* No.1045248. Began 1994; ecumenical. No magazine. Turnover £50,000 to year end Apr 98. Opening to the public locked places of worship.
Web: www.merseyworld.com/faithful/html_file/octhead.htm
Email: oct@reallyuseful.co.uk
☎ 020 7240 0880 Fax 020 7240 1204

Orthodox Christian Books Ltd, 7 Townhouse Farm, Alsager Road, Audley, Stoke-on-Trent ST7 8JQ
Managing Director: Nicholas Chapman. Executive staff 4, Other staff 2. Began 1993; Orthodox. Turnover n/a. European distributors, book wholesalers, mail order retail (over 2,000 titles); cassettes, CDs, greeting cards.
Email: orthbook@aol.com
☎ 07000 790 330 Fax 01782 723 930

Parish Pump, PO Box 236, Macclesfield SK10 4GJ
Editor: Rev Taffy Davies. No full-time staff. Began 1999; interdenominational. Turnover none. Internet based magazine, editorial and graphic resource site for church magazines.
Web: www.parishpump.co.uk
Email: mail@parishpump.co.uk
☎ 01625 582 297 Fax 01625 582 297

Peniel Pentecostal Church, 49 Coxtie Green Road, Pilgrims Hatch, Brentwood CM14 5PS
Bishop: Rev Dr Michael S B Reid. Ordained and lay staff 34, Serving ministers 9. *CC* No.279287. Began 1976. No magazine. Turnover n/a.
Web: www.peniel.org
Email: mbsr@peniel.org
☎ 01277 372 996 Fax 01277 375 046

Posters Plus, 7 Belvedere Drive, Belvedere Hill, St Saviour, Jersey JE2 7RN
Administrator: Mrs Yvonne Coppock. No other staff. Began 1999; interdenominational. No magazine. Turnover n/a. Using books, articles and practical workshops to encourage creative poster-making as a means of evangelism.
☎ 01534 728 434

ʜe John Ray Initiative, Fach Gynan, Moelfre, Oswestry SY10 7QP
Secretary: Dr John Sale. No full-time staff. *CC* No.1067614. Began 1998; interdenominational. No magazine. Turnover £31,500 to year end Aug 98. Promoting environmental sustainability based on Christian principles and the wise use of science and technology.
Web: www.jri.org.uk
Email: johnsale@aol.com
☎ 01691 791 494 🖷 01691 791 404

he Reader, Church House, Great Smith Street, London SW1P 3NZ
Chairman, Editorial Committee: Nigel Holmes. No full-time staff. Began 1904; Anglican. (Previously The Reader and Lay Worker). Turnover n/a. Circulation 10,000 quarterly. Magazine re-launch February 2000.
Email: nigel@gt-corby.demon.co.uk
☎ 020 7898 1415 🖷 020 7898 1421

'he Reformed Liberal Catholic Church (Old Catholic), Diocese of England & The Channel Islands, 15 Falkland Road, Chandlers Ford, Eastleigh SO53 3FN
Diocesan Bishop: Rt Rev Richard Palmer. Other staff n/a, Serving ministers n/a. Began 1999. Magazine: *The Cornerstone* (Circulation n/a half-yearly). Turnover n/a.
☎ 023 8025 4726 🖷 023 8025 4726

Release Foundation, Oakwood Court, Sprint Hill, Arley, Coventry CV7 8FF
Training Director: Rev Christopher Spicer. Executive staff 1, Admin staff 1. *CC* No.1073329. Began 1998; interdenominational. No magazine. Turnover: first year of operation. Serving churches through an innovative learning process; enabling Christians to recognise and release God-given potential.
Web: www.releasefoundation.com
Email: enquiries@releasefoundation.com
☎ 01676 540 808 🖷 01676 540 606

Ship of Fools, PO Box 26245, London W3 9WH
Editor: Mr Simon Jenkins. No full-time staff. Began 1998; ecumenical. Turnover n/a. Internet magazine and online community: humour, satire, comment and discussion about Christianity in today's world.
Web: ship-of-fools.com
Email: editor@ship-of-fools.com
☎ No telephone 🖷 020 8752 0949

The Spire Trust, 60 Green Lane, Purley CR8 3PJ
National Director: Mr Michael Kirkwood. Executive staff 2. *CC* No.1067308. Began 1997; interdenominational. Magazine: *Spire update* (2,000 half-yearly). Turnover £90,000 to year end Dec 98. Working with local churches to provide support for pupils' spiritual development in secondary schools.
Email: 101623.2255@compuserve.com
☎ 020 8668 8850 🖷 020 8668 8850
Also at: Spire Greater Manchester, 28 Rothiemay Road, Flixton M41 6LP
Email: spire.gtr.mcr@talk21.com
☎ 0161 746 8081 🖷 0161 746 8081
And: Spire Southwest, Pitt Meadow, St Dominic, Saltash PL12 6SX
☎ 01579 350 940 🖷 01579 350 940

The Spring, The Lodge, Highmoor Hall, Highmoor, Henley-on-Thames RG9 5DH
The Administrator: n/a. Executive staff 1, No other full-time staff. *CC* No.1021038. Began 1995; interdenominational. No magazine. Turnover n/a. Offering retreats, quiet days; day seminars on arts and crafts, music, personal development, spirituality.
☎ 01491 641 167

Star Tours & Holidays, 50 Vivian Avenue, Hendon, London NW4 3XH
Executive Manager: Mr Chris Jones. Staff n/a. Began 1985; non-denominational. No magazine. Turnover n/a. Offering Israel tailor-made tours for Christian, youth, schools and special interest groups.
Web: www.travelink.uk.com/startours.htm
Email: startours@travelink.uk.com
☎ 020 8931 8811 🖷 020 8931 8877

Terra Nova Publications Ltd, PO Box 2400, Bradford-on-Avon BA15 2YN
Publisher Director: Rev Peter Byron-Davies. Full-time staff 2. Began n/a; interdenominational. Turnover n/a. Charismatic evangelical books. Books published 1998:2.
Email: terranovapublications@email.msn.com
☎ 01225 868 723 🖷 01225 864 755

Wales Lausanne Cymru, 23 Cherry Tree Road, The Bryn, Pontllanfraith, Blackwood NP2 2PY
Chairman: Mr Ron Spillards. No full-time staff. Began n/a; interdenominational. No magazine. Turnover n/a. Furthering in Wales the purposes of the International Lausanne movement.
☎ 01495 223 255

***Worldwide Harvest Ministries**, 41 Marlow Road, Maidenhead SL6 7AQ
President: Rev Eric Cowley. Admin staff 1. *CC* No.1005119. Began 1990; interdenominational. Magazine: *Newsletter* (Circulation n/a every four months). Turnover £16,203 to year end Dec 98. Evangelisation and church planting through Gospel crusades.
Web: www.worldwideharvest.org
Email: wwhuk@compuserve.com
☎ 01628 621 727 🖷 01628 777 084

X

TABLE 2: LARGEST ORGANISATIONS BY TURNOVER/INCOME

Organisations listed in the UK Christian Handbook and which reported their Turnover/Income, as exceeding £2 million
Where an organisation gave a band for its Turnover/Income, the midpoint has been taken for this Table.
Turnover /Income is given in millions.
These organisations form 3% of the addresses in the Handbook but account for 75% for the total income.

Ecclesiastical Insurance Group plc	£191.4
Church Commissioners	£135.3
Church of Scotland Board of Stewardship and Finance	£90.0
Salvation Army	£78.8
Help the Aged	£60.0
The Presbyterian Church in Ireland	£50.0
Christian Aid	£37.9
NCH Action for Children	£37.6
Salvation Army Social Services	£34.0
Church of Scotland Board of Social Responsibility	£33.5
Shaftesbury Housing Group	£32.0
The Children's Society	£26.0
YMCA, England	£25.5
Send The Light Ltd	£25.5
Springboard Housing Association Ltd	£24.9
Methodist Homes for the Aged	£24.6
Tearfund	£23.8
The Shaftesbury Society	£19.5
SDA Architects Ltd	£18.0
YWCA of Great Britain	£18.0
World Vision UK	£17.9
Shared Interest	£17.2
Nugent Care Society	£14.2
Church of Scotland General Trustees	£14.0
Catholic Fund for Overseas Development (CAFOD)	£14.0
Trinity Care plc	£13.8
Barchester Green Investment	£13.8
Key Travel	£13.5
Stewardship Services (United Kingdom Evangelization Trust Inc-UKET)	£11.9
Autosave (UK) Ltd	£10.8
Congregational and General Insurance plc	£10.7
Bible Society (The British and Foreign Bible Society)	£10.1
Society for Promoting Christian Knowledge (SPCK)	£10.1
ETS Tours for Churches	£10.0
Christian Tours (UK) Ltd	£10.0
Barnicoats	£10.0
Church Army	£8.2
Ansvar Insurance Company Ltd	£8.0
John Grooms	£8.0
Methodist Insurance plc	£7.3
Mission Aviation Fellowship	£7.1
Bolsius (UK) Ltd	£7.0
Traidcraft plc	£7.0
Hospitaller Order of St John of God	£7.0
St Christopher's Hospice	£7.0
Lion Publishing plc	£6.5
Scripture Union	£6.4
Church Mission Society	£6.1
Operation Mobilisation	£6.0
Church of England Diocese of Liverpool	£6.0
United Society for the Propagation of the Gospel	£5.9
Adullam Homes Housing Association Ltd	£5.8
Church of England Diocese of Gloucester	£5.7
Mission Care	£5.5
MasterSki	£5.0
St Cuthbert's Care	£5.0
M Wood Insurance Services Ltd	£5.0
Ethical Financial Ltd	£5.0
International Care and Relief (ICR)	£5.0
Church of England Diocese of Bristol	£5.0
World Emergency Relief	£4.9
BMS, Baptist Missionary Society	£4.8
OMF International (UK)	£4.6
Methodist Church World Church Office	£4.5
Battersea Churches and Chelsea Housing Trust	£4.5
ECHO International Health Services Ltd	£4.5
Catholic Institute for International Relations	£4.4
The Christian Children's Fund of Great Britain	£4.3
John Grooms Housing Association	£4.2
McCabe Pilgrimages	£4.0
Unigraph (UK) Ltd	£4.0
Allchurches Investment Ltd Management Services	£4.0
Mildmay Hospital UK	£4.0
The Leprosy Mission	£3.9
Pilgrim Homes	£3.8
The Churches Conservation Trust	£3.8
Church Urban Fund	£3.7
Universities and Colleges Christian Fellowship (UCCF)	£3.7
BibleLands	£3.5
British & International Sailors' Society	£3.5
Christian Publishers' Representatives	£3.5
PROSPECTS for People with Learning Disabilities	£3.5
Echoes of Service	£3.5
Salvationist Publishing and Supplies Ltd	£3.5
L'Arche	£3.5
Father Hudson's Society	£3.5
London City Mission	£3.4
Trinity Hospice, Clapham	£3.3
Pontifical Missionary Societies	£3.3
Catholic Children's Society	£3.2
Scope Productions Ltd	£3.2
Scottish Catholic International Aid Fund (SCIAF)	£3.2
Wycliffe Bible Translators	£3.1
The Missions to Seamen	£3.1
Field Lane Foundation	£3.1
Church of Scotland Board of World Mission	£3.1
HCPT The Pilgrimage Trust	£3.1
SIM UK (Society for International Ministries)	£3.0
Sovereign Giving	£3.0
Macedonian (Evangelical) Trust	£3.0
UCB Europe	£3.0
Clifford Frost Ltd	£3.0
St Christopher's Fellowship	£2.9
Boys' Brigade	£2.7
FEBA Radio	£2.7
Maxco Trust	£2
Church of Scotland Board of National Mission	£2
Newbold College	£2
Catholic Children's Rescue Society	£2
SGM International	£2
Youth With A Mission UK	£2
The Gideons International in the British Isles	£2.
Campsie Litho Ltd	£2.
Saint Mary's Hospice	£2.
Falmouth Beach Resort Hotel and Conference Centre	£2.
Alliance Music	£2.
CWR (Crusade for World Revival)	£2.
CAHA Christian Alliance Housing Association Ltd	£2.
The Christian Distributors' & Shippers' Association (CDSA)	£2.
The Flight Bureau	£2.
Royal National Mission to Deep Sea Fishermen	£2.5
The Good News Press Ltd	£2.5
West London Mission	£2.5
Echoes of Service	£2.4
International Fellowship of Evangelical Students	£2.4
The Corporation of the Church House	£2.4
The Langley House Trust	£2.3
Methodist Local Preachers Mutual Aid Association	£2.3
Burrswood Christian Centre for Healthcare and Ministry	£2.3
Toc H	£2.3
Wigwam Acoustics Ltd	£2.3
ECL Ltd	£2.3
Church Pastoral Aid Society	£2.2
Evangelical Alliance	£2.2
Kingdom Faith Church Offices	£2.2
Aid to the Church in Need	£2.1
World Association for Christian Communication	£2.1
Methodist Holiday Hotels Ltd, trading as Epworth Hotels	£2.1
Surecar Consultants	£2.1
Open Doors with Brother Andrew	£2.1
Christian Publicity Organisation	£2.0
Belfast Central Mission	£2.0
Castle Craig Clinic	£2.0
YMCA, St Helens	£2.0
Worldwide Group	£2.0
Byrom Clark Roberts Ltd	£2.0
AFD Computers/AFD Software Ltd	£2.0
C Goodliffe Neale Ltd	£2.0
Scripture Union Scotland	£2.0
YMCA, Romford	£2.0
Sarner International Ltd	£2.0

Total: 149 organisations in 1999
(compared with 144 in 1997)

INDEXES

COUNTIES & POSTCODES

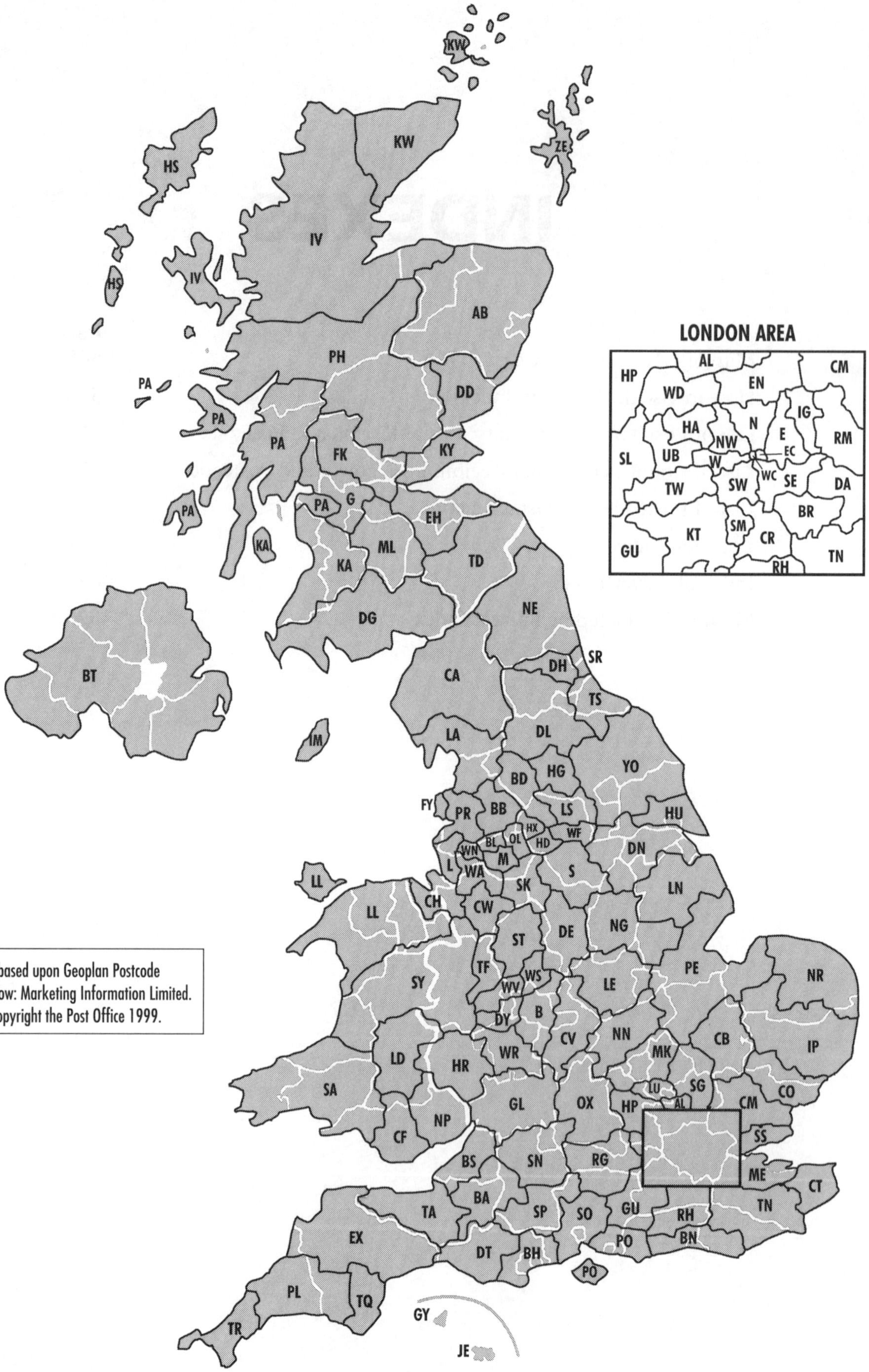

© Postcode maps based upon Geoplan Postcode Boundaries © Yellow: Marketing Information Limited. © Postcodes are copyright the Post Office 1999.

HOW TO USE THE LOCATION INDEX

OSTAL REGIONS

ıis Location Index is based on Postcodes rather than Counties, ecause of the confusion between geographical Counties and ocal Government Administrative Areas. It uses the Post Town ıd Postcode for each entry in the *Handbook*. Each address has een checked to ensure that these are included.

o retain an indication of which part of the UK an organisation is ased in, Royal Mail's Postal Regions have been used as the foun-ation of the Location Index. Postal Regions are specific to Royal Iail and are not identical either to Counties or to Local Govern-ıent Regions. The Postal Regions are:

	Page	Postcodes within the Region
ngland		
Anglia	581	AL, CB, CM, CO, EN, IG, IP, LU, MK, NR, PE, RM, SG, SS, WD
London	585	E, EC, N, NW, SE, SW, W, WC
Midlands	592	B, CV, DE, DY, LE, NG, NN, ST, WS, WV
North East	597	BD, DH, DL, DN, HD, HG, HU, HX, LN, LS, NE, S, SR, TD, TS, WF, YO
North West	600	BB, BL, CA, CH, CW, FY, L, LA, M, OL, PR, SK, SY, TF, WA, WN
South Central	604	GU, HA, HP, OX, PO, RG, SL, SN, SO, SP, UB
South East	609	BN, BR, CR, CT, DA, KT, ME, RH, SM, TN, TW
South West	613	BA, BH, BS, DT, EX, GL, HR, PL, TA, TQ, TR, WR
Channel Islands	617	GY, JE
Isle of Man	617	IM
Northern Ireland	617	BT
Scotland	619	AB, DD, DG, EH, FK, G, HS, IV, KA, KW, KY, ML, PA, PH, TD, ZE
Wales	623	CF, CH, LD, LL, NP, SA, SY

Organisations with an address in the **Republic of Ireland** but which serve Northern Ireland are also included (Page 619).

AIDS TO FINDING PLACES BY POSTCODE

1. Map The map on the previous page shows the correlation between Counties and Postal Regions. This map has been created specifically for the *Handbook*, and cannot be guaranteed to be totally accurate. We would be grateful if users of the *Handbook* would notify us of any errors so that they can be corrected in the next edition.

2. List of Post Towns. The list which starts below gives in alphabetical order each Post Town which has an organisation listed in the *Handbook*, showing the 'old' County under which it was listed in previous *Handbook* Location Indexes, followed by the Postal Region in which that town is located. Within each Postal Region in the Location Index, Postcodes are listed in alpha/numeric order using the first half of the Postcode (eg **Anglia** AL1 St Albans), so the list therefore also includes the two letters (eg AL).

Please note:
Some Postcodes may be found in an unexpected region!
Organisations at the same postal address are grouped together.
Three Postcodes straddle a national border and are therefore listed under two countries:

CH can be found in England (North West) and Wales
SY can be found in England (North West) and Wales
TD can be found in England (North East) and Scotland

3. List of 'old' Counties. The list on Page 575 gives the 'old' County name, and shows which Post Towns and Postcodes may be found within each.

4. List of Postcodes by Postal Region, on Page 580

POST TOWNS BY COUNTY, POSTAL REGION & POSTCODE

Post Town	'Old' County	Postal Region	Postcode
Aberdare	Mid Glamorgan	Wales	CF
Aberdeen	Aberdeenshire	Scotland	AB
Aberdovey	Gwynedd	Wales	LL
Abergele	Clwyd	Wales	LL
Abertillery	Gwent	Wales	NP
Aberystwyth	Dyfed	Wales	SY
Abingdon	Oxfordshire	South Central	OX
Accrington	Lancashire	North West	BB
Alcester	Warwickshire	Midlands	B
Alderley Edge	Cheshire	North West	SK
Aldershot	Hampshire	South Central	GU
Alfreton	Derbyshire	Midlands	DE
Alnwick	Northumberland	North East	NE
Alresford	Hampshire	South Central	SO
Alston	Cumbria	North West	CA
Alton	Hampshire	South Central	GU
Altrincham	Cheshire	North West	WA
Ambleside	Cumbria	North West	LA
Amersham	Buckinghamshire	South Central	HP
Ammanford	Dyfed	Wales	SA
Andover	Hampshire	South Central	SP
Anstruther	Fife	Scotland	KY
Appleby-in-Westmorland	Cumbria	North West	CA
Arbroath	Angus	Scotland	DD
Ardrossan	Ayrshire	Scotland	KA
Armagh	Co Armagh	Northern Ireland	BT
Arthog	Gwynedd	Wales	LL
Arundel	West Sussex	South East	BN
Ascot	Berkshire	South Central	SL
Ashbourne	Derbyshire	Midlands	DE
Ashford	Kent	South East	TN
Ashington	Northumberland	North East	NE
Ashtead	Surrey	South East	KT
Ashton-under-Lyne	Greater Manchester	North West	OL
Attleborough	Norfolk	Anglia	NR
Aviemore	Inverness-shire	Scotland	PH
Axminster	Devon	South West	EX
Aylesbury	Buckinghamshire	South Central	HP
Aylsham	Norfolk	Anglia	NR
Ayr	Ayrshire	Scotland	KA
Bala	Gwynedd	Wales	LL
Baldock	Hertfordshire	Anglia	SG
Ballachulish	Argyll	Scotland	PA
Ballycastle	Co Antrim	Northern Ireland	BT
Ballyclare	Co Antrim	Northern Ireland	BT
Ballygowan	Co Down	Northern Ireland	BT
Ballymena	Co Antrim	Northern Ireland	BT
Ballymoney	Co Antrim	Northern Ireland	BT
Banbridge	Co Down	Northern Ireland	BT
Banbury	Oxfordshire	South Central	OX
Banchory	Kincardineshire	Scotland	AB
Bangor	Co Down	Northern Ireland	BT
Bangor	Gwynedd	Wales	LL
Banstead	Surrey	South East	SM
Barking	Essex	Anglia	IG
Barnard Castle	Co Durham	North East	DL
Barnet	Hertfordshire	Anglia	EN
Barnsley	South Yorkshire	North East	S
Barnstaple	Devon	South West	EX
Barry	South Glamorgan	Wales	CF
Barton-upon-Humber	South Humberside	North East	DN
Basildon	Essex	Anglia	SS
Basingstoke	Hampshire	South Central	RG
Bath	Avon	South West	BA

Post Towns by County, Postal Region & Postcode

Post Town	'Old' County	Postal Region	Postcode
Battle	East Sussex	South East	TN
Beaconsfield	Buckinghamshire	South Central	HP
Beaumaris	Gwynedd	Wales	LL
Beccles	Suffolk	Anglia	NR
Beckenham	Kent	South East	BR
Bedford	Bedfordshire	Anglia	MK
Belfast	Co Antrim	Northern Ireland	BT
Belper	Derbyshire	Midlands	DE
Belvedere	Kent	South East	DA
Benfleet	Essex	Anglia	SS
Berkhamsted	Hertfordshire	South Central	HP
Berwick-upon-Tweed	Northumberland	North East	TD
Beverley	North Humberside	North East	HU
Bewdley	Worcestershire	Midlands	DY
Bexhill-on-Sea	East Sussex	South East	TN
Bicester	Oxfordshire	South Central	OX
Bideford	Devon	South West	EX
Biggar	Lanarkshire	Scotland	ML
Biggleswade	Bedfordshire	Anglia	SG
Billericay	Essex	Anglia	CM
Billingshurst	West Sussex	South East	RH
Bingley	West Yorkshire	North East	BD
Birkenhead	Merseyside	North West	L
Birmingham	West Midlands	Midlands	B
Bishop Auckland	Co Durham	North East	DL
Bishop's Stortford	Hertfordshire	Anglia	CM
Blackburn	Lancashire	North West	BB
Blackpool	Lancashire	North West	FY
Blackwood	Gwent	Wales	NP
Blaenau Ffestiniog	Gwynedd	Wales	LL
Blairgowrie	Perthshire	Scotland	PH
Blandford Forum	Dorset	South West	DT
Blaydon-on-Tyne	Tyne and Wear	North East	NE
Bo'Ness	West Lothian	Scotland	EH
Bognor Regis	West Sussex	South Central	PO
Boldon Colliery	Tyne and Wear	North East	NE
Bolton	Lancashire	North West	BL
Bonnyrigg	Midlothian	Scotland	EH
Bootle	Merseyside	North West	L
Bordon	Hampshire	South Central	GU
Borehamwood	Hertfordshire	Anglia	WD
Boston	Lincolnshire	Anglia	PE
Bourne	Lincolnshire	Anglia	PE
Bournemouth	Dorset	South West	BH
Bracknell	Berkshire	South Central	RG
Bradford	West Yorkshire	North East	BD
Bradford-on-Avon	Wiltshire	South West	BA
Braintree	Essex	Anglia	CM
Braunton	Devon	South West	EX
Brecon	Powys	Wales	LD
Brentford	Middlesex	South East	TW
Brentwood	Essex	Anglia	CM
Bridgend	Mid Glamorgan	Wales	CF
Bridgnorth	Shropshire	Midlands	WV
Bridgwater	Somerset	South West	TA
Bridlington	North Humberside	North East	YO
Bridport	Dorset	South West	DT
Brighouse	West Yorkshire	North East	HD
Brighton	East Sussex	South East	BN
Bristol	Avon	South West	BS
Broadway	Worcestershire	South West	WR
Bromley	Kent	South East	BR
Bromsgrove	Worcestershire	Midlands	B
Broughton-in-Furness	Lancashire	North West	LA
Buckfastleigh	Devon	South West	TQ
Buckhurst Hill	Essex	Anglia	IG
Buckie	Banffshire	Scotland	AB
Buckingham	Buckinghamshire	Anglia	MK
Bude	Cornwall	South West	EX
Builth Wells	Powys	Wales	LD
Bungay	Suffolk	Anglia	NR
Burgess Hill	West Sussex	South East	RH
Burnley	Lancashire	North West	BB
Burton-on-Trent	Staffordshire	Midlands	DE
Bury	Lancashire	North West	BL
Bury St Edmunds	Suffolk	Anglia	IG
Buxton	Derbyshire	North West	SK
Caernarfon	Gwynedd	Wales	LL
Caerphilly	Mid Glamorgan	Wales	CF
Calne	Wiltshire	South Central	SN

Post Town	'Old' County	Postal Region	Postcode
Camberley	Surrey	South Central	GU
Cambridge	Cambridgeshire	Anglia	CB
Camelford	Cornwall	South West	PL
Campbeltown	Argyll	Scotland	PA
Canterbury	Kent	South East	CT
Canvey Island	Essex	Anglia	SS
Cardiff	South Glamorgan	Wales	CF
Cardigan	Dyfed	Wales	SA
Carlisle	Cumbria	North West	CA
Carluke	Lanarkshire	Scotland	ML
Carmarthen	Dyfed	Wales	SA
Carnforth	Lancashire	North West	LA
Carrickfergus	Co Antrim	Northern Ireland	BT
Carshalton	Surrey	South East	SM
Castle Douglas	Kirkcudbrightshire	Scotland	DG
Castletown	Isle of Man	Isle of Man	IM
Castlewellan	Co Down	Northern Ireland	BT
Caterham	Surrey	South East	CR
Chard	Somerset	South West	TA
Chatham	Kent	South East	ME
Chatteris	Cambridgeshire	Anglia	PE
Cheadle	Cheshire	North West	SK
Cheddar	Somerset	South West	BS
Chelmsford	Essex	Anglia	CM
Cheltenham	Gloucestershire	South West	GL
Chepstow	Gwent	Wales	NP
Chesham	Buckinghamshire	South Central	HP
Chessington	Surrey	South East	KT
Chester	Cheshire	North West	CH
Chesterfield	Derbyshire	North East	S
Chichester	West Sussex	South Central	PO
Chippenham	Wiltshire	South Central	SN
Chipping Norton	Oxfordshire	South Central	OX
Choppington	Northumberland	North East	NE
Chorley	Lancashire	North West	PR
Christchurch	Dorset	South West	BH
Cinderford	Gloucestershire	South West	GL
Cirencester	Gloucestershire	South West	GL
Clacton-on-Sea	Essex	Anglia	CO
Cleethorpes	South Humberside	North East	DN
Clevedon	Avon	South West	BS
Clitheroe	Lancashire	North West	BB
Clynderwen	Dyfed	Wales	SA
Coalville	Leicestershire	Midlands	LE
Cobham	Surrey	South East	KT
Colchester	Essex	Anglia	CO
Coleraine	Co Londonderry	Northern Ireland	BT
Colwyn Bay	Clwyd	Wales	LL
Colyton	Devon	South West	EX
Coniston	Cumbria	North West	LA
Consett	Co Durham	North East	DH
Conwy	Gwynedd	Wales	LL
Cookstown	Co Tyrone	Northern Ireland	BT
Corby	Northamptonshire	Midlands	NN
Corwen	Clwyd	Wales	LL
Cottingham	North Humberside	North East	HU
Coulsdon	Surrey	South East	CR
Coventry	West Midlands	Midlands	CV
Craigavon	Co Armagh	Northern Ireland	BT
Cramlington	Northumberland	North East	NE
Cranleigh	Surrey	South Central	GU
Crawley	West Sussex	South East	RH
Crediton	Devon	South West	EX
Crewe	Cheshire	North West	CH
Crieff	Perthshire	Scotland	PH
Cromer	Norfolk	Anglia	NR
Crowborough	East Sussex	South East	TN
Croydon	Surrey	South East	CR
Cullompton	Devon	South West	EX
Cupar	Fife	Scotland	KY
Cwmbran	Gwent	Wales	NP
Dagenham	Essex	Anglia	RM
Dalbeattie	Kirkcudbrightshire	Scotland	DG
Dalgety Bay	Fife	Scotland	KY
Dalmally	Argyll	Scotland	PA
Dalry	Ayrshire	Scotland	KA
Darlington	Co Durham	North East	DL
Dartford	Kent	South East	DA
Darvel	Ayrshire	Scotland	KA
Daventry	Northamptonshire	Midlands	NN

st Town	'Old' County	Postal Region	Postcode
al	Kent	South East	CT
eside	Clwyd	Wales	CH
rby	Derbyshire	Midlands	DE
ereham	Norfolk	Anglia	NR
ewsbury	West Yorkshire	North East	WF
dcot	Oxfordshire	South Central	OX
inas Powis	South Glamorgan	Wales	CF
ingwall	Ross-shire	Scotland	IV
oncaster	South Yorkshire	North East	DN
ollar	Clackmannanshire	Scotland	FK
orchester	Dorset	South West	DT
orking	Surrey	South East	RH
ornoch	Sutherland	Scotland	IV
ouglas	Isle of Man	Isle of Man	IM
over	Kent	South East	CT
ownpatrick	Co Down	Northern Ireland	BT
riffield	North Humberside	North East	YO
roitwich	Worcestershire	South West	WR
ronfield	South Yorkshire	North East	S
udley	West Midlands	Midlands	DY
umbarton	Dunbartonshire	Scotland	G
umfries	Dumfriesshire	Scotland	DG
unbar	East Lothian	Scotland	EH
unblane	Perthshire	Scotland	FK
undee	Angus	Scotland	DD
unfermline	Fife	Scotland	KY
ungannon	Co Tyrone	Northern Ireland	BT
unkeld	Perthshire	Scotland	PH
unmow	Essex	Anglia	CM
unoon	Argyll	Scotland	PA
uns	Berwickshire	Scotland	TD
unstable	Bedfordshire	Anglia	LU
Durham	Co Durham	North East	DH
Dwygyfylchi	Gwynedd	Wales	LL
East Grinstead	West Sussex	South East	RH
East Molesey	Surrey	South East	KT
Eastbourne	East Sussex	South East	BN
Eastleigh	Hampshire	South Central	SO
Ebbw Vale	Gwent	Wales	NP
Edgware	Middlesex	South Central	HA
Edinburgh	Edinburgh	Scotland	EH
Egham	Surrey	South East	TW
Elgin	Morayshire	Scotland	IV
Ellesmere Port	Cheshire	North West	L
Ely	Cambridgeshire	Anglia	CB
Emsworth	Hampshire	South Central	PO
Enfield	Middlesex	Anglia	EN
Enniskillen	Co Fermanagh	Northern Ireland	BT
Epping	Essex	Anglia	EN
Epsom	Surrey	South East	KT
Erith	Kent	South East	DA
Exeter	Devon	South West	EX
Exmouth	Devon	South West	EX
Falkirk	Stirlingshire	Scotland	FK
Falmouth	Cornwall	South West	TR
Fareham	Hampshire	South Central	PO
Faringdon	Oxfordshire	South Central	OX
Farnborough	Hampshire	South Central	GU
Farnham	Surrey	South Central	GU
Faversham	Kent	South East	ME
Felixstowe	Suffolk	Anglia	IG
Ferndown	Dorset	South West	BH
Fishguard	Dyfed	Wales	SA
Fivemiletown	Co Tyrone	Northern Ireland	BT
Fleet	Hampshire	South Central	GU
Fleetwood	Lancashire	North West	FY
Flint	Clwyd	Wales	CH
Folkestone	Kent	South East	CT
Fort William	Inverness-shire	Scotland	PH
Fortrose	Ross-shire	Scotland	IV
Fraserburgh	Aberdeenshire	Scotland	AB
Freshwater	Isle of Wight	South Central	PO
Frinton-on-Sea	Essex	Anglia	CO
Frome	Somerset	South West	BA
Gairloch	Ross-shire	Scotland	IV
Galashiels	Selkirkshire	Scotland	TD
Garvagh	Co Londonderry	Northern Ireland	BT
Gateshead	Tyne and Wear	North East	NE

Post Town	'Old' County	Postal Region	Postcode
Gerrards Cross	Buckinghamshire	South Central	SL
Gillingham	Kent	South East	ME
Glasgow	Glasgow	Scotland	G
Glastonbury	Somerset	South West	BA
Glenrothes	Fife	Scotland	KY
Glossop	Derbyshire	Midlands	DE
Gloucester	Gloucestershire	South West	GL
Godalming	Surrey	South Central	GU
Gosport	Hampshire	South Central	PO
Grange-over-Sands	Cumbria	North West	LA
Grantham	Lincolnshire	Midlands	NG
Gravesend	Kent	South East	DA
Great Missenden	Buckinghamshire	South Central	HP
Greenford	Middlesex	South Central	UB
Greenock	Renfrewshire	Scotland	PA
Grimsby	South Humberside	North East	DN
Guernsey	Channel Islands	Channel Islands	GY
Guildford	Surrey	South Central	GU
Guisborough	North Yorkshire	North East	TS
Gullane	East Lothian	Scotland	EH
Haddington	East Lothian	Scotland	EH
Hailsham	East Sussex	South East	BN
Halesowen	West Midlands	Midlands	B
Halifax	West Yorkshire	North East	HX
Halstead	Essex	Anglia	CO
Haltwhistle	Northumberland	North East	NE
Hamilton	Lanarkshire	Scotland	ML
Hampton	Middlesex	South East	TW
Harlow	Essex	Anglia	CM
Harleston	Norfolk	Anglia	IP
Harpenden	Hertfordshire	Anglia	AL
Harrogate	North Yorkshire	North East	HG
Harrow	Middlesex	South Central	HA
Hartlepool	Cleveland	North East	TS
Harwich	Essex	Anglia	CO
Haslemere	Surrey	South Central	GU
Hassocks	West Sussex	South East	BN
Hastings	East Sussex	South East	TN
Havant	Hampshire	South Central	PO
Haverfordwest	Dyfed	Wales	SA
Hawick	Roxburghshire	Scotland	TD
Hayes	Middlesex	South Central	UB
Haywards Heath	West Sussex	South East	RH
Heathfield	East Sussex	South East	TN
Helensburgh	Dunbartonshire	Scotland	G
Helston	Cornwall	South West	TR
Hemel Hempstead	Hertfordshire	South Central	HP
Henfield	West Sussex	South East	BN
Henley-on-Thames	Oxfordshire	South Central	RG
Hereford	Herefordshire	South West	HR
Herne Bay	Kent	South East	CT
Hertford	Hertfordshire	Anglia	SG
Hessle	North Humberside	North East	HU
Hexham	Northumberland	North East	NE
Heywood	Lancashire	North West	OL
High Wycombe	Buckinghamshire	South Central	HP
Highbridge	Somerset	South West	TA
High Peak	Cheshire	North West	SK
Hinckley	Leicestershire	Midlands	LE
Hitchin	Hertfordshire	Anglia	SG
Hockley	Essex	Anglia	SS
Hoddesdon	Hertfordshire	Anglia	EN
Holsworthy	Devon	South West	EX
Holt	Norfolk	Anglia	NR
Holyhead	Gwynedd	Wales	LL
Holywood	Co Down	Northern Ireland	BT
Honiton	Devon	South West	EX
Hook	Hampshire	South Central	RG
Hope Valley	Derbyshire	North East	S
Horley	Surrey	South East	RH
Hornchurch	Essex	Anglia	RM
Horsham	West Sussex	South East	RH
Houghton le Spring	Tyne and Wear	North East	DH
Hounslow	Middlesex	South East	TW
Hove	East Sussex	South East	BN
Huddersfield	West Yorkshire	North East	HD
Hull	North Humberside	North East	HU
Hungerford	Berkshire	South Central	RG
Hunstanton	Norfolk	Anglia	PE
Huntingdon	Cambridgeshire	Anglia	PE

Post Towns by County, Postal Region & Postcode

Post Town	'Old' County	Postal Region	Postcode
Hyde	Cheshire	North West	SK
Hythe	Kent	South East	CT
Ilford	Essex	Anglia	IG
Ilfracombe	Devon	South West	EX
Ilkeston	Derbyshire	Midlands	DE
Ilkley	West Yorkshire	North East	LS
Ingatestone	Essex	Anglia	CH
Inverness	Inverness-shire	Scotland	IV
Inverurie	Aberdeenshire	Scotland	AB
Ipswich	Suffolk	Anglia	IP
Irvine	Ayrshire	Scotland	KA
Isleworth	Middlesex	South East	TW
Jersey	Channel Islands	Channel Islands	JE
Johnston	Renfrewshire	Scotland	PA
Keighley	West Yorkshire	North East	BD
Kelso	Roxburghshire	Scotland	TD
Kendal	Cumbria	North West	LA
Kenilworth	Warwickshire	Midlands	CV
Keswick	Cumbria	North West	CA
Kettering	Northamptonshire	Midlands	NN
Kidderminster	Worcestershire	Midlands	DY
Kidlington	Oxfordshire	South Central	OX
Kilbirnie	Ayrshire	Scotland	KA
Killin	Perthshire	Scotland	FK
Kilmarnock	Ayrshire	Scotland	KA
Kilwinning	Ayrshire	Scotland	KA
King's Lynn	Norfolk	Anglia	PE
Kings Langley	Hertfordshire	Anglia	WD
Kingsbridge	Devon	South West	TQ
Kingston upon Thames	Surrey	South East	KT
Kingswinford	West Midlands	Midlands	DY
Kingussie	Inverness-shire	Scotland	PH
Kirkby Lonsdale	Cumbria	North West	LA
Kirkby Stephen	Cumbria	North West	CA
Kirkcaldy	Fife	Scotland	KY
Knighton	Powys	Wales	LD
Knutsford	Cheshire	North West	WA
Kyle	Ross-shire	Scotland	IV
Kyleakin	Isle of Skye	Scotland	IV
Lanark	Lanarkshire	Scotland	ML
Lancaster	Lancashire	North West	LA
Lancing	West Sussex	South East	BN
Larbert	Stirlingshire	Scotland	FK
Larne	Co Antrim	Northern Ireland	BT
Latheron	Caithness	Scotland	KW
Launceston	Cornwall	South West	PL
Leamington Spa	Warwickshire	Midlands	CV
Leatherhead	Surrey	South East	KT
Ledbury	Herefordshire	South West	HR
Leeds	West Yorkshire	North East	LS
Leicester	Leicestershire	Midlands	LE
Leigh	Lancashire	North West	WN
Leigh-on-Sea	Essex	Anglia	SS
Leighton Buzzard	Bedfordshire	Anglia	LU
Leiston	Suffolk	Anglia	IP
Leominster	Herefordshire	South West	HR
Lerwick	Isle of Shetland	Scotland	ZE
Letchworth	Hertfordshire	Anglia	SG
Lewes	East Sussex	South East	BN
Leyburn	North Yorkshire	North East	DL
Lichfield	Staffordshire	Midlands	WS
Lightwater	Surrey	South Central	GU
Lincoln	Lincolnshire	North East	LN
Lingfield	Surrey	South East	RH
Liphook	Hampshire	South Central	GU
Lisburn	Co Antrim	Northern Ireland	BT
Liss	Hampshire	South Central	GU
Littleborough	Lancashire	North West	OL
Littlehampton	West Sussex	South East	BN
Liverpool	Merseyside	North West	L
Livingston	West Lothian	Scotland	EH
Llanbedr	Gwynedd	Wales	LL
Llandrindod Wells	Powys	Wales	LD
Llandudno	Gwynedd	Wales	LL
Llandysul	Dyfed	Wales	SA
Llanelli	Dyfed	Wales	SA
Llangollen	Clwyd	Wales	LL

Post Town	'Old' County	Postal Region	Postco
Llanidloes	Powys	Wales	SY
Llanrwst	Gwynedd	Wales	LL
Llanwrda	Dyfed	Wales	SA
Llanymynech	Powys	Wales	SY
Loanhead	Midlothian	Scotland	EH
Lochcarron	Ross-shire	Scotland	IV
Lochwinnoch	Renfrewshire	Scotland	PA
Lockerbie	Dumfriesshire	Scotland	DG
London	London	London E, EC, N, NW, SE, SW, W, WC	
Londonderry	Co Londonderry	Northern Ireland	BT
Loughborough	Leicestershire	Midlands	LE
Loughton	Essex	Anglia	IG
Lowestoft	Suffolk	Anglia	NR
Ludlow	Shropshire	North West	SY
Lurgan	Co Antrim	Northern Ireland	BT
Luton	Bedfordshire	Anglia	LU
Luston	Herefordshire	South West	HR
Lutterworth	Leicestershire	Midlands	LE
Lydney	Gloucestershire	South West	GL
Lyme Regis	Dorset	South West	DT
Lymington	Hampshire	South Central	SO
Lyndhurst	Hampshire	South Central	SO
Lynton	Devon	South West	EX
Lytham St Annes	Lancashire	North West	FY
Macclesfield	Cheshire	North West	SK
Maidenhead	Berkshire	South Central	SL
Maidstone	Kent	South East	ME
Maldon	Essex	Anglia	CM
Malmesbury	Wiltshire	South Central	SN
Malpas	Cheshire	North West	SY
Maltby	South Yorkshire	North East	S
Malvern	Worcestershire	South West	WR
Manchester	Greater Manchester	North West	M
Mansfield	Nottinghamshire	Midlands	NG
March	Cambridgeshire	Anglia	PE
Margate	Kent	South East	CT
Market Drayton	Shropshire	North West	TF
Market Harborough	Leicestershire	Midlands	LE
Marlborough	Wiltshire	South Central	SN
Maryport	Cumbria	North West	CA
Matlock	Derbyshire	Midlands	DE
Meifod	Powys	Wales	SY
Melksham	Wiltshire	South Central	SN
Melton Mowbray	Leicestershire	Midlands	LE
Mere	Wiltshire	South West	BA
Mexborough	South Yorkshire	North East	S
Middlesbrough	Cleveland	North West	TS
Middlewich	Cheshire	North West	CW
Midhurst	West Sussex	South Central	GU
Milton Keynes	Buckinghamshire	Anglia	MK
Minehead	Somerset	South West	TA
Mirfield	West Yorkshire	North East	WF
Mitcham	Surrey	South East	CR
Mitcheldean	Gloucestershire	South West	GL
Mold	Clwyd	Wales	CH
Monmouth	Gwent	Wales	NP
Montgomery	Powys	Wales	SY
Montrose	Angus	Scotland	DD
Morden	Surrey	South East	SM
Morecambe	Lancashire	North West	LA
Morpeth	Northumberland	North East	NE
Motherwell	Lanarkshire	Scotland	ML
Musselburgh	Midlothian	Scotland	EH
Nairn	Inverness-shire	Scotland	IV
Nantwich	Cheshire	North West	CW
Nelson	Lancashire	North West	BB
Nethy Bridge	Inverness-shire	Scotland	PH
New Malden	Surrey	South East	KT
Newark	Nottinghamshire	Midlands	NG
Newbury	Berkshire	South Central	RG
Newcastle	Co Down	Northern Ireland	BT
Newcastle	Staffordshire	Midlands	ST
Newcastle upon Tyne	Tyne and Wear	North East	NE
Newcastleton	Roxburghshire	Scotland	TD
Newent	Gloucestershire	South West	GL
Newmarket	Suffolk	Anglia	CB
Newnham	Gloucestershire	South West	GL
Newport	Gwent	Wales	NP

st Town	'Old' County	Postal Region	Postcode
ewport	Isle of Wight	South Central	PO
ewport	Shropshire	North West	TF
ewport Pagnell	Buckinghamshire	Anglia	MK
ewquay	Cornwall	South West	TR
ewry	Co Down	Northern Ireland	BT
ewton Abbot	Devon	South West	TQ
ewtown	Powys	Wales	SY
ewtownabbey	Co Antrim	Northern Ireland	BT
ewtownards	Co Down	Northern Ireland	BT
orth Berwick	East Lothian	Scotland	EH
orth Walsham	Norfolk	Anglia	NR
orthallerton	North Yorkshire	North East	DL
orthampton	Northamptonshire	Midlands	NN
orthwich	Cheshire	North West	CW
orthwood	Middlesex	South Central	HA
orwich	Norfolk	Anglia	NR
ottingham	Nottinghamshire	Midlands	NG
uneaton	Warwickshire	Midlands	CV
akham	Leicestershire	Midlands	LE
ban	Argyll	Scotland	PA
kehampton	Devon	South West	EX
ldbury	West Midlands	Midlands	B
ldham	Lancashire	North West	OL
magh	Co Tyrone	Northern Ireland	BT
ngar	Essex	Anglia	CM
rmskirk	Lancashire	North West	L
rpington	Kent	South East	BR
ssett	West Yorkshire	North East	WF
swestry	Shropshire	North West	SY
tley	West Yorkshire	North East	LS
xford	Oxfordshire	South Central	OX
xted	Surrey	South East	RH
aignton	Devon	South West	TQ
aisley	Renfrewshire	Scotland	PA
eacehaven	East Sussex	South East	BN
embroke	Dyfed	Wales	SA
enarth	South Glamorgan	Wales	CF
enmaenmawr	Gwynedd	Wales	LL
enrith	Cumbria	North West	CA
Penryn	Cornwall	South West	TR
Penzance	Cornwall	South West	TR
Pershore	Worcestershire	South West	WR
Perth	Perthshire	Scotland	PH
Peterborough	Cambridgeshire	Anglia	PE
Peterhead	Aberdeenshire	Scotland	AB
Peterlee	Co Durham	North East	SR
Petersfield	Hampshire	South Central	GU
Pewsey	Wiltshire	South Central	SN
Pinner	Middlesex	South Central	HA
Pitlochry	Perthshire	Scotland	PH
Plymouth	Devon	South West	PL
Pontefract	West Yorkshire	North East	WF
Pontypool	Gwent	Wales	NP
Pontypridd	Mid Glamorgan	Wales	NP
Poole	Dorset	South West	BH
Port Isaac	Cornwall	South West	PL
Port Talbot	West Glamorgan	Wales	SA
Porthcawl	Mid Glamorgan	Wales	CF
Porthmadog	Gwynedd	Wales	LL
Portree	Isle of Skye	Scotland	IV
Portrush	Co Antrim	Northern Ireland	BT
Portsmouth	Hampshire	South Central	PO
Potters Bar	Hertfordshire	Anglia	EN
Poulton-le-Fylde	Lancashire	North West	FY
Poynton	Cheshire	North West	SK
Prescot	Merseyside	North West	L
Prestatyn	Clwyd	Wales	LL
Preston	Lancashire	North West	PR
Prestwick	Ayrshire	Scotland	KA
Princes Risborough	Buckinghamshire	South Central	HP
Prudhoe	Northumberland	North East	NE
Pulborough	West Sussex	South East	RH
Purley	Surrey	South East	CR
Pwllheli	Gwynedd	Wales	LL
Radlett	Hertfordshire	Anglia	WD
Rainham	Essex	Anglia	RM
Ramsey	Isle of Man	Isle of Man	IM
Ramsgate	Kent	South East	CT

Post Town	'Old' County	Postal Region	Postcode
Randalstown	Co Antrim	Northern Ireland	BT
Rayleigh	Essex	Anglia	SS
Reading	Berkshire	South Central	RG
Redcar	Cleveland	North East	TS
Redditch	Worcestershire	Midlands	B
Redhill	Surrey	South East	RH
Redruth	Cornwall	South West	TR
Reigate	Surrey	South East	RH
Retford	Nottinghamshire	North East	DN
Rhyl	Clwyd	Wales	LL
Richmond	North Yorkshire	North East	DL
Richmond	Surrey	South East	TW
Rickmansworth	Hertfordshire	Anglia	WD
Riding Mill	Northumberland	North East	NE
Ringwood	Hampshire	South West	BH
Ripley	Derbyshire	Midlands	DE
Ripon	North Yorkshire	North East	HG
Robertsbridge	East Sussex	South East	TN
Rochdale	Lancashire	North West	OL
Rochester	Kent	South East	ME
Rochford	Essex	Anglia	SS
Romford	Essex	Anglia	RM
Romsey	Hampshire	South Central	SO
Ross-on-Wye	Herefordshire	South West	HR
Rossendale	Lancashire	North West	BB
Rotherham	South Yorkshire	North East	S
Royston	Hertfordshire	Anglia	SG
Rugby	Warwickshire	Midlands	CV
Rugeley	Staffordshire	Midlands	WS
Ruislip	Middlesex	South Central	HA
Rushden	Northamptonshire	Midlands	NN
Ruthin	Clwyd	Wales	LL
Ryde	Isle of Wight	South Central	PO
Rye	East Sussex	South East	TN
Ryton	Tyne and Wear	North East	NE
St Albans	Hertfordshire	Anglia	AL
St Andrews	Fife	Scotland	KY
St Asaph	Clwyd	Wales	LL
St Austell	Cornwall	South West	PL
St Davids	Dyfed	Wales	SA
St Helens	Merseyside	North West	WA
St Ives	Cornwall	South West	TR
St Leonards-on-Sea	East Sussex	South East	TN
Saffron Walden	Essex	Anglia	CB
Sale	Cheshire	North West	M
Salford	Lancashire	North West	M
Salisbury	Wiltshire	South Central	SP
Saltburn-by-the-Sea	Cleveland	North West	TS
Saltcoats	Ayrshire	Scotland	KA
Sandbach	Cheshire	North West	CW
Sandown	Isle of Wight	South Central	PO
Sandwich	Kent	South East	CT
Sandy	Bedfordshire	Anglia	SG
Sawbridgeworth	Hertfordshire	Anglia	CM
Scarborough	North Yorkshire	North East	YO
Scunthorpe	South Humberside	North East	DN
Seaford	East Sussex	South East	BN
Seaham	Co Durham	North East	SR
Seahouses	Northumberland	North East	NE
Seaton	Devon	South West	EX
Sevenoaks	Kent	South East	TN
Shaftesbury	Dorset	South Central	SP
Sheffield	South Yorkshire	North East	S
Shepperton	Middlesex	South East	TW
Sherborne	Dorset	South West	DT
Sheringham	Norfolk	Anglia	NR
Shetland	Isle of Shetland	Scotland	ZE
Shrewsbury	Shropshire	North West	SY
Sidcup	Kent	South East	DA
Sidmouth	Devon	South West	EX
Sittingbourne	Kent	South East	ME
Skelmersdale	Lancashire	North West	WN
Skipton	North Yorkshire	North East	BD
Sleaford	Lincolnshire	Midlands	NG
Slough	Berkshire	South Central	SL
Solihull	West Midlands	Midlands	B
South Croydon	Surrey	South East	CR
South Petherton	Somerset	South West	TA
South Queensferry	West Lothian	Scotland	EH

Post Towns by County, Postal Region & Postcode

Post Town	'Old' County	Postal Region	Postcode
South Shields	Tyne & Wear	North East	NE
South Wirral	Merseyside	North West	L
Southall	Middlesex	South Central	UB
Southampton	Hampshire	South Central	SO
Southend-on-Sea	Essex	Anglia	SS
Southminster	Essex	Anglia	CM
Southport	Merseyside	North West	PR
Southsea	Hampshire	South Central	SO
Southwell	Nottinghamshire	Midlands	NG
Spalding	Lincolnshire	Anglia	PE
Stafford	Staffordshire	Midlands	ST
Staines	Middlesex	South East	TW
Stalybridge	Cheshire	North West	SK
Stamford	Lincolnshire	Anglia	PE
Stevenage	Hertfordshire	Anglia	SG
Stirling	Stirlingshire	Scotland	FK
Stockport	Cheshire	North West	SK
Stocksfield	Northumberland	North East	NE
Stockton-on-Tees	Cleveland	North East	TS
Stoke-on-Trent	Staffordshire	Midlands	ST
Stone	Staffordshire	Midlands	ST
Stonehaven	Kincardineshire	Scotland	AB
Stornoway	Isle of Lewis	Scotland	HS
Stourbridge	West Midlands	Midlands	DY
Stourport-on-Severn	Worcestershire	Midlands	DY
Stowmarket	Suffolk	Anglia	IP
Stratford-upon-Avon	Warwickshire	Midlands	CV
Stroud	Gloucestershire	South West	GL
Sudbury	Suffolk	Anglia	CO
Sunbury-on-Thames	Middlesex	South East	TW
Sunderland	Tyne and Wear	North East	SR
Surbiton	Surrey	South East	KT
Sutton	Surrey	South East	SM
Sutton Coldfield	West Midlands	Midlands	B
Sutton-in-Ashfield	Nottinghamshire	Midlands	NG
Swadlincote	Derbyshire	Midlands	DE
Swaffham	Norfolk	Anglia	PE
Swanage	Dorset	South West	BH
Swanley	Kent	South East	BR
Swansea	West Glamorgan	Wales	SA
Swindon	Wiltshire	South Central	SN
Tain	Ross-shire	Scotland	IV
Talybont	Gwynedd	Wales	LL
Tarbert	Argyll	Scotland	PA
Tamworth	Staffordshire	Midlands	B
Taunton	Somerset	South West	TA
Tavistock	Devon	South West	PL
Teddington	Middlesex	South East	TW
Teignmouth	Devon	South West	TW
Telford	Shropshire	North West	TF
Templecombe	Somerset	South West	BA
Tenby	Dyfed	Wales	SA
Tewkesbury	Gloucestershire	South West	GL
Thame	Oxfordshire	South Central	OX
Thatcham	Berkshire	South Central	RG
Thetford	Norfolk	Anglia	IP
Thirsk	North Yorkshire	North East	YO
Thornton Heath	Surrey	South East	CR
Thurso	Caithness	Scotland	KW
Tilbury	Essex	Anglia	RM
Tipton	West Midlands	Midlands	DY
Tiverton	Devon	South West	EX
Tonbridge	Kent	South East	TN
Torquay	Devon	South West	TQ
Torrington	Devon	South West	EX
Totland Bay	Isle of Wight	South Central	PO
Towcester	Northamptonshire	Midlands	NN
Tranent	East Lothian	Scotland	EH
Tring	Hertfordshire	South Central	HP
Trowbridge	Wiltshire	South Central	SN
Truro	Cornwall	South West	TR
Tunbridge Wells	Kent	South East	TN
Turriff	Aberdeenshire	Scotland	AB
Twickenham	Middlesex	South East	TW
Tywyn	Gwynedd	Wales	LL
Uckfield	East Sussex	South East	TN
Ullapool	Ross-shire	Scotland	IV
Ulverston	Cumbria	North West	LA

Post Town	'Old' County	Postal Region	Postcode
Upminster	Essex	Anglia	RM
Upton-upon-Severn	Worcestershire	South West	WR
Uxbridge	Middlesex	South Central	UB
Ventnor	Isle of Wight	South Central	PO
Wadebridge	Cornwall	South West	PL
Wakefield	West Yorkshire	North East	WF
Wallasey	Merseyside	North West	L
Wallingford	Oxfordshire	South Central	OX
Wallington	Surrey	South East	SM
Walsall	West Midlands	Midlands	WS
Walsingham	Norfolk	Anglia	NR
Walton on the Naze	Essex	Anglia	CO
Walton-on-Thames	Surrey	South East	KT
Wantage	Oxfordshire	South Central	OX
Ware	Hertfordshire	Anglia	SG
Warley	West Midlands	Midlands	B
Warminster	Wiltshire	South West	BA
Warrington	Cheshire	North West	WA
Warwick	Warwickshire	Midlands	CV
Watchet	Somerset	South West	TA
Watford	Hertfordshire	Anglia	WD
Welling	Kent	South East	DA
Wellingborough	Northamptonshire	Midlands	NN
Wells	Somerset	South West	BA
Welshpool	Powys	Wales	SY
Welwyn	Hertfordshire	Anglia	AL
Welwyn Garden City	Hertfordshire	Anglia	AL
Wembley	Middlesex	South Central	HA
West Bromwich	West Midlands	Midlands	B
West Byfleet	Surrey	South East	KT
West Drayton	Middlesex	South Central	UB
West Linton	Peeblesshire	Scotland	EH
West Malling	Kent	South East	ME
West Wickham	Kent	South East	BR
Westbury	Wiltshire	South West	BA
Westcliff-on-Sea	Essex	Anglia	SS
Westerham	Kent	South East	TN
Westgate-on-Sea	Kent	South East	CT
Weston-super-Mare	Avon	South West	BS
Wetherby	West Yorkshire	North East	LS
Weybridge	Surrey	South East	KT
Weymouth	Dorset	South West	DT
Whitby	North Yorkshire	North East	YO
Whitchurch	Hampshire	South Central	RG
Whitchurch	Shropshire	North West	SY
Whitehaven	Cumbria	North West	CA
Whitland	Dyfed	Wales	SA
Whitley Bay	Tyne and Wear	North East	NE
Whitstable	Kent	South East	CT
Wickford	Essex	Anglia	SS
Widnes	Cheshire	North West	WA
Wigan	Lancashire	North West	WN
Wigton	Cumbria	North West	CA
Willenhall	West Midlands	Midlands	WV
Wilmslow	Cheshire	North West	SK
Wimborne	Dorset	South West	BH
Winchester	Hampshire	South Central	SO
Windermere	Cumbria	North West	LA
Windsor	Berkshire	South Central	SL
Winscombe	Somerset	South West	BS
Wirral	Merseyside	North West	L
Wisbech	Cambridgeshire	Anglia	PE
Wishaw	Lanarkshire	Scotland	ML
Witham	Essex	Anglia	CM
Witney	Oxfordshire	South Central	OX
Woking	Surrey	South Central	GU
Wokingham	Berkshire	South Central	RG
Wolverhampton	West Midlands	Midlands	WV
Wolverton	Buckinghamshire	Anglia	MK
Woodford Green	Essex	Anglia	IG
Wooler	Northumberland	North East	NE
Worcester	Worcestershire	South West	WR
Worthing	West Sussex	South East	BN
Wrexham	Clwyd	Wales	LL
Yelverton	Devon	South West	PL
Yeovil	Somerset	South West	BA
Ynys Môn	Gwynedd	Wales	LL
York	North Yorkshire	North East	YO

COUNTIES BY POSTAL REGION, POSTCODE AND POST TOWNS

ld' County	Postal Region	Postcode	Post Towns
berdeenshire	Scotland	AB	Aberdeen
			Fraserburgh
			Inverurie
			Peterhead
			Turriff
ngus	Scotland	DD	Arbroath
			Dundee
			Montrose
rgyll	Scotland	PA	Ballachulish
			Campbeltown
			Dalmally
			Dunoon
			Oban
			Tarbert
von	South West	BA	Bath
		BS	Bristol
			Clevedon
			Weston-super-Mare
yrshire	Scotland	KA	Ardrossan
			Ayr
			Dalry
			Darvel
			Irvine
			Kilbirnie
			Kilmarnock
			Kilwinning
			Prestwick
			Saltcoats
Banffshire	Scotland	AB	Buckie
Bedfordshire	Anglia	LU	Dunstable
			Leighton Buzzard
			Luton
		MK	Bedford
		SG	Biggleswade
			Sandy
Belfast	Northern Ireland	BT	Belfast
Berkshire	South Central	RG	Bracknell
			Hungerford
			Newbury
			Reading
			Thatcham
			Wokingham
	South Central	SL	Ascot
			Maidenhead
			Slough
			Windsor
Berwickshire	Scotland	TD	Duns
Buckinghamshire	Anglia	MK	Buckingham
			Milton Keynes
			Newport Pagnell
			Wolverton
	South Central	HP	Amersham
			Aylesbury
			Beaconsfield
			Chesham
			Gerrards Cross
			Great Missenden
			High Wycombe
			Princes Risborough
Caithness	Scotland	KW	Latheron
			Thurso
Cambridgeshire	Anglia	CB	Cambridge
			Ely
		PE	Chatteris
			Huntingdon
			March
			Peterborough
			Wisbech
Channel Islands	Channel Islands	GY	Guernsey
		JE	Jersey
Cheshire	North West	CH	Chester
			Crewe
		CW	Middlewich
			Nantwich
			Northwich
			Sandbach
		L	Ellesmere Port
		M	Sale

'Old' County	Postal Region	Postcode	Post Towns
		SK	Alderley Edge
			Cheadle
			High Peak
			Hyde
			Macclesfield
			Poynton
			Stalybridge
			Stockport
			Wilmslow
		SY	Malpas
		WA	Altrincham
			Knutsford
			Warrington
			Widnes
Clackmannanshire	Scotland	FK	Dollar
Cleveland	North West	TS	Hartlepool
			Middlesbrough
			Redcar
			Saltburn-by-the-Sea
			Stockton-on-Tees
Clwyd	Wales	CH	Deeside
			Flint
			Mold
			Abergele
			Colwyn Bay
			Corwen
			Llangollen
			Prestatyn
			Rhyl
			Ruthin
			St Asaph
			Wrexham
Co Antrim	Northern Ireland	BT	Ballycastle
			Ballyclare
			Ballymena
			Ballymoney
			Carrickfergus
			Larne
			Lisburn
			Lurgan
			Newtownabbey
			Portrush
			Randalstown
Co Armagh	Northern Ireland	BT	Armagh
			Craigavon
Co Down	Northern Ireland	BT	Ballygowan
			Banbridge
			Bangor
			Castlewellan
			Downpatrick
			Holywood
			Newcastle
			Newry
			Newtownards
Co Durham	North East	DH	Consett
			Durham
		DL	Barnard Castle
			Bishop Auckland
			Darlington
		SR	Peterlee
			Seaham
Co Fermanagh	Northern Ireland	BT	Enniskillen
Co Londonderry	Northern Ireland	BT	Coleraine
			Garvagh
			Londonderry
Co Tyrone	Northern Ireland	BT	Cookstown
			Dungannon
			Fivemiletown
			Omagh
Cornwall	South West	EX	Bude
		PL	Camelford
			Launceston
			Port Isaac
			St Austell
			Wadebridge
		TR	Falmouth
			Helston
			Newquay

Counties by Postal Region, Postcode and Post Towns

'Old' County	Postal Region	Postcode	Post Towns
			Penryn
			Penzance
			Redruth
			St Ives
			Truro
Cumbria	North West	CA	Alston
			Appleby-in-Westmorland
			Carlisle
			Keswick
			Kirkby Stephen
			Maryport
			Penrith
			Whitehaven
			Wigton
		LA	Ambleside
			Coniston
			Grange-over-Sands
			Kendal
			Kirkby Lonsdale
			Ulverston
			Windermere
Derbyshire	Midlands	DE	Alfreton
			Ashbourne
			Belper
			Derby
			Glossop
			Ilkeston
			Matlock
			Ripley
			Swadlincote
	North East	S	Chesterfield
			Hope Valley
	North West	SK	Buxton
Devon	South West	EX	Axminster
			Barnstaple
			Bideford
			Braunton
			Colyton
			Crediton
			Cullompton
			Exeter
			Exmouth
			Holsworthy
			Honiton
			Ilfracombe
			Lynton
			Okehampton
			Seaton
			Sidmouth
			Tiverton
			Torrington
		PL	Plymouth
			Tavistock
			Yelverton
		TQ	Buckfastleigh
			Kingsbridge
			Newton Abbot
			Paignton
			Teignmouth
			Torquay
Dorset	South Central	SP	Shaftesbury
	South West	BH	Bournemouth
			Christchurch
			Ferndown
			Poole
			Swanage
			Wimborne
		DT	Blandford Forum
			Bridport
			Dorchester
			Lyme Regis
			Sherborne
			Weymouth
Dumfriesshire	Scotland	DG	Dumfries
			Lockerbie
Dunbartonshire	Scotland	G	Dumbarton
			Helensburgh
Dyfed	Wales	SA	Ammanford
			Cardigan
			Carmarthen
			Clynderwen
			Fishguard
			Haverfordwest
			Llandysul
			Llanelli
			Llanwrda
			Pembroke
			St Davids
			Tenby
			Whitland
		SY	Aberystwyth
East Lothian	Scotland	EH	Dunbar
			Gullane
			Haddington
			North Berwick
			Tranent
East Sussex	South East	BN	Brighton
			Eastbourne
			Hailsham
			Hove
			Lewes
			Peacehaven
			Seaford
		TN	Battle
			Bexhill-on-Sea
			Crowborough
			Hastings
			Heathfield
			Robertsbridge
			Rye
			St Leonards-on-Sea
			Uckfield
Edinburgh	Scotland	EH	Edinburgh
Essex	Anglia	CB	Saffron Walden
		CM	Billericay
			Braintree
			Brentwood
			Chelmsford
			Dunmow
			Harlow
			Ingatestone
			Maldon
			Ongar
			Southminster
			Witham
		CO	Clacton-on-Sea
			Colchester
			Frinton-on-Sea
			Halstead
			Harwich
			Walton on the Naze
		EN	Epping
		IG	Barking
			Buckhurst Hill
			Ilford
			Loughton
			Woodford Green
		RM	Dagenham
			Hornchurch
			Rainham
			Romford
			Tilbury
			Upminster
		SS	Basildon
			Benfleet
			Canvey Island
			Hockley
			Leigh-on-Sea
			Rayleigh
			Rochford
			Southend-on-Sea
			Westcliff-on-Sea
			Wickford
Fife	Scotland	KY	Anstruther
			Cupar
			Dalgety Bay
			Dunfermline
			Glenrothes
			Kirkcaldy
			St Andrews
Glasgow	Scotland	G	Glasgow

·d' County	Postal Region	Postcode	Post Towns
›ucestershire	South West	GL	Cheltenham
			Cinderford
			Cirencester
			Gloucester
			Lydney
			Mitcheldean
			Newent
			Newnham
			Stroud
			Tewkesbury
·eater Manchester	North West	M	Manchester
		OL	Ashton-under-Lyne
·vent	Wales	NP	Abertillery
			Blackwood
			Chepstow
			Cwmbran
			Ebbw Vale
			Monmouth
			Newport
			Pontypool
·wynedd	Wales	LL	Aberdovey
			Arthog
			Bala
			Bangor
			Beaumaris
			Blaenau Ffestiniog
			Caernarfon
			Conwy
			Dwygyfylchi
			Holyhead
			Llanbedr
			Llandudno
			Llanrwst
			Penmaenmawr
			Porthmadog
			Pwllheli
			Talybont
			Tywyn
			Ynys Môn
·ampshire	South Central	GU	Aldershot
			Alton
			Bordon
			Farnborough
			Fleet
			Liphook
			Liss
			Petersfield
		PO	Emsworth
			Fareham
			Gosport
			Havant
			Portsmouth
		RG	Basingstoke
			Hook
			Whitchurch
		SO	Alresford
			Eastleigh
			Lymington
			Lyndhurst
			Romsey
			Southampton
			Southsea
			Winchester
		SP	Andover
	South West	BH	Ringwood
Herefordshire	South West	HR	Hereford
			Ledbury
			Leominster
			Luston
			Ross-on-Wye
Hertfordshire	Anglia	AL	Harpenden
			St Albans
			Welwyn
			Welwyn Garden City
		CM	Bishop's Stortford
			Sawbridgeworth
		EN	Barnet
			Hoddesdon
			Potters Bar
		SG	Baldock
			Hertford

'Old' County	Postal Region	Postcode	Post Towns
			Hitchin
			Letchworth
			Royston
			Stevenage
			Ware
		WD	Borehamwood
			Kings Langley
			Radlett
			Rickmansworth
			Watford
	South Central	HP	Berkhamsted
			Hemel Hempstead
			Tring
Inverness-shire	Scotland	PH	Aviemore
			Croy
			Fort William
			Inverness
			Kingussie
			Nairn
			Nethy Bridge
Isle of Lewis	Scotland	HS	Stornoway
Isle of Man	Isle of Man	IM	Castletown
			Douglas
			Ramsey
Isle of Shetland	Scotland	ZE	Lerwick
			Shetland
Isle of Skye	Scotland	IV	Kyleakin
			Portree
Isle of Wight	South Central	PO	Freshwater
			Newport
			Ryde
			Sandown
			Totland Bay
			Ventnor
Kent	South East	BR	Beckenham
			Bromley
			Orpington
			Swanley
			West Wickham
		CT	Canterbury
			Deal
			Dover
			Folkestone
			Herne Bay
			Hythe
			Margate
			Ramsgate
			Sandwich
			Westgate-on-Sea
			Whitstable
		DA	Belvedere
			Dartford
			Erith
			Gravesend
			Sidcup
			Welling
		ME	Chatham
			Faversham
			Gillingham
			Maidstone
			Rochester
			Sittingbourne
			West Malling
		TN	Ashford
			Sevenoaks
			Tonbridge
			Tunbridge Wells
			Westerham
Kincardineshire	Scotland	AB	Banchory
			Stonehaven
Kirkcudbrightshire	Scotland	DG	Castle Douglas
			Dalbeattie
Lanarkshire	Scotland	ML	Biggar
			Carluke
			Hamilton
			Lanark
			Motherwell
			Wishaw
Lancashire	North West	BB	Accrington
			Blackburn
			Burnley

Counties by Postal Region, Postcode and Post Towns

'Old' County	Postal Region	Postcode	Post Towns
			Clitheroe
			Nelson
			Rossendale
		BL	Bolton
			Bury
		FY	Blackpool
			Fleetwood
			Lytham St Annes
			Poulton-le-Fylde
		L	Ormskirk
		LA	Broughton-in-Furness
			Carnforth
			Lancaster
			Morecambe
		M	Salford
		OL	Heywood
			Littleborough
			Oldham
			Rochdale
		PR	Chorley
			Preston
		WN	Leigh
			Skelmersdale
			Wigan
Leicestershire	Midlands	LE	Coalville
			Hinckley
			Leicester
			Loughborough
			Lutterworth
			Market Harborough
			Melton Mowbray
			Oakham
Lincolnshire	Anglia	PE	Boston
			Bourne
			Spalding
			Stamford
	Midlands	NG	Grantham
			Sleaford
	North East	LN	Lincoln
London	London	E, EC, N, NW, SE, SW, W, WC	
Merseyside	North West	L	Birkenhead
			Bootle
			Liverpool
			Prescot
			South Wirral
			Wallasey
			Wirral
	North West	PR	Southport
		WA	St Helens
Mid Glamorgan	Wales	CF	Aberdare
			Bridgend
			Caerphilly
			Porthcawl
		NP	Pontypridd
Middlesex	Anglia	EN	Enfield
	South Central	HA	Edgware
			Harrow
			Northwood
			Pinner
			Ruislip
			Wembley
	South Central	UB	Greenford
			Hayes
			Southall
			Uxbridge
			West Drayton
	South East	TW	Brentford
			Hampton
			Hounslow
			Isleworth
			Shepperton
			Staines
			Sunbury-on-Thames
			Teddington
			Twickenham
Midlothian	Scotland	EH	Bonnyrigg
			Loanhead
			Musselburgh

'Old' County	Postal Region	Postcode	Post Towns
Morayshire	Scotland	IV	Elgin
Norfolk	Anglia	IP	Harleston
			Thetford
		NR	Attleborough
			Aylsham
			Cromer
			Dereham
			Holt
			North Walsham
			Norwich
			Sheringham
			Walsingham
		PE	Hunstanton
			King's Lynn
			Swaffham
North Humberside	North East	HU	Beverley
			Cottingham
			Hessle
			Hull
		YO	Bridlington
			Driffield
North Yorkshire	North East	BD	Skipton
		DL	Leyburn
			Northallerton
			Richmond
		HG	Harrogate
			Ripon
		TS	Guisborough
		YO	Scarborough
			Thirsk
			Whitby
			York
Northamptonshire	Midlands	NN	Corby
			Daventry
			Kettering
			Northampton
			Rushden
			Towcester
			Wellingborough
Northumberland	North East	NE	Alnwick
			Ashington
			Choppington
			Cramlington
			Haltwhistle
			Hexham
			Morpeth
			Prudhoe
			Riding Mill
			Seahouses
			Stocksfield
			Wooler
		TD	Berwick-upon-Tweed
Nottinghamshire	Midlands	NG	Mansfield
			Newark
			Nottingham
			Southwell
			Sutton-in-Ashfield
	North East	DN	Retford
Oxfordshire	South Central	OX	Abingdon
			Banbury
			Bicester
			Chipping Norton
			Didcot
			Faringdon
			Kidlington
			Oxford
			Thame
			Wallingford
			Wantage
			Witney
		RG	Henley-on-Thames
Peeblesshire	Scotland	EH	West Linton
Perthshire	Scotland	FK	Dunblane
			Killin
		PH	Blairgowrie
			Crieff
			Dunkeld
			Perth
			Pitlochry
Powys	Wales	LD	Brecon

d' County	Postal Region	Postcode	Post Towns
			Builth Wells
			Knighton
			Llandrindod Wells
		SY	Llanidloes
			Llanymynech
			Meifod
			Montgomery
			Newtown
			Welshpool
nfrewshire	Scotland	PA	Greenock
			Johnston
			Lochwinnoch
			Paisley
ss-shire	Scotland	IV	Dingwall
			Fortrose
			Gairloch
			Kyle
			Lochcarron
			Tain
			Ullapool
xburghshire	Scotland	TD	Hawick
			Kelso
			Newcastleton
lkirkshire	Scotland	TD	Galashiels
ropshire	Midlands	WV	Bridgnorth
		SY	Ludlow
			Oswestry
			Shrewsbury
			Whitchurch
	North West	TF	Market Drayton
			Newport
			Telford
merset	South West	BA	Frome
			Glastonbury
			Templecombe
			Wells
			Yeovil
		BS	Cheddar
			Winscombe
		TA	Bridgwater
			Chard
			Highbridge
			Minehead
			South Petherton
			Taunton
			Watchet
South Glamorgan	Wales	CF	Barry
			Cardiff
			Dinas Powis
			Penarth
South Humberside	North East	DN	Barton-upon-Humber
			Cleethorpes
			Grimsby
			Scunthorpe
South Yorkshire	North East	DN	Doncaster
		S	Barnsley
			Dronfield
			Maltby
			Mexborough
			Rotherham
			Sheffield
Staffordshire	Midlands	B	Tamworth
		DE	Burton-on-Trent
		ST	Newcastle
			Stafford
			Stoke-on-Trent
			Stone
		WS	Lichfield
			Rugeley
Stirlingshire	Scotland	FK	Falkirk
			Larbert
			Stirling
Suffolk	Anglia	CB	Newmarket
		CO	Sudbury
		IG	Bury St Edmunds
			Felixstowe
		IP	Ipswich
			Leiston
			Stowmarket
		NR	Beccles

'Old' County	Postal Region	Postcode	Post Towns
			Bungay
			Lowestoft
Surrey	South Central	GU	Cranleigh
			Farnham
			Godalming
			Guildford
			Haslemere
			Lightwater
			Woking
	South East	CR	Camberley
			Caterham
			Coulsdon
			Croydon
			Mitcham
			Purley
			South Croydon
			Thornton Heath
		KT	Ashtead
			Chessington
			Cobham
			East Molesey
			Epsom
			Kingston upon Thames
			Leatherhead
			New Malden
			Surbiton
			Walton-on-Thames
			West Byfleet
			Weybridge
		RH	Dorking
			Horley
			Lingfield
			Oxted
			Redhill
			Reigate
		SM	Banstead
			Carshalton
			Morden
			Sutton
			Wallington
		TW	Egham
			Richmond
Sutherland	Scotland	IV	Dornoch
Tyne and Wear	North East	DH	Houghton le Spring
		NE	Blaydon-on-Tyne
			Boldon Colliery
			Gateshead
			Newcastle upon Tyne
			Ryton
			South Shields
			Whitley Bay
		SR	Sunderland
Warwickshire	Midlands	B	Alcester
		CV	Bedworth
			Kenilworth
			Leamington Spa
			Nuneaton
			Rugby
			Stratford-upon-Avon
			Warwick
West Glamorgan	Wales	SA	Port Talbot
			Swansea
West Lothian	Scotland	EH	Bo'Ness
			Livingston
			South Queensferry
West Midlands	Midlands	B	Birmingham
			Halesowen
			Oldbury
			Solihull
			Sutton Coldfield
			Warley
			West Bromwich
		CV	Coventry
		DY	Dudley
			Kingswinford
			Stourbridge
			Tipton
		WS	Walsall

Postcodes by Postal Region

'Old' County	Postal Region	Postcode	Post Towns
		WV	Willenhall
		WV	Wolverhampton
West Sussex	South Central	GU	Midhurst
		PO	Bognor Regis
			Chichester
	South East	BN	Arundel
			Hassocks
			Henfield
			Lancing
			Littlehampton
			Worthing
		RH	Billingshurst
			Burgess Hill
			Crawley
			East Grinstead
			Haywards Heath
			Horsham
			Pulborough
West Yorkshire	North East	BD	Bingley
			Bradford
			Keighley
		HD	Brighouse
			Huddersfield
		HX	Halifax
		LS	Ilkley
			Leeds
			Otley
			Wetherby
		WF	Dewsbury
			Mirfield
			Ossett
			Pontefract
			Wakefield
Wiltshire	South Central	SN	Calne
			Chippenham
			Malmesbury
			Marlborough
			Melksham
			Pewsey
			Swindon
			Trowbridge
		SP	Salisbury
	South West	BA	Bradford-on-Avon
			Mere
			Warminster
			Westbury
Worcestershire	Midlands	B	Bromsgrove
			Redditch
		DY	Bewdley
			Kidderminster
			Stourport-on-Severn
	South West	WR	Broadway
			Droitwich
			Malvern
			Pershore
			Upton-upon-Severn
			Worcester

POSTCODES BY POSTAL REGION

AB	Scotland
AL	Anglia
B	Midlands
BA	South West
BB	North West
BD	North East
BH	South West
BL	North West
BN	South East
BR	South East
BS	South West
BT	Northern Ireland
CA	North West
CB	Anglia
CF	Wales
CH	North West
CH	Wales
CM	Anglia
CO	Anglia
CR	South East
CT	South East
CV	Midlands
CW	North West
DA	South East
DD	Scotland
DE	Midlands
DG	Scotland
DH	North East
DL	North East
DN	North East
DT	South West
DY	Midlands
E	London
EC	London
EH	Scotland
EN	Anglia
EX	South West
FK	Scotland
FY	North West
G	Scotland
GL	South West
GU	South Central
GY	Channel Islands
HA	South Central
HD	North East
HG	North East
HP	South Central
HR	South West
HS	Scotland
HU	North East
HX	North East
IG	Anglia
IM	Isle of Man
IP	Anglia
IV	Scotland
JE	Channel Islands
KA	Scotland
KT	South East
KW	Scotland
KY	Scotland
L	North West
LA	North West
LD	Wales
LE	Midlands
LL	Wales
LN	North East
LS	North East
LU	Anglia
M	North West
ME	South East
MK	Anglia
ML	Scotland
N	London
NE	North East
NG	Midlands
NN	Midlands
NP	Wales
NR	Anglia
NW	London
OL	North West
OX	South Central
PA	Scotland
PE	Anglia
PH	Scotland
PL	South West
PO	South Central
PR	North West
RG	South Central
RH	South East
RM	Anglia
S	North East
SA	Wales
SE	London
SG	Anglia
SK	North West
SL	South Central
SM	South East
SN	South Central
SO	South Central
SP	South Central
SR	North East
SS	Anglia
ST	Midlands
SW	London
SY	North West
SY	Wales
TA	South West
TD	Scotland
TD	North East
TF	North West
TN	South East
TQ	South West
TR	South West
TS	North East
TW	South East
UB	South Central
W	London
WA	North West
WC	London
WD	Anglia
WF	North East
WN	North West
WR	South West
WS	Midlands
WV	Midlands
YO	North East
ZE	Scotland

LOCATION INDEX

Note: Entries at the same postal address are grouped together

LOCATION INDEX

Location Index

Location Index

LOCATION INDEX

LOCATION INDEX

LOCATION INDEX

LOCATION INDEX

Location Index

Location Index

LOCATION INDEX

Location Index

LOCATION INDEX

LOCATION INDEX

South West

Location Index

LOCATION INDEX

Location Index

REPUBLIC OF IRELAND

SCOTLAND

WALES

Location Index

LOCATION INDEX

INDEX OF ADVERTISERS

MAIN INDEX

ıe Main Index includes the following items for all the organisa- ns listed in the *Handbook*:

Names, alternative names, known old names and commonly ed abbreviations of organisational names.
Names of all people listed.
Ecclesiastical titles by town eg; 1) Bath, Archdeacon of 2) bernethy, Presbytery of. Where the title relates to a Diocese it is ot included separately eg; Bishop of Bath and Wells cannot be und under Bath in the Main Index, but instead under Church of ıgland Diocese of Bath and Wells.
Magazine titles, unless the title is so similar to the organisation ımes that they appear in the same place in the index eg; *dministry Update* is not listed separately from Administry.
Imprints of publishers.
Subject areas of work. Subjects are only listed when they appear ther than in the relevant category eg; computers are not listed by ıbject if the organisation concerned is in the Computer and Busi- ess Service category. The word used as a subject entry will be ound in the description of work of one or more organisations on ıe page number given.

– Names of organisations which have closed or not been traced in the past 10 years, with the year it occurred. Where the date of closure is not known the year 1999 has been inserted.
– To help distinguish organisations of similar name, the town is given for Bookshops, Conference Centres, Guest Houses and Hotels, and other similar organisations (unless the town name appears in the name of the organisation eg Gloucester Cathedral Bookshop is listed as it stands, whereas The Cathedral Bookshop in Carlisle is listed as The Cathedral Bookshop, Carlisle). Towns are otherwise listed in the Location Index and in the list on Page 569.
– Advertisements are listed for the relevant organisation. These are also listed in the Index of Advertisers on Page 626.
– Category names (in bold) eg; Elderly people is a subject entry, but **Elderly People (Residential Homes for)** is a category

The index is constructed on the word principle, that is the order of entries is determinied by the alphabetical sequence of the word in each entry rather than the letters, recognising spaces between words. Thus Alpha Book Shop comes before Alpha Bookroom, since Book precedes Bookroom word for word.

INDEX

Index

MAIN INDEX

MAIN INDEX

MAIN INDEX

MAIN INDEX

C

MAIN INDEX

MAIN INDEX

MAIN INDEX

MAIN INDEX

MAIN INDEX

MAIN INDEX

D

MAIN INDEX

MAIN INDEX

MAIN INDEX

MAIN INDEX

MAIN INDEX

MAIN INDEX

MAIN INDEX

K

MAIN INDEX

MAIN INDEX

I

', Mc, Mac are all treated as Mac. and the ext letter in the name determines the position the entry. Other names come after

MAIN INDEX

MAIN INDEX

O

MAIN INDEX

MAIN INDEX

MAIN INDEX

MAIN INDEX

Index

MAIN INDEX

MAIN INDEX

MAIN INDEX

S

MAIN INDEX

MAIN INDEX

MAIN INDEX

MAIN INDEX

U

V

MAIN INDEX

MAIN INDEX

X

Y

Z